THE OXFORD HANDBOOK OF

CYBER SECURITY

THE OXFORD HANDBOOK OF

CYBER SECURITY

Edited by
PAUL CORNISH

OXFORD
UNIVERSITY PRESS

Great Clarendon Street, Oxford, OX2 6DP,
United Kingdom

Oxford University Press is a department of the University of Oxford.
It furthers the University's objective of excellence in research, scholarship,
and education by publishing worldwide. Oxford is a registered trade mark of
Oxford University Press in the UK and in certain other countries

© Oxford University Press 2021

The moral rights of the author have been asserted

First Edition published in 2021

Impression: 1

All rights reserved. No part of this publication may be reproduced, stored in
a retrieval system, or transmitted, in any form or by any means, without the
prior permission in writing of Oxford University Press, or as expressly permitted
by law, by licence or under terms agreed with the appropriate reprographics
rights organization. Enquiries concerning reproduction outside the scope of the
above should be sent to the Rights Department, Oxford University Press, at the
address above

You must not circulate this work in any other form
and you must impose this same condition on any acquirer

Published in the United States of America by Oxford University Press
198 Madison Avenue, New York, NY 10016, United States of America

British Library Cataloguing in Publication Data
Data available

Library of Congress Control Number: 2021940009

ISBN 978–0–19–880068–2

DOI: 10.1093/oxfordhb/9780198800682.001.0001

Printed and bound in the UK by
TJ Books Limited

Links to third party websites are provided by Oxford in good faith and
for information only. Oxford disclaims any responsibility for the materials
contained in any third party website referenced in this work.

In Memoriam David Upton

CONTENTS

Foreword. Sir David Omand GCB	xiii
List of Figures	xix
List of Tables	xxi
List of Contributors	xxiii

Introduction   1
PAUL CORNISH

PART I. CYBER SPACE: WHAT IT IS AND WHY IT MATTERS

1. The Origins of Cyberspace   7
   DAVID J. PYM

2. Opportunity, Threat, and Dependency in the Social Infosphere   32
   GREG AUSTIN

3. A Political History of Cyberspace   49
   MADELINE CARR

4. Cyber Power in International Relations   66
   TIM STEVENS AND CAMINO KAVANAGH

5. Ethical Standards and 'Communication' Technologies   82
   ONORA O'NEILL

PART II. SECURITY IN CYBER SPACE: CYBER CRIME

6. Cybercrime: Thieves, Swindlers, Bandits, and Privateers in Cyberspace   89
   RODERIC BROADHURST

7. Making Sense of Cybersecurity in Emerging Technology Areas   109
   CLAIRE VISHIK, MICHAEL HUTH, LAWRENCE JOHN, AND MARCELLO BALDUCCINI

viii CONTENTS

8. Assessing Harm from Cyber Crime 127
   EVA IGNATUSCHTSCHENKO

9. Toward a Vulnerability Mitigation Model 142
   JOSÉ EDUARDO MALTA DE SÁ BRANDÃO

PART III. SECURITY IN CYBER SPACE: EXTREMISM AND TERRORISM

10. Managing Risk: Terrorism, Violent Extremism, and
    Anti-Democratic Tendencies in the Digital Space 163
    ALEXANDER CORBEIL AND RAFAL ROHOZINSKI

11. Cyberweapons 173
    SANDRO GAYCKEN

12. Intentions and Cyberterrorism 187
    FLORIAN J. EGLOFF

13. Technology: Access and Denial 201
    CAITRÍONA HEINL

PART IV. SECURITY IN CYBER SPACE: STATE-SPONSORED CYBER ATTACKS

14. Cyber Espionage 223
    JON R. LINDSAY

15. Cyberwar *Redux* 239
    BEN BUCHANAN

16. On Cyber-Enabled Information Warfare and Information
    Operations 251
    HERBERT LIN AND JACLYN KERR

17. The Deterrence and Prevention of Cyber Conflict 273
    PAUL CORNISH

PART V. TECHNICAL AND CORPORATE CYBERSECURITY

18. Stepping out of the Shadow: Computer Security Incident Response
    Teams in the Cybersecurity Ecosystem 297
    NICOLE VAN DER MEULEN

19. Cybersecurity Information Sharing: Voluntary Beginnings and a Mandatory Future 314
STUART MURDOCH

20. Data Privacy and Security Law 328
FRED CATE AND RACHEL DOCKERY

21. The 'Insider Threat' and the 'Insider Advocate' 348
MIKE STEINMETZ

PART VI. PERSONAL CYBERSECURITY

22. Personal Protection: 'Cyber Hygiene' 361
DAVE CLEMENTE

23. Online Child Safety 377
JOHN CARR

24. Educating for Cyber (Security) 395
ROGER BRADBURY

25. Cybersecurity, Human Rights and Empiricism: The Case of Digital Surveillance 409
JONATHON PENNEY

PART VII. NATIONAL CYBERSECURITY

26. Securing the Critical National Infrastructure 429
DAVID MUSSINGTON

27. The Role of Defence in National Cybersecurity 447
MIKA KERTTUNEN

28. Cybersecurity Capacity Building 463
LARA PACE AND PAUL CORNISH

PART VIII. GLOBAL TRADE AND CYBERSECURITY

29. Cybersecurity, Multilateral Export Control, and Standard Setting Arrangements 479
ELAINE KORZAK

30. Cybersecurity, Global Commerce and International Organizations 497
DAVID FIDLER

CONTENTS

31. Global Trade and Cybersecurity: Monitoring, Enforcement, and Sanctions 514
    FRANZ-STEFAN GADY AND GREG AUSTIN

PART IX. INTERNATIONAL CYBERSECURITY

32. Semi-Formal Diplomacy: Track 1.5 and Track 2 531
    NIGEL INKSTER

33. States, Proxies, and (Remote) Offensive Cyber Operations 543
    TIM MAURER

34. Getting Beyond Norms: When Violating the Agreement Becomes Customary Practice 562
    MELISSA HATHAWAY

35. International Law for Cyberspace: Competition and Conflict 578
    THOMAS WINGFIELD AND HARRY WINGO

PART X. PERSPECTIVES ON CYBERSECURITY

36. Community of Common Future in Cyberspace: The Proposal and Practice of China 597
    TANG LAN

37. Look West or Look East? India at the Crossroads of Cyberspace 616
    ARUN MOHAN SUKUMAR

38. Cybersecurity in Israel: Strategy, Organization, and Future Challenges 631
    LIOR TABANSKY

39. The Evolving Concept of the Japanese Security Strategy 649
    YOKO NITTA

40. Contextualizing Malaysia's Cybersecurity Agenda 659
    ELINA NOOR

41. The Russian Federation's Approach to Cybersecurity 672
    ANTON SHINGAREV AND ANASTASIYA KAZAKOVA

PART XI. FUTURE CHALLENGES

42. Rethinking the Governance of Technology in the Digital Age 687
    JOËLLE WEBB

43. Maturing Autonomous Cyber Weapons Systems: Implications for International Cybersecurity 702
    CAITRÍONA HEINL

44. The Future Human and Behavioural Challenges of Cybersecurity 723
    DEBI ASHENDEN

45. The Future of Democratic Civil Societies in a Post-Western Cybered Era 735
    CHRIS DEMCHAK

46. Future Normative Challenges 751
    ENEKEN TIKK

47. 'Cybersecurity' and 'Development': Contested Futures 769
    TIM UNWIN

48. Project Solarium 1953 and the Cyberspace Solarium Commission 2019 785
    MIKE STEINMETZ

Conclusion 798
    PAUL CORNISH

Index 807

FOREWORD

SIR DAVID OMAND GCB

The publication of this *Oxford Handbook* could not be more timely. Security problems are multiplying in cyberspace at the same time as recognition is dawning of our vulnerability to cyber exploits and cyberattacks, and the large costs that they can impose on governments and businesses. Not only is there an urgent need to apply in practice the analysis of cybersecurity contained in the chapters of this *Handbook*, there is an overdue need to invest more in research into the gaps in our knowledge and understanding, apparent too from the chapters here, to enable us to be prepared for the inevitable development of the threat landscape and the malicious skills of those who populate it.

Recognition of the dependence of modern societies on the digital world of the Internet and the Web it carries, and of the Big Data it generates, has come not before time. Our reliance has crept up on us little by little. Our understanding of the consequent risks we are running has not kept pace, and has become divorced from our actual risky behaviours online. The private sector technology companies were the first to recognize the huge commercial advantages of using the open Internet to communicate directly to customers, building global businesses by being able to ignore the artificiality of national borders. Other businesses, including the financial sector, quickly followed to gather marketing information, communicate with customers and the supply chain, and dramatically cut down transaction costs through disintermediation. Yes, there were losses due to traditional frauds being able to be conducted at scale and new forms of digital crime but at first these would have seemed bearable in comparison with the benefits. As losses have mounted, with the easy gains already taken, that complacency is being shaken.

As mobile devices proliferated at ever decreasing real cost, the everyday life of the citizen was not far behind in being transformed by the connectivity of the Internet and the Web with access to family and friends on social media coming to dominate everyday interactions. Upcoming generations can scarcely imagine life without the connectivity of this portable digital environment. Again, the reported online bullying, cyber stalking and trolling at first mostly happened to others; now the prevalence of such personally damaging and destructive behaviour online has grown to disturbing proportions. Russia has demonstrated how digital subversive campaigns can be mounted against the United States and European nations by interfering in elections, exacerbating tensions in society, and undermining confidence in Western democracy.

The development of the Dark Net, exploiting the natural anonymity baked into the founding protocols of the Internet, has led to a proliferation of criminal websites offering for easy sale every type of illegal recreational drug, guns and other weapons, stolen personal details, and cyber exploits to enable further criminal fraud and extortion at the expense of the public. The grooming of youngsters for sexual exploitation on social media is now a major preoccupation of the police, along with trying to inhibit the sharing of child pornography and online streaming of extreme child abuse, often from the other side of the world, exploiting the borderless characteristics of the Internet. Terrorist groups have used a range of social media to stream violent propaganda at potential recruits, in ways that make it hard for the Internet companies to detect and remove it.

In addition, most governments have added to national Internet dependency, taking advantage of the speed and scale of data technology to cut out back offices and provide citizens with direct access to official services ranging from registering to vote and licensing motorcars to lodging tax returns. The cost reductions, and gains in convenience to have the service online, were just too attractive to be delayed in order to allow the massive investments in designing in security, staff training and developing the technical assistance that would have been needed to give a high assurance of data security. Just in time, as the Internet of Things begins to exhibit its potential, we have an overdue greater recognition on the part of elected governments that there are downsides for the citizen as well as upsides to the digital revolution.

It was entirely predictable that the wave of digital communications and data storage technology that developed in the 1990s and 2000s, and is currently cresting and breaking over us, would bring problems to those used to swimming in shallower waters. Many companies and individuals alike are now finding themselves out of their technical depth. For many small and medium-sized companies, the cost of paying for the cyber equivalents of lifeguards and rescue helicopters on standby in case of trouble is proving prohibitive.

In a historical perspective, those with criminal intent have always been quick to exploit technology for their own selfish benefit, whether using that revolutionary invention, the motor car, to enable fast getaways from robberies or when commercial aviation came along to escape jurisdiction, not to mention the use of plastic explosives to blow safes. Today, there is no need for the criminal to flee across borders because attacks can be mounted over the Internet from anywhere on the globe. Again, in the past, criminals could usually only plan and mount one attack at a time; today, the same attempted fraud can be directed at thousands of customers. And the really big heists do not require the swag to be carted away because the digital proceeds can be transferred at the touch of a key through a string of money-laundering accounts.

The ambition of cybercriminals (and their state sponsors in some cases) continues to amaze, both in its audacity and its global reach. Such was the attempt (thankfully only partially successful) to hack the Swift interbank payment system to defraud a number of central banks of some $951 million. That attack has been ascribed by cyber investigators to North Korea (the sum involved would represent one month of Republic's gross domestic product and would no doubt have been a welcome addition of foreign exchange funds for intelligence and subversive activity overseas). That attack appears to have had insider help, a reminder that cybersecurity is as much about people, and managing them well and with care, as it is about technology. The case also reminds us that the boundary between criminal and state activity is not clear-cut. Russian attackers inserted the NotPetya worm into tax preparation software aimed at a Ukrainian target but it escaped into the wild, did over $1billion's worth of damage to global companies, and almost destroyed the world's largest shipping container company, Maersk. Digital interference in another country's internal affairs is now commonplace. The pre–election hack into the US Democrat National Committee, and the subsequent release of stolen emails, intended to sway the 2016 US presidential election away from Hillary Clinton and towards Donald Trump, was a covert action firmly attributed to the Russian authorities and an example of the modern weaponization of digital information. And that attack should also serve to emphasize the value of being able to harness digital and other intelligence sources to assist with the attribution of exploits and attacks. The 2016 attack on the French TV5 Monde television channels, now attributed to Russia, was, for example, conducted with malware compiled in such a way as to try (unsuccessfully in the end) to divert blame on to the so-called 'Cyber Caliphate' linked to the Islamic State.

A profession that has always fastened early onto new technological advances is that of secret intelligence. UK naval intelligence was quick to exploit the early development of radio transmissions during the First World War to listen in to the enemy and to geo-locate warships and military units. During the Second World War, it was the advent of proto-computers for deciphering, and the application of mathematics to cryptanalysis, that revolutionized signals intelligence. During the Cold War, it was the development of microelectronics that led to the huge investment in spy satellites. Now we have the global Internet and the World Wide Web, and all the opportunities they offer for bulk access to the communications, and patterns of communication, of the targets of intelligence activity, as well as access through computer network exploitation to the stored data of every kind of organization. The first documented massive computer raid on classified information, Moonlit Maze, was a sophisticated Russian attack on the databases of the US military and research and development sector dating back to the early 1990s and lasting for several years before detection. A hard lesson of the need for cybersecurity protection for national defence networks. Nevertheless, subsequent Chinese so-called 'advanced persistent attacks' (APTs) on US and European industry and commerce exposed significant cybersecurity weaknesses in the private sector but not before huge losses of intellectual property had occurred. Finally, the US and Chinese presidents reached an agreement that neither side would conduct cyber espionage on the other for the commercial gain of their national companies, with a comparable agreement reached between the UK and China —rare examples of international cyber norms being agreed.

The increasingly urgent demands today are for intelligence on terrorists, proliferators, and criminals, and these have led to an upsurge in intelligence requirements being authorized for information about people as individuals, rather than the more traditional objects of intelligence attention to support defence and foreign policy. The demand is for the identities, associations, movements, locations, and financing of those who directly mean us harm, and where better to look for such information than the packet-switched networks of the global Internet, in social media use, or in data at rest in bulk personal databases. A cybersecurity dilemma arises at once between the need for the authorities to access such information for public safety and to uphold the law, and the calls for the strongest possible protection against the hacking of mobile phones, tablets, and other devices, and for strong end-to-end encryption to protect the privacy of the individual user and promote confidence in the integrity of the Internet.

The dynamic demand and supply interaction between the need for timely information about people of intelligence and law enforcement interest, and the intelligence opportunities offered by digital technology, often using the very same methods that commerce itself uses to derive marketing information on its customers, has created a strong set of surveillance tools.

The very power of these capabilities, and their potential for misuse in the wrong hands, has led to a significant strengthening in many Western democracies of the constitutional, judicial, and Parliamentary oversight protections for the privacy of individuals and for the maintenance of free speech (in the UK, principally through the Investigatory Powers Act 2016). In totalitarian and less democratic states, the abuse of digital surveillance against dissidents and political opponents is already apparent.

In the long run, a major danger facing the democracies is loss of confidence in the Internet as a secure medium for doing business, communicating with government, and conducting a fulfilling private life. That observation directly translates into the priority now being given by many governments to cybersecurity—for example, in the UK, through the 2016 creation of the National Cyber Security Centre. No one can promise the certainty of future trust in the Internet, and certainly not the elimination of the many cyber risks that exist today. And new risks are certain to emerge—for example, as terrorist groups and malign individuals come to recognize the harm they can inflict on advanced Internet-dependent societies with relatively simple cyberattack tools, many of which are already available to be bought on the Dark Web (for untraceable Bitcoin payment of course).

Most nations are now searching for cybersecurity strategies that will better enable them to manage all these risks. Most strategies contain the elements summed up in the recent euphonious UK cybersecurity strategy of *Defend* against cyber threats, *Deter* all forms of aggression in cyberspace, and *Develop* an innovative, growing cybersecurity industry, underpinned by scientific research and development, with a self-sustaining pipeline of talent providing the skills to meet public and private sector needs.

How such laudable goals are to be met is uncharted territory. Some nations, such as France and Germany, have chosen deliberately to present their centres of cyber expertise as organizationally separate from their intelligence communities, presumably in the hope of increasing public credibility in the security advice being given and to minimize the risk that the search for zero-day exploits to gather digital intelligence will take precedence over securing commonly used software. The alternative view, being taken by the United States and the United Kingdom among others, is that, while good cyber hygiene by companies and the public can secure some 80% of the required security, protecting against the really damaging exploits and attacks requires the information that only digital intelligence can gather, including that to support offensive cyber operations. That logic points to an organizational model that allows national deep cyber expertise to be exploited for both intelligence and cybersecurity purposes.

The policy implications of cybersecurity issues do not naturally fall to any single government department. Home affairs and interior ministries, justice ministries, defence and foreign affairs, finance, trade and business departments all have important interests at stake Nor is adequate cybersecurity in one country scarcely conceivable in the connected global Internet. Again, this is relatively uncharted territory for the machinery of government and for international organizations.

Governments are naturally uneasy with a situation in which no one is in charge of the global phenomenon that is the Internet. Yet, its very success and rapidity of growth is down to the founding fathers' insistence on 'running code and rough consensus' with the open protocols of the Internet, allowing any compliant network to work seamlessly into the whole and, most recently, for the millions of apps and Internet clouds to spring up for mobile devices, giving users unparalleled computing power at their fingertips. The interests of cybersecurity as interpreted by some states could quickly put a dampener on the flow of such innovation.

A useful conceptual distinction can be made between *cyber exploits*, where the intention is to penetrate networks for the purpose of intelligence gathering, and *cyberattacks*, with the intent to corrupt, deny, or destroy key information (including that in control systems). The coming Internet of Things poses real risks of malicious attacks for financial gain or for malicious damage, as do the myriad control systems that are present at every level of the critical national infrastructure and its key suppliers, almost all of whom are in the private sector. Putting to one side the apocalyptic fantasies of the complete collapse of urban civilization as a result of cyber war, the opportunities for sabotage for the purposes of intimidation, or to place significant obstacles in the way of a state trying to defend itself, add a new dimension to the concept of friction in war. The management of these issues, as many of the chapters in this *Handbook* discuss, is going to involve a combination of more responsible behaviour by employees and citizens generally, and the introduction of more secure technologies, some of which are still to be developed. What is clear is that no set of security measures that significantly impede people doing their jobs, or enjoying their social lives to the full, is going to succeed because all that will do is encourage even more insecure workarounds.

The Oxford Handbook of Cybersecurity comes, therefore, at the right moment and I hope for all our sakes that it will be widely read, digested, and acted upon in the years to come.

LIST OF FIGURES

1.1.	The Greek hydraulic semaphore	13
1.2.	A replica of one of Chappe's semaphore towers in Nalbach, Germany	14
1.3.	Spread of the Chappe Telegraph, 1793–1854	15
1.4.	Telegraph Connections (Telegraphen Verbindungen), 1891, *Stielers Hand-Atlas*, Plate No. 5, 'Weltkarte in Mercators projection'	17
1.5.	Undersea telecommunications cables	18
1.6.	The TCP/IP model and the OSI reference model	20
1.7.	How the Internet implements cyberspace	21
1.8.	Internet users in 2015 as a percentage of a country's population	21
1.9.	Reasoning about systems and reasoning about system models	26
7.1.	Evolution of cyberattacks	110
7.2.	Cybercriminals and the law	115
7.3.	Anticipated threat themes	117
7.4.	Leveraging Ontologies	119
7.5.	Cybersecurity Metrics and the OODA Loop	123
9.1.	Cyber Incident Lifecycle	144
9.2.	General Model for Vulnerability Mitigation	154
12.1.	Categorization of cyber terrorism	188
26.1.	A Cybersecurity Risk adaptive framework	430
33.1.	Three main types of relationships	550
46.1.	Existing instruments related to state use of information and communication technologies by topic. Source: compiled on the basis of Tikk, E. (2018). 'National Cybersecurity Legislation: Is There a Magic Formula?'. In *Cybersecurity Best Practices*, edited by Bartsch M. and Frey S. Springer Fachmedien, Wiesbaden.	757
46.2.	Existing instruments related to state use of information and communication technologies by venue. Source: compiled on the basis of Tikk, E. (2018). 'National Cybersecurity Legislation: Is There a Magic Formula?'. In *Cybersecurity Best Practices*, edited by Bartsch M. and Frey S. Springer Fachmedien, Wiesbaden.	757
46.3.	Normative gap analysis	758
47.1.	Conceptualizing the intersection between cybersecurity and development	771
47.2.	Active mobile-broadband subscriptions per 100 inhabitants by level of development. Source: ITU (2018a).	772

LIST OF TABLES

2.1	Headline descriptions of classes of dependence for critical infrastructure	43
6.1	Stolen credit cards – market values circa 2013–2015	96
27.1	An assessment of defence sector's contribution to national cybersecurity.	455
31.1	Microsoft's proposed norms	524
33.1	Non-state proxies based on organizational structure	546
43.1	Examples of arguments for possible military or economic advantages and disadvantages of advanced automation/maturing autonomous physical and cyber systems that require validation	709
43.2	Several technical risks associated with maturing autonomy in cyber systems	712

List of Contributors

Debi Ashenden is Professor of Cyber Security at the University of Portsmouth, UK, and the University of Adelaide, Australia.

Greg Austin is Head of the Programme on Cyber, Space and Future Conflict at the International Institute for Strategic Studies (IISS), and Professor of Cyber Security, Strategy, and Diplomacy at the University of New South Wales.

Marcello Balduccini is Assistant Professor, Department of Decision and System Sciences at Saint Joseph's University, Philadelphia.

Roger Bradbury is Emeritus Professor of Complex Systems Science at the Australian National University.

José Eduardo Malta de Sá Brandão is Deputy Director of International Studies, Political and Economic Relations at the Institute for Applied Economic Research (IPEA), Brazil.

Roderic Broadhurst is Professor of Criminology at the Australian National University Cybercrime Observatory.

Ben Buchanan is Assistant Teaching Professor at Georgetown University School of Foreign Service.

John Carr OBE is Secretary to the Children's Charities' Coalition on Internet Safety, and Visiting Senior Fellow at the London School of Economics and Political Science.

Madeline Carr is Professor of Global Politics and Cybersecurity, and Director of the Research Institute in Socio-technical Cyber Security (RISCS), Department of Computer Science at University College London.

Fred Cate is Vice President for Research, Distinguished Professor, and C. Ben Dutton Professor of Law at Indiana University, and Senior Policy Advisor to the Centre for Information Policy Leadership.

Dave Clemente is Head of Cyber Risk Research, Deloitte, UK.

Alexander Corbeil is Digital Fellow at Concordia University and Sessional Lecturer at Carleton University, Ottawa.

Paul Cornish is Visiting Professor, LSE IDEAS, at the London School of Economics.

Chris Demchak is Professor and Grace Hopper Chair of Cyber Security at the Cyber and Innovation Policy Institute (CIPI), and Senior Cyber Scholar in the Strategic and Operational Research Department (SORD) at the US Naval War College.

Rachel Dockery is Senior Research Fellow in Cybersecurity and Privacy Law at Indiana University Maurer School of Law.

Florian J. Egloff is Senior Researcher at the Center for Security Studies (CSS), ETH Zurich, and Research Associate at the Centre for Technology and Global Affairs (CTGA), University of Oxford.

David Fidler is Senior Fellow for Cybersecurity and Global Health, Council on Foreign Relations, Washington DC.

Franz-Stefan Gady is Research Fellow at the Institute for International Strategic Studies, London.

Sandro Gaycken is Director of the Digital Society Institute at ESMT Berlin and Director of the NATO Science for Peace and Security Programme (Cyberdefence Projects).

Melissa Hathaway is President of Hathaway Global Strategies LLC and former cyber advisor to President George W. Bush and President Barack Obama.

Caitríona Heinl is Executive Director of the Azure Forum for Contemporary Security Strategy, Ireland, and Adjunct Research Fellow at the School of Politics and International Relations (SPIRe), University College Dublin.

Michael Huth is Professor of Computer Science, Department of Computing, at Imperial College London.

Eva Ignatuschtschenko is a former Research Fellow at the Global Cyber Security Capacity Centre, Oxford Martin School, University of Oxford.

Nigel Inkster CMG is Senior Advisor at the International Institute for Strategic Studies, London.

Lawrence John (Major, USAF, retired) is Distinguished Analyst and Industrial Base Systems Engineer at Analytic Services Inc.

Camino Kavanagh is Senior Visiting Fellow at the Department of War Studies, King's College London.

Anastasiya Kazakova is Public Affairs Manager at Kaspersky, Moscow.

Jaclyn Kerr is an Affiliate at the Center for International Security and Cooperation, Stanford University.

Mika Kerttunen is Senior Research Scientist at the Department of Software Science, Tallinn University of Technology.

Elaine Korzak is Visiting Assistant Professor of Cybersecurity at Middlebury Institute of International Studies at Monterey, Palo Alto, California.

Tang Lan is Research Professor and Deputy Director of the Institute of Information and Social Development, China Institutes of Contemporary of International Relations (CICIR), Beijing.

Herbert Lin is Senior Research Scholar (Center for International Security and Cooperation) and Hank J. Holland Fellow (Hoover Institution), Stanford University.

Jon R. Lindsay is an Associate Professor at the Georgia Institute of Technology, School of Cybersecurity and Privacy, and in the Sam Nunn School of International Affairs.

Tim Maurer is Senior Fellow and Co-Director of the Cyber Policy Initiative at the Carnegie Endowment for International Peace, Washington DC.

Stuart Murdoch is the Founder and CEO of Surevine, London.

David Mussington is Professor of the Practice, School of Public Policy, University of Maryland College Park.

Yoko Nitta is Senior Fellow and Russia Study Group Chair at the Japan Society for Security and Crisis Management (JSSC), Tokyo.

Elina Noor is Visiting Fellow at the Institute of Strategic and International Studies, Malaysia.

Onora O'Neill is an Emeritus Honorary Professor of Philosophy at Cambridge, and has been a crossbench member of the House of Lords since 2000.

David Omand GCB is Visiting Professor in the War Studies Department, King's College London. and a former UK Security and Intelligence Coordinator, Permanent Secretary to the Home Office, Director of GCHQ, and Deputy Under Secretary of State for Policy at the UK Ministry of Defence.

Lara Pace is an independent analyst, has worked with government, academia, and multilaterals in more than 60 jurisdictions.

Jonathon Penney is Research Fellow at Citizen Lab, University of Toronto, and at the Berkman Klein Center for Internet and Society, Harvard University.

David J. Pym is Professor in Department of Computer Science and Department of Philosophy, UCL, and Institute of Philosophy, University of London.

Rafal Rohozinski is Principal, SecDev Group, Ottawa.

Anton Shingarev is Vice President for Corporate Relations, Yandex, and Visiting Scholar at the Higher School of Economics, Moscow.

Mike Steinmetz is Principal, Digital Executive, Limited. Director and General Partner at College Hill Ventures PBC, and Adjunct Professor at Boston College and Woods College. He was formerly State Cybersecurity Officer and Homeland Security Advisor for the State of Rhode Island.

Tim Stevens is Senior Lecturer in Global Security at the Department of War Studies, King's College London.

Arun Mohan Sukumar is Head of Cyber Initiative, Observer Research Foundation, Mumbai.

Lior Tabansky is Head of Research Development at the Blavatnik Interdisciplinary Cyber Research Center, Tel Aviv University.

Eneken Tikk is affiliate researcher of the Erik Castrén Institute of the University of Helsinki and Executive Producer, Cyber Policy Institute, Jyväskylä, Finland.

Tim Unwin CMG is Emeritus Professor of Geography and Chairholder of the UNESCO Chair in ICT4D at Royal Holloway, University of London.

Nicole van der Meulen is an expert in cybersecurity and former security advisor for the Dutch Banking Association.

Claire Vishik is a Fellow and GMT CTO at the Intel Corporation.

Joëlle Webb is a former Fellow at the Weatherhead Center for International Affairs, Harvard University, 2016–18.

Thomas Wingfield is Deputy Assistant Secretary of Defense for Cyber Policy, United States Department of Defense.

Harry Wingo is a Faculty Member at the College of Information and Cyberspace, National Defense University, Washington, DC.

INTRODUCTION

PAUL CORNISH

CYBER security has come to occupy a prominent position in public policy debates (nationally and internationally), in corporate risk analysis, and in the private lives of individual people. Vast amounts of public and corporate effort and investment are devoted to making cyber space more secure from a spectrum of security threats and challenges, including nuisance hacking, insider security breaches, criminality (ranging from low-level theft through to serious, organized activities involving data theft, sexual abuse, and large-scale financial fraud), commercial espionage, political subversion, national security espionage, terrorism and political extremism, and inter-state conflict. Many of these challenges are familiar and need little elaboration. Others are relatively novel, such as the undermining of democratic institutions and their associated legal and electoral processes, the vulnerabilities of health implantables, and the governance of algorithmic decision making. For its part, the public is reminded endlessly of the need for 'cyber hygiene' and hears news almost daily of another cyber 'hack' or 'attack' against national or corporate interests, of foreign interference in domestic politics, and even apocalyptic warnings of imminent 'cyber war'.

Yet, in spite of these risks and anxieties, the world is becoming ever more deeply dependent on the digital environment. When dependency of any sort is unmanaged and unmitigated, it can soon become the basis of vulnerability. In other words, a vicious spiral is created: as societies, governments, corporations, and individuals become more dependent on the digital environment, so they also become increasingly vulnerable to misuse of that environment, and particularly so when there is an inability or reluctance to close or even merely to manage the vulnerability. Vulnerability is increasingly a function of much of what goes on in the digital environment and, when mitigation is lacking, that vulnerability becomes increasingly brittle, possibly even critical. As well as the threats, hazards, and risks listed earlier, the users of cyber space have therefore become, in a sense, a threat to themselves.

In this ostensibly hazardous, even menacing, environment, it is scarcely surprising that a considerable industry should have developed to provide the means with which to make cyber space more secure, stable, and predictable: threat monitoring and intelligence reporting; hardware and software security; penetration testing; online awareness training; and consultancy of every conceivable sort. The case for the cyber security industry seems compelling enough. On the one hand, the 'threat picture' includes adversaries who are highly skilled, aggressive, and fast-moving while, on the other hand, that which they threaten is becoming ever more valuable to its users. A cynic might argue that cyber *in*security has become a rather compelling and self-serving business case in that, for as long as cyber space is not secure, there is commercial opportunity in managing that insecurity without resolving it. If the cyber security industry is vigorous and expansive, similar things might be said of another sector that has also been developing rapidly. Research and analysis of cyber security as a phenomenon in national and international public policy now receives considerable attention around the world in the media, in think tanks, and in academia. The coverage is wide-ranging and varies in style, quality, and coverage from the highly technical to the policy-analytical to what might, again, be described as self-servingly alarmist.

Cyber security is concerned with the identification, avoidance, management, and mitigation of risk in, or from, cyber space—the risk of harm and damage that might occur as the result of everything from individual carelessness to organized criminality, to industrial and national security espionage, and, at the extreme end of the scale, to disabling attacks against a country's critical national infrastructure. But this account represents a rather narrow understanding of security and there is much more to cyber space than vulnerability, risk, and threat. As any university lecture on international and national security would point out, the pursuit of security *from* financial loss, physical damage, etc. should not be seen as an end in itself. Security must also be *for* something: more than simply the avoidance or elimination of risk, security is also essential for the maximization of benefit. This important point is often explained by analogy. When we lock our front door to protect our house, ourselves, and our property from thieves and predators, we take this action not because we see ourselves as an agent of law enforcement but in order that we can enjoy what we have, live as we choose, and grow as we need. Security, including cyber security, is protective but it is also liberating and enabling. This applies at every level—individually, nationally, and globally—and it could scarcely be more positive and constructive.

It makes little or no sense to approach cyber security from a narrow perspective, categorizing and analysing cyber security according to this or that functional perspective or political level, concerned only with protection from threat, danger, harm, and loss. The security of cyber space is as much technological as it is commercial and strategic; as much international as regional, national, and personal; and as much a matter of hazard and vulnerability as an opportunity for social, economic, and cultural growth. Consistent with this outlook, the *Oxford Handbook of Cyber Security* takes a comprehensive and rounded approach to the still evolving topic of cyber security. The structure of the *Handbook* is intended to show that cyber security is far more than a matter of threat, vulnerability, and conflict, serious though these matters are; that it manifests on many (if not all) levels of human interaction; and that an understanding of cyber security requires us to think not just in terms of policy and strategy but also in terms of technology, economy, sociology, criminology, trade, and morality. Accordingly, contributors to the *Handbook* include experts in cyber security from around the world and from a wide range of perspectives: former government officials, private sector executives, technologists, political scientists, strategists, lawyers, criminologists, ethicists, security consultants, and policy analysts.

With a Foreword by Professor Sir David Omand GCB, former UK Security and Intelligence Coordinator and Director of the UK Government Communications Headquarters (GCHQ), the *Handbook* comprises 48 chapters organized in 11 parts. Part I—'Cyber Space: What it is and Why it Matters' sets out the origins, character, and dynamics of cyber space and explores certain of the moral, intellectual, and practical questions it poses. Parts II to IV are concerned with cyber space as an environment of vulnerability, threat, and confrontation of three different (though often overlapping) types: 'Cyber Crime' (Part II); 'Extremism and Terrorism' (Part III); and 'State-Sponsored Cyber Attacks' (Part IV). Having examined prominent challenges and threats to security in and from cyber space, the *Handbook* then turns its attention to security-seeking responses and practices, at various levels: 'Technical and Corporate Cyber Security' (Part V); 'Personal Cyber Security' (Part VI); 'National Cyber Security' (Part VII); 'Global Trade and Cyber Security' (Part VIII); and 'International Cyber Security' (Part IX). The penultimate set of chapters—Part X: 'Perspectives on Cyber Security'—analyses the approach to cyber security in six countries—the People's Republic of China, India, Israel, Japan, Malaysia, and the Russian Federation. A complete account of national perspectives would, of course, require the inclusion of almost 200 chapters, which would exceed by some pages the capacity of this *Handbook*. It is hoped, nevertheless, that these six chapters will help to offset any bias that might be perceived in the *Handbook* in favour of European and North American views and preferences and, more importantly, will capture something of the wealth of experience of cyber security that has been gained around the world in a variety of environments and circumstances. Finally, in Part XI: 'Future Challenges', the *Handbook* invites seven authors to suggest what technological and human challenges might lie ahead.

PART I

CYBER SPACE: WHAT IT IS AND WHY IT MATTERS

CHAPTER 1

THE ORIGINS OF CYBERSPACE

DAVID J. PYM

DEFINING CYBERSPACE

ACCORDING to *The Oxford English Dictionary* (OED)[1]:

cyberspace |ˈsʌɪbəspeɪs|
noun [mass noun]
the notional environment in which communication over computer networks occurs. *I stayed in cyberspace for just a few minutes.*

According to *The Oxford Dictionary of Science Fiction* (Prucher 2007):

the entirety of the data stored in, and the communication that takes place within a computer network, conceived of as having the properties of a physical realm; ...

My purpose here is to unpack and explain these definitions, which are wholly consistent with each other. In contrast to the approach of Hook and Norman (2002), who achieve an enormously impressive coverage of relevant material, my guiding principle is to explore the sense in which cyberspace is a 'space', a concept that is well understood in mathematics and physics, and the understanding of which in those fields is alluded to in the term 'cyberspace'.

The modern world is more-or-less wholly dependent for its operation on networks of communicating computers. These computers come in all shapes and sizes. They may be small devices embedded in everyday objects such as watches and household appliances, or cars, or personal laptops and workstations, or vast datacentres supporting the infrastructure of cloud computing. What is central to their function is communication—that is, the transmission of data—over local networks, wider corporate or government networks, or the Internet itself.[2]

In more detail, the Internet consists of a global network of networks that connect computers around the world and use a collection of communications protocols, including TCP/IP (Transmission Control Protocol/Internet Protocol, the basic language that the connected computers use to communicate with one another), and others such as OSPF

(Open Shortest Path First), BGP (Border Gateway Protocol), and RIP (Routing Information Protocol), which together describe how *data* should be decomposed into packets (the basic units of data handled by the protocol), addressed, transmitted, routed, and received. Data (which can be treated as a singular, plural, or mass noun) consists of blocks ('bits' and 'bytes') of binary numbers. Data itself has no inherent meaning, but data is used to *represent* features of physical or abstract worlds; that is, *information*.[3,4]

When thinking of the Internet, it is often tempting to conflate it with the World Wide Web (WWW). While this is quite understandable in many ways—and the distinction is often blurred in common discourse—it is a conceptual mistake. The WWW—with its language of Universal Resource Locators, or URLs—organizes data representations of information in a highly structured way and is just one of many applications that are supported by the Internet.[5]

The distinction between data and information—which is directly analogous, though not identical, to the distinctions between syntax and semantics that are made in logic and linguistics—is very important in our context. While it is data that the Internet processes, and which is used in the WWW to represent information in structured ways, it is information to which human beings relate.

Indeed, the WWW is often described as being an 'information space', but what is the concept of a *space* that is being invoked here? In fact, the concept of space is quite delicate. It is in mathematics—in particular, in geometry and topology—that it has been richly developed. The idea starts with the familiar three-dimensional environment, in which everyday objects have relative position and direction, and its more-or-less intuitive generalization to the four-dimensional environment, often called 'space-time' in which such objects also have relative position in time.

Although a formal mathematical definition is not needed for our purposes, the mathematical concept has quite strongly influenced the informal concept that I shall need. According to the OED[1]:

> space |speɪs|
> noun [mass noun]
> ...
> Mathematics: a mathematical concept generally regarded as a set of points having some specified structure. One of the most important examples of the mathematical concept is that of *topological space*.

Topological spaces are a way of describing geometrical properties and spatial relationships that are unaffected by the continuous change of shape or size of figures. An important example of a topological space is *metric space* in which there is assigned a distance—with, essentially, the familiar intuitive meaning of physical distance—between each pair of points.

These ideas of proximity translate not only to the network architecture of the Internet, but also to the data-representation of information in the WWW (though the situation is quite complicated and here I am simplifying matters greatly).

For our present purpose, the concept of space that is useful, and which builds on the mathematical ideas mentioned earlier, derives from a key concept in computer science—namely, *distributed systems* (Collinson, Monahan, and Pym 2012). According to the OED[1]:

> distributed system |dəˈstrɪbjudəd ˌsɪstəm|
> noun
> a number of independent computers linked by a network.

THE ORIGINS OF CYBERSPACE   9

Examples of distributed systems include the following:

- The Internet itself—a vast collection of interconnected networks of computers. Individual computers connected to the Internet interact by passing messages, which they do by employing a common means of communication (which will be described later on in this chapter).
- Intranets—localized parts of the Internet that are managed by identified organizations that, typically, enforce local management and security policies to control access and use. Intranets are connected to the wider Internet by special-purpose computers called 'routers', which also employ the common means of communication.
- Cloud computing infrastructure—vast data centres, consisting of hundreds of thousands of servers, provide storage and computer services for vast quantities of data that are fed from the intranets of large numbers of clients who are logically and physically widely distributed. A key problem here, and in distributed systems more generally, is to maintain the consistency of the different copies while simultaneously maintaining the robustness of the service: see, for example, the CAP (Consistency, Availability, Partition-tolerance) theorem in the theory of distributed systems, also known as 'Brewer's theorem' (https://en.wikipedia.org/wiki/CAP_theorem), which establishes that only two of the CAP properties can be maintained simultaneously. Handling this problem is important in maintaining the experience of cyberspace.
- Mobile and ubiquitous computing (and the Internet of Things)—laptops, phones, cameras, and wearable devices such as watches and spectacles, as well as cars, domestic appliances, smart meters, and electricity substations. Indeed, almost everything on which modern society depends is integrated into distributed systems. They reside on local networks that communicate with other local networks and devices, either directly ('peer-to-peer') or via network-based servers, all employing the common means of communication.
- The global banking system—the intranets belonging to each of the world's banks must not only provide services locally (logically locally, even if not physically locally) to the banks' own customers but must also communicate with one other in order to support the transactions upon which the world's commerce depends.
- Online games with multiple players—each player's local, or home, computer runs a client copy of the game, which communicates with the central game server, which communicates with other players' local games, and coordinates the overall interaction between all the players.

From a mathematical perspective, the basis of computer science and to which I shall return later, the key concepts of distributed systems are the following (Anderson and Pym 2016; Barwise and Seligman 1997; Caulfield and Pym 2015; Collinson, Monahan, and Pym (2012); Coulouris et al. 2011):

- *Locations*: a collection of linked places, be they physical or virtual, that constitutes the basic architecture of a system. Individual computers, file stores, and so on exist at locations within a distributed system, but locations are also the places within computers where the CPU (Central Processing Unit) and other components reside.
- *Resources*: the entities that a system uses—consumes, creates, moves—in the course of its operations. Examples of resources include the memory locations where data is stored, the

processor cycles available to perform computations, and human operators required to manage and maintain systems.

- *Processes*: the collection of activities, which are mostly concurrent, that constitutes a system's operations, and so delivers its services. Examples of services include a bank's customer-facing website, streaming films, and the multitude of system-level services provided by a computer's operating system in order to perform computations, manage the keyboard and screen, manage a computer's memory and storage, send and receive email, etc.

Additionally, a specific system, described using these components, resides within an *environment*, and resource transfers between the system and its environment characterize the service that the system provides.

So, here the relevant 'space' consists in the distribution of resources around the locations of the system and the presence of processes that manipulate those resources. This definition might seem a bit restrictive but, in the distributed systems metaphor, the presence and activities of a human being (using a computer, posting to Facebook, downloading a file, and so on) simply amounts to the presence of a process.

The term 'cyberspace' is derived from 'cybernetics' and 'space', and the meaning of the term depends essentially, though quite implicitly, on the distributed systems metaphor. The term 'cybernetics' was introduced in the late 1940s by Norbert Wiener (1948, 1950). According to the OED[1]:

cybernetics |sʌɪbə'nɛtɪks|
plural noun [treated as sing.]
the science of communications and automatic control systems in both machines and living things.

ORIGIN 1940s: from Greek *kubernētēs* '*steersman*', from *kubernan* '*to steer*'.

There are several aspects of this definition that are important for the idea of cyberspace. That it refers to 'automatic control systems' may perhaps seem rather restrictive, but I think that should be seen as a consequence of the perspective of the age of the definition: in the 1940s, although the idea of automated control of machines was well understood, the scope of the information technological revolution that was to come had not been anticipated. It mentions also communications. As I have described, the concept of communication, and a common means of supporting it, is a key aspect of distributed systems.

So, now I have all the components, I need to return to the OED definition of cyberspace given earlier. Let us try to understand this rather concise definition using the concepts we've considered so far. First, what are 'computer networks'? The appropriate metaphor here—which I have already discussed at some length is that of distributed systems. Computers, be they servers, workstations, laptops, phones, controllers embedded in cars, aeroplanes, or refrigerators—or even entire data centres—are resources that reside at locations.

Second, what does 'communication over' mean? Computers residing at locations communicate with other such devices residing at other locations using wired and wireless connections. These connections transfer data between located devices using the TCP/IP protocol.

Last, what is meant by the 'notional environment'? It seems that this is where the presence of human interpreters becomes essential. The distributed systems metaphor completely accounts for the infrastructure and its processing of data, so the 'notional environment' can only be something that is experienced by the users of the infrastructure.

Users provide the interpretations of data and its movement around the infrastructure that constitute the 'information environment'. Now, in principle, every data item is a discrete entity and the collection of all such items in the (albeit vast, massively interconnected) infrastructure of the Internet is finite and so can be counted.

From the perspective of the users, however, things look very different. This is for two reasons. First, end-users (as opposed to users who are systems professionals) primarily perceive information, not data. A picture received on a phone may be a finite collection of pixels, but it represents an image of the physical world of substances and qualities. Second, the exchange of information mediates communication between humans, in a shared social space that is created by the technology and its users, and that communication is almost never wholly captured by the data that is exchanged.

Only with this last component is the definition of cyberspace—and its characterization as a mass noun—really meaningful.

The origin of the word 'cyberspace' does not lie in hard science. Rather, it was coined in science fiction, by William Gibson, first in a short story, 'Burning Chrome', in 1982 and reused a little later in his celebrated novel, *Neuromancer*, in 1984. Not only does Gibson introduce the term but he also offers a definition:

> A consensual hallucination experienced daily by billions of legitimate operators, in every nation, by children being taught mathematical concepts ... A graphic representation of data abstracted from the banks of every computer in the human system. Unthinkable complexity. Lines of light ranged in the nonspace of the mind, clusters and constellations of data.

It can be seen that Gibson's definition, albeit expressed in a novelist's style, anticipates more-or-less all our analysis: a highly complex distributed system, the representation of data, and the presence of human minds. Indeed, it seems to capture very directly the experiences of humans who engage in 'immersive' or 'virtual reality' games with other players who may be physically located in many distributed locations, but who together inhabit a shared environment of data that they collectively, and consistently, interpret as the 'world' of their game.

Cyberspace is also an important component of conflict in the modern world (Rid 2013; Singer and Friedman 2014) and, consequently, the world's military and defence agencies have considered the significance of what is increasingly known as the 'cyber *battle*space' for their strategies and operations. Indeed, some of them have even attempted to formulate their own definitions—for example, the US Department of Defense in 2008 (Schachtman 2008):

> a global domain within the information environment consisting of the interdependent network of information technology infrastructures, including the Internet, telecommunications networks, computer systems, and embedded processors and controllers.

Here, it is important to understand that the use the term 'domain' refers not to what is usual in computer science, where it describes a collection of addresses within the Internet, such as everything with a '.com' or '.uk' suffix, but rather it refers to a domain of warfare, the other four being land, sea, air, and space. Again, it is clear that a distinguishing feature of the cyber domain is its combination of the virtual/digital and the physical.

In summary, then, what have I described about cyberspace so far?

- First, that it is a concept that builds on the physical and logical infrastructure provided by the Internet.
- Second, that, while the Internet processes data, it is information—that is, interpreted data—that is the medium of cyberspace.
- Third, that the interpretation of data, and the processing of information, are performed by humans, who are themselves essential components of cyberspace. Together, the human participants inhabit the shared *social space* that is an essential component of cyberspace.
- Fourth, that there is an essential interplay between—indeed, a merging of—the physical and the virtual.

So far, I have concentrated on unpacking the concepts that constitute cyberspace and their associated language. These concepts have, however, a substantial backstory through human history, and it is long and rich.

Before embarking on the story, I should note that it is not possible in a short chapter such as this one to represent fully and acknowledge all of what is a vast literature. Accordingly, the sources I reference are intended only to be suggestive of the literature, and I apologize unreservedly to anyone who feels unjustly treated. I note also that I am not a professional historian and I make no claim to historical completeness in this article.

Cyberspace in the Ancient and Early Modern World: Beacons and Semaphores

Travelling between widely separated cities, by walking, riding horses, and sailing in ships takes a long time. Messages sent by these means are therefore slow to arrive. For example, during the negotiation of the Treaty of Westphalia in Münster and Osnabrück in 1648, it took two weeks for a letter to reach Stockholm.[6] Consequently, governments and others throughout history have sought ways of communicating more rapidly.

Perhaps the simplest form of rapid long-distance communication is the *beacon*, a fire lighted on a hill to give warning of, say, an approaching enemy. A sequence of beacons on a chain of hills can give rapid warning over long distances—it takes just a few minutes to light a fire, and the signal then travels at the speed of light—but, of course, the language of communication is rather restricted.

In the fourth century BCE, the Greek military strategist Aineias Taktikos described a partial solution, the 'Greek hydraulic telegraph'—as explained at, for example, https://en.wikipedia.org/wiki/Hydraulic_telegraph, where more detail and further references can be found.[7] Fire torches were used, by the sender, to initiate and synchronize, with the receiver, a connection between operators at observation points on hills with clear lines of sight between them. Each hill had an identical container, with a valve or spigot at the bottom, filled with water and with a vertical rod floating in the water. The rods were marked with codes at points along their length. The set-up is depicted in Figure 1.1.

FIGURE 1.1. The Greek hydraulic semaphore

Once the connection was synchronized, each operator would open the valve until the water had emptied to the point marking the required code, at which point the operators would close their valves and simultaneously lower their torches. The length of time the sender's torch remained raised determined a specific, predetermined message. In principle, such a system could be used to send messages in full written language, but, in practice, it would seem likely that the need for efficiency would dictate a small, fixed set of possible messages.

Does the technology of beacons and semaphores, as developed from the Greek world, support something that corresponds to the concept of cyberspace? First, there is an underlying physical infrastructure, chains of torch beacons and data-processing water containers, which form a network of communication routes. This network supports logical connections between the individuals wishing to communicate with other individuals at other locations. Second, while the system of beacons and containers transmit data from location to location, it is the humans who send the messages (not the operators of the infrastructure) and who interpret the data, giving it meaning as information. Last, there is indeed an essential interplay between the physical and virtual. I think I must conclude that the fourth century BCE had a form of cyberspace.

A major advance in the development of cyberspace occurred in late seventeenth-century France. 'Le système Chappe', developed by Claude Chappe (see, for example, https://en.wikipedia.org/wiki/Claude_Chappe and also Standage's delightful book, *The Victorian Internet* (1998), was a nationwide semaphore network used for (relatively complex) government and military communications. At its greatest extent, it connected Paris to Amsterdam and Calais to the north, to Mainz, Strasbourg, and Venice to the east, to Marseille, Perpignan, and Bayonne to the south, and to Nantes, Brest, and Cherbourg to the west.

Chappe's system was a network of towers (see Figures 1.2, 1.3), each of which supported two arms that rotated into different positions. The positions included codes for letters and numbers as well as for control signals used to verify the correctness of the reproduction of the messages as they passed from one tower to the next.

Somewhat later, in 1838, an English civil engineer called Francis Whishaw also proposed a hydraulic telegraph. Whishaw's hydraulic telegraph[8] was based on the levels of water observed in vessels connected by water-filled pipes: a change in level at one end, representing

FIGURE 1.2. A replica of one of Chappe's semaphore towers in Nalbach, Germany

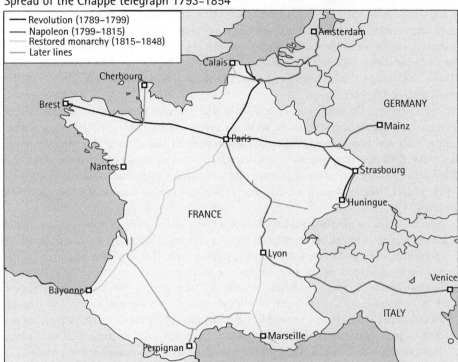

Map of France showing the spread of the Chappe telegraph. Information provided by Jean-Claude Bastian, telegraphe-chappe.com

FIGURE 1.3. Spread of the Chappe Telegraph, 1793–1854

the sent message, is reflected at the receiving end of the pipe with no perceptible time delay. This proposal represents a possible improvement in both speed and reliability, but essentially the same sense of a cyber space as the Greek version.

Amusingly, the term 'semaphore' persists in the modern world of information technology in the theory and practice of concurrency, in which two computer programs execute at the same time while attempting to use shared resources. In this context, a semaphore refers to a variable, or other abstract data type, that is used to control access to a resource between concurrently executing processes.

Some Key Concepts

Before considering cyberspace in the modern world, in the sections that follow, it is important to mention three of its other key precursors, all of which have contributed to its technological and social infrastructures:

- *The commercially available printing press*: Printing presses have existed in China and Korea for around 1,800 years, but it is perhaps Gutenberg's introduction of a commercially available, and well-promoted, service that marks the entry of printing into a 'space' of communication. Copies of single handwritten manuscripts, representing resources of knowledge and typeset using 'standard' characters, could be mass produced and circulated widely. Thus, knowledge could be shared around many distinct locations, commented on, modified, and further shared.
- *Postal services*: Although commercial printing presses provided a means of mass-producing information resources, so that they might be consumed by many different individuals residing at many different locations, the realization of this sharing requires a process for circulating copies of manuscripts. Postal services provided the first reliable such processes and, in so doing, adumbrate some concepts that are important in modern cyber space. These include the following (with no particular historical period or timeline implied):
    - *Addresses*: the sender of a package writes a code on the package that specifies the destination and recipient of the package; the service provider interprets the code in order to execute the process of delivering the package: for this to work, addresses must be written in an agreed, or at least recognizable, format;
    - *Routing protocols*: packages might be collected from widely distributed starting points, such as letter boxes, then taken to a local collecting point and combined into large groups of packages that are moved to a distant collecting point (possibly involving many such steps), from where individual packages are delivered to their final destinations; to make this work, the provider of the postal services must implement processes that collect, sort, and distribute packages; and
    - *A supporting infrastructure*: the service provider must provide the equipment (postage stamps, letter boxes, bags, vehicles, buildings, etc.) and personnel to collect, sort, and distribute the packages; the provider may also make use of other services, such as stage coaches, trains, and aeroplanes, and must agree terms of service with them.

A postal service, viewed as a service to its users, also has two key features:
- *Mass availability*: the service is available to all who are able to purchase the tokens, such as stamps, required to access the service;
- *Service guarantees*: state actors, such as monarchs or governments, might provide guarantees, with supporting policies, that packages will be delivered to their intended destinations and recipients, and that they will be undamaged in transit.
- *Telephone systems*: Such systems also provide examples of the importance of the concepts of addresses, routing protocols, and supporting infrastructure. It also demonstrates mass availability and, at least implicitly, service guarantees.

Agar's *The Government Machine* (2016) provides an excellent general contextual discussion for this perspective, exploring the mechanization of government work in the United Kingdom from the nineteenth to the early twenty-first century.

The Beginnings of Cyberspace in the Modern World: Semaphores and Telegraphs

A key technology of the Victorian period, the telegraph system developed in the 1830s and 1840s by Samuel Morse, provides another example of the importance of the concepts of addresses, routing protocols, and supporting infrastructure. It also demonstrates mass availability and, at least implicitly, service guarantees.

According to the OED[1]:

> telegraph, n. — a system of or instrument for sending messages or information to a distant place; v. — to signal (from French *télégraph*)

I have explained that the idea of an optical telegraph dates from the ancient world. Perhaps the most well-known early precursor to the Internet, however, and certainly the one with the strongest resemblance, is the telegraph system developed in the nineteenth century. The history of this 'Victorian Internet' has been elegantly and captivatingly described in Standage's (1998) book, which, as we shall see, helps us to understand its significance for the origins of the concept of cyberspace.

Figure 1.4 illustrates the major global telegraph connections around the world in 1891. Compare with the modern map of telecommunications cables given in Figure 1.5:

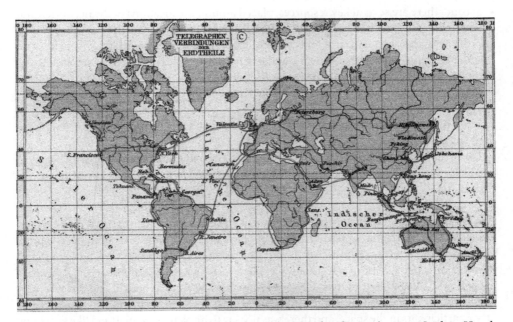

FIGURE 1.4. Telegraph Connections (Telegraphen Verbindungen), 1891, *Stielers Hand-Atlas*, Plate No. 5, 'Weltkarte in Mercators projection'

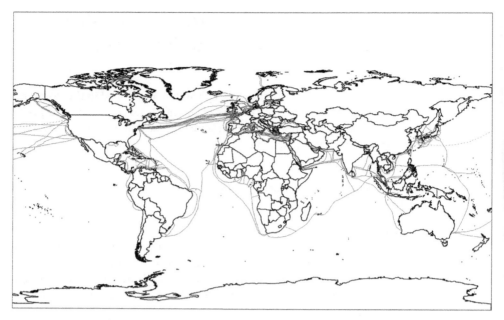

FIGURE 1.5. Undersea telecommunications cables

- First, there is an underlying network infrastructure;
- Second, there are several key resources, placed around the locations of the network infrastructure, upon which the operation of the telegraph depends—namely:
  - the network cables used to connect different points around the world;
  - the electrical devices that generate and receive the electrical signals that are used to encode messages for transmission across the network;
  - the human operators of the devices who translate between natural language and the encoded messages;
  - the paper used to write down messages to be encoded and messages that have been decoded.
- Third, the communication of messages between points on the telegraph network occurs as a collection of concurrent processes that utilize the resources present at locations around the network.

The telegraph system of the nineteenth century thus came very close to delivering a cyberspace. Many of the features of cyberspace that I have identified were present in the telegraph system—network infrastructure, key resources, and concurrent processes—but one aspect that was missing, at least in a sufficiently explicit form, was that of the shared social space created by the technology and its users. Although messages could be sent and received very efficiently, there was no way to post information that could be read and contributed to by other participants in the space; and there was no way to implement something like Facebook using the telegraph system.

The Infrastructure of Modern Cyberspace

The technology supporting worldwide data communications did not significantly advance from the telegraph (wired and wireless) until the early stages of the development of what would become the Internet. Indeed, as can be seen in Figure 1.5, the pattern of connectivity even now reflects that of the wired telegraph network (Figure 1.4).

The ARPANET—which stands for Advanced Research Projects Agency Network (https://en.wikipedia.org/wiki/ARPANET), after the United States' Advanced Research Projects Agency (https://en.wikipedia.org/wiki/DARPA) that funded its development—was the seed that would eventually grow into the Internet. It was proposed in 1968 and established in 1969, with the first link being between UCLA and Stanford University. Famously, the first message sent between the two sites was 'LO'—the first two characters of 'LOGIN'; the connection failed before the command could be completed.[9]

The ARPANET was an early 'packet-switching' network—in which transmitted data is grouped into blocks, called 'packets', that are of a suitable size (depending on things like the network's 'bandwidth') for transmission across a network—that implemented the TCP/IP protocol, upon which the modern Internet depends. Packet switching (https://en.wikipedia.org/wiki/Packet_switching) stands in contrast to 'circuit switching' (https://en.wikipedia.org/wiki/Circuit_switching), as used in early telephone networks, in which dedicated circuits are established between two points (e.g. two telephone service subscribers) that wish to communicate. Circuit switching, which does not require the overhead of decomposing messages into packets and recomposing after transmission, could be used in the Internet. However, it makes much less efficient use of the available network capacity (or 'bandwidth').

Recalling our discussion of semaphore and telegraph systems, it can be seen that although they also required a notion of packet in order to send and receive messages—words are coded as delineated sequences of coded letters, Morse code (https://en.wikipedia.org/wiki/Morse_code) —they all really worked by establishing circuits between the communicating locations, as with early telephone networks. Packet switching is perhaps the key conceptual advance of the Internet over the telegraph networks.

The TCP/IP protocol is one example, a very important example, of a specification of a network communications protocol—recall from our discussion of distributed systems the essential need for 'common means of communication'—that is tailored to the underlying physical technology that supports its operation. Such technology is not unique, however, and the Open Systems Interconnection (OSI) model provides a standardized reference—it describes the essential features of the infrastructure of the Internet. Figure 1.6 illustrates how the components of these protocols are built up, from the physical layer, providing underpinning infrastructure, through logical organizational layers, to the application layer, providing services to users. The TCP/IP model can be seen as an implementation of the OSI model—for example, the general 'Network' layer described in the OSI model is implemented by the Internet in the TCP/IP model.

Figure 1.6 depicts how, in a somewhat simplified and quite widely described form, the Internet can be seen as implementing cyberspace. To see this, first recall our summary of

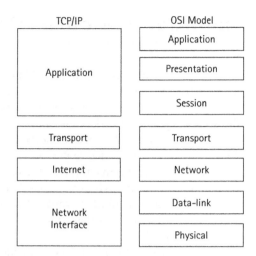

FIGURE 1.6. The TCP/IP model and the OSI reference model (many similar diagrams may be found in the literature)

cyberspace at the end of the first section. Note that, for the purposes of this discussion, I am taking cyberspace to be represented by the medium of the WWW and its use by humans.[10] Does this implementation of cyberspace deliver what we expect? Recall what we learned about cyberspace in the first section:

- First, that it is a concept that builds on the physical and logical infrastructure provided by the Internet;
- Second, that, while the Internet processes data, it is information—that is, interpreted data—that is the medium of cyberspace;
- Third, that the interpretation of data, and the processing of information, are performed by humans, who are themselves essential components of cyberspace;
- Fourth, that there is an essential interplay between—indeed, a merging of—the physical and the virtual.

The first point is clearly supported by this picture: the communication between a web browser and web server, both of which have physical location as well as logical location, is implemented by a sequence of flows of data over a physical network, but that physical network supports interpretations of that data relative to a logical architecture, which organizes the information into useful systems (of knowledge, understanding, and so on). The second and third points reside in the users' interpretations as information of the data that flows between the web browser and the web server. Finally, the fourth point summarizes the overall relationships between the components of the diagram in Figure 1.7: data and information have both physical and logical locations; data is processed at physical locations, around the loop between browser and server, but interpreted at logical locations by the human users—in, we might say, *Bewusstseinslagen*.[11]

Within cyberspace itself, as implemented by the Internet, the structural organization provided by the distributed systems model is not always the most helpful. Rather, it is sometimes more useful to infer information about cyberspace in terms of what the statistical

THE ORIGINS OF CYBERSPACE 21

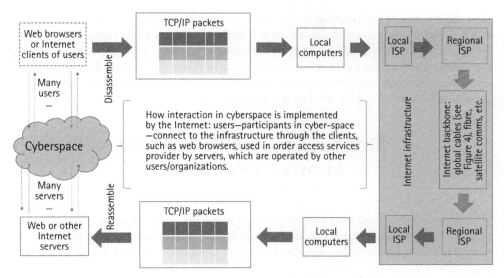

FIGURE 1.7. How the Internet implements cyberspace (many similar diagrams may be found in the literature)

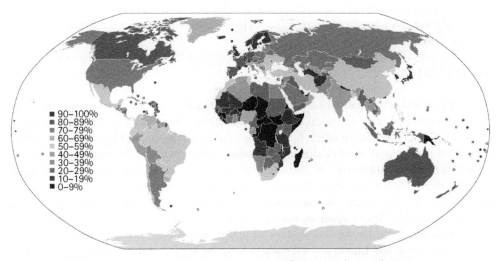

FIGURE 1.8. Internet users in 2015 as a percentage of a country's population

structure of the data and its flows tell us about patterns of use. In this context, topological modelling approaches such as that suggested in Ohmori and Kunii (2007) may also be helpful.

Examples of this kind of analysis include answering questions about the density of Internet use in different countries around the world (see, for example, Figure 1.8), which social networking sites are more popular in which countries, from where most phishing attacks originate, and with what levels of intensity, and so on. Figure 1.8 illustrates Internet users in 2015 as a percentage of a country's population.

How did a world of communication based on semaphores and Morse code sent over telegraph cables become a world dependent on Internet-supported cyberspace? The answer really is the story of the development of modern computer science (though see Isaacson 2014 for a useful perspective): I cannot hope to do justice to that in this chapter. Rather, I hope to provide a conceptual framework for understanding and reasoning about cyberspace that is applicable to all these stages in the history of cyberspace.

Modelling and Reasoning about Cyberspace

This section is primarily intended for those readers with a more mathematical, or at least philosophical, background and, in particular, for those with an interest in logic. Nevertheless, I hope that all readers who are willing to encounter a little formalism will be able to appreciate the value of the perspective I describe.

As I have described, *distributed systems* provide a model of computation in which information-processing devices are located on networks and communicate with one another, and with their environments, and coordinate their actions by passing messages between one another and between themselves and their environments. The resulting interaction of these components of systems and their environments delivers the systems' services to their clients.

Mathematically, distributed systems can be described using the following concepts, as described in Section 1:

- *Locations*: Mathematically, locations are described using topological structures that give a useful account of the (physical or virtual/logical) notion of 'place' and 'connections between places'. The leading example is perhaps directed graphs, but mathematically other structures can also be used (Collinson, Monahan, and Pym 2012). The concept of location, and its intended mathematical characterization in this context, provides the topological component that is a core part of the concept of space discussed earlier.
- *Resources*: Mathematically, resources are modelled by abstract algebraic structures called 'partial monoids'. These gadgets are sets that come with an operation, which has a unit or neutral element, for combining some, but not all, of their elements (used in Collinson, Monahan, and Pym (2012) and Ishtiaq and O'Hearn [2001]). Perhaps the most important example of such a monoid is given by the set of *natural numbers* (with 0) less than or equal to a specified maximum, *max*. Combination is addition, with unit 0. The combination of two numbers m and n is defined just in the case that $m + n$ is less than *max*. Another important example is given by the 'stack' and 'heap' in computer memory (RAM) (Ishtiaq and O'Hearn 2001).
- *Processes*: Mathematically, processes are described using structures called 'transition systems' and an important class of examples of transition systems are described by 'process algebras' (Anderson and Pym 2016; Collinson, Monahan, and Pym (2012); McKinsey and Tarski 1944).

The key idea is that the state of a system is described by a triple L, R, E consisting in the configuration of the system's locations, L, the distribution of its resources, R, around its locations, and a description, E, of the processes that are currently executing. When an action occurs during that execution, the resources are manipulated, perhaps being consumed, created, or moved to new locations.

Again, as described in Section 1, systems exist within environments with which they interact (i.e. they are part of an ecosystem). This interaction is typically described in terms of the incidence of events in and out of the model.

- *Environment*: Mathematically, the incidence of actions from the environment upon a model and, conversely, the incidence of actions from a model upon the environment can be represented simply using probability distributions. Perhaps the paradigmatic example of this is the arrival of entities, be they people or packets of data, in a queue, where the arrivals at the queue are described using the negative exponential distribution (Ross 2014), which has just one parameter, the 'arrival rate'.

With this machinery in place, I have, mathematically speaking, all I need to describe the logical and physical architecture of the Internet—that is, the infrastructure of cyberspace:

- *Locations* in the Internet are given by a range of examples that are relevant for my discussion:
  - The physical network graph: Figures 1.3, 1.4, and 1.5 give examples of network graphs; the global scale network connects regional and national networks, which, in turn, connect organizational and domestic networks.
  - The virtual network graph: organizations may be distributed across the world and yet appear to be a single network location—for example, a multinational corporation may have physical presence in many countries, but its networks may all be part of the same family of IP addresses, so that they appear as part of the same network location even though they are in many different physical locations.[12]
  - The locations of the human users of the Internet, participants in cyberspace, and the devices with which they interact and upon which the services they use depend.
- *Resources* in the Internet are things like computers, some providing computation, some providing network management, and some providing storage; peripheral devices, such as printers and scanners; security devices such as IDSs and IPSs;[13] and people, such as programmers, system administrators, and end users (the participants in cyberspace).
- *Processes* in the Internet are the things that happen. For one example, an individual computer's operating system is a program that executes continuously in order to provide all the computer's services to its users: screen, keyboard, network connection, application execution, and so on; for another, the services provided by the network of servers and routers that support the operations of an Internet service provider; and, for another, the human resources, financial, and other business processes followed by the users of information and management systems.

And, finally:

> *Environment* in this context provides a way for the modeller to focus on a particular part of the Internet, or indeed of cyberspace, while retaining an appropriate representation of the rest of the network on that specific part. While the part of interest is modelled in detail, using the concepts of location, resource, and process as described earlier, the interaction of that part with the rest of the network is modelled simply in terms of the incidence of events across the boundary of the part modelled in detail.

Although I have described a framework for describing the underlying conceptual and technical infrastructure of cyberspace, I have not yet provided a way to describe cyberspace itself: even if we consider that humans and their interaction with the architecture, and, indeed, other humans, can be described using located resources and processes, we still lack a natural way to talk about the interpretation of data and how humans reason about it. For that, we are going to take our final step: to *logic*.

Logic is the science of reasoning. It is studied within computer science, mathematics, and philosophy. It means the same thing in all these areas, although they each tend to emphasize different aspects of its study. They interact with one another very fruitfully. In computer science, in particular, it is important to become accustomed to the idea that there is no single, all-encompassing system of logic that is well adapted to all the different kinds of reasoning that are needed.[14,15] The discussion in Pym (2019) of the use of logic as a modelling technology may be useful for some readers.

Mathematical models of distributed systems of this kind are closely associated with ideas from logic. Logic is the science of reasoning and one of its key ideas is that of *truth*.

In logic, truth is a very precisely defined concept. It relies on a few key ideas: syntax, semantics, and interpretation. Syntactic entities are interpreted as semantic entities, just as data is interpreted as information. Truth is a property of a logical formula (which is a syntactic entity) relative to a *model*. A model is a mathematical structure that describes relationships between semantic entities.

In modal logic (Blackburn, de Rijke, and Venema (2001), which is perhaps the key tool in the logician's kit for reasoning about action, the ideas of *necessity* and *possibility*, so-called 'modalities', can be expressed. The key to understanding these ideas comes from some beautiful work initiated by Saul Kripke (1963), the application of which in systems modelling is discussed in, for example, Anderson and Pym (2016); Caulfield and Pym (2015); Collinson, Monahan, and Pym (2012); Simon (1996).

The main idea is that truth is defined relative to a *world*. The concept of a world is philosophically quite delicate, but for our present purpose we can think of it as a state of knowledge or the state of a system. A collection of such 'possible worlds' that might be taken as a place to give meaning to formal logical expressions can be seen as a space in the sense that we have already discussed. In fact, this kind of semantics can be formulated explicitly in terms of topological spaces, which are perhaps the prototypical mathematical example of the concept of a space (Tarski 1969; McKinsey and Tarski 1944).

What is most important for my story here is that the set of all worlds, W, must come with a partial ordering[16] on its set of elements, so that we define truth relative to models M of the form $(W, \leq)$.

Given a world w in the set W,

$$w \vDash_M \phi$$

denotes that the logical formula ϕ is 'true in the state w'. For example, if w is a state in which there are precisely three apples and two oranges, then the formula *More (Apples, Oranges)*, which is intended to mean that there are more apples than there are oranges, is true at w. But, if w is any state in which there are at least as many oranges as apples, then the formula is not true there.

Suppose now that our states are ordered as follows: $w \leq v$ just in the case that v has more apples than w.

In general, $w =_M \square\phi$ denotes that the formula ϕ is *necessarily* true at the state w in the model M. This is defined as follows: $w \vDash_M \square\phi$ just in the case that, for *every* state v such that $w \leq v$, it is the case that $v \vDash_M \phi$. So, in our little example of apples and oranges, the formula $\square$*More (Apples, Oranges)* is true if w is a state in which there are precisely three apples and two oranges because any state that is beyond w must have more apples than oranges. Note that we may choose to consider many possible models. Different models will, in general, have different sets of possible worlds.

Similarly,

$$v \vDash_M \Diamond\phi$$

denotes that the formula ϕ is *possibly* true at the state w in the model M. This is defined as follows:

$w \vDash_M \Diamond \phi$ just in the case that, for *some* state v such that $w \leq v$, it is the case that

$$v \vDash_M \phi$$

So, now supposing that states are ordered so that $w \leq v$ just in the case that either v has more apples than w or v has more oranges than w, then there is state beyond w at which

More (Oranges, Apples)

is true, so that

$\Diamond$ *More (Oranges, Apples)*

is true at w.

What has logic got to do with cyberspace? Just about everything, actually, if one believes that logic provides a good, or at least useful, account of human reasoning. Moreover, computers are inherently machines that implement logic. Assuming that at least, then logic provides the essential link between people and the systems that support cyberspace, as described in Figure 1.9.

The diagram indicates the relationship between reasoning about systems (including about other humans within the system) and logical reasoning about mathematical models of the system. The ideal situation is when this diagram 'commutes'—that is, for a given system, the logical formalization of human reasoning about its properties corresponds exactly to logical reasoning about a formal model of the system. Such a situation is very rare indeed, and really

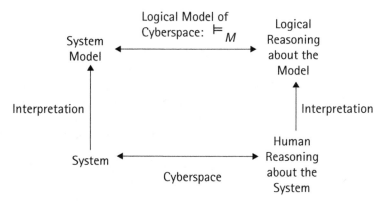

FIGURE 1.9. Reasoning about systems and reasoning about system models

only works out in the context of very specific reasoning tools (see, for example, discussions in Apt, de Boer, and Olderog 2010; Ishtiaq and O'Hearn 2001; Caulfield and Pym 2015; Pym, Spring, and O'Hearn 2018; and Simon 1996).

I have already given an example of a model in the context of distributed systems. It is built out of descriptions of the system's locations, resources, and processes. Triples of locations, resources, and processes are the states of the model of a system. The ordering of the states is then given by the evolution of the model as *actions* occur (Anderson and Pym 2016; Collinson, Monahan, and Pym 2012; and Milner 1989).

Actions are the basic building blocks of processes,[17] one of the core components in our model of the infrastructure of cyberspace. When actions occur, the state of a system changes. For one example, a computer program may perform a 'write' action to put value, a number representing a *resource*, to a memory, *location*. For another example, a human user of a computer may give the 'print' command, so causing data to be copied from the computer's memory to the printer, followed by the consumption on ink and paper and resources, and the creation of a document.

Thus we have $L, R, E \leq M, S, F$ just in the case that L, R, E can evolve to become M, S, F by some action. The notion of logical truth supported by such a mode, written as $L, R, E \vDash_M \phi$, is read as 'the process E, executing with respect to resources R, at location L, has property ϕ.'

Then we can define versions of the necessity and possibility modalities that are parametrized by actions. The counterpart to the necessity modality is $[a]\phi$, which is read as 'the formula ϕ is necessarily true after the action a'. Similarly, the counterpart to the possibility modality is $\langle a \rangle \phi$, which is read as 'the formula ϕ is possibly true after the action a'. More formally, we define them as follows:

- $L, R, E \vDash_M [a]\phi$ holds just in the case that, for *every* evolution of L, R, E to M, S, F by the action a, we have that $M, S, F \vDash_M \phi$ holds;
- $L, R, E \vDash_M \langle a \rangle \phi$ holds just in the case that, for *some* evolution of L, R, E to M, S, F by the action a, we have that $M, S, F \vDash_M \phi$ holds.

THE ORIGINS OF CYBERSPACE   27

These definitions explain how logical reasoning about (the data held by) systems interacts with the actions performed by the system. In particular, they begin to explain, in terms of *information* processing, how humans interact with the system and other humans.

In order to see an example of all this, think about the picture of the implementation of cyberspace given in Figure 1.6. Suppose a user, sitting at a computer in their home, is using a web browser to access an online store (let us call it 'BigRiver'). The user is looking at the webpage for Oxford University Press's *Handbook of Cybersecurity* and clicks on the 'Buy now' button. If the user's bank account has sufficient funds and if the BigRiver website has given the correct information about the availability of the book, then, provided everything works as it should, the book will be sent to the user. We can describe this situation logically as follows:

$$home\_computer, bank\_account, BigRiver\_website \vDash_{Cyberspace} (buy\_now)\ book\_sent$$

That is, located at their home computer, with the resources available in their bank account, while running the BigRiver website process, the user may click on the 'Buy now' link and it is possible, if all goes well, that the book will be sent to their specified address.

Note that this logical assertion describes a state of affairs in the part of the diagram described as 'Cyberspace'. We could use similar logical assertions to describe the (many) states of affairs that must obtain in other parts of the diagram in order for the assertion about Cyberspace to be realized.

At this point, the reader might be forgiven for thinking that the logical language that explains all this is rather impoverished. I would agree, although I would note that, in fact, the framework I have suggested, as developed, for example, in Anderson and Pym 2016; Apt, de Boer, and Olderog 2010; Caulfield and Pym 2015; Collinson, Monahan, and Pym 2012; and Milner 1989, can express a great deal, albeit somewhat tediously. A challenge for the community of logicians, if logic is to demonstrate what I believe is its full potential as a modelling technology, is to develop concise and powerful representations of logical reasoning.

In fact, the world of (modal) logics for reasoning about actions (performed by agents) is much richer than I have so far suggested and includes *epistemic logics*, for reasoning about agents' knowledge of systems, *doxastic logics*, for reasoning about agents' beliefs, and *temporal logics*, which incorporate a representation of time (system events, such as the sending and receiving of messages, which occur at relative points in time). All these systems of logic build on the basic ideas sketched earlier. *The Stanford Encyclopaedia of Philosophy* (https:// plato.stanford.edu) provides a great deal of information about these systems of logic, and there is a vast literature in computer science that is concerned with their use in reasoning about systems.

Perhaps the most important of these many possibilities for our story are the epistemic and doxastic logics. Roughly speaking, in these logics, modalities are parametrized not by actions but rather by agents, who of course can perform actions. Agents may be humans or system processes, and epistemic and doxastic logics (again, see the Stanford Encyclopaedia) allow us to reason about their knowledge and beliefs. Exploring the use of these logics, and their relationships with tools from behavioural economics (e.g. Baltag and Renne 2016), game theory (e.g. Binmore 2007), and psychology (e.g. Kirchler and Hoelzel 2017), to reason about the behaviour of agents in cyberspace would be another chapter in exploring the origins of cyberspace.

Of course, individuals and organizations do not always behave 'logically' when they interact with one another and with the systems that support cyberspace. They behave in ways that others may consider to be irrational. This observation does not really undermine the perspective presented here. It has very little to do with logic in the sense that I have described, which is about the mechanism by which conclusions are drawn from chosen assumptions. Some assumptions may lead to what may be described as 'irrational' behaviour, even though the logical mechanisms may be perfectly sound.

SUMMARY

I have sought to explain the origins of 'cyberspace' historically, linguistically, and conceptually. I have explained how the idea of cyberspace derives from a complex combination of physical and logical structure, which supports complex interactions between and among humans and information-processing machines, and I have given a conceptual and mathematical framework for modelling the conceptual and technical infrastructure of cyberspace.

I have also explained how logic can provide tools, based on our approach to modelling the infrastructure of cyberspace, for capturing how humans and other agents reason about cyberspace, and so, to some extent at least, how they experience cyberspace. Experience, of course, involves more than logical reasoning alone. Exploring that dimension would be yet another chapter in exploring the origins of cyberspace.

I have explained how the essential features of cyberspace have been part of the human experience, 'a consensual hallucination experienced daily by billions of legitimate operators' as Gibson (1982) put it, for a very long time and, as the science fiction writers continue to predict, we can expect that there is much more to come. I have not discussed questions of security in cyber space—that is the topic of the rest of this handbook. Again, Standage's 1998 book (Chapter 7, 'Codes, Hackers and Cheats') provides a delightful starting point.

ACKNOWLEDGEMENTS

I am warmly grateful to Tristan Caulfield and Jonathan Spring for their thorough and thoughtful advice on drafts of this article.

NOTES

1. *The Oxford English Dictionary* (OED), https://en.oxforddictionaries.com/definition/cyberspace
2. https://en.wikipedia.org/wiki/Internet
3. It is not my purpose here to explore the definition of 'information'. The literature on the subject is substantial. For our purposes, the usual understanding of a generally well-educated reader—see, for example, the definition provided in the OED—will suffice. For a philosophically sophisticated discussion that is beyond the scope of this article, see, for

example, L. Floridi. 2011. *The Philosophy of Information*. Oxford University Press. See also C. Zins. Conceptual approaches for defining data, information, and knowledge. '*Journal of the American Society for Information Society and Technology*', 58 (4). https://doi.org/10.asi.20508

4. TCP/IP: https://en.wikipedia.org/wiki/Internet_protocol_suite

   OSPF: https://en.wikipedia.org/wiki/Open_Shortest_Path_First
   BGP: https://en.wikipedia.org/wiki/Border_Gateway_Protocol
   RIP: https://en.wikipedia.org/wiki/Routing_Information_Protocol

5. The distinction between the WWW and the underlying Internet is an essential one, but there would be no WWW in its current form without the underlying communications architecture. Some of the key concepts of the WWW—for example, the concept of *hypertext* and the underlying ideas of *distributed systems* (Coulouris et al. 2011; Simon 1996)—have, as described in Berners-Lee's research proposal (1989, 1900) and book (2000), prior histories in computer science. The linking of hypertext to the Internet through 'http' (HyperText Transfer Protocol) and URLs and HTML (HyperText Markup Language) are Berners-Lee's definitive contributions.

6. The Treaty was a huge diplomatic effort: 176 negotiating teams representing 194 agents; the French brought a 150-strong entourage, including pastry chefs, priest confessors and dancing instructors. The negotiators had constantly to check with their capital: a letter took 2 weeks to reach Stockholm, 4 weeks to reach Madrid: R. Boyes, 'Treaty that created 'the soil of despair', *The Times*, 24 October 1998. I am grateful to Paul Cornish for this reference.

7. 'Telegraph' means 'distance writing' in Greek.

8. https://en.wikipedia.org/wiki/Hydraulic_telegraph

9. The SAGE (Semi-Automatic Ground Environment) missile defence system, which was developed by MIT's Lincoln Laboratory and which operated in the United States from the late 1950s to the 1980s, is also a seed (https://en.wikipedia.org/wiki/Semi-Automatic_Ground_Environment).

10. For our present purposes, I refrain from considering AI alternatives to humans as interpreters of data to yield information.

11. *German*: a state of consciousness or a feeling devoid of sensory components (Merriam Webster).

12. An IP address is a numerical label (a sequence of numbers representing a 32-bit or 128-bit number) assigned to each device connected to a network that uses the Internet protocol (IP) for its communications. An organization may, for example, own all of the IP addresses that begin with a given sequence of numbers.

13. Intrusion Detection Systems and Intrusion Prevention Systems: (https://en.wikipedia.org/wiki/Intrusion_detection_system).

14. That is not to say that many things expressible in one kind of logic cannot be expressed in another; rather, that it may not be convenient to do so.

15. In addition to the classical propositional and predicate logic that is routinely to taught to undergraduates in computer science, mathematics, and philosophy, we can add, among other things, modal, temporal, and epistemic systems, and their higher-order, intuitionistic, and substructural variants. The many volumes of the *Handbook of Philosophical Logic* and the *Stanford Encyclopaedia of Philosophy* (https://plato.stanford.edu) provide starting points for exploring these topics.

16. A partially ordered set formalizes the intuitive concept of an ordering of the elements of a set. A 'partial order' on the set relates pairs of elements of the set in such a way that the

relationship been the elements of the pair is reflexive (every element is related to itself), anti-symmetric (no two elements precede each other in the ordering), and transitive (if the higher of one pair is below the lower of another pair, then the lower of the former pair is below than the higher of the latter pair). Not all pairs of elements of the set need be related by the order; such pairs are 'incomparable' in such an order.

17. Technical note: for an elegant explanation of the structure of processes, including concurrency, non-determinism, and recursion, see Robin Milner's *Communication and Concurrency*.

BIBLIOGRAPHY

Agar, J. 2016. *The Government Machine*. Cambridge, MA: The MIT Press.

Anderson G., and D. Pym. 2016. 'A Calculus and Logic of Bunched Resources and Processes', *Theoretical Computer Science* 614: 63–96.

Apt K., F. de Boer, and E.-R. Olderog. 2010. *Verification of Sequential and Concurrent Programs*. Dordrecht: Springer.

Baltag A., and B. Renne. 2016. 'Dynamic Epistemic Logic'. In *Stanford Encyclopedia of Philosophy*, edited by E. Zalta (principal editor). https://plato.stanford.edu/entries/dynamic-epistemic/

Barwise J., and J. Seligman. 1997. *Information Flow: The Logic of Distributed Systems*. Cambridge: Cambridge University Press.

Berners-Lee T. (1989 March; 1990 May). 'Information Management: A Proposal'. CERN, W3C Archive, https://www.w3.org/History/1989/proposal.html

Berners-Lee, T. 2000. *Weaving the Web: The Original Design and Ultimate Destiny of the World Wide Web*. New York: Harper Business.

Binmore, K. 2007. *Playing for Real: A Text on Game Theory*. New York: Oxford University Press.

Blackburn, P., M. de Rijke, and Y. Venema. 2001. *Modal Logic*. Cambridge: Cambridge University Press.

Caulfield, T., and D. Pym. 2015. 'Modelling and Simulating Systems Security Policy', *Proc. SIMUTools 2015*, ACM Digital Library, doi: 10.4108/eai.24-8-2015.2260765.

Collinson, M., B. Monahan, and D. Pym. 2012. *A Discipline of Mathematical Systems Modelling*. London: College Publications.

Coulouris, G., J. Dollimore, T. Kindberg, et al. 2011. *Distributed Systems: Concepts and Design*. Harlow: Pearson.

Garson, J. 2016. 'Modal Logic'. In *Stanford Encyclopedia of Philosophy*, edited by E. Zalta (principal editor). https://plato.stanford.edu/entries/logic-modal/

Gibson, W. 1982. 'Burning Chrome', *Omni* 4 (10): July.

Gibson, W. 1984. *Neuromancer*. New York: Ace.

Hafner, K., and M. Lyon. 1998. *Where Wizards Stay Up Late: The Origins of the Internet*. New York: Simon & Schuster.

Hook, D., and J. Norman. 2002. *Origins of Cyberspace*. Novato, CA: History of Science.com.

Isaacson, W. 2014. *The Innovators: How a Group of Inventors, Geniuses, and Geeks Created the Digital Revolution*. London: Simon & Schuster.

Ishtiaq S., and P. O'Hearn. 2001. 'BI as an assertion language for mutable data structures', *Proceedings of the 28th ACM SIGPLAN-SIGACT Symposium on Principles of Programming Languages*: 14–26. ACM Digital Library.

Kirchler E., and E. Hoelzel. 2017. *Economic Psychology: An Introduction*. Cambridge: Cambridge University Press.

Kripke, S. 1963. 'Semantical Considerations on Modal Logic', *Acta Philosophca Fennica* 16: 83–94.

McKinsey, J.C.C., and A. Tarski. 1944. 'The Algebra of Topology', *Annals of Mathematics* 45: 141–91.

Milner, R. 1989. *Communication and Concurrency*. Hoboken, NJ: Prentice Hall.

MIT Artificial Intelligence Laboratory 1998. 'The JAIR Information Space', MIT Artificial Intelligence Laboratory, 10 June. http://www.ai.mit.edu/projects/infoarch/jair/jair-space.html.

Ohmori K., and T.L. Kunii. 2007. 'The Mathematical Structure of Cyberworlds', *Proceedings of the 2007 International Conference on Cyberworlds*. IEEE Computer Society, doi: 10.1109/CW.2007.19

Prucher J. 2007. *Brave New Worlds: The Oxford Dictionary of Science Fiction*. Oxford: Oxford University Press.

Pym, D. 2019. 'Resource Semantics: Logic as a Modelling technology', *ACM SIGLOG News*, April, 6 (2): 5–41.

Pym, D., J. Spring, and P. O'Hearn. 2018. 'Why Separation Logic Works', *Philosophy of Technology*, doi: org/10.1007/s13347-018-0312-8

Rid. T. 2013. *Cyber War Will Not Take Place*. London: Hurst and Company.

Ross S. 2014. *Introduction to Probability Models*. 11th edition. London: Academic Press.

Schachtman. N. 2008. '26 years after Gibson, Pentagon defines "cyberspace"', *Wired* 5 May, https://www.wired.com/2008/05/pentagon-define/

Schofield. H. 2013. 'How Napoleon's semaphore telegraph changed the world', *BBC News*, 17 June, http://www.bbc.co.uk/news/magazine-22909590

Shuler. R. 2002, 2005. 'How Does the Internet Work?' http://www.theshulers.com/whitepapers/internet_whitepaper/

Simon, H. 1996. *The Sciences of the Artificial*. Cambridge, MA The MIT Press.

Singer P., and A. Friedman. 2014. *Cybersecurity and Cyberwar: What Everyone Needs to Know*. New York: Oxford University Press.

Standage T. 1998. *The Victorian Internet*. London: Weidenfeld & Nicolson.

Tarski A. 1969. *Logic, Semantics, Metamathematics: Papers from 1923 to 1938*. Oxford: Clarendon Press.

van Ditmarsch, H., J.Y. Halpern, Wiebe van der Hoek et al. (eds). 2015. *Handbook of Epistemic Logic*. London: College Publications.

Wiener N. 1948, Hermann and Cie, eds, *Cybernetics or Control and Communication in the Animal and the Machine*. Paris: Technology Press. https://www.abebooks.co.uk/servlet/BookDetailsPL?bi=30332016088&searchurl=an%3Dwiener%2Bnorbert%26bi%3Dh%26sortby%3D17%26tn%3Dhuman%2Buse%2Bbeings%2Bcybernetics&cm_sp=snippet-_-srp1-_-image1

Wiener N. 1950. *Cybernetics and Society: The Human Use of Human Beings*. Boston, MA: Houghton Mifflin.

Wilkinson N., and M. Klaes. 2012. *An Introduction to Behavioral Economics*. Basingstoke: Palgrave.

The Mechanics' Magazine, Museum, Register, Journal, and Gazette, 7 October 1837–31 March 1838.

CHAPTER 2

OPPORTUNITY, THREAT, AND DEPENDENCY IN THE SOCIAL INFOSPHERE

GREG AUSTIN

INTRODUCTION

THE previous chapter described the revolutionary emergence of a suite of combined technologies (information and communications) as a powerful enabling force for many areas of human activity. These technologies and their exploitation have created a whole new ecosystem of human endeavour. This chapter looks at the social constructions of that information ecosystem—the infosphere. Using very broad sweeps, the chapter looks first at pre-political conceptualizations of cyber space as a moral sphere by scholars, technologists, and futurists. This overview sets the scene for a brief discussion of opportunities and threats that have shaped security in cyber space. The final section of the chapter offers an original analysis of the issue of dependency, which may be one of the more under-appreciated characteristics of the cyber age.

Terminology in this field remains problematic. To many readers, the term 'cyber security' implies a focus on protection of machines, systems, networks, the information they hold, and the communications systems that propagate the information. By contrast, the concept of 'security in cyber space' opens up a broader perspective, and implies consideration of social impacts arising outside the technological and physical perimeters of cyber space. The main social characteristic of defence of the new domain may not be the security of the zeros and ones that constitute the data, but protecting the political, economic, commercial, and personal power that results from new technological possibilities.

We can even go much further, as many do, and see 'knowledge' as the higher power compared with 'information'. Security of the knowledge ecosystem that depends on cyber space may be a far broader concept yet. These wider views lead us well beyond the idea of cyber security as a professional occupation, encompassing people with advanced technical skills, to a view of security in cyber space as the far bigger challenge—politically, economically, and militarily—of securing the information society, the knowledge economy, and our digital daily life.

The idea of security for the emerging information ecosystem finds endorsement in annual resolutions of the United Nations (UN) General Assembly, beginning in 1998, on 'Developments in the field of information and telecommunications in the context of international security'. It also finds strong endorsement by states beginning in 2002, when the UN convened the World Summit on the Information Society. This process saw the information society as global in scope and revolutionary in its impact on state power. These characteristics imply a new global obligation to protect a society 'where everyone can create, access, utilize and share information and knowledge' to 'achieve their full potential' in 'improving their quality of life' (United Nations 2003).

Is the Information Age a Revolution?

If the information ecosystem is a social order, then it follows that this order itself is valuable and demanding of protection independently of the machines, networks, and other technologies on which it depends. As the ancient philosopher Plato reminds us in *The Republic*, the security of exchange provides the primary reason for forming a society and constituting a state. The same concept exists in the Eastern tradition: 'only when families are regulated are states well governed; only when states are well governed is there peace in the world' (Confucius, *The Analects*). In any social order, stakeholders compete for position and for defence of norms that protect their positions. Norms, security and enforcers, heroes and villains, costs and benefits, winners and losers, are a part of any social order.

Plato and Confucius were both religious. In the modern era, we must understand that the social order of the infosphere, and its security, can still have an idealist or even religious orientation, or even an atheistic or materialist orientation.

In addition to being a type of social order that inherently creates, or at least demands, security relationships, the infosphere has another quality that is especially important when we consider what those security relationships might involve. This is the relationship between information, knowledge, and power that is captured in the twin adages: 'information is power' and 'knowledge is power'. Philosophical sources that have contemplated the relationship of knowledge and power before the modern era are numerous, and include sources from Asian writers and folk wisdom before the rise of Greek and Roman philosophy in Europe. Thomas Hobbes, in his original English version of *Leviathan* (1656), saw the sciences as 'small powers' but, when the Latin version was published in 1668, it omitted the word 'small' to make the phrase '*scientia, potentia est*' (subsequently taken as meaning 'knowledge is power') (Bell 1973). If these thinkers are right, and in my view history proves them to be correct, then security in the information age involves political dimensions of state power domestically and internationally, the underpinnings of corporate power and wealth, and the quality of citizen empowerment and independence.

It should be noted though that these earlier versions of the concept that knowledge is power saw it as only one of many forms of power. Hobbes is particularly relevant for this, because he included a list of sources of power (affability, prudence, nobility, friendship, and even reputation for power). The question posed by the information age is whether by its character it assigns knowledge as the dominant form or source of power relative to others. This is addressed later in this section.

Because knowledge (synthesized and processed information) delivers political and social power, ethical (values-based) framings are both possible and inevitable in understanding the security of the infosphere. Any security concept for the infosphere can and must include active defence of the values and norms that any social group attaches to the infosphere, whether these relate to the common needs of humanity, the often-conflicting self-interest of states, business imperatives, or personal privacy. Moreover, any practical concept of security in cyber space will be dependent on at least seven quite distinct contexts: privacy and civil surveillance, freedom from harassment, resilience of the digital economy and individual businesses, protection against cyber crime, state-on-state espionage, political subversion (including activity related to globally distributed terrorism), and cyber-enabled warfare. These contexts, and others, are addressed in subsequent chapters.

The first challenge in approaching the security impacts of the information age is to answer the question of whether it is truly transformational of almost everything, as was the industrial revolution, or whether it is merely one additional aspect of a modern technological society in which information and communications technologies (ICTs) sit alongside other enabling technologies. Building on his 500-page book on post-industrial society written in 1973, Bell later used a number of shorter formats to predict, correctly it seems, that knowledge exchange would become the primary foundation of all economic and social exchange in a world that had become an information society (Bell 1976).

In a rather prescient insight, Bell also warned that the change in scale provided by the information age would of necessity dictate a change in institutions.[1] He said a 'major political problem' in the post-industrial society will be its information policy. He mused on whether one of the new institutions would be an information utility (perhaps as Facebook, Google, and Twitter subsequently emerged). He then predicted that the 'politics of information handling will arise from the nature of information itself'. As I see it, this is precisely the situation the world is confronting as it struggles with problems like political hacking and so-called 'fake news'.

One of the most insightful analysts, however, was a Japanese technologist, Yoneji Masuda. He gave us the term 'computopia', in this way anticipating comprehensive and profound effects of ICTs and their use (Masuda 1981). He foresaw 'the realisation of a society that brings about a general flourishing state of human intellectual creativity, instead of affluent material consumption'.[2] He anticipated e-democracy, the globalization of a new renaissance, a shattering of previous conceptions of privacy (a 'Copernican turn'), the emergence of a new concept of time value (meaning a paradigmatic shift in economic and social valuations of time spent on a task or activity), and a new intensity in system innovation—all premised on the complete objectification and commodification of information.

There are scholars who take a less transformationalist view. Frank Webster's *Theories of the Information Society* challenges the idea of the information society as a dominant new paradigm supplanting other modes of social relationships. In his chapter, 'What is an Information Society?', he portrays the information society as a means of instrumentalizing certain novel aspects of social change without redefining human reality (Webster 2006). He leans closer to the idea of an informatization of life that stems from the continuity of established forces.

Robert Hassan's *The Information Society* is critical of both camps: the 'boosters' and the critics of the information society idea. He focuses his gaze on the conjunction between neo-liberal globalization (capitalism) and the 'revolution in the development and application of computer-based technologies' (Hassan 2008). He suggests that the information society has created not just 'pathways of possibility' but also a 'democratic vacuum' that will need to find a new controlling impulse from within, or 'we will continue to accelerate towards destinations unknown'.[3] Manuel Castells (2012), in *Networks of Outrage and Hope*, argues that politics has been forever transformed in certain dimensions, for better or for worse, by the new information technologies and their mass application, especially in social media forms. He foresees 'the uncertainty of an uncharted process of political change'.[4] Established institutions may hold on to power, especially if they can co-opt the more popular themes of activists, but the more citizens can convey their messages, the more their consciousness is raised. It also carries the implication, he says, that 'the more the public sphere becomes a contested terrain, ... the lesser will be the politicians' capacity to integrate demands and claims with mere cosmetic adjustments'.

Against this background of divergent views, a framework offered by Floridi and Sanders (2002) is particularly useful in laying out four possible discrete approaches to characterizing the information society, and these can be used to understand the security dimension:

- a professional approach, seeing the field of information technology as something akin to medicine or law, and therefore demanding a set of professionally bounded information ethics;
- a radical approach, seeing the information age as transformative and novel—'absolutely unique issues, in need of a unique approach';
- a conservative approach—we only need a 'particular applied ethics, discussing new species of traditional moral issues';
- an innovative approach (one step down from the radical approach) that 'can expand the metaethical discourse with a substantially new perspective' (p. 2).

Floridi and Sanders opt for the 'innovative approach' and conclude that the ethical issues raised by the information age 'are not uncontroversially unique' but 'are sufficiently novel to render inadequate the adoption of standard macroethics'.[5] While that is a philosophical and ethical analysis, it is directly useful for policy. Floridi (2005) sees a practical application of his ethics: it 'provides the conceptual grounds that then guide problem-solving procedures'. One implication of his approach is that, while not everything changes fundamentally, all in policy is affected sufficiently by the information society that it ought to be re-evaluated from that perspective.

In later works, Floridi appears to go further and approaches the transformationalist view. He suggests that the world is undergoing a transition of its mode of existence and survival every bit as radical as the transition from prehistory to history (Floridi 2012). He says that it is detaching us from future generations.[6] Floridi predicts that the world will become 'in-creasingly *synchronised* (time), *delocalised* (space) and *correlated* (interactions)' (Floridi 2013). He warned against seeing this as the 'friendly face of globalization', suggesting that we should have no expectation about the degree to which this new world would be widespread or inclusive. In a later chapter, he posits a profound impact (dislocation) on our values and ethics: 'Innovative forms of agency are becoming possible; new values are developing and old ones are being reshaped; cultural and moral assumptions are ever more likely to come into contact if not into conflict.[7] This process carries a risk of fragmentation of group values. As Paul Cornish observes on this point, 'ethics is profoundly inter-personal, and might therefore become increasingly difficult as the information society atomises to the individual level'.[8]

At the most abstract (philosophical) level, this single unifying characteristic has been described as 'distributed morality'.[9] In social science terms, as opposed to moral philosophy, this might be described as distributed authority. The mass availability of computational systems and universal, ubiquitous, and instantaneous access to information carries with it a diffusion of power to a new multitude of agents.

Floridi (2013) offers four imperatives for responding the infosphere from a moral perspective, and I have adapted them to the policy domain as follows:

- accept its political imperatives (assign a social value to information and how it is used, as well as to the machines that produce and disseminate it)
- grasp the centrality of distributed political morality (pre-existing moral and political authority becomes disaggregated, and a reaggregated collective responsibility emerges);
- recognize that the enablers of information dissemination and reaggregation on a special political significance;
- regard the welfare of information itself as a central reference point of policy.

This leads to an argument that ICTs work as powerful political enablers and help distributed authority to emerge. Noting that moral enablers for the information age do not need to be only ICT-based, Floridi suggests that 'Agents (including most importantly the State) are better agents insofar as they not only take advantage of, but also foster the right kind of moral facilitation properly geared to the right kind of distributed morality'.[10] He says that this elaboration by information ethics helps us to realize that 'in ethics [generally], moral facilitation is a much more influential, macroscopic and perhaps necessary phenomenon—not merely limited to computer ethics contexts—than we suspected in the past'.[11]

To summarize, the philosophy of information ethics suggests the following useful reference points for analysing both the ethical and political aspects of an information society:

- The information age is ethically (and politically) transformative, for better or for worse.
- The new ethics (and new politics) flow from the character of the infosphere (informational ecosystem).
- In the infosphere, all informational objects have a potential moral (and a political) value.
- A moral (and politically desirable) action can be one that contributes to the flourishing of the infosphere without doing harm to any aspect of it.
- Making a moral (and politically desirable) difference may depend on the aggregation of individual information acts.
- Distributed morality (and distributed political authority) may be the hallmark of information ethics (and political life): we participate in an infosphere, a social milieu in which the diversity of sources of potential moral authority is unprecedented.
- ICTs work as moral enablers in the process of distributing morality (and political authority) away from the government to the citizen.
- The process of moral facilitation is central to the health of the infosphere.

One inescapable conclusion from this broad philosophical perspective is that cyber security as a professionally bounded and technologically oriented set of concepts, research, technologies, and practices cannot be separated easily from broader conceptions of the security in cyber space of individual people, their community groups, the businesses that underpin their daily life, their national governments, and a globalized infosphere.

TRANSFORMATIONAL SECURITY: FOR BETTER AND FOR WORSE

We can understand the opportunity presented by the information age in many ways, most of them now being familiar elements in daily discourse, as well as continuing sources of wonder: from the Internet, the world wide web, and the role of social media in the Arab spring, to driverless cars, robotics, laser surgery, nanotechnologies, and exploration of deep space. Speed, ubiquity, and the global reach of ICTs now support and improve daily existence in ways previously imagined only by science fiction writers.

What is the common social element of all these amazing innovations that enhance and enrich human existence? It is the empowerment of billions of people to do old things better and faster, or in completely new ways, and to create new things to do on a vast scale. This is distributed (disaggregated) power, which brings with it a distribution or dilution of pre-existing social political power.

Alongside the opportunities, the threats are as daunting. As Floridi, Hassan, and Castells make plain, the information revolution does not have an inevitably positive moral character. The dangerous side of the new age has been seen in mass surveillance for suppression of political dissent, development of a cyber arms race, cyber attacks across international borders, cyber bullying of children ending in suicide, large-scale cyber crimes, and cyber espionage for political influencing in democratic elections. Some of the world's leading scientists and technologists, such as Bill Gates and Steven Hawking, have warned of a threat to the very existence of humanity from advanced artificial intelligence (Cellan-Jones 2014). The UN is scrambling to agree controls on lethal autonomous weapons systems, even as primitive versions are already being deployed by major states in limited roles, such as perimeter defence of Russian nuclear missile sites or in internal security surveillance in China.

The common social element of all these information innovations that diminish and degrade human existence is the novel form of reaggregation of the distributed (disaggregated) power. It is the re-concentration of social and political power outside pre-existing institutions. This reaggregation creates a reordering of previously assured social realities facilitated by new ICTs. The reaggregation has created new ways of hurting people, society, and a country's national interests as much as it has enhanced them. As an example, we might cite the emergence of the Donald Trump campaign and presidency as a new institution independent of and outside the Republican Party as a result of information age phenomena: the combined effect of Facebook, Twitter, and traditional media (such as CNN), aggravated by the manipulation of leaked information from intelligence agencies, both Russian and American.

If disaggregation and subsequent reaggregation of authority and power are in fact common elements to both the good and bad sides of the information age, what then is the practical significance of this insight for security in cyber space? It means that we must better understand not only the role of the enablers and facilitators (adapting Floridi's terminology) but also the processes that correspond uniquely to specific types of information that the enablers and facilitators are trying to leverage to create new social outcomes that affect our security. This dictates a novel requirement to study two stages of this new moral facilitation: first, what processes work most powerfully to support political and social exploitation of novel types of information; and, second, how skilful are particular enablers or facilitators in mastering those processes.

DEPENDENCE AS AN OUTCOME OF INFORMATION ENABLEMENT

One important real-world outcome from new forms of information enablement may be that of dependence created between the users of reaggregated information (in a physical product or a social communication) and the enablers. This means that the potential of ICTs to achieve new things can only be realized through the creation of a new state of dependence for the user upon the unrevealed processes underpinning the product or communication. In simple terms, dependence is, for social actors, a state of reliance on something or someone. In the material (non-social) world of objects, such as chemicals, solar systems, or electronic ICT signals, dependence is a relationship between an outcome and a necessary precondition. New forms of dependence affect the human operation and exploitation of ICTs at all levels.

The previous paragraph assumes a common sense meaning to the word 'dependence', which is often used interchangeably with 'dependency'. There is a more complex approach, albeit slightly esoteric, that adds depth to our understanding of the character of dependency in the information age. Caporaso (1978), writing in the 1970s about this topic in international political economy, felt that the generic term 'dependence' served little useful purpose. He called out a difference between the use of 'dependency' as a term meaning absence of actor autonomy and the term 'dependence' used in the sense of a highly asymmetric form of interdependence. He saw these as quite different phenomena.

Caporaso suggested that dependence, seen as an asymmetric relationship, was opposite to *interdependence* (a more balanced mutual satisfying relationship) rather than *autonomy*. The former implies mutual control, while the latter implies self-control. He arrives later at the important observation that it may be 'impossible to reduce dependency to a single, unidimensional concept'.[12] He suggested that it might be best viewed as a 'synoptic term for a body of theory' that addresses qualitatively different dependence types. This overarching approach also allows a necessary complementary lens, in addition to dependence and dependency.[13] This lens is less about objective analysis of either of those two conditions and much more about knowledge of the dynamic system in which the dependence or dependency exists. For political economy, this was in his view, 'integration of knowledge about the state and private sector within a single country which is then analysed with an external environment'.

Caporaso's ontology is directly applicable to dependence and dependency in the information age, and therefore to security in cyber space. The need for a 'whole of system approach' to understanding dependence in political economy finds reflection in the view of Hathaway and Klimburg (2012) that a 'whole of system approach rather than a whole of nation approach is the more mature form of cybersecurity'. Returning to this theme in another paper, Klimburg and Healey (2012) observe that the 'complicated international dimension of cyber security has not always been fully understood'. Cornish suggests that the growing interdependencies 'should defeat any notion that cyber-security is divisible: between foreign and domestic; between military and civil; and between governments and other intergovernmental or indeed non-governmental actors' (Cornish 2009).

Here are four examples of dependence that redefine security in the information age at the individual, community, national, and international levels. These examples are meant to be only illustrative of the very large number of cyber space dependencies, billions upon billions (10^n) of which that might be catalogued. All new risk arising in cyber space at any level can be expressed as a function of new dependencies.

Example 1: A single person is newly dependent and disempowered through committing large amounts of personal information into the care and trust of new ICT machines, their operators, and their users in circumstances (often in foreign countries) where the individual has also surrendered (or never had) the power to revoke access to, or re-privatize, the personal information.

Example 2: A community (or a corporation) locks itself into complex dependency when it agrees to computerized management of essential services such as water supply and electricity where there is no mapping or public disclosure of the parameters that will lead to interruption of supply, and where resilience strategies have not been put in place to compensate for sudden and/or sustained loss of authorized computerized control.

Example 3: A country has extreme dependency on ICTs when the overwhelming share of its public services (in finance, health, transportation, food supply, policing, and military defence) are delivered or coordinated through tens of thousands of unique computerized systems.

Example 4: The security or prosperity of groups of states (the international level) have a high dependency on ICTs when their critical services, or their armed forces, are built on physical systems that depend on global supply chains involving several countries for delivery of secure and assurable operation of the systems.

These dependencies exist regardless of whether or not the computerized systems involved have high degrees of inherent security. The dependency arises from the information character of the social exchange resulting from the technologies, but not from the technologies themselves. Dependency is not alleviated by better cyber security of the systems. Risk of certain types of threats arising from the dependency may be alleviated by better cyber security but systemic dependencies cannot be attenuated in that way. As Rinaldi et al. (2001) note, higher degrees of complexity in ICTs increase the degree of dependency and, as a result, 'more complex, and more extensive interdependencies lead to increased risks [and] greater requirements for security'.

That said, the inherent insecurity of many computerized systems and their vulnerability to attack become aggravating factors that exploit the dependency but, in social and political terms, the dependency is a different and pre-existing phenomenon from the phenomenon of vulnerability even if, as Cornish notes: 'where there is dependence there is also vulnerability'

(Cornish 2011). For security in cyber space, dependency must be mapped independently of assessments of vulnerability of threat. This is essential to develop in advance some sort of mitigation: 'where interconnectedness and dependency are not managed and mitigated by some form of security procedure, reversionary mode or redundancy system, then the result can only be a complex and vitally important communications system which is nevertheless vulnerable to information theft, financial electronic crime, malicious attack or infrastructure breakdown'.[14]

The list of dependencies studied by moral philosophy and science, including social science, is long. It includes topics like religion dependence, drug dependence, gender dependence, oil dependence, or even more complex structural approaches like co-dependence. In respect of the information age, the term 'dependency' is used in several different ways. Most often, it refers to 'Internet dependency' or 'digital dependency' of individual people who appear addicted (unable to function emotionally) without being connected to the world wide web or some form of computerized device.

Beyond the psychological level, the subject of information age dependency has been largely ignored by social scientists, including in management studies involving cyber security, other than to refer to it as a vulnerability and then move on to a discussion of threats. In English at least, the scholarly study of information age dependency has been confined largely to the United States, and in that case it has been centred on a few locations: Idaho National Laboratory, Argonne National Laboratory, Sandia National Laboratory, and, to a lesser extent, Carnegie Mellon University. This is a classic case of a phenomenon long visible in universities where social and political reality, especially around new technologies, races ahead of the institutional capability of social science researchers in those or other universities to respond.

At the same time, in terms of the response of policy communities globally, the United States seems to be relatively alone in its focus on the subject. The Department of Homeland Security (DHS) has included the management of external dependencies as item eight in its ten points for planning for a 'cyber resilience review' (CRR) since 2009 (US Department of Homeland Security 2014). By 2016, Carnegie Mellon University had produced a resources guide on this subject 'to help organizations implement practices identified as considerations for improvement' during a CRR. This and the work of the three national laboratories comprise the bulk of research and analysis on the topic of cyber dependency.

This is a remarkable gap in global research and analysis even though the concept of dependency is a foundational premise for all security in the information age. In a literature review for the Australian Centre for Cyber Security, Thakur (2016) found that most of the research work had been done in respect of critical infrastructure resilience. Even then, 'in contrast to the gravity of the vulnerability, the research reviewed reveals a lack of comprehensive information and analysis of cyber dependency that might clearly define the implications of it' even in the case of critical infrastructure resilience.[15] Thakur noted some 'comprehensive modelling tool applications', but saw these as 'mainly theoretical or limited to closed environments'. She argued that there was an 'absence of practical scenarios and multi-infrastructure analyses' and that the challenge for researchers was novel: 'scholars will need live and extensive cooperation from the operators of infrastructure and essential services, both nationally and globally, to reach the next level of comprehensive modelling and simulations that can provide insights into cyber dependencies'.

At the international level, a study on US/China relations in cyber space finds that there has been little comprehension in either country of the impact of cyber dependency on their broader security interests (Austin and Gady 2012). It gives a brief overview of the level of dependence, but this was captured succinctly and authoritatively in a July 2016 statement by China's President Xi Jinping when he said that 'our country is under others' control in core technologies of key fields' (Xinhua 2016). This was a staggering admission given that it had been Chinese policy for decades to work toward a self-sufficient high-tech industry, including in ICTs, and that China remained, in Xi's own words, with weak foundations in science and technology.

We can ask, as the Austin and Gady (2012) report does, whether China's level of dependence on a globalized ICT industry and international digital communications platforms is so high that it is forced to pursue cooperative behaviour on global cyber space issues rather than put at risk its international economic ties? The report also asks whether China's economy can remain unaffected by the cascading effects of an extreme cyber attack on US economic targets of the sort that Americans fear that China might undertake. It concludes that 'China is most likely obliged to cooperate in cyberspace rather than risk the fabric of its economic ties' and that 'China's economy is almost certainly not immune from serious damage that could be brought on by a US cyber attack'.[16]

More importantly, the report concludes that such questions could not be answered with a high degree of certainty because there were then few studies on the subject of shared cyber dependencies across international borders.[17] That remains the case today with few studies documenting such dependency in any detail, and even fewer analysing its transformative potential on geopolitics or economic power.

There is wide recognition of the general condition of dependency. For example, a RAND Corporation report recounts discussions between Chinese and Americans on the issue of China's dependence on the United States in the Track 2 talks sponsored by the Center for Strategic and International Studies beginning in December 2009 (Harold et al. 2016). The RAND report also concludes that China may have more to lose in economic terms than the United States if cyber disputes are allowed to escalate: 'Chinese representatives cited numerous ways in which their country was dependent on US capabilities'.[18]

This new form of mutual dependence, the mingling of interests and activities in cyber space affairs, is so profound that it has been called 'entanglement' and, in broad terms, this characteristic is shared among all countries. It is not possible to know how transformational the Internet may have been on geopolitics because there are no clear data on just how intermingled the critical elements of economic life have become.

The military security dimension of this dependence is a novel challenge. In the case of the United States and China, elements of the civil infrastructure almost totally reliant on the cyber domain (mobile communications, the Internet, electricity grids, landlines, undersea cables, banking) are also inter-mingled with military assets. The military power of states is now becoming more cyber dependent than ever, though the depth and implications of this dependence vary widely from country to country.

One of the best studies of international cyber dependence that begins to approach the granular level necessary is a 2010 report on the Reliability of Global Undersea Communications Cable Infrastructure (ROGUCCI) that was supported by several international stakeholders, such as the Institute of Electrical and Electronic Engineers, cable repair companies, cable-owning companies, and financial market representatives (Rauscher

2010). Published by the EastWest Institute in support of the goal of promoting greater co-operation on cyber space security, the report aimed to document the reliability of the global cable network, assess the potential implications of failures in it (with a focus on the financial services sector), and make recommendations for enhanced security and resilience.

The ROGUCCI report is especially noteworthy because it points to the cross-domain character of cyber dependencies: engineering and maintenance problems can carry consequences for international relationships in business and politics, and even in personal relationships. Delays in diplomatic approval for foreign cable repair ships to enter the territorial sea of a host country to repair an undersea cable can have serious repercussions for the transactions relying on that access. The report notes that the overwhelming share, possibly as much as 85% of all Internet traffic, passes through undersea cables. While some localities are blessed with multiple undersea or land-based cables carrying Internet traffic, many are not, and there are worrying concentrations (single points of failure) in the global network around the northern Arabian Sea and in the Luzon Strait.[19]

Several years prior to the cable study, in 2007, the US government became concerned about such international dependencies in a range of critical infrastructures, including ICT-related, and set up the Critical Foreign Dependencies Initiative (CFDI). As part of this process, it asked its embassies to report on those facilities in their host country that might be considered critical for the national security or economic prosperity of the United States. Based on the responses, the DHS compiled a prioritized list of these dependencies, which included 'over 300 assets and systems in more than 50 countries' (US Department of Homeland Security 2014). In many cases, the landfall stations of the undersea cables in foreign countries were included, as was other telecommunications infrastructure. But at that time and since, as Arce (2015) points out, there has been little consistent analysis of the character of the vulnerabilities and risks (what I would call the 'dependencies'). He also notes an 'absence of cyber entities in the list'.[20] The main enduring significance of this list might be that it highlighted the 'discontiguous and non-traditional character' of US vulnerabilities.

In 2014, in a report on global financial market infrastructures, the Bank for International Settlements described the management of dependencies ('complexities and interdependencies') as the biggest security vulnerability in the cyber domain (Bank for International Settlements 2014). By October 2016, the Group of Seven (G7; 2016) of the most developed economies was emphasizing the need for greater attention to inter-sectoral dependency involving financial services. It called on jurisdictions to 'identify … interconnections, dependencies, and third parties … prioritise their relative importance, and assess their respective cyber risks'.

If indeed the cyber age is transformational of nearly everything, and if it is a multi-level (cross-domain) problem involving states, international organizations, private corporations, citizens, and communities, and if the study of one of its most fundamental aspects (dependency) is at an early stage, then we have some way to travel in understanding (rather than simply observing) the social construction of security in cyber space. The pleasant surprise the world experienced when social media played such a powerful role in the Arab Spring can now be contrasted with the dismay and uncertainty many people feel—after the apparent deceit surrounding Brexit and Donald Trump's 'alternative facts'—about the manipulation of cyber space and its information platforms in bringing into question the very legitimacy of democratic political processes in Western liberal democracies. The depth of surprise and dismay about the negative impacts on politics of the information age is directly attributable to the lack of prior granular study of the dependency of power holders and their challengers upon the relevant types of cyber age phenomena.

Cyber Dependency: A Deeper Look

As dependency studies have improved, there has been a broadening of the lens as to what is involved. Table 2.1 compares the headline categories for the different types of dependency, in the specific case of critical infrastructure, from two different studies. Of special note, the cyber dependency is seen as sitting alongside other non-cyber dependencies, almost in a mutually exclusive position, without significant reflection on how the cyber age might transform the mitigation potential (or vulnerability potential) associated with non-cyber types of dependency.

There has been substantial development of the concept of dependency based in part on this early work. In an ideal world, assuming perfect knowledge, the end point of study of any type of dependency might be similar to that proposed by Petit et al. (2015) in respect of critical infrastructure. This goal is a comprehensive 'understanding of all dependency and interdependency dimensions' in a way that 'allows decision makers to anticipate and characterize, in real time, how all dependency and interdependency dimensions influence the resilience and protection of a critical infrastructure system, of a region, and, ultimately, of the Nation' (p. 24).

On the one hand, it is easy to agree with the view of a European Union directive that concluded that many of the dependencies are difficult to analyse in any detail: 'participation in the global infrastructure ecosystem is inherently predicated on acceptance of a measure of unknowable risk'.[21] On the other hand, as mentioned earlier, Carnegie Mellon has developed a manual ('resource guide') on external dependency management for cyber space. While

---

Table 2.1 Headline descriptions of classes of dependence for critical infrastructure

Rinaldi et al.[a]	Pederson et al.[b]
Physical	Physical
Cyber	Informational
Geographic	Geospatial
Logical (seen as human decisions or actions)	Policy/procedural
	Societal

[a] S.M. Rinaldi, J. Peerenboom, and T. Kelly. 2001. 'Identifying, Understanding, and Analysing Critical Infrastructure Interdependencies', *IEEE Control Systems Magazine*, December, 11–25, 19.
[b] P. Pederson, D. Dudenhoffer, S. Hartley et al., 'Critical Infrastructure Interdependency Modeling: A Survey of U.S. and International Research', Idaho National Laboratory, http://cip.management.dal.ca/publications/Critical%20Infrastructure%20Interdependency%20Modeling.pdf

recognizing difficulties in data acquisition, the guide assumes that it is possible to identify, prioritize, monitor, and track external dependencies, even if 'organisations have a limited ability to directly monitor and control the vulnerabilities and threats introduced'.[22]

It is of considerable philosophical and ontological import that the analytical processes themselves, intended to enhance security and resilience in cyber space, demand (if only for the purposes of dependency analysis on a continuing and timely basis), the creation of entirely new sets and types of social relations, at some or all levels of social organization (individual, community, national, and international). For example, at the international level, in the interests of promoting cyber security, leading intergovernmental groups and international organizations, such as the BIS mentioned earlier, have called on states to share information on their dependencies, but this has involved a process of trust building and new relationship creation, both of which have become even more difficult under the pressure of escalating international tensions over cyber intrusions or abuse.

Understanding dependency is not just an information problem. It is a knowledge problem and furthermore a knowledge *management* problem, and both these sets of challenges also introduce new social realities and constructs. On the first point, the mapping of dependencies and the study of the linkages require the 'combination of multiple areas of expertise'.[23] The need to create, marshal, and exploit these diverse levels of expertise is itself a new phenomenon that creates new social structures as well as new opportunities and tensions between communities and states.

The second point about knowledge management of dependency is profoundly more interesting and challenging. How can a single political leader or corporate manager visualize any dependency that is constituted by phenomena that are highly divergent in character, plane of action, and speed of manifestation. Many cyber dependencies are simultaneously constituted, on the one hand, by a global geographic scope in terms of Internet-based systems that they use (and the physical human activities set in train by the systems) and, on the other hand, by invisible, atomic level electronic pathways and data that can produce system failures in milliseconds under multi-vector, multi-phase attacks, or malfunctions. According to specialists from the Argonne National Laboratory in the United States, writing in 2015, no scalable approach, standardized capability, or combination of capabilities to undertake such a mapping currently exists.[24] The authors propose 'a critical infrastructure dependency and interdependency assessment framework' that can evolve over time, be based on flexibility in approach, and 'allow the implementation of innovative capabilities that will reflect the evolution of technical capabilities and of critical infrastructure protection and resilience policies'. Even after the processes to collect the relevant data and analyse them are executed, the process of synthesizing and communicating them presents a novel challenge. Just one part of this challenge is the question of visualization of the map of dependencies in a way that is meaningful to decision makers who have had no part in the data collection or analysis, bearing in mind that the visualization is operating across a potentially large geographic scale at the same time as needing to incorporate assessments of non-tangible electronic activity. The authors say that 'Development of GIS visualization capabilities is vital for the analysis of critical infrastructure dependencies and interdependencies, especially in visualizing cascading and escalating failures at the regional level' (beyond a small locality involving one or two assets). They foreshadow a capability that can integrate results for generating forecasts of pathways of cascading, escalating, and common-cause failures in a way that can address second- and third-order dependencies.[25]

Thus, the process of addressing dependency in cyber space creates new information products with hitherto unseen levels of sophistication and complexity. Arguably, the need for new products designed to map and understand highly entangled dependency may actually aggravate it, thereby frustrating the very logic and purpose of such dependency study.

The proposition that the concept of cyber dependency analysis is in its infancy, as suggested by Petit et al. has been borne out by initial results from the roll-out of a campaign by the DHS to get the country's corporations attuned to the management of their external dependencies. We can source DHS work in this area to around 2009 and possibly earlier but, by January 2015, in reporting results of a joint DHS/Carnegie Mellon survey, Gaiser and Haller (2013) concluded, based on a sample of US enterprises, that the country's maturity in this area of activity on a scale of 0–5 was probably below 1. And the United States is by far the most advanced country in understanding of cyber dependencies.

In general terms, security in cyber space remains very weak at best and in most places is non-existent. This applies as much to our dependency at the personal level on unverified sources of information and on emails as it does at the national level to management of critical infrastructure and preparations for cyber-enabled war. As Cornish observed, 'complete dependence on the cybered world is generating a complacency and fatalism like that caused by the complete vulnerability to MAD',[26] a reference to the nuclear warfighting doctrine of mutual assured destruction.

CONCLUSION: TOWARDS POLITICAL FRAMING OF THE INFOSPHERE

For all the wonders of the information age, the dangers may for now be greater. This prospect arises from one simple consideration foreshadowed by Bell in 1976. We do not have a social and political design that can keep up with the pace and character of change in the information age. Security in cyber space has only recently become a serious national and international policy consideration, and smaller communities and individual citizens are just beginning to come to terms with the issues. This chapter argues that there is an inevitable linkage between these four levels of analysis. It also argues that the infosphere has created new social and political realities that are potentially transformative. Of these, issues of dependency are among the most important but also among the least studied. The primary challenge in policy terms is for institutional and social renovation that addresses the challenges of distributed political authority and the ethical and practical implications of the reaggregation of data. As Bell characterized it, we need more scientists (including social scientists) to compensate for the 'talented tinkerers' in technology. The social science of security in cyber space is only at an embryonic stage of development and is not keeping pace with the extraordinary work of both the gifted scientists and the talented tinkerers.

NOTES

1. Bell, 'Welcome', 49.
2. Masuda, *Information Society*, 3.
3. Hassan, *Information Society*, 22–3.
4. Castells, *Networks*, 239.
5. Floridi and Sanders, 'Mapping the Foundationalist debate', 1.
6. Floridi, 'Hyperhistory', 130.
7. Floridi, *Ethics of Information*, 296.
8. Personal communication with the author.
9. Floridi, *Ethics of Information*, 261–76.
10. Floridi, *Ethics of Information*, 275. As I read it, Floridi is not postulating what may be right or wrong in particular cases but rather that in the information age a judgement on the moral worth of an enabling act depends on how well it conforms to the inherent moral character of the information process, which is its power to create a desirable kind of distributed morality.
11. Floridi, *Ethics of Information*, 274.
12. Caporaso, 'Dependence', 19.
13. Caporaso, 'Dependence', 43.
14. Cornish, 'Vulnerabilities', 1.
15. Thakur, 'Cyber Dependency', 1.
16. Austin and Gady, 'Cyber Detente', 19.
17. Austin and Gady, 'Cyber Detente', 20.
18. Harold et al., 'Getting to Yes', 50.
19. Rauscher, 'Proceedings', 102.
20. Arce, 'WikiLeaks', 10.
21. Cited in Clemente, David. 2013. *Cyber Security and Global Interdependence: What is Critical*. London: Chatham House, p. 9.
22. Carnegie Mellon University, 'CRR Supplemental Resources Guide', 5.
23. Petit et al., 'Critical Infrastructure Dependencies and Interdependencies', 33.
24. Petit et al., 'Critical Infrastructure Dependencies and Interdependencies', 29.
25. Petit et al., 'Critical Infrastructure Dependencies and Interdependencies', 27.
26. Cornish, 'Vulnerabilities', 3.

REFERENCES

Arce, Daniel G. 2015. 'WikiLeaks and the risks to critical foreign dependencies', *International Journal of Critical Infrastructure Protection* 11, December: 3–11, 9.

Austin Greg, and Franz Gady. 2012. 'Cyber Detente between the United States and China', New York/Brussels/Moscow: EastWest Institute. https://www.eastwest.ngo/idea/cyber-detente-between-united-states-and-china.

Bank for International Settlements. 2014. 'Cyber Resilience in Financial Market Infrastructures'. Committee on Payments and Market Infrastructures, November: 4.

Bell, Daniel. 1973. *The Coming of Post-Industrial Society: A Venture in Social Forecasting*. Basic Books.

Bell, Daniel. 1976. 'Welcome to the Post-Industrial Society', *Physics Today*, February, 43–7, 46.

Caporaso, James A. 1978. 'Dependence, Dependency, and Power in the Global System: A Structural and Behavioral Analysis', *International Organization* 32 (1): 13–43, 18.

Carnegie Mellon University. 2016. 'CRR Supplemental Resources Guide. Vol. 8. External Dependencies Management', Version 1.1. https://www.us-cert.gov/sites/default/files/c3vp/crr_resources_guides/CRR_Resource_Guide-EDM.pdf.

Castells, Manuel. 2012. *Networks of Outrage and Hope*. Cambridge: Polity .

Cellan-Jones, Rory. 2014. 'Stephen Hawking Warns Artificial Intelligence Could End Mankind', BBC News, 2 December. http://www.bbc.com/news/technology-30290540 .

Cornish, Paul. 2009. 'Cyber Security and Politically, Socially and Religiously Motivated Cyber Attacks'. Report no: EP/EXPO/B/AFET/FWC/2006-10/Lot4/15, PE 406.997. Brussels: European Union (Directorate-General for External Policies of the Union), p. 28.

Cornish, Paul. 2011. *The Vulnerabilities of Developed States to Economic Cyber Warfare*. London: Chatham House, p. 11.

Floridi, Luciano. 2005. 'Information Ethics, Its Nature and Scope'. *Computers and Society* 35 (2). https://dl.acm.org/doi/fullHtml/10.1145/1111646.1111649.

Floridi Luciano. 2012. 'Hyperhistory and the Philosophy of Information Policies'. *Philosophy & Technology* 25 (2): 129–31.

Floridi, Luciano. 2013. *The Ethics of Information*. Oxford: Oxford University Press, p. 9.

Floridi, Luciano, and Jeffrey W. Sanders. 2002. 'Mapping the Foundationalist Debate in Computer Ethics'. *Ethics and Information Technology* 11: 1–9, 2.

G7 (Group of Seven). 2016. 'G7 Fundamental Elements of Cybersecurity for the Financial Sector'. https://www.gov.uk/government/uploads/system/uploads/attachment_data/file/559186/G7_Fundamental_Elements_Oct_2016.pdf.

Gaiser, R., and J. Haller. 2013. 'Methods and Tools for External Dependencies Management'. Carnegie Mellon University, PowerPoint presentation, slide 13.

Harold, Scott, Martin C. Libicki, and Astrid Cevallos. 2016. *Getting to Yes with China in Cyberspace*. Santa Monica, CA: RAND Corporation. http://www.rand.org/pubs/research_reports/RR1335.html, pp. 49–50.

Hassan, Robert. 2008. *The Information Society*. Cambridge: Polity, p. 219.

Hathaway, Melissa, and Alexander Klimburg. 2012. 'Preliminary Considerations: On National Cyber Security'. In *National Cyber Security Framework Manual*, edited by Alexander Klimburg, 1–43, 29–31. Tallinn: Cooperative Cyber Defence Centre of Excellence. http://www.bbc.com/news/technology-30290540.

Hobbes, Thomas. 1656. *Leviathan or the Matter, Forme, & Power of a Commonwealth Ecclesiasticall and Civill*. English edition. Prepared for the McMaster University Archive of the History of Economic Thought, by Rod Hay.

Klimburg, Alexander, and Jason Healey. 2012. 'Strategic Goals and Stakeholders'. In *National Cyber Security Framework Manual*, edited by Alexander Klimburg, 66–107, 100. Tallinn: Cooperative Cyber Defence Centre of Excellence.

Masuda, Yoneji. 1980. *The Information Society as Post-industrial Society*. Tokyo: Institute for the Information Society. Reprinted 1981: Washington DC: World Future Society, pp. 146–56.

Petit F., W. Buehring, D. Verner et al. 2015. 'Analysis of Critical Infrastructure Dependencies and Interdependencies', Global Security Sciences Division, Argonne National Laboratory. https://www.researchgate.net/profile/Frederic_Petit/publication/299525808_Analysis_of_Critical_Infrastructure_Depefndencies_and_Interdependencies/links/56fd450a08aeb723f15d67cf.pdf?origin=publication_list, p. 24.

Rauscher, Karl F. 2010. 'Proceedings of the Reliability of Global Undersea Cable Communications Infrastructure Study and Global Summit. The Report'. Institute of Electrical and Electronics Engineers and the EastWest Institute. Issue 1. http://www.ieee-rogucci.org/files/The%20ROGUCCI%20Report.pdf.

Rinaldi, S.M., J. Peerenboom, and T. Kelly. 2001. 'Identifying, Understanding, and Analysing Critical Infrastructure Interdependencies', *IEEE Control Systems Magazine*, December, 11–25, 19.

Thakur, Moha, 2016. 'Cyber Dependency at a Domestic and International Level: Literature Review'. Australian Centre for Cyber Security, University of New South Wales, Discussion Paper #4.

United Nations. 2003. 'Declaration of Principles. Building the Information Society: A Global Challenge in the New Millennium'. Document WSIS-03/GENEVA/DOC/4-E, 12 December.

US Department of Homeland Security. 2014. 'Cyber Resilience Review Fact Sheet'. https://www.us-cert.gov/sites/default/files/c3vp/crr-fact-sheet.pdf.

Webster, Frank. 2006. *Theories of the Information Society*. Third edition. Routledge, pp. 8–31.

Xinhua. 2016. 'President Xi Says China Faces Major Science, Technology Bottleneck', 1 June. http://news.xinhuanet.com/english/2016-06/01/c_135402671.htm.

CHAPTER 3

A POLITICAL HISTORY OF CYBERSPACE

MADELINE CARR

INTRODUCTION: A SHORT BUT INTENSE HISTORY

DIGITAL technologies are so prevalent now, and so intertwined with many aspects of our lives, that it is easy to forget just how rapidly they have emerged and how profoundly they have had an impact upon us. Technological transformations always have implications for the way people work, play, live, and die. The first and second industrial revolutions (mechanization of the textile industry in the late 1700s and steel/electricity in the latter half of the 1800s) brought about the complete reorganization of societies from self-sufficient, largely agrarian communities into urbanized, interdependent communities. Unlike previous technological shifts that were absorbed slowly over many decades or even centuries, these periods of intense change had significant impact upon people's lives within a single generation.

Looking back, of course we can identify a whole range of political decisions, pressures, expectations, and power that facilitated and promoted the industrial revolutions—quite distinct from science or technology. In large part, these political levers also shaped the way those transitions emerged and developed. We now find ourselves living through the third Industrial Revolution: the Information Age; and, arguably, embarking upon the fourth: the Internet of Things. Benefitting from historical examples and equipped with the understanding that politics not only shapes the way technology develops but also that technology itself may have significant implications for how political practices are carried out, we can take a more analytical and critical approach to this latest transformation. This chapter highlights some of the ways that politics and digital technologies have affected one another over the past quarter-century—specifically in the context of cyber security. In doing so, it argues that power shifts in what may seem to be largely technical domains often have quite significant correlations in global politics. For this reason, they are worth observing and analysing with some care.

There are a number of ways that an awareness of the political history of cyberspace can help us understand and interpret technological change and its implications for society. First, it can help us to understand why certain technological decisions were taken—for example, the adoption of one standard over another. This is particularly interesting in terms of cyber security where we have observed the deliberate adoption of some protocols, practices, and standards that were recognized—even at the time—as difficult to secure (Willemssen 2001). Sometimes, these decisions have been taken wholly within the technical community, with no obvious link to political preferences. In other cases, these decisions have actually been the subject of intense political debate. And in yet other cases, while politics may not have been a direct or overt influence, we might observe some underlying tensions or preferences that we can trace back to political ideals and values.

The second way that an awareness of the political history of cyberspace can help us understand and interpret technological change and its implications for society is by providing background to contemporary political debates. Negotiations in the United Nations over cyber norms, proposals to limit state aggression in cyberspace, and talks between heads of states about cooperation in fighting cyber threats all take place today on the back of considerable dispute, contestation, and also some cooperation at a political level. Without understanding something of the political history, these negotiations can be misinterpreted or appear disconnected from the context that has informed them.

Finally, the political history of cyberspace can be useful in articulating exactly how political actors can shape the future of technology. In most histories of cyberspace or the Internet, the focus is on technological milestones or developments. This is important but it often serves to mask the motivations and intentions of political actors who seek to influence technological developments and adoption. All these aspects of the complex intersections between technological developments and global politics are essential to considerations of how power might be redistributed in the future, and what that might mean for global peace and security.

Chapter 4 further develops these points through a series of steps. First, some of the key political events that ultimately shaped and promoted the development of the Internet are outlined. These help to illustrate the ways that technological developments are linked to, and sometimes embedded within, political tides and currents. The second section runs through some of the evolutions of political perceptions of cyber security threats. Observing both change and continuity in these perceptions helps us put current approaches into some perspective, and avoids the two reductionist arguments that either 'everything is different now' or 'it is the same as it ever was'. The chapter then turns to some of the ongoing debates about how to conceptualize this technology—particularly with relevance to the political implications it evokes. It is necessary to have some understanding of these in order to engage with the final section, which looks at which remedies have been proposed thus far—including those that have had some success as well as those that have not moved forward. Essentially, the chapter calls for much more careful and comprehensive engagement with the interrelationship between technological developments and political forces. Without a better understanding of these dynamics, it will be unlikely that we will move through this technological shift with any better prospect of delivering positive, human-centred outcomes for society than was the case in the first two industrial revolutions.

THE POLITICAL EVOLUTION OF INTERNET TECHNOLOGY

This edited volume very usefully dedicates several chapters to the much-needed examination of perspectives on cyber security from non-Western countries. This has been a real deficit in the past few decades of scholarship and one that it is essential to address if we are to better understand the complexities of global cyber security. Cyberspace has such broad implications and intersects with the human condition, politics, the economy, military power, and other global affairs in such important ways that it is not at all surprising that not all communities regard its benefits and challenges in the same way. Some political cultures place more emphasis on state security and others on personal security. Some countries are deeply reliant upon cyberspace while others are much less so. And, crucially, it is not at all clear that state power in the Information Age can be as clearly recognized and exercised as it was in the Industrial Age, which means that our ideas about which states are powerful and which are vulnerable may need reconsideration (Carr 2016a). In order to come to grips with the implications of cyberspace for questions about power, equity, legitimacy, and vulnerability in the future of global politics, we must engage much more comprehensively and honestly with non-Western views than we have in the past three decades.

This chapter, however, dealing as it does fairly narrowly with the political history of cyberspace, focuses largely on the United States. While there was certainly plenty of activity of both a political and a technical nature taking place in other states, throughout the latter half of the past century, the bulk of activity in both these domains was definitely in the United States. This was in part a consequence of heavy investment by the US government, excellent research institutions, and also the political vision of some key actors. There can be little question that, in the early second half of the twentieth century, the United States displayed considerable leadership on Internet technology. Crucially, it also dedicated concentrated attention to the integration of emerging technologies with a vision for how best to strengthen and project US power. To understand the political history of cyberspace, it is therefore necessary to engage in some depth with the political history of cyberspace in the United States. The critical lesson here is that, when states successfully link their strategic ambitions to technological investment, this can profoundly affect their global power status. This is a point worth keeping in mind as one reads through the subsequent chapters in this volume—particularly those that delve into non-Western states.

Catalyst: Sputnik Crisis

There had been a long-standing and strongly held belief in the US that technology and power were connected. Manufacturing technology had transformed the fortunes of the US through the first and second industrial revolutions. Transport and communications technologies had been essential to colonizing the west and uniting the expansive landmass into one 'United States'. In addition, military technology had allowed the United States to establish its dominance over the Western hemisphere through the Monroe Doctrine. This belief in technology as linked to state power meant that confidence in US global leadership was severely undermined by one event in the late fifties.

On 4 October 1957, the USSR successfully launched the Sputnik satellite into orbit. The Sputnik success was a profound shock to the US, which also had the (less ambitious) Vanguard satellite programme underway but still a long way from maturity (Killian 1977). It was clear that the USSR had surpassed the US in a critical technological moment which, in the context of the Cold War, had very serious implications. Satellite technology was expected to be married eventually to missile technology—potentially to allow for nuclear strikes from space (Dickson 2001). The United States government responded by investing heavily in the establishment of both the National Aeronautics and Space Administration (NASA) and the Defence Advanced Research Projects Administration (DARPA; Abbate 2000). DARPA (or 'ARPA' as it was renamed) would become a central source of funding for academics and industry researchers focused on networking and related technologies. The very proactive support channelled through ARPA was fundamental to the United States emerging as a global leader in information technology (IT)—a point often overlooked in assertions more common today that technological innovation is the domain of the private sector.

The Cold War Research

Throughout the remainder of the Cold War years, the United States continued to invest enthusiastically in technology. While there was no way that the transformative effects of the Information Age could be anticipated back then, the computational power to solve complex problems and process data was seen as essential to most areas of science and technology that might underpin a return to global technological dominance for the United States. For this reason, harnessing this computational power for as many projects as possible was regarded as efficient resource management, and finding a way to get the most out of expensive computers that were typically housed in universities or large research institutes became a priority. Networking these computers would allow better access and support more work, and it was funded generously by ARPA on that basis.

It is important to note that, while the US government saw the links between strategic competition with the USSR and investment in technology that could be channeled to developing a military advantage, the researchers funded to carry out this work were certainly not all motivated along those lines. They were largely mathematicians, physicists, programmers, and engineers who developed research projects along the lines of their own interests while making use of available funding.

One of the projects to emerge from this research funding was a proposal to develop a secure and resilient communications system that was envisaged to enhance the second strike capability of the United States in case of a nuclear attack. The existing telephone system was a 'hub and spokes' model, which meant that, if the 'hub' (the exchange) was disabled, the system as a whole would be incapacitated. It seems a prosaic concern today, but the reality was that, in the event of a nuclear strike on the United States, a phone call would be necessary to launch a retaliatory attack and thus the 'second strike' capability rested upon a vulnerable communications system.[1] At the height of the Cold War, this was certainly a valid concern and, thus, the project was funded. It contributed to the development of networking technology, in concert with the many other funded research projects undertaken through those years.

Although computer scientists around the world were working on developing networking protocols at the same time, in the United States, this government funding was fostering a core group of talented researchers including Robert Kahn and Vinton Cerf who would later be credited with developing the important Transmission Control Protocol/Internet Protocol (TCP/IP; Cerf and Kahn 1974). This concentrated post-Sputnik investment in US technology research had exactly the desired effect: there emerged a concentration of skills and knowledge that gave the United States an edge and allowed it to shape the future of computer networking to a large extent.

Clinton/Gore Initiatives and Vision

By the beginning of the 1990s, a number of important changes had taken place that were significant for the political history of cyberspace. The Cold War had concluded with the dissolution of the USSR and a new team of Democrats had moved into the White House. Bill Clinton and his vice-president Al Gore formed a cohesive and effective political partnership. Clinton's ambitions to turn the world beyond the Iron Curtain into a truly global marketplace for the United States married neatly with Gore's long-standing belief in the future of IT (Gore 1989). Together, they formulated a powerful plan to use the internet to deliver US goods and services to the world, and to spread democracy and human rights—both in an effort to reshape the post-Cold War global order (Clinton 1993).

As was the general trend in many Western states in the 1980s and 1990s, the Clinton/Gore administration had a strong preference for private sector ownership of critical infrastructure—of which information and communications infrastructure was one component (Carr 2016b; Legrand 2014). Although the internet had been government funded and directly or indirectly managed by the state from its inception, the Clinton/Gore vision was very much one in which both the infrastructure and the management (what came to be known as 'governance') of the Internet would eventually be taken over by the private sector. However, it was not entirely clear in those early days just what the business case for the provision of Internet access might be and the private sector was cautious about committing investment. It was only after years of government investment, management, and strong political belief in the future of the internet that private organizations began to see that there was, indeed, commercial benefit to be harnessed. In keeping with the Clinton/Gore vision, by the mid-1990s, the internet was both commercialized and privatized.

These dominant political ideas in the United States would further shape the way this technology developed with lasting consequences for cyber security. The preference for openness, interoperability and innovation without permission were arguably fundamental to the success of the internet—and they also helped to build in some of the intractable security problems with which we now contend.

The Evolution of Cyber Threats

As information and communications technology developed and as states' reliance on this technology increased in scope and sophistication, the imagination and innovation of malicious actors in cyberspace meant that threats and attack vectors continued to evolve at a relentless pace. Consequently, ideas about what constituted cyber security vulnerabilities, and who the primary threat actors were, also changed. Looking back at the ways that cyber security has been perceived by politicians over the past 30 years provides some interesting insights into how the field has developed and evolved. It also provides some perspective on change and continuity that might help us anticipate future trends.

Early cyber threat actors were typically computer enthusiasts or engineers—very often motivated by proving either that they had the skills to break into a system believed to be secure (a kind of self-aggrandizement) or that the security flaws that they were able to exploit should be taken more seriously (a 'public good' motivation). This activity often took the form of intrusion and the proliferation of malware like the Morris worm or the Love virus was indicative. These were regarded as serious and concerning but they were predominantly viewed through a law enforcement lens and not a political or global conflict lens. Both these activities obviously continue today on a vast scale, but they are now augmented by much more sophisticated practices that move beyond criminality and into the domain of political conflict.

Early website defacement

In the very early years of thinking about cyber security as a national security concern, there was a focus on website defacement. This tended to take place in the context of existing political tensions. Pakistan and India, or Palestine and Israel, were common cases of website defacement. Although it seems relatively inconsequential today, politically motivated attacks on websites were initially seen as a new domain of political conflict. There was a kind of anxiety that stemmed from the realization that these attacks were difficult to trace back to a particular person, that they could arise from beyond the state borders, and that they could be used to inflame political conflict in the physical world or politically influence civil society.

Cyber Pearl Harbour

These same anxieties featured in the next wave of perceived cyber threats: distributed denial of service (DDoS) attacks on critical infrastructure. Critical infrastructure vulnerabilities had been a concern for policy makers almost from the beginning of the internet. As critical infrastructure like utilities, transport, and communication were denationalized and sold off to private sector owners and operators, and as networking technology developed, the inevitable happened. The industrial control systems used to control critical infrastructure were networked. This allowed for remote monitoring and management, and was seen as one way to enhance efficiency and cut costs. However, for various reasons, these systems were relatively vulnerable to attack. They tended to be built on outdated and insecure operating systems, and it could be both costly and risky to install software patches and updates—a fundamental element of contemporary cyber security practices (the May 2017 'Wannacry' NHS incident is a key example of this). This led to the use of the term 'Cyber Pearl Harbour'—particularly in the United States—to depict the political anxiety about a potentially devastating surprise attack on the homeland. The perpetrators of such an attack were expected to be a mix of actors: determined non-state criminally or politically motivated groups (including terrorists) or possibly states.

In 2007, in the midst of a diplomatic row with Russia over the relocation of a military memorial in Tallinn, Estonia experienced just such an attack, causing disruption to governmental websites and many services like news dissemination, banking, and law enforcement. Although this DDoS attack has never been conclusively attributed to the Russian state, the political context that enveloped it led many to believe that this was indeed a state-based attack. Estonia's appeal to NATO for support brought into focus the alliance's inability to deal with this new security threat under Article Five of its founding treaty and it prompted a wave of new thinking about how cyber insecurity could be understood within conventional international relations and international law frameworks.

The experience gained by both Estonia and NATO prompted governments, alliances, and regional groupings to consider much more carefully how exactly they might respond, cooperate, and work to mitigate cyber attacks in the future. The development of cyber security doctrine and policies intensified in many states and NATO established the Cooperative Cyber Defence Centre of Excellence (CCD CoE), which has subsequently produced some leading research on these issues, including the *Tallinn Manual on the International Law Applicable to Cyber Warfare* (Schmitt 2013).

Stuxnet

In 2010, another significant cyber incident took place that further shaped perceptions of the politics of global cyber security, especially in relation to critical infrastructure. Iran reported that it had suffered a targeted cyber attack on the industrial control system at its Natanz nuclear enrichment facility. The Stuxnet 'worm', as it came to be known, facilitated the physical damage of a set of centrifuges at the facility, reportedly disrupting the Iranian nuclear programme. This incident was significant because it was the first publicly reported example of a cyber attack causing physical damage to what could be regarded as a military asset. Once again, technical attribution has not been possible (at least not within the public domain) but, as in the Estonian case, the political context led many to conclude that the perpetrators were identifiable. In this case, the attack was believed to come from a joint programme between the United States and Israel—an account that has been comprehensively documented by *New York Times* journalist David Sanger but not officially verified by either state.

Internal challenges

While attention had been somewhat diverted to state-based activity as the source of threats in cyberspace, a new internal security concern emerged in the United States that had implications for global politics. In 2010, the whistle-blower website WikiLeaks made available a large number of US classified documents to major media outlets—documents mainly relating to the Iraq war that had been exfiltrated from a military network by Bradley (later Chelsea) Manning—then a US soldier serving in Iraq. Three years later, the Central Intelligence Agency IT contractor Edward Snowden also released classified details—this time about the extent of the US intelligence community's surveillance capability and practices. Not surprisingly, there are quite polarized views about whether these acts were commendable or condemnable. Although there are some important distinctions between the two cases, both of them reinforced the growing sense that many people are conflicted about issues such as information transparency, secrecy, and privacy—both at an individual and a state level. In the context of the Information Age when so much data can be stored on such physically small devices, it appears to be increasingly difficult for states to conceal much. Choosing what to conceal and what to reveal has been a fundamental element of statecraft and, thus, these challenges of controlling information, data, and secrets are being regarded as cyber security concerns in global politics to a new and enhanced degree.

The Future of Cyber Security Threats

Of course, the cyber security concerns of yesterday and today might not necessarily be the concerns of tomorrow. This brief summary of changing threat perceptions over the past few decades makes that abundantly clear. We have some insight into what will possibly become a further cause for concern, but predicting the trajectory of technological change and especially predicting the way that humans will interact with changing technology has always been more of an art than a science. There are many anticipated vulnerabilities that researchers, analysts, and policy makers are already focusing on, and others will emerge over time. Some of the issues that look set to feature in the future of international security are to be found in the developments of what is called the 'Internet of Things (IoT)' or the 'fourth industrial revolution'.

The Internet of Things refers to the increasing proliferation of embedded sensors in devices, in our environment, even in our bodies—that collect and transmit data that is then analysed and often used to produce real-world effects. There are expectations of significant benefits in the collection of the vast data sets that will be possible as a consequence of networking the hundreds of billions of devices that are expected to comprise the Internet of Things by 2025 (Statista, 2021). These benefits include not only economic value but also considerable research potential. For example, the collection of data from implantable medical devices can provide a scale of valuable research material otherwise impossible to collect through conventional means. However, there are many questions about the rights, liabilities, and responsibilities of personal data. Who will own the data generated by implantable devices? The person in whose body it resides? The medical practitioner who implants and monitors it? The company that manufactures and maintains the devices? And to what extent can people give consent to the use of their data when, in the Internet of Things, one is not always aware that one is sharing data or even interacting with a device?

Intrinsic to the cyber security concerns evolving around the Internet of Things are the 'real-world effects'. Devices that are connected can be compromised. Security researchers have already demonstrated how cars can be hacked and intentionally crashed. The same security implications apply to implanted or ingested medical devices and anticipated autonomous transport systems like international shipping. Also intrinsic to these evolving cyber security concerns is the growing and ever more critical reliance on data integrity and data privacy. If systems at both the micro (our bodies) and macro (critical infrastructure) levels increasingly rely on the automated collection and analysis of data, it becomes ever more important that we can rely upon the integrity and availability of those data streams. Another interesting dynamic here is the renewed challenge of DDoS attacks, briefly regarded as of little real concern due to the fact that they are not sustainable over a long period of time and do not usually cause lasting damage or facilitate theft. However, every insecure and connected device is an entry point to the network through which malicious actors can access and disrupt legitimate activity. Given that many Internet of Things devices are so small and so simple that they cannot support security mechanisms like passwords or software updates, there is some concern that these hundreds of billions of (largely unsecured) devices are rapidly causing the decay of whatever network security we have managed to achieve to date. And once these devices are coordinated into a DDoS attack (we witnessed the first one in late 2016[2]), the potential for widespread disruption escalates quickly.

It is not possible (or necessary) to describe every past or current cyber security vulnerability here. Nor it is possible to provide much certainty about the future of cyber security—although many chapters in this volume will offer considerable insight into that very question. In seeking to anticipate future security vulnerabilities and to mitigate against them, an understanding of the historical trends and political perceptions of cyber security can help provide an awareness of both change and continuity. We can see that some threats relate to concerns about the resilience of the state, some relate to civil society concerns about privacy and security, and others combine both.

MAJOR (AND ONGOING) DEBATES ABOUT CONCEPTUALIZING CYBER SECURITY

Although there has been general agreement that the problems and opportunities of cyberspace require coordination and cooperation across sectors, across borders, and across levels of governance, putting this into practice has been quite difficult. There are many reasons why, including the problems of coordinating domestic law and applying international law, the difficulties of conclusively attributing malicious activity in cyberspace, and the wide range of (sometimes competing or conflicting) interests that need to be accommodated. Also relevant, and perhaps less discussed, are quite fundamental differences in how key principles or concepts are understood and internalized by different state actors. These differences can quite significantly shape approaches to cyber security and the differences discussed later have been key factors in attempts to fashion a more coherent global approach to cyber security. It is important to note, however, that, although these factors are presented as dichotomies here, this can also dangerously over-simplify complex positions and considerations that further shape the approaches of state actors as well as the interactions between them. In reality, most political actors are not situated neatly at either end of these polarized positions but, rather, somewhere in the grey area between them.

Cyberspace as Borderless or Sovereign?

Internet technology heightened and intensified discussions that emerged from the globalization literature about the utility and ongoing relevance of the Westphalian system of states (Eriksson and Giacomello 2006). This (non)alignment of the territorial state with the internet is one of the divisive issues that underpin a lot of debate about global cyber security. There are two powerful reasons why some argue for the promotion and protection of a universal online experience for all those who access the internet. First, it has come to be regarded as a human right that all people should have access to the most comprehensive knowledge base ever conceived. If only some had this privilege, they would surely benefit disproportionately to those who did not—thereby entrenching the 'digital divide'. The second reason is that it is believed by some that the very act of connecting civil society through the internet could be a mechanism by which to promote peace and unity—through a newly connected 'global civil society' that would be able to circumvent or supplement conventional great power politics for the betterment of humankind. These ideas have been very firmly grounded in the United States, the European Union, Canada, Australia, and other 'like-minded' states which tend to refer to cyberspace as a 'global commons' or 'global public good'. Indeed, these ideas were eventually folded into US foreign policy under Secretary of State Hillary Clinton who combined them in the US 'Internet Freedom' doctrine (Clinton 2010) and, in 2012, Internet Freedom was declared a universal human right by the United Nations (UN Human Rights Council 2012).

For many other states, the perceived necessity of controlling both the content available online and activity carried out online, has led to a reassertion of sovereign principles of state authority. These states regard cyberspace as very much an extension of territorial space and, therefore, subject to the same levels and dimensions of state control as physical space. Of the great powers, sovereignty in cyberspace has been promoted most assertively by China and Russia but it also resonates strongly with many others—particularly post-colonial states. For these states, any relinquishment of sovereign control can be regarded as an unwelcome throwback to pre-independence. Contrary to some suggestions that this is simply the view of oppressive or autocratic regimes, it can be quite a complex issue that eludes a binary narrative of 'free' or 'not free' (Cornish 2015). In fact, civil society in these countries can often be supportive of firmer state control because they regard economic growth and national autonomy as indicators of governmental legitimacy (Mueller and Wagner 2014).

Information Security Versus Cyber Security

Related to the conceptions of cyberspace as borderless or sovereign is a second conceptual polarization: that of information security versus cyber security. At the great power level, these two concepts again tend to define the Chinese/Russian and the US approaches respectively. The United States prefers the term 'cyber security' to indicate a more confined mandate limited to infrastructure and applications. 'Information security', which Russia and China use, encompasses content as well—particularly content that could be politically or socially destabilizing. For those states, controlling politically or socially charged information is seen as essential to maintaining internal cohesion and it is therefore linked to national security. States that favour 'cyber security' as the defining concept argue that the 'information security' approach can be a mechanism for political oppression and is antithetical to the principles of a free, open internet that they favour. The problem of defining and enforcing jurisdiction in cyberspace remains deeply problematic.[3] Questions about who can or should control information continue to be debated, contested, and reconsidered as the implications of cyberspace shift and change.

These debates, of course, link back to the tensions over cyberspace as borderless or sovereign but they also relate to questions about the public/private layers of responsibility and authority in controlling internet infrastructure and content. The complexity of these arguments played out in a very stark and significant way during the 2016 US elections when there were allegations that Russia intervened to shape the election outcome. This suggestion that one state could potentially manipulate information in another state to pursue its own interests is one that has been raised many times at the United Nations—initially by Russia in 1998 and repeatedly over subsequent years by both the Russians and the Chinese (Tikk-Ringas 2016).

Security versus Privacy

Unlike either of the above conceptual tensions, different understandings of security and privacy are not as easily ascribed to particular states. Rather, they involve complex, intertwined and sometimes conflicting ideas that are distinct to actors, sectors, and contexts. Both security and privacy are abstract and deeply subjective concepts. For some actors, and in some contexts, privacy and security are indivisible. Surveillance and the self (or state) censorship that it evokes are fundamental threats to security. If individuals cannot enjoy a private life, free from scrutiny, there can be further negative implications for the political health of a state. Civil society's capacity to hold the government to account can be undermined and potentially lead not only to an individual sense of insecurity but a broader, national, and even international insecurity.

For others, online privacy or anonymity facilitates antisocial or even criminal behaviour. The challenges of connecting malicious activity to an individual actor can seriously undermine the efforts of law enforcement and can erode the sense of personal or professional accountability that, to some extent, moderates behaviour in a positive way. By this view, transparency is more important to security than privacy: the fact that the internet allows actors to shield their identity behind an avatar, a user name, or a re-routed IP address leads to a level of risk-taking and undesirable behaviour that can undermine the security of others.

Related to this are differing views about the appropriate role of the private sector in internet governance and cyber security. Again, many Western states that prefer minimal government involvement have regarded the private sector as better equipped to drive the direction of internet technology (though this is beginning to be challenged now).[4] This is generally for several reasons. First, they tend to view the private sector as being in possession of superior technical expertise. Second, there is a prevailing view that private sector ambitions are somehow more legitimate and perhaps more impartial than those of governments. Others have significant concerns about, first, how the private sector actors use the information they collect and whom they sell it on to, and second, the extent to which they themselves cooperate with governments that wish to make use of that data. (For a more comprehensive overview of three different approaches to data governance, see Carr and Llanos, 2021.)

These complex approaches to security and privacy, and to the interplay or relationship between them, cannot be untangled here. Security studies (and critical security studies) and psychology are both rich fields that seek to understand these and other related concepts, and it would be impossible to devote anything but the most cursory attention to them here. However, an awareness of some of the nuances and divergent views of these concepts is essential to keep in mind when engaging with this material. Not only can these terms have different meanings for different actors in different contexts but, most problematically, they are often conflated and assumed to mean the same thing. 'Cyber security' and 'information security' are equally meaningless terms unless we first unpack the meaning behind 'security'.

PROPOSED REMEDIES: FAILED, STALLED AND ONGOING

In considering the complex intersections between technological developments and global politics, it is useful to examine the ways that states have attempted to pursue a global, coordinated approach. While multilateral coordinated efforts (at least in the political domain) have been relatively slow to eventuate, what did develop quite quickly were domestic cyber security strategies. Here again, the United States led the way. Cyber security began to appear in the *US National Security Strategy* in 1998 under the Clinton presidency. In 2000, Clinton released the first *National Plan for Information Systems Protection* (Clinton 2000) and, in 2003, President Bush released *The National Strategy to Secure Cyberspace* (Bush 2003). Other states began to follow this lead, initially addressing cyber security through national security strategies and then, relatively quickly, producing dedicated cyber security strategies.

These national cyber security strategies provide insight into how governments have perceived and interpreted cyber security as an issue of national interest. They are useful for understanding how ideas about the politics of cyber attacks have changed over time, which big debates have developed and dominated the political discourse, and how future security concerns are taking shape. These are all central to the politics of cyber security. While these national policy documents continue to proliferate and provide insight into the commonalities and distinctions in state views on cybersecurity, a number of international initiatives have also been developed or proposed to try to address collectively the challenges of cybersecurity.

International Code of Conduct for Information Security

At quite an early stage, states began to anticipate the challenges that cyberspace might pose for global security. Concerns about the potential for 'information weapons' and the 'threat of information wars' were raised at the UN by Russia as early as 1998.[5] However, the considerable challenges of integrating this rapidly evolving technology into existing concepts and practices of international relations mean that, despite decades of diplomatic effort, few resolutions on cyberspace and global security have been reached. In 2011, four states proposed for consideration by the UN a new *International Code of Conduct for Information*

Security for consideration by the UN.[6] Russia, China, Tajikistan, and Uzbekistan argued that it was necessary to clarify the rights and responsibilities of states in protecting information infrastructure. The proposal placed a heavy emphasis on sovereign control and domestic legal jurisdiction. It also called for a multilateral mechanism to resolve international disputes in cyberspace.

The United States criticized the proposal for its emphasis on 'information security' rather than their preferred term of 'cybersecurity'. In 2015, the proposal was revised to incorporate some of the feedback from the international community and reintroduced to the UN by an expanded group of states that now included Kazakhstan and Kyrgyzstan. Significantly, this group now constituted the full membership of the Shanghai Cooperative Organization. The revised proposal was unable to attract more widespread support though these debates continue through the UN Group of Governmental Experts process discussed in more detail elsewhere in this chapter.

Budapest Convention

In 2001, the Council of Europe introduced the Convention on Cybercrime (the Budapest Convention) and opened it for signature by all states. This remains the only international treaty on cyber security. It has had some success but has also encountered some persistent challenges. The aim of the treaty is to enable more effective cooperation between states (specifically, between law enforcement agencies within states) in investigating and prosecuting cyber crime, which is often initiated in one state and has effects in another. To do this, states must align their criminal codes so that there is a common agreement on what constitutes a crime in different jurisdictions. At the time of writing, the Budapest Convention has been ratified by 54 European and non-European states.

Some key states that have not signed or ratified the Budapest Convention include the BRICS (although, in 2001, South Africa signed but never ratified the treaty). Russia, China, Brazil, and India are among the states that have objected for two main reasons. First, for some states, the Budapest Convention raises concerns about the relinquishment of sovereign control. The Russians, in particular, have said they will not assent to permitting foreign law enforcement agencies to conduct internet searches inside their borders (Markoff and Kramer 2009). The second reason why some states have objected to the Budapest Convention has to do with procedural rather than substantial issues. The treaty was developed and implemented largely within the European context although there were a number of participant and observer states from outside Europe involved in the process. Some states are unwilling to sign up to a treaty that they had no voice in drafting. This need to balance inclusiveness with efficacy that can sometimes only come from working in a smaller group will also likely become an issue for the UN Group of Governmental Experts (UNGGE) that has been working in small groups to develop a set of proposed 'cyber norms'.

United Nations Group of Governmental Experts

As noted in this chapter, Russia raised concerns about the militarization of cyberspace at the UN General Assembly in 1998 (Inkster 2015). In response to this, the United

Nations established the UNGGE to explore developments in the field of information and telecommunications in the context of international security under the Committee for Disarmament and International Security (First Committee).[7] Its goal has been to agree some norms of responsible state behavior in cyberspace that could be universally accepted. The UNGGE comprises the five permanent members of the Security Council and a small group of other states that apply to take part. It convened for the first time in 2004–5 with 10 additional states but the group failed to produce a consensus report. It then reconvened in 2009–10 (10 additional states), 2012–13 (10 additional states), 2014–15 (15 additional states), and 2016–17 (20 additional states and still underway at time of writing). The 2014–15 UNGGE produced an important consensus report in which the participants identified 11 proposed norms for responsible state behaviour in cyberspace.[8] Among these are norms that *prohibit* certain behaviour, including 'states should not knowingly allow their territory to be used for internationally wrongful acts using ICTs and states should not conduct or knowingly support ICT activity that intentionally damages critical infrastructure'. In addition, there are norms that speak to best practice or expectations of actions that states should take. These include the normative claims that 'states should take appropriate measures to protect their critical infrastructure' and that 'states should respond to appropriate requests for assistance by other states whose critical infrastructure is subject to malicious ICT acts'.

At this stage, these norms are only *proposed* norms and considerations on how best to implement them continue. One line of discussion involves more specificity about what exactly the 11 norms entail in practice. Another involves considering how they might be more widely adopted. Presumably, the 20 states involved in delivering the 2015 consensus report agree to adhere to those norms but they now need to be internalized by the rest of the international community. An update is due in 2021 that will develop this further.

The UNGGE norms process is arguably slow and is frequently criticized by external actors, especially in the private and technical sectors, for being too disconnected from the day-to-day realities of cyber security. However, it could be argued that the norms process is an essential step for international coordination and cooperation on cyber security, and that the consensus report and the 11 proposed norms are actually quite a significant achievement—given the range of complex factors that inhibit states aligning more closely over cyber security. Indeed, over the past 25 years, neither technical nor legal solutions have proven much more effective. Despite a hugely expensive and profitable cyber security technical industry, we currently find ourselves as insecure as, or possibly more insecure than, ever before. In terms of legal solutions, the application of international law to cyberspace has proven deeply problematic. At this point, and despite much effort, there is no agreement on what exactly constitutes an armed attack in cyberspace or the use of force—two critical elements of the international laws of armed conflict.[9] Consequently, in the absence of much promise from either a legal or a technical perspective, states instead engage in that slow, laborious, and often frustrating practice of discussion and negotiation about agreed norms of what is and is not acceptable behavior (Carr 2017).

While the slow progress on this is frustrating for many, it is less surprising for those who study other issues of global security cooperation. There have been some important cyber security initiatives put forward by states that, when scrutinized, serve to highlight how the persistent injection of power politics has slowed down any potential progress on international cooperation. In fact, while cyber security is increasingly recognized as a serious threat to national and global security, it is rarely the end goal. Rather, the promotion of a broader set of interests and goals specific to powerful states provides the context within which cyber security is navigated and negotiated. Put simply, some international cyber security proposals and initiatives have been subsumed by broader political agendas rather than evaluated on the basis of the quality of the content or ideas behind them. Given the extent of the growing implications for cyber insecurity, this could be regarded as a failure of states to adequately balance the perennial forces of great power politics with the pursuit of common or shared security goals.

Conclusion

In essence then, we come full circle back to an analysis of how political factors interact with technological developments—in a multidimensional way. As with any historical analysis, the purpose is to develop a better understanding of the context in which we move forward. The problems of cyber security are not simply technological. Rather, they are embedded in the ways that we choose to integrate that technology into a whole range of social, legal, economic, military, and political practices and processes. They are shaped by us and shape us. They are perceived differently in some ways and consistently in others. They cannot be resolved by technology or law alone because they spill out well beyond the borders of either of those domains.

One thing that is clear, however, is that, although politics may certainly be an impediment to better cyber security on one level, it will never be separated from it. Technological change responds to the needs of powerful actors—both state and non-state. It rarely develops in a context completely disconnected from perceived 'problem solving' (or threats) and how those problems are perceived and promoted is a function of power dynamics—within societies, within states, and within the international system. In order to ensure that the great opportunities of the third and fourth industrial revolutions are distributed in line with principles of equity, justice, and human rights, it is essential that we develop much more awareness of the political dynamics behind these movements. Doing so may allow us to deliver outcomes more conducive to global prosperity and harmony than those of the first and second industrial revolutions that have arguably institutionalized an unprecedented concentration of wealth as well as extraordinary benefits.

Notes

1. Abbate, Inventing the Internet, 40.
2. The Mirai attack first emerged on the website of security professional Brian Krebs. It is believed to have been predominantly comprised of unsecured CCTV cameras: Krebs, B. 2016. 'KrebsOnSecurity Hit With Record DDoS'. *Krebs on Security*. 21 September.
   For analysis, see Carr, M. 2013. 'Internet Freedom, Human Rights and Power', *Australian Journal of International Affairs* 67 (5): 621–37.
3. See the Internet & Jurisdiction Project: http://www.internetjurisdiction.net.
4. International Code of Conduct for Information Security, 2011: https://www.rusemb.org.uk/policycontact/49

5. Tikk-Ringas, *Evolution of the Cyber Domain*, 117.
6. International Code of Conduct for Information Security, 2011: https://www.rusemb.org.uk/policycontact/49
7. UN Resolution: A/RES/53/70, *Developments in the field of information and telecommunications in the context of international security*, Resolution Adopted by the General Assembly [*on the report of the First Committee (A/53/576)*], 4 January 1999.
8. UN General Assembly. 2015. *Group of Governmental Experts on Developments in the Field of Information and Telecommunications in the Context of International Security.*
9. Schmitt, *Tallinn manual.*

References

Abbate, J. 2000. *Inventing the Internet*. Cambridge, MA: The MIT Press: 36.

Bush, G.W. 2003. *The National Strategy to Secure Cyberspace*. Washington, D.C.: The White House.

Carr, M. 2016a. *US Power and the Internet in International Relations: The Irony of the Information Age*. Basingstoke: Palgrave MacMillan.

Carr, M. 2016b. 'Public-Private Partnerships in National Cyber Security Strategies', *International Affairs* 92 (1): 43–62.

Carr, M. 2017. 'Cyberspace and International Order'. In *The Anarchical Society at 40: Contemporary Challenges and Prospects*, edited by H. Suganami, M. Carr, and A. Humphreys. Oxford: Oxford University Press.

Carr, M. and Jose Tomas Llanos. 2021. 'Global Governance Challenges'. In *Global Governance Futures*, edited by Thomas G. Weiss and Rorden Wilkinson. Abingdon: Routledge.

Cerf, V., and R. Kahn. 1974. 'A Protocol for Packet Network Intercommunication'. *IEEE Transactions on Communications* 22 (5): 637–48.

Clinton, W. 2000. *Defending America's Cyberspace: National Plan for Information Systems Protection*. Washington D.C.: The White House.

Clinton, President W.J. 1993. 'Technology for America's Economic Growth: A New Direction to Build Economic Strength', *The Bottom Line* 6 (3/4): 4–17.

Clinton, W. 2000. *Defending America's Cyberspace: National Plan for Information Systems Protection*. Washington D.C.: The White House.

Clinton, H. 2010. 'Remarks on Internet Freedom', The Newseum, Washington, D.C. 21 January.

Cornish, P. 2015. 'Governing Cyberspace Through Constructive Ambiguity', *Survival* 57 (3): 153–76.

Eriksson, J., and G. Giacomello. 2006. 'The Information Revolution, Security and International Relations: (IR)relevant Theory?', *International Political Science Review* 27 (3): 221–44.

Gore, A. Jr. 1989. 'The Information Superhighways of Tomorrow', *Academic Computing Magazine* 4 (3): 30–.

Inkster, N. 2015. 'Battle for the Soul of the Internet', *Adelphi Series* 55.456: 109–42.

Killian, J.R. 1977. 'Sputnik Fever', *The Sciences* 17 (6): 6–9.

Legrand, T. 2014. 'Of Citadels and Sentinels: State Strategies for Combating Cyber-Terrorism'. In *Cyber-Terrorism*, edited by T. Chen, L. Jarvis, and S. Macdonald, 137–54. London: Springer.

Lionel Sujay Vailshery, "IoT and non-IoT connections worldwide 2010-2025", Statista, March 8, 2021. https://www.statista.com/statistics/1101442/iot-number-of-connected-devices-worldwide/

Markoff, J., and Kramer, A.E. 2009. 'In Shift, US Talks to Russia on Internet Security', *The New York Times*, 13 December: A1.

Mueller, M., and B. Wagner. 2014. 'Finding a Formula for Brazil: Representation and Legitimacy in Internet Governance', *Internet Policy Observatory* 8.

Nordrum, A. 2016. 'Popular Internet of Things Forecast of 50 Billion Devices by 2020 Is Outdated', *IEEE Spectrum* 18.

Schmitt, Michael N. 2013. *Tallinn Manual on the International Law Applicable to Cyber Warfare*. Cambridge: Cambridge University Press.

Tikk-Ringas, E. (ed.). 2016. *Evolution of the Cyber Domain: The Implications for National and Global Security*. London, IISS: 117.

UN Human Rights Council 2012. 'The promotion, protection and enjoyment of human rights on the Internet'. https://www.ohchr.org/EN/HRBodies/HRC/RegularSessions/Session20/Pages/ResDecStat.aspx.

Willemssen, Joel. 2001. Testimony at the 'How Safe is our Critical Infrastructure?' hearing before the Governmental Affairs Committee, United States Senate, 12 September.

CHAPTER 4

CYBER POWER IN INTERNATIONAL RELATIONS

TIM STEVENS AND CAMINO KAVANAGH

INTRODUCTION

THE conduct and practice of international relations are inextricably bound up with notions of power. Conventionally, power is understood as something to be obtained and wielded in pursuit of individual or collective goals. For this reason, strategy, both political and military, is considered the 'art of creating power', of generating more through one's actions than one began with (Freedman 2013, xii). National resources—territorial, material, financial—are converted into diverse means with which to coerce or convince an opponent to align their interests with yours, or to defeat their objections if they refuse. Resources grant you the 'power to' do something, through which you can develop 'power over' others. Historically, an important source of national power has been access to technology, from the superior military technologies of great empires to the consumer technologies of today's economic giants. Each has granted states potentially decisive opportunities to extend control and influence over others, which, while rarely uncontested, have led to transformations in international political and economic order.

The emergence of the global Internet has thrown these political and economic considerations into sharp relief. The history thus far of this remarkable technology confirms that states are no longer the sole significant actors in the international system. A host of commercial and non-state actors has seized the opportunities of the Internet to promote and pursue their own agendas, and to generate new webs of power and influence in a hyperconnected world. As a response to this renewed challenge to the primacy of state sovereignty, states have responded in multiple ways to reassert themselves in and through this complex environment, some seeking to maintain the status quo, others to disrupt it. The twin dynamics of power diffusion and decentralization have also revived reflection on the nature and character of power in international politics. How should we adjust our understanding of national power with respect to the transnational and supranational Internet? Do our theories of power need revising for this radical technological milieu? What other conceptions of power should we consult to understand better the workings of power in contemporary international relations? Marrying 'power' with 'cyber', the buzzword of the early twenty-first century, what is or might be 'cyber power'?

PERCEPTIONS AND MEANINGS OF CYBER POWER

Contemporary policy and media references to cyber power tend to stress the coercive implications of the term. They refer often to cyber power as the ability to use or threaten to use the resources of cyberspace to achieve strategic goals against the wishes of others. States that develop this capacity are in turn referred to as 'cyber powers'. Such a cyber power might wish, for example, to develop military cyber capabilities as a component of national cyber power, to be used against an adversary in what Clausewitz, the nineteenth-century military philosopher, would recognize as an act of force to compel an enemy to do one's will. Of course, national cyber power framed in this way is not reserved for military contexts alone. One well-known definition that proposes a more nuanced understanding of cyber power suggests that it is 'the ability to use cyberspace to create advantages and influence events in all the operational environments and across the instruments of power' (Kuehl 2009, 38). As such, it 'is not created simply to exist, but rather to support the attainment of larger objectives ... across the elements of national power—political, diplomatic, informational, military, and economic'.[1] This reflects the embedded nature of information technologies, both as physical artefacts and as the essential enablers of public and private life, inside and outside cyberspace. Adopting cyberspace as a 'domain' recognizes it as a separate warfighting domain but also as an environment that cuts across, supports, and draws together the conventional domains of land, sea, air, and space; so too with cyber power and its role in facilitating activities across the spectrum of social, economic, and political actions.

This is seen very clearly in considerations of cyberspace and soft power. Soft power describes the ability to shape the preferences of others without the coercive use of force (Nye 2004). It is the basis of modern public diplomacy and strategic communications, of interdependence through mutually beneficial trade networks, and of adherence to common values. These are inherently informational endeavours to persuade others to align their interests with one's own and, as such, rely on the information technologies of the day for their prosecution and eventual outcomes. On account of its global reach and ubiquity, the Internet has emerged as the platform par excellence for attempts by state and non-state actors to develop soft cyber power (Nye 2011, 113–51). These include activities as diverse as governmental attempts to develop norms of online behaviour, corporate advertising, and terrorist propaganda. Each leverages the Internet to disseminate messages on a global scale to multiple audiences. These forms of 'soft' cyber power can be combined with 'hard', coercive cyber power within an overarching strategy of 'smart power' through cyber means.[2]

These accounts, although they resonate with our experience of international relations, are incomplete. They persistently refer to cyber power as something that derives almost naturally from the marshalling of appropriate material resources: given enough resources, cyber power will follow. On the contrary, there is no logical connection between a particular asset or capability and the generation of cyber power, or indeed any other form of power. The possession of a gun might indicate intent, but it is no guarantor of persuasive or coercive success, any more than knowledge of a vulnerability in an adversary's computer network delivers effect in and of itself. Similarly, highly developed 'latent cyber capacity' does not necessarily translate into 'cyber power' (Valeriano et al. 2018, 59–61). Power, if it is anything, is a product of interaction between two or more actors, not a given attribute or possession of those actors. It is only through such relations that power emerges as a means of shaping the material and cognitive conditions in which an actor operates or makes decisions (Barnett and Duvall 2005). Viewed in this fashion, the nature of those relations determines a range of types of power beyond the hard and soft distinction, useful shorthand though that may be. Four forms of power have direct relevance for discussions of cyber power: compulsory, institutional, structural, and productive (Betz and Stevens 2011, 35–53).

Compulsory power exists in relationships between actors that facilitate the direct control by one actor over another. It is compulsory in its ability to compel one actor to abide by the wishes of another and may be derived from the actual or threatened use of force or other forms of coercion. It is the most familiar form of power generally and, in discussions of cyber power, it is the desired endpoint of developing and using offensive cyber capabilities to generate strategic effect, while denying the same to the adversary. Evidence suggests that states are restrained in their use of these tools (Valeriano and Maness, 2015). This is partly because the precise effects of their use are poorly understood. Uncertainty as to their effects constrains their deployment, states preferring not to embark upon actions that might be perceived as destabilizing or escalatory (Buchanan 2016). Existing norms around legitimate use of force also constrain states' recourse to this example of compulsory cyber power. It is also likely that cyber coercion is less effective than is commonly perceived. The former US Secretary of Defense, for instance, confessed to being 'disappointed' at the effectiveness of military 'cyber weapons' against Islamic State in Iraq and Syria (Carter 2017, 33). This does not stop states in possession of such capabilities from using them or from threatening to use them. Nor does it prevent others from developing them, due to their perceived efficacy, including a presently hypothetical category of cyber terrorists.

Institutional power arises in relationships mediated by institutional forms like international organizations, standardization regimes and even the Internet itself. Actors exert indirect control by designing the architecture and rules of institutions in ways that prioritize their own interests over others. The most obvious example is the United Nations, designed principally by the victorious allies of World War II, who guard vigorously their decades-long permanent membership of the Security Council, despite shifts in the balance of global politics. A similar observation can be made of the Internet, the architecture, protocols, and standards of which were designed by the United States, which retains significant, if often diffuse, influence over many of the core design aspects through technical institutions like the Internet Engineering Task Force (IETF) and the Internet Corporation for Assigned Names and Numbers (ICANN). Unsurprisingly, these arrangements are often subject to criticism from actors who perceive institutional imbalances, leading to pressure to reform the governance structure of certain institutions (e.g., non-renewal by the US government of its contract with ICANN regarding oversight of the Internet Assigned Numbers Authority [IANA], allowing its responsibilities to transition to the global multi-stakeholder community Internet Society 2016); the founding of alternative institutions (e.g., the Global Commission on Internet Governance or the Global Commission for the Stability of Cyberspace); and to 'forum shopping' to find institutions more amenable to the pursuit of their national interests. Even institutional models that attempt to short-circuit these problems, like 'multi-stakeholder Internet governance', still appear to serve the interests of major powers rather better than their less influential counterparts (Carr 2015). This may be the case but most international institutions also offer opportunities for lesser powers to develop institutional power with respect to major states. This has particularly been the case with efforts to shape norms of behaviour in cyberspace.

Structural power is a less obvious form of power but very evident in international relations. It illustrates that power is not simply a commodity to be possessed and deployed unilaterally but instead derives from actors' interrelationships. Structural power determines what actors can and cannot do within international structures such as global capitalism. In this example, global capitalism is a social structure that allocates privileges and capacities unequally, leading to relations of dominance and subjection that facilitate some actors' capacities to pursue their interests while suppressing those of others. These structures are often slow to change: once established, they are difficult to modify. They are also rarely referenced overtly by dominant actors: structural power operates whether it is deliberately mobilized or not. In some ways, the very notion of information societies that informs most national cyber security strategies, particularly in the West, is predicated on economic structures that confer advantage on countries with existing information-technological capacities. This is not to suggest that emerging economies like India cannot overcome historical structural constraints, but structural power does not create an even playing field for their efforts. That the world's five biggest firms by market capitalization deal in information products and services (Apple, Alphabet, Amazon, Facebook, Microsoft) indicates how the global economy has shifted in recent years. That all five are American suggests strongly an instance of structural cyber power that favours the United States in multiple ways.

Productive power is perhaps the most important facet of power. If we understand it as discursive power, it is the circulation of ways in which knowledge and meaning are constructed and which actors and actions are thereby legitimized, delegitimized or excluded. It works through diffuse informational fields, producing and reproducing identities, norms, customs, and understandings, which in turn enable or limit specific actors' capacities to determine their own fates. In our time, the naming of an actor as 'terrorist'—and, therefore, a priori illegitimate—illustrates how powerful the political effects of this form of power can be. It is apparent how productive cyber power might work to promote particular views about how the Internet should be governed along lines congruent with specific national interests and identities; how soft power can shape actors' decision-making processes; what centres of authority are considered legitimate; who is able to speak at all about particular issues. The dominant understanding of cyber power as 'compulsory', which privileges state sovereignty, is itself an instance of productive power. It restricts discussions about Internet and cyberspace norms and governance to state actors and collective security organizations, sidelining the potentially useful contributions of civil society. Productive power is more than mere words: it is the matrix that underpins and binds together all other forms of power.

ASSESSING CYBER POWER

This nuanced approach—parsing actor relationships and interactions across multiple dimensions of power—provides a useful framework for analysing power dynamics in and through cyberspace. It allows for the identification of different capabilities or processes (means) that can be leveraged under one or more of dimensions of cyber power in pursuit of given goals (ends). Moreover, the framework allows for a deeper analysis of the relational aspects of power: the actors or types of actors involved (scope), and the specific topic or issue (domain) over which one or more dimensions of cyber power are being leveraged, which in turn can help ascribe context (scope and domain) to the relationship.

This approach avoids the limitations of classic analyses of power focusing largely on material resources, predominantly population, territory, wealth, and military assets. The idea of 'quantifiable power', based largely on assessing the resources of a given state, assumes that 'a state's power position can be derived from its sources of power, and that power can be possessed, stored, and collected' (Van Haaster 2016). Despite shifts in academic understanding, this materialist framing of power still tends to permeate the thinking of decision makers and policy scholars. For instance, US cyber power is often perceived by other less-technologically sophisticated states in quantifiable terms: unfair from a developmental perspective and threatening from a national security perspective. This perception has historic roots, intrinsically tied to questions of sovereignty. During the Cold War, newly independent states became increasingly concerned with the technological divide between them and the major powers, a disparity rendered more salient by the superpowers' huge investments in science and technology during the first decades of the Cold War, and by growing economic interdependence. Developing (and many developed) states feared a future of increasing technological and economic dependence, one they were unwilling to accept. Hence the decades-old call for the transfer of tangible resources (technology, in particular) as a means to bridge socio-economic imbalances and related inequities.

However, assessing power in mere quantifiable terms is incongruent with the reality that greater material power does not necessarily produce successful outcomes in and of itself because it fails to capture 'the relation in which abilities are actualized' (Guzzini 2013, 65). As Nye has noted, power resources are 'simply the tangible and intangible raw materials or vehicles that underlie power relationships, and whether a given set of resources produces preferred outcomes or not depends upon behaviour in context'.[3] Assessing and discerning power is therefore highly complex. How, then, to assess cyber power with all its additional complexities?

If cyber power involves 'the variety of powers that circulate in cyberspace and which shape the experiences of those actors (state and non-state) who act in and through cyberspace',[4] assessing cyber power solely from a material or quantifiable perspective is both impractical and misleading. For one, the commercialization of the Internet and the low barriers of access to tools for the rapid collection, production, and dissemination of information appear to be redistributing power relations among states and between states and non-state actors, and contributing to 'fundamental changes in the nature of power' itself (Dunn Cavelty 2018, 306). While predictions that such shifts in power relations would usher in the end of the Westphalian state have proved inaccurate, in many jurisdictions the new technologies have given a broad range of actors a new capacity to challenge traditional structures of power, evidenced in the new forms of bottom-up governance that have emerged across societies and sectors.

Similarly, scholars in the 1990s hailed the 'revolutionary' military potential of cyberspace (Langø 2016). Yet, as with other predictions of revolutionary change spurred by information technologies, it has become clear that any strategic and tactical advantages that come with superior cyber resources and capabilities have to be weighed against the reality that states rarely choose the character of battles they fight. Also, when highly dependent on information technologies, they are equally, if not more, vulnerable to attack (as well as influence) by a range of actors, including those with significantly fewer resources and capabilities. Finally, imbalances in soft cyber power capabilities are often raised by different actors in international negotiations over norms to govern online behaviour, yet these capabilities themselves are of no value if deployed in isolation from other elements of power, and without consideration of their relationship to other actors.

Any international interaction is likely to reveal several forms of power shaping decisions and outcomes. 'Power' in the round is an aggregate rather than discrete entity, with internal dynamics and contradictions, not to mention contestations. If cyber power is the object or outcome desired by an actor, how that comes about can only be explained by looking at the relational aspects of power, rather than just the material capabilities through which power is conventionally understood.

OPERATIONALIZING CYBER POWER

Theorizations of cyber power have tended not to be as expansive as the framework outlined above. Since the 1990s, cyber power theory has remained resolutely focused on the nation state and its hypothetical role in supporting national goals and other elements of national power. In practice, too, cyber power has been viewed as a resource to be marshalled as a component of national strategy, whereby the means of cyber capability can be translated into the aims and ambitions of the state in question. At the same time, cyber power is more often implicit than explicit in national strategy. In 2011, the US *International Strategy for Cyberspace* broke open this black box, signalling that it viewed cyberspace as a new domain through which it could leverage all components of national power, be they political, diplomatic, informational, military, or economic. Since then, national cyber security strategies have proliferated, their nature and scope shifting in tandem with perceptions of the threat environment and with how cyberspace itself is defined. Indeed, today, the development and publication of a national cyber security strategy is increasingly seen as a norm of responsible behaviour, an essential capacity-building measure, and as enhancing confidence among states and between states and other actors in cyberspace, even if in reality few states have the resources and capabilities to operationalize and execute such broad-brush strategies once adopted.

The following provides insights into how the four elements of cyber power—compulsory, institutional, structural, and productive—manifest in different national strategies. Strategies evidently serve to link means to ends, which in the case of cyber power refers to the cyber capabilities and the relationships required to influence the behaviour of others. Operationalization of strategy requires the existence of institutions, resources, and so forth, through which said capabilities are channelled to execute or implement strategy.

Compulsory Cyber Power and Strategy

Compulsory power is manifest in various ways and can be leveraged by different actors—not just the state—in pursuit of their goals and interests. It might involve capabilities such as controlling or manipulating 'the behaviour of a machine or network of machines in order to change the behaviours of an individual or collective human actor[5]' as well as the deployment of non-material resources.

Capabilities aimed at controlling or manipulating machines for a specific strategic purpose are often referred to as 'offensive cyber capabilities', those external cyber actions aimed at either denying service or manipulating information for disruptive, damaging, or potentially even lethal effect. States generally do not refer to these capabilities in explicit fashion, preferring to develop an impression of strategic ambiguity, although the UK and the Netherlands, in particular, have articulated their development of, and willingness to deploy, offensive cyber capabilities. The justification often put forward for developing these capabilities is that states should seek to maintain their traditional control over the legitimate use of coercive force, including with regard to cyberspace (Belk and Noyes 2012).

Estimates suggest that scores of countries are developing offensive cyber capabilities but only a handful has used them for coercive purposes (Lewis 2018, 29). States have generally demonstrated restraint in deploying these capabilities, avoiding anything that could be interpreted as the use of force and, in particular, significant physical destruction or casualties (generally viewed as criteria for assessing the severity of an attack).[6] Moreover, it is unclear whether coercive cyber power would in itself produce the desired effect (i.e., compelling a rival to change behaviour for strategic advantage). Rather, such use of compulsory cyber power would need to be accompanied by other coercive instruments, whether diplomatic, economic, or military. The few known cases of offensive use (i.e., against infrastructure targets in Iran, Ukraine, and Germany) have demonstrated that significant planning, resources, and intelligence are required for their deployment. Uncertainty as to their effects, which could be potentially destabilizing and escalatory, is another reason why states have demonstrated restraint. Furthermore, while these kinds of external cyber actions may well represent a new form of coercive action, some observers argue that their role in strategy is misplaced and that it is the 'cognitive and informational capacity' of cyber power that will need to be addressed in future strategy.[7]

Compulsory cyber power can also include deploying non-material resources to affect the actions of others. Coercive actions such as the threat of military force, or non-forcible countermeasures in response to an internationally wrongful act or acts of retorsion—also referred to as 'negative sanctions'—are just some of the available tools of coercive cyber power that have slowly been woven into national strategy documents. Some of these tools relate to the deterrent and compellent effects strongly implied in, for example, the UK's National Cyber Security Strategy's focus on enhancing sovereign offensive cyber capabilities to deter and deny the actions of adversaries[8] or the US *International Strategy for Cyberspace* (White House 2011). The former stressed that it will deploy such capabilities 'at a time and place of [its] choosing, for both deterrence and operational purposes, in accordance with national and international law',[9] while the latter is more specific, stressing that the United States might invoke its inherent right to self-defence in response to 'certain aggressive acts in cyberspace' against it or its allies and that it would use all necessary means—diplomatic, informational, military, and economic—to this end.[10] The US 2015 Department of Defense (DOD)'s *Cyber Strategy* included a more comprehensive and detailed articulation of the 2011 strategy, of DOD's role in defending the United States against cyber attacks, as well as details of how the DOD intended to integrate its coercive cyber capabilities into military operations (US Department of Defense 2015). Rather than serving as a deterrent, however, the transparency of US military doctrine, policy, roles, and missions in cyberspace has often been viewed by other states as a justification for bolstering US military capabilities and capacities (resulting in further reciprocal action), while others have seized on it as an opportunity to promote a competing—and equally loaded—narrative centered on the 'peaceful use of cyberspace' and 'peaceful coexistence'.

States have also leaned on numerous institutions to signal such forms of coercive cyber power. For instance, in 2015, the UN Group of Governmental Experts (UNGGE) on Information Telecommunications in the Context of International Peace and Security included in its consensus report a reaffirmation of the applicability of international law to cyberspace. It also included a somewhat guarded reference to Article 51 of the UN Charter that 'States have an inherent right to take measures consistent with international law and as recognized in the UN Charter' in response to a serious incident involving information communications technologies (ICTs). Likely indicative of how difficult it was to reach agreement on the issue, the UNGGE also recognized 'the need for further study on this matter'.[11] Coercive action (or the threat thereof) as a response to malicious ICT activity by one state against another remains a highly disputed matter in ongoing normative discussions within the United Nations, influenced by disparities in attribution capabilities as well as other political and technical issues.

NATO, too, has affirmed that Article 5 of its charter relating to collective defence could be invoked in response to a cyber attack against one of its members (Kavanagh 2017). The Group of 7 (G7)'s Ise-Shima Principles include recognition of the inherent right of individual or collective self-defence as recognized in Article 51 of the UN Charter 'in response to an armed attack through cyberspace'. The G7 2017 Lucca Declaration specifically takes up a number of the international legal questions that reportedly impeded consensus in the 2017 GGE, notably the use of non-forcible countermeasures in response to an internationally wrongful act—in this case malicious ICT activities that do not amount to an armed attack—committed by another state directly or via proxies.[12]

Some states lean on public reporting of malicious cyber activity involving states or state-backed activity as a signalling mechanism, as part of a broader deterrence and risk management strategy, and aimed at shaping adversary thinking about the costs of engaging in or backing such activity. The Joint Technical Alert issued by the UK's National Cyber Security Centre (NCSC), the US Department of Homeland Security (DHS), and the Federal Bureau of Investigation (FBI) alerting industry and other relevant actors to 'Russian state-sponsored cyber actors targeting network infrastructure devices' is a case in point.[13] Other incidents for which the UK has named and shamed state actors include the NotPetya ransomware attack for which it attributed responsibility to the Russian military. Observers have critiqued the 'naming and shaming' approach, however, especially if not accompanied by consequences or penalties such as sanctions, that can induce the perpetrator to cease the malicious activity (Lewis 2016).

Certainly today, sanctions or the threat thereof are the coercive tool most used either by states unilaterally or through regional organizations in response to, or to deter, malicious cyber activity, even if the legitimacy and effectiveness of these measures are contested. For instance, in line with its 2011 *Strategy for Cyberspace*, the United States has issued indictments against Chinese People's Liberation Army (PLA) officers in response to China-backed cyber industrial espionage campaigns; it has leveraged sanctions against North Korea in response to the country's alleged cyber operations against Sony Pictures;

and it has censured Russia for its alleged interference in the 2016 US presidential elections. In line with the resulting regime, sanctions can now be imposed on 'individuals and entities responsible for (or complicit in) malicious cyber-enabled activities that "harm or significantly compromise" the provision of critical services; "significantly disrupt" the availability of a computer or network of computers; or "cause a significant misappropriation" of funds, resources, or intellectual property' (Moret and Pawlak 2017, 2). It also covers foreign interference (directly or by proxy) in US elections, including any activity 'undertaken with the purpose of influencing, undermining confidence in, or altering the result or reported result of, the election. Or undermining public confidence in election processes of institutions' (Presidential Document 2018, Sec. 8, (f)). The United States has also used the threat of sanctions to deter individuals or entities from providing material support—including ICT support—to al-Qaeda and ISIS. Following from the Joint Technical Alert issued in response to Russian-backed activity targeting network infrastructure devices, there appears to be greater appetite in the UK, too, to ensure greater consequences for malicious activity. This is particular evident in the call to apply international sanctions against countries that exploit cyberspace for illegal purposes.[14]

On the other side of the Atlantic, the European Union recently adopted a 'Cyber Diplomacy Toolbox' signalling that its member states will lean on existing measures within the Common Foreign and Security Policy, including, if necessary, 'restrictive measures' (i.e., sanctions) to influence the behaviour of potential aggressors in cyberspace. Although the deterrent measure is part of a broader cyber diplomacy package, it is still unclear how it combines with other EU policy instruments (e.g., diplomacy, law enforcement, bilateral and multilateral cooperation, cooperation with the private sector, and defence), as well as other necessary processes and procedures for the effectiveness of sanctions (or the threat thereof) to be assured.[15]

There has been a strong emphasis in strategy on the threat of coercive cyber action targeting critical national infrastructure. There has been much more ambiguity in strategy on how coercive cyber action should be deployed as a means to induce changes in behaviour. The overall effectiveness of coercive cyber action use remains unclear. Given existing norms constraining the use of force as well as the red lines voiced unilaterally or in international processes such as the UNGGE, the perceived risks associated with their use and the high costs involved, states have tended to rely on non-material forms of compulsory cyber power or, increasingly, on informational and cognitive forms of cyber action to compel changes in behaviour.

Institutional Cyber Power and Strategy

Institutional cyber power is generally manifest through 'the indirect control of a cyberspace actor by another, principally through the mediation of formal and informal institutions'.[16] It is expressed when one or several actors influence the way intermediary institutions work in a way such that they 'guide, steer and constrain the actions (or non-actions) and conditions of existence of others'.[17] It can involve influencing behaviour through bodies such as the United Nations, setting norms, and standards, or influencing foreign audiences via media institutions.

Over the past decade, the most common form of institutional cyber power is that of setting norms and standards. The US 2011 *International Strategy for Cyberspace* placed significant emphasis on norms of state behaviour in cyberspace, grounding these in five core principles—namely, upholding fundamental freedoms, respect for property, valuing privacy, protection from crime, and the right to self-defence.[18] The effectiveness of this 'soft form of cyber deterrence'[19] is indicated by the fact that many of these norms and principles—or at least efforts to promote their adoption or adherence—have become central to discussions on cyberspace and cyber security at the international (UN First Committee and its GGEs) and regional (NATO, EU, OAS, Organization of American States; Organization for Security and Co-operation in Europe (OSCE), ASEAN Regional Forum (ARF)) levels as well as in specialized institutions (G7, G20) and national strategies.[20] The national cyber security strategies of numerous countries (e.g., Australia and the Netherlands) specifically mention the norms recommended by the UNGGE. They are, however, challenged by the growing strength of China's normative power, exemplified in its 2017 *International Strategy of Cooperation on Cyberspace*, and other joint efforts with Russia via a growing range of institutions (e.g., the Asian–African Legal Consultative Organization, the Conference on Interaction and Confidence Building Measures in Asia, the Forum of China and the Community of Latin American and Caribbean States, the China–Arab States Cooperation Forum and the Shanghai Cooperation Organisation).[21] These denounce, inter alia, the US and Western normative emphasis on coercive action in cyberspace even if they, too, lean on compulsory cyber power to respond to or deter opponents, whether they are international or national, state or non-state.

Media institutions are also leveraged as a means for channelling institutional power in cyberspace.[22] Today, this is likely the most discussed form of institutional cyber power, particularly in light of Russia's alleged strategy of interference in the US elections and its use of social media platforms such as Facebook to this end, assumed to be part of a broader political strategy to 'neutralize' the West through a range of overt and covert means (Galeotti 2018). Since the early 2000s, strategic communications and public diplomacy have become key features of Western strategy, the cyber element growing in response to the online activities of groups such as al-Qaeda and ISIS. Western political actors, too, use this form of institutional cyber power in their campaign strategies, leveraging media institutions to manipulate electorates for political gain. The Cambridge Analytica debacle, in which the data of some 800,000 Facebook users was reportedly used as a tool in the electoral campaign of US President Donald Trump, the pro-Brexit campaign in the UK, and a number of other political processes across the globe, demonstrate how institutional cyber power is leveraged in strategy to influence behaviours. There are close links here between technological platforms being used for the development of institutional power and the productive, cognitive-epistemic power of the messages disseminated through such technologies (see later).

Structural Cyber Power and Strategy

Structural cyber power influences how structures or networks function, working both 'to maintain the status quo and to disrupt it'.[23] As discussed previously, the nature of the information societies that inform national cyber security strategies is predicated on structures (both economic and normative) that, to a large degree, confer advantage on countries with existing information-technological capacities, particularly the United States. China, in particular, views these and related forms of structural power as unfair, representing, in its view, an era in international relations that no longer exists. It also views some of these structural forms of power as a threat to the ruling status of the Communist Party of China (CPC): the experiences of the Arab Spring and other forms of online subversion have accentuated such perceptions and their concomitant threat to regime security.

China is using a range of policy measures, including the *National Cybersecurity Law*, the *International Strategy of Cooperation on Cyberspace*, and the *National Strategy for Cyberspace Security*—each underpinned by the principle of national sovereignty—to challenge the status quo, particularly as it relates to US technological dominance. This intent was confirmed ahead of the CPC's 19th Party Congress in 2017, when the Cyberspace Authority of China (CAC) published an article in the Party's leading theory journal, *Qiushi*, outlining 'the major elements of General Secretary Xi Jinping's strategic thinking on one of Chinese cyberspace policy's watchwords: 网络强国 (*wǎngluò qiángguó*)' which refers to 'building China into a national power in cyberspace' (Kania et al. 2017). The article outlined the institutions, capabilities, and governance capacity required to operationalize and execute this strategy: 'managing Internet content and creating "positive energy" online; ensuring general cyber security, including protecting critical information infrastructure; developing an independent, domestic, technological base for the hardware and software that undergird the Internet in China; and increasing China's role in building, governing, and operating the Internet globally'.[24]

The strategic intent outlined in China's *International Strategy* and by the CAC is evidenced in evolving mega-projects such as the Belt and Road Initiative which serves not just to connect China to the rest of the world (or, rather, the rest of the world to China), but to underpin this world with Chinese infrastructure, including China-made IT products and services. Indeed, China aims to use its Internet, ICT, manufacturing, and financial sectors to 'take the lead in going global' by identifying and competing for new markets, including through capacity building.

Congruent with these efforts, China aims to reform what it calls the 'Global Internet Governance System'—also viewed as an unfair distribution of resources—through a number of actions, including by 'vigorously promoting [further] reform of ICANN to make it a truly independent international institution, increase its representations and ensure greater openness and transparency in its decision-making and operation'.[25] China intends to play an increasingly important role in setting technical standards—a key element of its international strategy—to displace the structural influence of what it calls 'the eight *guardian warriors*' of US Internet hegemony (Cisco, IBM, Google, Quantum, Intel, Apple, Oracle, and Microsoft) (Harold et al. 2016, 29. It has made significant progress in penetrating hardware markets (e.g., through Huawei, ZTE, and Xiaomi), and continues to make inroads—albeit at a much slower pace—in global software markets. Indeed, its ability 'to invent and reinvent new things for devices and computers to do', or rely on structural network effects that can 'leverage prior market success', are elements of structural cyber power that China does not yet have at its disposal.[26] Nonetheless, these calculated efforts by China to disrupt a status quo largely established by different actors in the United States over the course of the past few decades will persist. This renders efforts by others to maintain or strengthen current structures and networks—largely played out through institutional cyber power—much more difficult in the coming years.

Productive Cyber Power and Strategy

Productive cyber power is one of the most important forms of cyber power today, representing a struggle to shape or control dominant narratives, binding together all other dimensions of power.

Competition between actors to shape such narratives emerges nationally and internationally within and between states, and between states and non-state actors. This has particularly been the case with regard to the dominant view that cyber power is 'compulsory', favouring states and sovereignty in both policy and strategy, in contrast to non-state actors who tend to be treated in text as 'passive intellectual capital'.[27] The top-down theories of cyber power of the 1990s played an important role in placing states and their strategic interests at the centre of debates on cyber power, the influence of early theorists evidenced in the nature of the cyber security strategies that have emerged over the past decade.[28]

A review by the Organisation for Economic Co-operation and Development (OECD) in 2012 confirmed this top-down approach, whereby cyber security strategies had become 'government-wide [...], encompass(ing) the economic, social, educational, legal, law-enforcement, technical, diplomatic, military and intelligence-related aspects of cybersecurity' (OECD 2012).[29] It also confirmed that a growing number of national strategies were placing a particular emphasis on sovereignty considerations in cyber security policy making at different levels of domestic policy: the strategic level (in response to cyber threats to the military, or foreign espionage); the organizational level (in reference to the inclusion of departments and militaries responsible for diplomacy, intelligence and military in intergovernmental coordination for policy making, or the designation of a national security agency as lead institution for cyber security coordination); and the operational level (e.g., intelligence bodies playing a key role as a source of information for situational awareness).

Sovereignty considerations were also evident at the international policy level in the sense that strategies increasingly stressed the need for international norms or rules of the road or confidence-building measures for cyberspace; the significance of international institutions (UN, NATO, OSCE) in these efforts; and the significance of cross-border cooperation for intelligence-sharing purposes. Business actors are viewed as important for providing input and supporting implementation of national strategies, but little is said of the role of academia or civil society, despite the fact that these have spurred much of the thinking that has shaped national cyber security strategy and cyber capacity-building policy over the past decade. Their role in track 1.5 and track 2 discussions, which also discuss questions relating to cyberspace and national, regional, and international policy and strategy, is also overlooked.[30]

China's national and international cyberspace policies and strategies have brought the conversation on sovereignty full circle (Cornish 2015). As with Russia and several other states, its focus on sovereignty goes beyond infrastructure and domestic policy issues to include a number of other factors, including content control, which it of which it continues to deem key to its legitimacy and survival. Indeed, China's narrative of identity and sovereignty (and its promotion in policy and strategy) is the matrix underpinning and binding together all forms of its cyber power. In common with its strategic allies and adversaries, China seeks to shape the narratives about what cyberspace is and should be, thereby legitimizing some actors and delegitimizing others. Ultimately, the aim is to translate these discourses of identity and legitimacy into institutional forms, whether these are international legal instruments or international organizations with authority to promote and proscribe particular categories of state and non-state actions in and through cyberspace. The most straightforward—but also most contested—means to do this is by establishing geopolitical hegemony and coercing or convincing states to adhere to the norms thus established. As the political and ideological factors influencing productive power are often deeply rooted in national culture and identity, it is dangerous to assume convergence between adversaries. This incommensurability grants productive power its potency, and suggests its potential intractability and potential for conflict.

CONCLUSION

This chapter suggests two important analytical points for future theory and practice of cyber power. The first is that cyber power does not exist in and of itself: if it is anything, it is a manifold of competing and mutually corroborating forms of power that derive from different capabilities, capacities, actors, institutions, and, ultimately, relationships between different aspects of international relations and the global economy. It is insufficient to view cyber power in anything but this expansive sense, even if alternative frameworks for its dissection and explanation may subsequently be developed. The second observation is closely related, in that we must wonder whether cyber power exists at all. Is it not merely another manifestation of 'power', howsoever we understand that term? This is especially pertinent, given that 'cyber' is frequently perceived as 'cross-cutting' other domains of interaction (land, sea, air, space), as inseparable from other forms of national power, and that, outside the military context, we do not normally speak of 'land power' or 'air power' in everyday international practices like diplomacy and commerce. Although we have offered an analytical perspective on the character of cyber power, is it really so different in nature from power in general?

We would submit that it is not, although the practices of international relations suggest that the quest for cyber power is worthy of analytical attention. As such, we must enquire after the reasons for this development and its implications for policy and strategy, particularly if the focus on 'cyber' distracts from understanding its articulations with other forms of national and collective power. It is certainly the case that the diversification of cyberspace actors and the distribution of capabilities affect our notions of cyber power, but these have yet to translate into significant, lasting shifts in the international system. This caution is a function of history yet to be told, and we do not underestimate the substantial influence of non-state actors, particularly of major technology firms. In this dynamic situation, it is more important than ever that we understand the derivation and operations of power in the international system. However, even these developments do not portend major transformation of the nature of power—cyber or otherwise—but in its character and empirical effects. The framework outlined in this chapter is offered as a means to begin to understand this shifting landscape but also to root cyber power in theories of power, understood as a relationship between actors who may or may not be states but include a whole range of agents, from international organizations to individual persons, and even down to computers themselves as they become increasingly capable of autonomous decision making.

NOTES

1. Kuehl, 'From Cyberspace to Cyberpower', 41–42.
2. Nye, *The Future of Power*, 207–34.
3. Guzzini, *Power, Realism and Constructivism*, 65.
4. Betz and Stevens, *Cyberspace and the State*, 44.
5. Ibid., 46.
6. Lewis, *Rethinking Cybersecurity*, 27.
7. Ibid.
8. UK National Cyber Security Strategy, 2016, 51.
9. Ibid.
10. White House, *International Strategy for Cyberspace*, 10, 14.
11. UN General Assembly, 'Report of the Group of Governmental Experts on Developments in the Field of Information and Telecommunications in the Context of International Security', UN document A/70/174, 22 July 2015.
12. Kavanagh, *The United Nations*, 2017.
13. See NCSC Advisory: Russian state-sponsored cyber actors targeting network infrastructure devices. 16 April 2018: https://www.ncsc.gov.uk/alerts/russian-state-sponsored-cyber-actors-targeting-network-infrastructure-devices
14. The Guardian, 'UK threatens to name and shame'.
15. Ibid.
16. Betz and Stevens, *Cyberspace and the State*, 47.
17. Ibid.
18. White House, *International Strategy for Cyberspace*.
19. Betz and Stevens, *Cyberspace and the State*, 47.
20. Department of Defense, *DoD Cyber Strategy*, 14.
21. CPC, *International Strategy of Cooperation*, ch. IV, para. 3.
22. Betz and Stevens, 2011: 47.
23. Ibid., 50.
24. Kania et al. 2017.
25. CPC, *International Strategy of Cooperation*, ch. IV, para. 4.
26. Harold et al., *Getting to Yes*, 29.
27. Dunn Cavelty, 'Europe's Cyber Power', 307.
28. Ibid.
29. OECD, Cybersecurity Policy Making'.
30. This is likely because no real assessment of the impact or outcome of track 1.5 and track 2 discussions has yet been produced.

REFERENCES

Barnett, M., and Duvall, R. 2005. 'Power in Global Governance'. In *Power in Global Governance*, edited by M. Barnett and R. Duvall, 1–32. Cambridge: Cambridge University Press.
Belk, R., and Noyes, M, 2012. *On the Use of Offensive Cyber Capabilities*. Report. Cambridge, MA.: Belfer Center for Science and International Affairs.
Betz, D.J., and Stevens, T. 2011. *Cyberspace and the State: Toward a Strategy for Cyber-Power*. London: Routledge for the International Institute for Strategic Studies.

Buchanan, B. 2016. *The Cybersecurity Dilemma: Hacking, Trust, and Fear Between Nations.* New York: Oxford University Press.

Carr, M. 2015. 'Power Plays in Global Internet Governance', *Millennium: Journal of International Studies* 43 (2): 640–59.

Carter, A. 2017. *A Lasting Defeat: The Campaign to Destroy ISIS.* Belfer Center Special report, October: https://www.belfercenter.org/sites/default/files/2017-10/Lasting%20Defeat%20-%20final_0.pdf

Communist Party of China (CPC). 2017. *International Strategy of Cooperation on Cyberspace.* 1 March: https://www.fmprc.gov.cn/mfa_eng/wjb_663304/zzjg_663340/jks_665232/kjlc_665236/qtwt_665250/t1442390.shtml

Cornish, P. 2015. 'Governing Cyberspace through Constructive Ambiguity', *Survival* 57 (3): 153–76.

Dunn Cavelty, M. 2018. 'Europe's Cyber Power', *European Politics and Society* 19(3): 304–20.

Freedman, L. 2013. *Strategy: A History.* New York: Oxford University Press.

Galeotti, M. 2018. 'I'm Sorry for Creating the Gerasimov Doctrine', *Foreign Policy*, 5 March: http://foreignpolicy.com/2018/03/05/im-sorry-for-creating-the-gerasimov-doctrine/

Guzzini, S. 2013. *Power, Realism and Constructivism.* Abingdon: Routledge.

Harold, W.H., Libicki, M., and Cevallos, A.S. 2016. *Getting to Yes with China in Cyberspace.* Report. Santa Monica, CA: RAND Corporation.

HM Government. 2018. *National Cyber Security Strategy 2016–2021*: https://assets.publishing.service.gov.uk/government/uploads/system/uploads/attachment_data/file/567242/national_cyber_security_strategy_2016.pdf

Internet Society, 2016. IANA Transition: https://www.internetsociety.org/iana-transition/

Kania, E., Sacks, S., Triolo, P. et al. 2017. 'China's Strategic Thinking on Building Power in Cyberspace: A Top Party Journal's Timely Explanation Translated'. *New America*, 25 September: https://www.newamerica.org/cybersecurity-initiative/blog/chinas-strategic-thinking-building-power-cyberspace/

Kavanagh, C. 2017. *The United Nations, Cyberspace and International Peace and Security: Responding to Complexity in the 21st Century.* UNIDIR report: http://www.unidir.org/files/publications/pdfs/the-united-nations-cyberspace-and-international-peace-and-security-en-691.pdf

Kuehl, D.T. 2009. 'From Cyberspace to Cyberpower: Defining the Problem'. In *Cyberpower and National Security*, edited by F.D. Kramer, S.H. Starr, and L.K. Wentz, 24–42. Dulles, VA: Potomac Books.

Langø, H-I. 2016. 'Competing Academic Approaches to Cyber Security'. In *Conflict in Cyberspace: Theoretical, Strategic and Legal Perspectives*, edited by K. Friis and J. Ringsmose, 7–26. Abingdon: Routledge,

Lewis, J.A. 2016. *Indictments, Countermeasures, and Deterrence. Commentary.* Washington, DC: Center for Strategic and International Studies: https://www.csis.org/analysis/indictments-countermeasures-and-deterrence

Lewis, J.A. 2018. *Rethinking Cybersecurity: Strategy, Mass Effect and States.* Washington, DC: Center for Strategic and International Studies: https://www.csis.org/analysis/rethinking-cybersecurity

Moret, E., and Pawlak, P., 2017. 'The EU Cyber Diplomacy Toolbox: Towards a Cyber Sanctions Regime?', EU Institute for Security Studies Issue Brief, July: https://www.iss.europa.eu/sites/default/files/EUISSFiles/Brief%2024%20Cyber%20sanctions.pdf

Nye, J.S., Jr. 2004. *Soft Power: The Means to Success in World Politics.* New York: PublicAffairs.

Nye, J.S., Jr. 2011. *The Future of Power: Its Changing Nature and Use in the Twenty-First Century.* New York: PublicAffairs.

OECD. 2012. *Cybersecurity Policy Making at a Turning Point: Analysing a New Generation of National Cyber Security Strategies for the Internet Economy:* https://www.oecd.org/sti/ieconomy/cybersecurity%20policy%20making.pdf

Presidential Document 'Imposing Certain Sanctions in the Event of Foreign Interference in a United States Election', Executive Office of the President, 14 September 2018: https://www.federalregister.gov/documents/2018/09/14/2018-20203/imposing-certain-sanctions-in-the-event-of-foreign-interference-in-a-united-states-election

US Department of Defense. 2015. *The DoD Cyber Strategy.* April. https://archive.defense.gov/home/features/2015/0415_cyber-strategy/final_2015_dod_cyber_strategy_for_web.pdf

The Guardian. 2018. 'UK threatens to name and shame state backers of cyber-attacks'. 23 May. https://www.theguardian.com/politics/2018/may/23/uk-threatens-to-name-and-shame-state-backers-of-cyber-attacks

Valeriano, B., and Maness, R.C. 2015. *Cyber War versus Cyber Realities: Cyber Conflict in the International System.* New York: Oxford University Press.

Valeriano, B., Jensen, B., and R.C. Maness. 2018. *Cyber Strategy: The Evolving Character of Power and Coercion.* New York: Oxford University Press.

Van Haaster, J. 2016, 'Assessing Cyber Power'. In *Cyber Power*, edited by N. Pissanidis, H. Rõigas, and M. Veenendaal, 7–21. Tallinn: NATO CCD COE Publications.

Valeriano, B., and Maness, R.C. 2015. *Cyber War versus Cyber Realities: Cyber Conflict in the International System.* New York: Oxford University Press.

White House. 2011. *International Strategy for Cyberspace: Prosperity, Security, and Openness in a Networked World.* Washington DC: White House. 17 May.

CHAPTER 5

ETHICAL STANDARDS AND 'COMMUNICATION' TECHNOLOGIES

ONORA O'NEILL

COMMUNICATION: CONTENT OR ACT?

THIS chapter is concerned with the responsibilities of technology companies for content posted on their platforms, and of governments for regulating online content that is damaging, or even menacing. I rather like that phrase 'menacing content', but in my view it suggests too narrow a focus for addressing ethical or regulatory issues that may arise when content is posted online. We need to consider not merely the *content* but the *posting*—the *speech acts* that are performed—and we need to consider not only speech acts that menace but a wide range of speech acts. Only by taking account of a wide range of *speech acts* (including misleading, mendacious, and malicious speech acts), that may be performed by various agents and agencies, can we work towards an adequate account of what should and should not be regulated, prohibited, or permitted.

Perhaps surprisingly, this is not a new topic. Ethical standards for communicative action have been discussed and disputed since antiquity. At least two of the Ten Commandments focus on ethical standards for communicative action: 'thou shalt not take the name of the Lord thy God in vain' and 'thou shalt not bear false witness against thy neighbour'. Today we may not see the prohibition of blasphemy as a central element of the ethics of communication, but we still see the prohibition of perjury and defamation as important.

However, discussion of the ethics of communication has now become remarkably narrow in some other ways, and often focuses selectively on a limited range of issues. Since the end of World War II, great emphasis has been put on relatively few standards that bear on communication, and little attention has been paid to others. The standards to which most attention has been devoted during the past 70 years include rights to *freedom of expression* and to *privacy*. Both these rights are included in the *Universal Declaration of Human Rights* and in the *European Convention of Human Rights*. Both are qualified rather than unconditional rights, so must be shaped and adjusted in daily practice by the demands of other rights, and by considerations of necessity and proportionality. Disagreements about ways in which the right to privacy may limit freedom of expression, and in which freedom of expression may limit privacy, have been staple topics of debate for many years. While some of the issues that have arisen were resolved with the implementation of the *General Regulation on Data Protection* on 25 May 2018, my guess is that the new legislation will secure only a temporary lull in this particular debate.

My reason for thinking this is simple, but fundamental. Data protection approaches seek to protect privacy on the assumption that it is possible to distinguish *personal content* from *non-personal content*, and to regulate the former while respecting freedom to express the latter. However, personal matters can quite often be inferred from data that are taken to be non-personal and are in the public domain. The hugely increased power of data analysis makes inferential identification of data subjects on the basis of data that are *not* seen as personal much more likely, and not merely blurs but threatens to undermine the basic distinction that data protection approaches seek to draw between *privacy violating* and *privacy respecting* uses of data.

As I see it, this problem arises because data protection approaches aim to regulate *types of speech content* rather than *types of speech act*. The difficulty of regulating speech content has been demonstrated time and again. Trying to prohibit specific *words* or *content* because they are thought blasphemous (or obscene, or politically taboo, or racist, or unacceptable in other ways) may seem easy, but has repeatedly ended in failure. Intelligent readers, listeners, and viewers grasp the forbidden content that writers, speakers, or broadcasters manage to convey very effectively without using the prohibited terms. The forbidden word or phrase, or other speech content, is indeed avoided, but the communicative act that was supposedly prohibited succeeds. A small amount of inventiveness, or euphemism, allowed Montesquieu to criticize the *ancien régime* in *Les Lettres persanes*, allows *Private Eye* to communicate supposedly secure or private content to its readers, and allows Chinese dissidents to discuss forbidden political topics. Rights to privacy matter, but the content-focused approach to them taken by data protection legislation is not only laborious but can be ineffective. If we seek to regulate, to prohibit, and to protect certain sorts of communication, we need to focus on communicative action, rather than on speech content. And we also need to do so for many, many other reasons.

New Technologies and New Regulation

How might we do better? Nobody has any doubt that we need to prohibit or protect, regulate or penalize, many sorts of speech act. The range is wide. We have reason to prohibit, regulate, or penalize communicative action that defrauds, deceives, or defames, or that breaches promises, privacy, agreements, contracts, or copyright—and many other types of speech act. We have reasons to protect communication that bears on political and scientific, as well as cultural and personal matters. But technological innovations have had, and continue to have, profound implications for the ways in which these aims can now be met.

This is not the first time that new communication technologies have put pressure on established ethical standards for communication. The oldest example of this problem of which I know was discussed by Plato, who reports that Socrates thought writing (then a newish technology, which many could not decipher) was a deceptive and defective way of communicating, because (unlike the spoken word) written words can be separated from their authors, with the result that nobody stands ready to interpret, explicate, defend, or vouch for their meaning, their truth, or their trustworthiness.[1]

The invention of printing provides a more recent and better-known example of the disruption of communicative practices by new technologies. It took over two centuries to develop the legislation, regulation, and cultures that support and regulate freedom to publish, while penalizing defamation, plagiarism, breach of copyright, passing off, and other unacceptable speech acts. Although copyright was written into law as early as 1710, with the passing by the British Parliament of 'The Statute of Anne' (8 Ann. c. 21), the law was often ineffective: when Charles Dickens toured the United States in 1842, he found that American printers were busy plagiarizing and selling his books.

Many of today's new technologies are commonly referred to as 'communication technologies'. This can mislead. As James Williams has pointed out, 'we persist in describing these systems as 'information' or 'communication' technologies, despite the fact that they are designed neither to inform us nor to help us communicate ... ' (Williams 2018). He argues that many of these systems and their uses have other purposes, and that they are now in considerable part organized to produce an 'infrastructure of industrialized persuasion ... and to open a door directly onto our attentional faculties'.[2]

Barely a decade ago, it was widely assumed that online technologies would benefit communication, and even democracy. In the future, it was then imagined, these technologies would allow anyone and everyone to post content, which would be accessible to and interpretable by a potentially unlimited audience, thereby achieving a version of the fuller communicative and democratic society that Jürgen Habermas had advocated when these technologies were in their infancy. Communication had previously been costly or impossible for many individuals and could be controlled by intermediating institutions, such as publishers, broadcasters, and the media, and indirectly by states and powerful companies. The new technologies would supposedly allow everybody to post content and everybody to reach whatever was posted directly, thereby eliminating these intermediaries and vastly extending communicative possibilities.

The reality has proved less benign. While it is easy, indeed all too easy, for more people to express themselves and to disseminate content online, the result does not reliably secure better communication because it can be hard for individuals to judge the content they encounter. The new technologies are splendid for *expressing content*, but not for *supporting the reception and judgement of content*. All too often, content is posted anonymously, leaving it unclear who is responsible for some speech act, whether what it claims is accurate, honest, or reliable, and who or what may be 'promoting' a given 'message'.

If we are to receive and interpret speech content effectively, we must judge the speech acts that convey it. This becomes much harder when we cannot identify *who* is communicating. Yet a great deal of online communication does not provide the necessary support for working out who produced specific speech content, or for telling what sort of speech act they were performing. Anonymous online content leaves many who encounter it unable to tell its source or judge its reliability. The term 'fake news' has now become as ubiquitous as the phenomenon, and can be genuinely hard to distinguish from competent reporting. Content that appears serious or reputable may have been invented, may have been targeted

THE ETHICS OF CYBER SECURITY   85

by unknown and interested parties, and may be repetitively circulated and recirculated by anonymous agents, or indeed algorithmically for undeclared purposes. Some of that content indeed arises from self-expression by individuals—particularly on social media. Some of it purports to be more than self-expression, but may in fact be just that. Some of it may have been created and circulated by interested parties who cannot be identified. Bloggers may use these technologies to post content while dispensing with journalistic standards; digital media may set aside the disciplines of editorial control or journalistic responsibility (Foer 2017); social media may provide networks for spreading algorithmically distributed content whose originators and credentials remain unknown to those who receive it.

As has been widely noted, these changes have led to both private and public harms. The private harms include not only those done by unlawful speech acts that have long been identified, but which have been facilitated by the enhanced anonymity provided by new technologies (e.g. fraud, defamation, intimidation, deception), but also harms that cannot so readily be dealt with by law enforcement, such as outing, trolling, cyber bullying, and other anonymous communicative action that harms lives, livelihoods, and reputations. The public harms arise when misinformation and disinformation are spread, promoted, and targeted for political and commercial purposes, which again can be done anonymously.

Can we reduce or even perhaps remedy these harms by regulating the posting of content on platforms provided by the Internet service providers (ISPs), by digital and social media companies, and by others? There are many suggestions that various platforms should be treated as publishers, thereby bringing them within the ambit of a range of existing legislation or regulation. I doubt whether this remedy would be easy, for several reasons. First, the companies that provide online services have concentrated power, but high mobility. If regulation is proposed, they will be uniquely well placed to relocate to jurisdictions that will not crimp their business—and if they do not take steps to avoid regulation, others may set up rival operations in more compliant jurisdictions. Second, the responsibilities of publishers are demanding: if the ISPs and other online companies were regulated as publishers, they would have to monitor *all* the content posted on them—not merely to take down specific sorts of content about which specific complaints are made. So far the companies themselves—understandably?—have indicated a limited willingness to change, such as (perhaps) taking down flagrantly unacceptable content when it is reported, or (perhaps) revealing more about who has paid for certain content. But a limited amount of taking down and a limited dose of transparency, that indicates a bit about who paid for what, may not achieve much. There are many players in this field and many data analytic companies who repackage and sell data on, and it can be far from simple to tell who is paying for what. After all, it appears that Facebook were not aware who was behind certain advertisements during the election of the President of the United States.

NOTES

1. Cf. 'When it has once been written down, every discourse roams about everywhere, reaching indiscriminately those with understanding no less than those who have no business with it, and it doesn't know to whom it should speak and to whom it should not. And when it is faulted and attacked unfairly, it always needs its father's [i.e. its author's]

support; alone, it can neither defend itself nor come to its own support'. Plato, *Phaedrus* 275d-e, tr. W. Hamilton, Penguin Books, Harmondsworth, 1973.

2. [2] Williams, *Stand Out of Our Light*, 87.

REFERENCES

Foer, Franklin. 2017. *World without Mind: The Existential Threat of Big Tech.* London: Jonathan Cape.

Williams, James. 2018. *Stand Out of Our Light: Freedom and Resistance in the Attention Economy*. Cambridge: Cambridge University Press, 87.

PART II

SECURITY IN CYBER SPACE: CYBER CRIME

CHAPTER 6

CYBERCRIME: THIEVES, SWINDLERS, BANDITS, AND PRIVATEERS IN CYBERSPACE

RODERIC BROADHURST

INTRODUCTION

THE Internet's decentralized and under-regulated form drives a transformative level of global connectivity and communication, compressing both time, distance, and place. It also offers anonymity: a desirable attribute for repeated illegal activities and enterprises. Cybercrime has now become ubiquitous and commonplace, with every day bringing news headlines of compromised computers, mass data breaches, crashed websites, and sophisticated scams. As connectivity increases with the Internet of Things (IoT), so will the opportunities for cybercrime. Malicious activity in cyber space has increased in sophistication, breadth of impact, and scale of damage, and is no longer exceptional. Cybercrime has become a mainstream form of crime—a parallel evolution caused by the expansion of networked technology and the vulnerabilities exposed by these developments.[1] While e-commerce markets developed, so did deep-web illicit markets such as online drug, stolen credential, illicit firearms, child exploitation, and hackers (malware-as-a-service) markets. Numerous criminal actors (thieves and swindlers) and enterprises (bandits and organized crime groups) engage in 'crime-ware' creation and distribution, combining social engineering, phishing, and identity theft with organizational efficiency to target vulnerable users.

As of June 2019, the Internet reached 55% of the world's population of 7.63 billion population. Access has grown rapidly from about 15% of the world's population in 2000 to 30% in 2010.[2] About 96% of the global population live in an area covered by a mobile wireless cellular network –opening up some of the least developed and remotest parts of the globe to leapfrog to modern information communication technologies (ICTs) and the world wide web. Disparity remains, because Internet adoption rates are about 36% in developing countries and 10% for the least developed countries, compared with 83% for the developed countries.[3] The digital divide also has another important dimension—the gap between those digital devices that are secure and those that are insecure. The disparity in security reflects the significant presence of insecure legacy (and pirate) software and hardware, as well as the costs of newer technologies.

The diffusion of new malware combined with the proliferation of innovative and adaptive forms of cybercrime and their rapid transnational deployment are difficult to counter. Understanding how best to minimize the impact of these cyber 'attacks', whether targeting computers themselves or enabled by computers, is often seen in terms of an innovation-to-obsolescence style 'arms race' between law enforcement and cybercriminals. The sheer diversity of the many forms of cybercrime such as ransomware, or the deceptions of phishing, to the disruption of weaponized code such as 'Stuxnet' will require different responses and strategies by law enforcement, industry, and government.[4]

The Australian Cyber Security Centre (ACSC)'s *Threat Report* (2016) highlights the emergence of cybercrime-as-a-service, introducing new business models to criminals, and increasing their spread and sophistication. In its 2016 assessment, the ACSC explained:

> The global cybercrime market is a low-risk, high-return criminal enterprise, with goods and services in strong supply and demand ... Anyone aiming to make an illicit profit can purchase infrastructure, delivery mechanisms, coding services, antivirus checking services, exploit kits, communication services, and 'cash out' and money transfer services ... The challenge lies in detecting the constantly evolving illicit activity, and determining its motivation, impact and mitigation strategies (p. 8).[5]

The Federal Bureau of Investigation (FBI) Cybercrime Division prosecutor Gavin Corn has also observed that networking among criminal groups has been greatly enhanced by the emergence of new encrypted applications:

> Cybercrime wasn't even a part of organized crime before, and now it's the epitome of it.

And:

> ... systems like TOR (The Onion Router) and other proxy systems that are designed to hide the location of internet connections and even servers—has been huge. This may be good for promoting freedom of speech but it makes investigating criminal cases much harder. Also, anonymous payment systems like Bitcoin that allow for the transfer of funds without revealing the identity of the persons behind the transactions pose a big challenge for us.[6]

This chapter discusses the prevalence, definitions, and scope of cybercrime including the dual role of 'weaponized' malware. It also outlines the short history of 'hacking' as well as the rise of online criminal networks and markets in the dissemination of malicious software. Various forms of cybercrime are described, including the use of deception in the exploitation of computer systems. The importance of international cooperation in the suppression of cybercrime is illustrated by the coordination required in response to the proliferation of child exploitation materials (CEM) and extremist violence. The chapter concludes with a summary of the challenges for law enforcement and the pressing need for broad partnerships in the prevention of cybercrime.

COST AND SCOPE OF CYBERCRIME

The estimated annual cost of global cybercrime was about US$445 billion in 2015 according to McAfee[7] while Lloyds, for example, estimated the cost of cybercrime in 2015 to be

$400 billion including the costs of disruption. The cost of cybercrime was estimated to have quadrupled between 2013 and 2015 and this trend is likely to continue, although the measurements of costs remain crude. Given the pace of digitization of consumers' lives, UK market analyst Juniper Research estimated that the annual cost of data breaches would also quadruple to about $2.1 trillion. Demand for cyber security products and services were also expected to increase from $75 billion in 2015 to $175 billion in 2020 for security counter measures while the insurance industry was projected to grow from $2.5 to $7.5 billion in 2020.[8] More recent estimates reinforce this rapid growth in the cost of counter measures, possibly reaching about $300 billion per year by 2024, while the costs of insurance against cyber-attacks was estimated in 2020 to be $8 billion (Columbus 2020).

The most common intrusion techniques were the combined use of deception and social engineering known as a phish[9] where cybercriminals trick victims into granting access to personal and bank account details. The Anti-Phishing Working Group (APWG) report for the last quarter of 2016 noted over 1.22 million attacks in 2016: an average of 92,564 phishing attacks per month compared with an average 1,609 per month in 2004. China, Turkey, and Taiwan are the countries most infected with malware, with nearly half the computers in China estimated to be compromised.[10] Victims who inadvertently post a picture of their first credit card or driver's licence to show friends are examples of how potential victims expose personal data that can be readily exploited by cybercriminals.

The scale and nature of cybercrime may be illustrated by data from just one jurisdiction— Australia—where in 2016 93% are Internet users and 73% Facebook users.[11] Victim studies show that fraudulent scams were the most reported type of cybercrime incidents reported to police. About two in five victims were aged between 20 and 40 and social network sites (SNS) were significant vectors for cybercrime offences (ACSC 2015). Annual losses were estimated to be about AU$1 billion mostly from credit card fraud and scams or swindles, many of which originated online. Data from the Australian Bureau of Statistics (2016) Personal Fraud Survey also confirm these trends, with 1.6 million Australians reporting being a victim of personal fraud and 126,300 victims of identity theft. Just over half the Australian population aged 15 and over were exposed to at least one scam, and 4% of these were victimised, either due to their supplying personal information, money, or both (Broadhurst 2017, 154).

Drawing from a large household panel study (Longitudinal Internet Studies for the Social Sciences [LISS]) of Dutch victims, Van Wilsem (2013) suggested that low self-control (manifested as impulsivity) contributed to online victimization and was a general risk factor in online victimization. However, using SNS and other social media predicted harassment rather than being hacked. An earlier victimization study, also drawing from the LISS panel, noted the overlap between digital and traditional crime rather than a displacement of crime to the virtual world. Online activities could result in traditional victimization and outdoor activities could result in digital threats or crime, and the research noted ' ... the pervasive influence of online activities on victimization experiences, both on the Internet and in "traditional" life' (Van Wilsem 2011, 125).

In the United States and other countries (e.g. Australia), laws require business to notify individuals in the event that their personal information is lost or stolen. A US survey in 2015 found that 26% of respondents, or an estimated 64 million US adults, recalled a breach notification in the past 12 months and 44% of those notified were already aware of the breach, but only 11% apparently ceased dealing with the business following the data loss.[12]

The IoT, combined with more businesses using social media, will increase the range and scale of cybercrime threat vectors, as new vulnerabilities in SNS arise. SNS users appear to take major risks when using social media, suggesting that they are unaware of the potential threats and the importance of securing their data. Online predators often collect sensitive information from SNS profiles and use the information to launch an attack. SNS users sometimes post information such as home addresses and holiday plans without understanding associated security threats.

Alarming as the scale of cybercrime events appears, these events are often misleadingly described as 'attacks' by the cyber security industry. Many so-called attacks are SPAM-borne attempts at controlling a computer or deceiving a user. This offender–victim engagement can be described as 'low-value, high-volume' crime usually devoid of physical harm—but costly to the victim in time, trust, and money. As a recent Australian cyber security threat report warned, the over-characterization of computer-related crimes as 'hacks' or 'attacks' misrepresents the 'low-tech' nature of most cybercrime. This distortion oversimplifies '... the spectrum of cyber security risk, vulnerability, and consequences; blurs the understanding of potential "red lines" in cyberspace; and undermines the development and application of proportionate nation state responses.'[13]

Social Engineering

The 'advance fee fraud' is a simple and often well-executed scam that attempts to extract information about users such as full name, phone number, residential address, and bank accounts. This information is then used to steal the victim's identity and money. In some cases, victims are persuaded to transfer so-called advance fees to facilitate a benefit. Classic examples include the unexpected inheritance; the philanthropist in search of a 'good Samaritan'; the business proposal; and the mysterious box full of cash (Broadhurst 2017, 159). The emergence of specific and carefully targeted forms of computer crime such as ransomware and sextortion can devastate victims. Ransomware emerged in 2012 and rapidly spread with the help of encryption, botnets (network of infected computers), and spammers disrupting all kinds of businesses, and it is commonly undertaken by organised crime groups. The method often uses a 'phish' to deceive users into inadvertently accessing malware that covertly installs on victims' computers, encrypts their crucial private data, and then 'offers' to help fix the 'problem' after payment of a recovery or decryption service fee. Common targets are medical clinic patient records, trade secrets such as an engineering plan, and small- and large-business client lists. Offenders often use untraceable cryptocurrencies such as Bitcoin for the transfer of funds.[14]

Laws and Definitions of Cybercrime

Cybercrime is a diverse criminal activity and there is no definitive typology. Even a single intrusion may require a number of distinct offences across a range of offence categories from identify theft, fraud, and child pornography. Law enforcement agencies have found it helpful to split cybercrimes into three broad groups for which a computer is:

a. the *instrument* used to commit the offence (e.g. a botnet-spreading malware spam);
b. the *target* of the offence (e.g. modification or theft of data, privileged access); or
c. *incidental* to the offence (e.g. investigative or forensic data).[15]

The scope of cybercrime or computer-related crimes may be described as listed below:

- Telecommunications theft and illegal interception.
- Piracy and copyright theft.
- Cyber-stalking, cyber-bullying, and harassment.
- Electronic money laundering and tax evasion.
- Electronic vandalism.
- Cyber-terrorism.
- Denial of service (DoS).
- Extortion; sales and investment fraud; forgery.
- Electronic funds transfer fraud and counterfeiting.
- Content crime (i.e. offensive materials, CEM).
- Espionage.
- Resource theft (i.e. illegal use of personal computers or other digital devices).

Theft of confidential personal information, or identity theft, entails use of a stolen, manipulated, or fabricated identity to facilitate the commission of a crime. It is an important predicate offence that can set in motion more serious offences such as credit card fraud and banking theft.[16]

The US Computer Fraud and Abuse Act 1986 (CFAA) makes it illegal to knowingly cause the transmission of a programme, information, code, or command and thereby intentionally cause damage to a protected computer; or to intentionally or recklessly access a protected computer without authorization and thereby cause damage or loss. The CFAA also makes it illegal to knowingly sell, buy, or trade passwords or other information used to access a computer with the intent to defraud the victims. The CFAA law applies to computers involved in interstate or foreign commerce, or operated by or for the US government, and designed to establish the connection between malware and hacking outcomes, such as data loss or manipulation. Most countries have now criminalized unauthorized access to computers and the spreading of malware, with few nations prohibiting the creation and supply of such software, as in the UK Computer Misuse Act 1990. The Australian Commonwealth Criminal Code Act 1995, No. 12 (as amended per the Commonwealth Cybercrime Act 2001) illustrates the usual scope of cyber offences identified:

1. unauthorized access to, or modification of, restricted data;
2. unauthorized impairment of electronic communication; and, as elsewhere,
3. seek to regulate the content by using a carriage service to menace, harass, or cause offence or distribute or display child sex abuse images and materials.

Laws in many other jurisdictions have applied these basic distinctions to the types of cyber-activity criminalized and they are often applied in conjunction with deception, dishonesty, and theft offences.

Practical responses include dedicated computer emergency response teams (CERTs), or computer security incident response teams, and policing or security agencies to coordinate national responses to vulnerabilities and wide-scale computer attacks, and to provide information on new threats to business and government. The Council of Europe (CoE)'s 2001 Cybercrime Convention ('Budapest Convention') has also been widely adopted and enables essential mutual legal assistance with respect to data preservation and extradition of suspects.

Cybercrime and Cyber Warfare

The quickening of the interaction between cybercriminal networks and hybrid forms of cyber war has elevated cybercrime as one of the means of undermining cyber-security and national security in the digital age. Applications of malicious software for espionage and sabotage are designed to control computers, insert spyware, and interfere with critical infrastructure such as energy, transport, and communication systems. Cyber attacks can also be crafted to disrupt industrial supervisory control and data acquisition (SCADA) systems that are the backbone of modern electricity grids and other essential services. In 2010, in a significant demonstration of the capacity of cyber war, the nuclear facility in Nantz, Iran, was the subject of the computer worm Stuxnet, which was allegedly designed by the Israeli and US governments to exploit zero-day vulnerabilities that allowed interference with the performance of the plant's centrifuges, a crucial element in the enrichment of uranium needed in the production of nuclear arms (Sanger 2012). Other examples include Chinese army espionage focused on US corporations including the theft of sensitive files held by US defence contractors.[17] Disruption to Internet communications via distributed denial of service (DDOS) attacks that flood email and other traffic were used by Russia against Estonia in response to perceived anti-Russian policies. The virus *Shamoon,* possibly launched by Iran, indiscriminately destroyed data on the computers at Saudi Arabia's state-owned oil company and affected business operations for several weeks.[18] These attacks constitute part of the so-called 'fifth domain' of modern war and conflict.

Cybercrime activities overlap with espionage, information warfare, and cyber-terrorism, disrupting nation states and corporations. Cyber-terrorists might raise funds via scams, and states might purchase zero-day exploits to deploy during a cyber attack on another state, a crime group, or other adversary. The blurring of the boundaries between crime, war, and violent extremism by state and non-state actors is a key factor in the development of more sophisticated malware—a cyber 'arms race'. These militarized versions can be dispersed into 'the wild', used by proxy actors or 'privateers' with a remit to engage in crime and espionage, and enhance the malware used by criminals to intrude and to evade detection. Cyber-security policy of many nations has emphasized the need for enhanced training in cyber-defence (or offence) and security, infrastructure protection, and partnership with private industry. These needs have become even more pressing with the impact of the Covid-19 pandemic.[19]

Malware

Malicious software or 'malware' is a term used to capture the range of computer code used to automate attacks against computer systems. The malware can take the form of viruses, worms, trojans, rootkits, adware, and spyware. They are costly for victims to remove and repair. Malware uses 'exploits' or flaws and vulnerabilities in computer programs to control or disrupt computer operating systems and functions. The exploit activates a payload—sometimes unintentionally downloaded by a deceived victim—that enables system changes and allows control through the malware. Malware can log keystrokes by the user and thus capture passwords and account details; delete or corrupt files; and access private files. It can also delete system calls and audits, and create backdoors in the infected system for remote control of the victims' computer by a botnet. Many hacks, malware compromises, or breaches of computer systems involve the exploitation of vulnerabilities or flaws in either the computer hardware or software code. These exploits—often errors in the software code—enable malware code to be inserted and thus compromise or control the operating system of the computer (Yugamuchi, et al. 2014). Since the mid-2000s, botnets have been used to manipulate multiple Internet-connected computers to disseminate malware, often exploiting and amplifying common vulnerabilities. Like worms and viruses, botnets infect other machines, but they can also deliver a payload like a Trojan. Botnets use these infected systems to engage in various types of attacks such as spam distribution or DDOS (Chon 2016). New macro-viruses and polymorphic viruses are increasingly problematic because polymorphic engines change the code of a virus each time it propagates and these are difficult to identify.

CASE: MALWARE AS A WEAPON?

On 11 December 2016, John Rivello, angry at journalist Kurt Eichenwald for his critical stories about the alleged potential criminal activities of Donald Trump, used the Twitterhandle @jew_goldstein to send an epileptogenic animated gif, (or Graphic Interchange Format [GIF]—a series of images that are combined to create a short animation) to Eichenwald's Twitter account. The tweet contained an animated strobe image embedded with the statement: 'You deserve a seizure for your post.' Upon viewing the flashing strobe image, Eichenwald had an 8-minute seizure that caused him to lose control of his bodily functions and left him incapacitated for several days. Eichenwald's wife contacted police. Rivello thought that Eichenwald deserved to be punished for his comments and texted friends saying, 'Spammed this [GIF] at [Eichenwald] let's see if he dies.'

Rivello was charged by the FBI with cyberstalking with the intent to kill or cause bodily harm. A Texas grand jury endorsed the notion that the GIF constituted a deadly weapon in the assault because it was designed to affect Eichenwald's physical condition. The FBI also charged Rivello with committing a hate crime because he attacked Eichenwald on the basis of his religious identity. The FBI identified Rivello, despite his use of a disposable cell phone and Twitter account with no identifying information.[20] The FBI search warrant showed that Rivello's iCloud account contained a screenshot of a Wikipedia page for the victim, which had been altered to show a fake obituary with the date of death listed as Dec. 16, 2016. Rivello's iCloud account also contained screenshots from epilepsy.com with a list of commonly reported epilepsy seizure triggers.

Cybercrime-as-a-Service:
Dark Markets for Malware

The underground market for 'bugs' that can exploit software vulnerabilities has existed since at least the 1990s, although informal sharing of these vulnerabilities goes back to the dawn of computing. Older readers may recall phone phreaking and the Massachusetts Model Railway Club's fostering of a hacker sub-culture in the 1960s. Since then, it has developed into a global market for the sale of exploits and exploit kits, and hacking tools such as Blackhole, Zeus, and Spyeye. Users of such 'off the shelf' malware are sometimes known as 'script kiddies' because only basic programming skills are required to use the malware. The Russian carding market, which developed in the 1990s as online forums for the sale of stolen credit cards and identities, developed into a sophisticated business enterprise mimicking online legal markets such as e-Bay.

The industrialization of the cybercrime market developed rapidly with the advent of VPNs and Tor in the mid-2000s (Anderson et al. 2013) The United Nations Office on Drugs and Crime (UNODC)'s 2013 *Comprehensive Study on Cybercrime* flagged the importance of these markets in the spread of monetized hacking tools. RAND's 2014 report on these hackers' markets notes: 'Black and gray markets for hacking tools, hacking services, and the fruits of hacking are gaining widespread attention as more attacks and attack mechanisms are linked in one way or another to such markets' (Ablon et al. 2014, ix). The report further observes that the markets have:

> ... emerged as a playground of financially driven, highly organized, and sophisticated groups. In certain respects, the black market can be more profitable than the illegal drug trade; the links to end-users are more direct, and because worldwide distribution is accomplished electronically, the requirements are negligible.[21]

Black-market prices of malware, stolen identities, and other trade tools used by cybercriminals include a number of the crime-as-a-service products listed in Table 6.1.[22]

Case: 'Dark Markets'—Cybercrime-as-a-Service

Botnet booter rental used to stress test networks or distract their target while undertaking an intrusion can be rented for US$60 per day or US$400 per week—discounts offered.

Table 6.1 Stolen credit cards – market values circa 2013–2015

Credit card types	U.S.	U.K.	Canada	Australia	EU
Basic or "Random"	$5-8	$20-25	$20-25	$21-25	$25-30
Plus, Bank ID#	$15	$25	$25	$25	$30
Plus, Date of Birth	$15	$30	$30	$30	$35
Plus Fullzinfo	$30	$35	$40	$40	$45

McAfee 2015: https://securingtomorrow.mcafee.com/mcafee-labs/hidden-data-economy-report-exposes-price-points-for-stolen-data/, accessed May 4, 2017.

Ransomware is widely advertised in black-market dark web bulletin boards with one service, the Radamant Ransomware Kit, originally posted in Russian, available for $1,000 per month.[23]

Compromised websites and servers are effective means for distributing malware and launching attacks. Access to these compromised sites can be purchased from a crime-as-a-service provider for as little as US$15 for stolen logins with related access to the victim's email fetching higher prices.[24]

Bulletproof hosting services (BPHS) help attackers keep their phishing sites and command and control infrastructure more resilient to takedowns and other law enforcement action. BPHS provide a set IP address, and hard disk space and memory. An account with an IP address, 100 GB of disk space, and 2 GB of RAM can cost as little as US$70, while basic once off use about US$5.[25]

Exploit kits are an effective means to launch intrusions and require low technical capability: common 'kits' include the basic 'Nuclear Exploit Kit' leased for $50 per day, $400 per week, or $600 per month, and the 'Sweet Orange Exploit Kit' leased from $450 per week, $1,800 per month.[26]

Stolen credit card credentials are also widely available in many different forms. For example, McAfee reports a US payment card number including the CVV2 at $5–$8 but with bank ID number at about $US15; and a card number with all details about the card and owner ('Fullz') may cost $30.[27]

Online payment services bank accounts, pricing for access to these accounts depends on the funds held. McAfee Labs reported in 2015 that a $400–$1,000 balance would cost $20–$50; a $1,000–$2500 balance $50–$120; a $2,500–$5,000 balance $120–$200; and a $5,000–$8,000 between $200 and $300.[28]

Healthcare data can also be purchased from illicit markets and enable insurance fraud, and a bundle of 10 Medicare numbers was reportedly offered for $4,700.[29]

These market innovations demonstrate how much traditional crimes such as theft and fraud have evolved with the help of digital technology. Some vulnerabilities have been reportedly sold for as much $900,000. According to Hacking Team's Vlad Tsyrklevich,[30] the zero-day exploit market offers a variety of prices for different exploits. Higher prices are paid for the more secure systems such as Apple iOS—iPhones but lower fees for older legacy operating systems like Windows XP. The market operates in an orderly way with testing and evaluation prior to purchase, and is similar to the carding business in that it seeks to create a stable, reliable service encouraging repeated use. Given the demand for legitimate penetration testing by the cyber-security industry, as well as national security agencies seeking to strengthen cyber arsenals for offensive purposes, the value of exploits has been greatly boosted. However, the secret acquisition of exploits (for offensive purposes) leaves many users unaware and at risk of the 'bug' or exploit. Secretive purchases of 0-day exploits also render legitimate 'bug' bounty projects run by the information technology industry less effective because these usually pay considerably less.

ONLINE OFFENDERS

One of the challenges for law enforcement is the cross-jurisdictional nature of cybercrime and the celerity of the methods used. Usually, the victim resides in one country and the offender in another, while the proceeds might be deposited in a third country. A careful cybercriminal operates from a safe haven (outside the international legal system), remains anonymous, and disguises the source of intrusion, making tracing difficult and often inconclusive. Hence, it is difficult to tell if a cybercrime was implemented by a teenager operating from their bedroom, by a nation state, or by a criminal network. Often, victims may not be aware of an offence, and many fail to report their victimization due to the belief that police can do very little to arrest offenders and recover losses. The low risk of detection and prosecution arises because of the limitations of cross-border policing, and accounts for the need for effective cross-national and international responses to combat cybercrime. Hence cybercrimes are attractive when compared with real-world offences because of easy access to technology, and the Internet, with a capacity to reach millions of potential victims (Broadhurst 2006).

Hacker Culture

Cybercriminals are commonly called 'black hats', those who contest them are referred to as 'white hats', and those who switch across the legal and the illegal are considered 'grey hats'. Hackers have a terrestrial existence with online and offline social connections. Hackers are those knowledgeable about computers and their systems, and apply their knowledge to gain unauthorized access to a computer. Hacking has been likened to a craft, which emphasizes skill, but also a 'transgressive craft' that draws on notions of resistance and hyper-individuality (Steinmetz 2016, 103). Hackers engage, learn, and act in the virtual world on web pages, forums, blogs, but also at hacker conferences. An individual hacker's skill, orientation, and level of knowledge can be gauged by the kind of terminology used to describe them. Highly skilled hackers are called 'crackers' or 'leets'. Novice hackers are referred to as 'lamers' and 'noobs', as well as 'script kiddies'.[31]

The skill of hacking is used to identify flaws in systems and can also serve a legitimate purpose (i.e. security testing and ethical hacking). The stress on secrecy, engagement with online communities, and the use of aliases by hackers is essential. The motivations for hacks have changed over time, from a problem-solving orientation and the thrill of hacking into a profitable tradecraft.[32] Combined with the reach of computer technology and the rise of e-commerce, differences between ethical hacking and malicious activities have blurred in helping to create both cybersecurity services and criminal enterprises.[33] Not all hacks are technical or code-based: they might also draw on deception, and increasingly sophisticated methods involve the blending of deception or 'social engineering'.

The word 'hacker' originally implied technological curiosity and ingenuity. Steven Levy's 1984 *Hackers: Heroes of the Computer Revolution* made one of the first references to inquisitive science students as 'hackers': those who explored the limits of technology. As an insurgent or saboteur-like sub-culture of hackers emerged, the legal response followed. In 1986, the US enacted the CFAA, making hacking computers a crime. Robert Morris, the creator of the eponymous worm was the first to be convicted under that Act in 1988, and this led to the establishment of the first computer security response team at Carnegie Mellon University (Rid 2016). The hacker culture, frequently associated with cybercrime, began to take shape in the 1980s along with the formation of many other loose networks, such as the *Legion of Doom* that crossed over from the era of telephone modems to the world wide web and the Internet).

Throughout the 1990s, malware became more complex and diverse with many government agencies repeatedly hacked. More digital devices had become available: MP3s became popular, leading to file-sharing sites and associated software that enhanced capacities for digital piracy. By 1999, chronic faults ('bugs') in Microsoft's Windows 98 operating system helped make cybercrime more common, as did vulnerabilities in other commercial software. By the 2000s, cybercrime had become normal, with spam emails, malware, scams, botnets, and the 'dark net' (e.g. Tor network was activated in 2002, followed by similar anonymization networks). The Anonymous 'hactivist' group was formed in 2003 and WikiLeaks was founded in 2006. Bitcoin appeared in 2009 although earlier versions of secure electronic money, such as DigiCash, created in the 1990s failed to take off because e-commerce markets were then immature. Block-chain crypto-currencies like Bitcoin, however, helped facilitate anonymous e-commerce and radically changed the nature of illicit markets when converging with novel encrypted markets such as *The Silk Road* in 2011 that offer a range of illicit drugs and services (Martin 2014). Underground illicit firearms e-markets have also emerged that facilitate crime and extremism via the sale of illegal or stolen weapons (and ammunition), including newer weapons with prices competitive with black-market street values. A RAND report estimated that 60% of the firearms listings on the dark web originate from the US but the largest and more valuable markets are found in Europe.[34]

The Silk Road was an exemplar of the online market for illicit drugs. The FBI removed it from the web in 2013 with the arrest of Ross Ulbricht, the system administrator who was convicted in 2015. However, many illicit markets emerged to capitalize on the model pioneered by *The Silk Road* (including versions 2.0 and 3.0, also subsequently disestablished by 2017) that mimicked eBay and Amazon. The alternative *Alpha Bay* and *Hansa* drug markets were also taken down in cross-border police operations (Dutch and US agencies) in 2017, closing a lucrative $1 billion market. The risks of arrest also helped to spread fear among criminal actors and undermine trust in underground markets to some extent. Nevertheless, these illicit markets are now established and flourishing in the encrypted realms of cyberspace. *Dream Market*, for example, established in late 2013, continued to operate as an underground Tor market with over 100,000 (mostly illicit drugs but also digital products and services) listings until April 2019 when it voluntarily closed.

Online Criminal Groups

Cybercrime can take different forms, and the pathway and means for offenders to engage in specific acts of cybercrime are diverse. Interaction among offenders and between offenders and victims can take place exclusively online, but they may also overlap (Van Wilsem 2011). However, cybercrime has an impact on the offline world of banks and financial institutions, businesses, and day-to-day Internet users.

There is growing research about offender behaviour and recruitment in cyberspace, and learning and imitation play important roles. In some cases, obsessive–compulsive behaviour is evident; in others, a sense of impunity—born of over-confidence in anonymity—is apparent. Greed may be only one of many motives, but other factors such as opportunity also play a role in the formation of online criminal networks. Little is known about organizational structure and relationships with other criminal enterprises or grey markets, or how trust is acquired in the virtual world (Broadhurst 2017). Some markets, such as that for CEM and hacking tools, require consumers to trade tools or illicit images before accessing the network, while open markets such as for illicit drugs use customer feedback and escrow services to enhance trust and encourage repeat purchases.

Among the first organized online criminal networks to emerge were those trading in CEM (see Chapter X). The Internet environment has facilitated and amplified the dissemination of pornography including CEM. Although the production of CEM has a long history, the anonymity offered by the Internet has amounted to an unprecedented facility for the widespread sharing and selling of images, as well as the live streaming of the sexual abuse of minors. It also facilitates the trading of child pornography via networks of those sexually attracted to children, and offers opportunities for child grooming and exploiting vulnerable children (UNODC 2015). The well-publicized 'Sweetie' sting operation in 2013, which depicted a fictional online vulnerable child, led to the arrest via the associated honeypot of around 1,000 offenders in three months.

In 2015, another large-scale CEM website, 'Playpen', with more than 150,000 members operating in TOR was taken over for two weeks by the FBI deploying 'new investigation techniques' that involved the hidden insertion of malware on the site in order to identify its customers. The operation resulted in the identification of 296 sexually abused children and 870 arrests by Europol and the FBI, including 25 CEM producers and 52 'hands-on' abusers in the US alone.[35] The case has been controversial because of the unprecedented techniques used to acquire and run the Playpen site, and procedural issues relating to jurisdiction and the validity of the search warrants used to 'capture' data. Law enforcement strategies often need to use such proactive methods to identify offenders and victims.[36]

McGuire (2012)[37] discussed the different types of organized crime present online including loosely organized communities with 'swarm' characteristics—namely, groups that cross between the online and offline, and structured hierarchies like the Mafia. Chabinsky[38] noted that, in a larger criminal enterprise, such as a credit card fraud, several specialized functions are needed, such as coders, distributors, hackers, fraud specialists, cashiers, tellers, executives, and money mules. A cybercriminal intending to send spam to victims around the world would need to create a simple virtual network to:

- acquire a list of victims' email addresses from a specialized harvester;
- rent a botnet from another specialized actor;
- join a spam affiliate program (e.g. Dark-Mailer, 7ReachLLC);
- include a link to an illegal market site on their spam emails; and
- receive a cut of the money that their victims spent to buy goods on the affiliate market.

CASE: ORGANIZED CRIME AND THE INTERNET

Koobface was a worm-based malware that targeted Web 2.0 social networks such as Facebook (the malware name is an anagram of Facebook). Koobface spread by sending messages to 'friends' of an infected Facebook account user. The message directed the recipient to a fake website where they were prompted to download a fake Adobe Flash Player update. Once the fake program was installed, Koobface controlled the computer's search engine and directed the user to affiliated illicit websites offering various scams such as false investments, fake antivirus (AV) programs, fake dating services, and the like. The Koobface botnet made money through pay-per-install and pay-per-click fees from these other websites. Data found in the botnet's command-and-control system suggested that the group had earned around $2 million a year. Financial enrichment was the group's raison d'être. Sophos identified five potential members of the Koobface gang, also referred to as 'Ali Baba & 4' who operated from Russian and Czech locations. One member was older than the others and possibly the leader, but the structure of the group was not fully understood. Members of the group had previously worked in online pornography and spyware, but they also attempted to conduct a legitimate mobile software and services business. The Koobface crime group was able to regularly upgrade and adapt the botnet, which included an effective traffic direction system that managed the activity on affiliate sites and boosted the Internet traffic to the botnet (e.g. targeting showbiz fans, online daters, casual porn surfers, and car enthusiasts). The overall structure of the botnet was resilient: it survived takedown attempts and countermeasures by Facebook and Google (Broadhurst et al. 2014).

INTERNATIONAL RESPONSES TO CYBERCRIME

Developments in the range and potency of cybercrimes have been met with an increase in penalties and the creation and/or modification of national cybercrime laws in many states. Given the transnational nature of much cybercrime, cross-national mutual legal assistance agreements to deal with the cybercrime have also been essential (UNODC 2013). The CoE's 2001 Cybercrime Convention is the key response and came into force in 2003. States outside Europe, notably the US, Japan, Chile, Canada, and Australia, have also joined (64 state parties thus far) with many other nations adopting similar law. However, a universal treaty for the suppression of cybercrime has not emerged because key states China and Russia have not signed up. Concerns about sovereignty and the role of state actors in information warfare have made consensus over the form of a universal (i.e. United Nations) treaty fraught. The CoE convention is influential in the response to cybercrime. In addition, the United Nations Convention on Transnational Organized Crime (UNTOC) that also came into force in 2003 plays a role, and has been ratified by 147 nations and 188 state parties. In 2010, the fifth Conference of Parties to the UNTOC identified cybercrime, and identity-related crimes, as new and emerging crimes of concern subject to the convention's international legal assistance protocols when conducted by an organized crime group.[39]

The CoE's Cybercrime Convention targets 'offences against the confidentiality, integrity and availability of computer data and systems'. It outlaws unauthorized access to computers or computer systems, as well as malicious software. The convention also specifically addresses DoS/DDoS).[40] The convention is an important means for international cooperation on legal interventions by providing for extradition of suspects, the disclosure and preservation of computer and traffic data, real-time traffic data collection, trans-border access to stored computer data (if publicly available), and the interception of content data (e.g. child abuse materials). Crucially, it reinforces law enforcement cooperation at all levels and supports a dedicated 24/7 response network, often drawing on established CERTs and other cross-agency law enforcement networks.

International Cross-Agency and Sector Cooperation

Many regulatory frameworks have emerged to address the global problems of cybercrime. They vary from state-centric approaches (as in cross-national cooperation among CERTs) to volunteer groups or alliances that foster cross-national government, industry, and academia collaboration. Such bottom-up approaches to enhancing private-sector cybersecurity have been crucial in the response to cybercrime. Non-profits such as Spamhaus and VirusTotal provide critical services monitoring malware. For example, the London Action Group tackles spam and the PhishTank (see www.phishtank.com/) is an anti-phishing clearing house associated with Cisco's OpenDNS in collaboration with the non-profit APWG, a global consortium of 2,000 businesses, non-governmental organizations (NGOs), academia, and law enforcement agencies, including the UNODC, Europol EC3, International Telecommunications Union, Organization for Economic Cooperation and Development, Organization for the Security and Cooperation in Europe, and the Organization of American States among others. As an industry association, the APWG has focused on encouraging a global response to cybercrime, and tracks the prevalence and scope of phishing attacks, coordinates responses to phishing, and advises governments and industry.

The suppression of Internet-driven CEM is a major challenge for law enforcement agencies across the globe and one example of the response to the transnational nature of cybercrime. However, effective alliances have been formed across nations to share intelligence and prosecute the most serious offences. The Virtual Global Taskforce (VGT) coordinates responses to multinational (CEM) cases. VGT was established in 2003 to help respond to and investigate serious CEM cross-border cases. Over 1,000 investigations have been completed to date. Fourteen agencies, including INTERPOL and Europol, are actively engaged, often in collaboration with the FBI's Violent Crimes Against Children unit, and police agencies in Australia, Italy, the UK, Switzerland, Canada, the Republic of Korea, the Netherlands, Colombia, the Philippines and the United Arab Emirates. INTERPOL's International Child Sexual Exploitation database, one of the key image databases used globally by police, has identified over 10,000 victims of child abuse since the current version was launched in 2009. Similar image databases and dedicated web search tools are also being developed to counter violent extremism, radicalization, and propaganda.

As Bergin and colleagues[41] noted: 'direct conversations with frontline fighters in Syria and Iraq, recruiters and facilitators are a keystroke away'. In response to repeated attacks by violent extremists, Facebook, Microsoft, Twitter, and YouTube announced in June 2017 the formation of the Global Internet Forum to Counter Terrorism (GIFTC). The goal of the GIFTC is to make the collective services of the forum members effective in removing terrorist and violent extremist content and communications. The GIFTC recognizes the need to respond to community standards and laws that prohibit hate speech, and to avoid potential litigation in Europe where hate speech, unlike in the United States, has long been criminalized. Measures in Germany effective from 1 July 2017 (and to be followed by France, the UK, and others) compel Internet services to remove such content or face significant fines. The GIFTC seeks to create a structure that promotes collaboration across the tech industry, civil society groups, academics, national governments, the European Union and the United Nations.[42] It aims to respond to changing terrorist and extremist tactics by commissioning of research, facilitating knowledge sharing, and developing the Shared Industry Hash Database for violent extremist images and machine learning to detect and remove violent extremist content.

How effective the GIFTC initiative will be in combatting online terrorist propaganda, recruitment, and operations awaits evaluation. One likely outcome will be the use of online services available outside the remit of the GIFTC and in jurisdictions that are not signatories to the CoE's Cybercrime Convention. Nevertheless, the recognition that apparent tolerance of hate speech and violent extremism by the new media requires intervention could galvanize these services to make self-regulation a feasible option.

The US National Institute for Standards and Technology (NIST) Cybersecurity Framework provides regularly updated cybersecurity best practices, and has helped improve the effectiveness of cybersecurity not only in the US but also in Canada, India, and Australia (Shackelford et al. 2016). Standards that mandate cybersecurity into the writing of programs, and applications that provide for automated regulatory reinforcement of such practices (e.g. password robustness), are essential. These will support changes in the culture of software engineers and contribute to the reduction of vulnerabilities. Common problems include such basics as buffer overflows, memory disclosure, null pointer dereference, integer overflows, and missing permission checks, all of which should be minimized by diligence at the programming stage (Yamaguchi et al. 2014). Other efforts against CEM, cyber-terrorism, and fraud have also been noted. These examples show the role that partnerships of NGOs can play in the prevention and mitigation of cybercrime.

CONCLUSION

Cybercrime has evolved from a *low-volume–high-value* crime once committed by an individual specialist offender to a mainstream *high-volume–low-value* crime, and 'organized and industrial like'[43] perpetrators are now more likely a skilled team of software engineers. It is not only the domain of organized crime groups but also networked crime groups of various forms, as well as state or quasi-state actors, that have an impact on the scale and sophistication of cybercrime. However, the overall burden of cybercrime and cyber security is not rationally distributed so that the costs of cybercrime can be catastrophic for some but not for others.

Constant hacker 'tinkering' leads to novel combinations with old, new, adapted, reassembled, and enhanced technologies that will continue to drive a cyber arms race—a game of cat and mouse between police and cybercriminals. Social engineering has become more personal and compelling, often able to deceive users into malware self-infection. Spear phishing has also come to exemplify cybercrime and draws on the increasing range of data available about individuals. No longer confined to email, diverse forms of spam continue to deliver malware, to disrupt or subvert automated services, and to launch DDOS attacks (Broadhurst 2017).

The increasing linkages across the IoT, such as large data collections ('Big Data'), cloud computing services, smartphones, SCADA systems, autonomous vehicles, emotional recognition, and other evolving forms of artificial intelligence (AI) yield ever more information about us and our behaviour. Now critical to successful crime (in the virtual and in the real world) is anonymity, and this is achieved via encryption and identity theft, in turn the principal precursor to many crimes in cyberspace. Underground markets (illicit drugs, CEM, arms and other contraband, piracy and malware toolkits) will continue to expand and diversify, and their disruptive effects will have an impact on more individuals and enterprises. These illicit markets attract privateers and proxy state actors as well as criminal actors of all stripes, and they are the crime rookeries or safe havens of the new digital age.

Holt and colleagues (2015) suggest that theft, swindles, and fraud will continue to increase, helped by large-scale data breaches, the extension of unwarranted access to computer operating systems (i.e. administrative privilege sprawl or creep), and identity theft. The widespread use of wearable devices and peripherals may also influence risk as our behaviour changes with our engagement with new technologies. Rare or theoretical events such as the cyber-jacking of aircraft, the interference with motor vehicle computer systems ('car-sploiting'), and power outages combined with more complex and self-exciting malware could emerge as common threats.

Finding the balance between a secure yet open Internet requires mitigating the negative effects of securitization (i.e. the justification of extreme measures in the name of national security) of cyber space so that the creative benefits provided by online resources such as Wikipedia are not lost. The steps already taken to secure the benefits of the new communication technologies through cross-national mutual legal assistance, national cyber security strategies, and community policing suggest how the impacts of cybercrime may be reduced.

In response to the challenges, law enforcement practices are compelled to adapt more rapidly than ever. A priority must be to increase the potency of deterrence. This will depend to a significant degree on the extent of mutual legal assistance, given the cross-border nature of cybercrimes. Mandating standards and guidelines for built-in cybersecurity of new products written into the code level (from O/S to 'apps') before release, combined with the promotion of crime prevention and cyber-safety awareness, must be central to the public–private partnerships needed to suppress cybercrime. The massive reach of the Internet inevitably enhances opportunities for cybercrime but it also offers the means to identify and counter threats, large and small, through effective forms of online community-style policing that have proven effective in addressing violence in the non-virtual world.

Notes

1. See Grabosky, 'Evolution of Cybercrime', 2017.
2. Miniwatts Market Group. 2019. 'Internet World Statistics', http://www.internetworldstats.com/stats6.htm
3. International Telecommunication Union, 2018: http://www.internetworldstats.com/stats.htm; https://news.itu.int/itu-statistics-leaving-no-one-offline/
4. See Broadhurst et al. 2017.
5. ACSC, '2016 Threat Report', 8.
6. 'Gavin Corn interviewed by Global Initiative', 27 February 2014: www.globalinitiative.net/gin-gavincorn/
7. McAfee, 2016. Net Losses: Estimating the Global Cost of Cybercrime: https://csis-website-prod.s3.amazonaws.com/s3fs-public/legacy_files/files/attachments/140609_McAfee_PDF.pdf.

8. Columbus, Louis. 5 April 2020. '2020 Roundup of Cybersecurity Forecasts and Market Estimates', *Forbes*; https://www.forbes.com/sites/louiscolumbus/2020/04/05/2020-roundup-of-cybersecurity-forecasts-and-market-estimates/?sh=21e8dbfe381d
   Morgan, Steve. 2016. 'Cyber Crime Costs Projected To Reach $2 Trillion by 2019', Forbes, 17 January. https://www.forbes.com/sites/stevemorgan/2016/01/17/cyber-crime-costs-projected-to-reach-2-trillion-by-2019/

9. The Anti-Phishing Working Group (APWG, n.d.) defines phishing as '... a criminal mechanism employing both social engineering and technical subterfuge to steal consumers' personal identity data and financial account credentials. Social engineering schemes use spoofed e-mails purporting to be from legitimate businesses and agencies, designed to lead consumers to counterfeit websites that trick recipients into divulging financial data such as usernames and passwords. Technical subterfuge schemes plant crimeware onto PCs to steal credentials directly, often using systems to intercept consumers online account user names and passwords—and to corrupt local navigational infrastructures to misdirect consumers to counterfeit websites (or authentic websites through phisher-controlled proxies used to monitor and intercept consumers' keystrokes).' http://apwg.org/, http://apwg.org/report-phishing

10. APWG, n.d.: http://apwg.org/, http://apwg.org/report-phishing

11. Miniwatts Market Group 2017, 'Internet World Statistics': http://www.internetworldstats.com/stats6.htm

12. The data survey was generated from the RAND American Life Panel, a US representative panel of more than 6,000 persons aged 18 and older who had agreed to participate in occasional Internet-based surveys. The survey was fielded between 14 May and 1 June 2015 to 2,618 adults with a response rate of 78%. See Ablon, Lillian, Paul Heaton, Diana Lavery et al., 2016. Consumer Attitudes Toward Data Breach Notifications and Loss of Personal Information. Santa Monica, CA: RAND Corporation: https://www.rand.org/pubs/research_reports/RR1187.html

13. ACSC, *Threat Report*, 5.

14. The Bitcoin trader Mt Gox went spectacularly bankrupt after the disappearance of 850,000 Bitcoins—the value of Bitcoins (then trading at over US$1,300) plummeted. Bitcoin recovered and is now reportedly dominated by Chinese players although the value of Bitcoins remains volatile.

15. United States Department of Justice (USDOJ). 1996. 'The National Information Infrastructure Protection Act of 1996, Legislative Analysis 1996': http//www.cybercrime.gov/1030analysis.html; USDOJ. 2015, July 15. 'Major Computer Hacking Forum Dismantled': https://www.fbi.gov/pittsburgh/press-releases/2015/major-computer-hacking-forum-dismantled

16. Broadhurst and Grabosky, 2005.

17. Mandiant, 2013, *Mandiant Intelligence Center Report (APT 1)*: https://www.fireeye.com/blog/threat-research/2013/02/mandiant-exposes-apt1-chinas-cyber-espionage-units.html

18. Nakashima, Ellen. 2012. 'When is a cyberattack an act of war?', *Washington Post*: https://www.washingtonpost.com/opinions/when-is-a-cyberattack-an-act-of-war/2012/10/26/02226232-1eb8-11e2-9746-908f727990d8_story.html

19. See Commonwealth of Australia, Department of Home Affairs. 2020. p. 7–9. *Australia's Cyber Security Strategy*: https://www.homeaffairs.gov.au/cyber-security-subsite/files/cyber-security-strategy-2020.pdf

20. At the time of writing, the case is pending trial in Dallas, Texas: 'Kang Cecilia. 2017. "A Tweet to Kurt Eichenwald, a Strobe and a Seizure. Now, an Arrest", *The New York Times*: https://www.nytimes.com/2017/03/17/technology/social-media-attack-that-set-off-a-seizure-leads-to-an-arrest.html

21. Ablon et al., 'Markets for Cybercrime Tools', ix.

22. Dark Reading online: http://www.darkreading.com/cloud/cybercrime-a-black-market-price-list-from-the-dark-web/

23. Abrams, L. 2015. 'Radamant Ransomware Kit for sale on Exploit & Malware Sites', 28 December. https://www.bleepingcomputer.com/news/security/radamant-ransomware-kit-for-sale-on-exploit-and-malware-sites/

24. Krebs, Brian (Dec 18, 2017) The Market for Stolen Account Credential; https://krebsonsecurity.com/2017/12/the-market-for-stolen-account-credentials/

25. Goncharov, Max. 2015. Criminal Hideouts for Lease: Bulletproof Hosting Services, TrendMicro Research: https://www.trendmicro.no/media/wp/wp-criminal-hideouts-for-lease-en.pdf

26. Dell SecureWorks 2016, Underground Hacker Markets: https://www.secureworks.com/resources/wp-underground-hacking-markets-report

27. McAfee. 2013. Hidden Data Economy: The Marketplace for Stolen Information: https://www.mcafee.com/us/resources/reports/rp-hidden-data-economy.pdf; McAfee, 2015: https://securingtomorrow.mcafee.com/mcafee-labs/hidden-data-economy-report-exposes-price-points-for-stolen-data/

28. McAfee, Hidden Data Economy, 2013, 2015.

29. Bowen, Chris. 2015. 'The seedy underworld of medical data trafficking', HealthcareITNews, July 8. http://www.healthcareitnews.com/blog/seedy-underworld-medical-data-trafficking

30. See https://tsyrklevich.net/2015/07/22/hacking-team-0day-market/

31. See Chon, *Cybercrime Precursors*.

32. Steinmetz, *Hacked*, 2016.

33. Chon, *Cybercrime Precursors*.

34. Persi Paoli, Giacomo, Judith Aldridge, Nathan Ryan, and Richard Warnes, 2017. *Behind the Curtain: The Illicit Trade of Firearms, Explosives and Ammunition on the Dark Web*. Santa Monica, CA: RAND Corporation: https://www.rand.org/pubs/research_reports/RR2091.html

35. ABC News. 2017. Child-porn website creator accidentally reveals IP address, leading to 870 arrests', 7 May. http://www.abc.net.au/news/2017-05-06/playpen-child-porn-site-creator-steven-chase-sentenced/8502626

36. Jayawardena, K., and R. Broadhurst. 2007. 'Online Child Sex Solicitation: Exploring the Feasibility of a Research "Sting" ', *International Journal of Cyber Criminology*, 1 (2): 228–48.

37. See also Broadhurst et al. 2014. 'An Analysis of the Nature of Groups', *International Journal of Cyber Criminology*, 8 (1): 1–20.

38. Chabinsky, S.R. 2010. 'The Cyber Threat: Who's Doing What to Whom?', 23 May. http://www.fbi.gov/news/speeches/the-cyber-threat-whos-doing-what-to-whom

39. UNODC, 'Emerging Crimes': http://www.unodc.org/unodc/organized-crime/emerging-crimes.html Note that trafficking in cultural property, environmental crime, piracy, organ trafficking, and fraudulent medicine were also featured as crime types subject to the convention.

40. The main headings of the Convention's substantive criminal law are illegal access; illegal interception; data interference; system interference; misuse of devices (computer viruses, etc.); forgery and fraud; child pornography; and copyright infringements.
41. Bergin et al., 'Gen Y jihadists', 18.
42. Seib, Philip. 2017. 'Facebook, Microsoft, Twitter, and YouTube Can't Stop Terrorism', 28 July. http://fortune.com/2017/06/28/global-internet-forum-to-counter-terrorism-policy-islamic-state-facebook-microsoft-twitter-youtube/; Twitter. 2017. 'Global Internet Forum to Counter Terrorism', 26 June. https://blog.twitter.com/official/en_us/topics/company/2017/Global-Internet-Forum-to-Counter-Terrorism.html
43. Anderson et al., 'Measuring the Cost of Cybercrime', 2013.

REFERENCES

Ablon, L., Libicki, M.C., and Golay, A.A. 2014. 'Markets for Cybercrime Tools and Stolen Data: Hackers' Bazaar'. RAND Corporation: http://www.rand.org/content/dam/rand/pubs/research_reports/RR600/RR610/RAND_RR610.sum.pdf

Anderson, R., Barton, C., Böhme, R. et al. 2013. 'Measuring the Changing Cost of Cybercrime'. In *The Economics of Information Security and Privacy*, edited by R. Böhme, 265–300. Berlin, Heidelberg: Springer.

Australian Bureau of Statistics, 2016. '4528.0—Personal Fraud, 2014–15', Canberra: http://www.abs.gov.au/ausstats/abs@.nsf/mf/4528.0/

Australian Cyber Security Centre (ACSC) 2016. '2016 Threat Report', Canberra: http://Users/u4661385/Desktop/ACSC_Threat_Report_2016.pdf

Bergin, A., Clifford, M., Connery, D., Feakin, T., Gleiman, K., Huang, and S. Yasmeen. 2015. 'Gen Y Jihadists Preventing Radicalisation in Australia', *Australian Strategic Policy Institute*: https://www.aspi.org.au/publications/gen-y-jihadists-preventing-radicalisation-in-australia/GenY_jihadists.pdf

Broadhurst, R., 2006. 'Developments in the Global Law Enforcement of Cyber-Crime', *Policing: An International Journal of Police Strategies and Management* 29 (3): 408–33.

Broadhurst, R., P. Grabosky, M. Alazab, B. Bouhours, and S. Chon, 2014. 'An Analysis of the Nature of Groups Engaged in Cybercrime', *International Journal of Cyber Criminology* 8 (1): 1–20.

Broadhurst, R.G. and P. N. Grabosky. 2005. 'Computer-related Crime in Asia: Emergent Issues'. In *Cyber-Crime: The Challenge in Asia*, edited by R.G. Broadhurst and P. Grabosky. Hong Kong: The University of Hong Kong Press.

Broadhurst, Roderic, Woodford-Smith, Hannah, Maxim, Donald, Sabol, Bianca, Orlando, Stephanie, Benjamin, Chapman-Schmidt, and Mamoun Alazab, 2017. 'Cyber Terrorism: Research Review', Australian National University, Cybercrime Observatory, Canberra, doi: 10.13140/RG.2.2.19282.96964

Broadhurst, R.G. 2017.'Cybercrime'. In *The Palgrave Handbook of Australian and New Zealand Criminology, Crime and Justice*, edited by A. Deckart and R. Sarre, 151–69. Basingstoke: Palgrave Macmillan.

Chon, Ki Hong, 2016. *Cybercrime Precursors: Towards a Model of Offender Resources* (Unpublished doctoral dissertation). Australian National University, Australia.

Grabosky, P. 2017. 'The Evolution of Cybercrime, 2006–2016.' In *Cybercrime Through an Interdisciplinary Lens*, edited by Thomas J. Holt, pp. 15–36. New York: Routledge.

Herzog, Stephen. 2011. 'Revisiting the Estonian Cyber Attacks: Digital Threats and Multinational Responses', *Journal of Strategic Security* 4: 49–60.

Holt, T.J., Bossler, A.M., and Seigfried-Spellar, K.C. 2015. *Cybercrime and Digital Forensics: An Introduction*. Routledge.

Levy, Stephen. 1984. *Hackers: Heroes of the Computer Revolution*. New York: Anchor Press/ Doubleday.

Martin, J., 2014. Lost on the Silk Road: Online Drug Distribution and the 'Cryptomarket'. *Criminology and Criminal Justice 14* (3), 351–67.

McGuire, M. 2012. *Organised Crime in the Digital Age*. London: John Grieve Centre for Policing and Security.

Rid, Thomas. 2016. *Rise of the Machines: The Lost History of Cybernetics*. New York: Scribe.

Sanger, D. E. 2012. 'Obama Order Sped Up Wave of Cyberattacks Against Iran', *The New York Times*, 1 June: http://www.nytimes.com/2012/06/01/world/middleeast/obama-ordered-wave-of-cyberattacks-against-iran.html?_r=0

Shackelford, S. J., Russell, S., and Haut, J. (2016). 'Bottoms up: A Comparison of "Voluntary" Cybersecurity Frameworks', *UC Davis Business Law Journal* 16: 217.

Steinmetz, K.F. 2016. *Hacked: A Radical Approach to Hacker Culture and Crime*. New York: New York University Press.

Sterling, B. 2002. *The Hacker Crackdown*. IndyPublish.com. (orig. 1994 Bantam Books).

UNODC (United Nations Office on Drugs and Crime). 2013. *Comprehensive Study on Cybercrime*. New York: United Nations: https://www.unodc.org/documents/organized-crime/UNODC_CCPCJ_EG.4_2013/CYBERCRIME_STUDY_210213.pdf

UNODC. 2015. 'Study on the Effects of New Information Technologies on the Abuse and Exploitation of Children': http//www.unodc.org/documents/organized-crime/cybercrime/Study_on_the_Effects.pdf

Van Wilsem, J.V. 2011. 'Worlds Tied Together? Online and Non-Domestic Routine Activities and Their Impact on Digital and Traditional Threat Victimization', *European Journal of Criminology* 8 (2): 115–27.

Van Wilsem, J.V. 2013. 'Hacking and Harassment—Do They Have Something in Common? Comparing Risk Factors for Online Victimization', *Journal of Contemporary Criminal Justice* 29 (4): 437–53.

Yamaguchi, F., Golde, N., Arp, D. et al. 2014. 'Modeling and Discovering Vulnerabilities with Code Property Graphs', *Security and Privacy (SP), 2014 IEEE Symposium*: 590–604.

CHAPTER 7

MAKING SENSE OF CYBERSECURITY IN EMERGING TECHNOLOGY AREAS

CLAIRE VISHIK, MICHAEL HUTH,
LAWRENCE JOHN, AND MARCELLO BALDUCCINI

TECHNOLOGY FORECASTING AND INNOVATION

Methodology for Predicting Trends in Cybersecurity

The term 'technology' can denote products and services developed based on scientific and engineering knowledge, but it may also refer to related knowledge and its integration to solve complex application problems (see National Infrastructure Commission 2016). Attempts to anticipate emerging technology areas and their impact are made routinely in the fields of policy, market analysis, research funding, and many more. Investments and policy decisions are made in anticipation of predicted developments. Research in the 'disruptiveness' of new technologies may focus on the disruption of markets by innovation as in (Govindarajan and Kopalle 2006) or, more frequently, on softer metrics, attempting to forecast future trends based on past evolution, statistics, or superficially logical considerations.

Such forecasts are rarely perfect, but they allow the broad community to define an area of focus for innovation. For example, in the United States, high-level research priorities in cybersecurity were established and tracked for a number of years, providing a relatively stable set of potentially disruptive technologies in cybersecurity and vocabulary for defining them.[1] The resulting report divides potentially disruptive technologies into several descriptive areas (e.g. 'moving target defence' and 'security of cyber-physical systems) and associates them with process-oriented activities, such as designed-in security, the establishment of scientific foundations of cybersecurity, or transition to practice. Although the resulting framework does not reliably forecast future technology environments, it allows us to talk consistently about technology innovation and its influence on trends in cybercrime when faced with cyber attacks of ever-increasing speed and scale. Can we do better than that? Later, we suggest approaches and provide examples to improve forecasts for disruptions in cybersecurity and for the evolution of cybercrime.

To understand the impact of emerging technologies on cybersecurity more accurately, we need a more formal and multidisciplinary approach. Traditionally, 'technology foresight' (Van Zwanenberg et al. 2009) is a structured activity, in which new possibilities of technological innovation are examined with a view toward harnessing the greatest economic or social value of future 'technology assessment'. Van Zwanenberg et al. focus on predicting the impacts of technology as used by humans (foresight), and on creating methodologies to inform the selection and deployment of technology (assessment). These two approaches, foresight and assessment, are often combined to yield 'strategic intelligence' (Kuhlmann et al. 1999). In the real world, planners must think frequently in terms of decades (foresight), but might also need to introduce new technology in the short- to medium- term (assessment). In increasingly smart cities, cybersecurity and crime are important aspects in both foresight and assessment activities.

In fast-emerging areas, where new threats, threat vectors, attack methods, and defensive capabilities emerge daily, it is a challenge to link these developments to cybersecurity and cybercrime. However, it is not a bleak picture, and, as we discuss later, second-order predictions, such as trends in cybersecurity, are somewhat easier to capture. Forecasting of longer-term technology trends has been shown to be no better than random selection of possibilities, unless a low baseline is taken, focusing on obvious requirements (Quinn 1967). Views such as 'security will continue to be important in electronic commerce' are likely to be correct, but they are obvious. We may not be able to anticipate even the *types* of technology that will exist at some future point, but some techniques could increase the likelihood of an actionable answer. Making well-founded assumptions about the technology environment in general makes it easier to predict impacts on the cybersecurity of citizens, systems, or entire infrastructures.

Cybersecurity and trends in cybercrime are typically secondary impacts of the introduction of innovative technologies: They can be addressed with greater confidence than

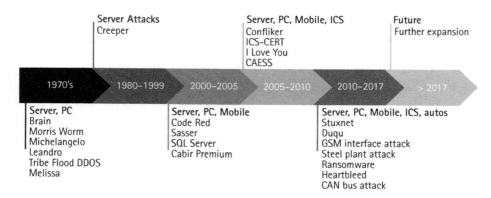

FIGURE 7.1. Evolution of cyberattacks

predictions for technology evolution in general. To illustrate, a prediction that flying autonomous vehicles will become common in 20 years (see NASA 2017) may be justified based on evolution of the technology up to now. But a more concrete prediction that 30% of new vehicles sold will be flying autonomous vehicles is hard to justify based on known technology and business trends. We lack scientific techniques to assess the probability of such a prediction. However, we have greater knowledge about the evolution of known cybersecurity and privacy threats (as illustrated in Fig. 7.1), and vulnerabilities for flying autonomous vehicles, based on what is known today. Although incomplete, this secondary assessment of cybersecurity could be more reliable than a more concrete technology prediction, because the secondary impacts of new technologies are more stable and depend more on the general technology environment than primary disruptive technologies.

Possible Techniques for Prediction of Future Technology

Let us consider specific techniques that can help anticipate cybersecurity and privacy concerns for innovative technologies with unknown usage models and evolution paths. How can we make sense of cybersecurity issues for technology environments that are too novel to be well understood or still evolving? Several approaches from adjacent research areas are available.

1. **Analysis based on past behaviours in similar environments**: this approach permits a reasonably reliable core assessment based on known facts and techniques, but does not offer structured methodologies to extract novel components and problems.

Studying past disruptive technological innovations may help us better understand how future disruptions or emerging technology with disruptive potential may influence the technological fabric that underpins modern societies and economies. As an example, the US government spent $1.5 billion in the late 1950s on developing a high-altitude strategic bomber, the XB-70 Valkyrie. However, the emergence of surface-to-air missiles that could reach high altitudes led to swift cancellation of the project and a complete change in US tactics. This apparent failure fostered research that created innovations in low observable design and coatings, greatly reducing the effectiveness of the aforementioned missile technology innovation (Rao and Mahulikar 2002). The Cold War environment did not exhibit either wide diffusion of emerging technology or capabilities analogous to current and emerging cybersecurity threats. It does not, therefore, qualify as a sufficiently similar environment. We must look to more recent use cases for guidance.

With regard to modern developments, such as Bitcoin (Nakamoto 2008) and blockchain technology, analysis based on past trends could point to expansion to other areas requiring robust transaction records for auditing or operations. Aerospace, automotive, and supply chains, among others, could use blockchain, and experience privacy and security issues detected for Bitcoin systems. We may suppose that sectors where blockchain is likely to be used will experience cybercrime trends informed by those detected for Bitcoin and/or for new sectors of blockchain use—with the necessary adjustment for new technology.

2. **Examining and combining analyses from different stakeholders**: this approach permits incorporation of societal and economic considerations, but can be imprecise.

The interpretation of the impact of technologies is partly a function of the objectives for the forecasting activity and the expertise of those who conduct it. Governments are interested in impacts on their societies and economies, including national security. International enterprises focus on financial impacts, their technological competitiveness, and impacts on trade and business models. Individuals are concerned with the impacts of emergent technology on their personal life and standard of living, in areas like food safety, online security, protection of personal data, and job prospects. Different technologies and stakeholders operate within different time horizons and tolerate different risks. In infrastructure-heavy sectors, such as telecommunications or manufacturing, longer-term analysis is needed than in areas such as software or consumer electronics, where planning horizons are shorter. In some areas, such as cyber-physical systems, time horizons vary between a lifespan of a few minutes (one-use medical sensors) and several decades (industrial control systems). But the essential technologies in these two areas are similar, leading to the need to develop models capable of evaluating both paradigms in one framework.

Continuing our blockchain example, examination of cybersecurity threats from different market and government sectors in which blockchain is used can help anticipate some of the cybersecurity vulnerabilities that are likely to be important, and apply already known or newly created mitigation techniques.

3. **Collecting 'signals' from the environment and analysing their impact**: signals can include diverse evidence of evolving characteristics of the technology environment, job advertisements, information on acquisition and alliances, research publications, and many other elements. The success of this approach depends heavily on the data quality and interpretation of these signals.

By collecting meaningful information over time on a wide range of topics, consistent trends can be constructed, including for cybersecurity. Although conclusions may not be immediately actionable, they can be improved by refining methods of signal interpretation. Artificial intelligence (AI) techniques could be added to this methodology, potentially offering deep or unusual insights into current and future trends.

To illustrate, signals and data from currently active blockchain markets, and analysis of those signals, could provide a practical, sometimes quantitative, foundation for more theoretical assumptions on the vulnerabilities of future blockchain systems described for the first two approaches.

4. **Creating models of disruptive technologies**: insights and results depend on the quality of the model and the viability of its assumptions, but they permit generalization of the methodology and evaluation of multiple scenarios.

Emergent technology may be disruptive in several ways. Innovation can make past technology obsolete, diminishing returns on prior investments. Or it can challenge past business models, including the rationale for existing service or product platforms. Note that none of the larger companies that produced computers based on analogue transistors survived the transition to digital transistors. Disruptions may also have important second-order effects. For example, if almost all cars are both powered by electricity and fully autonomous, opportunities for energy savings through coordinated road usage and planned recharging may increase. However, this may increase preference for cars over public transportation, potentially increasing energy demands (see National Infrastructure Commission 2016). Such insights can be refined through modelling, and can assist theory development not only for the primary environment (autonomous cars) but also for emerging cybersecurity and privacy concerns in an environment with predominantly autonomous vehicles.

Continuing our blockchain example, insights gleaned from approaches 1–3 (two theoretical approaches and one data-driven validation mechanism) are likely to provide enough useful information and strong assumptions to shape a model of a blockchain-enabled environment. In such a model, we can explore different use cases within a single framework to enable examination of future impacts on cybersecurity and privacy, and trends in cybercrime for this space.

5. **Ontology[2]-based analysis**: Knowledge-engineering[3] techniques can support structured analysis of components of innovative environments. They can also enable reasoning about the relationships within these environments; finding hidden connections and constraints; and understanding how the same technology can be used for different scenarios, ranging from digital business and e-government to cybercrime.

The intrinsic complexity of modern technology environments makes it hard to understand how innovative elements have an impact on other environments and technology users. Traditional approaches provide silo-based analysis but, without finding hidden connections, we cannot assess hypothetical situations that do not yet exist or have not yet been detected. What cybercriminal threats are there for a passenger in a flying autonomous vehicle? How can an old public ledger affect the security of an account created 20 years later? Reasoning algorithms in ontologies can help find answers to these questions.

Returning to blockchain, an ontology and its reasoning engine can draw from the techniques described earlier, while highlighting implicit relationships and constraints not noticed before. We may thus identify a lack of alignment between requirements in regulatory frameworks in some areas (e.g. aerospace) and capabilities of blockchain systems, or their potential ability to protect against or create the foundations for certain types of cybercrime.

Trend Forecasting and Cybercrime

The connection between innovative technologies and novel opportunities for cybercrime should be understood using a number of approaches. Because cybercrime covers a wide range of activities where information technology facilitates criminal purposes, the connection between the new technologies and the new forms of cybercrime is important. The same ecosystems are used for digital business and by cyber criminals (Kraemer-Mbula et al. 2013). Thus, a better understanding of emerging technologies and business models should also lead to a better potential to anticipate mitigations for cybercrime.

Quantum computing and post-quantum cryptography provide an example of the connection of emerging technologies and new types of cyber threats, and, consequently, cybercrime. The ability of quantum computing (Shor 1995) to potentially compromise existing digital signature solutions suggests that emergent technologies may not only threaten the cybersecurity of present systems but may also compromise the integrity of past commercial or legal transactions, potentially damaging the trustworthiness vital to a nation's social contract. Digital signatures and authentication enabled by asymmetric cryptography rely on the fundamental assumption that only a signatory can produce a signature while anyone can verify it. For this assumption to hold, the task of synthesizing a signing key from a verification key and a message must be too complex to perform in any reasonable amount of time by a state-of-the-art computer. Thus, these schemes are particularly vulnerable in a quantum computing environment. To make things worse, they are as pervasively used as asymmetric cryptographic algorithms for data encryption. The emerging problem with this technology is widely known, providing additional time and opportunities for cybercriminals to develop new techniques.

When fundamental changes in a paradigm are envisioned, as in post-quantum cryptography (Bernstein 2009), ontological analysis can identify impacts on complex systems or legal and regulatory environments. Extending this example to blockchain, ontological views of blockchain systems and post-quantum cryptography, informed by the outcomes of other forms of analysis, permit the developers to better understand the effect of fully functional quantum computers on blockchain systems and the effect of this paradigm change on cybercrime.

To summarize, we cannot rely on proven approaches to identify and analyse emerging technology environments, and their cybersecurity and privacy properties. But cybersecurity and privacy threats and vulnerabilities identified for older, yet similar, environments can be a useful guide because they represent derivative rather than primary insights. A number of techniques could improve the outcomes for anticipating disruptive technologies. An aggregation of these methodologies could improve the outlook.

Disruptive Technology and Regulatory Frameworks

New technology environments have a profound effect on the efficacy and content of regulatory and legal frameworks, which are also influenced by the need to combat cybercrime. However, this influence is delayed. Consider the evolution of the concept of anonymity in the modern technology environment. Anonymity is an important foundation for privacy and data protection, but the ability to achieve relative anonymity online is also an enabler of cybercrime.

Anonymity has gained importance largely due to European legislation on personal data protection. Anonymous data are not 'personal data' and are therefore outside the field of application of, for example, the European Union General Data Protection Regulation. But is anonymity absolute? It cannot be in some contexts. A writer can be anonymous to readers but not to the publisher. The multifaceted nature of anonymity is much more prominent in modern digital contexts.

Data can be considered personal if a data subject is identifiable. The subject need not be directly identified, but can be identifiable in principle—for instance, through aggregation of data sources. As the number of potentially related data sources and diverse identifiers increases, the ability to re-identify a user through multiple data sources also grows. European Union regulators adopted[4] the idea of 'reasonableness' as a foundation for the establishment

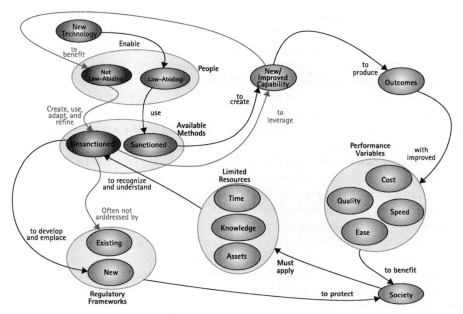

FIGURE 7.2. Cybercriminals and the law

of whether the data should be considered personal or anonymous. The reasonableness test relies on the amount on effort needed to re-identify a data subject.[5]

However, the complexity of the digital processes is likely to lead to further dilution of the strict definition of anonymity. It will become more difficult to interpret issues related to autonomy in the context of the latest technologies—for example, determining the appropriate level of anonymity within distributed ledgers or whether the distributed nature of many blockchain systems could violate requirements for, and place restrictions on, international data flows. In consequence, legal and regulatory approaches require continuing evaluation and modification of requirements to match the computing environment. It will also be necessary to reconcile, via technology adjustment and regulatory actions, the need to avoid re-identification to support data protection for users with the need to trace and combat cybercrime. Such assessments can be informed by conceptual models, where Fig. 7.2 shows such a model of the relationships between cybercriminals and the law.

Disruptive Technology and Threat Landscapes

A disruptive technology could dramatically change the cybersecurity threat landscape, yield effective new countermeasures against cybersecurity attacks, or influence the ecosystem in which cybersecurity attacks are realized and monetized. For example, the invention of Bitcoin (Nakamoto 2008, Narayanan et al. 2016) has the potential to make the flow of financial assets traceable, making it harder for cybercriminals to act through a combination of social and cyber attacks. But the pseudo-anonymity that Bitcoin affords to its users raises the interest of cybercriminals in Bitcoin transactions because such transactions may be hard to connect to legal actors. However, intelligent data analysis allows for the identification of particular Bitcoin users or operators of its clusters (Meiklejohn et al. 2016). This is an innovative environment with some features not previously encountered. The assessment of its impact on cybersecurity must draw from techniques described earlier to be comprehensive and reasonably pragmatic. Similar to anonymity, the legal and regulatory aspects of cybersecurity with regard to blockchain-enabled environments are expected to gradually evolve, as will the regulatory frameworks for virtual currencies. Society will have to anticipate and resolve a range of issues as new technologies take hold, such as the use of blockchain-based cryptocurrencies for cybercrime.

Anticipating gradual evolution of technology is easier than guessing the fundamentally new directions of distinctive innovations such as a digital transistor or software-defined radio, because incremental processes founded on known principles are easier to capture. However, it is important to understand that, while technology disruption through incremental change may be less opaque to researchers, in some situations, secondary properties with regard to cybersecurity and privacy may abruptly lose their incremental nature. Thus, gradual change in the general technology environment may lead to abrupt deterioration or improvement in security, limiting the usefulness of analytical tools developed to reflect an earlier state of a similar technology environment. To overcome consequences of abrupt changes resulting from originally incremental developments, good-quality metrics and advanced risk models may be leveraged.

We illustrate such gradual improvement in the use of military-grade Global Positioning Systems (GPS). The evolution of the features of the technology was obvious in military systems. But when GPS technologies became mature enough and cheap enough to support mass location services on non-dedicated devices, security and privacy concerns associated with location tracking emerged, requiring a separate solution.

Today, a growing number of organizations view threat landscapes in a more general way, in an attempt to predict the areas of focus for threats rather than specific threats and their precise or relative impacts. In part, this is due to the complexity of today's computing environment. But, in addition, the emphasis on the big picture is driven by the realization that it embeds the foundation, from which the details could be captured and addressed. Figure 7.3 illustrates this approach and shows a summary of the 2019 threat landscape released by the Information Security Forum (ISF).[6]

The need for generalization is obvious in both cybersecurity threat and technology forecasting. Analysis through knowledge representation provides an opportunity to examine not only the components of the big pictures but also the connections both between them and within the broader context of deployment or use.

KNOWLEDGE REPRESENTATION AND TECHNOLOGY TREND PREDICTION

In multidisciplinary subjects like cybersecurity, knowledge representation approaches could be useful in assessing current and emerging technology spaces for both research and technology deployment. Ontology-based reasoning can help us obtain a multidimensional

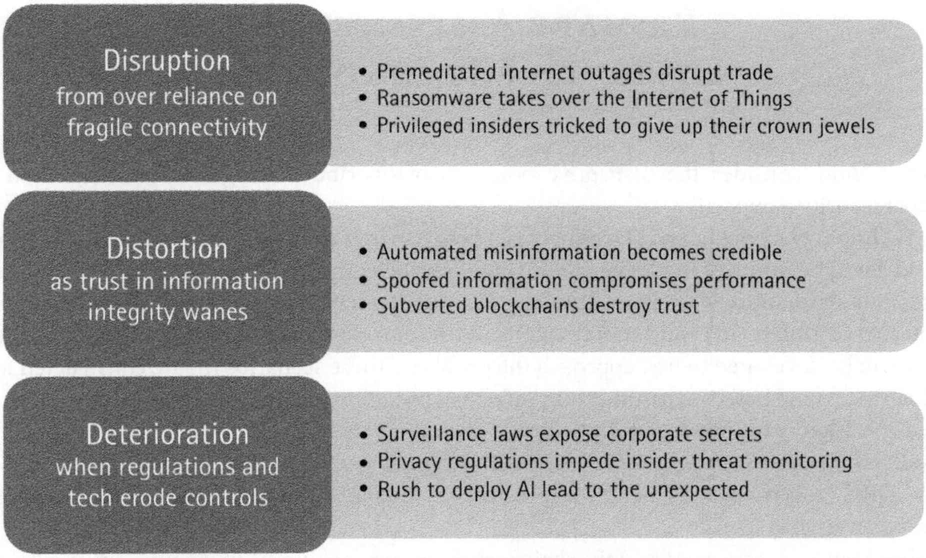

Disruption from over reliance on fragile connectivity	• Premeditated internet outages disrupt trade • Ransomware takes over the Internet of Things • Privileged insiders tricked to give up their crown jewels
Distortion as trust in information integrity wanes	• Automated misinformation becomes credible • Spoofed information compromises performance • Subverted blockchains destroy trust
Deterioration when regulations and tech erode controls	• Surveillance laws expose corporate secrets • Privacy regulations impede insider threat monitoring • Rush to deploy AI lead to the unexpected

Based on "Threat Horizon 2019: Disruption, Distortion. Deterioration," Information Security Forum, London, 2017.

FIGURE 7.3. Anticipated threat themes

view of the subject, incorporate consistent constraints, understand dependencies, and draw informed conclusions.

How can we make sense of cybersecurity in a way that can enable multiple and potentially contrasting contexts, including the legitimate use of technology on the one hand and cybercrime on the other? At a high level of abstraction, the idea is to create a landscape of existing technologies, using their distinguishing features to locate them as points in a multidimensional space of concepts. Current trends can then be identified by studying the relative density of points in this space. Higher-density areas denote technologies that are heavily investigated, or where investment is stronger, while lower-density areas correspond to technologies that have received less interest. Extrapolations can be carried out to determine future trends—possibly by studying how density has changed over a period of time.

But how can we concretely lay out these multidimensional points in such a concept space? Essential for a successful exploration of a complex landscape is the ability to link concepts based on their similarity and dependencies, so that more strongly related technologies are closer to each other in the space and can be considered part of a single set from a high-level view.

With ontologies and ontology-based reasoning, it is possible to capture the arbitrary relationships among concepts and, most notably, class–subclass relationships. An ontology-based approach could permit researchers and practitioners to link together disparate content that draws from similar premises (Iannacone et al. 2015), allowing technologists to reuse, share, and propagate knowledge. We think this approach, which offers mature reasoning capabilities, can be used very effectively to make more informed technology predictions.

Primary Assessment of Disruptive Technologies

Let us now consider the disruptive potential of distributed ledger technology from a cybersecurity perspective.

Technology foresight and assessment can help to better understand the opportunities and risks for cybersecurity in blockchain by highlighting complex dependencies and risks that are difficult to notice without an ontology. We will illustrate this for the use of blockchain in Internet of Things (IoT) and supply chains. With some possible future scenarios to consider that can be developed to first approach the problem. These scenarios (S) are constructed for illustration, and based on assumptions informed by past behaviour.

S1: All key workflows of supply chains including their CIA (confidentiality, integrity, availability) cybersecurity properties, the making of payments, KYM (know your machine) and GRC (governance, risk, and compliance) are mediated through blockchain technology based on open systems.

S2: Many workflows of supply chains, such as the making of payments, are mediated through open blockchains. Some other workflow aspects, such as GRC, cybersecurity, and IoT-facilitated cyber insurance, will be mediated through blockchains, in which nodes that elect the next block in the chain are controlled by stakeholders in these supply chains.

S3: The paradigm of open blockchains, in which everyone is free to join the network, is not adopted by industries to support aspects of workflows for their supply chains. But blockchain technology is fruitfully and judiciously used to make supply chains more flexible, auditable, secure, and cost effective.

What is the perceived likelihood of these scenarios and what might be the cybersecurity ramifications of their realization based on the analysis of past behaviour?

Scenario S1 is unlikely because of risks associated with open blockchains: their currencies may not be valid, their governance models may not align with GRC requirements, and open blockchains may not be scalable enough. Confidentiality is a potential issue because transactions and their history would be public, enabling de-anonymization of transactors (Meiklejohn et al. 2016).

Scenario S2 appears more likely to us. It is prudent to confine higher-risk aspects to blockchains that have access control (including control of the construction of the blocks) and confidentiality designed into them. And there are cybersecurity concerns about using open blockchains to create and maintain currencies. Smart payment contracts, a key innovation of blockchain, require complex run-time systems that are subject to conventional cyber attacks: the denial of service attack on Ethereum in 2016 (Siegel 2016) illustrates the risks of using a cryptocurrency with limited level of assurance.

Scenario S3 is also likely: developers of cryptocurrencies such as Ethereum are interested in better control of blockchains, through a combination of private and open approaches, to reduce the risks of cyber attacks. Cybersecurity may also be enhanced through advances in privacy-preserving distributed storage, cryptographic support, more advanced protocols, and other technologies.

Figure 7.4 illustrates a simplified ontology as it might be used in the analysis of the scenarios. One of its top-level concepts is 'Ledger', which is refined into 'DistributedLedger'

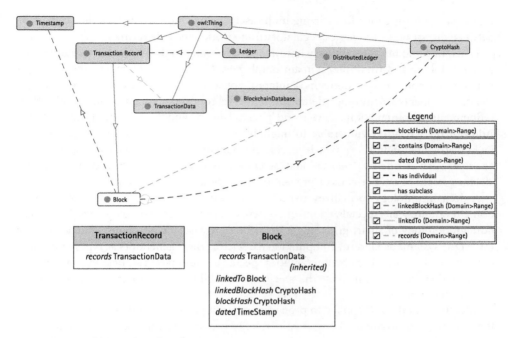

FIGURE 7.4. Leveraging Ontologies

and in its subclass 'BlockchainDatabase'. A ledger 'contains' one or more 'TransactionRecord' items, each 'recording' a set of 'TransactionData'. 'Block' is a subclass of 'TransactionRecord' and, as such, inherits relation 'records'. It also extends its superclass by relations specific to the workings of blockchains (i.e. 'linkedTo' and 'linkedBlockHash'), which point to the previous block and store its hash, 'blockHash', which records the hash of the current block, and to 'dated', which stores its timestamp. The hierarchical structure of the ontology enables both a high level of abstraction (e.g. viewing blockchain databases as any other ledger), and considering high-granularity details (e.g. using ontology-based reasoning to extract a blockchain from a database by leveraging the 'linkedTo' relation). It would not be difficult to extend the ontology further by adding a representation of access control and trustworthiness elements in blockchains, as well as additional dimensions to cover privacy, anonymity, threat agents, and cybercrime.

From Likely Scenario to an Ontology

Similar scenarios are frequently developed to understand the elements of a field or a use case. How can ontologies help here? As shown in Figure 7.4, an ontology is a hierarchical specification of classes of objects from a domain of interest, including their properties and relationships. As such, ontologies enable a principled organization of knowledge.

The general-purpose, hierarchical nature of ontologies, their broad applicability, and the fact that all relevant information has an explicit, machine-accessible representation, make ontologies well suited for formalizing multidisciplinary concerns, such as the connection between disruptive technologies, regulatory frameworks, and cybercrime.

When tackling multidisciplinary knowledge, it is useful to divide the formalization into upper ontology and (multiple) domain ontologies. An upper ontology encodes concepts that are common across all domains of interest. For securing cyber-physical systems, for instance, an upper ontology might define the high-level concept of 'system component', with its refinements of 'computational device' and 'physical device', and the concept of 'vulnerability'. Additionally, a relation 'vulnerable-to' might be used to associate a system component with its known vulnerabilities. A high-level concept 'activity' can be defined as a super-class of concepts such as 'offence', 'analysis', and 'defence' to map out a research taxonomy. In turn, 'defence' might be a super-class of 'prevention', 'detection', and 'mitigation'.

A domain ontology formalizes a specific knowledge domain. Concepts captured by a domain ontology are specializations of concepts from the upper ontology. For example, a domain ontology of smart grids might describe supervisory control and data acquisition (SCADA) systems as kinds of computational devices, power generators as types of physical devices, and list a number of vulnerabilities specific to the smart grid. Relation 'vulnerable-to' could then be used to indicate the specific vulnerabilities of smart grid components and types of cybercrime.

Inference can then be applied to propagate relevant properties and relations throughout the ontology. For example, if a new vulnerability is discovered that affects certain system components, one can determine which components are directly vulnerable. A notion of a component being 'affected by' the vulnerability, either directly or indirectly (connected to some other component that is affected by it) can then be analysed through inference to identify, across the ontology, any component that is affected by a vulnerability. This approach may be used in different contexts to study different dependencies and relations (e.g. between regulatory changes and cybercrime, or technology deployment and cybercrime).

This representation and reasoning framework is especially suited for situations in which knowledge from multiple fields must be captured at the same time. The aforementioned ontology would allow one to study exploits that may affect both the power system and the braking system in a connected vehicle, and also illustrate how cybercriminals might use this vulnerability. Multidisciplinary knowledge can be incrementally and seamlessly integrated, and sophisticated questions about the modelled systems can be answered by means of general-purpose inference mechanisms without the need to develop dedicated algorithms.

Knowledge representation permits us to capture relationships, constraints, and dependencies—important not only in forecasting future trends but also in obtaining insights about completely different environmental contexts, such as digital business and cybercrime. As an example of this, consider the notion of value chain, a sequence of activities that are performed to produce a product or service and bring it to the market. The general concept of value chain can be easily captured by an ontology, in which activities are linked, by a relation 'depends-on', to the activities they depend on. In a business context, a value-chain ontology can enable the identification of bottlenecks and the evaluation of the effects of new suppliers. However, this ontology can also be applied to studying illegal activities. Kraemer-Mbula et al. (2013) observed the existence of a cybercrime value-chain vulnerability *detection → infection and distribution → exploitation*: by applying the value-chain ontology to illegal activities, dependencies among the various illegal activities can be studied, leading to insights into critical links in the chain and methods for blocking them.

It is worth stressing that all this is made possible by the semantic nature of the approach. Having precisely defined semantics allows associating ontological languages with inference mechanisms that perform automated, provably correct reasoning. These inference mechanisms enable, for instance, expanding a class–subclass relationship into an ancestor/descendant one. In the value-chain example, the inference mechanisms' ability to propagate dependencies through a value chain is the key to identifying bottlenecks and critical illegal activities.

FROM KNOWLEDGE MODELS TO RISK MODELS

A comprehensive understanding of cybersecurity requirements brought forward by disruptive technologies is not an end goal. Anticipating and producing mitigation in novel environments and for novel uses of technologies is more important. Risk-based methodologies are helpful here.

Risk Engineering

Traditionally, risk assessments are done for specific, isolated aspects of an environment. Sometimes these aspects are very narrow, such as the functionality of a system component for a strictly defined use case, or a reputational risk from a premature release of a potentially disruptive computing device. At other times, these assessments are broader, examining the risks from different threat agents or from actions by people, and the effects of poor processes and new technologies on government systems, examined along these three separate axes: people, processes, and technologies.

The management of multi-domain risks reflecting the complexity of the computing environment can be improved if information and communication technology (ICT) systems themselves are engineered by explicitly reflecting risks of their use, be it in isolation or in a specific operational context. This approach requires that systems have specifications that articulate risks—be they informal, semi-formal or formal, qualitative or quantitative, given in textual form or within a mathematical model. The body of knowledge associated with various aspects of cybersecurity comprises ways of expressing such risk specifications and analysing the consequences of changing the risk picture. This technique can be also applied to cybercrime.

There is relatively little work on making such specifications composable to scale, or on specifying risks that stem from the combination or interaction of different aspects of systems, such as safety and security. This is where risk engineering can help. Risk engineering can be defined as 'incorporation of integrated risk analysis into system design and engineering processes' (Huth et al. 2016).

Although full definitions of risk engineering methodologies are wanted, it is clear that they must support an integrated picture of risks, including, at least, the domains of security, privacy, safety, reliability, and resilience (NIST 2017). Success in this area requires several obstacles to be overcome. As mentioned earlier, one challenge is the creation of a comprehensive semantic framework to enable a consistent terminology and ability to reason about the environment based on shared views. A multi-domain ontology can accommodate this requirement. To illustrate this need, even elementary terms, such as 'incident', have different definitions within different risk communities: for safety, 'incident' denotes an event that does not have safety-critical consequences whereas, for security, it refers to a serious breach.

Another obstacle is lack of a consistent approach to metrics that objectively assess risk and impact, a serious problem when an integrated risk model is considered. To illustrate, failure probabilities in the risk domain of safety are extremely small. But probabilities of a breach in security and privacy, where diverse and evolving attacks must be taken into consideration, are much larger. Thus, successful risk engineering requires integrated, multi-scale risk metrics.

Yet another challenge is risk composition, the ability to measure integrated risks that meaningfully compose risk parameters in multiple domains.

Risk engineering techniques offer advantages for several types of analysis, but especially when applied to an environment experiencing incremental changes, gradually leading to escalation of initially moderate risks. Risk engineering permits us to model and anticipate necessary mitigations for several connected risk domains. To invoke our blockchain example once again, risk engineering helps evaluate, in an integrated fashion, safety, security, and privacy risks introduced by the use of blockchain techniques in autonomous vehicles employing blockchain as a mechanism to support operational data integrity. Subject risks could also include analysis of risks from cybercriminal activity.

Examining cybercrime in isolation from the legitimate use of similar technologies during their life cycle is not likely to be constructive. Only when cybercrime and technology in general are evaluated based on the same models, including risk models, can we devise a forward looking rather than reactive approach to cybersecurity and cybercrime.

Cybersecurity Metrics

One of the most serious challenges in cybersecurity is the development of consistent and actionable metrics that could provide insights useful in many areas, such as trends in cybercrime or technology development. Performance management professionals live by the maxim 'measure what matters'. From this viewpoint, the purpose of metrics is to *provide actionable insights to decision makers*. This maxim is valid for technical and socio-technical systems. Cybersecurity metrics must, therefore, be guided by knowledge of what cybersecurity-related insights decision makers need, both on the security of systems they design or deploy and on the protection of these systems from cybercrime. These metrics will be constrained by the availability (at supportable cost) of suitable data or reliable proxies, and by the timeliness and ease of use of the assembled information.

Understanding impacts is important for creating meaningful metrics based on the cost-effectiveness of investments and operations, safety of persons and assets, legal liability, and similar characteristics. A recent report (Kelley et al. 2016) cited 'reducing average incident response and resolution times' as the primary cybersecurity challenge of the executives surveyed. As a practical matter, metrics capable of enabling reliable estimation of direct and indirect impacts of system compromise will be essential to informed decision making.

Perfect cybersecurity capabilities would obviate the need for responses by enabling decision makers to prevent incidents. But, as Figure 7.5 illustrates, decision makers prefer capabilities that enable them to 'observe, orient, decide, and act' before their adversaries are able to complete the same cycle. While effective cyber reconnaissance and attack campaigns can take months or years to come to fruition, the fact that cyber capabilities operate at machine speed materially affects both the practical usefulness of metrics and the value of research to create them.

In recent years, cybersecurity research and development activity has progressed from an emphasis on *reactive cybersecurity*, which seeks to create and improve tools and processes that can help analysts detect, respond to, mitigate, and recover from cyber threats, toward *proactive cybersecurity*. Proactive cybersecurity focuses on creating a 'science of cybersecurity' that enables the stakeholders to predict and, ideally, prevent cyber incidents before they happen, and understand when previously compromised nodes will once again become secure.

Reactive cybersecurity capabilities typically centre on detecting anomalies in a system's contents, environment, or behaviour. Unfortunately, those who rely on reactive cybersecurity frequently find themselves at a disadvantage, because their strategies and tactics are constantly disrupted by threat actors finding innovative ways to discover, create, and exploit vulnerabilities.

Proactive cybersecurity draws from metrics-based concepts, such as 'cybersecurity dynamics' developed by Shouhuai Xu and colleagues[7], and relies on 'risk-based security metrics' (Thuraisingham et al. 2016) that can evolve with the changing environment and proactively account for attack-countermeasure-response dependencies. Recent reports (NIST special publications 800–30, 800–37, 800–39, 800–53, and 800–53A) developed additional dimensions for risk-based and other types of cybersecurity metrics and guidelines (Ross, Feldman, and Witte 2016, 5).

Decision makers must know *in advance* whether devices attempting to connect with their networks are sufficiently trustworthy. '[M]easures of trustworthiness are meaningful only to the extent that (a) the requirements are sufficiently complete and well defined, and (b) can be accurately evaluated' (Neumann 2004, viii; Ross, McEvilley, and Oren 2016,1). When coupled with cyber hygiene efforts, reliable metrics of the trustworthiness of a device or environment would offer significant benefits, including protection against cybercrime. Metrics enabling prediction of future failures as a result of attacks are highly valuable, as would be the ability to account for the uncertainty caused by gaps in available data (Newmeyer 2015).

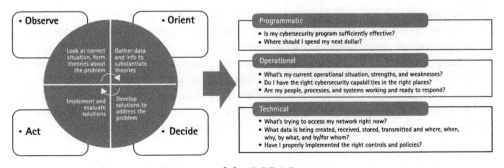

FIGURE 7.5. Cybersecurity Metrics and the OODA Loop

Many efforts noted earlier recognize that systems designed for reactive cybersecurity make inherent assumptions that may misinterpret or miss useful signals due to interpretational bias. Data-driven AI could also suffer biases as a result of the specific learning processes employed, but adversarial machine learning techniques (Huang et al. 2011) may help mitigate this.

How can this concrete wisdom from practitioners be applied to improving the quality of predictions for cybersecurity and cybercrime trends in future technology environments? The challenge lies in adapting the operational signals and related metrics traditionally used in cybersecurity to the techniques for disruptive technology forecasting. Optimized cybersecurity metrics for current systems allow us to quantify some parameters of predictive models for disruptive technology, understand the meaning of environmental signals, and improve the building blocks for the ontology supporting more reliable forecasting. Further, such metrics could help improve methodologies for integrated risk engineering and, therefore, contribute to better cybersecurity and improved protections against cybercrime.

Conclusions

In Principled Assuredly Trustworthy Composable Architectures,[8] Peter Neumann states:

> [T]here are no easy answers ... [C]omplexity must be addressed through architectures that are composed of well-understood components whose interactions are well understood, and also through compositions that demonstrably do not compromise trustworthiness in the presence of certain untrustworthy components.

In an ideal system, trustworthiness results from the intrinsic logic of the system understood by all its stakeholders. For cybersecurity, this state may never be achievable. But in order to protect our digital infrastructures and combat cybercrime, we need to be ahead of attackers, understand the current state of the ecosystem and its evolution, and comprehend trends in disruptive information technologies to enable us to anticipate and mitigate cybercrime.

In this chapter, we provided some recipes, techniques, methodologies, and examples that can help technologists and regulators more reliably anticipate the technology trends and develop necessary cybersecurity protections. Most important is to develop cybersecurity models that are broadly applicable and usable for full technology lifecycles and varied use cases as well as for the analysis of cybercrime. Today, use fragmentation in this area makes consistent analysis and reliable forecasts impossible.

Among the tools that can help us make sense of disruptive technologies and render insights to combat cybercrime, several directions of analysis, evaluated in this chapter, appear to be productive. Broader methodological approaches, such as reliance on knowledge representation, development of risk engineering, and creation of objective metrics should be key areas of focus in the multidisciplinary technology community.

Notes

1. See, e.g. NITRD: 'Report on Implementing Federal Cybersecurity Research and Development Strategy,' June 2014, http://www.nitrd.gov
2. According to Wikipedia, 'In computer science and information science, an ontology is a formal naming and definition of the types, properties, and interrelationships of the entities that really or fundamentally exist for a particular domain of discourse. It is thus a practical application of philosophical ontology, with a taxonomy. An ontology compartmentalizes the variables needed for some set of computations and establishes the relationships between them.' See https://en.wikipedia.org/wiki/Ontology_(information_science)
3. According to Wikipedia, 'Knowledge engineering (KE) refers to all technical, scientific and social aspects involved in building, maintaining and using knowledge-based systems.' See https://en.wikipedia.org/wiki/Knowledge_engineering
4. See Article 29 Working Party Opinion adopted on 10 April 2014 at https://ec.europa.eu/justice/article-29/documentation/opinion-recommendation/files/2014/wp216_en.pdf
5. The Article 29 Working Party Opinion 5/2014 on Anonymization Techniques adopted April 10 2014, p. 6 (https://ec.europa.eu/justice/article-29/documentation/opinion-recommendation/files/2014/wp216_en.pdf) describes the reasonableness test as follows: 'It should be recalled here that anonymisation is also defined in international standards such as the ISO 29100 one—being the "Process by which personally identifiable information (PII) is irreversibly altered in such a way that a PII principal can no longer be identified directly or indirectly, either by the PII controller alone or in collaboration with any other party" (ISO 29100:2011). Irreversibility of the alteration undergone by personal data to enable direct or indirect identification is the key also for ISO. From this standpoint, there is considerable convergence with the principles and concepts underlying the 95/46 Directive. This also applies to the definitions to be found in some national laws (for instance, in Italy, Germany and Slovenia), where the focus is on non-identifiability and reference is made to the "disproportionate effort" to re-identify (D, SI). However, the French Data Protection Law provides that data remains personal data even if it is extremely hard and unlikely to re-identify the data subject—that is to say, there is no provision referring to the "reasonableness" test.'
6. Based on Information Security Forum, 'Threat Horizon 2019: Disruption, Distortion, Deterioration', London, 2017.
7. See https://xu-lab.org/team/
8. Neumann (2004, 151).

References

Bernstein, D. J. 2009. 'Introduction to post-quantum computing.' In *Post-Quantum Computing*, edited by D.J. Benstein, J. Buchanan, and E. Dahmen, 1–14. Heidelberg: Springer-Verlag.

Govindarajan, V. and Kopalle, P.K. 2006. 'The Usefulness of Measuring Disruptiveness of Innovations Ex Post in Making Ex Ante Predictions', *Journal of Product Innovation Management* 23: 12–18.

Huang, L., Joseph, A.D., Nelson, B., Rubinstein, B.I.P., and Taylor, J. D. 2011. 'Adversarial Machine Learning', *Proceedings of 4th ACM Workshop on Artificial Intelligence and Security*, ACM, 43–58.

Huth, M., Vishik, C. and Masucci, R. 2016. 'From Risk Management to Risk Engineering: Challenges in Future ICT Systems.' In *Handbook of System Safety and Security: Cyber Risk and Risk Management, Cyber Security, Threat Analysis, Functional Safety, Software Systems, and Cyber Physical Systems*, edited by E. Griffor, 131–175. Cambridge, Mass.: Elsevier

Iannacone, M., Bohn, S, Nakamura, G. et al. 2015. 'Developing an Ontology for Cyber Security Knowledge Graphs,' *Proceedings of the 10th Annual Cyber and Information Security Research Conference (CISR '15)*, 1–4. New York: ACM Digital Library.

Kelley, D., Dheap, V., Jarvis, D. et al. 2016. *Cybersecurity in the Cognitive Era: Priming Your Digital Immune System*. Somers, NY: IBM Institute for Business Value.

Kraemer-Mbula, E. Tang, P., and Rush, H. 2013. 'The cybercrime ecosystem: Online innovation in the shadows?' *Technological Forecasting and Social Change* 80.3: 541–55.

Kuhlmann, S., Boekholt, P., Guy, K. et al. 1999. 'Improving Distributed Intelligence in Complex Innovation Systems'. Final Report of the Advanced Science and Technology Policy Planning Network (ASTPP), Fraunhofer Institute Systems and Innovation Research.

Meiklejohn, S. Pomarole, M. Jordan, G. et al. 2016. 'A fistful of Bitcoins: characterizing payments among men with no names.' *Communications of the ACM* 59 (4): 86–93.

Nakamoto, S. 2008. 'Bitcoin: A Peer-to-Peer Electronic Cash System.' https://bitcoin.org/bitcoin.pdf

Narayanan, A., Bonneau, J., Felten, E. et al. 2016. *Bitcoin and Cryptotechnologies: A Comprehensive Introduction*. Princeton, NJ: Princeton University Press.

NASA 2017. *NASA Aeronautics Strategic Implementation Plan 2017 Update*, NASA Aeronautics Research Mission Directorate.

Neumann, P. G., 2004. 'Principled Assuredly Trustworthy Composable Architectures', Final report to DARPA. Menlo Park, CA: SRI International

Newmeyer, N., 2015. 'Changing the Future of Cyber-Situational Awareness,' *Journal of Information Warfare* 14 (2): 32–41.

National Infrastructure Commission (NIC). 2016. 'The Impact of Technological Change on Future Infrastructure Supply and Demand'. London: NIC.

NIST (National Institute of Standards and Technology) 2017. *NIST Special Publication 1500-201, Framework for Cyber-Physical Systems: Volume 1, Overview*. Gaithersburg, MD: NIST.

Quinn, J.B. 1967. 'Technological forecasting.' *Harvard Business Review* 45 (2): 89–106.

Rao, G.A., and Mahulikar, S.P. 2002. 'Integrated review of stealth technology and its role in airpower', *Aeronautical Journal* 106 (1066): 629–41.

Ross, R., Feldman, L. and Witte. G. (eds). 2016. 'Rethinking Security through System Security Engineering', *ITL Bulletin for December*, NIST Information Technology Laboratory: http://csrc.nist.gov/publications/nistbul/itlbul2016_12.pdf

Ross, R., McEvilley, M., and Oren. J.C. 2016. *NIST Special Publication 800-160, Systems Security Engineering: Considerations for a Multidisciplinary Approach in the Engineering of Trustworthy Secure Systems*. Gaithersburg, MD: National Institute of Standards and Technology.

Shor, P.W. 1995. 'Polynomial-Time Algorithms for Prime Factorization and Discrete Logarithms on a Quantum Computer', *SIAM Journal on Computing*, 26(5): 1484–1509.

Siegel, D. 2016. 'Understanding the DAO Attack', *Coin Desk*, 25 June: https://www.coindesk.com/understanding-dao-hack-journalists/

Thuraisingham, B., Kantarcioglu, M., Hamlen, K. et al. 2016. 'A Data Driven Approach for the Science of Cyber Security: Challenges and Directions', *Proceedings of the IEEE 17th International Conference on Information Reuse and Integration*, 1–10. Piscatawy, NJ: IEEE.

Van Zwanenberg, P., Ely, A. and Stirling, A. 2009. 'Emerging Technologies and Opportunities for International Science and Technology Foresight', *STEPS Working Paper* 30, Brighton: STEPS Centre.

CHAPTER 8

ASSESSING HARM FROM CYBER CRIME

EVA IGNATUSCHTSCHENKO

INTRODUCTION

HARM, or the potential for harm, is a key notion in deciding whether an act is considered to be either criminal or non-criminal in legal-philosophical theory (Mill 1869, 13–47; Feinberg 1984, 31–6. Similarly, a concept of harm can inform the identification of unlawful activities in the online space. In this regard, harm can be understood as the adverse effect on victims of cyber crime, resulting from illegal conduct online or through information and communications technology (ICT). In an online environment, harm can also be the result of unintentional or accidental actions, rather than malicious activity. However, this article focuses on harm caused deliberately by criminal activities in cyber space.

Building a robust and comprehensive conceptual framework of harm is a prerequisite for a durable assessment of the impact of cyber crime and, thus, cyber risk. In contrast to other related concepts, such as 'impact', 'consequence', 'loss', and 'cost', the term 'harm' places the emphasis on the human victim (i.e. the individual or groups of individuals that are harmed). Contrary to the terms 'loss' and 'cost', harm also comprises non-financial effects, such as psychological or physical damage that can be caused by cyber crime. By using the term 'harm', it is clear that the impact of cyber crime is not an abstract phenomenon that affects computers or systems only or predominantly, but that these technical functions have an observable real-world impact on individuals and other victims. Perceptions of harm may vary according to individual susceptibility and resilience, which also determine the severity of harm experienced in each instance of cyber crime.

Within cyber security debates, harm has not yet entered common terminology, because discussions primarily focus on impact, in particular within cyber risk management frameworks. (Center for Strategic and International Studies 2014). There is neither a commonly agreed upon definition of harm, nor a common understanding of what comprises impact, cost, loss, or other concepts, because conclusive research and data to determine the effects of cyber crime are still lacking. A harmonized framework that allows for the identification of the full spectrum of harm would inform the analysis of cyber risks at any level and in any sector. Such a framework needs to recognize the constantly and rapidly changing landscape of cyber crime, as new technologies and operating methods emerge.

An understanding of the full spectrum of potential harm that can arise as a result of cyber crime is important in order, first, to detect and assess harm in all its manifestations. Even if one would be concerned only about the financial implications of cyber crime, whether in relation to a specific offence or the accumulated costs for a nation or at the global level, the costs would amount to more than just the mere loss of money—for instance, as a result of a hacked bank account or online fraud. Additional costs might be incurred to the health system due to the psychological harm that victims might suffer after an incident. If the crime involves a large number of victims, they might decide to move their business or accounts to another bank, causing further financial and reputational damage to the affected bank. In some cases, this might culminate in bankruptcy and have broader financial implications for the economy as a whole. Using current data and methodologies, the total costs of cyber crime can only reasonably be calculated through anecdotal or incident-based studies, because more evidence is needed to verify links between different forms of harm and associated costs (Anderson et al. 2013, 267–8).

Second, an enhanced understanding of harm can facilitate the mitigation of harm from cyber crime at all levels. Much of the attention of law enforcement agencies has been dedicated towards the detection, deterrence, and prosecution of offenders. A shift of focus towards the reduction of harm places the emphasis on the victim and the reduction of negative impact to victims, while countering cascading effects that could lead to a loss of trust or opportunity costs if victims discontinue their use of online services or technologies altogether. Rather than countering the most prevalent types of cyber crime, which might lead merely to a shift of criminal activity to other opportunities, law enforcement could prioritize those types of cyber crime that result in the most significant harm or mitigate harm that is caused by multiple forms of crime, thereby benefitting from multiplier effects.

Third, prioritizing investments in cyber security requires an understanding of where harm is most serious and disruptive. Investments into the technical, educational, and policy elements of cyber security require a substantial amount of resources, for organizations and nations alike. However, the return of investment is in many cases unclear. Rather than assessing the effectiveness of cyber security capacity-building initiatives in terms of the decrease of cyber attacks, which may after all be attributable to insufficient reporting and detection of incidents, these initiatives can instead be gauged in terms of the reduction of harm to individuals. This approach would inform more effective cyber risk management.

While the nature, scale, and magnitude of harm from cyber crime differ depending on the respective type of offence, among other factors, this chapter discusses elements of a broader conceptual framework that can facilitate the assessment of any given type of ICT-facilitated crime and proposes a human-centric approach to cyber security through harm mitigation.

Harm from Crime Versus Harm from Cyber Crime

Harm from cyber crime is not necessarily more severe than harm from traditional types of crime without a digital element. However, the difference from harm caused by more traditional types of crime, such as fraud, homicide, human trafficking, is the increased reach, scope, and volume that is enabled by committing offences through the Internet or other new technologies. While traditional forms of crime were often limited to a specific geographical space and targeted at specific victims, the evolution of technologies allows perpetrators to target a large number of victims at the same time, almost independently of geographical location. The Internet has thus created the potential for a global attack surface. Compared with traditional forms of crime, the required resources are also often much more limited in the case of cyber-enabled crime (Wall 2007, 31-48). A straightforward Internet connection might be all that is needed to launch a large-scale criminal attack against a significant number of victims.

In the same way that technologies have changed the modus operandi of crime, they have also changed the harm experienced by victims of such crimes. For example, harassment or intimidation in a school environment can have severe effects on the victim, even if it does not involve the Internet or social media. However, these effects are in most cases limited to the school location and, thus, are physically contained. In such cases, children are able to leave school and find a safe area at home. Harassment and intimidation conducted through the Internet and social media, on the other hand, are independent of time and space, allowing the perpetrator virtually to intrude into the victim's home and private space. As a consequence, the victim may see no other option than to withdraw from social media, specific websites, or technological devices, in order to escape from the threatening behaviour of the abuser (Carpenter 2014, 143).

Even though, from a criminological perspective, cyber crime follows opportunity in the same way that it does for traditional forms of crime, and even though motivations to commit crime have not changed fundamentally since the development of the Internet,[1] the relationship between the input (i.e. the intent of cyber criminals) and the output (i.e. the harm experienced by victims) is complex and varies significantly depending on the type of crime. Research suggests that factors such as online reputation, the potential for addictive behaviour, or a perceived absence of guardians online may serve as factors that create a pathway into cyber criminality (Aiken et al. 2016, 13–14). There also appears to be a strengthening link between different motivational patterns—for instance, as organized criminal groups are increasingly engaged in cyber crime (Malby et al. 2013, 44–9). Even if motivations could be determined with reasonable certainty, the separation that cyber crime creates between offenders and victims can lead to misconceptions or false assumptions on the part of the offenders as to the outcome of their actions. For example, an offender who physically attacks a victim on the street receives immediate feedback on the implications of their actions and is thereby able to perceive the harm caused. Within the online environment, equivalent direct feedback is often missing. Various layers of anonymity online further exacerbate the asymmetric relationship between victims and offenders.

Another difference between conventional forms of crime and cyber crime are the differing levels of resilience and preparedness among potential victims. While, in an offline environment, some victims may have an understanding of how to protect themselves from becoming victimized—for example, by installing enhanced protection measures in their home— the technical nature of online interactions leaves some victims feeling defenceless. There is also a lack of understanding regarding the nature of attacks. When money is physically stolen from a wallet, there is a tangible loss of monetary value and a perception of the way it was lost. On the other hand, if money is lost due to fraudulent online activities, the harm might be just as immediate but is often much less tangible and comprehensible. Victims may feel a loss of power and control in these situations, which can be more persistent than the financial damage caused by online fraud or theft. The lack of understanding as to what led to a particular incident and how to protect against repeat victimization may be of greater concern to the victim than the direct financial impact of the crime.

Assessing Harm from Cyber Crime

Evaluations of the impact of cyber crime have predominantly focused on estimating the financial or economic implications, either to determine the costs of particular instances or types of cyber crime, or to calculate the accumulated costs of cyber crime to nations or globally. However, methodologies used to quantify the costs of cyber crime differ in their scope (i.e. the scale and geographical coverage of analysis) and inclusiveness (e.g. whether costs to prepare for or mitigate attacks are considered or not). As a result, depending on the applied methodology, estimations of the cost of cyber crime vary significantly. For example, one source estimates the cost of cyber crime to the UK at the national level at £27 billion annually (Detica and the UK Cabinet Office, 2011: 24). In addition to direct losses due to cyber crime, the Detica/Cabinet Office report also considered costs related to the anticipation of, and response to, cyber crime, as well as costs that are more difficult to quantify, such as reputational harm. However, the report has been widely criticized and dismissed for methodological errors and the resulting exaggeration of the costs of cyber crime in the UK.[2] Relying on reported incidents by Action Fraud, another calculation by Get Safe Online and the National Fraud Intelligence Bureau estimated the cost of fraud and cyber crime in the UK at £11 billion in 2015.[3]

Some organizations have attempted to calculate the global costs of cyber crime. McAfee calculated the annual cost of cyber crime to the global economy at $400 billion (Center for Strategic and International Studies 2014, 2). According to a Ponemon Institute report, which used a benchmark sample of 237 small to large organizations across different industries, the average cost of cyber crime for organizations is $9.5 million annually across the globe (Ponemon Institute, 2016: 4–7). Some authors advocate for estimating a range of potential losses rather than aiming at a single number for assessing the costs of cyber crime, while recognizing the challenges associated with purely quantified approaches to assess indirect and intangible costs of cyber crime (Center for Strategic and International Studies 2013, 18.

Through a combination of different datasets and methodologies, Anderson et al. (2013, 294–6) suggest that, within the UK, the cost of 'genuine cyber crime', such as online banking fraud, advance-fee fraud, is significantly lower (ranging from $1 million to $50 million depending on the type of cyber crime) than the cost of 'transitional cyber crime', such as online payment card fraud, which was estimated to cost the UK $210 million in 2010. In an assessment of the minimum, medium, and maximum costs of cyber crime, Romanosky (2016, 3–9) makes a similar distinction between different types of cyber crime, rather than calculating a single value. Across these quantifications, the lack of a common framework for distinguishing cyber crime from other forms of crime, together with a divergent sense of what should constitute the costs of cyber crime, decrease the comparability of results overall.

Because of differences in what is, or is not, considered to be a cost resulting from cyber crime, the absence of large-scale datasets, and variations in methodologies, a robust assessment of the cost of cyber crime is difficult to achieve using current datasets and methodologies. However, beyond a purely financial estimation of the cost of cyber crime, the quantification of impact is essential in the context of risk analysis and management, in particular with a view to developing cyber crime insurance products. Even though insurance companies are increasingly turning to insure against cyber crime losses, and there is a clear need for insurance products, traditional methodologies to calculate other forms of risk seem only to be partially applicable to cyber risk (Institute of Risk Management 2014, 7–11; Filkins 2016, 3–5.

The main challenge of cyber risk quantification is the lack of historical data that could allow for the determination of probability distributions. Moreover, the fact that loss of intellectual property, customers, stock market value, and reputational damage can exceed the insurable loss by many times is widely acknowledged in the cyber crime insurance industry (Institute of Risk Management 2014, 11; Peckman, 2014: 1–2). Solutions for these limitations are still pending. In order to address the challenges, an alternative approach was suggested by the World Economic Forum and Deloitte. By adapting a value-at-risk model for cyber space, they developed a conceptual proxy model for cyber risk exposure (World Economic Forum and Deloitte 2015, 11–14). This model builds on a probabilistic risk measure commonly used in the finance sector, which considers the organizational portfolio and a specified time frame to calculate the probability of losses exceeding the value-at-risk threshold value. In the adapted cyber value-at-risk model, vulnerability, assets, and the profile of attackers were identified as components of cyber risk modelling for organizations. Another noteworthy contribution towards more granular quantification of cyber crime is the European Union-funded project called 'Economic Impact of Cyber Crime (E-CRIME)', conducted by an international consortium of 10 partners from law enforcement, private sector, research institutes, and academia, which concluded in March 2016 and focused on the economic impact of cyber crime on five major non-ICT sectors (Wright 2017).[4]

In light of the challenges associated with a quantification of the impact of cyber crime, some reports criticize the application of fiscal calculation models and instead advocate alternative approaches. An example of such an alternative methodology is a study conducted at the University of Haifa, Israel, on lethal and non-lethal cyber terrorism, using simulated cyber attacks in experimental manipulations. While more indicative than conclusive, the study not only offers insights into the role of cyber threat perception for the impact on psychological well-being, public confidence, and political attitudes, but also shows that novel approaches can give a more in-depth understanding of harm beyond financial losses in off-line and online environments (Gross et al. 2017).

Various other authors have recognized the need to assess harm more broadly than through purely financial calculations. A research report on economic cyber crime, commissioned by the City of London Corporation with a view to the enhancement of cyber crime policing, made reference to social harm, reputational harm, and harm to the quality of life or health of individuals (Levi et al. 2015, 18–51). Similarly, Fafinski et al. (2010, 16–18) acknowledge the value of a mapping and measuring exercise of the various manifestations of harm for cyber crime policing. The Internet Organised Crime Threat Assessment (IOCTA) 2016 by the European Police Office (EUROPOL) acknowledges harm from cyber crime beyond the financial impact, such as potentially long-term emotional damage, up to suicide, in the case of sexual coercion and extortion online, or reputational harm in the case of airline ticket fraud or chief executive officer (CEO) fraud (European Police Office 2016, 25–33). The report further mentions the potential for severe physical damage to infrastructure due to new technological developments—in particular, in the context of the Internet of Things (IoT; European Police Office 2016, 39–54. However, despite the growing recognition of the less tangible aspects of cyber crime, a comprehensive framework to assess harm from cyber crime in all its manifestations is still lacking.

CHALLENGES

The development of a comprehensive and robust framework for assessing harm from cyber crime, whether for specific instances or accumulated to national or global levels, faces several challenges.

Intangible Factors

Individuals and entities will perceive harm in different ways, depending on their disposition, previous victimization, and other external factors. The severity of harm from cyber crime experienced by individuals might be governed by such considerations as age, technological capabilities, personal experiences, religious beliefs. For organizations, their size and turnover, the level of dependence of their daily operations on ICT, and their technological capabilities are all among the factors that may influence the severity of harm perceived and experienced. While some of these factors can be measured relatively reliably—for example, by testing systems for vulnerabilities—other less tangible aspects relating to cultural, psychological, and behavioural influences are more difficult to determine. Yet, disregarding the intangible factors may result in a distorted assessment of harm.

Intangible types of harm, such as emotional harm, are similarly difficult to measure through quantitative methodologies. Instead, proxy measures, such as the costs incurred by the healthcare sector due to care provided for victims of cyber crime, could be included. However, this approach assumes that a clear distinction can be made between victims of cyber crime on the one hand and victims of more traditional crime on the other. Moreover, with each applied level of abstraction, the reliability and accuracy of results become more limited. Harm to broader society, including socio-economic, cultural, or political consequences, is even more difficult to measure. The 2016 United States election interference through cyber attacks on the Democratic National Committee and the leaking of documents demonstrates how difficult and challenging it can be to link harm to specific criminal acts, particularly when those acts might have broader societal implications (ICA 2017, ii.)

Availability and Reliability of Data

Another challenge to the accurate assessments of harm is the lack of data. This in turn can be attributed to the under-reporting of cyber crime, and a lack of information sharing among and across industry sectors and between the private and public sectors more broadly. The applicability of models and measurements to determining the extent of harm caused by cyber crime relies on there being datasets reliable enough to indicate the nature and scale of harm experienced by victims, in addition to statistical information on the number of affected victims, the type of cyber crime, modus operandi, etc. However, in contrast to many conventional forms of crime, victims of cyber crime are often not aware that they have been victimized, or they only realize that they have been affected at a later stage and may be reluctant to report the incident because of shame, a lack of knowledge, or other reasons. Even though there is increasing availability of reporting mechanisms in many countries, these mechanisms often only capture information on the type of crime, rather than going into detail on the impact it had on the victim. Most importantly, such mechanisms rely on a common reference framework to ensure consistent gathering and sharing of information and comparability of data. Given the fast pace of technological development, efficient mechanisms to gather data on harm from cyber crime have to include an element of anticipation. In particular, the increasing use of connected devices, the IoT, is changing the cyber crime threat landscape and the ways in which harm might be caused and experienced. Considering the rapid evolution of smart connected devices, which allow for the remote control of the heating system, lighting, etc. in smart homes or constantly track location, health status, lifestyle, or other sensitive information (Jing et al. 2014, 2493–5), it is not difficult to build scenarios of risks and potential harm associated with the misuse or manipulation of IoT.

Classification of Cyber Crime and Harm

Without a common classification framework of types of cyber crime and harm from cyber crime, gathered data will not be comparable and will therefore be of limited significance and validity. Currently, countries do not apply a standardized or coordinated approach to capturing cyber crime in their national crime statistics. Cyber crime may not even appear as such in statistics, because it may be submerged into other categories of conventional crime (Finklea and Theohary 2015, 3–5). For example, online fraud might be registered in statistics under general fraud. With the increasing proliferation of technologies in both developed and developing countries, almost any crime will have a digital element in the future and the range of ICT-facilitated crime seems likely only to expand.

The Need for a Common Framework

Even though it is a challenging endeavour, there is a clear need to work towards a robust assessment of harm from cyber crime. A lack of certainty regarding the extent of harm from cyber crime might lead to over-investment in certain cyber security capabilities that do not have the desired impact. On a broader scale, an enhanced understanding of harm from cyber crime would facilitate cyber security policy making and either substantiate or revise assumptions about decisions made to prioritize one cyber security investment over another. Reliable harm metrics would further support the development of a cyber crime insurance market. Current approaches to calculating insurance premiums generally do not cover the indirect losses from cyber crime, such as reputational damage, even though these can often exceed the direct losses that do tend to be covered by insurance products (Institute of Risk Management 2014, 11). A consistent framework for identifying and measuring harm in its full scope could support the tracking of cyber risk over time. This would facilitate the accumulation of historical data, making it possible, in turn, to gauge the effectiveness of risk mitigation techniques and, eventually, to extend available insurance coverage.

HARM SPECTRUM

Harm from cyber crime can be conceptualized through multiple spectra, which allow for a harm assessment across a continuum of multiple dimensions: duration, immediacy, magnitude, scale, and nature.

Duration

Harm can affect victims of cyber crime on different timescales. In some cases, harm might be experienced shortly after the incident, but then subside quickly. For example, the financial loss from online fraud is often instant, but limited to the one-time loss of monetary value. In other cases, harm can extend from short-term into long-term effects, such as psychological damage after being exposed to cyber bullying for an extended period of time. Some forms of harm may only manifest in the long term and are therefore harder to predict or assess.

Immediacy

An associated spectrum is how directly harm is experienced by victims. Direct harm is easier to observe and measure, which is often the case for financial or physical types of harm. Harm can also appear to be more indirect or hidden, which may be the case for some forms of socio-cultural or political types of harm. Indirect harm may occur long after a cyber event or may be the result of another more direct type of harm. For example, the erosion of consumer trust due to a single or repeated cyber attacks on a business (i.e. direct harm) may have severe implications for the operations and turnover of the business, which appears less directly linked to the incident(s). On an individual level, reputational damage caused by cyber crime might have cascading indirect effects, such as the inability to find a new job, which can lead to difficulties to sustain the family and may cause psychological distress.

Magnitude

In addition to duration and immediacy, experiences of harm also differ in their magnitude. Individual or organizational victims of the same incident can experience harm of different magnitude, depending on the variations in their susceptibility, as discussed earlier. Some forms of harm may not have a disruptive effect on daily operations and can, thus, be tolerated by the victim. For example, a minor financial loss may not represent a significant disruption. However, the difference between a minor and a major financial loss will vary across individuals, organizations, and nations. The most severe type of harm from an instance of cyber crime is not in all cases suffered by the direct or immediate victim. When personal user information of the dating website Ashley Madison, designed for people looking for extra-marital relationships, was leaked after a hacking attack, the impact on users of the website ranged from resignation, loss through blackmail, divorces, and even suicide (Mansfield-Devine 2015, 12–14). Arguably, even though the attack was directed at the website operators, the indirect effects on the users of the website were more severe as a consequence of the leaked information.

Scale

The scale in terms of number of victims or targets of cyber crime can differ substantially. One cyber crime incident can result in harm to thousands or more victims at the same time. The Ashley Madison data breach caused the release of personal information concerning up to 37 million users, including credit card transactions data and personal details, such as sexual preferences (Mansfield-Devine 2015, 10). In this case, cascading effects led to an even higher number of individuals being harmed, because the incident did not only affect the users of the website but also their families and relationships. Other instances, such as cyber bullying or 'revenge porn', are more targeted and typically involve a small number of victims.

Nature

The nature of harm differs depending on the type of cyber crime and the interplay of the factors outlined earlier. In 'Cyber Harm: Concepts, Taxonomy and Measurement' (Agrafiotis et al. 2016, 30–32). a taxonomy of harm is proposed based on six interrelated types of harm: physical, psychological, economic, political, reputational, and cultural. Additional types of harm could be added, such as environmental harm, if cyber attacks were to cause physical damage to certain types of infrastructure such as reservoirs, dams, and floodgates. Analysing harm within these different categories allows for a more structured and comprehensive assessment and makes it possible to take into account both tangible and non-tangible aspects of the problem of cyber harm.

Opportunity Costs

Finally, one aspect that is not captured earlier is the loss of opportunity due to cyber crime. Opportunity costs are often associated with a loss of trust and confidence in the use of on-line services and social media. Victims of cyber crime may feel hesitant to engage with technologies after an incident has occurred, because of fear of repeated victimization or a perceived lack of protection. Such opportunity costs can be persistent and affect victims over long periods of time until confidence is re-established (Center for Strategic and International Studies 2014, 17; Center for Strategic and International Studies 2013, 12–13). As a result, victims may not be able to have access to valuable services and benefits offered online, such as online retail, communication with social contacts, the pursuit of business opportunities, and the search for job vacancies. This loss of opportunity can in turn result in other types of harm, such as financial cost, reduced innovation, or even psychological damage caused by a sense of social marginalization.

HARM AND TRUST

The idea of trust underpins all analysis of harm from cyber crime. Relationships online, whether between individuals, between customers and businesses, or between citizens and the government, are formed and maintained on the basis of trust. Equally, maintaining established relationships online requires building and consolidating trust. The significance of trust in the context of the Internet and cyber security is scarcely a new issue, having been discussed for more than 10 years (Dutton and Shepherd 2003; Mansell and Collins 2005). However, our understanding of how trust is gained and lost in online environments is limited because of cultural differences in how trust is conceptualized and expressed, and the constantly changing ICT landscape. The erosion of trust is located at the outer layers of the harm spectrum discussed earlier, and is often one result of the cascade of effects following individual cyber crime incidents (Fenech and Hamilton 2015, 1–3).

A loss of trust may affect individuals, organizations, or nations. It can be observed most prominently at an organizational level in the form of the loss of customers after a large-scale data breach, such as in the cases of TalkTalk[5] or Target[6] . A loss of trust can also affect the broader institutional frameworks of a nation. Cyber crime can lead to the erosion of citizens' trust in the very foundation of the institutions that sustain the operations of societies. In particular, cyber crime targeted at government institutions, the electoral system, digital government services, or the health care system can have a grave impact on the operation of the nation as people begin to question the ability of the state to protect its citizens online. Over time, individuals can lose their confidence to engage with online services and media. This distrust can culminate in a fear that online services are simply no longer safe. As a consequence, individuals may choose to withdraw from certain parts of cyber space—or perhaps even its entirety.

On the other hand, dependence on digital technologies to complete mundane personal, organizational and societal tasks is deepening. This dependence creates a new, enforced form of trust. If vital services, such as tax payments or health services, are no longer available offline, users may not have the option to withdraw from cyber space completely, because they require the online services to function in society, even if they intrinsically distrust the security of the services. In particular, as IoT devices gradually integrate physical objects seamlessly into information systems, disengagement from the Internet will become increasingly difficult (Yan et al. 2014, 120). On the other hand, a lack of trust in the IoT can make consumers hesitant to purchase new connected devices, thereby limiting the extent to which they can benefit from the potential of the IoT.

The consequences of an erosion of trust can manifest across the spectrum of harm. Individuals may feel helpless, distressed, or anxious because they perceive a high risk of becoming a victim of cyber crime. At their most serious, such distress and anxiety might culminate in mental disorder. A lack of trust can have financial implications because of lost opportunities, as discussed earlier. A loss of trust in the Internet could conceivably have effects outside cyber space—for example, when employees or consumers begin to distrust a company's capability to put appropriate protective measures in place. Harm can also be caused to the democratic principles and institutions that nations rest upon, in particular when cyber crime targets politicians, government institutions, or democratic processes.

One example of how trust can be undermined online is the emergence of fake news (i.e. articles or stories that are deliberately distributed through the Internet but are partially or entirely inaccurate): a concern that was widely discussed in public media in 2016. For example, before the presidential elections in the United States at the end of 2016, a story emerged, suggesting that Pope Francis had endorsed presidential candidate Donald Trump. Despite a press conference in October 2016, during which Pope Francis stated that he had not even spoken about the elections, the story had triggered 960,000 Facebook engagements by November 2016.[7] The spread of fake news resulted in the declaration of the term 'post-truth' as the word of 2016 by Oxford Dictionaries.[8] Even though the distribution of false information is by no means a new phenomenon, the pervasiveness, speed, accessibility, and persistence of fake news through ICT is unprecedented. As a consequence, citizens have begun to distrust information from websites that they previously accessed for reading news items. In an environment where information accessed online may not be reliable, the erosion of trust can destabilize social structures.

Capacity building, in particular by deploying more advanced security technologies and encryption techniques, can help promote user trust in the security of businesses. However, this trust can erode quickly if incidents occur and cause harm, despite the improved capabilities (Gehem et al. 2015, 52–3). Once trust is lost, it cannot easily be restored. Moreover, our understanding of how trust and confidence building differs from offline environments is limited. It is thus important to consider underlying human trust in systems and their security beyond the strictly technological requirements when developing cyber security capacities. In order to mitigate a cascade of harm that might lead to a catastrophic erosion of trust, cyber security needs to focus on harm mitigation alongside the prevention of cyber crime instances. Unsurprisingly, the issue of trust has gained traction in academic and business discourse, whether in the context of data protection,[9] cyber security (McClimans et al. 2016), crime (Mansell and Collins 2005), or the IoT (Yan et al. 2014).

Harm Mitigation: Building a New Cyber Security Framework

The significance of harm in a cyber security context lies with the transforming effects of a human-centric harm mitigation approach. Effective cyber risk mitigation requires both the reduction of the likelihood of cyber crime incidents and the mitigation of harm from such incidents. Cyber security measures to date have been focusing on the reduction of likelihood, predominantly through technology-centric measures, such as access control systems, encryption techniques, or intrusion detection systems. Harm mitigation instead focuses on human-centric measures. This human-centric approach is not limited to mitigating harm experienced by individual victims but can also reduce harm to entities. For example, raising awareness on phishing attacks among all staff members of a company can avoid harm suffered by the company as a whole, if it decreases the success rate of such attacks. A comprehensive assessment of harm in its full scope forms the basis of effective harm mitigation. In order to gather the necessary data that take account of the spectrum of harm associated with different types of cyber crime, a robust classification framework needs to be developed. A cyber harm model, as proposed in 'Cyber Harm: Concepts, Taxonomy and Measurement' (Agrafiotis et al. 2016, 41–4), which can inform evaluations of cyber security capacity, is a first step towards such a framework.

Designing preventative and counteractive measures against cyber crime based on harm mitigation principles changes how cyber security capacity is built. Rather than focusing only on preventing or discouraging unwanted conduct, harm mitigation prioritizes the protection of victims by increasing their resilience. This approach could have a transformative effect on capacity building. For example, an in-depth harm assessment could enable law enforcement agencies to shift their focus from countering and preventing the most prevalent types of cyber crime: a preoccupation that might result in a diversion of criminals to other forms of crime, rather than truly solving the problem. Instead, they would be able to address those types of cyber crime that cause the most significant forms of harm (i.e. types of harms at the further end of the spectrum discussed earlier).

A harm mitigation approach also involves preparing for instances of cyber crime, because it recognizes the inability to prevent all occurrences of cyber crime, all the time. Redundancy efforts that increase the reliability of digital systems, such as backups or fail-safes, and emergency response plans, which include a clear communication and disclosure strategy, are essential to ensure efficient operations after an incident has occurred. Establishing lines of authority and responsibility, and a decision-making process that determines in advance what information will be shared when, how, and with whom can assist organizations to be prepared for crisis situations, avoid unnecessary escalation, and limit reputational damage (Kulikova et al. 2012, 103–6).

Harm can also be mitigated by decreasing the value of criminal proceeds. For example, data breaches can be mitigated before and after the incident has occurred by cancelling compromised credit cards, providing identity theft insurance, issuing credit freezes for victims, or monitoring behavioural anomalies for suspicious activities (Wolff and Lehr 2016, 17–18). The establishment of laws and regulations to compel organizations to establish, monitor, and upgrade cyber security measures that have been identified as best practice can assist in the general harm mitigation effort, as can the encouragement of information sharing across economic and industrial sectors.

At the individual level, harm mitigation is about empowering end users to implement proactive measures not only to protect themselves online but also, more fundamentally, to take responsibility for their own online security and privacy. Through targeted and tailored awareness raising programmes that take into account socio-economic and cultural factors, education across all ages on both the benefits and the potential risks associated with online activities, and the establishment of trust and confidence in online services, individuals can be enabled to make informed decisions online and thus become more resilient to potential cyber threats.

A human-centric approach to cyber security, which emphasizes harm mitigation in addition to risk reduction, distributes the responsibility for cyber security across all actors instead of solely holding internet service providers, the government, or other actors responsible. It also shifts cyber security from being a technology issue to one that is recognized as a societal and organizational challenge, the response to which could require a change in structures, processes, and behaviour. A comprehensive harm assessment would allow for strategic investments to be made into those areas of cyber security that mitigate the most significant harm, while also facilitating risk reduction. Rather than trying to avoid all instances of cyber crime, cyber security capacity building would seek to build an enabling environment for all stakeholders, one that facilitates an understanding of cyber risks and encourages protective measures to be taken that would mitigate cyber harm, in order to make use of the full potential that ICT holds for development and innovation.

NOTES

1. Motivations for committing crimes offline or online are predominantly the same, in most cases focusing on personal gain. However, come cyber criminals have other motives, such as building a reputation online. For a discussion of the motives of cyber criminals, see Kirwan, G. and Power, A. 2012. The Psychology of Cyber Crime: Concepts and Principles. Hershey: IGI Global.
2. See, for example, Brewster, T., 'Government-Backed Report Gets the Cost of Cyber Crime Wrong': http://www.silicon.co.uk/workspace/cyber-crime-small-business-attacks-800m-lies-116963
3. Get Safe Online, 'Fraud & Cybercrime Cost UK Nearly £11bn in Past Year': http://www.getsafeonline.org/news/fraud-cybercrime-cost-uk-nearly-11bn-in-past-year
4. A list of all deliverables of the E-CRIME Project is available at: https://cordis.europa.eu/docs/results/607/607775/final1-e-crime-final-report.pdf
5. Lewin, J., 'Cyber Attack Cost TalkTalk up to £60m and 101k Customers': http://www.ft.com/content/410f5477-d061-3cd4-a064-5563c91bd7fb
6. Silver, H., 'The Impact of Target's Data Breach on Consumer Trust': http://connexity.com/blog/2014/05/the-impact-of-targets-data-breach-on-consumer-trust
7. Ritchie, H., 'Read All About It: The Biggest Fake News Stories of 2016': http://www.cnbc.com/2016/12/30/read-all-about-it-the-biggest-fake-news-stories-of-2016.html
8. Oxford Dictionaries, 'Oxford Dictionaries Word of the Year 2016 is … ': https://www.oxforddictionaries.com/press/news/2016/12/11/WOTY-16
9. Orange, 'The Future of Digital Trust: a European Study on the Nature of Consumer Trust and Personal Data': https://www.orange.com/en/content/download/25973/581975/version/2/file/Report%20-%20My%20Data%20Value%20-%20Orange%20Future%20of%20Digital%20Trust%20-%20FINAL.pdf

REFERENCES

Agrafiotis, I., Bada, M., Cornish, P. et al. 2016. 'Cyber Harm: Concepts, Taxonomy and Measurement', *Saïd Business School WP 2016–23*. http://dx.doi.org/10.2139/ssrn.2828646

Aiken, M., Davidson, J., and Amann, P. 2016. *Youth Pathways into Cybercrime*. Washington, DC: Paladin.

Anderson, R., Barton, C., Böhme, R., Clayton, R., van Eeten, M.J.G., Levi, M., Moore, T. and Savageet, S. 2013. 'Measuring the Cost of Cybercrime'. In *The Economics of Information Security and Privacy*, edited by R. Böhme, 265–300. Berlin and Heidelberg: Springer.

Carpenter, L.M. 2014. 'Cyberbullying: Implications for the Psychiatric Nurse Practitioner', *Journal of Child and Adolescent Psychiatric Nursing* 27 (3): 142–8.

Center for Strategic and International Studies. 2013. *The Economic Impact of Cybercrime and Cyber Espionage*. Santa Clara: McAfee.

Center for Strategic and International Studies. 2014. *Net Losses: Estimating the Global Cost of Cybercrime. Economic Impact of Cybercrime II*. Santa Clara: McAfee.

Detica and the UK Cabinet Office. 2011. *The Cost of Cyber Crime*. Surrey: Detica Limited.

Dutton, W.H., and Shepherd, A. 2003. *Trust in the Internet: The Social Dynamics of an Experience Technology*. Oxford: Oxford Internet Institute, University of Oxford.

European Police Office. 2016. *Internet Organised Crime Threat Assessment (IOCTA) 2016*. The Hague: European Police Office.

Fafinski, S., Dutton, W.H., and Margetts, H. 2010. *Mapping and Measuring Cybercrime*. Oxford: Oxford Internet Institute.

Feinberg, J. 1984. *Harm to Others: The Moral Limits of the Criminal Law, Vol. 1*. New York: Oxford University Press.

Fenech, C., and Hamilton, L. 2015. *The Deloitte Consumer Review: Consumer Data under Attack—The Growing Threat of Cyber Crime*. London: Deloitte LLP.

Filkins, B. 2016. *Quantifying Risk: Closing the Chasm between Cybersecurity and Cyber Insurance*. Swansea: SANS Institute.

Finklea, K., and Theohary, C.A. 2015. *Cybercrime: Conceptual Issues for Congress and U.S. Law Enforcement*. Washington, DC: Congressional Research Service.

Gehem, M., Usanov, A., Frinking, E. et al. 2015. *Assessing Cyber Security: A Meta-Analysis of Threats, Trends, and Responses to Cyber Attacks*. The Hague: The Hague Centre for Strategic Studies.

Gross, M.L., Canetti, D., and Vashdi, D.R. 2017. 'Cyber Terrorism: Its Effects on Psychological Well-Being, Public Confidence and Political Attitudes', *Journal of Cybersecurity* 3 (1): 49–58.

ICA. 2017. *Assessing Russian Activities and Intentions in Recent US Elections*. Washington DC: Intelligence Community Assessment.

Institute of Risk Management. 2014. *Cyber Risk*. London: The Institute of Risk Management.

Jing, Q., Vasilakos, A.V., Wan, J. et al. 2014. 'Security of the Internet of Things: Perspectives and Challenges', *Wireless Networks* 20 (8): 2481–501.

Kulikova, O., Heil, R., van den Berg, J. and Pieters, W. 2012. 'Cyber Crisis Management: A Decision-Support Framework for Disclosing Security Incident Information', *International Conference on Cyber Security, Washington, D.C.*: 103–112.

Levi, M., Doig, A., Gundur, R. et al. 2015. *The Implications of Economic Cybercrime for Policing*. London: City of London Corporation.

Malby, S., Mace, R., Holterhof, A. et al. 2013. *Comprehensive Study on Cybercrime*. New York: United Nations.

Mansell, R., and Collins, B.S. (eds). 2005. *Trust and Crime in Information Societies*. Cheltenham: Edward Elgar.

Mansfield-Devine, S. 2015. 'The Ashley Madison Affair', *Network Security*, September 2015: 8–16.

McClimans, F., Fersht, P., Snowdon, J. et al. 2016. *The State of Cybersecurity and Digital Trust 2016: Identifying Cybersecurity Gaps to Rethink State of the Art*. Chicago: Accenture and HfS Research, Ltd.

Mill, J.S. 1869. *On Liberty*. London: Longman, Roberts & Green.

Peckman, A. 2014. *Cyber Risk Quantification—Five Ways Organisations Can Benefit From Quantifying Cyber Risks.* London: Aon UK Limited.

Ponemon Institute. 2016. *2016 Cost of Cyber Crime Study & the Risk of Business Innovation.* Traverse City: Ponemon Institute LLC.

Romanosky, S. 2016. 'Examining the Costs and Causes of Cyber Incidents', *Journal of Cybersecurity*, August: 1–15.

Wall, D. 2007. *Cybercrime: The Transformation of Crime in the Information Age.* Cambridge, UK: Polity.

Wolff, J., and Lehr, W. 2016. 'Ex-Post Mitigation Strategies for Breaches of Non-Financial Data', TPRC 44: The 44th Research Conference on Communication, Information and Internet Policy 2016.

World Economic Forum and Deloitte. 2015. *Partnering for Cyber Resilience Towards the Quantification of Cyber Threats.* Cologne/Geneva: World Economic Forum.

Wright, D. 2017. 'Project Final Report: Economic Impacts of Cybercrime', https://cordis.europa.eu/docs/results/607/607775/final1-e-crime-final-report.pdf.

Yan, Z., Zhang, P., and Vasilakos, A.V. 2014. 'A Survey on Trust Management for Internet of Things', *Journal of Network and Computer Applications* 42: 120–34.

CHAPTER 9

TOWARD A VULNERABILITY MITIGATION MODEL

JOSÉ EDUARDO MALTA DE SÁ BRANDÃO

INTRODUCTION

CYBERSPACE cuts across organizational boundaries and national frontiers, reaching out to connected devices and people everywhere, even on the oceans and in outer space. As defined by the National Institute of Standards and Technology (NIST; Kissel 2013, 58), cyberspace is 'a global domain within the information environment consisting of the interdependent network of information systems infrastructures including the Internet, telecommunications networks, computer systems, and embedded processors and controllers'. In this context, cyber security is 'the ability to protect or defend the use of cyberspace against cyber attacks' (Kissel 2013, 58).

Increasingly, public services, objects of personal use, and devices embedded in the human body will be connected, bringing an unimaginable interaction. While the technologies and Internet services evolve, the security of users, service providers, and critical infrastructure becomes more threatened. The cybercrime and cyber arms race are growing by exploiting new software vulnerabilities. Cybercrime is already a reality in everyday life for people and corporations. Its growth has led to increased cybersecurity costs for businesses and governments. The production of cyber weapons is a new problem that can be compared to a nuclear arms race. For now, at least, the consequences of a 'cyber arms race' cannot usefully be compared to a nuclear arms race. But the proliferation of connected devices may soon make this comparison worryingly valid. There are two noteworthy markets for the production of malware and cyber weapons: a formal market, with corporate clients, resellers, and governments; and a black market in which the actors involved in cybercrime also operate.

A typical cyber security incident might combine a wide range of elements. While it will never be possible to achieve complete control over these different elements, it should be possible to control the most decisive elements to manage the security incident more effectively and at a more tolerable level. The first step in cyber incident management is to understand the procedures used in an attack and to analyse the process steps. It becomes possible to identify those elements that should be addressed to mitigate the risks and impacts of cyber attacks. But this is not a simple task and cannot be addressed solely from a technological standpoint. The solution must involve multisector cooperation involving governments, the private sector, and cybersecurity researchers. The aim of this chapter is to demonstrate how the elements of a cybersecurity incident can be analysed systematically, and to suggest an alternative way to mitigate the causes and consequences of such incidents.

CYBER SECURITY INCIDENTS

Each of the elements that combine to form the operational process of a cyber security incident can be identified using classification models. These models, or taxonomies, make it possible to group objects with common characteristics and to create categories. But the creation of a taxonomy is not a simple undertaking: in some specific attacks, specialists can identify a closer than expected interdependence between certain elements such that the classification exercise might lose coherence.

In the first place, it is necessary to understand how cyber attacks occur. There are many publications on computer security that attempt to model cyber attacks, each one produced by a different research group and aiming at a specific goal. The AVOIDIT (Simmons et al. 2009) taxonomy aims to provide a vulnerable defender with details as to what an attack would encompass, and the effect of an attack on a targeted system. AVOIDIT classifies an attack in terms of Attack Vector, Operational Impact, Defence, Information Impact and Target. Conversely, Uma and Padmavathi (2013) attempt to classify cyber attacks in terms of other characteristics, such as severity, purpose, and legality, in order to provide an understanding of the motivation behind such attacks: information that might help programmers to develop security devices and mechanisms appropriate to the mode of attack.

Alternatively, a more conceptual model based on the perspectives of policy makers, and technical and legal actors, was developed by Happa and Fairclough (2016). This model identifies four classes of elements: attributes of attack; value of attack; impact of attack; and mitigation of attack. Cyber conflicts are object of study by Applegate and Stavrou (2013). Their taxonomy analyses a cyber security incident in terms of *events* or *entities*, further classified using the categories and subcategories of *actions* and *actors*. Attack agents and attack types are also the subject of research undertaken by Meyers et al. (2009), where different types of adversaries are listed and characterized. The European Union (EU) Agency for Network and Information Security produces its own taxonomy for cyber threats, covering some aspects of attack characteristics (ENISA 2016).

One of the earliest attempts to develop a taxonomy of cyber security incidents described an operational sequence of five elements connecting *attackers* with their *objectives* (Howard 1997). This work drew upon the analysis of safety incidents reported by the CERT Coordination Center and Sandia National Laboratories (CERT-CC) between 1989 and 1995. Next, Howard and Longstaff (1998) extended the proposal, structuring a cyber security occurrence in three parts: incident, attacks, and event. Despite being one of the first works in the area, the model of Howard and Longstaff is the most useful for the purposes of this chapter.

The Life Cycle for Cyber Incidents

The cyber incident life cycle is composed of seven elements, as shown in Figure 9.1 [1].
Agents (or attackers) are actors who attempt one or more attacks to achieve their *Objectives*. *Attacks* involve events caused by using *Attack Tools* to exploit *Vulnerabilities*. The logical end of an attack is an *Unauthorized Result*. The *Event* is a discrete change of state or condition of a system or device. These changes occur from actions that are directed against a specific *Target*.

The value of this model is that it helps us to define the operational processes in the life cycle of a cyber security incident, in which an attacking *Agent* uses *Tools* to exploit *Vulnerabilities*, causing *Actions* on a specific *Target* to obtain *Unauthorized Results*, thereby achieving its *Objectives*.

In theory, a cyber attack—like any other process—could be contained by interdicting one or more of the key steps in the critical path. Unfortunately, none of the cyber attack steps can be entirely eliminated. The challenge, therefore, is to identify which step or steps offer the most efficient way to reduce the incidence and mitigate the consequence of the attacks. For this purpose, each element of the incident life cycle must be analysed, as follows.

Attack Agents and Objectives

The first element of the security incident life cycle to be considered is the Attack Agent. The conflict analysis conducted by Applegate and Stavrou (2013) proposes a new subdivision for the attacking Agent, incorporating both non-state actors and state actors. The classification of non-state actors can itself be subdivided into the following categories:[2]

- Hackers—attackers who attack computers for challenge, status, or the thrill of obtaining access.
- Spies—attackers who attack computers for information to be used for political gain.
- Terrorists—attackers who attack computers to cause fear for political gain.
- Corporate raiders—employees (attackers) who attack a competitor's computers for financial gain.
- Professional criminals—attackers who attack computers for personal financial gain.
- Vandals—attackers who attack computers to cause damage.
- Voyeurs—attackers who attack computers for the thrill of obtaining sensitive information.

FIGURE 9.1. Cyber Incident Lifecycle

- Non-governmental organizations (NGOs)—attempting to promote an ideological position.
- Militia—a civil military force to supplement a regular army.
- Hacktivists, political activists—to promote a political cause.

State and parastatal actors undertaking political activity fall into three broad categories:

- Government organizations—departments and agencies of government.
- State military forces—state defence institutions.
- Militias—civil and reserve military forces.

Each Agent can be subdivided into further subcategories, depending on the level of explanation and detail desired.

The legal classification of Objectives can include cybercrime, cyber espionage, cyber terrorism and cyberwar.[3] Other objectives behind attacks include: challenge, status, thrill; political gain; financial gain; damage; enemy destruction.[4]

To deal with the objectives of the attacks and the agents involved, Ranum´s Law of making people behave must be applied: 'You cannot solve social problems with software.'[5] An attack can only be contained by addressing the attacker's motives: a social, rather than a technological problem.

ATTACKS TOOLS

The second element of the cyber incident life cycle is the Tool used to execute the attacks. Howard and Longstaff point out some examples of Attack Tools usually adopted:[6]

- Physical attack tools—a means of physically stealing or damaging a computer, network, its components, or its supporting systems.
- Information exchange—a means of obtaining information either from other attackers or from the people being attacked.
- User command—a means of exploiting a vulnerability by entering commands to a process through direct user input at the process interface.
- Script or program—a means of exploiting a vulnerability by entering commands to a process through the execution of a file of commands (script) or a program at the process interface.
- Autonomous agent—a means of exploiting a vulnerability by using a program, or program fragment, which operates independently from the user.
- Toolkits—a software package that contains scripts, programs, or autonomous agents that exploit vulnerabilities.
- Distributed tool—tool that can be distributed to multiple hosts, which can then be coordinated to anonymously perform a simultaneous attack on the target host.
- Data tap—a means of monitoring the electromagnetic radiation emanating from a computer or network using an external device.

Another example of Attack Tool classification can be found in the taxonomy created by the NIST Software Assurance Reference Dataset Project (SAMATE).[7] This project lists classes of tools that seek to improve the quality of software, but could also be used by attackers to scan for vulnerabilities:

- Source code security analysers, byte code scanners, binary code scanners.
- Web application scanners.
- Network scanners.
- Dynamic analysis tools.
- Web services network scanners.
- Database scanning tools.

As can be seen, most of these listed tools are 'dual use' in that they are valuable to legitimate users, system administrators, security analysts, and security researchers. These capabilities make important contributions to the operation, development, and maintenance of legitimate systems' security and network infrastructures. Even if it were possible to eliminate these tools, which it is not, it would clearly be unwise to seek to do so.

VULNERABILITY

The third element of the security incident life cycle is vulnerability. According to NIST[8], vulnerability is best understood as 'Weakness in an information system, system security procedures, internal controls, or implementation that could be exploited or triggered by a threat source'. Some sources, such as MITRE[9], differentiate between vulnerability and exposure. An information security 'vulnerability' might be a mistake in software that could be used by a hacker to gain direct access to a system or network. An information security 'exposure', on the other hand, is a system configuration issue or a mistake in software that allows access to information or capabilities that can be used by a hacker indirectly, as a stepping-stone into a system or network. There are clearly overlaps between the two terms and for the purposes of this chapter both expressions will be considered synonymous.

Vulnerability alone would not pose a danger if it were not possible to exploit it. This element is the most technical, and there are several studies focused on the classification and treatment of vulnerabilities. Although vulnerabilities are often created by people, they can be identified and treated manually or automated. This makes this element the least difficult to mitigate and will be more detailed in the next sections.

ATTACK ACTIONS

The 'Event' stage combines the fourth and fifth elements of the cyber incident life cycle: Actions taken against the Target. The Event is basically a set of processes and activities.

To analyse the element of Action, it is necessary to examine it in fine detail. The techniques cited by Howard and Longstaff[10] give a general notion of the constituent elements, but do not allow more detailed analysis. It can be quite difficult to separate Actions from Attack Tools, for example.

One reasonably complete classification system is the Common Attack Pattern Enumeration and Classification (CAPEC™).[11] The dictionary created by MITRE Corporation classifies attacks into two elements: *mechanisms* of attack and *domains* of attack. The taxonomy of mechanisms of attack can be adopted in the classification of Attack Actions by the 16 techniques identified in the dictionary:

- Gather information—focus on the gathering, collection, and theft of information by an adversary.
- Deplete resources—focus on the depletion of a resource to the point that the target's functionality is affected.
- Injection—uses the ability to control or disrupt the behaviour of a target through crafted input data submitted using an interface functioning to process data input.
- Deceptive interactions—also known by the term 'spoofing'—malicious interactions with a target in an attempt to deceive and convince the target that it is interacting with some other principle and, as such, to take actions based on the level of trust that exists between the target and the other principle.
- Manipulate timing and state—exploits weaknesses in 'timing' or state', maintaining functions to perform actions that would, otherwise, be prevented by the execution flow of the target code and processes.
- Abuse of functionality—a broad class of attacks on which the agent manipulates one or more functions of an application to alter the intended result or purpose of the functionality, and thereby affect application behaviour or information integrity.
- Probabilistic techniques—used to explore and overcome security properties of the target that assume strength due to the extremely low mathematical probability that an attacker would be able to identify and exploit the very rare specific conditions under which those security properties do not hold.
- Exploitation of authentication—involves the exploitation of weaknesses, limitations, and assumptions in the mechanisms a target utilizes to manage identity and authentication.
- Exploitation of authorization—used to actively target exploitation of weaknesses, limitations, and assumptions in the mechanisms a target utilizes to manage access to its resources or authorize utilization of its functionality.
- Manipulate data structures—used to manipulate and exploit characteristics of system data structures to violate the intended usage and protections of these structures.
- Manipulate resources—focus on the agent's ability to manipulate one or more resources, or some attribute thereof, to perform an attack and thereby affect application behaviour or information integrity.
- Analyse target—uses the 'analysis of a target' system, protocol, message, or application to overcome protections on the target or as a precursor to other attacks.
- Gain physical access—a set of techniques to exploit weaknesses that enable an adversary to achieve physical access to the target.
- Execute code—focus on the use of malicious code to achieve a desired negative technical impact.

- Alter system components—used in a system to achieve a desired negative technical impact. The manipulation of the components can be logical or physical and be done during the manufacture or distribution.
- Manipulate system users—focus on the manipulation of a user in an attempt to achieve a desired negative technical impact. It includes the influence via social engineering techniques.

The domains of attack include:

- Social engineering—the manipulation and exploitation of people.
- Supply chain—attacking the supply chain life cycle by manipulating computer system hardware, software, or services for the purpose of espionage, theft of critical data or technology, or the disruption of mission-critical operations or infrastructure.
- Communications—the exploitation of communications and related protocols.
- Software—the exploitation of software applications.
- Physical security—used to exploit weaknesses in the physical security of a system in an attempt to achieve a desired negative technical impact.
- Hardware—focus on the exploitation of the physical hardware used in computing systems.

It should be noted that the classifications of actions presented are not the only ones possible. Depending on the target of the attack, actions that are more specific can be taken. This is the case of WASC Threat Classification[12] and OWASP TOP-10 (OWASP 2013), which can be used to address actions on websites and web applications. The WASC Threat Classification, created by the Web Application Security Consortium[13], is a cooperative effort to clarify and organize the threats to the security of a website. The OWASP Top Ten represents a broad consensus about the 10 most critical web application security flaws.

Attack Target

The Target is the sixth element of the cyber incident life cycle. Howard and Longstaff[14] classify the attack targets in terms of computer infrastructures, communication networks, and their processes.

Targets can also be classified in terms of value at risk,[15] including information values, social values, assets, and reputation. Technological advancements applied in social and infrastructure areas create new potential targets, such as the components of national infrastructures. In the UK, 'national infrastructure' is defined by the government as:

> Those critical elements of infrastructure (namely assets, facilities, systems, networks or processes and the essential workers that operate and facilitate them), the loss or compromise of which could result in:
>   1. major detrimental impact on the availability, integrity or delivery of essential services—including those services, whose integrity, if compromised, could result in significant loss of life or casualties—taking into account significant economic or social impacts; and/or
>   2. significant impact on national security, national defence, or the functioning of the state.

National infrastructure in the UK is defined in terms of 13 sectors: communications; emergency services; energy; financial services; food; government; health; transport; water; defence; civil nuclear; space; and chemicals.

Within this framework, the UK has also adopted the idea of '*critical* national infrastructure'. The government uses a 'criticality scale' to identify those assets within the 13 sectors, 'the loss or compromise of which would have a major detrimental impact on the availability or integrity of essential services, leading to severe economic or social consequences or to loss of life.' These assets are known as the 'Critical National Infrastructure' (CNI). It is important to note, not only that the goal is to prevent 'severe economic ... consequences' but also that the CNI can be both physical (e.g. sites, installations, pieces of equipment) and logical (e.g. information networks, systems). So, communication is not simply one of the 13 infrastructure sectors—it is also a key, critical enabler underpinning the whole system.

The United States lists 16 critical infrastructure sectors, while 8 sectors are adopted in Australia, 10 in Japan, 10 in Canada, 12 in the European Commission (CIPSEC 2016, 24), and 5 in Brazil (Ministério da Defesa 2012, 134). A summary list of the main critical infrastructure sectors is as follows:

- Chemical industry and research.
- Commercial facilities.
- Communications.
- Critical manufacturing.
- Energy, dams, and hydroelectrical supply.
- Defence industrial base.
- Emergency services.
- Food and agriculture.
- Government facilities.
- Healthcare and public health.
- Information technology (IT).
- Nuclear reactors, materials, and waste.
- Transport systems.
- Water and wastewater systems.

Regardless of the taxonomy adopted, all related sectors are highly dependent on information and communication technologies.[16] And the same view is at the heart of the EU Network and Information Security directive: 'Network and information systems and services play a vital role in society. Their reliability and security are essential to economic and societal activities, and in particular to the functioning of the internal market' (European Union 2016, 1).

Attack Results

The seventh element of the cyber incident life cycle is the Result on the targeted. Usually, the results are classified in terms of impact on the information security principles of integrity, confidentiality, and availability. An example of this is the FIRST Common Vulnerability Scoring System (CVSS), which makes it possible to calculate both the risks of a specific vulnerability in a target, or a set of potential targets, and the possible effects resulting from the compromise of one or more principles of information security. However, as other elements, information security is not the only way to classify the results and impacts of an attack. The taxonomy model of Simmons et al. (2009) separates the results into 'Operational Impact' and 'Informational Impact', while the Howard and Longstaff model[17] also includes 'Increased Access' and 'Theft of Resources'.

One other way to classify the results is the matrix model proposed by Mpofu and Chikati (2015, 211), which separates the direct and indirect effects related to the integrity and confidentiality of information. Then there is the model devised by Uma and Padmavathi,[18] which includes: obstruction of information; counter international cyber security measures; retardation of decision-making processes; denial in providing public services; abatement of public confidence; and damage to the reputation and legitimate interests of the country.

The resilience of critical infrastructures can also be used to classify the severity of an attack. The terms 'unavailability' and 'disruption' can be applied to any of the sectors discussed earlier, while other effects will be particular to both attack and target. The results of cyber attacks over critical infrastructures might also include the terms 'disease', 'poverty', 'unemployment', 'recession', 'lack of food', 'death', 'war', 'immobility', 'darkness', 'lack of water', and 'terror'. This is an open area of research that still needs further study, especially in terms of the impacts related to the profusion of the Internet of Things (IoT), and to the social and human impacts that are rarely evaluated in technology studies.

VULNERABILITY TAXONOMIES

Vulnerability classification is also a difficult task. As with the elements of the attack cycle, there are several forms of classification. Howard and Longstaff[19] give as an example the classification of software vulnerabilities proposed by Krsul (1998, 103). The Krsul system is based on the three stages of software: design, implementation, and configuration. A more complete list of the most popular classifications is presented by Meunier (2008):

- Classification by software development life cycle (SDLC) phase.
- Classification by genesis.
- Classification by location in object models.
- Classification by affected technology.
- Classification by errors or mistakes.
- Classification by enabled attack scenario.
- CLASP (comprehensive, lightweight application security process) classification.
- Seven Pernicious Kingdoms classification.
- Classification by exploitability.
- Classification by disclosure process.
- Configuration issues, exposures, system vulnerabilities and 'proper' vulnerabilities.

The most common vulnerability classifications are concerned with the time when the vulnerability is introduced into the SDLC. The taxonomy can, for example, involve the steps of analysis, design, implementation, deployment, and maintenance. However, this approach implies that there should be a different classification for each software engineering model, analysing the vulnerabilities in each of its phases.

Classification by Genesis (Landwehr et al. 1994, 214–15) sees vulnerabilities being divided into intentional and inadvertent. Intentional vulnerabilities can be subdivided further into malicious and non-malicious, while inadvertent vulnerabilities are given other classifications.

The classification based on location in object models categorizes vulnerabilities according to the model object or 'entity' to which they belong. Vulnerabilities can be divided, for example, on the network architecture layer, elements of an operating system, or the sides of a client-server interaction. Affected technologies are also a basis of classification. Programming languages, protocols, and communication formats are common approaches to creating taxonomies. A widely used taxonomy of this kind is OWASP TOP-10[20], which presents the most important vulnerabilities for web applications.

Errors known to have led to vulnerabilities have been categorized by their cause, the nature and scale of their impact, and the type of change or fix necessary to remove the error.[21] Attack scenario is also a way to assess vulnerabilities by focusing on the type of attack. Examples of this classification include the attacks listed in CAPEC. Others are more specific, such as SQL-injection, cross-site scripting (XSS) or cross-site request forgery (CSRF), also adopted by OSAWP TOP-10.

The CLASP[22] is a set of activities aiming to improve security. It provides an organized and structured approach for moving security concerns into the initial stages of the SDLC. The classification has five top levels: range and type errors; environmental problems; synchronization and timing errors; protocol errors; and general logic errors.

The Seven Pernicious Kingdoms (Tsipenyuk et al. 2005) approach classifies causes, consequences, and adverse practices of software security. A vulnerability can belong to several categories simultaneously, or be classified differently depending on the abstraction level used. It has eight top levels: input validation and representation; Application Programming Interface abuse; security features; time and state; error handling; code quality; encapsulation; and environment.

Vulnerability can also be classified in terms of exploitability Muenier[23]introduced the classification of vulnerabilities depending on whether they are latent, potential, or exploitable. A *latent* vulnerability consists of vulnerable code that is present in a software unit and would usually result in an exploitable vulnerability if the unit were to be re-used in another software artefact. However, the vulnerability is not currently exploitable because of the circumstances of the unit's use in the software artefact. A *potential* vulnerability is caused by a bad programming practice recognized to lead to the creation of vulnerabilities. However, the specifics of its use do not constitute a vulnerability. A potential vulnerability can become exploitable only if changes are made to the unit containing it. This classification model can be very useful and is adopted in the CVSS to calculate the risks associated with a specific vulnerability.

The classification by disclosure process indicates whether a vulnerability has been disclosed. Unknown public vulnerabilities are known as 'Zero-day'. These vulnerabilities are also presumably unknown to the vendors. Zero-day vulnerabilities are the main source for the creation of cyber weapons and have high value in the black market. Software developers also pay rewards to researchers who find new vulnerabilities, sometimes reaching as high as $500,000.[24]

The last form of classification listed includes configuration issues, exposures, system vulnerabilities, and 'proper' vulnerabilities. This type of classification is based on the premise that what constitutes a vulnerability in a system may not be considered a vulnerability when the same system is deployed in the context of a different security policy. Vulnerability is context-dependent, in other words. One example would be vulnerability caused by configuration failures. A specific setting may be correct in a certain environment, but it may violate security policy in a different one. An example of such a classification is the MITRE Common Configuration Enumeration (CCE)[25], which relates configuration failure models to specific products and operating systems. Unfortunately, this database was last updated in 2013.

As discussed earlier, identification and classification of vulnerability are not trivial tasks. At the most basic level, some of the taxonomies outlined earlier share similar terms and elements, while others are more genuinely complementary. Based on the differences and similarities between taxonomies, the MITRE Corporation created the 'Common Weakness Enumeration' (CWE)[26], 'a unified, measurable set of software weaknesses that enables more effective discussion, description, selection, and use of software security tools and services that can find these weaknesses in source code and operational systems as well as better understanding and management of software weaknesses related to architecture and design'. The CWE makes a relationship of vulnerabilities between different taxonomies, allowing its application in several models of software development and identification of risks. Among the related models are CLASP, Seven Pernicious Kingdoms and OWASP TOP 10. CWE also has the advantage of displaying examples of vulnerability source code, allowing developers to learn from the indicated errors. The CWE has become an international standard through Recommendation ITU-T X.1524 (International Telecommunication Union 2014).

VULNERABILITY DATABASES

MITRE Corporation's 'Common Vulnerabilities and Exposures' (CVE*)[27] is currently the main vulnerability reference. It is not a vulnerability database but a dictionary of common names (i.e. CVE identifiers) for publicly known cybersecurity vulnerabilities. It was launched in 1999 to provide reference points for data exchange so that information security products, services, and databases can communicate with each other. Having been adopted by the US government[28] and by the International Telecommunication Union[29], CVE has become the public and market standard. IT products developers, cyber security products vendors, and independent researchers all include the CVE identifiers in their security advisories. The CVE identifier includes the CVE prefix + year + N arbitrary digits (CVE-YYYY-NN ... N)— for example, CVE-2017-0012345. Until 2014, the identifiers had only four arbitrary digits, but currently there are no limits to that numbering. The CVE has a rigorous process for the identification of vulnerabilities. The process of creating a CVE identifier begins with the discovery of a potential security vulnerability or exposure. The information is then assigned a CVE identifier by a CVE numbering authority (CNA)[30], and posted on the CVE website by the CVE editor.

CNAs are organizations that are authorized to assign CVEs to vulnerabilities affecting products within their distinct and acknowledged scope, for inclusion in first-time public announcements of new vulnerabilities. The participation is voluntary and the benefits of participation include the ability to publicly disclose a vulnerability with an already assigned CVE ID, the ability to control the disclosure of vulnerability information without pre-publishing, and notification of vulnerabilities in products within a CNA's scope by researchers who request a CVE ID from them. CNAs are organized in a federated structure[31]:

> CNAs are categorized as Primary, Root, and Sub-CNAs. Multiple Sub-CNAs may operate under the oversight of a Root CNA, while the Root CNAs operate under the oversight of a single, Primary CNA. Sub-CNAs only assign CVEs for vulnerabilities in their own products or their domain of responsibility, hereinafter referred to as scope. Root CNAs manage a group of Sub-CNAs within a given domain or community, train and admit new Sub-CNAs, and are the assigners of last resort (i.e., no Sub-CNA exists for the scope) within that domain or community. The Primary CNA operates the CVE Program, manages Root CNAs and Sub-CNAs, trains and admits new Root CNAs and Sub-CNAs, and is the assigner of last resort for requesters that are unable to have CVEs assigned at the Sub- or Root CNA levels.

The CVE serves as a reference for the current main vulnerability database, the NIST National Vulnerability Database (NVD).[32] It is a repository of standards-based vulnerability management data. These data enable automation of vulnerability management, security measurement, and compliance. NVD includes databases of security checklists, security-related software flaws, misconfigurations, product names, and impact metrics. NVD uses CVE, CCE, CWE, CVSS, and other security dictionaries. This interconnection between dictionaries enables developers and researchers to identify and learn from faults. It also allows consumers to calculate the potential impact of the vulnerability on their IT environment, as well as to find fixes or countermeasures to mitigate vulnerabilities.

VULNERABILITY MITIGATION MODEL

The lack of disclosure and vulnerability correction are important drivers in the rich market of exploits, where development costs and risks are still low when compared with the costs of conventional crime and weapons. To succeed, Attack Tools need to exploit unknown security holes for users and administrators of potential targets. Cyber weapons, for example, are only effective while exploiting unknown failures. When vulnerabilities are disclosed and corrected, attacking tools quickly begin to lose their effectiveness. Vulnerabilities, like risks, rarely disappear completely: but they can be mitigated. It is possible to reduce the impact of criminal activities on society, for example, and to stop the cyber arms race. The development of vulnerability mitigation mechanisms will limit the severity and consequences of attacks, and will ensure that greater cost and risk will be borne by the attacker.

There is frequently a tension between software developers and cybersecurity researchers. Vendors often underestimate security risks to protect the reputation and image of companies and their products. On the other hand, those researchers who simply do not trust software companies have, in many cases, acted irresponsibly by exposing vulnerabilities and exploits without due caution. The state tends to support corporations in disputes of this nature. It is not unusual to see proposals to criminalize the disclosure of vulnerabilities or publication of products that allow exploits. However, the research and development of security products involves knowledge and assessment of failures: 'know-how', which is difficult to contain. Databases such as NVD aid researchers and prevent vendors from claiming that vulnerabilities discovered by researchers are not exploitable in normal use or that the risks are insignificant.

A model for protocol and rules for the responsible disclosure of vulnerabilities was that proposed by Christey and Wysopal (2002). The model did not become a standard: the lack of state regulation or self-regulation mechanisms for supervision and rules enforcement made the proposal ineffective. Nevertheless, this model has served as the basis for the best practices currently adopted by the scientific community. The general model of vulnerability mitigation presented in Figure 9.2 is an adapted and updated version of the Christey and Wysopal approach. The main proposal is for multisector cooperation to create an independent, trustworthy, and secure vulnerability database, based on a new vulnerability report protocol devised in accordance with researchers, companies, governments, and society.

The general model is based on the participation of the whole of society. It has a trustworthy, common vulnerability database, with secure communication protocols for contact between researchers, companies, and software developers, including open source initiatives. The interactions must be regulated and audited by governments and international organizations. The main strategy involves multisector cooperation, security research, and market regulation for hardware and software security. To make all this possible, the following requirements must be met:

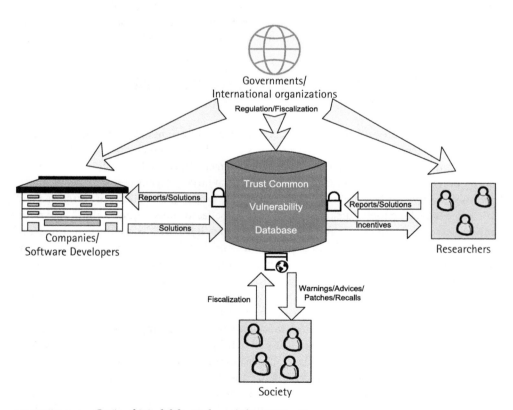

FIGURE 9.2. General Model for Vulnerability Mitigation

- Researchers must use the database to communicate their findings and talk with the companies.
- Companies must use the database to collect new vulnerabilities and quickly report any corrections.
- Consumers must use the database as a source of security information.

The vulnerability mitigation model must begin with the most interested part: society itself. Consumers need to be protected and informed of the risks associated with technology products. For many common consumer products, such as cars and home appliances, vendors are required to fix defects to avoid accidents, damage, or prejudice to consumers. The recall of products, with information given about the risks involved, is widely divulged and supervised by national and international consumer protection organizations. However, this situation is not common in the technological world. The general rule is the *non-disclosure* of risks and the release for sale of new versions that fix failures of previous versions, forcing consumers to purchase new products. For as long as this business model is accepted by society, it will be difficult for companies to strive for developing secure software products.

While products involved 'harmless' software and equipment, there was little or no social pressure for change. But this is changing rapidly. IT products now involve connected devices in the IoT, channels, and networks of communication, and public and financial services. It may not be obvious, but such technologies already connect lives that depend on cyberspace. Sensitivity to risk in these areas is becoming sharper.

As with models associated with risk, when the perception of risk is greater than the perception of advantage, society's tendency is generally to seek the least risk. Therefore, it is not in the interest of companies that the risk is exposed. In the information age, such behaviour has become unhelpful and some companies have perceived that misinformation may be more dangerous than correct and immediate information. As far as consumers are concerned, a dependable, risk-based model would have to include several reliable information disclosure mechanisms, warnings, recalls, and automatic software patches.

Another issue to consider is the relationship between researchers and the private sector. Companies that have security quality programs have already seen that rewards for identifying vulnerabilities improve their productivity and motivate their teams, which is good for marketing. On the other hand, the researchers see responsible partners in these companies, and the possibility of financial and professional gains are unquestionable incentives of this cooperation.

The fourth key element of an effective vulnerability mitigation model is the participation of the state and international organizations. Most national governments—but by no means all—have already understood that exclusively unilateral governance and regulation of cyberspace is not possible: international cooperation in cyber security is essential; local laws of market regulation and consumer protection need to be in line with international law and practice to take effect.

The last element is essentially technological. The vulnerability database does not need to be unique and centralized: it can be a federated set of databases maintained by companies, non-profitable organizations, and governments. The design of the database(s) must allow for the reliable implementation of the protocols of responsible disclosure of vulnerabilities, keeping safe the information exchanged between researchers and companies until the time specified for the disclosure. An important aspect to consider is the government and society monitoring, applying punishments, if necessary. This will depend on international agreements and the national regulations need to follow these agreements.

The vulnerability mitigation model therefore creates important social and political challenges, including, but not limited to:

- responsibilities for creation, maintenance, and audit of the technical infrastructures;
- incentives, responsibilities, and obligations for researchers, companies, consumers, and governments;
- international cooperation;
- international and national regulation; and
- incentives for consumer participation.

Technical studies will also be needed to enable the implementation and deployment of procedures, communication protocols, and other information infrastructures, such as:

- vulnerability database design and implementation;
- secure protocols for researchers' and vendors' communication;
- secure storage and access; and
- Automatic and secure patch mechanisms.

These requirements are easy to list but they represent a serious challenge for researchers and organizations working on cyber security.

Conclusions

Cybersecurity incidents can be explained in terms of a sequence of elements linking the attacking agents to their objectives: the attacking *Agent* uses *Tools* to exploit *Vulnerabilities*, causing *Actions* on a specific *Target* to obtain *Unauthorized Results*, achieving their *Objectives*.

Cyber security can be improved by stopping the flow of the attack by mitigating one or more elements that make up the process. Unfortunately, most of these elements have characteristics that limit the opportunities for mitigation. The least difficult element to mitigate is vulnerability. The current model of vulnerability mitigation has behaved for the corporate environment, which can pay for specialized tools and consulting. There is a profusion of security systems that use public vulnerability databases, such as NVD. Others employ proprietary bases, with Zero-day vulnerability information available to those who can pay. This is an excellent business model, but inaccessible to the public. A new model is necessary to prevent cybersecurity incidents on a broader, more inclusive level. The main proposal for vulnerability mitigation is multisector cooperation to create an independent, trustworthy, and secure vulnerability database, based on a new vulnerability report protocol developed in accordance with researchers, companies, governments, and society. However, this is not an easy task. The proposal creates some social, political, and technical challenges: challenges that open new perspectives and opportunities for research and international cooperation.

NOTES

1. Howard and Longstaff, *A Common Language*, 12.
2. See Howard and Longstaff, *A Common Language*, 15; Applegate and Stavrou, *Towards a Cyber Conflict Taxonomy*; Meyers et al., *Taxonomies*, 8.
3. Uma and Padmavathi, 'A Survey', 393–4.
4. Howard and Longstaff, *A Common Language*, 15–17.
5. The phrase was used for the first time by Marcus Ranum in 1993, in a discussion about the limits of firewalls on security: https://en.wikipedia.org/wiki/Marcus_J._Ranum. See also Ranum, M.J., 2000. The Network Police Blotter; login: THE MAGAZINE OF USENIX & SAGE, 25 (8): 30–4.
6. Howard and Longstaff, *A Common Language*, 13–14.
7. NIST, SAMATE—Software Assurance Metrics and Tool Evaluation: https://samate.nist.gov/Main_Page.html
8. Kissel, *Glossary*, 212.
9. MITRE, Common Vulnerabilities and Exposures Terminology: https://cve.mitre.org/about/terminology.html
10. Howard and Longstaff, *A Common Language*, 10.
11. MITRE, Common Attack Pattern Enumeration and Classification: http://capec.mitre.org
12. See WEBAPPSEC, 2010.
13. WASC, Web Application Security Consortium, http://www.webappsec.org/
14. Howard and Longstaff, '*A Common Language*, 10–11.
15. Happa and Fairclough, 'A Model', 179.
16. CIPSEC, Report on Taxonomy, 24.
17. Howard and Longstaff, *A Common Language*, 14–15.
18. Uma and Padmavathi, 'A Survey', 391.
19. Howard and Longstaff, *A Common Language*, 14.
20. See OWASP 2013.
21. Meunier, 'Classes of Vulnerabilities', 4.
22. OWASP, Comprehensive, Lightweight Application Security Process (CLASP): https://www.owasp.org/index.php/CLASP_Concepts
23. Meunier, 'Classes of Vulnerabilities', 7–8.
24. Exodus Intelligence, Zero-Day Vulnerabilities: https://rsp.exodusintel.com
25. NIST, Common Configuration Enumeration (CCE): https://nvd.nist.gov/cce/index.cfm.
26. MITRE, Common Weakness Enumeration (CWE): https://cwe.mitre.org
27. MITRE, Common Vulnerabilities and Exposures (CVE®): https://cve.mitre.org/about/
28. See Mell, P., and Grance, T. 2002. *NIST Special Publication 800–51: Use of the Common Vulnerabilities and Exposures (CVE) Vulnerability Naming Scheme*, Gaithersburg, MD: National Institute of Standards and Technology.
29. See ITU, *Common Vulnerabilities*.
30. MITRE, CVE numbering authority (CNA): https://cve.mitre.org/cve/cna.html

31. MITRE, Common Vulnerabilities and Exposures (CVE) Numbering Authority (CNA) Rules, 4: https://cve.mitre.org/cve/cna/CNA_Rules_v1.1.pdf
32. NIST, National Vulnerability Database: https://nvd.nist.gov

REFERENCES

Applegate, S.D., and Stavrou, A. 2013. *Towards a Cyber Conflict Taxonomy.* Tallinn, NATO CCD COE Publications.

Christey, S., and Wysopal, C. 2002. *Responsible Vulnerability Disclosure Process*, s.l.: Fremont, CA: Internet Engineering Task Force.

CIPSEC. 2016. *D1.3. Report on Taxonomy of the CI Environments*, s.l.: CIPSEC Consortium.

ENISA. 2016. *ENISA Threat Taxonomy*, s.l. European Union Agency for Network and Information Security.

European Union. 2016. Directive (EU) 2016/1148 of the European Parliament and of the Council of 6 July 2016—concerning measures for a high common level of security of network and information systems across the Union. *Official Journal of the European Union*, 19 July.

Happa, J. and Fairclough, G. 2016. 'A Model to Facilitate Discussions About Cyber Attacks'. In *Ethics and Policies for Cyber Operations: A NATO Cooperative Cyber Defence Centre of Excellence Initiative*, edited by M. Taddeo, and L. Glorioso, 169–85. Cham: Springer International Publishing,

Howard, J. 1997. *An Analysis of Security Incidents on the Internet, 1989–1995*, Pittsburgh, PA: Carnegie Mellon University.

Howard, J.D., and Longstaff, T.A. 1998. *A Common Language for Computer Security Incidents*, Albuquerque, NM: Sandia National Laboratories.

International Telecommunication Union (ITU). 2012. *ITU-T X.1524–Common Weakness Enumeration*, s.l.: ITU.

International Telecommunication Union (ITU). 2014. *ITU-T X.1520–Common Vulnerabilities and Exposures*, s.l.: International Telecommunication Union (ITU).

Kissel, R. 2013. *Glossary of Key Information Security Terms.* Gaithersburg: National Institute of Standards and Technology.

Krsul, I.V. 1998. *Software Vulnerability Analysis*, Ph.D. Dissertation, Computer Sciences Department. Lafayette, IN: Purdue University.

Landwehr, C.E., Bull, A.R., McDermott, J.P. et al. 1994. A Taxonomy of Computer Security Flaws. *ACM Computing Surveys* 26 (3): 211–54.

Meunier, P. 2008. 'Classes of Vulnerabilities and Attacks'. In *Wiley Handbook of Science and Technology for Homeland Security*, s.l., edited by J.G. Voeller, John Wiley & Sons, Inc.

Meyers, C., Powers, S., and Faissol, D. 2009. *Taxonomies of Cyber Adversaries and Attacks: A Survey of Incidents and Approaches.* Livermore, CA: Lawrence Livermore National Laboratory.

Ministério da Defesa. 2012. *Política Nacional de Defesa e Estratégia Nacional de Defesa*, Brasília: Ministério da Defesa.

Mpofu, N., and Chikati, R. 2015. 'Strategy Matrix for Containing Cyber-Attacks'. In *The Proceedings of the 10th International Conference on Cyber Warfare and Security—ICCWS 2015*, s.l., edited by J. Zaaiman, and L. Leenen, 207. Academic Conferences Limited.

OWASP (Open Web Application Security Project). 2013. *OWASP Top 10–2013*, s.l.: https://www.owasp.org

Simmons, C., Ellis, C., Sajjan, S. et al. 2009. *AVOIDIT: A Cyber Attack Taxonomy*, s.l. Memphis, TN: University of Memphis.

Tsipenyuk, K., Chess, B., and McGraw, G. 2005. Seven Pernicious Kingdoms: A Taxonomy of Software Security Errors. *IEEE Security & Privacy* 3 (6): 81–4.

Uma, M., and Padmavathi, G. 2013. A Survey on Various Cyber Attacks and Their Classification. *International Journal of Network Security*, 15(5), pp. 390–396.

WEBAPPSEC (Web Application Security Consortium). 2010. *The WASC Threat Classification v2.0*, s.l.: http://www.webappsec.org/

PART III

SECURITY IN CYBER SPACE: EXTREMISM AND TERRORISM

CHAPTER 10

MANAGING RISK: TERRORISM, VIOLENT EXTREMISM, AND ANTI-DEMOCRATIC TENDENCIES IN THE DIGITAL SPACE

ALEXANDER CORBEIL AND RAFAL ROHOZINSKI

INTRODUCTION

ON 19 August 2014, a video surfaced on the Internet. In it, a balaclava-clad British terrorist stood next to a kneeling American conflict reporter named James Foley. Foley, who had disappeared almost two years before in Syria, was dressed in an orange jumpsuit, reminiscent of those worn by Iraqi prisoners held by the American army in Abu Gharib. Before executing Mr Foley, the British member of the so-called Islamic State (IS) demanded that the United States end airstrikes against the group in Iraq.

The content of the video was not novel: the predecessor to ISIS, al-Qaeda in Iraq, had disseminated similar beheading videos. Rather, it was the quality with which the video was produced. The use of high-definition cameras, the staging, and rehearsal all mimicked the quality and painstaking time put into a Hollywood production. The video was also disseminated publicly, having been posted to YouTube, among other platforms, purportedly first by the IS media team. On Twitter, IS's recommended hashtag for the video, '#NewMessageFromISIStoUS' surpassed 2,000 tweets by the end of the day.[1] IS's Hollywood-styled execution video went mainstream, with news coverage amplifying the organization's reach, its brutality, and the direct threat to America.

Such a media spectacle would not have been possible without the affordances created by the Internet in general and, in particular, social media. Traditionally, such videos would be costly to produce and enjoy limited circulation. Terrorist supporters in the 1980s and 1990s would have viewed them on VHS cassettes, physically bought and passed around hand to hand or delivered by mail. Those adherents to al-Qaeda in Iraq in the early 2000s would have downloaded them through bespoke online forums dedicated to sharing terrorist content. In 2014, social media facilitated easy access, with users stumbling upon or being served up execution videos of James Foley or Steven Sotloff, another American journalist, through mainstream platforms such as Twitter. One study found that, out of a randomly selected group of 3,000 US residents, 20% had watched at least part of one of the beheading videos of either James Foley or Steven Sotloff, while 5% viewed one in its entirety.[2]

The Internet has transformed the way the people create, consume, and interact with information. Within a short two decades, the Internet went from a sleepy network connecting scholars and researchers to the infrastructure underpinning globalization. As of 2019, more than 50% of the world's population has had access to broadband Internet. There are more cell phones on the planet then there are human beings, and the growth of these technologies is fastest in low- income and developing countries where previously access to basic information communication technologies (ICTs), such as telephones, was limited. By some estimates, by 2012, three out of five new Internet users were coming from countries considered fragile, or where governance had failed (SecDev Group 2012).

The rapid uptake of these technologies has resulted in a social revolution with multiple dimensions. The first is what could be termed 'open empowerment' (Muggah and Rohozinski 2016). More people, in more places, can now access information and communicate in a manner that overcomes structural barriers of geography, income, and fragile or near non-existent governance. This had positive consequences: cutting out the middleman and other rent-seeking activities that often drove inequalities between primary producers such as farmers and fisherman and markets in urban areas. It also helped bring transparency and accountability to public administration and, in some cases, reduced low-level corruption. Friction-free access to global supply chains and markets also brought into being new economic activities.

The speed, scale, and global pervasiveness of the Internet means that the information it carries can be amplified globally and have significant and real-world impact. The Internet can also be used to efficiently and effectively circumvent social controls and legitimate political institutions. It is within this space—the gap between the possibilities that the Internet has brought into being and the institutional lag in developing new practices, norms, rules, and institutions—that malign and harmful uses of the Internet have come to the fore.

Laissez-Faire Versus Regulate: The Internet in Its Teenage Years

At its core, the Internet is a transport mechanism. As a result, messages are spread, unimpeded from one individual to another, or to many. Such communications are only curtailed when there are established rules and barriers that prevent them from spreading. Social media at once gave rise to the phenomenon of mass personal communication, but also linked it with an underlying economic incentive to quantify and monetize people's use of, and interaction with, the Internet. This twin phenomenon led to the massive, rapid development of websites and online platforms such as Facebook and YouTube. To help facilitate and protect the development of the Internet, a laissez-faire approach was applied to the regulation of, and liability for, user-generated content. The epitome of this laissez-faire approach is still engrained in Section 230 of the US Communications Decency Act, which protects sites that host content from being liable for what their users post. The more people created and shared content, the greater and more valuable the underlying data that could be repackaged and sold, creating the basis of a new, global advertising market. This facilitated the growth of astronomically larger data collection and marketing efforts, using ever more granular data to map and quantify user behaviour for economic benefit.

Social media companies and their supporters argued against regulation. Old rules and institutional arrangements were sufficient to both protect the right to communicate and to deal with its excesses (or so the argument went). What the proponents of this argument missed, however, was that opening access for anyone to produce, publish, and share information across these platforms, social media companies *disempowered* the checks and balances (particularly the editorial processes present in newsrooms) that helped to ensure the promotion of legitimate and authoritative voices. It is this filtering of information—*gatekeeping*—that underpinned the stability of democratic systems, and the suppression of fringe and toxic ideas. For example, in the pre-Internet age, white supremacists in the United States would face a slew of barriers to spreading their beliefs: they would need to pool resources in order to have even a relatively limited number of their newsletters printed; publications would be sent through the mail; letters or articles seeking publication in newspapers would need to go through an editorial board before they were accepted into print publication; even access to radio or television would ultimately need economic support and, importantly, editorial approval. If successful, the circulation of fringe narratives would still be relatively limited. With the Internet, and especially social media, those with anti-democratic, hateful, and violent ideas no longer needed to go through these arduous editorial and logistical processes and raise a significant amount of funds: they could publish directly to an audience, and cheaply.

For terrorists, the Internet has been attractive in much the same way that other novel communications technologies have benefitted their predecessors. Terrorism is, at its core, a form of violent communication (Schmid 2005). While modern terrorists have followed a now predictable pattern of adopting communication technology, it is the inherent affordances provided by the networked structure of the Internet that have allowed the online space to be manipulated by these actors to such great effect. Gabriel Weimann (2015) attributed the significant presence of modern terrorism on the Internet to two trends: 'the democratization of communications driven by user-generated content on the internet, and the growing awareness of modern terrorists of the potential of using the internet as a tool for their purposes.' The former is inherent to the Internet: it lacks a *gatekeeper* or *gatekeepers* who can make editorial decisions about which content is accessible to the public. This reality underpins the current state of terrorist and violent extremist activity online. This democratization is a by-product of the lack of official institutions playing a robust and traditional media gatekeeper role on the Internet. In effect, there are little by way of authorities that control the dissemination of information on the Internet in a manner that can significantly curtail the flow of terrorist communications and content online, or other nefarious activities for that matter. To emphasize, according to Weimann, it is 'The nature of the network—its international character and *chaotic structure*[3], its global reach, its simple access, and the anonymity it offers …' that provides such a rich environment for violent extremist and terrorist activity online (2006, 16). Terrorism scholar Alex Schmid wrote that, 'demonstrative, brazen acts of violence are often produced primarily to gain entry into a news system … ' (2005,

139). Further, the way this news system picks up, disseminates, and sometimes provides saturated coverage to certain acts of violence enters the terrorist calculus and co-determines the strategy of many terrorist groups. While this is still very much the case, the calculus of terrorists and violent extremists has somewhat changed with the advent and widespread adoption of social media. Terrorists and violent extremists no longer rely on influencing editorial decisions in newsrooms to reach a wide, diverse, and transnational audience as they did since the early 1900s. Instead, these organizations and individuals are themselves the content developers and disseminators, honing not only their destructive capabilities but their media savvy to reach various audiences simultaneously: enemies, the general public, supporters, potential adherents, and traditional media outlets (which may greatly amplify their message), among others.

The consequence is that violent actors, terrorists, and white supremacists (among others) have found in the Internet a megaphone to propagate, press the letters, and reach audiences that were previously inaccessible. The volume, virility, and substance of this content raise the level of concern to a point where it is now being addressed by policy makers globally. The growing alarm has occurred in several stages. The success with which IS leveraged the Internet for recruitment, and as an enabler to military operations in Syria and Iraq between 2014 and 2016, raised alarm bells as to the extent to which social media space was empowering local and regional insurgent groups.[4] The extent to which social media was leveraged as a tool to mobilize populations, such as in the expulsion and genocide against the Rohingya in Myanmar, or in political messaging during the UK Brexit campaign and Russian interference in the 2016 US elections, raised concerns further and brought the issue of regulating social media companies into the political limelight.[5]

The universal challenge faced by policy makers resides in crafting a careful balance that preserves democratic rights and freedoms, such as the freedom of speech, with the need for community safety and societal well-being, as well as economic development and a political atmosphere conducive to digital innovation. These three functions do not always sit well together. For example, while significant agreement exists that terrorist groups should not be allowed to use the Internet for recruitment and mobilization, the challenge remains in agreeing upon what constitutes a terrorist group and what related types of speech should be removed from platforms (e.g. that which glorifies terrorism as opposed to all content produced by a terrorist organization and its supporters), under what authority (i.e. national laws or platforms' terms of service), and to what geographical extent (i.e. at the national or global level). For the 'like-minded countries'—liberal democracies sharing a commitment to an open, free, and transparent Internet—the development of regulations governing content moderation comes with the risk of *normalizing censorship* and diminishing the freedom of speech, which these countries define as a fundamental human right.

Arguments for regulation have also run up against an absence of scholarship that could conclusively prove that mobilization to violence through the Internet was a significant and pervasive phenomenon. As one example, 'filter bubbles', a term coined by Internet activist Eli Pariser[6]—have been criticized as 'overblown' by scholars such as Elizabeth Dubois and Grant Blank, who have argued that most individuals have habits that help them avoid echo chambers in the online space. According to Dubois and Blank (2018), rather than relying on a single source, users actively check additional sources and encounter different perspectives as part of a diverse media diet, which may be a protective factor against radicalization to violence.

The academic arguments notwithstanding, the ability of Internet and social media users to propagate ideas, without reference to the facts, expertise, or research, has had an impact well beyond the bounds of political campaigns and violent extremist movements. One of the best examples is to be found in the anti-vaccine movement, which is predominantly made up of well-meaning individuals who oppose the vaccination on the basis of pseudoscientific information shared among online communities. According to a study conducted at George Washington University,[7] the offline impacts of this activity are immense and frightening. In the United States, from 1 January to 31 May 31 2019, there were 981 individual cases of measles in 26 states: the greatest number of cases reported since 1992 and since measles was declared eliminated in the United States in 2000.[8]

Introducing gatekeeping functions on the Internet is not one that can be left for the markets to decide alone. The Internet has reached its teenage years and can be said to be as rowdy and difficult to govern as a high school student. Deciding how to respond—preserving the Internet's ability to fuel economic dynamism and growth, while constraining its more negative social impacts—is a careful balancing act, one in which governments, corporations, and civil society have an important stake.

THE STATE AND INDUSTRY RESPOND

In reaction to government pressure to address violent extremist and terrorist activity on-line, four of the largest technology companies—Google, Facebook, Microsoft, and Twitter—launched the Global Internet Forum to Counter Terrorism (GIFCT) in June 2017. The GIFCT's expressed purpose was to prevent terrorists from exploiting these companies' platforms and those of other members, many of which are either their subsidiaries or sub-stantially smaller platforms. To do so, GIFCT focused on three areas of effort: employing and leveraging technology; sharing knowledge, information, and best practices; and conducting and funding research.[9] One of the major achievements of GIFCT was the creation of the shared industry hash database. Hashes are effectively digital fingerprints of images and videos made from a unique set of pixels in each image or video. These hashes are shared among members of the hash-sharing database and used to identify terrorist content on their platforms for removal and, in some cases, to block re-upload. By mid-2019, the database contained more than 200,000 hashes.

GIFCT was welcomed by governments that wanted to see a more concerted effort by in-dustry to address this cross-platform problem in an effective manner. It also provided the framework for larger, more-established companies to provide their smaller counterparts with the knowledge, training, and, in some cases, technology to combat terrorist use of their platforms. In addition to these smaller technology companies, GIFCT also worked with the civil society, academia, and multilateral institutions such as the European Union and United Nations to enhance work to prevent and counter terrorist use of the Internet. In 2019, the organization claimed major successes on behalf of its leading members: YouTube stated that 98% of the videos it removed were flagged by machine-learning algorithms; Twitter claimed that 93% of the accounts flagged for the promotion of terrorism were the result of internal tools; for its part, Facebook stated that 99% of IS and al Qaeda-related content was removed before users had flagged it.[10]

But GIFCT also laid bare the limits of industry self-regulation to address this issue. Successive G7 Interior Ministers' meetings from 2017 to 2019 highlighted the frustration with industry efforts up to that point, particularly a lack of transparency to government officials and the general public. The 2019 G7 Interior Ministers' outcome document, *Combating the Use of the Internet for Terrorist and Violent Extremist Purposes*, threw a spotlight on these vexations. In it, the authors wrote, ' ... the results and effectiveness on content removal remain varied, especially when it comes to smaller platforms.'[11] Interior Ministers of the world's seven largest advanced economies called on industry to more swiftly identify and remove all terrorist content; take proactive measures against exploitation; ensure larger company support for smaller platforms; address algorithmic processes that lead users to more extreme content; and work closely with law enforcement when necessary. These requests made to industry and others outlined in the document were underpinned by the need to ensure transparency and open communication with government as well as, in all efforts, the protection of human rights and fundamental freedoms.

The 2019 outcome document and the two that preceded it from G7 Interior Ministers' meetings in Ischia, Italy and Toronto, Canada, showed substantial government frustrations with industry in general and the GIFCT members in particular. Company communication with governments was piecemeal and uneven, and information provided in the public domain differed from company to company with no standard metrics. For example, Twitter's transparency report lumped together the promotion of terrorism with 'soliciting bounties for serious violence' and 'affiliating with and promoting organizations that use or promote violence against civilians to further their causes'.[12] In contrast, Facebook's transparency report provided a specific section for terrorist propaganda, though only actions against that propaganda emanating from IS, al-Qaeda, and affiliates.[13] This lack of standardization and clarity of definitions and metrics made it difficult to understand both how platforms dealt with this issue on their own and the cumulative effect of platform actions.

Platforms were also slow to adapt proactive measures to address terrorist exploitation. The development of new applications and services did not prioritize a duty of care for the user. Functionalities were first determined by their profit-making ability interwoven with user experience. Ensuring that the same users were not subject to, or influenced by, violent extremists and terrorists, among various other types of nefarious content and activity, was less than a second-order priority. As will be shown, this applied most importantly to the livestream feature on Facebook.

Companies are understandably protective of their algorithmic processes: the underlying technical infrastructure that serves users with content is based on engagement. The longer a platform keeps users engaged, the more advertising revenue it collects. These algorithmic processes, can, in some cases, drive users to more extreme content. Zeynep Tufekci from the School of Information and Library Science at the University of North Carolina observed in a *New York Times* opinion piece that YouTube was at minimum contributing to political polarization in the United States, and likely to provoke radicalization to violence as well. In engaging with Republican and Democratic candidate content during the 2016 election, Tufekci was continually recommended more extreme material by the YouTube algorithm. Interested in Donald Trump? One would then end up being recommended Holocaust denial videos. What about Bernie Sanders? Sustained engagement with pro-Sanders videos led to recommendations of leftist conspiracies including that the US government was behind the September 11 attacks.[14] Tufekci also noticed this with other types of content. Users were never 'extreme' enough for YouTube's recommendation algorithm. No matter the topic, the algorithm would bring users to increasingly extreme material. For instance, those users searching for vegetarian recipes would soon be introduced to vegan ones; users looking to learn more about running were quickly shown videos of Iron Man marathons. Content served to users is that which will keep them engaged, not necessarily the content that they want or prefer. Of course, companies were reluctant to allow for any oversight of these recommendation algorithms given that they are at the core of their businesses, driving user engagement with their platforms.

Lastly, larger company support, particularly from the leading GIFCT members, was piecemeal to smaller technology companies. These smaller platforms lack the technical expertise, resources, and staff to address terrorist exploitation of their platforms. Understandably, the business model for smaller platforms does not include funding to address terrorist exploitation, which from a commercial perspective is not the company's main focus. Yet, for a substantial number of smaller companies, terrorists made extensive use of their platforms. This was for a number of reasons. Many of these platforms were effective, particularly when combined with more mainstream platforms. They complemented the larger platforms and allowed for more flexibility and wider dissemination and reach of content. Other companies found themselves exploited by terrorists as an alternative to larger platforms. Simply, as larger platforms started to crack down on terrorist activity, those actors found more fertile and less repressive ground on less-than-mainstream platforms with similar affordances provided by larger platforms. For example, as YouTube worked to remove terrorist videos from its platform, individuals who had previously posted to YouTube ended up on video-sharing sites such as Vimeo.

Account removals help to diminish the reach of terrorists and violent extremists on social media platforms. This in turn has an impact on the group's or individual's ability to recruit, or spread propaganda, and forces these actors to spend time reconstructing their online networks (Stern and Berger 2015). Terrorism is a form of violent communication (Schmid 2005, 139). Thus, increasing the ability of online platforms to limit the spread of terrorist and violent extremist propaganda and activity through account removals and other moderation activities makes it more difficult for these actors to spread their message. But content moderation is not a panacea. These measures must be combined with various strategies to limit user exposure to content that is both illegal and harmful, while applying the appropriate protections for human rights and fundamental freedoms. Those at high risk may require online interventions by trained practitioners to nudge them to the appropriate psychosocial support programmes. Alternative and counter-narratives that contradict and push back against the hateful and violent ideologies are also required. These are but a few of the options that must be combined to push back against violent extremist and terrorist content and activity online. But most lie well beyond the capacity of small actors and outside the commercial interests of the Internet giants.

The expression of violent extremism and terrorism in the online space is, importantly, symptomatic of real-world conditions at the level of communities, groups, and individuals. These risk factors must be dealt with in the physical realm, including the societal level, where governments and elected officials must promote societal cohesion through their words, actions, and policies. At the individual level, pre-emptive social and economic measures in the pre-criminal space are needed to support those at high risk of joining or carrying out violence on behalf of terrorist organizations or violent extremist ideologies. For those who pose a significant national security risk, on-the-ground work is required by law enforcement and intelligence agencies. Overall, politicians, influencers, and traditional media must not stoke fears regarding immigration, technological development, and societal change but rather help adjust and prepare the general public for ongoing and future socio-economic and political change.

Conclusion

These negative, divisive, and at times destructive uses of the Internet should not be seen as outweighing the Internet's potential—or as a corruption of the principles of empowerment and democratization that some have argued are at the normative core of the Internet. Rather, these phenomena should be seen as a stage in the maturing of this global infrastructure: a time when new rules and norms need to be considered. It is apparent that a new social contract must be devised in order to define the roles and responsibilities of state and corporate institutions beyond the current confines of a Westphalian nation state system.

Most importantly, governments and relevant stakeholders must work together to establish an appropriate gatekeeper function, backed by significant regulation. At its basic level, the re-empowerment of gatekeepers for public communications will help societies re-establish the parameters of free speech and acceptable discourse in a democratic setting. Public institutions, including governments and traditional media as well as civil society, academia, and technology companies have a strong role to play in this process. Together, they must balance their competing interests and responsibilities, and allow for the public space to discuss today's and tomorrow's pressing issues, all while diminishing the voices of hate and those who incite violence. Educational institutions must also play a significant role in providing critical thinking and digital literacy skills not only to youth but also to adults, particularly those who have come online in information-scarce environments. In countries such as Myanmar, where more than 97% of the population moved online within a year and a half[15], gatekeeping and digital literacy are critical to ensure that the new power to communicate, receive, and share information does not lead to negative social outcomes including exclusion, persecution, and mob violence.

Gatekeeping functions are more difficult to conceive of, and implement, in a mature democratic society where the varied interests of constitutional rights, freedom of commerce, as well as the interests of political parties align around the new data economy. Getting the right balance of regulation, human rights, and incentives is important, and will mean rewriting the social contract for the digital era. Getting it wrong could mean, at best, an Orwellian turn that diminishes rather than increases basic rights and freedoms.

These are weighty questions, and ones with huge consequences, that place an inordinate burden on the decision makers of the present. While it is easy to be outraged by the excesses of terrorism and of marginal views gaining mainstream audiences, it is important to recognize that these are ultimately transient phenomena. The Internet and social media have brought immense socio-economic and political benefits not only in democratic contexts but in authoritarian ones as well. Any regulatory effort to curtail the spread of violent extremist, terrorist, and dangerous marginal views should ensure the appropriate protections for human rights and fundamental freedoms the world over, and to the furthest extent possible, while also ensuring that the Internet continues to be an engine for economic growth.

NOTES

1. 'Militant Group Says It Killed American Journalist in Syria', *The New York Times*, 19 August 2014.
2. 'Who Watches ISIS Beheading Videos in the U.S.? Men, Christians and The Fearful, Say Psychologists', *The Washington Post*, 19 March 2019.
3. Italian revolutionary Carlo Pisacane (1818–1857) wrote that deeds generated ideas. During the Paris Commune of 1871, French anarchist Paul Brousse (1844–1912) expanded upon this idea and called upon his countrymen to emulate their Italian counterparts by engaging in 'propaganda by the deed': political assassinations, bombings, riots, militant general strikes, and prison breakouts. These acts were meant to be defiant, to embarrass governments, and to expose the hypocrisy of political leaders and elite institutions. By doing so, it was believed that the general public would become aware of the weakness of their governments and the righteousness of the assailants' cause, bringing about substantial and lasting political change in favour of the revolutionaries. With this understanding, terrorist organizations have taken advantage of each new communications and, for that matter, transportation technology to spread their message even further. These technologies shrunk time and space, and made it easier to spread novel ideas of political transformation. Anarchists, active from the 1880s to the 1920s, benefitted from turn-of-the-century inventions such as the telegraph, daily newspapers, and railroads. Technological developments would come to benefit subsequent waves: Anti-Colonialist (1920s–1960s), New Left (1960s–1990s) and the Religious Wave (1979). These technological developments included the television, low-cost air travel, and, more recently, the Internet.
4. Violent extremist and terrorist actors are among some of the earliest adopters of the Internet. According to Gabriel Weimann, by 1998, about half of the 30 foreign terrorist organizations classified under the US Antiterrorism and Effective Death Penalty Act of 1996 maintained websites. By 2000, virtually all of them had an established presence on the Internet. Those espousing violent white supremacy have been just as willing to adopt new technologies to further their cause. Stormfront, one of the most prominent white supremacist websites was founded by Ku Klux Klan Grand Wizard and Nazi Party member Don Black in 1995. By the time Stormfront was temporarily taken offline in reaction to the Unite the Right rally in Charlottesville, Virginia, from 11 to 12 August 2017, it had garnered more than 300,000 registered users.
5. This targeted messaging process, or narrowcasting, aims messages at specific segments of the public defined by values, preferences, demographic attributes, or subscription. On Facebook, Russia's Internet Research Agency has achieved this through targeted clusters of advertisements which made it appear as if users were receiving advertisements from legitimate social movements. These advertisements would then entice individuals to join a group which espoused stereotypical political beliefs meant to closely align with their own closely held ideological beliefs. Upon entrance into the relevant Facebook group, individuals would be delivered content meant to amplify fault lines and erode trust in one's fellow citizens, government institutions and the democratic process. Such activities

by the IRA were ideologically agnostic, and groups created by this Kremlin propaganda machine before, during and after the 2016 election churned out divisive content related to race, gay rights, gun control and immigration.

6. A 'filterbubble' is a situation in which an Internet user encounters only information and opinions that conform to and reinforce their own beliefs, caused by algorithms that personalize an individual's online experience.

7. Caitlin O'Kane, 'Russian trolls fueled anti-vaccination debate in U.S. by spreading misinformation on Twitter, study finds': https://www.cbsnews.com/news/anti-vax-movement-russian-trolls-fueled-anti-vaccination-debate-in-us-by-spreading-misinformation-twitter-study/.

8. Centres for Disease Control and Prevention, 'Measles Cases in 2019': https://www.cdc.gov/measles/cases-outbreaks.html

9. Global Internet Forum to Counter Terrorism, 'About our Mission': https://gifct.org/about/.

10. Global Internet Forum to Counter Terrorism, 'About our Mission': https://gifct.org/about/.

11. G7 Interior Ministers, 'Outcome Document: Combating the Use of the Internet for Terrorist and Violent Extremist Purposes': https://www.elysee.fr/admin/upload/default/0001/04/287b5bb9a30155452ff7762a9131301284ff6417.pdf.

12. Twitter, 'Twitter Rules Enforcement': https://transparency.twitter.com/en/twitter-rules-enforcement.html

13. Facebook, 'Community Standards Enforcement Report': https://transparency.facebook.com/community-standards-enforcement#terrorist-propaganda

14. Zeynep Tufekci, 'YouTube, the Great Radicalizer': https://www.nytimes.com/2018/03/10/opinion/sunday/youtube-politics-radical.html

15. 'Internet Use Is on the Rise in Myanmar, but Better Options Are Needed', 22 September 2017: https://www.forbes.com/sites/chynes/2017/09/22/internet-use-is-on-the-rise-in-myanmar-but-better-options-are-needed/.

REFERENCES

Muggah, Robert, and Rafal Rohozinski (eds). 2016. *Open Empowerment: From Digital Protest to Cyber War*. Ottawa: SecDev Foundation.

Schmid, Alex. 2005. 'Terrorism as Psychological Warfare', *Democracy and Security*, 1 (2): 139.

SecDev Group. 2012. *Cyberspace 2.0 Socio Economic Drivers Of Cybersecurity*. Ottawa: Government of Canada.

Stern, Jessica, and J.M. Berger. 2015. *ISIS: The State of Terror*. New York: HarperCollins, p. 142.

Weimann, Gabriel. 2006. *Terror on the Internet: The New Arena, the New Challenges*. Washington, DC: Potomac Books Inc.: p. 16.

Weimann, Gabriel. 2015. *Terror in Cyberspace: The Next Generation*. New York: Colombia University Press: p. 18.

Dubois Elizabeth, and Grant Blank. 2018. 'The myth of the echo chamber': http://theconversation.com/the-myth-of-the-echo-chamber-92544.

CHAPTER 11

··

CYBERWEAPONS

··

SANDRO GAYCKEN

WHAT IS A CYBERWEAPON?

IN everyday experiences with low-end cybercrime, cyberattacks seem to have specific shapes—a trojan, a virus, a worm, a botnet, an implant, a side channel, or a denial of service attack. The terms suggest a certain materiality or constant features of cyberattacks, but this is true only in a limited way. What the terms rather describe are specific cuts and combinations of automized attack processes, or even only specific effects of attacks. These can be realized in many different ways and can have a large variety of consequences, intended or not. Any materiality or constant characteristic gets even harder to pin down when assessing high-end attacks, which are less automized than low-end attacks, and which try explicitly to avoid constant features or specific patterns.

Accordingly, it seems hard to define what a cyberweapon is. This poses a problem. It has implications on important issues such as the applicability of international humanitarian law or the conceptualization of cyber arms control. However, defining and describing cyberweapons is in fact not too difficult, once cyberattack cycles are dissected and analyzed. This chapter will explain this attack process, focusing on the specific, more relevant case of high-end cyberattacks, propose a clear-cut definition of cyberweapons, and explore some ideas for cyber arms control and functional cyber norms.

WHAT IS A CYBERATTACK?

Attacking a computer is basically programming a computer without the consent or knowledge of its users, administrators, or vendors, mostly against their interests, under a specific set of conditions and requirements, and with limited overall access. And, just like programming, attacking a computer is a process with different stages. There is a variety of classifications out there on how this process can be described but, by and large, five stages have to be mastered for a successful cyberattack.

First, the target system has to be understood. A reconnaissance process must explore the technologies at play: their configurations; their specific versions and states; their interconnections, hierarchies and dependencies, levels of protection and accessibility; their roles regarding functionality and safety; but also any technology vendors, suppliers, operators, administrators or developers, and their functions and relations. The more of the target is known and understood, the better. One aim of the reconnaissance process is to spot human and technical weaknesses, but the process also serves to create a complete set of specifications for the attack development process. If parts of the attack meet technical systems that they do not work on, those systems could do what computers frequently do when software tries to work in unknown environments: they crash. Any crash poses a risk for an attacker, because it causes administrators to search for the reason. And should the attack be discovered, the attacker loses initiative, momentum—in many cases, parts of their effort and knowhow—and alerts the defender.

Second, the target has to be accessed. Gaining access can use a) purely technical attacks—for instance, exploiting browser, hardware, enterprise resource planning software), or security vulnerabilities, b) social engineering as an attempt to remotely gain access through human users, administrators, or developers—for instance, by trying to trick an employee into leaking credentials or executing an attack, or c) human insiders, hired or blackmailed into cooperation, providing direct access. In many cases, specific combinations of different access methods are required. Attacks on high-value military targets with isolated high-security networks, for instance, usually require a combination of a human insider on administrator level (which is easy to get because this kind of personnel is still not considered highly critical and is not subject to strong clearance regulations) and a sophisticated, multi-stage technical attack, while avoiding automization, common patterns, or common social engineering techniques because these can be detected easily in such environments and would alarm the target. Depending on the difficulty of access, and the number and quality of the target's protective layers of, the access phase can require a set of different approaches and techniques, either coupled as a package and executed in a determined pattern, or injected sequentially.

Now the technical part of an access attack usually involves a first phase of programming (an exception being purely disruptive attacks, which can use more simple methods). Code has to be written in a specific way and injected in a specific vulnerable situation in order to infiltrate the target. This code, exploiting one of the many hundred thousands of vulnerabilities of a normal system, is commonly called an 'exploit'. What hackers mostly try to go for with their attack code can be described as 'recontextualization'. They use quite normal computational processes in the target system, but put them in a context that changes the impact of the process in a way that enables the hacker to enter the system and reprogram it more substantially. This pattern also applies in later stages of the hack. Whenever a new step of the attack is realized, the attacker has to use entirely normal system functions and computational orders, but tries to execute them in a context that changes the function of that specific part of the system in favour of the attacker—and best in ways and places least anticipated by the defender. In the more challenging cases, the attacker has to engage in a systematic development process, designing different elements of that context to make their attack work.

This recontextualization is a first challenge of any definition of a cyberweapon. It is simply impossible to define specific bits of code as weapons. The systemic context always has to be understood and considered alongside it. Recontextualization is also one of the many reasons why defence in cybersecurity is so incredibly difficult. What defence mostly tries to do is to find very common patterns of attempts to recontextualize a system. But, if confronted by a more knowledgeable adversary, who does not have to use well-known attack patterns, defensive technology usually cannot successfully guess the outcome. It cannot be given too much space to guess outcomes either. In a way, any normal operator of the system 'recontextualizes' the system too when working with it, so highly sensitive guessing tends to create too many false positives—an unsolvable structural dilemma of information technology (IT) security.

Another problem right here is Turing's halting problem. Turing posed the question whether a normal computer, running on a Turing language, would be able to predict all outcomes of possible combinations of algorithms and inputs that are theoretically possible, or, in other words, if there is an algorithm for all algorithms. The answer was the theoretical proof, deducted from the principles of the Turing machine, that this is not possible. A normal computer can always generate a surprising new outcome, a new context, and, if confronted with new combinations of algorithms or inputs, an infinite number of contexts is possible. For a hacker, this means that there are infinite options to create malicious contexts through an introduction of new algorithms and inputs, and that no security mechanism can ever be developed that detects and blocks each possible malicious recontextualization. And, in contrast to marketing promises from the IT-security industry, this is no vacuous, wacky assumption but a rock-solid theoretical principle, a condition for any standard computer. Two very important research streams in IT security are focusing on this problem and trying to build systems with better languages and limited contextuality—parts of high assurance computing and the langsec movement, a group of philosophers, logicians, and computer scientists who aim to craft a computer language with unique meanings for expressions and a finite number of contexts. Unfortunately, this research is little known, because it faces a lot of resistance from the IT industry, which has no interest in anybody designing entirely new systems to compete with their insecure old dinosaurs.

Third, having gained access to the system, the attacker has to gain a sufficient level of control over it. They have to be capable to move freely between different levels of access or subnetworks and subsystems of the system (frequently called 'lateral movement'), to monitor, administer, and manage the system with privileges sufficient to achieve all operational targets, and, in addition, to remain undetected and to stay as long as necessary or possible (called 'persistence'). These attempts are frequently working on different technological bases with different conditions—focusing, for instance, on lower system levels like the firmware or the operating system in order to gain high levels of access and full control over higher system layers, and to remain undetected. Accordingly, a new programming phase has to be started, including and introducing different bits of software into the target system to achieve the targets of this particular attack phase. Requirements also differ to some extent. To achieve persistence, elegant attack vectors and minimal attack code should be used, and a number of anti-security measures must be in place, including some thorough and fine-grained attacks on security and safety functionalities, because the attacker usually has an interest to keep them running smoothly but without causing problems for their attacks. Multiple heterogeneous entities should be established inside the system: in other words, many different access points and control mechanisms. If this can be achieved, the attacker will still be inside the system, even if one or two of their attacks are actually discovered.

These first three phases, 'recon', 'access', and 'control' usually thrive on an important feature of commercial software: vulnerabilities. Vulnerabilities are a specific fraction of programming errors or structural issues inside software, which enable an attacker to access and abuse that software into doing their bidding. Some of these vulnerabilities only enable limited access or functions, but roughly 30% of vulnerabilities (a surprisingly constant number across different types of software with little to no security quality assurance in programming) offer full access to the target, so called 'critical vulnerabilities'. However—and there are many misconceptions on this in the literature—vulnerabilities are not cyberattacks: they are an opportunity and sometimes a condition for a cyberattack, and will not be able to function as a cornerstone to identify cyberweapons.

The fourth phase of a cyberattack is the operative phase, the 'real deal' for the attacker. Once access and control are established, the attacker can go after their targets. They can start to search for desired data or processes in the system and conduct an operation on those targets. Any such cyberoperation can basically do four different things: it can monitor and exfiltrate data, it can manipulate or delete data, it can disrupt or delay processes, or it can deny access. This may not sound too intriguing but, because these different types of activities can be combined and applied in high granularity deep inside highly complex computational processes, any IT-based process can be observed, manipulated, hindered, disrupted, delayed, or denied in a myriad of different ways, most of which are not predictable. Good cybertacticians excel in combining different actions on highly granular variants of data and processes in order to achieve their operative goals in a highly stealthy and efficient manner. Hackers usually call this 'elegance'—to achieve an operational target with minimum effort and in novel and unpredictable ways.

In this phase of the attack, the attacker may again do some own coding and apply some self-designed software. Attackers mostly call this the 'payload', but this rather applies to automated attacks and the use of the term is not very coherent. Some hackers would also consider this an exploit or part of the overall exploit, even though no specific vulnerabilities have to be present at this stage. The coding would again follow the tactical pattern of elegant recontextualization. The attacker will use the existing software environment and standard functionalities of the system under control, and create a novel context to wreak havoc. To monitor, collect, and exfiltrate data, they will use standard data processing and communication techniques. To manipulate or sabotage a system, they only have to switch off safety functions or tinker with operative data. This is mostly not too hard, because most complex technologies come with a safety handbook, detailing all the things one should not do to that technology. An attacker can use this as a guide, only having to do some additional tuning and customizing to realize the most stealthy way to cause damage in precisely the way required. To disrupt or delay processes, the attacker can use a number of different standard functions and techniques, contradicting and blocking each other to cause a large variety of issues. The more complex an IT environment, the easier it is to cause such inconveniences, because most such systems have a natural tendency to be complicated and easily disturbed. The denial of access, too, can be caused by a number of standard measures and usually does not even require any specific software design process.

In many circumstances, attackers could consider it useful at this stage to build a whole attack system into the target system to ease their activities. In some sophisticated attacks, whole darknets had been built into target systems by attackers, with encrypted traffic, multiple manipulations of security features, and dedicated exfiltration points, in order to optimize access, control, and human insider efficiency.

The fifth and final phase of closing applies if the attacker wants to close the operation on the system. This may be desirable in some military contexts, for legal, tactical, or strategic purposes, but also in some criminal contexts. If a target is fully exploited, and there is nothing left to do, leaving traces or attack code behind is an unnecessary risk. If an operation is to be closed, the attacker may want to clean up the system by deleting all traces of their activities and all mechanisms that have been implemented.

This is the attack process. We can now describe important features of the development of a cyberattack in order to get a better idea of what cyberweapons are. In a proper attack development, just as in proper software development, the whole process is controlled, tested, and tuned before deployment, multiple times under varying conditions, as realistically as possible. Usually, this is even done with much higher scrutiny than ordinary software development quality assurance processes, in order to assure proper functionality and to minimize risks of premature discovery or malfunction. This testing is the most time-consuming process in attack development. But, even after deployment, some parts of the process may be iterative and have to be repeated in loops because conditions and opportunities may be different from anticipated, may have changed or, as certain complex effects turn up, create undesirable side effects or reduce the reliability of the attack. In a very unreliable and rather useless way, Turing's halting problem also works for the defender.

Another intrinsic part of the attack development process is the design of an attribution story. If the attacker wants to pin the attack on someone else, either to simply avoid attribution to themself or to escalate tensions in a certain direction by sailing under a false flag, pretending to be the favourite enemy of their victim or just someone they want to blame for the attack, they can craft every part of the attack to look as if it is coming from a specific actor. Unfortunately, this is not hard at all, and almost full control can be achieved regarding digital traces, despite promises to the contrary from the IT-security industry. The reasons will be explained in greater detail in the next paragraph.

Another important element in an attack is the level and locale of automizing. Not everything in the process has to be manual. Attackers have a lot of 'hacking tools' at their disposal to help them in reconnaissance or in the design of their bits of code for access and control. In addition to using these tools for reconnaissance and design, attackers may want to automize parts of the attack in the target. Any such automizing poses a risk, because the automized mechanism may interfere with something in an unprecedented fashion and be easier to detect but, in sufficiently granular cases, automizing can work well and save a lot of time and effort. A special case of automizing is a 'fire-and-forget' attack. In this case, the attacker cannot establish a reliable feedback channel to the target, or may not want to do so to avoid any risk of attribution, so they have to anticipate the whole attack process and automize every part of it. The attack is then being 'fired and forgotten', because the attacker cannot interact with it or control it anymore once it is in the target. An example is an isolated high-security network. In these cases, attackers cannot establish a standing feedback channel through a network connection, and most of the time not even indirect feedback channels through hops on and off laptops that are being carried in and out of the otherwise isolated target (this is also called a 'sneaker' attack). In such cases, attacks are frequently carried into the target network by an insider, who cannot risk interacting with the attack in the target, such that a sneaker attack has to function entirely automatically. Depending on the complexity of the target system and the complexity of the task the attack has to carry out, it can be very demanding and risky to carry out fire-and-forget attacks. The attack may not work and cause something entirely different to malfunction with unknown consequences, it may be detected and attributed, or, depending on the reliability of the isolation of the attack vector, it may escape and carry out its attacks in entirely different scenarios.

A famous example of such a failed containment is Stuxnet. Stuxnet was an act of sabotage, allegedly carried out by the United States in an operation called 'Olympic Games', aimed at a nuclear production site in Iran, which was rumoured to produce basic nuclear materials for the Iranian a-bomb. The attack hit the centrifuges of the facility, forcing them to accelerate quickly in between normal operation, so the delicate technologies would break and the enrichment of weaponizable uranium would not succeed. The attack had to be a fire-and-forget attack, because there was no direct access to the centrifuges. While effective, this feature turned into a problem because Stuxnet could not be contained successfully. It somehow escaped its original target and found many other facilities working on the same conditions, in turn executing its automized sabotage procedures and causing a lot of collateral damage. Much of it was an accident, but criminals also picked up the lost attack code and utilized it for their own malicious purposes. This accidental proliferation of high-value attack code into the criminal world happens very quickly whenever attacks become public. It also happened with the BlackEnergy code, an attack launched allegedly by Russia against a Ukrainian power plant, shutting it off for a short time to show off cyberpower. Only days after the attack was known publicly, criminals used it to attack trains and mining. This rapid proliferation of fire-and-forget attacks poses a very high risk for cybersecurity at large, because it puts very big cyberguns into the hands of just any kind of potential cyberattackers, while defenders frequently require weeks or months to develop workarounds or patches.

The case also demonstrates that dual use problems are a particular concern for cyberattacks. The underlying problem at this point is the fact that military units and the defence complex at large do not use specific military-off-the-shelf (MOTS) IT, but standard commercial-off-the-shelf (COTS) computers. MOTS systems once existed, but were too bulky and expensive. Therefore, weapon platforms, command and control environments, fighter jets, and a-bombs today are more or less run on the very same technologies that run hospitals, economies, and kindergartens. Accordingly, almost all attacks on military IT can work on critical civil IT as well.

DEFINING A CYBERWEAPON

Now, how can a description of a cyberweapon be derived? A weapon should be a thing with a potential to cause coercive effects through the threat of damage or harm in a rational and informed victim. When trying to apply this to an identification of cyberweapons, a few adjustments have to made.

A first demand is rather trivial: as could be seen, a cyberweapon is partially an immaterial and informational thing—the code used to attack—and partially a process. Accordingly, the term 'thing' in this definition should be adjusted to 'pieces of code or data and distinct informational processes'.

The next and less trivial problem is the recontextualization element of exploits. This element renders it hard to categorically identify an exploit code as an exploit code. There are no specific words or single lines of code that could be considered 'always malicious'. A few highly archetypical patterns of code and programming could be identified as 'mostly likely malicious' but, at any rate, the context has to be taken into account. In order to be recognized as a cyberweapon, a malicious recontextualization must have taken place or be highly likely through the code or the prepared attack process. In a first step, it suffices to say that the recontextualization must be illegitimate and enable sufficient malicious use or disruption of the target against the interest of its owner, supplier, or vendor. An important addition at this point should be that this interest must be rational and in security (not one of denial or marketing, which are common, security-degrading interests in the IT industry, often preferring to ignore problems rather than solve them).

Finally, another problem turns up. The vast majority of cyberattacks are either minor to medium nuisances, created by petty criminals or by activists, or they are intelligence collection and espionage of one sort or another. These cases, however, should explicitly not be considered attacks with a cyberweapon. If the definition of a cyberweapon would be set as wide to accommodate any kind of malicious cyberactivity, misinterpretations, false flag manoeuvres, and escalations would become very likely and pose an additional and very high risk, higher than the original risk in many cases. A cyberattack should only be considered an attack with a cyberweapon if it clearly has the potential to create a lot of damage or personal harm. So the context has to be somewhat enlarged from the technical, tactical level mentioned earlier to a strategic, political level.

At this point, a few notorious difficulties turn up. This kind of enlarged context requires additional external elements to be considered. Specifically, two come to mind: intent and effect. Intent would be a strong defining element of a cyberweapon. If it is known that the attacker has or had the intent to cause high damage or personal harm, the attack—whether successful or not—should be considered an attack with a cyberweapon.

Effect is a little less convincing. If an incident factually did cause a lot of damage or personal harm, it could be an attack with a cyberweapon, but it could also have been an accident. So a little bit of intent will have to be identified as well in order to define a cyberweapon—at least sufficient indicators to exclude an accident.

Now identifying intent is far from trivial in cyberattacks. It can only be determined if the attacker and their plans are known, or if the attack was unmistakably and necessarily aiming for damage or harm. Knowing the attacker and their plans is almost impossible because of the attribution problem in cybersecurity. The IT-security industry may pretend it has solved this issue, but it has not, and it cannot. The underlying systematic problem of any attribution is the simple fact that any digital evidence is digital, whether collected in local forensics from a victim or from the attacker through hackbacks. Anything digital is necessarily devoid of unique physical indicators and can always be crafted or forged in a fashion to make an analyst believe a certain attribution story. The only way to harden digital evidence is to create a hard cross-reference to physical evidence of some sort. Law enforcement can realize this in cybercrime cases by seizing a criminal's machines at their actual home, harbouring criminal data or executing criminal activities. Intelligence agencies can realize this as well, if they can utilize HUMINT (Human Intelligence, an insider) to get first-hand insights into an adversary's cyber capabilities or plans, enabling them to map an attack back to the attacker through previously unknown and sufficiently unique techniques or through specifically predicted actions. Any other evidence without hard cross-references, however, is essentially worthless and can always be contested. It may help analysts to gain an understanding by collecting more and more indicators, but it will never suffice to initiate legal or strong political countermeasures. And even gaining an understanding through indicators may be something an (entirely different) attacker may simply use to misguide them, to teach them what to look for, such that they look the wrong way in the future.

Another clear case of intent could be present if the code and the programming done can be clearly identified as belonging to one specific attack, and if their only purpose could have been sabotage or disruption of the target in order to create substantial damages or harm. This, again, is difficult. In many cases, only pieces of an attack can be found, while sufficient effects may not be visible (yet), and a forensic understanding of what the attack intended to do is hard to create. In most cases, an attack entailing access, monitoring, and exfiltration will only have been espionage, so will not be a case of an attack with a cyberweapon, but the very same techniques may also have been a reconnaissance process for an ensuing attack or already the first stages of an ongoing attack executed somewhere deep in the system or executed automatically if the reconnaissance part identifies a certain trigger. In other cases, a simple reconnaissance procedure by a petty criminal or a teenager may cause a critical system to crash and cause huge damages and harm. Industrial control systems and the programmable logic controllers (PLCs, tiny computers running smaller functions inside machines behind them), for instance, are often easily disturbed and a simple portscan, a minimally invasive standard procedure to find out which kind of Internet connectivity a computer has, can cause a denial of service condition and crash the system. Even safety-critical PLCs crashed in tests and did not recover upon reboot. So intent should definitely go into the definition of a cyberweapon, but it is something one should not hope for because attribution is difficult.

Accordingly, the definition of cyberweapons will have to be further refined by examining the context. To include context, a third criterion for the definition of a cyberweapon should be that a 'cyberweapon system' is being used. A weapon system, in military terms, is anything that directly and causally interacts with a weapon and enables it to be effective or more efficient. A sighting telescope attached to a gun is a good example. The gun is turned into a weapon system by it, consisting of the telescope and the gun in unison, as both together determine the effectiveness and efficiency of the weapon, and thus its potential and its character. This enlargement can now help to refine the definition of cyberweapons by including the attack context. First, it can be stated that any cyberweapon is always an attack system and must be understood as a system. Now, if one wants to find out whether the attack system was a weapon system or just an intelligence system, the systemic effects and functions can be taken into account. If the parts of the attack doing reconnaissance only collect intelligence on the target without any concrete or ad hoc use in an act of sabotage or disruption, the attack was an intelligence system. But if the reconnaissance part is functionally and in a unique way connected to an act of sabotage or disruption, it must be considered the sighting telescope of a cyberweapon system—a part of a weapon.

This can now be turned into a condition for what is a cyberweapon: to identify a cyberattack as an attack with a cyberweapon, all parts of the attack must be in a clear and unique functional and procedural connection to the part of the attack causing damage or harm.

A final question may concern the quality of the damage. Many cyberattacks can cause substantial immaterial harm, in some cases being even very hard to measure. A 'Black Friday' hack at a stock exchange could ruin a country, but the damage caused immediately is not in any way similar to the effects of any physical weapon, such as a missile. Information operations or single surgical hacking attacks such as BlackEnergy in Ukraine can influence politics in democratic countries or enrage or frighten citizens to cause coercion, chaos, damage, and harm but, again, cause and effect are different from real physical weapons. So should only material damages be accounted for or should immaterial damages also be a legitimate criterion to define cyberweapons? And should those immaterial damages be measurable and quantifiable or should that not be a requirement? Are they illegal intelligence activities or acts of war, falling under the law of armed conflict? These questions should be kept in mind as relevant, and will be discussed in the nearer future in great detail, but they cannot be answered from a definition of cyberweapons alone anyhow—apart from the fact that policy makers may prefer to answer them on a case-to-case basis and including other strategic concerns.

A definition of a cyberweapon could now be as follows: a cyberweapon system is a recontextualization of parts of an IT system against the interest of its owner, supplier, or vendor, realized through a subsystem of code or data and distinct informational processes, which contribute functionally and procedurally to an intentional creation of damage or harm.

IMPLICATIONS FOR ARMS CONTROL

It is of high importance to enforce an international regime of cyber arms control. Cyberwar is a game, which can be played by a lot of actors, from superpowers to small nations to larger rogue organizations. It enables most of these actors to cause terrible disruptions, escalations, and uncertainties, where only larger powers, embedded into rigid strategic traditions and professional strategic cultures and structures, can be more or less trusted to handle these new tools with sufficient care. Accordingly, the proliferation of cyberweapons poses a significant risk to international peace and stability, and must be strongly regulated. However, current approaches to regulate this proliferation are clearly insufficient and can only be considered a first stage in this process. At present, only a rather blunt and imprecise definition of 'intrusion software' is set[1] to describe cyberweapons to be controlled, referring to an undefined variety of hacking tools, and aiming rather at prohibiting the proliferation of surveillance tools to authoritarian states. This is certainly very important, but harnessing cyberweapons is, too. Also, the definition is not helpful once extended, because many of these intrusion tools are an indispensable part of security. Many tools qualifying for the definition are in regular use for testing and enhance defensive security significantly.

The definition of cyberweapon systems derived in this chapter, by contrast, seems to have the disadvantage that it is not very concrete. It may seem hard to identify particular products or companies to put under arms control. But this is not the case. In fact, a few very hard items and conditions can be derived from it.

First, parts of a cyberweapon system bearing a clear and unmistakable potential for the creation of harm or substantial damage, like exploits designed specifically to interfere with safety environments, are clear pieces destined for arms control. They should not be banned categorically, because such exploits do not have to be purely malicious—they are not 'always arms'. They can be highly important in a normal security context as well. Reported vulnerabilities should be patched according to an assessment of their criticality. However, vendors frequently prefer to patch the cheap and shameless vulnerabilities, and tend to lower the criticality of difficult and expensive vulnerabilities. An exploit can help at this point. It can demonstrate the criticality level of a vulnerability, thus leading to a proper vulnerability management process. Accordingly, such exploits should not be banned. However, they have to be disclosed responsibly in a legally organized process, and must be monitored and controlled by arms control mechanisms. With a little research effort, a mutually exclusive and collectively exhaustive list of relevant exploit characteristics could be derived and communicated. The concrete code does not have to, and could not, be included, but a set of possible offensive functions in a possible set of specified safety contexts can be formulated.

Second, parts of a cyberweapon system, which could be used to cause harm or substantial damage, but which could also be used for other purposes such as intelligence collection, should also be of concern for arms control, but need to be evaluated with greater care. This will apply to a lot of attacks and to many tools, in particular those that can be used for the development of exploits, such as metasploit, a famous toolbox for hackers, but harmless parts such as non-interfering vulnerability discovery tools could be excluded. In these cases, the specifications of the contexts in which the system could become a weapon have to be explicated and, if the system aims to be an intelligence system, explicitly avoided. This can be done either by strong local containment or by adding extra safety and reliability functionalities, any conditions being inherent technical conditions of the attack, without which it cannot execute. The contexts, conditions of strong local containment, and the safety functionalities can be derived and listed for the purpose of arms control. Many such parts will be tough to control, though, because they will be beyond direct legal access on the criminal hacker black market. But at least, if specific black market parts can be identified to bear a potential to become a weapon, these could be prosecuted under a different legal regime and with higher effort and different leverage.

Third, if a company or military unit specializes in the creation of cyberweapon systems— in other words, if the intent is clear and explicated—their cyberweapon systems can be controlled, considered, and verified for their potential impact and can use contexts designed directly for that actor.

Fourth, sets of capabilities can be identified in hacking companies or hacking units that bear the potential to create cyberweapon systems. In these cases, the capabilities could also be used to design intelligence systems only or, even better, to simply design security appliances, testing techniques, or secure systems. A rather large grey area unfolds at this point, which will have to be explored in detail to identify cases eligible to come under arms control. The case will be stronger if the capabilities include explicit abilities or tools to develop exploits. Then, high scrutiny should be applied.

These are some basic conceptual proposals that can be applied to cyber arms control. As mentioned earlier, they will require a compilation of specific lists of conditions that have to be met for specific contexts. In many cases, these will be multiple conditions that have to be present in unison. At any rate, compiling such lists should be undertaken with great care and high independent expertise, and with the joint expertise of offence and specialized system engineers of critical target systems, less of defence or—even worse—of policy scholars. Thus far, the latter have only confused the problem and delayed progress.

Another problem to be discussed here is the dual use issue in its specific shape in cyber regarding its implications for arms control. It has two dimensions to it. First, hacking tools or according capabilities are having an important effect for defensive and civil security, but can also be utilized to craft cyberattacks. These tools have to be assessed in detail for their specific potentials to wreak havoc, and cost–benefit calculations should assess whether they are beneficial or detrimental to security at large. If they should be put under arms control, a few options could be considered. Only the more powerful tools could be put under arms control regimes, demanding specific licences and procedures, while the less powerful tools or reduced variants of the powerful ones could be opened and recommended for everyone, or even made mandatory to use for companies, given good usability, to enhance their security. The more simple move to issue an outright ban of such tools or allow only the IT industry to use them internally will certainly have significant negative effects on security and will likely be little effective anyhow, because the ban would have to be global and capable of drying out the black market as well. Else, those tools will simply keep reappearing in exactly the places no one wants them to be. The other dimension of the dual use problem in cyber has already been mentioned. It is the widespread use of COTS-IT in military environments, which is also being used in critical civilian infrastructures. This fact would also have to be considered in cyber arms control, because such technologies should not be attacked or have to be contained with high reliability. Some ideas for that will be given later. But it could also be demanded (and would be a good move anyhow) that military units switch from COTS-IT to architecturally unique MOTS-IT in their more critical environments, so attacks on those cannot interfere with civilian critical infrastructures, if they escape their containment, and cause collateral damage. It could even be discussed whether military units under attack have complicity if a cyberattack aimed at them causes collateral damages in civilian IT structures because the target has used COTS-IT. The attacker could argue that they hid behind the equivalent of a human shield by using widespread, dual use, vulnerable technology, thus being in violation of international humanitarian law as described in rule 97 of the International Committee of the Red Cross. Interpreted this way, MOTS-IT could become a legal requirement for any kind of military IT, to solve the significant problem of cyber collateral damage from another angle.

Implications for Functional Cyber Norms

In addition to, and in support of, arms control, some conditions can be derived for the development of cyberweapons, which can feed into the ongoing process of cyber norms development. Cyberweapons should fulfil a number of conditions if they want to be 'clean' and responsible in the conduct of cyberwarfare, complying to the law of armed conflict and acknowledging the difficulties of offensive cyberoperations.

Counterproliferation

First, cyberweapons should include mechanisms in their design to prohibit leakage or proliferation into the black market or any recycling by adversary forces. This should be an inherent interest to any offence team anyhow, but it has not been an explicit part of the development process in offence on many occasions. A couple of measures can be recommended as best practice: anti-reverse engineering techniques and strong encryption should be included to make it harder to analyse the code. Beacons could be included, sending signals to the original author of a piece of code to identify stolen parts that are being recycled by other forces. Any part of an attack that is not in use should either be exfiltrated or delete itself immediately. Code could be designed to work only one time or only upon an additional trigger, so more factors are introduced in attack execution, making it harder for thieves to recycle the attack without knowing the trigger. In some bad cases of proliferation, teams and mechanisms should be ready for 'code rescue' missions, trying to recover the code and eliminate all traces of it or spread non-functioning variants to decrease trust in its use.

Containment

Second, cyberweapons should include strong mechanisms for containment. An attack should not be able to escape its target and wreak havoc on other structures. This applies in particular to highly automized attacks. Strong localization is a very good measure to achieve containment. Strong localization would be realized through a set of technical functions inside the attack, which are necessary for the attack to execute, as well as a trigger that executes the cyberweapons only if specific sets of local conditions are present at the target. Such local conditions could be specific places and times, unique configuration settings, version numbers, hardware serial numbers, unique technical addresses, operator names, and passwords. If five or six such conditions are sufficiently unique and defined as trigger in unison, high certainty can be achieved that the attack only executes in the target and nowhere else.

Authentication

Third, cyberweapons could be signed by their developers so they can be authenticated in use if, for instance, they are applied in a purely and clear-cut military scenario where bits and bytes should wear a uniform. Any such signatures should be one-time only, or set to expire after the operation and crafted in a way that they cannot be spoofed. Bookkeeping methods can be used for this, creating exact lists of activities, applying blockchain technology, so the bookkeeping cannot be spoofed. Or, as Dave Aitel from Immunity once recommended, watermarking with cryptographic hashes could be used, creating unique labels for attacks, which again are very hard to spoof. In addition, any obfuscation or false flag activities should be forbidden, especially anything involving the criminal black market, to avoid misinterpretations and proliferation. Copycats or false flag attacks could be identified more easily this way: a concern that will be quite high in the coming years.

Operative Care

Fourth, more generally, operative care must be exercised to avoid collateral damage. Intelligence units simply doing reconnaissance or collection must exercise great care when entering systems with a potential for harm or substantial damages, such as weapon systems, stock exchanges, or critical infrastructures. Each step of their process must be checked against lists of known interactions in the given context, and potentially difficult or hard-to-predict steps should be avoided. If they are not, the intelligence system may turn into a weapon system without their actor's intention and cause significant trouble, both for the victim and for the attacker. The safety of reconnaissance and collection should be researched and documented in great detail to distinguish safe techniques from dangerous ones and to prove operative care to decision makers before operations or in cases of unfortunate incidents. This also applies to the development of cyberweapons. Any phase, including the attack itself, must be checked and tested for unintended interactions and catastrophic failure. An internationally acknowledged testing methodology could be developed to warrant a high level of quality, thus leading to a low level of collateral damage. Recovery and mitigation strategies should be designed alongside more controversial parts of an attack, to enable the attacker to abort the attack and return the target into a fail-safe state if things should get out of hand. Safety technologies in widespread use in critical civilian infrastructures must be mapped and their specifications must be known to exercise operative care.

Accident Communication

Fifth, cyber intelligence systems causing harm or substantial damage accidentally should be communicated as such immediately to avoid escalations and to help mitigate harm. Because of the sensitive nature of any such incident, the communication should, if possible be anonymous and directed at the United Nations or appropriate technical agencies such as ENISA or IAEA. False flag activities could also be reported in such a way, if detected successfully.

Avoidance of High-Criticality Targets

Targets with very high criticality, such as nuclear warfare command and control environments, should not be attacked at all. All the more essential technologies of such environments must be consolidated on a top secret and internationally acknowledged black-list of specifications for which no attack shall ever be built. Military units will have to decide whether they want to let others know which components they built into this environment. At least some common, dual use components could be communicated, as long as they are unavoidable, and the list need only include general technical specifications, not concrete locations, configurations, set-ups etc. This demand is of highest importance, given various announcements of states such as South Korea, which want to establish such capabilities,[2] and given the aforementioned problems of offence to properly predict and contain fire-and-forget attacks. Because attacks on nuclear command and control would have to be fire-and-forget and these attacks are also highly unreliable, they must be banned! Previous attempts at this have been unsuccessful, because they were lacking a clear language and a specification of sets of conditions that can qualify as nuclear and only nuclear, but the international nuclear security community must undertake this effort now.

CONCLUSION

As can be seen, it is possible to define cyberweapons and to propose some steps to achieve cyber arms control and functional cyber norms. Two problems remain. First, many attacks will be in a somewhat gray area, difficult to interpret and to define. This is simply due to the structure of the battlefield and the conditions for offence and cannot be resolved any further. Second, if definitions and norms are to be effective, the attacker must play along. Much of what happens in cybersecurity, however, is executed either by criminals or by secret services, who simply don't play by the rules because they don't have to. In light of these caveats, we may be able to define cyberweapons, but it will only spare us a certain fraction of the overall trouble in global strategic cybersecurity.

Nonetheless, the derived definition and the proposals regarding arms control and cyber norms can be of help. They can help to clarify matters that are still very blurry right now, to create a common language for agreements, to formulate details for any actual implementation of arms control concepts or norms, to delineate research gaps to be filled for more complete definitions, to find alternative solutions to associated problems such as the humanitarian requirement to move from COTS-IT to MOTS-IT to avoid complicity in collateral damage, and they can help to determine some important red lines in strategic cyberwarfare, which may have a beneficial impact on rogue forces and sharpen control over them.

NOTES

1. Intrusion software is defined as 'software' specially designed or modified to avoid detection by 'monitoring tools', or to defeat 'protective countermeasures', of a computer or network capable device, and performing either or both of the following:
   a) The extraction of data or information, from a computer or network capable device, or the modification of system or user data.
   b) The modification of the standard execution path of a program or process in order to allow the execution of externally provided instructions. Source:http://cyberlaw. stanford.edu/publications/changes-export-control-arrangement-apply-computer-exploits-and-more
2. See http://thediplomat.com/2014/02/s-korea-seeks-cyber-weapons-to-target-north-koreas-nukes/

CHAPTER 12

INTENTIONS AND CYBERTERRORISM

FLORIAN J. EGLOFF

INTRODUCTION

THE missile came out of nowhere. Events had finally caught up with him. Junaid Hussain had been working out of an Internet café in Raqqa, Syria. Propaganda and outreach, recruitment and radicalization over the Internet were his specialties. He also possessed hacking skills from his days in the hacktivist collective, TeaMpoisoN. In recent months, he had had several successes. He had managed to encourage a shooting in Garland, Texas, and was in contact with a potential assailant in Ohio. He had also been working on recruiting Ardit Ferizi, a long-time member of the Kosova Hacker's Security collective.

In turn, Ardit now seemed convinced of Islamic State in Iraq and the Levant's (ISIL) cause. He had first provided support to their propaganda by administering an ISIL video webpage. He had then moved on to providing a hacked database with US service members' personally identifiable information (PII). In his conversations with Junaid, he had emphasized using the information to hit their enemy strongly.[1] Junaid had promised to do so, and ISIL had later released the PII of circa 1,300 military and government personnel as a 'kill list'.[2]

Junaid had tried to convince Ardit to join him in Syria, but Ardit was less convinced of the cause than Junaid had thought. Ardit had been studying at University in Malaysia, trying to make some money by extorting the companies he had been hacking. He had been involved in political website defacement, a relatively widespread practice for voicing political messages on the Internet. His operational security was lax. His relationship with ISIL had suddenly brought him into the purview of the US security apparatus and he was not ready for it. A month after Junaid had been killed in a drone strike, Ardit was arrested and later extradited to the United States. He was charged with a combination of hacking and material support for terrorism, the first such combination in the United States. He was sentenced to 20 years in prison.

Junaid and Ardit could easily be depicted as cyberterrorists. After all, they engaged in hacking for a terrorist organization. This chapter will lay out why that depiction is not appropriate. It will proceed in several steps. First, it will set up a definition of cyberterrorism, which will limit the universe of cases and explain why Junaid and Ardit's actions are not classified as cyberterroristic acts. Second, the chapter will introduce the claims made by intelligence officials about terrorists' intentions when using cyberspace. It then interrogates to what extent this matches the literature on terrorist motivations and intentions, and whether cyberspace is an attractive means for carrying out terrorist attacks. Finding that a cost–benefit analysis does not favour cyberspace as a means of carrying out terrorist acts, the chapter asks two questions:

> Q1: What would have to happen for the current generation of terrorists to view cyber attacks as an attractive strategy of terror?
> Q2: What could motivate people with more advanced cyber capabilities to choose a strategy of terror to engage in the political process?

The chapter closes with the analysis of a hypothetical case that would match the definition of cyberterror: a religiously inspired version of the Ashley Madison hack.

Definition of Cyberterrorism

Terrorism is a subcategory of political violence. Within terrorism, cyberterrorism is a special case (see Figure 12.1). Hence, to define acts of cyberterrorism, it is pertinent to start with the debate in terrorism studies on how to define their subject of study. This definitional debate is contentious and it seems unlikely that it will soon come to a conclusion.

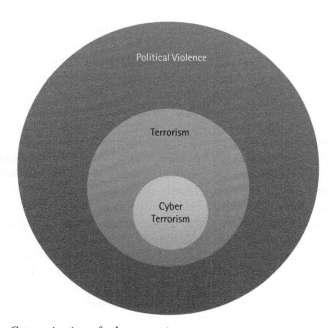

FIGURE 12.1. Categorization of cyber terrorism

Nevertheless, the debate does have important and useful features such as Richard English's definition:

> Terrorism involves heterogeneous violence used or threatened with a political aim; it can involve a variety of acts, of targets, and of actors; it possesses an important psychological dimension, producing terror or fear among a directly threatened group and also a wider implied audience in the hope of maximizing political communication and achievement; it embodies the exerting and implementing of power, and the attempted redressing of power-relations; it represents a subspecies of warfare, and as such it can form part of a wider campaigns of violent and nonviolent attempts at political leverage (English 2009, 24).

This definition highlights a few key elements of terror that are important for this chapter:

- Violence or the threat thereof.
- Political aim.
- Intent to produce terror (i.e. fear) in and beyond the target (psychological dimension).
- Multiple audiences (signal achievement and political messaging).
- Exert power.
- Subspecies of warfare and part of a wider political struggle.

The late Charles Tilly further clarified that terrorism is a strategy employed by a diverse set of actors to achieve a diverse set of agendas:

> It is one-sided, often pitting either relatively powerless people against very powerful enemies, or vice versa: powerful people, especially armies or governments, against the powerless. It deploys violence and threats of violence in the narrow sense of immediate damage to persons or objects rather than, say, shame or eternal damnation (Tilly 2005, 26).

Importantly, Tilly highlighted that terrorism is primarily a strategy, rather than simply an act, an event, or a grievance. Defining this strategy allows for the categorization of a set of practices as acts of terrorism. The categorization can entail a whole range of practices including assassination, abduction, hijacking, sabotage, mass destruction, and discriminate and indiscriminate mass casualty attacks (Drake 1998, 5). The labelling of the actor that engages in the strategy of terrorism as terrorist is, however, much more controversial, because the actor may engage in many other forms of political practices, besides using a strategy of terrorism. Hence, just because someone belongs to a terrorist organization does not mean that all their actions should be classified as terroristic acts. Furthermore, a strategy of terrorism can be used by any actor (also by states) against any target. The constitutive element of terrorism is its 'primary purpose of generating a wider psychological impact beyond the immediate victims or object of attack for a political motive' (Richards 2014, 230).

So, what is cyberterrorism?[3] In the narrow sense, one can capture the phenomenon best when restricted to those actions where 'cyberspace becomes the means of conducting the terrorist act. Rather than committing acts of violence against persons or physical property, the cyberterrorist commits acts of destruction and disruption against digital property' (Denning 2007, 124). Excluded from this definition are physical attacks against cyber infrastructure: only digital attacks count. Arguably, threats of physical violence issued through cyberspace that would not be actualized through cyberspace are also excluded. Furthermore, '[t]o fall in the domain of cyberterror, a cyber attack should be sufficiently destructive or disruptive to generate fear comparable to that from physical acts of terrorism.' (Denning 2007, 125)

Equipped with these definitions, an ensuing critical question is whether disruption or destruction of digital property can ever be 'sufficiently destructive or disruptive' to generate a level of fear comparable to a conventional terrorist attack. Uncontroversially, analysts have found that the disruption of critical infrastructures does qualify, because it is possible to imagine attacks against these infrastructures with horrific consequences. However, 9/11 has left many analysts with a skewed picture of terrorism. Many terrorist attacks are operating on a much smaller scale, and are carried out as part of wider violent and non-violent political campaigns. Hence, we should not restrict our definition of cyberterrorism to only large disruptive events. Smaller disruptions or destruction could also qualify as cyberterrorist attacks if they can generate terror in the psychological sense.

One might object to the inclusion of acts where no physical violence occurs. After all, many strategies of terror include horrific acts of violence. Hence, to dilute the category by including non-physical actions might stretch the concept too far. However, this is less of a difficulty than might be supposed. Rather, to capture the potential novelties of cyberterrorist acts, this chapter adopts a conception of violence that also includes psychological harm (Krause 2009; Krause 2016).[4] Hence, neither the violation nor the threat of the violation need be targeted against a body. It does not even have to have a physically destructive impact. Rather, a logical destruction (deletion of data) or disruption (e.g. by alteration of data) can still qualify as violent acts. This point is crucial, because it includes phenomena such as the mass deletion of a threatened group's digital data (and therefore digital identity) as a possible form of cyberterrorism. The lower threshold for the psychological harm could be for the harm (e.g. trauma) to have made a significant measurable impact.

The definitions give a first indication as to the intentions that might drive a strategy of terror. Acts of terror are symbolic actions. Terrorism scholar Mark Juergensmeyer (2003, 124) calls them 'performance violence'.[5] The act itself has performative social functions. Therefore, in order for a terror act to be successful, it has to be recognizable by the audiences as an act of terror. The audiences include both the targets of the political violence and third parties, as well as potential supporters of the political project pursued.

Now let us go back to Junaid and Ardit and consider their kill lists. As a result of their actions, the PII of circa 1,300 people were released as a 'kill list'.[6] Such lists, including the details of Americans to be targeted, have since become a recurring phenomenon. However, to date, no case is known to the author of someone being physically attacked because of being on such a list. The US government alleges that 'the harm to those government employees and officers [on the list] was real. Those targeted individuals must live in a perpetual state of fear that they may be attacked'.[7] This is a case where hacking led to the exposure of the personal information of US citizens, who were then threatened with physical violence and suffered psychological harm. Is this cyberterrorism?

Some might argue that they can be classified as acts of cyberterrorism, due to the provenance of the data; the data were acquired through hacking. This is too short-sighted: one does not usually classify terrorist events based on where the targeting information is from. Others might argue that the means of delivery of the threat matters: ISIS published the threats in cyberspace. Again, this fails to acknowledge that one would not usually classify terrorists, who air their threats on TV, as TV-terrorists. Rather, it is the type of violence that is threatened that informs classification. Is the harm to be induced by cyber means? One has to differentiate between the harm caused by the threat, and the harm that is threatened. If the intent is just to induce harm by threatening (rather than carrying out violent attacks against people), then one could classify the publication of people's data on kill lists as cyberterror. However, it is analytically more coherent to follow a restrictive definition of cyberterrorism by only including harm that is (or is threatened to be) induced by cyber means (e.g. the threat of publicizing PII versus the threat of being physically targeted because of such a publication).

To summarize, the definition of cyberterrorism requires the intended effect to generate fear (terror) beyond the immediate target through the cyberterrorist act itself and to be performed in pursuit of a greater political project. This definition captures a narrow category of potential intentional acts in cyberspace but adopts a wide definition of violence. As a result, the definition captures a genuinely new, possibly less ostentatious, form of terrorism, while excluding other cyber operations that are either not intended to generate fear for political purposes, or not capable of doing so.

Having delineated the concept of cyberterrorism, and concluded that Junaid and Ardit do not, under this concept, qualify as cyberterrorists, this chapter now interrogates terrorists' intentions in using cyberspace.

Intentions of Terrorists

This section introduces the claims of intelligence community officials about the use of cyberspace by terrorists. It then details the academic research on terrorist intent and asks why terrorists would use cyberspace as a means for actualizing terrorist intent.

Intelligence assessments on the use of cyberspace by terrorists

The US, UK, and Australian intelligence assessments point to the sophisticated use of the Internet for propaganda, recruitment, and operational planning. From the US worldwide threat assessment, one learns that terrorist groups have low cyber capabilities. It points to the risk that low-level cyber attacks may garner media attention, which may exaggerate their capabilities (Clapper 2015, 5). The UK assessment acknowledges that ISIL does not have the capability to attack UK infrastructures through cyber attacks (Martin 2016),[8] but claims 'we know they want it, and are doing their best to build it' (Osborne 2015). The Australian assessment is the most specific in that it assesses no 'significant disruptive or destructive effect for at least the next two to three years' (Australian Cyber Security Centre 2016, 9). Hence, there is a mix of assessments, with some agencies purporting intent but not capability, while others simply point to the continuing low capabilities of terrorists. It remains unclear to what extent the assessment of intent was based on a terrorist group having made material investments and acted upon that intent.

Tilly (2004) cautioned against including intentions as part of the definition of terrorism because 'solid evidence on motivations and intentions rarely becomes available for collective violence'. However, absence of solid evidence is not sufficient a reason for excluding what much of the literature on terrorism has identified as key elements defining terrorist strategies. For example, in a reflection on the study of terrorism, Richard English (2016) lists the goals behind terrorist violence as:

> the undermining of opponents; the setting of a political agenda in pursuit of the redress of grievances; the provocation of an over-reaction from an enemy; the coercion of a population; the gaining of otherwise unobtainable publicity for a cause; the building of support and the sustaining of resistance; the out-manoeuvring of rivals; the securing of revenge upon enemies; and the obtaining of renown or fame or other psychologically rewarding goods (p. 5).

Based on extensive reviews of first-hand accounts of terrorists, Louise Richardson (2006, 75) differentiated between short-term organizational and long-term political objectives. The long-term objectives of the terrorist groups she tracks (note: for Richardson, only substate groups count) include territorial gain (e.g. independence and secession by ethno-nationalists), overthrow of capitalism (social revolutionaries), remaking society (Maoists), or replacing secular law with religious law (fundamentalist groups). She also acknowledges that there are hybrids (e.g. Hamas, Hezbollah). As short-term objectives, she identified exacting revenge (TWA 847, Oklahoma City), generating publicity (9/11), achieving specific concessions (e.g. release of comrades), causing disorder (and thereby undermining the legitimacy of the state), or provoking repression (and hoping for retaliation) (Richardson 2006, 78).[9] She points to organizational dynamics as a possible determinant of action—for example, the show of strength against another group. She collates the reasons for engaging in a strategy of terror that recurred across the observed terrorist groups in three categories: revenge, renown, and reaction (Richardson 2006, 88–103).

Are the Identified Intentions Better Pursued in a Cyber Attack or in a Physical Attack?

Long-term goals do not seem to predetermine the exact means chosen to deliver terrorist violence. Rather, short-term objectives seem much more influential on operational decisions.[10] One starting point for understanding terrorist strategists is to do a cost–benefit analysis comparing cyber attacks with physical attacks. Maura Conway's (2014) research addressed this trade-off, using vehicle-borne improvised explosive devices (VBIEDs) as comparators.[11] Reflecting on whether the possibility of a cyberterrorist attack would also be a likely outcome, she raised four factors of interest: cost, complexity, destructive potential, and theatricality. First, Conway argued that the cost of cyber attacks is higher than traditional attacks: VBIED attacks are cheap. In comparison, the cost of a cyber attack is hard to estimate. To start with, there is a question of what level of destruction or disruption would be equivalent. For an impact similar to that of a car- or truck-bomb device, it would be necessary to take control of a critical system or infrastructure and surmount any safety-critical controls built into it, a step that would require precise knowledge of a cyber-physical system.

Giacomello (2004) looked at potential attacks on a hydroelectric dam or an air traffic control system, and priced them between $1.3 million and $3.0 million in 2004. An assumption in this calculation was that terrorists would be outsourcing the attack (i.e. paying people competitive salaries). Conway (2003) made a strong argument against such a hypothetical, however: the operational security risks of recruiting unknown people on the Internet, the small market of hackers willing to engage in killing operations, the high risk of double agents motivated by financial reward, and the lack of evaluative capability by the terrorists all make this scenario less likely. Hence, if an actor wanting to engage in terror is able to attract the necessary expertise, it is likely that cost is not the decisive factor against using cyber attacks.

Second, operational complexity also poses a significant challenge to terrorists. VBIEDs and small arms are tried and tested. They are simple and reliable to deliver. Supply chains, while partially monitored by law enforcement, are accessible not least because of the dual-use nature of many of the materials needed. Training can be delivered easily and quickly. Target reconnaissance is assisted by modern technology and the affordability of travelling. Many countermeasures can be identified without revealing the terrorists' intention. Finally, destructive impact is almost guaranteed and can be assured by having a variety of means of delivering impact (guns, explosives, etc.).

In comparison, the ability to attract or generate the talent with the necessary capabilities to plan and execute a cyber-physical attack has not yet been demonstrated by a non-state actor. Even if people with the knowledge and skills to attack cyber-physical systems were recruited, the organization would need to engage in in-depth target intelligence, with the risk of compromising the operation before it started. Ideally, the threat actor would have to rebuild the target environment to develop and test the attack capability, a feature that implies access to both the target and sensitive supply chains. Hence, for an organization that has traditional attacks as their current modus operandi, switching to high-impact cyber-physical attacks might well be too costly and too risky. However, the same cannot be said about using hacking for propaganda purposes, or as an enabler for traditional attacks. The US intelligence community assessed that terrorist groups continue to experiment with hacking, but the techniques used so far are based on low technical capabilities (Clapper 2015).

Third, destruction is easier to achieve with non-cyber attacks, but the impact achieved through a cyber-physical attack could be more severe. Direct destruction caused by VBIEDs, both in human lives and to property is limited by the place of the blast and the radius of the specific delivery mechanism. Indirect destruction, in terms of economic and social impact, depends on the specific target chosen. For cases of cyber-physical attacks, some estimates exist. Giacomello (2004) used an estimate of the impact of a power interruption in billions of dollars. Overall, it is possible to imagine scenarios where the destructive impact of targeting the critical infrastructure of a highly network-dependent society could outweigh a traditional terrorist attack. Hence, in terms of potential severity, cyber attacks may prove to be of interest to terrorist groups.

Fourth, the theatricality or the media impact factor of a conventional terrorist attack largely outweighs the cyber attack scenarios. This goes back to the definition of acts of terrorism as performative acts. Terrorist violence is a form of symbolic violence. It carries a message that needs to be understood by its audience. The current generation of terrorists has defined what a terrorist act looks like in the public imagination. The acts themselves are high-impact media events that cannot be ignored by their respective audiences. Looking at what are claimed to be acts of cyberterror by the media today, there seems to be much hype and little terror (i.e. fear). Conway argued that, even if there were larger-impact events, it is unclear that the public would recognize them as such. Missing are the spectacular live media coverages of power outages (Conway 2014, 11). Finally, going back to Richardson's 'renown' and 'reaction' motivations of terrorists, there is the risk that a cyber-terrorist event would be misconstrued as an accident (Conway 2012, 297). This is a serious risk to terrorists, who want to force a message onto their audiences. Terrorists would have to figure out how to credibly claim responsibility for the attack. How could terrorists prevent victims from construing a cyber attack as part of a state–state conflict, rather than a terrorist act?

The four factors combine to offer reasons for an actor pursuing a terrorist strategy not to opt for using cyberspace as a medium of attack. They offer one explanation for the absence of a significant cyberterrorist attack. However, counterarguments exist. Juergensmeyer (2014), for example, argues that:

> [s]trategy implies a degree of calculation and expectation of accomplishing a clear objective that does not jibe with such dramatic displays of power as the destruction of the World Trade Center towers. These creations of terror are not done to achieve a strategic goal but to make a symbolic statement (p. 131).

Some of the religious terrorists he observed were interested in performance violence with performative effects (i.e. changing the perceptions of the audience through the act). Hence, the cost–benefit logic, the immediate death count, and the direct impact may be less important than the message sent through the selected target and its media impact. Different actors using terrorist strategies vary in their ideology, degree of strategic planning, and target selection (Drake 1998, 45). Interestingly, Juergensmeyer also points to attacks without the attackers taking credit (e.g. 9/11), where the attack itself is sending a strong enough message (e.g. identifies the government as a target). Hence, despite the reasons offered in the cost–benefit analysis against the choice of cyberspace as a means of terror, there may still be people who do see a symbolic value in using it and are actively working on exploiting it.

Thus, it is worth asking about vectors of change that could influence the adoption of cyberspace as a means of terror. Two questions are pertinent. First: 'What would have to happen for the current generation of terrorists to view cyber attacks as an attractive strategy of terror?' The answer to this question will identify patterns of change that could alter the assessment of intent. Having assessed this, the article then poses a second question: 'What would motivate people with more advanced cyber capabilities to choose a strategy of terror to engage in the political process?' The answer to the second question ties in with the first one. It focuses on the issue of cyberterrorism requiring relatively rare human skillsets. As such, focusing on the possibility of new forms of terror emerging from people with that specific skillset is another way of gauging future sources of cyberterror. Both analyses would make it possible to model indicators that could be used for a continuous threat assessment.[12]

Q1: What Would Have to Happen for the Current Generation of Terrorists to View Cyber Attacks as an Attractive Strategy of Terror?

First, the parameters of theatricality could change. It is possible that terrorists would value highly the potential propaganda benefit of carrying out even a moderately difficult cyber attack.[13] Having become used to seeing conventional terrorist attacks on television, it is possible that a new form of terrorism would, at least temporarily, induce more fear. The first high-impact cyberterrorist event may be rewarded with a very loud media echo.

Second, as societies become ever more dependent on networks, the potential for disruption is increasing—for example, by attacking society's trust in the Internet (Valeri and Knights 2000). The cheap availability of bandwidth and networked devices leads to a deeper penetration of people's lives by technology (e.g. the Internet of Things). This enlarges the breadth and depth of the attack surface and creates novel opportunities for causing harm. It also increases the ability to have meaningful impact beyond attacking large infrastructure. While cyber-physical attacks used to be confined to attacks on industrial control systems, they are moving closer to having an effect even at the level of the consumer. Consequently, the ability to instil fear by exploiting a seemingly intimate environment at scale (e.g. private homes) is growing. Terrorist organizations adopting new strategies may take lessons from the criminal space, where sextortion is a growing category of crime.[14]

Third, research on terrorist innovation has identified four triggers that make a terrorist organization more likely to adopt new technological measures:

a) The 'presence of an inherent ideological predetermination toward using modern technologies or the need to innovate in order to obtain the capability to match the level of violence associated with the respective ideological and strategic preferences' (Dolnik 2007, 173). For example, Aum Shinrikyo had a technology-enabling ideology with a specific focus on scientifically self-produced weapons (e.g. chemical or biological weapons). Today, the high-tech equivalent of a technology-enabling ideology could be political movements inspired by the techno-anarchist ideology. Should a technically capable political terrorist group emerge, this could cause concern, especially because new terrorist organizations may be able to operate under the radar of the security agencies for some time.

b) The 'emergence of competition with other organizations operating in the same operational theatre' could trigger innovation (Dolnik 2007, 174). Competing organizations with strong ideological overlap could have a leadership clash, which could raise the likelihood for one organization to use innovation as a source of advantage. An example of this would be the competition 'among the Taliban, ISIL's branch in South Asia, and al-Qa'ida' (Rasmussen 2016). Similarly, the shrinking of the territory of Islamic State could put pressure on the different jihadi groups operating in Syria. As foreign fighters return or move elsewhere, competition for leadership of the jihadi movement could generate pressures for innovation. This could mean that some splinter group of the jihadi movement will specialize in cyber attacks.

c) The 'presence of government countermeasures' could force terrorists to innovate (Dolnik 2007, 174–175). This could be the case for a terrorist organization operating locally under closely surveyed territory. Given the strong government countermeasures against ISIL, they are cycling through different technological solutions for operational planning. However, due to the openness of liberal societies, the means of carrying out physical attacks are not denied by government countermeasures, and are not likely to be.

d) The 'incidental or unintended acquisition of a particular human or material resource' could trigger new technological adoption (Dolnik 2007, 175). This could be the case of a hacker joining an existing terrorist organization, which, if its ideology allows it, might try to profit from the new capabilities gained. Junaid Hussain joining ISIL is a case in point. However, with the jihadist ideology focusing on martyrdom, being a hacker seems less attractive. In addition, adopting an innovative approach is risky: people choosing a strategy of terror may seriously misjudge their capabilities (Drake 1998, 178). For example, someone trying to attack a critical infrastructure might at the same time identify themselves as a target to intelligence agencies.

Finally, while demographic change will raise the general technical literacy of terrorist groups, performing cyber attacks is not a generalist skillset. In order to have the skillset necessary, and short of a democratization of advanced attack tools, terrorist groups would have to make a concerted recruitment or investment effort. Why such specialists would support a strategy of terror is the focus of the next section.

Q2: What Would Motivate People with More Advanced Cyber Capabilities to Choose a Strategy of Terror to Engage in the Political Process?

Having identified the drivers of change that would contribute to a currently existing terrorist organization adopting cyberspace as their means of attack, this section explores the integration of people with potentially offensive skillsets into the political process. Some hacking collectives have a history of engaging in the political process through hacking. However, in order to delineate terrorism, the question is to what extent such practices have become part of the normal political process. For example, the disruption of the Church of Scientology by various hacking collectives in 2008 (Operation Chanology) could be viewed as legitimate political involvement by a protest movement. The boundaries of legitimacy of hacking as a political tool are still fluid, however. How likely is it that people with offensive cyber skillsets might choose a strategy of terror? What factors would contribute to such a process?

One potential source of hacking as a means of terror could be states using strategies of terror against specific subgroups of their population. They may use offensive cyber capabilities to terrorize political dissidents, for example. So far, some states have opted to combine cyber espionage with physical retribution (intimidation, detention, interrogation, incarceration), the digital practices of which are well documented by Citizenlab's research.[15] However, in the future, it is possible to imagine states using offensive capabilities as a means of terror—for example, by wiping out a minority group's digital imagery.

Individuals with offensive cyber skillsets are exposed to the same paths of radicalization as everyone else.[16] The presence of an ideological predetermination was mentioned earlier as an enabling factor for engaging in technologically demanding practices of terrorism. Such enabling ideologies are currently present in the techno-anarchist underground. Should offshoots of these groups radicalize and opt for a militant political strategy, they could pose a serious cyber threat to their opponents. For example, hacks against GammaGroup and HackingTeam, two companies that sell surveillance equipment and services to various governments including repressive regimes, were claimed to be performed by a hacker (or group of hackers) with the moniker Phineas Fisher. The hacker(s) claimed to be acting to rectify injustices committed by the customers of the two companies. Phineas Fisher further offered various revolutionary anti-capitalist and anti-statist ideas as the motivation for engaging in hacking governmental targets. These arguments resonate with the history of techno-anarchism in parts of the hacker community. One of their ways of engaging politically is to use cyberspace to make political concerns heard. In this discourse, the perceived unfairness of the long prison sentences of the US Computer Fraud and Abuse Act and the governmental anti-encryption stance is confirming the anti-state ideology, thereby increasing the risk of radicalizing a subset of skilled hackers.

A Hypothetical Account of the Ashley Madison Hack

So what then could a cyberterrorist attack look like? This last section will give a hypothetical reprise of the hacking of Ashley Madison to illustrate the harm that can be created through the release of socially prohibited private data. Ashley Madison is an online dating service targeted at people in committed relationships. In 2015, a hacker (or hackers) with the moniker 'The Impact Team' leaked large amounts of illicitly attained user data. Their stated aim was to take Ashley Madison and a similar related site (Established Men) permanently offline. In their manifesto, they claimed: 'Too bad for those men, they're cheating dirtbags and deserve no such discretion. Too bad for ALM [Ashley Madison], you promised secrecy but didn't deliver. We've got the complete set of profiles in our DB [database] dumps, and we'll release them soon if Ashley Madison stays online.'[17] A month later, they made good their threat and released the user data. They tried shaming the users by addressing their acquaintances:

> Chances are your man signed up on the world's biggest affair site, but never had one. He just tried to. If that distinction matters. Find yourself in here? It was ALM that failed you and lied to you. Prosecute them and claim damages. Then move on with your life. Learn your lesson and make amends. Embarrassing now, but you'll get over it.[18]

The details of who is behind the Impact Team and their motivations are still unclear. However, for the sake of argument about cyberterrorism, consider for a moment that this hack was undertaken by a morally conservative, religious extremist, who, by releasing the names of users tried to punish users and instil fear into potential users to change their behaviour. Setting this hypothetical scenario against the various definitions of cyberterrorism discussed earlier, it could be argued that the Ashley Madison hack complies with all constitutive criteria of terrorist acts:

> *Violence*: as argued above, violence can be psychological. The intended disruption of social relationships through the publication of names can be considered as violence, because the release of the data could, and did, lead to traumatic effects, and has reportedly led to suicides.
>
> *Political aim*: there is a clear aim to impose a religiously derived moral standard (assumption set by the hypothetical scenario).
>
> *Psychological dimension*: intent to instil fear in the targets and beyond. The hackers threaten that, if their victims engage in such practices in the future, similar public shaming may occur to them.
>
> *Multiple audiences*: not only do they address the targets, but they signal to their own supporters that they will enforce their desired moral standard.
>
> *Exert power*: there is an asymmetric power relationship between the individual user, who deems the service to be an intimate arrangement, and the attackers, who publish the intimate data on a great number of people.
>
> *Part of a wider political struggle*: it could be seen as part of a wider political campaign to instil a certain set of moral values onto a population.

Hence, while the actual Ashley Madison hack might not have been an act of terrorism, the hypothetical scenario demonstrated how this new type of terrorism may become possible.

This leads to several insights. While Ardit and Junaid may have appeared to be cyberterrorists at first, upon closer analysis they were found not to be. The term 'cyberterrorism' should therefore be used with caution. Restrictively defined, it can capture potentially novel behaviour that can be the basis of a terrorist strategy. While this may not correspond with a traditional understanding of terrorist attacks and could be far from the doomsday scenarios often portrayed by the popular press, the possibilities to use cyberspace to instil fear beyond the immediate victims or targets for political purposes are growing.

Conclusion

This chapter has raised several points of contention. It has suggested that, just because someone is part of an organization that uses a strategy of terror, not all their actions are necessarily terrorist acts. Rather, terrorist acts are a specific subset of political violence, whose primary purpose is to induce fear in a target audience beyond the immediate targets of the violence. The violence does not have to be physical but can also be psychological. Cyberterrorism was found to be the use, or threat of use, of cyberspace to deliver such violence through the disruption or destruction of digital data.

This chapter has discussed the motivations of terrorists, speculating as to the reasons why cyberterrorist attacks have not yet been seen. The chapter then discussed definitions of terrorism before introducing various intelligence agencies' claims that terrorists want to carry out cyber attacks but have so far lacked the capability. Intelligence assessments remain unclear as to whether any terrorist group has acted upon their intent and, if so, to what extent. Conway's cost–benefit analysis then showed there to be reasons why terrorists do not choose cyberspace as a means of attack for terrorism. Two vectors of change were identified: the current generation of terrorists turning to cyberspace as a means of terror, and potential new terrorists emerging with improved cyber capabilities. Both analyses enabled a better assessment of the types of scenarios that might give rise to cyberterrorism. Finally, the hypothetical scenario of a religiously inspired Ashley Madison hack demonstrated the potential and possible novelty of a cyberterrorist attack.[19]

Notes

1. *United States of America vs. Ardit Ferizi*, 1:16-cr-042 (2016). PageID 395–7.
2. *United States of America vs. Ardit Ferizi*, 1:16-cr-042 (2016). PageID 395–7.
3. For an excellent literature overview, see Maura Conway. 2012 'What Is Cyberterrorism and How Real Is the Threat?'. In *Law, Policy, and Technology: Cyberterrorism, Information Warfare, and Internet Immobilization*, edited by Pauline C. Reich and Eduardo Gelbstein (Hershey, PA: Information Science Reference), 279–307, 286–88. For an analysis of the cyberterror threat framing, see Cavelty, Myriam Dunn. 2008. 'Cyber-Terror—Looming Threat or Phantom Menace? The Framing of the US Cyber-Threat Debate', *Journal of Information Technology & Politics* 4 (1): 19–36.
4. The WHO definition of violence includes psychological harm: see https://perma.cc/ FQN8-73HM. See also discussion of virtual violence in Conway, 'What Is Cyberterrorism?', 286–8, and psychological perspective in Mizen, Richard. 2003. 'A Contribution Towards an Analytic Theory of Violence', *Journal of Analytical Psychology* 48 (3): 285–305.
5. A point made in Conway, 'What Is Cyberterrorism?', 297.

6. On kill lists, see SITE Intelligence Group. 2016. 'Special Report: Kill Lists from Pro-Is Hacking Groups', Bethesda, MD. https://perma.cc/TZG9-4ZK3
7. *United States of America vs. Ardit Ferizi*, 1:16-cr-042 (2016). PageID 378.
8. *UK National Cyber Security Strategy 2016 to 2021*. 2016. London: HM Government, 19. https://perma.cc/X9UP-S7QB
9. Drake, *Terrorists' Target Selection*, 39.
10. There is a debate about the extent of the rationality of terrorism. Some argue for social determinants, see e.g. Abrahms, Max. 2008. 'What Terrorists Really Want: Terrorist Motives and Counterterrorism Strategy', *International Security* 32 (4): 78–105. Others argue for rational strategic logic applying at the leadership level, see e.g. Pape, Robert Anthony. 2005. *Dying to Win: The Strategic Logic of Suicide Terrorism*. 1st edn. New York: Random House.
11. Maura Conway thereby draws on and updates Giacomello, Giampiero. 2004. 'Bangs for the Buck: A Cost-Benefit Analysis of Cyberterrorism', Studies in Conflict & Terrorism 27 (5).
12. On the difficulty of disentangling indicators of intent versus capability, see Schuurman, Bart, and Quirine Eijkman. 2015. 'Indicators of Terrorist Intent and Capability: Tools for Threat Assessment', *Dynamics of Asymmetric Conflict* 8 (3): 215–31.
13. UK National Cyber Security Strategy 2016 to 2021, 19.
14. National Crime Agency. 2016. 'Sextortion (Webcam Blackmail)', National Crime Agency. https://perma.cc/J6KQ-UEAM
15. For detailed reports on the digital targeting of political dissidents, see https://citizenlab.org/publications/; https://perma.cc/98M7-F3RK
16. On pathways and routes from radicalization to terrorism, see Koehler, Daniel. 2016. *Understanding Deradicalization: Methods, Tools and Programs for Countering Violent Extremism*. London: Routledge, Ch. 3. See also Horgan, John. 2008. 'From Profiles to Pathways and Roots to Routes: Perspectives from Psychology on Radicalization into Terrorism', *The ANNALS of the American Academy of Political and Social Science* 618 (1): 80–94.
17. The Impact Team, 'Impact Team Manifesto', 2015: https://perma.cc/8AU2-UJ2U
18. The Impact Team, 'Time's Up', Wired, 2015. https://perma.cc/AVP3-2YKB
19. The author thanks the members of the University of Oxford Cyber Studies Working Group for their valuable comments and insights.

REFERENCES

Australian Cyber Security Centre. 2016. *2016 Threat Report*. Canberra: Government of Australia. https://perma.cc/8HPE-98PK

Clapper, James. 2015. 'Worldwide Cyber Threats'. Hearing at the US House of Representatives Permanent Select Committee on Intelligence. 114th Congress. Washington DC: Government Printing Office. https://perma.cc/36N4-YLDP

Conway, Maura. 2003. 'Hackers as Terrorists? Why It Doesn't Compute', *Computer Fraud and Security* 12 (December): 10–13.

Conway, Maura. 2012. 'What is Cyberterrorism and How Real Is the Threat?'. In Law, Policy, and Technology: Cyberterrorism, Information Warfare, and Internet Immobilization, edited by Pauline C. Reich and Eduardo Gelbstein (Hershey, PA: Information Science Reference), 279–307.

Conway, Maura. 2014. 'Reality Check: Assessing the (Un)Likelihood of Cyberterrorism'. In *Cyberterrorism: Understanding, Assessment, and Response*, edited by Thomas M. Chen, Lee Jarvis, and Stuart MacDonald, 103–22. New York: Springer.

Denning, Dorothy E. 2007. 'A View of Cyberterrorism Five Years Later'. In *Internet Security: Hacking, Counterhacking, and Society*, edited by K. Himma. Sudbury, MA: Jones and Bartlett Publishers.

Dolnik, Adam. 2007. *Understanding Terrorist Innovation: Technology, Tactics and Global Trends*. London: Routledge.

Drake C.J.M. 1998. Terrorists' Target Selection. Basingstoke, UK: Macmillan Press."

English, Richard. 2016. 'The Future Study of Terrorism', *European Journal of International Security* 1 (2) (5 October): 135–49.

English, Richard. 2009. *Terrorism: How to Respond*. Oxford: Oxford University Press.

Giacomello, Giampiero. 2004. 'Bangs for the Buck: A Cost-Benefit Analysis of Cyberterrorism', *Studies in Conflict & Terrorism* 27 (5) (9 January): 387–408.

Juergensmeyer, Mark. 2014. 'Killing before an Audience. Terrorism and Group Violence'. In *The Causes and Consequences of Group Violence: From Bullies to Terrorists*, edited by James Hawdon, John Ryan, Marc Lucht et al., 125–40. Lanham: Lexington Books.

Juergensmeyer, Mark. 2003. *Terror in the Mind of God: The Global Rise of Religious Violence*. 3rd edn. Berkeley, CA; London: University of California Press.

Krause, Keith. 2009. 'Beyond Definition: Violence in a Global Perspective', *Global Crime* 10 (4): 337–55.

Krause, Keith. 2016. 'From Armed Conflict to Political Violence: Mapping and Explaining Conflict Trends'. Daedalus 145 (4) (9 January): 113–26.

Martin, Ciaran. 2016. 'A New Approach for Cyber Security in the UK' (speech presented at the Billington Cyber Security Summit, Washington DC, 13 September).

Osborne, George. 2015. 'Chancellor's Speech to GCHQ on Cyber Security'. Speech presented at the GCHQ, Cheltenham, UK, 17 November.

Rasmussen, Nicholas J. 2016. 'Testimony Presented at Hearing before the Senate Homeland Security and Governmental Affairs Committee "Fifteen Years after 9/11: Threats to the Homeland"'. 114th Congress. Washington DC: Government Printing Office. https://perma. cc/7QGG-D3BE

Richards, Anthony. 2014. 'Conceptualizing Terrorism', *Studies in Conflict & Terrorism* 37 (3): 230.

Richardson, Louise. 2006. *What Terrorists Want: Understanding the Enemy, Containing the Threat*. 1st edn. New York: Random House

Tilly, Charles. 2005. 'Terror as Strategy and Relational Process', *International Journal of Comparative Sociology* 46 (1–2) (1 April): 11–32.

Tilly, Charles. 2004 'Terror, Terrorism, Terrorists', *Sociological Theory* 22 (1): 5–13.

Valeri, Lorenzo, and Michael Knights. 2000. 'Affecting Trust: Terrorism, Internet and Offensive Information Warfare', *Terrorism and Political Violence* 12 (1) (3 January): 15–36.

CHAPTER 13

TECHNOLOGY: ACCESS AND DENIAL

CAITRÍONA HEINL

INTRODUCTION

CHAPTER 11 outlines the nature of cyber weapons and attack vectors, and Chapter 12 analyses the motivations and intentions of non-state actors like terrorists or extremists in the cyber field. This chapter therefore considers factors that may afford these groups opportunity to access offensive cyber means and how this threat might be best managed. It acknowledges that other terrorism-related areas identify a risk in focusing too narrowly on the technology, rather than dealing with motivations and intentions effectively (Bobbitt 2008, 404). Similarly, recommendations from law enforcement authorities include preventing criminals from becoming involved in the first place (EUROPOL 2016, 13). The main thrust of this chapter, however, is more in line with thinking that sees value in focusing on solutions and minimizing opportunities for violence from occurring rather than countering extremism itself (Conway, MacDonald, and Mair 2016, 35). The concept of cyber terrorism is discussed briefly, including current perceptions on the degree of terrorist access to offensive cyber means. Several factors that could affect, to varying degrees, such proliferation of tools and techniques include the following:

1. Rising complexity and vulnerabilities in the cyber domain.
2. Maturing skills.
3. The nexus with criminal groups and hacktivists.
4. Levels of resilience.
5. Media exposure.
6. International negotiations on state behaviour vis-à-vis cyber weapon proliferation.

Recognizing that there is no universal agreement on definitions of either terrorism or cyber terrorism, this chapter further highlights an additional difficulty whereby the very concept of 'cyber terrorism' is in fact misunderstood and mischaracterized.[1] This gap should be addressed more closely in order to enable the development of more effective policies. Some confusion is apparently caused by descriptions that blur the lines with other acts like hacktivism and terrorists' use of the Internet to facilitate conventional terrorism.[2] Furthermore, the degree of severity needed for an act to be viewed as cyber terrorism is still contested.[3] Confusing these different lines of inquiry, however, could affect proper understanding of the threat and thus affect policy development.[4] For the purposes of this chapter, the concept of cyber terrorism includes neither hacktivism nor terrorist use of the Internet to facilitate conventional terrorism. Although hacktivism, for example, can include social and political disturbance, acts are generally disruptive rather than causing the widespread fear and destruction that might be expected of cyber terrorism.[5]

Chapter 10 covers the use of the Internet for activities that include recruitment, planning, radicalization, spreading propaganda, intelligence gathering, training, and raising funds. Although the present chapter does not describe these activities as cyber terrorism per se, tackling them effectively should also limit the operational effectiveness of cyber terrorism activities.[6] In other words, this should reduce the chances of terrorist groups using cyber tools and techniques successfully. For example, a special meeting of the United Nations (UN) Security Council Counter-Terrorism Committee on preventing information and communications technology (ICT) exploitation for terrorist purposes (while respecting human rights and fundamental freedoms) convened in 2016 in response to growing concern over the threat to countries by the exploitation of ICTs, in particular the Internet and social media, for terrorist purposes.[7] It, too, described the Internet as a front line in the fight against terrorism.[8] Moreover, because these terror networks operate globally, they require a global response: groups like Islamic State in Iraq and the Levant (ISIL/Da'esh) and al-Qaeda carry out cross-border attacks as well as using the Internet to finance and incite acts of terror.[9]

In short, cyber terrorism can be understood to include attacks that can cause much more than mere inconvenience to victims, instead causing physical violence or serious damage to property or critical infrastructure (CI) in order to terrorize people beyond the immediate victims.[10] The oft-cited Denning test describes cyber terrorism as:

> the convergence of cyberspace and terrorism. It refers to unlawful attacks and threats of attacks against computers, networks and the information stored therein when done to intimidate or coerce a government or its people in furtherance of political or social objectives. Further, to qualify as cyberterrorism, an attack should result in violence against persons or property, or at least cause enough harm to generate fear. Attacks that lead to death or bodily injury, explosions or serious economic loss would be examples. Serious attacks against critical infrastructures could be acts of cyberterrorism, depending on their impact. Attacks that disrupt nonessential services or that are mainly a costly nuisance would not (Klein 2015, 24).

THREAT LANDSCAPE: PROJECTIONS ON THE STATUS OF TERRORIST GROUP ACCESS TO OFFENSIVE CYBER MEANS

In the past, there has been criticism about the dearth of strategic doctrines (like those relating to mutual nuclear deterrence in the Cold War) as well as a lack of international law and new institutions for global problems like terrorism.[11] Online counterterrorism efforts are equally criticized for lacking in such strategic thinking (Weimann 2015, 178). More recently, some government officials caution that it is unwise to assume that these terror groups do not think strategically themselves.[12]

Even though the subject of cyber terrorism has been examined since the late 1990s and early 2000s, it is still not fully understood as a strategic concept and there is even further debate about whether the actions of these groups can be deterred—in fact, some believe that acts of cyber terrorism, especially by non-state actors, cannot be deterred or eliminated and they recommend managing the cyber risk instead.[13] US government documents note that there is no universally applicable approach for deterring or responding—rather, the unique traits of a particular threat will assist in deciding the most suitable tools to be used.[14] Thus, a good example of one framework, that is still being developed by the State Department, outlines that deterrence could be best achieved through both 'deterrence by denial' (in other words, reducing incentives to use cyber capabilities by persuading a group that their objectives can be denied) and 'deterrence by cost imposition' (in other words, threatening or using actions that penalize or cost those who conduct malicious cyber activity).[15] Deterrence by denial can include policies or regulations to increase security and resilience; incident response capabilities; law enforcement authorities; cyber threat information-sharing mechanisms; public private partnerships; international cooperation; and diplomatic channels.[16] Deterrence by cost imposition, on the other hand, could include response options such as diplomatic tools (such as building cybersecurity and improving capacity to combat cybercrime in developing countries); law enforcement tools to investigate and prosecute; economic tools for state-affiliated actions by groups; economic sanctions against actors themselves and country-specific tools; military capabilities; and intelligence capabilities.[17] In the case of terrorist actors, however, some groups may not be highly concerned about such repercussions following an act of cyber terrorism. Alternatively, groups like al-Qaeda and the so-called Islamic State (IS) are said to act strategically and rationally, which means that deterrence might be a way to influence their actions.[18]

Following the September 2011 attacks, there was much policy interest as well as academic literature on the likelihood of cyber terrorism. More recently, following the public disclosures surrounding Operation Olympic Games and the Stuxnet worm as well as the activities of the so-called Islamic State, the subject has again risen to prominence. Notably, some terrorism experts argue that terrorist groups are constantly seeking to raise the threshold: causing more death, injury, and destruction, and attracting more media attention with each attack (Davies 2005, 240) As a result, terrorist organizations are expected to seek ever more powerful weapons.[19] The well-known author, Philip Bobbitt, has even highlighted several questionable assertions about twenty-first-century terrorism, which include the following:

1. Terrorists will be confined to low-technology weapons for the foreseeable future.

2. Because they will be so confined, they are at most a modest threat to modern societies' stability.

3. Rather than preparing for the remote possibility that terrorists will conduct a truly catastrophic attack, focus should be on more likely assaults.[20]

On the other hand, some scholars contend that, although cyber terrorism may occur in the future, the more imminent threat lies instead in the exploitation of the Internet to raise funds, research targets, and recruit. By this view, online crime, hacktivism, and cyber warfare are more urgent cyber-related challenges.[21] My own position is that this line of thinking could negatively affect policy development, especially if too much emphasis is laid on the unlikelihood of cyber terrorism occurring in the near future. Instead, while developing policies to counter the exploitation of the Internet or ICTs and other cyber threats, a number of different responses (such as enhancing resilience) could simultaneously reduce the chances of terrorist access and use of tools and techniques.

The intelligence community assesses cyber threats to national and economic security to be increasing in frequency, scale, sophistication, and severity of impact, and that a range of actors and methods will be encountered.[22] Yet, the likelihood of a *catastrophic* attack from any particular actor is considered to be remote.[23] Rather than a 'cyber Armageddon' scenario debilitating the entire national infrastructure, continuous low- to moderate-level cyber attacks from a variety of sources over time are envisaged, causing cumulative costs to economic competitiveness and national security.[24] Similarly, much of the current thinking across law enforcement and intelligence community public sources seems to assess that these non-state actor terrorist groups do not yet possess the capabilities or capacity for high-impact disruptive cyber attacks against CI. The extent to which extremist groups currently use cyber techniques to conduct attacks appears to be limited—while they might use the Internet for recruitment, propaganda, and incitement, there is currently little evidence that their cyber attack capability extends beyond common website defacement.[25] Nonetheless, the possibility exists. Concern remains about potential terrorist attacks against CI and its control systems.[26] For example, such groups are showing interest in these attacks by trying to recruit, and to develop, expertise, and groups like al-Qaeda have apparently expressed prior interest in conducting a major cyber attack.[27] The European Cybercrime Centre (EC3)'s Internet Organised Crime Threat Assessment for 2016 noted that, in addition to topics covered in previous years, it now included an examination of the use of cyber techniques by terrorist groups.[28] The US intelligence community similarly notes that terrorist organizations have expressed interest in developing offensive capabilities.[29] In the case of groups like IS more recently, their social media skills can sometimes be confused with the capacity and capabilities for a high-impact cyber-enabled attack against CI.[30] Nevertheless, IS's aims to commit violent acts means that experts are now more likely to accept that these concerns are more justified.[31]

The future consequences of the United States' announcement in 2016 that its Cyber Command would, for the first time, launch offensive cyber operations against IS may need further examination too. It is not clear whether these actions may end up catalyzing groups like IS to then bolster their defences to a greater extent as well as escalate their endeavours in offensive cyber operations. One of the benefits highlighted by this campaign was to 'rattle' IS's commanders even more as they had started to realize that sophisticated hacking efforts were manipulating their data, and a decision was taken that a 'bit of boasting' might lessen the group's trust in its communications in order to deter some of their activities.[32] There is a chance, though, that, by using an implant to attack, the IS militants might then stop using a communications channel or perhaps even use one that is harder to find, penetrate, or decrypt—in other words, balancing 'the collection entities against the disruption entities' is difficult.[33] Significantly, however, the skills and organizational capabilities for offence and defence in this field can be rather similar.[34] Defence will also require understanding how to compromise computer systems and one way to protect systems is to engage in penetration testing, such as controlled offensive operations on one's own systems.[35]

Members of the international cyber policy community, while now publicly recognizing the increasing likelihood of such incidents, are calling for action to address this challenge.

They explain that, '[t]he use of ICTs for terrorist purposes, beyond recruitment, financing, training and incitement, including for terrorist attacks against ICTs or ICT-dependent infrastructure, is an increasing possibility, that, if left unaddressed, may threaten international peace and security'.[36] The following sections thus explore several factors that could further enable the access to offensive cyber means by terrorist groups, and include recommendations to mitigate these risks whenever possible.

GROWING VULNERABILITIES AND COMPLEXITY

Two variables that can affect an attack's impact include the characteristics and countermeasures of the system or network.[37] In terms of the characteristics of systems or networks, continuing and increasing acceleration of previous cybersecurity trends are expected, including increasing vulnerabilities caused by the deepening complexity of the Internet of Things (IoT) as well as new systems being developed that do not have adequate security.[38] In addition, concerns traditionally focused on problems at an attacked facility, or the possible cascading effects on other facilities and processes dependent on the attacked facility.[39] The introduction of IoT across CIs can only increase the complexity and interdependencies between CI sectors, thereby exacerbating the danger of cascading effects. It is of course possible that interdependency could make CI structures harder, rather than easier to take down (yet more information becoming available online and sophisticated software tools for network analysis could apparently counter this possibility).[40]

Similarly, increasing use of artificial intelligence for cybersecurity will add further complexity, as will the growing likelihood of data manipulation if it can cause physical impact, reduce trust in systems, and have an impact on decision making.[41] The growing use of commercial off-the-shelf software for CI is also often cited as increasing the chances of vulnerabilities that can be exploited.[42] Moreover, while vulnerabilities still remain in key CI sectors, yet more are being introduced through the internationalization of critical supply chains and service infrastructure as well as in civilian and government systems, particularly because devices are developed without appropriate security.[43]

Cybercrime exploits that are already well known (sometimes 'decade-old' techniques, vulnerabilities, and attack vectors) are becoming popular again.[44] Simple threats could thus be used in standard operating systems, especially if organizations do not fix them (organizations strongly invested in security would not necessarily be vulnerable in this case).[45] Unfortunately though, more complex threats can find and exploit vulnerabilities in multiple organizations simultaneously, and these experts can find vulnerabilities that are not well known.[46]

Some examples of countermeasures that could be used to mitigate those vulnerabilities that malicious actors might abuse, include the following:

1. Technology-oriented (e.g. firewalls, intrusion detection systems, encryption, hardware security tokens, and biometrics).
2. Process-oriented (policies and procedures like access control policies, authentication procedures, and configuration management practices).

3. People-oriented (e.g. background checks, training requirements, physical barriers, and monitoring software).[47]

Likewise, a number of guidelines are being developed globally to deal with responsible vulnerability disclosure. Some analysts, for example, advocate that hackers or hacktivists should even have a 'safe space' for the responsible reporting of flaws discovered while undertaking potentially criminal activity albeit without a wider malicious intent.[48] And industry has previously proposed that states should have policies for handling product and service vulnerabilities that incorporate a strong mandate to report such vulnerabilities to vendors rather than stockpile, buy, sell, or exploit those vulnerabilities.[49]

The 2014 White House framework is an example of one such approach to the vexed question of whether (and when) government should withhold knowledge of a vulnerability. The Framework argues that, in the majority of cases, the responsible disclosure of a newly discovered vulnerability would be in the national interest. Building large stockpiles while leaving the Internet unprotected is not regarded as in the national security interest, however, although government should still reserve the right to use vulnerabilities for intelligence. For the purposes of this chapter, the White House Framework raises several pertinent questions:

1. How much harm could a criminal group cause with knowledge of a known vulnerability?
2. How likely is it that such a vulnerability can be discovered by a criminal group?
3. Can the vulnerability be patched or otherwise mitigated?[50]

Other initiatives of a broadly similar nature include the work of the new OASIS Common Security Advisory Framework Technical Committee on enabling interoperability among products and machine-readable security advisories to advance a standard format for vendors to disclose cybersecurity vulnerabilities.[51] The area is still evolving, however. A situation might arise, for example, where vulnerability disclosures could be so extensive in some industrial control systems as to require years of remedial work, at great cost. Given the technical and financial challenges of compliance, it should be no surprise that security industry representatives are sometimes concerned about public vulnerability disclosures.

'Bug bounty programs'—in other words, programs that reward finding and reporting bugs such as vulnerabilities and exploits in software products—could be an alternative approach. Such initiatives are often used in the United States and they seem to be gaining traction elsewhere—they are being developed in France as a way to detect vulnerabilities and security flaws, while Italian law enforcement highlight their cost efficiencies for companies.[52] If such programs are to be effective as a method to deny access to crime groups though, calls for adequate supervision should be heeded.

The members of the 2015 UN Group of Government Experts (GGE) further recommend in their consensus report that (among other voluntary non-binding peace-time norms), states should first consider reasonable steps to ensure supply chain integrity for the security of ICT products. The goal would be to prevent the proliferation of malicious ICT tools and techniques, and the use of harmful hidden functions. Second, the GGE recommends responsible reporting of ICT vulnerabilities and sharing associated information on available remedies to limit or even eliminate potential threats to ICTs and ICT-dependent infrastructure.[53] It seems likely that the GGE and other forums will continue to examine how to operationalize these and similar recommendations related to vulnerability and disclosure.

TERRORIST FINANCING

Some terrorist groups may perceive that conducting cyber attacks is less expensive than acquiring conventional weapons. But 'less expensive' does not mean 'cheap'. High-impact, cyber-enabled incidents may be substantially more expensive than expected, given the need for, inter alia, high-level expertise, tools, intelligence, and coordination. This thinking runs counter to the argument that an individual malevolent actor might only require a computer and Internet access to cause a catastrophic incident. This would also mean that there should be less risk of a 'lone wolf terrorist' launching a devastating high-impact cyber attack. Countering terrorist funding, whether it is obtained through offline or online means (including cybercrime and cyber-enabled crimes), as well as accessing or moving funds could make it more difficult for these groups to obtain offensive cyber tools and techniques. Nevertheless, even though there are numerous tools to counter such terrorist financing, the international community is concerned that they are not being implemented.[54] If these countermeasures are to be effective, they will have to be implemented soon.

Payment systems, like Bitcoin, can provide anonymity that could facilitate criminal-to-criminal payments.[55] Yet analysis of online terrorism financing suggests that, so far, although pre-paid cards and unregistered charities make money trails difficult to follow, terrorist groups do not seem to have made use of virtual currencies like Bitcoin (at least not with the same frequency as criminal organizations).[56] Furthermore, terrorist groups have yet to transfer to more encrypted forms of money transfer.[57] This raises a familiar dilemma: if policies are too aggressive, they may push groups to 'submerge', using methods that are harder to track.[58]

SKILLS: RECRUITMENT AND TRAINING

To conduct a cyber attack requires analytical skills (analysis of a target to find critical nodes and vulnerabilities, or connections to other targets) as well as technical capabilities (knowledge of computer software and hardware).[59]

Groups like al-Qaeda have previously called for those with expertise to target websites and information networks (hacking has been described as one way to jihad).[60] As far back as 2001, there was evidence that their operatives were educated in engineering and computer systems: downloaded features of dams were possibly used to plan or simulate failures; and research time was spent on software and programming instructions for digital switches running power, water, transport, and communications grids.[61] The author, Gabriel Weimann, further observes that US government reports in 2005 noted that terrorist groups were trying to recruit people with mathematics, computer science, and engineering skills while 2011 reports cited interest in an 'e-jihad center' for jihadists with expertise in hacking, networking, and programming language with study areas like Supervisory Control and Data Acquisition Systems (SCADA), machine and assembly languages, and knowledge of hacker websites.[62]

In addition, while trying to recruit in universities and companies, it seems that funding, ideology, religion, and blackmail have all become important factors.[63] For example, a co-opted anti-establishment ideology might be especially attractive for young hackers.[64] Displaced populations are also said to be possible targets for recruitment.[65] It is, however, apparently very difficult to conduct complex and coordinated attacks. To exploit different vulnerabilities across many organizations might require a team of experts to analyse the network and system vulnerabilities of each target, modelling the interrelationship between targets and the consequences of a multi-target attack.[66] For complex attacks (or a series of sustained and well-targeted advanced attacks), terrorist groups would require several highly educated or experienced computer scientists, engineers, or self-taught hackers either from within their own ranks or hired externally.[67] It seems, however, that it has been difficult for them to recruit or train for these purposes in the past.[68] These types of attack cannot be carried out by a single hacker or a small team of amateurs.[69] Instead, a team (or multiple teams) qualified in several technical areas like networks, operating systems, programming languages, infrastructure topologies, and control systems, intelligence gathering and analysis, and planning would be required.[70] Very strong planning and coordination skills are needed and it would be necessary to coordinate multiple attack vectors, for which a sophisticated test-bed might be required, with all the attendant acquisition and maintenance costs.[71] In the case of IS currently, it is apparently only centralized and highly coordinated at the top levels of its leadership, whereas lower levels are decentralized.

For more advanced attacks that may cause significant economic damage but are still not catastrophic, analysts argue that terrorist groups would require at least one attacker capable of writing or modifying programs and possessing a working knowledge of networks, operating systems, and possibly defensive techniques (perhaps even the technical capabilities akin to a Microsoft-certified systems engineer). More sophisticated analysis and planning would also be needed.[72] On the other hand, simple but highly effective cyber attacks, such as web defacement, could be conducted against a specific target by an individual with no more than basic computer skills and analytical capabilities (and by downloading additional tools if needed), and without the need for significant resources or organizational structures.[73] IS publications have begun to teach information security as well as operational security, and terrorists may continue to benefit from the next generation of recruits who are knowledgeable in information technology (IT), social media, and online research.[74] Some groups are seemingly creating online libraries with training materials, including for cyber terrorism, where experts answer questions on message boards or in chatrooms (like the online forum Qalah/Fortress discussion area known as 'electronic jihad' with links to latest hacking techniques).[75] Jihadist hackers are showing 'gradual sophistication in their attack modes and intended attack impacts' and more young jihadists are becoming better at identifying vulnerabilities.[76] The US intelligence community similarly assesses that terrorist groups continue to experiment with hacking, which might then be a foundation for developing more advanced capabilities.[77] Growing connectivity and the availability of low-cost devices globally may even exacerbate these trends.[78]

Furthermore, like state actors, terrorists would likely require operational tradecraft beyond this need for sophisticated cyber-related intelligence and coordination—the tradecraft that states generally need for complex cyber attacks that are normally the preserve of nation states includes some additional requirements such as human and signals intelligence capabilities.[79] The trends do not bode well in this regard either. It is expected that terrorists and transnational organized crime actors will continue to use and perhaps even improve their intelligence capabilities that include human, cyber, and technical means like technical surveillance to both facilitate activities and avoid detection.[80] By way of example, in conventional terrorism analysis, as well as training to ensure that they have the desired skills, suicide bombers might spend extended periods (even years) researching and using sophisticated intelligence before choosing a target.[81]

Such activities may, however, present opportunities for law enforcement and intelligence authorities to identify their plans and prevent their obtaining or using offensive means. For example, when they conduct research, reconnaissance, or development, there will be a point of breach and a point of discovery, and, because they will most likely be on a network, it could be possible to spot their actions.[82] In addition, those planning high-value attacks are more likely to conduct online research.[83] In other words, as they use the Internet or other ICTs for intelligence gathering or to develop their expertise, their activities might be picked up by authorities. Analysts additionally advocate counter-measures such as creating 'noise' to reduce the effectiveness of communications, like harming the flow of information.[84] Technological tactics could include damaging websites, redirecting users to spreading viruses and worms, blocking access, hacking, and total destruction (some of these attacks cannot be stopped by encryption and not all are stopped by firewalls), as well as tactics like spreading false technical information about weapons systems or messages to confuse operatives.[85] The US Cyber Command campaign against IS is reported to include goals such as disrupting the group's ability to spread its message, attract recruits, circulate commanders' orders and general daily functions, as well as to imitate or alter messages in order to redirect militants to dangerous locations and interrupt financial transfers.[86]

The Nexus with Criminal Groups and Hacktivists

Although terrorist groups are currently perceived to have low-level abilities in cyber, this situation could quickly change if capable actors are recruited or hired.[87] For instance, cybercrime tools and services on the Darknet could afford 'ample opportunities' for this to change.[88] EUROPOL reports conclude that the crime-as-a-service model that underpins cybercrime is now mature, providing tools and services from entry-level to top-tier players and any other seekers, including actors such as terrorists.[89]

Cybercriminals have a significant role in the international development, modification, and proliferation of malicious software.[90] However, they are generally motivated by profit rather than ideology.[91] In other words, this reduces the chances of their recruitment by an ideologically or politically motivated terrorist group that hopes to benefit from their expertise or to use their tools and techniques. Fortunately, the majority of reported attacks are not regarded as sophisticated—although cybercriminals apparently display a high level of sophistication in tools, tactics, and processes in some areas, many attacks are successful because of low digital hygiene, a lack of security-by-design, and low user awareness.[92]

In order to counter this crime-as-a-service model, it is essential to tackle key groups or individuals who provide these highly specialized services and tools in support of other areas of cybercrime (such as cyber-enabled terrorism).[93] In particular, countermeasures include focusing on the developers, vendors, and buyers of payload malware; developers, vendors, and buyers of enabling/facilitating malware like exploit kits, droppers (programs designed to install malware), and spam; providers of Distributed Denial of Service (DDoS) attack services and counter-antivirus services (as well as taking down botnets, like those deployed to distribute other malware and conduct DDoS attacks).[94] Botnets may, for example, be designed to disrupt in different ways and it is possible for a terrorist group to rent botnet services from cybercriminals if they do not possess the technical skills to develop their own.[95] In addition to focusing on key criminal actors, tools, and services, other suggestions include identifying preventive actions and working with people at risk of such criminal activity.[96] Other ideas include extraditions for prosecution to signal that these criminals will be penalized, or initiatives like the US State Department Transnational Organized Crime Rewards Program for information leading to arrest or conviction of Internet-based criminals.[97]

European law enforcement observes that policy makers, legislators, academia, and training providers, as well as law enforcement itself, should work in a more agile manner so as to adapt to the changing cyber landscape. It considers that current responses are untimely and ineffective on account of existing frameworks, programs, and tools that hinder fast responses.[98] More resources are requested by EUROPOL to increase response capacities by recruiting (and retaining) experts with specialized skills and knowledge, as well as to develop or acquire special purpose tools for digital forensics, big data analytics, and blockchain investigations.[99] To reduce duplication, there are further calls to develop a global 'cyber security eco-system' in order to, inter alia, identify stakeholders and map networks, identify links to legal and regulatory frameworks, and facilitate easier capacity building.[100] International cooperation is often cited as vital for cybercrime investigations and to prevent the development of safe havens.[101] Continuing intelligence sharing and stronger collaboration between law enforcement, academia, and the private sector are often specified too—for example, law enforcement may deal with the payload malware that causes actual damage or loss, and the Internet security industry may be more aware of 'upstream' malware threats like droppers or exploit kits that enable such attacks.[102]

Lastly, politically or ideologically motivated hackers sometimes attempt to access national CI systems too.[103] Hacktivists' skills can range from beginner to expert. Like terrorist groups, they are often driven by political, religious, or socio-economic causes, but they generally aim to disrupt rather than kill or terrorize.[104] Whereas hackers do not have political agendas (and may not even possess the skills and knowledge for serious harm), those with such skills are perceived not to use them.[105] Hacktivist groups are less likely to be motivated by profit, which means it could be less likely that they would be hired by a terrorist group (but there could be a risk of recruitment if they began to share a similar cause). Alternatively, scenarios that cannot be discounted include a possible chance that hacktivists alone escalate their actions for their own extreme ideological reasons, or that terrorist sympathizers might conduct low-level cyber attacks for a terrorist group.[106] The nexus with these groups should therefore continue to be monitored.

RESILIENCE IS KEY

Strengthening cyber defences and the resilience of systems, especially CI, can prevent or reduce the impact of incidents. It is possible to mitigate the malicious use of tools and techniques, and negate efforts to cause terror and widespread damage.

The US State Department notes the importance of cybersecurity due diligence, arguing that cybersecurity is critical to global security and that all countries have a responsibility to protect their own networks and information infrastructure so that they are secure and resilient.[107] Recommendations to heighten security can include adopting best practices; strengthening Computer Security Incident Response Teams (CSIRTs); public private collaboration; public awareness campaigns; enhancing response processes and procedures (such as the speed with which administrators can patch an exploited vulnerability and have the system work again, as well as measures for continuity of operations or back-up alternatives); and the resilience of the affected population.[108]

Although many experts and reports advocate enhanced resilience, it can be both expensive and time consuming.[109] If organizations are to use such guidance to enhance resilience, the challenges they face in terms of burdensome efforts and cost should be more readily addressed by both the public and private sectors in the near term. Again, security-by-design principles can be beneficial, too. One example of relevant guidance is the National Institute of Standards and Technology (NIST) security-focused engineering guide to help individuals building any piece of technology from smartphones to industrial control equipment so that security is prioritized at every stage of the design process (even when it may be more difficult to achieve this in IoT). In short, improving cyber resilience and mitigating the consequences following an attack could mean that an adversary, such as a terrorist group, will decide that such an attack will not cause the intended effects, or that it is not worth the cost.[110]

MEDIA RESPONSIBILITY

Terrorism experts traditionally warn against dangers associated with exaggerated media exposure, whereby overreaction can cause the very fear that terrorists may desire.[111] Similarly, in the cyber field, media reporting on cyber attacks has been somewhat sensationalized in recent years. Hacktivist actions are sometimes described as cyber terrorism, and a 'marginally successful attack at a major facility or service' can create much publicity as well as increase public anxiety.[112] It is important to reassure the public of the resilience of systems and CI in the wake of these risks, so that these groups' capabilities are not exaggerated. Awareness-raising campaigns may, for instance, be one method to better inform the public, and both government and academia can assist in this endeavour. Such counter-measures are necessary because media impact and the psychological projection of fear and intimidation are regarded as key components of terrorism.[113]

International Negotiations on State Behaviour vis-à-vis Proliferation of Cyber Weapons

Possible limitations on cyber operations continue to be negotiated by the international community. The 2015 UN GGE norms suggest that countries may be more likely to commit to limitations on the targets of cyber operations rather than support bans on the development of offensive capabilities or on specific means of cyber intervention.[114] The cautiousness of some states about banning offensive means could lead to a situation where some offensive means become available to terrorist groups. The rationale behind the 2015 GGE recommendations for norms of state behaviour, as well as confidence and capacity-building measures, is to provide an international standard of behaviour for responsible like-minded states to prevent hostile actors from engaging in malicious cyber activity, and to create a platform for states to preserve stability in response to state and non-state bad actors.[115] The US State Department argues that, as an increasing number of states commit to refrain from certain activities, states may be willing to join together against hostile actors to ensure that there are consequences for their behaviour.[116]

States may sometimes pre-position malware and access to target systems over a long period of time.[117] Thus, in preparing for future operations or creating access for purposes of state espionage, this could mean that nefarious actors can sometimes take advantage of weaker security too. This could perhaps occur when criminal actors have access to similar tools, tactics, and expertise. Stockpiling vulnerabilities for later exploitation leaves CI vulnerable to attack.[118] Equally, states' 'cyber weapons' could be re-used or modified once released. Therefore, there are requests for policy makers to concentrate more on understanding the potential for non-state actors to exploit cyber weapons that are developed by states, and how to mitigate the spread of malicious code.[119] In addition, state sponsorship could be another avenue for terrorists to obtain capabilities, especially where such states have the resources, personnel, and motives to launch complex cyber attacks (although countries with the most advanced cyber capabilities are considered unlikely to support terrorist groups, and those supporting such groups were, in the recent past at least, more limited in their cyber capabilities).[120]

Within discussions on international cyber stability that were held by the United Nations Institute for Disarmament Research (UNIDIR) in advance of the 2016–17 GGE, Chinese representatives outlined how to promote a peaceful and secure cyberspace, suggesting that in future the international community should identify and prioritize key issues like cyber terrorism.[121] In a separate UNIDIR report summarizing the findings of this group of workshops in 2016, the editors' background note explains that, although the 2015 GGE report recognizes the need to address possible terrorist attacks against ICTs or ICT-dependent infrastructure, previous GGEs limited themselves to calling for more state-to-state cooperation.[122] It then specifies that detailed recommendations on topics like terrorism and crime are more suitable for other UN bodies (GGEs have fallen under the UN First Committee).[123] It does not seem clear, however, whether all state parties, like the Chinese expert in this instance, agree that this should be the case and whether it could affect the outcome of negotiations. Nevertheless, these discussions on how states should operationalize the 2015 UN GGE norm to prevent the proliferation of malicious ICT tools and techniques, and the use of harmful hidden functions, are continuing.[124] Future norms discussions (like those under the 2016–17 GGE) may thus address the non-proliferation of malware and protect the IT supply chain.[125]

Central issues now under discussion are an exports control and a non-proliferation approach vis-à-vis an arms control approach—in other words, controlling the spread of dual-use tools that can be used for malicious purposes rather than banning capabilities and tools entirely.[126] In one of the 2016 UNIDIR meetings, the Russian representative recommended establishing basic rules of behaviour, rather than taking a non-proliferation or a technology control approach, given the significant challenges in achieving effective controls because of these tools' dual-use nature.[127] The European Union representative supported the development of positive norms to encourage responsible behaviour in the cyber domain, emphasizing that 'focusing on the regulation of behaviour rather than tools is all the more important due to the lack of a clear system of verification in cyber operations'.[128] Other parties, such as the International Committee of the Red Cross, argue that an explicit ban on cyber weapons may be more effective if it becomes apparent that cyber technologies cannot be used in accordance with international humanitarian law.[129] Industry has its own set of proposals: that states commit to non-proliferation activities; that they exercise restraint in developing cyber weapons, ensuring that those developed incorporate principles such as precision, and that they are limited and not reusable; and that states do not target ICT companies to insert vulnerabilities or back doors.[130]

Analysts observe that there can be no single solution to the proliferation of malicious cyber tools. Instead, a global web of measures is needed, including informal and formal, binding and voluntary, governmental and non-governmental, and domestic and international.[131] It seems to be difficult to apply traditional control measures to the field of cyber where, for example, possession of conventional weapons is more readily verifiable (hence the argument that the international community focus on behaviour rather than controlling objects).[132] Lessons from other mechanisms offer guidance but no perfect solutions—the Global Initiative to Combat Nuclear Terrorism is a voluntary regime that seeks to build capacity and cooperation among states to combat nuclear terrorism; and the Proliferation Security Initiative is a global framework of states to disrupt transfers of weapons of mass destruction, their delivery systems, and related items to and from states and non-state actors of proliferation concern.[133]

According to these UNIDIR reports, ICT characteristics mean three things. First, challenges arise in controlling the spread of tools that can be used for malicious purposes, including the relative ease and speed with which capabilities can be transferred and used. Second, the dual-use nature of many of these tools means that they can be used to strengthen cybersecurity too. Finally, they are ubiquitous technologies.[134] The existing mechanism under heated discussion that could be most applicable to cybersecurity is the Wassenaar Arrangement, which regulates transfer of conventional weapons and related dual-use goods and technologies. Participating states recently agreed to establish controls on malicious cyber tools but the items under these definitions are still debated because, for example, legitimate products might be included.[135] Moreover, it is uncertain whether the Wassenaar Arrangement would be effective for managing access to software products that are not linked to military hardware.[136]

These discussions gave rise to a number of expert recommendations.[137] First, it would be advisable for states to prevent a situation whereby production moves to less regulated or illicit markets. Second, it will be necessary to identify end uses or end users to which governments could restrict exports, while allowing a 'positive list' enabling sales for legitimate uses or users. Third, market-based mechanisms like bug bounty programs should be considered. And, finally, hardware and software should be designed in such a way that products cannot be modified for malicious purposes.

To conclude, these questions continue to be addressed globally. Both the cybersecurity and terrorism policy communities can inform the policy gaps identified throughout this chapter with both cyber and non-cyber solutions. It will be important for these communities to be brought together in forums devoted to exploring such key questions. The recently launched Transatlantic Cyber Policy Research Initiative (TCPRI) is an example of one such forum that could include these research questions in its future focus on policy challenges. The TCPRI aims to enhance cooperation between civil society, academia, and the private sector to deal with threats that include malicious cyber activity by criminals, states, proxies, and terrorist organizations. Similarly, initiatives like the Cyberterrorism Project, established in 2011, which already brings such experts from different disciplines and institutions together, could focus specifically on the more granular questions because it comprises experts from both the cyber and terrorism policy communities.[138] Recent workshops, organized by the ICT4Peace Foundation, on private sector engagement in responding to the use of the Internet and ICT for terrorist purposes, similarly recommend that further research be conducted on these types of questions through a separate research programme.[139] Initiatives of this sort might also limit the duplication of effort between the two communities that may sometimes arise. For example, extensive policy work has already been conducted on the protection of CI, including the work of the UN GGE (even if its main focus is not on terrorism but on state use of ICT).[140] There are, of course, a number of experts who already have expertise in both the fields of terrorism and cybersecurity who could be ideally placed to work on these questions.

Notes

1. Kenney, M. 2015. 'Cyber-Terrorism in a Post-Stuxnet World', Foreign Policy Research Institute, winter: 111–28; Lachow, I. 2009. 'Cyber Terrorism: Menace or Myth?'. In *Cyberpower and National Security*, edited by F.D. Kramer, S.H. Starr, and L.K. Wentz, Chapter 19. Sterling, VA: Potomac Books, Inc.; Kavanagh, C., Carr, M., Bosco F. et al. 2017. 'Responding to Terrorist Use of the Internet and Cyberspace', In *NATO Science for Peace and Security Series—E: Human and Societal Dynamics*, edited by Maura Conway, Lee Jarvis, Orla Lehane, Stuart Macdonald, Lella Nouri, p. 1. For a deeper discussion on definitions, see European Parliament, 'Understanding Definitions of Terrorism'. 2015. https://www.europarl.europa.eu/thinktank/en/document.html?reference=EPRS_ATA(2015)571320.
2. Kenney, 'Cyber-Terrorism', 111.
3. Conway et al., 'Advanced Research Workshop', 16.
4. Kenney, 'Cyber-Terrorism', 126; Lachow, 'Cyber Terrorism'.
5. Kenney, 'Cyber-Terrorism', 120.

6. Lachow, I. 'Cyber Terrorism'. Comments, Cybersecurity Panel, Raisina Dialogue, New Delhi, January 2017.
7. https://www.un.org/press/en/2016/sc12620.doc.htm
8. https://www.un.org/press/en/2016/sc12620.doc.htm
9. https://www.un.org/press/en/2016/sc12620.doc.htm
10. Kenney, 'Cyber-Terrorism', 122.
11. Bobbitt, *Terror and Consent*, 18.
12. Remarks, M.J. Akbar, Minister of State, Ministry of External Affairs, India. Raisina Dialogue. 17 January 2017.
13. Remarks, M.J. Akbar, Minister of State, Ministry of External Affairs, India. Raisina Dialogue. 17 January 2017; Clapper, J. (Director of National Intelligence). 2015. 'Statement for the Record: Worldwide Threat Assessment of the US Intelligence Community', Senate Armed Services Committee, p. 1.
14. United States Department of State 2016. 'Department of State International Cyberspace Policy Strategy', March. Public Law 114–113, Division N, Title IV, Section 402, p. 20.
15. Department of State, International Cyberspace Policy Strategy, 20.
16. Department of State, International Cyberspace Policy Strategy, 21.
17. Department of State, 'International Cyberspace Policy Strategy', 21, 23.
18. Klein, 'Deterring and Dissuading Cyberterrorism', 27.
19. Davies, *Terrorism*, 240.
20. Bobbitt, *Terror and Consent*, 6.
21. Kenney, 'Cyber-Terrorism', 127.
22. Clapper, 'Statement for the Record 2015,' 1; Department of State, 'International Cyberspace Policy Strategy', Section 402.
23. Clapper, 'Statement for the Record', 2015, 1; Department of State, 'International Cyberspace Policy Strategy', Section 402.
24. Clapper, 'Statement for the Record', 2015, 1; Department of State, 'International Cyberspace Policy Strategy', Section 402.
25. EUROPOL, 'IOCTA 2016', 11.
26. Weimann, *Terrorism in Cyberspace*, 149; Kavanagh et al., 'Responding to Terrorist Use', 1, 21.
27. Weimann, *Terrorism in Cyberspace*, 149, 152; Kenney, 'Cyber-Terrorism', 124.
28. EUROPOL, 'IOCTA 2016', 16.
29. Clapper, J. (Director of National Intelligence). 2014. 'Statement for the Record: Worldwide Threat Assessment of the US Intelligence Community', Senate Armed Services Committee, p. 2.
30. Kavanagh et al., 'Responding to Terrorist Use', 14–15.
31. Kavanagh et al., 'Responding to Terrorist Use', 14–15. The article cites the work of the Global Initiative to Combat Nuclear Terrorism in 2016 and vulnerabilities of the global submarine fibre optic cable system to terrorist attack.
32. https://www.nytimes.com/2016/04/25/us/politics/us-directs-cyberweapons-at-isis-for-first-time.html?_r=0
33. https://www.nytimes.com/2016/04/25/us/politics/us-directs-cyberweapons-at-isis-for-first-time.html?_r=0
34. Slayton, R. 2017. 'Why Cyber Operations Do Not Always Favor the Offense', February, *International Security*, Policy Brief, p. 3.
35. Slayton, 'Why Cyber Operations', 3.

36. Group of Governmental Experts on Developments in the Field of Information and Telecommunications in the Context of International Security. 2015. 'Report of the Group of Governmental Experts on Developments in the Field of Information and Telecommunications in the Context of International Security', United Nations General Assembly, A/70/174, p. 6.
37. Lachow, 'Cyber Terrorism'.
38. EUROPOL, 'IOCTA 2016', 7; Clapper, J. (Director of National Intelligence). 2016. 'Statement for the Record: Worldwide Threat Assessment of the US Intelligence Community', Senate Armed Services Committee, p. 1.
39. Weimann, *Terrorism in Cyberspace*, 157–9; Clapper, 'Statement for the Record', 2015, 1.
40. Lachow, 'Cyber Terrorism'.
41. Clapper, 'Statement for the Record 2016', 1–2.
42. Lachow, 'Cyber Terrorism'.
43. Clapper, 'Statement for the Record 2016', 1–2.
44. EUROPOL, 'IOCTA 2016', 8.
45. Lachow, 'Cyber Terrorism'.
46. Lachow, 'Cyber Terrorism'.
47. Lachow, 'Cyber Terrorism'.
48. Conway et al., 'Advanced Research Workshop', 39.
49. Microsoft. 2015. 'International Cybersecurity Norms: Reducing Conflict in an Internet-Dependent World', 12.
50. https://obamawhitehouse.archives.gov/blog/2014/04/28/heartbleed-understanding-when-we-disclose-cyber-vulnerabilities
51. https://www.helpnetsecurity.com/2017/01/20/disclose-cybersecurity-vulnerabilities/
52. Conway et al., 'Advanced Research Workshop', 27.
53. Group of Governmental Experts, 'Report', 7–8.
54. Findings, 2016 joint special meeting of the Security Council Counter-Terrorism Committee, the 1267/1989/2253 ISIL (Da'esh) and Al-Qaida Sanctions Committee and the Financial Action Task Force.
55. Conway et al., 'Advanced Research Workshop', 11.
56. Conway et al., 'Advanced Research Workshop', 26.
57. Conway et al., 'Advanced Research Workshop', 26.
58. Conway et al., 'Advanced Research Workshop'.
59. Lachow, 'Cyber Terrorism'.
60. Weimann, *Terrorism in Cyberspace*, 164.
61. Weimann, *Terrorism in Cyberspace*, 164.
62. Weimann, *Terrorism in Cyberspace*, 165.
63. Weimann, *Terrorism in Cyberspace*, 170.
64. Weimann, *Terrorism in Cyberspace*, 170.
65. Clapper, 'Statement for the Record 2016', 6.
66. Lachow, 'Cyber Terrorism'. An attack could be conducted without modelling.
67. Lachow, 'Cyber Terrorism'.
68. Lachow, 'Cyber Terrorism'.
69. Lachow, 'Cyber Terrorism'.
70. Lachow, 'Cyber Terrorism'.
71. Lachow, 'Cyber Terrorism'.
72. Lachow, 'Cyber Terrorism'.

73. Lachow, 'Cyber Terrorism'.
74. Kavanagh et al., 'Responding to Terrorist Use', 4; Clapper, 'Statement for the Record 2016', 6.
75. Weimann, *Terrorism in Cyberspace*, 168.
76. Weimann, *Terrorism in Cyberspace*, 168.
77. Clapper, 'Statement for the Record 2015', 3.
78. Weimann, *Terrorism in Cyberspace*, 170.
79. Hung, H. 2016. 'Cyberspace: Demystifying the Domain and Thinking Clearly about the Future', Presentation RSIS Singapore.
80. Clapper, 'Statement for the Record 2016', 10.
81. Davies, *Terrorism*, 246.
82. Hung, 2016.
83. Conway et al., 'Advanced Research Workshop', 35.
84. Weimann, *Terrorism in Cyberspace*, 180.
85. Weimann, *Terrorism in Cyberspace*, 183, 190.
86. https://www.nytimes.com/2016/04/25/us/politics/us-directs-cyberweapons-at-isis-for-first-time.html?_r=0
87. Hung, Presentation RSIS Singapore, 2016.
88. EUROPOL, 'IOCTA 2016', 11.
89. EUROPOL, 'IOCTA 2016', 7.
90. Clapper, 'Statement for the Record 2014', 2.
91. Clapper, 'Statement for the Record 2014', 2; Clapper, 'Statement for the Record 2015', 2.
92. EUROPOL, 'IOCTA 2016', 8.
93. EUROPOL, 'IOCTA 2016', 8.
94. EUROPOL, 'IOCTA 2016', 15.
95. Weimann, *Terrorism in Cyberspace*, 156.
96. EUROPOL, 'IOCTA 2016', 8–9.
97. Department of State, International Cyberspace Policy Strategy, 22.
98. EUROPOL, 'IOCTA 2016', 9.
99. EUROPOL, 'IOCTA 2016', 9.
100. EUROPOL, 'IOCTA 2016', 9.
101. Department of State, International Cyberspace Policy Strategy, 21; Kavanagh et al., 'Responding to Terrorist Use', 10; EUROPOL, 'IOCTA 2016', 14 (although many countries support international harmonization of substantive and procedural cybercrime laws through the Council of Europe Budapest Convention, this instrument is criticized for lacking wider legitimacy and universality, and signatories still need to implement it fully).
102. EUROPOL, 'IOCTA 2016', 10, 12–13.
103. Clapper, 'Statement for the Record 2015', 2.
104. Hung. 2016; Weimann, *Terrorism in Cyberspace*, 51.
105. Weimann, *Terrorism in Cyberspace*, 151.
106. Weimann, *Terrorism in Cyberspace*, 151; Clapper, 'Statement for the Record 2015', 3.
107. Department of State, International Cyberspace Policy Strategy, 4.
108. Department of State, International Cyberspace Policy Strategy, 4; Lachow, 'Cyber Terrorism'.
109. Lachow, 'Cyber Terrorism'.
110. Klein, 'Deterring and Dissuading Cyberterrorism', 35, 37.
111. Davies, *Terrorism*, 241.

112. Kenney, 'Cyber-Terrorism', 118; Weimann, *Terrorism in Cyberspace*, 154–5.
113. Kenney, 'Cyber-Terrorism', 122; Conway et al., 'Advanced Research Workshop', 17.
114. Clapper, 'Statement for the Record 2016', 3.
115. Department of State, International Cyberspace Policy Strategy, 4, 15.
116. Department of State, International Cyberspace Policy Strategy, 4, 15.
117. Hung, Presentation RSIS Singapore, 2016.
118. Slayton, 'Why Cyber Operations', 3.
119. Kenney, 'Cyber-Terrorism', 127.
120. Lachow, 'Cyber Terrorism'.
121. United Nations Institute for Disarmament Research (UNIDIR). 2016. 'Taking Security Forward: Building on the 2015 Report of the GGE'. UNIDIR Cyber Stability Seminar 2016, p. 16.
122. United Nations Institute for Disarmament Research (UNIDR) and Center for Strategic & International Studies (CSIS). 2016. 'Report of the International Security Cyber Issues Workshop Series'. UNIDIR and CSIS, p. 5.
123. UNIDIR and CSIS, 'Report', 5.
124. UNIDIR, 'Taking Security Forward', 9.
125. UNIDIR and CSIS, 'Report', 14.
126. UNIDIR and CSIS, 'Report', 18–20.
127. UNIDIR, 'Taking Security Forward', 4.
128. UNIDIR, 'Taking Security Forward', 9.
129. UNIDIR, 'Taking Security Forward', 7.
130. Microsoft, 'International Cybersecurity Norms', 20; Kenney, 'Cyber-Terrorism', 127; UNIDIR and CSIS, 'Report', 8.
131. UNIDIR, 'Taking Security Forward', 11.
132. UNIDIR, 'Taking Security Forward', 11.
133. UNIDIR and CSIS, 'Report', 18–20.
134. UNIDIR and CSIS, 'Report', 18–20.
135. UNIDIR and CSIS, 'Report', 18–20.
136. UNIDIR and CSIS, 'Report', 18–20.
137. UNIDIR and CSIS, 'Report', 18–20.
138. http://www.cyberterrorism-project.org/
139. http://ict4peace.org/preliminary-insights-into-the-private-sectors-response-to-terrorist-use-of-the-internet-and-ict/
140. http://ict4peace.org/wp-content/uploads/2016/12/Private-Sector-Engagement-in-Responding-to-the-Use-of-the-Internet-and-ICT-for-Terrorist-Purposes-1.pdf

BIBLIOGRAPHY

Bobbitt, Philip. 2008. *Terror and Consent: The Wars for the Twenty-First Century*. London: Allen Lane.
Conway, M., MacDonald, S., and Mair, D. 2016. 'Advanced Research Workshop Supported by the NATO Science for Peace and Security Programme: Terrorists' Use of the Internet—Assessment and Response (Final Report). Cyberterrorism Project Research Report 6.
Davies, B. 2005. *Terrorism: Inside a World Phenomenon*. London: Virgin Books Ltd.
EUROPOL. 2016. 'IOCTA 2016: Internet Organised Crime Threat Assessment'.

Klein, J. 2015. 'Deterring and Dissuading Cyberterrorism', *Journal of Strategic Security* 8 (4): 23–38.

Risen, J. 2006. *State of War: The Secret History of the CIA and the Bush Administration.* London: Simon & Schuster UK Ltd.

Theohary, C., and Rollins, J. 2015. 'Cyberwarfare and Cyberterrorism: In Brief', March, Congressional Research Service.

Weimann, G. 2015. *Terrorism in Cyberspace: The Next Generation.* Washington, DC: Woodrow Wilson Center Press.

PART IV

SECURITY IN CYBER SPACE: STATE-SPONSORED CYBER ATTACKS

CHAPTER 14

CYBER ESPIONAGE

JON R. LINDSAY

INTRODUCTION

NOTHING in cybersecurity makes sense except in the light of intelligence.[1] Information technologies expand the opportunities for surveillance and subversion, and cyber operations rely on deception to steal information or exert influence, or defend against such activities. The rise of cybersecurity as a national security concern, moreover, is not only a byproduct of technological development but also a reflection of the expanding role of intelligence agencies in society and the covert dimension of statecraft. Indeed, the ubiquity of information technology augurs a new golden age of espionage.

Much of the confusion about cybersecurity arises from treating computer network operations as something other than intelligence, or misunderstanding the nature of intelligence. Technical wizardry and futurist speculation is prominent in cybersecurity discourse, but technology alone is insufficient for understanding why threats emerge where and when they do, and whether hacking can shape political outcomes. The technical aspects of cyber operations are easier to study because we have more data about them. The political aspects are harder to game because strategy is interactive and social systems behave unpredictably (Jervis 1998). The most worrisome scenarios of cyber catastrophe—failure of a major metropolitan power grid in winter, meltdown of a nuclear power plant, paralysis of air traffic control, etc.—may be technically possible but politically improbable if the actors who are capable of inflicting such harm donot expect that it might benefit them (Rid 2012; Gartzke 2013; Lawson 2013).

The most dramatic fears are unlikely to be realized. Nevertheless, states have been relentless in exploring new ways to gather information and exert influence. Cyberspace is important for military operations and policing, to be sure, but this just reflects the prominence of intelligence in modern warfighting and law enforcement. Cybersecurity matters for non-state actors, too, in no small part because firms and individuals find themselves on the receiving end of foreign intelligence services. If cyber threats are an intelligence problem, furthermore, then cyber defence must look to not only technology for protection but also to counterintelligence, and, unavoidably, all the ethical dilemmas that come with it.

State Intelligence and Cybersecurity

The modern intelligence enterprise arose in response to opportunities created by the second industrial revolution and the information age. The telegraph, telephone, and wireless radio, anticipating the Internet, enhanced the potential for states and firms to monitor and control their affairs, and thus to eavesdrop on others, which in turn encouraged the development of cryptography and cryptanalysis. Railways, automobiles, ships, aircraft, and spacecraft extended the reach of commerce and war, and offered novel vantage points for surveillance. As weaponry became more lethal and precise, projecting power across longer distances in shorter times, intelligence became vital for targeting and countermeasures. Scientific progress opened up new ways of using the electromagnetic and acoustic spectra to learn about the world, resulting in a proliferation of intelligence disciplines—human (HUMINT), signals (SIGINT), imagery (IMINT), acoustic (ACINT), measurement and signature (MASINT), open source (OSINT), etc.—each requiring particular expertise and investment (Beniger 1986; Headrick 1991; Nickles 2003).

With more things to know about, more ways to know about them, and more ways to interfere with the knowledge of others, the difficulties of understanding and acting on intelligence increased dramatically. Military units employed more of their workforce in information specialties and invested more of their budgets in electronic systems, while civilian intelligence agencies played a greater role in foreign policy. Through two centuries of economic globalization, information infrastructure and the art of intelligence grew up together. Information technology enhances control, and intelligence contests it.

Ubiquitous networks create new collection and influence opportunities, and cyber operations can support or be supported by traditional intelligence disciplines. Human agents, for example, can upload malware to hard-to-reach networks, and they can leverage privacy technology for clandestine communication. Analysis depends on the fusion of multiple sources and types of intelligence, and the collaboration of distributed agencies but greater information sharing heightens the insider threats posed by moles, leakers, and careless employees. The people, satellites, aircraft, ships, and economic infrastructure that enable intelligence activities all rely on data networks that skilled attackers can exploit. Yet, intelligence risks are also counterintelligence opportunities. Deceivers must worry about being deceived.

Intelligence is notoriously hard to define. One textbook points out that 'intelligence' might refer to the processes of collecting and analysing information or conducting covert action, the products that result from processes as reports or operations, or the specialized organizations that produce them (Lowenthal 2014, Ch. 1.). Innovation in software and hardware can create new kinds of intelligence processes and products, and mobilize new organizations as targets, collectors, intermediaries, or consumers. Military intelligence not only supports battlefield operations but also fields sophisticated technical platforms (satellites, ships, aircraft) that provide intelligence for political customers, too. Civilian intelligence can operate covertly in foreign areas with special authorities in peacetime when military intervention is too risky or infeasible. A Central Intelligence Agency (CIA) historian reviews a number of unsatisfactory definitions before offering his own: 'Intelligence is secret, state activity to understand or influence foreign entities' (Warner 2002).

Intelligence differs from journalism or scholarship, even though it shares some analytic methodology, because of the extreme secrecy surrounding its sources, methods, and communication with its policy audience. Expertise in secrecy enables intelligence services to not only inform policy but also execute it. The same tradecraft that is useful for breaking in and stealing information can also be useful for sowing disinformation or organizing a conspiracy. Moreover, covert action is more likely to succeed when operatives have reliable intelligence about their target. The science and art of deception are difficult and expensive to master, and failure can be embarrassing or worse if the target retaliates. Thus the most sophisticated intelligence actors tend to be well-funded and experienced state agencies backstopped by the state's other instruments of power. Even so, nonstate actors may engage in secret statecraft as well, and cyberspace gives them more ways to do so.

DIRECTION—THE POLITICAL OBJECTIVE

Intelligence, as used here, is the use of secret means for strategic ends. This formulation highlights two general problems, one operational and one political. The operational problem is the design, execution, and protection of clandestine collection and/or covert action using technical and/or human means.[2] Yet actors do not conduct cyber operations for their own sake but rather in pursuit of some political or economic goal, in a social system of other actors with their own goals. The political problem is the evaluation of the costs and benefits of conducting the operation given the expected reaction of other actors affected by it. Both problems must grapple with uncertainty, and different actors may be more or less able to manage them.

Any organization that uses a computer is a potential target for cyber operations, so long as a competitor can imagine a use for its data. Many people are left alone in cyberspace despite being vulnerable for the simple reason that they are not wealthy or useful enough to attract attention. States may use cyber espionage for many purposes: to gather information about national security threats, to gain insight into foreign decision making, to support military targeting and operations, to advance the competitive position of domestic firms, to influence or intimidate civilian populations, to monitor and track dissidents, to steal or extort financial resources, etc.

The same organization, moreover, might be targeted for quite different reasons. Cyber operators might penetrate a foreign firm to steal its intellectual property or negotiating positions to provide their own firms with an unfair commercial advantage; or they might target the same firm to learn about a government's policies indirectly through firm communications with government officials, or to gain access to technologies to facilitate follow-on espionage operations. The US National Security Agency (NSA) targeted the Chinese telecommunications giant Huawei not to steal its intellectual property for economic gain but to learn how to hack into Huawei equipment used by other targets around the world (Sanger and Perlroth 2014). Intellectual property pilfered from a defence firm might, likewise, be used for economic espionage or to devise military countermeasures. The target of an intrusion also need not be the target of influence. For example, Russia hacked the Democratic National Committee and obtained embarrassing internal emails during the 2016 US election, but then it covertly released them through WikiLeaks and other public outlets to damage Hillary Clinton in the eyes of the electorate (Sanger, Lipton, and Shane 2016).

The political and operational dimensions of cybersecurity come together in targeting. Targeting is often described as a cycle that includes the articulation of requirements, analysis of target systems and selection of targets, execution of intelligence or military operations, assessment of operational effects, and the adjustment of requirements for follow-on targeting.[3] The intelligence cycle is a type of targeting cycle that includes direction ('the important bit'), collection ('the cool bit'), analysis ('the geeky bit'), and dissemination ('the boring bit'; Panjandrum 2012). Covert action depends on a similar planning process. The canonical phases are present in particular intrusions against specific targets as well as extended operations against multiple targets coordinated with other types of operations. Targeting requirements—priorities, objectives, constraints, rules-of-engagement, intentions, values, etc.—play a critical role throughout in specifying not only what to target, but also what to avoid, particularly if compromise or collateral damage might lead to undesirable reactions from targets or third parties.

Most high-profile cyber operations are not one-off events but rather campaigns that unfold over months or years, belying the popular belief that hacking occurs 'at Internet speed'. An initial penetration is usually followed by reconnaissance in the target network that may take hours or weeks before any data of value are discovered. Sophisticated operators seek persistence to facilitate repeat collection and influence. For example, Chinese operators target particular industries that Beijing has identified as priorities for economic development, seeking a shortcut through economic espionage, and remaining active in corporate networks for extended periods of time. The US–Israeli campaign against the Iranian nuclear program that culminated with the Stuxnet attack on enrichment was preceded by years of reconnaissance and testing, and malware developed from the same toolkit was deployed against other targets in the Middle East for intelligence collection. The Russian influence campaign against US elections, and ongoing operations against Ukraine, integrated network penetrations against a number of different organizations with overt and covert propaganda activity.

One reason why states have advantages in cybersecurity is that intelligence campaign planning requires experience and effort to synchronize activity across time, targets, and other lines of operations. Targeting supporting counterintelligence likewise requires a campaign mentality (Bejtlich 2015). The term 'advanced persistent threat' (APT), coined initially as a euphemism for Chinese intrusion sets, now usually refers to a bureaucratic state actor with the resources and patience to conduct espionage campaigns. The coordination of means and ends can be as, if not more, challenging than the tactical problems of collection or influence that receive more attention.

Indeed, the integration of policy and operations is often honoured in the breach. Principal-agent problems can distort civil-military relations, leading security agencies to work at cross-purposes with political goals, which may be ill-defined (Junio 2013). Policy-intelligence relations might be too distant, which causes intelligence to be ignored or allows agencies to go rogue, or to be too cozy, which then causes intelligence to be politicized to sell preferred policies, or prevented from asking sensitive questions (Rovner 2011). For instance, Russia's intelligence agencies compete for the attention of President Vladimir Putin without coordinating with each other, and thus military intelligence (GRU) or civilian agencies (the Soviet KGB split into the FSB and SVR) might run operations against the same target. Collusion with Russian criminal networks may further distort targeting aims (Galeotti 2016). The Chinese People's Liberation Army (PLA) consolidated space, cyber, and electronic warfare capabilities in a new Strategic Support Forces command in 2015 in an effort to centralize control over vital military and intelligence capabilities and, presumably, to rein in the PLA's wide-ranging economic espionage campaign throughout the previous decade, which had become a major irritant in China's relationship with the United States (Costello 2016).

To understand an adversary, therefore, and to counter it effectively, it is important to understand its interests and objectives, as well as the level of integration of its executing agencies. The cyber operations of different countries take on a different character because they focus on different goals. China seeks to stabilize the control of the Communist Party by censoring dissident expression and using commercial espionage to boost legitimacy-enhancing growth. Russia's operations aim to destabilize its geopolitical competitors by sowing chaos in the media and civilian communication. The United States seeks sophisticated clandestine capabilities to improve its global situational awareness and military power projection. The differential emphasis across these three states on control, chaos, or capabilities, respectively, produces a different suite of targets and activities. National targeting habits, embodied in campaigns, can thus aid attribution. Cyber defence should aim to combat the purpose and direction of an offensive cyber operation, not simply the technology of implementation.

COLLECTION—THE TECHNICAL OPERATION

Popular treatments of cybersecurity, and intelligence generally, emphasize the technical magic of collection. The gadgets and tricks that spies use to infiltrate a hostile organization and return with valuable data are inherently fascinating, but all collection is useless without effective direction, analysis, and dissemination. The collection phase in cyber intelligence is easier to study because the discovery of intrusions and malware infections provides abundant data, whereas the secretive organizations that control them from afar are more inscrutable. Computer scientists, naturally, tend to study the technical means and methods used to penetrate networks so that they can engineer tools and techniques to make penetration more difficult. The political direction or downstream use of any compromised data is of secondary concern to the tactical operator or the technical researcher.

Cyber tradecraft has clear analogues with traditional espionage. Just as a case officer tries to spot and recruit people in proximity to, or with insider access to, a target facility, so the cyber operator looks for vulnerable servers and workstations within a target organization that can be infected with spyware. It may take a lot of time to identify vulnerabilities in a particular target, especially if guarded by security systems. A common burglar may rattle doorknobs looking for any unlocked house to burgle, but a heist against a particular bank takes a lot more planning. Low-level spies may report on 'atmospherics' in a town or the movement of troops, but the best spy has access to specific information in an organization. Most cybercrime, similarly, looks to exploit any unguarded host or bank account, but cyber espionage targets a particular organization or person. The skilful, patient, determined adversary will almost always be able to find a way in, but this research (and development) process takes some time (Herley 2013).

A case officer might use the personal contacts of one spy to access other individuals with better placement—for example, recruiting a secretary to gain access to an executive. Likewise, the cyber operator uses an initial foothold in a network to move laterally to other more sensitive parts. Just as a case officer manipulates people to gain access and placement to her target by playing on their emotions, desires, and preconceptions, the cyber operator may use social engineering to trick gullible computer users into revealing their credentials or installing malware. One Russian group (known as APT-29 and likely the FSB) used a humorous video of monkeys as clickbait (F-Secure Labs Threat Intelligence 2015). Another Russian group (known as APT-28 and likely the GRU) crafted convincing spear-phishing emails containing links, disguised via the URL-shortening service Bitly that redirected users to a spoofed login page for the Gmail cloud email service, which in turn granted the Russians access to emails from the Democratic National Committee and Hillary Clinton campaign in 2016 (SecureWorks Counter Threat Unit Threat Intelligence 2016).

Traditional espionage with human agents is inherently difficult and risky. Spies must be identified, recruited, managed, supported, and continuously evaluated. Captured spies may be imprisoned or executed, and the spectacle can become a diplomatic crisis (e.g. the capture of Francis Gary Powers shot down over the Soviet Union). To plant electronic bugs, take pictures, remove documents, or simply engage in conversation, a human spy must physically navigate to the target without triggering suspicion and then transfer the acquired information back to base. The Boeing employee Dongfan Chung, who spied for China between 1979 and 2006, had 250,000 pages of sensitive material in his house at the time of his arrest (Office of the National Counterintelligence Executive 2011). Today these same data would fit onto a single compressed data file that could be quickly and securely transmitted through the Internet with little personal risk to the remote operator. The compromise of a cyber operation might result in the loss of access to a network (because defenders can reconfigure settings) or the forfeit of some particular malware (because discovery enables vendors to issue patches that close the exploited vulnerabilities), but the operator can simply try again with another method or move on to another target.

Although the risk to the *operator* is much reduced in cyber espionage, all the familiar risks to the *operation* remain. Communication between a case officer and an agent usually relies on cut-outs (trusted intermediaries who can pass on encoded and/or encrypted messages), dead drops (caches for hiding purloined documents and further instructions), and safe houses (protected hideouts for face-to-face meetings or refuge). Cyber operators, similarly, rely on elaborate command and control (C2) arrangements to send and receive data to malware on infected hosts. One system, known as Hammertoss and run by APT-29, relied on an algorithm to auto-generate new Twitter accounts every day (FireEye Threat Intelligence 2015). The infected host checked to see if the designated account included a tweet from APT-29, which provided a decrypt key and a hyperlink to a stock image stored in the cloud service GitHub. APT-29 used steganography to hide encrypted commands in the image that instructed the malware to take its next steps. Stuxnet used another innovative C2 system to pass information to infected hosts on a stand-alone ('air gapped') local area network in Iran. Through peer-to-peer messaging, Stuxnet could infect USB keys and maintenance files that spanned the gap via witting or unwitting human users, so infected hosts could receive instructions and pass status updates to American or Israeli operators (Falliere, O Murchu, and Chien 2011).

Cut-outs and dead drops protect a spy handler, but they can also become a liability if they are discovered by counterintelligence agents who stealthily monitor them in an attempt to unravel the network. Similarly for offensive cyber operations, C2 is the weak link. CitizenLab at the Munk School of Global Affairs, University of Toronto, discovered a Chinese operation targeting the Tibetan Government in Exile when one of its researchers happened upon an exposed C2 server with a list of compromised hosts in India (Deibert et al. 2009). Just as a case officer travels the streets looking for hostile surveillance before attempting a meeting with a source, perhaps employing disguises or other ruses to throw off counterintelligence detection, an APT intrusion may change its behaviour or even delete itself to elide specific antivirus, firewall, and intrusion-detection systems. To frustrate tracking via C2, one enterprising Russian operation hijacked the downstream bandwidth from a satellite-based Internet service provider (ISP) (Tanase 2015).

For all its technical nuance, cyber espionage is still an intelligence operation and intelligence requires planning, preparation, and a support team for logistics and assistance, to say nothing of legal or deterrent resources in case something goes wrong. The technology of collection changes but the organizational and strategic challenges remain. State intelligence agencies are more likely than individual hackers to have the experience and capacity to address enduring operational challenges. Maintaining cover for a sensitive operation is inherently difficult, and even skilled operators can make mistakes and leave behind clues. Just as it may take years to put in place a network of cut-outs, safe houses, and trained agents to run a productive spy ring, it takes some time to develop malware toolkits, perform target reconnaissance, and set up C2 infrastructure. States that are willing to make these investments will also think twice about risking it all with too aggressive or hasty an operation.

ANALYSIS AND APPLICATION— FOLLOWING THROUGH

Cyber espionage collects an immense amount of data. The security firm Mandiant observed APT-1, identified as PLA Unit 61398 in Shanghai, remove hundreds of terabytes from 141 organizations in 20 major industries over several years, including 6.5 terabytes from a single firm in a 10-month period (Mandiant 2013). General Keith Alexander, the commander of US Cyber Command and Director of the NSA in 2012, described the broad-based Chinese campaign of economic espionage as 'the greatest transfer of wealth in history' (Alexander 2012).

Yet, a transfer of wealth, or the creation of any type of political advantage, requires more than a transfer of information. Even in cybercrime, stealing credentials to access a bank account is much easier than monetizing the theft, which requires creative money-laundering schemes (e.g. employing human mules to visit cash machines or make small online purchases) lest banks simply reverse a fraudulent transaction. The follow-through requirements are even greater for the state seeking to create and exploit a political advantage over competitors that have the power to retaliate. An intelligence organization needs to be able to recognize and evaluate valuable information, and then get it to a manager who is willing and able to act on it. Furthermore, that action has to be able to make a difference in the market or international politics. Intelligence cannot provide a competitive advantage in business or diplomacy unless a policy maker or commander can understand and use it effectively.

Organizations today put a lot more of their value (plans, communications, blueprints, etc.) online than ever before, but they also generate a lot more useless data than ever before. There may be more needles in the haystack, but the haystack is growing too. Intruders usually copy and remove far more data than they need, or they fail to take the right data, because they lack the time or ability to analyse the data's usefulness on the spot. Machine-learning techniques can help to triage and sort data, but making sense of the take ultimately requires a human analyst.

Because the technical skills of intrusion differ from analytical methods, there is almost always a division of labour in intelligence organizations. The metrics of success in a collection unit might include the number of targets penetrated, the number of hosts compromised, and the number of gigabytes exfiltrated, but these measures of performance do not translate simply into measures of effectiveness, such as whether or not a decision maker acted on the information and improved their outcomes. In the absence of effective analysis and policy application, bureaucratic dynamics could drive up collection activity without translating all those data into improved competitive advantage.

Little is publicly known about the analysis of data acquired through sensitive cyber exploitation operations.[4] Whereas collection techniques may be exposed when malware or C2 infrastructure is compromised, the adversary conducts analysis far away in secret. A lot more is known about the analysis that supports cyber defence because security firms like Mandiant (now FireEye) and Kaspersky publish reports about the latest malware techniques to highlight their technical prowess. They focus on reverse-engineering malware or figuring how a network was compromised, and may venture to build an attribution case. Defensive analysis is *about* cyber means, whereas offensive analysis focuses on data gathered *by* cyber means, which is usually about something else entirely (e.g., intellectual property, war plans, etc.). Exploiting the take, moreover, usually requires other sources of intelligence (HUMINT, IMINT, SIGINT, etc.) to provide context and evaluate cyber data. The general problems of intelligence analysis, no matter the upstream source of data, should be relevant here as well. These include cognitive biases, methodological errors, miscommunication between collectors and analysts, detection of deception by the target, separating signal from noise, ill-defined requirements, and pathological relationships between intelligence producers and consumers.[5]

Hackers can steal text, but they cannot steal context. A lot of organizational capability, especially firms at the higher end of the value chain or advanced militaries, is embodied tacitly in the people and practices that enable it to innovate (Zahra and George 2002). Without the relevant knowledge, a purloined document may be hard, if not impossible, to interpret. Many cities and countries have attempted to replicate the miracles of Silicon Valley or Cambridge, Massachusetts, but these regions are innovative ecosystems, not just collections of firms and data. Context recovery is a long-standing problem for economic espionage. In the eighteenth century, France stole drawings and manuals from England, and then lured skilled England craftsmen, and yet still had serious trouble assembling machinery into factories that could rival the English ones (Harris 1998). Official Chinese statistics on licit foreign technology transfer report that the cost of back-end analysis and absorption relative to front-end acquisition increased from 5% to 45% between 1991 and 2011, suggestive of an increasingly difficult analysis and dissemination problem (this can be expected to be greater for illicitly acquired foreign data) (State Statistics Bureau, and Ministry of Science and Technology 2011). Chinese military modernization draws on many sources of intelligence, and open technical data and exchanges, with cyber espionage constituting just a small part of the effort, and still China struggles to match Western capabilities (Cheung 2016; Hannas, Mulvenon, and Puglisi 2013).

COVERT ACTION—AMBIGUOUS INFLUENCE

For all their technical prowess and analytical acumen, intelligence agencies are fundamentally specialists in secrecy and deception. Cyber espionage mainly aims to steal data from firms, governments, and others, but the same methods useful for clandestine collection can also be used to alter or corrupt data. Stolen data can be used not only to improve decision making by policy makers and commanders, but also to influence foreign opinion through blackmail or propaganda. The NSA software toolkit used to build Stuxnet was also used to build spywares known as Flame, Duqu, and Gauss, which were discovered on computers in the Middle East (Global Research & Analysis Team 2015). All these tools made their way through protected networks, and send and receive data, via a clandestine C2 network, but they did different things when they found their target. Spyware just spies, but Stuxnet used its software payload to infect the programmable logic units that drove Iranian centrifuges, causing them to spin near their mechanical limit and thereby heightening the breakage rate.

The category of covert action conflates a wide range of activity ranging from the secret sharing of intelligence with allies, the use of overt and covert (dis)information channels to influence public opinion, the organization or infiltration of dissident opposition, blackmail, assassination, arming and training proxy forces, sabotage of infrastructure and resources, and secret wars (Johnson 1992). Cyber operations are most useful at the lower end of this spectrum to manipulate information and opinion. The Russian campaign to influence the 2016 US presidential election combined a number of different measures including intelligence collection against both Republican and Democratic campaigns through cyber as well as HUMINT means, the release of embarrassing internal documents from the Democratic Party through cut-outs like the WikiLeaks website and the Guccifer 2.0 online persona, the generation of fake news and its propagation through bogus social media accounts, overt Russian media reporting, and, potentially, collusion with or blackmail of some members of the Republican campaign.[6] A number of complex interactions resulted in the surprising election of Donald Trump (including, but not limited to, economic dislocation, a polarized electorate, a chaotic media environment, mistakes by the Clinton campaign, and Trump's unique personality), so it would be premature to give too much credit to Russian active measures.

Covert action may also involve the physical disruption of control systems (e.g. Stuxnet) but the planning is difficult and carries greater risk of adverse consequences, so such activity is much rarer than propaganda and hacktivism. Stuxnet is also notable for its deliberate restraint. Designed to slightly degrade but not catastrophically interrupt enrichment, the operation might never have been discovered but for mistakes in the code that alerted Iranian operators and copied the worm into other countries. Stuxnet, moreover, is perhaps better understood as an American effort to reassure Israel and dissuade it from bombing Iran, an instance of secret diplomacy (Lindsay 2013).

Covert action gets more attention than information gathering, just as collection gets more attention than analysis. Yet, as discussed earlier, the economic and political utility of stolen data is ambiguous because of the complexity of analysis and application. Likewise, the political effects of covert action are ambiguous because of the constraints of conspiracy and the complexity of political interaction. Whether stealing data or manipulating opponents, the operational problem of getting in and/or out of a protected target, with some plausible deniability, while avoiding retaliation, is difficult. The difficulties tend to mount for more politically valuable targets, which are likely to be better defended. Another reason why it makes sense to consolidate covert action in collection agencies is that sensitive operations require detailed intelligence for target reconnaissance, operational planning, and effects assessment. 'Olympic Games' was a collection operation for years before Stuxnet started breaking centrifuges. The fungibility of exploitation can make it difficult to determine whether a discovered intrusion is intended merely for collection or is the prelude to covert action, which can heighten the security dilemma between adversaries (Buchanan 2017).

Plausible deniability makes covert action attractive but it is also self-limiting. Broad conspiracies are difficult to keep secret from domestic critics and competitors. The opprobrium of conspiracy or surveillance can even alienate supporters of the ostensible political goal of an action. Furthermore, successful attribution by the target can provoke a response that negates the benefit of the covert action. North Korea attempted to coerce Sony into withholding release of the satirical film *The Interview* by releasing embarrassing emails previously stolen from Sony servers and threatening terrorist attacks on movie theatres, but attribution by the US government and the ensuing controversy encouraged millions of people to watch a movie that critics panned (Haggard and Lindsay 2015). Similarly, if the costs of paying the ransom to unlock a system encrypted by cybercriminals exceed the costs of replacing it and/or initiating a law enforcement response, then anonymous coercion fails.

The resort to covert action often reflects a desire to keep conflicts limited. Plausible deniability in cases where attribution is obvious (e.g. the Russian incursion into Ukraine or interference with the US election) works not necessarily to hide the identity of the attacker but rather to provide an excuse for the defender to not respond forcefully (Carson 2016). One reason why cyber attacks seem so difficult to deter is that attackers intentionally target them below some threshold where they expect retaliation to be more likely. Ironically, most cyber insecurity is a consequence of deterrence working well where it is needed most (Lindsay 2015).

Counterintelligence—Deception for Defence

Because cyberspace increases the opportunities for intelligence collection and covert influence, it also heightens the importance of counterintelligence. If intelligence is the use of deceptive tradecraft to gain access to denied areas and manipulate people (and machines), then counterintelligence is the use of deception against the deceivers. A determined intelligence adversary constantly evolves its tools and techniques to find and exploit new vulnerabilities. Therefore, network defenders must continuously adapt as well. Static defences are inadequate in a contest of intellectual manoeuvre.

A computer that can send or receive no data is perfectly secure, but perfectly useless. Networked productivity inevitably carries some risk. Information assurance (IA) aims to manage risks to the confidentiality, availability, and integrity of enterprise data. IA includes operational security (OPSEC) to hide valuable data from observation as well as defensive counterintelligence to detect and respond to intrusions. Network administrators improve OPSEC by employing firewall, intrusion detection, and antivirus systems, and keeping application patches up to date. Information controls such as background checks, classification, and compartmentalization restrict access to sensitive data to people who have a validated 'need to know', which reduces data exposure and facilitates counterintelligence investigation. Workforce education improves OPSEC by cajoling employees to choose strong passwords, not store them in plain text, change them often, use encrypted circuits, not respond to phishing emails, report suspicious activity, and generally improve their 'cyber hygiene'. Loose tweets sink fleets.

OPSEC can lock out casual miscreants, but it is insufficient against a skilled APT or insider threat that can fake signals of trustworthiness. Defensive counterintelligence employs more active measures to detect, track, and ensnare an intruder. Even the most careful attackers sometimes make mistakes that raise suspicions. Traditional counterintelligence agents conduct investigations, leverage analysis from multiple intelligence streams, and run sting operations to catch, not just a single spy, but also their handlers and other spies. One way to limit the potential damage of an ongoing penetration while improving intelligence about it is to provide forged or innocuous data to the spy to see what they do. Arrests then offer interrogation opportunities that can help unravel the spy ring. In cybersecurity, similarly, defenders can patiently monitor data traffic patterns, isolate malware samples in sandbox networks, correlate locally observed activity with data from other intrusions, and assemble a multisource understanding of the threat, all while balancing risk and mitigating damage.

Whereas OPSEC aims to keep threats out, counterintelligence draws them in to learn more about their tools, C2, operators, and intentions. Network security monitoring employs silent alarms, logs, and baited files or honeypots to gather data about the threat (Bejtlich 2013). An APT breach is rarely a one-off event but rather part of an extended campaign in particular political circumstances. Security researchers thus have multiple opportunities to reverse engineer the same malware, follow its digital footprints, and make inferences about its origin. Because malware toolkits and C2 infrastructure take time to develop, attackers tend to reuse them. Attacks against coherent target sets that align with particular national objectives further contribute to a recognizable modus operandi for particular APT groups. Ironically, the agencies most skilled at evading detection through the use of sophisticated tradecraft may be more easily identified if they are detected. The US NSA is rarely caught in the act, for example, but when Kaspersky identified the Equation Group there was no reasonable alternative explanation for the expert coding, targeting patterns, and suggestive connections to Stuxnet and the Snowden leaks. Experienced professionals who respond to a breach learn to quickly recognize the tell-tale habits of familiar APTs, even as a solid attribution case takes time to assemble (Rid and Buchanan 2015).

Offensive counterintelligence, also described as active defence or hack-back, takes the fight to the adversary. Cyber analogues to double-agent and disinformation operations include attaching poisoned code to files that the intruder carries back to its networks, planting faulty data to confuse analysts or mislead foreign targets, or redirecting and interfering with C2 traffic. Defensive deception can administer a targeted retaliation even without attribution because, as in a minefield, the very act of transgression selects the target that needs to be punished. Network security monitoring might also provide targeting data to enable offensive cyber operations against the adversary's networks or other punishment, such as targeted economic sanctions or diplomatic retaliation (Bodmer et al. 2012).

The offensive advantages of cyberspace diminish in the face of an active counterintelligence posture. OPSEC employs deception to hide data from intruders. Defensive counterintelligence uses deception to monitor, understand, and trap an intruder. Offensive counterintelligence uses deception to actively harm the intruder or its home networks. Deception improves denial by making compromise of the offensive intrusion more likely, and deception improves deterrence if the attacker fears that compromise will lead to further consequences (Gartzke and Lindsay 2015).

Conclusion—A New Era of Espionage

Intelligence is the use of deceptive means for the strategic ends of statecraft, and cyberspace both expands the opportunities for and amplifies the challenges of intelligence. Understanding the technology of intrusion is necessary but not sufficient for understanding cybersecurity. Strategists who know nothing about the Internet, furthermore, have much to teach about cybersecurity. The ancient Chinese Sunzi states, 'The way of war is a way of deception', but also emphasizes, 'Only the enlightened ruler, the worthy general, can use the highest intelligence for spying, thereby achieving great success' (Tzu 2002, 6, 94) The ninth-century commentator Du Mu adds, 'Just as water, which carries a boat from bank to bank, may also be the means of sinking it, so reliance on spies, while productive of great results, is often the cause of utter destruction.'[7] These potentials and pitfalls are general considerations for deception, whatever the technology in play.

An intelligence framework helps to clarify a number of popular misconceptions about cybersecurity. Many people believe that cyber offence has the advantage over defence. There are countless access vectors and vulnerabilities available for determined attackers to exploit, while defenders have an impossible coordination problem across vendors, administrators, users, and regulators. As we have seen, however, planning and executing a complex operation is not trivial, and defensive deception raises the chances that offensive deception will fail. A cyber attacker's reliance on deception to do anything whatsoever is too often conflated with offensive advantage. A contest of wits is different from a contest of strength. In traditional espionage, the human spy is cheaper than the security services looking for them (so a dollar buys more offence than defence), but dangers of operational failure and potential retaliation lurk everywhere. Simply getting in, furthermore, does not produce a competitive advantage without follow-through analysis and application of the take. Hacking games of capture the flag emphasize the speed of compromising a tactical objective, but actual intelligence operations are lengthier campaigns for political or economic objectives in a complex and unpredictable social context.

It is also widely assumed that cyberspace levels the playing field, devolving power away from states. As described in previous chapters, terrorists, criminals, and dissidents can use readily available Internet tools to steal data and harass state regimes (and each other). Counterintelligence, once the exclusive purview of state agencies, is now de rigueur for private organizations targeted by APTs. Defensive tradecraft diffuses from the government (former intelligence officers have started private security firms like Mandiant and CrowdStrike) and is spontaneously reinvented (as with a group of scientists who trained their graduate students to masquerade as customers for counterfeit pharmaceuticals to study suspicious spammers) (Kanich et al. 2011). Indeed, cyberspace democratizes deception.

Nevertheless, it takes more than just a successful network intrusion to capitalize on a stratagem or conspiracy, and to insure against its failure. Intelligence is a process, often a campaign, conducted by a human organization, often multiple organizations, in political and economic circumstances, often fraught with risk. The intelligence agencies of advanced industrial countries possess distinct advantages in this context and pose the biggest threats to state and non-state actors alike.

Military metaphors are inevitable in any contest between attackers and defenders, but they can be misleading in cybersecurity. Cyber operations thrive in the grey zone between peace and war, intelligence and combat, and civilian and military affairs. Military cyber operations, discussed in the following chapters, are almost always clandestine (stealthy) but not necessarily covert (deniable). SIGINT from computer networks can support precision targeting and provide early warning. Disinformation can support ruses and feints or bait enemies into an ambush. The disruption of military command and control, in the electronic warfare tradition, can create tactical windows of opportunity and degrade enemy decision making. Yet, all these operations work indirectly through subterfuge and manipulation, not directly through brute force. Indirect action can provide leverage in unconventional conflict, but it can also blunt effectiveness when proxies—human or machine—misbehave.

The ethical controversies of cybersecurity, finally, are not simply novelties of the Internet age, but rather are symptomatic of the uneasy relationship between counterintelligence and democracy. Counterintelligence carries connotations of authoritarian surveillance, police infiltration of civil society, secret sanctions against domestic enemies of the regime, and debilitating paranoia. Intelligence is sexy but counterintelligence is creepy.[8] The democratization of deception extends the reach of states and social media firms into the private lives of citizens. Digital globalization depends on increasing social trust (e.g. people are willing to shop and bank online), but, ironically, that very trust creates more opportunities for the play of deception. Modern APTs, much like traditional spies before them, make use of everyday infrastructure and social roles to disguise dead drops, cut-outs, safe houses, and the rest of their C2 apparatus. Open connections and flexible technologies enable innovation for productive and destructive ends alike. Overreaction to the threat, however, could compromise economic productivity and democratic society (Zittrain 2006).

During the Cold War, it was easier for the Soviets to spy in the United States than vice versa. Soviet agents could easily enter and move through an open democracy, and useful information could be readily obtained through open sources. On the other side of the Iron Curtain, paranoid police states inhibited foreign espionage, but also undermined their own economic vitality. Just as Soviet intelligence could run 'illegals' who hid for years in plain sight living as Americans, APTs can now install implants that remain undetected for years within the networks of vital firms and critical infrastructure. Easily accessible satellite maps, corporate webpages, news archives, and social media sites provide open troves of targeting information. A more monitored, controlled, and compartmented Internet might curtail these cyber threats, but at what price? We should be wary of undermining the trust and creativity that make the Internet worth having in the first place.

NOTES

1. Paraphrasing Dobzhansky, Theodosius. 1973. 'Nothing in Biology Makes Sense except in the Light of Evolution.' *American Biology Teacher* 35 (3): 125–129.
2. *Clandestine* activity hides the activity itself while *covert* activity hides the identity of the actor. Uniformed commandos operate clandestinely but not covertly. Unattributed propaganda is covert but not clandestine. Cyber operations that are hidden in the network and hard to attribute if discovered are both clandestine and covert.
3. E.g. US Army. 2015. *FM 3-60: Targeting*. Washington, DC, Department of the Army.
4. NSA documents leaked by Edward Snowden offer some insight into the automated processing of some collection programs, but the role of the human analysts remains obscure.
5. Lowenthal, *Intelligence*, Ch. 6.
6. Sanger, Lipton, and Shane, 'The Perfect Weapon'.
7. Sun-tzu, *Art of War*, 325.
8. There is a reason why James Bond works for MI6 and not MI5.

REFERENCES

Alexander, Keith. 2012. 'Cybersecurity and American Power: Addressing New Threats to America's Economy and Military', Keynote address. American Enterprise Institute, Washington, DC, 9 July. http://www.aei.org/events/2012/07/09/cybersecurity-and-american-power/

Bejtlich, Richard. 2013. *The Practice of Network Security Monitoring: Understanding Incident Detection and Monitoring*. San Francisco, CA: No Starch Press.

Bejtlich, Richard. 2015. 'Strategic Defence in Cyberspace: Beyond Tools and Tactics'. In *Cyber War in Perspective: Russian Aggression against Ukraine*, edited by Kenneth Geers, 15 9–70. Tallinn: NATO Cooperative Cyber Defence Centre of Excellence.

Beniger, James R. 1986. *The Control Revolution: Technological and Economic Origins of the Information Society*. Cambridge, MA: Harvard University Press.

Bodmer, Sean, Max Kilger, Gregory Carpenter et al. 2012. *Reverse Deception: Organized Cyber Threat Counter-Exploitation*. New York: McGraw-Hill.

Buchanan, Ben. 2017. *The Cybersecurity Dilemma: Hacking, Trust and Fear Between Nations*. New York: Oxford University Press.

Carson, Austin. 2016. 'Facing Off and Saving Face: Covert Intervention and Escalation Management in the Korean War', *International Organization* 70 (1): 103–31.

Cheung, Tai Ming. 2016. 'Innovation in China's Defense Technology Base: Foreign Technology and Military Capabilities', *Journal of Strategic Studies* 39 (5–6): 728–61.

Costello, John. 2016. 'The Strategic Support Force: Update and Overview', The Jamestown Foundation, *China Brief* 16 (19).

Deibert, Ron, Arnav Manchanda, Rafal Rohozinski, Nart Villeneuve, and Greg Walton. 2009. *Tracking GhostNet: Investigating a Cyber Espionage Network*. Citizen Lab, Munk School of Global Affairs, University of Toronto, and SecDev Group.

Falliere, Nicolas, Liam O Murchu, and Eric Chien. 2011. 'W32.Stuxnet Dossier.' White Paper. Symantec.

FireEye Threat Intelligence. 2015. 'HAMMERTOSS: Stealthy Tactics Define a Russian Cyber Threat Group'. Milpitas, CA: FireEye, Inc.

F-Secure Labs Threat Intelligence. 2015. 'The Dukes: 7 Years of Russian Cyberespionage'. White Paper. Helsinki: F-Secure.

Galeotti, Mark. 2016. 'Putin's Hydra: Inside Russia's Intelligence Services'. Policy Brief. London: European Council on Foreign Relations.

Gartzke, Erik. 2013. 'The Myth of Cyberwar: Bringing War in Cyberspace Back Down to Earth', *International Security* 38 (2): 41–73.

Gartzke, Erik, and Jon R. Lindsay. 2015. 'Weaving Tangled Webs: Offense, Defense, and Deception in Cyberspace', *Security Studies* 24 (2): 316–48.

Global Research & Analysis Team. 2015. 'Equation: The Death Star of Malware Galaxy'. Securelist, Kaspersky Labs. 16 February. https://securelist.com/blog/research/68750/equation-the-death-star-of-malware-galaxy.

Haggard, Stephan, and Jon R. Lindsay. 2015. 'North Korea and the Sony Hack: Exporting Instability Through Cyberspace', 117. *AsiaPacific Issues*. Honolulu, HI: East-West Center.

Hannas, William C., James C. Mulvenon, and Anna B. Puglisi. 2013. *Chinese Industrial Espionage: Technology Acquisition and Military Modernization*. New York: Routledge.

Harris, J.R. 1998. *Industrial Espionage and Technology Transfer: Britain and France in the Eighteenth Century*. Aldershot: Ashgate Publishing.

Headrick, Daniel R. 1991. *The Invisible Weapon: Telecommunications and International Politics, 1851–1945*. New York: Oxford University Press.

Herley, Cormac. 2013. 'When Does Targeting Make Sense for an Attacker?', *IEEE Security & Privacy* 11 (2): 89–92.

Jervis, Robert. 1998. *System Effects: Complexity in Political and Social Life*. Princeton, NJ: Princeton University Press.

Johnson, Loch K. 1992. 'On Drawing a Bright Line for Covert Operations', *American Journal of International Law* 86 (2): 284–309.

Junio, Timothy J. 2013. 'How Probable Is Cyber War? Bringing IR Theory Back in to the Cyber Conflict Debate', *Journal of Strategic Studies* 36 (1): 125–33.

Kanich, Chris, Neha Chachra, Damon McCoy et al. 2011. 'No Plan Survives Contact: Experience With Cybercrime Measurement.' Berkeley, CA: Usenix. https://www.usenix.org/legacy/events/cset11/tech/final_files/Kanich.pdf

Lawson, Sean. 2013. 'Beyond Cyber-Doom: Assessing the Limits of Hypothetical Scenarios in the Framing of Cyber-Threats', *Journal of Information Technology & Politics* 10 (1): 86–103.

Lindsay, Jon R. 2013. 'Stuxnet and the Limits of Cyber Warfare', *Security Studies* 22 (3): 365–404.

Lindsay, Jon R. 2015. 'Tipping the Scales: The Attribution Problem and the Feasibility of Deterrence against Cyber Attack', *Journal of Cybersecurity* 1 (1): 53–67.

Lowenthal, Mark M. 2014. *Intelligence; From Secrets to Policy*. 6th edn. Los Angeles: CQ Press.

Mandiant. 2013. 'APT1: Exposing One of China's Cyber Espionage Units.' White Paper. http://intelreport.mandiant.com/Mandiant_APT1_Report.pdf

Nickles, David Paull. 2003. *Under the Wire: How the Telegraph Changed Diplomacy*. Cambridge, Mass.: Harvard University Press.

Office of the National Counterintelligence Executive. 2011. 'Foreign Spies Stealing US Economic Secrets in Cyberspace.' Report to Congress on Foreign Economic Collection and Industrial Espionage 2009–2011.

Panjandrum. 2012. 'Mice and Men: Disseminating Intelligence Product'. *IMSL Insights*. 8 July. http://intelmsl.com/insights/intelligence-101/mice-and-men-disseminating-intelligence-product/

Rid, Thomas. 2012. 'Cyber War Will Not Take Place', *Journal of Strategic Studies* 35 (5): 5–32.

Rid, Thomas, and Ben Buchanan. 2015. 'Attributing Cyber Attacks', *Journal of Strategic Studies* 38 (1–2): 4–37.

Rovner, Joshua. 2011. *Fixing the Facts: National Security and the Politics of Intelligence*. Ithaca, NY: Cornell University Press.

Sanger, David E., and Nicole Perlroth. 2014. 'N.S.A. Breached Chinese Servers Seen as Security Threat', *The New York Times*, 22 March.

Sanger, Eric, Lipton, David E., and Scott Shane. 2016. 'The Perfect Weapon: How Russian Cyberpower Invaded the U.S.', *The New York Times*, December 13.

Tzu SecureWorks Counter Threat Unit Threat Intelligence. 2016. 'Threat Group-4127 Targets Hillary Clinton Presidential Campaign.' Atlanta, GA: SecureWorks.

State Statistics Bureau, and Ministry of Science and Technology. 2011. *China Yearbooks on Science and Technology Statistics*. Vol. 1991–2011. Beijing: China Statistics Press.

Stefan Tanase. 2015. 'Satellite Turla: APT Command and Control in the Sky'. *Securelist, Kaspersky Labs*. 9 September. https://securelist.com/blog/research/72081/satellite-turla-apt-command-and-control-in-the-sky/

Sun. 2002. *The Art of War: The Essential Translation of the Classic Book of Life*. Translated by John Minford. New York: Penguin Books.

Warner, Michael. 2002. 'Wanted: A Definition of "Intelligence"', *Studies in Intelligence* 46 (3).

Zahra, Shaker A., and Gerard George. 2002. 'Absorptive Capacity: A Review, Reconceptualization, and Extension', *Academy of Management Review* 27 (2): 185–203.

Zittrain, Jonathan L. 2006. 'The Generative Internet', *Harvard Law Review* 119 (7): 1974–2040.

CHAPTER 15

···

CYBERWAR *REDUX*

···

BEN BUCHANAN

CYBERWAR is fashionable again. It took a while to get to this point. The 1990s and 2000s yielded a series of dire warnings about the looming cyber threat, first under the moniker of a 'Digital Pearl Harbor' and then as a 'Cyber 9/11'.[1] Former national security officials published books portending of the danger, with provocative titles like 'America the Vulnerable' (Brenner 2011). A 2007 test that destroyed a power generator, and the 2010 discovery of the Stuxnet worm that wrecked Iranian centrifuges, added explosive visuals and international intrigue to the new menace.[2]

Then came an interregnum. 2013 brought the arrival of academic scepticism. The widely read books of this period carried titles like *Cyber War Will Not Take Place*, while scholarly journal articles warned of the 'myth' of cyberwar (Rid 2013; Gartzke 2013). Absent many observable cyberwar activities—indeed, absent actual deaths—doubt about the prospects and dangers of cyber conflict started to solidify. In particular, it seemed unlikely that cyberwar would ever become war in the purest sense: politics by violent means, an instrument used to settle scores between nations.

Several events changed the calculus again, ushering in a new era of worrying about cyber conflict. At the very end of 2014, North Korean hackers launched a devastating attack on Sony (Schmidt, Perlroth, and Goldstein 2015). In 2015, for the first time ever (in public, at least), a cyber attack caused a power outage, plunging a quarter-million Ukrainians into darkness (Lee, Assante, and Conway 2016; Cybersecurity & Infrastructure Security Agency 2016; Zetter 2016). Around the same time, Iranian hackers wiped thousands of computers in Sands Casino (Elgin and Riley 2014). In 2016, in the midst of one of the most combative American presidential elections ever, Russian intelligence services used network intrusions and spoofed messages to gain access to the Democratic Party's files and emails. They then dripped these files out to the media and WikiLeaks over a series of months, perhaps with an appreciable effect on the ultimate election result (Rid 2016; Entous, Nakashima, and Miller 2016). Eight days before the vote, the Obama administration's reportedly stern warning to the Russians over a secure Cold War-era communications channel marked an important milestone (Sanger 2016a). Cyberwar was back.

This chapter takes as its inspiration David Kilcullen's influential article 'Counterinsurgency *Redux*' (Kilcullen 2006). That piece, published in 2006, noted the renewed interest in counter-insurgency sparked by the ongoing Iraq War. But it also warned against over-interpreting history and over-weighting seemingly foundational notions. The new form of counter-insurgency, the *redux*, as played out in the battlefields of Iraq and Afghanistan, was meaningfully different from what early counter-insurgency theorists had conceptualized. The initial ideas and practices were not always the best way to grasp the new threat.

So it is with cyberwar. By articulating a *redux* notion of cyberwar, this chapter argues that, as discussion of cyberwar returns to prominence, it is best not to repeat the period of hype and exaggeration. The *redux* version of cyberwar denotes a return of the concept but also, most importantly (and unlike Kilcullen's usage), a reduction of it. Indeed, it is wise to deploy the term 'cyberwar' as classically understood very carefully, if at all. Many of the critiques about cyber capabilities falling short of all-out war retain their merit. Instead, what many refer to as cyberwar is best conceptualized as modern versions of sabotage, espionage, and subversion.

This chapter proceeds in three steps. First, it recapitulates the debate about whether or not cyber capabilities are able to reach the level of war. This section raises concerns about whether cyber capabilities are violent, instrumental, and political enough to resolve contests of wills between nations. The question is an important one, but it is theoretical. There is no doubt that cyber capabilities can play a role in conflict, even if they do not resolve the conflict on their own. It then makes sense to look less at theoretical questions of what is war and more at what exactly cyber capabilities can do.

The second section attempts to do just this, establishing a *redux* understanding of what cyberwar looks like. It re-introduces older notions of spying, sabotage, and subversion, each of which has a rich history. Unifying these ideas—showing how cyber attacks on computer systems can achieve the military goal of sabotage, for example, or how network intrusions enable modern espionage—provides a framework for more realistically conceptualizing cyber operations. To make this section more practical, it is populated with several examples of what appear to be actual state-sponsored activities. These operations provide examples of important trends. If the cyberwar *redux* view is correct, then these will be representative of how future cyber conflict evolves.

The conclusion of the chapter attempts to guide the debate going forward. Though cyber operations are slower-changing than is often assumed, there is no doubt that new capabilities are developed and deployed over time. In order to better make sense of new evidence as it arrives, it is best to have a framework for determining whether or not the cyberwar *redux* view is correct, or whether the fears of a broader and more devastating cyberwar are more realistic. The conclusion therefore presents some provisional field observations. These observations can serve as tests of future evidence to determine if the cyberwar *redux* view holds merit going forward.

Cyberwar or Not?

By at least one account, high-level cyberwar fears began with a movie. *WarGames*, released in 1983, depicted teenage hackers as they broke into the United States' military's computer networks and played what they thought was a game but which turned out to be a simulation of nuclear exchange. The result was very nearly a fictional World War III. President

Reagan, upon seeing the film, is said to have asked his military advisers whether such a thing was possible. It was a question that would be repeated again and again over the next few decades: could this sort of penetration of American computers really happen?

The initial answer to Reagan, from then-Chairman of the Joint Chiefs of Staff John Vessey, was that the movie's plot was not as far-fetched as one might assume (Kaplan 2016, 1). The dangers were real. It is an answer that has turned up time and again in Washington commissions, as different administrations wrestle with the possibility of a massive cyber attack against the United States' critical infrastructure, against military capabilities, or against another nation.[3] Even if such things are not possible now, the argument usually goes, they are on their way. As the title of one famous RAND study warned, 'Cyberwar is coming!' (Arquilla and Ronfeldt 1993).

Influential books have portrayed a variety of circumstances of cyberwar, envisioning the harms that might occur: at a moment of political crisis, or in a shooting conflict, lights flicker, markets crash, trains and planes collide, and weapons fail. It is worth quoting at length one of these scenes, written by former United States cybersecurity coordinator Richard Clarke, in order to demonstrate the enormous fears of what cyberwar might entail:

> Within a quarter of an hour, 157 major metropolitan areas have been thrown into knots by a nationwide power blackout hitting during rush hour. Poison gas clouds are wafting toward Wilmington and Houston. Refineries are burning up oil supplies in several cities. Subways have crashed in New York, Oakland, Washington, and Los Angeles. Freight trains have derailed outside major junctions and marshaling yards on four major railroads. Aircraft are literally falling out of the sky as a result of midair collisions across the country. Pipelines carrying natural gas to the Northeast have exploded, leaving millions in the cold. The financial system has also frozen solid because of terabytes of information at data centers being wiped out. Weather, navigation, and communications satellites are spinning out of their orbits into space. And the U.S. military is a series of isolated units, struggling to communicate with each other. Several thousand Americans have already died, multiples of that number are injured and trying to get to hospitals (Clarke and Knake 2010, 67).

It was inevitable that, after several decades of these kind of predictions, but almost no physical damage from cyber attacks and zero deaths, the sceptics would have their say. Two related critiques emerged. First, the actual dangers of cyberwar are overstated: cyber capabilities are not able to do the amount of harm that those sounding the alarm feared. As a technical matter, developing these capabilities—or, as some would have it, cyber weapons—appears to be a daunting proposition. Gaining access to computer systems is, for a well-resourced intruder, straightforward enough. The spate of cyber espionage incidents confirms as much, even against systems that are or should be relatively secure.

Yet, should an intruder seek to have a destructive physical effect—the kind often associated with war—this is where the hard work often begins. In general, the more damaging a cyber attack is designed to be, the more tailoring of the malicious code is required (Rid and McBurney 2012). Cyber capabilities that seek to achieve specific tailored outcomes require a significant amount of customization to their target. This is very much unlike many conventional weapons, which can be retargeted easily or which function in a variety of environments. As one researcher of cyber capabilities said, 'You can make a general-purpose fighter plane and it will function more or less the same in the Pacific as in the Atlantic … The same is not true for going after a Russian cyber-target versus a Chinese target.'[4] All this required specific preparation has a net effect of reducing the amount of cyber capabilities a state will be able to bring to bear, limiting the overall damage that can be done by cyber means.

A second critique is that cyber capabilities are not capable of resolving the kinds of matters states usually settle with war. The great military theorist Carl von Clausewitz wrote that, 'War is an act of force to compel the enemy to do our will' and, most famously, that war is politics by other means (von Clausewitz 1976, 75, 605). Cyber capabilities, the critique contends, are not violent enough to achieve this forcing function. If they are not capable of imposing deadly costs on an adversary, they are likely to fade in relevance compared with traditional killing operations in a battle of wills between nations. Simply put, if cyber capabilities cannot damage the enemy in such a devastating way as to force acquiescence, then they are something short of war.[5]

Even in a hypothetical future in which some kinds of cyber operations might be capable of actually causing deaths in a scalable manner, these concerns about instrumentality make it unlikely that states will choose cyber means to resolve their conflicts. Many of the most damaging cyber attacks, such as the Stuxnet operation against Iran or the blackout in Ukraine—both discussed in greater detail in the next section—have been conducted with at least some ambiguity about the perpetrator. This ambiguity can make political instrumentality a significant challenge. It is hard to persuade an adversarial state to change its decision making out of fear if the force used is invisible or the desired end state is unclear.

Neither of these critiques argues that cyber capabilities are irrelevant or unimportant. They are a key tool of statecraft, and can even contribute in certain respects to a state's warfighting abilities. But, by themselves, they do not resolve the political matters ordinarily resolved by traditional conflict. For the sceptics, the conclusion is clear: 'Cyber war has never happened in the past, it does not occur in the present, and it is highly unlikely that it will disturb our future.'[6] Instead, a more nuanced approach is needed.

Spying, Sabotage, and Subversion

Once one moves away from the theoretical question of whether cyber capabilities live up to early conceptions of cyberwar, it is possible to consider more practically what they can and cannot do. This sort of examination reveals that these cyber means have great value before and during a conflict, even if their use does not amount to war on their own or even if they are more likely to be deployed in conjunction with other capabilities. Indeed, a persuasive cyberwar sceptic, Thomas Rid, argues that cyber capabilities matter and are important, but are best understood as modern versions of three age-old concepts: spying, sabotage, and subversion.

There is little doubt about the value of cyber capabilities in carrying out espionage both before and during a conflict. Using network intrusions, the United States apparently gathered information on more than 120 world leaders, presumably gaining valuable insight into these individuals' intentions and strategies (Wilson and Gearan 2013). Nor is the United States alone in this effort. Chinese network intruders took terabytes of data from American military networks, including detailed information on American capabilities (Feng 2015). These sorts of hacking operations are not violent, are not overtly political, and—because of their intended secrecy—do not seek to coerce the potential adversary towards a preferred political end. They are impactful and important, but they are espionage, not war.

It has long been a truism that states have spied on one another. Sometimes they have sought to use information collected, or fabricated, as a means of causing disruption in other states.[7] This is subversion, defined as 'the deliberate attempt to undermine the trustworthiness, the integrity, and the constitution of an established authority or order'.[8] Violent and non-violent subversion can be carried out by a variety of actors, such as terrorist groups, but also by foreign nations. Even in vitally important matters, subversion holds a time-honoured spot in the playbook of geopolitics: by one count, the United States and Soviet Union combined to try to influence, overtly or covertly, foreign elections in 117 cases between 1945 and 2000 (Levin 2016). Undermining regimes, either via revolution at home or interference abroad, is nothing new.

Cyber operations can enable subversion. States can obtain secret and potentially embarrassing information, and then dump that information online. The most visible case of this is the series of breaches of the Hillary Clinton campaign and the Democratic National Committee in 2016, likely orchestrated by Russian operators.[9] States can also edit this dumped information to try to push a preferred narrative (Groll 2016). This sort of publication of information is hardly war in the canonical sense of political theory, but it may well be effective; the American intelligence community has apparently concluded that the Russian activities were done not just with the goal of causing disruption, but of electing Donald Trump.[10] This technique is yet another way in which non-conflict cyber activities are significant and impactful, even though they do not meet the old theories of cyberwar.

Sabotage is the final category of activity. It, too, has long held an important place in military affairs. For example, from the period of January 1942 to February 1943, German archival records indicate that there were 1,429 instances of sabotage of rail lines by French saboteurs. In the critical first months of 1944, these saboteurs destroyed three times as many locomotives as Allied airstrikes did (Douthit 1988). But, even outside conflict, sabotage has been a valuable tactic. During a tense period of the Cold War, the Central Intelligence Agency (CIA) ran an operation to sabotage Soviet technology acquisition. The operation was broad, as 'Contrived computer chips found their way into Soviet military equipment, flawed turbines were installed on a gas pipeline, and defective plans disrupted the output of chemical plants and a tractor factory. The Pentagon introduced misleading information pertinent to stealth aircraft, space defense, and tactical aircraft' (Weiss 1996, 125). It remains for historians to uncover the full effects of such activities, but there can be no doubt that they were an attempt at sabotage.

The concept of sabotage is useful in understanding many cyber attacks. Activities in this category include those that, by deliberately weakening an enemy's computer systems, cause some kind of harm or enable another operation to do so. An early famous example is the series of denial of service cyber attacks often attributed to Russia against Estonia in 2007. These attacks, which appear to have been launched as a protest after Estonia moved a statue of a Soviet soldier, took down some government websites for a period of time but caused no deaths or permanent damage (Davis 2007). A similar series of denial of service attacks against American banks in 2012, likely carried out by Iran as a response to Stuxnet, fits in the same category. The effect of these attacks was to disable access to a few banks' websites for a few hours, but nothing more (Perlroth and Hardy). Once again, these attacks fall short of war: though they are political, they are not violent and not particularly instrumental. They might be viewed more as cyber diplomacy—aggressive as it is—or as a very weak form of sabotage than as cyberwar. Far from coercing the target into a less desirable position, none of these attacks even merited a military response at all.

This holds true even if the attacks become slightly more violent. There are a few that fit this description. Primarily, these kinds of attacks affect the availability or integrity of the targeted computer systems. In 2012, attackers potentially of Iranian origin wiped 30,000 computers at the Saudi oil giant Aramco (Fisher 2012). In 2014, Iran is believed to have carried out a wiping operation against computers in Sands Casino in retaliation for critical comments made by the casino's owner, Sheldon Adelson.[11] Also in 2014, North Korean attacks on Sony, apparently in response to the movie *The Interview*, wiped machines at the film studio (Sanger and Schmidt 2015; Baumgartner 2014). Once again, though, the critique appears to hold: while the attacks were probably political in motivation, their violence was limited to computers and their instrumentality was virtually non-existent. It is difficult to point to strategic shifts in policy as a result of these operations, save for additional American sanctions on North Korea, which probably were not the desired outcome when the North Koreans chose to launch their attacks.

A next category of attacks is instrumental, but not directly violent or political. This includes the cyber operation that reportedly enabled a 2007 Israeli airstrike against a Syrian nuclear facility. By blinding the Syrian radar, the cyber capability apparently permitted the Israeli jets to remain undetected (Leyden 2007). Yet, the instrumentality here is not towards political ends but towards military ones. Israel appears to have destroyed the facility and ended the Syrian nuclear programme, but it claims no public credit for the operation. While the airstrike itself was violent, it is best viewed as something closer to covert action, in which one state stealthily sabotages the capability of another rather than attempting political coercion. Cyber capabilities can enable this sort of targeted military operation. Indeed, to the extent that special operations forces can utilize them, they may be well suited to this task.[12]

Cyber means can also, in certain circumstances, carry out covert sabotage missions on their own. Stuxnet, the reportedly American–Israeli attack on Iran, is the canonical example of this. The operation destroyed several thousand Iranian centrifuges in a covert fashion, and probably slowed down the Iranian nuclear programme, though physicists disagree on how much, if at all.[13] But the United States and Israel did not claim the attack as theirs. The goal of the operation appears to have been to delay the Iranian programme and perhaps to introduce doubt in the mind of Iranian engineers who could not determine why centrifuges were breaking. The attack only became public by accident, when the worm escaped the Iranian facility. That the operation was arguably less effective once it became public—because the Iranians now knew the cause of the centrifuge failures—and that the operation did not diminish the Iranians' willingness to develop their nuclear programme reinforces the broader point: Stuxnet was more an example of covert sabotage than of declared war.

This leads to a final possibility: the perception of vulnerability to a cyber attack might have a long-term political effect. For example, reports of the negotiations between the United States and Iran on the nuclear deal indicate that the spectre of future Stuxnet-like attacks on a renewed nuclear programme was an unspoken threat of future sabotage (Sanger 2016b). But to what degree these threats influenced the final deal seems deeply uncertain. Similarly, the United States Defense Science Board has warned of the possibility of foreign cyber attacks crippling American military capabilities in conflict: '[T]he United States cannot be confident that our critical Information Technology systems will work under attack from a sophisticated and well-resourced opponent utilizing cyber capabilities in combination with all their military and intelligence capabilities ... ' (2012, 4). This is naturally a significant concern for strategic and operational planners.

It is possible that such worries might make the United States less willing to go to war with a state like China or Russia with developed cyber capabilities, for fear that it would be less able to win. But, once again, this seems deeply speculative and indirect. If the best case for the instrumentality of cyberwar is that it subtly leads to different political choices, then it once again looks more similar to covert action than to war.

CONCLUSION: OBSERVING (OR FALSIFYING) CYBERWAR *REDUX*

This chapter has attempted to show what modern cyber capabilities are not: the much-hyped vision of strategic and catastrophic cyberwar. It has also, in line with other scholars, tried to show what they are: new versions of old techniques such as spying, sabotage, and subversion. What remains is to distil some provisional observations about this *redux* understanding of cyberwar.

Such a distillation of insights serves two important purposes. First, it provides distinct characterization for what cyberwar *redux* looks like. In the same way that the vivid, though hypothetical, visions of catastrophic cyberwar defined the early days of the concept, these field observations can lend detail to the *redux* version. Second, it provides a roadmap to falsifiability. If several of these observations are persistently disproven by events, it is likely the cyberwar *redux* concept needs re-examination. As Kilcullen wrote in his 'Counterinsurgency *Redux*' article, fortunate or not, the modern age provides a live experiment of the subject matter of counter-insurgency; the same is true for the use of cyber capabilities.[14]

What Happens Before Conflict in Cyber Operations Shapes How Conflicts Unfold

If the *redux* theory of cyberwar is right, it is what happens before conflicts begin that is of enormous significance in cyber operations. This importance can take a number of forms. Espionage by cyber means appears to be an important component of statecraft. This activity yields information on the strategies, intentions, and capabilities of other states. It also enables better defensive preparation and counterintelligence operations. Perhaps most worryingly for some, this information collection is what enables the development of tailored and highly damaging cyber capabilities—what military strategists call 'operational preparation of the environment'.[15] All this intelligence work either directly or indirectly affects if and how conflicts emerge and resolve. In short, how states do pre-conflict cyber espionage—and how they react to other states doing the same—will be a key part of statecraft in the future. But such information collection is not war.

Indeed, subversion before conflict can also shape if and how conflicts unfold. Political leadership matters a great deal, and it is possible that subversion efforts can determine who holds office. To what degree the Russian activities in 2016 achieved this is a matter to be debated by historians, but a general concept can be theorized: to the extent that cyber capabilities enable subversion as well as espionage, they can have an enormous, though non-violent, effect. Even if they are not able to swing elections, the events of 2016 showed that leaked emails and files are very capable of driving news cycles and getting attention.

Cyber Capabilities Will Not on Their Own Serve as Effective Deterrents Through Significant Punishment

There is great hand-wringing over the subject of cyber deterrence. The challenge of cyber deterrence is often interpreted as the difficulty in convincing another state to not use a particular cyber capability, for fear either of the capability's failure (called 'deterrence by denial') or of retaliation ('deterrence by punishment').[16] Perhaps even more challenging, and less likely to successfully be achieved in practice, is deterrence via a cyber capability. To achieve this, one state threatens to use a cyber capability to impose significant costs on another state should the second state pursue a particular undesired course of action.

Cyber deterrence solely via cyber-imposed costs is likely to fail. Establishing a cyber deterrent is very difficult, because developing significant and tailored cyber attack capabilities requires large amounts of time-consuming preparatory work. In many cases, such work is primarily useful only for a particular target and cannot be easily retargeted. The net effect, all else being equal, is to make development of significant punishment capability the realm only of the most advanced states with the largest budgets and the most developed capabilities. To put it more provocatively, in most circumstances, there are cheaper and more effective ways to establish deterrence than through cyber means. On this point, the United States' so-called doctrine of equivalence, in which it reserves the right to respond to a cyber attack with a kinetic one, is relevant, as are the economic sanctions and indictments of foreign cyber operators.[17] In order to have a credible deterrent, American policy makers do not just look at the country's extensive cyber means, but beyond: this fits the notion of cyberwar *redux* quite well.

Cyber Capabilities Will Not Resolve Conflicts Between Nations on Their Own

The 2007 cyber attack on Estonia, in which websites were taken offline, was sometimes referred to as 'Web War One'.[18] As discussed, this does not do justice to the concept of war. Most significantly, there is no evidence that cyber operations can, on their own, bring an end to a conflict. The same concerns about punishment in the context of deterrence apply to punishment in the context of war as well.

Once again, this is not to diminish the relevance of cyber operations. There is great and long-ongoing debate about whether some activities that obviously do amount to war, such as strategic bombing, can end them (Pape 1996). Just because a capability cannot on its own end a war does not mean it is not vitally important. It is not difficult to imagine cyber operations playing a significant role in future conflicts. They might be used to sabotage critical infrastructure, to gather crucial information about an adversary's plans, to subvert foreign support for conflict, and much more. They might substantially aid military operations that take territory or topple governments. They may even, in the most extreme circumstances, begin conflicts, as when a state responds to a cyber attack with a kinetic one. But, if the cyberwar *redux* theory is right, they will rarely provide the decisive blow that ends a war.

Conflict Is a More Useful Framing than Cyberwar

There may arise a situation in which the cyberwar *redux* theory is partially wrong: in contrast to what has been argued thus far, cyber attacks may be scalable, potent, and perhaps instrumental. But, even in such a hypothetical world, it is deeply unlikely that cyber attacks will be the only method of war with this level of power. It would take an enormously potent cyber attack to not just inflict damage on an adversary but to do so much harm, or threaten so much future harm, so as to deter a kinetic response. Put differently, even a true cyberwar is unlikely to remain such for long. Policymakers will probably see fit to respond to significant violence by cyber means with traditional forms of military violence.

In a hypothetical world in which cyber attacks can achieve these ends, the useful lens of analysis is not a hazy notion of cyberwar but the traditional concept of conflict. Should cyber capabilities reach the point where they are just as impactful and instrumental as other forms of weaponry, it will be of limited value to speak of escalation from cyber to kinetic, just as it is currently odd to speak of escalation from air to sea. Similarly, it will make little sense to talk of cyberwar, just as one does not speak today of air war and naval war. Even in conflicts that do primarily take place in one domain, the recognition first and foremost is that it is the conflict and its ends that are the most important, not the means. Any notion of cyberwar, however fantastical, should be tempered in the same way.

Kilcullen closes 'Counter-insurgency *Redux*' by warning of 'cut and paste' approaches. Instead, he argues, careful observations, not pre-conceived notions and solutions, must guide the fight against insurgency. So it is with the use and deterrence of cyber capabilities. This chapter has set out to ground the cyberwar discussion on firmer territory, refining and reducing it based on actual rather than hypothetical cases, and providing paths to falsifiability. As scholars and practitioners debate and carry out activities in the digital domain, they should hold themselves to the same standard. Even if not war, cyber operations are too important to be overtaken by hype.

NOTES

1. Former Director of National Intelligence Michael McConnell warned of 'the cyber equivalent of the collapse of the World Trade Center' while former CIA Director Leon Panetta warned of a 'cyber Pearl Harbor': Bumiller and Shanker 2012. 'Panetta Warns of Dire Threat of Cyberattack on U.S.', *New York Times*, 11 October. http://www.nytimes.com/2012/10/12/world/panetta-warns-of-dire-threat-of-cyberattack.html; Taylor, P. 2012. 'Former US Spy Chief Warns on Cybersecurity', *Financial Times*, 2 December. https://www.ft.com/content/ed7ff098-3c4d-11e2-a6b2-00144feabdco.
2. For more, see Zetter, K. 2014. *Countdown to Zero Day*. New York: Crown.

3. For a famous example from the 1990s, see President's Commission on Critical Infrastructure Protection 1997 'Critical Foundations', October. https://fas.org/sgp/library/pccip.pdf

4. Quoted in Nakashima. 2012. 'Pentagon to Fast-Track Cyberweapons Acquisition', *Washington Post*, 9 April. http://www.washingtonpost.com/world/national-security/pentagon-to-fast-track-cyberweapons-acquisition/2012/04/09/gIQAuwb76S_story.html

5. For one attempt to argue that they are still war, see Stone, J. 2013. 'Cyber War *Will* Take Place!', *Journal of Strategic Studies* 36 (1): 101–8. For a broader discussion, see Cornish, P., Livingstone, D., Clemente, D. et al. 2010. *On Cyber Warfare*. London, Chatham House.

6. Rid, *Cyber War*, xiv.

7. Rid, *Cyber War*, Ch. 6.

8. Rid, *Cyber War*, 116.

9. Sanger, 'White House Confirms'; Rid, 'All Signs Point'.

10. Entous et al., 'Secret CIA Assessment'.

11. Elgin and Riley, 'Now at the Sands Casino'.

12. For a discussion of special operations and other forces, including their use of some in-theater cyber capabilities, see Naylor, S. 2015. *Relentless Strike: The Secret History of Joint Special Operations Command*. New York: St. Martin's Press; Harris, S. 2014. @ *War: The Rise of the Military-Internet Complex*. New York: Eamon Dolan/Houghton Mifflin Harcourt.

13. For more on Stuxnet, see Zetter, 'Inside the Cunning, Unprecedented Hack'. For one example of dissent on the effectiveness of the worm, see Barzashka, I. 2013. 'Are Cyber-Weapons Effective? Assessing Stuxnet's Impact on the Iranian Enrichment Programme' *RUSI Journal* 158 (2): 48–56.

14. Kilcullen, 'Counter-insurgency *Redux*', 9.

15. For greater discussion of these notions and the potential effects on escalation, see Buchanan, B. 2017. *The Cybersecurity Dilemma*. New York: Oxford University Press, Chs 2–4.

16. For more on the challenges of cyber deterrence, see Buchanan, B. 2014. 'Cyber Deterrence Isn't MAD; It's Mosaic', *Georgetown Journal of International Affairs*, International Engagement on Cyber IV: 130–40.

17. For more, see Gorman, S., and Barnes, J.E. 2011. 'Cyber Combat: Act of War', *Wall Street Journal*, 31 May. http://www.wsj.com/articles/SB10001424052702304563104576355623135782718.

18. Davis, 'Hackers'.

REFERENCES

Arquilla, J., and Ronfeldt, D. 1993. 'Cyberwar Is Coming!', RAND Corporation. http://www.rand.org/pubs/reprints/RP223.html

Baumgartner, K. 2014. 'Sony/Destover: Mystery North Korean Actor's Destructive and Past Network Activity', Kaspersky Lab, 4 December. http://securelist.com/blog/research/67985/destover/

Brenner, J. 2011. *America the Vulnerable*. New York: Penguin.

Clarke, R., and Knake, R. 2010. *Cyberwar*. New York: HarperCollins.

Cybersecurity & Infrastructure Security Agency. 2016. 'Cyber-Attack against Ukrainian Critical Infrastructure', Industrial Control Systems Emergency Response Team, Department of Homeland Security. https://ics-cert.us-cert.gov/alerts/IR-ALERT-H-16-056-01

Davis, J. 2007. 'Hackers Take Down the Most Wired Country in Europe', *Wired*, 21 August. http://archive.wired.com/politics/security/magazine/15-09/ff_estonia?currentPage=all

Defense Science Board. 2012. 'Resilient Military Systems and the Advanced Cyber Threat', Department of Defense. http://www.acq.osd.mil/dsb/reports/ResilientMilitarySystems. CyberThreat.pdf

Douthit, H.L. 1988. *The Use and Effectiveness of Sabotage as a Means of Unconventional Warfare-an Historical Perspective from World War I through Vietnam*. Wright-Patterson Air Force Base, Ohio: Air Force Institute of Technology.

Elgin, B., and Riley, M. 2014. 'Now at the Sands Casino: An Iranian Hacker in Every Server', *Bloomberg*, 11 December: http://www.bloomberg.com/bw/articles/2014-12-11/iranian-hackers-hit-sheldon-adelsons-sands-casino-in-las-vegas

Entous, A., Nakashima, E., and Miller, G. 2016. 'Secret CIA Assessment Says Russia Was Trying to Help Trump Win White House', *Washington Post*, 9 December. https://www.washingtonpost.com/world/national-security/obama-orders-review-of-russian-hacking-during-presidential-campaign/2016/12/09/31d6b300-be2a-11e6-94ac-3d324840106c_story.html

Feng, B. 2015. 'Among Snowden Leaks, Details of Chinese Cyberespionage', *The New York Times*, 20 January. http://sinosphere.blogs.nytimes.com/2015/01/20/among-snowden-leaks-details-of-chinese-cyberespionage/

Fisher, D. 2012. 'Saudi Aramco Confirms Scope of Malware Attack', ThreatPost, 27 August. https://threatpost.com/saudi-aramco-confirms-scope-malware-attack-082712/76954

Gartzke, E. 2013. 'The Myth of Cyberwar: Bringing War in Cyberspace Back Down to Earth', *International Security* 38 (2): 41–73.

Groll, E. 2016. 'Turns Out You Can't Trust Russian Hackers Anymore', *Foreign Policy*, 22 August. https://foreignpolicy.com/2016/08/22/turns-out-you-cant-trust-russian-hackers-anymore/

Kaplan, F. 2016. *Dark Territory*. New York: Simon & Schuster.

Kilcullen, D. 2006. 'Counter-insurgency *Redux*', *Survival* 48 (4): 111–30.

Lee, R., Assante, M., and Conway, T. 2016. 'Analysis of the Cyber Attack on the Ukrainian Power Grid', Electricity Information Sharing and Analysis Center, 18 March. https://media.kasperskycontenthub.com/wp-content/uploads/sites/43/2016/05/20081514/E-ISAC_SANS_Ukraine_DUC_5.pdf

Levin, D.H. 2016. 'When the Great Power Gets a Vote: The Effects of Great Power Electoral Interventions on Election Results', *International Studies Quarterly* 60 (2): 189–202

Leyden, J. 2007. 'Israel Suspected of 'Hacking' Syrian Air Defences', *The Register*, 4 October. http://www.theregister.co.uk/2007/10/04/radar_hack_raid/

Pape, R.A. 1996. *Bombing to Win*. Ithaca, NY: Cornell University Press.

Perlroth, N., and Hardy, Q. 2013. 'Bank Hacking Was the Work of Iranians, Officials Say', *The New York Times*, 8 January. http://www.nytimes.com/2013/01/09/technology/online-banking-attacks-were-work-of-iran-us-officials-say.html?_r=0

Rid, T. 2013. *Cyber War Will Not Take Place*. Oxford/New York: Oxford University Press.

Rid, T. 2016. 'All Signs Point to Russia Being Behind DNC Hack', *Vice*, 25 July. https://motherboard.vice.com/read/all-signs-point-to-russia-being-behind-the-dnc-hack

Rid, T., and McBurney, P. 2012. 'Cyber-Weapons', *RUSI Journal* 157 (1): 6–13.

Sanger, D. 2016a. 'White House Confirms Pre-Election Warning to Russia over Hacking', *The New York Times*, 16 November.

Sanger, D. 2016b. 'Diplomacy and Sanctions, Yes. Left Unspoken on Iran? Sabotage', *The New York Times*, 19 January. www.nytimes.com/2016/01/20/world/middleeast/diplomacy-and-sanctions-yes-left-unspoken-on-iran-sabotage.html

Sanger, D., and Schmidt, M. 2015. 'More Sanctions on North Korea after Sony Case', *The New York Times*, 2 January. http://www.nytimes.com/2015/01/03/us/in-response-to-sony-attack-us-levies-sanctions-on-10-north-koreans.html?_r=0

Schmidt, M., Perlroth, N., and Goldstein, M. 2015. 'F.B.I. Says Little Doubt North Korea Hit Sony', *The New York Times*, 7 January. http://www.nytimes.com/2015/01/08/business/chief-says-fbi-has-no-doubt-that-north-korea-attacked-sony.html?_r=0.

von Clausewitz, C. 1976. *On War*. Princeton, NJ: Princeton University Press.

Weiss, G.W. 1996. 'The Farewell Dossier', Langley, VA: Central Intelligence Agency, Center for the Study of Intelligence. https://www.cia.gov/static/887689795bd91ed08ca926a2f6278ee4/The-Farewell-Dossier.pdf

Wilson, S., and Gearan A. 2013. 'Obama Didn't Know About Surveillance of U.S.-Allied World Leaders until Summer, Officials Say', *Washington Post*, 28 October. http://www.washingtonpost.com/politics/obama-didnt-know-about-surveillance-of-us-allied-world-leaders-until-summer-officials-say/2013/10/28/0cbacefa-4009-11e3-a751-f032898f2dbc_story.html

Zetter, K. 2016. 'Inside the Cunning, Unprecedented Hack of Ukraine's Power Grid', *Wired*, 3 March. http://www.wired.com/2016/03/inside-cunning-unprecedented-hack-ukraines-power-grid/

CHAPTER 16

ON CYBER-ENABLED INFORMATION WARFARE AND INFORMATION OPERATIONS

HERBERT LIN AND JACLYN KERR

INTRODUCTION

FROM the standpoint of traditional military conflict, the United States is unmatched by any other nation. Other nations have taken note of US conventional military prowess and sought other 'asymmetric' methods for confronting the US and other Western nations—that is, they seek to confront the US and other Western nations by targeting their weaknesses and vulnerabilities. Cyber warfare is one asymmetric counter to Western (and especially US) military advantages that depend on the use of cyberspace (Lynn 2010).

'Cyber warfare' spans a broad spectrum. At the high end, cyber conflict threatens critical national infrastructure (e.g. information technology (IT) systems that are vital to society or national interests, such as the computers controlling the electric grid or air traffic control systems; undetected alteration of financial data held by major financial institutions; and computerized weapons systems unable to hit their targets because they have lost their ability to access GPS).

Much high-end cyber conflict amounts to war by any standard. In turn, war has connotations of hard power: armed conflict, violence, death and destruction, shooting, kinetic weapons, and clear transitions between war and peace. The patron saint of war is von Clausewitz, who wrote that 'War ... is an act of violence to compel our opponent to fulfill our will' (1984, 90), and that, in war, 'the fighting forces must be destroyed'.[1]

But not all cyber conflict resembles war in the Clausewitzian sense. Lower-level cyber conflict involves credit-card fraud; intellectual property theft involving blueprints, business data, and contract negotiating positions; compromises of personal information such as credit reports and medical data; and denial of service attacks that prevent rightful users from accessing online resources. Such activities can have significant effects on nations over time, but they do not rise to the level of war.

This chapter extends the spectrum of cyber conflict to a domain that is not even necessarily home to activity that is illegal under either domestic or international law but that nevertheless has profound threat implications for modern democracies—that domain is cyber-enabled information warfare and influence operations.

Information Warfare and Influence Operations

Information warfare and influence operations (IWIO) is the deliberate use of information by one party on an adversary to confuse and mislead an adversary, and ultimately to influence the choices and decisions that the adversary makes. IWIO is a hostile, non-kinetic activity, or at least an activity that is conducted between two parties whose interests are not well aligned along some important dimension. At the same time, IWIO is not warfare in the Clausewitzian sense (nor in any sense presently recognized under the laws of war or armed conflict): it is better characterized as hostile or adversarial psychological manipulation. IWIO has connotations of soft power: propaganda, persuasion, culture, social forces, confusion, deception. The patron saint of IWIO is Sun Tzu, who wrote that 'The supreme art of war is to subdue the enemy without fighting' (Tzu).

Note that IWIO is a methodology or an approach to how one party (Party A) might deal with another party (Party B) seen as an adversary. Party A and Party B can be nations, non-state actors, or domestic populations, and in principle IWIO could entail an adversarial relationship in any combination (that is, nations against other nations, against non-state actors, or against its domestic population; non-state actors against nations, against other non-state actors, or against its domestic population; or populations against their home nations, against non-state actors, or against other domestic populations). In principle, IWIO is also an approach that Party A can use on a third party (Party C) to induce hostility and adversarial action from Party C against Party B.

The Information Environment

The battlespace of IWIO is the information environment. This is the aggregate of individuals, organizations, and systems that collect, process, disseminate, or act on information.[2] It has three interrelated dimensions—physical, informational, and cognitive/emotional—in and through which individuals, organizations, and systems continually interact:

- The physical dimension is composed of command and control systems, software, key decision makers, and supporting infrastructure that enable individuals and organizations to create effects.
- The informational dimension specifies where and how information is collected, processed, stored, disseminated, and protected.[3]

- The cognitive/emotional dimension encompasses the minds and emotions of those who transmit, receive, and respond to or act on information.

STRATEGY AND A THEORY OF VICTORY IN INFORMATION WARFARE AND INFLUENCE OPERATIONS

In IWIO, victory is achieved by A when A succeeds in changing B's political goals so that they are aligned with those of A. Such alignment is not the result of B's 'capitulation' or B's loss of the ability to resist—on the contrary, B (the losing side) is openly willing. That is, IWIO victory shares the Clausewitzian focus on the opponent's will, but not its focus on destroying military forces.

IWIO mostly uses words and images to persuade, inform, mislead, and deceive so that the adversary does not use the (fully operational) military assets it does have, and the military outcome is the same as if those military assets had been destroyed. IWIO operations also provides additional options for action when it is undesirable for some reason to refrain from using kinetic military operations. Most importantly, IWIO takes place below legal thresholds of 'use of force' or 'armed attack', and at least in an international legal sense does not permit the victim to respond with the use of military force in self-defense.

The targets of IWIO are the adversary's perceptions, which reside in the cognitive dimension of the information environment. IWIO focuses on damaging knowledge, truth, and confidence, rather than physical or digital artefacts; the former reside in 'brain-space' rather than 3-D space or cyberspace. IWIO seeks to inject fear, anger, anxiety, uncertainty, and doubt into the adversary's decision-making processes. Successful IWIO practitioners alter adversary perceptions and are able to predict how altered perceptions increase the likelihood that the adversary will make choices that are favourable to the IWIO practitioner.

IWIO seeks to influence individuals, organizations, news media, government agencies, political leadership, and segments of society. Furthermore, these entities are not only military entities—there are no 'non-combatants' that enjoy immunity from IWIO attack. IWIO attacks the legitimacy of entities larger than ad hoc groups of individuals—government and other institutions that promote a larger societal cohesion (e.g. schools, news media) are particularly important targets from this perspective.

IWIO originators may also find that the sowing of chaos and confusion in an adversary for its own sake serves their interests. For example, an adversary whose government is in chaos and whose population is confused is unlikely to be able to take decisive action about anything, at least not without extended delay, thus affording the IWIO user more freedom of action. Sowing chaos and confusion is thus essentially operational preparation of the information battlefield—shaping actions that make the information environment more favourable for actual operations should they become necessary. In addition, introducing sufficient chaos into the information environment may reveal targets of opportunity that can be exploited.

Operations in Information/Influence Warfare

How Information Warfare and Influence Operations Achieves Their Objectives

IWIO activities seek to affect (change) the information environment in any one, or all, of its three dimensions (physical, informational, and cognitive/emotional) in ways that provide advantages over the adversary. IWIO can be (and mostly has been) conducted outside the explicit context of military operations (e.g. when traditional military operations are not going on) by entities without affiliation to military forces or military command and control.

IWIO is primarily psychological in nature, conveying selected information and indicators to adversary audiences to influence their emotions, motives, objective reasoning, and ultimately the behaviour of adversary governments, organizations, groups, and individuals. Their purpose is to induce or reinforce adversary attitudes and behaviour in ways favourable to the originator's objectives.[4]

The key term in the definition of IWIO is the conveyance of *selected* information to adversary audiences. The selected information may be mostly false, mostly true, or some mix of the two, and 'selected information' stands in contrast to 'all relevant information', a phrase that might be used in normal discourse regarding, for example, honest educational efforts. In IWIO, information is selected for conveyance on the basis of whether it will influence the audience's attitudes and behaviour in a favourable manner, rather than on whether it contributes to a fair, balanced, or objective presentation in which the audience can decide for itself. (Of course, it may be in the interest of the originator to make it appear that the operation is all of the latter.)

IWIO may be white, grey, or black.[5] White operations clearly and correctly identify the originator: a white operation publicly associated with Nation A is in fact conducted by Nation A. Grey operations are not publicly associated with any actor at all. Nation A may originate an operation but, if the operation is grey, no national actor is identified. Black operations are publicly associated with a nation or actor other than the true originator: thus, black operations are by definition 'false-flag' operations. If Nation A originates a black operation, Nation A may construct it so that it is publicly associated with Nation C.

Depending on the purpose of the operation and the risks entailed, a white, grey, or black operation may be more suitable. For the US, grey or black operations targeting certain audiences (e.g. US citizens) are constrained by law and/or policy.

IWIO may also involve deception. Deceptive operations can be executed to induce adversaries to take (or fail to take) specific actions that will advantage the IWIO originator and/or disadvantage the adversary. Deceptive operations seek to reinforce the adversary's preconceived beliefs; focus the adversary's attention on unimportant activities so that important activities go unnoticed; create the illusion of strength where weakness exists;

overload the adversary's information collection and analytical capabilities; and reduce the adversary's situational awareness.

The impact of IWIO can be significantly increased in two types of use:

1. *When IWIO is used to channel or influence other preexisting forces in society*: here, the actual large-scale impact is the direct result of economic forces, cultural forces, social forces, psychological forces, and organizational or bureaucratic forces, rather than any specific impact resulting directly from a particular operation.
2. *When IWIO is used in a pre-existing atmosphere of uncertainty and doubt*: the side using IWIO knows what its intentions are, what it hopes to accomplish, and what its future plans and moves are. By contrast, a doubtful or uncertain adversary is likely to dither in determining the scope and nature of the actual threat, and what should be done about it. Dithering consumes valuable time, during which the IWIO attacker can create new facts on the ground and may even change the adversary's strategic calculus.[6]

IWIO is not likely to be a supremely powerful instrument of conflict in the same sense as nuclear weapons. Because IWIO is primarily psychological in nature, there will always be people in a target population that are immune to its effects—this is most true in populations that have strong institutions and traditions dedicated to the rule of law, and relatively sane and trustworthy (i.e. not corrupt) political leaders. However, in instances when IWIO only need to change the behavior of a small number of people (e.g. in close electoral contests), IWIO can prove decisive.

The Psychological Basis for Information Warfare and Influence Operations

COGNITIVE BIASES

IWIO usually takes advantage of cognitive biases in human beings. These biases result from human use of intuitive reasoning strategies rather than analytical strategies. One of the most important intuitive reasoning strategies are heuristics, which substitute simple judgements for complex inferential tasks, resulting in cognitive biases that sometimes lead to erroneous conclusions (Nisbett and Ross 1980).

For IWIO purposes, some of the most important heuristics are the availability heuristic (people judge events or objects as frequent, probable, or causally powerful by the ease with which examples of those events or objects can be brought to mind);[7] the representativeness heuristic (people categorize events or objects on the basis of their resemblance to the underlying category characteristics); the anchoring heuristic (people give excessive weight to initial estimates in subsequent adjustments of those estimates); and the affect heuristic (people judge the risks and benefits of an event or a course of action depending on the positive or negative feelings that they associate with it; Finucane et al. 2000).

A variety of cognitive biases arise from the use of these heuristics. Here are a few illustrative examples:

- Fluency bias arises when the ease with which an individual processes information about an idea, object, or event fuels the expectation of being able to give a positive response to it. Simplistic and one-sided messaging takes advantage of the fluency bias.
- Confirmation bias is an individual's preference for seeking and interpreting new information in ways that are consistent with their beliefs, attitudes, and decisions, and to steer away from inconsistent information (Sweeny 2010). Media channels such as Fox News play to this bias for individuals with a right-of-centre orientation, and similarly MSNBC for those with a left-of-centre orientation.
- Illusory truth bias is an individual's perception of greater truth for statements that are more familiar—for example, as the result of repetition. IWIO thus often conveys the same message repeatedly.
- Loss aversion bias is an individual's greater sensitivity to loss than to gain (Kahneman and Tversky 1979). In many instances, people will take reckless gambles to recoup a loss but proceed cautiously when trying to improve their situation. IWIO thus often emphasizes how bad a situation is to prime people to act more recklessly.
- Recency bias is a tendency to rely upon memories that are easily accessed, which can encourage the use of recently presented information even when it is inaccurate (Benjamin et al. 1998).

Biases such as these (a more complete list can be found in Jonathan Baron's work, *Thinking and Deciding* (2007)) are vulnerabilities in the cognitive armour of otherwise rational and analytical individuals, and designing IWIO against these vulnerabilities is likely to enhance its effectiveness.

EMOTIONAL BIASES

The cognitive biases described suggest how the judgements and conclusions of actual human beings may differ from those of the hypothetical maximally rational person because of a reliance on fallible mental heuristics. But emotional factors also affect the judgements and conclusions that people make. Emotional biases can be seen when an individual has a motivation for believing (i.e. an emotional investment) in a particular answer or outcome or view that prevents them from achieving the benefits of rational consideration.

For example, a variety of studies have found that individuals are uncomfortable (an emotional reaction) about inconsistencies between their behaviour and their beliefs or attitudes, and are motivated to eliminate those inconsistencies (Festinger 1957). A most common way to do so is for them to change their perception of inconsistency regarding their behaviour. They may rationalize their behaviour so that they can see the behaviour as consistent with their beliefs and attitudes, or avoid exposure to information that challenges their beliefs and seek information that bolsters their beliefs.[8]

People are also more likely to arrive at conclusions that they want to arrive at (i.e. conclusions that they are motivated to reach; Kunda 1990). Their reasoning is also motivated by a desire to protect their status within an affinity group whose members share defining cultural commitments (Kahan 2017).

People subject arguments that are favourable to their own position to a less rigorous and critical analysis compared with arguments that are unfavourable (Taber and Lodge 2006). In the political context, an individual's emotional stance towards a political candidate is more important than their view about that candidate's policies (Lavine et al. 1998) or the facts known about the candidate (Westen 2007).

Findings such as the preceding suggest that IWIO that stimulates the emergence of strong emotion such as fear, ethnocentrism, and pride are likely to make those targeted more resistant to factual information and less willing to engage in reflective rational consideration.

A Typology of Information Warfare and Influence Operations

This paper takes note of three distinct kinds of IWIO: propaganda operations, chaos-producing operations, and leak operations.

PROPAGANDA OPERATIONS

A debate exists within the social science literature about the definition of 'propaganda'. Some scholars assert that all types of mass persuasion constitute propaganda.[9] Others define propaganda as 'The organized attempt through communication to affect belief or action or inculcate attitudes in a large audience in ways that circumvent or suppress an individual's adequately informed, rational, reflective judgment' (Marlin 2002).

These contrasting definitions have in common an emphasis on conveying information to large audiences to influence opinion, attitudes, and emotion in ways that help the originator. In this context, Hitler's ideas on propaganda remain relevant today—propaganda should attract broad public attention, provide the most simple formulations of essential ideas, focus on appealing to the emotions of the public rather than their reasoning powers, and repeat the conveyed messages continually (Hitler 1925, Ch. 6).

There is also no requirement that the information conveyed be true. Hitler was an advocate of 'the big lie',[10] believing that the broad masses would 'more readily fall victims to the big lie than the small lie, since ... It would never come into their heads to fabricate colossal untruths, and they would not believe that others could have the impudence to distort the truth so infamously.'

CHAOS-PRODUCING OPERATIONS

Chaos-producing operations are those that confuse and disrupt by means of misinformation for no purpose other than the creation of chaos. Such operations disorient without seeking a specific behavioural outcome but serve useful purposes by lowering an adversary's situational awareness and increasing the uncertainty in the environment.

For example, on 11 September 2014, St. Mary Parish in Louisiana was the subject of a well-coordinated and professionally produced IWIO chaos-producing operation claiming that a powerful explosion had occurred at the local Columbian Chemicals plant (Chen 2015). This operation included hundreds of Twitter accounts documenting the disaster, still images and videos of the explosion and flames, text messages to many local residents, a screenshot of CNN's home page discussing the event, and a YouTube video in which ISIS claimed credit for the attack.

It was all fake. The perpetrator had gone to enormous efforts to stage this operation, simply to create some hours and perhaps days of chaos and concern in the St. Mary Parish. Had this been a one-time event, it could have been a mere blip on the national scene, the equivalent of 'a tasteless prank', in the words of the director of the St. Mary Parish Office of Homeland Security and Emergency Preparedness. But it was not—rather, it was one of several such events orchestrated in the second half of 2014.

Although chaos-producing operations and propaganda operations share a lack of concern for truth, the latter are conducted to convey a particular political point of view to the target audience. The former have no such goal—taken in isolation and by themselves, they are not political at all, at least not explicitly.

Chaos-producing operations also have the important virtue that their messaging need not be consistent—for myriad messages to be inconsistent with each other helps rather than hurts the spread of chaos. Moreover, inconsistent messages need not be coordinated with each other—which means they can be produced in large volume very rapidly by a variety of different sources.

Leak Operations

If the information conveyed is mostly true, an IWIO is most similar to a leak of information. Leaks convey information to the target audience that the adversary might wish to keep out of public view and, when disclosure occurs in the context of revealing secret information, it gains notoriety and attracts attention disproportionately to its actual importance. Paraphrasing an editorial in the *New York Times* (Poniewozik 2016), there is a difference between treating a piece of information as newsworthy *even though* it was leaked and treating a piece of information as newsworthy *because* it was leaked. It is also worth noting that WikiLeaks in particular has skillfully exploited this phenomenon and can entice even mainstream media into reporting on any claim that Wikileaks wishes to make, because of the expectation that some leaked documents will underlie that claim.[11]

A mix of true and false information may be more efficacious than pure truth or pure lies. Pure truth may be inconvenient in the sense that true statements may not be available to support the message that the IWIO wishes to convey.[12] A listener who recognizes lies as lies is likely to become more sceptical of subsequent statements, whereas a listener who recognizes statements as true is more likely to believe that subsequent statements are true—one aspect of a cognitive bias known as 'truth bias' in cognitive and social psychology.[13] This phenomenon is also manifested even when people have good reason to refrain from assuming truth.

Cyber-Enabled Information/ Influence Warfare

Modern IT—computers and communications technology (i.e. the 'cyber' portion of 'cyber-enabled IWIO'—affords IWIO practitioners a variety of new opportunities. Unlike information technologies of the past (e.g. books, films), modern information technologies effectively separate information (represented as ones and zeros—as bits) from the physical substrate (e.g. paper) needed in the past to convey information. The following characteristics of today's information environment are noteworthy:

- High connectivity. In early 2021, the number of Internet users globally approached 4.7 billion people,[14] and nearly every user on the Internet is connected to every other one through a relatively small number of links.
- Low latency. Users who are directly linked can be notified in milliseconds of new communications and information, rather than the hours or days that characterized radio, telephone, or newspaper communication.
- Anonymity. Information represented in digital form can always be physically separated at some point from identifying information, at which point any party can be associated with it.
- Low cost. The marginal cost of conveying more bits of information is essentially zero in most instances today using modern IT, which more or less eliminates volume as a constraint on the information people can send and receive.
- Multiple distribution points. There are numerous content providers on the Internet, ranging in size from single individual teenagers and automated bots to government agencies, that supply information.
- Many-to-many bi-directional communications. Consumers and content providers easily engage in reciprocal dialogue, and the lines between consumer and provider are often indistinct.
- Disintermediation. Today's information environment is far less reliant on established intermediaries than the environment of a few decades ago. In the past, intermediaries such as newspapers played editorial roles that helped their readers to manage, interpret, and evaluate large volumes of information. Today, more users depend on the newsfeeds of social media and technological tools to filter and sift information, but these tools lack serious editorial judgement.
- Insensitivity to distance and national borders. It is just as easy to send information across the ocean as across the street, and national borders are much more porous to information than they are to physical objects.
- High availability of personal information. Large quantities of personal information of individuals are available to interested parties, either for free or for a nominal price.
- Information insecurity. All information is subject to risks related to compromises of confidentiality, integrity, availability, and authenticity, but digitally recorded information arguably suffers these risks to a greater degree. A full discussion of such risks is beyond the scope of this chapter, but it suffices to say that recording information digitally often engenders a false sense of security (likely because protecting bits of information

is different from protecting a physical artefact storing bits), and people continue to be surprised when the security of their information is compromised.

These characteristics of the information environment writ large have a number of important implications for the prosecution of IWIO.

Perhaps the most significant observation about cyber-enabled IWIO is that, unlike the cyber warfare described elsewhere in the *Handbook*, cyber-enabled IWIO need not be particularly sophisticated to be effective, as happened in the Russian email hacks described below. Furthermore, and as described on page 255, the impact of cyber-enabled IWIO can be enhanced by channelling larger forces to amplify their effects. At the same time, enhanced impact does not come for free—planning for and predicting psychological, legal, organizational, societal, and economic effects, especially on a large scale, is an exercise in predicting second-order effects—that is, effects that go beyond the technical effects of a cyber operation. This constitutes a significant expansion of the space that planners of an IWIO attack must account for—and IWIO defenders as well.

For example, IWIO originators can engage in a very high tempo of operations—it is fast, easy, and cheap to send out tweets and Facebook notifications, and tsunamis of information can be generated rapidly with little warning. Responses to noteworthy events in the real world can also be issued rapidly. Rapid response and a high tempo of operations means that the IWIO originator can obtain first-mover advantages that allow them to set the initial terms of the messaging narrative.

A high tempo of operations is particularly useful for IWIO chaos-producing operations. A great deal of experience with the Internet over the past several decades suggests that information suppression by removing it is a difficult if not impossible task. Attempts to remove information often (and arguably usually) lead to drawing more attention to that information, because it is impossible to destroy all copies of digitally stored information once a copy has become public. But another method to suppress a message that is almost as effective is to drown it out with competing messages (i.e. by creating messaging chaos with a flood of mutually inconsistent messages) instead of trying to remove it.

High connectivity also means that even actors whose voice would have been small before the rise of the Internet now have megaphonic reach to large audiences. Communities of like-minded 'fringe' individuals are much easier to form under such circumstances, where such individuals can and do receive social reinforcement for their views.

High connectivity has particular relevance to today's political campaigns, which are a mix of 'official' campaigns controlled by candidates and unofficial (and formally unrelated) 'informational' campaigns conducted by supporters (and opponents) of those candidates. The Internet has encouraged the proliferation of politically oriented websites in the United States and elsewhere, established by private citizens, which are not subject to government regulation regarding campaign financing or fairness, and some of these sites are as influential as any traditional political or media outlet.

IWIO originators can operate in relative anonymity, which eliminates the possibility of negative social consequences from engaging in such activities and reduces social inhibitions about engaging in such behaviour. Free of inhibitions, the number of individuals willing to engage in IWIO expands.

IWIO originators can leverage their large numbers to intimidate parties expressing views contrary to theirs. Most ordinary citizens are easily identifiable through publicly available information and thus anyone can reach them. Critical public postings often generate a flood of personally abusive and threatening but anonymous communications to the poster. Such communications can be psychologically intimidating to the poster and inhibiting to others who might otherwise express their views. In some cases, posters have had their physical safety threatened.

Disintermediation helps the IWIO originator. Those who use the online equivalents of traditional information intermediaries, and rely on their editorial services to cope with the information deluge, have at least some tools to cope with some IWIO because they continue to be exposed to useful and factual information from multiple points of view. But those who rely on social media and search engines to filter the information ocean are less likely to be exposed to information that contradicts their prior beliefs. These users are exposed preferentially (or almost exclusively) to information that conforms to their own individual predilections, and hence they reinforce their existing confirmation biases.

Today's information environment enables crowdsourcing—the use of large numbers of individuals, acting in loose cooperation and often without central guidance, to achieve certain purposes. IWIO originators can draw on the cooperation, witting or unwitting, of individuals whom they have been successful in influencing. In many instances, it only takes a retweet or a 'like' to achieve a many-fold amplification of the message embedded in an IWIO that has influenced an individual.

Because IWIO operations can easily cross borders, IWIO operators can take advantage of different laws in different geographic regions, engaging in IWIO targeted against one national jurisdiction from the comparative safety of another jurisdiction that allows such behaviour. In addition, IWIO originators can operate from the territories of their target nation with minimal infrastructure and gain protective benefits that the target nation confers upon its residents.

The easy availability of multiple distribution points gives rise to automated social chatbots that can be used in IWIO. A social chatbot is a computer program that generates content for, and interacts with, human users on social media but conceals its identity as a non-human entity. Chatbots have had a measurable impact on political dialogue (Bessi and Ferrara 2016).

Lastly, IWIO can exploit weak information security. Such operations can obtain information meant to be confidential, or forge or alter print, audio, and video documents. The products of these operations can then be disseminated strategically to support the IWIO originator's objectives. An example of this approach was the Russian hacking operation conducted in 2016 to access confidential emails of the Democratic National Committee (DNC) and key staffers of Hillary Clinton's campaign.

AN EXEMPLAR PRACTITIONER OF INFORMATION/INFLUENCE WARFARE—RUSSIA

In the lead-up to the US presidential election of November 2016, the American media audience was barraged by a display of confidential information and correspondence stemming from hacked private and organizational emails and other records, most notably from the DNC and John Podesta, a key member of the Clinton campaign. After months of speculation concerning Russian involvement in the hacking, which led to the release of private documents and data on the sites WikiLeaks, DCLeaks, and Guccifer 2.0, in early October 2016, the Obama administration formally announced its belief that the Russian Federation was behind the disclosures and that these were intended to interfere with the US election cycle.[15]

For those familiar with Russian politics, the strategic release of 'compromising material' concerning political rivals did not appear so unusual, with so-called *kompromat* having been used to tarnish reputations and undermine opponents' messages for years. Recent Russian examples included leaked recordings of private phone conversations by opposition leaders and video footage of prominent critics in bed with prostitutes. The international deployment of such a tactic to influence the domestic politics of another country, while a little more novel, likewise drew upon a rich history of Russian military strategy and was particularly exemplary of recent developments in Russian military strategic thinking.[16]

THE RUSSIAN ART OF STRATEGY

Russia has long excelled at some aspects of the use and manipulation of information discussed in this chapter. Soviet era theories of 'reflexive control', cybernetics, and *maskirovka*—focusing on the use of information, deception, and psychological manipulation have influenced the development of current approaches to military strategy.

In recent years, Russia has further refined an explicit strategic approach to the use of IWIO campaigns to achieve political and military goals at home and abroad. Asymmetry, ambiguity, indirect or deniable actions, and sophisticated information campaigns have become integral components of the country's military strategy—exemplified by what has been described as 'next generation warfare' or 'non-linear warfare'.

Elements of this strategy have been evident since Russian conflicts with Estonia (2007) and Georgia (2008), and have grown increasingly apparent in the Russian handling of the Crimea annexation and ongoing conflict in Ukraine, the Russian involvements in the Syrian civil war, and Russian meddling in the US election in 2016.[17] Aspects of the same approaches have likewise been used against protest movements, opposition leaders, and independent media within the country's own domestic sphere.

Explicit formulations of the current turn in Russian military doctrine have emerged in recent years, indicating a period of significant strategic thought concerning the role of information. In a December 2013 article in a professional military journal, chief of the general staff, General Valery Gerasimov, laid out a vision of the current geostrategic and military-technological challenges facing Russia, perceived threats, and potential strategic adaptations to respond to these global challenges.[18] The article, which focused particularly on the novel type of threat posed by events such as the Arab Spring and the Color Revolutions in states of the former Soviet Union, suggested that the rules of war and the relationship between overtly military and non-military 'means' in 'achieving political and strategic goals' had changed and that Russia's own approach must also adapt to these new forms of 'modern warfare'. 'The focus of applied methods of conflict,' Gerasimov explained, 'has altered in the direction of the broad use of political, economic, informational, humanitarian, and other non-military measures—applied in coordination with the protest potential of the population.' These non-military measures were, in turn, to be 'supplemented by military means of a concealed character, including informational conflict and the actions of special operations forces.'

Gerasimov spoke explicitly of the need to find and exploit vulnerabilities even of the most militarily powerful opponents. 'We must not copy foreign experience and chase after leading countries,' he argued, 'but we must outstrip them and occupy leading positions ourselves.' He describes the use of 'information spaces' as playing a critical role in this process, '[opening] wide asymmetrical possibilities for reducing the fighting potential of the enemy.'

This approach stresses the importance of 'cognitive-psychological forms of influence' in addition to 'digital-technological' mechanisms[19]—that is, information/influence war in addition to what we understand in the West as cyber war. These tools are likewise to be applied regardless of binary distinctions between wartime and peacetime. They can be used to deter, delay, or compel opponent actions. They can also help to influence perceptions, combined with special operations and diplomatic and economic forms of influence, as well as nuclear and conventional military deterrence. But the overriding preference is to reduce the need for outright use of military force to achieve desired strategic goals.

Adamsky argues that 'it is difficult to overemphasize the role that Russian official doctrine attributes to the defensive and offensive aspects of informational struggle in modern conflicts', a point reinforced by Gerasimov's view that the appropriate ratio of non-military to military operations is 4 to 1 (i.e. the former is of greater importance than the latter).

As a strategy of influence, rather than of brute force, Russia's next generation warfare approach both de-emphasizes kinetic force and relies heavily on the 'information struggle' as a core component of successful military campaigns. It can likewise be used against both individual actors and organizations, and even entire populations within opponent countries, internationally, and at home. In a turn modelled upon Western use of soft power and public diplomacy for the promotion of democratic values, the strategy seeks to shape and leverage popular opinion and protest potential in targeted populations as one lever in achieving strategic influence on rival countries.

IWIO In Action: Russian Annexation of Crimea

Russia's 2014 annexation of Crimea from neighbouring Ukraine demonstrated the country's developing approach to the use of IWIO in conflict and pre-conflict situations. Integrated campaigns of media and social media coverage sought to influence public opinion on the topic, both in Russia and Ukraine and the international community. Special operations and false-flag or unattributed actions (black and grey operations) involving 'polite people' and 'little green men' (Shevchenko 2014) were paired with official denial of Russian military involvement, causing other countries to pause before attributing the source of personnel and weapons observed in Crimea and other regions of Ukraine experiencing protest and violence. As the question of attributing actual Russian military involvement loomed, in the face of official Russian denials, there was also uncertainty as to whether any Russian actions in Crimea or Ukraine more broadly rose to the level of acts of war to which some international response might have been appropriate.

As the events in Crimea were orchestrated as a rapidly unfolding peaceful protest for independence and referendum concerning the region's return to Russia, Russian media coverage and diplomatic rhetoric emphasized the democratic nature of the transition (denying comparisons with prior infamous land grabs in European history). Meanwhile, lacking absolute certainty as to the nature of the threat or absolute binding security arrangements with Ukraine, Western states that had stood in solidarity with the Maidan protesters and rebuked Russian aggression stalled, concerned over escalating the crisis. By the time the nature of Russian activities in Ukraine became clearer, the annexation of Crimea was a fait accompli.

Domestic and regional Russian media coverage and viral social media during the crisis played on the emotions and biases of particular populations, emphasizing the 'Russianness' of the local Crimea population, the supposed threat of violence towards Russian speakers in the region, and the role of soldiers as peacekeepers protecting the Russian-ethnic population from the menace of Ukrainian nationalist extremist violence. Coverage varied from the plausible to the implausible (such as a story describing the crucifixion of a three-year-old Russian toddler), but was artfully mixed with real stories and footage. Nightly news footage showed long caravans of trucks bringing 'humanitarian aid' to the beleaguered regions, and Western resistance to such efforts was portrayed as an effort to obstruct assistance to fellow Russians facing ethno-national oppression and atrocities.

While the irredentist logic of the land grab was less acceptable to Western audiences, other arguments were emphasized in international statements and media output, relying upon the rhetorical tactic of 'what-about-ism' where Crimea's 'protection' was compared with US- and NATO-led efforts in Kosovo or Libya, and emphasizing the illegitimacy of the 'coup' that had recently displaced the democratically elected President of Ukraine, Viktor Yanukovich, placing Crimea (and the rest of Ukraine) under supposedly illegitimate and anti-Russian rule.

VULNERABILITIES OF LIBERAL DEMOCRACIES TO INFORMATION WARFARE AND INFLUENCE OPERATIONS

Liberal democracies are particularly vulnerable to IWIO for a number of reasons. First and foremost, liberal democracies are inherently open societies, at least by comparison with many of the other nations of the world. They make available to their publics more information about their societies, and that information tends to be more truthful and accurate. They have media outlets for carrying information to the public that are more independent than in authoritarian nations. Most importantly, they are subject to periodic, peaceful regime change according to the outcome of popular elections. Elections and political campaigns are thus particularly lucrative targets for IWIO.

Democracies are willing to do certain things in war that they are unwilling to do in peacetime and vice versa. Law, regulation, and societal institutions (both government and nongovernment) are often organized around this distinction, and thus democracies must make explicit decisions about transitioning between the two. They do not do well (and often do not take decisive action) in responding to hostile actions taken against them that fall below the threshold of war—and IWIO is premised on just such actions. By contrast, authoritarian states that believe in a continuous struggle with other nation states do not organize themselves this way, and are able to develop institutions that operate in an integrated manner and with equal facility and authority across these conditions.

Democracies also tend to believe in the rule of law. For example, the US operates under the auspices of the First Amendment to the US Constitution, which guarantees freedom of speech and expression against government intervention except under very limited and specific conditions. Domestic political speech and expression receive the highest levels of protection, even when such speech is factually inaccurate and inflammatory. And governments generally do not assert extraterritorial control over content hosted outside their borders.

Another exacerbating factor within the US government and especially within its military institutions is that information operations—deception, psychological operations, and so on—are somehow considered less important because of its unchallenged traditional military strength. For example, Steven Metz observes that 'the American military is not as strong at psychological precision [i.e. psychological operations] as it should be, in part because technological advantages appear to make psychological effectiveness unnecessary' (2000, 78).

Such sentiments are at least suggestive of a public reticence towards IWIO, at least by the US. But, irrespective of policy judgements about whether such operations are appropriate or helpful against adversaries of the US, so-called mirror-imaging of an adversary—attributing to an adversary our own values and sentiments—may well contribute to an insensitivity and lack of awareness of adversary efforts in this regard.

RESPONDING TO INFORMATION WARFARE AND INFLUENCE OPERATIONS

Citizens in modern societies live an IT-enabled information deluge. A fast-moving information deluge is the ideal battleground for using IWIO. Rapid information flow gives recipients (i.e., the targeted populace) little time to process and evaluate new information. Large volumes of information are cognitively disorienting and can be confusing. Opportunities for emotional manipulation abound.

Any coherent response strategy to IWIO involves two critical elements: identifying IWIO when it is in use and taking action to counter it or its effects.

Identifying Information Warfare and Influence Operations as They Occur

One of the most insidious effects of IWIO is that words and images do not have the same kind of obviously destructive effect on a society as do kinetic weapons or even cyber weapons. Indeed, successful IWIO by actor X against society Y should be able to persuade large segments of society Y that X is not their adversary.

One point of departure for recognizing IWIO is knowing the parties that have something to gain from it. As described earlier, Russia has adopted an approach to conflict that emphasizes IWIO as a domain of strength. But non-state actors such as the Islamic State also demonstrate high degrees of media sophistication in promulgating their messages and advancing their causes. Even political movements have caught on to the power of IWIO, as one can see in the rise of the alt-right in the US and Europe. Since the Internet and cyberspace point the way towards a much more powerful IWIO, cyber-enabled IWIO is a useful tool for many different types of adversary, and a useful instrument for political combat and competition.

A second characteristic of IWIO is efforts to undermine the legitimacy of the institutions that provide societal stability and continuity. In normal times, citizens argue over politics and the meaning of various events. Under IWIO attack, citizens do not even agree on the events that have happened—each side has its own version of the facts to drive its own narratives. IWIO also attacks institutions, such as established media outlets that adhere to journalistic standards and ethics, that seek to inform the public.

A third signal could be the automated detection and identification of IWIO weapons in use. For example, the rapid emergence of large numbers of automated social chatbots all promulgating similar political messages could signal the start of a concerted IWIO campaign. Research is underway to identify such chatbots automatically (Ferrara et al. 2016).

Countering Information Warfare and Influence Operations

As noted earlier, users who have abandoned traditional intermediaries (and their online equivalents) tend to be exposed preferentially (or almost exclusively) to information that conforms to their own individual preferences. These individuals are not what the Founding Fathers of the US had in mind when they placed their trust in a well-informed citizenry.

Because these parties are the most likely targets of IWIO, what can be done to protect them when they do not know they are being targeted and have no particular wish to be protected from IWIO that reinforce their prior beliefs and attitudes?

It is instructive first to consider some ideas that are nevertheless unlikely to help very much. For example, 'naming and shaming' is probably ineffective against many nation states conducting IWIO, especially those that have chosen to engage in international relations in ways that are not consistent with the behavioural norms of liberal democracies. Nor is naming and shaming effective against parties that engage in white IWIO.

The US response to the Soviet use of IWIO in the Cold War—the US launched Radio Free Europe/Radio Liberty and Voice of America to provide alternative information sources to those behind the Iron Curtain—is another model. These broadcast services operated as independent journalism outlets providing truthful information generally unfiltered by the US government, though of course they were not seen that way by the Soviets.

But it is hard to imagine such an approach helping very much today. One reason is that the target audiences of IWIO are today often the liberal democracies, where individuals have—and are supposed to have—considerable freedom as well as the legal right to choose their own information sources. Any approach to countering IWIO will have to be careful about excessive government control over private-sector content provision.

Also, the velocity of information flow gets in the way of thoughtful reflection. Russia, foreign terrorist groups, and extreme political movements use cyber-enabled IWIO that encourage and celebrate the public expression of raw emotion—anger, fear, anxiety—and thereby channel powerful destructive and delegitimizing forces against existing institutions such as government and responsible media. Moreover, users of IWIO techniques are under no obligation to be consistent in their messaging, which means that they can promulgate messages much more rapidly than if they had to ensure consistency. Against this rapid-fire information deluge, the pace of communication vehicles operating during the Cold war would be completely inadequate in countering the hostile narratives offered today.

A second important reason is that any effort to coordinate and synchronize government-wide communications will take time. The desire for government-wide coordination is understandable—responses to IWIO benefit from consistency, and uncoordinated responses may well be mutually inconsistent. But rapid response—made especially important because responding to adversary IWIO is by definition reactive—is arguably incompatible with coordination through an entity as large as a national government. If so, rapid government responses to adversary IWIO will almost certainly have to be grey in nature rather than white.

On the citizen side, efforts to improve civic participation and engagement are always important to pursue. But the scale of the effort needed to move the needle towards thoughtful and informed civic engagement is enormous, especially in light of the fact that people are known to resist the absorption of knowledge and information that disturbs their prior beliefs about the world.

Consider, for example, the phenomenon that people are generally predisposed to believe in ideas that they hear, and reject them only after exerting mental effort to evaluate them (Gilbert 1991). Rapp et al. (2014) have found that encouraging the retrieval of accurate knowledge during reading can reduce the influence of misinformation; however, such retrieval is effortful and individuals are less likely to undertake such effort if left to their own devices. Thus, if refuting a lie requires that the lie be repeated, refutation may well backfire since the repetition of the lie may well reinforce it.

Research on the psychology of communications suggests that people can be 'inoculated' against fake news. Such inoculation consists of simultaneous delivery of an initial message and also a pre-emptive flagging of false claims that are likely to follow and an explicit refutation of potential responses (Banas and Rains 2010).

This is easier said than done, however, and many other common-sense techniques to reduce reliance on misinformation apparently offer even less promise.[20] Individuals warned about the potential falsity of a statement are not less reluctant to rely on that statement subsequently. Waiting so that people can no longer easily recall misinformation also does not help, because the reliance of many readers on misinformation increases over time. Presenting materials more slowly and decreasing the complexity of text content, both of which should reduce processing burdens that can impede careful evaluation, do not help substantially either.

If solutions lie neither with government nor with individual citizens, perhaps the private sector can play a meaningful role. Some major private sector actors have indeed acknowledged a degree of responsibility to counter certain kinds of IWIO. For example, Facebook is deploying a new protocol for its users to flag questionable news sites. Google bans fake news websites from using its online advertising service. Twitter, YouTube, and Facebook shut down accounts that they determine are promoting terrorist content.

Many argue that such measures are helpful but inadequate to stem the rising tide of misinformation conveyed through cyber-enabled IWIO. For example, a recent Facebook letter from Mark Zuckerberg states that 'Our approach will focus less on banning misinformation and more on surfacing additional perspectives and information, including that fact checkers dispute an item's accuracy.'[21] But one must wonder about the value of the latter approach given the cognitive biases and requirements for effortful mental processing described earlier.

Others would advocate more intrusive or aggressive steps, such as cutting off prominent users who are 'obviously' disseminating misinformation. The interaction between private companies and end users is generally governed by the Terms of Service (TOS) agreement rather than by law—for the most part, private companies have no legal responsibility to protect the expression of all points of view. So far, goes the argument, these companies have interpreted TOS agreements narrowly, so narrowly that a lot of misinformation and inflammatory rhetoric does flow because their enforcement efforts are inadequate. But these private companies also respond to shareholders' and advertisers' concerns and, in the end, understandably intend to make a profit from their efforts—and that profit generally increases as more people generate more message traffic. What is 'obviously' misinformation to one user may not be obvious to others, and broad interpretations of TOS agreements run the risk of antagonizing a large part of their customer base, with all the financial consequences that such action might entail.

To sum up, some of the approaches described earlier have some promise of having some valuable defensive effect against IWIO. But, taken as a whole, the discussion of this section suggests that there are no good comprehensive solutions for countering IWIO in free and democratic societies. Development of new tactics and responses is therefore needed.

Conclusion

IWIO is one of the oldest forms of conflict known to humanity, and democracy itself has an ancient pedigree as well. In its older forms, democracy has rested on an underlying foundation of an enlightened, informed populace engaging in rational debate and argument to sort out truth from fiction and half-truth in an attempt to produce the best possible policy and political outcomes.

But even before Twitter and Facebook and the World Wide Web, the match between this idealized view of democracy and reality has been questioned by a number of scholars.[22] And, if the match between ideal and reality was not entirely perfect in those days, today's information environment and cyber-enabled IWIO have certainly rendered it much more questionable. The institutions of democracy are also poorly adapted to dealing with IWIO, and especially cyber-enabled IWIO because of its speed and reach.

Cyber-enabled IWIO is a new kind of threat to democratic nations—a threat that evades established laws and conventions and turns the strengths of democracies—namely, their openness and guaranteed freedoms—against them. In this regard, the threat from IWIO is much like the threat from traditional cyber weapons that affect the confidentiality, integrity, and availability of information and information systems—cyber weapons pose a greater threat to nations that are more advanced users of IT than to less-developed nations.

Lastly, it is worth noting that the cyber aspect of cyber-enabled IWIO is critical, but it need not to be particularly sophisticated for cyber-enabled IWIO to be effective. Cyber-enabled IWIO takes advantage of fundamental characteristics of modern IT—namely, vulnerabilities that will always be present in any kind of IT regardless of sophistication—and that in turn allows the IWIO attacker to control larger forces that have little to do with cyber per se. The significance of this point is that, wherever good responses to IWIO are to be found, a better, stronger, and more robust cybersecurity posture per se is not likely to be much help.

Disclaimer

"The views expressed in this article are those of the author and do not reflect the official policy or position of the National Defense University, the Department of Defense or the U. S. Government"

Notes

1. von Clausewitz, *On War*, Ch. 1.
2. This definition is identical to the US Department of Defense's definition of the information environment, but the various dimensions of the information environment are somewhat different. See US Department of Defense, *Joint Publication 3–13, Information Operations*, 27 November 2012, Incorporating Change 1, 20 November 2014. http://www.dtic.mil/doctrine/new_pubs/jp3_13.pdf
3. The definition of information in this context is the ordinary common-sense meaning of the term: information is 'facts provided or learned about something or someone'. As such, information is understood to have semantic content—i.e. a humanly understood meaning. This definition is different from Shannon's information: the latter refers to bit-encoded information and is devoid of semantics (see Claude Shannon and Warren Weaver. 1949. *The Mathematical Theory of Communication*. Urbana and Chicago: University of Illinois Press.

4. This definition of IWIO operations is almost identical to the definition of 'military information support operations' found in US Department of Defense, *Joint Publication 3–13.2, Military Information Support Operations*, 7 January 2010, Incorporating Change 1, 20 December 2011. https://publicintelligence.net/jcs-miso

5. Appendix A, FM 3-05.30, Psychological Operations, Army Field Manual, 2005, https://fas.org/irp/doddir/army/fm3-05-30.pdf

6. The advantages of orienting oneself to ground truth and then making decisions more rapidly than the other side are the foundation of OODA-loop theory, the combat paradigm in which one side in a conflict observes, orients, decides, and acts (and then repeating the cycle). The side that can execute this loop more rapidly usually gains significant advantages over the other side. See Frans Osinga. 2005. *Science, Strategy and War: The Strategic Theory of John Boyd*. Delft, The Netherlands: Eburon Academic Publishers

7. Tversky, Amos, and Daniel Kahneman. 1974. 'Judgment under Uncertainty: Heuristics and Biases', *Science* 185 (4157): 1124–31; 27 September. http://science.sciencemag.org/content/185/4157/1124. A popularized version can be found in Kahneman, Daniel. *Thinking Fast and Slow* 2011. New York: Farrar, Straus & Giroux. The original Tversky and Kahneman article reports on the availability, representativeness, and anchoring heuristics.

8. See, for example, Hart, William et al. 2009. 'Feeling Validated Versus Being Correct: A Meta-Analysis of Selective Exposure to Information', *Psychological Bulletin* 135 (4): 555–88 http://psycnet.apa.org/journals/bul/135/4/555.pdf and Kate Sweeny et al., 'Information Avoidance'.

9. See, for example, Pratkanis, Anthony, and Eliot Aronson, 2001. *Age of Propaganda: The Everyday Use and Abuse of Persuasion*, New York: Henry Holt, p. 11.

10. Hitler, *Mein Kampf*, Ch.10.

11. Cf. Zeynep Tufekci. 2016. 'WikiLeaks Isn't Whistleblowing', *New York Times*, 4 November, https://www.nytimes.com/2016/11/05/opinion/what-were-missing-while-we-obsess-over-john-podestas-email.html.

12. As digital forgery tools become more effective, the lack of useful 'true statements' will become less important—forged documents containing exactly the right information will become available.

13. Vrij Aldert. 2008. *Detecting Lies and Deceit: Pitfalls and Opportunities*. West Sussex, UK: John Wiley and Sons. A second aspect of truth bias is that people are more likely to correctly judge that a truthful statement is true than that a lie is false.

14. Statista, "Global Digital Population as of January 2021," https://www.statista.com/statistics/617136/digital-population-worldwide/

15. See, for example, Sanger, David E. and Charlie Savage, 2016 'U.S. Says Russia Directed Hacks to Influence Elections', *New York Times*, 7 October. https://www.nytimes.com/2016/10/08/us/politics/us-formally-accuses-russia-of-stealing-dnc-emails.html.

16. A good single-article press account of Russian activities in IWIO can be found in MacFarquhar, Neil. 2016. 'A Powerful Russian Weapon: The Spread of False Stories', *The New York Times*, 28 August. https://www.nytimes.com/2016/08/29/world/europe/russia-sweden-disinformation.html.

17. See Keir, Giles. 2016. *Handbook of Russian Information Warfare*, November. Rome, NATO Defense College. http://www.ndc.nato.int/news/news.php?icode=995; also Adamsky, Dmitry (Dima). 2015. *Cross-Domain Coercion: The Current Russian Art of Strategy*. November. Paris: Institut Français des Relations Internationales. http://www.ifri.org/sites/default/files/atoms/files/pp54adamsky.pdf

CYBER-ENABLED WARFARE AND OPERATIONS   271

18. The original Gerasimov article can be found at http://vpk-news.ru/sites/default/files/pdf/ VPK_08_476.pdf A non-authoritative English translation of this article done by Robert Coalson can be found at https://www.facebook.com/notes/robert-coalson/russian-military-doctrine-article-by-general-valery-gerasimov/10152184862563597/

19. Adamsky, *Cross-Domain Coercion.*

20. The techniques described in this paragraph are taken from Rapp, David N. 2016. 'The Consequences of Reading Inaccurate Information', *Current Directions in Psychological Science* 25 (4): 281–5. This paper also contains the original citations backing these claims.

21. Mark Zuckerberg, 'Building Global Community'. https://www.facebook.com/notes/mark-zuckerberg/building-global-community/10103508221158471/

22. See, for example, Ingber, Stanley. 1984. 'The Marketplace of Ideas: A Legitimizing Myth', *Duke Law Journal* 1 (1): 1–91. http://scholarship.law.duke.edu/dlj/vol33/iss1/1; Wonnell, Christopher T. 1986. 'Truth and the Marketplace of Ideas', *UC Davis Law Review* 19 (3): 669–728, spring; Weissberg, Robert. 1996. 'The Real Marketplace of Ideas', *Critical Review* 10 (1): 107–21. http://dx.doi.org/10.1080/08913819608443411

REFERENCES

Banas, John, and Stephen A. Rains. 2010. 'A Meta-Analysis of Research on Inoculation Theory', *Communication Monographs* 77(3): 281–311, September.

Baron, Jonathan, 2007. *Thinking and Deciding.* 4th edn. Cambridge, UK: Cambridge University Press.

Benjamin, Aaron et al. 1998. 'The Mismeasure of Memory: When Retrieval Fluency Is Misleading as a Metamnemonic Index', *Journal of Experimental Psychology: General* 127 (1): 55–68.

Bessi, Alessandro and Emilio Ferrara. 2016. 'Social bots distort the 2016 U.S. Presidential election online discussion', *First Monday* [S.l.], November. ISSN 13960466. http://journals.uic.edu/ojs/index.php/fm/article/view/7090/5653

Chen, Adrian. 2015. 'The Agency', *New York Times Magazine*, 2 June. https://www.nytimes.com/2015/06/07/magazine/the-agency.html

Ferrara, Emilio et al. 2016. 'The Rise of Social Bots', *Communications of the ACM* 59 (7): 96–104, July.

Festinger, Leon. 1957. *A Theory of Cognitive Dissonance.* Evanston, IL: Row & Peterson.

Finucane, Melissa et al. 2000. 'The Affect Heuristic in Judgments of Risks and Benefits', *Journal of Behavioural Decision Making* 13: 1–17.

Gilbert, Daniel. 1991. 'How Mental Systems Believe', *American Psychologist* 46 (2): 107–19, February.

Hitler, Adolph. 1925. *Mein Kampf.* http://www.greatwar.nl/books/meinkampf/meinkampf.pdf

Lynn III, William J. 2010. 'Defending a New Domain: The Pentagon's Cyberstrategy', *Foreign Affairs*, September/October.

Kahan, Dan. 2017. 'The Expressive Rationality of Inaccurate Perceptions', *Behavioural and Brain Sciences* 40: e6. https://papers.ssrn.com/sol3/papers.cfm?abstract_id=2670981

Kahneman, Daniel, and Amos Tversky. 1979. 'Prospect Theory: An Analysis of Decision Under Risk', *Econometrica* 47: 263–91.

Kunda, Ziva. 1990. 'The Case for Motivated Reasoning', *Psychological Bulletin* 108 (3): 480–98, November. http://psycnet.apa.org/psycinfo/1991-06436-001

Lavine, Howard et al. 1998. 'On the Primacy of Affect in the Determination of Attitudes and Behaviour: The Moderating Role of Affective-Cognitive Ambivalence', *Journal of Experimental Social Psychology* 34: 398–421.

Marlin, Randal. 2002. *Propaganda and the Ethics of Persuasion*. Peterborough, Ontario: Broadview Press, p. 22.

Metz, Steven. 2000. 'Armed Conflict in the 21st Century: The Information Revolution and Post-Modern Warfare', 1 March, p. 78, Director of Research, Strategic Studies Institute, US Army War College. http://www.strategicstudiesinstitute.army.mil/pubs/download.cfm?q=226

Nisbett, Richard, and Lee Ross. 1980. *Human Inference: Strategies and Shortcomings of Social Judgment*. Englewood Cliffs, NJ: Prentice-Hall.

Poniewozik, James. 2016. 'Just Because It's Hacked, Doesn't Mean It's Important', *The New York Times*, 18 October. https://www.nytimes.com/2016/10/18/arts/wikileaks-hillary-clinton-hacked.html

Rapp, David et al. 2014. 'Reducing Reliance on Inaccurate Information', *Memory and Cognition* 42 (1): 11–26, January. http://link.springer.com/article/10.3758%2Fs13421-013-0339-0

Shevchenko, Vitaly. 2014. ' "Little Green Men" or "Russian Invaders?" ', *British Broadcasting Company*, 11 March. http://www.bbc.com/news/world-europe-26532154

Sweeny, Kate et al. 2010. 'Information Avoidance: Who, What, When, and Why', *Review of General Psychology* 14 (4): 340–53. http://psycnet.apa.org/journals/gpr/14/4/340.html

Taber, Charles, and Milton Lodge. 2006. 'Motivated Skepticism in the Evaluation of Political Beliefs', *American Journal of Political Science* 50 (3): 755–69, July. http://www.jstor.org/stable/3694247

Tzu, Sun, *The Art of War*, trans. and ed. S.B. Griffith, 1963. Oxford: Oxford University Press.

von Clausewitz Carl, Michael Howard, Peter Paret et al. 1984. *On War*. Princeton, NJ: Princeton University Press.

Westen, Drew. 2007. *The Political Brain: The Role of Emotion in Deciding the Fate of the Nation*. New York, PublicAffairs, pp. 103–112.

CHAPTER 17

THE DETERRENCE AND PREVENTION OF CYBER CONFLICT

PAUL CORNISH

INTRODUCTION

DETERRENCE, as a theoretical proposition, is not difficult to grasp: the *Concise Oxford English Dictionary* defines it as 'Preventing by fear'. But, if deterrence can be defined in *principle*, it can only be understood in *practice* and, most importantly, in *context*. Thus, we might say that, in principle, deterrence could operate in many human activities and relationships, ranging from the private matter of bringing up children to the public measures taken by society to control crime. Yet, we would expect the character and style of deterrence to differ in each case: deterrence should be calibrated and proportionate. The schoolchild contemplating some misdemeanour might be dissuaded by the knowledge that they might be placed in detention rather than have time to play with their friends. Conversely, for the adult criminal, it might be the prospect of another custodial sentence that acts as an incentive not to reoffend. In both cases, the principle behind deterrence is plain to see: the fear of adverse consequences serves to prevent unacceptable behaviour. Described in this way, deterrence has probably been a feature of human interaction for as long as humans have been interacting. Today, even if the word itself might not be in everyday use, its central premise could scarcely be more familiar.

But, if deterrence is a thoroughly straightforward, familiar, and even commonplace phenomenon, it is not without its subtleties. While the enduring purpose of deterrence is prevention, the preferred means to that end—'fear'—has both practical and psychological dimensions, the arrangement of which, as just suggested, is determined by context and by prevailing circumstances. Deterrence amounts to a promise, whether explicit or implicit, to impose a cost on a given action such that the potential perpetrator is convinced that the expected benefits of the action will be outweighed by the probable costs incurred and will therefore choose not to act as planned or threatened. In traditional deterrence theory, prevention can be achieved both by fear of punishment and by fear of failure: by *punitive* (or counter-offensive) measures that would be undertaken in response to a transgression and intended to inflict some pain, damage, or loss upon the transgressor; or by a *denial* (or defensive) posture intended to impress upon an adversary that the complexities of the defences would be technologically insurmountable and/or the costs of overwhelming the defenses (however measured—human, financial, reputational, and diplomatic) unbearably high. Importantly, the first of these—deterrence by punishment—has a transactional quality while the second—deterrence by denial—could be said to be more unidirectional.

For deterrence to function in this traditional way, several elements must be in place. These are sometimes described as the 'three Cs' of deterrence theory. First, the deterring party must have the *capability* to impose the costs that have been promised or threatened. Second, the deterrer's promise must seem *credible* to the potential miscreant. Credible deterrence requires that the deterrer has both the acknowledged capability and the will—personal, political, or moral—to carry out the promise that has been made, and that this promise can then be *communicated* to, and understood by, the wrongdoer. Deterrence is therefore interactive—a relational activity, in which both sides must employ a broadly compatible rationality. Deterrence is a negotiation, of sorts, in which each side's position is understood by the other, and in which a mutually acceptable outcome—a tolerable status quo—is both available and desirable.

In the middle and latter decades of the twentieth century, we became especially familiar with dynamic, interactive, mutual deterrence as a component of the highly evolved politico-military strategies of the Cold War. For some, these strategies were opaque and inaccessible; they were derided by critics as requiring almost 'theological' levels of abstraction in order to be understood, or considered to be so absurdly over-engineered as to invite satire of the sort seen in Stanley Kubrick's *Dr Strangelove*. For others, however, deterrence was the most strategically, technologically, and psychologically sophisticated, and enduringly relevant, characteristic of the Cold War. The essential components of deterrence, in theory and in practice, were clearly articulated and more or less open to scrutiny. A potential aggressor's cost–benefit calculation might be influenced either by the threat of a punitive response or by the realization that the defender's preparations were so advanced and effective that the costs of carrying out the aggression would be too great. Moreover, each side engaged in the mutual strategic posturing of the Cold War was considered to have the necessary *capability*; each side's position was considered to be *credible*; and, in one way or another, each side *communicated* its position to its adversary. And it all worked, supposedly, insofar as a level of mutual strategic stability was sought and achieved, and there was no nuclear war.

The theory and practice of Cold War deterrence is sometimes perceived, if rather uncritically, to be a model for strategic stabilization in the digital era. As this chapter will argue, however, while there are lessons to be learned from the Cold War, there are also points at which its relevance becomes questionable, and even hazardous if pursued too enthusiastically. To enable a more critical comparison to be drawn, to assess where the Cold War experience could be relevant to the development of cyber deterrence and, conversely, where it might not, the first section of this chapter summarizes the principal tenets of Cold War strategic deterrence.

Some words of caution are due. Comparing different models and moments of deterrence across time and space, and between different technological contexts, will always be a difficult exercise, largely because the practice of deterrence is seldom, if ever, susceptible to scientific validation. While the general theory of deterrence is not difficult to comprehend, it is rather more challenging to establish practical cause and effect: how, when, and why deterrence 'worked' (or, indeed, failed) in a given set of circumstances. Because deterrence (as *prevention*) is concerned essentially with a non-event, the problem of establishing negative proof arises. Throughout human history, when an aggressor has taken stock and decided not to proceed, it is possible—but not certain—that deterrence will have played a part in that decision. This uncertainty is a feature of deterrence in general (even when it comes to explaining why, in its centre at least, the Cold War remained cold) and seems likely to persist in cyberspace, particularly when the activity to be deterred is taking place covertly, below what is often described as the 'threshold' of armed conflict. The second section of the chapter discusses several dilemmas and peculiarities that arise in the cyber sphere, including the difficulty of conducting deterrence as a mutual exercise in strategic stabilization, before examining, in the third section, what options there might be for the deterrence of adverse or aggressive behaviour in cyberspace. A final word of caution is that this chapter is primarily concerned with deterring adverse behaviour in cyberspace by states—a difficult enough prospect, as will be shown. But the deterrence of illegal, predatory, or aggressive behaviour in cyberspace by so-called 'non-state actors' (e.g. nuisance hackers, fraudsters, organized criminals, and political extremists and terrorists) is likely to be a still more challenging prospect.

COLD WAR DETERRENCE: FIVE LESSONS

With the invention of atomic and nuclear weapons in the mid-twentieth century, and the beginning of the Cold War, it became critically important that strategic conflict should be prevented and that deterrence should contribute to that goal. The evolution and maintenance of a framework of mutual strategic nuclear deterrence was not quite as automatic or as simple as is sometimes supposed, however. While a comprehensive history of Cold War deterrence would be neither feasible nor useful for the purposes of this chapter,[1] it is possible to draw lessons from that history to illustrate important similarities and differences between Cold War and cyber deterrence.

The first such lesson was the realization, early in the Cold War, that an atomic or nuclear counter-offensive (i.e. punitive) deterrent posture could compensate for strategic and operational disadvantages. After their use against Japan in August 1945, there was for some years a tendency to see atomic weapons as 'super-bombs', and as a means to extend and amplify existing doctrines of strategic air power. Atomic weapons were thought to have other advantages, too. They were considered, for example, to be unusually efficient in that they offered very much more 'bang for the buck' than an expensive conventional force posture. More significantly, it was also believed that these weapons could compensate for (or, in current politico-military jargon, 'offset') weaknesses in conventional forces, particularly useful at a time when the conventional military strength of the Soviet Union was thought to have remained overwhelming while the United States and its European allies had demobilized rapidly after World War II. An offset strategy is best understood as the use of technological superiority to compensate for perceived imbalances and weaknesses in a military force vis à vis certain advantages held by a likely adversary. In this respect, the 'offset' could be seen as an attempt to re-establish the capability, credibility, and communications upon which any successful deterrence posture must be based. The first such strategy was developed in the early 1950s, in the form of Eisenhower's New Look Strategy, whereby increases in nuclear capability (including at the tactical and operational levels) would offset the Soviet Union and Warsaw Treaty Organisation (WTO or Warsaw Pact)'s conventional military advantages. The Second Offset Strategy was a product of the 1970s and 1980s when doctrinal and technological developments such as 'Follow-On Forces Attack' and 'Airland Battle 2000' would enable non-nuclear attack against Soviet and WTO-armed echelons deep in their own territory.

The notion that one technology or another can offset disadvantages in a country's force posture is still alive in the security and strategy debate today, most clearly in the form of the US Third Offset Strategy, developed under the Obama administration. While the implementation of the strategy became very uncertain under the Trump administration, its stated goal was to acquire 'the means to offset advantages or advances in anti-access area denial weapons and other advanced technologies that we see proliferating around the world'.[2] By exploiting its technological advantage, the US would deter and defeat the use of these asymmetric systems and weapons by its adversaries, drawing upon 'five key areas' of research and development: autonomous learning systems, human–machine collaborative decision making, assisted human operations, advanced manned–unmanned systems operations, and network-enabled autonomous weapons and high-speed projectiles (Ellman, Samp, and Coll 2017).

For the purposes of this chapter, the offset idea is relevant to the challenge of cyber deterrence in two ways. First, whatever the fate of the Third Offset Strategy, the emphasis on data and intelligence, on information- and decision-making networks, and on automated/artificial processing and communication is unlikely to diminish. In other words, functions that might loosely be termed 'cyber' will play a part in the future deterrence posture of the United States (and its allies). Indeed, the summary of the 2018 US Department of Defense Cyber Strategy is explicit in this regard—'During wartime, US cyber forces will be prepared to [...] offset adversary strengths ... '[3] Second, none of this will have been lost on the adversaries of the US (and its allies). For these adversaries, the merit of a 'counter offset' strategy will surely be obvious, encouraging them to develop cyber power in order to compensate for their own disadvantages and to counter-deter their adversaries.

The second lesson concerns the shift from the unilateral, even rather primitive, flavour of early deterrence thinking, to the expectation that deterrence should serve as the basis for mutual stability between adversaries. As the Cold War advanced, and as atomic and then nuclear weapons were developed, together with evermore sophisticated and longer-range delivery systems, the foundations of deterrence thinking received ever closer attention. Capability alone—the 'super-bomb' idea—was not sufficient: with weapons of this scale, credibility and will mattered increasingly. And as the vulnerability to attack became mutual, so communication became ever more important. Deterrence became far more elaborate and could no longer be considered a unilateral advantage possessed by one side over the other. More than a relational activity, and certainly much more than simply a stand-off between adversaries, deterrence therefore became *mutual* and, in this highly evolved form, was henceforth, arguably, the central purpose of the Cold War as a whole. The goal of mutual stability is also one that is pursued in the cyber environment although, as will be suggested later in this chapter, mutual deterrence does not translate easily into cyberspace given, among other things, the difficulty of establishing the identity, location, and motivation of the adversary.

The difficulty of developing a complex strategic framework in the absence of clear evidence as to its validity was a feature of the atomic/nuclear era just as it is in cyberspace—the third lesson to consider. It is often claimed that, for four decades after its creation in 1949, NATO's deterrent posture 'worked' because the Cold War in Europe never became 'hot'. The Soviet Union and its allies in the WTO never attacked the NATO treaty area. As noted earlier in this chapter, however, the difficulty with this claim, and with deterrence thinking generally, is the problem of negative proof. It will always be difficult, practically and logically, to isolate the reasons why aggression or war did *not* take place and equally difficult, therefore, to be confident that preventive deterrence had succeeded as the cause, so to speak, of a non-event.

At this point, an interesting paradox emerges. Mutual deterrence became critical to Cold War strategic stability, yet this vitally important idea could never be analysed too closely, nor tested in practical terms, for fear of revealing its fragility or, worse still, of precipitating the very strategic crisis it was intended to prevent. Mutual deterrence could not fail, but neither could it be tested.[4] In *Strategy in the Missile Age* (1959), Bernard Brodie pointed to the difficulties of deterrence in the nuclear era: 'We expect the system to be always ready to spring while going permanently unused' (1959). How could Cold War strategists therefore be confident that the elaborate (and vital) system of mutual strategic deterrence would function as planned, if they had no possibility of experimentation and of knowing whether this punitive capability or that defensive posture would influence their adversary as decisively as required? The paradox of mutual deterrence was enough of a challenge during the Cold War, when adversaries, their intentions, and their capabilities were all more or less recognizable. But, as this chapter will show, the paradox seems likely to be still more problematic in the much less transparent cyber era.

The fourth lesson points to an important distinction between the Cold War strategic experience and its digital aftermath. Cold War deterrence was not expected to be the single, exclusive solution to the problem of establishing strategic stability. As the Cold War progressed, deterrence became one mechanism among a range of ideas, tools, and processes that reached their maturity during the Cold War, such as conflict prevention, management, and mediation, confidence building measures, and arms control agreements. If we are interested in preventing conflict and achieving a level of stability and predictability in cyberspace, and if our instinct is to look to the Cold War for some sort of a model to follow, or perhaps even a template to apply, then it seems reasonable to ask whether derivations of these highly evolved, Cold War mechanisms might also be effective in the cyber environment? The answer is that they might be effective, but only after thought and adaptation. These ideas were formed in the unusual context of the Cold War and should not be expected to survive in a new environment without careful nurturing. The purpose of conflict prevention, for example, is to reduce unpredictability and to emphasize the *management* of delicate, tense, or deteriorating situations over the *reaction* to unexpected crises for which little or no preparation has been made. In the context of the Cold War, a hasty or disproportionate reaction to a sudden event was considered to be a high-risk situation that might result in an extremely costly conflict. But, as will be discussed later in this chapter, the prospect of cyber conflict breaking out with no warning questions the assumption that the 'sudden event' is both exceptional and avoidable. Similar doubts can be raised about mediation, a classic tool both of conflict prevention and conflict management. In the cyber environment, however, the difficulty with early mediation is that it requires parties to a 'tense or deteriorating situation' to identify themselves as such, something that need not always happen in cyberspace. If they are to be effective, conflict prevention and mediation require a level of transparency, trust, and communication, all of which can prove to be in scarce supply in a cyber era characterized by 'plausible deniability'. Finally, conflict prevention and mediation also require early warning and preparation time if they are to be effective, whereas a cyber crisis might develop in a matter of minutes and hours rather than days, weeks, and months.[5]

Another echo of the Cold War is confidence building measures (CBMs). Could 'cyber CBMs' help to generate a more transparent and cooperative climate in cyberspace, making interaction less unpredictable and making it possible to understand and anticipate an adversary's or competitor's motives? Regional organizations such as the ASEAN Regional Forum, the Organization of American States and the Organization for Security and Co-operation in Europe (OSCE) have all considered the value of CBMs in the prevention of conflict in cyberspace, with the latter having produced a list of no fewer than 16 CBMs designed for states to limit and manage the risks of conflict arising from the use and misuse of information and communication technologies. Yet, CBMs depend for their success upon the political support of the respective governments, whether bilaterally or as members of a regional organization. In the case of the OSCE, with arguably the most developed regional approach to CBMs in cyberspace, that support has nevertheless not always been apparent. The Cold War also saw the evolution of a more ambitious form of CBM, intended not merely to encourage transparency and confidence but also to produce security—CSBMs, in Cold War parlance. When circumstances are conducive, CSBMs can make a significant contribution to conflict prevention and stability: the 1972 United States–Soviet Union Incidents at Sea Agreement is often cited in this regard. But if they are to succeed, CSBMs, like their less sophisticated forerunner, require mutual self-restraint among adversaries and competitors: a commodity that, again, is too little in evidence in cyberspace at present.

The fifth and final lesson is arguably the most compelling to be drawn from this brief survey of Cold War deterrence: that the underpinning rationale for deterrence can very quickly lose familiarity, credibility, and authority. The end of the Cold War has been described as the 'bonfire of the certainties'[6]—a particularly apt expression when it comes to the consideration of deterrence in Europe. A body of ideas, capabilities, and untestable assumptions that had for several decades been at the heart of security policy in and for Europe, deterrence was unceremoniously consigned to history in the early 1990s. It was not only that the highly elaborate, mutual strategic deterrence of the Cold War was considered suddenly to have become irrelevant but that politico-military deterrence itself was thought to be obsolete. In retrospect, this judgement was nothing but complacent: the past 25 years have shown that strategic deterrence is still required and there should in any case have been no reason to suppose that the basics of deterrence had become any less valid with the end of the Cold War than they had been throughout the previous millennia of human history. But the damage had been done. Post-Cold War optimism was accompanied by deep scepticism with regard to the relevance and efficacy of deterrence—a mood that largely disabled deterrence thinking, planning, and preparation. As one former Chairman of the US Joint Chiefs of Staff, General Martin Dempsey, observed 'As an alliance [i.e. NATO] we've taken deterrence for granted for 20 years now, but we can't do that anymore.'[7] The lesson here is that our experience of the Cold War has left us with two assumptions that are as incompatible as they are incorrect: first, that future threats can and should be deterred in the way Cold War adversaries were deterred—because, supposedly, 'it worked'; and, second, that we will never need to defend ourselves in the same way again and that, as a result, deterrence is obsolete. While strategic credibility forms one part of its interior logic (as one of the so-called '3Cs'), deterrence itself, as a general concept, requires, rather than blind faith, domestic political conviction and public confidence if is to be authoritative and persuasive in practice—in the cyber context as in any other.

CYBER DETERRENCE: THE PROBLEM

The underlying premise of deterrence is straightforward: within a given context or set of circumstances, deterrence works by promising to impose costs on a given action, either by making success more difficult or by threatening a punitive response. An adversary, if acting rationally, should then be convinced that the benefits of the action will be outweighed by the costs incurred or the punishment received, and will then choose not to act as intended. Explained in this way, deterrence seems to be such a commonplace and obvious proposition that we should expect to find evidence of it in operation in most, if not all, cases of competitive interaction among humans, including in cyberspace. By this simple logic, the purpose of *cyber* deterrence should be to convey the message that the benefits expected from adventurism or aggression will be outweighed by the costs and/ or punishments imposed. Cyber deterrence would then be understood to be a credible and communicable strategic posture combining passive and active elements—the capacity both to resist and to respond.

But this would be to assume that the general principles, and perhaps even the past practices of deterrence can be put to use 'out of the box', in any set of circumstances, with little or no adaptation required and without much accompanying thought. This section of the chapter asks what it is about cyberspace that makes deterrence (as we have so far understood it) difficult. There are two main areas to consider: strategic context and strategic communication. The relationship between the activity of deterrence and the historical, political, and geographical context in which it is practised cannot be accidental or incidental: deterrence must represent and be responsive to its strategic context if it is to be credible and to succeed in its aim of preventing conflict. The forms of strategic deterrence that evolved in the course of the Cold War were, self-evidently, born of that particular strategic context. Although there are today occasional voices warning of a 'new' Cold War (usually involving liberal democracies on one side and, on the other, Russia and/or China), few could argue (at least not convincingly) that the 'old' Cold War that began in the late 1940s is, to all intents and purposes, still under way. Yet, if the Cold War was a discrete moment in strategic history, the twenty-first-century strategic context seems much more resistant to convincing and durable description.

Strategic communication, the second point to consider, is as important to deterrence in theory as it is in practice: communication between actual or potential adversaries is vital if deterrence is to succeed and endure. Yet the nature of cyberspace—opaque in the uses to which it is put, globally distributed, multi-functional, non-hierarchical, and unpredictable— makes strategic communication between actual or potential adversaries extremely difficult in some circumstances. Who is the adversary, what do they want, and can they be drawn into rational conversation and negotiation?

Strategic Context

How should we describe strategic competition, confrontation, and conflict in the twenty-first century: the context in which cyber operations and cyber deterrence might be practised? Disturbingly, cyber capabilities (or 'weapons') and therefore cyber operations seem available to almost anyone with an aggressive, hostile, or predatory intent. It has long been recognized that 'cyber threats' might come from many quarters and on many levels including states, ideological and political extremists and terrorists, organized criminal groups, online child abusers, fraudsters, identity thieves, and nuisance hackers.[8] As noted earlier, however, whether cyber deterrence will be possible in all these instances remains to be seen.

The two 'Tallinn Manuals', published in 2013 and 2017 respectively, offer valuable guidance insofar as they show how and when cyber operations could be classified as 'armed conflict'. Although these volumes do not have the force of international law, they were prepared by internationally respected legal and technical experts at the invitation of NATO, and are widely considered to be authoritative. The first of these volumes—'Tallinn 1.0', as it has become known—argues that, in the event of a recognizable international armed conflict in which cyber operations have a role, such as that which took place between Georgia and Russia in 2008, then the law of armed conflict would apply to those cyber operations just as it would to other, conventional operations undertaken in the course of that conflict. The second volume, convened to consider 'the public international law governing cyber operations during peacetime', noted that, although 'cyber operations [that occur in the context of armed conflict] will typically be more worrisome from a national security perspective than those that occur in peacetime, States have to deal with cyber issues that lie below the use of force threshold on a daily basis'.[9] The authors' response to the challenge set for them was to argue that a cyber operation taking place in peacetime (below the threshold of armed conflict) could nevertheless constitute a use of force, to which the law of armed conflict would apply, 'when its scale and effects are comparable to non-cyber operations rising to the level of a use of force'.[10] Thus, if a cyber operation is undertaken *in furtherance of* (Tallinn 1.0) or even merely *in relation to* (Tallinn 2.0) 'on-going kinetic hostilities amounting to an armed conflict',[11] or if a cyber operation has an effect comparable or equivalent to a 'kinetic' operation, then that cyber operation falls into the category of armed conflict. These classifications provide valuable guidance, at least, as to the strategic context in which cyber operations might take place and what it is, therefore, that cyber deterrence would seek to prevent. Deterrence in these circumstances would appear to be feasible.

The Tallinn volumes are less helpful, at least for the purposes of this chapter, when it comes to the example of Estonia in 2007. Although Estonia, a recognized sovereign country, was the 'target' of 'persistent cyber operations', because these operations did not 'rise to the level of an armed conflict', the authors of the Tallinn manuals argued that they were not governed by the law of armed conflict.[12] That argument prompts an obvious and important question—if not an armed conflict, as traditionally defined and understood, then what *was* the strategic context within which the cyber campaign against Estonia took place? Estonia subsequently sought to frame the attacks as criminal activities of computer sabotage and interference with computer networks, and to prosecute the perpetrators for violations of the Estonian penal code. This effort was largely unsuccessful, however, because several of the suspected attackers were not resident in Estonia and therefore not subject to Estonian law enforcement.

The Estonia case points to a broader and deeper problem concerning cyber conflict and cyber deterrence. Many cyber operations fall within a rather murky category of activities, which, although they take place in peacetime, could nevertheless be described as *conflict*, and even considered *aggressive*. As David Omand (2020) has observed, 'most day to day malign cyber activity is ... well below what might be considered the threshold of an armed attack'. Omand deploys a memorable acronym to describe this malign activity—CESSPIT, or Crime, Espionage, Sabotage and Subversion Perverting Internet Technology. Yet, because conflict of this sort cannot be described as *armed*, it does not fall within the familiar strategic context of *armed conflict*. And, because there seems to be no effective alternative strategic context in which deterrence might function (e.g. international crime), deterrence is of limited use if, as suggested earlier, we insist that it must represent and be responsive to a strategic context. In these circumstances, adversaries might actually feel encouraged to act, rather than deterred from doing so. And, if these adversaries can ensure that their aggressive, peacetime, cyber operations can avoid being classified as armed conflict, then traditionally minded countries will have been wrong-footed by their own categorizations and unable to deter or to react effectively.

If the received wisdom concerning armed conflict can only provide us with a partial understanding of the twenty-first-century strategic context, and has too little to say about areas of conflict and competition in which cyber operations will play an important part, then what is the new wisdom that might be the basis for a new, twenty-first-century strategic context? There have been several attempts to find a new way to account for twenty-first-century conflict, but without convincing results. It has become fashionable to resort to expressions such as 'next generation', 'sub-threshold', 'hybrid', and 'grey zone' warfare. Yet, expressions such as these, for all their modishness, bring little if any clarity to the discussion: they seem instead to achieve precisely the opposite. To speak of 'generations' is to suggest that modes of armed conflict evolve in more or less discrete and recognizable phases, and that the sought-after wisdom lies simply in identifying where we (and our adversaries) lie on the evolutionary continuum. But the history of armed conflict has rarely if ever followed a neat and predictable course and seems even less likely to begin doing so in the early twenty-first century, given the pace and scope of technological change. 'Sub-threshold' suggests that dividing lines are useful when we know that technology has the effect of dissolving boundaries of all sorts and in all places: it implies that 'armed conflict' is a clear and valid discriminator, when it would appear not to be; and it suggests that activities that are 'sub' are somehow subordinate or peripheral, when that is certainly not the case. 'Hybrid warfare' is a confused term: a hybrid animal is one that is not only descended from its parents but also, importantly, different from its parents. Thus, a mule is neither a 'hybrid donkey' nor a 'hybrid horse'—it is a mule. 'Hybrid warfare' could also be said to be a category error: the distinctive feature in much of what is often described as 'hybrid' warfare is that it is *not* 'warfare'—if anything, it is political competition that has been 'hybridized', absorbing some military methods, rather than vice versa. And, if 'warfare' is allowed to persist in explanations of the twenty-first-century strategic context, it can also too easily lead to the assumption that the response should be the task of armed forces—the experts, after all, in warfare. Yet, where cyber operations are concerned, a military response might be the least appropriate, desirable, or effective. Similarly, the idea of 'grey zone' conflict tries to persuade us that the binary, monochrome understandings ('peace' *versus* 'war') that have for long governed our analysis of armed conflict can now be discarded in favour of a third option. But, on closer inspection, this radical alternative seems to do little more than allow for the binary options it seeks to replace to remain valid, albeit at different times and in different places. The 'grey zone' is indeed a category that cannot exist—how is it possible to describe the mid-point between 'peace' and 'war' other than in terms of 'peace' and 'war'? Lucas Kello's idea of 'unpeace' makes the point more honestly and plausibly, and without descending into complete taxonomic confusion:

> Let us leave at the wayside the two oppositional notions of war and peace, neither of which captures the essence of the contemporary situation. Let us resist, too, the urge to discard the distinction between war and peace. Instead, let us refer to the costly but nonviolent, incessant though often imperceptible hostilities in the new domain as a new state of affairs—a situation of *unpeace*, or mid-spectrum rivalry lying below the physically destructive threshold of interstate violence, but whose harmful effects far surpass the tolerable level of peacetime competition and possibly, even, of war (Kello 2018, 78).

For the purposes of this chapter, the difficulty with much of the language invented to describe the twenty-first-century strategic context is that it seeks to describe that context by exclusion, as something that cannot properly be explained using familiar terms of reference. Yet the new context is not sufficiently familiar or coherent to describe in its own terms: 'We don't know how to describe this environment other than in terms that we don't think can describe it.' In other cases, when familiar terms of reference *are* permitted, the result is no more illuminating. One such case is the tendency to describe the twenty-first century as an 'era of persistent competition'—but when have humans not been in competition, in one way or another? Another, popular expression is 'political warfare'—but when has warfare not been 'political' and, in any case, is warfare not meant to have some political purpose and to end in some politically recognizable conclusion? If, as I have argued, deterrence must embody, and operate within, a strategic context, then this loose language must make cyber deterrence more difficult to conceive and achieve. How can deterrence be shaped by, and function in, an environment that is not only unfamiliar but also, apparently, resistant to description in ways that can withstand scrutiny and which, in short, make sense?

Strategic Communication

As far as the development of deterrence is concerned, the shortcomings of the twenty-first-century strategic context are seen most clearly in the problem of strategic communication.[13] Deterrence is relational: it amounts to one party acting upon the risk calculus of another. Even if a deterrence posture is said to be 'adversary agnostic' (i.e. to have no specific adversary in mind, at least initially), it cannot function and would make no sense without at least the possibility of an adversary. In a way, 'adversary agnostic' simply means that the deterrence posture is waiting for a person, organization, or state to take on the mantle of an adversary, thereby entering into a relationship in which they can be deterred. It is possible, of course, that 'adversary agnostic deterrence' could be enough to persuade someone or something not to become an adversary, but this is probably best understood as pre-deterrence, or positioning. Until an adversary steps forward, there can be no strategic relationship and the adversary's cost–benefit calculus cannot be influenced by deterrence, at least not in the Cold War models with which we are most familiar. The Cold War saw basic, relational deterrence evolve into *mutual* deterrence. But, however complex and evolved it is, the central point about deterrence is that it involves communication between adversaries: whether relational or mutual, deterrence is a correspondence, or perhaps a negotiation, between parties who are knowingly and willingly part of that conversation.

One paradox of the information age is that, while the distribution of data around the world is unprecedented in scale and in the speed of transmission, too little of that exchange could be recognized as 'conversation'. Cyberspace allows communication without conversation insofar as it can permit surprisingly high levels of anonymity, opacity, and deniability. This characteristic of cyberspace can be explained in terms of the 'four zeros': 'zero day'; 'zero source'; 'zero effect'; and 'zero intent':

- The 'zero day' vulnerability is a deficiency in computer software that has been left unrepaired by the supplier and might be unknown to the user. 'Zero day' (or 'day zero') refers to the moment when the supplier becomes aware of the deficiency and begins to repair (or 'patch') it. But that is also the moment when hackers and other adversaries might become aware of the vulnerability. A race then begins: the supplier seeks to patch the problem as soon as possible while the adversary seeks to attack or 'exploit' the vulnerability using malicious software ('malware') developed specifically for that purpose. The significance of the 'zero day' for deterrence is that it limits (if not removes altogether) the time that a defender would ordinarily expect to require in order to identify, analyse, and respond to (or pre-empt) an impending attack, not least by signalling a sharpening of a deterrent posture.
- The 'zero source' challenge concerns the difficulty, in some circumstances, of establishing beyond doubt the identity of an adversary or attacker. This is often known as the problem of 'non-attribution': a situation in which an adversary might conduct hostile activities in cyberspace confident in the knowledge that, for technical or other reasons, his identity cannot be established and/or will not be revealed. Some argue that attribution is much less of a problem than is often supposed: the most sophisticated electronic intelligence systems are entirely capable of identifying the source of an attack and even, as will be discussed later in the chapter, of establishing the names and identities of the attackers. But if not a technical problem, attribution certainly remains a political and diplomatic problem, allowing attackers to hide behind the veil of so-called 'plausible deniability'. As with 'zero day', the 'zero source' problem questions the possibility either of establishing a manageable relationship with certain adversaries or of legitimately anticipating the attack. Both are important elements in the practice of deterrence.
- 'Zero effect' refers to the character of cyber attacks and intrusions. Whereas, in the past, we have associated conflict with violence and destruction—or at least with the possibility of such—a cyber attack might take place covertly, silently, and with few if any obvious consequences. An attack could take place with no indication that it has happened or that it is still taking place. This creates an obvious difficulty for deterrence because neither side in such a conflict would have reason to conduct a cost–benefit calculus or

to enter into negotiation. In these circumstances, there would be no obvious need for deterrence.

- Finally, 'zero intent' refers to the lack of clarity as to the adversary's intentions. Is the adversary's behaviour a nuisance, hostile, or, worst of all, 'warlike'? (Cornish et al. 2010) What is the adversary's rationale and what do they value how far are they willing to go? Without this knowledge, it is difficult for the defender to know where and how the adversary's values and ambitions can be held at risk, and to ensure that a threatened deterrence response would be timely, discriminate, and proportionate. A response that could not satisfy all three of these criteria might not qualify as a credible deterrent.

Taken together, these 'four zeros' suggest that cyberspace is not always the medium for open conversation, and for the free and transparent distribution of ideas and information that the originators of the Internet and the world wide web might have had in mind. And, for the purposes of this chapter, the four zeros also suggest that the idea of deterrence as the outcome of a rational conversation between adversaries might not easily be achieved, in all circumstances.[14] The paradox of communication without conversation has one further twist. What most distinguishes the twenty-first-century strategic environment from its Cold War predecessor is without doubt the development of cyberspace as both a medium of communication and a platform for strategic competition and conflict. We have thus come to the point where one of the essential '3Cs' of deterrence—communication—has itself become a battleground: the means to deter conflict have, for some, become the means to pursue it. This helps to explain, in part, why theories of cyber deterrence are in certain cases inclined to the deterrence of *actions* rather than *actors*—a shift that is discussed in the next section of the chapter.

Cyber Deterrence: The Options

Cyber deterrence is the subject of rich debate. For reasons discussed elsewhere in this chapter, some take the view that cyber deterrence is simply not possible. For others, however, cyber deterrence need not be a lost cause if it can respond to the difficult questions posed by the four zeros just discussed. For example, can an adversary and/or an attack be identified in a timely manner and, if not, are 'adversary agnostic' forms of cyber deterrence available? What quality of communication and rational conversation is possible or can be expected? If little or none, could cyber deterrence be designed in such a way that it encourages conversation? What is the target of the cyber deterrent posture—the hostile actor, the hostile action, or some amalgam of these? And what is the best form of deterrence to adopt—punishment, denial, or some other method? A comprehensive review of the cyber deterrence debate is not necessary in this chapter—further information is available elsewhere in this *Handbook*. Nevertheless, the various deterrence options currently under discussion can be grouped usefully into three sets of ideas and policies. Adapting and updating the 'punishment' and 'denial' terminology of the Cold War era of strategic deterrence, the three types of cyber deterrence can be described as Punitive Deterrence, Constructive Deterrence, and Protective Deterrence.

Punitive Deterrence

Punitive Deterrence options are those that draw upon familiar (particularly Cold War) practices, revised and reapplied to the digital era. Typically involving a credible threat to respond to (and, by that means, prevent) adverse behaviour, these options tend to assume known, predictable, and large-scale adversarial actors (e.g. states), to whom hostile intentions and actions can be attributed, and with whom something like rational conversation and negotiation can be expected. It is at least conceivable that a balanced relationship might develop between states in cyberspace, whereby adversarial ambitions and practices are stabilized by mutual deterrence, as they were during the Cold War. One state might acquire (and declare) the means for a large-scale computer network attack (CNA), above the 'threshold' of armed conflict, while its adversary in turn develops computer network defence (CND) coupled with counter-offensive cyber means.[15] However, the fact that a Cold War-style adversarial balance of this sort has not yet been established—and perhaps not even been pursued—could suggest that states see cyberspace as an as yet underdeveloped strategic environment, too unpredictable and unstable to take the highest level of strategic risks. The advantages of cyber power might, instead, be seen in lower-level, less overt postures. This possibility suggests that Punitive Deterrence of adversary states will have to be more agile and nuanced than in the past, able to respond at whatever level of hostility, with a variety of means (military, legal, diplomatic, economic) and in ways that are proportionate to the ambition and scale of the attack.

'Extended deterrence' is a more direct example of the reapplication of traditional deterrence thinking.[16] During the Cold War, the US 'nuclear umbrella' was widely considered to have restrained any ambitions the Soviet Union might have had to use its preponderant conventional armed forces to capture the territory of US allies in Europe. Something broadly equivalent seems feasible in the cyber era: 'In a conflict, cyber security will be as or more important in forward theaters as it will be in the United States. Most US allies and partners do not have the same cyber capabilities as the [US Department of Defense], yet it will be their infrastructures and national capabilities that US forces will be relying on for numerous tasks.'[17] Variations on the theme of extended deterrence include the 'triadic' or indirect deterrence of third parties and/or non-state actors.[18]

Another legacy of the Cold War is the idea of 'intra-conflict deterrence'. Once a conflict is underway, it can be driven by the dynamic of escalation—rather than accept loss or defeat, each side will use ever more powerful means to claim decisive advantage. The problem with the escalatory dynamic, however, is that it has no in-built stopping point—a characteristic considered to be particularly dangerous in the context of the Cold War nuclear confrontation. Punitive cyber deterrence offers two loose parallels to Cold War thinking: 'intradomain deterrence', where a cyber intrusion on one level might be met with a cyber response on a higher level; and 'cross-domain deterrence', where states might respond to a cyber attack by physical means in non-cyber strategic 'domains'—land, sea, air, and space—or might use non-military responses such as diplomacy and economic sanctions. Much of this discussion is speculative, however: there is as yet little experience of de-escalating a conflict in cyberspace and, in the context of the four zeros, it is difficult to see how escalation can be controlled, and by whom (Cornish 2018). 'De-escalation of a cyber conflict', writes Robert Axelrod (2017), 'can be substantially more difficult than de-escalation of a conventional military conflict. [...] The unpredictable effects of cyber weapons', he argues, 'can not only make escalation hard to contain, but may also make de-escalation difficult to achieve.'

The final Punitive Deterrence option to consider was not much in evidence during the Cold War but is becoming characteristic of the cyber environment. In February 2013, Mandiant, a US information security company, published a report entitled *APT1: Exposing One of China's Cyber Espionage Units* (Mandiant Intelligence Centre 2013). The report accused the Chinese People's Liberation Army of orchestrating an 'advanced persistent threat' against the United States and elicited the following response from the Chinese Ministry of Defence: 'It is unprofessional and groundless to accuse the Chinese military of launching cyber attacks without any conclusive evidence.'[19] There certainly did seem to be a shortage of 'conclusive evidence' in the published report—a photograph of air-conditioning units on a building in Shanghai was hardly technical proof of the involvement of the Chinese military in cyber espionage. This exchange was, nevertheless, an accurate reflection of the 'don't attribute; say nothing' mood that had dominated for so long. Yet, just 12 months or so later, in May 2014, the US FBI went so far as to publish the photographs of the five People's Liberation Army (PLA) officials it would subsequently indict for cyber espionage.

In April 2017, another hacking group—designated APT10 or 'Red Apollo'—was discovered by UK-based private sector companies (PwC and BAE Systems) working in conjunction with the UK government's National Cyber Security Centre. APT10 was described as one of the biggest cyber espionage campaigns ever mounted: attacking large security, defence, and technology companies in order to steal intellectual property (IP) from smaller companies in their supply chain. According to one report, forensic analysis of the timings of the attack, as well as the tools and techniques used, led investigators to conclude that the group was state-sponsored and based in China (Milliman 2017). Although it was not known at first who was behind APT10 or why it targeted certain organizations, in December 2018, the US Department of Justice charged two individuals—both associated with the Ministry of State Security—for their involvement in APT10 (Yang and Bland 2018). The mood had clearly changed in the course of just a few years—the consequence, not of technological developments but of a new willingness politically to 'tell it like it is' and to expose individual cyber attackers no matter what the security, intelligence, and diplomatic ramifications might be. Although in important respects the 'attribution problem' will remain, this change of mood gives substance to the view that a political, rather than a technological, standard of evidence can and should be used, and that governments and the private sector should be encouraged not just to form judgements but to discuss them more openly (Cornish 2012). Elisabeth Braw and Gary Brown describe this as a shift towards 'personalized deterrence' whereby deterrence will focus more closely 'on what individual hackers or attackers are most likely to value, and bases deterrence on that individual cost-benefit analysis' (Braw and Brown 2020).

Constructive Deterrence

Whereas Punitive Deterrence is concerned with preventing the hostile behaviour of (known) actors, and presupposes a level of conversation with those actors, Constructive Deterrence is 'adversary agnostic' and is concerned to show that the core principle of deterrence—the prevention of conflict—can apply, even in the absence of conversation with an adversary.

The possibilities of anonymous, more-or-less non-attributable or 'plausibly deniable' hostile activity might suggest to some actors that their interests can be pursued with impunity. Constructive Deterrence, however, tries to suggest that such behaviour could be an irrational act of self-harm. In a sense, therefore, Constructive Deterrence is unilateral communication (or signalling) whereby mutually beneficial, reciprocal behaviour is encouraged, which might, in time, become the foundations of a stable deterrence relationship between adversaries.

The most obvious form of Constructive Deterrence incorporates the idea of interdependence (or 'entanglement') and a shared sense of the unintended consequences and damage that might be caused by large-scale attacks against complex national networks (Nye 2016/17). Because neither attacker nor defender can be fully aware of the interdependencies, strengths, and vulnerabilities within these networks, the consequences could, conceivably, be out of proportion to the strategic purpose of the attack or, just as conceivably, fall far short of achieving a decisive effect. And an uncontrollable attack of this sort could also be met in kind, implying a shared vulnerability to yet more unpredictable consequences arising from the response. As Tang and Zhang observe, the fact that complex networks are interconnected globally should also give pause for thought: 'a retaliatory attack on another country's networks has the potential of harming the security of one's own networks' (Lan and Xin 2010) 'Damage limitation' is then the basis for a more enlightened state of affairs 'where all parties have a shared interest in the relationship not becoming too fraught, with international norms of good conduct chilling bad behaviour by the consideration that we all have to coexist and do business together'.[20]

If this 'shared interest' is not quite at the level of the mutual deterrence conversation of the Cold War, it is at least a step in that direction. Momentum towards this goal of self-limiting, reciprocal behaviour is boosted by various derivations of the Constructive Deterrence idea. For example, 'normative deterrence' argues for mutually beneficial taboos against attacking certain types of targets such as a country's critical civilian infrastructure or its Computer Emergency Response Team (CERT) and might seek international agreement, in the United Nations or elsewhere, on some framework for rules-based cooperation;[21] 'associative deterrence' highlights the risk of reputational damage that might attach merely from being connected to a cyber attack of some sort;[22] 'ideational deterrence' suggests that hostile behaviour might result in the perpetrator's political position becoming subject to damaging criticism, perhaps a campaign of delegitimization (Knopf 2010); and, finally, 'legal deterrence', which argues that domestic and international law are becoming steadily more consolidated and authoritative with respect to the misuse of cyberspace (Burton 2018).

While Constructive Deterrence, in its various forms, is an argument for or, perhaps, an invitation to rational self-restraint, it would be a mistake to assume that to be 'adversary agnostic' means that Constructive Deterrence must be entirely passive and non-kinetic. In the first place, as the US Defense Science Board has observed, these delicate normative frameworks and highly cultivated ideas can provide 'the basis for international legitimacy for imposing sustained costs on violators' (Department of Defense 2017). These 'sustained costs' could be economically and even physically destructive, and need not require an adversary to be known or named for the threat to be made. This declaratory aspect of Constructive Deterrence, which might also be described as 'latent cross-domain deterrence' amounts to reserving the right to respond in force, whoever the attacker might be. In 2016, for example, NATO's Warsaw Summit Communiqué described cyber defence as 'part of NATO's core task of collective defence' and recognized cyberspace 'as a domain of operations in which NATO must defend itself as effectively as it does in the air, on land, and at sea.'[23] NATO governments, and others, have taken a similar position. The 2018 US Cyber Strategy, for example, insists that 'Should deterrence [of malicious cyberspace activity] fail, the Joint Force stands ready to employ the full range of military capabilities in response.'[24]

Protective Deterrence

When the identity and ambitions of a hostile actor cannot be confidently identified (the pre-condition of Preventive Deterrence), and/or where there is little or no scope even for 'uni-lateral' communication with the unknown adversary, then Protective Deterrence becomes significant. Protective Deterrence takes the enduring obligation to ensure the defence and security of national territory and physical infrastructure (docks, railways, power stations, etc.), adds elements of Cold War-style 'deterrence by denial', and then adapts and extends these familiar ideas into the digital environment of the twenty-first century. In this envir-onment, it is imperative to protect not just the physical but also the digital infrastructure upon which developed economies are so dependent and which must be made resilient to attack. Protective Deterrence switches our attention from deterrence of an adversarial *actor* to deterrence of a hostile *action* and, through the idea of resilience, enhances deterrence by turning the digital environment into more of a strategic asset than a liability.

The proposition that a national digital infrastructure should be protected against the actions of spies, extremists, saboteurs, and hackers is scarcely controversial. Each country addresses this task in its own way but with common themes. In the UK, for example, the na-tional infrastructure comprises 13 sectors including water, defence, energy, communications, and health. The *critical* national infrastructure (CNI) comprises those assets, facilities, systems, networks, processes, and even workers, 'the loss or compromise of which would result in ... Major detrimental impact on ... essential services' and/or 'Significant impact on national security, national defence, or the functioning of the state.'[25] Importantly, the CNI can be both physical (e.g. sites, installations, items of equipment) and logical (e.g. informa-tion networks and communications systems). Thus, as well as being one of the 13 infrastruc-ture sectors, communication is also a key, critical enabler underpinning the whole system. A similar view informs the European Union's Network and Information Security Directive, which begins with the following words: 'Network and information systems and services play a vital role in society. Their reliability and security are essential to economic and societal activities.'[26] By this interpretation, protection of the digital infrastructure is a goal in itself. It is not required to be validated by some mutual deterrence framework and least of all should it be held hostage to conversation, particularly with an adversary who might be implacably and terminally committed to their cause and utterly uninterested, therefore, in any form of negotiation.

The case for protection of the digital infrastructure might be self-evident but its imple-mentation is not simple. It is often argued that in cyberspace the offence–defence balance is weighted heavily in favour of the former. There are so many 'attack surfaces' and 'attack vectors' in any national digital infrastructure that not even the most robust, comprehen-sive defensive system could guarantee protection against all attacks and intrusions: 'Offence is the position of strength, as anonymous attackers rarely have to face the consequences of their actions, whereas the static defender must successfully parry every blow.'[27] This imbalance between defence and offence has in turn led some to doubt the deterrent value of cyber defence: deterrence by denial 'has failed to substantively alter the motivational calculus of determined cyber attackers' (Korns 2009, 100); 'deterrence by defence is guaranteed to be ineffective in cyberspace' (Taddeo 2018).

Yet deterrence *without* defence seems implausible. Could a deterrent posture credibly seek to prevent a cyber adversary's hostile behaviour if that adversary were able to hold at risk the defender's critical digital infrastructure? Martin Libicki (2009) goes as far as to argue that defence (as the basis of deterrence by denial), plays a 'greater role' than deterrence by punishment. In the same vein, the 2016 version of the UK National Cyber Security Strategy suggests a very close relationship between a protection, denial, and deterrence:

> We will pursue a comprehensive national approach to cyber security and deterrence that will make the UK a harder target, reducing the benefits and raising the costs to an adversary—be they political, diplomatic, economic or strategic. We must ensure our capability and intent to respond are understood by potential adversaries in order to influence their decision-making. We shall have the tools and capabilities we need: to deny our adversaries easy opportunities to compromise our networks and systems; to understand their intent and capabilities; to defeat commodity malware threats at scale; and to respond and protect the nation in cyberspace (HM Government 2016, 47, 6.1.3).

If cyber defence is essentially compromised, yet at the same time essential to the success of cyber deterrence, then an obvious dilemma presents itself. One way out of that dilemma lies in the idea of resilience. The *Concise Oxford Dictionary* defines resilience as 'recoiling; springing back; resuming its original shape after bending, stretching, compression etc.' There is, plainly, a protective or defensive flavour to these words, which explains why the tools and techniques of cyber defence often make an appearance in discussions of cyber resilience: encryption and 'hardening' of data; accurate user identification and message authentication; personnel security (the problem of the 'insider threat'); penetration testing; anti-malware security updates and 'patching'; and ensuring adequate levels of redundancy in systems and that reversionary modes of operation are available, known, and practised. But resilience in cyberspace can be more broadly conceived as a tool for vulnerability management and mitigation, enabling the cyber defender to become more agile than static and thereby restoring deterrent credibility.

In a world of fast-moving, asymmetric cyber threats, to 'spring back' to a position that has just been shown to be vulnerable to attack could, at best, be described as 'dumb resilience'. But resilience can be more than resistance and restoration of the (compromised) status quo ante. 'Smart resilience' embodies the more useful idea of 'bouncing *forward*' to a different, more advantageous position. This can be achieved, in part, through technical and managerial measures such as in-built redundancy and operational recovery plans. But it might be possible for resilience to be 'smarter' still—perhaps even 'dynamic'—whereby the defender becomes more agile and adaptable, and can regain and hold the initiative by identifying and then managing their vulnerabilities. The starting point for dynamic resilience is for the defender to have a clear understanding of their own cyber vulnerabilities and interdependencies, and of the harms that they might face in and from cyberspace (Cornish et al. 2016). From that position of knowledge (which the attacker is unlikely to have), the defender can assess and reassess the value/vulnerability calculus to their advantage, whenever there is a case for doing so. In other words, rather than surrender the initiative to the aggressor, it is the defender who decides, on their terms, what is at stake, and when, retaining the ability and the initiative to change the analysis and reprioritize, as often as necessary.

Dynamic resilience positions the defender to understand and manage their own risk profile more promptly and effectively than the adversary can threaten it. Artificial intelligence (AI) and machine learning could be key to this task: auditing networks for compromises and vulnerabilities, identifying and testing critical interdependencies, and ensuring that the digital CNI has sufficient redundancy and the capacity for 'graceful degradation'.[28] The potential of AI for vulnerability management was tested in the 2016 DARPA Cyber Grand Challenge, in which teams competed to 'create automatic defensive systems capable of reasoning about flaws, formulating patches, and deploying them on a network in real time'. The rationale was clear: 'By acting at machine speed and scale, these technologies may someday overturn today's attacker-dominated status quo' (Fraze n.d.). The value of AI for the management of vulnerability is also recognized in the 2018 US Cyber Strategy, with reference to the use of 'cyber enterprise solutions' operating at 'machine speed', as well as 'large-scale data analytics', 'to identify malicious cyber activity across different networks and systems' and to then 'leverage these advances to improve our own defensive posture'.[29]

No network or system can be made absolutely invulnerable to intrusion and attack. It is certain that there will be a vulnerability of some sort, somewhere. This probably serves as an invitation to probe and test a system's defences. Yet, with its emphasis on resilience and, increasingly, on the role of AI, Protective Deterrence shows that cyber defence can be active and dynamic: in effect, updating 'deterrence by denial' by using digital means to deal with digital threats. But Protective Deterrence goes beyond simply denying success (or, indeed, victory) to the attacker. The deterrence of conflict, of any sort, is a matter not just of influencing the adversary's rational cost–benefit analysis: it is also a matter of ensuring that initiative is not lost to the adversary. Contrary to the received wisdom, Protective Deterrence shows that cyber vulnerabilities can be identified, managed, and redistributed in such a way that the attacker cannot expect to hold the initiative. As a result, Protective Deterrence also ensures that both Punitive Deterrence and Constructive Deterrence are meaningful and credible. Resilience, notes Nye, is essential 'to assure that cyber and noncyber military response options are available for retaliation'.[30]

Conclusion

There is no reason to suppose that the principles of deterrence should not apply in cyberspace as in any other environment in which human beings interact, and there is mounting evidence that the prevention of hostile and predatory activity—the purpose of deterrence— is essential if cyberspace is to be maintained as a stable, secure, and productive environment. Yet, while deterrence can be defined in principle and discussed in abstract, it can only be understood in practice and in context. To adapt an insight from Clausewitz, the nineteenth-century philosopher of war, while deterrence has a settled nature, it can nevertheless take many forms. It can be tempting to confuse one form of deterrence (i.e. the Cold War strategic variant) with deterrence's enduring nature, and then to assume that that particular form must by default have become universally and unalterably applicable. The comparison often drawn between cyber deterrence and its Cold War predecessor generally fails to appreciate that the Cold War experience serves best in a figurative rather than a literal way. And, if the Cold War can be a useful simile, we make best use of it by accepting that not all of that experience is, or needs to be, transferable. The Cold War experience embodies expectations of rational conversation and assumptions of state-centric, territorially focused strategy, not all of which is suitable for all circumstances. Ultimately, deterrence is shaped by context and in that context it must work, and be seen to work. Colin Gray's withering critique of arms control—'Arms control is feasible only when it is not needed' (1993, 343) (and, by inference, necessary when it is not feasible)—warns against devising a theoretical framework that, however elegant, might prove to be ineffective, irrelevant, or unnecessary.

The four zeros discussed in this chapter show why the Cold War model of deterrence does not translate automatically or easily into cyberspace, where the strategic context is so opaque and fluid and where mutually beneficial interaction can be so hard to establish. This is not to dismiss the Cold War experience completely, however. It is reasonable to draw upon the Cold War model in those cases where a cyber conflict between states could be the equivalent of, and classified as, armed conflict under international law. But the Cold War model is much less useful when the cyber conflict, so-called, takes place in time of relative stability, cannot be said to be armed, and does not directly involve states. This chapter has examined various options for cyber deterrence, grouped into three categories—Punitive Deterrence, Constructive Deterrence, and Protective Deterrence. Some options show the relevance of the Cold War experience, while others show the need for fresher thinking. What is clear is that none of the options or types of deterrence discussed here can provide a complete answer to the problem of cyber deterrence. It follows that, at least for the present, cyber deterrence is likely to be an amalgam of types and techniques depending on the prevailing circumstances. As Ben Buchanan observes, 'different actors and even different acts are subject to varying kinds of deterrence'. Buchanan (2014, 130) calls for a 'mosaic strategy'—a 'multi-faceted strategy to approach the cyber domain'. This is the challenge of cyber deterrence. Rather than pursue a singular, monolithic model of deterrence such as that of the Cold War era, in the cyber era, governments must have the capacity and the confidence to draw upon different deterrent options as circumstances (and adversaries) demand.

NOTES

1. For a sophisticated and concise introduction to the topic, see Martin, Laurence. 1981. *The Two-Edged Sword: Armed Force in the Modern World*. (The Reith Lectures; 1981). London: Weidenfeld & Nicolson.
2. See Deputy Secretary of Defense Bob Work, 'The Third U.S. Offset Strategy and Its Implications for Partners and Allies'. Speech, Washington, DC: 28 January 2015: https://www.defense.gov/News/Speeches/Speech-View/Article/606641/the-third-us-offset-strategy-and-its-implications-for-partners-and-allies
3. US Department of Defense (DoD) 'Cyber Strategy 2018 (Summary)', p. 1: https://media.defense.gov/2018/Sep/18/2002041658/-1/-1/1/CYBER_STRATEGY_SUMMARY_FINAL.PDF

4. Joseph Nye makes a similar point when writing of the 'usability paradox'—'If the weapons could not be used, they could not deter.' Nye, J.S. 2011. 'Nuclear Lessons for Cyber Security?', *Strategic Studies Quarterly* (winter): 24.

5. See Kavanagh C. and P. Cornish. 2020. 'Cyber Operations and Inter-State Competition and Conflict: The Persisting Value of Preventive Diplomacy', EU Cyber Direct: https://eucyberdirect.eu/wp-content/uploads/2020/09/rif-preventive-diplomacy.pdf.

6. 'Bonfire of the certainties'—an expression coined by G. (now Lord) Robertson in a speech at Chatham House in 1990.

7. M. Dempsey, interview, Atlantic Council, 28 September 2015. http://www.atlanticcouncil.org/blogs/natosource/general-dempsey-nato-has-taken-deterrence-for-granted

8. See Cornish P. et al. 2009. *Cyberspace and the National Security of the United Kingdom: Threats and Responses*. London: Chatham House.

9. Schmitt M. (ed.). 2017. *Tallinn Manual 2.0 on the International Law Applicable to Cyber Operations*. Cambridge, UK: Cambridge University Press, p. 1.

10. Schmitt, *Tallinn Manual*, Section 14, 'The Use of Force', Rules 69, p. 330.

11. Schmitt, *Tallinn Manual*, Section 14, 'The Use of Force', Rules 69, p. 376.

12. Schmitt, *Tallinn Manual*, 75–6.

13. The term 'strategic communication' has acquired a number of meanings and usages. For the purposes of this chapter, it is taken simply to mean communication between strategic adversaries in peace and/or conflict.

14. A counterpoint to the four zeros can be found in an article by Mike McConnell, former Director of the US National Security Agency, in which he advocated Cold War-style cyber deterrence based on four elements—'attribution', 'location', 'response' and 'transparency': 'How to win the cyber war we're losing', *The Washington Post*, 28 February 2010: https://cyberdialogue.ca/wp-content/uploads/2011/03/Mike-McConnell-How-to-Win-the-Cyberwar-Were-Losing.pdf

15. Cornish et al., *Cyberspace*, 4–5.

16. See D.J. Trachtenberg, 'US Extended Deterrence: How Much Strategic Force Is Too Little?', *Strategic Studies Quarterly* (Summer 2012).

17. Kramer, F.D., R.J. Butler, and C. Lotrionte. 2017. *Cyber and Deterrence: The Military-Civil Nexus in High-End Conflict*. Washington, DC: Atlantic Council, p. 18. See also DoD, Cyber Strategy', 4.

18. See Atzili, B. and W. Pearlman. 2012. 'Triadic Deterrence: Coercing Strength, Beaten by Weakness', *Security Studies* 21 (2): 301–35.

19. Mandiant, *APT1*, 1.

20. Omand, 'Future of Deterrence'.

21. See J.S. Nye, 'Nuclear Lessons for Cyber Security?', *Strategic Studies Quarterly* (winter 2011).

22. See P. Cornish, 'Deterrence and the Ethics of Cyber Conflict' in M. Taddeo and L. Glorioso (eds), *Ethics and Policies for Cyber Operations* (Springer International Publishing, 2017).

23. NATO. 2016. *Warsaw Summit Communiqué*, 9 July, para. 70: https://www.nato.int/cps/en/natohq/official_texts_133169.htm

24. DoD, *Task Force on Deterrence*, 4.

25. CPNI, 'Critical National Infrastructure'. https://www.cpni.gov.uk/critical-national-infrastructure-0

26. NIS Directive (EU) 2016/1148, 6 July 2016, *Official Journal of the European Union* (L 194/1, 19 July 2016), p.1 para (1). https: https://eur-lex.europa.eu/legal-content/EN/TXT/PDF/?uri=CELEX:32016L1148&from=EN//eur-lex.europa.eu/eli/dir/2016/1148/oj

27. Cornish et al., *On Cyber Warfare*, 37.
28. Graceful degradation is defined as 'the ability of a computer, machine, electronic system or network to maintain limited functionality even when a large portion of it has been destroyed or rendered inoperative. The purpose of graceful degradation is to prevent catastrophic failure'. https://searchnetworking.techtarget.com/definition/graceful-degradation
29. DoD, 'Cyber Strategy, 4.
30. Nye, 'Deterrence and Dissuasion', 56.

REFERENCES

Axelrod, R. 2017. 'How to De-Escalate a Cyber Conflict', Roundtable on Military Cyber Stability paper, August. http://www-personal.umich.edu/~axe/cyber-de-escalation.pdf.

Braw, E. and G. Brown. 2020. 'Personalised Deterrence of Cyber Aggression', *The RUSI Journal*, 18 March.

Brodie, B. 1959. *Strategy in the Missile Age*. Santa Monica, CA: RAND Corporation, p. 273.

Buchanan, B. 2014. 'Cyber Deterrence Isn't MAD; It's Mosaic', *Georgetown Journal of International Affairs: International Engagement of Cyber IV*, p. 130.

Burton, J. 2018. *Cyber Deterrence: A Comprehensive Approach?* April. Tallinn: NATO Cooperative Cyber Defence Centre of Excellence.

Cornish, P. 2012. 'Digital Détente: Designing a Strategic Response to Cyber Espionage', Public interest report, summer. Washington, DC: Federation of American Scientists.

Cornish, P. et al. 2016. *Cyber Harm: Concepts, Taxonomy and Measurement*. August. Oxford: Saïd Business School Research Papers, RP 2016–23.

Cornish, P. 2018. *Military Operations in Cyberspace*. Wilton Park Conference Report, September), pp. 4–6, 10. www.wiltonpark.org.uk/wp-content/uploads/WP1635-Report.pdf

Cornish, P. et al. 2010. *On Cyber Warfare*. London: Chatham House, p. 12.

Department of Defense (DoD). 2017. *Task Force on Deterrence*. February. Washington, DC: Defense Science Board, p. 11.

Ellman, J., L. Samp, and G. Coll. 2017. *Assessing the Third Offset Strategy*. March. Washington, DC: Center for Strategic & International Studies, p. 3.

Fraze, D. (n.d.). 'Cyber Grand Challenge (CGC) (Archived)', Defense Advanced Research Projects Agency. https://www.darpa.mil/program/cyber-grand-challenge.

Gray, C. 1993. 'Arms Control Does Not Control Arms', *Orbis*, summer, p. 343.

HM Government. 2016. *National Cyber Security Strategy 2016–2021*. London: HMSO, p. 47, para. 6.1.3.

Kello, L. 2018. *The Virtual Weapon and International Order*. London: Yale University Press, p. 78.

Knopf, J.W. 2010. 'The Fourth Wave in Deterrence Research', *Contemporary Security Policy* 31 (1), April: 10.

Korns, S.W. 2009. 'Cyber Operations: the New Balance', *Joint Force Quarterly* 54: 100.

Lan, Tang and Zhang Xin. 2010. 'Can Deterrence Work?'. In *Global Cyber Deterrence: Views from China, the U.S., Russia, India and Norway*, edited by A. Nagorski, 1. New York: EastWest Institute.

Libicki, M. 2009. *Cyberdeterrence and Cyberwar*. Santa Monica, CA: RAND Corporation, p. 7.

Mandiant Intelligence Centre. 2013. *APT1: Exposing One of China's Cyber Espionage Units*. February. Washington, DC: Mandiant.

Milliman, R. 2017. 'Huge Hacking Operation Uncovered Targeting Victims' Supply Chain', *SC Magazine*, 4 April.

Nye, J.S. 2016/17. 'Deterrence and Dissuasion in Cyberspace', *International Security* 41 (3): 48.

Omand, D. 2020. 'The Future of Deterrence', The 2020 Michael Quinlan Lecture, Strand Group, King's College London, 21 January. https://thestrandgroup.kcl.ac.uk/event/the-eighth-sir-michael-quinlan-memorial-lecture.

Taddeo, M. 2018. 'How to Deter in Cyberspace', *Hybrid CoE Strategic Analysis* 9 (June–July): 3.

Yang, Yuan and B. Bland. 2018. 'Who is the Chinese Group Blamed For Cyber Attacks on the West?', *Financial Times*, 21 December: https://www.ft.com/content/9ecc3232-04fa-11e9-99df-6183d3002ee1.

PART V

TECHNICAL AND CORPORATE CYBER SECURITY

CHAPTER 18

STEPPING OUT OF THE SHADOW: COMPUTER SECURITY INCIDENT RESPONSE TEAMS IN THE CYBERSECURITY ECOSYSTEM

NICOLE VAN DER MEULEN

INTRODUCTION

ON 2 November 1988, a graduate student by the name of Robert Tappan Morris managed to change the Internet for ever (Lee 2013). Morris developed and subsequently released one of the first computer worms. The 'Morris worm', as it is commonly known, is often referred to or commemorated as the first computer worm because it managed to attract significant media attention. The historical significance of the event is plentiful, especially as Morris himself was the first to be convicted of a felony under the US Computer Fraud and Abuse Act.[1] For the purposes of security, however, Lee describes the event's impact best when he writes: 'Before Morris unleashed his worm, the Internet was like a small town where people thought little of leaving their doors unlocked. Internet security was seen as a mostly theoretical problem, and software vendors treated security flaws as a low priority.'[2] Therefore, the impact of the Morris worm was significant not only in terms of the damage it caused but also in changing the perspective people had on the Internet and, in particular, its security. The event also led to the establishment of the first Computer Emergency Response Team (CERT)—namely, the CERT/Coordination Center, better known as CERT/CC, which explains the relevance of the Morris Worm for this chapter. Important to note is how the terms 'CERT' and 'Computer Security Incident and Response Team' (CSIRT) are often used interchangeably. CERT/CC, however, advocates for the use of the term CSIRT because the CERT acronym is registered in the US Patent and Trademark Office for exclusive use by the Software Engineering Institute (SEI) at Carnegie Mellon University.

After the establishment of CERT/CC following the Morris worm incident, many others followed. Today, the Forum for Incident Response and Security Team (FIRST) has a total of 403 CSIRT member teams from 84 different countries.[3] For many years, CSIRTs were only known within the technical community. They focused on vulnerabilities, incident response, and technical developments relevant to the field of computer security. Yet, as society's dependency on digital technology continued to grow and security risks became more pronounced, so did the importance of CSIRTs. Over the past decade in particular, CSIRTs have become a subject of conversation in the policy world, which has allowed them to step out of the shadow and into the public eye. This public presence also means that they are confronted by contemporary challenges, including (potential) conflicts of interests. Simultaneously, the services offered by CSIRTs have evolved and matured. These developments require a reflection on CSIRTs and, in particular, their role within the contemporary cyber ecosystem. This chapter aims to describe some crucial aspects of CSIRTs as a means to contextualize the challenges they presently face.

Historical Background

The introduction already briefly alluded to the connection between the launch of the Morris worm in November 1988 and the introduction of CERT/CC, just 15 days later. The Morris worm caused unexpected and unintended damage. Morris subsequently attempted to undo the destruction caused by his worm by sending anonymous instructions that detailed how to stop the worm and prevent reinfection (Guidoboni and Meltzer 1990). The institutional infrastructure at the time was ill equipped to implement his instructions. As a result, the incident led to significant damage. The reaction to the incident was considered 'isolated and uncoordinated, resulting in much duplicated effort, and in conflicting solutions'.[4] This observation led the US Defense Advanced Research Project Agency (DARPA), a Federal agency under the US Department of Defense (DoD), to request the SEI at Carnegie Mellon University to establish the first CSIRT. This led to the establishment of CERT/CC.

During the following years, similar initiatives began to surface as other academic and military CSIRTs emerged in the United States. Almost a year after the Morris worm, in October 1989, the Worms Against Nuclear Killers, commonly known as the 'WANK Worm', incident highlighted the need for improved coordination and cooperation between CSIRT teams. This led to the introduction of FIRST in 1990, which has as its primary purpose 'to enable incident response teams to more effectively respond to security incidents by providing access to best practices, tools, and trusted communication with member teams and to otherwise engage in all lawful activities consistent with these purposes'.[5]

A number of years after the introduction of CERT/CC in the United States, different CSIRTs emerged in Europe. Introduced in 1992 in the Netherlands as a research CSIRT, CERT-NL (now SurfCERT) became the first CSIRT in Europe (ENISA 2006, 6). Other comparative initiatives soon followed, including DK-CERT in Denmark and DFN-CERT in Germany (Clark et al. 2014). The introduction of research CSIRTs demonstrates that there are different types of CSIRTs. This observation is furthermore illustrated through the introduction of CERT-EU. The European Union institutions decided—after a pilot phase of one year and a successful assessment by its constituency[6] and its peers—to set up a permanent Computer Emergency Response Team (CERT-EU) for the EU institutions, agencies, and bodies. On 11 September, 2012, CERT-EU was created to strengthen operational resilience to incidents and threats against wider European networks (CERT-EU 2013).

Perhaps the most important distinction to make in general, and for this chapter specifically, is between national and other CSIRTs. CSIRTs that play a national role have a distinct position because they have a national interest to protect and are more directly involved in the challenges discussed later in this chapter. Their connection to national security, as well as their relationship with law enforcement and intelligence agencies, is at the forefront of their evolving nature. Even so, this is not to say that other types of CSIRTs are completely disengaged from national security developments. CSIRTs have to work together, both within and across borders. As a result, even CSIRTs that are not national CSIRTs will be indirectly involved in the challenges discussed within this chapter.

SERVICES OFFERED BY A COMPUTER SECURITY INCIDENT RESPONSE TEAM

Even though CSIRTs vary in terms of level of maturity and target constituency, on a more abstract level, three lines of services have been identified. The nature of these services must be closely understood; the challenges faced by the CSIRT community as their work becomes more political relate directly to these services. The CSIRT handbook identifies three primary lines of service: reactive, proactive, and security quality management. To reach a more long-term goal, a fourth line of service has been introduced: long-term resilience.[7]

The CSIRT handbook defines reactive services as those 'triggered by an event or request, such as a report of a compromised host, wide-spreading malicious code, software vulnerability, or something that was identified by an intrusion detection or logging system. Reactive services are the core component of CSIRT work' (Killcrece et al. 2003). Incident response—a part of the reactive services—are the reason CSIRTs came into existence, as demonstrated by the Morris Worm incident. Reactive services go beyond incident response, however, to include among their main features alerts and warnings, incident analysis, and incident coordination.

Proactive services form the counterweight to reactive services, and place the CSIRT more in charge of influencing computer security and preventing incidents. These services maintain a strong focus on assisting constituents to prepare, protect, and secure their systems.

Such proactive services are a line of service which developed over the years as CSIRTs evolved and matured. The European Network and Information Security Agency (ENISA) already noted this evolution in 2006 when it acknowledged how CSIRTs went beyond mere reactive services to include proactive services as described earlier. This turned CSIRTs into complete security providers.[8] ENISA continues by stating that '[t]he term 'CERT' was soon considered insufficient. As a result, the new term 'CSIRT' was established at the end of the 1990s.'[9]

Several years later, in 2010, Fafinski underlines the same development as he acknowledges how CSIRTs have widened the scope of their services from purely reactive emergency response towards the more proactive provision of security services including preventive services (Fafinski 2009).

Information sharing and dissemination are integral parts of reactive as well as proactive services. The Dutch National Cyber Security Centre (NCSC), for example, provides factsheets and other 'knowledge' products on a wide variety of topics that are publicly available. These factsheets can focus on existing threats and developments, or incidents that have taken place. The notion of proactive services has become more pronounced and valued as there is an increasing focus on the acquisition of threat intelligence and the preparation of threat assessment documents to guide policy making. The Organisation for Economic Cooperation and Development (OECD) underlines how CSIRTs maintain a growing responsibility to provide the evidence base necessary for policy making and to meet the hunger for reliable information (OECD 2015). In the Netherlands, for example, the Dutch Cyber Security Threat Assessment has been published annually since 2011 and is sent to Parliament to set the tone with respect to cyber security in the political scene. It is important to note in this case that the development of the assessment requires the involvement of a wide variety of partners affiliated with the Dutch NCSC. Therefore, the information included in the assessment extends beyond the information gathered by the NCSC in its capacity as a national CSIRT. Intelligence agencies, law enforcement, as well as organizations within critical infrastructure sectors, all provide input as well as reviewing the document prior to its publication.

The last category of the original three lines of services focuses on service quality management. These are not specific to CSIRTs but have been included as a facet of their potential range of services. The focus of this line of services is more long term and includes risk analysis, business continuity, and disaster recovery planning.

The fourth line of service, which focuses on long-term resilience, is evidentiary of a more mature approach to security. As digital developments continue to take place and society in general becomes more dependent on digital technology, resilience increases in importance. The inclusion of long-term resilience also demonstrates the connection between CSIRTs—in particular, national CSIRTs—and the broader policy-making agenda in the area of cyber security, where the focus on resilience reigns. The question, after all, is no longer if an incident will take place but when.

Entering the Public Policy Arena

For many years, CSIRTs were detached from public policy discussions. They managed to embrace working in the shadows within a close-knit community. Their entrance into the public policy arena, arguably, caused them to have to step into the public eye. This transition from shadow to 'spotlight' occurred in a gradual manner. Several high-level EU policy documents put great emphasis on explaining the strategic importance of strengthening CSIRTs. The 2010 Digital Agenda for Europe reiterates the notion that, in order to promote a sense of trust and security among Europeans using cyberspace, 'a well-functioning and wider network of Computer Emergency Response Teams (CERTs) should be established in Europe' (European Commission 2010, 17). The agenda further underlines that both national and EU CSIRTs play a decisive role in protecting critical information infrastructure against a wide range of cyber threats in a real-time fashion. In this respect, the agenda also reaffirms the need for close 'cooperation between CERTs and law enforcement agencies ... to help prevent cybercrime and respond to emergencies, such as cyber attacks'.[10]

The 2013 EU Cyber Security Strategy acknowledged that gaps still exist across the European Union especially in terms of national capabilities, of coordination in cases of cross-border incidents, and of private sector involvement and preparedness.[11] As a result, the strategy called for EU legislation to set out common minimum requirements for Network and Information Security (NIS) at a national level that would oblige Member States to do the following:

- designate national competent authorities for NIS;
- *set up a well-functioning CERT*; and
- adopt a national NIS strategy and a national NIS cooperation plan.[12]

In this respect, the NIS Directive calls upon all EU Member States to set up CSIRTs that are able to handle incidents and respond to threats. This call demonstrates two important aspects of the CSIRT community. First, despite the growing number of CSIRTs around the world after the introduction of CERT/CC, not every EU Member State possessed a national CSIRT prior to the Commission's call. Second, the main focus of the call to set up CSIRTs is focused on handling incidents and responding to threats illuminating the essence of CSIRTs as crucial players in reactive services. Significantly, the Directive also stipulates that 'Member States shall ensure that CERTs have adequate technical, financial and human resources to effectively carry out their tasks.'[13]

This demonstrates the benefit of the increased political attention paid to CSIRTs. Skierka et al. describe how CSIRTs in developed countries have been able to benefit from the increased political attention in the form of enhanced investment (Skierka et al. 2015). Whereas, prior to this political attention, CSIRTs generally struggled to provide a business case for their services, such struggle appears to be a part of the past both for government as well as commercial CSIRTs. For less developed countries, investment remains a challenge as noted by the authors.[14]

In addition to ensuring that all Member States maintain competent CSIRTs, the NIS Directive also prescribes the requirement for national competent authorities to cooperate within a network. The intention of this network is to enable secure and effective coordination. This includes 'coordinated information exchange as well as detection and response at EU level'. The NIS Directive highlights the anticipated benefits of such a network when it states '[t]hrough this network, Member States should exchange information and cooperate to counter NIS threats and incidents on the basis of the European NIS cooperation plan' (European Commission 2013). This policy reference is particularly relevant with respect to the ways policy makers intend to formalize existing relationships between CSIRTs. The original informal nature of CSIRTs and their community is a defining feature of their existence and their culture. As will be seen in the section on the culture of the CSIRT community, attempts to formalize or externally alter these relationships generally leads to friction and failure.

Since the launch of the cyber security policy initiatives in 2013, the EU has continued to work on the topic. With respect to the role of CSIRTs, the developments with respect to the CSIRTs network as well as the evolving role of ENISA bear mentioning. ENISA's establishment occurred in 2004, prior to the current urgency surrounding the topic of cyber security (European Commission 2004). ENISA was originally created as a purely complementary entity to help prevent, address, and respond to network information and security problems in the EU. The Agency has since undergone various changes. The duration of its mandate was extended in 2008 (European Parliament and Council of the European Union 2008) and in 2011(European Parliament and Council of the European Union 2011). When the Framework Directive of 2002 (European Parliament and Council of the European Union 2002) was amended in 2009 (European Parliament and Council of the European Union 2009, the boundaries of ENISA's mandate expanded significantly: 'The Commission, taking the utmost account of the opinion of ENISA, may adopt appropriate technical implementing measures with a view to harmonizing measures.'[15] ENISA is focused on capacity building and has garnered a greater role as a result of the passage of the NIS Directive:

> ENISA is also asked to proactively support the cooperation among the CSIRTs ... ENISA is expected to take the initiative to guide the CSIRT group in the fulfilment of its duties. The Agency will organise meetings of the CSIRTs Network, and provoke discussion by proposing discussion topics. It will also provide its expertise and advice both to the Commission and Member States, either in the form of guidance or in answer to specific requests (ENISA 2016).

The role of ENISA is presently—as of January 2018—a topic of discussion, as the European Commission has introduced a draft regulation—known as the 'Cybersecurity Act'. The legislative proposal tabled by the Commission—as part of resilience measures—aims to strengthen ENISA. ENISA is expected to play a broader role, following the adoption of the NIS Directive, in the EU cybersecurity landscape, but is arguably constrained by its current mandate and resources. The Commission has presented a reform proposal, including a permanent mandate for the agency, to ensure that ENISA can go beyond providing expert advice to also perform operational tasks (European Commission 2017).

Beyond the EU, the United Nations Group of Governmental Experts (UNGGE) on Developments in the Field of Information and Telecommunications in the Context of International Security, which is leading the international community's efforts in negotiating global cyber security norms at the UN, made several references to national CSIRTs in its 2015 report. In that report, the UNGGE seems to echo similar calls made within the EU when it recommends that states should 'Establish a national computer emergency response team and/or cybersecurity incident response team or officially designate an organization to fulfil this role' (UNGGE 2015). The UNGGE's recommendation is persuasive because the transnational nature of cyber-related threats requires CSIRTs to communicate among each other to exchange information and coordinate a response. If a country does not have a (national) CSIRT, it can complicate the actions taken by other CSIRTs to respond to an incident. Moreover, from a focus on proactive services, information about threats faced by different countries is relevant to the production of a critically important transnational threat landscape. The development of a transnational threat landscape, however, is complex because the decision about what constitutes a threat has become more subjective due to the increasingly political nature of cyber security. An action from a nation state may constitute a threat, even if such an action is carried out with the intention of enhancing national security. This connects to the discussion on the definition of cyber security further on in the chapter.

In sum, the entrance of CSIRTs as a topic of public policy has enhanced their importance and is paving the way for the introduction of more CSIRTs across the globe. At the same time, the policy discussions will influence the way CSIRTs operate and may do so in an undesirable manner. How this can happen will be discussed in the subsequent sections, which will also shed light on the contemporary challenges faced by CSIRTs.

CULTURE OF THE COMMUNITY

When becoming acquainted with the CSIRT community, trust will likely be the concept most often mentioned, especially in relation to the CSIRT culture. CSIRTs operate on the basis of trust and, as such, they embody the notion of a 'security community'. As Sundaramurthy et al. (2014) describe, gaining trust within the CSIRT community is vital. CSIRTs generally contact those colleagues from other CSIRTs whom they have had previous contact with and whom they know personally. As noted by ENISA, ' . . . cooperation and collaboration takes place in a practical, informal manner between operators who have trusted relationships rather than because of any strictly formalised legal agreement' (ENISA 2011). According to ENISA, this way of working has been regarded as an asset of the CSIRT community, because there is an intrinsic motivation to cooperate rather than an external source forcing them to do so. These trusted relationships, which have often been built up over time, are considered key to speedy and effective collaboration (even in a cross-border context). The value of trust—and the dependency upon this fundamental value if collaboration is to be effective—is also specifically recognized by Arkush et al. when they write, '[i]n the case of a mandatory requirement as proposed in the NIS Directive, it is expected by the experts that the initial level of trust between participants who haven't built interpersonal relationships before might be relatively low which will impede the willingness to share information' (Arkush et al. 2014). The challenge then for the involvement of policy makers and their attempts to formalize relationships between and among CSIRTs is to understand and incorporate the culture of trust. This also requires understanding why trust is such a fundamental value in the CSIRT community. Information exchange is an essential part of CSIRT activity and cooperation. Such information is often sensitive and therefore there is a necessity to trust the person the information is exchanged with. The CSIRT member sharing the information wants to be certain it will not fall into the 'wrong' hands.

ENISA identifies various ways to assist in building and maintaining trust, including the following:

- The provision of timely and specific data.
- The need for participants to share information which is of equal value.
- Information shared must be relevant to participants' concerns.
- Sharing information at a suitable level.

Other incentives mentioned by ENISA to build trust re-emphasize the need for personal relationships, consistency of membership of groups CSIRTs participate in, and regular face-to-face meetings.

The culture of the CSIRT community deserves attention because it is crucial to understanding why it is that, in light of the involvement of policy actors, certain approaches to 'reform' the CSIRT community may not prove to be successful. ENISA describes how the introduction of a European CSIRT coordination centre in 1998 failed.[16] The idea behind the centre was that it would assume an authoritative role to manage and guide actions between CSIRT teams at the national level across Europe. This important attempt at European-level coordination, led by an authoritative and otherwise respected organization, nevertheless came unstuck simply because CSIRTs were willing to work with EuroCERT only on the basis of equal partnership. In other words, national CSIRTs proved unwilling to take orders, or even to accept much in the way of top-down coordination. EuroCERT lasted no longer than two years.[17] As noted in a (very) brief history of EuroCERT, one of the problems was that each team delivered a different set of services, which made it very difficult to define a scope for EuroCERT that would satisfy the needs of all sponsors without overlapping with work that others were already doing for their own constituencies.[18] Moreover, the need of acceptance to submit to an external authority—e.g. to give up direct personal links—was also observed as a problem, perhaps precisely because it was counterintuitive considering personal links based on trust are the fundaments of the CSIRT community and its cooperation. This 'experiment', for lack of a better term, is an important experience to have in mind when examining other, more recent attempts to establish a platform for CSIRT coordination in the EU. As Arkush et al. describe, 'These problems, which eventually led to the failure of EuroCERT, tell much about what is acceptable to such bodies in the field of Network and Information Security (NIS) in Europe.'[19]

Central to the CSIRT community is a bottom-up rather than a top-down approach. Most of the practices that are currently accepted have been introduced by members of the community or by the community at large. This flexibility and open-mindedness is illustrative of a second quality of the CSIRT community: the informal and occasionally ad hoc way in which CSIRTs work. The CSIRT community's preference to date for a bottom-up, grassroots-style approach must be acknowledged in any effort to develop CSIRT collaboration. The CSIRT working culture, as described, might also explain the resistance often seen towards the development of a European platform, which is perceived as a more top-down type of initiative.

Besides trust, another crucial feature embodied by the CSIRT community is the ability to identify a shared interest or stake. The primary focus of the community is a more secure Internet infrastructure. The focus on information sharing underpins this shared interest. CSIRTs share information both with each other and with their constituents in order to enhance the security of the Internet as well as the systems that connect to it. This is evident through the regular issuance of advisories about vulnerabilities, threats, new types of malware, etc.

Yet, as cyber security has become increasingly politicized, security is no longer an objective concept or goal, because threats as well as means of protection have become more political. As Morgus et al. write, 'When it comes to cybersecurity, law enforcement agencies, intelligence agencies and national CSIRTs (nCSIRTs) share a high-level goal: securing networks. However, how highly each of these actors prioritize network security differs. At times, the tactics for providing network security can directly compete with each other' (Morgus et al. 2015, 13). To explore this tension, the next section of the chapter focuses on the transformation from computer to cyber security, the relationship between CSIRTs and other government institutions, and the treatment of vulnerabilities by CSIRTs.

Contemporary Challenges

From Computer to Cyber Security

Over a decade ago, Nissenbaum identified two distinct perspectives on what was then called 'computer security' (Nissenbaum 2005). The first approach had its roots in the technical community, while the second perspective approached the topic primarily from a national security perspective. Many years later, these two perspectives also return in the story of CSIRTs and their evolving role, because these two perspectives can potentially lead to a culture clash, especially since different interests are at stake.

The term 'computer security' is part of the name of CERTs and CSIRTs. This observation ought not to go unnoticed. In contemporary times, the policy world focuses almost exclusively on cyber security or sometimes even just 'The Cyber'. US President Trump has often been quoted when referring to 'The Cyber'. Trump's usage of the Cyber was even considered an assault on the English language (Wagner 2016). He is, however, as Wolff notes, hardly the first—let alone only—person or politician to do so (Wolff 2016). Why is this a potential problem? Felten describes how the transition from information security to cyber security reflects a different mindset and approach to the problem. The involvement of the military allowed for the introduction of the concept of cyber rather than information or computer security (Felten 2008).

Broeders (2015) describe how the engineers' approach of CERTs, focused largely on keeping the network 'healthy', and the cooperation of CSIRTs at the international level is experiencing difficulties from national security stakeholders, such as intelligence services and military departments. The convergence of these different perspectives on security is undesirable, according to Broeders because the partial interest of national security collides with the collective interest of ensuring the security of the network as a whole. He therefore argues for an effort 'to clearly differentiate at the national and international level between Internet security (security of the Internet infrastructure) and national security (security through the Internet) and have separate parties address these different forms.' Dunn Cavelty (2013) previously identified similar concerns. Levin and Goodrick present the problem in terms of contending policy areas:

> The more countries focus on their cybersecurity from cyberwar, the more they do that at the expense of cooperation on cybercrime. Worries of cyberwar cause countries to align and re-trench in their traditional international blocs, at the expense of international treaties that attempt to foster new forms of cooperation against cybercrime (2013, 130).

As the OECD notes, a lack of specificity with respect to how cybersecurity is defined, along with an emergence of sovereignty considerations, 'may lead to re-couch all cybersecurity issues into the language of "national security" and warfare, preventing balanced policy making and fostering the adoption of drastic solutions such as network monitoring instead of other practical solutions more respectful of citizens' rights.'[20] How governments define cyber security, therefore, is a crucial element of how they approach the topic itself. Morgus et al. indicate how at the global level significant disagreement exists about what constitutes a threat. This observation relates to the statement of the OECD since Morgus et al. describe how 'In some authoritarian systems, a cybersecurity threat is not only an actor that could cause damage through malicious code, but also an individual who publishes content online.'[21]

These definitional dilemmas, especially at a global level, introduce challenges for CSIRT cooperation because perspectives both between as well as within countries may differ about the security objective. Potential concerns over human rights violations may mean that certain CSIRTs are reluctant or refuse to share information.[22]

The Relationship with Other Governmental Institutions

The relationship between CSIRTs and other governmental institutions, especially law enforcement and intelligence agencies, has begun to receive increased attention. This is in part the case because of the redefining of computer to cyber security, as previously noted, but also because there is a growing move toward cooperation between these different agencies. Morgus et al. identify three options for structuring these relationships.[23] The first option the authors present is arguably best understood as a framework or 'meta-option' enabling a variety of flavours with respect to the relationship between the different entities. This option is to maintain the status quo, in which many different types of relationship can exist. They describe how, under the status quo, most likely some form of contact exists. More precisely, Morgus et al. contend that based on their research 'it is reasonable to assume that the majority of nCSIRTs, have links to both the law enforcement and intelligence communities, whether formally or informally.'[24] While the status quo allows for flexibility, the approach also maintains significant disadvantages. As Morgus et al. describe, the status quo can lead to uncertainty at an international level because there may be a lack of transparency about the relationship between the CSIRT, law enforcement, and intelligence agencies. Such a lack of insight into the relationship can be particularly problematic because it may lead to a state of distrust from other CSIRTs.

The second option is to formalize the relationship between the different institutional entities. This option essentially aims to remove the uncertainty that maintaining the status quo introduces. By formalizing the relationship between law enforcement, intelligence, and CSIRTs, there is more transparency, which can subsequently lead to greater trust among CSIRTs. In the Netherlands, for example, the national CSIRT—or better known as the 'NCSC'—maintains a liaison model. These liaisons from essential public and private parties make up the 'inner circle' of the partnership, as structured within the NCSC. The liaison collaboration is basically based on trust, reciprocity, common interests and added value, and cooperation. According to the NCSC:

> The liaison parties themselves establish the latitude of the liaison input and the degree in which knowledge and information is shared. They maintain this in accordance with statutory frameworks. The liaison takes care of the link between his/her own organisation and the NCSC, and arranges the required expertise from his/her own organisation. A powerful tool of the liaison collaboration is to seek links in times of peace, so that faster action can be taken in times of crisis. In this way the partnership benefits the most.[25]

As Morgus et al. note, however, even in the case of a formalization of the relationship between nCSIRTs and law enforcement and intelligence agencies, questions remain about the nature of the relationship.[26] The relationship can be unidirectional, from other actors to the CSIRT or vice versa, or bidirectional. The latter is the case in the Dutch example, where reciprocity is a fundamental principle of the collaboration.

The third option is to disassociate national CSIRTs from law enforcement and intelligence agencies altogether. Complete disassociation appears undesirable from a cyber security perspective, because information exchange between the different organizations can allow a more comprehensive threat landscape to emerge. This is, for example, the case in the Netherlands with respect to the Dutch Cyber Security Threat Assessment. A more formal relationship might therefore be considered desirable: one that sets boundaries and agrees permissions. This formalization might then, also, be more consistent with the Internet security/national security differentiation proposed by Broeders. Internet security and national security may overlap and intersect, but they may also conflict. In the case of a situation where Internet and national security collide, it is important for CSIRTs to maintain their 'independence' and to ensure that they focus on their primary objective of Internet security. Whether this can be realized in practice is difficult to say, because national security may have to take priority from a national government perspective. There are other areas where CSIRTs may encounter themselves in a conflict of interest, which may restrict their independence. Examples include political activities such as censorship or collection of digital intelligence for reasons other than securing networks and systems.[27] Other parties—for example, government agencies—may request them to engage in such activities leading to a conflict of interest.

Vulnerabilities

Information sharing in general is a crucial aspect of the role played by CSIRTs. This also includes information sharing about vulnerabilities. In computer security, vulnerabilities are flaws or mistakes in computer-based systems. They may exist in software or hardware. These vulnerabilities form an essential ingredient for perpetrators to take advantage of to commit cyber-related attacks. A vulnerability can be resolved through a 'patch', comparable to the application of a band aid to a wound. An unpatched vulnerability basically provides a perpetrator with an open door to enter. Information about vulnerabilities is sensitive if a 'patch'—or another means to resolve the vulnerability—has not yet become available. Vulnerabilities where a form of resolution is absent are commonly referred to as 'zero day vulnerabilities', or 'zero days'. The existence of zero day vulnerabilities has therefore become a particularly important topic within the realm of cyber security.

With regard to CSIRTs and vulnerability handling, their role is diverse depending on the type of CSIRT. Certain CSIRTs can provide assistance as coordinators of vulnerability handling—i.e. those who have discovered a vulnerability can call upon them to assist in the disclosure of the vulnerability. This is helpful, for example, when the discoverer of a vulnerability contacts the vendor but does not receive an answer, or is experiencing other difficulties that require assistance. Alternatively, the discoverer may want to remain anonymous. CSIRTs may also become involved when the disclosure of a vulnerability is particularly complex because various parties are involved that need to be informed.

Besides involvement as a coordinator, CSIRTs also provide advisories to their constituents in which they indicate which vulnerabilities have been discovered, and when, and where the vendor has made an update available. CSIRTs also use their expertise to assess the level of urgency and risk associated with the vulnerability and its remediation.

Through the introduction of certain powers—such as the ability to remotely infiltrate devices—for public agencies, predominantly in the realm of law enforcement and intelligence, the question of vulnerability discovery and particularly disclosure has become increasingly contentious. From an information or computer security perspective, the main aim is to resolve vulnerabilities after they are discovered and reported to the vendor. From a national security as well as a law enforcement perspective, vulnerabilities that are unknown to the vendor can be used as tools to carry out operations, either to investigate cybercrimes and locate perpetrators or to gather intelligence from foreign counterparts. News stories about assistance from, for example, CERT/CC have heightened the urgency of the issue (Skierka and Hohmann 2016).

In the Netherlands, the introduction of legislation to provide law enforcement with the ability to infiltrate devices remotely led to an extensive public discussion. Part of that discussion concerned the treatment of vulnerabilities, in particular zero day vulnerabilities. The ability to use vulnerabilities for national security or law enforcement purposes leads to an inherent conflict of interest and goes against the fundamental notion of a more secure Internet. If an agency wants to use a zero day after all, the incentive is to keep it as an undisclosed vulnerability for which an exploit can be developed and used. The counterargument often offered by the law enforcement and intelligence community is that, without the ability to use unrevealed, commonly referred to as 'unknown', vulnerabilities, they are basically handicapped with respect to carrying out their actions, whether these actions are to do with investigation or with the protection of the national interest. End-to-end encryption leaves little to no room for interception. Moreover, law enforcement and intelligence agencies do not even necessarily need to use zero days because many revealed vulnerabilities can be taken advantage of as well if users have failed to install updates and subsequently patch their systems.

The complexity of the matter increases when CSIRTs become involved, because their involvement means that they can no longer be perceived as independent or as organizations that will operate with a primary focus on achieving a more secure Internet. This is particularly problematic in light of the role that some CSIRTs have with respect to the coordination of vulnerability disclosure.

The Way Forward?

The challenges introduced require critical reflection as well as answers. During this process, a new development has occurred throughout the past decade: the introduction of NCSCs, or in some cases the evolution of governmental or national CSIRTs into NCSCs. Clark et al. argue that governments can reasonably be expected to have (or acquire) the capacity to stimulate and facilitate a safer cyber landscape. On that basis, national CSIRTs should develop into NCSCs, according to the authors. This development has, for example, occurred in the Netherlands, the Czech Republic, Finland, as well as in the UK and Ireland. NCSCs can be given much more extensive responsibility in comparison to national CSIRTs, particularly with respect to their relationship with the private sector. NCSCs would be expected to collaborate with the private sector through knowledge facilitation and innovation stimulation, through research and education. The Dutch example is an illustration of this as the transformation from a national CSIRT to an NCSC meant the organization expanded its focus to include critical infrastructure. To speak, as Clark et al. do, of the *expansion* of CSIRTs could be rather misleading, however. Clark and his co-authors note that, while the original focus of the typical CSIRT was on its constituents at both the national and the municipal level, that focus has now widened to include critical infrastructure broadly defined. Rather than expansion, it might be more accurate to describe this as a process of substitution or transformation, whereby concern for the critical infrastructure has been elevated at the expense of policies and activities concerned with the municipal level. In the UK, the development and launch of the NCSC in February 2017 was in some respects a reorganization of a complicated bureaucratic picture in which lines of authority and responsibility in different aspects of cyber security were not as clear as they could have been. This demonstrates how a transformation into an NCSC aims to resolve the complexity of cyber security—in particular, the different players involved at the governmental level.

While Clark et al. welcome the evolution from CSIRT to NCSC, challenges nevertheless remain.[28] As previously described, the relation between CSIRTs, law enforcement, and intelligence agencies is complex due to the inherent nature of the different organizations. These organizations have different concerns and interests: differences that may lead to conflicts of interest. When CSIRTs transform or evolve into NCSCs, their connection with law enforcement and intelligence agencies becomes more pronounced and this may complicate their relationship with other national CSIRTs. This is especially the case because information sharing may become compromised, or at least there may be a feeling that existing relationships of trust are in danger. This is most closely felt in the area of vulnerability handling where the exchange of information about vulnerabilities might be essential in counter-intelligence operations or in the investigation of high-profile cybercrime cases. In the UK, the NCSC, for example, is part of GCHQ, which demonstrates a close connection between the NCSC and its partner or—perhaps better said—parent organization. This then provides the NCSC with a particular image and may challenge relations with fellow CSIRTs more sceptic of the intersection between national CSIRTs and intelligence agencies.

The benefits of having a broader connection between the different public and private agencies involved in cyber security should not be overlooked. In the Dutch example, the NCSC maintains liaison officers from a wide variety of public sector agencies including law enforcement, the public prosecutor's office, intelligence agencies, and the tax administration office as well as the radio communication agency. From the private sector, the NCSC has a banking liaison. The importance of such a tightknit network is that it allows the Centre to be a coordination hub that enhances information sharing and dissemination.

Conclusion

Thirty years ago, as a result of the Morris worm, the first CSIRT was introduced. The following three decades witnessed the introduction of an increasing number of CSIRTs, as well as a growing role for them to play in the cyber security ecosystem. From the EU to the UN, policy actors have begun to understand the essential nature of CSIRTs and have also highlighted their strategic importance in various policy documents. CSIRTs have evolved from predominately reactive to more proactive and strategic services. Previously, CSIRTs garnered little (public) attention; they worked in the background to exchange information in an effort to enhance cyber security and assist their peers and constituents to respond to security incidents. Morgus et al. note (almost with a sense of relief) how 'CSIRTs existed long before international diplomatic statements called for them.'[29]

The CSIRT community and culture are founded on trust, informality, and a bottom-up approach, whereas the tendency of policy makers is to formalize relationships and to do so through a top-down tactic. Moreover, CSIRTs have always held security as a shared interest. The involvement of other government actors, however, has led to the inclusion of different perspectives on which elements of security to emphasize. This is evident in the definitional dilemmas introduced with the concept of cyber security, the relationship between CSIRTs and other government agencies such as law enforcement and intelligence, as well as the treatment and usage of vulnerabilities. These elements illustrate the growing complexity CSIRTs are faced with in an ever-changing cyber ecosystem.

Moving forward, the evolution of CSIRTs into NCSCs requires critical reflection in order not to lose the core characteristics of CSIRTs and their qualities. Independence is essential to ensure that they do not become the victim of a conflict of interest between national security and Internet security.

As computer security has evolved into cyber security, so have CSIRTs 'evolved from loosely organized groups of system administrators to highly trained organizations with diverse capabilities, relying on complex technology to track, analyse, manage, and remediate security incidents' (Horne 2014, 13). With greater capability also comes greater responsibility.

NOTES

1. 18 U.S.C. § 1030.
2. Lee, 'How a grad student'.
3. As of January 2018.
4. FIRST n.d. 'FIRST History'. https://www.first.org/about/history
5. FIRST n.d.
6. 'Constituents' is a term used within the CSIRT community and refers to the organizations or people CSIRTs provide their services to.
7. Clark et al. 'A Dutch Approach'.
8. ENISA, 'CERT Cooperation'.
9. ENISA, 'CERT Cooperation'.
10. European Commission, 'Communication'.
11. European Commission, 'Communication'. 5.
12. European Commission, 'Communication'. 5, emphasis added.
13. European Commission, 'Communication'. 5.
14. Skierka et al. 2015.
15. European Parliament and Council of the European Union 2009.
16. ENISA, 'CERT Cooperation'.
17. ENISA, 'CERT Cooperation'.
18. ENISA, 'CERT Cooperation'.

19. Arkush et al. *Feasibility Study* (emphasis in original), 14.
20. OECD, 'Cybersecurity Policy Making'.
21. Morgus et al., 'National CSIRTs', 14.
22. Morgus et al., 'National CSIRTs'.
23. Morgus et al., 'National CSIRTs'.
24. Morgus et al., 'National CSIRTs', 22.
25. NCSC n.d. 'Liaisons'.
26. Morgus et al., 'National CSIRTs'.
27. Morgus et al., 'National CSIRTs'.
28. Clark et al., 'A Dutch Approach'.
29. Morgus et al., 'National CSIRTs'.

REFERENCES

Arkush, A.C., Cano, P., Bouckaert, V. et al. 2014. *Feasibility Study and Preparatory Activities for the Implementation of a European Early Warning and Response System against Cyber-Attacks and Disruptions.* Brussels: European Commission, DG Communications Networks, Content & Technology, 27 January.

Broeders, D. 2015. *The Public Core of the Internet: An International Agenda for Internet Governance.* WRR Scientific Council for Government Policy, Policy Brief 2.

CERT-EU. 2013. 'RFC 2350'. http://cert.europa.eu/static/RFC2350/RFC2350.pdf

Clark, K., Stikvoort, D., Stofbergen, E., et al. 2014. 'A Dutch Approach to Cybersecurity Through Participation', *IEEE Security & Privacy*, 12 (5): 27–34.

Dunn-Cavelty, M. 2013. 'From Cyber-Bombs to Political Fallout: Threat Representations with an Impact in the Cyber-Security Discourse.' *International Studies Review* 15: 105–122.

ENISA. 2011. 'A Flair for Sharing—Encouraging Information Exchange Between Certs—A Study into the Legal and Regulatory Aspects of Information Sharing and Cross-Border Collaboration of National/Governmental CERTs in Europe'. https://www.enisa.europa.eu/publications/legal-information-sharing-1/at_download/fullReport

ENISA. 2016. ENISA's Position on the NIS Directive. https://www.enisa.europa.eu/publications/enisa-position-papers-and-opinions/enisas-position-on-the-nis-directive

European Commission. 2004. 'Establishment of the European Network and Information Security Agency.' Regulation (EC) no. 460/2004.

European Commission. 2010. 'Communication from the Commission to the European Parliament, the Council, the European Economic and Social Committee and the Committee of the Regions', 26 August. https://ec.europa.eu/digital-single-market/en/news/digital-agenda-europe-communication-commission-26082010

European Commission. 2013. 'Proposal for a Directive of the European Parliament and of the Council Concerning Measures to Ensure a High Common Level of Network and Information Security Across the Union', 7 February.

European Commission. 2017. 'Regulation on ENISA, the "EU Cybersecurity Agency", and on Information and Communication Technology Cybersecurity Certification (the "Cybersecurity Act"). COM(2017) 477.

European Network and Information Security Agency (ENISA). 2006. 'CERT Cooperation and Its Further Facilitation by Relevant Stakeholders'. https://www.enisa.europa.eu/

publications/cert-cooperation-and-its-further-facilitation-by-relevant-stakeholders/at_download/fullReport

European Parliament and Council of the European Union. 2002. 'Common regulatory framework for electronic communications networks and services (Framework Directive)'. Directive 2002/21/EC, 7 March.

European Parliament and Council of the European Union. 2008. 'Amending Regulation (EC) No 460/2004 establishing the European Network and Information Security Agency as regards its duration'. Regulation (EC) no. 1007/2008, 24 September.

European Parliament and Council of the European Union. 2009. 'Amending Directives 2002/21/EC on a common regulatory framework for electronic communications networks and services, 2002/19/EC on access to, and interconnection of, electronic communications networks and associated facilities, and 2002/20/EC on the authorization of electronic communications networks and services'. Directive 2009/140/EC, 25 November.

European Parliament and Council of the European Union. 2011. 'Amending Regulation (EC) No 460/2004 establishing the European Network and Information Security Agency as regards its duration.' Regulation (EU) No 580/2011, 8 June.

Fafinski. S. 2009. 'Memorandum by Dr Stefan Fafinski'. http://www.publications.parliament.uk/pa/ld200910/ldselect/ldeucom/68/68we06.htm

Felten, E. 2008. 'What's the Cyber in Cyber-Security?' https://freedom-to-tinker.com/2008/07/24/whats-cyber-cyber-security/

Guidoboni, T.A., and E. R. Meltzer. 1990. *UNITED STATES of America, Appellee, v. Robert Tappan MORRIS, Defendant-Appellant*. United States Court of Appeals, Second Circuit. Argued 4 December 1990. Decided 7 March 1991.

Horne, B. 2014. On Computer Security Incident Response Teams. *IEEE Security & Privacy*, 12(5), 13–15.

Killcrece, G., Kossakowski, K.P, Ruefle, R. et al. 2003. 'State of the Practice of Computer Security Incident Response Teams'. http://resources.sei.cmu.edu/asset_files/TechnicalReport/2003_005_001_14204.pdf

Lee, T.B. 2013. 'How a grad student trying to build the first botnet brought the Internet to its knees'. *Washington Post*. https://www.washingtonpost.com/news/the-switch/wp/2013/11/01/how-a-grad-student-trying-to-build-the-first-botnet-brought-the-internet-to-its-knees/

Levin, A., and P. Goodrick. 2013. 'From Cybercrime to Cyberwar? The International Policy Shift and Its Implications for Canada.' *Canadian Foreign Policy Journal* 19 (2): 127–43.

Morgus, R., Skierka, I., Hohmann, M. et al. 2015. 'National CSIRTs and Their Role in Computer Security Incident Response'. https://static.newamerica.org/attachments/11916-national-csirts-and-their-role-in-computer-security-incident-response/CSIRTs-incident-response_2-2016.eea78f5a4748443d8000903e300d5809.pdf

Nissenbaum, H. 2005. Where Computer Security Meets National Security. *Ethics and Information Technology* 7 (2): 61–73.

Organisation for Economic Co-operation and Development (OECD). 2012. 'Cybersecurity Policy Making at a Turning Point'. http://www.oecd.org/sti/ieconomy/cybersecurity%20policy%20making.pdf

OECD. 2015. Guidance for Improving the Comparability of Statistics Produced by Computer Security Incident Response Teams (CSIRTs). https://www.oecd.org/officialdocuments/publicdisplaydocumentpdf/?cote=DSTI/ICCP/REG(2013)9/FINAL&doclanguage=en

Skierka, I., Morgus, R., Hohmann, M. et al. 2015. 'CSIRT Basics for Policy-Makers'. https://static.newamerica.org/attachments/2943-csirt-basics-for-policy-makers/CSIRT%20Basics%20for%20Policy-Makers.7694665e821048ef85a6007eb5a29105.pdf

Skierka, I., and Hohmann M. 2016. 'Germany Needs an Independent Digital Emergency Response Team'. http://www.gppi.net/publications/data-technology-politics/article/germany-needs-an-independent-digital-emergency-response-team/

Sundaramurthy, S.C., McHugh, J., Ou, X.S. et al. 2014. 'An Anthropological Approach to Studying CSIRTs'. *IEEE Security & Privacy* 12 (5): 52–60.

United Nations Group of Governmental Experts (UNGGE). 2015. 'Group of Governmental Experts on Developments in the Field of Information and Telecommunications in the Context of International Security'. http://www.un.org/ga/search/view_doc.asp?symbol=A/70/174

Wagner, M. 2016. 'Braggadocious, Hilary and "The Cyber": The Biggest Language Fails from the Presidential Debate'. http://www.nydailynews.com/news/politics/5-language-grammar-fails-presidential-debate-article-1.2808401?utm

Wolff, J. 2016. 'Cyber Is Not a Noun. When You Use It That Way, It Sounds Like You Don't Know What You're Talking About'. http://www.slate.com/articles/technology/future_tense/2016/09/cyber_is_not_a_noun.html

CHAPTER 19

CYBERSECURITY INFORMATION SHARING: VOLUNTARY BEGINNINGS AND A MANDATORY FUTURE

STUART MURDOCH

INTRODUCTION

THE history of information sharing on security incidents and breaches will of course go back to the very dawn of the computer age, and attempts to secure and respond to breaches in the security of electronic telecommunications go back to the beginnings of the technology that underpins the development of the information age. An article by Paul Marks in the Christmas edition of the *New Scientist* magazine in 2011 describes how the very first public demonstration of—purportedly secure—wireless telecommunications by Marconi in 1903 were 'hacked', for reasons of commercial subterfuge, by a music-hall magician, Nevil Maskeleyne.

In this chapter, we will chart the evolution of cybersecurity information sharing from the first initiatives to organize voluntary efforts to respond to early threats to computer security, through to the current legal and contractual mechanisms to make the reporting of cybersecurity mandatory.

THE MORRIS WORM

The efforts to organize and coordinate collaboration on cybersecurity, certainly at a national level, can perhaps be traced back to 1988 and the response to the so-called 'Morris Worm'.

Both the ad hoc way in which collaboration happened in response to a security incident in the early days of the computer industry, and the events that led up to the first attempts to make that more organized, are luridly described in Clifford Stoll's book, *The Cuckoo's Egg* (1990). The main part of that book deals, in an accessible 'thriller/crime fiction' style, with how Stoll, an astronomer working as a systems administrator in the Lawrence Berkeley National Laboratory in California detected—and helped coordinate the response to—a significant computer espionage incident in 1986. The epilogue (certainly in editions printed post-2005) describes the events surrounding the Morris Worm that led to the formation of those organizations and structures that continue to form the architecture of organized cyber security information sharing we know today.

The Morris Worm is often classified as the first Internet worm. For the purposes of this introduction, it will be sufficient for us to describe the difference between a virus and a worm in the following way: a virus is designed to affect one system, such as a computer, whereas a worm is designed to infect a network and/or all the systems on it.

The Morris Worm was launched in 1988 by Robert Tappan Morris while a graduate student at Cornell University. Ironically, he was the son of Robert Morris, who worked in the National Computer Security Centre (NCSC)—part of the US National Security Agency (NSA). Morris Junior has the ignominious reputation of being the first person to be convicted[1] under the United States' first 'anti-hacking' law, which was an attempt to respond to information security breaches through the legal system, the 1986 Computer Fraud and Abuse Act.

Morris claimed that he designed the worm in order to try and determine the size of the Internet at the time. Others disputed this, suggesting that correspondence from Harvard student Paul Graham asking for an update on 'the brilliant project' implied others knew in advance about the planned outcome. At the time, some saw the impact of Morris's worm as bringing to an end a golden period of trust that pervaded the early spirit of the computer industry. Indeed, it led to his username 'rtm' being changed to 'rtfm' by another user on the MIT ITS network[2]

Because of a flaw in the way the worm was coded (or by design), the program allowed multiple copies of itself to be created on each infected computer. This caused the infected computer to run so slowly as to be unusable. As part of the subsequent legal process, the US Government Accountability Office tried to estimate the impact of the Morris Worm. It was estimated that around 10% of the computers connected to the Internet at the time, which was estimated to be 60,000, were infected and the financial impact of removing the virus was calculated to be between $100,000 and $10,000,000.

The main part of Stoll's book describes his persistence in hunting down, and ultimately successfully uncovering, the international espionage that lay behind the hackers he had discovered on his academic network. In the absence of any mechanisms or procedures, he personally coordinated and instigated a response from US national security, telecoms providers, and their international counterparts. So, when the Morris Worm hit, those sometimes-reluctant actors from the 1986 episode, turned to him for support to help diagnose and respond to this new incident. The way the response to the Morris Worm was coordinated at the time is described in the short epilogue of his book.

COMPUTER EMERGENCY RESPONSE TEAM/COORDINATION CENTRE

The Morris Worm led to an official effort to organize the ability to respond to these types of incident at a national level for the first time. The Defence Advanced Research Projects Agency (DARPA) of the US Department of Defense funded the establishment of CERT/CC—the Computer Emergency Response Team (CERT) Coordination Centre (CC).[3]

The decision was made to house the CERT at Carnegie Mellon University (CMU) in Pittsburgh, Pennsylvania, which had previously been awarded the contract by the US Department of Defense in 1984 to run the Software Engineering Institute (SEI) (which it has been re-awarded six times since, most recently in 2014.)

The CERT at CMU has, over time, come to focus on responsibility for three key areas in relation to cyber security information sharing:

1. Responsibility for coordination of major national incidents that are not the responsibility of any other incident response team (e.g. the US Department of Homeland Security (DHS)'s Cybersecurity and Infrastructure Security Agency (CISA) has responsibility for US federal networks).
2. A Certificate Numbering Authority (CNA) for the assignment of unique identifiers (Common Vulnerability and Exposure—CVE identifiers) to vulnerabilities in products.
3. Establishing standards for how other CERTs might be run.

Initially the name 'CERT' was simply an abbreviation of Computer Emergency Response Team. More recently, the SEI has taken the position that CERT should no longer be considered to be an abbreviation. The SEI at CMU hold the trademark for CERT and, in the past, have tried to prevent others from using the CERT name without having been granted permission by SEI. Some teams choose to seek approval from the SEI to become an authorized user of the trademarked CERT name as an indicator that they have auditably met the baseline standards required by the SEI for the use of that name. Those CERTs that have met that standard have permission to advertise the fact on their website using an officially approved certificate for that purpose.

The fact that the CERT name was protected led those teams fulfilling the same function, but which had not gone through the process of seeking permission for the use of the CERT name, to create an alternative identifier, CSIRT (Computer Security Incident Response Team),—which the SEI itself says should be considered to be synonymous with CERT. Throughout this chapter, we will use CERT and CSIRT to mean the same thing.

The approval process,[4] which organizations seeking to become a CERT need to follow, requires them, in the first place, to complete a form with certain key information, and then to be audited by an auditor authorized by the CERT who will check whether those processes are in place and being fulfilled.

While the CERT division of the SEI to this day maintains its reputation globally for having established those standards and continues to exercise its official responsibility for the matters identified earlier, within the first year of its existence, it became apparent that there was a need to establish another process for coordination on cyber security incidents.

FORUM OF INCIDENT RESPONSE AND SECURITY TEAMS

That organization became the Forum of Incident Response and Security Teams (FIRST). It started out in 1990 as an entirely North American organization, coordinating responses across the wide geography with multiple time zones that makes up the United States. By 1992, it had its first international members from Europe and it 592[5] member organizations (here referred to as CSIRTs even if some are authorized users of the CERT name) in 98 countries.

In a similar way to those wishing to use the CERT name, teams that wish to become members of FIRST must complete forms sharing information with FIRST. They must also undergo a site inspection to ensure that the processes for incident response that are in place meet with the standards set by FIRST. Key information required includes:

- The jurisdiction of the CSIRT—which Internet domains it is responsible for (e.g. the UK NCSC, established in 2016, was originally the CSIRT responsible for the gov.uk domain in the UK).
- Mandatory contact information—the CSIRT joins FIRST in order to identify itself as a team with responsibility for certain networks. It therefore necessarily shares publicly the ways in which those who need to can contact it to collaborate on cybersecurity matters (e.g. email address, website, physical address, phone numbers). The FIRST annual convention, held in 2018 in Kuala Lumpur, had over 800 registered attendees from CSIRTs from more than 60 countries across the globe.

Both the CERT division of the SEI at CMU and FIRST have a global reputation for their activities, and the teams that make up the membership of the latter very often fulfil national or state level responsibilities.

INFORMATION SHARING AND ANALYSIS CENTERS

In 1998, during the Clinton Presidency (the year in which he was impeached) in the United States, a Presidential Decision Directive (PDD) NSC-63[6] was enacted. Entitled 'Critical Infrastructure Protection', the PDD called for (or, to quote the document directly, 'strongly encouraged') the 'creation of a private sector Information Sharing and Analysis Center (ISAC)'.

While the wording of the directive could be interpreted as imagining that there would be only one such ISAC, cutting across all Critical National Infrastructure (CNI) sectors, within the space of a year, the Financial Services ISAC (FS-ISAC)[7] had been established, closely followed by a long tail of other sectoral ISACs. A voluntary organization, the National Council of ISACs[8], brings together these bodies. At the time of writing, the National Council reported a membership of 25 ISACS (from the original FS-ISAC, through the influential Health ISAC (H-ISAC), the (Retail and Hospitality ISAC) RH-ISAC, and the IT-ISAC, to other smaller, more recently formed ISACs.

At the time of writing, the FS-ISAC reported membership of over 7,000 organizations, with 17,000 individual members, making it the largest single information-sharing organization. The membership of the FS-ISAC, while originally having been formed of organizations in the United States, is now to be found from over 35 countries across the globe. An unofficial survey estimated the membership of all the other ISACs combined to be not much more than 4,000, making the FS-ISAC by far the dominant entity for cyber security information sharing in the United States, and the largest such sector-specific information-sharing organization in the world.

The PDD had 'encouraged' the operators of CNI (in the United States, predominantly private sector) to coordinate their activities through an ISAC but had little to say about collaboration with those public sector organizations that had responsibility for information security matters.

CRITICAL NATIONAL INFRASTRUCTURE

In the United States, the National Computer Security Centre (which might have been the first to use the NCSC acronym, increasingly adopted by national cyber security centres globally including in the UK, albeit with a different meaning), which operated out of Fort Meade, the headquarters of the NSA, had responsibility for the information security standards of federal government networks. The Federal Bureau of Investigations (FBI) established InfraGard in Cleveland, Ohio, in 1996.[9] Through its national network of 56 field offices, it endeavoured to establish links between federal government and local representatives of critical infrastructure organizations who, with the right security vetting, could have access to classified intelligence on relevant matters.

In line with many other economies with a mature national cybersecurity strategy, the United States stated what it considered to be Critical National Infrastructure. It identified 16 sectors in Presidential Policy Directive 21 of 2013 (White House 2013), with elections infrastructure being added as a subsector of the existing government facilities sector after President Trump was elected President in 2016. Those sectors include chemical; commercial facilities; communications; critical manufacturing; dams; defence industrial base; emergency services; energy; financial services; food and agriculture; government facilities; healthcare and public health; information technology; nuclear reactors, material, and waste; transportation systems; and water and wastewater systems. In 2009, the US CISA, which at the time of writing was the national authority in the United States, established the Cybersecurity Information Sharing and Collaboration Program (CISCP)[10] to cover the 16 sectors of Critical National Infrastructure.

By comparison, the UK has identified 13 sectors through the government's Centre for the Protection of National Infrastructure (CPNI)[11]: chemicals; civil nuclear; communications; defence; emergency services; energy; finance; food; government; health; space; transport;

and water. In Japan, the National centre for Incident readiness and Strategy for Cybersecurity (NISC 2018), part of the Cabinet Office, identifies 14 and includes credit card infrastructure as distinct from the rest of finance.

INFORMATION SHARING AND THE CYBERSECURITY INFORMATION SHARING PARTNERSHIP

On 25 November 2011, the year before the London Olympic Games, a revised national cyber security strategy was published by the UK government (Cabinet Office 2011). That strategy referenced the existing private sector initiatives that had encouraged the establishment of more formal mechanisms for secure, trusted information sharing on cyber security matters for UK entities. It set as its objective to harness 'the wider private sector joint working initiative on cyber security'. Known as 'Project Auburn', this initiative resulted in the creation of a public–private partnership (the Cybersecurity Information Sharing Partnership—CiSP), which sought to build on the experience of the United States. It was formed intentionally from the start as a cross-sector partnership, in contrast to the ISAC models in the United States that had organized themselves quite quickly (despite the wording of the original directive that had led to their creation) into sector-specific ISACs.

WARNING ADVISORY AND REPORTING POINTS AND INFORMATION EXCHANGES

The CiSP was built on two prior models for information sharing. The first of these were the WARPs (Warning Advisory and Reporting Points), which had been promoted by the UK National Infrastructure Security Co-ordination Centre (NISCC, established in 1999), the forerunner to CPNI, created in 2007. These were regional (e.g. for local/regional government) for the main part, but other WARPs existed within central government departments (e.g. the Ministry of Defence). The WARPs were for the most part moved to form part of the CiSP at an early stage. The second model, which continues to exist, is the Information Exchange. Information Exchanges (there were around a dozen at the time of writing) form around particular industry sectors (e.g. civil nuclear). In addition to being hosted on CiSP, they meet physically to a regular schedule (e.g. quarterly) to discuss some matters face to face and further build trust. Indeed, it was for the Information Exchanges that CPNI invented the Traffic Light Protocol (TLP)[12] , which is now the standard at version 1.0 (managed by FIRST) for the way cybersecurity information handling rules are expressed.

The CiSP community was officially launched by the UK Cabinet Office, the very heart of UK Government, at Chatham House in London at the end of March 2013. One year later, at the end of March 2014, CERT-UK was formed, with responsibility for hosting that partnership.

On 16 November 2015, the establishment of the UK NCSC was announced by the then Chancellor of the Exchequer, the Rt Hon George Osborne MP (HM Treasury 2015). The NCSC built on the expertise of CERT-UK and brought in GovCERT, which had responsibility for Government networks in the UK, and elements of CPNI (mentioned earlier) with its mission to protect the national infrastructure of the UK.

The NCSC reports to the Director of the Government Communications Headquarters (GCHQ), and as such the information sharing by participants in the CiSP community is exempt from Freedom of Information Act (FOIA) requests.[13] The implication of this is that legal counsel from the majority private sector participants in the community have fewer grounds to object to requests to share information relating to incidents or breaches from their network defenders—the technical staff within their organization responsible for monitoring and maintaining the security of their networks.

At the time of writing, the CiSP community in the UK had over 12,000 members from over 4,000 organizations drawn from over 25 sectors including all 13 CNI sectors. It had public sector participation from the outset (e.g. from law enforcement through the 10 Regional Organized Crime Units—ROCUs.) This made it the largest national cross-sector cyber security information sharing community globally and, as such, represented a key case study for cyber security information sharing.

INFORMATION SHARING AND ANALYSIS ORGANIZATIONS

Subsequent to the establishment of the CiSP in the UK, and in order to enhance cyber security information sharing in the United States, in 2013, President Obama signed an Executive Order (number 13691), which sought to address two consequences of the way in which partnership had evolved in the United States. It called for the establishment of Information Sharing and Analysis Organizations (ISAOs)—these organizations would be horizontal, whereas ISACs had evolved to be vertical (for industry sectors). ISAOs might therefore be established for specific geographies (with the Arizona state level ACTRA[14]— Arizona Cyber Threat Response Alliance—for example, declaring itself as the first ISAO), or for cross-cutting industries (such as the legal sector, which represents clients from multiple CNI sectors). ISAOs were also designed to encourage more public–private sharing, where some of the ISACs had minimal sharing with the relevant federal agencies.

A contract was awarded to the University of Texas, San Antonio, in October 2015 to run the ISAO Standards Organization[15], which was designed to establish the way ISAOs were to be run (in the way that the SEI sets standards for CERTs globally). In particular, the new organization would address concerns about the way in which sensitive information about cyber security breaches, or incidents that private sector operators of critical infrastructure might otherwise have been reluctant to disclose, would be protected and, likewise, the way in which classified information, which only the federal government had permission to aggregate, could be shared with those organizations.

With a background of significant breaches of sensitive information held by the US federal government, including the US Office of Personnel Management and the Internal Revenue

Service, the Obama Administration sought to reassure the private sector with a guarantee of further protections in the shape of the Cybersecurity Information Sharing Act[16], which came into law in October 2015. At the time of writing, the impact of this had yet to be measured.

AUTOMATED INDICATOR SHARING

The Cybersecurity Information Sharing Act also led to other initiatives within US federal government—particularly the CISA, in the DHS —relating to the automatic (machine-to-machine) sharing of cyber security information. This imagined a model in which private sector participants would install software on their networks (adhering to the 'Trusted Automated eXchange of Indicator Information—TAXII™ standard[17]), which would receive Indicators of Compromise (IOCs) in the standard Structured Threat Information eXpression (STIX™) format[18]. These would be used, automatically, to protect the networks of those participants. The hope was that the private sector participants would reciprocate, allowing those same agents in their networks to share relevant information, automatically, back to federal government.

The uptake of this initiative, Automated Indicator Sharing (AIS)[19], has not yet been at the level hoped for by the federal government in the United States. This might be illustrated by the challenges that were communicated by Ann Beauchesne, in her capacity as Senior Vice President for National Security and Emergency Preparedness at the US Chamber of Commerce. In her keynote speech to the inaugural ISAO Standards Organization conference on 31 October 2017, she highlighted some of the key concerns of her members (private sector organizations across the whole United States) (ISAO Standards Organization 2017). Those focused on two interrelated concerns:

- An inability to express information handling rules that ensured control of with whom the information would be shared.
- A lack of clarity of which international entities with whom the US Government was sharing that information (e.g. organizations in Japan).

MANDATORY INFORMATION SHARING

An alternative approach to incentivizing information sharing is to make it mandatory. In many—if not all—states, operators in key sectors of CNI will already have in place a reporting regime that makes it mandatory for them to notify the relevant authority of incidents. These regimes will encompass a broad range of conditions for reporting, including, for example, resilience and safety. What is changing is the extent to which those regulations now begin explicitly to cover both cyber security incidents and breaches.

We will use four examples to demonstrate the steady increase in the level of explicitly mandatory cyber security information sharing: the Defence Industrial Base (DIB) in the United States; the UK implementation of the European Union (EU) Network and Information Security Directive (NISD); the Cyber Security Reporting Requirements[20] for the Department of Finance of the State of New York; and the Food and Drug Administration (FDA) in the United States.

United States Defence Industrial Base

Companies that supply the US Department of Defense (DoD), either directly or as part of a supply chain, have to sign up to Federal Acquisition Regulations (FARs), which form part of their contractual obligations. These FARs cover a wide variety of concerns, but FAR 55.204-21 and the defence-specific DFARs 252.204-7012 address cybersecurity information sharing (Department of Defense 2016). This represents an increase in the amount and type of information that has to be shared with the DoD by a supplier. The mechanism for suppliers notifying the DoD is via the DIB online portal.[21] While this covers mandatory information notification, the defence industry established its own parallel mechanism for voluntary sharing among its members, in order to facilitate more detailed information exchange within a trusted group than is necessary to simply comply with the obligations of the DoD, their common customer. This was via the Defense Security Information Exchange (DSIE)[22] . It was reported at the NSA Information Assurance Symposium in Washington DC in 2015, by a senior representative of the DoD, that the increase in the amount of mandatory sharing was leading to a decrease in the volume and breadth of sharing as suppliers restricted their sharing to that required to comply with the FARs/DFARs and no more. This same phenomenon has been observed within CISA, part of the US Department of Homeland Security (DHS) where, as operators of critical infrastructure were obliged to share information in compliance with the Cyber Information Sharing and Collaboration Program (CISCP) initiative, those who were doing the reporting were shifting from technical network defenders to legal counsel.

United Kingdom Network and Information Systems Regulations 2018

The Network and Information Systems Regulations 2018[23] , the UK transposition of the EU NISD, entered into force on 10 May 2018, at the same time as the much more widely known General Data Protection Regulation (GDPR). In the same way that GDPR makes it mandatory to notify breaches of Personally Identifiable Information (PII), so the NISD makes it mandatory to give notification of cyber incidents. It requires each EU Member State to put in place one or more competent authorities (CAs) to whom operators of essential services (a category that overlaps with CNI) have to give notification of cyber incidents.

In the UK, the government department that has been responsible for transposing the NISD into UK law is the Department for Digital, Culture, Media and Sport. It identified at least one CA for each essential service sector: drinking water; energy; digital infrastructure; health; transport; and the digital service providers whom the operators must notify. The CAs have an additional obligation to forward aggregate information to the EU for dissemination to Member States. As an example, the CA for the water sector is the Department for Environment, Food and Rural Affairs, but the responsibility for handling incident notifications has been delegated to the Drinking Water Inspectorate because this body already has in place mechanisms for handling other (non-cyber) incidents. Some concerns have begun to emerge about this state of affairs:

1. UK regulators are not permitted to join the CiSP collaboration environment, in order to reassure members that they can share information on cyber breaches without fear of triggering liability proceedings. One consequence of this is that the built-in incident reporting mechanism cannot be used for mandatory reporting (e.g. to comply with NIS regulations) to those regulators because they are not in the CiSP.
2. Second, there is concern over the burden of having to report multiple times. In the UK, a cyber breach that resulted in a loss of PII and affected safety might need to be reported to the relevant Network and Information Systems (NIS) CA; the Information Commissioners Office (ICO); and the Health and Safety Executive. If the operator also wants to contribute to the broader security of the sector in which they operate, they will also want to share information in the CiSP.
3. Third, there is no CiSP-like platform or mechanism in place to allow cross-sector information sharing from the outset between CAs.
4. Finally, the CAs are already sufficiently concerned about how voluntary incident reporting will be affected by the existence of mandatory reporting requirements, that they have started to consider putting in place parallel mechanisms to remind operators that they would like them to share more than is strictly necessary to comply with the NIS regulations.

New York State Department of Financial Services

Turning our attention back to the United States, but in a move that has global consequences, the Department of Financial Services (DFS) of the State of New York put in place a set of Cyber Security Reporting Requirements[24] , which came into force in March 2017. These regulations make incident reporting mandatory for all those bodies operating under a licence issued by the DFS. Given that Wall Street, the global financial centre, is in the State of New York, this means that a significant number of financial organizations from across the globe will be affected by these requirements to report on incidents. Depending on the gravity of the situation, the time limit for incident reporting might be as little as 72 hours.

United States Food and Drug Administration

Lastly, we consider some further incentives that are in place to improve cybersecurity information sharing in another sector in the United States—namely, health. In some cases, the FDA classes software as a medical device that requires a licence. If a medical device (including software) fails because of a cybersecurity issue, the FDA can revoke the licence that it had granted to allow the device to be used for medical purposes (and might therefore damage the market for the product in the United States), and it can 'name and shame' and publish details of the breach, leaving the supplier open to litigation.

In order to incentivize information sharing, the FDA says that it will be more lenient with those companies that can demonstrate that they have actively participated in an information-sharing exchange (such as the H-ISAC) (US Food and Drug Administration 2016). The FDA might not take enforcement action if the company concerned can demonstrate that, by their involvement in an information exchange, they were taking a proactive approach to post-market cybersecurity. Similar incentive schemes have been discussed elsewhere, including in the UK and Israel.

THE FUTURE OF INFORMATION SHARING

It seems highly likely that, in future, market forces will increasingly be brought to bear, shaping the information-sharing environment accordingly. Cyber insurance policies, for example, might offer reduced premiums to policy holders who are members of an information-sharing partnership (just as, in the UK, insurers offer reduced premiums for home insurance to home owners who are part of a Neighbourhood Watch scheme).

The examples discussed earlier illustrate the need for regulators of critical infrastructure sectors to consider the impact of the way in which they mandate reporting to ensure that they do not unwittingly create perverse disincentives, reducing the amount or type of voluntary sharing, and that they do not create silos that affect cross-sector sharing. Both possible outcomes would have an effect opposite to that which they were hoping to encourage.

NATIONAL CYBER STRATEGIES

Most advanced economies already have a national cyber security strategy and some have been through a number of iterations: the third UK strategy, for example, was published on 1 November 2016. The EU NISD makes it mandatory for each member state to have an appropriate national cybersecurity strategy. Emerging economies are also being supported in order to put in place their own national strategies. With the interconnectedness of the global digital economy and the networks that power it, there is recognition that threats originating in those emerging economies can affect domestic citizens and businesses elsewhere in the world, including in the advanced economies. One widely adopted model for improving the maturity and effectiveness of cyber security strategies is the Global Cybersecurity Capacity Maturity Model for Nations (CMM) from the Global Cyber Security Capacity Centre hosted within the Oxford Martin School at the University of Oxford (GCSCC 2016). That model makes it clear that information sharing is a foundational element of any cyber security strategy, and is essential to the development of a fully mature and robust strategy. As noted earlier, key attributes of a national strategy, as defined by the NIS Directive, include mandatory information-sharing responsibilities, and the nomination of a single named CSIRT as the point of contact for international information sharing.

Conclusion

The history of computing demonstrates that, while there have always been those who pose a threat to our information systems, there have equally always been those who will voluntarily cooperate in order to defend against, and respond to, the threat. Organizations, like FIRST and CiSP, founded on those voluntary drivers, have been successful in amplifying that voluntary effort, benefitting the security of specific industry sectors, and the local and wider economy.

'Mandatory sharing' is something of a contradiction in terms and regulations mandating incident reporting will necessarily result in organizations reporting just the information required to comply with the regulation to the authority.

In order to preserve—and build on—the positive will to collaborate to confront the cyber threat, industry needs the following:

- *The burden of mandatory reporting to be minimal.* Regulators need a common mechanism to ensure that organizations do not need to report the same incident multiple times and in different ways (e.g. to both the ICO for GDPR and CAs for NIS.)
- *Guaranteed liability protections.* Those volunteering sensitive information about incidents and breaches for the common good should be encouraged and incentivized to do so. This could take the form, as touched on above, of guaranteed protections from investigation, liability proceedings, and public information requests.
- *Enforcement of information handling rules.* Organizations need to be able to assert the rules about whom they are happy for their information to be shared with, and to have the right to expect that those rules will be enforced. Whether the information is shared across the boundary from the organization's own network with their industry sector regionally, across multiple industry sectors, nationally or ultimately even internationally, mechanisms including the industry standard Traffic Light Protocol (TLP) or the richer Information Exchange Policy (IEP) standard will form the basis of how those rules are expressed.

Information sharing is not an optional extra a 'nice to have'. It is the foundation stone of cybersecurity strategy and it is increasingly becoming mandatory, particularly for CNI operators. Getting information sharing right, and not creating perverse outcomes as the unintended consequences of clumsily implemented regulation, is essential to the security of citizens, and our ability to go about our business online in our almost entirely interconnected digital economies.

Notes

1. *United States v. Morris* (1991), 928 F.2d 504, 505 (2d Cir. 1991). https://scholar.google.com/scholar_case?case=5513862414516396668
2. The Jargon File, 'RTM'. http://catb.org/jargon/html/R/RTM.html
3. CMU, SEI, 'The CERT Division'. https://www.sei.cmu.edu/about/divisions/cert

4. CMU, SEI, 'Steps in the Process for Becoming an Authorized User'. https://resources.sei. cmu.edu/library/asset-view.cfm?assetID=51636
5. FIRST, 'FIRST Members Around the World'. https://www.first.org/members/map
6. 'Critical Infrastructure Protection (Presidential Decision Directive PDD-63). https://fas. org/irp/offdocs/pdd/pdd-63.htm
7. Financial Services ISAC, 'Sharing Timely, Relevant and Actionable Intelligence Since 1999'. https://www.fsisac.com/who-we-are
8. National Council of ISACs, 'Member ISACs'. https://www.nationalisacs.org/member-isacs-3
9. InfraGard, 'Factsheet'. https://www.infragard.org/Files/INFRAGARD_Factsheet_10-10-2018.pdf
10. US Department of Homeland Security, 'Cyber Information Sharing and Collaboration Program (CISCP)'. https://www.cisa.gov/ciscp
11. Centre for the Protection of National Infrastructure, 'Critical National Infrastructure'. https://www.cpni.gov.uk/critical-national-infrastructure-0
12. FIRST, 'Traffic Light Protocol (TLP)—Version 1.0' https://www.first.org/tlp/
13. National Cyber Security Centre (NCSC). 'UK CiSP Terms and Conditions v5.0'. https://www.ncsc.gov.uk/information/cyber-security-information-sharing-partnership--cisp-
14. Arizona Cyber Threat Response Alliance, https://www.actraaz.org/
15. ISAO Standards Organization. 'About us'. https://www.isao.org/about/
16. Congress.Gov, 'Cybersecurity Information Sharing Act of 2014'. https://www.congress. gov/bill/113th-congress/senate-bill/2588
17. OASIS, 'Introduction to TAXII'. https://oasis-open.github.io/cti-documentation/taxii/intro
18. OASIS, 'Introduction to STIX'. https://oasis-open.github.io/cti-documentation/stix/intro. Structured Threat Information Expression (STIX^{TM}) was an initiative to agree one common standard for the automated exchange of cyber threat intelligence at a time when there were various competing standards such as the Incident Object Description Exchange Format and the OpenIOC.
19. Cybersecurity & Infrastructure Security Agency or CISA, 'Automated Indicator Sharing (AIS)'. https://www.cisa.gov/ais
20. ISAO Standards Organization, 31 October–1 November 2017, '2017 International Information Sharing Conference'. https://www.isao.org/past-events/iisc2017/
21. DOD, 'DIBNet portal'. https://dodcio.defense.gov/Portals/0/Documents/DIB%20Fact%20Sheet.pdf
22. DSIE, 'Defense Security Information Exchange'. https://ndisac.org/resource-library/ndisac-overview/
23. 'The Network and Information Systems Regulations 2018'. https://www.legislation.gov.uk/uksi/2018/506/made

24. New York State, Department of Financial Services, 'Cybersecurity Requirements for financial services companies'. https://www.dfs.ny.gov/system/files/documents/2019/02/dfsrf500txt.pdf

REFERENCES

Cabinet Office. 2011. 'The UK Cyber Security Strategy', 25 November. https://www.gov.uk/government/publications/cyber-security-strategy

Department of Defense. 2016. 'Safeguarding Covered Defense Information and Cyber Incident Reporting', October. https://business.defense.gov/Portals/57/Safeguarding%20Covered%20Defense%20Information%20-%20The%20Basics.pdf

GCSCC (Global Cyber Security Capacity Centre, University of Oxford). 2016. 'Cybersecurity Capacity Model for Nations (CMM)'. 31 March. https://cybilportal.org/wp-content/uploads/2020/05/CMM-revised-edition_09022017_1.pdf

HM Treasury. 2015. 'Chancellor Sets Out Vision to Protect Britain Against Cyber Threat in GCHQ Speech', 17 November. https://www.gov.uk/government/news/chancellor-sets-out-vision-to-protect-britain-against-cyber-threat-in-gchq-speech

ISAO Standards Organization. 2017. '2017 International Information Sharing Conference', 31 October–1 November. https://www.isao.org/past-events/iisc2017/

Marks, Paul. 2011. 'Dot-Dash-Diss: The Gentleman Hacker's 1903 Lulz', New Scientist, 24 December.

NISC. 2018. 'Summary of the Cybersecurity Policy for CIP' (4th edn), revised 25 July. https://www.nisc.go.jp/eng/pdf/cs_policy_cip_eng_v4_summary.pdf

Stoll, C. 1990. The Cuckoo's Egg. New York: Pocket Books.

US Food and Drug Administration. 2016. 'Postmarket Management of Cybersecurity in Medical Devices', 28 December. https://www.fda.gov/downloads/MedicalDevices/DeviceRegulationandGuidance/GuidanceDocuments/ucm482022.pdf

White House, Office of the Press Secretary. 2013. 'Critical Infrastructure Security and Resilience (Presidential Policy Directive 21)', 12 February. https://obamawhitehouse.archives.gov/the-press-office/2013/02/12/presidential-policy-directive-critical-infrastructure-security-and-resil

CHAPTER 20

DATA PRIVACY AND SECURITY LAW

FRED CATE AND RACHEL DOCKERY

History and Context of Data Security Laws

Legal obligations to protect the security of data have their foundation in data protection law. In 1980, for example, the Committee of Ministers of the Organization for Economic Cooperation and Development (OECD) adopted Guidelines on the Protection of Privacy and Transborder Flows of Personal Data.[1] The OECD Guidelines were designed to 'represent a consensus on basic principles which can be built into existing national legislation' and to 'serve as a basis for legislation in those countries which do not yet have it.'[2] In this aspiration, they have undoubtedly succeeded because most of the dozens of national and regional privacy regimes adopted after 1980 claim to reflect the OECD Guidelines. Among the eight foundational principles that make up the OECD Guidelines is the security safeguards principle:

> Personal data should be protected by reasonable security safeguards against such risks as loss or unauthorised access, destruction, use, modification or disclosure of data.[3]

Security has been recognized in every significant codification of data protection law since. For example, the European Union (EU)'s 1995 Council Directive on the Protection of Individuals with Regard to the Processing of Personal Data and on the Free Movement of Such Data (Data Protection Directive)[4] includes specific obligations reflecting what European regulators have described as 'the security principle', under which 'technical and organisational security measures should be taken by the data controller that are appropriate to the risks presented by the processing.'[5]

The same is true of the EU's recent Regulation of the European Parliament and of the Council on the Protection of Natural Persons with Regard to the Processing of Personal Data and on the Free Movement of Such Data, and Repealing Directive 95/46/EC (better known as the 'General Data Protection Regulation', or 'GDPR').[6] Article 32 of the GDPR specifies:

> Taking into account the state of the art, the costs of implementation and the nature, scope, context and purposes of processing as well as the risk of varying likelihood and severity for the rights and freedoms of natural persons, the controller and the processor shall implement appropriate technical and organisational measures to ensure a level of security appropriate to the risk ...[7]

US law has followed a similar approach. In 1998, the Federal Trade Commission (FTC) reported to Congress on key privacy principles.[8] After reviewing the 'fair information practice codes' of the United States, Canada, and Europe, the Commission concluded: 'Common to all of these documents are five core principles of privacy protection.'[9] Included among these five was integrity/security:

> [D]ata [must] be accurate and secure. To assure data integrity, collectors must take reasonable steps, such as using only reputable sources of data and cross-referencing data against multiple sources, providing consumer access to data, and destroying untimely data or converting it to anonymous form.[10]

Other nations' data protection laws, as well as regional agreements, have also included this principle. To take only one example, the Asia-Pacific Economic Cooperation (APEC) forum adopted privacy principles in 2004. The APEC Privacy Framework (2004) includes nine principles. Among these is the security safeguards principle:

> Personal information controllers should protect personal information that they hold with appropriate safeguards against risks, such as loss or unauthorized access to personal information, or unauthorized destruction, use, modification or disclosure of information or other misuses. Such safeguards should be proportional to the likelihood and severity of the harm threatened, the sensitivity of the information and the context in which it is held, and should be subject to periodic review and reassessment.[11]

The connection between privacy and security is intuitive because privacy depends absolutely on security. No obligation to provide privacy, whether entered into voluntarily or compelled by law, will be meaningful if the data to be protected can be accessed or stolen by unauthorized third parties. Similarly, privacy and cybersecurity are often advanced by common tools, such as encryption, data minimization, and limits on collecting, retaining, and transferring personal data.

Nonetheless, linking privacy and security presents challenges as well—not surprisingly given the obvious tensions between the two. Many measures employed to enhance cybersecurity pose a risk to privacy. For example, proposals to enhance cybersecurity by requiring identity verification, reducing online anonymity, and sharing potentially personal information about cyberattacks all create risks for personal privacy. In addition, data protection laws focus only on personally identifiable information, while cybersecurity is also concerned with securing economic data such as trade secrets and company databases, government information, and the systems that transmit and process information. Increasingly, these include systems that control critical infrastructure, such as transportation, finance, utilities, manufacturing, and other key economic sectors.

Another challenge reflected in many security requirements is the imprecise and often subjective nature of privacy, and what constitutes a privacy harm. This challenge is reflected with the frequent use of the words 'reasonable' and 'appropriate' to describe necessary security measures in these laws. These words have allowed for important flexibility, but they have also limited the impact and precision of security requirements.

As a practical matter, despite the prominence of security obligations in data protection legislation, these were often downplayed or ignored entirely until recent years. Only as cybersecurity threats became more pressing did regulators begin actively enforcing the security obligations found in most data protection laws. More recently, legislative bodies and regulators have begun adopting cybersecurity-specific obligations. However, as described in greater detail throughout this chapter, even these have often mirrored or been combined with privacy protections—sometimes to the detriment of effective cybersecurity.

The following sections examine major categories of cybersecurity law.

Unfair or Deceptive Practices Legislation: Privacy and Security

In the United States, the FTC, which has broad responsibility for consumer protection and other areas, has relied on the 1914 statute that created it for authority to address both privacy and security practices. Section 5 of the Federal Trade Commission Act grants the FTC broad general authority to enforce against 'deceptive' or 'unfair' practices affecting commerce. Although privacy and security were undoubtedly not in the drafters' minds in 1914, the FTC has used the statute not merely to prosecute 'deceptive' privacy and security activities—primarily companies making promises that they failed to live up to—but also to require that companies comply with basic cybersecurity standards on the basis that the failure to do so would be 'unfair'. Under federal law, an 'unfair' practice must result in an injury to consumers that is 'substantial', 'not outweighed by any countervailing benefits to consumers or competition', and not something they could 'reasonably have avoided'.[12]

The use of the Section 5 'unfairness' power has been controversial for many reasons, not the least of which is that the FTC does not have general authority to issue regulations concerning security or privacy, so it can only indicate what it believes the basic standards are through after-the-fact litigation. However, it has employed Section 5 to target suspect security practices in more than 50 cases. In 2015, the US Court of Appeals for the Third Circuit upheld the FTC's authority under Section 5.[13]

The law in many US states grants similar authority to state attorneys general. Unfair or deceptive practice litigation is often used to prescribe penalties for non-compliance with breach notification laws, as now described.

Breach Notification Laws: Notice and Liability

United States State Breach Notification Laws

One of the earliest responses to rising data breaches was the adoption of breach notification laws requiring victims of security breaches to notify consumers when their personal information had been accessed. All 50 states now have some form of a breach notification law. California adopted the first in 2003[14] and, in 2018, Alabama and South Dakota became the last remaining states to enact breach notification legislation.[15]

Although each state's approach differs slightly, most state breach notification laws define personal information and security breach; describe the conditions that trigger required notification (such as number of affected individuals); explain who, when, and how to notify;

and prescribe penalties for non-compliance. Similar to many other states, the Massachusetts breach notification law defines 'breach of security' as the 'unauthorized acquisition or unauthorized use of unencrypted data or encrypted electronic data and the confidential process or key that is capable of compromising the security, confidentiality, or integrity of personal information'.[16] The law further defines personal information as 'a resident's first name and last name or first initial and last name in combination with any 1 or more ... data elements that relate to such resident', such as a social security number, driver's licence number, bank or credit card information, or passwords.[17] The definition of personal information varies from state to state, and defining this term with the advent of big data is one of the challenges legislators face today.

When breaches occur in a manner that compromises personal data, most states require notification without unreasonable delay. A safe harbour is sometimes built in for situations where it is unlikely that any harm will occur, such as the case where stolen data is encrypted. Although not every state sets forth notification requirements via statute, notifications generally include a description of the incident, the type of information compromised, the company's mitigation procedures, and contact information to receive further information or advice. In at least 14 states, companies who detect data breaches must notify the state attorney general or other state agencies.[18] In at least 30 states, companies must also notify consumer-reporting agencies if the breaches meet certain conditions.[19] Liability for non-compliance varies, but enforcement usually includes administrative fines or civil penalties, civil causes of action, or penalties related to state unfair or deceptive practices legislation.

United States Federal Breach Notification Laws

Unlike the comprehensive breach notification laws of individual states, federal security breach notification laws focus on industry-specific uses and the variation in the type of information collected by companies. Under federal law, certain sectors are legally obligated to protect personally identifiable information as a result of legislation in the credit, financial services, healthcare, government, and Internet sectors. This is largely a reflection of the United States' sectoral approach to privacy.

The two most noteworthy sectors with required breach notifications are health and financial services. The Health Insurance Portability and Accountability Act (HIPAA), originally designed to improve healthcare efficiency in the United States, developed privacy and security rules when federal healthcare reimbursement requests were moved to an electronic system.[20] As healthcare providers continued to adopt electronic systems, Congress enacted the Health Information Technology for Economic and Clinical Health Act (HITECH) in 2009, requiring covered entities to conduct risk assessments whenever a breach of unsecured, unencrypted information was detected.[21] If there is a significant risk of financial, reputational, or other harm, the entity must notify affected individuals within 60 days of discovery.[22] If the breach affects more than 500 individuals, the entity must also notify the Department of Health and Human Services.[23] Furthermore, if more than 500 affected individuals are living in the same jurisdiction, the entity must notify the media as well.[24] The FTC promulgated mirroring regulations under the Health Breach Notification Rule, and violations are considered an unfair or deceptive trade practice.[25] These requirements indicate the seriousness with which the US federal government views personal health information.

Whereas HITECH specifically enumerates breach notification requirements, the federal Gramm-Leach-Bliley Act (GLBA) imposes no such direct requirement on the financial sector. However, the GLBA creates privacy protections regarding financial information and specifically prohibits disclosure of financial information to a third party without providing notice to customers.[26] Pursuant to this requirement of the GLBA, regulators promulgated the Interagency Guidance on Response Programs for Unauthorized Access to Customer Information and Customer Notice, which is similar to many of the state breach notification requirements discussed earlier. This Guidance requires that financial institutions disclose security breaches to customers, the primary federal regulator, and appropriate law enforcement.[27]

In early 2017, the Office of Management and Budget created guidelines for responding to data breaches within federal departments and agencies. The memorandum defines personally identifiable information, provides notification content requirements and methods, and outlines a risk of harm analysis.[28] Subsequently, US-CERT issued the Federal Incident Notification Guidelines, which detail notification requirements and impact assessments.[29]

Although the current approach to breach notification at the US federal level is sector-specific, there appeared to be some legislative traction for a comprehensive federal breach notification law. The Data Security and Breach Notification Act was introduced in the House of Representatives in April 2015. In January 2017, the House Energy and Commerce Committee reported on the proposed legislation and recommended passage, noting that the 'patchwork of State laws creates confusion for consumers looking for consistency and predictability in breach notices, as well as complex compliance issues for businesses as they secure their systems after a breach.'[30] The bill has not been further considered, but breach notification will likely be a component of any proposal for a comprehensive federal privacy law.

Other National and Regional Breach Notification Laws

Breach notification laws have been adopted widely around the globe. Some countries take a sector-specific approach, while others have laws that span across all sectors. For example, South Korea's Personal Information and Protection Act (PIPA) requires that affected individuals, as well as the most relevant regulators, be notified of any breach of personal information.[31] PIPA defines personal information as data related to a living person, such as a name, resident registration number, photos, or other information that can identify an individual.[32] Additionally, the definition includes non-identifying information that can become identifying when combined with other information.[33] Penalties for non-compliance range from fines to civil liabilities.[34]

The EU has also adopted a comprehensive breach notification law as part of its GDPR. The GDPR requires notification of the relevant supervisory authority within 72 hours of breach discovery.[35] If the breach is 'likely to result in a high risk to the rights and freedoms of natural persons', breach notification must occur 'without undue delay'.[36] If there are 'appropriate technical and organizational measures' in place, such as encryption, the GDPR does not require breach notification as long as there is no evidence that the protection measures have been compromised.[37] The GDPR replaced the patchwork of breach notification laws that existed under the e-Privacy Directive, whereby only telecommunications and Internet service providers were required to notify national authorities and affected individuals of data breaches unless a national law applied.[38] All the countries in the EU and European Economic Area (EEA) have adopted and incorporated the GDPR breach notification requirements in their national law.

Many other countries around the world have some form of breach notification requirement, either specifically required for all companies, required for specific sectors, or required under government regulations. These countries include Brazil, Canada, Costa Rica, Ghana, Indonesia, Japan, Malaysia, Mexico, Taiwan, Uganda, the United Kingdom, and Uruguay—to name a few.[39] Other countries have no breach notification requirement, but may have guidelines suggesting that companies notify individuals affected by security breaches.[40]

DATA DESTRUCTION LAWS

In addition to providing notifications when security breaches occur, many jurisdictions have laws that regulate the disposal of personally identifying information, prescribe potential liability, or otherwise impose regulations on the destruction of data. As of January 2019, at least 35 states in America provide regulations for the disposal of personal information, often incorporated into data breach laws.[41] So-called data destruction laws apply to governments, businesses, or both, and are often passed to ensure that disposal of information leaves the information unreadable or undecipherable by any means. Some states, such as Arizona,[42] only apply data destruction laws to paper records, although the majority also address electronic data destruction or disposal. Massachusetts requires that covered entities meet 'minimum standards for proper disposal' to ensure that 'personal information cannot practicably be read or reconstructed'.[43] Penalties in each state range from fines to public and private rights of action.

Under US federal law, the FTC's Disposal Rule requires proper disposal or destruction of consumer information contained in a consumer report to protect against 'unauthorized access to or use of the information in connection with its disposal'. [44] This Disposal Rule was passed in 2010 under the Fair and Accurate Credit Transactions Act (FACTA). To comply with this regulation, covered entities must take 'reasonable' steps to ensure proper disposal. Examples of 'reasonable' means of disposal include burning or shredding papers containing consumer report information, destroying or erasing electronic files or media containing consumer report information, or hiring a document destruction contractor.[45]

Although specific data destruction rules are useful, comprehensive data protection laws and guidelines can create implicit disposal rules as a result of data protection obligations. For example, under the EU's GDPR, destruction of personal data is included in the definition of 'processing'.[46] When processing data, organizations must take adequate measures to protect against unauthorized disclosure, which includes taking reasonable measures when destroying or erasing data. In Singapore, although there is no law that specifically enumerates responsible data disposal methods, the general obligation to secure personal data led to the creation of guidelines for destruction of data in a physical medium[47] and sanitization of data in an electronic medium.[48]

Focus on Critical Infrastructure and Information Sharing

Whereas breach notification and data destruction laws focus on protecting personal information, critical infrastructure and information sharing emphasize protecting systems from infiltration and damage. Infrastructure has been an important military target throughout history. As the world becomes more digital, infrastructure is increasingly controlled and monitored electronically. At the same time, attacking electronically controlled infrastructure is cheaper, less dangerous for the attacker, and more easily concealed. Because infrastructure is often connected to a network, it is also easier for attackers to connect their attacks to multiple sectors. Examples of cyberattacks on infrastructure include the 2013 Iranian-backed attack on New York financial institutions, the 2014 power and Internet outage in North Korea, and the 2015 attack on the Ukraine power grid. The reason for focusing on critical infrastructure is obvious: 'Contaminated water sanitation systems may injure thousands before any issue is detected; vulnerable electric grids may leave cities black for days; and disrupted financial systems may cripple economies' (Shackelford and Craig 2014).

Global Emphasis on Critical Infrastructure Protection

According to a 2008 OECD report, 'critical infrastructure has gained prominence as a concern for essential security interests'.[49] Although critical infrastructure definitions and covered sectors vary across different countries, the most frequent sectors are banking and finance; government services; telecommunications and information communication technology; emergency response services; energy; health; food and water supplies; and transportation systems.[50] Some countries expand on these to include chemicals, manufacturing, defence, or legal and judicial systems.[51] One argument against this critical infrastructure approach is that definitions are often over- or under-inclusive. Defining critical infrastructure too broadly can reduce the effectiveness of the approach; defining it too narrowly can leave out critical sectors—for example, as the United States did by omitting voting from its list of critical infrastructure prior to 2017.

The US approach to protecting critical infrastructure from cyberattacks began in 1998 with President Clinton's Presidential Decision Direction No. 63. The intent was to put measures in place to safely and swiftly eliminate vulnerability to physical and cyberattacks on critical infrastructure.[52] The USA Patriot Act of 2001 further emphasized critical infrastructure, defining it as 'systems and assets, whether physical or virtual, so vital to the United States that the incapacity or destruction of such systems and assets would have a debilitating impact on security, national economic security, national public health or safety, or any combination of those matters'.[53] As the United States continued to see an increase in attacks and feared a disruption in power, water, communication, or other critical systems, President Obama issued Executive Order (EO) 13,636 and Presidential Policy Directive-21 (PPD-21) in an effort to bring consistency in the approach to protecting critical infrastructure, expand information sharing, and promote collaboration.

EO 13,636 directs the executive branch to develop a voluntary cybersecurity framework, promote and provide incentives for the adoption of that framework, increase the fluidity of information sharing, and otherwise explore how existing frameworks can be used to promote stronger cybersecurity. As noted by the order, 'It is the policy of the United States to enhance the security and resilience of the Nation's critical infrastructure and to maintain a cyber environment that encourages efficiency, innovation, and economic prosperity while promoting safety, security, business confidentiality, privacy, and civil liberties.'[54] PPD-21 enumerates 16 areas of critical infrastructure: chemical; commercial facilities; communications; critical manufacturing; dams; defence industrial base; emergency services; energy; financial services; food and agriculture; government facilities; healthcare and public health; information technology; nuclear reactors, materials, and waste; transportation systems; and water and wastewater systems.[55] Some critique this approach as over-inclusive, because not everything within these sectors is 'critical'.

EO 13,636 directed the National Institute for Standards and Technology (NIST) to develop the voluntary NIST Framework, encouraging companies to develop and implement comprehensive cybersecurity systems. The Framework provides a set of common vocabulary that aligns policy, business, and technical approaches to addressing cyber risks. The framework consists of standards, methodologies, and procedures that help businesses identify, protect against, detect, respond, and recover from cyber threats.[56] In 2016, 70% of businesses viewed the NIST Framework as a best practice, but 50% saw adopting the Framework as a barrier because of the high level of investment needed.[57]

In May 2017, President Trump signed an Executive Order on Strengthening the Cybersecurity of Federal Networks and Critical Infrastructure.[58] The order requires federal agencies to implement the NIST Framework to assess and manage their cybersecurity risks, including risks due to botnets and other automated distributed attacks.[59] Trump's order placed emphasis on 'an open, interoperable, reliable, and secure internet that fosters efficiency, innovation, communication, and economic prosperity, while respecting privacy and guarding against disruption, fraud, and theft'.[60] The overall spirit of the order was to bolster US cybersecurity systems and continue the ongoing trend of protecting critical infrastructure. Passed in late 2018, the Cybersecurity and Infrastructure Security Agency (CISA) Act furthered this trend by establishing CISA as an agency under the Department of Homeland Security (DHS), tasked with supporting security efforts for critical physical and cyber systems.[61]

The United States is not unique in its desire to identify, secure, and protect sectors that are vital to national security. Six years after the first US policy directive on critical infrastructure, the EU announced an emphasis on critical infrastructure beginning in June 2004, and proposed the European Programme for Critical Infrastructure Protection (EPCIP) as well as the development of a Critical Infrastructure Warning Information Network (CIWIN).[62] The first task of the EPCIP was to create a framework designed to protect infrastructure that was critical from a regional European perspective, although national critical infrastructure may receive some support in special cases. According to the Communication from the Commission of European Communities, 'European Critical Infrastructures constitute those designated critical infrastructures which are of the highest importance for the Community and which if disrupted or destroyed would affect two or more MS, or a single Member State if the critical infrastructure is located in another Member State.'[63] The EU Commission's Work

Programme for 2020 included addressing additional measures to strengthen the resilience of critical infrastructure.[64]

Because the EPCIC provides limited support to national critical infrastructure, many European countries have independent laws that further defend and protect their critical infrastructure. For example, Germany's IT Security Act of 2015 requires public and private critical infrastructure operators to develop cybersecurity systems, report cyber incidents to the Federal Office for Information Security, and designate a contact person (Gabel and Schuba 2015). The United Kingdom's Centre for Protection of National Infrastructure (CPNI) is tasked with measuring infrastructure using a 'criticality scale', determining which sectors are national priorities and providing security advice to those sectors (Stoddart, 2016: 1081). Unlike the United States, the UK has avoided deeming everything that falls within national infrastructure to be 'critical'. Instead, the UK defines 'Critical National Infrastructure' as:

> Those critical elements of national infrastructure (facilities, systems, sites, property, information, people, networks, and processes), the loss or compromise of which would result in major detrimental impact on the availability, delivery or integrity of essential services, leading to severe economic or social consequences to loss of life.[65] (Stoddart, 2016: 1079)

Thus, the UK approach to critical infrastructure looks not only at critical sectors but also what is 'critical' within those sectors.

Although this discussion of critical infrastructure has largely focused on Western countries, this trend of identifying and protecting critical sectors is not an exclusively Western concept. For example, the Chinese government emphasized protection of critical infrastructure as early as 1994, with Decree No. 147 requiring security systems for 'state affairs, economic construction, national defense, and the most advanced science and technology'.[66] China's 2016 Cybersecurity Law, discussed in greater detail later, also based regulations on categories of critical infrastructure.[67] In March 2014, the Republic of Ghana released its National Cyber Security Policy & Strategy, which provided a framework for protecting critical infrastructure sectors.[68] In January 2017, the Australian government created the Critical Infrastructure Centre to improve cyber preparedness and manage public–private coordination.[69] Critical infrastructure protection frameworks are prominent around the globe.

Global Emphasis on Information Sharing

In addition to conducting risk assessments and implementing more effective cybersecurity systems, governments around the world have searched for ways to expand information sharing. Cybercriminals often share information, whereas private businesses, for competitive or marketing reasons, do not. This discrepancy has created a need for sharing information regarding cyber threats and threat mitigation techniques in an effort to even the playing field between good and bad actors. While national security experts view this public–private partnership as an essential part of security in the digital age, privacy professionals have concerns about protecting personal information within an information-sharing framework.

Information sharing emerged as a national issue in the United States after the 9/11 Commission Report revealed that a lack of information sharing among agencies created a vulnerability in national security (Kean and Hamilton 2014, 394). Following that report, various executive orders required some extent of information sharing among government agencies, but Congress extended this directive to private businesses in 2015. Unlike most cybersecurity regulation that comes through executive orders, the Cybersecurity Information Sharing Act of 2015 (CISA) created information-sharing requirements through bipartisan legislation.[70]

Under CISA guidelines, companies may send information to the Automated Indicator Sharing portal, which is managed by the DHS and then shared with seven other federal agencies.[71] CISA encourages sharing of threat indicators, such as data about malware or other exploits hackers are able to use, as well as effective defensive measures to provide other companies with direction on how to handle such threats.[72] Although companies are explicitly required to protect personal information, CISA provides immunity for companies that are not grossly negligent with personal information.[73] By developing information-sharing systems, the goal is to increase the costs for cyber adversaries who will not be able to use the same hack after that technical information is shared.

Similar to the US plan to facilitate information sharing, the EU also implemented a development plan for the CIWIN, an information-sharing platform intended to aid in exchanging best practices for security. The voluntarily shared information is used for the sole purpose of protecting critical infrastructure, such as improving understanding about interdependencies, facilitating the exchange of incidents and best practices, conducting threat and risk assessments, and developing more effective approaches to training, research, and development.[74] The Commission specifically stated that proprietary or sensitive information needed to be adequately protected and that privacy rights must be respected.[75] The GDPR provides more comprehensive guidance on information collection, use, and storage in an effort to ensure greater privacy protection for European citizens, including in the information-sharing context.[76]

Whereas protection of critical infrastructure is something privacy advocates generally support, the trend of information sharing raises more difficult privacy considerations both in the United States and in Europe. Senator Ron Wyden criticized CISA, noting that such a programme needs 'adequate privacy protections' or else it becomes 'a surveillance bill by another name.'[77] CISA requires companies to remove personal information prior to sharing information and also that the government notifies entities when information unrelated to a cyber threat is shared.[78] It also creates oversight with privacy and civil liberties officers as well as time limitations for retention of data.[79]

However, many privacy advocates find these inadequate. The limited liability components of the bill excuse businesses from violations of privacy laws other than in the most extreme circumstances. Furthermore, many opponents argue that sharing this information does little to no good while creating additional privacy risks. Privacy advocates stress that information-sharing laws, and personal data protection laws in general, need to be clear in how to protect personal data due to the 'large volumes of personal data ... collected and stored by intermediaries' and the 'worrying trend of States obliging or pressuring these private actors to hand over information of their users' (Fry 2015).

OTHER UNITED STATES CYBERSECURITY LAWS

Computer Fraud and Abuse Act

Although the trend in cybersecurity legislation focuses on cybersecurity preparedness and defence, a separate approach involves having a body of criminal laws that specifically address computer crime. In the United States, the most significant of these laws is the Computer Fraud and Abuse Act (CFAA). The CFAA was originally enacted in 1984, but it has since been amended nine times. Originally, the law was designed to protect only a limited number of computers in the federal government and those used by financial institutions.[80] In what has proven to be the most significant amendment, the term 'protected computer' was expanded in 1996 to include any computer 'which is used in interstate or foreign commerce or communication, including a computer located outside the United States that is used in a manner that affects interstate or foreign commerce or communication of the United States'.[81] This definition extends the Act to nearly every computer because it includes every device connected to a network.

Offences under the CFAA include trespassing on a government computer, trespassing to obtain information on any protected computer, causing or intending to cause computer damage, committing computer fraud, making extortionate threats, trafficking in computer passwords, and committing computer espionage.[82] The Act punishes conspirators with equal force, and provides for both civil and criminal penalties—both of which have grown over time.[83] While the broad language in the Act has been criticized as over-inclusive, the Department of Justice published a memorandum describing eight factors to consider when determining whether to use the CFAA for prosecution.[84] Although this is just one of many federal and state laws working to combat cybercriminal activity, it was one of the first and remains one of the most significant.

State Statutes

While the US federal government has been loath to adopt substantive cybersecurity requirements, US states have begun enacting laws imposing both procedural and substantive obligations. The first major comprehensive state cybersecurity legislation was passed by Massachusetts and came into effect in 2010. The Standards for the Protection of Personal Information of Residents of the Commonwealth placed an emphasis on the importance of businesses protecting personal information. To achieve this goal, businesses were required to adopt minimum cybersecurity standards through a 'comprehensive information security program'.[85] Not only do the regulations create a duty to protect personal information, but they also set forth computer system security requirements as a floor for information security programs. Most significantly, the regulation requires '[e]ncryption of all transmitted records and files containing personal information that will travel across public networks, and encryption of all data containing personal information to be transmitted wirelessly'.[86] This requirement disregards the physical location of the device, requiring encryption even if the device does not leave the premises of the business.

Whereas the Massachusetts law takes an omnibus approach to cybersecurity, other states gear regulations toward sectors where sensitive personal information is most commonly stored. The most stringent of these sector-specific regulations took effect in New York in March 2017. Pursuant to the state's Financial Services Law, the New York State Department of Financial Services adopted regulations for the banking, insurance, and financial services industries and set minimum cybersecurity standards that exceed those required by the GLBA or those of any other state. Some key requirements of that law include 'continuous monitoring or periodic penetration testing and vulnerability assessments',[87] implementation of multi-factor or risk-based authentication,[88] and encryption of non-public information 'held or transmitted by the Covered Entity both in transit over external networks and at rest'.[89]

The New York and Massachusetts regulations are only two examples of how US state legislatures are trending toward increased cybersecurity measures. In 2019 alone, nearly 300 cybersecurity-related pieces of legislation were considered by US states, with 31 states enacting new legislation.[90] These substantive data security laws are wide-ranging in scope, including topics such as increasing required security measures for government or businesses, funding cybersecurity training or research, addressing cybersecurity risks with emerging technologies, or creating task forces on cybersecurity. All US states have statutes defining and penalizing computer crimes, with at least 20 states criminalizing spyware and 23 criminalizing phishing.[91] At least 26 states have passed laws regarding denial of service (DoS) attacks, and more states are considering laws that specifically address ransomware.[92]

California, after passing one of the nation's first cybersecurity laws in 2003, continues to lead the nation for both cybersecurity and privacy legislation, passing multiple laws in the past few years to bolster the state's cybersecurity preparedness.[93] The most robust of these laws is the California Consumer Protection Act (CCPA), passed in June 2018 and going into effect in early 2020. The CCPA is the most comprehensive privacy law in the United States, comparable to the GDPR in the EU. The law creates some new rights for California citizens—namely, the right to 'see what data companies have gathered about them, have that data deleted, and opt out of those companies selling it to third parties' (Edelman 2020)'. The CCPA also recognizes a business' 'duty to implement and maintain reasonable security procedures and practices appropriate to the nature of the information to protect the personal information'.[94] Failure to do so creates a civil right of action with defined statutory damages.

CHINA CYBERSECURITY LAW

Although China has recognized the importance of protecting computer information systems since 1994, the passage of the China Cybersecurity Law is a recent example of a nation passing omnibus cybersecurity legislation. The law came into effect in June 2017 and includes 'safeguards for national cyberspace sovereignty, protection of critical information infrastructure and data and protection of individual privacy'.[95] The law provides specific requirements for the protection of personal information and individual privacy, and sets minimum security requirements for network operators. The law also provides limitations on transferring sensitive information overseas. As mandated by Article 37:

> Personal information and important data collected and generated by critical information infrastructure operators in the [People's Republic of China] must be stored domestically. For information and data that is transferred overseas due to business requirements, a security assessment will be conducted in accordance with measures jointly defined by China's cyberspace administration bodies and the relevant departments under the State Council.[96]

In addition to ensuring that businesses are operating responsibly to preserve and protect sensitive data, the Cybersecurity Law further mandates that critical network equipment and other cybersecurity products or services must receive certain security certifications prior to sale or use.[97] Penalties for non-compliance with the law include suspending of or closing business activities, shutting down websites, revoking certificates or licences, or fines.[98] Through these omnibus provisions, the Chinese government has taken a significant and controversial step toward increasing the nation's cybersecurity efforts.

New Challenges to Data Privacy and Security Law

Data privacy and security law is a rapidly evolving field. New technologies breed new challenges, and governments around the world must work to keep up with new developments to manage the threats or vulnerabilities that are created. While most governments and companies have a tendency to treat privacy and security as separate concepts, developments in technology are inevitably intertwined with both privacy and security concerns. This last section will comment on the major issues that legislators and policy analysts around the world are currently faced with addressing.

The Aggregation Problem: Big Data and Personal Information

Many of the privacy protections for individuals and security requirements for companies hinge on protection of personally identifiable information. The lines between what is personal and what is not personal have blurred with the emergence of big data. Information that once seemed completely harmless to the individual now has significant privacy implications due to the correlations and inferences that can be discovered through aggregated data. For example, data indicating whether a particular conference room in a library is occupied would not seem to contain any personal information but, when combined with cell phone records or GPS locations, this data can easily be re-identified and linked to an individual. The problem of re-identification will only expand as big data grows in both scale and capabilities, and this will continue to cloud the definition of personally identifiable information. In light of this phenomenon, legislatures are faced with the question of what data should be protected and how to define what data is personal.

Emerging Technology

New innovations in artificial intelligence (AI) and other digital technologies also pose challenges to both privacy and cybersecurity. AI applications hold tremendous potential to improve efficiency and quality of everyday life in a number of sectors—including healthcare, transportation, agriculture, scientific research, and others (Cate and Dockery 2018). AI can be helpful for cybersecurity and privacy—because many companies use AI technologies in their intrusion-detection systems to help them detect and respond to potential security breaches (Columbus 2019). AI is also the backbone of Polisis—an application that helps individuals understand privacy policies and tries to create consistency in user preferences across online platforms (Greenberg 2018). At the same time, AI poses many challenges for traditional data protection principles that rely on individual control of data, data minimization, and collection limitations. AI often requires large amounts of data to be useful; the precise purpose for the data is not always understood at the outset; and limiting the retention of data can harm efforts to harness the benefits of these technologies.

Encryption

In an effort to protect information from unauthorized access, many individuals and companies are turning to encryption, which transforms plaintext into unintelligible ciphertext that cannot be deciphered unless someone has the encryption key. This development has sparked widespread debate in privacy, information security, law enforcement, and intelligence. Encryption helps protect important information from hackers and bad actors, and it is also used to protect and to verify identity in online transactions. However, encryption can keep information from law enforcement and intelligence agencies even if they have a lawful right to access. A number of countries are considering limits on encryption or are requiring mandatory back doors for law enforcement and intelligence authorities. Opponents adamantly caution that such steps would create vulnerabilities that bad actors could inevitably exploit.

Although encryption is an important step in protecting both privacy and security, encryption alone is not enough to consider information secure. Many breach notification laws contain safe harbours for encrypted data that can create a false sense of security. For example, encryption is often badly implemented, or passwords that protect decryption keys are easily compromised (such as taped to the back of a laptop or in another easily accessible place). Privacy advocates try to frame security with encryption as a floor rather than a ceiling, noting that further protection is necessary in order to truly protect individual privacy.

Individual and Organizational Incentives

Cybersecurity often appears to suffer from non-existent or misaligned incentives. The volume and complexity of code and the pressure to get new products to market mean that many software products are sold with errors. Responsible developers issue patches, usually without charge, for security vulnerabilities, but large institutions are often hesitant to install those patches for fear that they may have unanticipated consequences. This contributed to the success of the WannaCry ransomware in 2017. More than 300,000 computers in Britain's National Health Service, Federal Express, DeutscheBahn, and other large institutions around the globe were affected in a matter of days. However, Microsoft patched the flaw more than two months before WannaCry appeared; the machines that were infected had not been updated.

The Internet of Things only exacerbates the absence of appropriate incentives. Computing code is being introduced into thousands of devices that are difficult to update—consider cars and airplane engines—or which will never be updated—such as light bulbs and consumer products. Yet, in 2016, hackers exploited the unsecured yet connected computing capacity of baby monitors and digital video recorders to create a botnet that launched a series of distributed DoS attacks on Dyn, a domain name system provider. Hundreds of major websites were affected by the attack including major media organizations, Amazon, Netflix, Starbucks, and other companies. The failure of manufacturers and users of baby monitors and digital video recorders created a platform from which devastating attacks could be suffered by others.

Despite the widely acknowledged failure of markets to provide appropriate incentives for good cybersecurity, governments have resisted creating those incentives through legal obligations, preferring to focus instead on voluntary initiatives, information sharing, and notices to individuals about security breaches. There are signs—such as the new state laws emerging in the United States and the national law in China—that this is beginning to change and, as it does, providers and users of digital technologies should expect more substantive legal requirements.

Jurisdiction

Internet law finds difficulty in establishing jurisdiction. Information sent via the Internet inevitably crosses many borders, which is the very nature of packet-switching. No one has jurisdiction over the Internet as a whole, but defining jurisdiction based on physical borders has difficulties that are unprecedented in other areas of law. Even when countries prescribe laws that apply to the Internet, rulings can be difficult to enforce because of the inevitable global scale. To highlight these jurisdictional issues, this section will present two circumstances where jurisdiction (or lack thereof) poses central issues for lawmakers and courts.

The first of these involves US law enforcement trying to execute a valid Fourth Amendment warrant on email servers of Internet service providers when the servers are located outside the United States. US courts are currently split on this issue. The Second Circuit ruled in 2016 that law enforcement officials in the United States could not compel disclosure of email information stored on Microsoft servers in Ireland with the use of a warrant, but instead had to go through the Mutual Legal Assistance Treaty between Ireland and the United States.[99] However, the Eastern District of Pennsylvania took a different approach, holding that Google must disclose information stored overseas on the cloud to law enforcement officials with a valid Fourth Amendment warrant.[100] Both courts gave extensive consideration regarding extraterritorial application of US law, with the latter concluding that overseas storage does not matter because disclosure is occurring in US territory. The Google court also noted that the information would not otherwise be subject to jurisdiction, because it is stored on the cloud and bounces around jurisdictions. The exceptional nature of the Internet begs the question of when it is appropriate, and what procedural mechanisms should be used, for law enforcement to access data stored overseas.

The second case involving important questions of jurisdiction is the emerging right to be forgotten in certain countries and regions, including the EU, Russia, Turkey, South Korea, and Nicaragua (Lynch 2016). Although European countries recognize a right to be forgotten, a question remains as to whether countries can enforce this individual right on a global scale. This debate rose to a level of international importance when French data protection officials asserted authority over Google and ordered them to de-list information from searches globally (Hern 2015). Google had already de-listed the information in France, but they refused to comply with the global order, arguing that France was asserting authority to sensor search results around the world and setting a dangerous international precedent.[101] The right to be forgotten fosters an important dialogue on how far a country can go toward protecting the privacy rights of their citizens. With the implementation of the GDPR in 2018, this question of jurisdiction only became greater, because the right to erasure codified what is colloquially referred to as 'the right to be forgotten.'[102] Because of the extraterritorial scope of the regulation,[103] this right has far greater reach than that which previous laws had allowed.

Conclusion

Although cybersecurity is often thought of as presenting primarily technical challenges, in reality the factors that contribute to weak security are as much related to individual and institutional behaviour and the incentives for changing that than to any technology. Economic and other market incentives for good cybersecurity behaviour are often too weak or misaligned to deliver effective resilience. Despite this widely recognized reality, policymakers and regulators have been hesitant to deploy laws and regulations, despite the fact that these are the basic elements of most nations' approaches to other broad societal challenges. Even where legal requirements exist—most commonly in data protection laws— there has been a widespread reluctance to enforce them aggressively. As the number and severity of cyberattacks escalate, this is slowly beginning to change, and we are witnessing both increased enforcement of existing laws and regulations as well as new requirements being considered, and in some cases adopted, around the globe. Law is unlikely to ever get ahead of cybersecurity or data protection challenges. The outstanding question is how close it can come to catching up.

Notes

1. *Guidelines* Governing the Protection of Privacy and Transborder Flows of Personal Data, OECD Doc. C(80)58/Final. 23 September 1980.
2. *Guidelines* on the Protection, Preface.
3. *Guidelines* on the Protection, 7–15.
4. Amended Proposal for a Council Directive on the Protection of Individuals with Regard to the Processing of Personal Data and on the Free Movement of Such Data, *Commission of the European Communities*, COM(92) 422 Final SYN 287. 15 October 1992.
5. Working Document on Transfers of Personal Data to Third Countries: Applying Articles 25 and 26 of the EU Data Protection Directive, *Working Party on the Protection of Individuals with Regard to the Processing of Personal Data*, 24 July 1998.
6. Regulation of the European Parliament and of the Council on the Protection of Natural Persons with Regard to the Processing of Personal Data and on the Free Movement of Such Data, and Repealing Directive 95/46/EC (General Data Protection Regulation), Council of the European Union, 6 April 2016 (hereafter GDPR).
7. Regulation of the European Parliament. art. 32.
8. Privacy Online: A Report to Congress, Federal Trade Commission, 1998: 7.
9. Privacy Online, 7.

10. Privacy Online, 10.
11. *APEC Privacy Framework*, 8–19.
12. Federal Trade Commission Act, 15 U.S.C. § 45(n).
13. FTC v. Wyndham Worldwide Corp., 799 F.3d 236 (3d Cir. 2015).
14. California Civil Code § 1798.29 (2003).
15. 2018 Security Breach Legislation, National Conference of State Legislatures, 8 February 2019.
16. Massachusetts Gen. Laws Ann. ch. 93H, § 1(a) (2007).
17. Massachusetts Gen. Laws Ann. ch. 93H, § 1(a) (2007).
18. See Computer & Internet Law—Privacy & Security: Personally Identifying Data Security, *LexisNexis 50-State Survey,* December 2016.
19. See Computer & Internet Law.
20. Health Insurance Portability and Accountability Act, H.R. Rep. No. 104–736 (31 July 1996), § 261, at 89.
21. See Report to Congress on Health IT Progress: Examining the HITECH Era and the Future of Health IT, Department of Health and Human Services, 2016.
22. 45 C.F.R. § 164.404(b) (2009).
23. 45 C.F.R. § 164.408(b) (2009).
24. 45 C.F.R. § 164.406(a) (2009).
25. 16 C.F.R. § 318 (2009).
26. Gramm-Leach-Bliley Act, 12 U.S.C. § 502(a) (2012).
27. Interagency Guidance on Response Programs for Unauthorized Access to Customer Information and Customer Notice, 70 Fed. Reg. 15,736, 29 March 2005.
28. Preparing for and Responding to a Breach of Personally Identifiable Information, Office of Management and Budget (3 January 2017).
29. US-CERT Federal Incident Notification Guidelines, Cybersecurity and Infrastructure Security Agency (1 April 2017), https://www.us-cert.gov/incident-notification-guidelines.
30. Data Security and Breach Notification Act of 2015, H.R. Rep. No. 114–908 (3 January 2017): 9.
31. Personal Information and Protection Act, art. 34(1) (29 March 2011): http://koreanlii.or.kr/w/images/0/0e/KoreanDPAct2011.pdf
32. Personal Information and Protection Act, art. 2(1).
33. Personal Information and Protection Act, art. 2(1).
34. Personal Information and Protection Act, art. 75.
35. GDPR, art. 33.
36. GDPR, art. 34.
37. GDPR, art. 34.
38. Directive of the European Parliament and of the Council of 12 July 2002 Concerning the Processing of Personal Data and the Protection of Privacy in the Electronic Communications Sector (Directive on Privacy and Electronic Communications), 2002/58/EC, 12 July 2002: art. 4.
39. *Global Guide to Breach Notifications,* World Law Group, 2016.
40. *Guide to Managing Data Breaches,* Personal Data Protection Commission, May 2015: https://www.pdpc.gov.sg/docs/default-source/other-guides/guide-to-managing-data-breaches-v1-0-(080515).pdf?sfvrsn=2
41. Data Disposal Laws, *National Conference of State Legislatures,* 2019.
42. Arizona Rev. Stat. § 44-7601(F) (2006).

43. Massachusetts Gen. Laws Ch. 931, § 2(b) (2007).
44. 16 C.F.R. § 682.3(a) (2004).
45. 16 C.F.R. § 682.3(b) (2004).
46. GDPR, art. 4(2).
47. *Guide to Disposal of Personal Data on Physical Medium*, Personal Data Protection Commission, July 2016.
48. *Guide to Securing Personal Data in Electronic Medium*, Personal Data Protection Commission, July 2016.
49. Protection of 'Critical Infrastructure' and the Role of Investment Policies Relating to National Security,' OECD, May 2008: 3.
50. Protection of 'Critical Infrastructure'.
51. Protection of 'Critical Infrastructure'.
52. Protecting America's Critical Infrastructure, PDD-63, 22 May 1998.
53. USA PATRIOT Act, 42 U.S.C. § 5195(e) (2001).
54. Improving Critical Infrastructure on Cybersecurity Exec. Order 13,363, 12 February 2013.
55. Critical Infrastructure Security and Resilience, Pres. Policy Directive-21, 12 February 2013.
56. Framework for Improving Critical Infrastructure Cybersecurity, NIST, 12 February 2014.
57. 'Trends in Security Framework Adoption: A Survey of IT and Security Professionals', Dimensional Research, March 2016.
58. Strengthening the Cybersecurity of Federal Networks and Critical Infrastructure, Exec. Order 13,800, 11 May 2017.
59. Strengthening the Cybersecurity § 2(d).
60. Strengthening the Cybersecurity § 3(a).
61. Cybersecurity and Infrastructure Security Agency Act, 6 U.S.C. § 652 (2018).
62. *Communication from the Commission on a European Programme for Critical Infrastructure Protection*, Commission of the European Communities, COM(2006) 786, 12 December 2006: 3 (hereafter 'Communication on CIP').
63. Communication on CIP, 4.
64. Communication from the Commission to the European Parliament, the Council, the European Economic and Social Committee and the Committee of the Regions, Commission Work Programme 2020, COM(2020) 37, 29 January 2020.
65. Critical National Infrastructure, 2017.
66. Regulations for Safety Protection of Computer Information Systems, Decree No. 147 (China, February 1994).
67. Overview of China's Cybersecurity Law, *KPMG*, February 2017: 3.
68. Ghana National Cyber Security Policy & Strategy, Ministry of Communications, March 2014. (Defining CI as sectors vital to national economic strength, national image, national defence and security, government function, and public health and safety).
69. 'Keeping Australia's Critical Infrastructure Secure', Attorney General Joint Media Release, 23 January 2017.
70. Cybersecurity Information Sharing Act, Pub. L. No. 114-113, §§ 101-11, 114th Cong. (2015) (hereafter 'CISA').
71. Privacy and Civil Liberties Final Guidelines: Cybersecurity Information Sharing Act of 2015, Dept. of Homeland Security & Dept. of Justice, 15 June 2016.
72. CISA, § 105.
73. CISA, § 106.
74. Communication on CIP, 2006: 6.

75. Communication on CIP, 2006: 6.
76. See N. Purtova (2017) 'Between GDPR and the Policy Directive: Navigating through the Maze of Information Sharing in Public-Private Partnerships,' *Working Paper*: 24.
77. Press Release: Wyden: Cybersecurity Bill Lacks Privacy Protections, Doesn't Secure Networks, Senator Ron Wyden, 12 March 2015.
78. Privacy and Civil Liberties Final Guidelines: Cybersecurity Information Sharing Act of 2015, Department. of Homeland Security and Department of Justice, 15 June 2016: 9.
79. Privacy and Civil Liberties Final Guidelines, pp. 11–12.
80. See Computer Fraud and Abuse Act, Pub. L. No. 99-474 (1986).
81. Computer Fraud and Abuse Act, 18 U.S.C. § 1030(e)(2) (2012) (hereafter CFAA).
82. CFAA, 18 U.S.C. § 1030(a)(1)-(7).
83. CFAA, 18 U.S.C. § 1030(c), (g).
84. 'Memorandum to the United States Attorneys and Assistant Attorney Generals for the Criminal and National Security Divisions', Office of the Attorney General, 11 September 2014.
85. 201 Mass. Code Regs. § 17.03(1) (2009).
86. 201 Mass. Code Regs. § 17.04(3) (2009).
87. 23 NYCRR § 500.05 (2017).
88. 23 NYCRR § 500.12 (2017).
89. 23 NYCRR § 500.15 (2017).
90. Cybersecurity Legislation 2019, National Conference of State Legislatures (10 January 2020).
91. See Greenberg, P. 2016. 'Trends in State Cybersecurity Laws & Legislation', National Conference of State Legislatures. https://iapp.org/resources/article/trends-in-state-cybersecurity-laws-legislation/
92. Computer Crime Statutes, National Conference of State Legislatures (24 February 2020).
93. Cybersafety, *State of California Office of the Attorney General* (2017), https://oag.ca.gov/cybersafety.
94. California Civil Code, § 1798.150(a)(1) (2018), SB-1121, California Consumer Privacy Act of 2018.
95. *Overview of China's Cybersecurity Law*, KPMG, February 2017: 7.
96. *Overview of China's Cybersecurity Law*, 12.
97. *Overview of China's Cybersecurity Law*, 13.
98. *Overview of China's Cybersecurity Law*, 14.
99. In the Matter of a Warrant to Search a Certain E-Mail Account Controlled and Maintained by Microsoft Corporation, 829 F.3d 197 (2d Cir. 2016).
100. In re Search Warrant No. 16-960-M-01 to Google, 2017 WL 471564 (E.D. Pa. 3 February 2017).
101. Hern, 'Google Says Non'.
102. GDPR, art. 17.
103. GDPR, art. 4.

References

Cate, F., and Dockery, R. 2018. 'Artificial Intelligence and Data Protection: Observations on a Growing Conflict', *Seoul National University Journal of Law & Economic Regulation* 11 (2): 107–130.

Columbus, L. 2019. '10 Charts That Will Change Your Perspective of AI in Security', *Forbes*, 4 November.

Edelman, G. 2020. 'California's Privacy Law Goes Into Effect Today. Now What?' *WIRED*, 1 January.

Fry, J. 2015. 'Privacy, Predictability, and Internet Surveillance in the U.S. and China: Better the Devil You Know?', *University of Pennsylvania Journal of International Law* 37: 419.

Gabel, D., and Schuba, M. 2015. 'Germany Rolls Out IT Security Act', *White & Case Technology*, 18 August.

Greenberg, A. 2018. 'An AI That Reads Privacy Policies So That You Don't Have To', *WIRED*, 9 February.

Hern, A. 2015. 'Google Says Non to French Demand to Expand Right to Be Forgotten Worldwide', *The Guardian*, 30 July.

Kean, T., and Hamilton, L. 2014. *The 9/11 Commission Report: Final Report of the National Commission on Terrorist Attacks Upon the United States.* New York: W.W. Norton & Company.

Lynch, G. 2016. 'Could a Right to Be Forgotten Online Kill Libraries?', Bloomberg Law: Privacy & Data Security, Bloomberg BNA, 17 October 2016. https://www.bna.com/right-forgotten-online-n57982078697/

Personal Data Protection Commission. 2016. *Guide to Disposal of Personal Data on Physical Medium*, July.

Personal Data Protection Commission. 2015. *Guide to Managing Data Breaches*, May.

Personal Data Protection Commission. 2016. *Guide to Securing Personal Data in Electronic Medium*, July.

Shackelford, S., and Craig, A. 2014. 'Beyond the "Digital Divide": Analyzing the Evolving Role of National Governments in Internet Governance and Enhancing Cybersecurity', *Stanford Journal of International Law* 50: 119.

Stoddart, K. 2016. 'UK Cyber Security and Critical National Infrastructure Protection', *International Affairs* 92: 1079.

CHAPTER 21

THE 'INSIDER THREAT' AND THE 'INSIDER ADVOCATE'

MIKE STEINMETZ

INTRODUCTION: WHAT IS THE INSIDER THREAT?

THIEVES, criminals, traitors: just a few of the titles assigned to a demographic of humans who enter and exit workplaces around the world having wilfully altered the confidentiality, integrity, and accessibility of critical digital systems and data. Add to that demographic the unskilled, unknowing, or untrained humans who unwittingly become a disruptive entity within the digital environment and a definition of the insider threat begins to emerge. Leadership around the world now has a clearly identifiable hazard labelled the 'insider threat'. The insider threat brings uncertainty into the workplace, disrupting controls on security, reducing both productivity and profitability within the private sector, and, within government, eroding confidence and the esprit de corps upon which our citizenship and loyalties are built at great sacrifice. Then, there is the act itself: dysfunctional and costly. Within government organizations, the hope is that such acts do not cause grave or serious harm to the government or, worse yet, loss of life. In the private sector, the reputational costs alone begin to mount as both government and private sector organizations ask the inevitable question: how could this have been prevented? That single question now drives research and a growing body of published work addressing the many aspects of the insider threat, the results of which present readers with daunting tasks: how to sort it all out, make sense of it, and take action? When does the thought (intention) to do something turn into a commitment to act? How wide is the gap between human intention and a human committing an act? Thinking of, or even discussing, a malicious act does not mean one would actually carry out such an act. However, does knowledge of such latent intent inform a useful dialogue that could serve to reduce the likelihood of an insider attack?

Technological advances that leverage the growing body of knowledge regarding behaviour-based analytics and big data analytics provide very promising approaches that both identify insider threats in finer, more useful detail and offer paths to remediation. A recent publication by the US Intelligence and National Security Alliance (INSA), 'assessing the mind of the malicious insider: using a behavioral model and data analytics to improve continuous evaluation' (Allen et al. 2017), provides the reader with a synthesis of the behavioural and psychological aspects of the malicious insider. The INSA publication (Allen et al. 2017) concludes with five recommendations to 'integrate behavioural models, employee management, and new technology to identify and mitigate insider threats before they progressed down the critical path to malicious acts'. As with the INSA paper, most of the more recent publications follow the rapidly maturing field of the psychology of the worker and the technical means by which behaviours can be identified digitally and then synthesized (Shaw and Stock 2011). Considering the amount of research regarding the psychology of the worker and dysfunctional behaviour in the workplace, it may now be possible to widen or enlarge the dataset, enabling a synthesis of all employee psychological and behavioural data incorporating the broader aspects of behavioural consistency and other personality and behavioural factors (Ajzen 2011). The larger dataset could then be analysed through advanced technology, so that compromise of company or government interests could be stopped or reduced before harm occurs. Studies and publications within the past 10 years present methods for predicting and changing deviant behaviours (Fishbein and Ajzen 2010). More recent white papers, such as the INSA papers published in 2014 and 2017, build on the considerable body of work published by E.D. Shaw, K.G. Ruby, and many others (Cappelli et al. 2013). Thus, both the behavioural paths open to the malicious insider, and the technological capabilities that can turn qualitative assessments of human behaviours into structured quantitative analytics that can operate within the digital environment and inform decision making, are continuing to evolve and mature.

Threat and Opportunity

Most reading this chapter would agree that the threat from an insider is not hypothetical: it is a real threat upon which there are abundant verifiable data. Bob Gourley, a former government chief technology officer and former leader of intelligence support to cyber defence policies in the United States, lists five basic threats in his book, *The Cyber Threat*: national governments, industrial spies and organized crime groups, terrorist and extremist groups, hackers and activists, and *trusted insiders* (Gourley 2014). Similarly, Frank Greitzer and Ryan Hohimer of the Pacific Northwest National Laboratory, in a paper entitled 'Modeling Human Behavior to Anticipate Insider Attacks', quote surveys from the US Department of Defense (beginning in 1997), detailing that more than half of security breaches 'were either employees or others internal to the organization' (Greitzer and Hohimer 2011). The threat would seem to be both severe and enduring, at least judging by the number of leading communications and Internet service providers drafting entire reports on the insider threat.

Greitzer and Hohimer pose a question that is especially germane to this chapter: 'Can we pick up the trail before the fact?' In other words, in the complex, fast-moving and continually evolving digital world, in which government and commercial organizations become ever more digitally dependent and inter-dependent, is there enough time and sufficiently accurate oversight to ensure timely and effective intervention and prevention of an insider attack?

This chapter will travel the road occupied by the current body of work before pausing to look back at the entire workforce and the factors affecting the entire workplace environment.

What we see when looking back indicates that science and technology have addressed some difficult and daunting topics, providing new capabilities and interesting frameworks that identify the complex behaviours associated with the insider threat. For Greitzer and Hohimer, picking up the trail before the fact means identifying the decisive behaviour before the dysfunctional act takes place. Their approach infers that there is indeed a trail to pick up. But, what if there are other indicators, early warnings, and trails (some more obvious than others, perhaps), that, when combined with a technological focus on the threat, will provide leadership with opportunities to create the future they wish to have rather than focusing so intensely on elements that they could have changed had they the knowledge and tools to do so? Leadership could better measure and shape the work environment enhancing employee commitment. Through better measurement and shaping leadership then creates a different work environment for employees. Failing to utilize every metric available, and every opportunity to shape the work environment, results in a missed opportunity. What opportunity is leadership overlooking?

LEADERSHIP

While observing the ever more intelligent displays of behaviour analysis and the evolving sophistication of the technology, it became clear that one element of the analysis was under-represented: what about all the other insiders? Gallup has been measuring employee attitudes within the workplace for a number of years. It analyses the data from its workplace surveys and divides employees into three groups: engaged, neither engaged or disengaged, and actively disengaged. Actively disengaged employees are characterized as 'employees [that] aren't just unhappy at work, they are busy acting out their unhappiness. Everyday these workers undermine what their engaged co-workers accomplish.' What about the employees who are engaged and committed, and do not indulge in challenging or threatening behaviour? Equally, what can be said of the large body of employees who are ambivalent? The malicious insider (most likely a person actively disengaged in the organization) is the employee with the lowest barrier to move from intention to volition to action (Fishbein and Ajzen 2010, 48–61). When examining the literature on organizational behaviour and citizenship, and then comparing that literature with the results produced by new technology that identifies and mitigates insider threats, it becomes clear that the technology and analytics approach sampled a workforce environment that was simply too narrow and/ or too functionally specific to tell a complete story. Intuitively at least, it must be the case that there are environmental elements of the workplace that could turn ambivalent workers into disengaged workers or, at worst, introduce levels of uncertainty and instability causing fully committed workers to question their previously unwavering commitment to an organization. In short, the phenomenon that was under-represented in much of the literature (whatever the author's discipline or initial perspective) was the effect of workplace dynamics on organizational behaviours (Colquitt, LePine, and Wesson, 2015). In these circumstances, as challenges evolve and as it becomes ever clearer that the responses to such challenges must be cross-domain in character, it becomes ever more necessary to grow the technological capability to identify and isolate the insider threat. Additionally, leadership must begin to identify and assess the many different behaviours that can be found in the workplace. Particular effort must be made to identify those environmental features of the workplace that underpin high levels of commitment, engagement, and corporate citizenship (Organ, Podsakoff, and MacKenzie, 2006). Finally, leadership must also address the largest demographic within any organization: those employees categorized as neither engaged nor disengaged, but ambivalent (Gallup, 2018).

WORKING ENVIRONMENT

Looking inside many different organizations (academic, national government, military, intelligence community, the private sector, and state government) reveals myriad individual and group behaviours taking place within them. Many, if not all, of the individual behaviours identified in the studies referenced in this chapter are readily observable in many workplaces, whatever the functional specialism. Similarly, it is relatively easy to see the merit of technological strides being made to identify behaviours before organizations incur harm. That said, while the growing technological capacity to identify a propensity to do harm is impressive, this is not the only important consideration. What must also be included in the analysis are those features of the working environment that relate to all employees and that are under the control of the leadership of the organization concerned. Employing some of the approaches to measuring uncertainty set out by Douglas Hubbard and Richard Seiersen in their book, *How to measure anything in cybersecurity risk* (Hubbard and Seiersen, Chs 10, 11, 2016), by taking a closer look at the workplace dynamics and the workplace environment (both of which, importantly, are under the control of the organization's leadership), it should be possible to improve at least the contextual element of our assessment of the possible behavioural path of every employee. It then becomes possible not only for the analyst to suggest a range of possible outcomes for any given employee or insider, but also for the organization's leadership to act on that advice. One such approach Hubbard and Seirsen use falls under their operations security metrics model where they describe the beneficial outcomes of employing prescriptive analytics. Their comparison with other analytical approaches is best represented in a direct quote from Chapter 10 of their book:

> ... in short, prescriptive analytics runs multiple models from both data and decision science realms and provides optimized recommendations for decision-making. When done in a big data and stream analytics context these decisions can be done in real time and in some cases take actions on your behalf—approaching artificial intelligence.

The benefits of prescriptive analytics increase with the need to run multiple models simultaneously; models which must embrace data and decision science, where near real-time actions could aid leadership decision making. An approach such as this assumes that everyone in the workplace is a part of the datasets: everyone is then an insider. With a closely defined sample set such as this, it then becomes possible to observe and then measure the propensity for individual dysfunctional behaviour based on both advanced technological means (such as UEBA [User and Entity Behaviour Analytics], employee [or any user] monitoring, and Data Centric Audit and Protection [DCAP]),[1] and, more traditional observations of organizational behaviour and organizational citizenship (Colquitt, LePine, and Wesson, 2015); Organ, Podsakoff, and MacKenzie, 2006). Such an approach is more than merely a 'prove good' approach (an approach that would assume all employees are bad) if leaders are willing not only to interrogate but also to act upon insider behaviours on the basis that these behaviours may be directly affected by workplace dynamics and environmental factors over which leadership has a decisive level of control. This crucial element of leadership responsibility for variables within the workplace environment—variables that can have the preferred effect of nudging employees in the direction of greater corporate citizenship and positive organizational behaviours—appears under-represented in the highly technical calculus of identifying the insider threat. To repeat, this is not to suggest that technological advancements have no place in the assessment of the insider threat. Far from it: this chapter takes precisely the opposite view, that the value of technology to identify the propensity to do harm is both impressive and necessary. Yet, while technology is a necessary component in the fight against the insider threat, it is not sufficient. There is no shortage of theoretical and practical works focusing on behaviours within the workplace, in which the psychological predisposition to display dysfunctional or negative behaviours is set out in detail. The work of Shaw and Stock in 2011 is just one of many. The central argument of this chapter, however, is to suggest that an organization's leadership can exploit the fact that it controls and can maximize those features of the workplace environment known to have a positive, affirming effect on employees. Leadership can then use advanced technological means to measure positive effects, rather than simply to warn against negative inclination.

The measurement of the effect of variables under leadership control would highlight the opportunity cost of *not* taking such measures. Alternatively, a *measurement of such effects* in a 'measurement-action-measurement' loop could be considered a hedge, reducing the risk of an insider moving from intention to volition. For leadership to be able to measure the effect of these measures on organizational behaviour and organizational citizenship, they must have available to them data that encompass the inevitabilities and broader effects of our socially and technologically connected world—to the extent, of course, that these data are available, comprehensive, and reliable. It is already the case that the ability of social media to extend the workplace into the private lives and spaces of employees is being fully leveraged as an element of leadership communication (Coine and Babbitt 2014). It is then both logical and necessary to consider how the digital extension of our workplace into other aspects of our personal and professional life might contribute to both our best and our worst behavioural inclinations— providing technological sanctuary for disinhibition (Lapidot-Lefler and Barak 2015) on the one hand and opportunities for positive social outcomes, such as crowdfunding for disaster relief, on the other. The evolution of technological solutions that locate, isolate, and identify complex insider threat behaviours must continue to evolve. However, there could be more dynamics at play in the workplace with respect to individual and group behaviours within an organization. Effective identification of those workplace dynamics and environmental influences, and the integration and synthesis of these dynamics and influences with modern technological solutions, might provide leadership with a higher-fidelity, more-rounded picture of the insider. Looking at all employees as insiders with the daily potential to adopt either more positive or more negative behaviours could provide leadership with a behavioural engineering method to systematically and reliably quantify the uncertainty residing within each individual every day. The only passably scientific and reliable way to quantify the full range of behaviours open to an individual (insider) is to break down and systematically reconstruct all the elements (or as many as possible) that could drive an individual's patterns of behaviour in the workplace.

INSIDER AMBIVALENCE

Only a continuous breaking down and rebuilding of the organizational model can provide a comprehensive and faithful account of the wide range of options open to a person (i.e. employee) on any given day. Here, John Boyd's work (Boyd 1976) continues to be germane. Any model that deliberately, or even merely knowingly, overlooks an element that could influence the behaviour of an insider risks being a casualty to the element overlooked. One such behaviour that is much less discussed (perhaps even overlooked) is *insider ambivalence* (Gallup 2018). What can be said of the co-worker whose inclinations are not readily classified and whom we might label ambivalent? What conclusions should be drawn with respect to insiders who do not display negative behaviours yet (given a certain sequence of personal or professional events or activities in their work or personal environment) might have the propensity to move from what we might label as neutral ambivalence to posing an insider threat? If it could be shown that workplace dynamics and environmental features—those factors that are under the control of the organization's leadership—could have the potential to change insider behaviour from one category to another, could there be a case for a deeper analysis to be made, or for some attempt to synthesize qualitative behavioural analysis with other more technical modalities? If so, then a committed effort by leadership to monitor an organization's environment and the (collective and individual) behaviours within it, could work in a pre-emptive manner to ensure, *at a minimum*, that the intent of the 'ambivalent insider' at least remains ambivalent rather than move across the line to negative volition (Fishbein and Ajzen 2010). Having taken this step, it should then be possible to monitor and modulate aspects of the work environment in order to change insider behaviours from ambivalent to committed. Leadership would then have the opportunity to focus on those features of the organization's working environment that most directly affect employee behaviours. Leadership could then couple data from these observations with other technological means to produce a more informed picture of the range of employee behaviours within their organization.

It is not uncommon to come across individuals with a high level of organizational commitment, and an admirably positive sense of organizational citizenship, nevertheless becoming increasingly ambivalent in response to environmental dynamics and factors under the control and discretion of the organization's leadership, and to sudden, unexpected changes in the organization's direction. Examples of the latter might include surprise announcements on a change in leadership—pending merger and acquisition, for example—or changes to salary bands, pension plans, and other internal reorganizations. In many cases, it is often less a matter of *what* happened than *how* and *why* it happened that is the focus of employee concern. Examples of sub-optimal internal communication of this sort, where the organization's leadership is also considered to be wholly responsible for the decision and its outcome, could include suspected discrimination based on gender, religion, or sexual orientation, or more hostile examples such as sexual harassment or verbal abuse. In cases such as these, it is also worth asking whether the leadership makes changes and/or announcements with as much concern for the internal reaction (of employees) as for the external reaction (of shareholders and other stakeholders). Does leadership fully understand the impact of their actions on employees' organizational commitment? While many, or even most, of these environmental dynamics and factors are under the control of the organization's leadership, some allowance should be made, by employees, shareholders, and other observers, for the fact that sometimes change is unavoidable, and sometimes it is the only way for an organization to improve (or, indeed, to survive). But these allowances cannot be made if the reasons for these decisions and changes of direction are not communicated properly, sensitively, and in a timely fashion. The 'What' can be unavoidable but the 'Why' cannot be beyond explanation, and the 'How' is in most cases under the control of an organization's leadership. A more reflective and better communicated approach of this sort can be a powerful tool in shaping the working environment for the better and future-proofing the organization's behaviour against the insider threat.

Next Steps

The first requirement is for more information about the study of organizational behaviour and organizational citizenship, and how these topics feature in organizational change management (Cameron and Green 2015). A review of select publications regarding the insider threat and the effect of social media on employees in the workplace would serve as a starting point to clarify some of the realities of the twenty-first-century workplace (e.g. Coine and Babbitt 2014; Wagner, 2015; Colquitt, LePine, and Wesson 2015; Organ, Podsakoff, and MacKenzie 2006). It would also be beneficial to provide examples of how organizations predict dysfunctional behaviour and, finally, which steps should be taken and what metrics are available with which to measure the desired change. This chapter proposes an approach that centres on an organization's working environment, which, if monitored and shaped, could contribute to a higher level of employee commitment to an organization. In theory, the combination of organizational behavioural analysis with a technological capacity for psychological profiling of insider behaviour should yield enough data for metrics development and verification of alternative methods (i.e. the combination with other disciplines and approaches) worthy of further study. In short, an organization should study its workplace environmental dynamics not narrowly, or in a defensive sense, but more expansively as they relate to *positive* organizational behaviour and organizational citizenship. The leadership of an organization should also examine their workplace environment as it relates to leadership actions under their direct control; examples are listed earlier. Leadership should better understand all changes in the workplace environment and their employee's perspectives upon the workplace. Leadership should consider how their decisions are viewed through the lens of all enagaged and critical observers, and particularly their own insiders. What is vitally important is for the leadership to consider—and explain—not just the 'What' but also the 'Why' and the 'How'. Before-and-after measurements should be taken so that leadership may determine what synthesized set of controls to employ in any future scenarios. Once those controls are in place, leadership may then determine what steps are needed to increase an employee's organizational citizenship and commitment. Not doing so suggests an opportunity missed: an opportunity that could have created greater insider advocacy.

CREATE THE DESIRED OUTCOME

Industry is working hard to create the policies and practices necessary to counter the insider threat: work that should be encouraged and facilitated wherever possible. That said, care must be taken to avoid falling into the trap of categorical thinking (Sapolsky 2018). In his book, *Behave: The Biology of Humans at our Best and Worst*, Dr Sapolsky describes the trap of categorical thinking in the following way: 'In other words, when you think categorically, you have trouble seeing how similar or different two things are. If you pay lots of attention to where boundaries are, you pay less attention to complete pictures.' While the focus on malicious or dysfunctional behaviour must continue, there is a risk that other workplace demographics might be overlooked. These demographics—representing the engaged/committed and dependable, together with the ambivalent and malleable—represent the largest set of employees inside any organization (Gallup 2018). All employees should be considered first as insiders and the task of the organization's leadership is then to identify where there is risk. When considered against a standard risk X–Y graph where the likelihood or probability of an event taking place is on the vertical axis [lowest to highest, bottom to top] and the impact of an event taking place within an organization is plotted on the horizontal axis [lowest to highest, left to right], low, medium, and high risk are then plotted on a line bisecting the right angle of the graph. 'Low' risk resides at the junction of the X–Y axis, 'medium' half-way up the bisecting line, and 'high' (or critical risk) depicted at the end of the line. The most critical risks are then found when plotted as high likelihood' and 'high impact'. Leadership can reduce risk by addressing each or both. In our example, leadership would now be focused on identifying and reducing the likelihood of someone becoming an insider threat, which would move the risk down vertically with the impact remaining the same (in this case). One can now visualize that, regardless of the intent (wilful or unwitting), the impact metric remains largely the same. However, the chance of that event happening has been reduced. Thus, when a cyber-related incident takes place, the impact can be the same whether committed by somebody actively disengaged from, and dysfunctional within, the organization (with a risk rating of 'high likelihood') or triggered by a person or circumstance previously assessed as 'low likelihood' but with a rapidly changing (and deteriorating) risk profile. The variable in these risk assessments is the dynamic that causes the movement in likelihood. And, for an individual, it is that variable that moves the person from intention to volition. Leadership would be well served to ask themselves what they can or should do every day to create an environment that increases those affirming, trusting, and positive aspects of the work environment, increasing organizational commitment, corporate citizenship, and employee satisfaction. These factors are largely found within the disciplines of organizational behaviour and behavioural engineering, and can be used in ways to create the company insider who is both engaged and committed. Leadership must view their overarching control of the dynamics of the workplace environment as an opportunity to turn insider ambivalents into insider advocates. By these means, the leadership of an organization can decrease workplace uncertainty and suspicion, providing more opportunity to create higher levels of commitment and corporate citizenship.

Conclusion

The first task for the leadership of organizations in both the public and private sectors should be to leverage investments made in technology that focus on locating the malicious insider. Those capabilities should then be merged with the other workplace modalities mentioned in this chapter. The result would provide a model for a more complete analysis of the workplace environment, how that environment reacts to the various dynamics found in the twenty-first-century workplace, and what effects it might have on the worker. The data and model will then show leadership gaps and opportunities. Some gaps will prove to be opportunities to create a more committed workforce. All opportunities that enhance organizational commitment and corporate citizenship are opportunities to create insider advocates.

Note

1. Gartner: https://blogs.gartner.com/avivah-litan/2018/04/05/insider-threat-detection-replaces-dying-dlp/

References

Ajzen, Icek. 2011. *Attitudes, Personality and Behavior*. Maidenhead, UK: McGraw-Hill/Open University Press.

Allen, Charlie, Katherine Hibbs Pherson, Doug Thomas et al. 2017. 'Assessing the Mind of the Malicious Insider: Using a Behavioral Model and Data Analytics to Improve Continuous Evaluation'. Intelligence and National Security Alliance. 4 April. https://www.insaonline.org/wp-content/uploads/2017/04/INSA_WP_Mind_Insider_FIN.pdf

Boyd, J. 1976. 'Destruction and Creation'. http://www.goalsys.com/books/documents/DESTRUCTION_AND_CREATION.pdf

Cameron, Esther, and Mike Green. 2015. *Making Sense of Change Management: A Complete Guide to the Models, Tools and Techniques of Organizational Change*. 4th edn. London: Kogan Page, Kindle edition.

Cappelli, Dawn, Zalmai Azmi, Steve Coppinger, et al. 2013. 'A Preliminary Examination of Insider Threat Programs in the U.S. Private Sector'. September. https://www.insaonline.org/wp-content/uploads/2017/04/INSA_InsiderThreat_WP.pdf

Coine, Ted, and Mark Babbitt. 2014. *A World Gone Social: How Companies Must Adapt to Survive*. New York: AMACOM, American Management Association, Kindle edition.

Colquitt, Jason A., Jeffery A. LePine, and Michael J. Wesson. 2015. *Organizational Behavior: Improving Performance and Commitment in the Workplace*. 5th edn. New York: McGraw-Hill Education, Kindle edition.

Fishbein, Martin, and Icek Ajzen. 2010. *Predicting and Changing Behavior: The Reasoned Action Approach*. New York: Psychology Press.

Gallup. 2018. 'State of the American Workplace'. https://news.gallup.com/reports/199961/state-american-workplace-report-2017.aspx

Gourley, Bob. 2014. *The Cyber Threat and the Role of Cyber Intelligence in Defending Your Organization*. Online publication: https://www.createspace.com/

Greitzer, Frank L., and Ryan E. Hohimer. 2011. 'Modeling Human Behavior to Anticipate Insider Attacks', *Journal of Strategic Security*, summer, 4 (2): 25–48, 1. http://dx.doi.org/10.5038/1944-0472.4.2.2

Hubbard, Douglas W., and Richard Seiersen. 2016. *How to Measure Anything in Cybersecurity Risk*. Hoboken, NJ: John Wiley & Sons, Inc.

Lapidot-Lefler, Noam, and Azy Barak. 2015. 'The Benign Online Disinhibition Effect: Could Situational Factors Induce Self-Disclosure And Prosocial Behaviors?' *Cyberpsychology: Journal of Psychosocial Research on Cyberspace*, 9 (2), Article 3. doi:10.5817/cp2015-2-3.

Organ, Dennis W., Philip M. Podsakoff, and Scott Bradley MacKenzie. 2006. *Organizational Citizenship Behavior: Its Nature, Antecedents, and Consequences*. Thousand Oaks, CA: SAGE Publications, Kindle edition.

Sapolsky, R.M. (2018). *Behave: The Biology of Humans at our Best and Worst*. Penguin Books, Kindle edition.

Shaw, E.D., and Stock, H.V. 2011. 'Behavioral Risk Indicators of Malicious Insider Theft of Intellectual Property: Misreading the Writing on the Wall.' https://zadereyko.info/downloads/Malicious_Insider.pdf

Wagner, Rodd. 2015. *Widgets: The 12 New Rules for Managing Your Employees as If They're Real People*. New York: McGraw-Hill Education, Kindle edition.

PART VI

PERSONAL CYBERSECURITY

CHAPTER 22

PERSONAL PROTECTION: 'CYBER HYGIENE'

DAVE CLEMENTE

INTRODUCTION

CYBERSECURITY is about protecting the confidentiality, integrity, and availability of data—whether these data are personally identifiable information, email, text messages, payment card details, intellectual property, or government secrets. The human element of cybersecurity is essential and cannot be ignored. Despite popular notions of the Internet as an abstract and impersonal environment, cybersecurity depends on the actions of the individual.

While automation and machine learning are becoming more advanced, there is no replacement for human experience, intuition, and decisions, and these remain key factors in the digital domain. Humans are often identified as the 'weak link' in cybersecurity. But they are also the creators of the Internet: its designers, maintainers, defenders, and attackers.

Governments and large corporations can muster significant resources to address their cybersecurity challenges, but individuals are forced to fend for themselves. This chapter is a modest attempt to redress this imbalance. It examines the basics of personal cybersecurity (often described as 'cyber hygiene'), including the protection of connected devices and personal data from malicious actors, and the consequences of poor security. It looks at a range of threat actors and their primary motivations, as well as factors that influence personal security decisions, such as perceptions or misperceptions of what is valuable.

This chapter connects discussions on security with growing debates on digital privacy and the ability to choose what personal information we want to share or keep hidden. It offers a set of tangible recommendations to help individuals make more informed cybersecurity decisions and maintain a level of cyber hygiene that is appropriate for them.

The debate on personal cybersecurity is often filled with contradictory advice, misunderstanding, and even misinformation. In many ways, this is not surprising, given humanity's brief experience with cybersecurity, relative to our long evolutionary experience with physical security (Schneier 2012). For example, the World Wide Web—the most popular and widely used application on the Internet—was publicly launched in 1993, and has turbocharged the growth in technology products and services that surround us today.[1] Rapid immersion in this new environment can be disorienting and confusing, leaving many people at a loss for trustworthy sources of information for safely navigating this indispensable environment.

It is becoming increasingly important to understand the personal implications of the Internet—its data-hungry nature, long memory, and security pitfalls—and this chapter aims to provide clarity for those wishing to manage their cyber risks more effectively.

Seeing the Big Picture

As the global economy becomes more dependent on the Internet, and as data breaches become more damaging to companies and individuals, the challenges of cybersecurity are receiving sustained attention from decision makers in both the public and the private sectors. These challenges include strategic issues of deterrence and international norm-building, as well as endemic issues such as financial fraud, identity theft, and online harassment.

These challenges reflect the unparalleled success of the Internet in enabling new ways of buying and selling, and facilitating the sharing of information with a minimum of friction, in ways that were difficult to imagine 30 years ago: 'The effect of the internet is to lower transaction costs; everything else is advertising' (Lewis 2012).

More than half the world's population is online and steadily conducting more of its daily activities via the Internet.[2] The global economy and its supporting financial infrastructure are now entirely dependent on the Internet, with little or no possibility for 'business as usual' without digital connectivity.

The ability to have non-digital contingency options—for example, using a cheque instead of a payment card—has diminished to the point where many of these options are viable only at a local level (as opposed to national or international), and sometimes not even that. Strong commercial motivations for growth and profitability mean that this trend will only continue, with business strategies eliminating non-digital contingencies and redundancies, and focusing instead on investment in Internet-enabled services such as cloud and mobile.

In many instances, the Internet and digital technology offer opportunities that the physical world cannot, making irrelevant any discussion of a non-digital backup option. Examples include transacting in cryptocurrencies, managing complex international supply chains in real time, or monitoring and identifying patterns of suspicious employee behaviour across large organizations. The Internet offers unprecedented scalability and flexibility but, as digital migration gathers pace across all sectors, the costs of disruption (either malicious or accidental) are also increasing, and personal cybersecurity is becoming a higher priority.

Security and Privacy

Privacy and security overlap on the Internet, and changes to one affect the other. One primary overlap occurs when the inner workings of Internet products and services are obscured from users, either intentionally or unintentionally, and communicated via privacy policies or terms and conditions that are lengthy and written in impenetrable legal language.

If companies are gathering personal information—and users remain unaware of this, or do not care—when these data are compromised, the effects can range from minor annoyance to identity theft and major financial fraud. Not only will the user suffer because of the insecure actions of the company, but they are also unlikely to receive notice that their data were compromised, or to know which company was at fault.

Most people use a variety of online services—for example, webmail, cloud storage or messaging—that cost nothing financially but which they pay for with data such as personal information or browsing habits. This reflects the dominant economic model of the Internet, by now so widely acknowledged that it is summed up in the cliché 'if you are not paying for it, you are the product'.

This exchange—of free services for personal data—is rarely transparent, and most people do not realize the extent of the data being collected about their online behaviour, browsing habits, shopping preferences, and contacts list—and sold and resold to a long chain of data brokers and advertisers.

Transparency around personal data collection is increasing (albeit from a very low threshold) because of an evolving European regulatory landscape and the European General Data Protection Regulation (GDPR). The GDPR gives significant data protection rights to citizens of European Union Member States, including access to personal data held by companies and governments, erasure of data, data portability, rights related to automated decision making and profiling, and numerous others.[3]

Despite the long-term improvements enacted by the GDPR, most users still have little idea of the type and volume of data they unwittingly hand over to companies (e.g. permissions given to a mobile application), and the security and privacy implications.

PRACTICALITIES OF PRIVACY

Surveys have shown that Internet users profess to value their privacy, but behave very differently in practice (Madden 2014). Despite this apparent contradiction, there are logical reasons for this behaviour.

First, for most people, most of the time, the Internet just *works*. Many online products and services are sufficiently reliable and appealing to continue attracting new users, who may not feel any ill effects from sharing their data with companies. Life on the Internet is easy if users do not care what company is collecting their browsing habits, targeting them with advertising, or following them across the web with increasingly sophisticated tracking methods.

Second, as noted earlier, there is a significant information asymmetry between users and companies that make a living from collecting personal data. Most people are unaware of the extent to which their personal data are being harvested, and have no easy method of getting clarification.

Third, many people may wish for greater privacy but consider the costs to be unreasonably burdensome and to require the abandonment of popular and convenient online activities (e.g. social media or online shopping). They may be fully aware of the data collection and feel this harms them in some way, but the practical barriers to change are too onerous and the trade-offs unpalatable: *personal data is often valued more highly by the company collecting it than the person it was collected from.*

Individuals may place little value in their browsing history, but billion-dollar companies are built on such data, so it clearly has value to someone. Personal data also have value to hackers and criminals, and here is where the poor data privacy habits of many companies can become a security problem. Business motivations make it tempting to collect as much data as possible, use what is immediately beneficial, and store the rest while searching for a way to use it. When a data breach is made public, it is often revealed that the breached company was collecting more personal data than realized by users, exchanging data with insecure third parties, or promising to delete data that it then retained indefinitely.[4]

TRADE-OFFS IN CYBERSECURITY

The challenges of protecting personal data are reflected in the tension inherent between the three preferences of the CIA Triad security model:

1. *Confidentiality*: A set of rules limiting access to information only to a set of authorized parties (often equated to privacy). This can be accomplished via encryption, passwords, biometric verification, or disconnected storage devices.
2. Integrity: Information is protected (throughout its entire life cycle) from modification by unauthorized parties (e.g. through file permissions or access controls).
3. Availability: Information is available to authorized parties when needed (e.g. through robust business continuity planning, hardware maintenance, and redundancy and fail-over options).

A company or individual cannot maximize all three of these at the same time. Instead, they must decide where their priorities lie and choose a product, service, or commercial strategy that offers the desired balance between the three.

For example, an individual can choose from a variety of free webmail services with high levels of availability (e.g. available 24/7) and integrity (e.g. emails will not be modified by unauthorized parties). In this case, a common trade-off is diminished confidentiality. The business models of many free webmail companies are dependent on scanning emails to target advertising more precisely at the interests of the account holder. Personalized advertising is often thought to be more effective at encouraging purchasing, and webmail companies can use this personalization to justify a higher price to advertisers. Confidentiality is reduced in exchange for increased availability and integrity: a trade-off that most people make every day, whether they realize it or not.

Another example is a large retail bank that strictly limits the ability of employees to access or amend the account records of high-net-worth customers. In this case, availability of the data is strictly limited and the priorities are integrity and confidentiality.

For companies, the primary challenge is to balance between these preferences while offering a competitive product to their chosen market demographic. For most people, availability of data is the overriding priority. They want to be able to access email, cloud storage, messaging, social media, and online banking easily, consistently, and without delay.

For more discriminating and security-conscious individuals, there is a growing range of products and services designed with privacy and security in mind, and which aim to give users more power over what personal data are collected and how this information is used. This variety is a welcome change but can be somewhat overwhelming for non-experts who want to secure themselves more effectively. The way forward is to conduct a realistic assessment of personal risk on the Internet.

Assessing Personal Risk

Before choosing from among the wide range of cybersecurity measures (with varying levels of time and resources required to use them), the first step is to consider what is at risk and its value. This will help to determine the appropriate amount of time and effort spent on protective measures.

Individuals often consider their personal data to be the data most valuable to them, and therefore the highest security priority. Criminals also see value in these data and other parts of an individual's digital life, including the following:

- Webmail and social media accounts, and contact lists—These are useful for gathering contact lists that, in turn, can be targeted with spam or malware (e.g. ransomware).
- Account credentials (e.g. PayPal, eBay, LinkedIn)—These have many uses, including for resale on criminal forums, sending credible-looking phishing messages to friends and followers, and gaining access to other accounts that the owner may access using the same password (it is good advice never to use the same password to access multiple sites).
- Bank account or credit card details—These are useful for bank transfer or payment card fraud, or for resale on online criminal markets.
- Reputation—Social media accounts can be hijacked and held to ransom or used to send spam to personal and professional contacts (Krebs 2012).

What is deemed valuable by a criminal may seem trivial to their victims. For example, a trail of seemingly innocuous personal details scattered across multiple social media platforms can provide criminals with the means to commit identity theft and open fraudulent lines of credit.

The examples noted earlier are only a small sample of what is valuable to criminals and other threat actors, and understanding this will help non-security experts to identify what needs to be protected.

Identifying Threat Actors

The next step to improve personal cybersecurity is to think about who would be interested in conducting a hacking attack, and why. A realistic assessment of this is essential when considering how much time and effort to invest in security. The primary threat actors include the following:

- *Amateur hackers* have low/medium capability (e.g. they are likely to buy their attack kits on the black market) and financial or ideological motivation (e.g. hacktivism).
- *Skilled hackers* have medium/high capability (e.g. they may create their own attack kits) and offer their professional services to the highest bidder (e.g. to organized crime).
- *Organized criminals* have high capability (e.g. they are likely to develop their own malware) and a high degree of patience along with financial motivation.
- *Insiders (benign)* are usually just trying to do their job, but lack security awareness or take shortcuts that make a data breach or other security incident more likely.
- *Insiders (malicious)* have valuable internal knowledge and may be disgruntled with their employer and/or be financially motivated.
- *Nation-state actors* have the highest capability, extensive funding, and a wide range of human and technical capabilities that can be combined effectively to achieve political aims.

In practical terms, most people will never be targeted by government intelligence agencies (although their data may be gathered by bulk collection, as discussed elsewhere in this *Handbook*). The insider threat is more pertinent to companies and governments, and less so to individuals (aside from those who may have upset their partner or a flatmate).

Amateur and skilled hackers, and organized criminals, have primarily financial motivations (and occasionally ideological). They pose the most immediate and persistent cybersecurity threat to individuals, and this is unlikely to change in the foreseeable future. Organized crime is also a persistent threat faced by companies across all sectors. Profit-focused attackers naturally focus on information that can be turned into cash, including financial data, payment card details, personally identifiable information, contact lists, intellectual property, and market-moving data. Some criminals freelance, the more effective ones are organized, and the most proficient ones even offer reliable customer service including guarantees, call centres, and tech support.

Some threat actors are demonstrating new levels of strategic planning, and one example of this was detailed in a 2016 US criminal case against a group of Ukrainian hackers. The hackers were accused of stealing more than 100,000 embargoed press releases (often detailing publicly traded companies' quarterly or annual earnings) over a five-year period. They then collaborated with a network of financial traders to buy or sell stocks based on this non-public information, reaping illicit profits estimated to exceed US$100 million (Newman 2016). This level of attack sophistication goes beyond what most individuals might be subjected to, but it gives an indication of how advanced non-state threat actors are becoming.

IDENTIFYING THREAT VECTORS

After identifying the most likely attackers, the next step is for an individual to better understand the most common threat vectors, or types of attack, they are likely to encounter. News reports regularly publicize exotic and niche attacks developed by security researchers, but many of these deserve the label of 'stunt hacking' (e.g. revealing a smartphone PIN code via a thermal fingerprint heat on the screen) (Waddell 2017). These attacks remain more theoretical than practical, they do not scale easily (e.g. from one-to-one to one-to-many), and they are unlikely to have any impact on most individuals.

Instead, the focus should be on dealing with the kind of attacks that are most prevalent and damaging. These attacks are rarely sophisticated or expensive, and hackers do not need to be highly skilled to be successful: They can often achieve their aims by exploiting technical vulnerabilities that are years old. This reflects the age and complexity of much of the software that runs the modern information and communications infrastructure, and the challenges faced by individuals trying to understand and manage the cyber risks they face: 'Looking for good software to count on has been a losing battle. Written by people with either no time or no money, most software gets shipped the moment it works well enough to let someone go home and see their family. What we get is mostly terrible' (Norton 2014).

Hackers are also adept at taking advantage of human nature through social engineering (i.e. manipulating or tricking people into taking an insecure action). Social engineering is a way of exploiting distraction, impatience, greed, laziness—as well as sympathy for a friend in need ('I've lost my wallet; please send money') or a desire to be effective at work ('the CEO has lost his password, please reset asap').

The human element comprises both the weakest link and the greatest point of strength in cybersecurity, depending on the individual and the circumstance. Human nature is one of the most consistently exploitable vulnerabilities in cybersecurity. While there is plenty of guidance on the most common and effective types of attacks (several of which are outlined later), the risks from human behaviour will require awareness training and close attention if they are to be managed effectively and efficiently (UK National Cyber Security Centre 2017).

PHISHING

Phishing is a common type of social engineering, and is one of the most popular and successful methods of cyberattack. Phishing is usually done via an email claiming to be from a recognized source, with the aim of tricking the recipient into opening a malicious link or attachment, or navigating to an infected website: 'Millions of accounts across the internet are regularly compromised when an attacker simply asks someone for their password' Alex Stamos (2016).

Hackers often compromise email or social media accounts and send phishing emails to everyone on the contact list, in an attempt to gain access to a computer or network. Phishing is easy to automate and far cheaper than crafting exotic exploits to hack into a network, making it useful for a wide variety of malicious actors. Individuals should be suspicious of unsolicited emails, and not click on links or open attachments contained in those emails if they have any doubt (CERT-UK 2015).

Ransomware

Phishing is being used increasingly as a method of delivering ransomware. Ransomware is a kind of malicious program that infects the victim's device and encrypts all the data, rendering the device unusable. The program then asks the victim to pay a ransom (e.g. £300 via a digital currency like Bitcoin) to unlock the data. This kind of attack is becoming widespread and is generating hundreds of millions of dollars annually in ransom payments.

Ransomware attacks affect hundreds of thousands of individuals around the globe, and cause significant business disruption for public and private sector organizations, including hospitals in the United States, local councils in the UK, and banks in India. Hackers can buy relatively inexpensive ransomware packages online, with some sellers even offering customer support to the aspiring criminals.

Getting the Basics Right

The range of possible personal cybersecurity measures is vast, but there is a finite number of basic measures that are important to consider. These basics of 'cyber hygiene' have remained largely constant, although they are evolving to keep pace with changes in technology.

Updates

Many hackers succeed thanks to technical vulnerabilities in a computer network or connected device. On some occasions, these vulnerabilities may be unknown to the device or hardware manufacturer, giving the hacker plenty of time to exploit the vulnerability before it is discovered and patched. However, it is far more common (and easier) for a hacker to exploit vulnerabilities that have been made public—for example, in home routers, PCs, and mobile devices (particularly ones that have not been updated by the owner).

It is crucial to check regularly for software updates, or heed manufacturer update notices. Security researchers and manufacturers regularly discover and publicly disclose vulnerabilities in major PC and mobile operating systems or popular applications. When a major update is released (e.g. for Android or iOS), users may need some time to become familiar with new security or privacy settings, or to change settings that may have reverted to default (Wi-Fi or Bluetooth might have been reactivated, for example).

Although many manufacturers release regular security updates, a significant proportion of people never install them, or only install them once their device is so outdated it no longer runs a preferred application without the update (e.g. some mobile banking apps). Many

Android smartphone owners are reportedly forced to wait weeks or months for an update to be made available to their device, and many of these phones are never patched.[5]

While many people have the luxury of owning well-supported devices, others are not so fortunate. This is an age where digital devices are often designed to be replaced after a pre-determined lifespan, also known as 'planned obsolescence'. This replacement cycle is due in part to the fact that rapid technology changes now render devices, such as telephones or automobiles, obsolete faster than was common through most of the twentieth century. There are also strong commercial motivations to encourage customers to upgrade regularly to the newest device (resulting in happy shareholders and consistent revenue for the company and its supply chain). However, this industry dynamic (or ethos) fails at least two groups (Hadhazy 2016):

1. Those who choose to use their devices beyond the manufacturer-supported lifetime. They may not wish to upgrade, but are forced to do so because their devices have become incompatible with services they wish to use (e.g. mobile banking).
2. Those who are forced to use an older device or operating system, either because they cannot afford the newer device/system or because the local infrastructure does not support it (e.g. inadequate 3G/4G mobile infrastructure).

These two groups are at a significant disadvantage when trying to protect themselves online. Their devices are probably running software that is approaching (or past) its end-of-life date, or is unsupported by the manufacturer. Their devices are therefore vulnerable to a wide variety of publicly known vulnerabilities. This is particularly applicable to buyers of used smartphones, and in 2016 it was predicted that at least 120 million smartphones were sold by their original owners.[6] For these owners and many others, it is crucial to download updates if they are available and to consider taking other security measures (such as those recommended in this chapter) to minimize the risks of using an outdated device.

Passwords

Passwords deserve their own chapter, given the lengthy and heated debate about them over the years. Keeping passwords safe, or merely remembering them, has proven to be such a difficult challenge that whole industries (e.g. biometrics) have arisen to alleviate the pain of password management. By itself, a password is said to be one 'factor' of authentication, out of a total of three possible factors:

1. Something the user *knows* (e.g. a password or PIN code).
2. Something the user *has* (e.g. a mobile phone or security key, the latter usually in the form of a special USB stick).[7]
3. Something the user *is* (e.g. biometric authentication, such as fingerprint or voice recognition).

Multi-factor authentication helps to increase security dramatically—for example, by using a password plus a code sent via text message to log into an account. This is becoming more common, but passwords are still the most common form of online authentication, and are used daily by most people. The only way to sign in to most online accounts is with a password, meaning that most regular Internet users might have several dozen accounts that require a password (Okyle 2015). Passwords are inescapable, at least for the present, making it advisable at least to get the basics right:

- Longer is stronger. But, with many passwords, this quickly becomes hard to remember, so ...
- Use a passphrase. This is a password that is a combination of words that are odd or humorous and therefore easily remembered. This also has the benefit of being longer than an average password.[8] Passphrases are strong, although some difficulty is added when a website requires numbers and special characters to be used. The next challenge is that individuals may have several dozen (or even a hundred!) long passwords. The temptation is to reuse the same ones again and again. Passwords should never be reused, however.
- Instead use a password manager (W. 2017). This is a heavily encrypted (and modestly priced) application that stores all an individual's passwords. It is necessary to remember only one strong password to open the program and access all other passwords. Many password managers offer a smartphone app, making it possible to synchronize passwords between desk-based computers, laptops, and mobile devices.
- Use two-factor authentication whenever possible. Two-factor authentication is offered by a growing number of websites and applications, and is often required when a user tries to log in from a new computer, mobile device, or browser.
- Change the default (manufacturer) passwords for all personal devices and network equipment—for example, PCs, routers, webcams, digital video recorders, smart TVs, and other connected devices. Tests have shown that unprotected devices (particularly ones that are not protected by a router) will be scanned and even compromised shortly after being connected to the Internet (McGill 2016). Changing default passwords helps to block malicious programs that scan the Internet looking for unsecured devices.
- Physical security still matters. For example, 'shoulder surfing' is still a common method to steal passwords in a public place.
- Login credentials should be set for all devices, particularly mobile devices. All modern mobile phones will accept a PIN code or password as a login, and many smartphones are equipped with fingerprint readers for biometric authentication.
- In addition to login credentials, most smartphones also allow a separate PIN code to be set to restrict access to data on the SIM card. The PIN code is usually set to a default by the service provider. It should be changed to something easily remembered, to prevent scammers from stealing a phone, moving the SIM card to a different phone, and dialling premium rate numbers (often set up by organized criminals) at the victim's expense (Tims 2016).

Security Software

- There is no excuse for not protecting a PC, laptop, or tablet with third-party antivirus or built-in security (e.g. Windows Defender, Apple Gatekeeper and file quarantine/malware check). These are either free (from the manufacturer) or reasonably priced.

PERSONAL PROTECTION: 'CYBER HYGIENE'   371

- Still better is to use several lines of defence—e.g. a router with a built-in firewall, together with antivirus on a PC/laptop, and (if possible) with all of them set to auto-install software updates from the manufacturer.
- Free antivirus programs are not recommended. Many collect personal data for advertising, lack the customer service and additional features of paid programs, and may cause problems with other computer programs (Quain 2017).

Browsing

- Browsers are not all created equal. Some focus on security (most of these are designed for PCs), while others offer built-in advertisement blocking and features that encourage minimal data use (designed for smartphones and data plans). Users should do their own research and decide what works best for their individual needs.
- Software, such as the Tor browser bundle or a virtual private network (VPN), can help to increase privacy and anonymity on the web, although usability can be more limited (e.g. the Tor browser does not come with Flash installed).[9]
- Ad blockers have increased significantly in popularity, motivated by several factors including the desire to reduce visual clutter, speed up browsing, and (for smartphones) reduce bandwidth and battery usage (Bilton 2015). There is also a security benefit from ad blockers. Hackers regularly try to plant advertisements with malicious software on legitimate websites, and ad blockers prevent a user's computer from being infected by this kind of 'drive-by' attack (Patrizio 2016).

Email

- Users should not click on links or open attachments they are not expecting to receive. This helps to prevent phishing, and is one of the most basic cybersecurity measures available. This guidance is relatively easy to follow with personal email accounts. It is much harder at work—for example, in human resource or finance departments where email attachments are a common occurrence.
- Phishing emails do not require perfect grammar or good design to trick recipients. The aim is simply to persuade the recipient to suspend good judgement for a split second. One example is phishing emails that look like an invoice for something the recipient didn't buy. Momentarily upset by thinking they may have been charged incorrectly, the recipient might click on the 'contact us' link and open a malicious link, thus carrying out the hacker's wishes.
- Users should consider using multiple email accounts for different purposes. For example, one account could be used for commercial interactions such as online shopping or newsletters, and another for personal communications and financial transactions. Temporary email accounts can also be useful when registering for a discount or service that might be used only once.

Messaging

- There is a variety of popular messaging applications (e.g. iMessage, WhatsApp, Signal) that have high security and reliability. These should be used in preference to other, less secure services such as standard SMS services.

Pirated Software

- Pirated software should not be downloaded. Not only is it illegal in most countries, but it is also an excellent way to install malware on a computer, leaving it completely vulnerable to hackers (Ducklin 2016). Pirated software is never advised, particularly with software such as an operating system, which is the foundation for everything that runs on a computer.

Backups

- With the cost of storage decreasing each year, there is no reason not to back up data regularly. Options include cloud storage services, or physical devices such as external hard drives or USB sticks, all of which are reasonably priced. At least one physical backup should be disconnected from the laptop or PC, and connected only when doing the backup. This preserves a clean copy of important data, in case a computer (and its connected backup) become infected with malware.
- More advanced users may wish to use a RAID array, which is virtualization technology that treats multiple hard drives (e.g. 4–5) as a single logical unit, to increase redundancy or performance. For example, the high redundancy configuration (RAID 1) means that, if one hard drive fails, the other drives will contain mirror images of the data. RAID is particularly useful with valuable data that are updated or accessed regularly.

BEYOND SECURITY AWARENESS

Much has been written over the past two decades about the need for greater cybersecurity awareness and for individuals to better understand the online threats they are likely to encounter. A lack of awareness has clear implications at the individual level—for example, a phishing email that results in financial fraud or data held hostage by ransomware. This same lack of awareness has far greater implications for the private sector— for example, a multinational company that has invested millions in cybersecurity, only to have an employee or contractor click on a malicious link and allow malware into the corporate network.

Many large and damaging data breaches have been attributed to security lapses at the individual level, with an attack via a targeted phishing campaign or infected USB stick left in a car park (Krebs 2015). As noted earlier, the human factor is often the weakest link. There is no need to use exotic and expensive attacks if an individual or employee can easily be persuaded to clink on a link or open an attachment.

Awareness has its place, and there is plenty of reputable guidance available.[10] But awareness also has limits. It is unreasonable to expect non-security experts to make complex security decisions—for example, to distinguish between a normal (safe) email and a sophisticated phishing email. Technical controls, such as those provided by a webmail company or corporate security team, are often required to achieve what the average user cannot, and to distinguish between the malicious and the benign.

There is also scope for improvement to user interfaces, particularly with error messages. What is a non-expert supposed to do when confronted with a message that says 'This website is using an invalid certificate'? How are they expected to know that this message is likely to be the result of a certificate that is either expired or from an unknown signer? Even if they had that context, how can they reasonably be expected to use that knowledge to assess the potential risks and decide on a course of action?

In many ways, security awareness was easier when Internet users were more culturally and socially homogenous (i.e. American). One example comes from security questions—the kind that might be required to reset a password or make changes to a user account. A popular security question used to be 'mother's maiden name', which, from the perspective of an American technology company, is a piece of information not readily available to the general public and therefore sufficiently confidential. However, this security question is useless in Italy, for example, where married women cannot change their maiden names. They may use their married name in social settings, but must use their maiden name in professional life and for government paperwork. There is much more work to be done in understanding and improving upon cybersecurity awareness, and much to be learned from research in behavioural psychology.

Conclusion

The challenges of managing cyber risks and maintaining good cyber hygiene are unlikely to diminish as attackers become both more numerous and more proficient. As long as the collection and monetization of data remain the dominant business model of the Internet, it will be difficult for individuals to 'opt out' of this collection to preserve their privacy or strengthen their security.

Public debates over privacy and security will increase in volume as the unconnected proportion of the global population steadily comes online, and the Internet reflects more accurately the cultural and linguistic diversity of the physical world.

This chapter has outlined some of the fundamental challenges of personal cybersecurity, including primary threat actors and threat vectors. It has provided a range of technical and non-technical security measures that can help individuals to manage their cyber risks and protect their data more effectively. At the individual level, cybersecurity does not have to be onerous, and neither, conversely, is it a hopeless endeavour. But personal cybersecurity does require some effort and thought. At the highest level, it requires choices to be made between the competing priorities of confidentiality, integrity, and availability. Ultimately, cybersecurity rests on individuals understanding that they have something of value that needs to be protected. Only through this realization will individuals be motivated to act and choose the security measures that work best for them.

The views and opinions expressed are those of the author and do not necessarily reflect the views and opinions of Deloitte.

NOTES

1. CERN. 'The Birth of the Web'. https://home.cern/science/computing/birth-web; Naughton, J. 2010. 'The internet: Everything you ever need to know', *The Guardian*, 20 June. https://www.theguardian.com/technology/2010/jun/20/internet-everything-need-to-know
2. Miniwatts Marketing Group. 'World Internet Usage and Population Stats; June 30, 2016—Update'. http://www.internetworldstats.com/stats.htm
3. UK Information Commissioner's Office (ICO), 'Overview of the General Data Protection Regulation (GDPR)'. https://ico.org.uk/for-organisations/guide-to-data-protection/guide-to-the-general-data-protection-regulation-gdpr/
4. The Register. 25 August 2015. 'What Ashley Madison did and did NOT delete if you paid $19 —and why it may cost it $5m+'. https://www.theregister.com/2015/08/25/us_class_action_ashley_madison/
5. University of Cambridge Computer Laboratory. 'Proportion of devices running vulnerable versions of Android', *AndroidVulnerabilities.org*. https://androidvulnerabilities.org/graph
6. Deloitte TMT Predictions 2016. 'Used smartphones: the $17 billion market you may never have heard of'. https://www2.deloitte.com/xe/en/pages/technology-media-and-telecommunications/articles/tmt-pred16-telecomm-used-smartphones-17-billion-market.html
7. One example is Yubico, who produce a security key accepted by many large companies and websites. https://www.yubico.com/
8. Xkcd. 'Password Strength'. https://xkcd.com/936/
9. 'What is Tor Browser?'. https://www.torproject.org/projects/torbrowser.html.en; Paul, I. 2017. 'How—and why—you should use a VPN any time you hop on the internet', *TechHive*, 18 January. http://www.techhive.com/article/3158192/privacy/howand-whyyou-should-use-a-vpn-any-time-you-hop-on-the-internet.html
10. In the UK, for example, online fraud and attempted fraud (such as phone scammers purporting to be security technicians requesting to log in to your computer) can be reported to Action Fraud, the UK's national fraud and cybercrime reporting centre. http://www.actionfraud.police.uk/

REFERENCES

Bilton, R. 2015. 'What Ad Blocker Users Say Makes Them Boycott Web Ads', *Digiday*, 15 October. http://digiday.com/publishers/motivations-ad-block-users/

CERT-UK. 2015. 'Phishing: What Is It and How Does It Affect Me?', National Cyber Security Centre. https://www.ncsc.gov.uk/guidance/phishing

Ducklin, P. 2016. 'Will a Visit to The Pirate Bay End in Malware?', *Naked Security*, 6 May. https://nakedsecurity.sophos.com/2016/05/06/will-a-visit-to-the-pirate-bay-end-in-malware/

Hadhazy, A. 2016. 'Here's the Truth About the Planned Obsolescence of Tech', *BBC Future*, 12 June. http://www.bbc.com/future/story/20160612-heres-the-truth-about-the-planned-obsolescence-of-tech

Krebs, B. 2012. 'The Scrap Value of a Hacked PC, Revisited', *KrebsOnSecurity*, 15 October. https://krebsonsecurity.com/2012/10/the-scrap-value-of-a-hacked-pc-revisited

Krebs, B. 2015. 'Inside Target Corp., Days After 2013 Breach', *KrebsOnSecurity*, 21 September. https://krebsonsecurity.com/2015/09/inside-target-corp-days-after-2013-breach/

Lewis, James A. 2012. 'Rethinking Digital Development (Effect of Internet Is to Lower Transaction Costs; Everything Else Is Advertising). What's Missing?', (@james_a_lewis), Twitter, 9 January, 1.36 p.m. https://twitter.com/james_a_lewis/statuses/156368736209747969

Madden, M. 2014. 'Public Perceptions of Privacy and Security in the Post-Snowden Era', 12 November, Pew Research Center. http://www.pewinternet.org/2014/11/12/public-privacy-perceptions/

McGill, A. 2016. 'The Inevitability of Being Hacked', *The Atlantic*, 28 October. https://www.theatlantic.com/technology/archive/2016/10/we-built-a-fake-web-toaster-and-it-was-hacked-in-an-hour/505571/

Newman, L.H. 2016. 'Press Releases Finally Get a Devoted Readership: Hackers', *Wired*, 10 August. https://www.wired.com/2016/08/press-releases-finally-get-devoted-readership-hackers/

Norton, Q. 2014. 'Everything Is Broken', *Medium*, 20 May. https://medium.com/message/everything-is-broken-81e5f33a24e1 - .disnlntwx

Okyle, C. 2015. 'Password Statistics: The Bad, the Worse and the Ugly', *Entrepreneur*, 3 June. https://www.entrepreneur.com/article/246902

Patrizio, A. 2016. 'How Forbes Inadvertently Proved the Anti-Malware Value of Ad Blockers', *Network World*, 11 January. http://www.networkworld.com/article/3021113/security/forbes-malware-ad-blocker-advertisements.html

Quain, J. 2017. 'Do You Really Need to Pay for Antivirus Software?', *tom's guide*, 30 November. https://www.tomsguide.com/us/antivirus-software-pay-or-free,news-18570.html

Schneier, B. 2012. *Liars and Outliers: Enabling the Trust that Society Needs to Thrive*. Indianapolis, IN: John Wiley & Sons.

Stamos, A. 2016. 'Addressing Security Blindspots through Culture', Facebook. 1 August. https://www.facebook.com/notes/alex-stamos/addressing-security-blindspots-through-culture/10154390896047929/

Tims, A. 2016. 'A Knife-Point Attack on Holiday, Mobiles Stolen ... Then a £5,789 Bill from Vodafone', *The Guardian*, 14 August. https://www.theguardian.com/money/2016/aug/14/knife-point-attack-on-holiday-mobiles-stolen-bill-vodafone

National Cyber Security Centre. 2017. 'Common Cyber Attacks: Reducing the Impact', 7 October. https://www.ncsc.gov.uk/white-papers/common-cyber-attacks-reducing-impact

W., Emma. 2017. 'What does the NCSC think of password managers?', National Cyber Security Centre blog, 24 January. https://www.ncsc.gov.uk/blog-post/what-does-ncsc-think-password-managers

Waddell, K. 2017. 'Your Hot Hands Can Give Away Your Smartphone PIN', *The Atlantic*, 9 March. https://www.theatlantic.com/technology/archive/2017/03/hot-hands-smartphones/519069/

Weblinks

A Few Thoughts on Cryptographic Engineering: https://blog.cryptographyengineering.com/
Communications of the ACM, BLOG@CACM: https://cacm.acm.org/blogs/blog-cacm/
CyberSecPolitics: https://cybersecpolitics.blogspot.co.uk/
Dan Geer (collected works): http://cyberlaw.stanford.edu/blog/2015/10/dan-geer-keynote-%E2%80%9Cintelligence%E2%80%9D-and-his-remarkable-body-work
Errata Security: http://blog.erratasec.com/
Krebs on Security: https://krebsonsecurity.com/
Light Blue Touchpaper, Security Research, Computer Laboratory, University of Cambridge: https://www.lightbluetouchpaper.org/
Memex 1.1: http://memex.naughtons.org/
Random Spaf Items: http://blog.spaf.us/
Schneier on Security: https://www.schneier.com/
UK National Cyber Security Centre: https://www.ncsc.gov.uk/

CHAPTER 23

ONLINE CHILD SAFETY

JOHN CARR

THIS chapter looks at the origins of the idea of online child safety, noting how it moved from an initial focus on largely criminal activities connected with child sexual abuse images (referred to as child pornography in many jurisdictions) and paedophile behaviour through to wider concerns about children being exposed to age-inappropriate content such as, but not limited to, legal adult pornography and violent or extremist materials. However, today the new technologies are so thoroughly integrated into so many different aspects of children's lives, a large part of the focus has started to shift towards trying to assess their impact on the overall quality of children's lives. Behavioural issues have become a key part of the online safety agenda, particularly around bullying, privacy, self-harm, and self-generated sexual images. Industry and regulatory responses are examined and certain definitional problems are touched upon.

BORN IN THE USA

Child Safety on the Information Highway[1] was the first of its kind. Published in the United States in 1994 and republished with minor revisions a further three times up until 2005, it was written by Larry Magid, a technology journalist from Silicon Valley.[2] Magid identified many of the advantages that were available to children who had access to the Internet, but he also highlighted issues of concern that still preoccupy parents, children, the media, governments, and Internet businesses:

- Exposure to inappropriate material.
- Physical molestation.
- Harassment and bullying.
- Viruses and hackers.
- Legal and financial.

If the list of categories were being drawn up today, such has been the growth in the importance of privacy[3] that it would warrant a separate heading, perhaps linked to a changed definition of 'legal and financial'. Cases such as the 'Cayla' doll[4], Barbie[5] and VTech computers[6] hint at a growing set of concerns around children within the wider framework of the 'Internet of Things'. In addition, there is a question mark around 'over use' or, controversially[7], 'addiction' to the Internet.

More recently, there has been a greater focus on, and concern about, the effects on young people of exposure to terrorist and other violent material online, and on the 'echo chambers'[8] that social media services can create[9], perhaps particularly when also linked to the 'fake news' phenomenon. Images and online environments that appear to promote or give access to information on suicide and other forms of self-harm have also become more prominent. This is part of a wider shift towards trying to assess the overall impact of the new technologies in general, and social media in particular, on the quality of children's lives.

However, in terms of the volume of ink spilt and the attention given to it by public authorities, children's advocates and technology companies, in the UK and most other countries, up to the time of writing, most of the dominant issues would easily fit within Magid's original definitions even if they might be expressed slightly differently. These form the principal focus of this chapter.

The Journey Begins

In the mid 1990s, a consumer-facing Internet industry began to emerge in the United States and fairly soon in other higher-income countries such as the UK. The nascent industry was then comprised principally of, fixed-line Internet access providers. Some of their wider promotional messaging emphasized that children's grades at school were improving because they had access to the Internet at home. This helped foster what became a widespread assumption—namely, that making more information available and presenting it in more interesting ways *must* lead to better educational outcomes. There was no evidence to support this conjecture but, unsurprisingly perhaps, technology companies did little to discourage it. This contrasted sharply with their insistence on 'seeing the evidence' when a measure was advanced that might not immediately help their bottom line.

Quite quickly, governments started promoting the Internet not only as a new, cheaper, and more efficient way of delivering all manner of public services, but also quite specifically as a way of improving education as we all advanced towards the high-tech future that clearly beckoned on the near horizon. Schools began to reshape the way teaching was carried out, and the nature of homework and class assignments changed, as did the manner in which both teachers and the administration communicated with parents and students themselves. Public policy therefore became not the sole driver but certainly an important one pushing children towards cyberspace.

What is a Child?

The United Nations Convention on the Rights of the Child (UNCRC) is the premier international instrument that sets the framework for child welfare and child development policies across the world. It defines a child as a person who is below the age of 18.[10] The United States is the only UN Member State not to have ratified the Convention[11]. While the parties to the UNCRC are, by definition, states, non-state parties (e.g. companies) are, by extension, also bound by it.[12]

It is important to note that the Convention was adopted in 1989. It is very much a 'pre-Internet' document[13] and it shows. Thus, while the principles and values reflected in the UNCRC remain valid and (likely) eternal, their practical application in cyberspace can be fraught with difficulty.

For example, Article 5 speaks of the need to have regard to the 'evolving capacities' of a child. This speaks of a time when important actors in a child's life would meet and deal with the child face to face: teachers, doctors, youth group leaders, shop keepers, and so on. If an issue about a child's capacities or age arose, the matter would be resolved through pre-existing knowledge, discussion, or observation, either on the spot or, in some instances, by engaging directly with a trusted third party or by asking for documentary evidence.

Article 5 accords with common sense and scientific knowledge. It recognizes that young people mature at different rates, but as yet there is no authoritative guidance available to indicate how a business operating in a remote environment, typically in very high volumes and at great speed, might carry out the individual, subjective assessment that would allow 'regard' to be had to a particular child's 'capacities', 'evolving' or otherwise.

A US Federal law, the Children's Online Privacy Protection Act 1998 (COPPA),[14] nevertheless blithely decreed that at the age of 13 a young person was fully competent to make their own decision about joining or using an online service, without the need to refer to their parents (or anyone else) and, once 'in', it seems it further assumed that the child was fully competent to make any and every decision the site or service might put before them.[15]

It should be noted that COPPA was enacted before Web 2.0 emerged, yet it continues to be the baseline nominally observed[16] by a great many social media services across the globe. The only significant variation from this standard occurred when the European Union adopted the General Data Protection Regulation (GDPR)[17] in 2016. This became operative in May 2018. The age of 13 remained the minimum age at which a child could decide for themselves whether or not to join a particular online service but, when the service relied on consent as the basis of joining, Article 8 gave Member States an option to stipulate a higher minimum age as long as it was between 13 and 16, with 16 being the default.

Thus, in countries such as the UK, which opted to remain with 13, nothing changed. In countries where 14, 15, or 16 was adopted, companies were required to obtain verifiable parental consent if they wished to allow a child below the minimum age to become an end user.[18] One of the consequences of these changes was that a number of companies chose to abandon consent as the basis for becoming an end user or, as in the case of Facebook, in effect they introduced a new category of membership that relied on the company's 'legitimate interests'.[19]

How is a site or service to know if someone is a child anyway? It is well established[20] that huge numbers of children misrepresent their age to social media companies so that they can 'hang out' with the older, 'cooler' kids. COPPA does not require businesses to carry out age verification; neither does the GDPR but it does require service providers to perform risk assessments.[21] These could lead them to conclude that age verification is required in particular circumstances, notwithstanding that in many parts of the world the problems associated with doing this may be substantial.

The date nature of Article 5 provides a particularly acute illustration of a difficulty that exists with the UNCRC in relation to the Internet, but it is by no means the only Article of that kind.[22]

The prospects for agreeing a major overhaul of the Convention to make it more 'Internet-savvy' are remote.[23] However, in March 2019,the UN's Committee on the Rights of the Child issued a consultation note[24] preparatory to publishing a 'general comment' intended to help states interpret the UNCRC having regard to the way the Internet had evolved and become so enmeshed in children's lives in all parts of the globe. "This was adopted in March, 2021 in the form of General Comment 25. It provides States with an updated interpretation of the UNCRC." https://docstore.ohchr.org/SelfServices/FilesHandler.ashx?enc=6QkG1d%2f PPRiCAqhKb7yhsqIkirKQZLK2M58RF%2f5FovEG%2bcAAx34gC78FwvnmZXGFUl9nJ BDpKR1dfKekJxW2w9nNryRsgArkTJgKelqeZwK9WXzMkZRZd37nLN1bFc2t The UK's Information Commissioner's Office also funded a research project that aimed to examine 'evidence gaps concerning children's conception of privacy online, their capacity to consent ... and their deeper critical understanding of the online environment'. This was the first research of its kind,[25] This led to the publication and adoption of the Age Appropriate Design Code which, following a transition perion take full legal effect in September 2021.

LEVELS OF ENGAGEMENT

From quite early in the history of the consumer-facing Internet,[26] it was known that children were major users. Several countries began systematically to research and document levels of engagement[27] but it was not until November 2015 that any sort of authoritative study appeared describing the position worldwide. 'One in Three'[28] was first published by the Global Commission on Internet Governance and the Royal Institute of International Affairs (Chatham House), and later by UNICEF. As the title suggests, it showed that one in three of all human Internet users on the planet were under the age of 18. In parts of the developing world, this has risen to almost one in two while in the UK and most of the EU it is around one in five.

In the developed world, the Internet is used in almost every school and in a very high proportion of people's homes. In the foreseeable future, the same will be true elsewhere in the world. Whatever people might imagine, believe, or want the Internet to be, it is without question *also* a children's and a family medium. Yet, it would be difficult to find any acknowledgement of this among some of the rarefied global bodies that discuss Internet policy.

LEVELS OF DISENGAGEMENT

Ironically, the same publishers of 'One in Three' only 12 months later also brought out 'One Internet'[29] . It makes occasional reference to child welfare in an online setting but the text is thin and its tone is hurried, perfunctory, and consequently disappointing. Moreover, 'One Internet' expressly endorsed the NetMundial statement[30] in the following terms: 'NETmundial ... mark(s) a major step by all stakeholder groups toward agreement on the basics of Internet governance, including agreement that Internet governance should be carried out through a distributed, decentralized and multi-stakeholder ecosystem.'

And this despite the fact the NETMundial final communiqué contains none of the following words, not even once: child, children, youth, or young. Specific references to persons with disabilities appear twice and there is a reference to the importance of achieving '... *geographic ... and gender balance ...*' [emphasis added] so it is not as if the authors were implacably opposed to recognizing specific interests. It is just that children were not seen as being one of them.

NetMundial neatly illustrates how even today, at the highest levels of business and government thinking as well as among particular types of non-governmental organizations, children's interests can be, and all too often are, marginalized, overlooked, or relegated to a second order of importance, sometimes even to the point where they can create dangers to children.[31] This is not to say that there are always easy or obvious solutions to some of the challenges thrown up by children's large-scale presence on the Internet but observers might be forgiven for believing that somewhere there must be a box marked 'too difficult' and that children are in that box.

INTERNATIONAL RECOGNITION

The First World Congress Against Commercial Sexual Exploitation of Children, held in Sweden in 1996, was the first recorded major public international gathering where reference was made to children being sexually exploited, or being placed in any kind of jeopardy, because of the Internet. In the final declaration and agenda for action, in the section on protection, the Congress spoke about the need to 'develop or strengthen and implement national laws to establish the criminal responsibility of service providers, customers and intermediaries in child prostitution, child trafficking, child pornography, including possession of child pornography, and other unlawful sexual activity'.[32]

In 2000, the UN General Assembly adopted the Optional Protocol on the Sale of Children, Child Prostitution, and Child Pornography. Language similar to that used at the First World Congress also appeared in the final declarations of the Second World Congress held in Japan in 2001.

In 2003, the United Nations initiated the World Summit on the Information Society (WSIS). This culminated in a final communiqué that was adopted in November 2005. Paragraph 90q proclaimed that governments of the world intended to find ways of 'incorporating regulatory, self-regulatory, and other effective policies and frameworks to protect children and young people from abuse and exploitation through information and communication technologies (ICTs) into national plans of action and e-strategies'.

Pursuant to paragraph 90q, 'Action Line' C5 was adopted, which aimed to 'build confidence and security in the use of ICTs', and on this basis in November 2008 the International Telecommunication Union (ITU) launched its Child Online Protection initiative. An early outcome was the publication, in November 2010, of a set of four guideline documents. UNICEF later became more fully engaged in the space and, in January 2016, the updated versions of two ITU guidelines were described as being a joint publication of the ITU and UNICEF. It seems likely that this partnership will continue with UNICEF being the lead in respect of child protection issues.

THE INTERNET GOVERNANCE FORUM

Another spin-off from the WSIS process was the creation of the Internet Governance Forum (IGF). This meets annually and is said to be the embodiment of the multi-stakeholder Internet governance model. The IGF is indeed a unique institution in that it creates a space where civil society organizations can meet and mix, in theory at least, on equal terms, with government representatives and industry leaders.

However, the IGF has no decision-making powers and, after an initial flurry of enthusiasm for the notion that dialogue alone can shape outcomes elsewhere, fewer and fewer senior people from industry now bother to attend. The same is the case with senior representatives of national governments.

Although there is usually a significant number of events within an annual IGF gathering that address child protection concerns, it is hard to detect any great interest in the issue among the IGF's leading lights. For example, there has only ever been one plenary session devoted to child protection matters and that was in 2009 when the IGF was held in Egypt. It happened because President Mubarak's wife insisted.

OTHER INTERNATIONAL RESPONSES

It is beyond the scope of this chapter to try to detail every online child safety initiative in every country in the world. The nearest anyone has ever come to completing such a gargantuan task is in the UNICEF-sponsored Global Resources and Information Directory (Grid)[33]. At the time of writing, it is not clear how well they have been able to sustain their ambition.

The Council of Europe has the power to draw up treaties and conventions that have legal force. It has been particularly energetic in relation to the online security agenda generally and also quite specifically in respect of the protection of children. The Budapest Convention on Cybercrime and the Lanzarote Convention on the Protection of Children against Sexual Exploitation and Sexual Abuse are key examples. In 2016, the Council also adopted its 'Strategy for the Rights of the Child (2016–21), which includes a major online component. In 2018, the Council adopted a comprehensive set of recommendations to 'better respect, protect and fulfil the rights of the child in the digital environment' to be followed by a detailed handbook providing guidance on implementation. This was published in November, 2020. https://rm.coe.int/publication-it-handbook-for-policy-makers-final-eng/1680a069f8.

The EU began its engagement with online child safety in 1997 when the Daphne Programme made grants available to NGOs involved in combatting next violence against women, children, and young people. 1999 saw the establishment of a tailor-made Safer Internet Programme, which, inter alia, inaugurated 'Safer Internet Day', a now global event that draws attention to a range of online child safety issues. In 2012, the EU adopted a new and comprehensive strategic policy document in the shape of its 'European Strategy to Deliver a Better Internet for our Children'. Self-regulation remained at the core of the EU's declared position but its hold seems to be weakening.

Just before the new strategy was put in place, in December 2011, the EU also adopted a Directive on 'Combating the sexual abuse and sexual exploitation of children and child pornography'. This sought to bring a degree of uniformity to how Member States tackled a number of important child protection issues. The Directive was an example of the EU intervening directly. In July 2020 the EU adopted a new strategy " For a more effective fight against child sexual abuse". Inter alia the strategy anticipates the establishment of a new European Centre as a focus for child protection activity in both the online and offline spaces. https://ec.europa.eu/home-affairs/sites/default/files/what-we-do/policies/european-agenda-security/20200724_com-2020-607-commission-communication_en.pdf

The adoption of the GDPR is further evidence of a shift away from self-regulation. The GDPR could have a major influence on the wider online child safety agenda, if only because of Article 35[34], which appears expressly to require the providers of all information society services to carry out impact assessments in respect of those services.

#WEPROTECT GLOBAL ALLIANCE

Initiated as #We Protect in the UK by Prime Minister David Cameron in 2014, two years later, this initiative was given a £50 million budget and metamorphosed into the #We Protect Global Alliance to End Child Sexual Exploitation Online. At that point, the US government and the EU also formally signed up. Seventy countries have joined the Alliance, as have 20 leading technology companies and 17 leading civil society organizations. It is dedicated to national and global action to end the sexual exploitation of children online[35]. A key output of the Alliance has been the production of the 'Model National Response Guidance Document' provides an ambitious blueprint for any country wishing to devise a comprehensive online child protection policy.

SUSTAINABLE DEVELOPMENT GOALS AND THE GLOBAL PARTNERSHIP TO END VIOLENCE AGAINST CHILDREN

Following on from the 'Millennium Development Goals'[36] adopted in 2000, in September 2015, the United Nations developed a series of 'Sustainable Development Goals'[37] (SDGs), which are meant to be completed by 2030. Several of these, in particular SDG 16, are of particular relevance to children. Linked to the SDGs, a 'Fund to End Violence Against Children'[38] was established, which by early 2019 had attracted in excess of US $68 million to finance a range of projects, including several directly addressing online concerns. The #We Protect Global Alliance very sensibly decided to work closely with the Global Partnership and Global Fund.

THE IMPORTANCE OF LANGUAGE

International cooperation is difficult to achieve at the best of times. Cultural and legal differences are ever present and national priorities will not always be aligned simultaneously. These differences and misalignments can lead to a lack of a common vocabulary for describing and therefore for acting or cooperating on solving a problem. For this reason, ECPAT International (formerly known as 'End Child Prostitution, Child pornography and Trafficking International) took the lead in convening a substantial number of major international players to draft what ultimately became known as the 'Luxembourg Guidelines'. The authors included INTERPOL, EUROPOL, the African Committee on the Rights and Welfare of the Child, Instituto Interamericano, ILO, UNICEF, Council of Europe, The International Centre for Missing & Exploited Children (ICMEC), ITU, UN Special Rapporteurs and Save the Children International. It is too early say how important this initiative is going to be although, to the extent that it is helping to standardize vocabulary, there is every reason to suppose that it will have a beneficial impact.

BULLYING

In terms of the broader online child safety agenda, bullying is the issue that is most likely to directly affect the largest number of children who use the Internet and its associated technologies.[39]

Bullying behaviour can manifest itself in a number of different ways[40], sometimes with truly catastrophic consequences[41]. Since time immemorial and in varying degrees bullying, typically linked in one way or another to school[42], has been an unpleasant feature of a great many young people's lives. However, before the rise of social media and the increasing ubiquity of smartphones, a young person who was being bullied would usually be able to find some sort of respite, a safe haven or sanctuary where the bullies' taunts or threats could not reach them. Those days are gone. In an 'always-on' world, bullies potentially have 'always-on' access to their victims. Moreover, whereas in the past when name-calling, whispered gossip, or offensive graffiti might have been among the major weapons used by bullies, there was limited scope for a wider audience to become engaged thereby magnifying the original insult. Technology has changed that situation beyond all recognition and, in doing so, has almost certainly made the experience of certain types of bullying all the more intense or hurtful and destructive. A humiliating picture or posting can be seen by the whole school in seconds and remain visible for a protracted period. The resilience or capacity of individual children to cope with the stresses of being bullied will vary considerably from child to child even within the same age group and there is some evidence that children with special needs are more likely to be victimized[43]. Being different always seems to attract attention.

A number of companies are promoting innovative technical solutions that can analyse data streams (e.g. postings on social media and messages or pictures sent from mobile devices[44]), with a view, in particular, to help determine whether a child is involved in or is a victim of bullying.

Every major social media site will have a mechanism for reporting bullying behaviour and for getting bullying messages or content taken down. Yet, in January 2017, the Children's Commissioner for England[45] reported:

> It is currently impossible to know how many children are reporting content, what they are reporting and how these reports are dealt with. When the Children's Commissioner requested

information from Facebook and Google about the numbers and types of requests it receives from minors to remove content neither was able to provide it.

In the face of a seemingly never-ending stream of media reports about a range of different harms being suffered by children arising from online bullying incidents, this lack of accountability and transparency to a substantial degree is behind the frequent calls for the UK to adopt a statutory regulatory framework. In response to this, in October 2017, the Government published a consultative Green Paper[46] on a new 'Internet Safety Strategy'. Publication of a draft Online Safety Bill, which following examination by a Pre Legislative Scrutiny Committee of both Houses of Parliament is expected to be published in early 2022.

In young people's lives, sites and services like Facebook, Instagram, Snapchat, YouTube and more recently Tik Tok are in positions analogous to that of a monopoly or near-monopoly public utility. If everybody in your school or social circle is on or using a site or service, the pressure to follow suit can be enormous. There is a compelling case, therefore, for a public interest institution with the necessary resources and legal powers to be able to reassure parents and children that these businesses' dominant market positions have not allowed a degree of lethargy or indifference to creep into their corporate habits. The creation of just such a body is one of the widely anticipated outcomes of the White Paper just referred to above and the legislation which will follow.

Exposure to Pornography

It is impossible to say with any degree of certainty how much and what type of pornography was around in pre-Internet days.[47] Neither can we reliably know whether more children are now seeing pornography than was the case in pre-Internet days, although there seems little doubt that that is the case. Nevertheless, in the EU Kids Online survey[48], nearly 10,000 children in over 20 countries were asked what kind of Internet content they found upsetting and the most frequently mentioned category was pornography, ranked first by 22% of respondents. Violent content was second, mentioned by 18%.

Much of the research into the harms associated with children's exposure to pornography predates the Internet, and there are substantial methodological and analytical problems associated with researching in this area. How, for example, does one isolate the 'narrow' Internet dimension of exposure to pornography from the effects of what many see as the wider 'pornified culture'[49] of modern society? Does one medium push or pull the other or are they symbiotic? Then there are the longitudinal and ethical dimensions. Which ethics committee would allow a cohort of children to be exposed to different types of pornography for varying lengths of time and then insist that the rest of the world waits until we see how the experience affected them? These difficulties have led different people to different conclusions. Some say 'unless and until we have convincing research-based evidence we should be slow to act for fear of inadvertently making things worse' whereas others argue 'if we have a reasonable apprehension that significant harm may be being done we cannot wait until we have absolute or near certainty, we must make the best judgments we can but be willing to revisit the question as and when convincing new evidence is presented'.

Historically, many of the groups or individuals that have been most heavily identified with attempts to restrict access to pornography by children have in one way or another started from a position informed by their own moral code, often linked in turn to strongly held religious beliefs or specific religious institutions. Yet, there is now a growing body of evidence that is emerging from clinicians and others without any obvious (or at any rate publicly acknowledged) ideological or religious bias.[50] This evidence appears to be confirming what many parents and policy makers have felt they knew intuitively. Exposure to pornography can do harm to children[51] and the harm can be severe.

In 2011, Frank La Rue, the UN's Special Rapporteur on the promotion and protection of the right to freedom of expression, acknowledged that there are certain 'exceptional types of expression' which may be legitimately restricted under international human rights law.'[52] These legitimate restrictions have to be designed, he argued, in order 'to protect the rights or reputations of others, or to protect national security, public order, or public health or morals'. La Rue also expressed concern that some regimes used child protection as a pretext for introducing wider forms of censorship.

Thus, the question is what proportionate steps can be taken to restrict children's access to pornography in ways that do not unreasonably interfere either with their or adults' rights? However, proportionality, like beauty, can be in the eye of the beholder.

A great many totalitarian regimes take a very direct and simple approach. They simply ban pornography, without exception. These regimes do not want anyone in the general population, irrespective of their age, to access what they define as pornography. By contrast, in liberal democracies where the rule of law prevails, any form of censorship is viewed with suspicion and every such restriction on private preference has to be justified.

In the United States, the Communications Decency Act 1996 failed to find a workable formula to limit children's access to pornography. Within the EU the Audio Visual Media Services Directive establishes obligations to limit access by children to several kinds of unsuitable content although its jurisdictional limits cast doubt on its likely effectiveness. https://digital-strategy.ec.europa.eu/en/policies/revision-avmsd

Since 2005, the UK's domestic mobile phone networks have restricted access to pornography sites unless and until the account holder was verified as over 18. The 'Big Four' domestic broadband suppliers also put in place a scheme providing filters.[53] Games consoles manufacturers and some hardware suppliers that target the children's market—for example, Kindle Fire for Kids—do likewise. Providers of wifi access in public spaces have a scheme that allows suppliers to block access to pornographic content. The legitimacy of such schemes was called into question by the EU's net neutrality rules[54] but the UK Parliament passed a law making it clear that it did not regard the provision of these kinds of filters as constituting an unlawful breach of those rules. However, none of these schemes addressed the root cause of the problem—namely, that commercial pornography publishers themselves took no steps to keep children off their sites.

At the 2015 General Election in the UK, the Conservative Party promised to introduce an age verification requirement for commercial publishers of pornography. The Conservatives won and in 2017 Parliament passed the Digital Economy Act, Part 3 of which fulfilled their promise. However in October 2019 the Government announced that it no longer intended to procede with implementing the Act. Instead the Government promised to deal with children's access to pornography in new and broader Online Safety Bill referred to above.

GROOMING

Occasionally, the media create the impression that the Internet is the most dangerous place in the world for children because of the presence of adult strangers who are paedophiles seeking to 'groom' children—that is to say, develop relationships with persons below the age of consent with a view to engaging them in illegal sexual activity.

Given the horrific nature and consequences[55] of child sex abuse, the ongoing public concern about grooming is entirely understandable. Sex crimes against children perpetrated by adults pluck at deep human emotions. When these get mixed up with underlying or background unease about strangers, new technologies, and the inordinate power of seemingly arrogant, unaccountable, profitable private companies, it creates a potent policy challenge and political dynamic.

Pre-Internet for an adult with a sexual interest in children to make contact with a child they did not already know could be exceptionally difficult, risky, and extremely time-consuming. Making contact with a child in an overseas jurisdiction could be even more complicated. Web 2.0 changed that for everyone and cheap international air travel meant hitherto remote locations came within easy reach. In some of these places, the law either permitted or was very relaxed about sexual acts between adults and minors, or there were no clear laws at all, maybe because local law enforcement agencies were under-resourced, indifferent, ignorant, or corrupt.

It is beyond the scope of this chapter to discuss in any detail the profiles of those convicted of grooming offences[56] save to say there is no common set of characteristics that would allow law enforcement or any other agency to identify a 'groomer' rapidly and reliably. They come in all shapes and sizes, from across the spectrum of age, education, income, and occupation.

In the UK, the National Society for the Prevention of Cruelty to Children (NSPCC) estimated that 5% of all children under the age of consent (16) have been sexually abused[57]. In March 2019, NSPCC also published the results of Freedom of Information requests made to 39 of the 43 police forces in England and Wales. Far from showing that grooming was in decline, these results showed an 'almost 50% increase in offences recorded in latest six months compared to same period in the previous year'. NSPCC further estimated that over 90% of sexually abused children were abused by someone they already knew—that is to say, someone within their 'circle of trust'. Historic data on arrests and convictions for child sex offences also bear this out. From a child protection point of view, therefore, in terms of sex abuse there is no doubt that the most dangerous place for a child is not the Internet: it is their family, school, and neighbourhood.

Of course this does not exclude the possibility of an Internet connection to child sex offending even within the circle of trust[58], but it would be reasonable to make the claim that child sex offending is still overwhelmingly carried out secretively with no visual or other record of it being made or shared with others, either online or in any other way.

From that point of view, there can be no question that, if the objective of public policy is to reduce the level of sex offending against children, the major focus should be on the circle of trust and helping children to recognize and resist inappropriate sexual advances or, if they occur, to feel empowered to report them at the earliest opportunity with a view to getting the abuse stopped and having the offender dealt with in an appropriate way. However, these actions should never be advanced as an alternative to focusing on an Internet dimension to child sex abuse. They are complementary and, while the state is the obvious principal actor in respect of the first type of abuse, Internet companies have a clear responsibility in the case of the second.

The mass media often refer to any adult (someone over the age of 18) who has sex with anyone under the age of consent to sex as a 'paedophile'. That does not correspond with the accepted clinical definition[59] , which describes paedophilia as a persistent sexual interest in prepubescent children. In fact, not all paedophiles are necessarily adults anyway. Many individuals who are eventually diagnosed as paedophiles were aware of their sexual attraction to prepubescent children when they were themselves young teenagers and some acted on that interest during their pre-adult, teenage years.[60]

CHILD SEX ABUSE: WHY DO THE IMAGES MATTER?

It would be preferable for there to be no child sex abuse in the first place and therefore for there to be no images of it to circulate on the Internet or anywhere else. However, absent that condition the question arises, what is to be done about the images once they do exist? Some have argued that it should be legal to possess such images[61] although that view is thankfully extremely rare.

An image is typically evidence of a serious crime that has harmed a child who needs to be found and helped. The perpetrators also need to be addressed. An image might enable the identification of one or more offenders who may have been involved in abusing the child or children depicted in the image or other children. Alternatively, they may be contemplating new crimes against children in the future. Moreover, publication and circulation of images is a gross abuse of a child's right to human dignity and privacy. Continued circulation puts the child in the image at risk of further harm and being aware that the image is still being viewed by any number of unknown persons is highly likely to impede their recovery. Continued circulation of images also helps sustain or create paedophile networks, thereby putting yet more children at risk. For all these reasons, securing the removal of an image from the Internet is extremely important. If an image cannot be deleted rapidly, whenever possible, access to it should be restricted until that has happened. A growing number of adult survivors of child sexual abuse whose images were distributed online are becoming increasingly vocal about the failings of an industry which allowed such distribution to continue substantially unhindered.

In 2012, the NSPCC sent out Freedom of Information requests to police forces in England and Wales. They asked how many child abuse images they had seized between March 2010 and April 2012. Five forces replied within the permitted time frame. Between them, these forces had seized 26 million images. Extrapolated across the whole of England and Wales, this suggested that in excess of 300 million such images were likely to have been in circulation during the period in question. This in turn further suggests that, globally, the number of sex abuse images moving around the Internet could be counted in the tens of billions.

ATTACKING THE PROBLEM

The challenge of preventing online child abuse images circulating in the first place, or continuing to circulate, has received a great deal of attention from technology companies, governments, and civil society organizations alike. This level of interest is in part procedural, reflecting the fact that the offence is easily identifiable and to some degree quantifiable. But there is also a deep moral revulsion at work: these images are graphic evidence of a horrific offence against children and the betrayal of their innocence.

As early as 1983, in a bulletin from the North American Man-Boy Love Association, we see evidence of an awareness among paedophiles of the possibilities presented by the new technologies. But leading Federal Bureau of Investigation (FBI) agent Ken Lanning acknowledges that it was not until around 1993 that law enforcement began to realize that the problems and challenges were changing, both qualitatively and quantitatively. This resulted in the FBI establishing the 'Innocent Images' programme.

The prominent English legal case *R v Arnold* (1994) saw the first reported prosecution in the UK for Internet-assisted offences relating to the possession of indecent images of children. In the mid-1990s, 'hotlines' were established in the UK, Holland, and Norway to allow anyone who found something they believed to be a child sex abuse image on the Internet to report it with a view to securing its removal from the Internet via a 'notice and take down procedure'. In 1998, the United States established its hotline and the following year a global association of hotlines—the International Association of Internet Hotlines (INHOPE)— was created with funding from the EU. Its aim was to coordinate information sharing and promote the growth of hotlines on a global basis. Today, there are over 40 hotlines on all 5 continents.

'Notice and take down' remained the sole basis on which hotlines operated for many years and it is still the case with most of them. However, in 2004, as more and more child abuse images started to be distributed via websites, following a collaboration between the UK's hotline, the Internet Watch Foundation (IWF) and British Telecom (BT), a system known as 'Cleanfeed' was announced.[62] This was a first among the liberal democracies. Cleanfeed allowed BT to block access to URLs notified to it by the IWF as containing child sex abuse images. Not long afterwards, every UK ISP and mobile phone network introduced a version of Cleanfeed and in 2011 the EU passed a Directive making it mandatory for every Member State to establish machinery to allow similar blocking systems to be operated. The practice of restricting access to URLs containing known child abuse images is now widespread. However, in most instances, the hotlines, including the IWF one, were still allowed only to respond to reports: they were not allowed to search proactively. For the IWF, this changed in 2016 when they were given a legal power to begin searching for images. Not unexpectedly, the number of illegal images they were dealing with started to climb dramatically, but not as dramatically as they would soon do in Canada.

In 2009, Microsoft announced PhotoDNA, a system to facilitate the detection of images that had already been seized and classified as illegal. PhotoDNA allocates a unique value to each image. This unique value, known as a 'hash', can be used to look for matches. This has two obvious and immediate advantages. The matching can be done by computers and therefore cover large volumes at great speed. This is now being widely used by law enforcement agencies[63] and, in 2018, by around 150 enterprises across the world[64] to detect images on their networks. In January 2017, the Canadian hotline announced that it had found a way to link PhotoDNA to a web crawler and in a six-week period it had processed over 230 million web pages, detecting 5.1 million that contained child abuse material displaying 40,000 unique images. Nothing on this scale had ever been achieved before and it may be a portent of even greater success in the future.

Companies are developing products that work in a similar way with video content, and work is progressing on developing tools to automate the identification of images that have not yet been seized and determined to be illegal. However, the fact that Microsoft reported that only 150 companies or other bodies are using PhotoDNA suggests a great many online businesses are not availing themselves of tools that are to work well known and widely available.

This raises the question of what else can be done? Here a problem arises with the issue of intermediary liability, or rather the lack of it. The author knows of no person of standing who would seek to abolish the principle of immunity for Internet intermediaries. It would simply be against natural justice to attempt to make anyone liable for something they could not have known anything about. Yet, there is no doubt that the principle of immunity for intermediaries has provided too many companies with an incentive to do nothing. It is a permanent alibi for inaction and evasion in connection with some of the most important threats to children—i.e. the continued spread of child abuse images.

Perhaps a lesson should be learned from the law and practice of data protection. Here it is universally accepted that states not only have a right to impose requirements on businesses in terms of minimum security and other standards but they also have a right to establish independent agencies to carry out inspections to determine how those standards are being observed by any organization that collects, processes, or stores personal data.

It is known that networks are being abused by a variety of lawbreakers in ways that harm children, and it is also known that inexpensive technical tools are available that can help to reduce the problem. Thus, the case for imposing cyber hygiene obligations in respect of a broad range of Internet businesses is clear.

In other words, while the principle of immunity from liability for any substantive criminal or civil wrongs should be maintained, companies ought to be required to take reasonable and proportionate steps to detect, eliminate, or mitigate any and all unlawful activity taking place on their network. They have a 'duty of care' that is not eliminated by the principle of intermediary immunity. At the very least companies should be expected to take reasonable and proportionate steps to enforce their own terms and conditions of service; otherwise, these terms and conditions are tantamount to being a deceptive practice. An independent inspectorate could have a role here to reassure the public that the designated standards are being observed by every relevant business active in cyberspace.

Several of these ideas were taken up in the Government's White Paper on Online Harms, published in April 2019. It now seems that the UK is heading towards the establishment of a statutory regulator with considerable powers to intervene to direct online businesses to behave in particular ways. Over the years, the Internet industry had many opportunities to avoid the prospect of statutory regulation in the UK but they failed to find a way. The doors of the last chance saloon have been nailed shut and sealed.

Notes

1. Sponsored by the then US Internet Service Providers Association http://www.scag.gov/wp-content/uploads/2011/03/infohwy.pdf
2. Magid later went on to found Connect Safely, which at the time of writing he still runs.
3. Propelled in part by the growth both of e-commerce and the 'Internet of Things' of which toys, for example, are a part.
4. CCFC report on Cayla dolls. http://www.commercialfreechildhood.org/internet-connected-toys-are-spying-kids-threatening-their-privacy-and-security
5. NBC news report on Barbie dolls. http://www.nbcnews.com/tech/gadgets/hello-barbie-goodbye-privacy-expert-says-connected-doll-has-security-n474446
6. Guardian report on VTech computers. https://www.theguardian.com/technology/2015/nov/30/vtech-toys-hack-private-data-parents-children
7. There is no consensus within the psychotherapy community as to whether the word 'addiction' can be properly used in this context.
8. The tendency only to meet, speak to, or learn from those people or sources with whom or which you already agree—thus limiting exposure to new ideas or perspectives.
9. Meaning that, through our 'likes' and our subscriptions to particular sites, newsfeeds or services, we can easily slip into a constantly reinforcing cocoon or bubble where alternative viewpoints are effectively banished and serendipitous encounters with different perspectives become rare.
10. Within individual jurisdictions, a person may be classed as an adult if they are below 18 providing a specific law declares a lower limit. Very few nations avail themselves of this possibility. A handful have legislated for an age of majority that is higher than 18 although that appears to conflict with the Convention.
11. However, the United States signed it in 1995. https://treaties.un.org/Pages/ViewDetails.aspx?src=IND&mtdsg_no=IV-11&chapter=4&clang=_en
12. See UN report, page 4, para 8. https://resourcecentre.savethechildren.net/sites/default/files/documents/7140.pdf
13. However, its Optional Protocol on the sale of children, child prostitution, and child pornography, adopted in 2002, does very much reflect some of the new realities of cyberspace.
14. https://www.ftc.gov/enforcement/rules/rulemaking-regulatory-reform-proceedings/childrens-online-privacy-protection-rule
15. The service would need to satisfy itself that each service offered was appropriate for 13-year-old children.
16. 'Nominally' because gigantic numbers of under 13s disregard the rule and the companies do little or nothing to police the boundary.
17. https://eur-lex.europa.eu/legal-content/EN/TXT/?qid=1532348683434&uri=CELEX:02016R0679-20160504
18. https://www.betterinternetforkids.eu/web/portal/practice/awareness/detail?articleId=3017751
19. https://ico.org.uk/for-organisations/guide-to-data-protection/key-data-protection-themes/children/
20. https://www.theguardian.com/media/2013/jul/26/children-lie-age-facebook-asa OK
21. https://ico.org.uk/for-organisations/guide-to-data-protection/guide-to-the-general-data-protection-regulation-gdpr/accountability-and-governance/data-protection-impact-assessments/

22. Article 12 decrees that children have a right to be heard in all matters affecting them. Articles 13 and 15 speak of a right to access information and freedom of expression and association as long as it is in the child's best interests.
23. However, a potential alternative was published in January, 2017, by Professor Sonia Livingstone http://blogs.lse.ac.uk/mediapolicyproject/2017/01/19/an-updated-uncrc-for-the-digital-age/
24. https://www.ohchr.org/EN/HRBodies/CRC/Pages/GCChildrensRightsRelationDigitalEnvironment.aspx
25. http://www.lse.ac.uk/media-and-communications/research/research-projects/childprivacyonline
26. Seen by many to have begun around 1995 when Microsoft issued and started to give away Internet Explorer.
27. e.g. see Ofcom, 'Internet Use and Attitudes', 20 July 2015. https://www.ofcom.org.uk/research-and-data/internet-and-on-demand-research/internet-use-and-attitudes
28. Livingstone, S., Carr, J. and Byrne, J. (2016). 'One in Three: Internet Governance and Children's Rights', Innocenti Discussion Paper No.2016-01, UNICEF Office of Research, Florence.
29. Carl Bildt and 28 others. https://www.oecd.org/about/secretary-general/launch-of-the-one-internet-report-of-the-global-commission-on-internet-governance.htm
30. Netmundial Declaration. www.netmundial.org
31. For example, ICANN allowed a Russian Registry to create a new domain aimed solely or very largely at children, without insisting on a range of basic security measures that would have deterred paedophiles from becoming owners or employees of any websites or services created under it.
32. First World Congress against Commercial Sexual Exploitation of Children, Declaration and Agenda for Action, Stockholm, 27–31 August 1996. https://www.ecpat.org/wp-content/uploads/legacy/stockholm_declaration_1996.pdf
33. The Family Online Safety Institute website is the principal data source. http://fosigrid.org/
34. http://www.privacy-regulation.eu/en/35.htm
35. www.weprotect.org
36. https://www.undp.org/content/undp/en/home/sdgoverview/mdg_goals.html
37. https://www.un.org/sustainabledevelopment/sustainable-development-goals/
38. http://www.end-violence.org/files/The_Fund_Story.pdf
39. https://www.nspcc.org.uk/preventing-abuse/child-abuse-and-neglect/bullying-and-cyberbullying/bullying-cyberbullying-statistics/
40. http://www.endcyberbullying.org/5-different-types-of-cyberbullying/
41. http://www.bullyingstatistics.org/content/bullying-and-suicide.html
42. It is beyond the scope of this chapter to discuss the equally serious phenomenon of adult-on-adult bullying.
43. http://repec.ioe.ac.uk/REPEc/pdf/qsswp1411.pdf
44. http://www.endcyberbullying.org/mit-media-lab-researchers-create-artificial-intelligence-to-flag-cyber-bullying/; https://www.newscientist.com/article/mg21428713-400-ai-systems-could-fight-cyberbullying/
45. http://www.childrenscommissioner.gov.uk/publications/growing-digital
46. https://www.gov.uk/government/consultations/internet-safety-strategy-green-paper
47. Agreeing on a precise definition of what constitutes pornography is not easy and can vary enormously between countries but in most surveys it is left to the respondent to decide what they regard as being pornographic.

48. https://www.lse.ac.uk/media-and-communications/research/research-projects/eu-kids-online
49. https://www.gov.uk/government/collections/bailey-review; http://www.publichealthpost.org/viewpoints/pornography-public-health-issue/
50. http://www.apa.org/monitor/nov07/webporn.aspx
51. https://www.childrenscommissioner.gov.uk/report/basically-porn-is-everywhere/
52. United Nations General Assembly, A/66/290, 10 August 2011, https://www.ohchr.org/documents/issues/opinion/a.66.290.pdf
53. https://www.internetmatters.org/parental-controls/
54. http://berec.europa.eu/eng/news_and_publications/whats_new/3958-berec-launches-net-neutrality-guidelines
55. Any examination of the life stories of prison populations, of people with criminal records, involvement in prostitution, or with drug addiction issues shows a significantly above-average presence of persons who have been sexually abused as a child or young teenager.
56. https://www.iicsa.org.uk/key-documents/3720/view/rapid-evidence-assessment-behaviour-characteristics-perpetrators-online-facilitated-child-sexual-abuse-exploitation.pdf OK
57. https://www.nspcc.org.uk/preventing-abuse/child-abuse-and-neglect/child-sexual-abuse/sexual-abuse-facts-statistics/
58. See, for example, the facts in the case of Paroline v. United States where the child's uncle had raped 8-year-old Amy and then posted the videos on the Internet: http://www.scotusblog.com/case-files/cases/paroline-v-united-states/
59. http://www.apa.org/pubs/books/4317136.aspx
60. https://www.nspcc.org.uk/preventing-abuse/child-abuse-and-neglect/grooming/ OK
61. http://falkvinge.net/2012/09/07/three-reasons-child-porn-must-be-re-legalized-in-the-coming-decade/ OK
62. http://www.theregister.co.uk/2004/06/07/bt_cleanfeed_analysis/ OK
63. http://www.theverge.com/2012/3/20/2886999/microsoft-licensing-photodna-child-pornography-matching-software-police OK
64. Correspondence between the author and Microsoft.

BIBLIOGRAPHY

Bartlett, J. 2015. *The Dark Net: Inside the Digital Underworld*. London: Windmill Books.

Davidson J., and Hamerton, C. 2016. *International Perspectives on Child Victimization*. London: Routledge.

Finklehor D., Wolak J., and Mitchell, K. 2006. *Online Victimization of Youth: Five Years Later*. Durham, NH: University of New Hampshire, Crimes Against Children Research Center.

Hooper, C-A. 2003. *Abuse, Interventions and Women in Prison: A Literature Review*. London: Home Office and Prison Service.

Lanning, Kenneth. 2011. *Love, Bombs and Molesters. An FBI Agent's Journey*. Kindle edition.

Livingstone, S., L. Haddon, A. Görzig, and K. Ólafsson. 2009. *EU Kids Online: Final Report*. London: EU Kids Online Network.

Livingstone, S., Carr, J., and Byrne, J. 2016. 'One in Three: Internet Governance and Children's Rights', Innocenti Discussion Paper No.2016–01. Florence: UNICEF Office of Research.

Martellozzo, E. 2013. *Online Child Sexual Abuse: Grooming, Policing and Child Protection in a Multi Media World*. London: Routledge.

Quayle, E. 2003. *Child Pornography: An Internet Crime*. London: Routledge.

Quayle, E. 2005. *Viewing Child Pornography on the Internet: Understanding the Offence, Managing the Offender, Helping Victims*. Lyme Regis, UK: Russell House Publishing.

Rumgay, J. 2004 *When Victims Become Offenders: In Search of Coherence in Policy and Practice*. London: Fawcett Society.

Seto, M. 2017. 'Multiple Indicators of Sexual Interest in or Pubescent Children as Predictors of Sexual Recidivism', *Journal of Consulting and Clinical Psychology, 85*(6), 585–595.

Social Exclusion Unit. 2002. *Reducing Re-offending by Ex-prisoners*. London: Office of the Deputy Prime Minister.

Wolak, J. 2008. 'Online "Predators" and Their Victims: Myths, Realities, and Implications for Prevention and Treatment', *American Psychologist, 63*(2).

Wortley and Smallbone 2012. *Internet Child Pornography: Causes, Investigation and Prevention*. Santa Barbara, CA: Praeger.

CHAPTER 24

EDUCATING FOR CYBER (SECURITY)

ROGER BRADBURY

INTRODUCTION

SOME years ago, I met a colleague at a University of California campus. He was an agricultural scientist of great distinction working at the leading edge of simulating the response of agro-ecosystems to climate change. He had been raised in China during the Cultural Revolution. And he had been sent as a little boy, with his parents, to a rural labour camp. They were to be re-educated for, as high school teachers and therefore intellectuals, his parents were class enemies. Their re-education consisted of hand-digging irrigation ditches for a vast cotton farm in an entirely unsuitable semi-arid region of China.

The work was arduous and long, and the little boy was expected to work with his parents. The conditions were primitive, if not barbaric. There was no school for the children in the camp. But there were many scholars there. A group of them, including some Academicians, organized to teach the children on the few rest days. There were no books or stationery. They taught the children in the dust, drawing and writing with sticks. My colleague learnt to read and write in this way. He learnt arithmetic and later geometry and algebra, and then calculus. He learnt the basic principles of physics, chemistry, biology, and geology.

When China's universities reopened in the early 1970s, only politically correct students chosen by party committees were admitted. It was not until 1977, under Deng Xiaoping, that entrance exams were re-established. At that time, my colleague gained entrance to Tsinghua University and blitzed his science degree. He was awarded a PhD scholarship to the United States, blitzed that degree too, and never returned to China.

The point of this anecdote for our purposes is not about the barbarity, cruelty, and stupidity of the Cultural Revolution and the Communist Party of China that spawned it. Nor is it about the nobility and grace of my colleague's teachers. Each of those points is self-evident. Rather, it is about the notion of education. For here, stripped of policies and programmes, syllabi and curricula, institutions and governments, is the essence of education: on the one hand, teachers, masters of their subjects, who love to teach; and, on the other, students, keen to learn, to understand. And, somewhere there, a body of knowledge and understanding that each in turn draws upon and contributes to. At its best, as seen in my anecdote, a love of learning comes for free with the body of knowledge and understanding.

I think this helps us place the problem of educating for cybersecurity in a proper context. And that is, ultimately, the subject of this chapter.

For context is all in understanding our problem. As I argued in an earlier essay on the nature of science (Bradbury 1999, 9), education is not an output of some mechanical process any more than it is an algorithm, procedure, or mechanism for generating such outputs. Rather, it is, like science, 'a body of knowledge about the world and a recipe for growing that body of knowledge, and a bunch of people busying themselves with that knowledge and that recipe all mixed up together'. But it is a special mix because 'each part can change the other. The knowledge can change the recipe, the recipe can change the people.' This recursiveness places science, and education, squarely within the frame of complex systems (Mitchell 2009), and it is with this frame in mind that my analysis will proceed.

THE GATHERING STORM

Why we need to understand this matter of cyber education is quite vexing. There is a deep anxiety in the Western world, and especially in the United States, about the way in which countries are responding to the societal challenges of cyberspace. At a superficial level, it manifests itself as anxiety about the fitness of the workforce to engage with cyberspace, and especially with cybersecurity. There are dire predictions about the shortfall in trained workers. And there are plenty of opportunists—both traditional education institutions and private firms—offering to provide training and education to solve the problem.[1] At a deeper level, the anxiety can be seen as a concern about the future of STEM (science, technology, engineering, and mathematics) education in the liberal democracies. This concern is most vividly on show in a series of reports—*Rising Above the Gathering Storm*—by the US National Academy of Sciences (Augustine 2007, 2110). In those, and similar reports (Royal Society 2014), senior educators warn that the West is falling behind and cannot provide the workforce to build the next generation of high technology industries—all of which will be cyber-enabled.

The solution that these educators propose is, unsurprisingly, more funding for education at all levels from pre-school to university, and a refreshed focus on STEM, especially to encourage more women and minority groups to take up a STEM career. Roadblocks are identified, and solutions proposed for each, often including the idea of more industry participation in the process.

The result has been a flowering of STEM education initiatives at all levels in the education systems of Western countries. And many of these earnest enterprises are built with cyber in mind.[2] Industry has been co-opted—usually willingly—to sponsor competitions or provide work experience.[3] No modern schoolchild can now escape.

But has anything really changed? Have we become more STEM-literate as a society? Have we become more aware of cyber challenges, especially in the area of cybersecurity? Was the education system sick in the first place and, if so, will the medicine work?

To understand these issues, I will take a different tack and, as indicated earlier, will analyse the problem from the perspective of complex systems science. I will seek a theory that is real and general (Levins 1970, 73). Real because of the particularities of human social systems—civilizations, if you will. And general because I wish to extract scientific explanation—a theory, perhaps—from embedding such systems in the more general class of living systems. This will allow me to argue that if we get 'educating for cyber' right, then 'educating for cybersecurity' comes for free.

I will anchor the argument in reality by examining the role of education in earlier social systems—the civilizations that were built on the Agricultural Revolution and the Industrial Revolution—and show how principles from complex systems science provide a general theory allowing us to understand how education will unfold through the Cyber Revolution.

In so doing, I hope to strip away the epiphenomena—the gathering storm and the like—and explain the underlying dynamics of education as a complex systems phenomenon.

But first I need to put some of those principles of complex systems science on the table.

WHAT AN UNDERSTANDING OF COMPLEX SYSTEMS BRINGS TO THE TABLE

Complex systems are those systems that are made up of many different interacting entities, each of which have many different attributes (Holland 2014). Good examples are ecosystems, nervous systems, organisms, economies, civilizations, tectonic plates, and the climate system. These typically show emergent properties and behaviours like tipping points and step changes that are not easily explicable from an understanding of their component parts (Holland 1998). This distinguishes them from simple systems, such as gases, where there may be many interacting entities, but these entities are broadly the same—they have the same attributes. Understanding the properties and the dynamics—that is, behaviour over time—of simple systems has been the mainstay of science since the Enlightenment. And that understanding, typically, is reductive. It explains the system-level phenomena in terms of the properties of the components. Thus, the system-level properties of gases—their temperature, pressure, volume, and so on—are explained by the properties of their constituent molecules.

But complex systems were refractory to science until the last half of the past century. Before that, analysis of complex systems was largely taxonomic—a natural history and classification of these systems. With the magnificent exception of Darwin's theory of evolution for living things, explanation of the dynamics of complex systems, especially of human systems, was the province of the humanities.

Since the 1940s with General System Theory (von Bertalanffy 1968), some powerful new mathematics, and the first computers, steady progress has been made in understanding complex systems natively, as it were (Allen and Starr 1982; Kauffman 1995). This work stands in strong contrast to the attempts by economists, through their so-called and fraught 'general equilibrium theory', to treat economies as simple dynamical systems like gases (Walras 1954).

No general theory of complex systems yet exists, but there is now at least a coherent view of many dimensions of complexity (Chaisson 2001). We know that their dynamics often feature stable points—states to which a system tends to return after small perturbations. We know also that some complex systems show stable cycles that are analogous to stable points, whereby the system repeatedly cycles through a series of states. And we know that, if these systems are perturbed too severely, they may reach a tipping point and jump to a new stable point or cycle.

We see these behaviours in all complex systems, but especially so in that class of complex systems called 'complex *adaptive* systems'—which include all living systems. Such systems can 'learn' from the past and use that information to adapt to new conditions. They are often Darwinian, as organisms are, or at least quasi-Darwinian as assemblages of organisms are. They winnow out information useful for their present situation and encode that information in genetic material if they are organisms or, if they are assemblages of organisms, in artefacts in their structures—such as physical networks in ecosystems, the architecture of a termite mound, or, say, books and buildings in civilizations.

Complex adaptive systems need energy to do all this—to maintain or return to a stable point or cycle, to learn and encode new information, and to adapt to change—just as all systems, simple and complex, do. And all systems, simple and complex, are constrained by the laws of thermodynamics, which have some interesting things to say about what can and cannot be in the lives of these systems.

In particular, in complex adaptive systems, there is a subtle interplay between information, knowledge, and learning on the one hand, and energy and its strange bedfellow, entropy, on the other. And understanding this interplay is crucial in understanding how education will play out in the cyber era because, in civilizations, education is one of the key ways in which information is passed through time.

By stripping education and learning of their accreted layers of institutions, syllabi, and curricula, we are left with a sparse description about the flow of information in complex systems. This allows us to think about education in the context of the dynamics of such systems, and, in particular, in the flows of energy that are at the heart of their dynamics.

So I will now describe how energy and entropy work in complex systems, and then I will consider how information, knowledge, and learning help organize the energy flows in the complex adaptive systems that are living systems. These include, of course, civilizations.

Energy and Entropy in Complex Systems

Entropy is a measure of the disorder of systems. All natural systems, left to themselves, tend to become disordered over time, and the most disordered state of any system is just the random movement and collision of a sea of its molecules. And, in this disordered state, the energy in the system (embedded in the random movements) cannot be harvested to do useful work. These concepts are captured in the laws of thermodynamics and they rule the behaviour of all dynamical systems—that is, systems that can change over time (Smil 2008).

It is important to emphasize the universality of that phrase 'rule the behaviour of all dynamical systems'. This means what it says. It refers to everything from the universe itself to its galaxies, from the solar system to the Earth's oceans and the climate, and from viruses and bacteria to humans, economies, and civilizations.

The first law of thermodynamics states that energy is always conserved, although it can be transformed from one sort of energy to another. The potential energy of water flowing through a hydroelectric station can be transformed into electrical energy flowing out on transmission lines, for example. But the second law of thermodynamics states that, at every transformation, entropy increases. The transformations are never completely efficient and some waste heat, some disorder, is produced. After the transformation, the entropy—the amount of disorder—in the whole system is more than before.

Thus, the fate of all dynamical systems is the same: a final state of complete disorder. We can see this if we create closed dynamical systems in the laboratory—that is, systems that are completely isolated from the rest of the universe, with their own fixed dollops of energy and matter, and some sort of energy transforming process. They run down over time, as their entropy increases, to a final steady state where nothing happens except the disordered collisions among their molecules. The laws of thermodynamics ensure that perpetual motion machines cannot exist.

But open systems, often called 'non-equilibrium systems', can cheat this fate, at least for a time, and use a flow of energy from *outside* their system to create *inside* their system a state of low entropy—a state of high order or organization. Living systems, including human social systems, are complex systems that have leveraged evolution to master this trick (Schrödinger 1944). The result is that the Earth now hosts a biosphere that is far from disorder. Its low entropy is maintained by the flow of energy from the sun cascading through ecosystems and creating subsystems that have become more ordered—more complex—through time (Morowitz 1968).

Entropy and Negentropy, Information and Education

At first glance, it may seem difficult to relate these ideas about energy flows and entropy in systems to ideas about information, knowledge, learning—ideas that we think of as especially human. But they are linked at a deep level. And that linkage has determined and constrained the role of education in human social systems for thousands of years. And will do so through the Cyber Age and beyond.

Claude Shannon, an American mathematician, described the link in 1948 (Shannon and Weaver 1949). Shannon redefined information as surprise and showed that it could be related to entropy. He argued that, if you send a message to someone, the more predictable it is, the less information it contains. And, conversely, the more surprising it is, the more information it contains. That is, a message consisting of a string of completely random words is completely unpredictable and so contains maximum information. But if a message's content can be guessed from just a portion of it, it has low information content. More broadly, the information content of a system is more or less the same as its entropy content.

This paradoxical formal definition of information is, however, not very helpful for our purposes. It does not describe what we might call 'useful' information. We need instead a more workaday description of information that increases as structure and order themselves increase in complex systems.

To meet this problem head on, Schrödinger proposed the idea of negative entropy.[4] later shortened by the information theorist, Brillouin (1953), to negentropy. Negentropy is reverse entropy (and is formally equivalent, in physics, to free energy or exergy). It increases as a system increases in orderliness.

As Liska and Heier (2013, 574) describe it:

> The ordered energy in a system that is available to do maximum work on its environment has been defined as free energy (often alternatively defined as exergy). From fluids to organisms to empires, local order arises in far-from-equilibrium open systems from inputs of free energy, thus countering the natural pull towards disorder described by the second law of thermodynamics.

We can say that a complex system exports entropy to keep its own entropy low. Or we could say, equivalently, that complex systems import and store negentropy. Thus, we can use the idea of negentropy in discussing how systems store, use, and transmit what we might call knowledge–that is, *useful* information.

In this formalism, a complex system has a store of negentropy, some of which is encoded in the structure of the system. This store, at its best, needs to grow and be passed through time. In the case of living systems, much of the negentropy is stored in the DNA of the organisms that create the living structures—cells, organisms, populations, and ecosystems—that constitute the system. And it is passed through time by reproduction of these structures, and it is adapted to changing circumstances by evolution.

Human social systems are a special case of living systems and they have developed new ways to store, use, and transmit negentropy. In particular, as I argue later, human social systems have growing stores of negentropy encoded as what humans call 'knowledge'.

It is characteristic of human social systems that their negentropy is stored in increasingly complex ways compared with other living systems. Through time, a growing body of knowledge is encoded in language itself, in cultural artefacts like buildings and images, in books, and nowadays in digital records. Each of these encodings requires algorithms to create, interpret, and apply them. Thus, what we think of as knowledge, or even know-how, is the body of knowledge stored as negentropy together with the algorithms to interpret and apply that knowledge. In its most evolved form, this is science.[5]

Education then becomes the process of passing on through time this store of negentropy and the algorithms for operating on it; and, in doing so, adding to it and curating it.

For a complex adaptive system like a civilization, education is a crucial process for ensuring the system's existence. Because such systems can learn and adapt, they use the algorithms to operate on the store of knowledge to solve problems relevant to their existence. In doing so, they often further complexify their systems. As Tainter (2006, 93) notes, 'we often respond by developing more complex technologies, establishing new institutions, adding more specialists or bureaucratic levels to an institution, increasing organization or regulation, or gathering and processing more information'. Such increased complexity will generate new knowledge but also new problems that cannot be solved with the current algorithms. So education is more than the passing on of today's information and algorithms: it is also the passing on of the meta-algorithms that allow us to create new knowledge and new algorithms for the new problems that have yet to arise. At their best, we see such meta-algorithms—algorithms for creating algorithms—as the core of mathematics, science, languages, philosophy, history, and the like.

THE PRINCIPLE OF MAXIMUM
ENTROPY PRODUCTION

We need to consider one more principle from complex systems science—the principle of MaxEP—to create a robust and general theoretical framework of the dynamics of information in complex systems. This will allow us to explore the special case of education in human social systems through time, leading us to education in the cyber age and beyond.

The principle of MaxEP (Harte 2011) describes the way in which open systems actually manage the trick of increasing their negentropy in the face of the second law. It suggests that sufficiently complex open systems—such as living systems—will configure themselves, when driven hard enough by an external force, to produce entropy at the maximum rate allowed by existing constraints (Haff 2014, 399). That is, they take in usable energy from a low entropy source, such as sunlight or electricity, and pass it through one or more energy transformations until that energy is shunted out of the system to a high entropy sink of low temperature, and unusable, heat. In doing so, they maximize the production of entropy through their system as they squeeze out as much utility as they can from the energy flow.

Thus, as external energy flows into a living system, the system will respond by altering its configuration through evolution, becoming more complex, more ordered, and with higher negentropy, to manage that flow in such a way that the outflowing energy has high entropy even as the entropy within the system is lowered. As living systems respond to MaxEP, they evolve to increase their negentropy.

But learning to manage the flow takes time. As living systems have evolved, they have become better at configuring themselves. They have complexified as evolution has discovered ever more subtle ways to maximize the flow of energy. At first, the external forces driving these systems were abiotic, and they learned to respond to temperature, salinity, and the like. Over geological time, biotic forces became more prominent as living things competed against each other for resources or preyed on one another as resources.

Haff has argued that a strong interpretation of MaxEP would suggest that the biosphere was one solution to the Earth's energy flows and was selected by entropy maximization.[6] There may be other solutions and it may be possible for complex adaptive systems to find other, better solutions that are potentially available to them. But this may not always happen. There may be hidden constraints that prevent that discovery. And, in any case, the search for solutions takes time. Thus, the Earth was more or less abiotic over most of its history, with a recognizable biosphere evolving only about half a billion years ago.

It seems clear not only that human social systems have found new solutions for the Earth's MaxEP that were unavailable to other living systems, but that those solutions too face constraints and take time to maximize their entropy production.

A Thermodynamic History of Education

Human social systems—civilizations—have found new solutions to the problem of maximizing entropy production. But each solution has been characterized by its own constraints and by the time it has taken for those systems to complexify sufficiently to approach the available upper limit of entropy production for that system. We can recognize three such solutions in history and each has involved the use of much more energy per person than the previous solution (Christian 2004).

The first solution, the Agricultural Revolution, was first explored about 5,000 years ago, as human societies first began to grow crops and domesticate animals. This created a large energy supply, in the form of domesticated grains, which was able to power the social system through human and animal muscles. Over time, human societies increased in both size and complexity as they found, through adaptation, maximum-entropy-producing states that were potentially available to them through this energy supply.[7] The components of this trend included growing populations, greater technical abilities, hierarchy, differentiation and specialization in social roles, greater scales of integration, and increasing production and flow of information.[8] By the Middle Ages, civilizations were harnessing more than 1,000 watts per person per day, compared with their hunter-gatherer forebears who were able to harness not many more than 100 watts per person per day[9].

The complexification of civilization through the Agricultural Revolution was an adaptive response to MaxEP. That is to say, it took time—some thousands of years, really—to fully explore the maximum-entropy-producing states that were potentially available, and the civilizational responses were always built from what was available at the time. While the adaptive path for any particular civilization was a series of local problems solved, one of the most common solutions involved increasing the production and flow of information.[10] But the differentiation of this task and its evolution into something resembling education came very late in the overall development of civilizations based on agriculture.

It was not until the Middle Ages, some thousands of years after the beginning of the Agricultural Revolution, that the first universities were founded. They slowly evolved from religious institutions—that is, structures that were at hand—in response to the problem of the need for an educated elite to manage the deeper complexification of their civilizations. Grammar schools and their like evolved some hundreds of years later in the Early Modern period, again built from religious institutions, as feeders for the universities, and again in response to the need for an educated elite. And dame schools also arose in these times in response to a need for what we now call primary education. Again, these were cobbled together from the older traditions of home instruction.

The second solution, the Industrial Revolution, began to be explored in the mid-eighteenth century. Human social systems began to exploit the pools of stranded energy resources—first coal, then oil, then natural gas—stored for millions of years in the Earth's crust. These resources represent a metastable accumulation of free energy that nature had not hitherto been able to convert to heat.[11]

Over time, civilizations complexified to reach up to this newly available solution to the Earth's MaxEP. And, as with the Agricultural Revolution, increasing the complexity of civilization took time, and it built on and from the pre-existing structures in the civilization. It was an adaptive process, solving problems as they arose, using the now-enlarging store of negentropy as the driver.

By the middle of the twentieth century, industrial civilizations were harnessing more than 10,000 watts per person per day, an order of magnitude over that available to individuals in agricultural civilizations.[12]

Over the couple of centuries of the Industrial Revolution, industrial civilizations complexified astonishingly as they responded to MaxEP. And education came to hold proportionally a much greater share of the negentropy of their systems as the problems to be solved became tougher and the 'returns' from that investment in knowledge and education diminished.[13]

Even though education was of crucial importance in solving the MaxEP challenges of the industrial age, it was late to the party. Universities through the nineteenth century were still focusing on a classical education with a heavy emphasis on Latin, Greek, and philosophy to create the generalists needed to run agricultural civilizations. It was not until the late nineteenth century that modern university faculties like science and engineering began to flower, heavily indebted in their structure to the traditional, even medieval, faculties they now joined. And it was also not until the late nineteenth century that compulsory primary education commenced, drawing on the structures and ideas of the standardized mass production of the early industrial age.

MAXEP AS A DRIVER OF EDUCATION

There are three distinct trends here that bear on our consideration of the role and future of education in the cyber age.

The first is that education responds to, rather than creates, the 'revolution'. Once the revolution begins, education accelerates it, but it does not initiate it. The revolution is a response to the discovery of a new, but still potential, MaxEP solution, and education is part of the complexification of the system needed to reach to, or converge on, that solution. Thus, there can be no theory of education free of the idea of MaxEP and the particularities of the problems to be solved at that time to reach MaxEP. Nor can there be any counter-theory of education—no Illichian counter-narrative[14]—beyond this adaptive and contingent process.

The second trend is that an education system, like all components of a complex adaptive system, is built from—really, cobbled together from—whatever structures are available at the time that the problem is 'perceived' and with whatever energy is available.[15] It necessarily needs only to be good enough to help solve the current problem even if it creates problems for the future. It is a blind evolutionary process.

And the third trend is that, to the extent that education both responds to and is also responsible for the deepening complexification of the civilization as the civilization reaches towards MaxEP, education itself becomes subject to diminishing returns. Progressively more energy is needed to create the next dollop of education negentropy in the system. This begins to limit the application of education to solving the current crop of problems.[16]

With those trends in mind, I turn now to the cyber age.

The Cyber Revolution as the Third Solution to MaxEP

The Cyber Revolution, sometimes described as the 'Information Age', can now be seen as a new solution to the Earth's MaxEP[17]. But, unlike the earlier solutions, it does not depend on tapping a store of energy in a new way (grains in the Agricultural Revolution, fossil fuels in the Industrial Revolution) to find a new solution to MaxEP. Rather, it depends on finding a new, more efficient way to create negentropy at a vastly lower cost in energy. The results are the same as in the earlier revolutions—a more complex civilization with a higher tempo driven by the application of more energy. And, so far—this revolution only got underway in the middle of the twentieth century—the increase in energy has been much smaller, perhaps only doubling or tripling the energy used per person during the Industrial Revolution.

The role of education in this revolution is closely following the pattern seen in the earlier revolutions.

First, education is following the revolution, not leading it. The first computers emerged in the 1940s and 1950s, but there were few if any university-level schools of computing then. Those schools started to emerge in the 1960s and 1970s, generally evolving out of university physics departments (and often called 'departments of computer [or computing] science') or out of engineering schools (and often called 'departments of information technology)'. And it has only been in the first decades of the twenty-first century that the broader aspects of the revolution—particularly the legal and policy aspects—have emerged.

Second, this education is a response to perceived problems created by the Cyber Revolution. And it is built from the system's existing components, often dating back to previous stages of the civilization. It needs only to be good enough to solve the problem—the 'gathering storm' say—even if it creates new problems for the future. Complex adaptive systems, which merely strive to continue to exist until the next moment, are masters of 'kicking the can down the road'. Thus, education in the Cyber Revolution harnesses the education structures of the Industrial Revolution—standardized mass production—and even of the Agricultural Revolution—a current fad for generalists who can understand, at least superficially, all the threads of the Cyber Revolution from the technical to the legal.

Third, because education is part of the deeper complexification of the civilization undergoing the Cyber Revolution, it is subject to diminishing returns—more energy is required for each extra dollop of education negentropy created. We can see this in the way that the cost of education in advanced societies is rising faster than the broad measures of system growth such as GDP. This makes it progressively harder for education to solve the future problems that it helped create.[18]

The Cyber Revolution and the Future of Education

Two probably conflicting processes are likely to dominate the future of education in today's advanced societies—societies that are in the vanguard of the Cyber Revolution.

The first is the further complexification of these societies as they reach towards the 'cyber' solution to MaxEP for the Earth. This carries with it diminishing returns of negentropy, particularly in education, for each marginal dollop of external energy. Coping with this rising complexification is a hard problem, one that has caused previous civilizations to founder, even if each complexification step is a rational response to the problems of the moment.[19]

The Western Roman Empire complexified, through the elaboration of its government and army, to solve its problems, which then required extra energy subsidies from the agriculture of conquered countries. The control of those new provinces required further complexification, which in turn required further energy subsidies, and so on. 'In the end the Western Roman Empire could no longer afford the problem of its own existence'[20]. Modern Europe has faced the same dilemma but has wriggled out of it twice by finding new energy sources. Late in the Agricultural Revolution, Europe's colonial project gave it access to new bioenergy sources. During the Industrial Revolution, it gained access to fossil fuels—the energy sources that still power the Cyber Revolution.

The second process is the likely emergence of a fourth solution to MaxEP for the Earth. Counting the Industrial Revolution and the Cyber Revolution as the first two 'industrial revolutions', this new solution will be the third industrial revolution following the Agricultural Revolution, although the Davos set seem to think it is the fourth (Schwab 2017). It will count as a revolution in our sense if it is able to reach towards a new level of MaxEP and, in so doing, create greater stores of negentropy on Earth and hence greater complexity.

The revolution, if it occurs, will be built on new abilities to manipulate materials, often at very fine scales, with the help of cyber technologies. We are promised a convergence of advanced biotechnologies, advanced material technologies and advanced cyber technologies. The early fruits of this cyber-enabled 'technology singularity' are things like 3D printing of heart tissue, synthetic biology, nano-machines, and quantum sensors.

It remains to be seen if the 'technology singularity' will constitute an authentic revolution—a step change in the search for new and better solutions to the Earth's MaxEP. It will require either the corralling of new, hitherto unexploited sources of energy as the Agricultural and Industrial Revolutions did, or the vastly more efficient creation of negentropy from existing sources of energy as the Cyber Revolution is doing. My guess is that it will become such an authentic revolution, and follow the path pioneered by the Cyber Revolution.

If these two processes do intersect, many of today's issues of education will become moot. The problems of cyber education will be steamrolled by the problems of the new revolution. And the solutions to these emerging problems will no doubt be built from the shards of today's hard-won solutions to the problems of educating for cyber.

Coda

Given the arguments earlier, what might a cyber education system look like in the near future—in what might be the twilight of the cyber age? Broadly, and perhaps sadly, it is likely to be more of the same: an embellished and complexified version of late industrial age education.

I suggest this because, while the future of any complex adaptive system is deeply unpredictable, complex adaptive systems evolve by exploring 'adjacent possibilities'—a narrower, highly contingent, and sometimes not-yet-realized set of possibilities sometimes brought into existence by the system in question moving into that neighbourhood of possible futures (Dennett 2017).[21] And this exploration takes time, time that the Cyber Revolution has not yet had—and may never have.

The Industrial Revolution moved our civilization into a neighbourhood of possible futures that were unreachable—indeed, they did not really exist as possibilities—by the Agricultural Revolution. And, lagging somewhat, the industrial age education system found adjacent possibilities in terms of its structure and dynamics that were similarly new and previously unreachable, even if they had been built, at least at first, by cobbling together earlier structures in new ways.

I see three processes constraining any civilizational revolution as that civilization seeks a new and better solution to the Earth's MaxEP, and these constraints each have an impact on the future of education for that complex adaptive system. I introduced and discussed each of them earlier, but it is useful to recap them here.

The first is that complex systems take time to explore the new possibilities opened up by new approaches to MaxEP. And, in particular, education, because this is situated deep in the negentropy dimensions of the system and is always a lagging response to a civilizational revolution. That means that in the early stages of a civilizational revolution, the education landscape will look very much like the late stages of the system's earlier phase. Today's cyber education—in terms of the structure of curricula, syllabi, and pedagogy—would look very familiar in any faculty of engineering or science of 50 years ago.

The second is that complex systems use what is at hand when they adapt to their new environment. Evolution is always a blind process of exploring and testing uses of structures and processes to fit the needs of a new environment. It is not surprising that early motor cars were called 'horseless carriages'. Nor is it surprising that the education structures and processes of the industrial age were cobbled together from those of much earlier times. Thus today's cyber education will be cobbled together from industrial age components.[22]

The third is that complex systems complexify to reach towards MaxEP. And, as new solutions to MaxEP become possible, the complexification increases. But it seems that this complexification cannot increase indefinitely within any one solution to MaxEP—the collapse of the Western Roman Empire in the agricultural age and the narrow escape of the Western European powers in the industrial age show the risks involved. Education is particularly vulnerable to increasing complexification, as can be seen by the steady increase in the years of required education in the Western world. It is now common in Western countries for compulsory pre-schooling, longer periods of primary and secondary schooling, and four-year university degrees followed by master's degrees to be seen as, at least, the aspirational norm. (In 1825 in the early industrial age, Charles Darwin enrolled at the University of Edinburgh at age 16 to study medicine, a one-year course! (Browne 1995, 34)). Today's cyber education is in the thick of this complexification.

In sum, the best that can be said about today's cyber education is that it has both the strengths and weaknesses of late industrial age education. It shows little evidence that it has, as yet, lifted itself to a new level as the cyber age explores a new level of MaxEP. And it shows much evidence that it is stuck in a late and, perhaps, limiting stage of complexification of industrial age processes.

And, worryingly, it is now running up against the next revolution without having sorted itself out as a fully evolved response to today's civilizational revolution.

Acknowledgements

I thank John Finnigan for our discussions over many years, across the physics–biology divide, on complex systems, and, most recently, on entropy.

Notes

1. E.g. SINET. https://www.security-innovation.org
2. E.g. in Australia, STEM, innovation, and cyber education are conflated in government education programmes. https://www.education.gov.au/support-science-technology-engineering-and-mathematics
3. E.g. Northrop Grumman sponsors school and university cyber competitions in the United States, United Kingdom, and Australia. http://www.northropgrumman.com/CorporateResponsibility/Pages/CyberPatriot.aspx
4. Schrödinger, *What is Life?*
5. Bradbury, 'Just What Is Science Anyway?'.
6. Haff, 'Maximum Entropy Production by Technology', 400.
7. Haff, 'Maximum Entropy Production by Technology', 402.
8. Tainter, 'Social Complexity and Sustainability', 93.
9. Christian, *Maps of Time,* 2004. These estimates (watts) are rates of energy use, not amounts of energy. I use them here for simple comparisons. They should be read, strictly, as the rate of energy use per person per second on average over a day.
10. Tainter, 'Social Complexity and Sustainability', 94.
11. Haff, 'Maximum Entropy Production by Technology', 400.
12. Christian, *Maps of Time.*
13. Tainter, 'Social Complexity and Sustainability', 94.
14. Ivan Illich was a prominent critic of the institutions of Western civilization in the second half of the twentieth century (Illich, I. 1971. *Deschooling Society.* New York: Harper & Row). He was particularly dismissive of the institutionalization of the modern—that is, industrial age—education system. He favoured de-schooling education as a way of de-institutionalizing society. His nostrums were infused with the liberation theology of the time and contained not a little romantic wistfulness for the noble savage. His ideas, needless to say, had no sense of the role of education in the evolution of civilization as a complex system.
15. Tainter, 'Social Complexity and Sustainability'.
16. Tainter, 'Social Complexity and Sustainability', 95.
17. Cf. Haff, 'Maximum Entropy Production by Technology', 400.
18. Tainter, 'Social Complexity and Sustainability'.
19. Tainter, 'Social Complexity and Sustainability'.
20. Tainter, 'Social Complexity and Sustainability', 97.
21. Kauffman, *At Home in the Universe,* 1995.

22. Even if with a twenty-first century politically correct veneer (OECD. 2018. *The Future of Education and Skills: Education 2030.* Paris: OECD).

References

Allen, T.F.H., and Starr, T.B. 1982. *Hierarchy: Perspectives for Ecological Complexity.* Chicago: University of Chicago Press.

Augustine, N.R. 2007. *Rising Above the Gathering Storm: Energizing and Employing America for a Brighter Economic Future.* Washington, DC: National Academy of Sciences.

Augustine, N.R. 2010. *Rising Above the Gathering Storm, Revisited: Rapidly Approaching Category 5.* Washington, DC: National Academy of Sciences.

Bradbury, R.H. 1999. 'Just What Is Science Anyway?', *Nature & Resources* 35 (4): 9–11.

Brillouin, L. 1953. 'Negentropy Principle of Information', *Journal of Applied Physics* 24 (9): 1152–63.

Browne, J. 1995. *Charles Darwin: A Biography.* London: Jonathan Cape.

Chaisson, E.J. 2001. *Cosmic Evolution: The Rise of Complexity in Nature.* Cambridge, MA: Harvard University Press.

Christian, D. 2004. *Maps of Time: An Introduction to Big History.* Berkeley, CA: University of California Press.

Dennett, D.C. 2017. *From Bacteria to Bach and Back: The Evolution of Minds.* New York: W. W. Norton & Company.

Haff, P.K. 2014. 'Maximum Entropy Production by Technology'. In *Beyond the Second Law: Entropy Production and Non-Equilibrium Systems*, edited by R.C. Dewar, 397–414. Berlin: Springer-Verlag.

Harte, J. 2011. *Maximum Entropy and Ecology.* Oxford: Oxford University Press.

Holland, J.H. 1998. *Emergence: From Chaos to Order.* Oxford: Oxford University Press.

Holland, J.H. 2014. *Complexity: A Very Short Introduction.* Oxford: Oxford University Press.

Kauffman, S. 1995. *At Home in the Universe: The Search for the Laws of Self-Organization and Complexity.* Oxford: Oxford University Press.

Levins, R. 1970. 'Complex Systems'. In *Towards a Theoretical Biology. 3. Drafts*, edited by C.H. Waddington, 73–88. Edinburgh: Edinburgh University Press.

Liska, A.J., and Heier, C.D. 2013. 'The Limits to Complexity: A Thermodynamic History of Bioenergy', *Biofuels, Bioproducts & Biorefining* 7, 573–81.

Mitchell, M. 2009. *Complexity: A Guided Tour.* Oxford: Oxford University Press.

Morowitz, H.J. 1968. *Energy Flow in Biology.* New York: Academic Press.

Royal Society 2014. *Vision for Science and Mathematics Education.* London: Royal Society.

Schrödinger, E. 1944. *What is Life?* Cambridge, UK: Cambridge University Press.

Schwab, K. 2017. *The Fourth Industrial Revolution.* New York: Crown Business.

Shannon, C.E., and Weaver, W. 1949. *The Mathematical Theory of Communication.* Urbana, IL: University of Illinois Press.

Smil, V. 2008. *Energy in Nature and Society: General Energetics of Complex Systems.* Cambridge, MA: MIT Press.

Tainter, J.A. 2006. 'Social Complexity and Sustainability', *Ecological Complexity* 3: 91–103.

von Bertalanffy, L. 1968. *General System Theory: Foundations, Development, Applications.* New York: Braziller.

Walras, L. 1954. *Elements of Pure Economics.* New York: Kelly.

CHAPTER 25

....

CYBERSECURITY, HUMAN RIGHTS, AND EMPIRICISM: THE CASE OF DIGITAL SURVEILLANCE

....

JONATHON PENNEY

CYBERSECURITY AND SURVEILLANCE

....

SURVEILLANCE has today become 'core' to state national security strategies (Sparrow 2014, 19). This is particularly so for cybersecurity. In a digital age of ubiquitous computing, Big Data, and new technologies empowering data analytics like artificial intelligence, automation, and machine learning, surveillance is no longer pursued simply for 'influence, management, protection or direction', but is now 'fundamental' to cybersecurity strategies dealing with digital threats (Wang and Tucker 2017, 145).

This is not surprising. Each of surveillance's primary purposes both historically and in contemporary times can, at least in theory, be seen to advance core aspects of most cybersecurity strategies (Lyon 2007).[1] First, surveillance is used to *maintain control*, a primary rationale for employers, law enforcement, and governments that have deployed surveillance practices.[2] Second, it provides for *social sorting*, useful for commercial enterprise seeking to manage and influence consumers.[3] Third, surveillance provides for *mutual monitoring*, which largely exists through peer-to-peer social networks, both in virtual and real contexts.[4] Cybersecurity primarily aims to identify and detect threats,[5] both digital and otherwise, and each of these purposes ostensibly advances those aims. Surveillance's *control* function can promote cybersecurity by helping limit the scope and diversity of digital threats that must be identified and detected over time. Its *social sorting* function also naturally advances threat identification and detection—for example, data gathered through mass digital surveillance programmes to sort and categorize populations so that certain individuals or groups can be treated differently, like subjecting identified threats to more targeted forms of surveillance and tracking.[6] And *mutual monitoring* through social networks provides new data sources—like social media platform data—and means of identifying threats through those sources.

In light of this, it is understandable why surveillance has been central to the 'securitization' of discourse in cybersecurity (Deibert 2015, 124–5). If the predominant framing or conceptualization for cybersecurity is the identification, detection, and prevention of national security threats (Stevens 2016, 37; Dunn Cavelty 2013),[7] with little concern for other dimensions of surveillance like its impacts on civil society or human rights, then expanding its scope, ubiquity, and prevalence makes perfect sense. If increasing surveillance means increased national security through threat identification, detection, and prevention, then the logical choice is for policy makers and government officials to expand its prominence and deployment in national security policy and strategies more generally. This is precisely what has happened.

But what if these assumptions are wrong—that, in fact, surveillance, and its impact on human rights and civil society, did not promote cybersecurity but, overall, actually undermined it? Critics of securitization have argued for new approaches to cybersecurity more focused on civil society or human rights,[8] not just because doing so may lessen the impact on human rights—a worthy goal—but also because there is good reason to believe that state surveillance practices may lead to less security, not more.[9] Yet, cybersecurity literature has largely remained atheoretical and overly technical, dominated by a national security focus and analyses (Eriksson and Giacomello 2014, 208).[10] Thus, gaps in research and literature persist, particularly on the impact of surveillance. This chapter addresses these gaps with a discussion of recent research on the impact of surveillance—both mass and targeted forms—and considers these insights and their implications for cybersecurity. A range of new interdisciplinary empirical studies on the impact and dimensions of surveillance, particularly online and digital forms, has yet to be considered in light of cybersecurity. This chapter aims to do this. Overall, it is suggested that such state-led digital surveillance, rather than guaranteeing cybersecurity, undermines it, both in the near term and the long term, in expected and unexpected ways.

Theories of Surveillance Impact

Surveillance today typically concerns activities and information practices that enable a nation state to track or 'manage' a population by monitoring individuals (Marwick 2012, 380), with heavy reliance upon electronic communications and related digital technologies (Nissenbaum 2009). Indeed, state surveillance has been central to the 'securitization' in cybersecurity, particularly the increasing sophistication and expansion of digital surveillance.[11] This modern expansion began after 9/11, through a plethora of anti-terror laws, ordinances, and surveillance infrastructure that governments subsequently enacted, and today it has expanded further with the emergence of Big Data and other forms of digital and informational tracking made possible through complex analytics and people's increasing reliance upon constant Internet connectivity, ubiquitous computing, and digital media globally.

There are different theoretical and empirical approaches to understanding the impact of such surveillance activities, which are often discipline specific. A predominant body of work on point is surveillance studies, a field largely founded and defined by sociologist and leading surveillance expert David Lyon.[12] Surveillance studies theory and research are deeply influenced by the work of Michel Foucault and his use of the 'panopticon' metaphor to understand surveillance and its impact on modern society.[13] Foucault's panopticism drew on the work of English philosopher and reformer Jeremy Bentham, whose 'panopticon' prison design—inmates in cells being subject to the *possibility* of constant surveillance by an invisible watcher in a central tower—offered a powerful metaphor for modern surveillance.[14] Here, the threat or possibility of always being watched helps 'discipline' or shape people's behaviour—encouraging self-censorship and docility, making populations easier to control them.[15] Today, surveillance studies theory has increasingly turned to the idea of 'surveillance culture', which focuses on how, in our era of digital technology and social media, surveillance is an everyday fact of life for everything we do,[16] and how people's own behaviour helps facilitate surveillance—like how our own clicks, social media engagement, or consumer behaviour, create data to facilitate a surveillance culture.[17]

Another emerging body of work exploring the impact of surveillance is chilling effects theory—an interdisciplinary theoretical account of how certain laws and regulatory state actions—namely, surveillance—can 'chill' or deter people from speaking or engaging in other legal, constitutionally protected, and even desirable activities (Schauer 1978; Penney 2016; Penney 2017). Indeed, with Internet regulation and censorship on the rise, states increasingly engaging in online surveillance, and state cyber-policing capabilities rapidly evolving globally, (Nye 2011; Zittrain 2018; Deibert 2013, Schneier 2015) concerns about how these new state practices—particularly digital surveillance—have an impact on, or 'chill', people's activities have taken on greater urgency and public importance. Though chilling effects theory is primarily based on a mix of legal, economic, and privacy theory and empirical research, chilling effect concerns have also been investigated and pursued in other disciplines like sociology and psychology (Kaminski and Witnov 2014) and in the contexts of surveillance studies.[18] Indeed, chilling effects theory explores empirically and theoretically in further depth different impacts of panopticism and surveillance culture that surveillance studies have highlighted.

Frederick Schauer (1978) and Daniel Solove (2006; 2007) offer the most commonly cited accounts of chilling effects theory, though leading intersecting works also informing the analysis here include surveillance studies,[19] privacy,[20] libel chill (Barendt et al. 1997), studies on self-censorship/self-presentation online (Das and Kramer 2013; Boyd and Marwick 2010), and different dimensions and dynamics of Internet regulations (Zittrain 2008; Benkler 2006; Seltzer 2010). Schauer treats 'chilling effects' as a form of 'deterrence', whereby people's fear of state sanction or punishment, legal risk and penalties, and uncertainty built into the legal system deter or 'chill' people from exercising their rights. That is, they self-censor or disengage from certain activities to avoid these uncertainties and risks of punishment.[21] Solove, informed by the insights of surveillance studies, extends Schauer's account in theorizing chilling effects associated with modern information practices like state surveillance and data collection, and how such activities promote a climate of self-censorship and risk comparable to 'environmental pollution'.[22] Chilling effects theory is often operationalized methodologically in empirical studies designed to measure how certain surveillance practices, whether mass or targeted, or knowledge thereof, may reduce, alter, dampen, and thus deter or chill, certain activities, particularly in online contexts where digital surveillance is at stake.

Though cybersecurity literature has focused little on the impact of surveillance, a range of new empirical studies from disciplines like law, sociology, communications, and privacy/surveillance studies, is emerging, providing new insights on point. These works often draw on surveillance studies theory or chilling effects theory as a framework to understand these impacts, though most are interdisciplinary in orientation and design, and draw on a range of theories and research in their analysis.

IMPACT ON CIVIL SOCIETY AND HUMAN RIGHTS

New research shows that surveillance has impacts on a range of fundamental human rights and freedoms, with important implications for civil society and deliberative democracy. These rights include freedom of expression as well as the right to seek, receive, and impart information and ideas, recognized and protected in the Universal Declaration of Human Rights (UDHR) and the International Convention on Civil and Political Rights (ICCPR).[23] For example, awareness of surveillance—or the threat of it—can have a substantial chilling effect on people's exercise of these rights, leading them to self-censor or avoid seeking or imparting certain sensitive information.[24] Surveillance can also be said to violate international rights against discrimination and protection for minorities,[25] in that it has an unequal or disproportionate impact on certain groups, including vulnerable minorities.

Chilling Speech and Promoting Self-Censorship and Conformity

Surveillance chills the exercise of free speech and expression overall, promoting self-censorship and conformity. Several new studies, consistent with chilling effects and surveillance studies theory, document these impacts, including in relation to both mass surveillance and more targeted or tailored forms. Stoycheff's 2016 study involved an experimental design whereby participant Internet users agreed to 'terms of agreement' that reminded individual participants that their subsequent online activities were subject to interception and surveillance (Stoycheff 2016, 302)—that is, if targeted, their activities could be surveilled and monitored. The study found that exposing participants to these 'terms of agreement' chilled their willingness to express their political views, with the greatest chilling effect on those who believed that their political views were not mainstream.[26] These findings support the notion of a 'spiral of silence', whereby individuals, due to fear of isolation, moderated their political expression to conform with what they perceived to be the more 'mainstream' views of the majority. In short, the study found that awareness of potential surveillance 'chilled' online speech, leading to self-censorship, with the potential for greater social conformity, and less political dissent, at a societal level.[27]

I made similar findings in my own 2017 published empirical study on surveillance chilling effects.[28] This study involved a survey, administered to more than 1,200 United States-based adult Internet users, designed to explore the impact of surveillance or digitally delivered targeted threats by comparing and analysing user responses to hypothetical scenarios that, in theory, may cause chilling effects or other forms of self-censorship. The findings suggested that, once people were made aware of different online threats, they were far less willing to speak about certain topics online, and were more cautious in their speech. For example, in terms of online speech, 62% of respondents indicated they would be 'much less likely' (22%) or 'somewhat less likely' (40%) to 'speak or write about certain topics online' due to such online surveillance by government. And 78% of respondents 'strongly' (38%) or 'somewhat' agreed (40%) that they would be more cautious about what they said online due to the surveillance.[29] The findings suggested a noteworthy chilling effect on speech and other expression online due to awareness of state surveillance. These findings are consistent with previous findings by Pew Internet, wherein Americans reported self-censoring and changing their online habits after learning about government surveillance programs through news reports about the Snowden disclosures (Pew Research Centre 2015a, 2014a, 2014b.

Stoycheff et al. (2018)'s more recent work further supports these findings via two experimental studies that, again, found that ' "perceived surveillance" chilled the intentions of participants to engage in online political activities'.[30] That 'restrictive chilling effect' held across samples of both Muslim American Internet users as well a broader sample of US Internet users.[31] This work, the authors concluded, supported earlier findings,[32] while contributing to a 'growing body of evidence' that mass surveillance is not innocuous as its supporters claim.[33] Rather, it has important implications for fundamental rights and freedoms.

Chilling Online Information Access, Engagement, and Content Sharing

Surveillance also has a negative impact on information access and a range of other forms of online engagement. My own 2017 study found that, once people were made aware of online threats like government surveillance, Internet users were less willing to engage in a range of other activities online, including being less likely to contribute to social networks online, less willing to share personally created content, and more cautious about what they searched for online.[34]

Similarly, two recent empirical studies, centred on Snowden's NSA/PRISM surveillance revelations in June 2013, provide evidence that mass government surveillance can have a widespread chilling effect on people's online activities—in particular, topics or information they read about or search for online. An MIT-based study by Marthews and Tucker (2014) analysed Google Search trends before and after June 2013, and found a statistically significant reduction in searches for privacy-sensitive topics. Similarly, Penney's 2016 study examined Wikipedia article traffic on topics that raise privacy concerns over a period of 32 months before and after Snowden's revelations in June 2013.[35] The study found not only a statistically significant immediate decline in traffic for privacy-sensitive Wikipedia articles after June 2013, but also a change in the overall secular trend in page views for these articles, suggesting not only immediate but also long-term chilling effects resulting from online surveillance revelations.[36] This conclusion was strengthened by the fact that the view counts for several comparator groups of Wikipedia articles, which would not raise privacy concerns, remained unaffected through the same period of time.[37]

Given how Google Search and Wikipedia are extremely popular online tools for millions of Internet users to attain information, these two studies raise significant civil society and democratic concerns about whether citizens, under mass surveillance, will continue to seek out information about controversial matters of public importance (like terrorism) in order to stay informed and engage in healthy democratic deliberation.

Unequal/Disparate Impact, Including Vulnerable Minorities

These surveillance effects may also have a negative impact on certain groups more than others, including a greater chilling effect on women and younger Internet users.[38] In every scenario examined in my own 2017 study, I found a statistically significant age effect where the younger the Internet user, the greater the impact or chilling effect on the user's on-line activities. This statistical association was strongest in the scenario involving government surveillance. There was also a gender effect, whereby women were more impacted in scenarios involving surveillance as well as a scenario involving a digitally delivered targeted threat (here, a legal threat). And Stoycheff's 2016 findings also suggested disproportionate impacts on those who believed their political views were not mainstream or dissented from the majority.[39] Certain professions and civil society sectors—such as journalists and human rights workers—may also be differentially impacted. A series of other recent qualitative and quantitative studies document how state surveillance impacts or chills journalistic practices while also dampening or rendering more difficult certain forms of activism (Myers West 2017; Lashmar 2017; Wahl-Jorgensen, Bennett, and Cable 2017; Dencik, Hintz, and Cable 2017; PEN America 2013, 2015).

CYBERSECURITY IMPLICATIONS

Though critiques of surveillance for impacting human rights or civil society are not new, systematic and interdisciplinary empirical research supporting those claims *is*, and the previous section aimed to assemble just some of those important and innovative works. However, these impacts do more than undermine human rights or harm civil society more generally: they also undermine cybersecurity. This section makes this case, with reference to emerging new empirical studies.

Surveillance Renders Populations More Vulnerable to Cybersecurity Threats

A society under surveillance is one far more vulnerable to cybersecurity problems and exploitation. The growing prevalence and centrality of surveillance in cybersecurity, and national security more generally,[40] is consistent with what Lyon calls 'surveillance culture'[41]—that is, the increasing ubiquity and prevalence of surveillance and surveillance practices within broader culture and day-to-day life.[42] A 'nefarious result' of surveillance culture is that people come to accept the ubiquity of surveillance as normal—a fact of everyday life (Bauman and Lyon 2013, 13).[43] This 'normalization' of surveillance, and acceptance of it, leads to a state of learned acceptance and helplessness that Wahl-Jorgensen

et al. call 'surveillance realism': 'Surveillance becomes normalised and, because of its pervasiveness, we do not question it. We are, in that sense, living in a state of "surveillance realism" where we "accept it as an inevitability of our world" and do not question or contest it.'[44]
In other words, surveillance realism means passivity and acceptance in the face of surveillance— one simply accepts it without taking steps to challenge it, or, in other cases, defend oneself from it.

This surveillance realism, and attendant learned helplessness and passivity in the face of surveillance, has been documented, as well as its very real and serious consequences for cybersecurity. Surveillance realism leads to a passive and docile population unwilling to take the necessary steps to challenge, resist, or oppose surveillance more generally. For example, Dencik and Cable's 2017 study based on multiple focus groups among UK citizens, as well as semi-structured interviews with political activists, found evidence of 'surveillance realism'. Here, a 'lack of transparency', 'knowledge' and 'control over' surveillance and data-gathering practices among participants led to feelings of 'widespread resignation' (though not consent) to 'status quo' surveillance (Dencik and Cable 2017, 764). Similarly, Mamonov and Koufaris' 2016 experimental study of the impact of surveillance on citizens, similarly found evidence that exposure to news about government surveillance led to 'learned helplessness'—exposure to an 'uncontrollable aversive stimulus' leads to deficits in motivation to act to address the issue, here being government surveillance. In other words, surveillance realism means citizens are not seeking out the necessary information or tools they need to protect themselves from surveillance and other cybersecurity threats.

Surveillance realism also has an impact on sound cybersecurity practices. In fact, Mamonov and Koufaris found that participants exposed to news about electronic government surveillance caused the participants to use weaker passwords compared with those exposed only to general government-related news stories.[45] The best explanation, the authors surmised, was learned helplessness about the inevitability of state surveillance. These findings were also consistent with van Schaik et al. who also found, in a 2017 study on risk perception and cybersecurity, that users who felt in control were more likely to use cybersecurity tools like security add-ons and anti-virus software (van Schaik et al. 2017).

The earlier discussed surveillance chilling effects found by Penney, Stoycheff, and others, also undercut cybersecurity. If surveillance chills citizens from speaking, sharing, or accessing information online or off, then they are likely also chilled from seeking out information about how best to protect themselves and their data from surveillance and collection.[46]

Surveillance Practices and Technology Promote Cybersecurity Vulnerabilities

Surveillance realism's passivity and learned helplessness also contributes to cybersecurity challenges and vulnerabilities in other ways. With a passive population willing to accept and not contest surveillance, surveillance realism leads to a permissive law, policy, and technological environment whereby new surveillance tools and technologies can be developed or deployed, with little scrutiny or critical assessment as to how these technologies have an impact on security.

A powerful criticism of digital surveillance and related technologies, for instance, is that it undermines cybersecurity by promoting and maintaining security vulnerabilities that can be exploited by criminals and foreign adversaries.[47] Cybersecurity's predominant national security culture emphasizes offensive capabilities, in addition to defensive, wherein states exploit vulnerabilities in software and hardware to attack others.[48] Targeted surveillance often involves either actively inserting 'back doors' and other security vulnerabilities in software and hardware or leaving known vulnerabilities unpublished or unreported to exploit later for offensive operations like hacking, cyber espionage, or surveillance. Snowden's revelations, for example, documented a number of instances where the National Security Agency took steps to insert vulnerabilities into commercial software and weaken encryption standards.[49] With states working covertly to weaken hardware and software security while stockpiling vulnerabilities rather than publishing or disclosing them to vendors, then citizens, journalists, activists, and even entire populations are less secure and safe.

Renders Populations Vulnerable to Disinformation, Propaganda, and Fake News

An emerging and increasingly complex civil society and national security challenge is the prevalence, spread, and consumption of misinformation, rumours, and 'fake news', by citizens, particularly in online contexts like social media network sites (Kwon and Rao 2017; Tufekci 2017).

Kwon and Rao's 2017 study is among the first to examine empirically how the 'threat' of Internet surveillance has an impact on the spread of rumour and disinformation among the general public online.[50] In two surveys conducted in South Korea, the authors found, counter intuitively, that citizens' concerns about government surveillance online actually 'increased their willingness to engage in cyber-rumour sharing'.[51] The authors hypothesized that state surveillance concerns led citizens to distrust government as an information gatekeeper, rendering them more likely to engage in rumour and misinformation as alternative information sources.

Another explanation might be found in the previously discussed studies finding that surveillance can have a noteworthy chilling effect on citizens' willingness to seek out controversial or privacy-concerning information and content online.[52] This means that citizens under state surveillance may be chilled from searching about controversial or contentious news stories to determine their truth or veracity, rendering them less able to critically assess rumours or misinformation and thus more likely to share or be duped or exploited. Moreover, earlier discussed studies by Stoycheff and Penney suggest that surveillance promotes self-censorship and a 'spiral of silence' among citizens: people less willing to speak out may also self-censor on controversial rumours or misinformation, thus also contributing to the problem.

Surveillance Can Encourage Dangerous Cybersecurity Practices

The threat of surveillance, both targeted and mass forms, can also encourage activists to adopt dangerous cybersecurity practices. Myers West's 2017 observational study of the impact surveillance and other threats had on activist communities revealed a tension between practices taken to protect communications from surveillance—like encryption and anonymizing tools—and the need (and importance) of greater visibility and transparency to reach a broader audience/affect the larger 'information environment'.[53] A 2016 study by Dencik, Hintz, and Cable, which included in-depth interviews with 'social justice activists', revealed similar tensions, with Snowden revelations leading more technology-savvy activists to adopt stringent measures and tools to protect privacy and anonymity, with other activist communities avoiding basic security measures out of need for transparency that they have 'nothing to hide' in terms of their aims and methods.

Undermines Reporting, and thus Public Awareness, on National Security Matters

There is also evidence that surveillance will make journalism and investigative reporting more difficult, meaning fewer news sources and less quality information for citizens, particularly on national security matters, which are often complex and require confidential government sourcing. In a qualitative study involving interviews with journalists after the Snowden revelations, Lashmar (2017) found that all participants believed that the existence of mass government surveillance would 'chill' and deter confidential sources from speaking with journalists. Wahl-Jorgenson et al.'s 2017 research also found that reporters struggled with the reality of mass government surveillance, leading them to focus mainly on surveillance of elites and other 'legitimating' narratives, rather than more complex stories centred on mass surveillance programmes.[54] Similarly, journalists also report self-censorship on certain topics post-Snowden.[55]

TOWARDS A RIGHTS-CENTRIC CYBERSECURITY

Critics of the narrow and often technical national security focus in cybersecurity literature have argued for new frameworks for cybersecurity centred on civil society or human rights. This chapter has supported those criticisms, with a discussion of surveillance and related research demonstrating how surveillance not only has a negative impact on human rights, but also undermines cybersecurity. How have cybersecurity experts and researchers missed these important impacts and implications of surveillance? There are likely several factors at play. First, until recently, cybersecurity literature has remained largely technical, national security focused, and unconcerned with either research in other fields relevant to cybersecurity or in interdisciplinary approaches that would incorporate insights from those disciplines and fields. Second, the literature has ignored the impacts on human rights and civil society argued in securitization studies. If you are not concerned with how cybersecurity has an impact on human rights, then you will also surely miss other related impacts on people. Third, cybersecurity has been atheoretical but also lacks systematic empirical work, supporting central cybersecurity claims.

A rights-centric approach to cybersecurity is required, one that is both interdisciplinary and empirical. Such an approach will require more cross-disciplinary research, but even that

Interdisciplinary Focus: Necessary but Insufficient Condition

Cybersecurity is no longer approached as a merely technical subject, but rather an 'exploding field' with a growing body of research from a range of disciplines beyond computer science, including political science, economics, law, international relations, and business management, among many others (Ramirez and Choucri 2016, 2216). [56] And today, cybersecurity also concerns technologies far beyond the computer, like the Internet and the Internet of Things, power grids, cars, and other 'cyber-physical systems'.[57]

This multi-technology and multi-disciplinary challenge has led to consistent calls for greater collaboration and interdisciplinary work between fields in cybersecurity over the years. Ramirez and Choucri recently conducted an extensive literature review and noted that a strong consensus among works commenting on the cybersecurity field as a whole agreed that more interdisciplinary work is needed, especially to formulate new cybersecurity approaches more focused on civil society or human rights.[58] In fact, as earlier noted, the notion that information security ought to be expanded to encompass broader 'political, societal, economic, and environmental sectors' first emerged in the 1990s.[59]

Years on, these calls for interdisciplinary approaches *have* led to important contributions to cybersecurity literature. The most noteworthy are studies drawing on securitization studies and framing theory to demonstrate and explore the 'securitization' of cybersecurity—in particular, understanding 'threat construction' concerning cyber threats and other issues, in order to justify expansion of related state measures or 'exceptional' responses outside the normal boundaries of politics.[60] Other important contributions have been works like Carr (2011) highlighting the role of people—namely, elected politicians—in this context, by showing how political conceptualizations of technology shape cybersecurity and technological outcomes.[61]

Despite these contributions, and this 'turn' to interdisciplinarity, however, cybersecurity remains predominantly framed in national security—even military—terms rather than civil society or human rights.[62] And cybersecurity literature itself remains, as noted earlier, decidedly narrow—both 'largely atheoretical' as well as 'dominated' either by 'technological or policy oriented analysis'.[63] Part of the challenge is the fact that interdisciplinary cybersecurity work often requires expertise across a range of complex fields, which is rare. Another reason, suggested by Ramirez and Choucri, is that the present lack of standardized 'cybersecurity terminology' has rendered cross-disciplinary collaboration more difficult. As terminology becomes more standardized and expertise more cross-disciplinary, additional interdisciplinary approaches will be possible, enabling more systematic study of how cybersecurity practices have an impact on human rights and longer-term security outcomes over time.

Individual-Focused Empiricism and Human Rights

But more interdisciplinary work is also not enough. Such work, while enriching the literature, would not necessarily be any more focused on human rights and other individual-level cybersecurity impacts than more technical traditional cybersecurity research. Rather, the underlying assumptions and tenets of cybersecurity's predominant national security tilt need to be systematically interrogated with citizen- and user-focused empirical and theoretical studies.[64] This is, in part, one of the key contributions of securitization studies to cybersecurity literature. For example, Dunn-Cavelty's work on how 'cyber doom' scenarios and other threats in cybersecurity discourse are employed to justify expanded state powers and measures was more compelling *because* the threat construction largely lacked any empirical foundation.[65] Cybersecurity research thus must not only be interdisciplinary, but also focused on individual-level impacts, particularly on human rights and cyber or information security. Dutton (2017, 9) recently made this point and called for more user-focused empirical studies in cybersecurity. Despite a realization that cybersecurity is no longer the exclusive domain of technical experts but instead involves a range of different actors and stakeholders, he notes that there have not been corresponding 'strong' programmes of research 'aimed at understanding the attitudes, values, and behaviour of users with respect to cyber security'.[66] Ultimately, he calls for more social science research in cybersecurity—particularly, 'qualitative or quantitative research on end-users ... '[67]

Of course, calls for greater and better empirical work in cybersecurity literature are not novel.[68] Equally, the term 'empirical' can be understood quite broadly, encompassing anything from technical studies on cybersecurity systems—which remain common in the literature—to broader empirical work on state cybersecurity practices. Dutton's call is for a more focused empiricism—one focused on users: that is, people—and interdisciplinary works specifically drawing on social science methods and research. This chapter has employed a user-focused discussion of digital surveillance and its impact on users to answer this call, as well as meeting the aforementioned need to address the narrow technical and policy-focused nature of existing cybersecurity literature. Specifically, through a human rights and civil society lens, this chapter has drawn on new insights from recent empirical and social science studies on the impact of forms of online surveillance, and explores its impact and implication for users online—in particular, their 'behaviour' as well as their rights and interests.

If cybersecurity is ever to shed this national security tilt, or at least acknowledge and encompass civil society or human rights issues and concerns, then its discourse and literature need to change. Researchers and practitioners must consider more systematically and empirically the impact that cybersecurity practices have on individuals and discrete groups, drawing not just on technical studies but also on well-designed social scientific investigations focused on human rights as well as broader security impacts.

Notes

1. Wang and Tucker, 'Surveillance and Identity', 145. See generally, Penney, Jonathon W. 2015. 'The Cycles of Global Telecommunications Censorship and Surveillance', *University of Pennsylvania Journal of International Law* 36 (3): 693.
2. Lyon, *Surveillance Studies*; Wang and Tucker, 'Surveillance and Identity', 145.
3. Lyon, *Surveillance Studies*; Wang and Tucker, 'Surveillance and Identity', 145–6.
4. Lyon, *Surveillance Studies*; Wang and Tucker, 'Surveillance and Identity', 145–6.
5. Wang and Tucker, 'Surveillance and Identity', 145–6.

6. Wang and Tucker, 'Surveillance and Identity', 145–6; Lyon, D. 2018. *The Culture of Surveillance*. Cambridge, MA: Polity Press, 16–17, 107–8; Comninos, A., and Seneque, G. 2014. 'Cyber Security, Civil Society and Vulnerability in an Age of Communications Surveillance'. In *Global Information Society Watch 2014: Communications Surveillance in the Digital Age*, edited by A. Finlay, 32. Melville, South Africa: Association for Progressive Communications.
7. Comninos and Seneque, 'Cyber Security'.
8. E.g. Deibert, R. 2012. 'Distributed Security as Cyber Strategy: Outlining a Comprehensive Approach for Canada in Cyberspace', *Journal of Military and Strategic Studies* 14 (2); Deibert, 'Cyberspace Under Siege'.
9. Dunn Cavelty, 2013; Deibert, 'Cyberspace Under Siege'.
10. Dunn Cavelty, 'From Cyber-Bombs to Political Fallout', 106.
11. Deibert, 'Cyberspace Under Siege', 124–5.
12. See, for example, Lyon, D. 2015. *Surveillance After Snowden*. Cambridge, MA: Polity Press; Lyon, D. (2006). *Theorizing Surveillance: The Panopticon and Beyond*. Cullompton, Devon: Willan Publishing.
13. Lyon, *Theorizing surveillance*, 3–4; Lyon, *The Culture of Surveillance*, 33–4.
14. Lyon, *Theorizing surveillance*, 3–4; Lyon, *The Culture of Surveillance* 34.
15. Lyon, *Theorizing surveillance*, 3–4; Lyon, *The Culture of Surveillance* 34.
16. Lyon, *The Culture of Surveillance* 2–4.
17. Lyon, *The Culture of Surveillance* 2–4.
18. See, for example: Lyon, *Theorizing surveillance*.
19. See, for example, Lyon, *The Culture of Surveillance*; 2015; Lyon, *Theorizing surveillance*; Graham and Wood, 'Digitising Surveillance', 2003.
20. See e.g. Nissenbaum, *Privacy in Context*; Acquisti, A. 2004. Privacy and Security of Personal Information. In *Economics of Information Security*, pp. 179–186. Springer, Boston, MA.
21. Schauer, 'Fear, Risk, and the First Amendment, 689.
22. Solove, 'A Taxonomy of Privacy', 487.
23. Article 19 of both the UDHR and ICCPR.
24. See Report of the Special Rapporteur on the promotion and protection of the right to freedom of opinion and expression, UN Doc A/HRC/32/38 (11 May 2016) at pp. 15 ('Kaye Report, 2016').
25. See Article 7 of the UDHR and Articles 26 and 27 of the ICCPR; Kaye Report, 2016, 15–16.
26. Stoycheff, 'Under Surveillance', 303–4.
27. Stoycheff, 'Under Surveillance', 306–7.
28. Penney, 'Internet Surveillance'.
29. Penney, 'Internet Surveillance'.
30. Stoycheff et al. 'Privacy and the Panopticon' 10.
31. Stoycheff et al., 'Privacy and the Panopticon' 10–11.
32. Specifically, Penney 'Chilling Effects', and Stoycheff 'Under Surveillance'.
33. Stoycheff et al., 'Privacy and the Panopticon', 10–11.
34. Penney, 'Internet Surveillance'.
35. Penney, 'Chilling Effects'.
36. Penney, 'Chilling Effects'.
37. Penney, 'Chilling Effects'.

38. Stoycheff, 'Under Surveillance', 303–7.
39. Stoycheff, 'Under Surveillance', 303–7.
40. Sparrow, 'Digital Surveillance', 19; Wang and Tucker, 'Surveillance and identity', 145.
41. Lyon, *The Culture of Surveillance*, 2–4.
42. Lyon, *The Culture of Surveillance*, 2–4.
43. Wahl-Jorgensen, et al., 'Surveillance Normalization', 256; Bauman and Lyon, 2013: 13.
44. Wahl-Jorgensen, et al., 'Surveillance Normalization', 256.
45. Mamonov and Koufaris, 'The Impact of Exposure', 62.
46. See Marthews and Tucker, 'Government Surveillance'; Penney, 'Chilling Effects'.
47. Deibert, *Black Code*.
48. Schneier, *Data and Goliath*.
49. Schneier, *Data and Goliath*.
50. Kwon and Rao, 'Cyber-rumor Sharing', 308.
51. Kwon and Rao, 'Cyber-rumor Sharing',
52. Marthews and Tucker, 'Government Surveillance'; Penney, 'Chilling Effects'; Penney, 'Internet Surveillance'.
53. West, 'Ambivalence'.
54. Wahl-Jorgenson et al., 'Surveillance and Identity'.
55. PEN America, *Chilling Effects, Global Chilling*.
56. Azmi et al., *Motives behind Cyber Security Strategy Development*; Eriksson and Giacomello, 'International Relations'.
57. Ramirez and Choucri, 'Improving Interdisciplinary Communication'.
58. Ramirez and Choucri, 'Improving Interdisciplinary Communication'.
59. See e.g. Buzan, *People, States & Fear*; Deibert, *Parchment, Printing and Hypermedia Communication*; Eriksson and Giacomello, 'International Relations'.
60. Eriksson and Giacomello, 'International Relations', 209; Lawson, S. (2013). Beyond Cyber-Doom: Assessing the Limits of Hypothetical Scenarios in the Framing of Cyber-Threats. *Journal of Information Technology & Politics* 10 (1): 86–103, 88.
61. Eriksson and Giacomello, 'International Relations'; Carr, 'Irony'.
62. Stevens, 'Politics of Time'; Comninos and Seneque, 'Cybersecurity'; Dunn Cavelty, 'From Cyber-Bombs to Political Fallout', 105; Nye, 'Cyberspace Wars'.
63. Eriksson and Giacomello, 2014: 208; Dunn-Cavelty, 'From Cyber-Bombs to Political Fallout', 106.
64. See e.g. Deibert, 'Distributed Security'; Deibert, 'Cyberspace Under Siege'; Kovacs, A., and Hawtin, D. 2013. 'Cyber security, cyber surveillance and online human rights', paper presented at the Stockholm Internet forum on Internet freedom for global development; Taddeo, 'The Struggle between Liberties and Authorities'; Deibert, 'Cyberspace Under Siege'; Liaropoulos, 'Cyberconflict and Theoretical Paradigms'.
65. Dunn Cavelty, 'From Cyber-Bombs to Political Fallout'.
66. Dutton, 'Fostering', 2.
67. Dutton, 'Fostering', 9.
68. See, for example, Lawson, 'Beyond Cyber-Doom'; Eriksson and Giacomello, 'International Relations'; Domingo, F.C. 2015. 'Cyber War Versus Cyber Realities: Cyber Conflict in the International System by Brandon Valeriano and Ryan C. Maness', *Journal of Information Technology & Politics* 12 (4): 399–401.

BIBLIOGRAPHY

Andrew, N.L. 2016. 'Reconceptualising Cyber Security: Safeguarding Human Rights in the Era of Cyber Surveillance', *International Journal of Cyber Warfare and Terrorism* 6 (2): 32–40.

Azmi, R., Tibben, W., and Win, K.T. 2016. 'Motives behind Cyber Security Strategy Development: A Literature Review of National Cyber Security Strategy', 27th Australasian Conference on Information Systems, December.

Barendt, P., Lustgarten, P., Norrie, K., and Stephenson, J. 1997. *Libel Law and the Media: The Chilling Effect*. Wotton-under-Edge, UK: Clarendon Press.

Bauman, Z., and Lyon, D. 2013. *Liquid Surveillance: A Conversation*. Cambridge, MA: Polity Press.

Bauman, Z., Bigo, D., Esteves, P. et al. 2014. 'After Snowden: Rethinking the Impact of Surveillance', *International Political Sociology* 8 (2): 121–44.

Bayerl, P.S., and Akhgar, B. 2015. 'Online Surveillance Awareness as Impact on Data Validity for Open-Source Intelligence?'. In *Global Security, Safety and Sustainability: Tomorrow's Challenges of Cyber Security*, 10th International Conference, ICGS3 2015, September 15–17, Proceedings, edited by H. Jahankhani, A. Carlile, B. Akhgar, et al., 15–20. Cham, Switzerland: Springer International Publishing.

Benkler, Y. 2006. *The Wealth of Networks: How Social Production Transforms Markets and Freedom*. New Haven, CT: Yale University Press.

Betz, D.J., and Stevens, T. 2013. 'Analogical Reasoning and Cyber Security', *Security Dialogue*, 44 (2): 147–64.

Boyd, D., and Marwick, A. E. 2010. 'I Tweet Honestly, I Tweet Passionately: Twitter Users, Context Collapse, and the Imagined Audience'. *New Media & Society* 13 (1): 114–133.

Brantly, A.F. 2014. 'The Cyber Losers', *Democracy and Security* 10 (2): 132–55.

Buzan, B. 1991. *People, States & Fear: An Agenda for International Security Studies in the Post-Cold War Era*, 2nd edn. Boulder, CO: Lynne Rienner.

Carr, M. 2011. *The Irony of the Information Age: US Power and the Internet in International Relations*. PhD dissertation, Australian National University, Canberra.

Carr, M. 2013. 'Internet Freedom, Human Rights and Power', *Australian Journal of International Affairs* 67 (5): 621–37.

Carr, M. 2016. 'Public–Private Partnerships in National Cyber-Security Strategies', *International Affairs* 92 (1): 43–62.

Cavelty, M.D., and Balzacq, T. 2016. *Routledge Handbook of Security Studies*. Abingdon, UK: Routledge.

Cavelty, M.D., and Van Der Vlugt, R.A. 2015. 'A Tale of Two Cities: Or How the Wrong Metaphors Lead to Less Security', *Georgetown Journal of International Affairs* 16: 21.

Das, S., and Kramer, A. 2013. 'Self-censorship on Facebook'. *Proceedings of the International AAAI Conference on Web and Social Media 2013*, 120–127.

Deibert, R. 1997. *Parchment, Printing, and Hypermedia Communication and World Order Transformation*. New York, NY: Columbia University Press.

Deibert, R. 2015. 'Cyberspace Under Siege', *Journal of Democracy* 26 (3): 64–78.

Deibert, R. 2016. *Cyber Security*. Abingdon, UK: Routledge.

Deibert, R. 2017. 'Digital Threats Against Journalists'. In *Journalism After Snowden: The Future of the Free Press in the Surveillance State*, edited by S. Khorana and J. Henrichsen, New York: Columbia University Press.

Deibert, R., Palfrey, J., Rohozinski, R. et al. 2012. *Access Contested: Security, Identity, and Resistance in Asian Cyberspace*. London: MIT Press.

Deibert, R., and Rohozinski, R. 2010. 'Cyber Wars', *Index on Censorship* 39 (1): 79–90.

Deibert, R.J. 2013. *Black Code: Inside the Battle for Cyberspace*. Toronto: Signal.

Dencik, L., and Cable, J. 2017. 'The Advent of Surveillance Realism: Public Opinion and Activist Responses to the Snowden Leaks', *International Journal of Communication* 11, 763–81.

Dencik, L., Hintz, A., and Cable, J. 2016. 'Towards Data Justice? The Ambiguity of Anti-Surveillance Resistance in Political Activism', *Big Data & Society* 3 (2). doi.org/10.1177/2053951716679678

Dunn Cavelty, M. 2013. 'From Cyber-Bombs to Political Fallout: Threat Representations with an Impact in the Cyber-Security Discourse', *International Studies Review* 15 (1): 105–22.

Dutton, W. 2017. 'Fostering a Cyber Security Mindset', *Internet Policy Review* 6 (1). doi.org/10.14763/2017.1.443

Eriksson, J., and Giacomello, G. 2006. 'The Information Revolution, Security, and International Relations: (IR)relevant Theory?', *International Political Science Review* 27 (3): 221–44.

Eriksson, J., and Giacomello, G. 2007. 'International Relations, Cybersecurity, and Content Analysis: A Constructivist Approach'. In *Introduction: Closing the Gap between International Relations Theory and Studies of Digital-age Security*, 1–25. Oxford: Routledge.

Eriksson, J., and Giacomello, G. 2014. 'International Relations, Cybersecurity, and Content Analysis: A Constructivist Approach'. In *The Global Politics of Science and Technology – Vol. 2*, edited by M. Mayer, M. Carpes, and R. Knoblich, 205–19. Berlin Heidelberg: Springer.

Graham, S., and Wood, D. 2003. 'Digitising Surveillance: Categorisation, Space, Inequality', *Critical Social Policy* 23 (2): 227–248.

Hardy, S., Crete-Nishihata, M., Kleemola, K. et al. 2014. 'Targeted Threat Index: Characterizing and Quantifying Politically-Motivated Targeted Malware'. Paper presented at the Proceedings of the 23rd USENIX conference on Security Symposium, San Diego, CA.

Kaminski, M.E., and Witnov, S. (2014). 'The Conforming Effect: First Amendment Implications of Surveillance, Beyond Chilling Speech', *University of Richmond Law Review* 49: 465.

Khorana, S., and Henrichsen, J. 2017. *Journalism after Snowden: The Future of the Free Press in the Surveillance State*: New York: Columbia University Press.

Kwon, K., and Rao, R. 2017. 'Cyber-Rumor Sharing under a Homeland Security Threat in the Context of Government Internet Surveillance: The Case of South-North Korea Conflict', *Government Information Quarterly* 34 (2): 307–16.

Lashmar, P. 2017. 'No More Sources?', *Journalism Practice* 11 (6): 665–88.

Lawson, S.T., Yeo, S.K., Yu, H. et al. 2016. 'The Cyber-Doom Effect: The Impact of Fear Appeals in the US Cyber Security Debate'. Paper presented at the Cyber Conflict (CyCon) 2016 8th International Conference.

Liaropoulos, A. 2014. 'Cyberconflict and Theoretical Paradigms: Current Trends and Future Challenges in the Literature'. *Proceedings of the 13th European Conference on Cyber Warfare and Security*, 3–4 July, pp. 133–139.

Lyon, D. 2007. *Surveillance Studies: An Overview*: Oxford: Polity Press.

Lyon, D. 2014. 'Surveillance, Snowden, and Big Data: Capacities, Consequences, Critique', *Big Data & Society* 1 (2). doi.org/10.1177/2053951714541861

Mamonov, S., and Koufaris, M. 2016. 'The Impact of Exposure to News About Electronic Government Surveillance on Concerns About Government Intrusion, Privacy Self-Efficacy, and Privacy Protective Behavior', *Journal of Information Privacy and Security* 12 (2): 56–67.

Marthews, A., and Tucker, C. 2014. 'Government Surveillance and Internet Search Behavior'. MIT Sloane Working Paper No. 14380.

Marwick, A.E. 2012. 'The Public Domain: Social Surveillance in Everyday Life', *Surveillance & Society* 9 (4): 378.

Michaelsen, M. 2017. 'Far Away, So Close: Transnational Activism, Digital Surveillance and Authoritarian Control in Iran', *Surveillance & Society* 15 (3/4): 465.

Nissenbaum, H. 2004. 'Privacy as Contextual Integrity', *Washington Law Review* 79: 119.

Nissenbaum, H. 2009. *Privacy in Context: Technology, Policy, and the Integrity of Social Life*. Palo Alto: Stanford University Press.

Nye, J. 2010. *Cyber Power. The Future of Power in the 21st Century*. Cambridge, Mass.: Belfer Center for Science and International Affairs.

Nye, J. 2011. 'Cyberspace Wars', *International Herald Tribune 28*.

PEN America. 2013. *Chilling Effects: NSA Surveillance Drives US Writers to Self-Censor*. New York: PEN American Center.

PEN America. 2015. *Global Chilling: The Impact of Mass Surveillance on International Writers*. New York: PEN American Center.

Penney, J. 2016. 'Chilling Effects: Online Surveillance and Wikipedia Use', *Berkeley Technology Law Journal* 31: 117–82.

Penney, J. 2017. 'Internet Surveillance, Regulation, and Chilling Effects Online: A Comparative Case Study', *Internet Policy Review* 6 (2). doi. org/10.14763/2017.2.692

Pew Research Center. 2014a. *Global Opposition to U.S. Surveillance and Drones, But Limited Harm to America's Image*. Washington, DC: Pew Research Center.

Pew Research Center. 2014b. *Social Media and the 'Spiral of Silence'*. Washington, DC: Pew Research Center.

Pew Research Center. 2014c. *Public Perceptions of Privacy and Security in the Post-Snowden Era*. Washington, DC: Pew Research Center.

Pew Research Center. 2015a. *Americans' Privacy Strategies Post-Snowden*. Washington, DC: Pew Research Center.

Pew Research Center. 2015b. *Americans' Attitudes About Privacy, Security and Surveillance*. Washington, DC: Pew Research Center.

Pfleeger, S.L., and Caputo, D.D. 2012. 'Leveraging Behavioral Science to Mitigate Cyber Security Risk', *Computers & Security* 31 (4): 597–611.

Prakash, B.A. 2015. 'Graph Mining for Cyber Security'. In *Cyber Warfare: Building the Scientific Foundation*, edited by S. Jajodia, P. Shakarian, V. S. Subrahmanian, V. Swarup et al., 287–306. Cham, Switzerland: Springer International Publishing.

Ramirez, R., and Choucri, N. 2016. 'Improving Interdisciplinary Communication with Standardized Cyber Security Terminology: A Literature Review'. *IEEE Access*, 4: 2216–2243.

Schneier, B. 2015. *Data and Goliath: The Hidden Battles to Collect Your Data and Control Your World*. New York: WW Norton & Company.

Schauer, F. 1978. 'Fear, Risk, and the First Amendment: Unraveling the "Chilling Effect"', *Boston University Law Review* 58: 685–732.

Seltzer, W. 2010. 'Free Speech Unmoored in Copyright's Safe Harbor: Chilling Effects of the DMCA on the First Amendment', *Harvard Journal of Law and Technology* 24: 171–232.

Solove, D.J. 2006. 'A Taxonomy of Privacy', *University of Pennsylvania Law Review* 154: 477–564.

Solove, D.J. 2007. 'The First Amendment as Criminal Procedure', *New York University Law Review* 82: 112.

Sparrow, E. 2014. 'Digital Surveillance'. In *Global Information Society Watch 2014: Communications Surveillance in the Digital Age*, edited by A. Finlay, Melville: Association for Progressive Communications.

Stevens, T. 2016. *Cyber Security and the Politics of Time*. Cambridge: Cambridge University Press.

Stoycheff, E. 2016. 'Under Surveillance: Examining Facebook's Spiral of Silence Effects in the Wake of NSA Internet Monitoring', *Journalism & Mass Communication Quarterly*.

Stoycheff, E., Liu, J., Xu, K. et al. 2018. 'Privacy and the Panopticon: Online Mass Surveillance's Deterrence and Chilling Effects', *New Media & Society*, doi.org/10.1177/1461444818801317

Taddeo, M. 2015. 'The Struggle Between Liberties and Authorities in the Information Age', *Science and Engineering Ethics* 21 (5): 1125–38.

Tufekci, Z. 2017. *Twitter and Tear Gas: The Power and Fragility of Networked Protest*. New Haven, CT: Yale University Press.

van Schaik, P., Jeske, D., Onibokun, J. et al. 2017. 'Risk Perceptions of Cyber-Security and Precautionary Behaviour', *Computers in Human Behavior* 75 (Supplement C), 547–59.

Wahl-Jorgensen, K., Bennett, L.K., and Cable, J. 2017. 'Surveillance Normalization and Critique', *Digital Journalism* 5 (3): 386–403.

Wang, V., and Tucker, J. 2017. 'Surveillance and Identity: Conceptual Framework and Formal Models', *Journal of Cybersecurity*.

West, S.M. 2017. 'Ambivalence in the (Private) Public Sphere: How Global Digital Activists Navigate Risk'. In 7th {USENIX} Workshop on Free and Open Communications on the Internet ({FOCI} 17).

Zittrain, J. 2008. *The Future of the Internet and How to Stop It*. New Haven, CT: Yale University Press.

PART VII

NATIONAL CYBERSECURITY

CHAPTER 26

SECURING THE CRITICAL NATIONAL INFRASTRUCTURE

DAVID MUSSINGTON

INTRODUCTION

CRITICAL infrastructures provide essential services for national economies and support to national security. States are increasingly aware of the vulnerabilities of these digitally dependent critical national infrastructures (CNIs). From the cyberattacks on Estonia in 2007 to the Black Energy cyber campaign against Ukraine's electric grid in 2015, we have seen states resort to cyber effects in pursuit of strategic objectives. The 2016 US Presidential elections underlined this now obvious trend. In each major case during this period, critical infrastructures have been targeted. The same period saw international attempts to define norms that would create the equivalent of 'keep out' zones, protecting critical infrastructures from deliberate targeting or disruption using cyber means. The UN GGE (Group of Governmental Experts) process represents the high point for these initiatives but has yet to show persistent positive impact. The ecosystem for information and communications technology (ICT) and critical infrastructures is global and creates interdependence between and among economic sectors and nations. These dependencies are a central concern for policymakers. And with the return of geostrategic competition among Great Powers, the possibility exists that differences in CNI vulnerability could be used by states for coercion in crises or interstate conflict. As a result, critical infrastructure cybersecurity has become a top priority policy problem, fostering the development of structured plans and institutions in many countries.

CRITICAL INFRASTRUCTURE RISK CONCERNS

Critical infrastructure vulnerabilities are created and spread through the private market, disseminating fragility in key systems and commercial technologies, and by the failure of society to prioritize security in basic system design and component selection over the addition of new product features. Inadequate patching or replacement of vulnerabilities in key systems further adds to the problem. Cyberattack capabilities pose an increasing challenge to infrastructure operators. These developments produced calls for programs and research into better cyber risk management, and metrics for evaluating threat and risk trends. CNI risk management varies in effectiveness between states and infrastructure sectors. Common features recur in national and sector approaches, however. Summarizing key elements, infrastructure cybersecurity programs typically prioritize:

1. Identifying and prioritizing key infrastructures.
2. Categorization of CNI elements (critical systems, key operators) into key sectors, using criteria from existing policies or infrastructure entity 'self-organization'.
3. Identifying key cyber risk mitigation responses on a spectrum from information sharing to reconfiguring operations and ownership.
4. Internalizing lessons learned from domestic or foreign experience in critical infrastructure disruption or targeting.

These interlocking functional goals constitute a framework for managing critical infrastructure cyber risks and effects. Figure 26.1 summarizes the resulting functional approach.
Resilience is a positive by-product of the effective performance of these functions. Countries adopt different policies and organizational responses to optimize the execution of each of them. No single model is perceived to perform better at managing cyber risks. However,

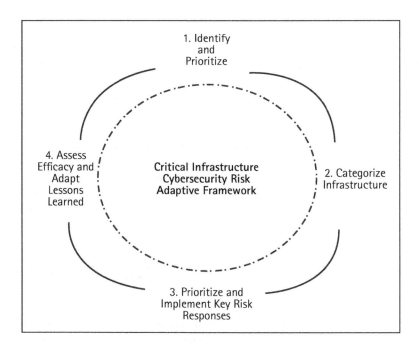

FIGURE 26.1. A Cybersecurity Risk Adaptive Framework

effective critical infrastructure resilience planning requires a structured approach. The following discussion analyses key concepts involved in national CNI policies and discusses the effectiveness of protections in an increasingly harsh threat environment.

CYBER RISK ADAPTATION

Because cyber risk conditions are dynamic, addressing them requires a systematic process of risk identification, assessment, and mitigation. This section elaborates on each of the phases involved and gives examples from countries adopting different but similar approaches to these tasks.[1]

Identifying Key Infrastructures

Most societies prioritize critical infrastructures according to their importance for economic growth and material well-being of citizens, and their contribution to protection of national security and public safety. Governments seek to advantage domestic operators of critical infrastructure services and products, and to reshape national product and services markets in a way that delivers goods and services at lower cost. Popular acceptance of government economic policies that appear to 'pick winners' varies, with the United States most resistant to overt interventions of this type, but with Western Europe much more willing to entertain mixed economic models allowing significant government control. For critical infrastructure cybersecurity, interventionist government policy is doubly difficult because of the global nature of ICT and supporting digital services (software) supply chains. For most countries, the option of a fully internal critical infrastructure services design and delivery process is simply not affordable. Instead, jurisdictions accept certain levels of risk, seeking to minimize particular dependencies while leaving unaddressed strategic entanglement with other countries and globalized industry.

For critical infrastructures, the question is whether foreign dependencies offer valuable redundancy in supply, or exploitable vectors that an attacker might use to achieve denials of service and other effects against targeted CNI. The answer is likely to be 'both'.

Example 1: United States

Critical Infrastructures and Key Resources
Critical infrastructures and key resources are defined under US law and in policy as:

> Critical infrastructure includes those assets, systems, networks, and functions—physical or virtual—so vital to the United States that their incapacitation or destruction would have a debilitating impact on security, national economic security, public health or safety, or any combination of those matters. Key resources are publicly or privately controlled resources essential to minimal operation of the economy and the government.[2]

Each administration since 2006 has amended this definition somewhat, varying the emphasis on risk factors from unaddressed vulnerabilities to the evolving tactics (or tools), techniques, and procedures (TTPs) of threat actors. US policy identifies 16 critical infrastructure sectors,[3] prioritizing their secure functioning and resilience as a national security issue. A number of executive actions and policy documents shape the implementation of this policy position—in particular, Executive Order 13636 and Presidential Policy Directive 21 (PPD-21) of February 2013 are of special importance because they set conditions under which infrastructure owners are directed to identify critical facilities and nodes in their operations—which could then be subject to mandatory risk mitigation actions.[4]

Foreign Investment Review and Critical Infrastructure

The United States operates a policy framework for tracking foreign technology acquisition and investment activity in sectors designated as important to US national security. Known as the Committee on Foreign Investment in the United States (CFIUS), the regime is not specifically concerned with critical infrastructures, but does pay special attention to ICTs and to special materials, energy, and transport systems and subsystems.[5] In the context of 5G technologies (addressed in the concluding section), a regime for detecting and responding to threats from foreign technology dependence or espionage has stark relevance.

USCYBERCOM and Persistent Engagement

The post-2016 maturation of USCYBERCOM as the Department of Defense element charged with protection of its own networks and with supporting the Department of Homeland Security (DHS) in its responsibilities for the protection of critical infrastructures against nation state threats is significant. The emergence of a new strategic approach to cyber operations[6]—Persistent Engagement—that envisions a *defend forward* concept of operations for cyber actions that are on the networks and critical infrastructures of both allies and adversaries. The events of the 2016 US Presidential Elections underline the implications of this perspective for critical infrastructure protection and the subtle militarization of risk judgements that could emerge. It is to be noted that civilian control and prioritization of critical infrastructures for protection is the binding approach in the US, Canada, and most of the core of the Western alliance. It is possible, however, that military cyber strategies could erode the utility of such a hard and fast division in roles and missions. The last section of this chapter develops this theme at greater length.

Example 2: United Kingdom

The United Kingdom identifies 13 national infrastructure sectors containing key assets and facilities.[7,8] Two key risk concerns drive UK policy on the security of key assets and facilities:

- Major detrimental impact on the availability, integrity, or delivery of essential services—including those services whose integrity, if compromised, could result in significant loss of life or casualties—taking into account significant economic or social impacts; and/or
- Significant impact on national security, national defence, or the functioning of the state.

Responsibility for protection of 'CNI IT networks, data, and systems' rests with the National Cyber Security Centre (NCSC). The Centre for the Protection of National Infrastructure works with the NCSC to provide guidance to the private sector on how to respond to threat information coming from the government.[9] The CNI encompasses both physical and logical systems or assets.[10] The UK government issues dated five-year national cyber strategies that articulate national goals for the country, encompassing both critical infrastructure cybersecurity and national defence perspectives. The most recent one covers the period 2016–21.[11] This document identifies a range of threat actors of concern, from cybercriminals to so-called 'script kiddies'. The list mirrors that considered by the United States and most other nations. It also outlines investments by the UK government to mitigate threats of concern and encourage private sector practices that reduce (not eliminate) risk situations of national importance.

Foreign Investment and 4G

Of late, the leading UK backbone telecommunications operator, BT, has made decisions to remove equipment designed and manufactured by China's Huawei from its core 4G network.[12] Long-running concerns with ICT supply chain risks from Huawei have culminated in changes to decisions about acceptable risks in equipment operation and remote access potential. The pending 5G transformation has elevated these concerns still further, creating an international controversy whereby the United States and UK (not to mention Europe) are following potentially divergent positions.[13] 5G issues are addressed directly in the concluding section.

In June 2018, the UK adopted a new regime for oversight of foreign investment in priority technology areas. A white paper published at the time proposed an extensive revision of timelines for notification of potentially problematic foreign investments in key technologies and possibly in CNI.[14] As the Latham and Watkins note relates, this development parallels measures under development since 2017 across the developed world, specifically in Germany and the United States.

Both the US and UK examples show the significance of policy overlap between technology security and foreign investment in key ICT technologies, and effective risk management on critical infrastructure cybersecurity. Most directly, foreign technology dependencies and supply chains diminish the risk awareness and policy levers available to governments to shape the technology portfolio in critical infrastructures. The long-lived nature of infrastructure system acquisitions (decades-long rather than the half-decade phasing of business IT purchasing) further weakens the effectiveness of government interventions—because the predictability of impact is so uncertain. Cross-sector risk management and resilience planning is impeded by limits on situational awareness, a situation made worse still by the disincentives to share information already identified.

Categorizing Infrastructure Elements

Infrastructure equipment, facilities, and supply relationships typically support a particular company, agency, or government utility.[15] Collectively, these are frequently called an 'enterprise'. Cybersecurity at this level is analogous to risk management in a commercial firm. Cost minimization and a desire to deflect risks on suppliers (or customers) operate to reduce the margins available for security and other 'cost centre' expenses.[16] Collections of enterprises, either linked together through corporate governance into common firms or consortia, are referred to as 'sectors'. Sectors are at a higher level of organization, encompassing individual firms and organizations, and are more typically the target for government regulation or direct oversight. Examples of sectors—or industries—include the communications sector, water and wastewater systems, transportation, banking and financial services, and healthcare.[17]

Addressing individual infrastructure networks, devices, and functionality—such as a critical oil refinery, an important data centre or a cloud application—allows policy to focus on particular service providers and products.[18] These can support high-priority services to the public, and merit special legal and emergency response plans and preparation.[19] Key responsibility for assuring redundancy and recovery in the case of service interruptions can be given to civilian governmental or military personnel and agencies. Equally, contingency contracts with private firms also offer a mechanism for assuring the availability of reserve capacity in the case of an emergency.

Example 3: US Critical Infrastructure Sector Identification

As noted earlier, the United States identifies 16 different critical infrastructure sectors in its national approach to cyber risk management.[20] The sectors are, respectively, the chemical sector; commercial facilities; communications; critical manufacturing; dams; defense industrial base; emergency services; energy; financial services; food and agriculture; government facilities (including elections); healthcare and public health; information technology; nuclear reactors, materials, and waste; transportation systems; and water and wastewater systems. US policy assigns sector lead agency roles (known as sector-specific agency [SSA] responsibilities) to single or dual federal agencies—with the DHS serving in that role for nine of the critical sectors and co-SSA for another two.

Cyber threat information is produced and distributed by the DHS in collaboration with the Office of the Director of National Intelligence (ODNI), and a complex of private sector cyber threat information companies and non-profit organizations. US CERT and the ICS-CERT functions are components of the Cybersecurity and Infrastructure Security Agency (CISA), a new entity created by federal legislation and initiating operations in November 2018.[21]

Example 4: Australian Critical Infrastructure Sector Identification

Australia identifies seven critical infrastructure sectors: energy, water services, communications, transport, food chain, health, and banking and finance.[22] Overall governance of critical infrastructure cybersecurity is provided by the Department of Home Affairs and its Critical Infrastructure Centre.[23] Australian policy identifies four key partners in cybersecurity and critical infrastructure risk mitigation, the private sector, commonwealth (i.e. national) government, state, and territory regulators. As such, there is *shared* governance—a variation on the pattern of risk oversight in the United States. The four partners are linked through information exchange mechanisms and a programme of risk assessments, modelling and analysis activities, and a focus on organization resilience—prioritizing business continuity planning and recovery.[24]

Cyber threat intelligence is provided by the Australian Cyber Security Centre (ACSC), an entity that became part of the Australian Signals Directorate (ASD) in 2018.[25] The model of cyber risk intelligence and governance resembles that adopted by the UK's NCSC, and encompasses Australia's CERT, convening groups to enhance public and private sector threat awareness, and promulgating guidance and assistance on cyber risk management.

Implementing Key Risk Responses

Responses to cyber risks take place at strategic, operational, and tactical levels. At the strategic level is broad priority setting created by enterprise-wide assessments of priority services, the vulnerability of key elements of critical infrastructure, and observed threat trends. At the operational level are protocols for infrastructure action that implement strategic priorities for safe and secure operation of key equipment and service relationships. These include contractual conditions for key suppliers, technical specifications for operating equipment and connectivity in a secure manner, and, finally, the conditions for restoration of services following system upgrades or recovery from disruptions (including denials of service or breaches). At the tactical level are cyber incident response procedures—forensic analysis requirements and practices—linking together law enforcement, military services, and contract support with subject matter expertise from academia. Interaction between the operational and tactical levels are frequent because resources (technical and human) from business operations commonly have a role in cyber incident response and diagnosis of root causes of system failures or breach.

Standards and protocols at each of the three levels are increasingly institutionalized in best practice codes, certification, and binding standards.[26] One differentiating factor in Western critical infrastructure cybersecurity policies is the use of mandates versus voluntary coordination in the implementation of risk management measures and best practices. The United States favours market solutions determined by the decentralized decisions of companies in all but a few instances (identified in Executive Order 13636 and in separate legislation), while Australia, the UK, and other Western nations adopt a different mix of policies combining mandatory risk prioritization, commercial best practices, and centralized cyber incident management.

Example 5: The UK Financial Services Sector

The Bank of England is the principal regulator of the cybersecurity risk management practices of the UK financial sector.[27] To achieve sector-wide consistency of risk management, record keeping and audit for cybersecurity, the Bank established the CBEST framework to test the cyber resilience of financial firms. CBEST tests are designed to be realistic and involve contractors conducting penetration tests of bank systems and key infrastructure elements. The aim is to evaluate the robustness of defences against a spectrum of threat actors—from criminals to nation states.

Threat intelligence companies figure prominently in the CBEST process and are accredited to the Bank of England as validated providers of cybersecurity services. These providers are then used to simulate threat actor behaviour—and provide insights into the protections in place at covered financial institutions. The issue is the existence and quality of cybersecurity best practices that reduce the incidence of risk to the financial system. Assessing individual institutions is the job of accredited cyber threat analysis firms. Three overarching questions are as follows:

- Does the firm have a board-approved cybersecurity strategy?
- How does it identify and protect its critical assets?
- How does it detect and respond to an incident, recover the business, and learn from the experience?

The point here is that the focus of policy appears to be on meeting static capacity metrics based in personnel numbers, budgets, or program scope. This is different from a focus on incident response *capabilities* that prioritizes resilience and reconstitution metrics and redundancy. Older policies prioritizing compliance over responsiveness to emerging threats are unlikely to succeed in an environment where complex threat and vulnerability conditions are changing unpredictably.

Example 6: US Energy Sector Rules—

The US electricity sector is subject to a multilevel and interlocking set of regulations on cybersecurity (NERC CIP v5)[28]. Widespread confusion exists on which rules are binding on which actors (at least, among some commentators). At the federal level a family of standards exists—governing cybersecurity risk management among so-called 'bulk electric power systems'. These entities generate and transmit electricity across state lines, selling power to public and private sector utilities that serve counties, cities, or other industrial customers. There is also a set of regional independent system operators, and regional transmission organizations that move power from one region to another through market transactions reconciling load with generating capacity. NERC-CIP v5 (North American Electric Reliability Corporation—Critical Infrastructure Protection (rules—Version 5) is the governing rule set for federally regulated electric power operators. Within states, public utilities commissions set operating rules for safety, security, and pricing for firms (investor-owned or cooperatives) that distribute power to industrial customers and consumers.[29]

Federal entities that generate and sell electric power use the National Institute of Standards and Technology (NIST) Cybersecurity Framework, the NIST Risk Management Framework (providing guidance on the selection of sector-relevant risk mitigations or controls), and the Federal Information Security Management Act (FISMA).[30] More detailed cyber risk management guidance is provided by NISTR 7628—Guidelines for SMART GRID Cybersecurity.[31] Additionally, NERC cybersecurity oversight makes a programme maturity judgement when auditing electricity providers. NERC rules focus on the strategic capacity of providers but make trend assessments based on more granular operational evaluations of performance through both investigations by inspectors general and auditors, but also through review of exercise results and performance after interruptions in electricity service following storms or natural disasters. Note that the SSA for the energy sector is the Department of Energy, but that the DHS is co-SSA for some resource providers involved—such as providers of natural gas.[32]

Efficacy Assessment and Risk Management: Internalizing Lessons Learned

Internalizing lessons learned from critical infrastructure incidents requires the exchange of information and the sharing of intelligence. A number of significant challenges confront this requirement. First are impediments to the sharing of classified information with non-cleared civilians and commercial operators. Fear of compromising 'sources and methods' prevents easy sharing with large numbers of individuals, requiring instead the granting of special access to smaller numbers of responsible officials—each of whom must undergo special background investigations. A follow-on concern arises, however: the difficulty of sharing 'within critical infrastructure entities' once top-level or specialized technical personnel are given access to classified insights. After all, the premise of their limited access is that they are designated as the single or small number of approved channels for the sharing of sensitive data.[33] Broader sharing is expressly forbidden, except under very narrowly documented conditions. This creates a structural barrier to the sharing of threat and vulnerability information that derives from possibly the best sources of such information: the intelligence communities of a nation state.[34]

Some sharing of technical cyber risk data occurs routinely among CERTs around the world—as they exchange information on malware, denial of service attack TTPs of advanced persistent threat actors and—selectively—on uncovered Zero Day vulnerabilities.[35] This process—reconciling vulnerabilities equities between the public and private sectors—is a fundamental aspect of internalizing lessons from cyber activities. Sharing is necessarily limited between the two communities. Technical exchanges of data do occur, however, and personnel from the respective communities share career paths that foster common methodologies for forensic analysis and making inferences that create 'norms of attribution' for the cyber domain.[36]

A second source of impediments to enhanced situational awareness is the use of non-disclosure agreements (NDAs) by private sector companies where, in the aftermath of a cyber incident or breach, those involved in responses are prevented from sharing insights because of a fear of reputational or financial damage if details are revealed.[37] While these arrangements typically constrain contractors brought in to deal with breaches or losses of PII (personal identification information), they are often also used to constrain the disclosure by employees of information that may relate to intellectual property, trade secrets, or otherwise confidential business records. Effectively these restrictions parallel those in the public sector that impede the sharing of possibly critical risk information. Linked together in critical infrastructures already subject to closer government oversight due to the importance of the products and services provided, classification and NDA use disadvantages the enterprise or sector-wide dissemination of risk situational awareness—weakening protection—and slows down responses to threat actor innovation in both tactics and attack tools.[38]

An additional concern is the potential loss of 'government-grade' cyberattack tools through either theft, operational breakdowns, or the actions of disloyal or corrupt insiders. Recent cases in the United States may be a case of failed collateral risk management. Tools developed by NSA or other US entities may have fallen into a foreign entity's or criminal's hands, subsequently used in ways that impeded clear attribution, empowering 'false-flag' attacks. It is not that risks are not inherent in the use of cyber tools for intelligence or military operations. These risks are unavoidable and must be weighed in operations or strategy against the gains from greater situational awareness and persistent access. The key issue is that attribution and conclusions regarding attacker 'intent' are fundamentally weakened in a proliferated environment where cyber weapons—malware, code bases, and exploit usage patterns—are disseminated rapidly by black and grey markets of global scope. For critical infrastructures, each of these trends means that protections are unlikely to keep pace with the dynamism of change on the attack or offence side. Similarly, private and government sector impediments to information exchange and insight sharing reinforce defence disadvantages in a manner likely to persist into the foreseeable future.

Achieving Critical National Infrastructure Resilience

Resilience is a fundamental element of an adaptive critical infrastructure cybersecurity posture. The ability to reconstitute key functionality and recover after disruptions is important enough to merit systematic examination. The next section provides a discussion of key factors important to the enhancement of resilience and its measurement.

An Overview of Key Factors

A number of factors contribute to an overall resilience posture. Among these are the capacity for making informed choices, effective planning for redundancies and support, management of dependencies that mitigate or transmit risk exposure, and effective threat management. Each of these factors is explored later.

Capacity

Resources for achieving better outcomes when addressing risk factors include adequate funding, human resources and training, information regarding risk conditions, and an effective threat tracking programme aligned with protections. Effective and interoperable risk management efforts by partners expand the ability of critical infrastructures to remain agile as threat conditions change. Leveraging the capacity of others also allows better performance with a lowered resource burden. Information sharing is an essential part of capacity because it allows for the deepening of capabilities across an organization or jurisdiction's component parts. This means that the efficiency of information sharing translates directly into greater resilience in critical infrastructures. The potential of information-sharing additions to add to protection capabilities almost never live up to their theoretical maximum, however.[39] For the reasons given earlier on lessons learned, the interests of government and private sector in information exchange are not structurally aligned, or at least the alignment at the operational or tactical levels does not translate directly into effective strategic collaboration.

Metrics for overall capacity include the cost of planning and exercises, the number and frequency of exercises of plans, and the number of staff permanently assigned to response and recovery tasks, or on call for contingency response.

Timing (or Timeliness)

Capabilities usable for resilience need to be available when needed. Aligning resources to requirements necessitates planning and contingency prioritization based on some means of assessing event likelihood. Techniques used for this purpose include scenarios and simulations, (historical) lessons learned analysis, forensic analysis of data breaches and malware incidents, among other events. A key insight in assessing the timing or timeliness of resource availability is the degree to which resilience and recovery are planned in the context of a clear threat model.[40] A threat model identifies and prioritizes actors or processes that undermine the availability, integrity, or confidentiality of critical infrastructures and/or the data and digital services that they deliver. This enables more efficient allocation of risk mitigation and cyber incident response resources against the most challenging threats to normal operations. Threat models also facilitate the design of metrics for assessing capabilities and performance against design basis threats.[41] Metrics for timing or timeliness include recovery time objectives or recovery performance objectives (RTOs and RPOs). These are typically embedded in contingency planning and service restoration programs—and frequently implement legal requirements for priority restoration of service.

Dependencies

Dependencies are relationships that require resources and expose potential vulnerabilities—human, financial, and/or technical—in the processing of key data and the provision of digital services. Connectivity—over fibre or cell tower—are both key dependencies for local network and Internet access and use. Dependencies can be one- or two-way. If, for example, an Internet service provider has a high bandwidth link over which customers deliver valuable applications, such as email, consumer banking, or VPN service, that link both enables interconnection and is a principal vehicle through which its operator generates income and profits. Equally, while users sending messages over a network link gain from its use, it is also a potential channel over which false information or malformed network packets can transit. Dependencies are also potential vectors (or channels) available to attackers or foreign intelligence agencies for cyberattacks or computer network exploitation. Accessibility of dependencies—for connectivity, financial support, and/or key applications—is synonymous with attack potential. In other words, dependencies are an exploitable attack surface and yet are unavoidable—by design. For resilience purposes, the density of dependencies carries with it both vulnerability concerns and redundancy advantages. Contingency plans and 'on-call' resources determine which potential is dominant. Metrics for awareness and management of dependencies include reporting requirements for contracts (financial cost, nationality of contractor), audit targets for periodic review of redundancy in key or service component supply, and frequency and completeness of background checks on key staff and employees.

Resourcing

Resilience plans require resources and practice in order to be implemented effectively. Exercises and rigorous planning are the primary means for ensuring success, via the validated adequacy of recovery and emergency preparedness capacity. Risk conditions are the driver for determining resourcing requirements. National policy priorities determine the methods and organizational imperatives (doctrine) for implementing resilience and recovery programs. Because doctrines can differ between countries, resource levels for critical infrastructure cybersecurity are an imperfect metric for comparing the adequacy of resource levels across jurisdictions.[42] Other factors are much more important in determining the protection or cyber defence potential of a nation's critical infrastructure. These factors include the context of a cyber incident, the suspected identity of involved threat actors, and the criticality of the target. Metrics typically revolve around budgets and performance during historical incidents or in simulated losses of service or disruptions to key customers. Budget justifications aligning identified stakeholders with resources to support continuous availability of services are the norm.

Plans and Courses of Action

Plans and courses of action implement strategies and risk judgements articulated by leaders. For the government, this means taking a set of ordered priorities and translating them into binding guidance on government agencies and, secondarily, on private sector service providers. Two alternatives can be described here: government entities (a) direct implementation of policy preferences through the allocation of legal sanctions, and human and material resources, to change the behaviour or risk exposure of a critical infrastructure; or (b) seek less direct oversight over private companies that provide key infrastructure services, and are directed through regulation to adhere to standards, practices, and contingency service delivery arrangements to maintain a satisfactory minimum base of operations. This second dimension also frequently mandates reserve requirements for critical parts and materials, and even funding for expedited restoration of service. Both governance regimes, (a) and (b), vary according to the degree for centralized control in a particular country. For example, disaster preparedness and response differ in a federal state (the United States), from patterns and practices in a unitary state (the United Kingdom). Both national examples, however, seek to execute similar functions in terms of prioritized restoration of key services and clear metrics for performance against which entities can be held accountable.[43]

CONCLUSION: SUMMARIZING CRITICAL NATIONAL INFRASTRUCTURE RISK CONCERNS AND CHALLENGES

Critical infrastructures are vulnerable to deliberate disruption through cyberattack. However, mitigations to these risks exist, and are deployed in different countries through organizations and technical specialists charged with the maintenance of key systems and services. Different countries have adopted more or less centralized government solutions to safeguarding critical infrastructure cybersecurity. The United States favours private sector cyber risk management, with the UK, much of Europe, Australia, and Canada favouring a more mixed approach integrating public and private sector efforts under an umbrella governing framework.

CNIs are defined by countries in different ways, but generally prioritize the same basic industries and services. Government services are a common top priority, with financial services, energy, and transportation frequent next-tier concerns. Dependencies for vital infrastructures are a policy concern and are frequently the target of government intervention. Among the topics that are central are the national origin of firms providing key components and services, ownership of key infrastructures, remote management of key systems or assets, and the reputation of service providers as effective managers of system availability, data integrity, and information confidentiality.

Threat information is considered sensitive and is produced by both public and private sector organizations. For governments, threat information is produced by intelligence organizations that implement classification systems for data and clearances to determine those to whom access is permitted. For the private sector (customers), vulnerability and operations information are often treated as trade secrets or as business proprietary data. This means that freely sharing lessons learned during cyber incidents is frequently not possible or is otherwise limited. Taken together, classification by governments, and non-disclosure constraints on information exchange by companies reduce public knowledge of risks to critical infrastructures and, by extension, awareness of the utility of mitigation alternatives.

Impediments to effective cyber risk management in critical infrastructures are products of vulnerable technologies, limited oversight by government authorities over supply chains, and a lack of well-integrated response, recovery, and resilience planning. Because critical infrastructure cyber disruptions are relatively infrequent, lessons learned for response and recovery come mostly from industry or business best practices, simulations, and exercises based on scenarios or interpretations of foreign cyber incidents and attacks. This gives the events of Estonia (2007), Georgia (2008), Iran (2010), Saudi Arabia/Qatar (2011), United States (2012), Ukraine (2015), and the NotPetya and WannaCry malware campaigns (2015 to the present) outsized influence in interpretations of relative risk and protection capabilities. The backdrop of large and recurrent data breaches hitting financial, consumer credit, and governmental data centres further adds to heightened risk awareness and concern.

The series of conflict and cyberattacks over the past decade raises the prospect of a greater military role in critical infrastructure cybersecurity than many currently envision. For the United States, the UK, and Canada, military cyber capabilities are emerging as the core of an 'active defence' approach to cyber operations. Interestingly, however, these countries do not closely link critical infrastructure cybersecurity plans and incident response protocols to their offensive cyber operations doctrines. It remains to be seen whether this separation in policy thinking and implementation is sustainable over the long term. Given the fragility of critical infrastructures and the high degree of peace-time cyber espionage activity, this issue appears ripe for future controversy and conflict.

Overlaps between critical infrastructure cyber risks and peer competition evidenced through espionage and the use of proxies (third party contractors) in intrusions are recurrent. The cases listed earlier involve frequent attacks on or through critical infrastructures. The attacks are mostly successful and validate the basic insight that—all things being equal—attackers hold a durable advantage over defenders. Considerable uncertainty remains, however, over the predictability and controllability of attacks targeting multiple interdependent infrastructures simultaneously. This topic is the subject of military planning and research in many countries' defence establishments.[44]

Global ICT supply chains represent perhaps the most challenging risk factor for critical infrastructures. Not only do critical infrastructures use commercial off-the-shelf (COTS) technologies, they are also one of the most enthusiastic consumers of SMART technologies connecting users and service providers over the Internet. The pending introduction of 5G technologies promises to enhance this challenge—as the principal suppliers of 5G technology are based in China, with a diminishing number of suppliers in North America and Western Europe. The United States has taken a position opposing the use of China-origin technologies and systems due to a perception of the risks to critical data and applications if untrusted devices and device architectures gain market dominance. So far, only Australia and the UK have articulated unqualified support for the initiative.

Western European countries are seeking a middle ground, with a post hoc review of network and asset risk factors—taking suppliers' guarantees of firmware provenance and quality and seeking to validate them.[45] In doing so, European governments are expressing a willingness to accept risk in the supply chain because of the anticipated prompt and long-term benefits of an accelerated 5G roll-out. Such a position mirrors largely implicit risk acceptance decisions adopted by *all* countries, at least those that choose to leave critical infrastructure investment and technical design details to specialists or for-profit entities with interests misaligned with those of the jurisdictions where they operate.

On aggregate, the vulnerabilities of critical infrastructures are probably increasing. Risk mitigation approaches are of some value but, for the reasons discussed in this chapter, protections are unlikely to keep pace with the exploitation possibilities available to cyberattackers. The deployment of 5G and Internet of Things technologies will worsen this problem further, expanding disruption possibilities for attackers without providing a parallel set of supply chain risk countermeasures to defenders. Faced with this reality, it is more important than ever that states adopt risk-oriented programs to mitigate threats posed by determined cyberattackers. These threats will worsen much more quickly than defence can improve. Collective action between the public and private sectors, and between like-minded countries, is the best means to prevail in an increasingly one-sided cyber game with aggressors.

NOTES

1. One popular best practice framework for managing cybersecurity risks is the National Institute of Standards and Technology (NIST) Cybersecurity Framework first promulgated in 2014. The NIST Framework provides an organizing scheme for risk response functions (identify, protect, detect, respond, recover), controls (mitigations) within each of the five functions, and a means of evaluating the maturity of risk management capabilities.
2. This definition comes from the 2006 National Infrastructure Protection Plan—contextually expressed in an annex that is updated periodically. See https://www.fema.gov/pdf/emergency/nrf/nrf-support-cikr.pdf

THE CRITICAL NATIONAL INFRASTRUCTURE   443

3. See critical infrastructure sectors as defined by the Department of Homeland Security (DHS) at https://www.dhs.gov/cisa/critical-infrastructure-sectors

4. For an elaboration, see its restatement in the summary of Executive Order 13800 on 8 May, 2018. https://www.nist.gov/itl/applied-cybersecurity/nice/resources/executive-order-13800/findings-and-recommendations

5. CFIUS is an interagency committee of the US Federal Government chaired by the US Department of the Treasury. In August 2018, the authorizing legislation for the committee changed its mandate to encompass a larger number of transactions, expanded timelines for investigations, mandatory declarations of foreign participation in transactions in covered technology areas, and experimentation in imposed restrictions. See the FAQ file on the Foreign Investment Risk Review Modernization Act (FIRRMA) passed on 13 August 2018. https://www.treasury.gov/resource-center/international/Documents/FIRRMA-FAQs.pdf

6. This approach is enunciated in the 2018 National Security Strategy: (https://www.whitehouse.gov/wp-content/uploads/2018/09/National-Cyber-Strategy.pdf) and the released summary of the US Department of Defense Cyber Strategy: (https://media.defense.gov/2018/Sep/18/2002041658/-1/-1/1/CYBER_STRATEGY_SUMMARY_FINAL.PDF)

7. The deployment of 4G cellular networking technology from China's Huawei highlighted the complex decision calculus of foreign technology dependence and economic costs. For 5G, the reversal of the earlier permitted market entry is doubly fraught with contradictions. See 'British Telecoms Giant BT Group to Strip Huawei from Core Networks, Limit 5G Access,' *South China Morning Post*, 5 December 2018. https://www.scmp.com/tech/gear/article/2176573/british-telecoms-giant-bt-group-strip-huawei-core-networks-limit-5g-access

8. See the policy statements of the UK's Centre for the Protection of National Infrastructure. (https://www.cpni.gov.uk/critical-national-infrastructure-0)

9. NCSC is a part of GCHQ.

10. See Cornish, Paul. 2017. *Integrated Deterrence: NATO's 'First Reset' Strategy GLOBSEC NATO Adaptation Initiative*, Bratislava: GLOBSEC Policy Institute, p. 12.

11. See (HM Government) National Cyber Security Strategy 2016–21. (https://assets.publishing.service.gov.uk/government/uploads/system/uploads/attachment_data/file/567242/national_cyber_security_strategy_2016.pdf)

12. See Fildes, Nic. 2018. 'BT to Strip Huawei Equipment from its core 4G Network,' *Financial Times*, 4 December. https://www.ft.com/content/c639aaf4-f7c9-11e8-8b7c-6fa24bd5409c

13. For a summary discussion of these risks and their meaning for national cyber strategies, see Melissa Hathaway OAS White Paper Series, Issue 2 Managing National Cyber Risk (Organization of American States), 2018. http://www.potomacinstitute.org/images/CRI/ENG-Digital-White-paper-issue-2.pdf

14. 'New UK National Security M&A Regime Expected in 2019', LEXOLOGY Latham &Watkins LLP, 11 January 2019. https://www.lexology.com/library/detail.aspx?g=9daff9bd-a2f8-47db-9afb-cf6526e11f8e)

15. Elements are different from sectors in that they constitute individual facilities, data sets, business processes, or even subject matter expertise—rather than of enterprises or groups of businesses.

16. For costs or losses typically resulting from cyberattacks or data breaches, see a representative summary by Varonis: https://www.varonis.com/blog/cybersecurity-statistics and Melissa Hathaway, Managing Cyber Risk: http://www.potomacinstitute.org/images/CRI/ENG-Digital-White-paper-issue-2.pdf

17. For the list of Department of Homeland Security critical infrastructures, see https://www.dhs.gov/cisa/critical-infrastructure-sectors; for the UK, see https://www.cpni.gov.uk/critical-national-infrastructure-0; and for Australia, see https://www.homeaffairs.gov.au/about-us/our-portfolios/national-security/security-coordination/critical-infrastructure-resilience

18. FIRSTNET in the United States (emergency preparedness communications for state agencies (law enforcement and public safety) is one example of hybrid forms of this requirement. For a summary description of FIRSTNET, see https://www.firstnet.gov

19. Executive Order 13636 Section 9 mandates the identification by infrastructure owners of critical facilities that merit extra levels of protection. See EO 13636, 19 February 2013. https://www.federalregister.gov/documents/2013/02/19/2013-03915/improving-critical-infrastructure-cybersecurity

20. The 16 critical infrastructures identified in the United States have different national government agencies responsible for their coordination. See https://www.dhs.gov/cisa/critical-infrastructure-sectors

21. See the CISA web presence at https://www.dhs.gov/CISA

22. https://publicwiki-01.fraunhofer.de/CIPedia/index.php/Critical_Infrastructure_Sector

23. For a discussion of the Critical Infrastructure Centre's role, see https://cicentre.gov.au

24. See the Critical Infrastructure Centre's Organizational Resilience page: https://cicentre.gov.au/tisn/resilience

25. ASD is Australia's counterpart to the US NSA and the UK GCHQ. For background, see the Australian Signals Directorate public web presence. https://asd.gov.au/infosec/acsc.htm

26. The NIST Cybersecurity Framework and the ISO 27001 series both offer standards and practice frameworks that align infrastructure cybersecurity with risk mitigations and technical risk judgments. Governments and private sector firms use these concepts to evaluate vulnerability and risk management across complex industry settings. See the NIST Cybersecurity Framework version 1.1 (https://www.nist.gov/cyberframework) and the ISO 27001 information security management standards (https://www.iso.org/isoiec-27001-information-security.html)

27. For background on CBEST, see https://www.bankofengland.co.uk/financial-stability/financial-sector-continuity/

28. The North American Electric Reliability Corporation (NERC) Critical Infrastructure Protection (CIP) Version 5 standards cover all bulk electric power generation and transmission companies involved in the interstate transfer of electricity. For a summary of NERC CIP controls, see https://www.velaw.com/uploadedfiles/vesite/resources/summarycipversion5standards2014.pdf

29. For background on NERC, its history and rules, see the organization's web presence at https://www.nerc.com

30. Federal entities covered by these rules and legislation include the Tennessee Valley Authority and the Bonneville Power Administration.

31. https://csrc.nist.gov/csrc/media/publications/nistir/7628/rev-1/final/documents/draft_nistir_7628_r1_vol2.pdf

32. See the Department of Energy Fact Sheet: https://www.energy.gov/ceser/activities/energy-security/emergency-preparedness/federal-authorities. Note that the Department of Homeland Security is the sector specific agency for the pipelines that transport natural gas to refineries and power-generating plants.

THE CRITICAL NATIONAL INFRASTRUCTURE 445

33. See Knake, Robert. 2018. 'Sharing Classified Cyber Threat Information with the Private Sector,' Digital and Cyberspace Policy Program (Council on Foreign Relations), 15 May. https://www.cfr.org/report/sharing-classified-cyber-threat-information-private-sector

34. The belief that foreign intelligence agencies are more informed about cyber threat activity than are commercial platform or software providers is itself flawed. The global scale of some platforms—such as those operated by anti-virus vendors, or by leading operating system developers such as Microsoft—gives access to a stream of data possibly without peer in the ICT or intelligence ecosystems.

35. The vulnerabilities equities process—through which states determine whether to share zero-day vulnerability insights with platform operators and software developers—offers a complex case in point. While governments purchase zero days in order to develop exploits based upon them, the balance of risk may favour disclosure when one of the following conditions pertains: (a) the risk of the use of a discovered vulnerability to national economic or critical infrastructure cybersecurity is great enough to warrant disclosure to domestic private sector partners; (b) the collateral risks of use of exploits based on zero days exceed the utility of keeping the exploit itself secret; or (c) where the exploits themselves are discovered 'in the wild', diminishing their utility and increasing the risk that they could be repurposed by other state actors or criminals. Optimizing decisions across these three dimensions is a function executed in different ways in different countries. The United States is the most public in discussing these dilemmas, but any advanced cyber-capable state necessarily confronts the same dilemma. See the unclassified Vulnerabilities Equities Process and Policy for the United States Government, 17 November 2017. https://www.whitehouse.gov/sites/whitehouse.gov/files/images/External%20-%20Unclassified%20VEP%20Charter%20FINAL.PDF

36. An increasingly important group of private sector cyber threat information and service providers has emerged. Many of these companies have relationships with government agencies. And frequently personnel formerly employed by government are principal staff or company founders. For a list of them, see the collection maintained by G2: https://www.g2.com/categories/threat-intelligence-services

37. On the problem of the overuse of NDAs, see, for example, Lobel, Orly. 2018. 'NDAs are Out of Control. Here's what Needs to Change,' *Harvard Business Review*, 30 January: https://hbr.org/2018/01/ndas-are-out-of-control-heres-what-needs-to-change

38. See ransomware success across geographic borders, and the persistence of criminal re-use of similar techniques. Innovation may be a market phenomenon: resort to new tools tracks the deployment of new protections. If the protections are absent or failing, defenders are unlikely to see new attack tools that may be held 'in reserve' for higher-value targets. These targets may be high-value government defence or intelligence assets. This sets up a situation where leaking government cyberattack tools can be used against critical infrastructure targets structurally disabled from agile or timely incident response. See Perlroth, Nicole, and Scott Shane. 2019. 'In Baltimore and Beyond, a Stolen N.S.A. Tool Wreaks Havoc,' *New York Times*, 25 May. https://www.nytimes.com/2019/05/25/us/nsa-hacking-tool-baltimore.html?action=click&module=Top%20Stories&pgtype=Homepage

39. For a summary of the limits to information-sharing productivity and reach, see Fischer, Eric A. 2016. 'Cybersecurity Issues and Challenges: In Brief', Washington DC: Congressional Research Service (CRS), R43831, 12 August. https://fas.org/sgp/crs/misc/R43831.pdf

40. Threat modelling is one of the most effective ways of optimizing response and recovery plans and responses. It allows for an efficient focus on infrastructure elements and assets at risk—using mission or service priorities to assure appropriate resilience levels.

41. For a discussion of the applicability of design basis threats to federal information security, see Federal Facility Security: Selected Agencies Should Improve Methods for Assessing and Monitoring Risks, (GAO-18-72), Government Accountability Office, October 2017. https://www.gao.gov/assets/690/687968.pdf.

42. For US homeland security doctrine, see the US National Infrastructure Protection Plan for 2013—NIPP 2013: Partnering for Security Infrastructure Security and Resilience. Washington DC: DHS, 2013: (https://www.dhs.gov/sites/default/files/publications/national-infrastructure-protection-plan-2013-508.pdf); and the analogous UK document, National Security and Strategic Defence and Security Review 2015, First Annual Report: (https://assets.publishing.service.gov.uk/government/uploads/system/uploads/attachment_data/file/575378/national_security_strategy_strategic_defence_security_review_annual_report_2016.pdf).

43. The Stafford Act is the source of the US federal authorities and defines the division of labour for emergency preparedness and response between the states and the federal government.

44. See, for example, the testimony of Lewis, James. 2018. 'Cyber Threats to our Nation's Critical Infrastructures', Statement before the US Senate Judiciary Committee, Subcommittee on Crime and Terrorism. United States Senate, Washington DC, 21 August. https://www.judiciary.senate.gov/imo/media/doc/08-21-18%20Lewis%20Testimony.pdf.

45. See Fung, Brian. 2019. 'How China's Huawei took the lead over US Companies in 5G technology', The Washington Post, 10 April. https://www.washingtonpost.com/technology/2019/04/10/us-spat-with-huawei-explained/?utm_term=.b17efc2d4b8a.

CHAPTER 27

···

THE ROLE OF DEFENCE IN NATIONAL CYBERSECURITY

···

MIKA KERTTUNEN

CYBERSECURITY has become by default a national and international agenda point. National policy and legislative measures are being crafted, manifested most visibly in over a hundred national cyber or information security strategies issued during the past 15 years.[1] Political attention is given, and financial and human resources are allocated, to such activities as countering cybercrime and cyberterrorism; protection of critical infrastructure, education, and public awareness; as well as subsequent research and development. Calls are made to incorporate (all) relevant stakeholders into national cyber policymaking and implementation.

Surprisingly little explicit consideration is given to the role of the defence sector in national cybersecurity policies and strategies. National cybersecurity strategies take account of defence sector undertakings in careful and modest terms, if at all. The argument to make more effective use of the competences and capabilities of the defence sector is three-pronged. First, cybersecurity questions are becoming routine aspects of foreign and security policy in which the military has an essential role. Second, the armed forces possess skills and capabilities that neither the public nor the private sector have. Third, the armed forces are developing capabilities to conduct protective, intrusive, and offensive cyber activities.

This chapter assesses the actual and potential role and tasks that could be undertaken by the defence sector and armed forces in national cybersecurity policy and strategy. More specifically, it seeks to identify areas of national cybersecurity where the competences and capabilities of the defence sector could be employed. The chapter models both national cybersecurity and military defence as systems, and then compares the capacity and opportunities of the defence sector with the requirements of national cybersecurity. These models, however, operate more as heuristic, conceptual, and logical tools and frameworks for analysis than as authoritative or normative descriptions.

The chapter opens by examining the nature of national cybersecurity. This political and administrative autopsy seeks to identify national objectives, levels of ambition, and measures to be taken, and classifies the key focus and functionality areas of national cybersecurity. The chapter then sets military involvement in the wider context of the civil-military relationship. After identifying three generic roles for the defence sector, the inquiry looks at the specific tasks and the types of operations the military can conduct.[2] Finally, the demand-side of cybersecurity will be set against the supply-side of defence competences and capabilities. The chapter ends with critical observations on the rationale and implications of deploying the military into national cybersecurity.

NATIONAL CYBERSECURITY

What is national cybersecurity? Security is a highly contextual notion raising questions such as security of what, for whom, and to what extent? In the context of information and communication technologies, security/insecurity covers objects and subjects from single devices to industrial processes, global military communications, regional adversary or global super-power relations, and the fundamental equation between haves and have-nots. Technical or information security alone is not sufficient for corporate purposes where, for example, customers' trust, public reputation, and continuity of operations are key expectations of security measures. Accordingly, national security needs and ambitions encompass both security *from* a wide range of risks and security *to* live the political, economic, and social life a given nation has chosen.

After the 2007 cyberattacks against Estonia, the dominant national and international information technology (IT) discourse shifted. Earlier governments had focused on digital agendas and the development of information societies. Now they started to formulate and publish cybersecurity strategies at an increasing pace. At the same time, a rather narrow and concrete focus on data protection, information assurance, and information security was replaced by the more encompassing and admittedly more obscure concept of cybersecurity. Obviously, the proliferation of smart and connected technologies has accelerated this quest for security.

Strategy, a political and administrative mechanism, is supposed to inform and educate domestic and foreign audiences as to a government's chosen policy. Strategy should provide policy guidance for national administration and organization, and should legitimize the direction and content of that policy. By communicating intentions, direction, and capabilities security and defence strategies can also have a deterrent effect[3] on known or potential adversaries.[4] Issuing a strategy is also an act of framing that, through discursive legitimatization, can expand security as a controlling mechanism into new areas of social and political life. National cybersecurity strategies define and determine what is considered security, and what are the appropriate and accepted security measures to be taken (Dunn Cavelty 2008, 24–40, 84–6). In this respect, national strategies both manifest and enhance the process of securitization, the discursive and political process to construct particular issues as security issues.[5]

Nations often only characterize cybersecurity in terms of objectives to be achieved or measures to be taken, without explicitly defining the policy context. National strategies speak either of information security or of a collection of cyber/technology-related challenges, risks, or threats. Alternatively, they might present cybersecurity as a strategic-level discussion. The understanding of cybersecurity differs markedly among all those who have discussed, defined, or described the concept (Luiif et al. 2013, 1–17; Luiif, Besseling and de Graaf 2013, 4–6).[6]

National strategies contain a bundle of ambitions and objectives. Safeguarding the security and functionality of the information and communication systems, and establishing legal frameworks, setting or re-setting regulatory authorities, and creating a national computer emergency response organization is common to all nations.[7] Such predominantly technical and material measures are often widened to, and supported by societal, procedural, and educational steps. When a single governmental agency—for example, a national computer emergency response team—is recognized as insufficient to cover all cyber-related issues, then whole-of-government responsibility, engagement and, cooperation becomes an obvious alternative approach. This then leads to the establishment of a cross-governmental coordinating body—for example, a cybersecurity committee. As the penetration of information and communication technologies deepens, and the related services evolve from simple to complex, then it becomes a national priority to raise public awareness, skills, and competences. In a similar way, the scope of security widens from governmental to include industrial and commercial systems.[8] Governments seek to integrate cyber affairs to support governmental policy areas, most notably in foreign, security and defence, economic, industrial, and development policies.[9] Robust, proactive and interventionist measures are incorporated to supplement the necessary protective and operational measures. Moreover, civil society, academia and the private sector have become natural stakeholders in the development of information societies and in the pursuit of security.[10]

In sum, national approaches to cybersecurity cover traditional threat-based and geopolitical security, including the following areas[11]:

- Establishment of legal and administrative frameworks including a national cybersecurity organization.
- Ensuring information security.
- Ensuring technical functionality and improving resilience:
  o Protection of governmental networks and systems.
  o Protection of national critical infrastructure defined as concrete infrastructure or as vital services or functions.
  o Development of material and organizational capabilities.
- Improving supply chain security and trust in products and services.
- Increasing skills and competencies through systematic workforce development and public awareness raising.
- Promoting national values and regional and global ambitions through cyber diplomacy, focusing especially on norms development, Internet governance, capacity building, countering cybercrime, and promoting responsible state behaviour.

National cybersecurity can be further operationalized into the following functional areas:

- Situational awareness to be able to grasp how the systems and networks are functioning, and their potential shortfalls. as well as how different threat actors and vectors operate within and can be repelled or removed from networks and systems.
- Protection of networks and systems for technical functionality, administrative effectiveness, and for specific reasons such as privacy or national security and secrecy.

- Robust deterrence and countermeasures to prevent malicious activities taking place or to limit their effects.
- Resilience as an ability to endure and, when needed, to adapt to restraining and limiting conditions as well to recover from them.
- Public awareness and competence to avoid unintended incidents and raise the threshold of malicious attacks.

Seen from a systemic-environment perspective, national IT-development strategies and cybersecurity strategies seek to create a socially and economically functional environment, which is technically and politically stable and secure from, yet hostile to, illegal and unauthorized use and exploitation. Ultimately, the question is of continuity management where two main schools of thought dominate thinking and discourse, one focusing on securing the functionality of systems and the other on controlling the content.

CIVIL-MILITARY RELATIONS

Civil-military relations scholarship offers two broad models: separation or integration of the two domains. Although the issue can be traced back to Sunzi's (Sun Tsu) maxims, Hamilton's and Madison's arguments in the *Federalist Papers* and von Clausewitz's ideals, Huntington's *The Soldier and the State* all set an explicit and dominant theoretical framework concerning civil-military relations.

Huntington's point of departure was the concern of civilian control over the military. He described the two worlds as fundamentally and functionally different, and saw military professionalism as a vehicle to drive and secure both civilian control and military performance. The Huntingtonian theory of civil-military relations thus prefers objective control from outside, regards subjective and intrusive control harmful, and creates a sharp division between politics and strategy as well as civilian and military roles and tasks (Huntington 1957). Janowitz's answer to Huntington, and to the problem of control, was the convergence of the two institutions. This would be achieved especially through conscription, adoption of civic values in the military, and interaction between the civilian and military elites. Janowitz also saw the tasks of the armed forces changing: the future requiring constabulary skills and fire fighters' versatility to fight in limited wars (Janowitz 1960).[12]

Post-Cold war societal and military changes have made civilian and military domains more dependent on each other. 'New wars', multi- and uni-lateral military interventions and the so-called 'war on terrorism' all developed in parallel with emerging digital technologies while asymmetric vulnerabilities also widened the scope of security.[13] Many liberal industrial countries redefined the role and tasks of the defence sector. Armed forces obviously continued to be responsible for the military defence of the nation as well as its military allies, but were increasingly expected to participate in international military cooperation and operations, such as peacekeeping, crisis response operations and assistance missions to civilian authorities in case of emergencies.[14] The men and women in uniform remained combatants, but were also expected to become diplomats, builders, constables, and communicators. Societal, commercial, and industrial practices also changed. During the Cold War, many West European (i.e. industrialized states) had based their defence on conscription, large force reserves, and mobilization. Armed forces expected to receive vast amounts of resources from society and industry: manpower, readily available material such as heavier vehicles, tools, and weapons systems produced in factories and logistic services. Globalized societies and just-in-time industries lack such a reserve-oriented mentality, however, and now civilian society expects to receive material and non-material goods and services from the military.

Military support to civilian authorities is more a rule than an exception. For example, the United States has issued a Joint Chiefs of Staff doctrine statement to guide the defence sector's support to civil authorities (following the name of the doctrine). The concept refers to employment of 'federal military forces, Department of Defense civilians, contract personnel, component assets, and National Guard forces in response to requests for assistance from civil authorities for domestic emergencies, law enforcement support, and other domestic activities, or from qualifying entities for special events'.[15] The Joint Chiefs' doctrine outlines cyber-related activities including the provision of assistance to state and local networks to ensure their continued operation in a disrupted or degraded cyber environment. US military services may be requested to support the remediation and creation of critical emergency telecommunication networks, which may also require providing cyberspace support services to secure critical information infrastructure (Joint Chiefs of Staff 2013, V-14). The doctrine also includes the defence industrial base within the Pentagon's responsibilities for critical infrastructure protection. This designation excludes commercial infrastructure, such as communications, transportation, power, and other utilities, the commercial infrastructure assets that are addressed by other sector-specific agencies such as the Department of Homeland Security in particular.[16] In a similar way, the Russian National Security Strategy has mandated the consolidation of federal and local efforts and resources with those of civil society more broadly (Kremlin 2015, #109).[17] Moreover, Russian military doctrine lists among the tasks of the armed forces the protection of important national, military, communication and transportation objects as well as the need to assist in the recovery from emergencies and the protection of important objects (Kremlin 2014, #32 h and q).

Liberal democracies have, however, been very cautious to grant the defence sector extensive mandates in such areas as intelligence and surveillance operations, in counter-terrorism, and in other operational areas considered to be especially sensitive. Liberal democracies tend to be highly cautious when there is a likelihood of violence, and are particularly sensitive to the prospect of intelligence-led intrusions into the functioning and freedoms of normal society. Totalitarian regimes, on the other hand, characteristically lean more heavily to the support of the military and intelligence services, but also expect the civilian sector to support the military and law enforcement activities.

Threat perceptions are again on the move. International interventions arguably had their day between the mid-1990s and mid-2010s. But now something closer to a traditional view of national defence has re-emerged, usually reflecting the reawakening of geopolitical tensions in Europe and elsewhere, and often under the guise of 'homeland' security and defence. What were in the past clearly distinct national, societal, and commercial fields have merged. Societies and industries have become fully dependent on constantly functioning information and communication systems. As individuals, organizations and businesses have become more dependent so their tolerance of any disturbances has decreased. Their vulnerability to attacks has thus increased as they have become more dependent and they increasingly sensitive to the possibility that any breakdown might be part of something larger and more disabling— perhaps even a hostile and politically motivated operation or campaign. As they confront these challenges, governments of all political colours are also facing constant pressure to reduce public spending. Cross-sectoral (and perhaps even cross-border) burden sharing is fast becoming more of a necessity than an interesting idea.

Acknowledging the key focus areas of national cybersecurity strategies, as well as the scope of expectations nations now have, it is possible to describe three different patterns for military participation in civilian affairs: independent actor, contingent contributor, and integrated stakeholder. These models follow the Huntington/Janowitz debate and differ mainly in the strength and independence permitted to the military.

Adjusted to the cyber realm, the roles that could be operationalized are as follows:

1. Independent actor: focusing on the protection of own systems, networks, and services for the purposes of information security, force protection, and the effectiveness of all military operations and activities, as well as on subsequent cyber military capability development for intelligence and both defensive and offensive cyber military operations.
2. Contingent contributor: offering technical capabilities and human resources to support civilian authorities during emergencies and cyber incidents at the request of civilian authorities and when, mandated, by national legislation and other regulations.
3. Integrated stakeholder: becoming an elementary part of coordinated national and governmental efforts for domestic and international purposes.

These roles are political-administrative abstractions that at best help to describe and categorize the position and strength of the military involvement. Political tolerance, national ambitions, and legal codes could limit the role the defence sector could have; or they could indeed expand that role. A particularly sensitive matter is the employment of armed forces in domestic operations. And, where the process of *securitization* is questioned, what might be perceived as a process of *militarization* is certain to provoke even more entrenched ideological and organizational resistance.[18] The following section therefore takes a closer look at military cyber operations, capabilities, and effects, which the militaries in general are able to deploy and employ.

MILITARY CYBER ACTIVITIES

Armed forces conduct military operations. This rather self-evident observation acknowledges armed forces as means to project state power—not the continuation of 'normal' politics as such, but nevertheless an elementary part of politics where the roles and explicit tasks of the armed forces signify national or at least governmental ambitions. The ability to conduct any meaningful military operations requires a vast spectrum of capabilities and supporting capability elements that, to a large extent, can also be used for non-lethal or non-offensive purposes.[19]

Defence forces are technically competent developers and operators of information and communication technology (ICT) in their operations and peacetime activities. As cyber policy is becoming part of foreign policy and especially national security policy, it seems inevitable that the ICT-competent defence sector should be included in national cyber policy. The trend is increasing although the pace has been modest. In 2011, the United Nations Institute for Disarmament Research assessed that, of the 68 states having cybersecurity programmes, some 32 included 'cyberwarfare in their military planning and organizations'. A year later, the survey found the number of states with national cybersecurity programmes to have grown to 114, of which 47 had programmes where the armed forces had 'some role'. The UNIDIR report notes that [only] 6 states had published military cyber strategies, 2 were planning to do so, and 30 had identified cybersecurity as a military concern or priority in policy documents (UNIDIR 2013, 1–2). The vast majority of the military efforts focus more on the protection of military networks and communications (i.e. modest defensive and functional measures), and on the establishment of military cyber command structures, rather than on developing battlefield operational capabilities (Pernik 2018).

To present, measure, and set criteria for military cyber capabilities, as well as assess the technical, tactical, operational, or strategic effect cyber-military operations may deliver, requires a clearer understanding of what constitutes military cyber capability and cyber operations. For example, armed forces have integrated ICTs to improve the operational effectiveness of conventional units, functions, and operations. Practically all units and functions employ advanced ICTs to a lesser or greater extent, because it is the current state of operational art and military affairs.

Accordingly, there is no unified understanding of what constitutes cyber military operations. The view the United States has taken since 2012 defines *cyberspace* operations as 'the employment of cyberspace capabilities where the primary purpose is to achieve objectives in or through cyberspace'. Cyberspace operations are categorized as offensive cyberspace operations intended to project power by the application of force in and through cyberspace; defensive cyberspace operations intended to defend friendly cyberspaces; and 'operations taken to design, build, configure, secure, operate, maintain, and sustain Department of Defence communications systems and networks in a way that creates and preserves data availability, integrity, confidentiality, as well as user/entity authentication and non-repudiation'.[20] By this view, more accurate intelligence, precise targeting, and the focused effects offered by modern digital ICTs would only be considered cyberspace operations if their effects took place in and through the cyber domain.[21]

That computer and electromagnetic technologies are merging has led the US Army to speak of *cyber-electromagnetic* activities integrating and synchronizing cyberspace operations, electronic warfare, and spectrum management operations. Cyberspace as a domain is understood to co-exist with the electromagnetic spectrum through telecommunications systems that use the spectrum and have converged into a worldwide network to create cyberspace. Separating cyberspace operations from other electronic operations that target ICT infrastructure, data networks, and the spectrum would not be operationally wise.[22]

Most importantly, these technical readings distinguish cyberspace operations from cognitive-psychological information operations. Information operations as defined by US joint doctrines are intended to 'influence, disrupt, corrupt, or usurp the decision making of adversaries and potential adversaries while protecting our own'. Cyberspace is considered to be but one medium through which information-related capabilities may be employed.[23] Previously in US thinking, 'cyber operations' (understood to be mainly computer network operations), were held to be a subset of information operations: a wider approach that continues to be taken by NATO and indeed by Russia and China, yet often without speaking of 'cyber'.[24]

Operations are conducted to create effects. Cyber effects can be many and various, depending on the level of war (i.e. strategic, operational, tactical, or technical), or the target-type, such as data, information service, or cyber-persona. In his Presidential Policy Directive (PPD-20) on cyber operations, President Obama outlined a typology of cyber effects useful for operational purposes. According to the Directive, cyber effects are '[T]he manipulation, disruption, denial, degradation, or destruction of computers, information or communications systems, networks, physical or virtual infrastructure controlled by computers or information systems, or information resident thereon'.[25] The military system is geared to develop, deploy, and employ capabilities able to create such effects. Although not explicitly stated in a publicly available document, similar thinking can be detected in Russian military doctrine: the Doctrine signed by President Putin commands the military to develop forces and means for information struggle.[26]

Yet the defence sectors' contribution to national cybersecurity does not need to be limited to operations, whether cyber or of any other sort. Defence as a system possesses qualities and capabilities that expand its military utility to broader civilian and national purposes. Armed forces, in particular, are deployable organizations equipped with leadership, operational, and technical competences and capabilities, manpower in readiness, material at hand (as devices and deployable systems) as well as vigorous education, training, and exercise regimes.

The implementation of national cybersecurity requires systematic work. Policy or strategy documents are not the end but the beginning of implementation. Like any other branch of public administration, or any supporting or supported private sector actor, the defence sector needs to have explicit mandates, procedures, and mechanisms of employment. A major strategy document can be a transparent and effective way to show how strategic objectives are to be operationalized, and how tasks are to be allocated between relevant governmental sectors and agencies. A more detailed division of objectives and responsibilities can be achieved in sectorial action plans.

The US Presidential Directive on national preparedness, for example, orders the national preparedness system to 'include an interagency operational plan to support each national planning framework'. Accordingly, each interagency operational plan is to 'include a more detailed concept of operations; description of critical tasks and responsibilities; detailed resource, personnel, and sourcing requirements; and specific provisions for the rapid integration of resources and personnel' (White House 2011). In the Netherlands, the defence organization's capabilities and manner of employment in cyber operations are being worked out in greater detail. The Dutch are also considering mechanisms to guarantee the availability of armed forces' cyber assets as part of their Intensification of Civil-Military Cooperation policy (Netherlands Ministry of Defence 2012). In Ireland, where the defence forces focus on protecting their own networks and users, the established culture of civil-military cooperation will be formalized by service level agreements, which 'will also include a mechanism for sharing technical expertise in the event of a national cyber incident or emergency' (Irish Department of Communications, Energy and Natural Resources 2015, 14). In Canada, the national cybersecurity action plan incorporates the Department of National Defence and the defence forces in the main pillars of the strategy, securing government systems and partnering to secure vital cyber systems outside the federal government.

The Canadian Plan defines specific actions, timelines, deliverables, status of action, and lead agencies (Government of Canada 2013).

Neither is it necessary to limit the deployment of cyber military support to domestic situations or national defence: military capabilities and effects can be relevant in international military operations. These operations might include peacekeeping, humanitarian operations, and disaster relief missions, as well as more robust crisis response operations or military interventions. As in the case of delivering humanitarian assistance, for example, or reconstructing ports, roads, and runways, the armed forces may be the first agency to deploy and run field communication systems as well as support local authorities to reinstate their information and communication networks and services.

The key capabilities the defence sector should, theoretically, be able to offer national cybersecurity are set out in the Table 27.1. The table connects the focus and functionality areas of national cybersecurity strategies with the generic competences and capabilities of the armed forces. The areas of cybersecurity shown follow the content and logic of contemporary national cybersecurity strategies. The capabilities the defence sector has at its disposal, and that should be employable and deployable, include both virtual and physical means and measures. Depending on national legislation and political considerations, they can be employed in domestic and international operations. As such, capabilities are not limited to either the virtual or the physical area of operations. Table 27.1 does not cover technical systems but speaks of capabilities as abilities to perform and create desired effects.

Table 27.1 An assessment of defence sector's contribution to national cybersecurity. Author's compilation.

Areas of cybersecurity	Capabilities (means and measures)
Situational awareness	Network and spectrum monitoring. Intelligence (operations) on e.g. cybercriminals, hacktivists, and foreign state actors. Information sharing.
Prevention	Deterrence by denial through network protection, information security, and defensive means. Deterrence by punishment through offensive means.
Preparedness	Training and exercises. Technical consultations. Readiness to be deployed.
Response	Defensive cyber-electromagnetic operations. Offensive cyber-electromagnetic operations.
Recovery and resilience	Deployment of back-up systems. Offering emergency or temporary communication services as well as manpower and material.
Public awareness and competence	Awareness and competence-raising, especially through conscription or some form of militia system. Education, training, and exercises. Information operations in support of national information campaigns.

In each area, the defence sector can—on one of the three levels discussed earlier— lead the effort (independent actor); act in support to other agents (contingent contributor); or give support to, and be supported by, other agents in a coordinated national effort (integrated stakeholder). For example, cyber-electromagnetic operations can be conducted independently to achieve military operational objectives, or mounted in support of law enforcement and emergency authorities. Similarly, the military, based on its competences and technical capabilities, can take a prominent role in organizing national (and international) cyber exercises.

CONCLUSION

Cyber affairs encompass all areas of societal life. Cybersecurity is a whole-of-society issue where every actor is a stakeholder, a potential target, and a risk factor at one and the same time. To establish, maintain, and update adequate security requires such wide competence and vast resources that no single agency possesses. Only few governments explicitly include the defence sector in the overall national cybersecurity plan. But keeping undefined the relationship between the cyber soldier and their state is of doubtful benefit. An explicit mandate is far better than an implicit but *de facto* one. The scope and strength of this role vary from the (Huntingtonian) separation to the (Janowitzian) integration of the military as modelled above in the three roles of independent actor, contingent contributor, and integrated stakeholder.

What the majority of nations do is to deploy their cyber military assets to support civilian authorities. This is justifiable by several input and output factors including the following:

- Harmonizing national and governmental efforts in the field of cybersecurity.
- Expanding and ensuring civilian political control of military cyber operations and capability development.
- Effective use of national resources without duplication.
- Increasing capacity and competence in preparation for and during cyber incidents.
- Strengthening national resilience during cyber incidents.

In sum, the question is of shared or contrasting interests and of shared or separated capabilities. How can all public competence and resources be harnessed to maximize the desired political impact while at the same time achieving desired standards of economic-administrative effectiveness and efficiency?

The horizontal and vertical proliferation of governmental cybersecurity policies and strategies is not unproblematic. Securitization and militarization of cybersecurity change the politics of input and go against the Utopian promise of cybernetics: the ideals of a stateless cyber world that epitomized the early years of connectivity, the Internet and a cosmopolitan cyber culture.[27] Appeals such as 'not taking the Internet from the people' signify not only an emphasis on the individual but also an inherent distrust of the government—or perhaps simply the fear by one elite that it might be about to lose control to another.

National cybersecurity is, and must remain predominantly, a civil concern. Cybersecurity measures and strategy need to first and foremost serve national information technology and IT society strategies. Similarly, the military has first and foremost a supporting, not supported, role. There is no need for a new military role, although there are several new tasks that could reasonably (and safely) be allocated to the defence sector. These new tasks would not contaminate the digital infrastructure. The civil digital environment can be protected in the same fashion and under the same political, legal, and administrative mandates as any other form of individual and societal life.

Despite their cyber-specific organizational, planning, and implementation skills, the armed forces should not be considered to be a jack-of-all-trades solution to complex cyber problems. Each societal and governmental sector should develop and employ its own approaches and capabilities. Even with a risk of treating the armed forces too romantically, as the epitome of an apolitical and virtuous institution, the defence sector and the armed forces are first and foremost configured for military missions and operations to defend the nation, its people, and interests. Although a wasteful duplication of effort is often feared, the greater risk would be the loss of effectiveness. When responsibilities are split across the spectrum of missions, the anticipated resources may not exist or be easily available and deployable, and the suitability and level of performance of such capabilities can be questioned.

In its fundamental goals and characteristics, online national security cannot differ from its traditional, off-line predecessor: the same underlying political principles must guide national and governmental activities regardless of the field. Civilian security authorities must have the principal role of leading and implementing national cybersecurity measures. The defence sector and respective military authorities should remain focused on the protection of their own networks and communications. The armed forces must be prepared to conduct cyber military operations under the same limitation and political, legal, and professional scrutiny as any other military operations. For their part, private actors should possess only very limited authority to override political freedoms for the sake of their security. Governments should set out clearly the roles their military forces (and private sector, when appropriate) are to have in national cybersecurity. The defence sector can offer vital support to civilian authorities and society if and when needed but must at all times be governed by clear and robust protocols.

A strong, even purist, view of the explicit but limited role for the defence sector is mostly applicable to liberal-pluralist democracies. It is presented here with an assumption and conviction that, despite any deficiencies, a liberal democratic governance model is the best model to safeguard civilian control of armed forces and individual human rights, as well as international peace and security. Incorporating the defence sector into mainstream cyber policy can actually help to extend political and civilian control over military cyber affairs. Quite obviously, totalitarian regimes are different. Given their questionable record in honouring universal human rights and even granting the political freedoms their constitutions theoretically provide, the involvement of the defence sector in national cybersecurity affairs raises many uneasy questions. Equally, there are many in liberal democracies who fear the state and its security apparatus extending their control mechanisms into the cyberspace (Deleuze 1995; Dillon and Reid 2001, 41–66; Diniz, Muggah, and Glenny 2014; Nyst 2016).

Concerns over the loss of privacy, 'mass surveillance', and a so-called 'Big Brother' society stem from the extensive security measures many governments have taken, and the detailed data that advanced technologies allow them to have. In totalitarian countries, the defence/security sector quite obviously plays a major role in national administration and governmental control apparatus: a fact that undermines the fundamental principles of rule of law and good governance as safeguards against any misuse of powers. Henkin's alarming comment on state behaviour that the development (and deployment) of technologies has enabled states to use methods that otherwise would have been considered illegal by international law is worth remembering in cyber affairs (Henkin 1979, 103–4).

Cybersecurity policies and strategies expand the space controlled by the executive. This expanding influence creates and legitimizes the state as an actor, indeed a sovereign actor, in cyberspace. The inclusion of the defence sector into national cybersecurity also updates the concerns of the 'military-industrial complex' described by US President Eisenhower in his farewell address. If the old weapons industry was able to shape American defence and military policy, the new cybersecurity industry has no less influence. The 'contract state' should therefore seek to implement strong political control in order to avoid unnecessary securitization and militarization of IT and cyber development policies, misuse of public mandate and funds, and ultimately abuses of power by any elite (Dunleavy and O'Leary 1987, 16, 23–37, 183–4). Paradoxically, increasing the role of the defence sector in cybersecurity can both secure democratic societies and make totalitarian ones even worse.

Notes

1. The 'man-bit-a-dog' type real news here is that, as of March 2019, almost half the countries do not have an explicit cyber or information policy, strategy, or doctrine. On national strategies, see Tikk, Eneken, and Kerttunen, Mika. 2019. *A Normative Analysis of National Cybersecurity Strategies*. Paris: EU Institute for Strategic Studies.
2. Defence sector refers to the ministry or department of defence and the related independent defence agencies or military or paramilitary organizations countries have. Alongside the armed/defence forces, these may include, for example, military intelligence services, cybersecurity and communications agencies, and border, coast, and national guards. This ontology of 'the military' excludes civilian intelligence agencies, such as the CIA, FSB, or GCHQ, and, for example, police, customs and other law enforcement organizations.
3. A deterrent effect can be achieved through either deterrence by denial or deterrence by punishment, both clearly communicated, cognitively understood and by capabilities credible state of mind of the adversary.
4. Strategy can be understood as a pattern or method of thinking, an administrative process, or a manifestation of policy in form of an issued instrumental document. Strategic thinking can be seen as a balanced calculation between ends, ways, and means, or in other words between objectives and resources. Strategy, as an administrative process, constitutes organized work to define objectives and design overarching and long-term policies and action plans as well as to implement, steer, and improve such policies and plans. Strategies, as manifestation of policies and plans to be effectively implemented, need to be communicated. It should also be noted that often the notions of strategy and doctrine are used interchangeably and in two hierarchical orders.
5. On the notion and theory of securitization, see especially Wæver, Ole. 1995. 'Securitization and Desecuritization'. In *On Security*, edited by Ronnie D. Lipschutz, pp. 46–86. New York: Columbia University Press; Buzan, Barry, Ole Wæver, and Jaap de Wilde. 1998. *Security: A New Framework for Analysis*. Boulder, CO: Lynne Rienner; and Dunn Cavelty, Myriam. 2008. *Cyber-Security and Threat Politics. US Efforts to Secure the Information Age*. Abingdon, UK: Routledge.

6. Tikk and Kerttunen, *A Normative Analysis*.
7. See, for example, the Lithuanian Government. 2011. *Programme for the Development of Electronic Information Security (Cyber-Security) for 2011–2019* (Resolution 796).
8. See, for example, Czech National Security Authority. 2015. *National Cyber Security Strategy of the Czech Republic for the period from 2015 to 2020*, https://www.enisa.europa.eu/topics/national-cyber-security-strategies/ncss-map/CzechRepublic_Cyber_Security_Strategy.pdf and Singapore's infocomm and cybersecurity masterplans where security thinking has developed from the protection of government networks and system to national critical infrastructure protection, and towards the 2016 national strategy, the first encompassing document in this field.
9. These internationalist agendas are not only manifestations of countries' foreign and security policy but export preferred forms of information strategies and global governance. Norm entrepreneurs and capacity-builders can critically be regarded to use the necessity of security to promote allied social order, systems of distributive justice, and political morphology of what it is to be a State. Such strategies may extend from technical security and law enforcement purposes to population management. See, for example, Dillon, Michael. 2015. *Biopolitics of Security. A political analysis of finitude*. London: Routledge, pp. 101–110; Nyst, *Travel Guide*, e.g. p. 63; of such biopolitical normativism, see, in particular, VII BRICS Summit, 2015. Ufa Declaration.
10. Dutch cyber policy is a prime example of such a holistic approach to cybersecurity. The 2012 Dutch national cybersecurity strategy defines cybersecurity in a rather technical manner as 'efforts to prevent damage caused by disruptions to, breakdowns in or misuse of ICT and to repair damage if and when it has occurred', but aims to make the Netherlands a global and progressive leader in cybersecurity. The strategy applies an integrated approach whereby the Dutch defence organization with its three core tasks of (i) protecting the integrity of national and Alliance territory, (ii) promoting stability and the international rule of law, and (iii) supporting civil authorities in upholding the law, providing disaster relief and humanitarian assistance, both nationally and internationally, is explicitly intertwined into national objectives. The broader scope is reflected in the name of the 2018 policy document: *A Cyber Security Agenda* (Netherlands Ministry of Defence, 2012, The Defence Cyber Strategy; Netherlands Ministry of Security and Justice. 2013. National Cyber Security Strategy 2. From Awareness to Capability.) p. 4.
11. The conceptual and epistemological difference in these approaches is that, whereas the traditional geopolitical approach takes security as given, material and secret, the postmodern-expressionist approach regards it as voluntaristic, normative, and visible.
12. See also Machiavelli, Niccolò. 1992 (1515). *The Prince*. Mineola NY: Dover Publications, Chapters 12 and 13; and Smith, Rupert. 2008. *The Utility of Force. The Art of War in the Modern World*. New York NY: Random House, pp. 269–80.
13. Dunn Cavelty, *Cyber-Security and Threat Politics*, pp. 84–6; Tikk-Ringas, Eneken (ed.) 2015. *The Evolution of Cyber Domain*. London: International Institute for Strategic Studies. Chapters 4–6, 10.
14. For example, Finnish (11.5.2007/551), Norwegian (Prob. 73 S; Innst. 388 S (2011–12) and Swedish (SFS 1994: 642) regulations are rather identical in defining the defence forces' domestic and international tasks.
15. Joint Chiefs of Staff. 2018. *Defence Support to Civil Authorities*. Joint Publication 3-28, p. 1.4. 29 October..

16. Joint Chiefs of Staff, *Defense Support*, IV–3; White House, 2011. The National Guard, for example, can offer cyber teams and squadrons to Federal Emergency Management Agency response regions to respond to large-scale emergencies and disasters at home. Guard units can also organize and run education and training as well as sensibilization and awareness activities (National Guard. 2016. 'National Guard Uniquely Positioned to Contribute in Cyber Realm', 19 October). The Guard's domestic mandate stems from the *U.S. Code 32: National Guard*. See, in particular, Chapter 9, 'Homeland Defence Activities' as well as State Active Duty, Title 32 and Title 10 duty statutes.

17. See also the Russian doctrine on information security (Kremlin, 2000. *Information Security Doctrine of the Russian Federation*, 9 September; https://www.itu.int/en/ITU-D/Cybersecurity/Documents/National_Strategies_Repository/Russia_2000.pdf. Kremlin 2016. *Decree on the Approval of the Doctrine of Information Security of the Russian Federation*, 5 December. https://www.mid.ru/en/foreign_policy/official_documents/-/asset_publisher/CptICkB6BZ29/content/id/2563163).

18. Militarization here refers to the discursive and political process constructing particular issues as military issues, thus requiring military response as well as the process of accumulating, organizing, and legitimizing military capacity (see Wendt, Alexander. 1989. *The States System and Global Militarization*. Ann Arbour, University of Minnesota).

19. The notion of capability refers to a direct means, methods, techniques, and devices designed to create cyber effects or effects in cyberspace. Supporting capability elements refer to means and measures that are needed (the direct) capabilities to exist, but which do not create cyber effects. Of the latter, financing, logistics, education, and leadership are perhaps the clearest examples. On views to capabilities and capability development, see, in particular, De Spiegeleire, Stephan. 2011. 'Ten Trends in Capability Planning for Defence and Security', *The RUSI Journal*, 156 (5): 20–8, Joint Chiefs of Staff. 2013. Cyberspace Operations, JP 3–12, 5 February and Joint Chiefs of Staff. 2018. *Cyberspace Operations*, JP 3–12, 8 June. For a threat-based discussion on the role of defence, see Wallace, Ian. 2013. 'The Military Role in National Cybersecurity Governance'. Seoul Defence Dialogue. 12 November.

20. Joint Chiefs of Staff, : (2013), *Cyberspace Operations*, v, vii.

21. cyberspace and information operations whereas some European countries still regard cyber operations as a subset of information opertations.

22. Headquarters Department of Army. 2014. *Cyber Electromagnetic Operations*, FM 3–38, 12 February, pp. 1–1 to 1–6. Electronic warfare refers to military action involving the use of electromagnetic and directed energy to control the electromagnetic spectrum or to attack the enemy. It consists of the functions of electronic attack, electronic protection, and electronic warfare support. Spectrum management operations are the interrelated functions of spectrum management, frequency assignment, host-nation coordination, and policy that enable the planning, management, and execution of operations within the electromagnetic operational environment.

23. Joint Chiefs of Staff, *Cyberspace Operations*, I–5 to I–6.

24. The 1998 joint information operations doctrine (JP 3-13 [October 1998]) does not mention the concepts of 'cyber', 'cyber operations' or 'cyber domain'. See also Giles, Keir. 2016. *Handbook on Russian Information Operations*. NATO Defence College, pp. 6–15 on 'Russian cyber' concepts.

25. White House, 2012, *U.S. Cyber Operations Policy*, PPD-20, a top-secret document acquired and published by *The Guardian* (7 June 2013) and available, for example, at the Federation of American Scientists website. The United States holds an official view that the document and its information is stolen federal property.

26. Kremlin, *Military Doctrine*, # 46c.

27. See, for example, Benedict, Michael. 1991. *Introduction to Cyberspace: First Steps.* Cambridge, MA: MIT Press.

BIBLIOGRAPHY

VII BRICS Summit, 2015. *Ufa Declaration.* http://www.brics.utoronto.ca/docs/150709-ufa-declaration_en.html.

Cyber Security Agency of Singapore. 2016. *Singapore's Cybersecurity Strategy.*

Government of Canada. 2013. *Action Plan 2010–2015 for Canada's Cyber Security Strategy.*

Deleuze, Gilles. 1995. 'Postscript on Control Societies'. In *Negotiations*, edited by Gilles Deleuze, and Claire Parnet. New York: Columbia University Press, pp. 177–182.

Dillon, Michael, and Julian Reid. 2001. 'Global Liberal Governance: Biopolitics, Security and War', *Millennium: Journal of International Studies* 30 (1). doi.org/10.1177/03058298010300010501

Diniz, Gustavo, Robert Muggah, and Misha Glenny. 2014. 'Deconstructing Cyber Security in Brazil', *Igarapé Institute Strategic Paper* 11.

Dunleavy, Patrick, and Brendan O'Leary. 1987. *Theories of the State. The Politics of Liberal Democracy.* New York: New Amsterdam Books.

Dunn Cavelty, Myriam. 2008. *Cyber-Security and Threat Politics. US Efforts to Secure the Information Age.* Abingdon, UK: Routledge.

Dunn Cavelty, Myriam. 2020. 'Cybersecurity between Hypersecuritization and Technological Routine'. In *Routledge Handbook of International Cybersecurity*, edited by Eneken Tikk and Mika Kerttunen, Abingdon, UK: Routledge, pp. 11–21.

Henkin, Louis. 1979. *How Nations Behave.* New York: Columbia University Press.

House of Representatives. 2012. *U.S. Code 32: National Guard.* Available at: https://uscode.house.gov/view.xhtml?path=/prelim@title32&edition=prelim.

Huntington, Samuel. 1957. *The Soldier and the State.* Cambridge, Mass.: Belknap Press.

Irish Department of Communications, Energy and Natural Resources. 2015. *National Cyber Security Strategy: Securing our Digital Future.* Available at: https://www.ncsc.gov.ie/pdfs/National_Cyber_Security_Strategy%202015-2017nb.pdf.

Janowitz, Morris. 1960. *The Professional Soldier.* Glencoe, IL: Free Press.

Joint Chiefs of Staff. 2018. *Defense Support to Civil Authorities*, JP 3–28, 29 October.

Kremlin. 2014. *The Military Doctrine of Russian Federation*, 19 December. Avialable at: https://rusemb.org.uk/press/2029.

Kremlin. 2015. *Russian National Security Strategy*, 31 December. Available at: http://static.kremlin.ru/media/acts/files/0001201512310038.pdf.

Luiif, H.A.M., Besseling, Kim, Spoelstra, Maartje et al. 2013. 'Ten National Cyber Security Strategies: A Comparison'. In *Critical Information Infrastructure Security*, edited by Sandro Bologna, Berhhard Hämmerli, Dimitris Gritzalis et al. Heidelberg: Springer-Verlag.

Luiij, Eric, Kim Besseling, and Patrick de Graaf. 2013. 'Nineteen National Cyber Security Strategies', *International Journal of Critical Infrastructure Protection* 9 (1/2): 3–31.

Machiavelli, Niccolò. 1992 (1515). *The Prince.* Mineola, NY: Dover Publications Available at: https://www.itu.int/en/ITU-D/Cybersecurity/Documents/National_Strategies_Repository/Netherlands_2012_NDL-Cyber_StrategyEng.pdf.

Netherlands Ministry of Defence. 2012. *The Defence Cyber Strategy.*

Netherlands Ministry of Security and Justice. 2013. *National Cyber Security Strategy 2. From Awareness to Capability*. Available at: https://www.enisa.europa.eu/topics/national-cyber-security-strategies/ncss-map/NCSS2Engelseversie.pdf.

Netherlands Ministry of Security and Justice. 2018. *National Cyber Security Agenda. A Cyber Secure Netherlands*. Available at: https://english.ncsc.nl/topics/national-cybersecurity-agenda/documents/publications/2019/juni/01/national-cyber-security-agenda.

Norwegian Parliament, Standing Committee for Foreign Affairs and Defence. 2012. *Innstilling fra utenriks—og forsvarskomiteen om Et forsvar for vår tid,* Prob. 73 S; Innst. 388 S. Available at: https://docplayer.me/10713906-Innst-388-s-2011-2012-innstilling-til-stortinget-fra-utenriks-og-forsvarskomiteen.html.

Nyst, Carly. 2016. *Travel Guide to the Digital World: Cybersecurity Policy for Human Rights Defenders*. London: Global Partners Digital.

Parliament of Finland. 2007. *Act on the Defence Forces, 551/2007*. Available at: https://finlex.fi/en/laki/kaannokset/2007/en20070551.

Pernik, Piret. 2018. *Preparing for Cyber Conflict: Case Studies of Cyber Command*. Tallinn: International Centre for Defence and Security.

Swedish Parliament. 1994. 'Förordning med instruktion för Försvarsmakten', SFS: 642.

UNIDIR. 2013. *The Cyber Index. International Security Trends and Realities*. Geneva: UNIDIR.

United Nations General Assembly. 2013. 'Development in the Fields of Information Technologies and Telecommunication in the Context of International Security', 68/98 (24 June). Available at: https://www.unidir.org/files/medias/pdfs/developments-in-the-field-of-information-and-telecommunications-in-the-context-of-international-security-2012-2013-a-68-98-eng-0-518.pdf.

United Nations General Assembly. 2015. 'Development in the Fields of Information Technologies and Telecommunication in the Context of International Security', 70/174 (22 July). Available at: https://undocs.org/A/70/174.

White House. 2011a. *International Strategy for Cyberspace*. Available at: https://obamawhitehouse.archives.gov/sites/default/files/rss_viewer/international_strategy_for_cyberspace.pdf.

White House. 2011b. *National Preparedness, PPD-8*. Available at: https://www.dhs.gov/presidential-policy-directive-8-national-preparedness#:~:text=Presidential%20Policy%20Directive%20%2F%20PPD%2D8%20is%20aimed%20at%20strengthening%20the,pandemics%2C%20and%20catastrophic%20natural%20disasters.

CHAPTER 28

CYBERSECURITY CAPACITY BUILDING

LARA PACE AND PAUL CORNISH

INTRODUCTION

THE purpose of cybersecurity capacity building is best explained by a simple analogy. In an imaginary case, a lake sits landlocked between five countries. The lake is an essential resource for the five countries that surround it, and it has become the distinctive feature of the social and cultural heritage of them all, and imperative for future life. For these different reasons, it is essential that the lake is kept healthy, clean, unpolluted, and accessible. Contrary to these expectations, however, country A (accidentally or otherwise), begins to pump in industrial effluent that dramatically reduces the cleanliness of the water, rendering it unsafe to drink and dramatically reducing fishing stocks. How might countries B, C, D, and E be affected, and how should they respond? Should each of them take immediate measures to clean up the pollution, ensure their access to fresh water, and prevent further toxic discharge? If so, are there rules in place to ensure that their individual response is reasonable, efficient, effective, proportionate, and, above all, guided by law? Should the four affected countries work together to muster their response to reverse the pollution and should they invite country A to join the clean-up operation? If the response is well calibrated and proves to be successful, what measures must these countries put in place to ensure that the lake does not suffer a similar event again? More broadly, how could these countries work together in the longer term to ensure the preservation of the lake's health, which is essential to the economies and the lives of the people in those countries and perhaps beyond? These questions all fall within the political theory known as *functionalism*, most often associated with David Mitrany for whom, writing in the early 1940s, thoughts of a 'saner future' persuaded him 'to look at things "functionally", to look for a prospect of some balance of beneficial mutual concert' (Mitrany 1975, 20).

Yet there are also awkward questions of liability and culpability to consider. If country A is held to be negligent and responsible for the pollution (whether by accident or by intent) then should some form of action—even *punitive* action—be taken against country A by the other four littoral states? What would be the position of those four states if they were to receive information that the perpetrator was in fact a criminal organization of some sort, exploiting weaknesses in country A's internal security apparatus. Would country A be held responsible? And if there were a suspicion that country A had engaged the criminal organization to act on its behalf in a 'plausibly deniable' way, how would this be proved and with what consequences?

This simple analogy translates relatively easily into the subject matter of this chapter. The *lake* is of course cyberspace: a shared utility, a resource vulnerable to interference and disruption and therefore to be secured and protected, an economic driver and a social platform. The analogy is possibly more convincing in reverse: as the singular driver of much of modern life, we might say that cyberspace is more obviously endowed with the properties of the lake than the lake itself. What might then be expected of 'digital functionalism' in this context? Who or what is responsible for keeping this essential resource clean, and what measures as a global community must be put in place, and by whom, to maintain its health? Who should set the rules of behaviour and what should be done about those who break those rules?

The list of questions is lengthy and there are few, if any, straightforward answers. Nevertheless, it is the purpose of cybersecurity capacity-building initiatives to address these questions (and others yet to be asked) in order to identify initiatives and behaviours that will not only be effective in protecting and maintaining cyberspace as a global resource but will also be within the capabilities of national governments around the world.

CONNECTIVITY: RISKS AND OPPORTUNITIES

Through fast-paced and seemingly unending technological advancement, the world has seen the uptake of smart technologies and their deployment globally across the public and private sector, and among thousands of millions of individual people. By January 2021, according to Internet Stats and Facts (2021), there were some 4.78 billion active Internet users in the world, an increase of about 40% over five years,[1] and, according to the International Telecommunications Union, there were almost 8.2 billion mobile-cellular telephone subscriptions around the globe.[2] These extraordinary rates of 'take-up' of digital means can only be described as revolutionary, not just technologically but also, and perhaps more significantly, in terms of politics, economics, and opportunity. And there seems no end in sight, no natural limit to this expansion. If, as is often argued, the expanding global communication infrastructure not only *shapes* but also *improves* all dimensions and all levels of human life—cultural, economic, religious, diplomatic, commercial, family, individual, non-governmental, and governmental, etc.—then it is clear why it should be so popular and the case for even greater digital expansion difficult to resist.[3] In the UK, for example, something like one-eighth of GDP has been reported to come from the digital economy, which is growing 2.5 times faster than other areas.

The premise of the World Economic Forum's Networked Readiness Index (NRI) is that information and communications technology (ICT) can be activist, progressive, and transformative, and that countries can be helped to 'leverage ICTs for increased competitiveness and well-being.'[4] The World Bank is similarly confident in the social and economic merits of digital transformation:

> Connectivity—whether the Internet or mobile phones—is increasingly bringing market infor-
> mation, financial services, health services—to remote areas, and is helping to change people's
> lives in unprecedented ways. New information and communications technologies (ICT), in
> particular high-speed internet, are changing the way companies do business, transforming
> public service delivery and democratizing innovation. With 10 percent increase in high speed
> Internet connections, economic growth increases by 1.3 percent.[5]

Just as the World Economic Forum report saw the need for 'new economic and social dynamics' to be 'managed if the digital transformation of industries and societies are to deliver long-term and broad-based gains', so the authors of an earlier World Bank study were clear that 'this great potential to contribute to growth and competitiveness' would be determined by the ability of governments to 'understand the opportunity and ensure that supportive conditions are in place through regulatory and policy reforms as well as strategic investments and public-private partnerships' (Qiang, Rossott, and Kimura 2009).

The result is not only unprecedented mass access to advanced communications (for better or, possibly, for worse), it also amounts to nothing short of a flood of data. It has been said that, every second, one hour of video is uploaded to YouTube: the equivalent of one decade's worth of video being uploaded every single day. By another account, YouTube's monthly uploads are roughly equivalent to all video transmissions by all US television networks over the past 30 years. There could be as many as 500 million Tweets sent each day and, according to the Radacati Group in 2020, some 258 billion emails could have been sent each day.[6] Soberingly, in 2010, Eric Schmidt (formerly Chief Executive Officer and then Executive Chairman of Google) claimed that every two days as much information was being created as throughout the history of humanity up until 2003: approximately five exabytes.[7]

Connections are also proliferating among machines and objects, and with them the flow of yet more data. The so-called Internet of Things (or, as some prefer, the Internet of *Everything*) amounts to networks of sensors, devices, and machines connected by an automated communications process in which data, measurements, and information are transmitted to a central point for collation, monitoring, analysis, and communication, all without the need for a human to be 'in the loop'. The variety of devices networked in this way seems limitless: communications equipment; domestic appliances; surveillance equipment; vehicles; health monitoring devices; energy management systems; environmental monitoring equipment; industrial management systems, and so on. According to Cisco, by 2020, there could be as many as 50 billion such devices connected to the Internet, each generating its own telemetry. If this huge figure is difficult to accept, even a more modest estimate, such as that made by the US Census Bureau, suggests that 'just' 20.5 billion devices could be connected in this way.[8]

Connectivity is clearly perceived to create opportunity, on all levels. But it also represents hazard, creating the potential for insecurity on all levels. The rapid advance of digital technology and the growth of the Internet have outpaced the capacity of nation states to ensure that cyberspace does not become polluted or misused, damaging the economy and the security of the population it serves. Nation states, historically responsible for the security of their people and the social and economic stability of their society, therefore find themselves in an unenviable position, whereby technological innovation and implementation are taking place at fast pace across the private sector and the global marketplace, but without the supervisory and regulatory frameworks that should be in place to ensure the safety of the billions of users who consume, and increasingly depend upon, these technological developments.

The rapid take-up of digital technology poses a number of practical and conceptual problems, which must be addressed if cybersecurity capacity building (discussed in more detail later) is to be effective. One practical challenge is the relative ease with which criminal actors have been able to exploit not only the opportunities offered by the Internet but also the absence of a convincing and effective regulatory framework. Financial crime has become a desk-based activity, requiring little of the paraphernalia and behaviour that would traditionally have been associated with the physical act of robbing a bank, for example. While it is true to say that some leaders have responded to this challenge by prioritizing the development and propagation of cybercrime law, there remain a significant number of jurisdictions around the world that have no legal frameworks or legal instruments in place whatsoever, with which to address criminal activity taking place electronically or via a digital means. Even then, the development and propagation of cybercrime law (otherwise known as 'computer misuse legislation') would not be sufficient.

Legal infrastructures around the world need the ability to talk to each other and to collaborate in order to eradicate safe havens within which cybercriminals can shelter. The harmonization of legislation is also required to expedite the prevention of evidence in order to successfully prosecute perpetrators in court. With almost 200 countries in the international system, each with their own constitutional traditions and legal culture, it would be highly ambitious to expect conformity to a common international code, even if such a thing were conceivable and practically possible. Nevertheless, it could be possible, at minimum, to emphasize the general need for national cybercrime legislation while also pursuing more focused and specific efforts such as agreement on the safe preservation and storage of electronic evidence.

Other challenges include the comprehensiveness of cybersecurity capacity building efforts. Arguably the greatest challenge of cybersecurity capacity building is that it requires what has become known in the jargon as a 'multidisciplinary approach', seeking the active participation of professionals from all relevant and/or affected disciplines, some of which might not have been accustomed to working with each other in the past. The delivery of effective and comprehensive cybersecurity capacity building requires the skills, insights, and experience of economists, policymakers, behavioural scientists, technologists, human and civil rights advocates, computer scientists, logistics specialists, political scientists, lawyers, philosophers, and many more. As well as comprehensiveness in participation, effective cybersecurity capacity building will also need to address the breadth of the geopolitical playing field. Cyberspace is not governed by any single entity (technical or political, national or international) and neither is it containable within any traditional geopolitical border. The global and borderless nature of the Internet presents immense opportunity for innovation, yet at the same time it provides a very attractive, and all-too-easily accessible avenue of for malign activity.

Having discussed the broad rationale for cybersecurity capacity building, its scope and modalities, the remainder of this chapter examines the practical politics of capacity building. What, precisely, do we mean by 'capacity' in this context? Who, or what, is responsible for capacity building, and what resources are available? How could cybersecurity capacity building become sustainable to keep pace with technological developments and how will it continue to develop as a discipline in itself across the globe?

What is Cybersecurity Capacity?

For the most part, cybersecurity capacity building professionals will hear terms such as 'sustainable', 'comprehensive', 'holistic', repeated incessantly on a daily basis, in relation to capacity building in cybersecurity. These terms are now engrained in the common international language of capacity building but what exactly do they mean?

As with the development of natural languages, there are also several toolkits, indexes, and reference materials that are now embedded in the capacity-building language. These reference materials include, among others, the Australian Strategic Policy Institute Cybersecurity Maturity Index; Estonia's National Cybersecurity Index; the Potomac Institute's Cyber Readiness Index; and the International Telecommunication Union's National Cybersecurity Strategy Guide (a development of the Cybersecurity Toolkit of 2008). These indexes and initiatives are all useful in understanding national existing capacities, although not all employ a comprehensive methodology and not all take a practical, in-country approach to capacity building. In several cases, the capacity assessment is undertaken remotely, with a strong emphasis on desk-based research and analysis.

The initial goal of these (and other) reference materials and guiding tools is to understand the existing capacities of a nation as a baseline for the development of a strategic approach to further national capacity building. This strategic approach should, in turn, enable active and secure participation in cyberspace. Although the outline and structure of each of these guides, indexes, and models vary, because they are developed through different methodologies, they all endeavour to reach more or less the same objective. The challenge common to cybersecurity capacity-building initiatives remains, however, the absence of a comprehensive international approach premised on the respect of human rights and international law. Both authors of this chapter were closely involved in the design, development, and implementation of one other capacity-building initiative—the Cybersecurity Capacity Maturity Model for Nations (CMM) created by the Global Cyber Security Capacity Centre (GCSCC) at the University of Oxford. The CMM was designed to address many of the tasks outlined earlier and serves as a useful illustration of the scope and complexities of cybersecurity capacity building.

Designed to be a vehicle for data collection for a very ambitious research programme, the CMM is based on software maturity assessment models developed by the Carnegie Mellon University in the 1970s. The CMM addresses cybersecurity capacity through five dimensions, or lenses (strategy and policy; awareness, education, and training; legal frameworks; and standards and technology) across five levels of maturity (start-up, formative, established, strategic, and dynamic). Fifty or so considerations of cybersecurity capacity emerge when the five dimensions are mapped across the five levels of maturity. In the breadth and robustness of its design, the CMM proved able to be deployed around the world, in different economies holding varying levels of cybersecurity maturity. The CMM was launched in 2014, following broad consultation with a range of international experts drawn from government, private sector, the tech community, and academia, and was deployed in over 70 countries in its first 5 years.

The uptake of the CMM is attributable to its having adopted a methodology designed to break through 'silos' and special interests, insisting on a comprehensive approach from the start of the assessment process. The CMM methodology embraces the multidisciplinary approach described earlier, and it is this that has driven the uptake of the CMM. A typical CMM review in-country will bring a range of stakeholders into specific focus groups to address two dimensions of the model—one directly related to the expertise in the room and another where stakeholders may or may not be able to contribute directly to the discussion and debate but have relatable expertise to the subject being discussed. The three-day exercise is in itself a capacity-building exercise insofar as its consultative approach introduces stakeholders from across the working spectrum to cybersecurity capacity, demonstrates what cybersecurity might mean for their country, and, more importantly, shows what role the specialist participants might have in improving the national cybersecurity landscape. The methodology is designed to broaden the conversation at a national level, and allows for new considerations and ideas to be explored for any particular national context. The methodology often allows for the inclusion of new concepts, which may not have been considered before the CMM review was initiated.

The five extant CMM dimensions and the factors they consider (and there might be a case to adapt the CMM further to cover emerging areas such as financial technology, artificial intelligence, and the media) show that the capacity-building effort must be sophisticated and comprehensive and that it will require a multi-ministry, public-private, multi-agency response if any progress is to be made.

In short, the CMM process serves as a model for cybersecurity capacity building to the extent that it encourages the participation of relevant and interested parties drawn from public, private, civil society, academia, and the technical community. The breadth of participation establishes a 'high and wide' stakeholder ownership of the capacity-building process in the country concerned. It is this element of engagement that makes the CMM unique—and successful. Above all, the CMM is more than merely an exercise or demonstration in understanding cybersecurity capacity. Much more ambitiously, the goal of the CMM is instead to ensure that policymakers understand the questions *they* should be asking and of whom. With this goal in mind, the output of the review is a report with specific recommendations to improve the maturity of cybersecurity capacity in the country, and the owner and audience of that report remains the commissioning government.

Agency, Responsibility, and Resources

To improve the prospects of success in cybersecurity capacity building, the approach taken must be multidisciplinary, holistic, and comprehensive and, importantly, must include all stakeholders in the exercise from the outset. Just as importantly, the capacity building must be located somewhere and authorized in some way. In the absence of an international body or authority, charged with overseeing and standardizing cybersecurity capacity building around the world, many different agencies from the development sector (traditional multilateral agencies as they are perhaps better understood) have been prompted to introduce a cybersecurity stream in their own programmes of work. In some cases, agencies have developed a dedicated cyber capacity-building programme consistent with their core mandate and core business. For example, an international organization charged to develop capacity within a given state's criminal justice system might reasonably see the case for a programme of cybercrime legislation development with supporting exercises and programmes around that theme. Indeed, to do otherwise—for an international organization working in the criminal justice sector to omit capacity building in cybercrime—would almost certainly be considered a disservice to the state concerned. Equally, an international organization with a mandate to develop capacity across law enforcement would reasonably be expected to develop a programme to train law enforcement agents on cybercrime investigations and the preservation of electronic evidence. In both these examples of capacity building—criminal justice and law enforcement—it has too often been the case, and particularly where cybersecurity capacity is concerned, that the approaches taken have been small in scale and incomplete, and have been applied as a general template, sometimes lacking sensitivity to the local cultural and political context.

The largely ungoverned, fragmented, and unsystematic nature of cybersecurity capacity building around the world has also meant that a market (of sorts) has emerged in which organizations of various backgrounds and disciplines have been able to create and project their own cyber programmes, causing a flood of initiatives and interventions to build cyber capacity across the world. This in turn has exacerbated the lack of coordination across the international community and has resulted in the duplication of efforts as well as avoidable overspending.

The fragmented international approach has resulted in a number of shortfalls and inefficiencies that must be addressed. Primarily, the demand for financial resources and expertise far outstrips the supply and, when these scarce resources are used ineffectively, the result is slow development and implementation of the requisite capacity. Second, government officials are often expected to contribute to capacity-building exercises in addition to their principal role in government: time spent away from their desks means less time furthering their national cybersecurity agenda, which must be of primary importance. And if untargeted interventions, or interventions with low impact, are undertaken by a number of governments, then the time away from developing national agendas is also duplicated and wasted.

With so many public, private, and civil society organizations now active in the field, for any national government beginning to think about cybersecurity capacity building— perhaps with limited resources and little knowledge as to 'what good looks like'—the task of understanding the various approaches on offer and choosing the organization(s) with which to collaborate could at least be confusing and at worst overwhelming. In such circumstances, it would be understandable if a government, beginning to consider its nation's cybersecurity, were to accept the first approach made to it. This is not, of course, a position to be encouraged because these random offers of assistance might not be consistent with the receiving country's national strategy. It might be argued, on the other hand, that *any* effort constitutes progress and should be welcomed as such. Yet it is vital that such assistance should be located in and validated by a national strategic plan. Otherwise, the capacity-building effort could prove to be an expensive (and perhaps wasted) effort for both the capacityobuilding organization and the receiving government.

Unsolicited offers of assistance—as well as undiscriminating acceptance of the same offers—might not be consistent with national priorities and might even have an undermining effect. As funding lines, budget spending targets are set in the headquarters of international organizations, often with little consultation with experts either within the donor organization or on the ground in the country or region concerned, it is not unusual to see the re-funding of the same capacity-building interventions and exercises, with the same participants attending multiple programme and budget meetings, causing a general duplication of effort and waste of scarce resource with little incremental progress.

FROM CONCEPT TO CORE: STRATEGY DEVELOPMENT, IMPLEMENTATION, AND CAPACITY-BUILDING INITIATIVES

By 2019, approximately one hundred countries had published a national cybersecurity strategy or had, at least, begun to speak openly of the widespread and urgent need for information security. This was a remarkable increase from the 20 or so countries that had a strategy in 2009. The obvious question that arises concerns the extent to which this increased activity has affected the overall security of cyberspace. Research of this complexity, and on this scale, would be a difficult undertaking, although there are individuals and organizations engaged on precisely this task. A more manageable line of inquiry might, instead, be to ask how and why improvements in national capacity and—most importantly—how the *implementation* of such strategies have contributed to the cybersecurity of the country concerned. More tangibly still, how has increased national capacity contributed to a country's ability to collect and process digital evidence, and constructively participate in the global combat of cybercrime?

Questions of this sort require access to data, much of which has only just begun to be collected and collated in a usable format. Other questions, more qualitative in nature, are easier to answer, particularly when examining the capacities and capabilities of the criminal justice system. Is the requisite legislation on the statute books? Has the legislation been meaningfully operationalized? Is there scope for productive international collaboration? And can digital evidence be collected and processed in a legally admissible format? In this regard, the Council of Europe's Cybercrime Programme Office (C-PROC) was established by the Council's Rule of Law Division in Bucharest in 2014 with the goal of 'assisting countries worldwide in strengthening their criminal justice capacities to respond to the challenges posed by cybercrime and electronic evidence on the basis of the standards of the Budapest Convention on Cybercrime'.[9] C-PROC is able to examine the effect of its capacity-building interventions around the world, using the ratification of the Budapest Convention as a relatively simple measurement of a country's readiness to collaborate internationally in the fight against cybercrime. As a result, the Council of Europe has become the lead international organization for capacity building in the criminal justice system, and particularly with respect to the harmonization of legislation to facilitate international cooperation on cybercrime. By 2020, no fewer than 65 states had ratified or acceded to the Convention, with a further three signatories yet to ratify.[10]

In some respects, capacity building to address cybercrime is a contained and therefore relatively straightforward challenge. The response to cybercrime is largely practical and tangible, involving improvements to the legislative infrastructure, increasing the capacity for investigation and law enforcement, and ensuring that the courts are able to manage the volume and technical sophistication of cybercrime prosecutions. It is a different proposition, however, to build capacity to meet other, less tangible requirements, such as the need for governments to select cyber defence priorities or for the public awareness of cybersecurity to be heightened. In its breadth, complexity, and ambition, qualitative research and analysis of this sort—as undertaken by the GCSCC at Oxford, by the Potomac Institute and others—is still foundational and more time is needed before we can be confident of the methodologies that have been developed and of the conclusions that have been drawn.

Rather than wait for research methodologies to be perfected, national governments have been busily developing their own strategies for information security and cybersecurity. At first, the aim of many of these strategies was to protect the critical national infrastructure, ensuring the provision of services to the public. But, as threat technologies continued to develop, and as organized cybercrime came to the fore, signifying the borderless nature of the challenge ahead, national strategies began to reflect the need for closer international collaboration in combating cybercrime. And, as the merits of multidisciplinary, multistakeholder and multi-agency approaches to cybercrime became more widely understood and accepted, so the case has been made more broadly for international collaboration across the range of cybersecurity capacity-building challenges. The value of an international component to capacity-building activities has been recognized increasingly in national cybersecurity strategies, as illustrated by the following examples of capacity-building initiatives driven either by national governments or regional organizations.

The United Kingdom

In the 2011 edition of its National Cyber Security Strategy, the UK government made a strong case for international collaboration in cybersecurity capacity building, dedicating a budget of £650 million to activities within the UK and as part of the UK's international development funding (Cabinet Office 2011). The UK was the first leading cybersecurity nation to make an announcement of this magnitude in relation to cybersecurity capacity investments. Not only did it promise to focus on traditional critical infrastructure but also to develop new markets for a thriving cybersecurity workforce to foster. Following the UK initiative, similar announcements were made subsequently by such governments as those of the Netherlands, Japan, Estonia, Singapore, and Australia. The UK also began what became known as the Global Conference on Cyberspace (GCCS), or the 'London Process', bringing heads of government together to discuss the opportunities of the Internet as well as to address the challenge of cybersecurity. Hungary, Korea, and the Netherlands hosted the next three conferences and the fifth conference, held in India, saw substantial agreement on the importance of capacity building in cybersecurity—known as the 'Delhi Communiqué'.[11]

The Netherlands

Established under the auspices of the 2015 GCCS in The Hague, the Global Forum on Cyber Expertise (GFCE) was intended specifically to advance implementation of cybersecurity capacity building and the sharing of relevant expertise around the world. At inception, membership included a significant number of governments and international private sector companies, all of whom agreed to contribute to support specific cybersecurity projects proposed by member states. The forum chose to focus on four key areas of cybersecurity capacity building and was, essentially, intended to be a global resource-driver. The intention was to provide states with expertise and financial support they would have otherwise not have had access to. The GFCE's work on capacity building was endorsed at the 2017 GCCS in Delhi, in the form of the Delhi Communiqué discussed earlier, and the organization aspires to become an 'effective global clearing house mechanism' with which to strengthen 'international cooperation on cyber capacity building'.[12] The GFCE is open to new participants and is currently focused on implementing a number of capacity-building initiatives. At its most recent Annual General Meeting in Addis Ababa, Ethiopia, in October 2019, the GFCE launched the Knowledge Portal for Cyber Capacity Building, known as 'Cybil', intended to be a 'one-stop shop knowledge portal.'[13]

Singapore

Inspired by the achievements of the UK and the Netherlands, in 2016, the government of Singapore announced a US$10 million fund for capacity building among ASEAN member states. Holding the Chairmanship of the ASEAN ICT Ministerial Forum, Singapore saw the ASEAN community as a vehicle for improving regional collaboration towards the goal of a more secure regional critical national infrastructure from which all ASEAN members—including Singapore—would benefit. In September 2019, the government of Singapore also announced the establishment of a regional capacity-building centre. The purposes of the ASEAN-Singapore Cybersecurity Centre of Excellence (ASCCE) will be to distribute cybersecurity knowledge, awareness, and training across the ASEAN community, and to develop the workforce required to sustain an ASEAN regional strategy for increased cybersecurity capacity. ASCCE is expected to be launched formally in 2020 in Singapore.

The Commonwealth

In 2011, the Commonwealth Secretariat received a mandate by Commonwealth Heads of Government at their meeting in Perth to build cybercrime capacity across the Commonwealth and beyond. The proposal presented to Commonwealth governments included an implementation-focused programme premised on the Commonwealth Secretariat's Computer Misuse Act. This Act had provided Commonwealth member countries with an off-the-shelf toolkit to develop and propagate legislation to combat cybercrime, in harmony with the Council of Europe's Budapest Convention. The Commonwealth initiative was also the basis of a partnership of over 35 international organizations with specific expertise that could contribute to national programmes to build counter cybercrime capacity. The partnership was funded by the Commonwealth Secretariat, Malta, and the UK, and the participating international organizations included the World Bank, the Organisation of American States, the International Telecommunication Union, the UN Office on Drugs and Crime, the Council of Europe, the Internet Watch Foundation, the Internet Corporation for Assigned Names and Numbers, the Commonwealth Telecommunications Organisation, and others. In 2018, Commonwealth Heads of Government announced a Cyber Declaration that set out cybersecurity capacity-building priorities and identified funds to support the initiatives. The Cyber Declaration, with its goal both to drive both the agenda for capacity building and to secure the resources necessary, is due to be reviewed at meetings of Commonwealth Heads of Government.

Cybersecurity Capacity Building: Sustaining the Effort

As the cybersecurity capacity-building agenda has advanced, so we have seen increased interest in international capacity building and a corresponding shift in emphasis away from narrower national interests and priorities. National governments have also demonstrated an increased willingness to commit financial resources to the international effort. These various national efforts have also, finally, been supported and amplified by regional and international organizations. The level and breadth of progress has been extraordinary, but obvious questions now arise: can the global capacity-building effort be more efficient and more strategic, and is it sustainable in the longer term? Cybersecurity capacity building and development is also a complex process, involving many stakeholders and many specialist disciplines. This complexity prompts one further question: how can the international community measure and demonstrate the progress that is being made?

Several governments have begun to consider these questions and are currently putting in place the mechanisms and funding models required to identify the metrics with which the impact of cybersecurity capacity-building initiatives could be demonstrated. 'Impact', in this context, would refer to a change (in one direction or another) in socio-economic indicators that most directly govern the quality of life of societies and individuals. It is also important to identify quantitative metrics, demonstrating a return on investment in capacity-building interventions and activity. In a resource-constrained climate, it will be essential for capacity-building delivery agents, whether public or private, to make a robust business case to justify the ever-increasing budgetary demand for cybersecurity capacity building.

If the international community is able to demonstrate the impact of cybersecurity capacity building, both qualitatively and quantitatively, then it should as a result be possible to produce convincing arguments for the allocation of scarce financial resource. Convincing arguments will always be required—it is in the nature of economics, after all, for financial resources to be considered a scarce, and therefore contested, commodity. And if expenditure on cybersecurity capacity building can be shown to be not only impactful but also efficient and consistent with the expectations of the (increasingly interested and involved) international community, then it is conceivable that the all-important, practical implementation of capacity-building initiatives will proceed at a faster pace than currently. What will also be required, finally, before cybersecurity capacity building can be considered durable, is for organizations working in this field—public, private, and third sector alike—to make significant improvements in efforts at collaboration, allowing for flexibility and adaptability when needed, and seeking coordination and deconfliction of activities whenever possible.

CONCLUSION

In the course of just a decade or so, cybersecurity capacity building has developed into a more or less discrete specialism—that, at least, is the impression some of its more ardent advocates and experts like to convey. But, if it has become a niche activity, it is one that nevertheless comes into contact with a surprisingly wide array of policy areas, ranging from national and international security to human rights and civil liberties, technological and industrial innovation, and socio-economic development. On this basis, if capacity building in cybersecurity ever was a distinct and autonomous activity, then its chances of remaining so are slim as it becomes part and parcel of the general political discourse. Returning to the analogy of the lake and the challenge it represents, is the functionalist initiative to keep the lake clean best seen as a narrow, self-help endeavour in the policy programme of each of the riparian countries, or will the collaborative effort become an essential component of any and all economic or developmental policies of the countries concerned? And, furthermore, will it not in time be necessary for any capacity-building endeavour, in any of the four countries—a new road, or a new energy plant—to consider the importance of the lake remaining clean?

As awareness of cybersecurity sharpens, and as our economic and social dependency on the Internet becomes ever more pronounced, so the security and prosperity of cyberspace will be at the heart of any evolving or new public policy debate around the world. What, for example, will be the cybersecurity dimensions of climate change, public transport, post-industrial economic development, and food and water security? Increased budgetary allocations for capacity building in cybersecurity, together with improved coordination among governments, international organizations and the public and third sectors, are all symptomatic of a shift in emphasis in which capacity building becomes less a niche and much more a norm.

NOTES

1. Internet Stats & Facts (2021).https://www.websitehostingrating.com/internet-statistics-facts/
2. International Telecommunications Union, 'Statistics: Global and Regional ICT Data, 2005–2018'. https://www.itu.int/en/ITU-D/Statistics/Pages/stat/default.aspx
3. Mary Meeker's annual 'Internet Trends' report provides a comprehensive analysis of Internet usage by societies and individuals. For the 2019 version, see https://www.bondcap.com/report/itr19/#internettrends
4. World Economic Forum, *Global Information Technology Report 2016*. http://reports.weforum.org/global-information-technology-report-2016/
5. 'Information Communications Technology for Development', *World Bank Live*. http://live.worldbank.org/information-communications-technology-development
6. Radacati Group, Email Statistics Report, 2016-2020. https://www.radicati.com/wp/wp-content/uploads/2016/03/Email-Statistics-Report-2016-2020-Executive-Summary.pdf
7. Exabyte: one quintillion, or one billion, billion, or 10^{18}. See https://techcrunch.com/2010/08/04/schmidt-data/

8. Quoted in Munich Security Conference. 2018. *Munich Security Report 2018: To the Brink— and Back?* Munich: Munich Security Conference Foundation, p. 51.
9. https://www.coe.int/en/web/cybercrime/cybercrime-office-c-proc-
10. https://www.coe.int/en/web/conventions/full-list/-/conventions/treaty/185
11. *Delhi Communiqué on a GFCE Global Agenda for Cyber Capacity Building*, 24 November 2017. https://dig.watch/sites/default/files/GFCE%20Delhi%20Communique.pdf
12. Global Forum on Cyber Expertise, 'About the GFCE'. https://thegfce.org/about-the-gfce/
13. Cybil: The Knowledge Portal for Cyber Capacity Building. https://cybilportal.org/

PART VIII

GLOBAL TRADE AND CYBERSECURITY

CHAPTER 29

CYBERSECURITY, MULTILATERAL EXPORT CONTROL, AND STANDARD SETTING ARRANGEMENTS

ELAINE KORZAK

INTRODUCTION

INFORMATION and communication technologies (ICTs) play a critical role in global economic activity. As a report by the World Economic Forum noted, the digital economy contributed '$2.3 trillion to the G20's GDP in 2010 and an estimated $4 trillion in 2016, [and] is growing at 10% a year—significantly faster than the overall G20 economy' (World Economic Forum 2015, 7). The digital economy marks that part of economic activity that is enabled by 'almost 3 billion connected consumers and businesses ... transact[ing] and interact[ing] every day using personal computers (PCs) and, increasingly, mobile devices'.[1] This tremendous impact is not confined to economic activity alone, with digitization also affecting developments across healthcare, education, energy, and many other fields.

The significance of ICTs is perhaps even more pronounced for developing economies. Growth rates of digital economic activities range from 15% to 25% annually in emerging markets, greatly outperforming those in developed countries.[2] Use of ICTs, and Internet access in particular, is increasingly seen as a major driver of economic growth as well as broader development efforts. The World Bank dedicated its 2016 Development Report to 'Digital Dividends'—the broader development benefits from using digital technologies (World Bank 2016). As 60% of the world's population is still to come online,[3] ICTs are set to be key enablers of the Sustainable Development Goals.

While the global trade in ICTs offers significant economic benefits, it has also raised novel and challenging issues. As one commentator put it, '[i]nformation technology has often been seen as a huge success story in global trade, but its rapid diffusion has introduced new risks' (Friedman 2013, 1). Developed and developing economies alike rely heavily on information and communication systems for the functioning of everyday life while these systems are vulnerable to a plethora of malicious activities from state and non-state actors. Threat profiles are rapidly expanding and evolving; global interconnectivity and interdependencies seem only to compound risks. Thus, with growing cybersecurity concerns, the questions arise whether and how the international community can mitigate these risks while continuing to promote the global trade in ICTs.

While a growing number of states have developed national cybersecurity strategies that seek to address these and other questions, this chapter examines international efforts in this regard. More specifically, it focuses on two trade mechanisms and their role in pursuing the policy imperatives of promoting international trade in ICTs while seeking to mitigate cybersecurity risks. The first mechanism, international standard setting and certification efforts, aims to *facilitate* international trade by providing benchmarks and assurances for security features. In contrast, the second mechanism, international export controls, explicitly seeks to *restrict* the trade in certain ICT goods for national and international security purposes. Both are ultimately aimed at enhancing the level of cybersecurity globally but differ significantly in their rationale and impact on trade—one being permissive and one being restrictive.

The first section of this chapter discusses international standard setting and certification efforts while the second part provides a detailed account of export control regimes. In doing so, the first section introduces the concepts of standards and certification, and surveys the landscape of cybersecurity standard setting, before providing a discussion of the major intergovernmental certification scheme, the Common Criteria Recognition Arrangement. The second section introduces the Wassenaar Arrangement and examines its recent experience in bringing two types of technologies, IP surveillance systems and intrusion software, under the purview of export controls.

The focus of analysis is on the role of multilateral and intergovernmental instruments in addressing cybersecurity concerns in global trade. Thus, the Common Criteria Recognition Arrangement and the Wassenaar Arrangement are discussed in detail and, in each case, key insights are identified with regard to the effectiveness and utility of the respective instruments. The chapter concludes by contrasting and comparing these insights to argue that past experience indicates a limited role for both instruments as trade mechanisms that seek to enhance cybersecurity. Further, any efforts to broaden both instruments are likely to be limited as well, in the case of the Common Criteria Recognition Arrangement due to a lack of trust among participants, and in the case of the Wassenaar Arrangement due to difficulties in defining technologies that should be controlled.

STANDARD SETTING AND CERTIFICATION

The Role of Standards and Certification

In general terms, a standard is described as 'a document, established by consensus and approved by a recognized body, which provides for common and repeated use, rules, guidelines or characteristics for activities or their results' and is 'aimed at the achievement of the optimum degree of order'.[4] Obviously, standards play a critical role in virtually all aspects of daily life. In the context of cybersecurity, they provide valuable guidelines to raise cyber defences and security across a multiplicity of organizations and countries (Purser 2014, 97). Standards for cybersecurity not only cover technical features but also extend to processes, procedures, and organizational structures that help enable effective cooperation among stakeholders. With regard to global trade activities, standards for cybersecurity play an important facilitating role. As the US government has stated:

> Given the increasingly global, complex, and interconnected nature of the world economy, characterized by rapid advances in technology and use of commercial off the shelf products to assure cybersecurity and resilience, the use of international cybersecurity standards for information technologies (IT) and industrial control systems (ICS) are necessary for the cybersecurity and resilience of all U.S. information and communications systems and supporting infrastructures.[5]

As previously alluded to, the increased reliance on ICTs coupled with global trade activities has introduced new risks. Globalized manufacturing and supply chains have introduced numerous concerns with regard to supply chain security. As the Cyber Security Strategy of the European Union points out, '[a] high level of security can only be ensured if all in the value chain (e.g. equipment manufacturers, software developers, information society services providers) make security a priority' (European Commission 2013, 12). International standards for cybersecurity are intended to help address these risks by stipulating certain requirements for security and resilience. In this way, cybersecurity standards can facilitate the international trade in ICTs by creating a level of trust regarding the reliability of products.[6] International standards for cybersecurity further promote economic activity trade by creating a level playing field for companies from different countries, fostering even-handed international competition.[7] Standards can provide users with the means to meaningfully assess and compare different products.[8]

Standards are often used in conjunction with certification or conformity assessments. Certification is an activity that 'provides demonstration that specified requirements relating to a product, process, system, person or body are fulfilled'.[9] In this way, cybersecurity assertions can be tested and certified. More specifically, 'testing and attestation of products, processes, and services against established cybersecurity standards may help provide a level of assurance that a product, process, or service's stated security claim is valid'.[10] Both standards for cybersecurity and assessment schemes are thus important instruments that can be used in the promotion of global trade in ICTs.

However, standards imposed on a national basis could, in particular, also be used to achieve the opposite effect—namely, to restrict trade by denying market access or by excluding certain competitors from the market. The World Trade Organization's Agreement on Technical Barriers to Trade, for instance, seeks to ensure that standards and conformity regulations are non-discriminatory and do not create unnecessary obstacles to international trade (World Trade Organization 2015). While the Agreement acknowledges that states can adopt regulations to fulfil legitimate objectives such as national security, it strongly advocates that national measures be based on international (rather than differing national) standards. According to Article 2(4), member states shall use international standards as a basis for technical regulations unless they would be 'an ineffective or inappropriate means for the fulfilment of the legitimate objectives pursued'.[11]

Standards for Cybersecurity

In light of the growing importance of standards and certification schemes, standards developing organizations (SDOs) have played an increasingly significant role in this ecosystem. In general terms, an SDO is 'any organization that develops and approves standards using various methods to establish consensus among its participants'.[12] Thus, organizations can differ drastically with regard to their organizational structures, membership, scope of work, and output.[13] In addition to government-driven or government-created standards organizations, SDOs include a large number of standards bodies that are driven by non-governmental actors—industry, academia, consumers, and other civil society entities.[14]

Globally, the number of SDOs active in the field of IT has increased so much that one of the tasks of the European Union Network and Information Security Agency (ENISA) is to 'track the development of standards for products and services on Network and Information security' (European Parliament and Council 2004). Currently, there are over 200 SDOs whose work is relevant for IT (International Cybersecurity Standardization Working Group 2015a, 7). However, only a relatively small number of these are developing standards for cybersecurity with even fewer working on international standards for cybersecurity that would be applicable across borders. Nevertheless, the list of organizations developing international cybersecurity standards is quite substantial, including the International Electrotechnical Commission (IEC), the Institute of Electrical and Electronics Engineers (IEEE); the Internet Engineering Task Force (IETF); the European Telecommunications Standards Institute (ETSI), the International Organization for Standardization (ISO), the International Society of Automation (ISA), the International Telecommunication Union (ITU), and the Alliance for Telecommunications Industry Solutions (ATIS) among others.[15]

As this list reveals, cybersecurity standards are developed by very diverse entities ranging from intergovernmental organizations to those with membership for individual professionals. Similarly, the scope, areas, and applications of standardization can differ greatly. Cybersecurity standards can cover cryptographic techniques, identity and access management, cyber incident management, network security, and IT system security evaluation across a set of different applications such as cloud computing or industrial control systems.[16] Together, SDOs are developing or maintaining 'many hundreds of cybersecurity standards projects'.[17]

A prominent example of standard-setting is the work of ISO, an international non-governmental organization founded in 1946 (International Organization for Standardization 2017). Its membership consists of 161 national standards bodies and it develops voluntary international standards on the basis of consensus covering nearly all industries.[18] Within this system, there are several entities relevant for IT and cybersecurity standards. In 1987, ISO and IEC established a Joint Technical Committee merging existing work on IT standards from both organizations: ISO/IEC JTC 1.[19] Over 2,000 technical experts are engaged in the work of this Joint Technical Committee, which currently has 18 subcommittees (SCs), one of them (SC 27) focusing on cybersecurity standardization.[20]

In sum, standards for cybersecurity are developed by a variety of mostly non-governmental actors touching upon a wide array of issue areas. Their impact can vary considerably, depending on a number of factors such as market relevance and speed of adoption, and is further mediated by their voluntary character. Promulgated standards are mostly non-binding agreements that different stakeholders can sign up to on a voluntary basis. In contrast, the following section discusses one of the few multilateral, government-driven initiatives in this area—the Common Criteria Recognition Arrangement.

The Common Criteria Recognition Arrangement

The Common Criteria (CC) were created in the 1990s after the US Department of Defense's Trusted Computer System Evaluation Criteria were merged with the European Information Technology Security Evaluation Criteria (ITSEC) (Kallberg 2012, 1). The CC describe a particular set of IT security evaluation criteria and were used as a basis for the certification of systems procured by governments for national security-related agencies.[21] The CC were later adopted as ISO/IEC 15408 standard.[22] As such, they provide the basis for the evaluation of security properties of IT products. They do not, however, offer a *guarantee* of security. Instead, the CC form an international standard for certification. They are used as the basis for an intergovernmental certification and recognition scheme, the Common Criteria Recognition Arrangement (CCRA). The CC and the corresponding Arrangement represent one of the very few international, intergovernmental approaches to conformity or certification schemes, particularly for certification of systems used by states in the national security context.

The Arrangement was originally created by the United States, the United Kingdom, Canada, France, and Germany, joined later by other states bringing the membership to the current 27 states.[23] In 2014, states ratified the latest revision of the 'Arrangement on the Recognition of Common Criteria Certificates in the field of Information Technology Security'.[24] The agreement provides that participating states will mutually recognize evaluation certificates issued against the CC.[25] As Kallberg summarizes, '[t]he idea is that once an IT-security product is certified as secure to use, the certification is mutually recognized within a group of signatories of the Common Criteria'.[26]

Requirements are defined in the form of 'Protection Profiles', which are an 'independent set of security requirements for a category of IT Products that meet specific consumer needs'.[27] Once vendors meet these requirements, the CC provide a framework within which to evaluate ICT goods:

> by matching security requirements to security assertions in a fashion that can be verified by independent testing labs.[28] The certificates issued are then recognized among the participants of the Common Criteria Recognition Arrangement. The independent testing labs, known as a Certification/Validation Body (CB), play a critical role and participating states have created numerous conditions to ensure a satisfactory performance.[29]

The CCRA also distinguishes between two types of participating states. There are authorizing members that can issue and accept CC certifications (such as the United States, United Kingdom, Germany, and India) whereas consuming members can only accept CC certifications (for example, Qatar, Israel, and Finland).[30] In the end, the certification process provides an Evaluation Assurance Level (EAL) ranking from 1 to 7 with 7 being the highest. However, the EAL is not an actual measurement of the level of security that a system provides: it is best understood as an indicator of the rigour of the evaluation process.[31]

Overall, the evaluations and their recognition seek to enhance trust and reliability in IT systems while creating efficiencies: 'In an ideal world, the need for internal certification and control in countries that buy IT-security equipment would be removed as they now can trust the authorizing countries' laboratory that the goods are safe from a security standpoint.'[32] Thus, IT systems can be procured without the need for further testing, which eliminates the burden of duplicate evaluations.[33] A stated objective of the Arrangement is further to improve the availability of evaluated, security-enhanced IT products.[34] Trust and confidence in the security performance of products are critical factors. As Friedman points out, '[t]o fully trust that a piece of software or hardware does what it claims to do, a country may be tempted to demand full access not just to the product, but the underlying source code, architecture and intellectual property'.[35] Standards and certification schemes such as the CCRA are geared towards addressing such concerns and removing them as potential obstacles to global trading relations. In this sense, the smaller the number of states that seek access to underlying source code, the more successful certification schemes such as the CCRA appear to be. If schemes such as the CCRA remove or reduce the need for internal control and certification, then they also serve a more general purpose of showing that trust among states can be built and maintained in this field.

However, the certification process can also be very time-intensive and expensive.[36] In light of the pace of technological change, the question arises whether 'rigid frameworks'[37] such as the CCRA can be adaptive and agile enough. As Kallberg points out, particularly less-central parts of the certification process are not necessarily up-to-date.[38] Moreover, only government organizations or agencies can participate in the Recognition Arrangement. Thus, definitions of Protection Profiles as well as CC requirements are promulgated predominantly by governmental actors. Limited industry input has been recognized as one of the issues during the 2014 revision process.[39] In contrast, the majority of the non-governmental SDOs described earlier seek to establish and maintain the relevance of their standards by seeking broad-based participation, particularly from industry.

Lessons Learned

Based on the survey of standards and certification schemes for cybersecurity, valuable insights can be gleaned regarding the utility of these mechanisms in global trade.

First, the landscape of relevant SDOs is highly competitive, raising the question to what extent the promulgated standards actually contribute to aiding global trade in ICTs. Both the number of SDOs as well as the number of standards issued by these organizations is considerable. Moreover, the landscape of SDOs is highly fragmented. Thus, the question arises whether the plethora of standards bodies might lead to competing or even contradictory sets of standards, a situation that could hamper global commerce. As one commentator put it, '[t]o some extent, these standards are competing with each other for adoption and it is often difficult for the end user to judge which is best for their particular requirements. Occasionally, it is necessary to mix and match standards from different families'.[40] A major challenge lies in ensuring the interoperability of standards promulgated by a wide variety of standards bodies. In any case, in light of the multiplicity of bodies and standards, meaningful engagement, and indeed effective use of international standards, requires considerable resources and commitment.

Second, the multiplicity of standards is promulgated predominantly by non-governmental actors with strong industry participation, and adoption is based on voluntary commitment. This means that certain cybersecurity concerns or requirements may not be addressed if they are not aligned with commercial interests.[41] Areas such as authentication (verifying the identity of a user) or billing (invoicing and receiving payments electronically) have been dominant since vendors and service providers have a business case interest in adopting security and resilience requirements.[42] However, states may find cybersecurity standards equally necessary in other areas that are not imminently relevant to the bottom line of commercial enterprises. It would thus be difficult to address these challenges exclusively, or even largely, through the promotion of standards that have been developed in the context of multilateral trade.

Third, while there is a variety of predominantly non-governmental SDOs, multilateral cooperation among governments is very limited in this area. The CCRA represents the major multilateral effort in this regard and, as shown earlier, it is not focused on standards but on certification. The member states purport that the CC and the Arrangement comprise the 'widest available mutual recognition of secure IT products'.[43] Yet its membership and scope are very limited. It comprises fewer than 30 countries with an even smaller number of states with certificate-issuing authority. The cost and time investment required for the evaluation have limited the products that go through this process, predominantly those for use by national security and law enforcement entities.

Fourth, the limited scope of government efforts embodied by the CCRA points to the critical role of trust in international standards and certification schemes. The number of states with certificate-issuing authority is limited and consists of a fairly homogenous group of states. The Arrangement originated in a small number of states that have been closely aligned through organizations such as NATO. It is, therefore, doubtful whether the trust necessary for the functioning of the CCRA can be maintained if countries with different historical and political backgrounds, interests, and alignments enter the Arrangement.[44] Somewhat ironically, the potential of this multilateral certification scheme to create trust and thereby facilitate global trade in ICTs is limited by the fact that trust is needed in the first place for the CCRA to function. Significant expansion of this instrument remains doubtful. Thus, the CCRA indicates a very limited role for multilateral, governmental certification schemes as mechanisms in facilitating global trade and addressing cyber-security concerns.

In light of these observations, the overall potential of standard setting and certification schemes as facilitative mechanisms in international trade of ICTs appears limited. With permissive efforts facing a number of obstacles, the following section of this chapter turns to export control regimes to examine the potential of restrictive trade mechanisms.

EXPORT CONTROLS

The Wassenaar Arrangement and the Role of Export Controls

This section examines a trade mechanism that is restrictive in its nature—namely, multilateral export control regimes and their use in the context of cybersecurity. National and multilateral controls on exports are typically used for items that are deemed sensitive or otherwise relevant for national policy objectives. That is, governments explicitly restrict trade under certain circumstances in order to pursue those policy objectives. National and international security are prominent policy concerns that have resulted in an elaborate multilateral system designed to manage the export of key items, chiefly those connected with weapons of mass destruction, in order to enhance international security and stability.[45] A part of this system, the Wassenaar Arrangement, deals specifically with the trade in conventional weapons and what are known as 'dual-use' items—products used for civilian purposes that can also have military applications. Cybersecurity concerns have only recently been considered in its context and the subsequent sections examine this experience in more detail.

As its name indicates, the Wassenaar Arrangement on Export Controls for Conventional Arms and Dual-Use Goods and Technologies addresses the global trade in conventional weapons and dual-use items (Wassenaar Arrangement on Export Controls for Conventional Arms and Dual-Use Goods and Technologies 2016). Its current membership of 41 states is predominantly North American and Western European but also includes a number of former Eastern bloc states, most notably the Russian Federation.[46] The self-proclaimed goal of the Wassenaar Arrangement is to 'promot[e] transparency and greater responsibility in transfers of conventional arms and dual-use goods and technologies' in order to prevent destabilizing accumulations and thus contribute to regional and international security.[47] To that end, the states participating in Wassenaar agree to coordinate and harmonize their export control policies with regard to conventional arms and dual-use items. The main mechanisms for this are two so-called 'Control Lists' created under the auspices of Wassenaar: a Munitions List and a List of Dual-Use Goods and Technologies.[48] Items placed on these lists are then to be regulated by the national export control regimes of the participating states. Wassenaar's Control Lists are updated periodically; changes to the Lists have to be agreed on the basis of consensus at a plenary meeting held annually.[49]

It is worth noting that the Wassenaar Arrangement and its provisions do not represent an export ban or prohibition of trade in certain goods or technologies. Rather, an inclusion of items in one of the two Control Lists simply indicates that states have committed to instituting a national export control policy. Companies seeking to sell such items to foreign entities are then required to obtain an export licence. Such a policy may undoubtedly result in a restriction of exports and a higher degree of control, but it does not constitute an outright ban. Further, Wassenaar represents a multilateral *arrangement* rather than an agreement as such. This means that it does not constitute an international, legally binding treaty or instrument for which the latter term is generally reserved. Wassenaar is a voluntary association of states governed by a set of policies and guidelines, most notably its 'Initial Elements'.[50] Thus, decisions reached within the Wassenaar Arrangement are not automatically legally binding for the participating states. Instead, the implementation of unanimous decisions reached within Wassenaar is entirely dependent on national governments. According to the Initial Elements, '[t]he decision to transfer or deny transfer of any item will be the sole responsibility of each Participating State'.[51] As a result, states are afforded considerable 'national discretion' in their implementation of the Arrangement's changes.[52]

Cybersecurity and the 2013 Additions to the Wassenaar Arrangement

While the Wassenaar Arrangement has covered technology transfers, including hardware and software, cybersecurity concerns have entered the Arrangement's discussions only recently. At its plenary meeting in December 2013, participating states adopted two changes that have proved to be highly controversial in cybersecurity discussions internationally. Reportedly at the initiative of the UK and France, the Arrangement agreed to include certain surveillance technologies as well as intrusion software in its export control regulations (Privacy International 2015, 2–3). This move was largely seen as a response to international controversy over the sale of such technologies to repressive regimes and their use in human rights abuses. However, the inclusion of these technologies under the Wassenaar regime has also stirred debate over unintended consequences that could end up lowering cybersecurity worldwide.

More specifically, the Wassenaar Arrangement agreed to two changes. First, with regard to surveillance technologies, participating states placed 'IP network communications surveillance systems or equipment, and specially designed components therefor' that perform certain functions on the Dual-Use List.[53] The second addition covered '[s]ystems, equipment, and components therefor, specially designed or modified for the generation, command and control, or delivery of "intrusion software".'[54] 'Intrusion software', in turn, is defined as ' "Software" specially designed or modified to avoid detection by "monitoring tools", or to defeat "protective countermeasures", of a computer or network-capable device' to either extract data or modify the standard execution path of a program.[55]

Both amendments aim at controlling (but not prohibiting) access to technology that in broad terms enables data collection and analysis, and reflect concerns over the development and growth of a particular market for 'spyware'. The Arab spring of 2011 revealed a web of trade relations of predominantly North American and Western European companies that supplied intelligence and law enforcement agencies in countries such as Libya and Bahrain with a variety of surveillance tools.[56] The revelations of spyware used by repressive regimes garnered international attention and criticism. Perhaps the most notorious case was that of the Italian-based company Hacking Team whose client relations were released after the company was, ironically, itself hacked (Kopstein 2015). It revealed sales of its products designed to access devices and collect data to entities in more than 20 countries, including Egypt, Saudi Arabia, and Sudan.[57]

A plethora of human rights organizations pointed to the detrimental impact of exporting such technologies.[58] Privacy International, for instance, argued that:

> [s]urveillance technologies are used by governments to target opponents, journalists and lawyers, crack down on dissent, harass human rights defenders, intimidate populations, discourage whistle-blowers, chill expression and destroy the possibility of private life ... In short, they are often part of a broader state apparatus of oppression, facilitating a wide variety of human rights violations including unlawful interrogation practices, torture and extrajudicial executions.[59]

By this view, the uncontrolled export of these types of technologies facilitated a broad range of human rights violations and should have been brought under the umbrella of international export controls.

The two amendments to the Wassenaar Arrangement were ultimately instituted against this backdrop. To most observers, the human rights motivation was critical in the lead-up to the changes to Wassenaar, as '[t]he driving force originally pushing for updated export controls were human rights groups who had grown increasingly concerned' (Maurer 2016, 2). Moreover, the amendments were proposed by the French and British governments, 'which were both particularly criticized for allowing the export of technologies to authoritarian governments that eventually used them for surveillance.'[60] However, the Wassenaar Arrangement, as a multilateral instrument of conventional and dual-use arms control, does not explicitly address or seek to regulate human rights concerns and it remains unclear to which extent the additions were driven by human rights motivations. The changes to the Arrangement have also been described in weapons-like language, as an effort to curtail the international proliferation of 'cyberweapons' (Shahani 2015). As such, the surveillance and intrusion technologies covered by the changes have been portrayed as a novel type of weaponry that could and should be regulated by the main arms control regime for conventional weapons.

Controversy over Implementation

As noted earlier, decisions reached within the Wassenaar Arrangement have to be implemented by individual participating states. While most participating states, including European Union member states, have implemented the 2013 additions,[61] the proposed rules led to a great deal of controversy in the United States. In May 2015, the US Department of Commerce's Bureau of Industry and Security (BIS) published its proposed rule for the US implementation of the 2013 additions of IP surveillance systems and intrusion software.[62] In response, a variety of actors across industry, academia, and civil society heavily criticized the proposed implementation.

One of the main points of criticism was that the proposed US rules were (unnecessarily) broad. Many observers argued that the rules went further than the original Wassenaar language as well as the language adopted by European states, resulting in an 'unworkably-broad set of controls' that would not only restrict repressive technologies but also technology commonly used in cyber defences (Cardozo and Galperin 2015). Much of the criticism was focused on BIS' 'intrusion software' regulation, as opposed to the proposed language on surveillance systems. Accordingly, the proposed rule regarding 'intrusion software' was too broad because it arguably covered a number of tools that are commonly used in security research. Thus, technology that is a legitimate part in enhancing the defences of computer networks and systems would be covered by export control requirements. The dilemma is summarized neatly by Moussouris 2015:

> There's a conundrum when it comes to exploits and other potentially malicious software. For human rights advocates, software like DaVinci from Hacking Team that bypasses security protections, hides from anti-virus and other malware detection tools, and spies on the victim, represent a threat to human life when used by repressive regimes. But for security researchers, the same offense techniques that are developed to bypass existing computer security measures are used in research to highlight weaknesses in order to fix the vulnerable software.

As a result, many companies argued that the proposed instrument would substantially affect their ability to conduct security assessments as well as restrict the availability of security tools (Internet Association 2015, 4–7). Export control regulations would introduce a significant regulatory burden for cybersecurity companies resulting in '[i]ncreased cost and reduced speed to market for these tools'.[63] Others feared that companies providing such security technologies may be put out of business entirely.[64] Similarly, 'the proposed rules create enormously complex hurdles for individual researchers who might otherwise be able to make a meaningful impact on overall security'.[65] With this, even civil society organizations that had initially lobbied for including surveillance systems and intrusion software in the Wassenaar regime voiced serious concerns over the planned US implementation due to the potentially adverse effects on cyber defence.

In addition to the arguably broad scope, the regulations proposed by BIS were also criticized for being unclear and open to interpretation.[66] The discussion surrounding the research and disclosure of vulnerabilities illustrates this point. While BIS reportedly sought to exclude vulnerability research and disclosure from the scope of the regulations, security professionals were nevertheless concerned with the potential inclusion of vulnerability research.[67]

All in all, the US implementation efforts have caused considerable concern that the Wassenaar additions could unintentionally hurt cybersecurity efforts globally by stifling research and tools that are vital for improving cyber defences. That is, provisions that were geared towards addressing the human rights violations enabled by the export of certain technologies could potentially lead to unintended consequences for efforts to increase cybersecurity worldwide. In light of the considerable criticism levelled at the Department of Commerce, BIS first announced its intention to revise its proposed regulation. In March 2016, it went further, stating that 'the United States has proposed in this year's Wassenaar Arrangement to eliminate the controls on technology required for the development of "intrusion software"'.[68] Since the plenary meeting of the Wassenaar Arrangement in December 2016 did not result in any changes with regard to the categories of surveillance systems and intrusion software, it remains to be seen how this issue will unfold in the future. For now, the 2013 additions remain a part of the Arrangement's Dual-Use List with an uneven implementation across its membership. While a majority of participating states have translated the provisions into their domestic export control regulations, arguably the most important participating state—the United States—still seeks to revise the intrusion software provision significantly. Perhaps most worryingly, it remains unclear whether the initial human rights concerns have been adequately addressed thus far, and what changes are required to that end.

Lessons Learned

Based on the experience of the 2013 additions to the Wassenaar Arrangement, valuable lessons can be identified regarding the use of multilateral export control regimes in the context of cybersecurity.

First, the continuing debate over the 2013 changes following the failed US implementation shows that international efforts have had, at best, mixed results. Particularly in the United

States, implementation efforts have left virtually all interested stakeholders sceptical as to the utility and effectiveness of national and multilateral export control regimes. Even civil society groups, which had initially advocated using the trade mechanism of export controls to address human rights violations, appeared alarmed by effects that could ultimately undermine cybersecurity globally. The criticism levelled at the Wassenaar changes showed that measures designed originally to address specific cybersecurity concerns could in the end have the opposite effect. And, even if adverse effects on security research and collaboration were contained, it remains unclear whether export controls have the desired effect of keeping these technologies out of the hands of actors who will use them for human rights violations. The case of Ahmed Mansoor, a pro-democracy activist in the United Arab Emirates who was targeted by commercially sold spyware as late as 2016, illustrates this point (Peterson 2016). Thus, the limited success of the Wassenaar Arrangement in restricting the trade in IP surveillance systems and intrusion software raises significant questions about the appropriateness and effectiveness of using such a trade mechanism.

Second, these concerns are compounded by the fact that the 2013 additions concerned only a very small set of technologies among the limited membership of the Arrangement. With 41 participating states, the Wassenaar Arrangement represents a fairly small as well as homogenous group of countries. And, even among this small group of states, the implementation of the 2013 changes has been uneven or lagging. In light of this, it is doubtful whether export control policies such as those instituted by Wassenaar could be extended to a larger group of states in a successful way. The experience of the 2013 changes and the continued controversy raise doubts. At the same time, the limited membership also means that developments beyond its membership could affect, or perhaps even undermine, efforts undertaken under the auspices of the Arrangement.

Third, the recent experience with the Wassenaar Arrangement shows that controlling cybersecurity-relevant technologies challenges fundamental assumptions underlying export control regimes, in particular the ability to define the items to be covered and the ability to monitor and control their transfer across borders. What the controversy surrounding intrusion software has shown is that it is exceedingly difficult to delineate offensive versus defensive technologies in the context of cybersecurity. As many of the critics have argued, the technology used to infiltrate dissidents' devices is hardly distinguishable from that used in penetration testing. Nevertheless, the assumption that there are workable definitions of those technologies to be controlled is the core of the export control regime approach. The Wassenaar controversy has shown that efforts to control arguably offensive technologies— spyware—could sweep up technologies legitimately used in the defence of IT systems. The difficulties in devising a definition could thus even lead to counterproductive effects and, as a consequence, undermine cybersecurity. Even if definitional questions are resolved, export controls rely on the ability to control transfers across national borders. The 2013 additions, however, and particularly the controversy surrounding vulnerability research and disclosure, raise the question whether seemingly intangible software that 'can be transferred via intangible mediums of transfer such as telephone calls, emails, and face-to-face conversations between individuals holding disparate passports' (Pyetranker 2015, 178) can be controlled in the same way if it is not tied to a tangible object inspected at a border. Arguably, '[d]esigned to manage tangible exports, conventional methods of export control can do little to prevent the spread of information from one person to another'.[69] Thus, fundamental assumptions underlying export controls are challenged, calling into question the appropriateness and effectiveness of the trade mechanism embodied by the Wassenaar Arrangement.

Fourth, and finally, the experience of the Wassenaar additions illustrates the complexity of cybersecurity, not only with regard to the technology involved but also with regard to the relevant stakeholders and issues. The Wassenaar Arrangement represents a rather tailored trade mechanism used to address concerns related to international security. It is also something of a legacy system, being the successor to the West's Co-ordinating Committee on Multilateral Export Controls, developed during the very early years of the Cold War. Thus, the Wassenaar Arrangement's focus on conventional weapons and dual-use items has meant that it has generally been understand in traditional strategic terms: as an arms control instrument at the disposal of states. However, the impetus for the 2013 changes came, at least partly, from a coordinated civil society campaign driven by human rights concerns that traditionally have been outside Wassenaar's purview. Further, the implementation of the 2013 changes has not only run into difficulties with industry but has also drawn criticism from the research community and other civil society actors. This multiplicity of actors and interests, and perhaps their misalignment, have shaped the experience of cybersecurity and export controls in the context of the Wassenaar Arrangement. On this basis, it would be fair to assume that any trade mechanism operating in the field of cybersecurity will in some way affect a multiplicity of stakeholders and will have to balance the different equities involved.

Conclusion

ICTs have become important drivers of economic growth for developed and developing economies alike. However, with the diffusion of ICTs, an increasing number of states have had to confront a variety of cybersecurity concerns. While states have at their disposal several national and international instruments with which to address these issues, this chapter focused on two distinct types of international or multilateral trade regulation mechanism. The first, international standard and certification efforts, are geared towards enabling global trade in ICTs by providing assurances regarding the security and reliability of products. In contrast, the second mechanism, export controls, aims to restrict trade under certain circumstances in the name of international security. The chapter focused on intergovernmental, multilateral initiatives taken under these two approaches—namely, the CCRA and the Wassenaar Arrangement.

A number of observations can be made with regard to the potential of these two mechanisms to mitigate cybersecurity concerns in the context of global trade. Although both mechanisms are very context-specific and have been used to address discrete sets of circumstances and aspects of cybersecurity, commonalities nevertheless reveal important implications. First, both the CCRA and the Wassenaar Arrangement illustrate the dearth of international and intergovernmental instruments in this area. In the context of standard setting and certification schemes, the CCRA represents the most prominent instrument between governments. Even so, as this chapter has shown, the competitive space of cybersecurity standard setting is dominated largely by non-governmental organizations. Similarly, the Wassenaar Arrangement represents the only major governmental agreement with regard to harmonizing export controls that has sought to address cybersecurity-related concerns. Thus, there are very few intergovernmental and international instruments, and with it government-to-government coordination and agreement in these fields.

Second, even the existing governmental mechanisms are very limited, both in terms of their scope and their membership. Both the CC and the Wassenaar Arrangement have a limited membership that only covers a fraction of the world's many states. Moreover, with a few exceptions, both instruments are also fairly homogenous in their composition of states, consisting of a core group of states from North America and Europe. In terms of scope, both arrangements seek to regulate a set of specific circumstances. The Wassenaar Arrangement seeks to harmonize national export control policies of certain conventional weapons and dual-use items if the participating states deem restrictions to be supporting regional or international security. The additions of 2013 were reportedly borne out of human rights concerns over the export of IP surveillance systems and intrusion software. Similarly, the CCRA covers the evaluation of products' security claims, not their actual security, among a select group of states. Its origins are found in assurances for products primarily procured for government agencies in the national security context. Thus, the items covered by both arrangements represent a fraction of the total of available ICT products and services. These limitations are somewhat exacerbated by the voluntary and informal character of both instruments. Participating states are expected to play a critical role in their effective implementation. Yet, neither participation nor compliance can be enforced because both instruments lack enforcement mechanisms.

Third, as this chapter has shown, the effectiveness of both arrangements has been questioned to varying degrees. In the case of the Wassenaar Arrangement, its first experience with cybersecurity-related or motivated controls resulted in a significant backlash as a result of the attempted implementation in the United States. The CCRA, on the other hand, has been criticized for its lengthy and cost-intensive process limiting the products and assurance levels that have been evaluated according to the CC.

Lastly, these observations raise serious doubts as to whether the instruments of standard setting and certification as well as export controls could be employed effectively on a broader basis. The question arises whether, given the experience with the two arrangements, these mechanisms could be scaled internationally. Even without their limited and fairly homogenous membership, as well as their relatively narrow scope, efforts to make use of the CCRA and Wassenaar to contribute to cybersecurity would have been demanding. Further, past experiences offer important insights with regard to potential obstacles to using these mechanisms more broadly. In the case of the CCRA, it seems likely that the level of trust among its participants will be a key determinant of the Arrangement's success and relevance. Any extension of the membership to include a larger and more diverse set of countries would challenge this. Somewhat ironically, a mechanism that is geared towards increasing reliability of products and, by extension, trust would be hampered in its enlargement efforts because trust would be initially required for it to function. In contrast, the discussion of the Wassenaar Arrangement has pointed to the limits of using export controls on a broader scale due to definitional uncertainty and the difficulties of technology monitoring. Discussion of intrusion software has revealed inherent difficulties in defining offensive versus defensive technologies. However, without a workable definition of these terms, any attempt to facilitate legitimate international trade in ICTs, while restricting the transfer of illegitimate technologies, will remain elusive. In summary, it would seem that the application of multilateral, intergovernmental trade mechanisms to cybersecurity concerns has enjoyed very limited success. Furthermore, efforts to broaden the membership and scope of these mechanisms seem likely to encounter considerable limitations.

NOTES

1. World Economic Forum 'Expanding Participation'.
2. World Economic Forum 'Expanding Participation'.
3. World Bank, 'World Development Report', 2–3.
4. International Cybersecurity Standardization Working Group of the National Security Council's Cyber Interagency Policy Committee, 2015a: 3.
5. International Cybersecurity Standardization Working Group, 'Interagency Report' 1.
6. Friedman, 'Cybersecurity and Trade', 25.
7. International Cybersecurity Standardization Working Group 'Interagency Report', 3.
8. Purser, 'Standards for Cyber Security', 98.
9. International Cybersecurity Standardization Working Group, 'Interagency Report', 4.
10. International Cybersecurity Standardization Working Group, 'Interagency Report', 4.
11. World Trade Organization, 'Technical Barriers, Article 2(4).
12. International Cybersecurity Standardization Working Group, 'Interagency Report', 3.
13. International Cybersecurity Standardization Working Group, 'Interagency Report', 3–4.
14. See Westby, Jody (ed.). 2004. *International Guide to Cyber Security*. Chicago, IL: ABA Publishing, 159–81.
15. See, for more detail, International Cybersecurity Standardization Working Group of the National Security Council's Cyber Interagency Policy Committee, 2015b. 'Supplemental Information for the Interagency Report on Strategic U.S. Government Engagement in International Standardization to Achieve U.S. Objectives for Cybersecurity. Volume 2'. http://nvlpubs.nist.gov/nistpubs/ir/2015/NIST.IR.8074v2.pdf
16. International Cybersecurity Standardization Working Group, 'Supplemental Information'.
17. International Cybersecurity Standardization Working Group, 'Interagency Report', 7.
18. International Organization for Standardization, 'About ISO'.
19. International Cybersecurity Standardization Working Group, 'Supplemental Information', 26.
20. International Cybersecurity Standardization Working Group, 'Supplemental Information', 26.
21. Friedman, 'Cybersecurity and Trade', 7–8. 'Arrangement on the Recognition of Common Criteria Certificates In the field of Information Technology Security', 2 July 2014, p. 12. https://www.commoncriteriaportal.org/files/CCRA%20-%20July%202,%202014%20-%20Ratified%20September%208%202014.pdf
22. See ISO/IEC 15408 Information technology—Security techniques—Evaluation criteria for IT security. http://www.iso.org/iso/catalogue_detail.htm?csnumber=50341
23. Authorizing members are Australia, Canada, France, Germany, India, Italy, Japan, Malaysia, the Netherlands, New Zealand, Norway, the Republic of Korea, Spain, Sweden, Turkey, the United Kingdom, and the United States. Consuming members are Austria, the Czech Republic, Denmark, Finland, Greece, Hungary, Israel, Pakistan, Qatar, and Singapore.
24. See 'Arrangement on the Recognition of Common Criteria Certificates'.
25. 'Arrangement on the Recognition of Common Criteria Certificates', Article 2.

26. Kallberg, 'Common Criteria', 1.
27. 'Arrangement on the Recognition of Common Criteria Certificates', 15.
28. Friedman, 'Cybersecurity and Trade', 8.
29. 'Arrangement on the Recognition of Common Criteria Certificates', Article 5.
30. 'Arrangement on the Recognition of Common Criteria Certificates', Article 1.
31. Kallberg, 'Common Criteria', 2.
32. Kallberg, 'Common Criteria', 2.
33. 'Arrangement on the Recognition of Common Criteria Certificates', Preamble.
34. 'Arrangement on the Recognition of Common Criteria Certificates', Preamble.
35. Friedman, 'Cybersecurity and Trade', 8.
36. Friedman, 'Cybersecurity and Trade', 8.
37. Kallberg, 'Common Criteria', 2.
38. Kallberg, 'Common Criteria', 2.
39. 'Arrangement on the Recognition of Common Criteria Certificates'. 'Twenty-six countries agree on reform to improve cyber security certification through international public-private collaboration', News release, 8 September 2014, https://www.commoncriteriaportal.org/news/.
40. Purser, 'Standards for Cyber Security', 100.
41. Purser, 'Standards for Cyber Security', 100.
42. Purser, 'Standards for Cyber Security', 100.
43. Arrangement on the Recognition of Common Criteria Certificates, 'Common Criteria'. https://www.commoncriteriaportal.org/
44. Kallberg, 'Common Criteria', 3.
45. The main export control regimes are the Nuclear Suppliers Group, the Australia Group, and the Missile Technology Control Regime. The Nuclear Suppliers Group focuses on restricting the proliferation of nuclear weapons while the Australia targets chemical and biological weapons.
46. Participating states are Argentina, Australia, Austria, Belgium, Bulgaria, Canada, Croatia, Czech Republic, Denmark, Estonia, Finland, France, Germany, Greece, Hungary, Ireland, Italy, Japan, Latvia, Lithuania, Luxembourg, Malta, Mexico, Netherlands, New Zealand, Norway, Poland, Portugal, the Republic of Korea, Romania, the Russian Federation, Slovakia, Slovenia, South Africa, Spain, Sweden, Switzerland, Turkey, Ukraine, the United Kingdom, and the United States.
47. Wassenaar Arrangement, Section I (1).
48. The Munitions List covers conventional weaponry such as machine guns and grenades. The Dual-Use List covers goods and technologies that are 'major or key elements for the indigenous development, production, use or enhancement of military capabilities'. See Wassenaar Arrangement on Export Controls for Conventional Arms and Dual-Use Goods and Technologies. 2020. 'List of Dual-Use Goods and Technologies and Munitions List', December. http://www.wassenaar.org/wp-content/uploads/2016/12/WA-LIST-16-1-2016-List-of-DU-Goods-and-Technologies-and-Munitions-List.pdf https://www.wassenaar.org/app/uploads/2020/12/Public-Docs-Vol-II-2020-List-of-DU-Goods-and-Technologies-and-Munitions-List-Dec-20-3.pdf
49. Wassenaar Arrangement, Sections III and VII.
50. See, generally, Wassenaar Arrangement, 'Guidelines & Procedures'.
51. Wassenaar Arrangement, 'Guidelines & Procedures', Section II (3).
52. Wassenaar Arrangement, 'Guidelines & Procedures', Section II (3).

53. For the full provision, see Wassenaar Arrangement, 'List of Dual-Use Goods' Section 5. A. 1. j.
54. Wassenaar Arrangement, 'List of Dual-Use Goods', Section 4. A. 5.
55. Wassenaar Arrangement, 'List of Dual-Use Goods', Section 4. A. 5.
56. The *Wall Street Journal* has provided a catalogue of trade relations available at http://graphics.wsj.com/surveillance-catalog/
57. Kopstein, 'Sketchy Government Agencies'.
58. See, for instance, the Coalition Against Unlawful Surveillance Exports (CAUSE). Human Rights Watch, 'New Global Coalition on Surveillance', Press release, 4 April 2014. https://www.hrw.org/news/2014/04/04/new-global-coalition-surveillance
59. Privacy International, 'Privacy International BIS Submission', 2.
60. Maurer, 'Internet Freedom', 2.
61. Maurer, 'Internet Freedom', 3.
62. The rule was proposed with a two-month comment period, an unusual step in the otherwise automatic implementation of changes agreed to in the Wassenaar Arrangement. US Department of Commerce, Bureau of Industry and Security, 'Wassenaar Arrangement 2013 Plenary Agreements Implementation: Intrusion and Surveillance Items', Proposed rule, 20 May 2015
63. Internet Association, 'Comments on BIS Implementation', 5.
64. Moussouris, 'You Need to Speak Up', 2015.
65. Internet Association, 'Comments on BIS Implementation', 4.
66. Internet Association, 'Comments on BIS Implementation', 4.
67. Moussouris, 'You Need to Speak Up', Also Internet Association, 'Comments on BIS Implementation', 6–7.
68. Letter by the US Secretary of Commerce, Penny Pritzker, 1 March 2016. https://www.bis.doc.gov/index.php/forms-documents/about-bis/newsroom/1434-letter-from-secretary-pritzker-to-several-associations-on-the-implementation-of-the-wassenaar-arrang/file
69. Pyetranker, 'An Umbrella', 178.

References

Cardozo, Nate, and Galperin, Eva. 2015. 'What Is the U.S. Doing About Wassenaar, and Why Do We Need to Fight It?', 28 May. https://www.eff.org/deeplinks/2015/05/we-must-fight-proposed-us-wassenaar-implementation

European Commission. 2013. 'Cybersecurity Strategy of the European Union: An Open, Safe and Secure Cyberspace', JOIN(2013) I final. http://eeas.europa.eu/archives/docs/policies/eu-cyber-security/cybsec_comm_en.pdf

European Parliament and Council. 2004. 'Regulation (EC) No 460/2004 establishing the European Network and Information Security Agency'. http://eur-lex.europa.eu/LexUriServ/LexUriServ.do?uri=CELEX:32004R0460:EN:HTML

Friedman, Allan. 2013. 'Cybersecurity and Trade: National Policies, Global and Local Consequences'. https://www.brookings.edu/wp-content/uploads/2016/06/Brookings CybersecurityNEW.pdf.

International Cybersecurity Standardization Working Group of the National Security Council's Cyber Interagency Policy Committee. 2015a. 'Interagency Report on Strategic U.S.

Government Engagement in International Standardization to Achieve U.S. Objectives for Cybersecurity. Volume 1' http://nvlpubs.nist.gov/nistpubs/ir/2015/NIST.IR.8074v1.pdf

International Organization for Standardization (ISO). 2017. 'About ISO', 7 February. http://www.iso.org/iso/home/about.htm

Internet Association. 2015. 'Internet Association Comments on BIS Implementation of the Wassenaar Arrangement 2013 Plenary Agreements on Intrusion and Surveillance Items', 20 July. http://internetassociation.org/wp-content/uploads/2015/07/Internet-Association-Comments-on-BIS-Implementation-of-Wassenaar-7.20.15.pdf

Kallberg, Jan. 2012. 'Common Criteria Meets Realpolitik. Trust, Alliances, and Potential Betrayal', *Selected Papers in Security Studies* 9, The University of Texas at Dallas. https://www.utdallas.edu/~bxt043000/Publications/Technical-Reports/UTDCS-13-12.pdf

Kopstein, Joshua. 2015. 'Here Are All the Sketchy Government Agencies Buying Hacking Team's Spy Tech', 6 July. https://motherboard.vice.com/en_us/article/here-are-all-the-sketchy-government-agencies-buying-hacking-teams-spy-tech

Maurer, Tim. 2016. 'Internet Freedom and Export Controls', Briefing before the Commission on Security and Cooperation in Europe, 3 March. http://carnegieendowment.org/files/Tim_Maurer_final_briefing_-_03.03.20162.pdf

Moussouris, Katie. 2015. 'You Need to Speak Up for Internet Security. Right Now', *Wired*, 16 July. https://www.wired.com/2015/07/moussouris-wassenaar-open-comment-period/

Peterson, Andrea. 2016. 'This Malware Sold to Governments Could Help Them Spy on IPhones, Researchers Say', *The Washington Post*, 25 August. https://www.washingtonpost.com/news/the-switch/wp/2016/08/25/this-malware-sold-to-governments-helped-them-spy-on-iphones/?utm_term=.a34cb444c88e

Privacy International. 2015. 'Privacy International BIS Submission'. https://privacyinternational.org/blog/1425/us-publishes-proposed-rules-implementing-2013-wassenaar-agreements

Purser, Steve. 2014. 'Standards for Cyber Security'. In *Best Practices in Computer Network Defense: Incident Detection and Response*, edited by M.E. Hathaway, 97–106. Amsterdam: IOS Press.

Pyetranker, Innokenty. 2015. 'An Umbrella in a Hurricane: Cyber Technology and the December 2013 Amendment to the Wassenaar Arrangement', *Northwestern Journal of Technology & Intellectual Property*, 13 (2): 153–80.

Shahani, Aarti. 2015. 'Commerce Department: Tighter Controls Needed for Cyberweapons', 20 July. http://www.npr.org/sections/alltechconsidered/2015/07/20/424473107/commerce-department-tighter-controls-needed-for-cyber-weapons

Wassenaar Arrangement on Export Controls for Conventional Arms and Dual-Use Goods and Technologies. 2019. 'Guidelines and Procedures, including the Initial Elements'. December, p. 3. https://www.wassenaar.org/app/uploads/2019/12/WA-DOC-19-Public-Docs-Vol-I-Founding-Documents.pdf

Wassenaar Arrangement on Export Controls for Conventional Arms and Dual-Use Goods and Technologies. 2016. 'List of Dual-Use Goods and Technologies and Munitions List', 8 December, http://www.wassenaar.org/wp-content/uploads/2016/12/WA-LIST-16-1-2016-List-of-DU-Goods-and-Technologies-and-Munitions-List.pdf

World Bank. 2016. 'World Development Report 2016: Digital Dividends'. http://documents.worldbank.org/curated/en/896971468194972881/pdf/102725-PUB-Replacement-PUBLIC.pdf

World Economic Forum. 2015. 'Expanding Participation and Boosting Growth: The Infrastructure Needs of the Digital Economy'. http://www3.weforum.org/docs/WEFUSA_DigitalInfrastructure_Report2015.pdf

World Trade Organization. 1995. 'Agreement on Technical Barriers to Trade'. https://www.wto.org/english/docs_e/legal_e/17-tbt_e.htm

CHAPTER 30

CYBERSECURITY, GLOBAL COMMERCE, AND INTERNATIONAL ORGANIZATIONS

DAVID FIDLER

INTRODUCTION

THE manner in which digital technologies have disseminated and become integrated into cross-border business produces a complex relationship between global commerce and cybersecurity. Private-sector dependence on networked computers creates vulnerabilities to cybercrime and economic cyber espionage. National security measures, such as electronic surveillance, generate cybersecurity problems for companies. Technological innovation, including the 'Internet of Things', increases risks in global commerce while exacerbating difficulties corporations face building cyber defences.

Thus, managing cybersecurity in global commerce has become important in international political economy. In other contexts, states use international organizations to pursue economic growth while protecting other interests, including national security. Some of the most successful regional and multilateral organizations focus on economic governance, such as the European Union (EU) and World Trade Organization (WTO), which support claims that institutions matter in international relations. This chapter analyses how states use international organizations to address cybersecurity issues affecting global commerce.[1]

Although states have brought these issues into international organizations, the results are not impressive. Global diffusion of cyber technologies and their commercial exploitation happened without direct involvement by international organizations. This phenomenon is unusual in the history of international political economy. Previously, states managed international uses of information and communication technologies (ICTs) through institutional action via, for example, the International Telecommunication Union (ITU). When cybersecurity problems proliferated in global commerce, international organizations were not well positioned to respond.

Responses to these problems in international organizations have proved inadequate, secondary to diplomacy in other contexts, or inconclusive. Despite action in many international organizations, cybercrime has grown. Governments' worries about terrorism and political threats from online activities make expanded surveillance and national cyber regulations a headache for companies, and international organizations provide no relief. Efforts against state-sponsored cyber espionage targeting corporations emerged in bilateral relations , were then supported at the intergovernmental level, but ultimately failed. Attempts by regional and multilateral organizations to foster better cybersecurity in critical infrastructure are underway but, at present, they face questions about their long-term impact.

Prospects for international organizations improving their contributions to cybersecurity are not good. Negotiations at the United Nations (UN) on cybercrime have not strengthened cooperation, and no international organization has tackled economic cyber espionage after bilateral efforts failed. Use of encryption by companies, criminals, and terrorists poses challenges for law enforcement and intelligence agencies, and discussions of this problem in international organizations have not generated productive cooperation. Geopolitical competition reinforces conflicts over Internet governance and cybersecurity, produces disagreements in international organizations, and fragments collective action through divergent approaches pursued in different venues. Finally, neither growing assertiveness by authoritarian governments nor rising populism in democratic countries bodes well for collective action on cybersecurity threats to global commerce.

Cybersecurity and Global Commerce

Analysing how international organizations address cybersecurity and global commerce requires clarifying what cyber threats companies face. Businesses encounter many challenges in cyberspace, but not all are cybersecurity problems. Privacy advocates criticize technology companies for exploiting users' personal information for profit. Governments investigate technology enterprises to prevent anti-competitive behaviour. Companies confront challenges protecting intellectual property in cyberspace. While important, these issues do not involve the security of cyber systems and digital information that companies use to conduct business. In global commerce, cybersecurity problems arise in three contexts.

Direct Threats

Cybersecurity threats typically slot into categories used in national security policy—crime, terrorism, espionage, and war. Within these, cybercrime and economic cyber espionage pose the most important cybersecurity threats to companies. Governments often express fears about terrorist cyber attacks against critical infrastructure but such attacks have not materialized for various reasons (International Law Association 2016). In addition, many companies that operate critical infrastructure, such as local electrical utilities, are not engaged in global commerce. Cyber warfare could damage transnational business, but what little is known about military use of cyber technologies in armed conflict does not suggest cyber warfare is, yet, a danger to global commerce.

Indirect Threats

Problems arise for companies from national security actions by governments that undermine the security of corporate cyber systems. To counter terrorism, conduct espionage, engage in counter-intelligence and fight crime, governments often intensify and expand surveillance and hacking operations in ways that can affect corporations. Such measures sometimes use digital means, such as 'zero-day' vulnerabilities, that exploit bugs in software that businesses use. The incentives governments have to keep such vulnerabilities secret rather than disclose them for patching mean that corporate cybersecurity can be compromised (Healey 2016). Government surveillance and hacking can also put pressure on companies to strengthen their cyber defences in order to protect user confidence and privacy. Such pressure has led companies to use encryption more extensively.

Vulnerabilities Created by Corporate Behaviour

Companies also experience cybersecurity problems because of private-sector behaviour. Technological change and corporate use of software largely transpire without much attention to the security of digital products and services. Businesses often fail to protect their computers and networks adequately. Commercial incentives to reorient innovation and bolster cyber defences have not been sufficient to reduce the risks businesses create for themselves (President's Commission on Enhancing National Cybersecurity 2016, 7).

INTERNATIONAL ORGANIZATIONS AND GLOBAL COMMERCE

International organizations have played major roles in the growth of trade, foreign direct investment, and global spread of new technologies. In the nineteenth century, states began standardizing telegraphy equipment and developing rules for cross-border telegraphic communications (International Telecommunication Union 2017a). After World War II, the Bretton Woods system of international economic governance functioned through multilateral institutions, such as the General Agreement on Tariffs and Trade (GATT). In the 1950s, countries in Western Europe started building institutions to facilitate the free movement of goods, services, capital, and labour that later became the EU. Over time, states produced new, or modified existing, multilateral and regional organizations to liberalize trade and investment, integrate new technologies into commerce, and deepen interdependence among countries.

International economic governance developed into a 'regime complex'—a web of diplomatic mechanisms supporting global commerce.[2] This regime complex provides evidence for theories of international relations that identify the contributions international organizations can make in world affairs (Keohane 1984). Institutionalist theories argue that international organizations can shape how states calculate their self-interests by reducing transaction costs for cooperation, increasing informational transparency, bolstering rule development and compliance, managing disputes, and deepening political commitment to collective action. International institutions help states lengthen 'the shadow of the future' (Axelrod 1984) by making cooperation more durable over time.

A regime complex can also produce synergies when activities of international organizations converge. For this chapter, the most relevant synergy emerges from the liberalization of trade and investment, and the dissemination of ICTs. Institutions facilitating trade liberalization, such as the GATT, created commercial incentives for ICTs to disseminate as globally as possible. These incentives informed the interest states showed in using the ITU to help make telegraphy, telephony, and radio operate across borders. The integration of ICTs into commercial operations helped businesses exploit opportunities generated by trade and investment liberalization.

Breaking with the Past: The Internet and Global Commerce

The Internet's emergence breaks with this pattern of international organizations benefiting global commerce through synergies between economic and ICT governance. The Internet developed, spread, and became an engine of economic activity without the direct involvement of international organizations. The ITU did not lead the standardization of the Internet protocols that allow computers to communicate and share information (Leiner, Cerf, and Clark et al. 1997). Nor did the ITU create the domain name system or the world wide web—innovations that increased the Internet's utility and accessibility (Kleinwächter 2007). Governance of Internet protocols, the domain name system, and the world wide web emerged in multi-stakeholder processes that involve governments but are not anchored in intergovernmental institutions (Post 2009).

The Internet's commercial potential became clear in the latter half of the 1990s, but international organizations tasked with economic governance did not have this objective on their agendas. Efforts to liberalize trade and investment accelerated in the early 1990s after the Cold War ended. By the mid-1990s, these efforts produced the North American Free Trade Agreement (NAFTA), the WTO, and the proliferation of bilateral investment treaties (BITs) (Gilpin 2001). These waves of economic liberalization were rolling before access to the world wide web made the Internet a powerful tool for global commerce in the latter half of the 1990s. Thus, NAFTA, WTO agreements, and BITs did not contain rules on electronic commerce or address the dependence of businesses on digital information and its cross-border transfer.

Further, the Internet as a tool of global commerce expanded in the 1990s without effective opposition from states in international organizations, including the UN's security, political, and economic organs. During the Cold War, the appearance of a transformative information technology would have sparked controversies, and the UN would have been a venue where disagreements played out. The end of the Cold War essentially eliminated political barriers to the Internet's dissemination and integration into global commercial activities. Thus, an unprecedented convergence of technological, political, and economic factors occurred. A radically different ICT gelled as geopolitical and ideological competition faded and economic globalization exploded.

ENTER CYBERSECURITY INTO GLOBAL COMMERCE

The manner in which the Internet globalized and societies became dependent on networked digital technologies generated concerns that this dependence rendered governments and companies vulnerable to malicious cyber activities. The technologies behind the Internet and their commercial use emerged with little attention paid to the security of cyber-enabled communications. As the twentieth century closed, policymakers and corporations began to worry about cybersecurity threats from state and non-state actors, and to identify ways to counter them. These efforts arose in many contexts, including international organizations.

However, global dependence on the Internet developed without a centre of gravity in the world of international organizations and without cybersecurity being a priority. As the security of digital communications and networks grew as a policy concern, political differences emerged among countries about what 'cybersecurity' means. The United States and European democracies focused cybersecurity policy on malicious actions threatening an open, global Internet supportive of private enterprise, democracy, and individual rights. This position bolstered the multi-stakeholder strategy for Internet governance and the concept of 'Internet freedom' (Clinton 2010).

By contrast, China, Russia, and other authoritarian countries framed the problem as one of 'information security', defined to include not only malicious cyber acts but also online activities threatening domestic political stability. This position was anchored in the notion of 'Internet sovereignty'—the primacy of a state's sovereignty over cyber activities in or affecting its territory, supported by the principle of non-intervention in its domestic affairs (Government of China 2010). Countries backing Internet sovereignty wanted to shift Internet governance from multi-stakeholder mechanisms to intergovernmental institutions, particularly the ITU.

Tensions between these perspectives began in the late 1990s and early 2000s, and escalated in UN-sponsored venues, including the World Summit on the Information Society, the Internet Governance Forum, and the Group of Governmental Experts on Developments in the Field of Information and Communication Technologies in the Context of International Security (UNGGE). Negotiations to revise the ITU's International Telecommunication Regulations ended acrimoniously when the United States and European countries rejected efforts to have the revised regulations address Internet governance issues, including the security of international telecommunication networks (Farivar 2012).

The 'Internet freedom' versus 'Internet sovereignty' conflict was not primarily about global commerce, but it created difficult politics for collective action on cybersecurity. The fight meant many countries opposed addressing cybersecurity in the ITU. States associated with Internet sovereignty did not participate in cybersecurity initiatives launched by the United States and its allies. The diplomatic friction and governance fragmentation adversely affected using international organizations to confront cybersecurity problems in global commerce.

Direct Threats to Cybersecurity in Global Commerce

To date, cybercrime and economic cyber espionage have been the major cybersecurity threats companies face. Cybercrime costs companies billions of dollars annually, and the problem has become so bad that many states consider cybercrime a national security issue. Economic cyber espionage involves state-conducted or state-sponsored espionage against foreign companies in order to obtain commercially valuable information that can help domestic enterprises become more successful. Economic espionage was a problem before the Internet transformed global commerce, but cyber technologies make it possible on an unprecedented scale. Like cybercrime, governments began to treat economic cyber espionage as a national security problem.

The approaches taken against cybercrime and economic cyber espionage have been different, but the outcomes achieved have been the same. Concerning cybercrime, states have used international organizations, developed international law, and watched cybercrime grow worse. By contrast, a new norm against economic cyber espionage emerged in bilateral agreements, was endorsed by a global economic governance regime, but did not survive the intensification of geopolitical competition among states.

Cybercrime

States began formulating international responses to cybercrime in the first decade of the twenty-first century, and regional and multilateral organizations have played leading roles.[3] In 2001, the Council of Europe (COE) and the Commonwealth of Independent States produced treaties on cybercrime, and the Association of Southeast Asian Nations (ASEAN) added cybercrime to its transnational crime agenda (COE 2001; Commonwealth of Independent States 2001; Lee 2016). The Shanghai Cooperation Organization included cooperation on cybercrime in its agreement on international information security in 2009; the League of Arab States adopted a cybercrime treaty in 2010; and the African Union addressed cybercrime in a cybersecurity convention finalized in 2014 (Shanghai Cooperation Organization 2009; League of Arab States 2010; African Union 2014). At the multilateral level, the International Police Organization (INTERPOL 2017) made cybercrime a priority. States parties to the UN Convention on Transnational Organized Crime (TOC Convention) extended it to cover cybercrime (Conference of the Parties 2010, 50). UNGGE reports have emphasized the importance of cooperation on cybercrime (UN Group of Governmental Experts 2013, 2015). These, and other, activities demonstrate that states have used international organizations more on cybercrime than on any other cybersecurity threat.

However, despite extensive involvement of international organizations, the cybercrime threat to global commerce continues to grow, as ransomware attacks during the COVID-19 pandemic illustrate. The COE Convention is the strongest treaty in this area, but a COE official admitted in 2016 that cybercriminals operate with 'virtual impunity in cyberspace' (Kleijssen 2016). This admission also calls into question efforts under INTERPOL and the TOC Convention. The impact of the treaties adopted by the Commonwealth of Independent

States, Shanghai Cooperation Organization, and League of Arab States is not clear, but these instruments are unlikely to have better records than the COE Convention, INTERPOL, and the TOC Convention. The African Union convention is not in force, and ASEAN cooperation on cybercrime has had limited effect.[4]

What explains this grim assessment? The growth of cybercrime suggests that states cannot rely on the criminal law strategies international organizations use (Brenner 2010, 215–18). The growth also highlights the fragmentation of collective action. The COE wanted its treaty to be a global instrument, but the number of states parties remains limited and concentrated within Europe (Council of Europe 2017). Countries in other regions decided to produce different agreements. This patchwork of regimes means that governments often have to use extradition and mutual legal assistance treaties, and few states have adapted these instruments to the challenges of cybercrime. These problems with the law enforcement approach inform why the United States started applying direct pressure on countries, such as Russia, to act against cybercriminals operating from their territories. In addition, many governments have not developed adequate law enforcement capabilities to address cybercrime effectively (Brown 2015, 56). Finally, companies have failed to improve their defences against cybercrime despite awareness of the threat.

Economic Cyber Espionage

Turning to economic cyber espionage, international organizations have played a less significant role as, states attempted to address on this threat.[5] Economic espionage was a problem in the pre-Internet era, but cooperation against it never developed. The United States prominently opposed economic espionage, claiming it did not conduct espionage against foreign companies in order to benefit American enterprises. The US government continued this opposition after the Internet made economic cyber espionage possible, but its identification of countries, particularly China and Russia, as practitioners of it produced no collective action (Shanker 2011, A4). The UNGGE has never addressed this issue in working on ICTs and international security since the early 2000s.

The United States explored bringing WTO cases against WTO members engaging in economic cyber espionage (Strawbridge 2016, 838). Such cases would have accused such members of stealing information protected by the WTO Agreement on Trade-Related Aspects of Intellectual Property Rights (TRIPS). However, it is not clear whether TRIPS or other WTO agreements permit claims against economic cyber espionage, or that the WTO was an appropriate forum for addressing this problem. In the event, the United States had filed no WTO complaints based on economic cyber espionage by the end of the Trump administration.

Instead, the United States acted unilaterally. It indicted members of the Chinese People's Liberation Army for conducting economic cyber espionage against US companies (Schmidt and Sanger 2014, A1). It threatened to sanction Chinese companies benefiting from economic cyber espionage against American enterprises (Nakashima 2015b).[6] According to US experts, these threats persuaded China to negotiate (Knake 2015). In 2015, President Obama and President Xi agreed not to engage in economic cyber espionage—a startling outcome given the acrimony between the two countries on this issue (Segal 2016). As surprising was

China's next move—making the same agreement with the United Kingdom and Germany (Mason 2015; Wu 2015).

These agreements created momentum for a global norm against economic cyber espionage, and the Group of 20 (G20) supported the norm (Nakashima 2015b). Although the G20's support is important, the norm did not emerge within international organizations. The G20's role was secondary to unilateral actions of the United States and bilateral agreements China made with the United States, United Kingdom, and Germany.

US analyses initially indicated that Chinese economic cyber espionage against US companies had declined, suggesting the agreement was working (Menn and Finkle 2016). However, the agreement did not survive the deterioration in US-China relations. Through its Clean Network program, the Trump administration countered Chinese economic cyber espionage by 'de-coupling' Chinese enterprises from telecommunication networks in the United States and like-minded countries.

Cyber Terrorism

The fear that terrorists will use cyber weapons to kill or injure people, damage property, spread fear in societies, or coerce governments has not, to date, come to pass.[7] The lack of terrorist cyber attacks explains why international organizations concerned about terrorism, such as the UN, have not taken steps to address this threat. Instead, UN efforts have highlighted terrorist use of the Internet to spread propaganda, radicalize and recruit people, and raise funds.[8]

Policy worries that terrorists might launch cyber attacks against critical infrastructure have been the most salient issue for commercial interests.[9] In many countries, the private sector owns or operates critical infrastructure. Governments have acted to improve cyber defences in domestic critical infrastructure (National Institute of Standards and Technology 2014), an objective countries have also pursued in bilateral relations and regional and multilateral organizations.[10] Regionally, the EU has imposed regulations on operators of critical infrastructure to improve cybersecurity (Wessel 2015).

In some critical infrastructure sectors important to global commerce, international organizations are involved in efforts to bolster cyber defences against malicious activities regardless of their source. This 'all hazards' approach covers not only cyber terrorism but also threats from criminals and governments. The International Civil Aviation Organization (ICAO) has adopted treaties that cover cybersecurity threats (Piera and Gill 2014). ICAO has also identified improving cybersecurity in civil aviation as a priority for the organization and its member states (Kaiser and Aretz 2013). The International Maritime Organization (IMO 2016) is addressing cybersecurity in its efforts on maritime security. Cybersecurity also arises in the International Cable Protection Committee's work on the security of submarine communication cables (von Heinegg 2013).

Cyber Warfare

States have analysed military use of cyber weapons in armed conflict, including within international organizations.[11] The UNGGE has debated—without reaching clear consensus—whether international humanitarian law (IHL) applies to use of cyber weapons in war (Grigsby 2015). By contrast, NATO members agree that IHL applies, and a NATO-sponsored research centre continues to analyse how this law functions in cyber warfare (International Group of Experts 2017). Debates about IHL and cyber warfare involve more than the problems military use of cyber weapons might cause for global commerce, problems which remain, at present, hypothetical. The US, British, and Australian governments acknowledged launching military cyber operations in the armed conflict against the Islamic State (Grigsby 2016). But, given little is known, analysing the implications of these operations for global commerce involves mere speculation.

IHL protects civilians, including their commercial activities, from military attack during war (International Committee of the Red Cross 2017). International lawyers have debated whether these rules adequately protect civilians from cyber warfare (Schmitt 2002). In keeping with IHL's development, international organizations, such as the UN, will not determine how IHL applies to military cyber operations. As already indicated, the UNGGE has not achieved consensus on whether this law applies to cyber weapons, let alone how it applies. State practice outside international organizations will determine what IHL means for military cyber operations, including operations affecting commercial activities during war.

INDIRECT THREATS TO CYBERSECURITY IN GLOBAL COMMERCE

Global businesses face cybersecurity problems created by government measures addressing national security threats, such as electronic surveillance and hacking operations. Governments do not necessarily intend to undermine private-sector cybersecurity, but law enforcement and intelligence activities against crime, terrorists, or spies have generated cybersecurity problems for companies. With national security measures and commercial activities having global scope, these indirect cybersecurity threats are important in global commerce. However, international organizations play little to no role in responses to such threats.

Edward Snowden's disclosures of US surveillance, intelligence, and covert operations in cyberspace provide examples of indirect cybersecurity threats in global commerce (Fidler 2015). Documents disclosed by Snowden revealed US efforts that, among other things, captured communications of Americans and foreign nationals on a large scale, intercepted intra-company communications outside the United States, tampered with digital-product supply chains, collected information on foreign companies to aid US trade negotiators, and hacked into foreign companies. Such revelations undermined confidence in US-based technology companies, angered companies targeted or affected by U.S. government activities, and produced foreign government reactions that harmed US companies.

The response of companies included measures to improve cybersecurity for customers and business operations. The most prominent step was increased use of encryption to protect consumer and corporate communications. Major US technology companies also banded together to advocate for reforms to US policies. However, international organizations were not venues for these efforts. Some activities in international organizations provoked by Snowden, such as on the right to privacy, supported steps to strengthen corporate cybersecurity (Cannataci 2016, 5). However, greater corporate use of encryption prompted law enforcement and intelligence officials in various countries to warn that encryption threatened their ability to enforce the law and protect national security.[12] Government officials aired these warnings in international organizations, such as the UN, but collective action has not emerged.

Snowden's disclosures also sparked concerns over government actions that could adversely affect cross-border data flows. After Snowden's leaks, the EU terminated its 'safe harbour' arrangement that allowed US companies to transfer data from the EU to the United States. The EU and the United States had to negotiate a new agreement to permit data flows to resume (US Department of Commerce 2017). More generally, 'data localization' laws threatened business operations reliant on transferring information across borders. Despite how critical such data transfers have become in global commerce, traditional rules on trade and foreign direct investment do not specifically protect cross-border data flows. The Trans-Pacific Partnership (TPP) agreement would have included the first-ever rules in a trade and investment agreement that directly addressed 'concerns over requirements that data be stored locally and prohibitions on the flow of data or information across borders' (Office of the US Trade Representative 2015). However, the United States rejected the TPP agreement after Donald Trump's election, which adversely affected collective action on the data localization problem.

Cybersecurity problems in global commerce also include worries associated with government discovery, purchase, stockpiling, and use of 'zero-day' vulnerabilities—flaws in software that can be exploited before they become known to, and fixed by, software vendors. Zero-day vulnerabilities have national security utility for governments. Law enforcement personnel, intelligence agencies, and military forces can exploit them to hack into computer systems for various purposes. However, not disclosing a zero-day vulnerability for potential use later exposes software users, including companies, to risks the flaw creates.[13]

This problem produced controversy in the United States, and the Obama administration developed an interagency mechanism—the Vulnerabilities Equities Process—to vet zero-day vulnerabilities known to the US government and, in most cases (according to the government), to disclose them for patching.[14] Information released by WikiLeaks in March 2017 revealed that the US Central Intelligence Agency 'was hoarding undisclosed [zero-day] vulnerabilities' (Newman 2017), which reignited the controversy over the government's handling of such vulnerabilities and threatened to make relations between the US government and Silicon Valley worse (Segal 2017).

Even though this controversy has dogged the US government's policies on zero-days, no other country discussed the problem as openly. Nor has the zero-day issue featured in the cybersecurity work of regional or multilateral organizations. One of the few examples comes from the Global Forum on Cyber Expertise's initiative that allows government and non-governmental members to share information and experiences about responsible disclosure of software vulnerabilities (Global Forum on Cyber Expertise 2016).

CORPORATE BEHAVIOUR AND CYBERSECURITY THREATS IN GLOBAL COMMERCE

The last category of cybersecurity threats relevant to global commerce emerges from the private sector itself. Innovation in digital technologies and company failures to build robust cyber defences contribute to cybersecurity vulnerabilities burdening commerce.[15] Criticisms that commercial pressures and incentives to deliver new software and digital services rapidly produce insecure products and services have gone largely unheeded. For example, cybersecurity vulnerabilities accompany the new wave of innovation cresting with products and services associated with the 'Internet of things' (Lohr 2016, B3). Proposals to hold companies accountable for selling insecure software and services typically envision national regulations rather than action through international organizations.

Similarly, corporate underinvestment in cybersecurity persists despite the threats of cybercrime and economic cyber espionage. National initiatives to increase information flows on cybersecurity threats between the public and private sectors have not sparked sustained improvements in private-sector cybersecurity. Nor have domestic legal requirements to report data breaches to government agencies. In the United States, the damage malicious cyber activities inflict on the private sector has produced interest in allowing companies to 'hack back' as an act of self-defence and deterrence, an idea that would go nowhere in cyber diplomacy. In international organizations, corporate responsibility for protecting the privacy of personal information receives attention, but the range of problems created by poor company cybersecurity extends beyond threats to privacy.[16]

Insecure software and services and inadequate private-sector cybersecurity practices disseminate with the world's deepening dependence on Internet-enabled technologies. Efforts to close the 'digital divide' in low-income countries infrequently address cybersecurity challenges, including those arising from insecure software and digital services and private-sector disinterest in cyber defences. Despite the global scale of these problems, regional and multilateral organizations have not contributed much to mitigating them. The ITU undertakes standardization work on ICTs and has a study group generating standards on the Internet of Things.[17] A 2016 ITU report identified security vulnerabilities as a problem with Internet-of-Things systems (International Telecommunication Union and CISCO 2016, 4), suggesting that Internet-of-things devices and services are going global without adequate attention to cybersecurity.

CONCLUSION: PROSPECTS FOR INTERNATIONAL ORGANIZATIONS AND CYBERSECURITY PROBLEMS IN GLOBAL COMMERCE

Looking ahead, a range of problems limit the contributions international organizations might make in improving cybersecurity in global commerce. First, extensive use of regional and multilateral organizations has not been effective against cybercrime, the biggest cybersecurity threat companies face. Policymakers and diplomats often stress the need to improve existing cybercrime regimes, but how more of the same will transform cooperation on cybercrime is not clear. UN negotiations on a new cybercrime treaty supported by China and Russia but opposed by the United States promise more controversy rather than greater legal harmonization and law enforcement collaboration.

Second, increasing the willingness of states to tackle cybersecurity threats in global commerce more seriously within international organizations would have to overcome the intensification of geopolitical competition and conflict over cyber issues. The acrimony over negotiating a UN cybercrime treaty demonstrates that China, Russia, and the United States cannot agree on a common framework on confronting cybercrime. Similarly, the fleeting progress on economic cyber espionage between the United States and China emerged in bilateral relations not regional or multilateral organizations. The intensification of the US-China rivalry, and its adverse impact on cooperation on economic cyber espionage, means that the G20's support for the norm against economic cyber espionage had no lasting significance.

Perhaps the most promising area for international organizations involves improving cybersecurity in critical infrastructure sectors important to global commerce. Such work is underway in, for example, civil aviation and maritime transport. The success the ICAO and IMO have had in raising international standards for safety and security in their sectors allows cybersecurity to slot productively into their activities. To date, the initiatives these organizations have taken on cybersecurity have not caused the controversies seen over the ITU's role in Internet governance and cybersecurity. The same describes actions taken by other international organizations with responsibilities in critical infrastructure sectors, such as the cybersecurity work within the International Atomic Energy Agency (2013).

Third, international organizations do not seem well suited to address the cybersecurity threats companies experience because of government national security measures, the pace of innovation in digital technologies, and corporate reluctance to build more robust cyber defences. Regional and multilateral organizations rarely prove effective in regulating how states protect their national security. Post-Snowden controversies about government surveillance, intelligence, and covert operations in cyberspace reinforce scepticism that international organizations can govern such practices. Similarly, like national governments, international organizations do not demonstrate much skill in keeping policy from falling behind technological change. Strategies to encourage or force improvements in private-sector cyber defences are likely to be national in scope, with the EU's legal mandates remaining a regional exception.

Fourth, contributions on cybersecurity from international organizations associated with trade and investment will be difficult to construct. The WTO has struggled with electronic commerce issues. Nothing on the horizon suggests it will advance this agenda in ways that support better cybersecurity in global commerce. Regional and bilateral trade and investment regimes also face challenges that limit what might be possible on cybersecurity within them. For example, recent trade treaties, such as the US-Mexico-Canada agreement and the US-China Phase One agreement do not address cybercrime or economic cyber espionage.

Fifth, President Trump transformed US trade policy, and trade's role in US foreign policy, through his 'America First' strategy (Fidler 2017). This approach embraces protectionism over the long-standing US commitment to liberalized trade and investment. This anti-globalization turn towards protectionism by an economic superpower damageed global commerce, even before the global economic disruptions caused by the COVID-19 pandemic. As countries struggle with protectionism in a post-pandemic world, cybersecurity problems in global commerce will not be a prominent issue in international political economy.

Finally, collective action across many issue areas, including cybersecurity, has to navigate not only difficult geopolitics but also shifts in domestic politics. The UK's exit from the EU, the continued impact of President Trump's America First agenda, and populist movements across the democratic world have democracies turning inwards. By contrast, authoritarian countries, led by China and Russia, are assertively reshaping international relations to suit their power and interests. These dynamics inform fears that the 'liberal international order' sustained by democracies since World War II might be in danger (Nye 2017). If so, managing cybersecurity threats in global commerce will not be a priority as countries adapt to a new world order.

NOTES

1. In this chapter, 'international organization' means intergovernmental institutions established through treaties, such as the World Trade Organization', and non-treaty regimes in which states engage in collective action, such as the Group of 20.
2. This definition follows Raustalia, K. and Victor, D. 2004. 'The Regime Complex for Plant Genetic Resources', *International Organization* 58 (2): 277–309: 'a regime complex is "an array of partially overlapping institutions governing a particular issue-area"' (278–79).
3. On cybercrime, see also Chapters 6 and 8 in this volume.
4. Lee, 'ASEAN Cybersecurity Profile', 2016.
5. On economic cyber espionage, see also Chapter [12] in this volume.
6. On sanctions, see also Chapter [32] in this volume.
7. On terrorism and cyberspace, see also Chapters [8–11] in this volume.
8. UN Counter-Terrorism Committee. 2016. 'Concept Note for the Special Meeting of the Counter-Terrorism Committee on "Preventing the Exploitation of Information and Communications Technologies for Terrorist Purposes, with Respecting Human Rights and Fundamental Freedoms"'. http://www.reuters.com/article/cyber-spying-china-idUSL1N19D00O. Government responses to terrorist exploitation of the Internet, such as intensified surveillance, can affect cybersecurity for commercial enterprises.
9. International Law Association, 'Final Report of the Study Group', 2016, 63–9. On cybersecurity and critical infrastructure, see also Chapter [26] in this volume.
10. International Law Association, 'Final Report of the Study Group', 2016, 64.
11. On cyber warfare, see also Chapter [13] in this volume.
12. Brown, 'Investigating and Prosecuting', 2015, 82.
13. On zero-day vulnerabilities, see Stockton, P. and Golabek-Goldman, M. 2013. 'Curbing the Market for Cyber Weapons', *Yale Law & Policy Review* 32: 101–28; Fidler, M. 2015. 'Regulating the Zero-Day Vulnerability Trade: A Preliminary Analysis', *I/S: A Journal of Law and Policy for the Information Society* 11: 405–83; Healey, 'The US Government', 2016.
14. Healey, 'The US Government', 2016.

15. On corporate cybersecurity, see also Chapter [18] in this volume.
16. On privacy, see also Chapter [20] in this volume.
17. International Telecommunication Union Study Group. 2017b. 'IoT and Its Applications Including Smart Cities and Communities (SC&C)'. http://www.itu.int/en/ITU-T/studygroups/2013-2016/20/Pages/default.aspx. On standardization, see also Chapter [30] in this volume.

References

African Union. 2014. Convention on Cyber Security and Personal Data Protection, EX.CL/846 (XXV).

Axelrod, R. 1984. *The Evolution of Cooperation*. New York: Basic Books.

Brenner, S. 2010. *Cybercrime: Criminal Threats from Cyberspace*. Santa Barbara: Praeger.

Brown, C. 2015. 'Investigating and Prosecuting Cyber Crime: Forensic Dependencies and Barriers to Justice', *International Journal of Cyber Criminology* 9 (1): 55–119.

Cannataci, J. 2016. *Report of the Special Rapporteur on the Right to Privacy*, UN Human Rights Council, A/HRC/31/64, 8 March.

Clinton, H. 2010. 'Remarks by the Secretary of State on Internet Freedom', 21 January. www.state.gov/secretary/20092013clinton/rm/2010/01/135519.htm

Commonwealth of Independent States. 2001. Agreement on Cooperation in Combatting Offenses Related to Computer Information.

Conference of the Parties. 2010. Report of the Conference of the Parties to the UN Convention against Transnational Organized Crime on Its Fifth Session, 18–22 October, CTOC/COP/2010/17.

Council of Europe (COE). 2001. Convention on Cybercrime, European Treaty Series No. 185.

Council of Europe (COE). 2017. 'Convention on Cybercrime'. http://conventions.coe.int/Treaty/Commun/ChercheSig.asp?NT=185&CM=1&DF=20/02/2015&CL=ENG

Farivar, C. 2012. 'The UN's Telecom Conference is Finally Over. Who Won? Nobody Knows', *Ars Technica*, 14 December. https://arstechnica.com/tech-policy/2012/12/the-uns-telecom-conference-is-finally-over-who-won-nobody-knows/

Fidler, D. (ed.). 2015. *The Snowden Reader*. Bloomington: Indiana University Press.

Fidler, D. 2017. 'President Trump, Trade Policy, and American Grand Strategy: From Common Advantage to Collective Carnage', *Asian Journal of WTO and International Health Law & Policy* 12 (1): 1–32.

Gilpin, R. 2001. *Global Political Economy: Understanding the International Economic Order*. Princeton, NJ: Princeton University Press.

Global Forum on Cyber Expertise. 2016. 'Coordinated Vulnerability Disclosure'. https://www.thegfce.com/initiatives/r/responsible-disclosure-initiative-ethical-hacking

Government of China. 2010. *White Paper: The Internet in China*, 8 June. http://en.people.cn/90001/90776/90785/7017177.html

Grigsby, A. 2015. 'The 2015 GGE Report: Breaking New Ground, Ever So Slowly', *Net Politics*, 8 September. http://blogs.cfr.org/cyber/2015/09/08/the-2015-gge-report-breaking-new-ground-ever-so-slowly/

Grigsby, A. 2016. 'Year in Review: Militaries Got More Cyber in 2016', *Net Politics*, 26 December. http://blogs.cfr.org/cyber/2016/12/26/year-in-review-cyber-bombs/

Healey, J. 2016. 'The U.S. Government and Zero-Day Vulnerabilities: From Pre-Heartbleed to Shadow Brokers'. (Report from Columbia University School of International and Public Affairs and Journal of International Affairs). https://jia.sipa.columbia.edu/sites/default/files/attachments/Healey%20VEP.pdf

International Atomic Energy Agency. 2013. *Nuclear Security Plan 2014–2017*, GOV/2013/42-GC(57)/19, 3 August.

International Committee of the Red Cross. 2017. 'Customary IHL—Rule 1. The Principle of Distinction between Civilians and Combatants'. https://ihl-databases.icrc.org/customary-ihl/eng/docs/v1_rul_rule1

International Group of Experts. 2017. *Tallinn Manual 2.0 on the International Law Applicable to Cyber Operations*, Cambridge: Cambridge University Press.

International Law Association. 2016. 'Final Report of the Study Group on Cybersecurity, Terrorism, and International Law', 31 July. http://www.ila-hq.org/en/study-groups/index.cfm/cid/1050

International Maritime Organization (IMO). 2016. 'Interim Guidelines on Maritime Cyber Risk Management', MSC.1/Circ.1526, 1 June. https://www.gard.no/Content/21323229/MSC.1-Circ.1526.pdf

International Police Organization (INTERPOL). 2017. *Cybercrime*. https://www.interpol.int/Crime-areas/Cybercrime/Cybercrime

International Telecommunication Union. 2017a. *Overview of ITU's History*. http://www.itu.int/en/history/Pages/ITUsHistory.aspx

International Telecommunication Union and CISCO. 2016. *Harnessing the Internet of Things for Global Development*. Geneva: International Telecommunication Union.

Kaiser, S. and Aretz, O. 2013. 'Legal Protection of Civil and Military Aviation against Cyber Interference'. In *Peacetime Regime for State Activities in Cyberspace*, edited by K. Ziolkowski, 319–48. Tallinn: NATO Cooperative Cyber Defence Centre of Excellence.

Keohane, R. 1984. *After Hegemony: Cooperation and Discord in the World Political Economy*. Princeton, NJ: Princeton University Press.

Kleijssen, J. 2016. 'Remarks at Technical Meeting of the UN Counter-Terrorism Committee Executive Directorate on Preventing the Exploitation of Information and Communications Technologies for Terrorist Purposes, while Respecting Human Rights and Fundamental Freedoms', 30 November. http://webtv.un.org/meetings-events/watch/session-ii-preventing-the-exploitation-of-information-and-communications-technologies-for-terrorist-purposes-while-respecting-human-rights-and-fundamental-freedoms-30-nov-2016/5229934173001

Kleinwächter, W. 2007. 'The History of Internet Governance'. In *Governing the Internet: Freedom and Regulation in the OSCE*, edited by C. Möller and A. Amouroux, 41–64. Vienna: Organization for Security and Cooperation in Europe.

Knake, R. 2015. 'Quick Reactions to the U.S.-China Cybersecurity Agreement', *Net Politics*, 25 September. http://blogs.cfr.org/cyber/2015/09/25/quick-reactions-to-the-u-s-china-cybersecurity-agreement/

League of Arab States. 2010. 'Arab Convention on Combating Information Technology Offences'. https://www.asianlaws.org/gcld/cyberlawdb/GCC/Arab%20Convention%20on%20Combating%20Information%20Technology%20Offences.pdf

Lee, S. 2016. 'ASEAN Cybersecurity Profile: Finding a Path to a Resilient Regime', Henry M. Jackson School of International Studies, 4 April. https://jsis.washington.edu/news/asean-cybersecurity-profile-finding-path-resilient-regime/

Leiner, B., V.G. Cerf, and D.D. Clark et al. 1997. 'Brief History of the Internet (Internet Society)'. https://www.internetsociety.org/internet/history-internet/brief-history-internet/

Lohr, S. 2016. 'Stepping Up Security for an Internet-of-Things World', *The New York Times*, 17 October: B3.

Mason, R. 2015. 'Xi Jinping State Visit: UK and China Sign Cybersecurity Pact', *The Guardian*, 21 October.

Menn, J. and Finkle, J. 2016. 'Chinese Economic Cyber-Espionage Plummets in U.S.—Experts', *Reuters*, 20 June.

Nakashima, E. 2015a. 'U.S. Developing Sanctions against China over Cyberthefts', *Washington Post*, 30 August.

Nakashima, E. 2015b. 'World's Richest Nations Agree Hacking for Commercial Benefit is Off-Limits', *Washington Post*, 16 November.

National Institute of Standards and Technology. 2014. 'Framework for Improving Critical Infrastructure Cybersecurity (Version 1.0)', 12 February. https://www.nist.gov/system/files/documents/cyberframework/cybersecurity-framework-021214.pdf

Newman, L.H. 2017. 'Security News This Week: A One Stop-Guide to Zero-Day Exploits', *WIRED*, 11 March. https://www.wired.com/2017/03/security-news-week-everything-know-zero-day-exploits/

Nye, J. 2017. 'Will the Liberal Order Survive?', *Foreign Affairs* 96 (1): 10–16.

Office of the US Trade Representative. 2015. *The Trans-Pacific Partnership Agreement—Electronic Commerce*. https://ustr.gov/sites/default/files/TPP-Chapter-Summary-Electronic-Commerce.pdf

Piera, A. and Gill, M. 2014. 'Will the New ICAO-Beijing Instruments Build a Chinese Wall for International Aviation Security?' *Vanderbilt Journal of Transnational Law* 47: 145–237.

Post, D. 2009. *In Search of Jefferson's Moose: Notes on the State of Cyberspace*. Oxford: Oxford University Press.

President's Commission on Enhancing National Cybersecurity. 2016. *Report on Securing and Growing the Digital Economy*. Washington, DC: President's Commission on Enhancing National Cybersecurity.

Schmidt, M. and Sanger, D. 2014. '5 in China Army Face U.S. Charges of Cyberattacks', *The New York Times*, 20 May: A1.

Schmitt, M. 2002. 'Wired Warfare: Computer Network Attack and *Jus in Bello*', *International Review of the Red Cross*, 84 (846): 365–99.

Segal, A. 2016. 'The U.S.-China Cyber Espionage Deal One Year Later', *Net Politics*, 28 September. http://blogs.cfr.org/cyber/2016/09/28/the-u-s-china-cyber-espionage-deal-one-year-later/

Segal, A. 2017. 'Wikileaks and the CIA: What's in Vault7?', *Net Politics*, 8 March. http://blogs.cfr.org/cyber/2017/03/08/wikileaks-and-the-cia-whats-in-vault7/

Shanghai Cooperation Organization. 2009. Agreement on Cooperation in the Field of International Information Security.

Shanker, T. 2011. 'In Blunt Report to Congress, U.S. Report Accuses China and Russia of Internet Spying', *The New York Times*, 4 November: A4.

Strawbridge, J. 2016. 'The Big Bluff: Obama, Cyber Economic Espionage, and the Threat of WTO Litigation', *Georgetown Journal of International Law* 47: 833–65.

UN Group of Governmental Experts. 2013. 'Report of the Group of Governmental Experts on Developments in the Field of Information and Telecommunications in the Context of International Security', UN Doc. A/68/98*, 24 June.

UN Group of Governmental Experts. 2015. 'Report of the Group of Governmental Experts on Developments in the Field of Information and Telecommunications in the Context of International Security', UN Doc. A/70/174, 22 July.

U.S. Department of Commerce. 2017. 'Privacy Shield Overview'. https://www.privacyshield.gov/Program-Overview

von Heinegg, W. 2013. 'Protecting Critical Submarine Cable Infrastructure: Legal Status and Protection of Submarine Communication Cables under International Law'. In *Peacetime Regime for State Activities in Cyberspace*, edited by K. Ziolkowski, 291–318. Tallinn: NATO Cooperative Cyber Defence Centre of Excellence.

Wessel, R. 2015. 'Towards EU Cybersecurity Law: Regulating a New Policy Field'. In *Research Handbook on International Law and Cyberspace*, edited by N. Tsagourias and R. Buchan, 430–25. Cheltenham: Edward Elgar Publishing.

Wu, W. 2015. 'Handshake to End the Hacking: China and Germany Pledge for Peace in Cyberspace by 2016', *South China Morning Post*, 9 November.

CHAPTER 31

GLOBAL TRADE AND CYBERSECURITY: MONITORING, ENFORCEMENT, AND SANCTIONS

FRANZ-STEFAN GADY AND GREG AUSTIN

INTRODUCTION

GLOBAL trade in information and communication technology (ICT) products reached an all-time high of US$3 trillion in 2019. This commerce is, however, tainted by growing concerns over the security and integrity of the exchanged goods because of a proliferation of sophisticated digital security threats, both from non-state and state actors (Office of the United States Trade Representative 2016). These concerns are multiplying as technology advances, not least through the arrival of the Internet of Things—machine-to-machine communication underpinned by billions of networks of sensors and cloud computing. Novel technologies such as this have created, and will continue to create, new vulnerabilities in critical information infrastructures across the globe.

As a consequence, to prop up cyber defences while encouraging the expanding global trade of ICT products, states are increasingly attempting to assert national security controls over their domestic digital economies, especially foreign inputs. As the dependency of the state on ICT products in civilian critical infrastructure and security operations increased, so did the desire to make them more secure via standards, best practices, laws, and new regulations. But a near equal driver has been a reversion to protectionism, an instinct to push toward the indigenization of ICT products to promote the domestic sector. After all, ICTs have become the new foundations of national power, at home, and on the world stage.

This increased securitization and protectionism has produced a number of barriers to international ICT commerce despite the July 2015 extension of the Information Technology Agreement (ITA) to reduce tariffs on ICT goods in the framework of the World Trade

Organization (WTO) (United Nations Conference on Trade and Development 2015). As Neutze and Nicholas (2013) observed: 'Barriers such as unique product requirements or service compliance could cause ICT providers to not participate in certain markets, or stop future developments of certain products because of shrinking markets.'[1] This easing of interest in participation in trade was further accentuated by the Trump administration's hostility towards free trade, its early abandonment of the Trans-Pacific Partnership (TPP) agreement, and suggestions that it might abandon the Transatlantic Trade and Investment Partnership (TTIP). Both these agreements contained e-commerce chapters to bolster the trade of ICTs (Fidler 2016). For its part, China attracted strong critical attention at a WTO meeting in July 2017 for possible barriers to trade in its new measures on encryption and cybersecurity (World Trade Organization 2017). One third of the new concerns about technical barriers to trade raised at this meeting related to high-technology products.

While relatively free from state interference in the 1990s and early 2000s, the global digital economy is now in the grips of an escalating push toward the 'nationalization' both of data and ICT manufacturing, with little regard to just how Quixotic this challenge may be. While unilateral measures may promote a sense of greater national control, they simply cannot address the global proliferation of ICT goods and services that can be appropriated for malicious and offensive purposes in cyberspace. Most states lack proper oversight and enforcement mechanisms. Even where states attempt multilateral export controls, such as through the Wassenaar Arrangement (discussed later), this similar lack of comprehensive monitoring and enforcement instruments remains a major constraint on state power in cyber-related trade.

This chapter reviews the shortcomings of existing international trade regimes both in mitigating the spread of malicious and offensive ICT products and in helping to establish responsible state behaviour in cyberspace. These shortcomings are aggravated by the broader challenge faced by states in universalizing norms, rules, and principles for the responsible behaviour of states in cyberspace, as proposed by the UN Group of Government Experts (GGE) on international security aspects of the trade in ICTs. This chapter also highlight the difficulties of applying trade sanctions to reinforce norms of responsible state behaviour.

The discussion focuses first on the efforts by states to deliver more security in cyberspace by putting up new barriers to international trade in related products (nationalization or indigenization). This is followed by a review of the enforcement regimes to prevent the trade in malicious ICT products or in other sensitive technologies' impacts on cybersecurity. The discussion addresses not just products (i.e. software) but also foundational knowledge (the computer science aspects of cybersecurity). This leads to a review of how the evolving normative regimes for cyberspace, represented by the work of the UN GGE, aggravates or ameliorates the challenges raised in earlier discussion. Discussion of norms requires some attention to be paid to the use of sanctions in ICT trade in response to malicious actions by other states in cyberspace.

The final section of the chapter looks briefly at an even broader question. Because the trade in illicit or sensitive software products is mostly a non-state transaction made somewhat non-transparent by the near instantaneous exchange enabled by the unique medium of cyberspace, the world faces a completely novel problem set. Non-state actors have a new power to trade in illicit or destabilizing software products and even foundational knowledge is beyond the exclusive control of government.

The chapter concludes that rule setting for this trade will be most effective to the extent that its private (non-state) participants are represented in, or can dominate, the crafting of new regimes for it.

The Nationalization Trend and Technology Sovereignty

The so-called 'Year Zero' in the nation state's battle over cyberspace, as the security expert Adam Segal argues, stretched from June 2012 to June 2013. It began with new revelations about the US role in the Stuxnet attack on Iran, the cyberattacks on Saudi Aramco with the Shamoon malware, and ended with the exposure of National Security Agency (NSA) surveillance and espionage programs by the former NSA contractor Edward Snowden. 'It was in 2012 that nation-states around the world visibly reasserted their control over the flow of data and information in search of power, wealth, and influence,' Segal notes (Segal 2016, 1). This reassertion of control was accompanied by a corresponding rise in trade protectionism ostensibly for national security reasons.

Trade protectionism in the name of national security is nothing new. For example, the Chinese multinational networking and telecommunications equipment and services company, Huawei, has been blocked twice (in 2007 and 2010) from acquiring US network-server and switch companies because of national security concerns by the US government (Cendrowski 2017). Australia also excluded the company from bidding on its new national broadband network in 2012 (Hiltzik 2014). But it was the Snowden revelations in particular that fuelled a resurgence of technological nationalism across the globe.

Among other things, in 2014, following the Snowden revelations of US surveillance activities in Germany, the German government cancelled a contract with the US telecommunication firm Verizon, in favour of a German competitor (Reuters 2014). The US tech company Cisco saw loss in market share in Brazil, China, and Russia (Castro and McQuinn 2015). China also removed a number of leading US tech companies from its Central Government Procurement Center's approved state purchase list in 2013, thereby restricting market access. In addition, on 1 June 2017, a stricter cybersecurity law had come into effect in China after almost two years of debate. The new law was designed to tighten state control over digital data and ICTs by mandating, among other things, to store user data in China. It was interpreted as a move by the Chinese government to rid the country of its dependencies on foreign ICTs and to nationalize the country's critical information infrastructure.[2]

European cloud service providers have also used the Snowden disclosures as a marketing ploy to advertise their own services and to push for data protectionism. 'Amid growing anti-U.S. sentiment, Europe has seen calls for data localization requirements, procurement preferences for European providers, and even a "Schengen area for data"—a system that keeps as much data in Europe as possible—as ways to promote deployment of cloud services entirely focused on the European market,' a 2015 study found.[3] The financial losses incurred by US cloud providers in foreign markets due to the Snowden revelations were estimated in excess of $35 billion by 2016.[4] The disclosures of the former NSA contractor also strengthened the so-called 'Brussels effect', which describes the European Union (EU)'s success in externalizing its regulations on other countries, including data protection laws potentially causing market entry barriers for US tech companies across the globe.[5]

At the same time, the past decade has seen a push toward the indigenization of ICT supply chains in an attempt to make ICT products more secure (Charney and Werner 2011). Brazil, the EU, Russia, the United States, China, and India have been particularly strong proponents of indigenous ICT innovation in this new environment.[6] Furthermore, governments have repeatedly pushed for access to source codes in ICT products imported into their domestic market, raising fears of intellectual property (IP) theft (Friedman 2013). The United States and other countries have created best practices in standards and processes, such as those found in the voluntary cybersecurity framework developed by the US National Institute of Standards and Technology (NIST) in collaboration with ICT industry representatives (EastWest Institute 2016). Country-specific standards, however, have become the most prevalent non-tariff barriers to ICT trade.[7]

Given the burgeoning importance of ICT for waging war and protecting internal security, another barrier to ICT trade is the possible invocation of national security exceptions under the General Agreement on Tariffs and Trade (GATT). According to article XXI, 'Nothing in this Agreement shall be construed to require any contracting party to furnish any information the disclosure of which it considers contrary to its essential security interests'.[8] Although invocation of this right has so far been very rare, the ambiguous wording leaves room for wide interpretation, particularly when it comes to the largely uncharted territory of cyber and cyber-enabled conflict. According to one study, article XXI lacks 'proper regulatory structures' and has 'clearly inconsistent and incoherent elements' (Yoo and Ahn 2016). These shortcomings could potentially be exploited by protectionist states seeking to promote their technological sovereignty.

Current International Regimes: Weak Enforcement and Monitoring Mechanisms

In the late 1990s, the issue of export controls on encryption tools and cyber technologies likely to cause harm to states was already a live topic.[9] As trade in ICT expanded in a spirit of free trade and open innovation, and states moved away from Cold War limitations on technology transfer, interest in controls on these tools dropped off. It was soon revived once states began to take up their military and espionage potential more fully, and once states and leading corporations began to appreciate their possible critical infrastructure impacts in a variety of scenarios. The market for malicious software, cyber weapons, hacking tools, and encryption techniques to hide from government has been expanding. After the Year Zero turning point identified by Segal, leading states intensified their focus on trade controls for certain cyber technologies.

For example, discoveries of new zero-day exploits were expected to rise from an average of one per week in 2015 to one per day by 2021—a good indicator for the burgeoning underground trade in this essential component of a sophisticated cyber weapon (Mello 2017). Before looking at enforcement mechanisms, it is worth illustrating the character of the problem with more detail on the trade in zero-days as an example, recalling that this is simply one of more than 20 generic types of cyber knowledge that can be exploited for harm.

Zero-day exploits are valuable commodities traded in the grey, dark, or white markets often facilitated by so-called zero-day brokers, which specialize in buying and selling the exploits to the highest bidder.[10] One example of such a broker in the grey market is the Italian-based company Hacking Team (HT). In 2015, the company itself was hacked and more than 400 gigabytes of the 'company's most sensitive data, including passwords, internal e-mails, exchanges with clients, and 80% of the company's source code, including the zero-day exploits that were in its arsenal', were stolen (Burkart and McCourt 2017).

The leaked data revealed that HT clients comprised law enforcement and security agencies in Egypt, Nigeria, Oman, Lebanon, Bahrain, India, Mexico, Ecuador, Thailand, South Korea, Russia, Italy, Hungary, and Switzerland. According to one report, clients in the United States included the Florida Metropolitan Bureau of Investigation, the Drug Enforcement Administration, and the Federal Bureau of Investigation.[11] Fees ranged from $400,000 to $2.4 million.

The HT case illustrates one of the major problems when it comes to regulating the trade in zero-day exploits. Governments, next to cybercriminals, are the principal customers in the market and are driving demand. And, as a RAND Corporation study indicates, the market is as healthy and vibrant as it is complex (Ablon and Bogart 2017). Thus, it appears highly unlikely that governments would impose stricter legal enforcement mechanisms domestically (e.g. the mandatory disclosures of zero-day exploits), given that it could potentially put national security at risk and shift the zero-day trade to the black market, thereby emboldening cybercriminals (Stockton and Golabe-Goldman 2013).

Given the acceleration of this digital arms race, what other mechanisms are currently in place for states and the international community as a whole to curb the trade in zero-day exploits and to deter their use? Existing multilateral trade treaties, standards agreements, and the role of international organizations have been discussed earlier. This section looks at two particular mechanisms—the Wassennaar Arrangement and the Agreement on Trade-Related Aspects of Intellectual Property Rights (TRIPS)—to illustrate the difficulty of limiting the trade in cyber weapons. The question of enforcement also prompts a discussion of sanctions by states that limit ICT trade as a response to harmful actions by other states in cyberspace.

The Wassenaar Arrangement on Export Controls for Conventional Arms and Dual-Use Goods and Technologies is a non-binding multilateral export control regime with 42 participating states. Parties to the arrangement pledge to enact national policies to better control the export of conventional arms and dual-use goods and technologies recorded in control lists via the issuance or denial of domestic export licences.[12] The arrangement was updated in December 2013 to include intrusion software and network communications surveillance systems, as well as associated software and hardware. The aim of the amendment was to prevent companies from selling surveillance technology to countries with poor human rights records.

However, US companies expressed concern over the broad regulatory language of the amendment, which they claimed would force Microsoft alone to apply for 3,800 export licences per year in order to share exploit code across borders with which to identify and mitigate security vulnerabilities (Reeve 2016). Some of the wording was clarified in December 2016 by the Wassenaar Plenary—the decision-making body for the

Arrangement—but the American government and the US private sector remain dissatisfied (Mulholland and Moussouris 2017). It is likely that this disagreement will be resolved before too long. Nevertheless, other problems with using the Wassenaar Arrangement or any other export control mechanism for cyber weapons will remain, for a number of reasons.

First, states have broad discretion in implementing the arrangement domestically, thus creating potential loopholes for blacklisted countries to obtain ICT. For example, implementing legislation varies between jurisdiction, enforcement agencies in different countries apply different priorities to monitoring and investigation, and multinational private sector actors can adjust their compliance behaviour depending on the jurisdiction. Second, it remains a challenging task to track the flow of code and data across borders. Technical solutions are available although, according to one study, none of these would be 'politically palatable' for Western democracies.[13] Third, significant cyber powers such as China and Iran are not party to the arrangement, although a number of dialogues on dual-use technologies have been held with Beijing over the past few years to align Chinese with Wassenaar export control lists. Fourth, and most importantly, as the study further notes, the arrangement 'is voluntary and lacks strong compliance monitoring and enforcement measures'.

Given that it appears difficult to curb the proliferation of cyber weapons for the foreseeable future via formal regimes for export control, states need to reach into the diplomatic toolbox for less direct methods to mitigate the effects of this unwanted trade rather than prevent it. As Malawer suggests, in the case of Chinese economic cyber espionage, there is a dispute resolution system available to the United States under TRIPS, which came into effect in 1995.[14]

While TRIPS does not specifically address cyber espionage for commercial gain, Malawer argues that it would be applicable to IP theft in cyberspace. He argues that provisions in TRIPS preclude member states from obtaining IP information from foreign firms and then passing it on to domestic companies. He cites the following language from the agreement: 'Each Member shall accord to the nationals of other members treatment no less favourable than that it accords to its own nationals with regard to the protection of intellectual property (. . .)' (Malawer 2015, 4). Malawer concludes that 'a successful action by the United States and compliance by China would be a limited but an important step in tackling the technological advances in cyber espionage and promoting a rules-based system of global governance'.[15]

Other scholars are less convinced that the WTO is a proper venue for pressing US claims against China. Fidler has pointed out that WTO members in the past have shown no interest in addressing economic espionage within the WTO. Their reticence acknowledges the legal difficulty in establishing that cyber espionage for commercial purposes violates existing agreements such as TRIPS. Furthermore, as well as highlighting difficulties in applying international law to commercial cyber espionage, he also cites problems in attributing a cyberattack 'without revealing counter-intelligence means and methods' (Fidler 2013).

While the debate on this subject will most certainly continue, no country has filed such a case against another country under the WTO dispute mechanism, and this appears to confirm Fidler's point. The United States has instead chosen other remedies including diplomatic dialogues, bilateral agreements, the indictment of members of the People's Liberation Army for malicious activities in cyberspace, as well the threat of sanctions, among other things, to cope with alleged Chinese cyberattacks (Gady 2016). It should also be noted that any commercial cyber espionage case under TRIPS would pertain just to WTO members (i.e. states) and cannot address other powerful non-state actors in cyberspace, such as cybercriminals.

As mentioned, states have been unwilling to move to directly limit the trade of zero-day exploits, with some governments preferring to explore a broader approach that does not leave them so exposed that they might be forced to surrender this tool. The broader approach includes rising interest in the imposition of sanctions against the peacetime use of malicious code for offensive purposes in cyberspace. The United States has been in the lead in this regard, and its closest allies appear to be following.

In 2013, a US bipartisan Commission on IP theft made several key conclusions.[16] One of the three items in its terms of reference was to 'document and assess the role of China in international intellectual property theft'. It accepted numerous sources of evidence that China (as a geography) accounted for between 50% and 80% of all theft of American IP. One of its main conclusions was that companies in China that benefit from IP theft are immune from domestic consequences and can only be deterred if they face sanctions in the market place (because the legal system was not delivering the needed results).

In May 2014, the United States Justice Department brought criminal charges against five Chinese military personnel for commercial espionage. At the same time, the Administration introduced very mild sanctions (import restrictions) by prohibiting the purchase by four US government agencies of computer or network equipment and services produced by entities owned , or controlled, by entities from China. In January 2015, the United States imposed sanctions on three North Korean organizations and 10 individuals in response to a cyberattack against Sony Pictures Entertainment (BBC News 2015). It is likely that, at that time, the United States also retaliated covertly in cyberspace against North Korea. On 1 April 2015, President Barack Obama issued an Executive Order establishing the first-ever economic sanctions regime in response to cyberattacks.[17] The order was in response to an increasing number of attacks from outside the country that threatened its national security or economic prosperity. One of the targets of the new sanctions order, though not named specifically, was Chinese state-sponsored commercial espionage aimed at stealing US trade secrets and proprietary technology. On 28 December 2016, Obama issued a new order updating the previous one, this time specifically targeting Russian hackers and organizations involved in providing material support to the hackers who had interfered in the US presidential election.[18] As a result of the US belief that the Russian government had directly initiated the hacking attacks, two of the organizations added to the sanctions list included the Federal Security Service and the Main Intelligence Directorate of the Russian General Staff. On 19 June 2017, the EU announced its intention to use a range of diplomatic measures, including sanctions ('restrictive measures') to retaliate for malicious cyber activities (European Council 2017).

As with economic sanctions in general, those associated with retaliation for cyberattacks may have a largely symbolic effect, as a demonstration of the imposing state's anger, rather than directly influencing the target state's behaviour. For example, the 2014 sanctions affecting the procurement of Chinese products by a small number of US government departments were never fully implemented: a result of the bilateral agreement at head of state level in September 2015 that neither country would undertake commercial cyber espionage. In this case, it might be concluded that the threat of sanctions in and of itself would not have weighed as heavily with the Chinese leaders as the threat from related activity of a breach in the technology transfer and investment relationship between the two countries.

However, it is almost impossible to determine the causal relationship between the threat of sanctions and a reduction in Chinese cyberattacks (FireEye 2016). This first set of cyber-related sanctions appears to have had little impact.

In the North Korea case, it seems that the Kim regime is continuing its cyberattacks (and missile launches) despite US sanctions, if its reported involvement in a global ransomware attack that occurred in 2017 is any indication (Perlroth 2017).

In the Russia case, because of the deterioration in its relations with the United States after the annexation of Crimea and support for armed insurgency in eastern Ukraine, sanctions imposed by the Obama administration in 2016 in response to hacking of the election and renewed by Congress in July 2017 have had an explosive diplomatic effect but have probably not dented Russian enthusiasm for continuing cyber harassment.

As far as non-state actors are concerned, in spite of occasional convictions for cybercrime, there have been few legal actions against individuals involved in trade in ICT products, such as malware (as opposed to stolen IP). In 2014, the US government revived its penalties for unauthorized export of encryption technology when it fined a subsidiary of Intel $750,000 in retaliation for export deals worth just over $2 million to 'governments and various end users in China, Hong Kong, Russia, Israel, South Africa, and South Korea' (Bureau of Industry and Security 2014).

CAN THE UN GGE NORMS HELP?

Given weak existing regimes and the apparent inability to control and monitor the trade in sensitive ICT, an argument could be made for a bottom-up, joint public-private approach centred around voluntary norms. The July 2015 report of the UN GGE on Developments in the Field of Information and Telecommunications in the Context of International Security gave a strong lead for new international commitments to make ICT more secure. This included provisions for the strengthening of global ICT supply chains. Given that exclusionary trade regimes such as the Wassenaar Arrangement will not suffice in mitigating the proliferation of cyber weapons, universalizing the proposed voluntary GGE norms into binding commitments may be one option. It is of considerable significance that the EU document supporting the June 2017 decision on sanctions, and other diplomatic tools to constrain malicious cyber activity, cited the GGE proposed norm to the effect that 'states should not knowingly allow their territory to be used for internationally wrongful acts using ICTs'.[19]

Section III of the July 2015 GGE report set out 'Norms, rules and principles for the responsible behaviour of States': voluntary, non-binding norms or principles for a more stable ICT environment.[20] Of particular relevance for international ICT trade, the document also includes the following recommendation: 'States should take reasonable steps to ensure the integrity of the supply chain so that end users can have confidence in the security of ICT products. States should seek to prevent the proliferation of malicious ICT tools and techniques and the use of harmful hidden functions'.[21] This norm is a restatement of a principle in international law that is already binding on states: the principle that states have an obligation not to permit activities on their territory that cause harm in the territories of other states. In the specific case of ICT supply chain security, it would mean that states cannot knowingly permit the insertion of firmware or malware into ICT products that will cause damage in the territory of another state.

However, there are several problems in using the GGE norms to help reduce the trade in compromised and malicious ICT. First, enforcement of this obligation by nation states has proven technically difficult, especially when dealing with sophisticated state-sponsored actors intent on such action. Second, it could be argued that the UN GGE is diluting a general principle of state responsibility by giving states some leeway to avoid the pre-existing (but only assumed) generalized obligation under international law. This pre-existing principle is that, if one state notifies another of harm against it coming from the territory of the second state, the latter has a responsibility to attempt to bring that harm to an end. The voluntary GGE norm is about states exercising due diligence rather than being responsible to prevent an undesirable outcome. Third, the language in the GGE report is unclear. For example, the norm talks about 'due diligence' and that states 'should take reasonable steps', but the GGE provides no clarity on what reasonable steps are. Furthermore, it is unclear what the GGE means by 'harmful hidden functions': does malware that simply exfiltrates information for cyber espionage purposes cause harm, even when international law does not regulate espionage in any serious way? Or, does harm include inserting a 'logic bomb' that does nothing unless activated?

Nevertheless, the GGE voluntary norm may still be useful. It has taken a general principle of international law and elaborated a new normative set of circumstances with potentially more binding force and more practical implications than the general principle. There are precedents for this. For example, the 2010 Beijing Treaty on aircraft hijacking requires states to criminalize certain forms of terrorist activity, including electronic or cyberattack, on their territory because it affects civil aviation, even though there are already obligations based on principle and arguably on norms to prevent (and arguably criminalize) terrorism or attacks on civil aviation. The current norms of the law of state responsibility are mainly post facto: they relate to 'when an international obligation is breached, the consequences that flow from a breach, and who is able to invoke those consequences (and how)' (Borelli 2020). So the GGE norm is imposing an additional preventive obligation, as does the 2010 Beijing Treaty on hijacking. According to this logic, the idea of a norm on supply chain integrity would be a significant innovation in international law.

PRIVATE SECTOR ROLE IN GLOBAL REGIMES FOR CONTROLLING SOFTWARE TRADE

As mentioned several times earlier, states are not alone in global ICT commerce. In fact, states might be seen as relative bystanders compared with the engaged interests of the private sector. It is this reality that has allowed Microsoft and other global corporations to take a leading role in the evolution of international regimes for regulating trade in malicious or potentially dangerous cyber products. It has been ever thus, with the regime complex for cyber activities articulated by Joseph Nye in 2014 demonstrating the accumulated weight of commercial interests over decades of work in various technical forums, such as the International Telecommunication Union (Nye 2014).

By 2010, when corporations like Microsoft, AT&T, Huawei, Goldman Sachs, and Deloitte threw their support behind the EastWest Institute's new global cybersecurity initiative, and in 2011 when leading corporations joined the London Process (Global Conference on Cyberspace), the pathway for corporate sector leadership in the regulation of trade in harmful cyber products had been firmly established. By 2016, when Microsoft released its white paper on this topic, specific and concrete actions became available to guide states and other actors (Charney, English, and Kleiner et al. 2016).

The list of proposed private sector norms was lengthy and was compared with proposed intergovernmental norms (Table 31.1)[22] :

In addition to these specific recommendations, there was a new principle afoot in the global ICT sector that had been missing until the Snowden revelations revealed the depth of private sector collusion with governments in cyberspace. Corporations found themselves repudiating hitherto 'patriotic' activities. The new principle was articulated by the Microsoft authors as follows: 'Industry cannot participate in offensive activities and help one customer attack another. This would undermine cyberspace itself and erode the very foundations of the global economy.'[23]

The global collaborative response to the WannaCry ransomware attack showed that these sorts of proposals are beginning to acquire traction. While the attack was based on the Eternal Blue vulnerability discovered by the US NSA and leaked by Russian hackers, Microsoft had moved to patch the vulnerability in March 2017. While hundreds of thousands of users around the world were affected, governments and the private sector from many countries showed a highly cooperative attitude. This can be seen in two reports on the Interpol website (Interpol 2017a, 2017b).

CONCLUSION: THE FUTURE OF MALICIOUS ICT TRADE

Criminals and states will continue to trade in malicious ICT products. As the cyber arms race between leading powers escalates and as cyber knowledge becomes distributed even more widely than it is today, trade in cyber weapons will proliferate, rather than be constrained. In some parts of the world, civil society activists and criminals (including terrorists) alike, will fight to preserve their access to encryption and other cyber tools. In this environment, collaborative resilience approaches (mutual support) among parties affected by serious cyberattacks will be essential, as Microsoft and the GGE have suggested. Such collaboration will be hampered by each new cyber campaign by states on each other, as is the case for now between Russia and the United States. There is, however, an international consensus emerging that states, corporations, and citizens (regardless of political systems and ideologies) have high stakes in the fundamental order in cyberspace. There is equal recognition by states that a growing class of scientific researchers and activist developers will be quick to circumvent collaborative interstate action and create novel dark spaces as quickly as governments open up the old ones.

Table 31.1 Microsoft's Proposed Norms

Desired impacts of Microsoft's proposed norms	Cybersecurity norms proposed by Microsoft for nation-states	Cybersecurity norms proposed by Microsoft for the global information and communication technology (ICT) industry
Maintain trust	States should not target global ICT companies to insert vulnerabilities (backdoors) or take actions that would otherwise undermine public trust in products and services.	Global ICT companies should not permit or enable nation-states to adversely impact the security of commercial, mass- market ICT products and services.
Coordinated approach to vulnerability handling	States should have a clear, principle- based policy for handling product and service vulnerabilities that reflects a strong mandate to report them to vendors rather than to stockpile, buy, sell, or exploit them.	Global ICT companies should adhere to coordinated disclosure practices for handling of ICT product and service vulnerabilities.
Stop proliferation of vulnerabilities	States should exercise restraint in developing cyber weapons and should ensure that any which are developed are limited, precise, and not reusable.	Global ICT companies should collaborate to proactively defend against nation- state attacks and to remediate the impact of such attacks.
Mitigate the impact of nation-state attacks	States should commit to non-proliferation activities related to cyber weapons.	Global ICT companies should not traffic in cyber vulnerabilities for offensive purposes, nor should ICT companies embrace business models that involve proliferation of cyber vulnerabilities for offensive purposes.
Prevent mass events	States should limit their engagement in cyber offensive operations to avoid creating a mass event.	No corresponding norm for the global ICT industry.
Support response efforts	States should assist private sector efforts to detect, contain, respond to, and recover from events in cyberspace.	Global ICT companies should assist public sector efforts to identify, prevent, detect, respond to, and recover from events in cyberspace.
Patch customers globally	No corresponding norm for nation- states.	ICT companies should issue patches to protect ICT users, regardless of the attacker and their motives.

Notes

1. Neutze, J. and J. Paul Nicholas. 2013. 'Cyber Insecurity: Competition, Conflict, and Innovation Demand Effective Cyber Security Norms', *Georgetown Journal of International Affairs*. 23 December 2013: https://www.georgetownjournalofinternationalaffairs.org/

online-edition/international-engagement-on-cyber-iii-state-building-on-a-new-frontier-2013

2. 'We've heard from companies that they feel these policies cite national security for protectionist purposes,' according to Jake Parker, Vice President, U.S.-China Business Council. Chin, Josh, and Eva Dou. 2017. 'China's New Cybersecurity Law Rattles Foreign Tech Firms', *The Wall Street Journal*, 7 November: https://www.wsj.com/articles/china-approves-cybersecurity-law-1478491064

3. Castro and McQuinn, 'Beyond the USA Freedom Act?

4. Castro and McQuinn, 'Beyond the USA Freedom Act?'

5. Gady, 2016: 16.

6. Neutze and Nicholas, 'Cyber Insecurity', 8.

7. Friedman, 'Cybersecurity and Trade?'

8. World Trade Organization, 'Article XXI Security Exceptions': https://www.wto.org/english/res_e/booksp_e/gatt_ai_e/art21_e.pdf

9. See, for example, Evans, Charles. L., 'US Export Control of Encryption Software: Efforts to Protect National Security Threaten the US Software Industry's Ability to Compete in Foreign Markets', *North Carolina Journal of International and Commercial Regulation* 19 (3): 469–90.

10. For a precise definition of black, gray, and white markets see: Fidler, Mailyn, 2014. 'Anarchy or Regulation: Controlling The Global Trade in Zero-Day Vulnerabilities', Doctoral dissertation, Master thesis. Stanford University, April, p. 5

11. Burkart and McCourt, 'International Political Economy'.

12. The Wassenaar Arrangement on Export Controls for Conventional Arms and Dual-Use Goods and Technologies: http://www.wassenaar.org/

13. Stockton and Golabek-Goldman, 'Curbing the Market for Cyber Weapons'.

14. World Trade Organization, 'Agreement on Trade-Related Aspects of Intellectual Property Rights': https://www.wto.org/english/tratop_e/trips_e/t_agm0_e.htm

15. Malawer, 'Chinese Economic Cyber Espionage'.

16. *Report of the Commission on the Theft of American Intellectual Property*, May 2013.

17. The White House. Executive Order 13694 of April 1, 2015. Blocking the Property of Certain Persons Engaging in Significant Malicious Cyber-Enabled Activities: https://www.treasury.gov/resource-center/sanctions/Programs/Documents/cyber_eo.pdf

18. The White House. Executive Order 13757 of December 28, 2016. Taking Additional Steps to Address the National Emergency with Respect to Significant Malicious Cyber-Enabled Activities: https://www.treasury.gov/resource-center/sanctions/Programs/Documents/cyber2_eo.pdf

19. Council of the European Union, Draft Council Conclusions on a Framework for a Joint EU Diplomatic Response to Malicious Cyber Activities ('Cyber Diplomacy Toolbox'), 9916/17, CYBER 91, RELEX 482, POLMIL 58, CFSP/PESC 476, 7 June 2017, http://data.consilium.europa.eu/doc/document/ST-9916-2017-INIT/en/pdf

20. United Nations General Assembly. 2015. 'Report of the Group of Governmental Experts on Developments in the Field of Information and Telecommunications in the Context of International Security', 22 July: http://www.un.org/ga/search/view_doc.asp?symbol=A/70/174.

21. United Nations General Assembly. 2015. 'Report of the Group of Governmental Experts on Developments in the Field of Information and Telecommunications in the Context of International Security', 22 July: http://www.un.org/ga/search/view_doc.asp?symbol=A/70/174.

22. Charney et al., 'From Articulation to Implementation', 7. Used with permission of the authors.
23. Charney et al., 'From Articulation to Implementation', 13.

REFERENCES

Ablon, Lillian, and Timothy Bogart. 2017. *Zero Days, Thousands of Nights: The Life and Times of Zero-Day Vulnerabilities and Their Exploits*. Santa Monica, CA: RAND Corporation, March. https://www.rand.org/pubs/research_reports/RR1751

BBC News. 2015. 'Sony Cyber-Attack: North Korea Faces New US Sanctions', 3 January: http://www.bbc.com/news/world-us-canada-30661973

Borelli, Silvia. 2020. 'State Responsibility in International Law'. In *Oxford Bibliographies in International Law*, http://www.oxfordbibliographies.com/view/document/obo-9780199796953/obo-9780199796953-0031.xml.

Bureau of Industry and Security. 2014. 'Intel Subsidiary Agrees to $750,000 Penalty for Unauthorized Encryption Exports', 8 October, https://www.bis.doc.gov/index.php/about-bis/newsroom/press-releases/107-about-bis/newsroom/press-releases/press-release-2014/763-intel-subsidiary-agrees-to-750-000-penalty-for-unauthorized-encryption-exports.

Burkart, Patrick, and Tom McCourt. 2017) 'The International Political Economy of the Hack: A Closer Look at Markets for Cybersecurity Software', *Popular Communication* 15(1): 37–54, January: http://dx.doi.org/10.1080/15405702.2016.1269910

Castro, Daniel, and Alan McQuinn 2015. 'Beyond the USA Freedom Act: How U.S. Surveillance Still Subverts U.S. Competitiveness', *Information Technology & Innovation Foundation*, June. http://www2.itif.org/2015-beyond-usa-freedom-act.pdf

Cendrowski, Scott. 2017. 'Is the World Big Enough For Huawei?', *Fortune*, 24 January: http://fortune.com/huawei-china-smartphone

Charney, Scott, and Eric T. Werner. 2011. 'Cyber Supply Chain Risk Management: Toward a Global Vision of Transparency and Trust', Microsoft, 26 July. https://query.prod.cms.rt.microsoft.com/cms/api/am/binary/REXXtT

Charney, Scott et al. 2016. 'From Articulation to Implementation: Enabling progress on cybersecurity norms', Microsoft: https://mscorpmedia.azureedge.net/mscorpmedia/2016/06/Microsoft-Cybersecurity-Norms_vFinal.pdf

EastWest Institute. 2016. 'Purchasing Secure ICT Products and Services: A Buyers Guide', 11. https://www.eastwest.ngo/sites/default/files/EWI_BuyersGuide.pdf

European Council Press Release 357/17, 'Cyber attacks: EU Ready to Respond with a Range of Measures, Including Sanctions', 19 June 2017, http://www.consilium.europa.eu/en/press/press-releases/2017/06/19-cyber-diplomacy-toolbox/?utm_source=dsms-auto&utm_medium=email&utm_campaign=Cyber+attacks%3a+EU+ready+to+respond+with+a+range+of+measures%2c+including+sanctions.

Fidler, David P. 2013. 'Economic Cyber Espionage and International Law: Controversies Involving Government Acquisition of Trade Secrets through Cyber Technologies', *American Society of International Law Insights* 17 (10) March: https://www.asil.org/insights/volume/17/issue/10/economic-cyber-espionage-and-international-law-controversies-involving

Fidler David. 2016. 'What a Trump Administration Means for U.S. Digital Trade', Council on Foreign Relations Blog, 15 November: http://blogs.cfr.org/cyber/2016/11/15/what-a-trump-administration-means-for-u-s-digital-trade-policy/

FireEye, 'Special Report: Redline Drawn: China Recalculates its Use of Cyber Espionage', June 2016: https://www.fireeye.com/content/dam/fireeye-www/current-threats/pdfs/rpt-china-espionage.pdf

Friedman, Allan A. 2013. 'Cybersecurity and Trade: National Policies and Local Consequences', Center for Technology Innovation at Brookings, September. https://www.brookings.edu/wp-content/uploads/2016/06/BrookingsCybersecurityNEW.pdf.

Fidler David P. 2013. 'Economic Cyber Espionage and International Law: Controversies Involving Government Acquisition of Trade Secrets through Cyber Technologies', *American Society of International Law Insights*, 17 (10), March: https://www.asil.org/insights/volume/17/issue/10/economic-cyber-espionage-and-international-law-controversies-involving.

Gady, Franz-Stefan. 2016. 'Are Chinese Cyberattacks Against US Targets in Decline?', *The Diplomat*, 22 June: http://thediplomat.com/2016/06/are-chinese-cyberattacks-against-us-targets-in-decline/

Hiltzik, Michael. 2014. 'Suspicions Keep Chinese Telecom Firm Huawei out of U.S. Market', *Los Angeles Times*, 4 December: https://www.latimes.com/business/hiltzik/la-fi-hiltzik-20141207-column.html

Interpol 2017a. 'INTERPOL Coordinating Global Law Enforcement Response to WannaCry Ransomware Attack', 19 May; https://www.interpol.int/News-and-media/News/2017/N2017-067

Interpol. 2017b. 'INTERPOL Gathers Cyber Experts to Assess Global Response to WannaCry Attack', 7 June. https://www.interpol.int/News-and-media/News/2017/N2017-072

Malawer, Stuart S. 2015. 'Chinese Economic Cyber Espionage', *Georgetown Journal of International Affairs*, Fall: http://www.globaltraderelations.net/images/Malawer.China_Cyber_Economic_Espionage_Lead_Article_Georgetown_Int_l_Affairs_J._June_2015_.pdf.

Mello Jr., John P. 2017. 'Bad Code and Black Hats Will Boost Zero-Day Attacks in 2017', *Cybersecurity Ventures*, 3 January. http://cybersecurityventures.com/zero-day-vulnerabilities-attacks-exploits-report-2017/.

Mulholland, Iain, and Katie Moussouris. 2017. 'Administration Should Continue to Seek Changes to International Cyber Export Controls', *The Hill*, 31 January. http://thehill.com/blogs/congress-blog/technology/316978-administration-should-continue-to-seek-changes-to

Nye Jr. Joseph S. 2014. 'The Regime Complex for Managing Global Cyber Activities', Belfer Center for Science and International Affairs, Harvard, p, 7, http://belfercenter.hks.harvard.edu/files/global-cyber-final-web.pdf

Office of the United States Trade Representative. 2016. 'U.S. and WTO Partners Begin Implementation of the Expansion of the Information Technology Agreement' July. https://ustr.gov/about-us/policy-offices/press-office/press-releases/2016/july/us-and-wto-partners-begin#.

Perlroth, Nicole. 2017. 'More Evidence Points to North Korea in Ransomware Attack', *The New York Times*, 22 May: https://www.nytimes.com/2017/05/22/technology/north-korea-ransomware-attack.html?mcubz=2&_r=0

Reeve, Tom. 2016. 'Wassenaar Arrangement "Inhibits International Cybersecurity Efforts"', *SC Magazine UK*, 21 July: https://www.scmagazineuk.com/wassenaar-arrangement-inhibits-international-cyber-security-efforts/article/530845/

Reuters, 'German Government Cancels Verizon Contract in Wake of U.S. Spying Row', 26 June 2014: http://www.reuters.com/article/us-germany-security-verizon-idUSKBN0F11WJ20140626

Segal, Adam. 2016. *The Hacked World Order: How Nations Fight, Trade, Maneuver, and Manipulate in the Digital Age*. Philadelphia, PA: PublicAffairs.

Stockton, Paul N., and Michele Golabek-Goldman. 2013. 'Curbing the Market for Cyber Weapons', *Yale Law & Policy Review*, 32 (1): http://digitalcommons.law.yale.edu/ylpr/vol32/iss1/11/

United Nations Conference on Trade and Development, 2015. 'Trade in ICT Goods and the 2015 Expansion of the WTO Information Technology Agreement', December: http://unctad.org/en/PublicationsLibrary/tn_unctad_ict4d05_en.pdf

World Trade Organization. 2017. 'Members Debate Cyber Security and Chemicals at Technical Barriers to Trade Committee', 14–15 June, https://www.wto.org/english/news_e/news17_e/tbt_20jun17_e.htm

Yoo Ji Yeong, and Dukgeun Ahn. 2016. 'Security Exceptions in the WTO System: Bridge or Bottle-Neck for Trade and Security?', *Journal of International Economic Law* 19 (2), June. https://academic.oup.com/jiel/article/19/2/417/2358168/Security-Exceptions-in-the-WTO-System-Bridge-or

PART IX

INTERNATIONAL CYBERSECURITY

CHAPTER 32

SEMI-FORMAL DIPLOMACY: TRACK 1.5 AND TRACK 2

NIGEL INKSTER

DIPLOMACY between states has existed as long as states themselves and has become a highly formalized process with internationally agreed rules—the 1961 Vienna Convention on Diplomatic Relations[1]—determining the basis on which diplomatic relations between states should be conducted. For much of recorded history, formal diplomacy has been conducted primarily on a bilateral basis but the establishment in the twentieth century of first the League of Nations and then the United Nations inaugurated a period of significant growth in institutionalized multilateral diplomacy at both a global and regional level. Formal diplomacy, often referred to as 'Track 1' to distinguish it from less formal mechanisms addressed later, has some clear and well-understood strengths that are particularly relevant in situations where states are in, or at risk of being in, conflict. These include the ability of states to exercise political power including the threat of the use of force; the capacity to access material and financial resources that provide leverage and flexibility in negotiations; the ability to deploy in-depth knowledge derived from national intelligence assets; the ability of diplomatic negotiators to draw on broad knowledge of their own states' foreign policies and those of the states with which they are negotiating.

State power can, however, serve as a barrier to negotiating success if it seeks to override the vulnerabilities of other states. Diplomatic missions are vulnerable to closure during periods of conflict between states, thus reducing communication and understanding in times of greatest need, and diplomats cannot speak against or engage in actions seen as potentially undermining the interests of the state they represent, thereby limiting their flexibility (Mapendere 2006). A further consideration in a world of ever greater public expectations of transparent government is that formal diplomatic engagements generate media expectations that may well lead diplomatic negotiators to adopt more hard-line positions than they otherwise might out of a perceived need to accommodate the expectations of domestic constituencies.

But, as politics became more participatory during the late nineteenth and early twentieth centuries, formal Track 1 diplomatic processes have been progressively supplemented by less formal processes referred to as 'public diplomacy' and 'Track 2' and 'Track 1.5'. The concept of public diplomacy began to emerge, articulated first by Woodrow Wilson, during and after World War 1, and was given conceptual definition in 1965 by Edmund Gullion, Dean of the Fletcher School of Law and Diplomacy at Tufts University (Cull 2006). The definition of public diplomacy has shifted substantially from the original Wilsonian connotation of diplomacy openly conducted towards the current concept in which governments seek to bypass political elites and communicate directly with populations. Such public diplomacy has evolved to a point where no self-respecting diplomat can be without a presence on social media. Western governments have for many years devoted significant resources to promoting their values and systems around the world and, in recent years, states in which the news is tightly controlled by the government, such as Russia and China, have begun to invest more in promoting their systems and values overseas, including through purchasing interests in Western news media and establishing broadcast and print media operations targeted at Western audiences. More recently, the Russian Federation has stated in its 2016 Foreign Policy Concept that 'promoting dialogue between Russia's academics and experts and foreign specialists on global politics and international security is one of the areas of public diplomacy[2]—in other words, linking public and Track 2 diplomacy (see later).

More directly germane to conflict-related transactional diplomacy are the concepts of Track 2 and Track 1.5 diplomacy. The concept of Track 2 diplomacy was first articulated in 1981 by US diplomat Joseph Montville and psychiatrist William Davidson in an article in *Foreign Affairs*. Montville and Davidson were writing during the height of the Cold War, an era of high strategic danger and instability during which contact of any sort between the United States and the Soviet Union was severely constrained. This translated into high levels of mutual suspicion and a propensity for these nuclear-armed adversaries to make worst-case assumptions about each other's capabilities and intentions—as evidenced by the conviction holding sway in the Soviet Politburo in the early 1980s that the United States was planning a nuclear first strike (Fischer 1997).

The concept underpinning the article was that of 'esteem needs' defined as a deep-rooted human instinct for affirmation and respect, which, if denied, can give rise to violent responses and conflict. Although the article was written against the backcloth of the Cold War, the principal examples cited involved the Israel–Palestine conflict and Cyprus, both of which seemed to epitomize the problems of respect or lack thereof. The authors expressed the hope that, by building a psychological dimension into diplomacy, the problems arising from unfulfilled esteem needs could be mitigated, thereby creating an enabling environment for conventional diplomacy. As they put it, 'Track 2 has as its objective the reduction or resolution of conflict, within a country or between countries, by lowering the anger or tension or fear that exists, through improved communications and a better understanding of each other's point of view.' (Davidson and Montville 1981–82). The authors characterized Track 2 diplomacy as 'always open-minded, often altruistic and strategically optimistic',[3] based on a belief that conflicts could be resolved. But they warned against a propensity by liberal intellectuals to believe that Track 2 could be seen as an alternative to conventional diplomacy. An approach based solely on Track 2 risked sending overly conciliatory messages to an adversary, suggesting that the other side was unwilling robustly to fight its corner and was hence potentially vulnerable. Track 2 diplomacy and conventional diplomacy needed to operate in tandem.

Track 2 diplomacy consists of a broad spectrum of activities ranging from academic conferences designed to address specific conflict-related diplomatic issues to much more generic people-to-people contacts designed to create a climate of greater mutual understanding, an example of the latter being the 'ping pong diplomacy' that preceded the Nixon administration's rapprochement with China in 1972. The impact of such activities can be difficult if not impossible to measure and Track 2 activities can often give rise to controversy. Some of the best-known examples of Track 2 diplomatic activity—though they were not so categorized at their inception—are the Pugwash Conferences on Science and World Affairs established in 1957 by Canadian philanthropist Cyrus Eaton to bring together scientists from around the world with the aim of 'the elimination of all weapons of mass destruction and of war as a social institution to settle international disputes'[4]. Through a series of private conferences and related research initiatives, Pugwash provided intellectual inputs during the Cold War to a succession of international arms control treaties, such as the Partial Test Ban Treaty, the Non-Proliferation Treaty, the Anti-Ballistic Missile Treaty, and the Biological Weapons Convention. But it also generated controversy, being seen in the West as a vehicle for the promotion of Soviet views and propaganda.[5] Pugwash exemplifies some of the strengths of Track 2 diplomacy: participants are not bound by any political constraints including electoral cycles, and they can express themselves freely and explore ideas and options that an official dialogue could not accommodate. By the same token, participants in Track 2 exercises may have influence with policymakers but do not by definition have the capacity to exercise power. At worst, Track 2 fora can lack credibility if they are seen as nothing more than talking shops or exercises in displacement activity.

A further—and arguably more effective—form of informal diplomacy is Track 1.5, which in effect seeks to split the difference between Track 1 and Track 2 processes. The origins of Track 1.5 are not clear but the concept seems to have emerged in the 1990s in the context of efforts to resolve post-Cold War unfrozen conflicts such as Abkhazia and Transdniestria. The US scholar A.S. Nan has defined Track 1.5 diplomacy as 'diplomatic initiatives that are facilitated by unofficial bodies, but directly involve officials from the conflict in question' (Nan 2005). The unofficial bodies will typically be either a philanthropic foundation or a think tank. Track 1.5 diplomacy seeks to leverage the strengths of both Track 1 and Track 2 diplomacy. The intermediary institutions that typically take the lead in orchestrating this form of diplomacy tend to enjoy a high level of trust on the part of their respective governments, which may well provide the financial and other resources required to enable such activities to take place. The intermediary organization is able to exercise its role precisely because it is familiar with the thinking of the governments concerned and has the requisite expertise on the issues to be addressed. Because it is not a formal party to a dispute, it can offer ideas and pursue lines of research that officials themselves could not, and it can serve as a lightning conductor by absorbing the blame if such initiatives are poorly received, enabling official participants to regroup and continue conversing with no damage having been done. Track 1.5 diplomacy can also be as discreet or as public as the parties involved see fit, which offers scope for greater flexibility. As with Track 2 diplomacy, impact can be hard to measure but one possible metric is the degree to which discussion initiated in Track 1.5 environment can become part of a Track 1 agenda.

Informal Diplomacy in the Cyber Domain

The early evolution of the cyber domain was not at first seen as something that required diplomacy of either a formal or an informal kind. The Internet was seen by many of its pioneers as a phenomenon that transcended and threatened to make redundant the traditional constraints of a bordered Westphalian world. This outlook was famously articulated by John Perry Barlow in Davos in 1996: 'Governments of the Industrial World, you weary giants of flesh and steel, I come from Cyberspace, the new home of Mind. I ask you of the past to leave us alone. You are not welcome among us. You have no sovereignty where we gather' (Barlow 1996). And even if US and other Western politicians eschewed such loftily expressed visions of cyber utopianism, the roll-out of the Internet, coinciding as it did with first the dissolution of the Warsaw Pact and then of the Soviet Union, seemed emblematic of an age in which ideological, political, and cultural divisions appeared redundant—as US historian Francis Fukuyama put it in a book with that title, *The End of History*.

If not cyber utopianism, then at the very least a spirit of cyber optimism informed the evolution of early arrangements for global cyber governance known as the multi-stakeholder model. This comprised a series of informal and quintessentially democratic collaborations between scientists and engineers, other interested stakeholders and the major—at that point almost exclusively US-based—technology companies to develop work on technical standards and interoperability. Implicit in such activities was a belief in a free open Internet with minimal constraints on information flows, a belief that broadly accorded with the views of the US government and its Western allies. Examples of the kind of organization that emerged under this dispensation are the Internet Society, a US-based not-for-profit organization whose purpose is 'to promote the open development, evolution and use of the Internet for the benefit of all people throughout the world', and the Internet Engineering Task Force, an informal body set up to promote voluntary Internet technical standards in particular relating to the Internet Protocol (IP) suite. This latter body, participation in which is open to all with the requisite technical qualifications, began under the aegis of the US government but now operates under the direction of the Internet Society.

But, while the United States and its allies were broadly content with the way in which the Internet was evolving, many other states, while seeing no alternative to adopting a technology that so obviously conferred major economic benefit, saw the phenomenon as politically disempowering and socially destabilizing. This was particularly true for authoritarian states whose instinct had always been to exercise tight control over their own information space, and to monitor and filter the information their populations were able to access. Such states were also acutely aware of the national security vulnerabilities implicit in dependence on technologies designed, manufactured, owned, and operated by companies based in the United States—an apprehension that crystallized in 2013 following the revelations by rogue National Security Agency (NSA) contractor Edward Snowden about the purported extent of NSA penetration of foreign communications networks (Harding 2014).

As Internet use became more pervasive and the related technologies ever more sophisticated, the Westphalian system sought to reassert itself. There was a growing recognition that, while the Internet was advertised as a borderless phenomenon, the infrastructure that comprised it was located within sovereign jurisdictions that not only had the possibility of policing it but also in some respects an obligation to do so, if only to ensure uninterrupted global functionality. International diplomatic discussions began about issues of global cyber governance and global cybersecurity although during the pre-Snowden period the United States, secure in the possession of a massive first-mover advantage, had little interest in such exercises beyond the preservation of the status quo. The issue that has dominated international discussion of global cyber governance has been the question of what role national governments should play relative to other stakeholders with a number of states, led first by Russia and then China, arguing for global cyber governance to become the preserve of the United Nations and with a preponderant role for national governments.[6]

One issue that has been at the centre of this debate has been the Domain Name System (DNS), the Internet's global address book that converts IP addresses—long streams of digits that enable computers to communicate with each other—into more easily memorable Internet addresses such as www.usa.gov. The fact that this system has been under the de facto control of the US government since its inception in 1983 has given rise to widespread dissatisfaction, in particular within states that fear that not having control over their top-level country domain names—.usa, .ru, .cn—makes them vulnerable to the risk of being cut off from the Internet. These states have accordingly pursued efforts to wrest ICANN from US government control. In 2016, the contract between ICANN and the US Department of Commerce lapsed and was replaced by a service-level agreement (SLA) between ICANN and the five regional Internet registries with the SLA overseen by a review committee. Other notable—and to date unsuccessful—efforts to erode US dominance of global cyber governance included the 2012 World Conference on International Telecommunications in Dubai, in which a greater role in Internet governance was sought for the International Telecommunication Union (ITU),[7] and the 2014 NetMundial conference organized by Brazil in the wake of the Snowden revelations.

The other key issue that has preoccupied diplomats has been the issue of global cybersecurity. Russia fired the starting-gun for this process with a letter from the then-foreign minister Igor Ivanov to the United Nations secretary-general in 1998 condemning the creation of 'information weapons' and warning of the threat of information war. The letter proposed that the topic of international information security be substantively discussed at the United Nations.[8] As a result of this initiative, a United Nations Group of Governmental Experts (UN GGE) was set up under the UN First Committee to look at ways of preventing developments in the cyber domain from posing a threat to international peace and security. This led to a prolonged exercise to identify norms of conduct in the cyber domain, which, as is the case for global governance, was informed by a competition between major stakeholder nations—the United States on the one hand, and Russia and China on the other—to promote their value systems in line with their political ambitions and strategic calculations.

Russia, in particular, sought to situate this debate within a traditional arms control context designed to limit the development of cyber weapons and to be enshrined in an international treaty. This was an approach the United States and its allies resisted on the grounds that, in contrast to nuclear or chemical weapons facilities, computers were far too widely distributed to allow for any kind of monitoring. The basic tension was between the United States and its main Western allies arguing for minimal restrictions on global information flows, a focus on network security, and a position that existing international law was adequate to regulate the cyber domain, versus Russia and China arguing for the rights of states to control information flows and the need for new international legislation to regulate this new domain.

This tension achieved an interim resolution in 2014 in that the UN GGE reached consensus to the effect that existing international law applied in the cyber domain and so too did the traditional concept of state sovereignty. This resolution raised arguably more questions than it answered, in particular in relation to how International Humanitarian Law, otherwise known as 'the Law of Armed Conflict (LOAC)' should apply with the United States yet again arguing for the status quo, and Russia and China arguing for a new law for new situations. This was followed by consensus in 2015 on a series of 'norms, rules and principles for the responsible behaviour of States' (CCDCOE 2015). Thinking about the practical applications of the UN GGE's findings has been a significant focus for semi-official diplomatic activity.

Track 1.5 and Track 2 Diplomacy in the Cyber Domain

The cyber domain is a farmyard in which all animals are emphatically not equal and it became clear from an early stage that three countries, the United States, Russia, and China were in a position to determine the strategic evolution of this domain due to their status as global geo-political actors, their advanced cyber capabilities, their possession of nuclear weapons, and their differences in values and ideology. Russia was the first to make a move towards semi-official diplomacy. In 2006, the Lomonosov Moscow State University began what has since become an annual gathering with the title 'State, Civil Society and Business Partnership on International Information Security' in the Bavarian town of Garmisch-Partenkirchen. In 2010, an International Information Security Research Consortium was established with the aim of promoting joint research activities between the annual conferences. Significantly, the Director of the Lomonosov Moscow University's Institute of Information Security Issues, Colonel-General Vladislav P. Sherstyuk, was a former KGB then FAPSI (Federal Agency of Government Communications and Information) signals intelligence specialist who, as adviser to the Russian National Security Council, had played a key role in developing Russian cybersecurity strategy. The other key Russian player at Garmisch has been Andrey V. Krutskikh, a professional diplomat who now has the title of Special Representative of the President of the Russian Federation for Issues of International Cooperation in the Field of Information Security. It seemed that, in setting up this event, Russia had hoped to create a venue in which ideas could be informally discussed with US counterparts but, faced with a progressive lack of US enthusiasm, this aspect of the exercise has declined in significance. The event has, however, attracted and continues to attract governmental, academic, and private sector participation from a range of countries including the United States, China, the United Kingdom, France, Germany, India, and Japan.

The agenda from the 2015 Garmisch meeting gives a good sense of the issues that are typically discussed at this venue:

'1. Proposals on Frameworks for Adaptation of International Law to Conflicts in Cyberspace;
2. Challenges of countering the threat of ICT use for interference in the internal affairs of sovereign states;

3. Improving the Information Security of Critical Infrastructures: Possible Initiatives;
4. Legal and Technical aspects of ensuring Stability, Reliability and Security of the Internet;
5. National Approaches and Priorities of International Information Security System Development.'[9]

These topics tend to be at the heart of most meaningful official and semi-official exchanges on cybersecurity though reflecting particular Russian preoccupations in respect of agenda item 2. The Garmisch exercise must in some ways be seen as a missed opportunity due primarily to a lack of US willingness to engage. But it has nevertheless created opportunities for serious exchanges on some of the most difficult security and governance issues in the international arena, even if attendance by Western countries at an official level has been relatively sparse.

Whereas Russia has taken a leading role in international negotiations on cyber governance and cybersecurity, China has arguably become more consequential in terms of how its relationship with the United States will shape the normative culture of the cyber domain. Having made the Internet available to its citizens only in 1996, China has grown to become the world's largest digital user community and has developed ambitious plans to integrate its real-world and digital economies via the Internet Plus strategy, and its national ICT champions such as Huawei, ZTE, Lenovo, and Xiaomi have become global brands. China began to attract significant US and Western attention starting in the mid-2000s as a result of a broad-spectrum industrial cyber espionage campaign that Western nations believed to be state-sponsored at worst and state-condoned at best (Inkster 2012). And, since 2012, when Xi Jinping became President and Chairman of the Chinese Communist Party, China has begun to adopt a more extrovert approach to discussions of international cyber governance and cybersecurity based on an unabashed assertion of cyber sovereignty and a more overt challenge to the United States' dominance in the cyber domain.

Partly in response to this challenge, the United States initiated direct Track 1 diplomatic discussions with China and, in 2009, these were supplemented by a Track 1.5 Dialogue. The conveners of this dialogue were on the US side the Center for Strategic and International Studies (CSIS), a respected non-partisan Washington think tank, and on the Chinese side the China Institutes of Contemporary International Relations (CICIR), a similarly respected Chinese think tank publicly described as coming under the State Council but which also functions as an open-source research institute for the Ministry of State Security. Publicly available information about the substance of these exchanges, described as Track 2 but in reality Track 1.5 and which take place twice-yearly alternating between Washington and Beijing, are necessarily sparse. Topics for discussion listed on the CSIS website have included principles, norms, and a lexicon for international security for cyberspace; dealing with cybercrime; securing global cyber infrastructure; confidence-building; responsible state behaviour; the applicability of sovereignty; international governance structures; rules for military conflict in the cyber domain; stability in cyberspace; and communications and co-operation to deal with cyber incidents. This agenda has also included discussion of a number of scenarios. Examples, taken from the CSIS website, are:

> Each country discovers evidence that its energy pipelines have been probed and mapped for possible cyber attack. Each suspects the other is responsible. How should a country respond to such reconnaissance efforts? What domestic preparations would it take? Who is responsible

for working with the energy companies in response to the probes? What additional actions (such as 'leave-behinds' in electrical networks) increase the likelihood of some kind of confrontation? Where are the areas for cooperation (if any)?

and

Chinese and U.S. authorities both found a serious vulnerability with a widely used IT product while the manufacturer is still unaware of the flaw. What are the consequences of such a discovery? What actions would each side take? What are national responsibilities and which agencies are responsible in each country? What communications channels are best for sharing any information?[10]

Following the United States' example, the United Kingdom entered into a similar dialogue in 2012 with the International Institute for Strategic Studies (IISS) leading for the UK. The European Union followed suit in 2013 with the Hague Centre for Strategic Studies in the lead, as did Australia in 2015, represented by the Australian Strategic Policy Institute (ASPI). In all cases, the Chinese lead was CICIR, which is the only institution authorized by the Chinese government to conduct such exercises. In each case, the rationale for Chinese engagement is somewhat different: the UK is seen as a major intelligence power, in particular thanks to the capabilities of its signals intelligence agency GCHQ and its membership of the Five-eyes intelligence alliance; the EU is seen as a valid interlocutor due to its status as a major trading bloc; and Australia is a major regional power, a member of the Five-eyes, and a strategic security partner of the United States.

It is difficult to say how much impact these dialogues have had, given the paucity of available information. But it is reasonable to suppose that, at the very least, these exchanges will have created a community of experts with a good understanding of each other's policies and strategies, and that the exchanges between them will have enabled each to clarify aspects of their interlocutor's views and positions. It may also be that the US–China dialogue played a role in the September 2015 agreement between the USA and China not to use their cyber capabilities to engage in industrial espionage, if only by helping to convey to a hitherto disengaged Chinese leadership an awareness of the extent to which allegations of Chinese cyber espionage had become a major irritant in bilateral relations. The same considerations may have informed a similar agreement reached between the UK and China the following month. As China drives forward an ambitious state-led cyber agenda in areas such as the Internet of Things (IoT), artificial intelligence (AI) and the development of quantum encryption and quantum computing, it seems inevitable that China's technologies will become more ubiquitous and hence that China's global influence on matters of cyber governance and cybersecurity will have greater capacity to become globally normative, and the need for engagement by other major powers all the greater.

OTHER EXAMPLES OF SEMI-OFFICIAL DIPLOMACY

The nature of the cyber domain with its wide range of public and private stakeholders positively demands wide-ranging diplomatic engagement and a number of international forums have been established to bring these entities together. One such initiative is the London

Global Conference on Cyberspace (GCCS), launched by the UK government in 2011 with successive iterations in Budapest (2012), Seoul (2013), the Hague (2015) with a further iteration taking place in India in November 2017.[11] The original London Conference took as its starting point the growing prevalence of malign cyber activity and the need for a greater focus on cybersecurity, and agreed a set of principles for governing behaviour in cyberspace. The key theme for the 2012 Budapest Conference was the need to reconcile freedom and security in cyberspace. By 2015, the Seoul Conference had a much expanded attendance of 1,600, with many more attendees coming from the developing world, and it gave rise to the Seoul Framework for and Commitment to Open and Secure Cyberspace. One of the issues addressed in this series of conferences has been the need to get the private technology sector more engaged in a security agenda that up to now has not, for understandable reasons, been a key driver of business development models. Failure by the private sector to take adequate account of security concerns could at its worst lead to growing levels of distrust in and disengagement from cyberspace by ordinary citizens.

This latter theme was addressed in a separate but related exercise when, in 2014, the World Economic Forum announced the creation of a Global Commission on Internet Governance chaired by former Swedish foreign minister Carl Bildt to provide a strategic vision for the future of Internet governance. The Commission, comprising 29 members from the policy, academic, and civil society communities from around the world, and supported by the UK think tank Chatham House and the Canadian think tank Center for International Governance Innovation (CIGI), produced a report in the summer of 2016 that offered three visions for a future Internet. These were:

'• A Dangerous & Broken Cyberspace
  The Internet breaks due to malicious activity, and overreaching government regulation. Basic human rights are violated, online privacy is non-existent and government surveillance follows. Criminal data breaches are the norm and cyber attacks become more frequent. The public loses its trust in the Internet and people simply stop using the network. Its potential is truly lost.
• Uneven & Unequal Gains and Stunted Growth.
  Some users are able to enjoy some of the many benefits offered by being connected, while others are permanently locked out. Freedom of expression suffers, as does access to knowledge because governments don't preserve the Internet's openness. As a result, more than three billion people are left off-line. Inequality and unrest spread, with minimal cooperation by governments across borders. Sharing and innovation are limited and stifled. Many are left behind
• Broad, Unprecedented Progress
  An open internet that enables unprecedented progress and opportunities for individual freedom, knowledge and innovation. Billions of new users join us online narrowing digital, social, and economic divides. GDP growth reaches upwards of $11.1 trillion by 2025. Government and industry collaborate across borders to manage the risks of online activity. This future requires concrete actions to ensure that the Internet becomes open, secure, trustworthy and inclusive for all.'[12]

It is of course in the nature of scenario planning that none of the options identified will be precisely the one that transpires: the aim rather is to encourage thinking about how to respond to these eventualities in the hope that this will provide a degree of preparation that can adapt to the actual situation that presents.

A relatively recent, but in the long term potentially significant, addition to what is fast becoming an endless array of international conferences on cybersecurity and cyber governance is China's World Internet Conference (WIC), which since 2014 has been held at the traditional water-village of Wuzhen, some 80 kilometres south-west of Shanghai. This event seems to have been conceived as a counter-balance to what has to date been a somewhat Western-centric London Conference, and designed to showcase China's cyber capabilities and promote China's vision for global cybersecurity and governance. Western take-up to date has been poor with few major Western technology companies being represented at anything other than a junior level and most Western governments being represented by relatively low-ranking members of their Beijing embassies. The first iteration of this conference was used by the then head of China's newly formed Cyberspace Administration of China (CAC), Lu Wei, vigorously to assert China's concept of cyber sovereignty and the 'multilateral'—i.e. government-centric—concept of cyber governance as a contrast to the established multi-stakeholder model. The following year, the conference was addressed by President Xi Jinping who spoke of the need for a 'multilateral, democratic and transparent system of Internet governance' adding that 'existing rules governing cyberspace hardly reflect the desires and interests of the majority of countries.'[13] The 2016 iteration of the conference was lower key than in the two preceding years. And, as had happened in the preceding year, there were panel discussions involving Chinese and foreign academics and other experts looking inter alia at issues of 'hard' security. Whether Western states will continue their thinly disguised boycott of the WIC remains to be seen. Given China's growing preponderance in the cyber domain, that may not prove a tenable long-term proposition, not least because China is practised at the art of presenting an absence of clearly articulated opposition to any proposal as indicating a consensus in favour of it.

Prospects for Further Semi-Official Diplomacy

In a world characterized on the one hand by growing geo-political uncertainty due to an unravelling post-World War II international order, and on the other by a suite of technologies evolving at an exponential rate, the need for effective diplomacy in the cyber arena has never been greater. National governments do undoubtedly have a key role to play, in particular those that possess significant cyber capabilities and significant international responsibilities, notably the five permanent members of the UN Security Council. But the challenge is significantly complicated by the plethora of other stakeholders whose equities need to be taken into account. Of particular importance is the alignment of the interests of states, whose ultimate purpose is to guarantee stability and security, with the interests of the private sector that owns and operates most of the global cyber infrastructure on which this stability and security increasingly depend. To date, the private sector has shown little interest in active engagement in the 'hard' security agenda outlined earlier. By the same token, this community has shown itself at best ambivalent about the privacy implications of the technologies it is developing and marketing, whether such capabilities have the potential to serve the interests of illiberal regimes or simply to alienate user communities through the creation, for supposedly benign purposes, of the kind of cyber panopticon decried by writers such as Evgeny Morozov (2011).

There is a pressing need for key states, notably the United States, Russia, and China to engage on all aspects of governance and security but in particular in the more challenging aspects of hard security, notably the potential for the cyber domain to serve as an enabler of security dilemmas and to have escalatory potential into the realms of space and nuclear weapons. These states in particular ought to be showing the way in terms of looking at the specifics of escalatory dynamics and developing models for managing such situations, as well as crisis communication systems and protocols that can operate in cyber time. Such things are difficult for states to do because they involve sensitive security issues and tend to argue for the exposure of capabilities where every instinct is to keep these concealed. In this context, it should be borne in mind that there are other major states in antagonistic relationships—the USA and North Korea; India and Pakistan; Saudi Arabia and Iran—any and all of which could see an incident beginning in cyberspace moving quickly to military confrontation and kinetic exchanges with consequences that will reach far beyond the borders of the states concerned. Such a state of affairs would seem to argue for the greatest possible extent of informed engagement, and the development of greater academic and practitioner expertise in this seemingly recondite but vitally important area. The more the situations described earlier can be given public exposure, the greater the incentive for states to act. The costs of well-considered para-diplomatic activity are remarkably small relative to the benefits that success might bring, which argues for continued investment in such exercises.

NOTES

1. http://legal.un.org/ilc/texts/instruments/english/conventions/9_1_1961.pdf
2. Foreign Policy concept of the Russian Federation, 30 November 2016. http://www.mid.ru/en/web/guest/foreign_policy/official_document/-/asset_publisher/CpHCkBZ29/content/id/2542248
3. Davidson and Montville, 'Foreign Policy', 146.
4. Principles, Structures and Activities of Pugwash for the Eleventh Quinquennium (2007–12).
5. Joseph Rotblat Russell and the Pugwash Movement, The 1998 Bertrand Russell Peace Lectures.
6. State Council White Paper 'The Internet in China' section VI, http://news.xinhuanet.com/english2010/china/2010-06/08/c_13339232_8.htm
7. Internet's future on the agenda at Dubai meeting, IISS Strategic Comments 2012 (44), 30 November 2012, http://www.iiss.org/en/publications/strategic%20comments/sections/2012-bb59/internets-future-on-the-agenda-at-dubai-meeting-907d
8. Evolution of the Cyber Domain: The Implications for National and Global Security, IISS Strategic Dossier 2015, p. 117.
9. Private information.
10. https://www.csis.org/programs/strategic-technologies-program/cybersecurity-and-governance/other-projects-cybersecurity-3

11. 'India to Host 5th Global Conference on Cyber Space Next Year', The Indian Express, 20 December 2016, http://indianexpress.com/article/india/india-cyber-space-4437148/
12. https://www.cigionline.org/
13. 'Xi Slams "Double Standards", Advocates Shared Future in Cyberspace', Xinhua 16 December 2015.

References

Barlow, John Perry 1996. 'A Declaration of the Independence of Cyberspace', 8 February, Electronic Frontier Foundation. https://www.eff.org/cyberspace-independence

CCDCOE (NATO Cooperative Cyber Defence Centre of Excellence). 2015. '2015 UN GGE Report: Major Players Recommending Norms of Behaviour, Highlighting Aspects of International Law', 31 August. https://ccdcoe.org/incyder-articles/2015-un-gge-report-major-players-recommending-norms-of-behaviour-highlighting-aspects-of-international-law/

Cull, Nicholas J. 2006. Public Diplomacy Before Gullion: The Evolution of a Phrase, 18 April, Los Angeles, CA: University of Southern California Center on Public Diplomacy. http://uscpublicdiplomacy.org/blog/public-diplomacy-gullion-evolution-phrase

Davidson, William, and Joseph Montville. 1981–82. 'Foreign Policy According to Freud', Foreign Policy, winter, 45: 146.

Fischer, Benjamin B. 1997. A Cold War Conundrum: The 1983 Soviet War Scare. Washington DC: Center for the Study of Intelligence. https://www.cia.gov/readingroom/docs/19970901.pdf

Harding, Luke. 2014. The Snowden Files. London: Guardian Books.

Inkster Nigel. 2012. 'China in Cyberspace'. In Cyberspace and National Security: Threats, Opportunities and Power in a Virtual World, edited by Derek S. Reveron, 200–1. Washington DC: Georgetown University Press.

Mapendere, Jeffrey. 2006. 'Track One and a Half Diplomacy and the Complementarity of Tracks', Culture of Peace Online Journal 2 (1): 67–8.

Morozov, Evgeny. 2011. The Net Delusion: How Not to Liberate the World. London: Allen Lane.

Nan, A.S. 2005. 'Track one-and-a-Half Diplomacy: Contributions to Georgia-South Ossetian Peacemaking'. In Paving the Way, edited by R.J. Fisher, 165. Lanham: Lexington Books.

CHAPTER 33

···

STATES, PROXIES, AND (REMOTE) OFFENSIVE CYBER OPERATIONS

···

TIM MAURER

In the shadow of the debate about whether cyberwar will or will not take place (Clarke and Knake 2011; Rid 2013), a rather state- and interstate-centric discussion, malicious non-state actors have become increasingly active in cyberspace. In 2014, Ari Baranoff from the US Secret Service stated, 'Many of the actors that we look at on a daily and weekly basis have capabilities that actually exceed the capabilities of most nation-states' (Cirilli 2014). And the impact these actors are having is significant. For example, in 2015, a single group of cybercriminals stole as much as US$1 billion from financial institutions worldwide over a period of two years.[1] It is no longer a matter of dispute that hackers can physically harm people and the risk is growing, as demonstrated by the March 2016 official warning[2] by the US government concerning the vulnerability of cars to hacking. As capabilities and number of actors proliferate, there is a case for taking a much closer look at non-state actors and the market for cyber capabilities.

Proxies are a particularly important subset of actors as part of this broader line of inquiry. If one follows media coverage of cyber incidents on a regular basis, one might think cyber proxies lurk behind every corner online. 'State-sponsored actor' has become the default description in news articles for many alleged perpetrators, especially when the incident first hits the news. However, this wording is often only a workaround for what continues to be a major problem for cybersecurity: the difficulty of attributing the action in a prompt, publicly and independently verifiable manner (Rid and Buchanan 2015). Because it is often not known for weeks, sometimes months, and occasionally never, whether a state, state-sponsored, or criminal actor is behind a malicious action online, journalists use 'state-sponsored' in those instances where it seems at least somewhat plausible that a state is involved in some way. It is the inability to attribute the incident to a state for certain at the time of publication that prompts journalists to use 'state-sponsored' to cover both a state *and* a state-sponsored actor as the potential source. A similar logic applies to cybersecurity industry reports that rarely attribute a specific malware or incident to a state as such: in some cases, arguably due more to business reasons than lack of evidence. They usually adopt a similarly vague approach, mentioning 'state involvement' much like the warnings of 'state-sponsored attackers' that Google started issuing in 2012 (Grosse 2012) followed by Facebook (Stamos 2016), Microsoft (Charney 2015), and Yahoo (Lord 2015) in late 2015.

More research on this issue is therefore necessary from an international security perspective. As Deborah Avant cautions in her seminal study on the market for force:

> [i]t is commonly assumed by international relations theorists that states, organised hierarchically, create military organisations that provide security ... This need not be the case, however. There is more than one way to organise security forces. Imagine a continuum moving from universal conscription at one extreme ... to purely market contracts at the other extreme. (Avant 2006, 507)

In the context of mobilizing cyber power, Alexander Klimburg even argues, specifically, 'To create an integrated national capability in cyber power, the non-state sector must be induced to cooperate with government' (2011). The market of cyber force is therefore a complex and dynamic relationship between the state and actors detached from the state that can target a third party beyond a state's border with unprecedented ease. Only hacking, also known as 'remote cyber operations' in the military bureaucracy's vernacular, makes global reach possible at such low cost.

Research identifies three main types of proxy relationships between a state and non-state actors: (1) delegation, (2) orchestration, and (3) sanctioning. First, delegation describes proxies on a tight leash held by the state and under the latter's effective control. Private security contractors, such as the contractors hired by US Cyber Command, are the best illustration of this relationship. Second, orchestration applies to proxies on a looser leash with the state. Their bond is not based on a contract but a shared ideological outlook that substitutes some of the contractual mechanisms to minimize the agency problem. The relationship between the Iranian government and students illustrate this category (Abbott et al. 2015). Third, the concept of sanctioning builds on the framework of passive support developed by counterterrorism scholars to describe the phenomenon where a state is aware of but turns a blind eye toward the activity of a non-state actor and indirectly benefits from the latter's actions. The cybersecurity equivalent are Russian hackers committing cybercrime without having to fear punishment from Russian security agencies as long as they operate beyond the borders of Mother Russia.

How to manage effectively both proxies and the market for cyber capabilities, both tools and services to the degree that they can be separated, is not only of interest for academic scholarship but also for practitioners and policymakers. States appear to change their systematic approach to engaging with proxies only very slowly over time, usually in the span of decades rather than years (Ahram 2011). The recent controversy over the agreement of 41 states to create 2 new export controls under the Wassenaar Arrangement on Export Controls for Conventional Arms and Dual-Use Goods and Technologies can be viewed as an attempt by states to gain greater control over the resources used to project force through cyberspace. Other examples are the specific requirements designed to minimize the agency problem in the US Cyber Command's 2015 solicitation to award contracts to private security firms.[3] Recent waves of arrests of members of the Anonymous hacktivist group in the United States and Europe as well as of hackers in China as part of the government's overall anti-corruption campaign (Areddy 2015) illustrate efforts to punish those who violate domestic laws. Meanwhile, the US government's recently unsealed indictments of Iranian hackers and members of the Syrian Electronic Army expose and shame foreign nations' proxies directed against another country.

PUTTING PROXIES INTO PERSPECTIVE

The international relations literature includes many varied meanings of proxies covering 'proxy warriors' (Ahram 2011a), 'proxy forces' (Salehyan 2010, 496), 'proxies' (Wyatt 2014; Dunér 1981, 'proxy war' (Cragin 2015; Newton 2006; Hughes 2015), and 'proxy warfare' (Dunér 1981. Meanwhile, there is not even agreement among scholars as to whether the use of proxies poses greater risks (Bobbitt 2003) or fewer risks (Wilner 2012, 22), with some even arguing that it could be 'risk free' (Hughes 2014a, 522). The related literature on mercenaries (Patterson 2009; Percy 2007), state-sponsored actors, privateers[4], and private security and military companies provides some useful insights, but there is no consensus on many of these terms either. Avant, for example, rejects the term mercenary altogether, arguing that its meaning has changed so much over time that it is no longer particularly useful as an analytical term. One distinguishing factor, though, is their respective domain. In other words, the discussion of mercenaries is about land-based proxies whereas studies on privateering are about proxies on the high seas. Jules Lobel also suggests that '[t]he covert action of today is the marque and reprisal of yesterday', (Lobel 1986, 1041) adding that '[b]oth involve the use of private individuals rather than public armed forces to engage in hostilities against other nations. Both are primarily utilized when war has not been formally declared. Both are often precursors to full-scale war.'[5]

Nevertheless, proxies are a useful prism through which to study states' relationships with non-state actors at a global level. To explain why, it is helpful to put Max Weber's famous quote in a broader historical and global context. To start, Joseph Nye reminded an audience at the Massachusetts Institute of Technology in November 2012 that 'Weber did not define the state as having "the monopoly over the use of force" but "the monopoly over the *legitimate* use of force."'[6] And, while a bedrock for the modern nation-state, sociologist Michal Mann has observed that 'most historic states have not possessed a monopoly of organised military force and many have not even claimed it' (Mann 1986). That is why Ariel Ahram (2011b) suggests that states be viewed 'as brokers, instead of monopolists'. In short, Weber's definition arguably best describes the modern nation-state as it emerged in Europe, including the separation of private and public. Efforts by governments to nudge other states toward a Weberian monopoly, together with the negative normative disposition in international regimes toward privateers (Thomson 1994), mercenaries[7], and proxies[8], reflects this historically dependent and imbued aspiration. Yet states in other parts of the world often have very different relationships with actors detached from the state. Examples of these alternative approaches include the Chinese government's ties with state-owned enterprises, the nexus between Russian government officials and criminal networks, and the Islamic Revolutionary Guard Corps in Iran. That is why Avant also cautions that her own and others' analysis of the private market for force 'refers to the world of advanced, industrialized countries where the state, government, and public revolve around some notion of collective good. In parts of the developing world, state institutions and international recognition of them function mainly as mechanisms for rulers to achieve personal (private) gain' (Avant

2005). That is why proxies in their different shapes and forms remain an important part of international security in need of scholarly attention and analysis, and can be viewed as an analytical umbrella term for these other, historically more bounded, terms.

What the work of these scholars has in common is that they all focus on actors that are legally not part of the government and therefore detached from the state to a certain degree. They differ in what motivates them, their organizational structure, the environment in which they operate, and in the historic conditions that lead to their rise and fall. The scholarship covering these actors is, at its core, an analysis of the relationship between them and the state, and how they have helped states to project power, complicated by the fact that they all exhibit different shades of the proxy phenomenon occurring at different points in time and across domains. I therefore define a proxy actor as an intermediary that conducts or directly contributes to an offensive action that is enabled knowingly, actively or passively, by a beneficiary.[9] This definition consists of two sides of one coin. One side of the coin focuses on the proxy side of the relationship whereas the other side focuses on the beneficiary side of the relationship.[10] One shortcoming of the definition is that it does not account for a potential change in the nature of the relationship. For example, Emile Hokayem offers the fascinating account of a conventional proxy outgrowing its role, which he sums up thus: 'Syria today is more pro-Hizballah than Hizballah is pro-Syria. Hizballah is no longer a card or a proxy; it has become a partner with considerable clout and autonomy' (2007).[11] An example in the context of cybersecurity is researchers' assessment that the Syrian Electronic Army's structure and relationship with the Syrian government evolved over time toward a more autonomous actor as the country descended into chaos (Perlroth 2013).

A range of non-state actors can act as proxies including (i) individual actors, (ii) groups of people that are organized informally and as a networked structure, as well as (iii) more formal, organized groups of people extending to hierarchical organizations outlined in Table 33.1. They include lone hacktivists, such as The Jester, or the individual hacker offering malicious hacking-for-hire services. When it comes to small groups of people, these include networks of politically driven hacktivists, curiosity-driven hackers, or profit-driven cybercriminals. These groups tend to be informal and usually have more of a flat, networked character than a hierarchical one (Powell 2003). Formal and hierarchical non-state actors include private military and security companies as well as militias and entities such as the Estonian Cyber Defense League.[12]

To assess the relevance of proxies in the broader context of cybersecurity and possible effects, one must first assess the capabilities of non-state actors generally that could

Table 33.1 Non-state proxies based on organizational structure

Organizational unit	Individual	Small, informal, networked group of people	More formal, hierarchical group of people
Examples	Individual hacktivist, individual cybercriminal	Network of hacktivists, network of cybercriminals	Organized cybercrime groups, militias, private companies

potentially act as such proxies. Some experts suggest that non-state actors are the biggest threat while others reject this argument, preferring to focus their interest on states instead. Unfortunately, both arguments are true. A small group of people, even an individual, can acquire the ability to cause harm, including physical harm, and, due to diffusion of reach, across vast distances. That does not mean that any script kiddie can cause a serious degree of harm. The important point here is that a small group of individuals, even a single individual, can cause significant levels of harm through malicious hacking and cause effects remotely. In the context of offensive cyber operations, harm is therefore not a major differentiator among non-state and state actors until the level of technical sophistication gets to a point that it requires the resources of a major state with the ability to gain access to specific technologies. That is why, today, some individuals have more sophisticated cyber capabilities than many nation-states. A higher level of sophistication enhances an actor's ability to target precisely and to do so stealthily.[13] In other words, to a certain extent, it is easier to cause widespread harm than limited harm.

The most powerful states do stand apart from other states and non-state actors today primarily for two reasons: first, the level of resources they have available and, second, the ability to gain access to certain technologies. In terms of resources, for example, the US National Security Agency's Tailored Access Operations are carried out by some 600 staff at what is called 'the Remote Operations Center' 24 hours a day, 7 days a week (Peterson 2013). The resources required to pay that number of highly skilled individuals to work such hours for a prolonged period of time are generally only available to a major state. With regard to an actor's ability to gain access to certain technologies, major states again stand out and differ from other state and non-state actors. Only major powers can gain access to certain systems, for example, by relying on human intelligence and covert agents to provide physical access for a cyber operation. As Andrey Nikishin at Kaspersky Lab acknowledged in his Black Hat 2016 conference presentation, 'most developed advanced persistent threats (APTs) are able to jump over air gap' (Nikishin 2016). There is no publicly known cyber incident involving a proxy actor where the proxy jumped the air gap. Proxies' activities have so far been limited to operations based on remote access: a reflection of proxies' technical and operational limitations. But it does not follow that proxies are not able to cause significant harm, especially given the number of critical infrastructure systems that remain without an air gap today.

But why do states use these non-state actors and why do these proxy relationships exist in the first place? Four conditions must be met for a state-non-state proxy relationship to occur.[14] First, actors detached from the state must be available to act as proxies. Second, the state must have an actual or perceived need for, or else receive an actual or perceived benefit from, a proxy's activity. Third, the state must have the ability to mobilize non-state actors to act as proxies, or the capability to put an end to a non-state actor's activities. Fourth, the proxy must see a benefit from the relationship.

1. *Proxy availability:* For a beneficiary to address an immediate need or to reap benefits through a proxy relationship, non-state actors must be available to act as proxies in the first place.[15] Privateering did not simply emerge out of thin air. Privateering required vessels. The degree to which European monarchs could use privateers to augment their own navy's power therefore depended on the number of ships that had been built. Moreover, the operational value of privateers depended on manpower, and the

number of men available and trained to operate the vessels. The same is true for proxies in cyber space. Unlike in the case of maritime privateering, however, it is less the quantity than the quality of manpower that matters. As the former head of the US Army Cyber Command, Lt. Gen. Rhett Hernandez, has pointed out, '[c]yberspace requires a world-class cyber warrior ... [W]e must develop, recruit and retain in a different way to today' (Apps 2012). A recurrent theme in interviews with technical experts, security researchers, and hackers around the world has been that their estimates of the number of the most sophisticated hackers range in the hundreds or low thousands rather than tens of thousands or more.

2. *Beneficiary's ability to mobilize (or capability to stop) a proxy:* Proxy availability is a necessary but not sufficient condition. The beneficiary must be able to mobilize the proxy as a resource (Holsti 1964, 185). While a central theme in the literature on power, Abbott et al. omit the condition of the orchestrator having the capacity and appropriate mechanism to act as an orchestrator in the first place, and to use an intermediary when available. This condition can explain cases of non-orchestration even when intermediaries were available—for example, the Ukrainian government's apparent inability to leverage effectively the various volunteer groups that spontaneously emerged following the conflict's escalation in 2014.[16]

3. *Beneficiary's benefit:* Proxy relationships must yield a benefit to both sides that is larger than the cost that the relationship brings with it, such as the associated loss of autonomy, cost of mobilization, or reputational costs. This cost–benefit calculus can change over time and influence the proxy relationship including its potential termination. Focusing on the beneficiary state, there are several potential factors that come into play. One of the most referenced factors is a need for capabilities,[17] either capabilities that the state does not possess at all or that the state does possess but wishes to augment.[18] Today, only a very small number of states have established a cyber command. In fact, it was not until 2010 that the US government formally declared cyber space to be a new operational domain and that US Cyber Command was stood up. It is therefore not surprising that a UN study published in 2013 found only six states having published military cyber strategies. Yet, the study also found that the number of states that had included cybersecurity in their military planning had risen from 32 in 2011 to 47 in 2012, demonstrating a world-wide trend to follow the US example (United Nations Institute for Disarmament Research 2011).

The general need for capabilities and expertise explains why states around the world can be found to rely on private actors to build and augment their cyber power. Even established cyber powers like the United States is actively seeking out skilled hackers and support from the private market for cyber capabilities. A good example is the recent contract awarded by the US government to six contractors that will support the establishment of US Cyber Command.[19] This illustrates that, apart from the initial need when a state creates a cyber-specific command or even service, a related factor driving some governments' search for private capabilities is the availability of cheaper capabilities as part of the broader privatization trend (Stanger 2009).

Political benefits are another reason states pursue proxy relationships. One of the most cited benefits in the literature on conventional proxies is the preference to avoid a direct conflict (Hughes 1014b, 26).[20] This preference can be the result of a state's sensitivity to casualties, or a state's aversion to casualties among its own military, to be exact.[21] A proxy relationship may also be the result of a benefit a state enjoys without having pursued it itself; a possibility expressed in the idea of passive support. For example, Eugene Dokukin, head of the Ukrainian Cyber Forces, shared the results of his group's actions with the government even though the group is independent of the government. This provides the state with a certain benefit even though it did not directly sponsor or encourage the activities, one possible explanation for why the government has been turning a blind eye to its activities.

4. *Proxy's benefit:* Proxy relationships consist of at least two actors and most of the same factors influencing a beneficiary's behaviour also apply to the proxy with both sides influencing each other.[22] Non-state actors are likely to act as proxies if they derive a benefit, either material or ideational support, including support augmenting existing capabilities[23] in case of the former, or the provision of a sanctuary and legal protections against extradition as an example of the latter. Shared goals may result in a proxy relationship even in the absence of such positive incentives, while negative incentives such as threat of arrest, disruption of funding, or other form of abandonment can also motivate the non-state actor's behavior.[24]

THREE IDEAL TYPES OF PROXY RELATIONSHIP

Three ideal types of proxy relationship —delegation, orchestration, and sanctioning— can be identified as shown in Figure 33.1. With respect to international law, the concept of delegation effectively captures the type of proxy relationships above the threshold of effective and overall control—what is described as 'state-sponsored' in the counterterrorism literature. Orchestration, on the other hand, essentially covers the broad spectrum of activities from financing to the provision of arms, intelligence, and logistical support below this threshold that is considered to constitute 'state-supported'. Sanctioning, finally, captures the discussion among international lawyers about state responsibility and due diligence (Becker 2006).[25] It is important to note that, given the lack of comprehensive empirical data and the highly secretive nature of this field, the examples used in this section are biased, relying as they do on existing publicly available, empirical data.

Delegation: Cyber Proxies on a Tight Leash

Delegation captures proxy relationships in their narrowest sense. A principal delegates authority to an agent to act on their behalf. Its basis in the law of agency and principal–agent theory is in fact the closest representation of the Latin roots of the word *proxy*, 'pro-curare'. From the condottieri of the Italian city-states, the historical ideal type of mercenary, to the private security companies that have been the focus of attention in the literature during the past two decades, contracts are the typical instrument to control the behaviour of the agent

Type of relationship	Beneficiary (actor a)	→	Proxy (actor b)	→	
Delegation	Principal	→	Agent	→	Target (actor c)
Orchestration "Blitz orchestration"	Orchestrator	→	Intermediary	→	
Sanctioning	Sanctioner	→	Sanctionee	→	

FIGURE 33.1. Three main types of relationships

to whom authority has been delegated.[26] Principal–agent theory is directly applicable to these types of relationship. The principal–agent problem also comes into play in other proxy relationships and has recently been applied beyond its usual arena of organizational theory in international relations.[27] Private security and military contractors (PSMCs) are the classic examples for delegation and principal–agent relationships. This model of the state relying on the private market is particularly pronounced in the United States, the United Kingdom, and other European and NATO countries, as well as Israel. This phenomenon has significantly increased in scope and scale as part of a broader trend of privatization that dates to the 1980s.[28] As part of this broader trend toward privatization over the past three decades, bringing with it the growth of a PSMC industry, private cybersecurity contractors emerged either as a subdivision of existing contractors or as wholly new stand-alone companies. In fact, Peter Singer already mentions in his 2003 book an article in the US Army's professional journal arguing that the US military 'hire specialized PMCs for specific offensive information campaigns, providing a surge capability instead of attempting to maintain limited-use, cutting-edge skills in the regular force, far removed from its core activity' (Singer 2003). (In 2014, the US Army awarded a US$125 million one-year contract for cyber operations; Defense Systems 2014).

Two factors have been driving this development. First, traditional defence contractors have been expanding their activities to also include cybersecurity. Second, smaller boutique firms and start-ups emerged and either grew in size and became independent firms or were bought by larger companies. These contractors are involved in both defensive and offensive cyber operations. The website of the company CACI, for example, states that its 'personnel analyze systems, networks, and platforms to facilitate cyber targeting for the purpose of identification and penetration of target environments, from data centres to platforms'.[29] Meanwhile, job advertisements of the firm SAIC include those for cyberspace operational planners expected to develop 'Offensive Cyber Space Operations and Defense Cyber Space Operations policy, plans, processes, procedures, and government directives' as well as 'lead the creation of strike packages, and the vetting and validation of targets' at Fort Meade. In short, Singer's image of contractors' offerings along the full length of the spear (except for its deadly tip) also appears to apply to offensive cyber operations. An open question remains what exactly constitute inherently governmental functions in the context of cyber operations, and which types of activities can and cannot be outsourced.

The United States, Israel, France, and the United Kingdom are all examples of countries that pursue this approach. Their political systems, legal traditions, and history draw a clear distinction between the public and private spheres, and these states have been under pressure to privatize and outsource state functions to save costs. For example, in April 2015, US Cyber Command solicited proposals to award contracts to private companies for up to US$475 million.[30] According to the solicitation, the US military was looking for outside expertise, tools, and administrative services including the provision of:

> technical expertise to assist in the deliberate planning, coordination, and synchronization of Offensive Cyber Operations (OCO), Defensive Cyber Operations (DCO), and operation of the DODIN [Department of Defense Information Network] ... Additionally, the Contractor shall assist in providing maneuver, fires and effects through the application of capabilities in and through the cyber domain.[31]

These developments, much like the creation of US Cyber Command itself, are closely watched around the world. For example, according to Li Zheng from the China Institute for Contemporary International Relations, a think tank affiliated with the Ministry of State Security, 'China is aware that the United States and other Western countries are actively using defence contractors such as Lockheed Martin, Boeing, Northrop Grumman, and Raytheon for cyber-weapon development and deployment' (Zhang 2012).

Orchestration: Cyber Proxies on a Loose Leash

Orchestration has been defined in organizational theory as the enlistment of:

> intermediary actors on a voluntary basis, by providing them with ideational and material support, to address target actors in pursuit of IGO [intergovernmental organization] governance goals ... The key to orchestration is that the IGO brings third parties into the governance arrangement to act as intermediaries between itself and the targets, rather than trying to govern the targets directly.[32]

This is obviously very similar to the discussion of proxy relationships. A strong ideological bond often reduces divergence and thus the need for other control mechanisms to mitigate the agency problem. A shared ideology offers a tremendous source of potential influence for the principal, but may also lead a state not to control the agent's attacks even if they are strategically costly.[33] Orchestration is therefore similar to delegation and principal–agent theory but addresses the limitations of the latter. The main difference between delegation and orchestration is that orchestration places a much stronger emphasis on the ideational dimension of the relationship complementing the principal–agent theory's focus on interest.[34] In fact, because of this difference, Abbott et al. argue that the correlated goals between the orchestrator and the intermediary 'are constitutive of their relationship', whereas they are not necessary for principal–agent relationships.[35] In other words, the orchestration framework is an attempt not to stretch the existing principal–agent model to accommodate various criticisms,[36] but to propose a new, complementary framework. This new framework is helpful to better capture some of the nuances of the various proxy relationships that exist today.

Iran is an excellent case study for a country whose government started focusing on cyber space only recently and subsequently established proxy relationships typical of orchestration. The massive protests in 2009 and the discovery of the Stuxnet malware in 2010 suddenly presented officials in Tehran with both internal and external threats enabled by a technology they had not made much of a priority beforehand. According to Hossein Mousavian, a former Iranian diplomat, 'The US, or Israel, or the Europeans, or all of them together, started war against Iran ... Iran decided ... to establish a cyberarmy, and today, after four or five years, Iran has one of the most powerful cyberarmies in the world' (Segal 2016). Yadollah Javani, a former senior Islamic Revolutionary Guard Corps (IRGC) official, boasted in the spring of 2011 that Iran has the world's fifth largest 'cyber army' and the former deputy representative of the Supreme Leader, Mojtaba Zolnoor, mentioned that Iran's cyber army had successfully hacked 'enemy sites' shortly thereafter. A year later, the IRGC commander-in-chief, Mohammad Ali Jaafari, made a similar statement and claimed that the hackers had targeted opponents to the regime while an IRGC commander in Tehran, Hossein Hamedani, explicitly referenced the existence of 'two cyber war centers' in Iran's capital (Bastani 2012). CrowdStrike states in its 2014 Global Threat Intel Report that the Iranian government started hosting hacking contests to identify skilled hackers.[37] The Iranian government is not merely tolerating and providing passive support to hackers operating out of its territories. It is aware of their activities and, similar to the finding of the International Court of Justice in 1980 regarding the US embassy takeover in 1979, 'failed altogether to take any "appropriate steps" to protect ... or to persuade or to compel them to withdraw'.[38]

Like the expansion of the security contractor model by the aforementioned governments, the Iranian government also relied on its existing approach and structures— namely, the Basij, dating back to the Iran–Iraq War during the 1980s. Originally paramilitary volunteers, the Basij volunteers became institutionalized and its armed units absorbed by the IRGC in 2007. *Forbes* reported in 2011 that '[t]he government of Iran has recently decided that the Basij, its volunteer paramilitary corps, must recruit more hackers to fight what it calls the "soft war" in cyber space according to a 29 November 2010 article in the *Iran* newspaper' (Carr 2011). According to the authors of a *FireEye* 2013 report focusing on Iran:

> There is increasing evidence to suggest that the hacker community in Iran is engaged in a transition from politically motivated defacements and denial of service attacks to cyber espionage activities. This model is consistent with the Basij's recruitment of paramilitary volunteer hackers to "engage in less complex hacking or infiltration operations" leaving the more technical operations to entities over which they have increasingly direct control. (Villeneuve et al. 2013)

The indictment of seven Iranian hackers by the US government unsealed in March 2016 provides unprecedented detail into this evolution in Iran, and the relationship between the state and private actors.[39] It also marks the first time the US government has indicted state-sponsored hackers in addition to its indictment of five Chinese military hackers in 2014. According to the US government, the seven Iranians 'were employed by two Iran-based computer companies ... which were sponsored by Iran's Islamic Revolutionary Guard Corps'. Several of the people indicted, all in their early or mid-twenties were publicly boasting about their web defacements only a year prior to becoming involved in the alleged malicious activity targeting US financial institutions. This timeline is reminiscent of the students' actions in 1979 taking over the US embassy and their actions being subsequently endorsed by Ayatollah Khomeini, thus illustrating the rather loose nature of the relationship and the importance of the ideological bond.

Sanctioning: Cyber Proxies on the Loose

A state sanctions a non-state actor's actions when the former knowingly chooses not to stop but to tolerate the latter's activities despite having the capacity to do otherwise.[40] There is, therefore, neither delegation nor orchestration by the beneficiary, yet the state's decision not to act in spite of its ability transforms the non-state actor into a proxy. A state's condonation of a non-state actor's malicious activity from its territory can be driven by different factors.[41] First, the activities of the non-state actor might enjoy considerable domestic sympathy, threatening political costs in case of a government crackdown. For example, as discussed earlier, the Iranian students who took over the US embassy in November 1979 were initially acting independently. Yet, they enjoyed domestic support and their activities were subsequently endorsed by Ayatollah Khomeini. Second, a state might tolerate the non-state actor as long as it does not pose a domestic threat. Third, sanctioning occurs when the cost imposed by the international community is low. As Daniel Byman points out, 'because passive support is far less open than active support, it often is viewed as more acceptable internationally—and thus has fewer diplomatic costs.'[42] A fourth factor might be a discrepancy between the state's projected capacity, or aspirational status, and its actual capacity and power. In other words, a state might be trying to project itself as a regional or even global power, implying that it has all the correlated domestic capacities. In reality, however, its capacity might be significantly more limited, and an ineffective attempt at cracking down on the non-state actor could expose this discrepancy and prove a source of embarrassment, if not a more significant vulnerability.

Sanctioning describes a situation whereby a state consciously but indirectly benefits from a malicious activity targeting a third party, which the state could stop. Countries in the former Soviet Union serve as the best illustrations of such relationships. Following the end of the Cold War and the lack of sustained economic growth, unemployment has risen and the economy has not been able to absorb the technically skilled labour. The economic crash in 1998 further exacerbated the problem with only an estimated 50% of Russian software companies surviving the downturn and cybercrime rising instead, according to *The Moscow Times* (Alvey 2001). Today, a cybersecurity job in the Ukrainian government for somebody in their twenties pays roughly US$3,000—per year, not per month. And while Samsung has one of its largest research and development centres in Kyiv, the private information technology (IT) industry is neither large nor attractive enough to absorb the skilled labour (Goal Europe 2013). In short, there is no shortage of labour skilled in IT and hacking in the region, but a mature industry is absent and government salaries of a few thousand dollars a year pale in comparison to reports of thousands or millions of dollars made in the latest cyber heist. According to Alexei Borodin, a 21-year-old hacker, 'People think: "I've got no money, a strong education and law enforcement's weak. Why not earn a bit on the side?"' (De Carbonnel 2013). Moscow-based cybersecurity company Group-IB estimated the size of the cybercrime market in Russia alone to be US$2.3 billion.[43]

Meanwhile, cybercrime expert Misha Glenny doubts that law enforcement is weak and that the government is unable to take action, at least in the Russian context. He argues that 'Russian law enforcement and the FSB (Federal Security Service) in particular have a very good idea of what is going on and they are monitoring it but as long as the fraud is restricted to other parts of the world they don't care.'[44] In fact, malware used by Russian and East European cybercriminals is often designed so that it 'purposefully avoids infecting computers if the program detects the potential victim is a native resident' (Krebs 2009). When hackers do target victims in Russia, the response is swift and harsh. In 2012, eight men were arrested by Russian police after stealing some US$4 million from several dozen banks including some in Russia (Krebs 2012). Meanwhile, Russian law enforcement agencies often do not respond to requests for assistance from foreign law enforcement agencies and frequently protest when Russian nationals are arrested abroad.[45] For example, when Vladimir Drinkman was arrested while vacationing in Amsterdam in 2012, the Russian government tried to block the US government's extradition request by filing its own extradition request, thereby at least delaying prosecution (Goldstein and Perlroth 2015).

Such sanctioning can turn into more proactive interest from the government. In 2001, an article published by Jane's Intelligence mentioned that the former head of the KGB office in London, Oleg Gordievsky, said at the Global Cyber Crime Conference in 1998 that:

> [t]here are organized groups of hackers tied to the FSB and pro-Chechen sites have been hacked into by such groups ... One man I know, who was caught committing a cybercrime, was given the choice of either prison or cooperation with the FSB and he went along.[46]

Avoiding arrest is therefore one of the benefits for a non-state actor to become a proxy. In return for their cooperation, the hackers not only benefitted from not having to go to prison, but the FSB actively defended them. Alexander Klimburg and Heli Tirmaa-Klaar mention that the malicious activity 'by hacker patriots against "pro-Chechen" websites in 2002–04 were described by the Tomsk FSB office as not being illegal and simply an "expression of their political position, which is worthy of respect."' They also mention that '[o]ther reports have indicated that the National Antiterrorist Committee (NAK) has tried to pressure these non-state hackers into collaborating with it' (Klimburg and Tirmaa-Klaar 2011). Similarly, several experts argue that the offensive cyber operations against targets in Georgia during the 2008 war between Russia and Georgia were carried out by Russian criminals in collaboration with the Russian government.[47] The short war on the ground lasted only five days from 7 to 12 August and occurred together with the blitz orchestration, the rapid mobilization of non-state actors to project coercive (cyber) power, of a distributed denial of service (DDoS) attack.

Conclusion

Proxy relationships vary across regions and states, and depend on the state's history and its internal and external threat perceptions.[48] Countries where prebendalism (Joseph 1987) reigns differ from the market-state that Philip Bobbitt describes.[49] Yet, what states have in common across the various proxy relationships is significant path dependence. States' relationships with cyber proxies are extensions of their conventional approaches to mobilizing capabilities to project coercive power in private hands. The contracting model in the United States and elsewhere historically did not stop at the door of intelligence agencies. The industry for 'spies-for-hire' (Shorrock 2008) grew as well and, as intelligence capabilities expanded to offensive cyber operations, so did this latter industry. The Chinese government extended its traditional system of militias to this new domain, whereas Iran fell back on old patterns when it suddenly faced new threats. Russia, on the other hand, illustrates how the state adjusts its proxy relationships at a time of contraction, fragmentation, and increasing corruption. Needless to say, states have relationships with a variety of proxies. Hacktivists exist in pretty much every country, as well as in cybersecurity firms. However, there are primary models for a state's engagement with non-state actors for coercive power. This group of countries therefore reflects the myriad ways states build and augment their ability to project power through non-state actors, each with their own challenges.

Another finding that emerges is that categorizing proxies based on intent is not particularly helpful even for ideal types. Not only do proxies' motives change over time, as demonstrated by the hacktivists in China—whose actions shifted from political to profit-driven over time—but proxies can have mixed motives simultaneously. For example, the indictment of the three members of the Syrian Electronic Army explicitly references their personal profit-driven and political ambitions. The video on the cybercriminal BadB's website also revealed a strong political undertone to the hacker's criminal behaviour as well as that of his collaborators. That is why typologies of proxies based on motivation proposed by some scholars (Borghard and Lonergan 2016) quickly face severe limitations when applied to real-world examples and risk distorting analyses of the phenomenon. The same is true for typologies of proxies based on whether the proxy targets are perceived as internal or external threat actors. Several proxy actors in a number of different countries have engaged in malicious cyber activity targeting both perceived internal and external threats, creating a methodological challenge for such typologies. Hence, this chapter defines proxy relationships in terms of degree of detachment and control vis-à-vis the state. In the absence of detailed, timely information (a function of uncertainties over attribution) the proposed three main categories of delegation, orchestration, and sanctioning can serve as useful approximations for analytical frameworks until the exact details of the relationship become known.

Interestingly, a common characteristic across the different types of proxy relationship is their covert nature of operating and their attempts to conceal their true identity. For example, private security contractors working for governments will hide their unauthorized access as well as, if not better than, a member of a militia unit in China. There is an important difference in that the most technically advanced states are more likely to achieve plausible deniability through technical means, whereas less technically advanced states might not have the technical capabilities to be as stealthy and therefore perhaps a greater incentive to rely on actors further detached from the state to achieve the same effect.

Ultimately, managing proxy relationships carefully is important for at least two reasons: first, due to escalatory risks and, second, because of the proliferation of capabilities. (A third reason, particularly for democratic societies, is accountability and transparency vis-à-vis relevant oversight bodies.) Meanwhile, the high degree of path dependence for a state's use of cyber proxies suggests that the lessons learned from states' relationships with conventional proxies provide insights for this new phenomenon. These lessons are rather sobering and suggest that the abilities for an external actor to significantly shift the type of proxy relationships from a long-term perspective are limited.[50] Building a normative regime and taboo is one of the first elements usually mentioned in the context of cyber proxies, especially in comparison with maritime privateers. However, a similar trajectory is unlikely in the foreseeable future. There is not only the predictably temporary shortage of expertise and capabilities within government, fuelling a short-term dependence on non-state actors and their capabilities, but also the long-term, systematic reorientation of the modern industrial state toward something commonly understood as the market-state, being more intertwined with non-state actors in at least part of the world. Meanwhile, countries where the state is not going through this transition are extending their existing models of leveraging non-state actors to project coercive power.

Acknowledging the reality that many states act as brokers, rather than in pursuit of an effective monopoly over the legitimate use of coercive power, therefore has important implications for how this issue is viewed from a global governance perspective. While a state may face significant challenges in affecting another state's proxy relationships, it can exercise greater control over its own relationships with cybersecurity companies, hacktivists, and those breaking the law either at home or abroad. Future research analysing and comparing various actions taken by different governments over the years can offer insights into the various tools states can use to manage their proxy relationships and to shape the private market of cyber capabilities more broadly speaking.[51]

Notes

1. 'Cybercrime ring steals up to \$1 billion from banks: Kaspersky,' *Reuters*, 14 February 2015, www.reuters.com/article/us-cyber security-banks-idUSKBN0LJ02E20150215 OK
2. 'Motor vehicles increasingly vulnerable to remote exploits' (Public Service Announcement, Alert No. I-031716-PSA), Federal Bureau of Investigation, 17 March 2016). www.ic3.gov/media/2016/160317.aspx
3. United States Cyber Command (USCYBERCOM) Omnibus Contract, Solicitation No. HC1028-15-R-0026 (2015), 16.
4. For a fascinating account and one of the earliest comprehensive discussions, providing quips about Great Britain from the perspective of a nineteenth-century American, see Francis R. Stark. 1897. *The Abolition of Privateering and the Declaration of Paris*. New York: Columbia University.
5. Lobel, 'Covert War', '1051.
6. 'Who Controls Cyberspace? A Puzzle for National Security and International Relations' (conference, Explorations in Cyber International Relations, Cambridge, MA, 6–7 November 2012), http://ecir.mit.edu/index.php/events/ecir-workshops/263-who-controls-cyberspace.
7. Percy, *Mercenaries*.
8. United Nations, 'Report of the Group of Governmental Experts on Developments in the Field of Information and Telecommunications in the Context of International Security' 22 July 2015, UN Doc. A/70/174.
9. For a detailed discussion for how to define proxies, especially in the context of international law, see Maurer, T. 2016. "Proxies' and Cyberspace', *Journal of Conflict and Security Law*, 21 (3): 384–403.
10. A recurrent theme in the literature on the use of state proxies is the discussion about how it differs from an alliance and what makes the state proxy different from an ally. This text does not offer a definitive answer how best to distinguish alliances from proxy relationships. It is clear that the aforementioned asymmetric nature in the proxy relationship is a necessary condition in spite of the difficulties of measuring it. Apart from considering it an open empirical question for each case, another approach would be to exclude formal alliances that are treaty-based from being considered proxies, as Michael

T. Klare suggests in 'Subterranean alliances: America's global proxy network,' Journal of International Affairs (1989): 104.

11. For additional studies focusing on Hizballah, Syria, and Iran, see Hughes, 'Syria', 522–38; Hadaya, S. 2013. 'A Proxy War in Syria', *International Affairs: A Russian Journal of World Politics, Diplomacy & International Relations*, 59 (6): 176. For an additional analysis focusing particularly on Iran's role in this context, see Caudill, S. 2008. 'Hizballah Rising: Iran's Proxy Warriors', *Joint Force Quarterly*, 49: 130–133.

12. See also Michael Schmitt and Liis Vihul. 2014. 'Proxy Wars in Cyber Space: The Evolving International Law of Attribution.'

13. I thank Morgan Marquis-Boire and an expert who prefers to remain anonymous for their input.

14. This builds on the general hypotheses identified by Abbott et al. in their work on orchestration.

15. Building on Abbott et al., *International Organizations*, 20; Salehyan, 'Delegation of War', 508.

16. Abbott et al.'s orchestrator capabilities hypothesis does not focus on the orchestrator's ability ...to orchestrate but their lack of certain capabilities.

17. Building on Abbott et al., *International Organizations*, 20; Salehyan, 'Delegation of War', 509.

18. See, for example, Wilner, 'Apocalypse Soon?', 21.

19. United States Cyber Command (USCYBERCOM) Omnibus Contract. Solicitation No. HC1028-15- R-0026, 2015.

20. Salehyan, 'Delegation of War', 494.

21. Hughes, *My Enemy's Enemy*, 25.

22. Holsti, 'Concept of Power', 182.

23. Salehyan, 'Delegation of War', 507.

24. Salehyan, 'Delegation of War', 507.

25. Tal Becker, Senior Fellow, Shalom Hartman Institute, https://www.hartman.org.il/person/tal-becker/

26. Abbott et al., *International Organizations*, 17; Byman, D. and S. Kreps. 2010. 'Agents of Destruction? Applying Principal-Agent Analysis to State-Sponsored Terrorism', *International Studies Perspectives* 11 (1): 3.

27. Byman and Kreps, 'Agents of Destruction'; Salehyan, 'Delegation of War'; Hanrieder, T. 2014. 'Gradual Change in International Organisations: Agency Theory and Historical Institutionalism', *Politics* 34 (4): 325; Byman and Kreps, 'Agents of Destruction', 12–13.

28. Stanger, *One Nation Under Contract*.

29. CACI International Inc., 'Cyber Security—Capabilities': http://www.caci.com/cyber_security/capabililites.shtml

30. United States Cyber Command (USCYBERCOM) Omnibus Contract, Solicitation No. HC1028-15- R-0026, 2015: 14.

31. United States Cyber Command (USCYBERCOM) Omnibus Contract, Solicitation No. HC1028-15- R-0026, 2015: 18.

32. Abbott et al., *International Organizations*, 3–4.

33. Byman and Kreps, 'Agents of Destruction', 12.

34. Abbott et al., *International Organizations*, 17.

35. Abbott et al., *International Organizations*, 18.

36. Abbott et al., *International Organizations*, 17; Byman and Kreps, 'Agents of Destruction', 5.

37. CrowdStrike. 2015. 'CrowdStrike 2014 Global Threat Intel Report', 67.
38. *Case Concerning United States Diplomatic and Consular Staff in Tehran (United States of America v. Iran)*, Order, 12 V 81, International Court of Justice (ICJ), 1981: 31–2.
39. The indictment makes clear that: 'As the introductory phrase signifies, the entirety of the text of the Indictment, and the description of the Indictment set forth herein, constitute only allegations, and every fact described should be treated as an allegation.'
40. This definition builds on Byman, D. 2005. 'Passive Sponsors of Terrorism', *Survival* 47 (4): 132–3, 136–9.
41. Byman, 'Passive Sponsors', 132.
42. Byman, 'Passive Sponsors', 133.
43. De Carbonnel, 'Hackers for hire'.
44. De Carbonnel, 'Hackers for hire'.
45. Krebs, 'Story-Driven Résumé'.
46. Alvey, 'Russian Hackers for Hire', 52–3.
47. See, for example, Carr, J. et al., 2008. *Project Grey Goose: Phase I Report: Russia/Georgia Cyber War—Findings and Analysis. Case Concerning United States Diplomatic and Consular Staff in Tehran (United States of America v. Iran)*, Order, 12 V 81, International Court of Justice (ICJ). 12 May 1981; Tikk, E., Kaska, K., and Vihul, L. 2010. *International cyber incidents: Legal considerations.* Tallinn: Cooperative Cyber Defence Centre of Excellence. For a sceptical view of the proxy relationship, see Deibert, R., Rohozinski, R., and Crete-Nishihata, M. 2012. 'Cyclones in cyberspace: Information shaping and denial in the 2008 Russia-Georgia war', *Security Dialogue,* 43 (1).
48. Ahram, *Proxy Warriors,* 551.
49. Bobbitt, *Shield of Achilles.*
50. Byman, 'Passive Sponsors', 136–9.
51. This chapter is based on Maurer Tim. 2018. *Cyber Mercenaries.* Cambridge, Mass.: Cambridge University Press.

REFERENCES

Abbott, K., P. Genschel, and D. Snidal. et al. (eds.) 2015. *International Organizations as Orchestrators.* Cambridge, UK: Cambridge University Press: 3–4, 17–18, 20.

Ahram, A. 2011a. *Proxy Warriors: The Rise and Fall of State-Sponsored Militias.* Stanford: Stanford University Press.

Ahram, A. 2011b. 'Origins and Persistence of State-Sponsored Militias: Path Dependent Processes in Third World Military Development', *Journal of Strategic Studies,* 34 (4): 551.

Alvey, R. 2001. 'Russian Hackers for Hire: The Rise of the Mercenary', *Janes Intelligence Review* 13 (7): 52–3.

Apps, P. 2012. 'Analysis: In Cyber Era, Militaries Scramble for New Skills', *Reuters,* 9 February. www.reuters.com/article/us-defence-cyber-idUSTRE8182HI20120209

Areddy, J. 2015. 'Xinjiang Arrests Nearly Doubled in '14, Year of "Strike-Hard" Campaign', *The Wall Street Journal,* 23 January. http://blogs.wsj.com/chinarealtime/2015/01/23/xinjiang-arrests-nearly-doubled-in-14-year-of-strike-hard-campaign/

Avant, D. 2005. *The Market for Force: The Consequences of Privatizing Security.* New York: Cambridge University Press: 24.

Avant, D. 2006. 'The Implications of Marketized Security for IR Theory: The Democratic Peace, Late State Building, and the Nature and Frequency of Conflict', *Perspectives on Politics* 4 (3): 507.

Bastani, H. 2012. 'Structure of Iran's Cyber Warfare'. Paris: Institut Français d'Analyse Stratégique.

Becker, T. 2006. *Terrorism and the State: Rethinking the Rules of State Responsibility*. Portland, OR: Hart Publishing: 5.

Bobbitt, P. 2003. *The Shield of Achilles: War, Peace, and the Course of History*. New York: Anchor Books: 331.

Borghard, E. and S. Lonergan. 2016. 'Can States Calculate the Risks of Using Cyber Proxies?' *Orbis* 60 (3).

Carr, J. 2011. 'Iran's Paramilitary Militia is Recruiting Hackers', *Forbes*, 12 January. http://www.forbes.com/sites/jeffreycarr/2011/01/12/irans-paramilitary-militia-is-recruiting-hackers/#55206d8072b9

Charney, S. 2015. 'Additional Steps to Help Keep Your Personal Information Secure', Microsoft on the Issues (official blog), 30 December. http://blogs.microsoft.com/on-the-issues/2015/12/30/additional-steps-to-help-keep-your-personal-information-secure

Cirilli, K. 2014. 'Hackers Have Powers Beyond Most Countries, Expert Says', *The Hill*, 20 October. https://thehill.com/policy/cybersecurity/221287-hackers-have-powers-beyond-most-countries-says-expert

Clarke, R. and R. Knake. 2011. *Cyber War: The Next Threat to National Security and What to Do About It*. New York: Ecco.

Cragin, R. 2015. 'Semi-Proxy Wars and U.S. Counterterrorism Strategy', *Studies in Conflict & Terrorism* 38 (5).

De Carbonnel, A. 2013. 'Hackers for Hire: Ex-Soviet Tech Geeks Play Outsized Role in Global Cyber Crime', *NBC News*, 22 August. www.nbcnews.com/technology/hackers-hire-ex-soviet-tech-geeks-play-outsized-role-global-6C10981346

Defense Systems, 2014. 'Army Awards $125 Million Contract for Cyber Operations', 15 October. https://defensesystems.com/articles/2014/10/15/army-netcom-nci-contract-cyber-operations.aspx

Dunér, B. 1981. 'Proxy Intervention in Civil Wars', *Journal of Peace Research* 18 (4).

El-Hokayem, E. 2007. 'Hezbollah and Syria Outgrowing the Proxy Relationship', *Washington Quarterly* 30 (2): 44.

GoalEurope. 2013. 'Nearshoring: Top 20 largest In-House R&D offices in Ukraine', 4 October. http://goaleurope.com/2013/10/04/nearshore-outsourcing-top-20-largest-rd-offices-in-ukraine/

Goldstein, M., and N. Perlroth. 2015. 'Authorities Closing In on Hackers Who Stole Data From JPMorgan Chase', DealBook, *The New York Times*, 15 March. www.nytimes.com/2015/03/16/business/dealbook/authorities-closing-in-on-hackers-who-stole-data-from-jpmorgan-chase.html

Grosse, E. 2012. 'Security warnings for suspected state-sponsored attacks', Google Security Blog, 5 June. https://security.googleblog.com/2012/06/security-warnings-for-suspected-state.html

Holsti, K.J. 1964. 'The Concept of Power in the Study of International Relations', *Background* 7 (3): 182, 185.

Hughes, G. 2014a. 'Syria and the Perils of Proxy Warfare', *Small Wars & Insurgencies* 25 (3): 522–38.

Hughes, G. 2014b. *My Enemy's Enemy: Proxy Warfare in International Politics*. Portland, OR: Sussex Academic Press: 25–6.

Hughes, G. 2015. 'A Proxy War in Arabia: The Dhofar Insurgency and Cross-Border Raids into South Yemen', *The Middle East Journal* 69 (1): 91–104.

Joseph, R. 1987. *Democracy and Prebendal Politics in Nigeria*. Cambridge, UK: Cambridge University Press.

Klimburg, A. 2011. 'Mobilising Cyber Power', *Survival* 53: 43, 56.

Klimburg, A., and H. Tirmaa-Klaar. 2011. *Cyber Security and Cyberpower: Concepts, Conditions and Capabilities for Cooperation for Action Within the EU*. Brussels: European Parliament, p. 60.

Krebs, B. 2009. 'Story-Driven Résumé: My Best Work 2005–2009', Krebs on Security (blog).

Krebs, B. 2012. 'A Busy Week for Cybercrime Justice', Krebs on Security (blog).

Lobel, J. 1986. 'Covert War and Congressional Authority: Hidden War and Forgotten Power', *University of Pennsylvania Law Review* 134 (5): 1041, 1051.

Lord, B. 2015. 'Notifying Our Users of Attacks by Suspected State-Sponsored Actors', Yahoo!: The Paranoid (official blog), 21 December. https://www.verizon.com/about/news/notifying-our-users-attacks-suspected-state-sponsored-actors

Mann, M. 1986. *The Sources of Social Power, Volume 1: A History of Power from the Beginning to AD 1760*. New York: Cambridge University Press: 11.

Newton, M. 2006. 'War by Proxy: Legal and Moral Duties of "Other Actors" Derived From Government', *Case Western Reserve Journal of International Law* 23 (2/3).

Nikishin, A. 2016. 'ICS Threats. A Kaspersky Lab view, predictions and reality'. Presentation at RSA Conference, 29 February – 4 March.

Patterson, M. 2009. *Privatising Peace: A Corporate Adjunct to United Nations Peacekeeping and Humanitarian Operations*. New York: Palgrave Macmillan.

Percy, S. 2007. *Mercenaries: The History of a Norm in International Relations*. Oxford: Oxford University Press.

Perlroth, N. 2013. 'Hunting for Syrian Hackers' Chain of Command', *The New York Times*, 17 May. www.nytimes.com/2013/05/18/technology/financial-times-site-is-hacked.htm

Peterson, A. 2013. 'The NSA has its own team of elite hackers,' *The Washington Post*, 29 August. https://www.washingtonpost.com/news/the-switch/wp/2013/08/29/the-nsa-has-its-own-team-of-elite-hackers/

Powell, W. 2003. 'Neither Market nor Hierarchy', *The Sociology of Organizations: Classic, Contemporary, and Critical Readings*: 104–17.

Reuters. 2015. 'Cybercrime Ring Steals up to $1 Billion from Banks: Kaspersky', 14 February.

Rid, T. 2013. *Cyber War Will Not Take Place*. Oxford: Oxford University Press.

Rid, T., and B. Buchanan, 2015. 'Attributing Cyber Attacks', *Journal of Strategic Studies* 38 (1–2): 4.

Salehyan, I. 2010. 'The Delegation of War to Rebel Organizations', *Journal of Conflict Resolution* 54: 494, 496, 507–9.

Segal, A. 2016. *The Hacked World Order: How Nations Fight, Trade, Maneuver, and Manipulate in the Digital Age*. New York: Public Affairs: 6.

Shorrock, T. 2008. *Spies for Hire: The Secret World of Intelligence Outsourcing*. New York: Simon and Schuster.

Singer, P. 2003. *Corporate Warriors: The Rise of the Privatized Military Industry*. Ithaca, NY: Cornell University Press: 63.

Stamos, A. 2016. 'Notifications for Targeted Attacks', Facebook Security, 16 October. www.facebook.com/notes/facebook-security/notifications-for-targeted-attacks/10153092994615766/

Stanger, A. 2009. *One Nation Under Contract: The Outsourcing of American Power and the Future of Foreign Policy*. New Haven, CT: Yale University Press: 93.

'Tal Becker', Shalom Hartman Institute.

Thomson, J. 1994. *Mercenaries, Pirates, and Sovereigns: State-Building and Extraterritorial Violence in Early Modern Europe*. Princeton, NJ: Princeton University Press.

Tikk, E., K. Kaska, and L. Vihul. 2010. *International Cyber Incidents: Legal Considerations*. Tallinn: Cooperative Cyber Defence Centre of Excellence.

United Nations. 2015. 'Report of the Group of Governmental Experts on Developments in the Field of Information and Telecommunications in the Context of International Security', UN Doc. A/70/174.

United Nations Institute for Disarmament Research. 2011. 'Cyber security and Cyberwarfare—Preliminary Assessment of National Doctrine and Organization'. http://unidir.org/files/publications/pdfs/cyber security-and-cyberwarfare-preliminary-assessment-of-national-doctrine-and-organization-380.pdf

Villeneuve, N., N. Moran, T. Haq et al., 2013. 'Operation Saffron Rose', FireEye: 3.

Wilner, A. 2012. 'Apocalypse Soon? Deterring Nuclear Iran and its Terrorist Proxies', *Comparative Strategy* 31 (1): 21–2.

Wyatt, C.M. 2014. 'Princes, Patriots, and Proxies: Great Power, Politics and the Assertion of Afghan Sovereignty', *Fletcher Security Review* 1 (2).

Zhang, L. 2012. 'A Chinese Perspective on Cyber War', *International Review of the Red Cross* 94: 805.

CHAPTER 34

GETTING BEYOND NORMS: WHEN VIOLATING THE AGREEMENT BECOMES CUSTOMARY PRACTICE

MELISSA HATHAWAY

INTRODUCTION

CRITICAL infrastructure sectors and services, such as electricity generation, gas and oil production, telecommunications, water supply, transportation, and financial services, are becoming uniquely vulnerable to malicious attacks because of their increased automation, interconnectedness, and reliance on the Internet. This infrastructure–Internet entanglement has become a strategic vulnerability for most countries around the world, which are realizing that this serious weakness can threaten their national security and, potentially, international peace and stability. This realization came to the forefront in 2007, when a malicious computer worm known as 'Stuxnet' was used to degrade and ultimately shut down Iran's nuclear facility in Natanz. The use of this military-grade cyber weapon against a state utility sparked intense and urgent conversations within the international community about the importance of norms of state responsibility in cyberspace to ensuring the future safety and security of the Internet and Internet-based infrastructures.

Cyber *insecurity* is both a sovereign issue and an international challenge. The volume, scope, scale, and sophistication of cyber threats to critical services and infrastructures are outpacing defensive measures, while data breaches, criminal activity, essential e-service disruptions, and property destruction are becoming commonplace. The Stuxnet source code was analysed by experts around the world and then replicated with new variants (e.g. Flame, Gauss, DuQu, Wiper), proliferated, and traded on the black market by both state and non-state actors (Hathaway 2012). Countries are now increasingly concerned about the immediate and future threats that could emanate from the misuse of ICTs, and that could jeopardize international peace and security similarly to terrorism, transnational organized crime, infectious diseases, environmental degradation, and nuclear, biological, chemical, and radiological weapons. This makes it all the more necessary to advance a dialogue on how best to limit the misuse of ICTs in the digital age and constrain harmful state behaviour in cyberspace.

CODIFYING RESPONSIBLE STATE CYBER BEHAVIOUR

The development of normative standards guiding state behaviour—and especially the 'norm of state responsibility'—is enshrined in the United Nations (UN) Charter (2001) (UN General Assembly 2001). By signing the UN Charter, states not only commit to respecting the sovereignty rights of other countries but also accept certain responsibilities, which include avoiding harm to other states. Under customary international law of state responsibility, states bear responsibility for malicious activity that is attributable to the state that violates international and legal obligations applicable to that state of an international legal obligation applicable to that state. Following the 9/11 attacks, the 'norm of state responsibility' under international law has been more broadly interpreted to include 'state responsibility for the actions of non-state actors that follow from the state's failure to meet its international obligations to prevent its territory from being used as a platform or sanctuary for the non-state actors to attack other states' (Lotrionte 2012).

A number of multilateral institutions have been promoting the responsible use of technology and advocating for normative or 'responsible' behaviour among nations. The first set of discussions on these matters was proposed by Russia in 1998. Russia introduced a draft resolution in the First Committee of the UN General Assembly proposing that member states inform the then Secretary-General Kofi Annan about their views and assessments of the 'advisability of developing international principles that would enhance the security of global information and telecommunications systems and help to combat information terrorism and criminality.'[1] Russia continued to push the importance of this issue with similar draft proposals and, in January 2002, the General Assembly asked Secretary-General Annan to establish a Group of Governmental Experts (GGE) to report on the potential threats in the sphere of information security and possible cooperative measures to address them.[2] The first UN GGE was established in 2004 and included 15 member states selected on the basis of equitable geographical distribution. They were expected to submit a report on the outcome of their study to the General Assembly at its sixtieth session in 2005. No consensus was achieved by the group, however, although the discussion did open the channel of communications among nations on the importance of cybersecurity as it contributes to international peace and stability—building on the common understanding of the UN Charter and customary law enshrined therein.

Since 2004, six GGEs have studied the threats posed by the misuse of ICTs in the context of international security. Four of these GGEs have studied the threats posed by the misuse of ICTs in the context of international security and how these threats should be addressed (UN Office for Disarmament Affairs 2019). Three of these iterations have resulted in the publication of substantive consensus reports with conclusions and recommendations.

For example, the second GGE (2009/10) was asked to identify initial measures and behaviours to protect critical national and international infrastructures from cyber harm, and to propose methods to reduce collective risks posed by malicious activities. The report, published in 2010, stated that the effects from the misuse of ICTs 'carry significant risk for public safety, the security of nations and the stability of the globally linked international community as a whole'.[3] The report also called for the development of confidence-building and risk-reduction measures, including discussion on the use of ICTs during conflict. It recommended that the member states undertake information exchanges on their respective national legislation and ICT security strategies, and conduct capacity building in less-developed countries.

The third GGE (2012/13) consisted again of 15 member states—although with a slightly different geographical distribution—and produced an important consensus document in 2013.[4] All five UN Security Council permanent members of the group (i.e. China, France, the Russian Federation, the United Kingdom, and the United States) asserted that 'international law, and in particular the Charter of the United Nations, is applicable and is essential to maintaining peace and stability and promoting an open, secure, peaceful and accessible ICT environment.' Beyond the UN Charter, the document specifically enumerated state sovereignty, human rights, and the law of state responsibility as among the applicable bodies of international law governing state use of ICTs.[5] The report concluded that 'states must meet their international obligations regarding internationally wrongful acts attributable to them'.

The fourth GGE (2014/15) consisted of 20 member states[6] and their consensus report officially endorsed and adopted a set of voluntary, non-binding norms of responsible state behaviour in cyberspace, explicitly building on the 2013 report.[7]

Three norms stood out in particular. The UN GGE member countries agreed that:

- 'A State should not conduct or knowingly support ICT activity contrary to its obligations under international law that intentionally damages critical infrastructure or otherwise impairs the use and operation of critical infrastructure to provide services to the public.'[8]
- 'States should not knowingly allow their territory to be used for internationally wrongful acts using ICTs.'[9]
- 'States should take appropriate measures to protect their critical infrastructure from ICT threats, taking into account General Assembly resolution 58/199 on the creation of a global culture of cybersecurity and the protection of critical information infrastructures, and other relevant resolutions.'[10]

These norms received international endorsement by the UN General Assembly in December 2015, and also by the G-7, G-20, and the Organization for Security and Cooperation in Europe (OSCE) in the following years.

In June 2017, the fifth GGE (2016/17)—which by then included experts from 25 member states[11]—concluded another round of deliberations. They had been tasked with studying 'existing and potential threats in the sphere of information security' and measures to address them, including 'norms, rules, and principles of responsible behaviour of states, confidence-building measures, and capacity-building'. More importantly, the Group was supposed to reach an agreement on *how* 'international law applies to the use of information and communications technologies by states'. However, this particular issue of how international law applies in cyberspace, and especially the applicability of the law of countermeasures and the inherent right of self-defence, became a deeply divisive topic. Rather than converging toward a common understanding and agreement, the Group failed to produce a consensus report. The United States expected 'clear and direct statements on how certain international law applies to states' use of ICTs, including international humanitarian law, international law governing states' exercise of their inherent right of self-defense, and the law of state responsibility, including countermeasures' (Markoff 2017). Other countries, however, rejected the inclusion of such provisions in a consensus report. The Cuban representative argued that recognizing self-defence rights in cyberspace would lead to a militarization of cyberspace that would 'legitimize ... unilateral punitive force actions, including the application of sanctions and even military action by states claiming to be victims of illicit uses of ICTs' (Rodriguez 2017). Instead, Cuba argued that the Group should be emphasizing the peaceful settlement of disputes and conflict prevention. In response, Western countries stated that the use of international legal frameworks precisely 'help reduce the risk of conflict by creating stable expectations of how states may and may not respond to cyber incidents they face' (Korzak 2017)' The failure of member states to reach an agreement on the matter, however, stalled the UN GGE process for almost two years, with some experts considering it defunct forever.

The same year, in September 2017, UN Secretary-General Antonío Guterres renewed calls for member states to work on an international framework for responsible state behaviour in cyberspace by stating that 'cyber war is becoming less and less a hidden reality—and more and more able to disrupt relations among States and destroy some of the structures and systems of modern life'. He acknowledged that traditional forms of regulations do not apply, signalling a need for strategic thinking, ethical reflection, and thoughtful regulation. The dialogue about responsible state behaviour in cyberspace was reinstated at the UN General Assembly plenary meeting in December 2018. Two different processes were launched to discuss the issue of security in cyberspace during the UN session running from 2019 to 2021. Russia proposed a resolution along the same lines of its previous ones on this matter, which ultimately resulted in the establishment of an (OEWG) on Information and Communication Technology Developments in the Context of International Security...that was comprised of the entire UN membership (UN General Assembly 2018). The group intended to further the development of norms and principles for responsible state behaviour in cyberspace, and to look for meaningful ways to implement them. It was intended that the group would deliver a final report at the seventy-fifth session of the UN General Assembly in September 2020. The OEWG's work was delayed by the COVID-19 pandemic and their final report was published in March 2021. Another resolution, proposed by the United States, established a new GGE on 'Advancing responsible state behaviour in cyberspace in the context of international security' UN General Assembly 2019. This group continued to study possible cooperative measures to address information security threats for the following two years and reached a consensus on their final report in May 2021. Their report built upon the previous GGEs, reaffirmed the 11 norms agreed on in 2015, and provided guidance on how to implement or adhere to each of these norms.

In May 2018, before the conclusion of the OEWG and the sixth GGE, Secretary-General Guterres had already noted ... that the UN GGE process had made progress on 'norms, rules, and principles of responsible behaviour of states' (UN Secretary General 2018). The internationally agreed norms established in 2015 remain important and should be the basis upon which the new UN initiatives must build. To make any tangible progress, each member state is going to have to learn about the importance of cybersecurity to their overall economic and national security well-being as well as how the misuse of ICTs can affect the stability of their sovereignty. The member states must commit not just in principle but in action to ensure the future safety and security of the Internet and Internet-based infrastructures. The world needs to move beyond declaratory statements because the disruptive and destructive activities in cyberspace are becoming commonplace.

THE DE FACTO NORMS

Despite the unanimous consensus on the high-level set of international norms for responsible state behaviour in cyberspace—endorsed by the entire UN General Assembly in December 2015 and reiterated in countries' declaratory policies even after the 2017 GGE—some of the key tenets in these norms have been consistently violated. There have been multiple instances of wrongful use of ICTs and harm caused to nations' critical infrastructures and services since the approval of the 2015 UN GGE agreement—some caused by signatories of the agreement itself. Moreover, there is a general unwillingness by member states to call out the wrongful use of ICTs by other countries for political or economic reasons and this has contributed to a new de facto norm—'anything goes.' This is dangerous because it increases the risks to international peace, security, and stability—the very things that the process has been trying to prevent since 2002.

Unfortunately, disrupting or damaging critical infrastructures that provide services to the public has become customary practice—the new normal. In the past four years and especially since the 2015 UN GGE agreement, there has been an alarming number of harmful incidents targeting critical infrastructures and vital national networks around the world. Citizen-essential services are being knocked offline, causing significant disruption to society and economic stress to companies and countries. Indiscriminate use of ICT weapons is affecting power, telecommunications, oil and gas, financial, healthcare and transportation systems, and infrastructures. No sector is untouched.

For example, in late December 2015, three Ukrainian regional electric power distribution companies were simultaneously targeted, bringing more than 50 substations offline and leaving more than 225,000 residents without power for up to six hours. The malicious software used in this attack damaged equipment and prevented engineers from remotely restoring power. Months later, the distribution centres were still running under constrained operations, affecting the quality of service to citizens and businesses (ICS-CERT 2016). Almost exactly a year later, Ukraine suffered another sophisticated attack against the Pivnichna electric substation outside its capital Kiev (Goodin 2017). The attacks against Ukraine were successful and quite instructive, especially because they were clear instances in which intentional damage against a state's critical infrastructure was perpetrated (Lee, Assante, and Conway 2016)—and likely conducted by a UN GGE member state—and the rest of the world did not publicly condemn these actions. And, while the UN GGE norms only apply during peacetime, some experts would say that this type of attack against a civilian target must still meet a necessary and proportional threshold, permissible during wartime under international law. Similar destructive malware has since been discovered in nuclear and electric power plants in Germany, South Korea, the United States, and elsewhere, and the leaders of those nations have remained largely silent.

At the end of 2016, Internet service providers (ISPs) and businesses around the globe were victims of a variety of disruptive and damaging distributed denial-of-service (DDoS) attacks. Even more worrisome is the fact that these types of DDoS attack (which are significantly above 200 gigabits per second) can be dangerous for network operators and cause collateral damage across cloud hosting environments, service providers, and enterprise networks (NetScout 2016). Attacks of this size can also impair the functionality of the entire Internet infrastructure—disrupting the free flow of goods, services, data, and capital across borders. Recent DDoS attacks have peaked at 1.7 terabits per second and there was a 200% increase in DDoS attacks in the first quarter of 2019 that averaged at least 100 gigabits per second.[12] The harm posed to nations by DDoS attacks underscores the importance of two of the international norms adopted by UN GGE, specifically that 'States should take appropriate measures to protect their critical infrastructure from ICT threats' and 'should not knowingly allow their territory to be used for internationally wrongful acts using ICTs'.

In 2016, individuals in the United States created and deployed a malicious software called 'Mirai' to turn Internet-connected devices into remotely controlled 'bots' that were then used to mount large-scale network attacks.[13] This malware infected over 600,000 vulnerable Internet of Things (IoT) devices (Cloudflare 2017). As part of this string of attacks, in October 2016, the Mirai malicious software was used to launch a DDoS attack against the Domain Name System (DNS) infrastructure and Internet provider Dyn in the United States (York 2016). The DNS is the 'telephone directory' for the Internet so, when Dyn was knocked offline, all its customers were too, including PayPal, *The New York Times*, Spotify, Airbnb, and others. Thousands of citizens and other businesses were adversely affected as well.

In November 2016, the Mirai software was used again in Europe, knocking nearly one million Deutsche Telekom customers offline (Auchard 2016). This time, the malicious software attempted to infect routers and thus affected a much broader part of the Internet's infrastructure. In March 2019, a new variant of Mirai emerged, which was now able to 'botnetize' just about any connected device and is attacking an alarming number of businesses. The Mirai attacks have highlighted various vulnerabilities and the lack of security of the IoT and the 'smart' devices it comprises. Between 2016 and 2017, IoT attacks increased by nearly 600% (Symantec 2019). These attacks also highlight why the Internet's security and stability are issues of international concern.

As countries continue to embrace the economic opportunities of becoming more connected to the Internet, and adopting and embedding more IoT devices in every part of life, they must also prepare for the misuse of these same ICT-based devices. Moreover, countries should be held accountable to the norm that 'States should not knowingly allow their territory to be used for internationally wrongful acts using ICTs.' Allowing infected devices within a country's territory to be harnessed to conduct illegal or illicit activity against another state is, in fact, a clear violation of this norm. States must demonstrate that they are willing to take the necessary steps to protect the security and mitigate the misuse of the Internet in their own countries. By funding and fielding results-based initiatives, a state can demonstrate its active vigilance and commitment to minimize and mitigate the damages caused by any misuse of ICT-based devices, and therefore become a steward for the promotion of safety, security, and stability in cyberspace. For example, states should invest in technologies and regulations that could be used to mitigate malicious rerouting of Internet traffic, and that would make it harder for machines (within a state's sovereign networked infrastructures) to be harnessed in a botnet and used in a scaled DDoS attack.

Sweden also suffered a series of attacks against its critical infrastructures in 2016. The attacks began with the purposeful sabotage of the radio mast owned and operated by the state-owned broadcasting company Teracom. Of particular importance, this mast supports the national command-and-control system of the country (*The Guardian* 2016). Swedish experts believe that the activity was a violation of the UN GGE norm of non-interference in the internal affairs of the state. It was also a clear violation of the norm against conducting activities that impair the use and operation of critical infrastructures. A few days later, air traffic control glitches were recorded in the computer systems at Stockholm's Arlanda and Bromma airports, as well as at the Landvetter airport in Gothenburg. At that time, aviation authorities said that a 'communications problem' with a radar system forced them to ground all planes (*NT News* 2016). While the radar problem was fixed several hours later, subsequent delays and disruptions raised fears about the ramifications of a potential compromise of Sweden's air traffic control system. The possibility of sabotage was later dismissed, but the events caused great concern among Sweden's leaders.[14] In March 2017, the Swedish government reintroduced military conscription and, in April 2019, the Swedish Defence Commission published a paper highlighting the fact that their military-strategic situation had deteriorated so much that Sweden must move to a wartime footing and increase its military capacity to include offensive and defensive cyber capabilities.[15]

Beginning in November 2016 and culminating in January 2017, Saudi Arabia fell victim to a series of critical infrastructure attacks that used the Shamoon 2 virus. The original Shamoon virus was first observed in 2012 and was designed to collect, disrupt, and damage targeted systems. The virus propagates through networked systems, compiles lists of files from specific locations on those systems, uploads files to the attacker, and then erases the master boot record of the infected system to render it inoperable. The Shamoon 2 virus is even more virulent and effective. In January 2017, the Saudi government issued a warning notice to all telecommunications companies alerting them that they had 'detected destructive electronic strikes against several government agencies and vital establishments'. The Saudi government went on to claim that this was a systemic attack on crucial government agencies, including the transport sector, and that the attacks were aimed at halting operations, stealing data, planting viruses, and damaging equipment by overwriting the master boot record (which makes attribution difficult because it erases the intruder's tracks) (Sewell 2016). These attacks have continued for months and are a clear violation of the norm that prescribes that a 'state should not conduct or knowingly support ICT activity contrary to its obligations under international law that intentionally damages critical infrastructure or otherwise impairs the use and operation of critical infrastructure to provide services to the public'. At the time of writing, members of the UN GGE have not publicly renounced the harm caused to the Kingdom of Saudi Arabia by these attacks.

The global financial services sector has also experienced a wide range of malicious activities ranging from DDoS attacks to breaches of core networks for the past several years. These successful intrusions have resulted in the loss of both personally identifiable information and real money, and have potentially allowed money laundering from other rogue states (e.g. North Korea). A number of breaches at major banks were caused by security weaknesses in the Society for Worldwide Interbank Financial Telecommunication (SWIFT) system—the international payment and messaging system used by banks and other financial institutions to request and approve money transfers. In January 2016, hackers were able to exploit the SWIFT system to steal US$12 million in at least 12 fraudulent money transfers from the Ecuadorian Banco del Austro's account at Wells Fargo to bank accounts across the globe. In February 2016, hackers were able to use this same electronic bank messaging technology to steal US$81 million—one of the biggest electronic heists in history—from the Bangladesh Central Bank's official account at the New York Federal Reserve Bank and to transfer it to accounts in the Philippines (it would have been US$1 billion if not for a mere typo in the SWIFT message sent). After intense investigation by law enforcement, SWIFT acknowledged that the scheme involved using malicious software to alter SWIFT software and tamper with a database recording the bank's activity over the network, which allowed attackers to delete outgoing transfer requests and intercept incoming requests, as well as to change recorded account balances—effectively hiding evidence of fraudulent transfers. The malware even interfered with a printer to ensure that paper copies of transfer requests did not give the attack away. The Philippine Central Bank admitted that its accounts were illegally used to enable a web of transfers and currency conversions, before moving the cash through casinos in Manila and junket operators (Barrett and Burne 2016).

It was not until April 2016 that SWIFT finally warned customers that it was aware of 'a number of recent cyber incidents' where attackers had sent fraudulent messages over its system and manipulated the SWIFT's Alliance Access server software (Finkle 2016), and started releasing mandatory software security updates. While the warning did not contain the names of any of the victims or discuss the value of any losses from the previous attacks, publicly available information reveals that at least a dozen other banks linked to SWIFT's global payments network (that had irregularities similar to those in the Bangladesh case) could have been victims of this software vulnerability (Bergin and Finkle 2016; Riley and Katz 2016), and some lost millions of dollars:

- Tien Phong Bank, Vietnam (thwarted attack in December 2015) (*RT News* 2016);
- Banco del Austro SA, Ecuador (lost US$12 million in January 2015) (Schwartz 2016);
- Bangladesh Central Bank, Bangladesh (lost US$81 million in February 2016) (Kovacs 2016); and
- Philippine Central Bank, Philippines (involved in the Bangladesh fraud).[16]

The forensic analysis of the malware used against the Tien Phong bank showed that the malware contained a 'target folder' that included the SWIFT codes for many other banks (Riley, Robertson, and Katz 2016), including:

- Industrial & Commercial Bank of China Ltd., China (world's largest bank by assets);
- Bank of Tokyo Mitsubishi UFJ Ltd., Japan (Japan's largest bank);
- UniCredit SpA, Italy (Italy's largest bank);
- Australia & New Zealand Banking Group Ltd.;
- United Overseas Bank Ltd., Singapore;
- Kookmin Bank, South Korea; and
- Mizuho Bank Ltd., Japan.

In May 2016, SWIFT publicly acknowledged that 'the Bangladesh fraud was not an isolated incident', and that they were aware of many attempts to compromise banks, obtain credentials to payment generation systems to send fraudulent payments, and obfuscate the statements/confirmations from their counter-parties (Liebbrandt 2016). They also stated that 'the threat is very persistent, adaptive and sophisticated—and it is here to stay', and that banks using the SWIFT network—which includes both central banks and commercial banks—had been hit with a 'meaningful' number of attacks, about one-fifth of them resulting in stolen funds since the Bangladesh heist.[17] The same month, security firm BAE Systems published a report warning about a global campaign exploiting the security weaknesses in the SWIFT's messaging system of financial institutions (Shevchenko and Nish 2016). The report showed that the malware used in the attacks against the Vietnam and Bangladesh banks was linked to the Lazarus hacking group with known affiliations to North Korea.

Banks around the world continue to be robbed of their money, undermining the integrity of public trust in the financial systems writ large. Some recent examples include:

- the Far Eastern International Bank in Taiwan, which lost almost US$60 million in October 2017;[18]
- the NIC Asia Bank, based in Kathmandu, Nepal, which lost US$4.4 million in fraudulent money transfers from its accounts to accounts in six other countries in November 2017;[19]
- the Russian bank Globex, which lost about US$6million in December 2017;[20]
- the National Bank of Kenya, which lost approximately US$287 thousand in January 2018;[21]
- India's City Union Bank, which lost US$2 million in February 2018 (*Reuters* 2018);[22]
- the Bank Negara in Malaysia, which detected and foiled unauthorized fund transfers using falsified SWIFT messages in March 2018;[23]
- the Banco de México (Banxico), which lost US$20 million in April 2018;[24]
- the Banco Chile, which lost US$10 million in May 2018;[25] and
- the State Bank of Mauritius (SBM), which lost US$20 million in October 2018.[26]

While many of the banks affected are private entities, all central banks and federal reserve banks are also critical infrastructures of nations. The malicious use of ICTs against the SWIFT system and the attacks on banks all around the world clearly show that states are not in compliance with the norm that requires them to 'take appropriate measures to protect their critical infrastructure from ICT threats'. The SWIFT vulnerability also highlights the need for states to cooperate, exchange information, assist each other, and prosecute the criminal use of ICTs over the Internet.

In May 2017, the world experienced a global attack by a very simple ransomware named WannaCry, which reached 150 countries within minutes and halted manufacturing operations, transportation systems, and telecommunications systems. In particular, the UK's National Health Service (NHS) was significantly affected. According to the UK National Audit Office, WannaCry hit at least 81 of the 236 NHS trusts—rendering medical equipment inoperable, and significantly affecting public health and safety (National Audit Office 2017). Australia, Canada, Japan, New Zealand, the United Kingdom, and the United States attributed the attack to North Korea and denounced it for its involvement in WannaCry, albeit seven months after the event (White House 2017). Clearly, when nearly one-third of a country's healthcare facilities are knocked offline, citizen safety is also put at risk. The attack, which intentionally damaged and impaired critical infrastructures and essential public services in many other countries, was later attributed to North Korea. In conducting this attack, North Korea blatantly violated the UN GGE norm of responsible state behaviour in cyberspace.

One month later, in June 2017, a destructive malware called NotPetya was released into the world's networked businesses by way of a software update for a widely used Ukrainian company's accounting program (doc.me). NotPetya contained a wiper program similar to those used against other countries (e.g. Stuxnet, Flame, Gauss, DuQu, etc.). Within minutes, the malware infected and destroyed tens of thousands of Internet-connected systems in more than 65 countries, including those belonging to government institutions, banks, energy firms, and other companies. Business operations halted in many companies, including A.P. Moller-Maersk (shipping), Merck (pharmaceuticals), Mondelez (confections), and DLA-Piper (legal services). Shipping giant A.P. Moller-Maersk was one of the companies most affected by this attack. The company is responsible for the management of 76 port facilities worldwide and roughly 20% of the world's container shipping capacity (*Reuters* 2017). It was figuratively and literally dead in the water after NotPetya spread across its entire global network. It took weeks for Maersk to resume operations, and the incident cost the company US$435 million to replace the entire information technology systems that powered its digital business (Moller-Maersk 2017). It also negatively affected Denmark's overall gross domestic product (GDP) as Maersk contributes at least 7% of the country's GDP. The primary and ancillary losses of NotPetya to the digital economy were significant and the harm (damage) to critical services and infrastructures took months to recover from.

Eight months later, in February 2018, Denmark, the United Kingdom, and the United States attributed this attack to Russia. Condemning the attack as an assault to society and the economy, British Defence Secretary Gavin Williamson stated that 'Russia is ripping up the rulebook by undermining democracy, wrecking livelihoods by targeting critical infrastructure and weaponizing information.' He also urged that 'we must be primed and ready to tackle these stark and intensifying threats' (Fortune 2018). Russia rebutted his accusations claiming that they were groundless (*France24* 2018).

As demonstrated, the world has witnessed an alarming number of harmful acts through the misuse of ICTs in recent years. States remain unchecked in their abuse and misuse of ICTs. They are unafraid of international naming and shaming much less any real consequences of retaliation. Even worse, they are arming themselves, preparing self-defensive measures, and anticipating conflict. In April 2019, the European Union (EU) urgently called for state actors to stop undertaking malicious cyber activities and stressed the need to respect the rules-based order in cyberspace. In May 2019, it adopted a framework:

> to impose targeted restrictive measures to deter and respond to cyber-attacks which constitute an external threat to the EU or its member states, including cyber-attacks against third states or international organisations where restricted measures are considered necessary to achieve the objectives of the EU Common Foreign and Security Policy (CFSP).[27]

The same month, in May 2019, NATO leadership declared that the Western military alliance was ready to use all means at its disposal to respond to cyberattacks after the UK shared details of malicious Russian activity being used against 16 of the 29 NATO members over the past 18 months.[28] Moreover, seven members of NATO had already declared to be standing ready to employ the full force of their cyber arsenal should one member fall victim to a particularly grievous cyberattack.[29]

Based on these events, threats to international peace and security are escalating. International agreement on what should be considered responsible state behaviour in cyberspace is in paralysis. The gross disregard of formal commitments by member states in a multilateral institution and its processes affirms that declaratory aspirations without action can undermine the best intentions of those same states, the integrity of multilateral agreements, and even subvert the UN process itself. All evidence suggests that states are not following their own doctrine of restraint, and that each disruptive and destructive attack further destabilizes our future safety and well-being. Dialogue is urgently needed to build confidence and restore trust among states. This requires obtaining consensus that states meet their international obligations regarding internationally wrongful acts attributable to them. It must also meet the expectation that states commit not just in principle but in action to ensure the future safety and security of their society's critical infrastructures and services.

FIVE STANDARDS OF CARE

If states want to resuscitate efforts to establish voluntary, non-binding norms of responsible state behaviour in cyberspace and make sure that in the future these norms become truly meaningful words that can achieve their desired goals, then their actions and practice must demonstrate those tenets. States must first and foremost negotiate with other countries on an equal footing, and agree on what exactly they want to govern in cyberspace (e.g. data protection and privacy; rules and standards dealing with telecommunications, trade, and finances; digital trade and the Internet economy; restricting and monitoring digital content; and countering extremism and fake news).

States must then demonstrate that they are willing to take the necessary steps to protect the security and prevent the misuse of the Internet in their respective countries. They must also outwardly condemn harmful acts conducted or condoned by other states. These results-based initiatives would demonstrate individual states' vigilance and commitment to minimize and mitigate the damages caused by any misuse of ICTs, and therefore to become stewards for the promotion of safety, security, and stability in cyberspace. The following five standards of care can be used to 'test' individual states' true commitment to the international norms of behaviour they have already ascribed to:

1. States should take the necessary measures to stop malicious rerouting of Internet traffic and make it harder for machines to be harnessed in a botnet and to participate in a scaled DDoS attack. Specifically, states should require:
- ISPs and the Internet Exchange (IX) community to do more to identify compromised devices, provide early warning of new infections, and offer managed security services to clean up the networked infrastructures to significantly reduce, if not eliminate, the infections;
- ISPs and the IX community to provide authentic and authoritative routing information, by adopting secure Border Gateway Protocol (BGP) routing procedures and protocols; and
- the Internet services community (e.g. manufacturers, distributors, suppliers, retailers, and others who make digital products and services) to provide authentic and authoritative naming information as part of their product interface or service. DNS trust must be established throughout the DNS hierarchy, from root servers to browsers (Hathaway 2016; Hathaway and Savage 2012).
2. States should focus on consumer protection and citizen safety, in order to mitigate the risks of next-generation threats now posed by the IoT, by introducing proactive

responsibility and accountability into the marketplace through product liability. Today's flawed products are disrupting businesses, damaging property, and jeopardizing economic and national security. States need to take the necessary steps to hold accountable manufacturers, distributors, suppliers, retailers, and others who make digital products and services available to the public for the security flaws in their offerings, in particular when the security flaws are easily prevented by commonly accepted good engineering principles at that time.

3. States should cooperate on investigations and provide technical, investigative, and financial assistance to other states that lack the domestic capacity to do so.

4. States should demonstrate a commitment to protecting their society against cybercrime by codifying domestic criminal legislation and using those laws to prosecute criminal offences both nationally and internationally.

5. States should build capacity to investigate cybercrime by training legislative authorities and investigative personnel.

Conclusion

Leaders around the globe have come to recognize that cyber insecurity is both a sovereign issue and an international challenge. The risks to critical infrastructure and services have been shown to adversely affect international peace, security, and stability. The UN GGE endorsed and adopted a set of norms for responsible state behaviour in cyberspace. To move from cyber insecurity to cyber stability, states need to enforce these norms, speak out, hold other states that violate them accountable, and take steps to adopt and implement the standards of care outlined earlier. Only with a concerted and coordinated effort across the global community will it be possible to change the 'new normal' of 'anything goes' and move forward to ensure the future safety and security of the Internet and Internet-based infrastructures.

If we fail to de-escalate today's tensions and close the gap of divergent views, the world will likely witness ongoing hostility and even open conflict. A state's inherent right to self-defence will be exercised. Moreover, states will most likely revert to what they can control and will regulate their sovereign cyberspace unilaterally by passing laws and regulations, and asserting new policies. This too will change the way states interact in commerce and politics. This dangerous situation makes it all the more necessary to advance a dialogue on how best to limit the misuse of ICTs in the digital age and constrain harmful state behaviour in cyberspace.[30]

Notes

1. UN General Assembly, Resolution (A/Res/53/70) (1999) [on the report of the First Committee (A/53/576)]. The resolution was adopted, see: https://undocs.org/A/RES/53/70

2. UN General Assembly, Resolution (A/Res/56/19) (2002): https://undocs.org/A/RES/56/19

3. Members included Belarus, Brazil, China, Estonia, France, Germany, India, Israel, Italy, Qatar, the Republic of Korea, Russian Federation, South Africa, the United Kingdom, and the United States. UN General Assembly, 'Report of the Group of Governmental Experts

on Developments in the Field of Information and Telecommunications in the Context of International Security' (A/65/201), 30 July 2010: https://undocs.org/A/65/201

4. Members included Argentina, Australia, Belarus, Canada, China, Egypt, Estonia, France, Germany, India, Indonesia, Japan, Russian Federation, the United Kingdom, and the United States. UN General Assembly, Group of Governmental Experts on Developments in the Field of Information and Telecommunications in the Context of International Security (A/68/98), 24 June 2013: https://undocs.org/A/68/98

5. UN General Assembly, Group of Governmental Experts on Developments in the Field of Information and Telecommunications in the Context of International Security (A/68/98), 24 June 2013, p.8. https://undocs.org/A/68/98

6. Members included Belarus, Brazil, China, Colombia, Egypt, Estonia, France, Germany, Ghana, Israel, Japan, Kenya, Malaysia, Mexico, Pakistan, the Republic of Korea, the Russian Federation, Spain, the United Kingdom, and the United States.

7. UN General Assembly, Group of Governmental Experts on Developments in the Field of Information and Telecommunications in the Context of International Security, (A/70/174), 22 July 2015: https://undocs.org/A/70/174

8. UN General Assembly, Group of Governmental Experts, para 13(f).

9. UN General Assembly, Group of Governmental Experts, para 13(c).

10. UN General Assembly, Group of Governmental Experts, para 13(g).

11. Members included Australia, Botswana, Brazil, Canada, China, Cuba, Egypt, Estonia, Finland, France, Germany, India, Indonesia, Japan, Kazakhstan, Kenya, Mexico, the Netherlands, the Republic of Korea, the Russian Federation, Senegal, Serbia, Switzerland, the United Kingdom, and the United States.

12. Neustar, https://ns-cdn.neustar.biz/creative_services/biz/neustar/www/resources/whitepapers/it-security/neustar-cyber-threats-and-trends-report-q1-2019.pdf?_ga=2.235 456769.1867608730.1558875227-1888682377.1558875227

13. The Mirai malicious software has two functions: it has an 'attack now' component that harnesses and channels traffic from an infected device and directs it toward a victim's server, and a 'go looking' function that uses traffic from an infected device to hunt for other insecure devices to infect.

14. Personal interview with Richard Oehme, Director, Office of Cybersecurity and Critical Infrastructure Protection, Swedish Civil Contingencies Agency, in Arlington, VA: 3 October 2016.

15. The Swedish Defence Commission's white book on Sweden's Security Policy and the Development of the Military Defence 2021–25: https://www.gov.se/49a295/globalassets/regeringen/dokument/forsvarsdepartementet/forsvarsberedningen/slutrapport-14-maj/defence-commissions-white-book-english-summary.pdf

16. Barrett and Burne, 'FBI'.

17. Bergin and Finkle, 'Exclusive'.

18. 'Lai Orders Information Security Review', *Taipei Times*, 8 October 2017.

19. 'NIC Asia Bank Seeks CIB Help to Down SWIFT Server Hacker', *The Himalayan Times*, 5 November 2017.

20. 'Hackers Steal $6 Million in SWIFT System Attack in Russia', *RadioFreeEurope*, 15 February 2018.

21. https://medium.com/@NicKanali/national-bank-of-kenya-loses-ksh-29-million-to-hackers-5885752ec1b8

22. 'India's City Union Bank CEO says suffered cyber hack via SWIFT system', *Reuters*, 18 February 2018.

23. http://www.bnm.gov.my/index.php?ch=en_press&pg=en_press&ac=4651
24. 'How Hackers Pulled Off a $20 Million Mexican Bank Heist', *WIRED*, 15 March 2019.
25. 'Chile to Seek Cybersecurity Advice after Hackers Rob Bank', *Business Times*, 13 June 2018
26. 'Fraudsters Duped State Bank of Mauritius by Hacking SWIFT System', *Mumbai Mirror*, 13 October 2018.
27. https://www.consilium.europa.eu/en/press/press-releases/2019/05/17/cyber-attacks-council-is-now-able-to-impose-sanctions/
28. https://www.securityweek.com/nato-warns-russia-full-range-responses-cyberattack
29. The seven NATO members that have pledged their offensive cyber weapons to the alliance are Estonia, Denmark, France, Germany, Netherlands, the United Kingdom and the United States.
30. This chapter is based on CIGI Paper No. 127 published by the Centre for International Governance Innovation in April 2017 entitled 'Getting Beyond Norms: When Violating the Agreement Becomes Customary Practice'.

REFERENCES

Auchard Eric. 2016. 'German Internet Outage Was Failed Botnet Attempt: Report', *Reuters*, 28 November. http://www.reuters.com/article/us-deutsche-telekom-outages-idUSKBN13N12K

Barrett, Devlinn, and Katy Burne. 2016. 'FBI Investigating Bangladesh Bank-Account Heist', *The Wall Street Journal*, 18 March www.wsj.com/articles/fbi-investigating-bangladesh-bank-account-heist-1458313232

Bergin, Tom, and Jim Finkle. 2016. 'Exclusive: SWIFT Confirms New Cyber Thefts, Hacking Tactics', *Reuters*, 12 December. www.reuters.com/article/ us-usa-cyber-swift-exclusive-idUSKBN1412NT

'Chile to Seek Cybersecurity Advice after Hackers Rob Bank', *Business Times*, 13 June 2018.

Cloudflare. 2017. 'Inside the Infamous Mirai IoT Botnet: A Retrospective Analysis,' 14 December. https://blog.cloudflare.com/inside-mirai-the-infamous-iot-botnet-a-retrospective-analysis/.

Finkle Jim. 2016. 'Exclusive: SWIFT Warns Customers of Multiple Cyber Fraud Cases', *Reuters*, 26 April www.reuters.com/ article/us-cyber-banking-swift- exclusive-idUSKCN0XM2DI

'Russia Blamed for "Costliest Cyberattack in History": What You Need to Know', *Fortune*, 16 February 2018.

'Kremlin "categorically" denies Russia behind NotPetya cyber-attack', *France24*, 15 February 2018

Goodin, Dan. 2017. 'Hackers Trigger Yet Another Power Outage in Ukraine', *Ars Technica*, 11 January. https://arstechnica.com/security/2017/01/the-new-normal-yet-another-hacker-caused-power-outage-hits-ukraine/

Guterres, António, UN Secretary-General. 2017. 'Secretary General's Address to the General Assembly.' 19 September. https://www.un.org/sg/en/content/sg/statement/2017-09-19/secretary-generals-address-general-assembly

Hathaway, Melissa. 2012. 'Leadership and Responsibility for Cybersecurity', *Georgetown Journal of International Affairs: Engagement on Cyber 2.0*, November .

Hathaway, Melissa. 2016. 'What Trump Can Do About Cybersecurity,' *Bloomberg View*, 30 November. www.bloomberg.com/view/articles/2016-11-30/what-trump-can-do-about-cybersecurity

Hathaway, Melissa, and John Savage, 2012. 'Stewardship of Cyberspace: Duties for Internet Service Providers', Cyber Dialogue Conference, Toronto: Munk School of Global Affairs, University of Toronto, March. www.cyberdialogue.citizenlab.org/ wp-content/uploads/ 2012/2012papers/ CyberDialogue2012_hathaway-savage.pdf

ICS-CERT. 2016. 'Cyber Attack Against Ukrainian Critical Infrastructure', 25 February. https:// ics-cert.us-cert.gov/alerts/IR-ALERT-H-16-056-0

Korzak, Elaine 2017 'UN GGE on Cybersecurity: The End of an Era?', The Diplomat, 31 July 2017.

Kovacs, Eduard. 2016. 'Custom Malware Used in \$81 Million Bangladesh Bank Heist', Security Week, 26 Aprilwww.securityweek.com/custom-malware-used-81-million-bangladesh-bank-heist

Lee, Robert M., Michael J. Assante, and Tim Conway, 2016. Analysis of the Cyber Attack on the Ukrainian Power Grid, Defense Use Case No. 5. Washington, DC: SANS Industrial Control Systems and the Electricity Information Sharing and Analysis Center. https://ics.sans. org/ media/E-ISAC_SANS_Ukraine_DUC_5.pdf

Leibbrandt, Gottfried. 2016. 'Gottfried Leibbrandt on Cyber Security and Innovation', Speech at the 14th annual European Financial Services Conference, Brussels, May. www.swift.com/ insights/press-releases/gottfried-leibbrandt- on-cyber-security-and-innovation

Lotrionte, Catherine. 2012. 'State Sovereignty and Self-Defense in Cyberspace: A Normative Framework for Balancing Legal Rights', Emory International Law Review 26 (2): 857

Markoff, Michele. 2017.'Explanation of Position at the Conclusion of the 2016-2017 UN Group of Governmental Experts (GGE) on Developments in the Field of Information and Telecommunications in the Context of International Security', 23 June. https://usun. usmission.gov/explanation-of-position-at-the-conclusion-of-the-2016-2017-un-group-of-governmental-experts-gge-on-developments-in-the-field-of-information-and-tele/?_ga=2 .165230527.167921373.1619943772-1795081959.1619943772

Moller-Maersk, A.P. 2017. 'Annual Report 2017'. http://investor.maersk.com/news-releases/ news-release-details/annual-report-2017

National Audit Office. 2017. 'Investigation: WannaCry Cyber Attack and the NHS', 27 October. https://www.nao.org.uk/wp-content/uploads/2017/10/Investigation-WannaCry-cyber-attack-and-the-NHS.pdf

'Swedish air traffic glitch solved,' NT News, 19 May 2016.

NetScout. 2016. 'Arbor Networks Releases Global DDoS Attack Data for 1H 2016', Arbor Networks press release, 19 July. www.netscout.com/ press-release/arbor-networks-releases- global-ddos-attack-data-for-1h-2016/

'Hackers Steal \$6 Million in SWIFT System Attack in Russia', RadioFreeEurope, 15 February 2018

Reuters. 2017. 'Global Shipping Giant Maersk is Reeling from the Ransomware Fallout'. Fortune, 29 June. http://fortune.com/2017/06/29/petya-goldeneye-maersk-ransomware-effects/

Riley, Michael, and Alan Katz. 2016. 'SWIFT Hack Probe Expands to Up to a Dozen Banks Beyond Bangladesh', Bloomberg Technology, 26 May. www.bloomberg.com/news/ articles/ 2016-05-26/swift-hack-probe-expands-to-up-to-dozen-banks-beyond-bangladesh

Riley, Michael, Jordan Robertson, and Alan Katz. 2016. 'Bangladesh, Vietnam Bank Hacks Put Global Lenders on Edge', Bloomberg, 17 May. www.bloomberg.com/news/ articles/2016-05-17/global-lenders-on-edge- as-hacks-embroil-growing-list-of-banks

Rodríguez, Miguel, 2017. 'Declaration by Miguel Rodríguez, Representative of Cuba, at the final session of the Group of Governmental Experts on Developments in the Field of Information and Telecommunications in the Context of International Security', 23 June. https://www. justsecurity.org/wp-content/uploads/2017/06/Cuban-Expert-Declaration.pdf

RT News. 2016. Vietnamese Bank Reports Another Hacker Attack On SWIFT Money Transfer System', 16 May. www.rt.com/ business/343196-vietnam-bank-attack-swift/

Schwartz, Mathew J. 2016. 'Another SWIFT Hack Stole $12 Million', Information Security Media Group, 20 May. www.bankinfosecurity.com/ another-swift-hack-stole-12-million-a-9121

Sewell, Chan. 2016. 'Cyberattacks Strike Saudi Arabia, Harming Aviation Agency', *The New York Times*, 1 December. www.nytimes.com/2016/12/01/world/ middleeast/saudi-arabia-shamoon-attack.html

Shamseddine, Reem, Jim Finkle, Maha El Dahan et al. 2017. 'Saudi Arabia Warns on Cyber Defense as Shamoon Resurfaces', *Reuters*, 23 January. www.reuters. com/article/us-saudi-cyber-idUSKBN1571ZR

Shevchenko, Sergei, and Adrian Nish. 2016. 'Cyber Heist Attribution', BAE Systems Threat Research Blog, 13 May. https://baesystemsai.blogspot.com/2016/05/cyber-heist-attribution.html

Symantec. 2019. 'Internet Security Threat Report', Volume 24. February. https://img03.en25. com/Web/Symantec/%7B984e78e2-c9e5-43b8-a6ee-417a08608b60%7D_ISTR_24_2019_ April_en.pdf?elqTrackId=3b60a2f23b38434c9ca9afa7ce30e0a8&elqaid=6820&elqat=2.

'Russia Under Suspicion after Sabotage of Swedish Telecom Mast', *The Guardian*, 18 May 2016. www.theguardian.com/world/2016/may/18/russia-under-suspicion-after-sabotage-of-swedish-telecom-mast

UN General Assembly, Group of Governmental Experts on Developments in the Field of Information and Telecommunications in the Context of International Security (A/70/174), 22 July 2015. https://undocs.org/A/70/174

UN General Assembly, 'Resolution adopted by the General Assembly on 27 December 2013' [on the report of the First Committee (A/68/406)], 68/243: 'Developments in the field of information and telecommunications in the context of international security', 9 January 2014. https://undocs.org/A/RES/68/243

UN General Assembly, 'Resolution adopted by the General Assembly on 5 December 2018'. (A/ Res/73/27), 11 December 2018. https://www.un.org/en/ga/search/view_doc.asp?symbol=A/ RES/73/27

UN General Assembly, 'Resolution adopted by the General Assembly on 22 December 2018.' (A/Res/73/266), 2 January 2019. https://www.un.org/en/ga/search/view_doc. asp?symbol=A/RES/73/266

UN General Assembly, 'Responsibility of States for Internationally Wrongful Acts', (A/Res/56/ 83, art. 1–8, Annex), 12 December 2001. http://legal.un.org/ilc/texts/instruments/english/ draft_articles/9_6_2001.pdf

UN Office for Disarmament Affairs, 'Fact Sheet: Development in the field of information and telecommunications in the context of international security', January 2019. https:// s3.amazonaws.com/unoda-web/wp-content/uploads/2019/01/Information-Security-Fact-Sheet-Jan2019.pdf

UN Secretary General, 'Securing our Common Future: An Agenda for Disarmament', 24 May 2018. https://www.un.org/disarmament/publications/more/securing-our-common-future/

White House, 'Press Briefing on the Attribution of the WannaCry Malware Attack to North Korea', 19 December 2017. https://www.whitehouse.gov/briefings-statements/press-briefing-on-the-attribution-of-the-wannacry-malware-attack-to-north-korea-121917/

'How Hackers Pulled Off a $20 Million Mexican Bank Heist', *WIRED*, 15 March 2019.

York, Kyle, 2016. 'Dyn Statement on 10/21/206 DDoS Attack', Dyn Company News, 22 October. http://dyn.com/blog/dyn- statement-on-10212016-ddos-attack/

CHAPTER 35

INTERNATIONAL LAW FOR CYBERSPACE: COMPETITION AND CONFLICT

THOMAS WINGFIELD AND HARRY WINGO

COMPETITION

PUBLIC international law governs the relations between states around the world, both during times of armed conflict and during 'peaceful' times when states compete on the global stage in all areas of human endeavour (economic, diplomatic, cultural, etc.).[1] International law applies in cyberspace and addresses the legality of cyber-related actions taken by countries, companies, associations, and citizens on the world stage. Cyberspace has been described as a new 'domain' that is radically different from the land and sea upon which international law developed, but such law either covers or is evolving to cover issues that have been under development for hundreds of years. Such coverage includes the international law principles of sovereignty, due diligence, jurisdiction, and state responsibility. International law also covers numerous specialized regimes: human rights, diplomatic and consular law, law of the sea, air law, space law, and international telecommunications law. Another developing area of international law and cyberspace concerns international peace and security with respect to cyber activities, but those issues lead right up to the threshold of conflict.

Sovereignty

The right of a state to exercise supreme authority over all persons and infrastructure within its geographical territory is a cornerstone principle of international law (Oppenheim 1992). It applies to cyberspace in times of peaceful competition.[2] States may engage in cyber activities beyond their borders, but must do so in a manner not inconsistent with international law. A state must not conduct cyber operations that violate the sovereignty of another state. For example, a state's internal sovereignty would be violated if another state frustrated its ability to conduct an inherently governmental function, such as conducting an election—the changing or deletion of electronic ballot information would likely constitute a violation (Schmitt 2017).

Sovereignty creates obligations for states, notably the requirement to comply with the principle of due diligence (Schmitt 2012). Since a state has dominion over its geographical territory, it has a duty to be vigilant in taking steps to prevent activities harmful to other states (or their citizens) being conducted from within its territory. This principle of due diligence presents challenges for states in that cyber activities are in many ways harder to detect than 'real-world' activities that might harm other states. The Tallinn 2.0 International Group of Experts asserts that feasible preventive measures satisfying due diligence include 'introducing information security policies, setting up computer emergency response teams (CERTs), and adopting appropriate domestic legislation requiring companies to report cyber incidents in order to be able to generate accurate threat assessments.'[3] Due to the transnational nature of most cyber problems, due diligence will often include information sharing and investigative cooperation with other states.

Violations of sovereignty generally involve two factors: breaching the territorial integrity of a state for a prohibited act, and interfering with an inherently governmental function within a state. Cyber espionage or more active intelligence activities on the territory of the target state are the simplest case and a clear violation of sovereignty. Remote operations, much more common in cyberspace, present a more complex picture for characterization. The Tallinn 2.0 International Group of Experts offers the most comprehensive and authoritative review of the topic.[4] The consensus of the experts is that most instances of physical destruction are violations of sovereignty, as are serious interferences with functionality. Trivial interferences with functionality, and other minor intrusions, probably do not rise to the level of a breach of sovereignty. In any case, sovereignty is simply the lowest of several thresholds in international law: prohibited intervention, unlawful use of force, and armed attack are discussed in the 'Conflict' section.[5]

Jurisdiction

The general principle of jurisdiction that allows a state to prescribe, enforce, and adjudicate with respect to persons, infrastructure, and activities within its territory, applies in cyberspace. In the case of prescriptive (legislative) jurisdiction, a state enjoys the authority to enact laws and regulations concerning cyber-related activities.

Whether a state may exercise extraterritorial jurisdiction over persons or infrastructure engaged in cyber-related activities is less settled, and turns on various factors such as the effects of the activities within the territory of the state.[6] There are five bases for extraterritorial jurisdiction, permitting a state to apply its laws beyond its borders. They include territorial (over cyber activities initiated or completed on a state's territory—which is not 'extraterritorial' at all—or having 'significant effects' within its territory, which contemplates a 'territorial' effect from beyond a state's territory); active nationality (over its citizens committing crimes); passive nationality (exercised by the state of the nationality of the victim of an offence taking place beyond its territory); protective (action, compatible with international law, to protect the state's security interests); and universal (over offences subject to universal jurisdiction). In practice, this legal determination of a claim to jurisdiction is simply the starting point for diplomatic and policy negotiations with the other concerned states. Since the most serious cyber operations are almost by definition transnational, extra-territorial jurisdiction is a key determination.

State Responsibility

A state bears responsibility under international law for a cyber-related act that is attrib-utable to that state and that breaches an international legal obligation (treaty obligation, customary international law, or general principles of law).[7] *Tehran Hostages* and other International Court of Justice cases have confirmed this principle.[8] Cyber activities carried out by persons or entities empowered by the domestic law of a state are attributable to that state.[9] Traditionally, the use of military vessels or aircraft were indisputably attributed to a State because these objects were so likely to be used solely by state organs. Today, cyber infra-structure may arguably be under the control of another state or foreign persons such that the requirements for responsibility might be defeated. If the basis for responsibility is that the offending activity originates from cyber infrastructure that is merely located in a state's ter-ritory (e.g. privately held, or under the jurisdiction of another state), then attribution—and therefore responsibility— may require even more evidence.[10]

Cyber operations conducted by non-state actors, such as private individuals or companies that are not attributable to a state, do not violate international law. As a result, such cyber activities will not trigger state responsibility. Yet, activities by non-state actors do fall under the principle of due diligence, so, even if not responsible in the international legal sense for such actions, a state must be vigilant to intervene if such actions originate from the state's ter-ritory, or from extraterritorial vessels, aircraft, facilities, or infrastructure under its jurisdic-tion. Whether cyber operations conducted by non-state actors may be attributed to a state depends on the factual relationship to the state, but attribution is likely where a non-state actor plays an essential role, such as in selecting targets. Acts that were not initiated by a state may nonetheless be attributed to that state to the extent it acknowledges and adopts the con-duct as its own, as was the case in the 'offline' conduct in the *Tehran Hostages* case.[11]

A state that is injured by another state's breach of its responsibility under international law may resort to self-help, which is permissible through several means: retorsion (un-friendly but legal actions in response to a perceived wrong); countermeasures (normally illegal, but permissible to persuade the injuring state to comply with its obligations); and plea of necessity (response to grave and imminent peril; also considered the complement of countermeasures when the target is a non-state actor).[12] With respect to meeting the re-quirement for a plea of necessity, the Tallinn 2.0 International Group of Experts provides the following examples:

> [A] cyber operation that would debilitate the State's banking system, cause a dramatic loss of confidence in its stock market, ground flights nationwide, halt all rail traffic, stop national pension and other social benefits, alter national health records in a manner endangering the health of the population, cause a major environmental disaster, shut down a large electrical grid, seriously disrupt the national food distribution network, or shut down the integrated air defence system would provide the basis for the application of this Rule.[13]

A plea of necessity, unlike countermeasures, does not require that the action of another state be unlawful, but it is limited in that a state invoking a plea of necessity may not seriously impair other states' essential interests—unless, of course, the actions of the non-state actor can be legally attributed to a state, returning us to the world of countermeasures.[14]

Espionage

Some peacetime cyber operations may not violate international law per se, but the manner in which they are conducted may do so. Espionage, for example, is permissible under international law, even if such activities violate the domestic law of a particular state. Cyber espionage by, or otherwise attributable to, a State raises new questions, however, because the speed and impact of espionage differs from such activities in the 'real world'. For example, probing military communications networks and data centres or the information and communication technology elements of another state's civilian critical infrastructure is different in cyberspace. It is conceivable that stealthy cyber operations may leave behind undetected code, or at least avenues for such code, that might enable devastating effects should the spying state, or its agents, so choose. Cyber espionage that allows a State to create easier and swifter transition from competition to conflict in the form of an armed attack does not, in itself, violate international law. A cyber espionage operation that causes harm, even if unintentional, will, however, be considered at least a violation of sovereignty.[15]

Human Rights

Around the world, the Internet is becoming an even more important part of individuals' public and private lives. There is general consensus that the international human rights that individuals enjoy in the 'real world' are also protected online.[16] Freedom of expression is protected under international law, but a state may restrict this freedom provided limitations are necessary to achieve a legitimate purpose.[17] The right to hold an opinion, unlike the right to free expression, is deemed so important by international law that a state may not restrict its exercise.[18] The right to privacy is protected under international law, but it is subject to limitations and its scope is still being determined.[19] Under international law, states are required to respect international human rights.[20] States are also required to protect the human rights of individuals from abuse by third parties.[21] The Tallinn 2.0 International Group of Experts noted that, while certain regimes (e.g. the Council of Europe) extend human rights to legal persons, customary international human rights are afforded only to natural persons.[22]

Diplomatic and Consular Law

Diplomatic missions (embassies) and consular offices, as well as diplomatic and consular staff, are entitled to privileges and immunities under international law.[23] For example, consider an embassy of state A (the 'sending state') located in the capital of state B (the 'receiving state'). State A enjoys inviolability for its premises and any cyber infrastructure there—equipment enabling cyber operations may not be accessed, including from off premises, without consent. Included in this principle is the receiving state's 'special duty' to protect the cyber infrastructure of the sending state.[24] The principle of inviolability has its limits, however. The receiving state would be justified in ignoring inviolability should the sending state use the cyberinfrastructure in its embassy to conduct cyber operations that could be seen as crossing the line from cyber espionage to preparation for an armed attack—for example, by preparing potentially devastating attacks against critical infrastructure.

Specialized Regimes: Sea, Air, Space, and Telecommunications

International law has evolved to keep up with technological developments, as demonstrated by several specialized regimes. The international law of the sea, a 'peacetime regime' that addresses cyber operations that emanate from or are carried out at sea, is reflected in the widely accepted Law of the Sea Convention.[25] Air law concerns operations in the airspace below outer space (generally understood to be between 80 and 120 kilometres above sea level), and developed out of the 1944 Chicago Convention on Civil Aviation.[26] International space law has been developing since the Cold War under the guidance of the United Nations (UN) Committee on the Peaceful Uses of Outer Space ('UNCOPUOS') and the *Outer Space Treaty*.[27]

The law of the sea regards as the 'high seas' all parts of the sea not within the exclusive economic zone (EEZ), a state's territorial waters or internal waters.[28] Cyber operations covered by aspects of the law of the sea involve operations on the 'high seas' (operations may be conducted only for peaceful purposes); the 'right of visit' (warships or other authorized state vessels may board a vessel without flag state consent if cyber means are used for piracy, slave trading, or unauthorized broadcasting); cyber operations within the exclusive economic zone (cyber operations must be for peaceful purposes). The law of the sea protects submarine cables, which carry most of the world's Internet traffic. A state may use its internal, prescriptive sovereignty to pass laws and regulations protecting undersea cables on the seabed of its territorial sea and internal waters, consistent with other states' right of innocent passage for their vessels. States may lay undersea cables in the exclusive economic zone of another state, and have the right to maintain such cables consistent with the right of the coastal state.

The international law concerning civilian air travel, which has developed for more than 70 years from baselines set at the Chicago Convention, covers cyber operations conducted from aircraft.[29] Air law provides that a state (1) may regulate aircraft over its national airspace, including those conducting cyber operations; (2) may conduct cyber operations, consistent with international law, above international waters; and (3) may not conduct cyber operations that jeopardize civil aviation.

The international law of space directs that any cyber operations by a state on the moon and other celestial bodies must be peaceful, and that any cyber operations in outer space must comply with restrictions on the use of force. Space law also directs states to conduct cyber operations in a manner that avoids interfering with other states' peaceful space activities.

International telecommunications law compels states to establish, maintain, and safeguard an international telecommunications structure.[30] A state has the right to suspend or stop cyber communications services within its territory, but it must provide immediate notice of such action.[31] A state may use radio stations, but such wireless cyber communications must not interfere with those of other States.[32] Telecommunications law exempts military radio installations, but it is generally agreed that this exemption would not extend to a 'dual-use' service (e.g. the United States' GPS navigation system, which the US Department of Defense operates but that serves both military and civilian purposes.[33]

CONFLICT

Despite the international legal mechanisms for managing competition and preventing conflict in cyberspace, conflict does arise—and it is only now rising to the level of use of force and armed attack. The once theoretical and purely academic literature of cybercrime, cyber espionage, and, especially, cyberwar must now be applied to real-world cases, and law and policy for the future of cyber security must be formulated with an understanding of these broadly accepted international norms.

Peaceful Settlement of Disputes

International law, both customary and treaty, prefers the peaceful settlement of disputes, and requires attempts at peaceful settlement when such disputes endanger international peace and security.[34] This norm is most clearly, and most authoritatively, stated in the Charter of the United Nations: '[t]he parties to any dispute, the continuance of which is likely to endanger the maintenance of international peace and security, shall, first of all, seek a solution by negotiation, enquiry, mediation, conciliation, arbitration, judicial settlement, resort to regional agencies or arrangements, or other peaceful means of their own choice'.[35] In either case, the means of dispute settlement may not themselves pose a threat to international peace and security.

The *Mavromatis* case provides the most widely accepted definition of a dispute: 'a disagreement on a point of law or fact, a conflict of legal views or interests between parties'.[36] Under international law, disputes must be specific assertions of fact or right rejected by an opposing party.[37] To fall under this prohibition, disputes may not be purely domestic,[38] or between states and non-state actors.[39] The threshold of 'threatening international peace and security' is an indefinite one. The United Nations Security Council may act pursuant to Article 39 and designate almost any situation a threat to international peace and security, but, short of such a designation, international law looks to the likely consequences of such an action. Cyber operations likely to lead to armed conflict are a clear example; less clear are actions that cause severe disruption within a state, irrespective of the likelihood to result in military action. Military action, or escalation, may be unlikely if the victim is in a significantly weaker position than the intruder, or when both the victim and the intruder are each so powerful that they are mutually deterring. Military action may also be less likely when two states have such extensive economic interconnections that they are effectively 'self-deterred' from a military response. Russia-Ukraine, Russia-US, and China-US are examples of each of these situations, respectively.

Examples of severe cyber disruption include attacks on critical infrastructure, such as communications, finance, or power generation, that rise above the level of a mere demonstration of power—i.e. that send a political message that does not involve the loss of life, significant property destruction, or widespread social unrest. The 2007 cyberattacks on Estonia may be seen as an example of such a political message. However, the early stages of the attack, which involved agitating the ethnic Russian minority in the country to violent if not life-threatening protest, show that even when cyber operations begin below the threshold, they have the capacity to rise above it.

International law requires that peaceful settlement be pursued 'in good faith'—i.e. with an eye toward success rather than mere appearance, and that such efforts do not include statements of fact that are demonstrably false.[40] Parties need not pursue all peaceful means, or pursue them indefinitely. Rather, they need only pursue peaceful means with a reasonable chance of success, and pursue them only so long as success is a realistic expectation.[41] After the good faith pursuit of such options, there is a general duty to refer threats to international peace and security to the United Nations Security Council.[42] Of course, if one of the 'Permanent Five' members of the Security Council (China, Russia, United States, United Kingdom, and France, each possessing veto power over Security Council resolutions), is itself a party to the dispute, the expectation of success will quickly become unrealistic.

Beyond this generalized duty, states may have accepted a more specific duty for compulsory dispute resolution under a particular treaty regime, such as the Optional Protocol to the Vienna Convention on Diplomatic Relations concerning the Compulsory Settlement of Disputes[43] or, more specific to the world of cyber operations, the Optional Protocol on the Compulsory Settlement of Disputes relating to the International Telecommunication Union instruments.[44] Any such treaty-based mechanism is in accordance with the requirement for peaceful dispute resolution.

Prohibition of Intervention

It is a general precept of international law that a state may not interfere in the internal or external affairs of another state. The very nature of sovereignty provides a general limit to such intervention, and it is more specifically declaimed in the UN Charter.[45] The key to evaluating the lawfulness of any such interference is the degree to which it is coercive—i.e. that it is intended to change the targeted state's behaviour.[46] The Tallinn 2.0 International Group of Experts asserts that intervention without coercion is mere interference, and is therefore not subject to this ban.[47] Internal affairs (that is, those not subject to international law), are referred to as *domaine réservé*, and are by definition unlawful subjects of another state's intervention.[48] At the very heart of a state's *domaine réservé* is its legitimate capacity to select and maintain the governmental system of its choice.[49] Such an unlawful intervention need not be directed at an organ of the state—the intent need only be to influence the state. Coercive acts against intermediate institutions, such as corporations, non-governmental organizations, media outlets, political parties, or other influential elements of civil society, could provide effective leverage for an unlawful intervention. However, international law intrudes upon the *domaine réservé* when permissible retorsions or countermeasures appropriately target institutions such as these to compel a return to compliance by the offending state. External affairs, to the extent they are the sole domain of the state, are protected as the *domaine réservé*. Such actions would include normal diplomatic and consular activities, and other customary foreign affairs powers of a state, such as negotiating or concluding treaties.

The recent example of presumed Russian interference in the recent US presidential elections brings this standard into focus. According to the Tallinn 2.0 International Group of Experts:

> coercion must be distinguished from persuasion, criticism, public diplomacy, propaganda ... retribution, mere maliciousness, and the like in the sense that, unlike coercion, such activities merely involve either influencing (as distinct from factually compelling) the voluntary actions of the target State, or seek no action on the part of the target State at all. As an illustration, a State-sponsored public information campaign via the Internet designed to persuade another State of the logic of ratifying a particular treaty would not amount to a violation of the prohibition of intervention. Similarly, if a State's Ministry of Foreign Affairs publishes content on social media that is highly critical of another State's internal and external policies, the activity is not coercive in nature and therefore does not constitute prohibited intervention. The key is that the coercive act must have the potential for compelling the target State to engage in an action that it would otherwise not take (or refrain from taking an action it would otherwise take).[50]

The crucial distinction here is that the *state* be the target of the coercion, rather than some element of the populace, and that the state be intended to take (or forbear taking) an action. Influence operations against segments of the target state's population, where the population was itself the target, would appear to be outside the ambit of this prohibition.

While these rules *supra* are an accurate statement of the international law prohibiting intervention, it is clear that the expansion of the 'infosphere' will shrink the traditionally domestic aspects of the *domaine réservé*—already, most information available on the Internet in most countries derives from an extra-national source.

Several other factors bear on characterizing an action as an intervention. Attempt is usually seen as an intervention, even if it is unsuccessful. Depending on the strength and credibility of the intervenor, a mere threat may rise to the level of an intervention if it has the desired effect. Interventions need not be accomplished directly: the use of intermediaries does not, in itself, absolve the intervening state. Espionage, as intelligence collection distinct from intelligence activities such as covert operations, is not a prohibited intervention. Unilateral economic sanctions, if conducted within the framework of otherwise lawful economic activity, are usually not considered interventions. Interventions legitimately justified as the protection of nationals abroad are not per se prohibited. A contextual analysis will determine if a genuine threat to a group of extra-nationals was threatened, or if the intervention was merely pretextual.[51] It is less clear if the international community not participating in a humanitarian operation would view cyber operations in support of that operation as a prohibited intervention.

Unless pursuant to a UN Security Council resolution or the lawful exercise of national self-defence, the prohibition of intervention is violated by any activity in cyberspace that rises to the level of a 'use of force'.[52]

Use of Force

The *jus ad bellum* is the body of international law that authoritatively prescribes the thresholds of 'use of force' and 'armed attack'. At the core of the *jus ad bellum* are articles 2(4) and 51 of the Charter of the United Nations. Article 2(4) prohibits the international use or threat of use of force absent a valid exception,[53] and Article 51 provides one such exception—national self-defence in response to an armed attack.[54] The other universally recognized exception is Chapter VII authorization from the UN Security Council, permitting (but not requiring) the use of armed force in defence of a specified mandate.[55]

As these thresholds and prohibitions apply to the use of force with any type of weapon,[56] the use of cyber means and methods of warfare call for the application of the same standards. The UN Charter does not define 'use of force' or 'armed attack'. In general terms, all military operations take place along a spectrum of intensity from minor border skirmishes to global thermonuclear conflict. Lower-end operations that do not immediately threaten loss of life or irreparable military harm to a state are considered uses of force—unlawful, but not serious enough to permit an armed response. Higher-end military operations—armed attacks—are considered serious enough to permit the activation of the inherent right of national self-defence, permitting an immediate armed response. Distinguishing mere uses of force from armed attacks, then, is perhaps the key question in the emerging law of cyber conflict. Because the *Nicaragua* case suggested a 'scale and effects' test to evaluate if an action rises to the level of an armed attack,[57] the Tallinn 2.0 International Group of Experts recommended that a similar quantitative and qualitative test be applied to determine if an action is a use of force.[58] Specifically, they endorsed the use of the widely known 'Schmitt Analysis' to make this determination.[59] This analysis involves eight separate evaluations of a novel cyber event: severity (loss of life or damage to property), immediacy (the speed with which consequences manifest themselves), directness (the proximity of cause to effect), invasiveness (the degree to which a state's interests are threatened by the penetration of a highly protected system), measurability (the quantifiability of damage), state involvement (the degree to which a government controls or directs the intrusion), presumptive legality (the lawfulness of the 'real world' analogy of the cyber action), and military character (whether a military organization is the attacker or the target).[60] Each of these factors can be given a low, medium, or high value and, when taken as a composite, allow for a principled characterization of a cyber event as clearly a use of force, clearly not, or perhaps somewhere in an ambiguous middle zone. At higher levels of intensity, cyberattacks causing damage comparable to kinetic attacks that have been characterized as 'armed attacks' may also be characterized as such, permitting a unilateral military response.[61]

Any exercise of lawful self-defence must comply with the *jus ad bellum* principles of necessity, proportionality, and imminence. This is often a cause for confusion, in that the *jus in bello* (described *infra*), which governs the actual conduct of hostilities, includes principles of necessity and proportionality with different definitions. Within the context of the *jus ad bellum*, necessity requires that all peaceful means with a reasonable chance of success be exhausted before resorting to armed force.[62] Proportionality under the *jus ad bellum* permits all the force required to defeat an attack, but no more. The quantum of force required is a military, not a legal, decision. Proportionality merely forbids the use of additional discretionary (i.e. punitive or recreational) force. There is no linkage between the level of force used in the attack and that permitted in the response: the amount of force required to defeat an attack may be substantially more, or less, than that of the precipitating attack.[63] The principle of imminence does not require the defender to 'take the first hit' before launching a lawful response, but it does limit the window of anticipatory self-defence. This limitation is less temporal than situational: assuming an attacker has the capability and the intent, then the most commonly accepted standard is that the defender be permitted to 'shoot first' if the opportunity is reasonably considered to be the last clear chance to intercept the attack. This is an especially challenging judgment in the areas of counterterrorism and cyberattacks in that the threats are discontinuous and may not provide an analytically convenient linear path from launch to execution. The determination of reasonableness is from the victim state's perspective, based on the information it has available at the time it chooses to launch its defensive response. In the case of the emplacement of a potentially destructive cyber weapon in a victim state's network, the likelihood of the conditions permitting its activation would be the principal determinant in the imminence of the attack, and therefore the lawfulness of an anticipatory defensive action.[64]

Law of Armed Conflict

The *jus in bello* is the body of law that controls the conduct of hostilities between belligerents in an armed conflict. While there has been very little acknowledged state practice in which cyber operations, by themselves, have risen to the level of armed conflict, cyber operations are now an inseparable part of military operations along the entire spectrum of conflict. The law governing these operations applies to these routine, multi-domain operations, and will apply to purely cyber operations just as it would to purely ground, air, or naval operations.

Early debate, first about the applicability of law to cyberspace, then of international law to cyberspace, and finally of the law of armed conflict to cyberspace, has largely been resolved. Current debate involves the precise contours of the application of the customary principles of international humanitarian law to cyber operations undertaken in the context of armed conflict. When particular situations are not specifically covered by explicit black-letter law, or even analogies from particular principles, customary international law provides a 'savings clause' in the form of the Martens Clause, first promulgated in Hague Convention IV[65] and since repeated in in the Geneva Conventions of 1949[66] and Additional Protocol I.[67] The Clause provides:

> Until a more complete code of the laws of war has been issued, the High Contracting Parties deem it expedient to declare that, in cases not included in the Regulations adopted by them, the inhabitants and the belligerents remain under the protection and the rule of the principles of the law of nations, as they result from the usages established among civilised peoples, from the laws of humanity, and the dictates of the public conscience.[68]

At the very least, all cyber operations in the context of armed conflict are governed by this general statement of principle, and the customary principles that have risen to the level of non-discretionary *jus cogens* international law.

Armed conflict may be characterized as international (between states) or as non-international (in which at least one party is an organized armed group). Either type of conflict may give rise to individual criminal responsibility for war crimes. Commanders bear the additional burden of all reasonable and necessary measures to prevent war crimes that they knew, or should have known, may occur.[69] This opens a fascinating question for the further development of the law as it applies to command responsibility for the target selections of artificial intelligence (AI) agents employed in combat. It is entirely foreseeable that the broad outlines of the law governing the conduct of hostilities will have to be programmed into—or taught to—these AI agents.

For humans, there are no restrictions on who may participate in an armed conflict, but such participation does permit all but protected medical and religious persons to be lawfully targeted by the opposing force. In addition to members of the armed forces and members of organized armed groups, civilians may be targeted in an armed conflict for such time as they directly participate in hostilities.[70] Of course, the degree of participation that qualifies as 'direct' has been left open to interpretation by states, but there are clear examples at the high end (fighters, intelligence assets, weapons delivery) that clearly meet the standard, and at the low end (commissary, administration, political support) that clearly do not. Furthermore, only those participants in an international armed conflict who comply with the requirements of lawful combatancy (wearing a fixed and distinctive emblem visible at a distance, carrying arms openly during an engagement, being subject to regular military discipline and membership in an organization that substantially complies with the law of armed conflict[71] receive combatant immunity and prisoner-of-war status. In the cyber context, with a large number of military operations being conducted from safely within friendly territory, the likelihood of capture is remote, and so the incentive to comply with these requirements is correspondingly small.

Numerous provisions of the *jus in bello* apply to the conduct of cyberattacks. Within the context of international law, attacks are 'acts of violence against the adversary, whether in offence or defence'.[72] Cyber operations that do not result in violence against a target, with resulting injury or loss of life to humans or damage or destruction of property, are per se not attacks.

When combatants are carrying out attacks, they are subject to several customary principles of the law of armed conflict. The first of these is distinction, which permits the intentional targeting of combatants and military objectives,[73] but forbids the intentional targeting of civilians and their property (or 'objects').[74] Included within this concept is the prohibition of cyber weapons that are indiscriminate by nature—that is, they are incapable of being directed against particular targets.[75] In addition, states are required to conduct initial weapon reviews at the time of development to ensure that new cyber weapons are not per se indiscriminate.[76] This prohibition includes cyberattacks intended to spread terror among the civilian population, such as attacks, or the threat of attacks, against critical infrastructure producing widespread and severe agitation in the populace.[77]

The principle of superfluous injury and unnecessary suffering forbids the use of cyber weapons that, through original design or later modification, cause additional damage or injury without any further military advantage.[78] This relates closely to the *jus ad bellum* principle of proportionality, *supra*, with its prohibition of punitive or recreational force.

The *jus in bello* principle of proportionality requires that the unintended but unavoidable harm to civilians and their property not be unreasonable in light of the anticipated concrete and direct military advantage to be gained.[79] Of course, the principle of distinction prohibits intentional cyberattacks against civilian targets, but many attacks result in some degree of collateral damage to surrounding civilian property or connected civilian networks. In practice, this becomes a balancing exercise—the more important the military objective, the larger the surrounding penumbra of permissible damage to civilian property. In the frequent case when cyber targets consist of dual-use military and civilian components, such targets themselves are lawful military objectives. However, the civilian component of such a dual-use object, and the damage that would be done to it, is the subject of the principle of proportionality.

The final customary principle is perfidy, which prohibits treachery, defined as '[a]cts inviting the confidence of an adversary to lead him to believe that he is entitled to, or is obliged to accord, protection under the rules of international law applicable in armed conflict, with the intent to betray that confidence'.[80] Put simply, the principle makes it illegal to feign non-combatant status for the purposes of launching an attack. In the kinetic world, this would involve assuming the identity of a non-combatant (civilian, prisoner, wounded, medical or religious personnel) before launching a treacherous attack. Other forms of military deception, often referred to as *ruses de guerre*, are permitted under the law of armed conflict.[81]

In competition and in conflict, states rely on international law to provide the rules of the road for routine transnational activities. States also look to international law for agreed-upon standards and thresholds against which to judge bad actors on the international scene. With no true international executive, legislature, or judiciary, international law is very much driven by the interests and limitations of states. All this remains true as the fundamental principles of international law are being applied to the new domain of cyberspace.

NOTES

1. Experts have proposed frameworks for understanding why States, particularly the most powerful, comply with international law. See, e.g. Koh, H.H. (1997). Faculty Scholarship Series. Paper 2101: http://digitalcommons.law.yale.edu/fss_papers/2101
2. See, e.g. Koh, H.H., Legal Advisor of the Department of State, International Law in Cyberspace, Address to the USCYBERCOM Inter-Agency Legal Conference (18 September 2012)('States conducting activities in cyberspace must take into account the sovereignty of other States, including outside the context of armed conflict.'): R http://www.harvardilj.org/2012/12/online_54_koh/
3. Tallinn Manual 2.0, at 46.
4. Tallinn Manual 2.0, at 17 to 27.
5. Tallinn Manual 2.0, at 17 to 27.
6. This effects doctrine is subject to overbreadth if taken too far, but the principle can be reasonably said to reflect customary international law. See, e.g. Oppenheim's International Law, at 472–475; Shaw, Malcolm N., International Law (7th edn., 2014), (hereinafter Shaw's International Law), at 499–505; American Law Institute Restatement (Third) of the Foreign Relations Law of the United States (1986), (hereinafter Restatement (Third)), Sec. 402(1)(c).
7. International Law Commission, Responsibility of States for Internationally Wrongful Acts, G.A. Res. 56/83 annex, U.N. Doc. A/RES/56/83 (Dec. 12, 2001) (hereinafter Articles of State Responsibility), Art. 1. See also UN GGE 2013 Report, para. 23; UN GGE 2015 Report, para. 28(f).
8. *United States Diplomatic and Consular Staff in Tehran (US v. Iran)*, 1980 ICJ 3 (24 May) at 30, para. 61: http://www.icj-cij.org/docket/files/64/6291.pdf

9. International Law Commission, Responsibility of States for Internationally Wrongful Acts, GA Res. 56/83 annex, UN Doc. A/RES/56/ 83 (12 December 2001), (hereinafter Articles on State Responsibility), Art. 4(1).

10. See Tallinn 2.0, at 91; Group of Governmental Experts on Developments in the Field of Information and Telecommunications in the Context of International Security, UN Doc. A/70/174 (22 July 2015), (hereinafter UN GGE 2015 Report), para. 28(f).

11. *United States Diplomatic and Consular Staff in Tehran (US* v. *Iran),* 1980 ICJ 3 (24 May), (hereinafter *Tehran Hostages* Judgment), para. 74. See also Articles on State Responsibility, Art. 11; see also Tallinn 2.0, at 99.

12. Tallinn 2.0, at 79–142; Articles on State Responsibility, chapeau to Chapter II of Part 3, para. 3 of commentary.

13. Tallinn 2.0, at 136.

14. Articles on State Responsibility, Art. 25(1)(b).

15. Tallinn 2.0, at 173.

16. See, e.g. The Promotion, Protection and Enjoyment of Human Rights on the Internet, para. 1, UN Doc. A/HRC/32/L.20 (27 June 2016).

17. Universal Declaration of Human Rights, GA Res. 217A (III), UN Doc. A/810 (10 December 1948)('UDHR'), Art. 19; ICCRP, Art. 19(2)(free expression); International Covenant on Civil and Political Rights, 16 December 1966, 999 UNTS 171 ('ICCPR'), Art. 19(3)(b)(restriction for legitimate purpose).

18. UDHR, Art.1; ICCPR, Art.19(1).

19. UDHR, Art. 12; ICCPR, Art. 17.

20. See ICCPR, Art. 2(1).

21. ICCPR, Art. 2(1).

22. Tallinn Manual 2.0, at 183.

23. See Vienna Convention on Consular Relations, 24 April 1963, 596 UNTS 261, (hereinafter Vienna Convention of Consular Relations); Vienna Convention on Diplomatic Relations, (*hereinafter* Vienna Convention on Diplomatic Relations), 18 April 1961, 500 UNTS 95.

24. Vienna Convention on Diplomatic Relations, Art. 21(1); *Tehran Hostages* Judgment, paras. 61–6.

25. See, generally, United Nations Convention on the Law of the Sea, 10 December 1982, 1833 UNTS 3 (hereinafter UNCLOS).

26. See, generally, Convention on Civil Aviation, 7 December 1944, 15 UNTS 295 (hereinafter Chicago Convention).

27. See, generally, Treaty on Principles Governing the Activities of States in the Exploration and Use of Outer Space, including the Moon and Other Celestial Bodies, 27 January 1967, 610 UNTS 205 (hereinafter Outer Space Treaty).

28. UNCLOS, Art. 86.

29. See, generally, Chicago Convention.

30. Constitution of the International Telecommunication Union, 22 December 1992, 1825 UNTS 331 (hereinafter ITU Constitution), Art. 38.

31. ITU Constitution, Articles 34 (Suspension of Services) and 35 (Stoppage of Services).

32. ITU Constitution, Articles, 45(1) and 1(2)(b).

33. International Radiotelegraph Convention, Berlin 1906, Art.21; Tallinn 2.0, at 298–9 (regarding GPS services and exemption).

34. See, e.g. European Convention for the Peaceful Settlement of Disputes, 29 April 1957, 320 UNTS 243 (hereinafter European Convention for the Peaceful Settlement of Disputes),

and Conference on Security and Co-Operation in Europe: Final Act (hereinafter Conference on Security and Co-Operation in Europe: Final Act), princ. V, 1 August 1975, 14 ILM 1292.

35. The Charter of the United Nations, Article 33(1).

36. *Mavrommatis Palestine Concessions (Greece v. UK)*, PCIJ (ser. A) No. 2, at 11 (30 August 1924).

37. The Charter of United Nations: A Commentary, at 192.

38. The Charter of United Nations: A Commentary, at 193.

39. Tallinn Manual 2.0, at 305.

40. The Charter of the United Nations, Article 33(1).

41. The Charter of United Nations: A Commentary, at 1150–1151.

42. The Charter of the United Nations, Article 37(1).

43. Optional Protocol to the Vienna Convention on Diplomatic Relations Concerning the Compulsory Settlement of Disputes, Arts. I–III(1), 18 April 1961, 500 UNTS 241.

44. Optional Protocol on the Compulsory Settlement of Disputes Relating to the Constitution of the International Telecommunication Union, to the Convention of the International Telecommunication Union and to the Administrative Regulations Art. 1, 22 December 1992, 1825 UNTS 3.

45. See the Charter of the United Nations, Articles 2(1), 2(3), and 2(4).

46. 'The element of coercion ... defines, and indeed forms the very essence of prohibited intervention ... ', *Military and Paramilitary Activities in and against Nicaragua (Nicar. v. US)*, 1986 ICJ 14 (27 June), (hereinafter *Nicaragua* Judgment), para. 205.

47. ' "[I]nterference" refers to "acts by States that intrude into affairs reserved to the sovereign prerogative of another State, but lack the requisite coerciveness ... to rise to the level of intervention. The term intervention ... is limited to acts of interference with a sovereign prerogative of another State that have coercive effect ... ', Tallinn Manual 2.0, at 313.

48. *Nationality Decrees Issued in Tunis and Morocco*, advisory opinion, 1923 PCIJ (ser.B) No. 4, at 24 (7 February).

49. 'The International Group of Experts agreed that the matter most clearly within a State's *domaine réservé* appears to be the choice of both the political system and its organisation, as these issues lie at the heart of sovereignty.' Tallinn Manual 2.0, at 313.

50. Tallinn Manual 2.0, at 318–19.

51. See, generally, Jackson Jesse. 1985. 'A Text Without a Context is a Pretext'. Statement on Nightline, 15 December.

52. *Nicaragua* Judgment, para. 205.

53. 'All Members shall refrain in their international relations from the threat or use of force against the territorial integrity or political independence of any state, or in any other manner inconsistent with the Purposes of the United Nations.', the Charter of the United Nations, Article 2(4).

54. 'Nothing in the present Charter shall impair the inherent right of individual or collective self-defence if an armed attack occurs against a Member of the United Nations, until the Security Council has taken measures necessary to maintain international peace and security. Measures taken by Members in the exercise of this right of self-defence shall be immediately reported to the Security Council and shall not in any way affect the authority and responsibility of the Security Council under the present Charter to take at any time such action as it deems necessary in order to maintain or restore international peace and security.', the Charter of the United Nations, Article 51.

55. 'Should the Security Council consider that measures [not involving the use of armed force] provided for in Article 41 would be inadequate or have proved to be inadequate, it may take such action by air, sea, or land forces as may be necessary to maintain or restore international peace and security. Such action may include demonstrations, blockade, and other operations by air, sea, or land forces of Members of the United Nations', the Charter of the United Nations, Article 43.

56. *Legality of the Threat or Use of Nuclear Weapons*, Advisory Opinion, 1996 ICJ 226 (8 July), (*hereinafter Nuclear Weapons* Advisory Opinion), para. 39.

57. *Nicaragua* Judgment, para. 195.

58. Tallinn Manual 2.0, at 331.

59. See Schmitt, Michael N. 1999. 'Computer Network and the Use of Force in International Law: Thoughts on a Normative Framework', 37 COLUM. J. TRANSNAT'L L. 885, 914.

60. Tallinn Manual 2.0, at 333 to 337.

61. See *Nicaragua* Judgment, para. 191.

62. See Tallinn Manual 2.0, at 349: '[W]hen measures falling short of a use of force cannot alone reasonably be expected to defeat an armed attack and prevent subsequent ones, cyber and kinetic operations that cross the use of force threshold are allowed under the law of self-defence.' *Id.*

63. See US Department of Defense, Office of The General Counsel, Law of War Manual (June 2015), para. 16.3.3.2.

64. See Tallinn Manual 2.0, at 352.

65. Convention (IV) Respecting the Laws and Customs of War on Land, 18 October 1907, 36 Stat. 2277, (hereinafter Hague Convention IV), pmbl.

66. Convention (I) for the Amelioration of the Condition of the Wounded and Sick in Armed Forces in the Field, 12 August 1949, 75 UNTS 31, (hereinafter Geneva Convention I), Art. 63; Convention (II) for the Amelioration of the Condition of Wounded, Sick and Shipwrecked Members of Armed Forces at Sea, 12 August 1949, 75 UNTS 85, (hereinafter Geneva Convention II), Art. 62; Convention (III) Relative to the Treatment of Prisoners of War, 12 August 1949, 75 UNTS 135, (hereinafter Geneva Convention III), Art. 142; Convention (IV) Relative to the Protection of Civilian Persons in Time of War, 12 August 1949, 75 UNTS 287, (*hereinafter* Geneva Convention IV), Art. 158.

67. Protocol Additional to the Geneva Conventions of 12 August 1949, and Relating to the Protection of Victims of International Armed Conflicts, 8 June 1977, 1125 UNTS 3, (*hereinafter* Additional Protocol I), Art. 1(2).

68. Hague Convention IV, pmbl.

69. Geneva Convention I, Art. 49; Geneva Convention II, Art. 50; Geneva Convention III, Art. 129; Geneva Convention IV, Art. 146; Additional Protocol I, Arts. 86–87; Hague Convention for the Protection of Cultural Property in the Event of Armed Conflict with Regulations for the Execution of the Convention, 14 May 1954, 249 UNTS 240, Art. 28; Second Protocol to the Hague Convention of 1954 for the Protection of Cultural Property in the Event of Armed Conflict, Art. 15(2); Statute of the International Criminal Court, 17 July 1998, 2187 UNTS 90, Arts. 25(3)(b) and 28.

70. Additional Protocol I, Art. 51(3) and Protocol Additional to the Geneva Conventions of 12 August 1949, and Relating to the Protection of Victims of Non-International Armed Conflicts, 8 June 1977, 1125 UNTS 609. (hereinafter Additional Protocol II), Art. 13(3).

71. Geneva Convention III, Art. 4A(2).

72. Additional Protocol I, Art. 49(1).

73. Military objectives are defined as 'those objects which by their nature, location, purpose or use make an effective contribution to military action and whose total or partial destruction, capture or neutralisation, in the circumstances ruling at the time, offers a definite military advantage'. Additional Protocol I, Art. 52(2).

74. Additional Protocol I, Art. 48.

75. Additional Protocol I, Art. 51(4)(b) and (c).

76. Additional Protocol I, Art. 36.

77. Additional Protocol I, Art. 51(2) and Additional Protocol II, Art. 13(2).

78. Additional Protocol I, Art. 35(2).

79. Additional Protocol I, Arts. 51(5)(b) and 57(2)(iii).

80. Additional Protocol I, Art. 37(1).

81. Additional Protocol I, Art. 37(2).

FURTHER READING

Buergenthal, Thomas, and Sean Murphy. 2013. *Public International Law in a Nutshell* (5th edn). St. Paul, MN: West.

Floridi, Luciano, and Mariarosaria Taddeo (eds). *The Ethics of Information Warfare*. Springer.

Garrie, Daniel, Rhea Siers, and Mitchell Silber. 2015–16. *Cyberwarfare: Understanding the Law, Policy, and Technology*. Thomson Reuters.

Geers, Kenneth (ed.). 2015 *Cyber War in Perspective: Russian Aggression against Ukraine*. CCDCOE.

Hooker, R.D. (ed.). 2016 *Charting a Course: Strategic Choices for a New Administration*, National Defense University.

Lemieux, Frederic (ed.). 2015 *Current and Emerging Trends in Cyber Operations: Policy, Strategy, and Practice*. Palgrave Macmillan.

Libicki, Martin. 2009 *Cyberdeterrence and Cyberwar*, Rand.

Moore, John Norton, Guy B. Roberts, and Robert Turner, *National Security Law & Policy* (3rd edn) 2015. Durham, NC: Carolina Academic Press.

Ohlin, Jens David, and Keith Olin, 2013 *Cyberwar: Law and Ethics for Virtual Conflicts*. Oxford.

Oppenheim, Lassa. 1992. *Oppenheim's International Law* edited by (Robert Jennings and Arthur Watts (9th edn) (hereinafter *Oppenheim's International Law*), at 564.

Osula, Anna-Maria, and Henry Roigas (eds.). 2016 *International Cyber Norms: Legal, Policy, and Industry Perspectives*, CCDCOE.

Schmitt, Michael N. 2012. 'International Law in Cyberspace: The Koh Speech and Tallinn Manual Juxtaposed'. http://www.harvardilj.org/wp-content/uploads/2012/12/HILJ-Online_54_Schmitt.pdf

Schmitt, Michael (gen. ed.). 2017. *The Tallinn Manual 2.0 on the International Law Applicable to Cyber Operations*. Cambridge University Press.

Spinello, Richard. 2013 *Cyberethics: Morality and Law in Cyberspace* (5th edn). Jones and Bartlett.

PART X

PERSPECTIVES ON CYBERSECURITY

CHAPTER 36

COMMUNITY OF COMMON FUTURE IN CYBERSPACE: THE PROPOSAL AND PRACTICE OF CHINA

TANG LAN

BENEFITTING from the rapid development of information and communication technology (ICT), China achieved a rapid evolution from a semi-industrial country to a digitized nation. For now, China's population of Internet users, the penetration of digital services, and the volume of its digital economy all rank among the highest in the world. Besides these immense advantages, ICT has acted as a powerful catalyst, bringing huge benefits to every aspect of Chinese society. Yet cyberspace has also created a new dimension of insecurity and disarray due to the increasing dependence on a brand-new interconnected ecosystem. The Chinese government has realized that cybersecurity is the most complicated and elaborate challenge, and has put it at the top of the policy agenda. China's approach, in which current international challenges are viewed through the prism of ancient wisdom, can provide an alternative for the world.

This chapter begins with an account of the current state of China's digitization and cybersecurity. The second part of the chapter examines the meaning of, and the necessity for, a 'community of common destiny' in cyberspace, before continuing to illuminate what China can do at the domestic and international levels to pursue this aim. The final section tries to analyse the implications of China's approach for the stability and security of international cyberspace.

BIG POWER AND WEAK MUSCLE IN CYBERSPACE

It is well known that the development of China's information infrastructure has been a remarkable achievement in the past decade, summarized by four features. The first is the ultra-high volume of Internet users. According to the biannual survey by the China Internet

Network Information Center (CNNIC), up to December 2016, China had 731 million Internet users. Internet penetration reached 53.2% of the population while mobile netizens accounted for 95.1% of the netizen total.[1] The number of Chinese netizens is now almost the equal of the total European population and continues to increase at a steady pace. Various applications including e-governance and business models have become an integrated part of ordinary life, and an enabler of a more streamlined and efficient public service, which in turn has helped to foster the rapid growth of the digital service. The second feature is China's increasing reliance on the information economy. As a proportion of China's gross domestic product (GDP), the value of this new economy has increased from 10% in 2002 to 30.1% in 2016. In real terms, the value of the information economy reached 22.4 trillion Yuan in 2016, an increase of 16.6% over 2015 figures when the information economy was responsible for 68.6% of China's GDP.[2] The information economy has, furthermore, maintained its high rate of growth when compared with the rest of the economy: an Information Economy Index proposed by one Chinese think tank indicated that China is one of the most dynamic information economies in the world.[3] It is predicted that the overall scale of China's digital economy will approach $16 trillion and could create 415 million jobs by 2035 (Boston Consultanting Group and Ali Research 2017). Beyond the obvious economic interest, the persistent high growth of the information economy is having a revolutionary influence on the Chinese innovation system and, more generally, on China's economic and social formation. The Chinese government takes the digital economy to be the most important catalyst of industrial upgrading and economic and social development. During the drafting and launching of China's thirteenth five-year plan in 2016, Big Data, Internet plus, smart manufacture, the Internet of Things (IoT), robotics, artificial intelligence, and strategic industry in general were all very clearly priority objectives.

The third feature is the increasingly leading role being played by the ICT sector. There are two indicators of this shift. The information technology (IT) industry is most innovative and active in China and China's Internet players are shifting the centre of gravity in the global digital economy. The best of China's ICT companies rival their Western counterparts in terms of overall scale, value, and innovative capability. In 2015, the overall capital investment value of China-based Internet businesses was $20 billion, exceeding the value of U.S.-based Internet businesses ($16 billion) for the very first time (PwC's Experience Center 2016). The pace of unicorn births (companies valued at over $1 billion at start-up) is startling: among the 10 wealthiest Internet companies in the world, 4 come from China. At the same time, new start-up companies are springing up like mushrooms after rain due to the Chinese policy of mass entrepreneurship and innovation. Moreover, China possesses competitive advantage in some areas of advanced technology. According to the World Intellectual Property Organization (WIPO), in 2015, China applied for almost 30,000 patents, ranking third globally (CNNIC 2016). Chinese research on artificial intelligence (AI), for example, has developed rapidly. Although there are disputes surrounding the development of AI in China, it is clear that the United States 'no longer has a strategic monopoly on the technology', and that 'artificial intelligence is only one part of the tech frontier where China is advancing rapidly' (Markoff and Rosenberg 2017; Zhang 2017) and showing huge potential. Some Internet giants like Baidu, Tencent, Alibaba, and Didi Chuxing established their own AI laboratories and have developed successful related business. Baidu has shown itself to be a real innovator when it comes to AI and machine learning, establishing itself 'as a truly global leader' (Marr 2017).

The fourth feature is the perception of high policy dividends. Digitization is considered to be the most effective approach to achieve the Chinese dream of national rejuvenation. Fostering the development of ICT and related industry has accordingly become a central theme in Chinese policy over the past three years. Strategies and initiatives like Made in China 2025, Internet Plus, Building Cyber Power and Big Data all shape a favourable environment for the development of the new economy. To exploit this positive trend, the Chinese administration has poured a great amount of money, manpower, and resources into this domain, and will continue to do so. In December 2016, China issued the thirteenth five-year plan for national informationization, which launched 12 priority actions including the deployment of next-generation information and network technology, the expansion of open data, and other initiatives all intended to make significant gains by 2020. The returns on investment in the IT revolution and the information economy further encourage the government to remain practical and open. At the same time, the demand from industries and individual users also prompts deeper and comprehensive reform, especially in regulatory policy. In the view of President Xi, cybersecurity and informationization will be a dominant activity during the whole period of *Shisanwu (十三五)*.

Just as China has a prominent position in the global economy, so there can be no doubt as to China's importance in cyberspace. But, beyond the impressive statistics, China still faces many challenges and often exposes its weaknesses when grappling with diverse challenges. Although there is not yet a unified metric with which to gauge a nation's cyber power, reputable research can be used to show that China is a large but not yet a strong player in cyberspace. According to the World Economic Forum's Networked Readiness Index (NRI) 2016, China's performance gave it a ranking of 59 among the 139 emerging and developing Asian economies reviewed. Yet, China still lagged behind most of the Western digitized countries, even some small nations such as Malaysia, Estonia, Qatar, Latvia, Cyprus, and Panama (Baller, Dutta, and Lavin 2016). In the International Telecommunication Union (ITU)'s annual ICT Development Index (IDI), China's IDI was 5.19 and ranked 81 among all 174 countries (ITU 2016). Other regional evaluations produce almost the same results for China. In the three cyber maturity reports in the Asian-Pacific region, China is usually ranked below developed countries such as the United States, Japan, South Korea, Australia, and New Zealand.[4] In specific areas such as users' skills, network management, and general resiliency, the United States 'enjoys substantial advantages, though Chinese performance is improving'. Chinese cybersecurity is regarded with suspicion and its civilian computers suffer from the world's highest rate of infection by malware (RAND Corporation 2016). The WuZhen Index, which judges AI ability among countries, shows that the number of AI companies, the scale of capital raised, and the number of investment pathways is respectively 4, 7, and 21 times higher in the United States than in China.[5] These assessments all use different methodologies and take into account different factors. Nevertheless, they amount to clear evidence of a persistent gap. China's leaders are clearly aware that their country has a long way to go in developing the new economy, and they are committed to promoting China's capacity in all areas including technology, economy, governance, and security.

In the first *National Strategy of Cyberspace Security*, China officially defined cyberspace for the first time. For China, cyberspace consists of the Internet, communication networks, computing systems, automatic control systems, digital devices, and the applications, services, and data carried on those systems. In the Chinese view, cyberspace is a new channel for information distribution; a new space for manufacturing and living; a new engine for economic development; a new medium for culture prosperity; a new platform for social governance; a new medium of exchange and cooperation; and a new territory of state sovereignty.[6] In China's view, security in cyberspace is much broader than simply a technical issue, and should be considered as a vast and complicated systems engineering problem.

Challenges caused by different threats emerge one after another. 'We are concerned about network security, including ideological security, data security, technical security, application security, capital security, channel security and others'.[7] The stability of the national critical information infrastructure, the core information system, and the public Internet service are all under constant attack. The National Computer Network Emergency Response Technical Team (CNCERT)'s annual report of Internet network security in China argues that, regardless of the strengthening of capability, some core infrastructure assets, such as fundamental network devices, the domain name systems (DNS), and the Internet of industry face huge risks. One popular industry control system, for example, has suffered infiltration from thousands of Internet protocol (IP) addresses outside China.[8] Moreover, the leakage of individual information, the spread of mobile malware, and the growth of such activities as DDoS-as-service also brought significant risks. Some security companies have analysed and published the details of several attacks on China. The 360 Cyber Threat Intelligence Center, for example, has detected 36 advanced persistent threat (APT) groups attacking China up to the end of 2016, with universities, private enterprise, government, and scientific research organizations (particularly ocean studies) receiving most attention.[9]

As one of few companies with the capability to monitor and analyse APT activity, 360's SkyEye Labs and Helios Team have released several reports of sophisticated attacks suffered by China, including OceanLotus (APT-C-00)[10] and APT-C-09[11]. 360's research implied that APT reliance on social engineering and spear phishing had developed over several years and was unlikely to come to an end.

The problem of cybercrime is becoming severe and is a major concern for Chinese citizens. One senior official repeatedly highlighted the importance and urgency of combating online crime, which accounts for one-third of the total amount of crime in China and is increasing by 30% every year.[12] Cybercrime has become a lucrative business, with staggering profits achieved in a relatively short time. According to a statistic released at the China Internet Security Conference, the annual value of the Black Industry Chain (online and offline crime) could exceed 115.2 billion yuan: a sum that would 'create millions of jobs' at a conservative estimate.[13] The evolution and features of cybercrime in China epitomize the unprecedentedly complicated nature of the cybersecurity landscape: the combination of existing challenges with emerging threats; the combination of traditional and untraditional security issues; and the combination of general crime with social and livelihood problems. In any interconnected society, vulnerabilities are pervasive. If networks and information systems, which have become the nerve centre of the whole economy and society itself, suffer attacks, disruptions, or significant events, the consequences could be catastrophic, gravely jeopardizing national security and public interest.

As it embraces the ICT revolution, another challenge confronting China is the shortage of appropriate governing capability. An objective law that no country can avoid when dealing with the challenges of ICT is that the speed and complexity of technological evolution always exceed people's expectation. The pace of change means that regulation tends to be reactive and inflexible, adjusting only with difficulty to the changing threat environment. There are many grey areas that are not sufficiently understood or supervised and, the practice of prioritizing the development and application of ICT over the requirements of security only makes the situation worse. This phenomenon is more prominent in those developing countries that stick closely to rigid and obsolete managing concepts—not unlike dealing with twenty-first-century threats with twentieth-century technology and nineteenth-century bureaucracy. The policy/regulatory lag, combined with deficiencies in legislation and law enforcement, and inefficiencies in administrative mechanisms, all result in an untidy and uncertain situation. Given the tendency of traditional unlawful and criminal activities to exploit ICT—for example, in rampant online drug production and trafficking, online gambling and pyramid selling, and online gun and ammunition selling—it is conceivable that various criminal preparations (both online and offline) might actually be permissible under existing law. All this makes it increasingly difficult for law enforcement and the judicial process to find appropriate legal measures, particularly to contain the source of crime and to destroy an entire criminal industrial chain. Taken together, neither traditional criminal law, nor specific legislation for the Internet, nor the rules of digital forensics and evidence can adjust sufficiently to meet these new challenges and provide a strong investigative and legislative basis for combating cybercrime (Jingjing 2017).

Another example of the same phenomenon is the exponential growth of the Internet finance or fintech sector.[14] This sector includes such activities as non-cash payment, cryptocurrencies, online capital raising, smart financial service, and block chain. The relevant authorities (including the China Banking Regulatory Commission, the People's Bank of China, and the Ministry of Industry and Information Technology) spent almost two years developing relevant regulations, while still encouraging many small businesses to undertake peer-to-peer (P2P) online margin lending, with value-at-risk amounting to $93 billion (Heinrich 2016).

To compound the challenge of effective regulation, the enormous capital data values circulating in the Internet finance sector also attract the interest of hackers.[15] Similar dilemmas accompany the rapid development of other sectors such as the share economy and artificial intelligence. Faced with these dilemmas, it can be all too easy for a vicious cycle to develop, whereby power delegation leads to market disorder, which, in turn, leads to calls for tighter control.

Although not all these problems will inevitably be components of the broader cybersecurity challenge, it is clear that each could adversely affect the functioning of the virtual information system and possibly harm the real national economy, and perhaps even the whole of society. It is for this reason that the Chinese government considers cybersecurity to be an unprecedentedly complicated challenge and one that is getting tougher because of the influence of 'barbarians from the outside', which has forced government to react rapidly and accelerate bureaucratic reform. During the drafting of the cybersecurity law, the Chinese government demonstrated an extraordinarily open posture, inviting public comment from many stakeholders including individual users and foreign vendors, the guiding principle being that the cybersecurity law should work in the interest of all stakeholders. In addition, as senior leaders consistently reiterated, the biggest danger China faces is to its core and fundamental technology, with the 'lifeline' of its technology supply chain being controlled by others. President Xi has compared this situation to having a house standing on others' property: although the house might be bigger and more attractive than others, it might not endure storms and heavy wind, and might not even withstand a single blow.[16] This reminds senior leaders to estimate calmly and objectively the gap between China and other developed countries. Senior leaders are urged to pay close attention to speeding up indigenous innovation in ICT and to grasp the initiative, making breakthroughs in frontier technologies that are internationally competitive, and establishing a secure and controllable ICT system.[17] In short, cybersecurity is seen as 'a major strategic issue concerning a country's security and development as well as people's life and work'.[18] China does not accept the trade-off of reducing security and stability in exchange for development.

The Foundation of China's Cybersecurity Concept

Acknowledging the two sides of the cyberspace coin, the Chinese government proposed a strategy to achieve national power in cyberspace: striving to exploit the opportunities and avoid the harms of cyberspace, and making the digital economy the primary goal of economic and social development. In 2014, China substantially restructured the administrative mechanisms responsible for its cyber affairs. The establishment of the Leading Group of Cybersecurity and Informationization marked a new period. With the party's general secretary acting as group leader, it was declared that 'there is no national security without cybersecurity'. The overall scheme would be to combine security and development: 'security and development are like two wings of one bird, we should plan, assign, foster and implement simultaneously'.[19] In the first meeting of the new group, President Xi put forward five indicators of a strong cyber power: possessing technology of the highest quality and under its own control; having a comprehensive information service and a flourishing online culture; having a sound information infrastructure to facilitate a fully reinforced information economy; having high-quality cybersecurity talents and specialists; and seeking dynamic bilateral and multilateral international cooperation. In sum, the goal is to popularize cyber infrastructure throughout China, to dramatically increase the capacity for indigenous innovation, to develop a complete, indigenous information economy, and to safeguard cybersecurity without compromise.[20] One document, the *National Strategic Outline of Informationization Development,* provided detailed objectives and a timeline from 2020 to the middle of this century.[21]

One of the pillars of strong cyber power is international cooperation. In other words, due to hyper-interconnectivity and unprecedented interdependence, it is acknowledged that the cybersecurity of China is bound together for good or ill with the security of other countries and the whole world. In his keynote speech[22] at the second World Internet Conference held in Wuzhen in December 2015, President Xi analysed the root of insecurity in cyberspace and resolved to build a community of shared future in cyberspace, setting out four basic principles and five propositions. The values of pursuing common, comprehensive, cooperative, and sustainable security, jointly shaping the future of the world, writing international rules, managing global affairs, and ensuring development outcomes are shared by all and embedded in the philosophy and behaviour of Chinese leaders, as demonstrated through a variety of initiatives around the world. The concept of a community of shared future was derived from the Five Principles of Peaceful Coexistence and has become the guiding principle and strategic aim of China's diplomacy, concentrating efforts to deal with common threats and global challenges to humanity, and building partnerships in the political, economic, security, cultural, and diplomatic spheres (Fan 2016).

The economic and political foundations of China's initiative are now all in place. In international law, a concept of 'international community' was raised by several pioneers to try to answer the question whether the international system should reflect Hobbes's 'state of nature', in which every nation pursues its own goals regardless of morality and justice, or Kant's 'homo sapiens' seeking to comply with a code of ethics of lasting peace. In *On the Law of War and Peace*, Grotius proposed a middle way between these two standpoints in the form of the 'international society'. In his view, international politics should be neither unending conflict among nations, nor the pursuit of a unanimously identified global interest. Instead, the relationships among states should be defined by coexistence and cooperation through shared business and diplomatic regimes, such as international law. The idea stemmed from the change of society caused by increased interaction and looming globalization. Thereafter, the broad concept was given more detailed shape by a number of scholars who gave particular attention to the changing foundations of society. The concept also drew upon Wolfgang Friedman's 'cooperative international law', which implied that the appearance of 'community interests' would go beyond the clash of interests among countries. In the digital era, the world encounters greater interconnection and closer interdependence than ever before. How countries choose to respond to the changing foundations of society is the challenge of the moment.

The economic and social foundations of coexistence and cooperation are already established and continue to strengthen. As mentioned earlier, China firmly chose to abide by the tendency of digitalization and devote to developing a new economy based on ICT. In fact, no country can ignore or resist this momentum. Originating in the 1990s, the profit the information revolution brought is obvious to all and its effectiveness doesn't show any sign of declining. The Internet 'has ingrained itself in daily life to the extent that most of us no longer think of it as anything new or special ... has become indispensable'. Besides China, lots of countries developed planning of a new economy, such as the European Union's digital single market, Singapore's Smart Nation, 'i-Japan', 'Digital India', the United Kingdom's digital strategy, Australia's broadband and big data strategy, and so on. At the Antalya and HangZhou G20 summits in 2015 and 2016, leaders recognized that we are living in the age of the Internet economy and acknowledged its driving force for global economic and sustainable growth. The digital economy of the G20 amounted to 4.1% of GDP or $2.3 trillion in 2010; its developed members' annual growth rate was expected to reach 8% over the following five years with the contribution to GDP rising to 5.7% in the EU and 5.3% for the G20. Furthermore, growth rates are expected to be more than twice as fast (at an average annual rate of 18%) in the developing market. Overall, the Internet economy of the G20 almost doubled between 2010 and 2016 (Boston Consulting Group, 2012, 3, 6).[23] The ICT revolution enabled the circulation and flow of capital, personnel, information, and data on every level globally. ICT led to tighter entanglement among disparate countries, with private sectors and ordinary people realizing the necessity for collaboration. Some scholars even consider this entanglement as a form of deterrence, with countries persuaded not to behave maliciously. 'It's no reason for China to take advantage of the asymmetrical strategy, because China is not the country that has nothing to lose ... To the extent that a state's economic growth becomes more dependent upon the Internet, the state may develop interests in systemic stability' (Nye 2016/17). Under the global cyber ecosystem, every nation, organization, and even person has the ability, theoretically, to launch a cyberattack directed at a certain country and system. The characteristics of cyberspace mean that the outcome of an attack can easily run out of control and overflow to other nation's territory. The biggest impetus to cooperation is creating a secure and trusted place to grow digital business collaboratively.

The political foundation has also consolidated. Most countries agree that lack of 'rules of the road' is the main reason for chaos, instability, and potential disorder in cyberspace. How these regulatory gaps should be filled is now the central concern for various platforms and policy agendas. In spite of the differences, disputes, and unsolved puzzles, the international community has made the first step and there is an initial non-binding framework to restrain national behaviour in cyberspace. Based on the 2015 report of the United Nations Group of Governmental Experts (UN GGE), there is consensus about responsible norms of state behaviour and about the basic principles of international law applicable in cyberspace, as well as several concrete measures for a country to build confidence, remain transparent, and make efforts to bridge the capacity divide. Some general principles of international law, such as state sovereignty and the international norms and principles that flow from sovereignty, including the injunctions not to interfere in a state's internal affairs, to settle international disputes by peaceful means, and to refrain from the threat or use of force, are all universally acknowledged as the 'ethical bottom line' and a fundamental obligation for national activity in cyberspace. In order to fulfil these obligations, many countries also undertake a great deal of practical cooperation at bilateral, regional, and international levels. One typical example is the agreement made by China and the United States in 2015, which undertook that 'neither country's government will conduct or knowingly support cyber-enabled theft of intellectual property, including trade secrets or other confidential business information, with the intent of providing competitive advantages to companies or commercial sectors', and established a high-level joint dialogue mechanism to 'review the timeliness and quality' of requests for information and assistance in criminal investigations (Office of the Press Secretary 2015). The G20 leaders' communique at Antalya Summit in 2015 also restated the norm against conducting or supporting the cyber-enabled theft of intellectual property and its support for robust and inclusive growth. Similar efforts are being undertaken across the world, driven by the common goal to ensure that humankind can continue to enjoy the benefits of ICT development.

There is one more incentive for cooperation: the imperative to deal jointly with abundant cyber threats. During recent years, the number of cyberattacks has increased markedly, causing significant disruption. Critical infrastructure assets, such as power grids and banks, are under constant sabotage. Vast quantities of personal information, including private health information, are being stolen and sold on the darknet as a lucrative business. Non-state actors, such as terrorists, are increasingly capable of using advanced cyber methods going far beyond online recruitment, propaganda, and training to the point of planning cyberattacks. The arbitrary definition of 'offensive' and 'defensive' results in the rampant proliferation of malicious technology. In the absence of operable, measurable, and proportionate supervisory mechanisms, there are lots of grey areas and loopholes that can easily be taken advantage of, such as what activity would constitute an intervention in another country's domestic affairs, what would constitute the violation of another's sovereignty, and how to restrain massive surveillance and find a balance between national security and the protection of private rights. No countries, organizations, or individuals can stay immune from such problems and challenges. In October 2016, Dyn, a DNS provider, suffered a large scale DDoS attack that paralysed its Internet service in Europe and North America. The methods of attack itself were by no means new. What was new was that IoT botnets enabled attackers to use malicious code to infect a great number of small Internet-connected items to overload the traffic. Millions of digital video recorders (DVRs) and cameras manufactured by a Chinese company inadvertently became the medium, using the vulnerabilities of an insecure default password. This incident demonstrated once again the importance of each element of the entire globalized ICT industry chain, including design, manufacture, delivery, and even users. China believes that no country can be secure while others are in turmoil, because threats facing some countries may threaten others too. This is particularly true in cyberspace. At both the national and the international levels, cybersecurity is undoubtedly a team effort.

China has identified itself as a force for world peace, a contributor to global development, and a defender of international order, and has been contributing its part to building and maintaining cyberspace accordingly. Just as President Xi said in his keynote speech at the United Nations Office at Geneva, 'China will do well only when the world does well, and vice versa.'[24] A nation's primary responsibility is to maintain its internal cybersecurity, while it also bears the obligation to contribute to international cybersecurity. Countries should pursue their own security on the basis of mutual self-interest, through common security on the basis of full respect for others. Chinese cyber policy and its practices repeatedly stress shared governance and shared interest, which is also the essence of the concept of community of shared future in cyberspace. 'With the theme focusing on peaceful development and the core message for win-win cooperation', China's first International Strategy of Cooperation on Cyberspace, released in March 2017, advocates the principles of peace, sovereignty, shared governance, and shared benefits. These four principles, accompanied by nine matched action plans, provide a guideline for China's participation in cyber international cooperation, aimed at encouraging other countries to build a peaceful, secure, open, cooperative, and orderly cyberspace as well as a multilateral, democratic, and transparent global Internet governance system.

CONSTRUCTIVE OR DESTRUCTIVE

China's decision to become a powerful actor in cyberspace prompted many questions and, in some cases, even worry that China would completely overturn existing principles of international politics and relations. In part, this is explained by cultural differences and by China's reluctance to tell its own story. But many foreign commentators, particularly in Western countries, tended to judge China in a biased way, often revealing deep prejudices and assumptions about China's intentions. When reporting on these developments in China, it was not unusual for foreign media to use such expressions as 'tighten control', 'controversial', and 'step backward' when describing the effects of Chinese policy.[25] Even without reading the Chinese legal position in full, some journalists labelled it as an 'evil law'. While it is acknowledged that there were flaws in China's policy, these were largely identified and criticized by domestic companies and experts. But the 'assumed adversary' rhetoric originating from the Cold War was not a good foundation for building cooperation and mutual trust.

Domestically, the importance of cybersecurity cannot be exaggerated. After the official launch of the Leading Group, the government and legislative organization hastened to introduce new policy and legislation to fill gaps and make improvements in order to keep pace with the fast-changing threat environment. It is estimated that there were 47 relative regulations and legislative measures to be enacted and put into practice since then. This high-level policy work, combined with numerous special operations, aimed at various kinds of illegal and harmful activities, including hacking, piracy, fake cell tower, and so on, when the government saw an urgent need to increase its defence capacity.

What informed this work, at all levels, was a new security concept. President Xi's speech made this new thinking explicit, setting out the five characteristics that will have a decisive influence on policy and practice. First, security is holistic, not fragmented; cybersecurity integrates with other security issues and even a slight change in the cyber environment will affect the whole national security picture. Second, cybersecurity is dynamic, not static; the source of threats and attacks will require very rapid analysis and assessment, and an appropriate response. Defensive measures that depend simply on the installation of layers of security devices or software are totally outdated: what is needed is a dynamic and comprehensive defensive concept. Third, cybersecurity is an open, not a closed, environment. Security can only be increased if it is based on this open environment, with advanced technology being absorbed through strengthening foreign exchange, cooperation, and interaction. Fourth, cybersecurity is relative, not absolute. Absolute security in cyberspace cannot be assured: even, if possible, the cost of attempting absolute security would be intolerable and might require unbearable sacrifices to be made elsewhere in society. Fifth, cybersecurity is mutual, not isolated. Protecting cybersecurity needs not only a whole-of-government approach but also a whole-of-society understanding, including netizens, civil society, the private sector, and government itself.[26] In sum, China is eager to build a secure, safe, open, cooperative, and orderly cyberspace based on respect for sovereignty and the rule of law.

China's efforts to bring about a community of shared future in cyberspace seeks to build upon the well-known foundations of international politics. One such foundation is the need to acknowledge and respect national sovereignty. The international community has reached consensus that the principles of state sovereignty apply in cyberspace, as demonstrated in GGE reports and in the two Tallinn manuals on the international law applicable to cyber warfare and cyber operations. Although there is still some vagueness about the application of existing international law to specific cyber activities, governments and legal experts have tended to agree that 'sovereignty is a foundational principle of international law ... various aspects of cyberspace and state cyber operations are not beyond the reach of the principle of sovereignty' (Schmitt 2017), and that 'a state may exercise control over cyber infrastructure and activities within its sovereignty territory' (Schmitt 2013). China is a strong supporter and promoter of sovereignty in cyberspace, even though it has been met with some misunderstanding as to its real intention. Although the term 'cyberspace sovereignty' was not created by China, China was the first serious user of the term. Some US cyber law scholars are thought to have been the first to propose the term in the late 1990s—scholars such as Timothy S. Wu, David Johnson, David Post, and Jack Goldsmith. Western theorists' attitude towards the idea has changed from total rejection to considered acceptance within certain parameters (Xinbao and Ke 2016).

How to define the scope of sovereignty jurisdiction and deal correctly with the relationship between regulation and freedom, rights, and obligations so as not to undermine innovation and the real value of the free flow of information, is now a hot topic within China. Cyberspace is a unique environment with dual features of the physical and the virtual, an environment that is simultaneously both sovereign territory and global commons. On the one hand, cyberspace acts as a global information channel enjoyed by all peoples and cannot be divided; no single country can own or dominate cyberspace. On the other hand, every country can and should exercise jurisdiction over cyber activities within its territory and exterritorially when appropriate and necessary. Cyberspace should be governed by nation states and by the international community jointly (Xinmin 2016). The key to this discussion is not whether sovereign states will merge according to some vision of the future cyber world, but in what ways sovereign states will exercise their power and influence in cyberspace. Some scholars argue that debate about the relevance of national sovereignty in cyberspace is the result of the dual features mentioned earlier, and reflects different priorities at the individual, national, and international levels. One analytical framework has tried to use a three-perspective theory to settle contradictions between cyber sovereignty and the spirit of the Internet, between human rights and the involvement of multi-stakeholders. This framework has sought to reconsider the exclusivity of traditional sovereignty and to produce a reasonable account of the relevance of sovereignty in the era of globalization. The conclusion to this work is that cyberspace is divisible into different layers. One way to settle the controversy is therefore to distinguish the different layers and then to identify an appropriate interpretation of sovereign exclusivity and transferability.[27]

In its national cybersecurity strategy, China outlines the implications of cyber sovereignty and focuses its argument on three aspects. The first is that sovereignty is inviolable and that states should respect others' rights to choose their methods of cyber development, cyber administration and Internet public policy independently. Every country has the right to develop legislation and policy based on the national situation and on its interpretation of international customs, taking necessary measures to protect public legal interest and order as entitled by domestic and international law. The second aspect concerns the equality of sovereignty. Each country, whether big or small, strong or weak, rich or poor, has an equal right to participate in the development of the international Internet governance system. 'Cyberspace is the common space of activities for mankind. The future of cyberspace should be in the hands of all countries.'[28] The third aspect is never to seek network hegemony and double standards, never to interfere in other nations' internal affairs and never to engage in, indulge, or support cyber activities that harm other countries' national security. China's proposal of cyber sovereignty does not mean thoroughly controlling everything in cyberspace and excluding non-state actors from a country's life and culture.

Unless its core interests are being challenged, China's policy is to comply with the law, in reasonable and predictable ways. For example, the protection of the stability of the regime and society is the biggest concern for the Chinese government. In the International Information Security Code of Conduct, China strongly opposed activity that would use ICT to interfere in the internal affairs of other states with the intention of undermining their political, economic, and social stability.[29] It is meaningless to discuss cybersecurity as an abstract or theoretical problem, as if the country itself simply did not matter or was no longer in existence. The protection of sovereignty, development, and national interest is at the root of China's current outlook. In that respect, China's position is scarcely different from that of any other state taking an active role in cyberspace.

For China, one concern is the risk that technology itself can bring, especially given China's acknowledged lack of core technology. For example, when Microsoft declared that it would no longer provide an upgrade service for Windows XP, many governmental institutions and industries had no choice but to accept exposure to risk. Thus, ensuring secure and controllable ICT applications and services is currently a major task for China. The cybersecurity law that became effective on 1 June 2017 requires operators and providers to correspond responsibly to assure the safety and credibility of their products and services, and entitles departments in charge to carry out a security review. In February 2017, the cyber administration of China issued a draft security review for public comment, identifying the scope of the review, the requirements for security and control, and the procedures and mechanisms of the review itself.[30] Unlike concerns about stealing intellectual property or digital protectionism[31], the security review aimed to prevent and manage risks that products and services might be controlled, disturbed, and interrupted; risks that occur when products and key components are developed, delivered, and maintained; risks that the providers might take commercial advantage of their privileged position to illegally collect, store, process, and use users' private information; risks that the providers might take advantage of the users' dependence to indulge in unfair competition or to harm users' interests; and, finally, other risks that might damage national security and the public interest.

Before developing this regulation, China has examined foreign best practice and international customs thoroughly. Some international technological standards have clear requirements governing the introduction of new products and services. The IT security evaluation criteria, for example, demand source code assessment of high-level IT products. When China proposes a similar review, its proposal is often opposed, with protection offered as an excuse; China finds this kind of double standard to be unacceptable (Xiaodong). Many countries worried that the regulation of cross-border data flow, data localization, and access to source code all implied that China would close the door and build barriers to exclude foreign companies. This would be an understandable concern but it is in fact groundless and exaggerated. Whether government officials, experts, or entrepreneurs, senior Chinese leaders all strongly oppose the notion that a 'made-in-China' notion should operate in cybersecurity. Locking its door against the world to develop technology is retrogressive and would even expose the country to huge risk. Ren Zhengfei, the founder of Chinese biggest IT provider Huawei, articulated a typical thought in China. Writing in an influential newspaper, he argued that 'national development and progress needs open technological system and environment, cutting itself off the outside world would just lead to more and more backwardness'. The success of Huawei is the result of this openness: excessive self-protection could not provide security, and isolation would undermine the value of cyber and information.[32] The toughest challenges China faces are not in the area of policy: they concern finding and maintaining the balance between competing priorities—security and development, openness and independence, freedom and regulation. In this regard, Chinese leaders are happy to listen to different opinions, whether from ordinary netizen or foreign governments, and they keep an open mind to adapt to the fast-changing world.

China has affirmed its commitment to a multilateral, democratic, and transparent global Internet governance system, echoing the aspirations and actions of the World Summit on the Information Society (WSIS) and its WSIS+10 review. In order to realize these goals, China supports equal participation and joint decision making within the framework of the United Nations, making full use of the representativeness of the world body and the role it has played in dealing with global threats. However, there has been some criticism that China's intention was to exclude non-state actors from participation in the process of Internet governance, even to the point of creating a dichotomy between the multilateral and the multi-stakeholder approaches. But these two models are not incompatible and the discussion should not be reduced to 'all or nothing'. National government is itself a multi-stakeholder collaboration and it is on this basis that national governments play their key role in protecting the stability and peace of the Internet, preventing conflict, combating criminals, and establishing a sound policy environment. The existing UN mechanism, although denounced because of its complicated procedure and inefficiency, is still a fair platform to allow every country to have a voice in decision making. It is also the proper platform to discuss issues involving international security and conflict. What is more, national governments cannot dominate cyberspace in the same way that they can influence land, sea, and air. The technological community has a leading role as far as the fundamental function of the Internet is concerned, and it is the private sector that makes the global ICT system possible and continues to lead the new technology revolution. In any case, the multi-stakeholder approach is no more than a methodology. The approach need not employ only one model and even then it should not be politicized: it should remain flexible and adaptable to different circumstances. Different stakeholders should contribute according to their expertise. In technological governance, for example, the technology community and the private sector should have the dominant role in a 'bottom-up' approach. As far as the distribution of basic Internet resources and the management of critical information infrastructure such as root servers are concerned, these should be the duty of Internet Corporation for Assigned Names and Numbers (ICANN) which should '(be) a truly independent international institution, increase its representations and ensure greater openness and transparency in its decision-making and operation'.[33] In an environment of increasingly serious cyber threats, governments should clearly take more responsibility and play a greater role. At the same time, deficiencies in the intergovernmental mechanism must not be ignored. Cyberspace is unlike any other, more traditional, domain of international politics: the private sector and the technology community make an indispensable contribution in preserving the stability of cyberspace, and cybersecurity relates to every person's immediate interest and ordinary life. The question then becomes how to listen to the input from non-state actors, especially global companies, and accommodate their perspectives in international norms and relevant international documents? Since 2015, Microsoft has made great efforts to present its views on international norms for cyber behaviour, with its senior executive recently proposing a Digital Geneva Convention (Smith 2017): a proposal that offered interesting and valuable thoughts on self-restraint and attribution. Other useful contributions include the EU's regulatory framework for the protection of private information.

Conclusion

Harper Lee made a well-known remark in her novel *To Kill a Mockingbird*: 'You never really understand a person until you consider things from his point of view ... Until you climb inside of his skin and walk around in it.' This remains a useful insight for those seeking to analyse and comprehend the reality of China's position regarding cyberspace.

Chaos and lawlessness in cyberspace are not in China's interest. The newest IT technology, services, and applications can all be popularized and promoted in China, almost simultaneously with developed countries. Sometimes, the speed of dissemination might even be faster, the degree of penetration deeper, and the impact on society stronger than elsewhere in the world. Nevertheless, at the level of policy-making, experience, and social governance, Chinese concepts and administrative mechanisms are considered to be obsolete and more rigid than in most developed countries. Driven by the Internet, Chinese society has experienced huge transformation and has changed gradually from a closed and opaque country with a highly asymmetrical distribution of information to one that is increasingly open and liberal, and in which the positive influence of new technology is willingly accepted. Some of these changes are readily visible, while others are more subtle and develop over a long period. China's leaders have clearly embraced digitization as one element of a new economy with which to achieve the goal of a powerful and prosperous state and a dynamic nation. As a late developer, China grapples with the problem of winning initiative and gaining advantage. But, where there are challenges, there are as many opportunities.

To understand both the policy background and the internal security requirement, it is essential to see China's cyber strategy vision as a whole. As a big player, it is beyond dispute that China should take greater responsibility to protect and maintain the stability of cyberspace, and its role should be constructive through providing public goods. From the Chinese perspective, there are many shortcomings in the existing international governance system. For that reason, China has vowed to be a norms *shaper* rather than simply a norms *implementer*, by proposing new thinking, by insisting that the UN should be the main forum for the governance debate, and by complying with the basic principles of international law including the UN Charter. One measure China advocates is to strengthen exchanges and prevent misunderstandings by conducting practical cooperation at various levels in various sectors such as the economy, capacity building, and law enforcement. As set out in the International Strategy of Cooperation on Cyberspace, China not only promises to safeguard the peace and stability of cyberspace and to establish a rules-based order in cyberspace, it also undertakes to:

> support enhanced cooperation and sharing of Internet technology. It calls for countries to work together to address technological difficulties and grow new industries and new business models through closer cooperation in network communication, mobile Internet, cloud computing, Internet of Things and big data. Personnel exchange will be further enhanced to expand the rank of professionals strong in innovation.

ICT has totally changed the human life, with its biggest impact being the upheaval caused to our ideology and modes of thinking. How to break the restrictions of old habits of thought and to be dynamic and innovative is a formidable challenge not only to China but to all the countries in the world. The Internet will continue to change in the next several years, perhaps even more so than it has in its first 30 years. Security should not be the purpose of this ICT revolution. Instead, cybersecurity should be simply the means to a better and more sustainable life for all. To prevent conflict in cyberspace, it has become popular to introduce the theory of strategic stability into this new domain. Although there are huge differences and incompatibilities between the cyber and the nuclear domains, there are some insights that can be used for reference. The theorist Thomas Schelling sought to find a focal point with which to achieve strategic collaboration during a conflict. He argued that a complete, uncompromising confrontation between national interests is rare. Schelling saw that a mixed-motive game or non-zero sum (or variable sum) game is the norm, and therefore that the possibility exists of pursuing common interest through coordination and cooperation. When the expectations of both sides in a conflict can focus on one point, then that point provides the rationale for both sides to seek to reach a stable outcome. In the hyper-interconnective and interdependent cyberspace, the Schelling Point is of considerable importance: it is crucial that all states should acknowledge the strength of Schelling's insight and act accordingly.

NOTES

1. 'Statistical Report on Internet Development in China', CNNIC, January 2017. The newest Chinese edition can found at: http://www.cnnic.net.cn/hlwfzyj/hlwxzbg/hlwtjbg/201701/P020170123364672657408.pdf. The last English edition was released in July, 2016, and can found at http://cnnic.com.cn/IDR/ReportDownloads/201611/P020161114573409551742.pdf

2. *The Development of Information Economy Report 2016*, ChinaInfo 100 Annual Report, 21 January 2017. http://www.chinainfo100.net/document/201701/article13455.htm; *White Paper of the Development of China Information Economy*, China Academy of Information and Communication Technology (CAICT), September, 2016, p.15, http://www.catr.cn/kxyj/qwfb/bps/201609/P020160918606005659368.pdf

3. *White Paper of the Development of China Information Economy*, China Academy of Information and Communication Technology (CAICT), September, 2016. http://www.catr.cn/kxyj/qwfb/bps/201609/P020160918606005659368.pdf. The paper also provided a definition of the information economy, including basic components such as the regular IT industry covering technology, products and services, and a more developed definition including the use of ICT to yield additional value and high productivity for traditional industries, including new retail, pan-entertainment, new finance, and new manufacture. The G20 HangZhou Summit also provided a definition of the digital economy in *G20 Digital Economy Development and Cooperation Initiative*, p. 1: http://www.g20.utoronto.ca/2016/160905-digital.html

4. *Cyber Maturity in the Asia-Pacific Region*, International policy Center of Australia Strategic Policy Center (ASPI), April 2014, September 2015, September 2016.

5. *Global Artificial Intelligence Development Report* (2016), WuZhen Think Tank, released before third World Internet Conference in WuZhen, HangZhou, China, 14 October 2016: http://sike.news.cn/statics/sike/posts/2016/10/219507990.html

6. *National Strategy of Cyberspace Security*, 27 December 2016: http://news.xinhuanet.com/politics/2016-12/27/c_1120196479.htm

7. 'Interview with Deputy Director of National Internet Information Office Wang Xiujun', People's Daily, 18 May 2014.

8. 2015 Internet Network Security Report, CNCERT, May 2016, p.16: http://www.cert.org.cn/publish/main/upload/File/2015annualreport.pdf

9. *2016 China Advanced Persistent Attack (APT) Research Report*, QiHu 360, pp. 5–6: https://ti.360./upload/report/file/28-2016APT-201702120743.pdf

10. 'Ocean Lotus (APT-C-00): Safari in the Digital Ocean, Sky Eye Labs, 29 May 2015: https://skyeye.360safe.com/get_apt_pdf/kTAvH8mZuLfdclsD/OceanLotusReport.pdf

11. Also named 'Hang Over', 'Viceroy Tiger', 'The Dropping Elephant', and 'Patchwork', this attack was exposed in 2013. Its operation could be tracked back to early in December 2009 and it has remained active. The APT aimed at stealing sensitive information from government, and scientific research and education organization: https://ti.360.com/upload/report/file/mkczzbg1.pdf, 4 August, 2016. Starting from 2015, the Helios team has published several reports on APT, details of which can be found at *2016 China Advanced Persistent Attack（APT）Research Report*, p. 56.

12. 'Meng Jianzhu: Enhance the Sense of Security of the Masses through Promoting the capability of combating new kind of crime', *China News*, 3 February 2017: http://news.xnnews.com.cn/gnxw2/201702/t20170203_2568978.shtml. Mr. Meng is the secretary of the Political and Judiciary Commission under the Central Committee of Communist Party of China.

13. 'The Black Industry Chain of Cybercrime Tended to Borderless', *Economic Information Daily*, 17 August 2016: http://finance.people.com.cn/n1/2016/0817/c1004-28642215.html

14. For more details about the Internet finance industry and its regulation in China, see McKinsey&Company. 2016. 'Disruption and Connection: Cracking the Myths of China Internet Finance Innovation', July: https://www.mckinsey.com/~/media/mckinsey/industries/financial%20services/our%20insights/whats%20next%20for%20chinas%20booming%20of%20fintech%20sector/disruption-and-connection-cracking-the-myths-of-china-internet-finance-innovation.ashx. Li Barbara. 2015. 'China Issues Comprehensive Regulations on Internet Finance', October. http://www.nortonrosefulbright.com/knowledge/publications/133500/china-issues-comprehensive-regulations-on-internet-finance.

15. *Survey Report of Cybersecurity of Whole Finance Industry in China(2016)*, 28 June, 2016: http://www.aqniu.com/industry/17160.html

16. 'President Xi Jinping's Remarks at the Symposium of Cybersecurity and Informationization', People's Daily, 26 April 2016, p. 3.

17. 'President Xi's Remarks at the Group Study of Politic Bureau Central Committee, People's Daily, 10 October 2016, p. 1.

18. 'President Xi's Remarks at the Group Study of Politic Bureau Central Committee, People's Daily, 10 October 2016, p. 1.

19. For details of leading group, see Yukai, Wang, 'History of Central Committee Leading Group of Cybersecurity and Informationization and Its Significance', 4 March 2014: http://theory.gmw.cn/2014-03/04/content_10565077.htm.

20. The meeting and remark of President Xi can be found at the official website of China Administration of Cyberspace, which is in charge of the ordinary works for leading groups, 27 February 2014: http://www.cac.gov.cn/2014-02/27/c_133148354.htm.

21. *National Strategic Outline of Informationization Development*, announced by general office of Central Committee Communist Party and State Council, 27 July 2016, http://finance.china.com.cn/news/gnjj/20160727/3832184.shtml.

22. The full text can be found at People's Daily, 17 December 2015, p. 2.

23. People's Daily, 17 December 2015, p.6.

24. 'Full Text: Speech by Xi Jinping at the United Nations Office at Geneva' , *XinHua*, 25 January 2107: http://www.china.org.cn/chinese/2017-01/25/content_40175608.htm.

25. There are some examples: Haour, Georges, 'Why China's New Cybersecurity Law Is A Threat To International Businesses And Innovation', November 2016, https://www.imd.org/publications/opinions/why-chinas-new-cybersecurity-law-is-a-threat-to-international-businesses-and-innovation/; Conger, Kate. 2016. 'China's New Cybersecurity Law Is

Bad News for Business', 6 November: https://techcrunch.com/2016/11/06/chinas-new-cybersecurity-law-is-bad-news-for-business/; 'China's New Cybersecurity Law Sparks Fresh Censorship and Espionage Fears', *The Guardian*, 7 November 2016: https://www.theguardian.com/world/2016/nov/07/chinas-new-cybersecurity-law-sparks-fresh-censorship-and-espionage-fears; Clover, Charles, and Sherry Fei Ju: 'China Cyber Security Law Sparks Foreign Fears', *Financial Times*, 7 November 2016: https://www.ft.com/content/c330a482-a4cb-11e6-8b69-02899e8bd9d1; 'The Noose Tightens: China Adopts a Tough Cyber-Security Law', *The Economist*, 10 November 2016: http://www.economist.com/news/china/21710001-foreign-firms-are-worried-china-adopts-tough-cyber-security-law; 'China Approves Law to Tighten Control on Internet Use', 7 November 2016, *CNBC*, http://www.cnbc.com/2016/11/07/china-approves-law-to-tighten-control-on-internet-use.html; Mozur, Paul. 2016. 'China's Internet Controls will Get Stricter, to Dismay of Foreign Business', *The New York Times*, 7 November: https://www.nytimes.com/2016/11/08/business/international/china-cyber-security-regulations.html; Chin, Josh, and Eva Dou. 2016. 'China's New Cybersecurity Law Rattles Foreign Tech Firms', *Wall Street Journal*, 7 November. https://www.wsj.com/articles/china-approves-cybersecurity-law-1478491064.

26. 'President Xi Jinping's Remarks at the Symposium of Cybersecurity and Informationization', People's Daily, 26 April 2016, p. 3.

27. Yeli Hao. 2016. 'Unity of Opposites in Cyber Sovereignty as per Three Perspectives', *Journal of Shantou University, Humanities & Social Science Edition* 6: 10. The author classified cyberspace into three layers: the Bottom Level (physical level includes cyber infrastructure); the Middle Level (applications) and the Top Level (core level comprising regime, law, political security and ideology, and the country's core interest). The first two levels are characterized by open and shared transferability. While the top level is inviolably exclusive, which means that it should be prohibited to challenge the core interests of a nation, at the same time it should also be prohibited to shake the foundation of the World Wide Web by abusing traditional sovereignty.

28. Keynote speech by President Xi at the second World Internet Conference, The full text can be found in *People's Daily*, 17 December 2015, p. 2.

29. Letter Dated 9 January 2015 from the Permanent Representatives of China, Kazakhstan, Kyrgyzstan, the Russian Federation, Tajikistan, and Uzbekistan to the United Nations addressed to the Secretary-General, A/69/723, 13 January 2015, p. 5.

30. The full text can be found at the official website of the Cyberspace Administration of China: http://www.cac.gov.cn/2017-02/04/c_1120407082.htm?from=groupmessage&isappinstalled=0. The deadline for public comment was 4 March 2017.

31. In recent years, more and more countries have tried to develop stricter regulation because of serious concerns over data and information security. This has placed a greater burden and increased responsibility on the private sector, as well as inconveniencing flow of data among countries. Together, these measures have stimulated a debate on digital protectionism, including the following argument: 'US commerce secretary warns of "digital protectionism"', 23 June 2016: http://www.business-standard.com/article/pti-stories/us-commerce-secretary-warns-of-digital-protectionism-116062300018_1.html; 'Fact Sheet: Key Barriers to Digital Trade', Office of the United Stated Trade Representative, March, 2016: https://ustr.gov/about-us/policy-offices/press-office/fact-sheets/2016/march/fact-sheet-key-barriers-digital-trade; Lund, Susan, and James Manyika, 'Defending Digital Globalization', *Foreign Affairs*, March–April, https://www.foreignaffairs.com/articles/world/2017-04-20/defending-digital-globalization

32. Zhengfei, Ren. 2016. 'Openness Is the Inevitable Road to Resolve Security', *Study Times*, 22 August.

33. Plan of Action, No. 4, International Strategy of Cooperation on Cyberspace, Ministry of Foreign Affairs of the People's Republic of China, 1 March 2017: http://www.scio.gov.cn/32618/Document/1543874/1543874.htm

BIBLIOGRAPHY

Baller, Silja, Soumitra Dutta, and Bruno Lavin (eds). 2016. 'Global Information Technology Report 2016', February. World Economic Forum, p. 16: http://www3.weforum.org/docs/GITR2016/GITR_2016_full%20report_final.pdf

Boston Consultant Group and Ali Research. 2017. 'Year 2035: 400 Million Job Opportunities in the Digital Age', January: http://www.bcg.com.cn/cn/files/publications/reports_pdf/BCG_Year_2035_400_Million_Job_Opportunities_in_the_Digital_Age_Jan_2017_CHN.pdf

Boston Consulting Group. 2012. 'The Connected World: The Internet Economy in the G20', March, p. 3: https://www.bcg.com/documents/file100409.pdf

CNNIC. 2016. 'The Evaluation Report of National Informationization Development', November, p. 18: https://www.cnnic.net.cn/hlwfzyj/hlwxzbg/hlwtjbg/201611/P020161118599094936045.pdf

Fan, Wang. 2016. 'The Academic Significance and Existing Practice of Community of Shared Future', *Contemporary World* 6, p. 4.

Heinrich, Erik. 2016. 'Small Business Loans In Minutes, Thanks To Startups', *The Globe and Mail*, 12 September: http://www.theglobeandmail.com/report-on-business/small-business-loans-in-minutes-thanks-to-startups/article31796302/

International Telecommunication Union (ITU). 2016. 'Measuring the Information Society Report', ITU, p. 12: http://www.itu.int/en/ITU-D/Statistics/Documents/publications/misr2016/MISR2016-w4.pdf

Jingjing, Li. 2017. 'On the Legislative Countermeasures for Checking Cybercrime', *Cybersecurity Technology and Application* (1).

Markoff, John, and Matthew Rosenberg. 2017. 'China's Intelligent Weaponry Gets Smarter', *The New York Times*, 3 February: https://www.nytimes.com/2017/02/03/technology/artificial-intelligence-china-united-states.html?_r=0

Marr, Bernard. 2017. 'How Chinese Internet Giant Baidu uses AI and Machine Learning', *Forbes*, February 13: http://www.forbes.com/sites/bernardmarr/2017/02/13/how-chinese-internet-giant-baidu-uses-ai-and-machine-learning/ - 612dc95c4e2b

Nye, Joseph. 2016/17. 'Deterrence and Dissuasion in Cyberspace', *International Security* 41 (3), winter: 60.

Office of the Press Secretary. 2015. 'Fact Sheet: President Xi Jinping's State Visit to the United States', 25 September, White House: https://www.whitehouse.gov/the-press-office/2015/09/25/fact-sheet

'Interview With Deputy Director of National Internet Information Office Wang Xiujun', People's Daily, 18 May 2014.

PwC's Experience Center. 2016. 'The Rise of China Silicon Dragon', June: http://www.pwc.com/id/en/Consulting/Asset/Consulting%20Publication/rise-of-china-silicon-dragon-apr-2016.pdf

RAND Corporation. 2016. 'The U.S.-China Military Scorecard: Forces, Geography, and the Evolving Balance of Power, 1996–2017', October, p. 259, p. xxviii.

Schmitt, M.N. (ed.). 2013. *Tallinn Manual on the International Law Applicable to Cyber Operations*, Cambridge: Cambridge University Press, p. 15.

Schmitt, M.N. (ed.). 2017. *Tallinn Manual on the International Law Applicable to Cyber Operations*, Cambridge: Cambridge University Press, p. 11.

'Ocean Lotus(APT-C-00): 'Safari in the Digital Ocean', Sky Eye Labs, 29 May 2015: https://skyeye.360safe.com/get_apt_pdf/kTAvH8mZuLfdclsD/OceanLotusReport.pdf

Smith, Brad. 2017. 'The Need for a Digital Geneva Convention', 14 February: https://blogs.microsoft.com/on-the-issues/2017/02/14/need-digital-geneva-convention/#DWlG4vRiGjvuUPdl.99

Xiaodong, Zuo. 'The G20's Initiative of Digital Economy and Cybersecurity', *Microcomputers and Its Applications* 35 (18): 2

Xinbao, Zhang, and Xu Ke. 2016. 'A Study on Cyberspace Sovereignty', *China Legal Science* 4 (33): 35–6.

Xinmin, Ma. 2016. 'Key Issues and Future Development of International Cyberspace Law', *Information Security and Communication Privacy* 11: 28–9.

Zhang, Sarah. 2017. 'China's Artificial-Intelligence Boom', *The Atlantic*, 16 February: https://www.theatlantic.com/technology/archive/2017/02/china-artificial-intelligence/516615

Zhengfei, Ren. 2016. 'Openness Is the Inevitable Road to Resolve Security', *Study Times*, 22 August.

CHAPTER 37

....

LOOK WEST OR LOOK EAST? INDIA AT THE CROSSROADS OF CYBERSPACE

....

ARUN MOHAN SUKUMAR

As a net importer of technology[1] and a net exporter of data, India faces a unique challenge. With the country's users and enterprises relying on supply chains based abroad, India's regulators are constrained to mitigate vulnerabilities in its digital ecosystem. Security testing for hardware is mostly done by the private sector, and India has found it difficult to set domestic testing standards given that the main suppliers of digital infrastructure come from jurisdictions without uniform technical specifications.[2] Mobile applications, on the other hand, are vetted in-house by the proprietors of popular platforms like Android and iOS, with minimal regulatory intervention—a phenomenon observed globally.[3] Both at the infrastructure layer and the application layer, therefore, India is reliant on external actors to ensure the integrity of its electronic data. Complicating this scenario is the absence of data localization laws in the country.[4] Most data harvested from Indian users by foreign companies is stored outside its borders.[5] As a result, the retrieval of electronic information for law enforcement purposes becomes difficult. Indian agencies, ranging from the National Intelligence Agency to the local constabulary, have to navigate a minefield of legal complexities to make available data hosted by a foreign company.[6]

The Indian state is therefore caught in a quandary. On the one hand, regulators cannot ensure the safety of a digital ecosystem driven by imported technology; on the other, cybercrimes that do occur cannot be effectively investigated and prosecuted for lack of access to electronic data. This is, essentially, the paradox of digitalization for India's economy. Framed generally, it may be asked: should open digital economies reconcile themselves to a persistent state of cyber insecurity? The question is pertinent not only for India but for most economies in the Asia-Pacific region, which is set to witness the fastest expansion in Internet connectivity anywhere in the world over the next decade.[7]

It is increasingly apparent that the rest of the world cannot emulate the trajectories of the United States or China, among the largest digital economies in the world. Both countries have managed to achieve self-sufficiency in digital infrastructure—relative to other major economies—as well as the content that flows through it. The United States has incubated

Internet giants that are today the guardians of nearly half the world's user-generated data.[8] While its digital infrastructure is no longer manufactured within the country's borders, most American companies tightly control their supply chains.[9] China's, on the other hand, resembles a closed digital ecosystem. Its digital infrastructure is produced indigenously, and a decades-long policy of protectionism has allowed domestic e-commerce, social media, and financial technology applications to edge out foreign competition in the Chinese market (Dai 2002).

In both jurisdictions, regulators retain considerable agency over the digital economy. Data-harvesting companies like Google, Facebook, or Twitter are incorporated in the United States, making even their extra-territorial operations answerable to its laws.[10] The United States also hosts the Internet Corporation for Assigned Names and Numbers (ICANN)—which backstops the Domain Name System (DNS)—as well as nine of the twelve 'root server' operators, who administer authoritative name servers for the DNS.[11] The data of Chinese citizens, and those who use Internet applications within China's borders, are held within the country on account of its data localization policies (Mayer Brown 2016). By circumstance and design, therefore, the United States and China have certain political and economic levers that enhance the states' capacity to regulate and secure cyberspace.

For the reasons mentioned earlier, these properties are not accessible to India and other emerging economies. India's calibration of its cybersecurity regulations, while preserving the openness of its digital economy, could be a test case for smaller countries struggling with the same limitations. Should India pursue data localization or require technology companies to use locally manufactured components, economies such as Brazil, Mexico, and Malaysia may be encouraged to replicate such regulations for their digital economies (*ANTARA News* 2016). India's 'digitalization paradox' could, therefore, become a global or regional phenomenon. This chapter explores how India has managed its external environment with a view to securing its own digital ecosystems. It will highlight India's engagement with the United States and China, the biggest players in its digital ecosystem. Both relationships reflect certain geopolitical realities, but also offer contrasting narratives. India and the United States have sought in recent years to align their views on the governance of common digital spaces, whereas New Delhi's outreach to China has been more instrumental and largely confined to interactions with specific Chinese companies that invest in the country. Mindful, however, of Beijing's potential to expand its influence in Asian economies by supplying their digital infrastructure and applications, India has acknowledged the need to engage China at a strategic level on 'cyber' issues. Its high-level interactions with the United States and China could lead India to a crossroads from where it has to choose one model of standards, rules, and norms for cybersecurity and Internet governance over the other.

INDIA AND THE UNITED STATES: BELATED NORM CONVERGENCE

The India–United States relationship on, cyber policy policies is notable for the convergence it has achieved in recent years. That India would collaborate with the United States in articulating norms on cybersecurity or the digital economy seems inevitable given the factors at play. Nearly 89,000 Indians live in Silicon Valley alone, and this community is at the forefront of innovations in digital technologies (Dave 2015). By one estimate, nearly 14% of start-ups in the Valley have had an Indian co-founder.[12] For major Internet companies like Facebook and Google, India is their second biggest market, where revenues have grown almost by half year on year.[13] Indian engineers, based at home and abroad, continue to be the mainstay of US corporations, as full-time employees, consultants, or bug bounty researchers.[14] Cybersecurity companies like Symantec and McAfee (Intel Security) maintain a significant presence in the Indian cities of Bangalore and Chennai that serve as research and development hubs for their global operations.[15]

Despite these factors, India and the United States struggled until recently to articulate a common framework for Internet governance and cybersecurity. To be sure, a government-to-government dialogue on cybersecurity has been ongoing since 2010, while a private sector-led working group on Information and Communication Technology (ICT-WG) has been meeting for nearly 10 years.[16] These platforms failed to achieve any significant breakthrough on cyber policy coordination, however, for three reasons. First, they focused on transactional, 'now and here' issues. While governmental dialogues on cybersecurity highlighted hurdles to ongoing criminal investigations, the India–US ICT working group confined discussions to work visas and investment flows.[17] Second, the dialogues themselves did not involve key stakeholders: for example, until 2015, the Indian delegation at the security dialogues did not feature nodal institutions tackling cybersecurity or critical infrastructure protection (The White House 2015a).

Start-ups from India and the United States continue to be marginally represented in the ICT working group, limiting their role in policy creation. Third, the dialogues themselves did not feed into high-level engagements between the leadership of both countries.

Beyond institutional reasons, there were also political factors that contributed to the lack of substantive collaboration between India and the United States on cyberspace. With its announcement of the Internet Assigned Numbers Authority (IANA) transition process in 2014, the United States National Telecommunications and Information Administration (NTIA) sought to transfer the oversight of critical DNS functions from the US Department of Commerce to a global, 'multistakeholder' body.[18] India and the United States then had divergent views on Internet governance, with New Delhi preferring intergovernmental forums to tackle global policy issues. In October 2014, India also proposed through the International Telecommunications Union (ITU) to create a system of Internet governance 'in which the naming and numbering of different countries are easily discernible'. The proposal also encouraged data localization for data 'originating and terminating' in the same country.[19]

These radical measures were shelved after opposition from the United States at the ITU Plenipotentiary Conference in Busan, South Korea.[20] But the Indian proposal reflected a great schism in the policy positions of both countries. New Delhi sought greater governmental say in the running of the DNS, whereas the United States pushed for a 'level playing field' for the private sector and the technical community in the matter. Both positions acknowledged certain economic realities. In India, the government has been the final arbiter of cyber policy since the Information Technology Act came into force in 2000, and continues also to be the biggest provider of welfare measures through e-governance programmes. For the United States, maintaining the primacy of its private sector in the development of global technical standards and protocols was crucial as it would affect their business interests abroad. For a while, it appeared that these differences would become acute as the IANA transition entered its final stages.

Then, at the ICANN 53 meeting in Buenos Aires, Argentina, India surprised the international community by roundly endorsing the multistakeholder model of Internet governance.[21] Several factors may have contributed to this decision, which was announced by the Minister of Electronics and Information Technology at ICANN 53. India had since 2014 created unique institutions to coordinate decision making across its ministries—the office of the National Cyber Security Coordinator in the Prime Minister's Office, for instance[22]— and likely felt confident that an endorsement of 'multistakeholderism' would not weaken the government's hands in articulating cyber policy. More importantly, the endorsement was a political signal from the Indian government that it sought to work with the United States in confronting mutual challenges in cyberspace.[23] India acknowledged, through this announcement, that it could better secure its open digital ecosystem by cooperating with the United States.

Barely a month after the ICANN 53 announcement, the United States and India formalized high-level engagement on cyberspace through its Strategic and Commercial Dialogue (SCD). The joint communique from the 2015 SCD proposed that both sides 'work together to promote cybersecurity, combat cyber crime, and advance norms of state behaviour in cyberspace'.[24] It also signed off on the creation of a Track 1.5 Cyber Dialogue.[25] The Track 1.5 process was convened by think tanks on either side, but saw participation both from the Indian Prime Minister's Office and the US White House.[26] India used this platform to discuss what one government delegate referred to in the meeting as the 'number one issue between both countries': retrieval of electronic information across borders. The first and second meetings devoted substantial attention to the proposed UK–US Data Sharing Agreement, and whether that could be a template for a similar instrument with India. New Delhi was using its new-found political convergence with the United States to meet some of its domestic security objectives. The Track 1.5 Dialogue was arguably the first time that US companies sat alongside both governments to discuss legal hurdles in handing over information to Indian law enforcement agencies.

Meanwhile, the SCD also encouraged both sides to negotiate a 'framework' agreement for the cyber relationship. The United States in 2015 had signed a landmark cybersecurity agreement with China, but it did not offer prescriptions for state behaviour in cyberspace on account of political differences between both countries (The White House 2015b). The Obama administration saw cyber cooperation with India as an important element in its pivot to Asia.[27] On its part, India saw the framework agreement as another opportunity to elicit cooperation from the United States in securing its digital infrastructure.[28] Consequently, at the 2016 iteration of the SCD, both sides signed this important agreement. India 'committed' to promote the 'free flow of information' in return for 'practical cooperation to mitigate cyber threats to the security of ICT infrastructure and information'. The agreement also sought to 'promote cooperation in [...] cybersecurity standards and security testing [...] and cybersecurity product development'. And, finally, the framework agreement also proposed joint strategies to preserve the integrity of digital supply chains.[29]

The India–US cyber relationship and its rapid progress in recent years reflects how New Delhi has confronted the 'digitalization paradox' through political engagement. In addition to high-level cooperation on cybercrime and supply chain integrity, both sides have also begun to discuss the security of the application layer. Mindful that encrypted messaging platforms like WhatsApp and Telegram are widely used in the country, India has also initiated discussions on encryption standards and policies with the United States.[30] These conversations have also resulted in both sides finding common ground on Internet governance principles.

WARMING UP TO CHINA

If it belatedly identified convergences with the United States, the Indian engagement with China on cybersecurity has struggled to find common ground. To be sure, Chinese device manufacturers have long been assumed to have a promising market in India: in 2015 Huawei was expected to corner 10% of the smartphone devices sold in the country by the end of 2017[31], while Xiaomi has achieved a market share of 8% in just under three years.[32] Their explosive growth in India is pegged to a surge in Internet penetration, but also to their affordability (more expensive Apple devices, used by nearly half the US population, have a market share of just 2% in India[33]). But the language barrier has been difficult for both countries to overcome: there is limited exchange of expertise between technical communities in India and China, and few common applications preferred by their respective users. Consequently, no intergovernmental channels have been created specifically to tackle cybercrime or discuss cybersecurity—in fact, at the time of writing, there is no institutionalized dialogue on cyber governance between the two states. The security of Chinese hardware has been a lingering concern. Huawei's investment proposals in India, for instance, have been vetted in the past for clearance from national security agencies.[34] To make up for its lack of agency over foreign manufacturers, India's onerous cybersecurity regulations have placed the burden of detecting malware in foreign and indigenous information technology (IT) equipment on domestic Internet service providers.[35] Given the increasing and already sizeable presence of Chinese players like Huawei, Xiaomi, and Oppo, this regulatory requirement may be unsustainable. But future conversations around supply chain integrity are likely to be had between the Indian government and China's businesses, which appear willing to tailor their security requirements to suit India's digital economy.[36]

Nevertheless, there is a strategic imperative for India to engage with the Chinese government, given that both countries will play a crucial role in shaping future cyber regimes. Over the next decade, Indian ICT enterprises and applications will look to expand their footprint, in Central and South East Asia as well as Africa, where digital ecosystems are booming. In many instances, they will compete directly with their Chinese counterparts: 'fintech' gateways like Alipay of China may clash with India's digital wallet offerings, while Indian telecom service providers such as Airtel may find themselves vying for market space alongside China Telecom.

The competition between Indian and Chinese companies to build the ICT ecosystem in Asia is not merely a matter of market revenues but also of strategic influence. Both New Delhi and Beijing will be mindful of the opportunity to establish themselves as the custodians of electronic data in the region. They also have reasons to cooperate. The absence of clear standards or technical protocols for digital ecosystems in the Asia-Pacific will hinder the interoperability of devices and applications, potentially leading to fragmented digital spaces in the region.[37] Such an outcome will be neither business- nor consumer-friendly. As their businesses intertwine, both India and China may be compelled to develop interoperable standards together.

The security architecture of digital payments systems is one such area necessitating co-operation between both countries. Digital wallets and card companies today rely on technical protocols that were developed at the turn of the twenty-first century. The Secure Socket Layer (SSL) and Secure Electronic Transaction (SET) protocols, for instance, were designed to provide 'point-to-point' and 'end-to-end' protection for the user's data and payment information, respectively.[38] SSL certificates validate the authenticity of the e-commerce vendor chosen by a user, while the SET guarantees the integrity of the business transaction between both. When protocols like SET were developed, they privileged speed over security, mindful that longer processing times for consumers could discourage them from transferring money over the Internet.[39] As a result, payment security protocols do not encrypt order information but only details about the payment itself.[40] Subsequent advancements in data analytics have ensured that the 'metadata' of orders is as valuable as the payment information itself because it reveals consumption patterns and user behaviour that is often the target of identity theft.

These protocols also assumed, crucially, that the user would have a functional understanding of digital payment gateways, and that these transactions would be conducted over relatively secure platforms. Neither assumption holds true for many Internet users in the Asia-Pacific region.

The SET protocol, for example, initially required users to have a digital certificate—ironically, this property would set back its adoption even in advanced economies like the United States.[41] It also conflated the electronic identity of the card with the physical identity of the user, thus discounting cases of fraud. (The 3-D Secure protocol developed by Visa in 2001 introduced an additional layer of authentication to mitigate this problem.)[42] In Asia, the digital ecosystem is characterized by communications and transactions over low-cost devices bought by first-generation Internet users. Customers transacting over mobile e-commerce platforms neither have a clear understanding of the security checks in place to protect their personal and financial data nor adopt devices that promise 'security by design'.[43]

The proliferation of vulnerabilities that target the weakest link in Asia's ICT supply chain—the end user—could therefore prompt India and China to jointly develop secure protocols for digital payments. These discussions may be initiated by the private sector in both countries, which have already begun to collaborate across businesses. The Chinese e-commerce giant Alibaba has invested a 40% stake in India's leading payments gateway, PayTM.[44] The business operations of most technology companies in India and China, currently confined to their domestic markets, will soon turn towards markets in Central and South East Asia. To ensure the security of their digital infrastructure and applications, these businesses have few options but to work together, for which the India–China relationship can give strategic direction.

Government-to-government engagement for rule setting on cybersecurity may take place through a 'trifecta' of institutions—the Asian Infrastructure Investment Bank (AIIB), the One Belt One Road initiative (OBOR), and the Regional Comprehensive Economic Partnership (RCEP). Taken together, these institutions will supply the political capital, lines of funding, and regulatory guidelines to create future digital ecosystems in Asia. Already, the AIIB has scouted for, or approved, infrastructure projects with key ICT elements in India, Bhutan, and Indonesia.[45] The Belt and Road initiative has a 'digital Silk Road' component aimed at strengthening 'e-commerce, industrial networks and Internet banking abroad'.[46]

E-commerce regulations are at the heart of RCEP negotiations, although countries are far from reaching meaningful consensus on foreign investment in their digital economies.[47] The progress achieved by these three institutions will not only affect India and China's own economies but also the business prospects of their ICT companies in Asia. As a result, New Delhi and Beijing may be compelled to cooperate sooner rather than later to jointly develop standards and protocols for interoperable digital technologies.

Like India's relationship with the United States, its engagement with China on cybersecurity and Internet governance has an important political dimension. The Belt and Road Project—presumably the vehicle for implementing many of the ICT projects that will be funded by the AIIB and other Asian institutions—is viewed with suspicion by New Delhi for fear of 'encirclement' by China.[48] The China-Pakistan Economic Corridor (CPEC), an extension of OBOR, criss-crosses Pakistan-Occupied Kashmir, which has been formally contested by India since 1947, its year of independence. India declared in 2017 that 'regional connectivity' plans should respect 'sovereignty' concerns of countries, indicating that it is yet to warm up to OBOR.[49] Citing this reason, it became the only major country to boycott the Belt and Road Forum summit organized by the Chinese government in May 2017.[50] Although New Delhi is an active member and beneficiary of the AIIB, the possibility of cybersecurity cooperation in ICT infrastructure projects funded by the bank appears bleak for now. Indian companies investing in AIIB's ICT projects with their Chinese counterparts, either at home or abroad, may be subjected to a vetting process by the government. Similarly, there is considerable opposition among Indian companies to throwing open the country's e-commerce sector for fear of being dominated by bigger players like Alibaba.[51] Calls for protectionism are likely to influence India's negotiating position during RCEP talks, making it difficult to reach common ground with China.[52] Both governments appear seized of the necessity, even desire, to cooperate at a strategic level, but it appears for now that short-term economic concerns and intractable political issues may slow down substantive engagement.

LOOK EAST OR WEST?

'Sovereignty' in cyberspace may be defined as the capacity of a state to:

1. Prevent large-scale cyberattacks on its territory, citizens, businesses, and institutions, as well as the use of its digital infrastructure for cyberattacks against another country. This property implies a legal obligation by states not to intervene in internal activities of another.
2. Investigate, prosecute, and punish the commission of cybercrimes in its territory and those committed on its citizens, businesses, and institutions outside its borders.
3. Regulate the terms of business of domestic and foreign players in its digital economy.

These metrics are not exhaustive but indicative of a state's overall ability to secure its digital ecosystem. India does not score well on all three counts. The country's digital infrastructure and the applications that ride on it are largely sourced from abroad, diminishing the regulatory agency of the state. Preparedness against cyberattacks may be enhanced by building the country's defence capabilities and resilience, both of civilian and military institutions.

Cybersecurity awareness among its citizens may also go a long way in detecting and tackling malicious activity taking place over India's networks. However, as long as the country relies on external digital supply chains, its government agencies or businesses will not be able to fully mitigate the risk of vulnerabilities introduced in its infrastructure. Similarly, to prosecute electronic crimes, Indian law enforcement agencies are reliant on information supplied by technology giants like Facebook, Google, or Twitter, who weigh them against privacy regulations in the United States. The absence of clear data protection standards also makes it difficult for the Indian state to regulate foreign businesses in its digital economy. For example, the terms and conditions for the use of iCloud, Apple's cloud computing service, makes it clear that the 'Agreement and the relationship between [the user] and Apple shall be governed by the laws of the State of California, excluding its conflicts of law provisions.' 'You and Apple agree to submit to the personal and exclusive jurisdiction of the courts located within the county of Santa Clara, California, to resolve any dispute or claim arising from this Agreement', states the agreement,[53] effectively precluding the role of Indian government agencies in regulating its conduct.

These limitations have often led the Indian state to propose extreme measures in the past, such as data localization and back doors to encrypted platforms.[54] To date, the licensee agreement between the central government's Department of Telecommunications and India's Internet service providers pegs the ceiling for bulk encrypted services at 40 bits[55]—an extraordinarily low encryption key length by industry standards, leading this rule to be observed only in the breach. India's landmark legislation to regulate its digital ecosystem, the Information Technology Act, was enacted in 2000. By conferring law enforcement agencies with wide powers to 'intercept, monitor or decrypt' and take down electronic communications, the Information Technology Act, through an amendment in 2008 to its Section 69, sought to enhance the regulatory capacity of the state.[56] However, this strategy has been upended by developments in secure communications technology, and also the judicial review of the law's provisions.[57] On the hardware front, India has until recently limited Chinese investment in ICT manufacturing[58], which has only resulted in greater imports.[59] Four out of the five leading smartphone manufacturers (by market share) in India are Chinese, none of whom have manufacturing hubs in the country.[60] In other words, India's domestic initiatives to police and secure its cyberspace have only been partially effective.

To regulate its digital ecosystem, therefore, India's management of its external environment becomes important. New Delhi's interactions with the United States and China on cybersecurity should be viewed in this context. As the largest suppliers of its ICT infrastructure and end-user applications, regulations in China and the United States—as well as the regional and global norms they promote—have a direct bearing on India's digital economy. Another factor driving this engagement is India's desire to be a 'leading power' in the Asia-Pacific that articulates rules of governance for the region's common spaces.[61]

As this chapter highlights, India has belatedly acknowledged the importance of diplomacy in the governance of its digital networks. Its challenge will be to balance relations with two powers that have divergent approaches to Internet governance. The aspirational or normative claims that animate India's cyber diplomacy with the United States are currently absent in its ties with China. India and the United States have found common ground in embracing the multistakeholder model of Internet governance, and committing to free and open digital spaces. The bilateral 'cyber framework agreement' is not only driven by core security interests on both sides, but also an understanding that New Delhi and Washington DC, as two big democracies, bear joint responsibility to foster free speech and expression online.

Despite the political baggage associated with the relationship, India's engagement with Beijing on ICT cooperation may be showing the green shoots of progress. Late in 2016, China signed an 'Action Plan' with India's Ministry of Electronics and Information Technology to connect its 'Internet Plus' initiative with the 'Digital India' programme. The Action Plan seeks to:

> take advantage of digitisation in all areas of [the] economy; expanding the interchange on the electronic manufacturing [sic] to jointly promote manufacturing technology; [promote] cooperation through the partnership of enterprises between the two countries in the area of high performance computing, smart cities, mobile telecommunication, DTV, tablet display, lighting display and other emerging areas.[62]

At the 2016 India-China Strategic Economic Dialogue, during which the Action Plan was signed, both sides noted that 'the complementary strengths of India and China in [the] ICT sector, specially computer hardware of China and computer software of India should be leveraged for competitive and economic advantage'.[63] These recent, high-level declarations suggest that ICT cooperation between both countries is mostly visualized through the co-creation of digital technologies. Baseline rules around supply chain integrity and Chinese investment in India must be clearly articulated before this goal can be realized. That said, it is likely that the domestic demand for creating affordable digital infrastructure, especially for Internet of Things (IoT) ecosystems, will spur both countries to enter into norm-setting agreements. Indian regulators will be mindful of the need to mitigate vulnerabilities in the IoT supply chain, for which cybersecurity cooperation with China will be critical.

India's engagement with the United States and China is born of a desire to secure its digital ecosystem, but this outreach is likely to have far-reaching consequences. Its continued high-level cooperation with the United States may draw India into political discussions on Internet freedom globally, which it has thus far eschewed. Security needs may even nudge India to sign multilateral instruments like the Budapest Convention on Cybercrime, placing it in the camp of Western powers like the United States and the European Union.

The opportunity to export jointly manufactured products to emerging markets in the Asia-Pacific, on the other hand, may prompt India and China to develop common technical protocols and standards. Prominent Indian businesses have already called for regulators to adopt investment measures because China has to protect its domestic e-commerce players, and calls to emulate the 'Chinese model' are likely to resonate with Indian start-ups.[64] And, finally, technical cooperation may create political 'spillovers', leading India to engage with Chinese initiatives along the Silk Road Economic Belt, or crafting a joint vision for ICT financing through the AIIB.

In any case, it is clear that India's decision to look East or look West will have strategic, perhaps permanent, consequences for the management of digital spaces in Asia. For emerging markets, which rely on imported ICT technology with little agency over their data, India presents a test candidate in the struggle between two competing approaches to securing digital networks.

NOTES

1. *Business Standard.* 2014. '65 Per Cent of Electronic Items' Demand Met by Imports: Report': http://www.business-standard.com/article/economy-policy/65-per-cent-of-electronic-items-demand-met-by-imports-report-114011300761_1.html
2. See ENISA. 'Supply Chain Integrity: An Overview of the ICT Supply Chain Risks and Challenges, and Vision for the Way Forward (2015)': https://www.enisa.europa.eu/publications/sci-2015. See Sharma, R.K. 2016. 'India must attain e-SWARAJ', ORF Issue Brief.
3. See generally, Future of Privacy Forum and the Center for Democracy & Technology, 'Best Practices for Mobile Application Developers': https://fpf.org/wp-content/uploads/Best-Practices-for-Mobile-App-Developers_Final.pdf; National Institute of Standards and Technology, US Department of Commerce, 'Vetting the Security of Mobile Applications': http://nvlpubs.nist.gov/nistpubs/SpecialPublications/NIST.SP.800-163.pdf
4. See generally, The Information Technology Industry Council, 'Data Localization Snapshot': https://www.itic.org/public-policy/SnapshotofDataLocalizationMeasures7-8-2016.pdf; Department of Science & Technology, Ministry of Science & Technology Government of India. 2012. 'National Data Sharing and Accessibility Policy': https://dst.gov.in/national-data-sharing-and-accessibility-policy-0
5. Vinit Goenka's blog, 'IT Sovereignty in India—The Data Centre Dimension': https://vinitgoenka.wordpress.com/2014/04/11/it-sovereignty-in-india-the-data-centre-dimension/; Internet and Mobile Association of India (IAMAI). 2016. 'Make in India—Conducive Policy and Regulatory Environment to Incentivize Data Center Infrastructure': https://www.medianama.com/wp-content/uploads/iamai-make-in-india-data-center-report-india.pdf
6. *The Hindu*, 'Locked Out—NIA Seeks U.S. Help to Crack Militant's iPhone': http://www.thehindu.com/news/national/locked-out-nia-seeks-us-help-to-crack-militants-iphone/article18516253.ece
7. Adobe Digital Dialogue, 'Asia Pacific Tops the World in Growth of Smartphone Traffic to the Internet': https://blogs.adobe.com/digitaldialogue/digital-marketing/asia-pacific-tops-world-growth-smartphone-traffic-internet/
8. Quartz, 'The US is Home to One Third of the World's Data—Here's Who's Storing it': https://qz.com/104868/the-us-is-home-to-one-third-of-the-worlds-data-heres-whos-storing-it/; BBC, 'Where in the World is My Data and How Secure is it?': http://www.bbc.com/news/business-36854292
9. *WIRED*, 'Apple Tightens Grip on Worldwide Supply Chain with Asia Hiring Spree': https://www.wired.com/2014/03/apple-tightens-grip/; Gartner, 'Gartner Announces Rankings of the 2016 Supply Chain Top 25': http://www.gartner.com/newsroom/id/3323617
10. *The Washington Post*, 'Google Must Turn Over Foreign-Stored Emails Pursuant to a Warrant, Court Rules': https://www.washingtonpost.com/news/volokh-conspiracy/wp/2017/02/03/google-must-turn-over-foreign-stored-e-mails-pursuant-to-a-warrant-court-rules/?utm_term=.c30399b8d88e
11. http://www.root-servers.org
12. http://www.forbes.com/sites/singularity/2012/10/15/how-indians-defied-gravity-and-achieved-success-in-silicon-valley/#1523a6926d1e

13. Malviya, Sagar. 2016. 'Facebook India Revenues Jump 43 Per Cent', *The Economic Times*: http://economictimes.indiatimes.com/tech/internet/facebook-india-revenues-jump-43-per-cent/articleshow/55675221.cms

14. YourStory, 'Facebook Paid $5M to Bug Bounty Hunters in 5 Years; India Leads in Payouts in 2016': https://yourstory.com/2016/10/facebook-bug-bounty-payout-india/

15. Rediff.com, 'McAfee's India R&D to Play Vital Role in Intel's Future': http://business.rediff.com/report/2010/aug/20/tech-mcafee-india-to-play-vital-role-in-intel-future.htm; Popkin, J., Iyengar, P., and Gartner Inc. 2007. *IT and the East*. Boston, Mass.: Harvard Business School Press, p. 106.

16. Embassy of India, Washington DC, USA, 'First Meeting of India-U.S Information and Communications Technologies Working Group, 7–8 December, 2005': https://www.indianembassy.org/archives_details.php?nid=481; Ministry of Electronics & Information Technology, Government of India, USA: http://meity.gov.in/content/usa

17. Observer Research Foundation, 'Revival of India-US ICT Working Group: Significance for India': http://www.orfonline.org/research/revival-of-india-us-ict-working-group-significance-for-india/

18. National Telecommunications & Information Administration, United States Department of Commerce, 'NTIA Announces Intent to Transition Key Internet Domain Name Functions': https://www.ntia.doc.gov/press-release/2014/ntia-announces-intent-transition-key-internet-domain-name-functions

19. International Telecommunication Union, India (Republic Of) Proposals for the Work of the Conference- Draft New Resolution on ITU's Role in Realizing Secure Information Society': http://cis-india.org/internet-governance/blog/india-draft-resolution-itus-role-in-securing-information-security/at_download/file

20. The Indian Express, 'Trapped in the web': http://indianexpress.com/article/opinion/columns/trapped-in-the-web/

21. The Internet Corporation for Assigned Names and Numbers,' Indian Minister of Communications & Information Technology Ravi Shankar Prasad': https://www.icann.org/news/multimedia/1453

22. See Sukumar, A., and R.K. Sharma. 2016. 'The Cyber Command: Upgrading India's National Security Architecture', Observer Research Foundation Special Report.

23. The Wire, 'The "I" in the Internet Must Also Stand for India': https://thewire.in/4688/the-i-in-the-internet-must-also-stand-for-india/

24. US Department of Commerce, 'Joint Statement on the First U.S.-India Strategic and Commercial Dialogue': https://www.commerce.gov/news/press-releases/2015/09/joint-statement-first-us-india-strategic-and-commercial-dialogue

25. US Department of Commerce, 'Joint Statement on the First U.S.-India Strategic and Commercial Dialogue': https://www.commerce.gov/news/press-releases/2015/09/joint-statement-first-us-india-strategic-and-commercial-dialogue

26. Observer Research Foundation, 'First US-India Track 1.5 Cyber Dialogue Held in Washington DC': http://www.orfonline.org/expert-speaks/first-us-india-track-1-5-cyber-dialogue-held-in-washington-dc/

27. The Hill, 'US, India pledge cyber cooperation as security threats rise': http://thehill.com/policy/cybersecurity/251150-us-india-pledge-cyber-cooperation-amid-rising-threats

28. International Telecommunication Union, India (Republic Of) Proposals for the Work of the Conference- Draft New Resolution on ITU's Role in Realizing Secure Information Society':http://cis-india.org/internet-governance/blog/india-draft-resolution-itus-role-in-securing-information-security/at_download/file

29. US Department of State, 'U.S.-India Strategic and Commercial Dialogue': https://www.state.gov/p/sca/ci/in/strategicdialgue/

30. US-India Business Council, 'U.S.-India Business Council Applauds Resumption of Cybersecurity Dialogue': http://www.usibc.com/press-release/us-india-business-council-applauds-resumption-cybersecurity-dialogue

31. *The Economic Times*. 2015. 'Huawei Revamps Offline Mobile Business to Clock 10% India Market Share': http://economictimes.indiatimes.com/tech/hardware/huawei-revamps-offline-mobile-business-to-clock-10-india-market-share/articleshow/48413415.cms

32. *The Indian Express*. 2016. 'Xiaomi is Number Three in India's Top 30 Cities: IDC': http://indianexpress.com/article/technology/mobile-tabs/xiaomi-idc-report-redmi-note-3-review-price-sales-3016596/

33. Gadgets Now, 'Apple's iPhone marketshare falls by 35% in India: Report': http://www.gadgetsnow.com/tech-news/Apples-smartphone-marketshare-falls-by-35-in-India-Report/articleshow/53569868.cms

34. Livemint, 'China's Huawei Gets Security Clearance to Manufacture in India': http://www.livemint.com/Companies/hjolfVmmxM24A8yFjKsaZM/Chinas-Huawei-gets-security-clearance-to-manufacture-in-Ind.html

35. Department of Telecommunications, Ministry of Communications and IT, 'Amendment to UASL': http://www.dot.gov.in/sites/default/files/AS%207-9-12_0.pdf

36. Marngain, Pramugdha. 2010. 'Huawei Takes Steps To Address Security Concerns', *The Economic Times*, 5 July: http://economictimes.indiatimes.com/industry/telecom/huawei-takes-steps-to-address-security-concerns/articleshow/6129013.cms

37. See Diogo, P., Reis L., and Lopes, N. 2016. 'Fragmentation is the Enemy of the Internet of Things', 19 February, Qualcomm: https://www.qualcomm.com/news/onq/2016/02/19/fragmentation-enemy-internet-things

38. SSL, 'What is SSL?': http://info.ssl.com/article.aspx?id=10241. See Ismaili, H., Houmani, H., and Madroumi, H. 2014. 'A Secure Electronic Transaction Payment Protocol Design and Implementation', *IACSIT International Journal of Engineering and Technology* 5 (5):172–80.

39. Gary Kessler, 2017. 'Internet Payment Systems: Status and Update on SSL/TLS, SET, and IOTP', 20 February: http://www.garykessler.net/library/is_payment_systems.html,accessed.

40. See Kawatra, N. and Kumar. V. 2011. 'Analysis of E-Commerce Security Protocols SSL and SET', *National Workshop-Cum-Conference on Recent Trends in Mathematics and Computing*: https://research.ijcaonline.org/rtmc/number12/rtmc1111.pdf

41. See Jarupunphol, P., and Buathong, W. 2013. 'Secure Electronic Transactions (SET): A Case of Secure System Project Failures', *IACSIT International Journal of Engineering and Technology* 5 (2): 278–82.

42. See Jarupunphol, P., and Buathong, W. 2013. 'Secure Electronic Transactions (SET): A Case of Secure System Project Failures', *IACSIT International Journal of Engineering and Technology* 5 (2): 278–82.

43. *The Times of India*. 2016.'None of Mobile Payment Apps in India Fully Secure, Warns Qualcomm': http://timesofindia.indiatimes.com/business/india-business/None-of-mobile-payment-apps-in-India-fully-secure-warns-Qualcomm/articleshow/55967778.cms; Kaspersky blog, '87% of Android Smartphones are Insecure and That's No Joke': https://blog.kaspersky.com/insecure-android-devices/10296/

44. Aulakh, Gulveen. 2015. 'Alibaba, Ant Financial Invest about $680 Million in Paytm, up stake to 40%', *The Economic Times*: http://economictimes.indiatimes.com/industry/banking/finance/banking/alibaba-ant-financial-invest-about-680-million-in-paytm-up-stake-to-40/

articleshow/49148651.cms; Livemint, 'Alibaba to Lead $200 Million Investment into Paytm's Online Marketplace': http://www.livemint.com/Companies/LkpKu4425fHKDXOG7yIKlN/Paytm-Ecommerce-in-talks-to-raise-up-to-200-million-from-A.html

45. Asian Infrastructure Investment Bank. 2017. 'India: Andhra Pradesh 24x7—Power for All Project': https://www.aiib.org/en/projects/approved/2017/_download/India/document/andhra_pradesh_co-financed_world_bank.pdf; Asian Infrastructure Investment Bank. 2016. 'Indonesia: National Slum Upgrading Project': https://www.aiib.org/en/projects/approved/2016/_download/indonesia/document/approved_project_document_national_slum_upgrading.pdf

46. ChinaDaily. 2015. 'Web Companies Asked to Support "digital Silk Road"': http://usa.chinadaily.com.cn/business/2015-07/18/content_21318972.htm

47. Peterson Institute for International Economics. 2016. 'China's Belt and Road Initiative—Motives, Scope, and Challenges': https://piie.com/system/files/documents/piieb16-2_1.pdf

48. Livemint, 'China may Invite India to "One Belt One Road" Meet, but Delhi Wary': http://www.livemint.com/Politics/iwSTA1EPSjrcnxbaoHghTO/China-may-invite-India-to-one-belt-one-road-meet-but-Delh.html

49. *The Wire*, 'Modi Criticises China's One Belt One Road Plan, Says Connectivity Can't Undermine Sovereignty': https://thewire.in/100803/modi-criticises-chinas-one-belt-one-road-plan-says-connectivity-corridors-cant-undermine-sovereignty/

50. *The Hindu*, 'India Skips BRF's Summit Ceremony': http://www.thehindu.com/news/national/india-skips-chinas-brf-summit-ceremony/article18450997.ece

51. TechCircle, 'Snapdeal investor Vani Kola joins Flipkart, Ola in "capital dumping" debate': http://techcircle.vccircle.com/2017/01/30/snapdeal-investor-vani-kola-joins-flipkart-ola-in-capital-dumping-debate/,

52. Livemint, 'Interest Groups Battle over E-Commerce': http://www.livemint.com/Opinion/tFc8uS22nsHRVQKn48YshL/Interest-groups-battle-over-ecommerce.html

53. Apple, 'iCloud Terms and Conditions': https://www.apple.com/legal/internet-services/icloud/en/terms.html

54. *The Hindu*, 'Government to Withdraw Draft Encryption Policy': http://www.thehindu.com/news/national/govt-to-withdraw-draft-encryption-policy/article7677348.ece

55. Ministry of Communications and IT, Government of India, 'License Agreement for Unified License': http://dot.gov.in/sites/default/files/Unified%20Licence_0.pdf

56. Ministry of Law and Justice, Government of India, 'Information Technology (Amendment) Act, 2008': http://meity.gov.in/writereaddata/files/itact2000/it_amendment_act2008.pdf

57. *The Hindu*, 'SC Strikes Down "Draconian" Section 66A': http://www.thehindu.com/news/national/SC-strikes-down-'draconian'-Section-66A/article10740659.ece

58. *Hindustan Times*, 'MHA Gives Security Clearance to Chinese Telecom Major Huawei': http://www.hindustantimes.com/business/mha-gives-security-clearance-to-chinese-telecom-major-huawei/story-GSrw4IonKXJKfkRGohozMN.html

59. *Business Standard*. 2014. 'Over 90% of Telecom Gear in India's Rs 50,000-cr Market is Imported': http://www.business-standard.com/article/companies/over-90-of-telecom-gear-in-india-s-rs-50-000-cr-market-is-imported-114042900254_1.html

60. Livemint, 'Chinese Smartphones Rout Indian Brands on Their Own Turf': http://www.livemint.com/Consumer/tfwRGY9Za1UYNjdHIkS82K/Chinese-smartphones-rout-Indian-brands-on-their-own-turf.html

61. Ministry of External Affairs, Government of India, 'IISS Fullerton Lecture by Dr. S. Jaishankar, Foreign Secretary in Singapore': http://mea.gov.in/Speeches-Statements.htm?dtl/25493/IISS_Fullerton_Lecture_by_Foreign_Secretary_in_Singapore
62. Ministry of External Affairs, Government of India, 'Agreed Minutes of 4th India-China Strategic Economic Dialogue': http://www.mea.gov.in/bilateral-documents.htm?dtl/27478/Agreed+Minutes+of+the+4th+IndiaChina+Strategic+Economic+Dialogue
63. Ministry of External Affairs, Government of India, 'Agreed Minutes of 4th India-China Strategic Economic Dialogue': http://www.mea.gov.in/bilateral-documents.htm?dtl/27478/Agreed+Minutes+of+the+4th+IndiaChina+Strategic+Economic+Dialogue
64. Quartz India. 2016. 'India's Startup Billionaires are Desperate to Make The Country Like Protectionist China': https://qz.com/858002/flipkarts-sachin-bansal-and-olas-bhavish-aggarwal-want-india-to-become-like-protectionist-china/

BIBLIOGRAPHY

ANTARA News. 2016. 'Indonesia Plans to Cooperate with India in Forming Digital Economy': http://www.antaranews.com/en/news/108360/indonesia-plans-to-cooperate-with-india-in-forming-digital-economy

Dai, X. 2002. 'Towards a Digital Economy with Chinese Characteristics?', *New Media & Society* 4 (2): 141–62.

Dai, X. 2002. 'Is China Making Life Difficult for Foreign Companies?', *South China Morning Post*: http://www.scmp.com/news/china/diplomacy-defence/article/1940397/china-making-life-difficult-foreign-companies

Dave, Paresh. 2015. 'Indian Immigrants are Tech's New Titans', *Los Angeles Times*, 11 August: http://www.latimes.com/business/la-fi-indians-in-tech-20150812-story.html

Diogo, P., Reis, L. and Lopes, N. 2014. 'Internet of Things: A System's Architecture Proposal', IEEE.

Mayer Brown JSM. 2016. 'China Passes Cybersecurity Law', 10 November, Mayer Brown JSM: https://www.mayerbrown.com/files/Publication/3c8214cb-f3a4-42c8-bc17-bb2f27da9af3/Presentation/PublicationAttachment/c1a4fdf2-9d57-40bb-8a83-c5b5f8902c82/161110-HKGPRC-CybersecurityDataPrivacy-TMT.pdf

The White House. 2015a. 'Joint Statement: 2015 United States—India Cyber Dialogue', 14 August: https://obamawhitehouse.archives.gov/the-press-office/2015/08/14/joint-statement-2015-united-states-india-cyber-dialogue

The White House. 2015b. 'FACT SHEET: President Xi Jinping's State Visit to the United States', 25 September: https://obamawhitehouse.archives.gov/the-press-office/2015/09/25/fact-sheet-president-xi-jinpings-state-visit-united-states

FURTHER READING

Anderson, Sydney. 2015. 'India's Gender Digital Divide: Women and Politics on Twitter', Observer Research Foundation: http://www.orfonline.org/wpcontent/uploads/2015/12/ORFIssueBrief_108.pdf

Bhairav, Acharya. 2015. 'Biometrics, Privacy, and Governance in India: the Unique Identity ('Aadhaar') Case' https://bhairavacharya.net/2015/12/03/biometrics-privacy-aadhaar/

Hathaway, Melissa. 2016. 'India: Cyber Readiness at a Glance', Potomac Institute for Policy Studies: https://www.potomacinstitute.org/images/CRI/CRI_India_Profile.pdf

Kathuria, Rajat, Mansi Kedia, Vatsala Shreeti et al. 2016. 'Quantifying the Value of an Open Internet for India', ICRIER: http://icrier.org/pdf/open_Internet.pdf

Mohanty, Bedavyasa. 2016. '"Going Dark"' in India: The Legal and Security Dimensions of Encryption', Observer Research Foundation: http://www.orfonline.org/research/going-dark-in-india-the-legal-and-security-dimensions-of-encryption/

Pal, Abhipsa, Sai Dattathrani, and Rahul Dé. 2017. 'Security in Mobile Payments: A Report on User Issues', Indian Institute of Management, Bangalore: http://www.iimb.ac.in/sites/default/files/iimb-csitm-security-issues-in-mobile-payment.pdf

Parsheera S., Ajay Shah, and Avifrup Bose. 2017. 'Competition Issues in India's Online Economy', NIPFP: www.nipfp.org.in/media/medialibrary/2017/04/WP_2017_194.pdf

Ranganathan, Nayantara. 2016. 'Watchtower: An Interactive Map of Cybersecurity Institutions in the Government of India', an Internet democracy project: https://internetdemocracy.in/2016/03/an-interactive-map-of-cybersecurity-institutions-in-the-government-of-india/

Saran, Samir. 2014. 'The ITU and Unbundling Internet Governance', Council on Foreign Relations: https://www.cfr.org/report/itu-and-unbundling-internet-governance

Sukumar, A.M., and Sharma R.K. 2016. 'The Cyber Command: Upgrading India's National Security Architecture', Observer Research Foundation: http://www.orfonline.org/wp-content/uploads/2016/03/SR_9_Arun-Mohan-Sukumar-and-RK-sharma.pdf

Thapar, Shuchita. 2016. 'Mapping the Cyber Policy Landscape: India', Global Partners Digital: https://www.gp-digital.org/wp-content/uploads/2017/05/India_mapping-report_final_2-1.pdf

Ranganathan, Nayantara. 2016. 'Watchtower: An Interactive Map of Cybersecurity Institutions in the Government of India', an Internet democracy project: https://internetdemocracy.in/2016/03/an-interactive-map-of-cybersecurity-institutions-in-the-government-of-india/

CHAPTER 38

CYBERSECURITY IN ISRAEL: STRATEGY, ORGANIZATION, AND FUTURE CHALLENGES

LIOR TABANSKY

CYBERSECURITY AND ISRAEL'S GRAND STRATEGY

THE essence of strategy remains designing an effective relationship between ends, ways, and means. 'Ends' are political objectives defined by the state's leadership. 'Ways' are the selected form of action. 'Means' refers to the resources at the state's disposal: people, gold, land, oil, trade, weapons, etc. Sir Lawrence Freedman writes: 'Strategy is about getting more out of a situation than the starting balance of power would suggest. It is the art of creating power' (Freedman 2013).

This chapter focuses on the highest level, known as the 'grand strategy' (Martel 2015). Although Israeli governments have so far avoided publishing formal national strategy documents,[1] Edward Luttwak correctly insists that 'All states have a grand strategy, whether they know it or not' (2009). Israel's political end remains in force: to develop a sovereign, secure, and prosperous Jewish nation state. Israel's grand strategy was developed in the decades before Israel's independence in 1948 and manifested throughout Israel's political thought, statecraft, and numerous wars and counterterrorism operations as well as in domestic social and economic policies (Tabansky and Israel 2015).

The focus here is on the two central, constant, strategic tenets: first, Israel can only rely on itself for national security and defence. Second, to counterbalance its overwhelming numerical inferiority in the region, Israel requires qualitative superiority (Breznitz 2007; Paikowsky and Israel 2009; Eilam 2011). Technical and tactical solutions can create the desired intelligence and battlefield superiority, giving a 'qualitative edge' to Israel. Yet, each advantage is bound to be short-lived. In its quest for qualitative edge, Israel has come to repeated outsized investments in numerous human, educational, scientific, and

Information, Technology, and Smart Power

Power, the currency of international relations, undergoes technology-driven change. The Tofflers elegantly presented how 'the Third Wave's' economy and war move away from industrial mass production to be based on production and control of information and knowledge (Toffler 1980; Toffler and Toffler 1993). Information is crucial for the modern world and information is qualitatively different from material resources (Ben-Israel and Tabansky 2011). Paul Romer, the recent co-recipient of the Nobel Prize in Economic Sciences, demonstrated that the development of knowledge is a new, potent source of endogenous growth and increasing productivity. Technology as input differs from what is familiar in the traditional economy: information is neither a conventional good nor a public good. Information is a non-rival, partially excludable good. Some of the implications bode well for Israel's quest for qualitative edge

> 'The main conclusions are that the stock of human capital determines the rate of growth, that too little human capital is devoted to research in equilibrium, that integration into world markets will increase growth rates, and that having a large population is not sufficient to generate growth' (Romer 1990).

Data, information, and knowledge increasingly drive economic growth, social progress, competitive advantage, and power. Cybersecurity thus enables and directly contributes to cyber power: '... the ability to use cyberspace to create advantages and influence events in other operational environments and across the instruments of power' (Kuehl 2009). Cyber power must be a smart power, combining hard- and soft-power resources into effective strategies.

Israel's main hard- and soft-power resources are now described in turn.

Hard Power: Non-Intelligence Cyber Operations

In the May 2019 round of fighting with the Hamas terrorist organization in the Gaza Strip, the Israel Defence Forces (IDF) responded to a cyberattack with an immediate kinetic air strike. According to the IDF spokesperson:

> After dealing with a Hamas cyber-attack in the cyber dimension, the IAF dealt with it in the physical dimension.

However, two offensive operations which happened over a decade ago are more remarkable and suggest that Israel has long developed and unleashed cyber innovative offense to attain its topmost strategic goal: prevent adversaries from gaining a nuclear weapon (Tabansky 2016).

Operation 'Olympic Games'

Operation Olympic Games, commonly attributed to the United States and Israel, demonstrated the real-world strike on high-value, heavily defended targets with bits alone (Sanger 2012). Stuxnet malware damaged the nuclear enrichment process at the Natanz facility in Iran by reprogramming the embedded Programmable Logic Controller (PLC) to spin the centrifuges' motors out of the safe range and eventually self-destruct (Langner 2011; Zetter 2014). Probably implanted in late 2007, the malware's infection modules were written specifically to stealthily infiltrate air-gapped[2] networks. The unique payload was tailored to physically destroy equipment while faking normal activity to the operator's monitor.[3] It was a precision-guided cyber weapon: additional modules identified the network configuration and devices of the Industrial Control System (ICS) and only triggered payload to execute if the target met every predetermined condition (Rid 2013). The covert sabotage rendered useless at least 1,000 of the 9,000 IR-1 centrifuges deployed at Natanz in late 2009 and early 2010 (Albright, Brannan, and Walrond 2010). The prolonged, unexplained failures likely eroded Iranian confidence and triggered costly reorganization throughout Iran's nuclear program. The cyberattack substituted the air raids that would have been necessary to deliver kinetic, physically destructive, ordnance with a stealthy, deniable, and effective alternative (Raas and Long 2007).

Operation 'Orchard'/'Outside the Box'

On 6 September 2007, eight Israeli Air Force (IAF) aircraft bombed and destroyed a building complex in Al-Kibar, near the city of Deir ez-Zor in eastern Syria. The building hid the construction of a graphite-cooled nuclear reactor: a nearly exact copy of the plutonium reactor in North Korea (Abrams 2013). The air strike on the Syrian nuclear reactor echoed the daring 1981 IAF raid, which destroyed the Osirak nuclear reactor in Iraq. Foreign sources assume that Israel infiltrated and temporary neutralized the air defence radars and communication systems in a cyberattack (Fulghum, Wall, and Butler 2007).

It could be that cyberattacks continue to help supressing the dense Syrian air defence. As Iranian encroachment in Syria has built up, the IAF has almost routinely bombed Iranian targets in Syria since 2017. In May 2018 alone, the IAF struck 50 airfields, weapons depots, intelligence sites, and other Iranian targets within Syria. The strikes against Iranian assets in Syria and weapon transfers to Lebanese Hezbollah continue despite the Russian military presence.

The Armed Forces and Military Cyber Power

Armed forces exist to defend the nation from foreign harm and cyberattacks have long become an instrument of power in international conflict:

> The Stuxnet method and its success thus changed the notion of vulnerability across increasingly internetted societies and critical infrastructures. The days of cyber spying through

software backdoors or betrayals by trusted insiders, vandalism, or even theft had suddenly evolved into the demonstrated ability to deliver a potentially killing blow without being anywhere near the target (Demchak and Dombrowski 2011, 33).

However, Israel's defence sector caters for its own cybersecurity and has no direct domestic cybersecurity mission. No public information on cyber capabilities of the *Mossad* or the *Shabak* is available. The IDF openly declared cyberspace an operational and strategic war-fighting domain in 2009. The areas of responsibility within the IDF were delineated in 2012, reflecting its organizational legacy. The Military Intelligence Directorate (*Agaf HaModi'in [Aman]*) was tasked with computer network attacks (CNAs) and exploitation (CNE), and the C4I Directorate (established in 2003 in place of the Signal Corps) was tasked with IDF's computer network defence (CND). *Aman* is an independent service: not part of the ground, navy or air force. Its Unit 8200 performs signal intelligence (SIGINT) and code decryption: similar to the American National Security Agency (NSA) or Britain's Government Communications Headquarters (GCHQ) missions. Israel's strategy puts a premium on early warning and qualitative edge: thus, Israel's intelligence has long investment in cyber technologies. As in the United States, Russia, or the United Kingdom, intelligence organizations pioneered cyber technology and operations, have amassed operational experience, and often possess superior capabilities. Foreign sources routinely assert that Unit 8200 contributed to Stuxnet, Flame, Duqu, and other sophisticated cyber campaigns.

In May 2017, the IDF renamed the C4I Directorate 'the C4I and Cyber Defense Directorate' (*Agaf Ha-Tikshuv VeHaHagana BiSvivat Reshet*). It aims to advance the networked IDF vision to enhance jointness, effectiveness, and efficiency. Moreover, a streamlined architecture enables foundational cybersecurity advances. The IDF Cyber Defense Division, headed by a Brigadier-General, is responsible for cybersecurity of the IDF's networks. The C4I and Cyber Defence Directorate will remain a central player in Israel's cybersecurity because it contains core resources and capabilities, including:

- developing system architecture and software for the IDF;
- creating cryptographic foundations for the IDF and Israel at large;
- training recruits to become professionals in Centre of Computing and Information Systems *(Mamram)* and the School for Computer Related Professions (*Basmakh*). (Breznitz 2002)

The IAF possesses significant resources, unique capabilities, advanced organization, and a service culture that is based on central command and control and communications (Amidror 2018). Air forces view combat as the application of advanced high technology in waging war and the airplane embodies the supremacy of advanced technology. Practically everything in the IAF depends on advanced information and communication technologies (ICTs). The need to develop and secure ICTs has therefore long been a requirement in force design and operation, contributing to the independent and separate cyber capabilities of the IAF. Modern systems, such as the *Eitan* Medium Altitude Long Endurance Unmanned Aerial Vehicle (MALE UAV) and the multi-tiered missile defence system that includes the Counter rocket, artillery, and mortar (C-RAM) *Iron Dome*, are only as good as their custom hardware, software, and networking. Consequently, the IAF has developed and controls its own functions, including software and hardware development and electronic warfare.

Facing the challenge of streamlining diverse branches and capabilities, the then IDF Chief of General Staff Lt. Gen. Gadi Eisenkot directed in June 2015 that a new joint cyber command should be established by the end of 2017 (Siboni and Elran 2015). The same Chief of General Staff reversed, or rather postponed in official parlance, this decision in early 2017.[4] Either way, the IDF capabilities serve only militarily purposes.

SOFT POWER: ISRAEL'S INNOVATION SYSTEM AT A GLANCE

Despite geopolitical challenges and the defence burden, Israel has matured into a rich and developed democracy: life expectancy is among the world's highest; gross domestic product (GDP) per capita is on par with Western Europe, after doubling in 25 years; public debt, external debt, and unemployment are low and the Shekel is stable.[5]

Israel's innovation system performance has driven this growth. As hi-tech business flourishes in Tel Aviv, Jerusalem, Haifa, and Be'er Sheva, it is easy to ignore the fact that Israeli efforts to spur innovation creation and absorption go before the nation's independence. Israel's innovation system stems from the long-standing foundations of Israel's national security strategy: defence self-reliance and the qualitative edge.

Digital transformation in general, and cybersecurity in particular, depend on innovation. All three are too often conflated with creating new technology. Defence adaptation as well as business administration studies demonstrate the crucial role of non-technological, organizational innovation. Innovation creation, diffusion, and adoption capacity also depend on cultural, social, and political aspects (Adamsky 2010; Grissom 2006; Roberts 2017; Watts and Murray 1996). This broader, non-technological innovation capacity is less tangible but crucial for the public sector in Israel to establish cybersecurity organizations and reshuffle policies, as well as for research and development (R&D)-intensive business.

Among the main characteristics of Israel's innovation system are:

- exceptionally high and growing R&D expenditure (at 4.9% in 2019, it was double the Organisation for Economic Co-operation and Development average), sustained for decades;
- Sustained high defense expenditure (at 5.5% of GDP in 2018) including defense R&D.
- public research universities nurturing high-quality human capital;
- robust collaboration between academia, industry, and government;
- well-developed venture capital industry;[6] and
- foreign funding dominates Business expenditure on R&D (BERD.)

GLOBAL MARKETS, AMERICAN INVESTORS

Public expenditure on R&D now accounts for only about 20%, but the Israeli government has not cut the budgets. Business expenditure on R&D (BERD) performed in Israel has grown dramatically, mostly through foreign investments by multinational corporations (MNCs) and venture capital (VC). Several hundred VC-backed start-ups attempt to innovate cybersecurity every given year. These are a fraction of roughly 6,000 Israeli start-ups.

Some MNCs span more than four decades: Intel, Applied Materials, Motorola, and IBM. the number of foreign MNCs with active R&D centres in Israel reached 360 in 2019; machine vision, artificial intelligence (AI), and cybersecurity are the main R&D clusters. Most MNCs have acquired Israeli companies for their technology and talent, transforming them through mergers and acquisitions into their own local research facilities. Foreign corporate investments (excluding exits) totalled $983 million in 196 deals in 2019.

Israeli-made innovation is firmly embedded in the global digital economy: Intel, Apple, IBM, Broadcom, and Qualcomm design chips in Israel. Google and Microsoft were the most active corporate buyers of Israeli companies in 2014–2019, acquiring ten and eight companies respectively.

Israel's 2014 non-defence cybersecurity exports were three times higher than the target the UK set for 2016 (Economist 2015). Israel attracts about 20% of the global private cybersecurity investment.[7] As early as in 2011, Prime Minister Netanyahu had made cybersecurity a top priority. These conditions support the innovation system and contribute to soft cyber power. However, increased China–United States tensions might reduce Israeli access to markets and capital.

HUMAN CAPITAL: SPILL-OVER EFFECTS OF MILITARY SERVICE

Israel maintains mandatory conscription of 18 year olds. Driven by the pursuit of qualitative advantage, The IDF has long developed an intricate system to assess the conscripts' potential and assigns a fitting training and career path to most. It has significantly contributed to the very share of scientists and engineers in Israel (Baram and Ben-Israel 2019). Those have receive valuable training must sign up to serve after the mandatory service, and are more likely to do reserve service. Through its numerous technological units, the IDF has long become the main stimulus for the diffusion of computer professions and technologies throughout the economy.[8] In addition to many self-developed in-house information technology (IT) courses, in 2012, the C4I Directorate introduced the Cyber Defender course, training soldiers in cyberdefense.

Israeli hi-tech workers possess very high military capital, constituting skills (human capital), social networks (social capital), and social norms and codes of behaviour (cultural capital). For instance, while not part of the official IDF code, IDF cultivates improvisation as a problem-solving skill in a resource-poor and uncertain environment (Swed and Butler

2015). For cyber development jobs, military service in the IDF technological units is a job market advantage that often equals a university degree.[9] The job market also demonstrates an institutional preference for those with military capital in general.

DEFENCE RESEARCH AND DEVELOPMENT AND INDUSTRIAL BASE

Driven by the qualitative edge principle, Israel's large and classified defence R&D carries out extensive thematic research. Israel's defence community has long perceived ICTs as an important broad force multiplier. The defence industrial base has developed original cybersecurity capabilities, often rivalling the best of commercial offerings. These are naturally funded publicly: the defence R&D expenditure was ILS 7.6 billion in 2017. The Ministry of Defence (MoD) R&D Directorate (*Maf'at*) coordinates between the IDF, Israel's defence industries (Rubin 2017), the Israel Space Agency, and the Institute for Biological Research. In addition to classified R&D, a dual-use, civilian, and defence cyber R&D plan called *MASAD* was launched in October 2012.

THREE PRINCIPLES SHAPING CYBERSECURITY IN ISRAEL

A state exists primarily to provide security and safety to its citizens: the excuse that 'it's the Internet!' no longer flies. Although cyber threats hardly rank as a top security concern, Israelis unmistakably expect the state to provide security. The first guiding principle is that the state must provide cybersecurity and increasingly improve it.[10]

Technically speaking, cybersecurity is feasible. One should deploy sensors throughout the endpoints and networks, process and fuse the collected Big Data to produce timely intelligence, and act upon it. Many of the capabilities are readily available and increasingly automated. However, moral and political dilemmas arise: Who can be trusted with sensitive information and metadata? Who should bear the additional costs? What policy instruments may be used to mitigate market failures? In June 2013, Edward Snowden began leaking classified documents he unlawfully obtained from the US NSA revealing numerous global surveillance programs often with the cooperation of telecommunication companies and Western intelligence services. These counterterrorism operations blatantly degraded citizens' rights to privacy and due process, and routinely undermined the security of the Internet. The ensuing scandal lingers on in cybersecurity debates. Israelis resist any resemblance of surveillance, enact laws that limit the authorities, and cherish the fundamental freedoms no less than other open societies. The second guiding cybersecurity principle is not only to preserve citizens' rights but also to prevent any appearance of security measures potentially infringing on basic liberties. Balancing fundamental freedoms and cybersecurity on a national scale is a delicate political art.

The deregulatory neoliberal economic policies Israel's leaders pursue to facilitate growth are the third constraint. Typical government policy instruments are top-down regulation and legislation. Yet, national cybersecurity measures that increase regulatory burdens will be turned down in Israel. The growing dominance of foreign-owned MNCs in the innovation system created a unique environment with dependencies as well as advantages.

The means and ways of Israel's national cybersecurity described later must deliver comprehensive cybersecurity while protecting basic liberties, refraining from hampering the markets and continuing to attract foreign investments.

THE 2011 NATIONAL CYBER STRATEGY OF ISRAEL AND ITS ROOTS

Israel's cybersecurity strategy acknowledges an unconformable truth: the pace of change in digital technology makes future threats unpredictable. Together with the lack of enforceable borders, this renders traditional defence obsolete. To secure the nation and gain advantage, Israel opts to develop and nurture a national innovation ecosystem that will repeatedly devise innovations and shape cybersecurity.

The Government Resolution 3611 'Advancing the national capacity in cyberspace' laid out the current national cyber strategy of Israel. The goals are:

- To work towards advancing national capabilities in cyberspace and improving management of current and future challenges in cyberspace.
- To improve the defence of national infrastructures essential for maintaining a stable and productive life in the State of Israel, and
- To strengthen those infrastructures, as much as possible, against cyberattack by advancing Israel's status as a centre for the development of information technologies while encouraging cooperation among academia, industry, and the private sector, government ministries and special bodies.[11]

Israel's national cyber strategy of 2011 seeks more than securing IT. Rather, Israel considers cybersecurity as the foundational enabler of the overarching driving force: digital transformation. The pursuit of sovereignty, security and prosperity depends on developing and harnessing digital transformation.

The definitions section clarifies the strategy's scope:

- Cyberspace: the physical and non-physical domain that is composed of part or all of the following components: automated and computerised systems, computer and communications networks, software, computerised information, content conveyed by computer, traffic and supervisory data and the users of such data.
- Cybersecurity: policies, security arrangements, actions, guidelines, risk management protocols and technological tools designated to protect cyberspace and allow action to be taken therein.
- Civilian Space: cyberspace that includes all the governmental and private bodies in the State of Israel, excluding 'special bodies': the Israel Defence Forces, the Israeli Police, Shabak (the

Israel Security Agency), Mossad (the Institute for Intelligence and Special Operations), and Malmab (the [MoD] Directorate of Security of the Defence Establishment.) (1)

The 2011 strategy remains in force in 2021. But its roots run deeper, and it builds upon earlier CIP policy.

The Evolution of Cybersecurity in Israel

In April 1995, the government resolved to establish a new department for securing 'sensitive information'.[12] Separately, the Accountant General's office in the Ministry of Finance launched an e-government project in 1996. To provide the government branches with ICT infrastructure and services, the *Tehila* (Government Infrastructure for the Internet Era) unit was established in 1997 and became a driving force in Israeli computing and IT security.

Circa 2001, the head of *Maf'at* elevated the cybersecurity concerns that had accumulated in defence over many years to the national government, which then tasked the National Security Council (NSC) to assess risks and outline strategies. Following the NSC staff work, Israel established the world's first state-guided Critical Infrastructure Protection (CIP) in 2002 and has grappled with the ensuing political dilemmas, investing in mission-specific cyber technologies and concepts of operations.

Israel's government was remarkably and uncharacteristically proactive with CIP: the strategic focus came before any cyber risk or threat had manifested. Even in 2020, most of Western CIP policies remained voluntary: an operator could choose whether or not to adopt and comply with the recommendations. The state of Israel took responsibility for cybersecurity of complex cyber-physical processes in the Special Government Resolution B/84 'The responsibility for protecting computerised systems in the State of Israel' of December 2002. The *Knesset* (Parliament) amended the 'Regulation of Security in Public Bodies Law of 1998' to include what today we refer to as cybersecurity: 'activities required to preserve those vital computerised systems, information stored in them, confidential information related to them, as well as preventing damages to those systems or the information in question' (Tabansky 2013). In parallel, the new 'National Unit for the Protection of Vital Computerised Systems' was tasked with overseeing the critical infrastructure operators. Neither the IDF nor the police were deemed suitable for civilian cybersecurity. The new unit known as '*Re'em*' (National Information Security Agency)[14] was placed within *Shabak* (Israel Security Agency), which enjoyed a solid legal foundation to operate domestically. The law authorised *Re'em* to access any system of the designated critical infrastructure (*Tamak*) operator to assess its risks and audit IT security. Moreover, *Re'em* can issue binding directives to supervised organizations, which then must finance the costs, and also ensure compliance.[15]

The process of designating a system as 'vital' allowed for deliberation. As tensions between security, liberty, and business concerns erupted, the banking sector argued that, if a clandestine security agency were known to reside in the banks' computers, then domestic and international business would plummet. Despite the sector's obvious systemic criticality, the appeal was accepted and the banks were never overseen by the *Shabak*. The Tel Aviv Stock

Exchange used the same argument but failed to convince. Notably, intelligence, defence, and defence industries were exempt from the new CIP arrangement, remaining responsible for their own protection. This division remains to date.

The 2010 discovery of Stuxnet was a global cybersecurity watershed and propelled changes in Israel's policy. Prime Minister Netanyahu requested Major-General (res.) Professor Isaac Ben-Israel, who at that time was the Chairperson of the National Council for Research and Development in the Ministry of Science, to lead a multi-stakeholder taskforce to review Israel's cybersecurity. The resulting 'National Cyber Initiative' launched in 2010 with the vision:

> To preserve Israel's standing in the world as a centre for information-technology development, to provide it with superpower capabilities in cyberspace, to ensure its financial and national resilience as a democratic, knowledge-based, and open society.[13]

For six months, eighty experts in eight subcommittees systematically reviewed both the challenges and opportunities for Israel. The findings focused on the gap between existing protections and the expanding threat landscape: Israeli cybersecurity was confined to the critical infrastructure and the defence establishment.

While the 2010 review found that this CIP arrangement was functioning well, it still left most of society exposed and the taskforce stressed that cybersecurity was critical to reaping the benefits of digital transformation. But the review identified several relevant areas of excellence in Israel throughout the innovation system: a vibrant high-tech industry; skilled human capital; world-class research university centres; and technological capabilities in the defence community and defence industry. Given existing capabilities, the taskforce recommended a cooperative strategy: enhancing collaborations between government, defence, research universities, and education and high-tech business sectors. The unclassified part of the report details concrete recommendations for capacity building (Tabansky and Ben-Israel 2015). The first was to coordinate national cybersecurity efforts.

The Israel National Cyber Directorate: Capacity Building and Operations

The Israel National Cyber Directorate (INCD) united two new cybersecurity organizations: the Israel National Cyber Bureau (INCB) established in 2011 and the National Cyber Security Authority (NCSA) established in 2015. Since the Government Resolution 3270 of 17 December, 2017, the INCD is responsible for both civilian capacity development and cybersecurity operations.[16]

The INCB was set up in 2011 in Resolution 3611 to:

1. advance defence and build national strength in the cyber field;
2. build up Israel's lead in the cyber field; and
3. advance processes that support the first two tasks (Prime Minister's Office 2013).

The INCB was designed as a civilian staff organization, devoid of intelligence, law enforcement, or defence missions. The deliberate recommendation to place the Bureau in the Prime Minister's Office was intended to improve the INCB's power in the disputes likely to arise.

Cyber capacity building remains a central function role for the Bureau and the INCD. It has supported new cyber research centres in Israeli universities since 2014; these had amassed 388 research teams by 2020.

The Government Resolution 2443 of 15 February 2015 established a government security operation centre (SOC) and the government cybersecurity unit (*Yahav*). It also required government ministries to allocate at least 8% of their ICT budgets to cybersecurity and to comply with ISO 27001 standard. Improving cybersecurity in the civilian government should lead by example and trickle down to the private sector.

In a separate capacity-building effort, the CyberSpark project aims to form a new cybersecurity cluster in the city of Be'er Sheva.[17] The larger policy goals are boosting the socio-economic periphery through deliberate development of a working environment attractive for high-skilled jobs and enlarging Israel's cybersecurity ecosystem. CyberSpark is a modern office compound that will house civilian and military units, Israeli start-ups, MNCs and co-working space, all within walking distance of the railway station and the local university. In 2020, it was partly built and already employs some 600 cyber professionals.

The INCB has encountered significant difficulties in its staff work to delineate authorities and responsibilities for operational cyber defence. It has proposed to establish a *civilian* (as in non-defence, non-intelligence) agency for civilian sector cybersecurity, including CIP. It reasoned that removing the clandestine intelligence agency from the civilian cybersecurity front is necessary to mitigate the looming clashes between security requirements and basic liberties. *Shabak* on the other hand argued that the *Shabak* Statute (2002) prevents abuses, and cited *Re'em's* operational success as well as its track record in keeping CIP separate from intelligence missions. *Shabak* promoted expanding *Re'em* to lead a national cybersecurity strategy similar to that of Israeli counterterrorism: forward intelligence-driven defence and defence-in-depth.

Unfortunately, in addition to substantial disagreements between various Israeli stakeholders, staff work had deteriorated into turf wars and was stalled for years (Ravid 2014). Prime Minister Netanyahu had to intervene, and again tasked Isaac Ben-Israel with finding a solution to the gridlock. *Shabak* has eventually lost the CIP mission: the primary reason was to better balance basic liberties and security. To lead the operational cybersecurity efforts, the government of Israel established a new government entity in February 2015: the NCSA (*Rashut Le'umit le-Haganat ha-Cyber*[18]) in the Prime Minister's Office. The CIP mission has been transferred to the NCSA. Unlike cybersecurity organizations worldwide, the NCSA was purposely set up as a civilian agency that has no law enforcement or intelligence missions. The unorthodox organizational design intends to manage liberty and security tensions as they arise and to enable the trust necessary to cooperate openly with the private sector. At the seventh annual CyberWeek held by the Blavatnik Interdisciplinary Cyber Research Centre of Tel Aviv University in June 2017, the NCSA held a one-day unveiling event. Mr. Baruch (Buki) Carmeli, Head of NCSA, laid out his vision for the NCSA before the 600-strong audience:

> Anyone in Israel knows that opening a tap will provide clean drinkable water. She does not need to inspect it because she knows that the Government took care of it. Same

with cyberspace. The Authority will ensure that anyone in Israel can use a safe and secure cyberspace.[19]

Aligning policy to the constraints and guiding principles, the NCSA and the INCB aim to work with the 'natural' regulators to introduce cybersecurity. A sectoral regulator enjoys an established legal authority, a cooperative deliberation mechanism with the sector's stakeholders, and a good understanding of the sector's business. Taken together, these features result in higher legitimacy than a new cybersecurity agency. Instead of competing with the likes of the Bank of Israel and Ministry of Finance, Ministry of Energy, and Ministry of Health, the INCD accepts that these are better suited to balance the business needs of the respective sector with national cybersecurity. Accordingly, sectoral SOCs for energy, government, and financial sectors have already started operation collocated with the national Cyber Event Readiness Team (CERT-IL) in Be'er Sheva. The CERT-IL began operations on 1 July 2014 as a civilian, public organization that develops national situational awareness, information sharing and incident response. The NCSA commissioned the development of 'CyberNet:' the custom information-sharing platform, offered to enterprises and sectoral SOCs to voluntarily share detailed threat information.[20] The members can indicate anomalies: CERT-IL can augment these with commercial data and state intelligence in order to improve national cyber situational awareness, and can share threat indicators as well as prioritized mitigations. By 2018, over two hundred large Israeli organizations joined the CyberNet; in January 2020, 1,400 Israeli Chief Information Security Officers (CISOs) had registered with it.

In addition to information sharing domestically and with dozens of foreign Computer Security Incident Response Teams (CSIRTs) worldwide,[21] the CERT-IL team proactively scans the public parts of the Israeli Internet for recent high-priority vulnerabilities. The team then contacts the vulnerable organizations, and provides actionable guidance and validated countermeasures. Overall, the INCD has succeeded in helping private and public Israeli civilian organizations to mitigate critical vulnerabilities, such as WannaCry or BlueKeep, faster and more efficiently than elsewhere.

As Dr Eviatar Matania completed two three-year terms as the Head of the Bureau and later the Directorate, Mr Yigal Unna took office at the beginning of 2018. The cyber technologies unit of the INCD integrates all the technological activities. The INCD published a 'National Cyber Security Strategy In Brief' booklet in September 2017, presenting the concept of operations and its three operational layers, called 'aggregate cyber robustness', 'systemic cyber resilience' and 'national cyber defence'. The three-layer approach aims to embrace the big roles of private organizations in achieving national cybersecurity.[22] The 2019 INCD Annual Report, however, presents four layers of national cybersecurity: resilience in face of attacks; operational response to attacks; nurturing scientific and industrial ecosystems; and international cooperation.

As the Western concerns with hostile influence operations exploded with the American investigation of Russian activities and intentions in the 2016 US Presidential Elections,[23] the web and social media platforms came under increasing scrutiny (Lazer et al. 2018; Svetoka and Reynolds 2016; Del Vicario et al. 2016, Zuboff 2019). Yet, the INCD remains clear and consistent regarding risks and threats to content: these exceed its mission.

Three Challenges to National Cybersecurity in Israel

As Israel's cybersecurity strategy embraces innovation, many future changes are expected in cybersecurity environment, missions, policies, and capabilities. Market cybersecurity proclamations tend to stress technological change and the resultant expansion of attack surface. However, the major national cybersecurity issue is one of balancing fundamental freedoms and cybersecurity. As long as security technologies can deduce our location, social network, mood, health, location, and so forth, the tensions such as between privacy and security are likely to persist (Mayer, Mutchler, and Mitchell 2016; Bond, Fariss, Jones et al. 2012). Thus, aside from inventing a radical privacy-preserving cybersecurity approach, three domestic challenges should keep Israel's cybersecurity stakeholders busy in the near decade.

Fortify the Legal Foundations

Primary legislation supported the 2002 CIP arrangement in the form of the Regulation of Security in Public Bodies Law (1998) and the *Shabak* Statute (2002). All subsequent progress described earlier was made through government resolutions, based on existing legislations. Faced with years-long primary legislation and political bargaining, Israel's governments opted to incrementally advance national cybersecurity more rapidly through executive power. However, government resolutions provide a weaker legal foundation, opening space for friction between various stakeholders. As the Ministry of Justice and the INCB were preparing a draft 'Cyber Law', the NCSA initiated cybersecurity operations and stakes grew higher. Lack of cooperation and turf wars between the NCSA and the security establishment was the topic of an August 2016 report prepared by a Knesset cyber defence sub-committee. In April 2017, the turf wars exploded in the televised leak of a letter from the heads of the Israeli security agencies to the Prime Minister and the Cabinet Ministers. Signed by the head of Mossad, the head of the Shabak, the IDF deputy chief of staff and the director-general of the Ministry of Defence, the letter lamented that granting the NCSA broad operational powers could severely harm their cyber operations and called for legislation that preserves the position of the undersigned security agencies.

In June 2018, the INCD presented the draft Cyber Law for public consultations.[24] The draft triggered public debate, especially with regard to the measures the INCD may require to detect, investigate, and respond to suspected cyberattacks.[25] The law stalled due to Israel's continued political deadlock: three election rounds between April 2019 and March 2020 resulted in stalemate. An unlikely power-sharing government was formed to deal with the pandemic.[26] Once the legislative process commences, dramatic yet groundless allegations of potential 'NSA-like' abuses and ruthless political bargaining are sure to re-emerge. The primary legislation will require substantial changes in draft Cyber Law and is unlikely to complete before the end of 2022.

Gain Cyber Situational Awareness

CERT-IL responded to 3,233 serious cyber incidents in 2019. Were these random or a part of persistent campaigns? How many systems in Israel are infected with a given malware? How many networks blocked incidents similar to the ones that CERT-IL responded to? What is the dwell time between breach and discovery? Effective defence demands answers to such questions, otherwise known as 'situational awareness'. However, no developed country can boast of a satisfactory understanding of what happens in its cyberspace in near real-time. Notably, Israel has already embarked on the mission. Much of the current activity, including organization design and new technological solutions, constitutes a high-stakes experiment in maintaining basic liberties while improving situational awareness. Israel's technical and non-technical innovation creation and adoption deserve close attention in the coming years.

Reassess the Cybersecurity Roles of the Israel Defence Forces

Israel's defence expenditure is still high at about 5% of GDP, with the IDF consuming the lion's share. How much of the defence expenditure contributes to national civilian cybersecurity? What return on (defence) investment does Israel get?

Comprehensive national cybersecurity requires frequent rebalancing of security instruments, including military roles and resources. The IDF is already investing considerable resources and highly talented personnel for a deep and broad development of military cyber capabilities. Yet organization and doctrine remain huge challenges.[27] What is clear is that the MoD and the IDF are not tasked with domestic cyber operations, such as CIP or situational awareness.

As in other democracies, military instruments are not to be routinely used domestically. However, rising cyber threats require different responses, including the new civilian cybersecurity organizations Israel established. Calls to reduce defence expenditure or to modify IDF's authority, missions, and force structure are routinely met with arguments presenting the non-cyber threats and concluding that the military needs are expanding. On the other hand, imminent adoption of artificially intelligent systems will exacerbate the breadth and criticality of cybersecurity risks and threats. Israeli leaders contemplating changes must support and accept innovation, while overcoming mounting political pressure.

Conclusion: Grand Strategy Should Drive Cybersecurity in the Age of Artificial Intelligence

Israel's experience suggests that each society and even small nations can gain and utilize cyber power. Common insights—such as high defence expenditure, compulsory military service, high threat awareness, and state-of-the-art technologies—offer only superficial accounts of Israel's experience. The root of Israel's achievements is that it has developed cyber power guided by its grand strategy, in particular by the self-reliance and qualitative edge principles.

Israel's national cybersecurity journey is far from complete. To pursue sovereignty, security and prosperity, Israel opts to develop and nurture a national innovation ecosystem that will adapt to the risks and opportunities of the profound global digital transformation and advance cyber power. So far, this strategy has served Israel and its allies well. Three major challenges remain: Cementing the current cybersecurity organization requires primary legislation; comprehensive near real-time cyber situational awareness remains an aspiration; and the IDF holds most defence resources but plays marginal roles in national cyber defence.

Israel proves that an ambitious grand strategy is the crucial factor in developing and utilizing cyber power towards comprehensive security and prosperity. Considering the immediate challenges and benefits of narrow AI, already apparent in smart intelligent systems or Industry 4.0, countries tackling cybersecurity challenges in order to maintain the status quo are unlikely to lead the way.

Cyber power grows in importance. Harnessing digital transformation, in particular narrow AI applications, requires further radical innovation. Israel must continue adhering to its grand strategy on the journey to security and prosperity in the coming age of AI.

NOTES

1. Such as the French *Le Livre Blanc sur la Défense et la Sécurité Nationale* or the American *Quadrennial Defense Review*.
2. In IT-security, air-gapped refers to a network secured to the maximum by disconnecting it, often physically, from other local networks and the Internet.
3. Zetter, *Countdown to Zero Day*. Langner, 'Stuxnet'.
4. http://www.israeldefense.com/en/node/29613
5. http://www.oecd.org/israel/
6. Israel has the largest share of early-stage and seed venture capital funding in GDP among OECD countries.
7. 'The State of Innovation: Operating Model Frameworks, Findings and Resources for Multinationals Innovating in Israel,' (PricewaterhouseCoopers Advisory Ltd., 2019).
8. Breznitz, *The Military as a Public Space*.
9. Swed and Butler, 'Military Capital'.
10. This resonates with the puzzle that public approval for political institutions in advanced liberal democracies declines despite rising government performance on almost every indicator. Political scientists hypothesize an 'expectations gap:' as life improves, public expectations for further progress rises faster than the system can deliver.
11. Israel, G. o. (2011). Government decision 3611: Advancing national capacity in cyber space. Jerusalem, Israel, PMO Secretariat, p. 1.
12. The ministerial committee for coordination and administration Decision 431/TM 9 April 1995.
13. Technology, T. S. C. o. S. a. (2011). The National Cyber Initiative—a special report for the Prime Minister Jerusalem, Ministry of Science and Technology National Council on Research and Development.

14. http://www.pmo.gov.il/ENGLISH/PRIMEMINISTERSOFFICE/DIVISIONS
    ANDAUTHORITIES/CYBER/Pages/Background.aspx
15. Tabansky, 'Critical Infrastructure'.
16. https://www.gov.il/he/departments/policies/dec_3270_2017
17. http://cyberspark.org.il/
18. Government Resolution 2444 of February 15, 2015. Prime Minister's Office. 'Cabinet
    Approves Establishment of National Cyber Authority', http://www.pmo.gov.il/English/
    MediaCenter/Spokesman/Pages/spokeCyber150215.aspx
19. https://www.youtube.com/watch?v=BCtwjpaFg4Q
20. https://www.gov.il/he/Departments/news/amar Revealed June 2016 at the Blavatnik
    Interdisciplinary Cyber Research Center's CyberWeek.
21. http://www.israeldefense.com/he/node/31498
22. However, the document has been promptly removed from the website. See also the
    two articles by the INCB leadership: Matania, Eviatar, Lior Yoffe, and Tal Goldstein.
    2017. 'Structuring the National Cyber Defence: In Evolution Towards a Central Cyber
    Authority', *Journal of Cyber Policy* 2 (1): 16–25; Matania, Eviatar, Lior Yoffe, and Michael
    Mashkautsan. 2016. 'A Three-Layer Framework for a Comprehensive National Cyber-
    Security Strategy', *Georgetown Journal of International Affairs* 17 (3): 77–84.
23. United States and Director of National Intelligence, 'Assessing Russian Activities and
    Intentions in Recent Us Elections,' in *Intelligence Community Assessment* (DNI, 2017).
24. https://www.gov.il/he/Departments/news/lawabstract
25. Israel's 2019-2020 political crisis has seen ridiculous allegations in the 'Gantz cell phone
    affair.' https://www.economist.com/middle-east-and-africa/2019/03/21/benny-gantz-
    must-convince-israelis-that-he-can-protect-them https://www.haaretz.com/israel-news/
    elections/.premium-former-mossad-chief-leaking-hack-of-gantz-s-phone-an-attack-
    on-democracy-1.7028086. https://en.wikipedia.org/wiki/2019%E2%80%9320_Israeli_
    political_crisis
26. https://en.wikipedia.org/wiki/2019%E2%80%9320_Israeli_political_crisis
27. Amidror, 'The Evolution and Development of the Idf.'

REFERENCES

Abrams, Elliot. 2013. *Tested by Zion: The Bush Administration and the Israeli-Palestinian
Conflict*. Cambridge, UK: Cambridge University Press.

Adamsky, Dima. 2010. *The Culture of Military Innovation: The Impact of Cultural Factors on
the Revolution in Military Affairs in Russia, the U.S., and Israel*. Stanford, CA: Stanford
University Press.

Albright, David, Paul Brannan, and Christina Walrond. 2010. *Did Stuxnet Take Out 1,000
Centrifuges at the Natanz Enrichment Plant?* Washington, DC: Institute for Science and
International Security.

Amidror, Yaakov. 2018. 'The Evolution and Development of the IDF". In *Routledge Handbook
on Israeli Security*, edited by Stuart A. Cohen and Aharon Klieman: London: Routledge.

Baram, Gil, and Isaac Ben-Israel. 2019. 'The Academic Reserve: Israel's Fast Track to High-Tech
Success', *Israel Studies Review* 34 (2): 75–91.

Ben-Israel, I., and D. Paikowsky. 2017. 'The Iron Wall Logic of Israel's Space Programme',
Survival 59 (4): 151–66.

Ben-Israel, Isaac, and Lior Tabansky. 2011. 'An Interdisciplinary Look at Security Challenges in the Information Age', *Military and Strategic Affairs* 3 (3) November: 21–37.

Bond, Robert M., Christopher J. Fariss, Jason J. Jones et al. 2012. 'A 61-Million-Person Experiment in Social Influence and Political Mobilization', *Nature* 489 (7415): 295–8.

Breznitz, D. 2007. 'Industrial R&D as a National Policy: Horizontal Technology Policies and Industry-State Co-Evolution in the Growth of the Israeli Software Industry', *Research Policy* 36 (9): 1465–82.

Breznitz, Dan. 2002. *The Military as a Public Space: The Role of the IDF in the Israeli Software Innovation System*. Haifa: Samuel Neaman Institute for Advanced Studies in Science and Technology/Mosad Shemuel Neaman Lemehqar Mitqaddem Bemadda, Uvtekhnologya, Technion, Israel Institute of Technology.

Del Vicario, Michela, Alessandro Bessi, Fabiana Zollo, et al. 2016. 'The Spreading of Misinformation Online', *Proceedings of the National Academy of Sciences* 113 (3): 554–9.

Demchak, Chris C., and Peter Dombrowski. 2011. 'Rise of a Cybered Westphalian Age', Strategic Studies Quarterly. Ft. Belvoir: Air Univ Maxwell Afb Al Defense Technical Information Center.

Economist. 2015. 'Cyber-Boom or Cyber-Bubble? Internet Security Has Become a Bigger Export Earner than Arms', *Economist*. http://nationalinterest.org/blog/the-buzz/cyber-superpower-netanyahu-reveals-bold-plans-israel-15038

Eilam, U. 2011. *Eilam's Arc: How Israel Became a Military Technology Powerhouse*. Portland, OR: Sussex Academic Press.

Svetoka, Sanda, and Anna Reynolds. 2016. 'Social Media as a Tool of Hybrid Warfare'. Nato Strategic Communications Centre of Excellence.

Freedman, L. 2013. *Strategy: A History*. Oxford: Oxford University Press.

Fulghum, David A, Robert Wall, and Amy Butler. 2007. 'Israel Shows Electronic Prowess.' *Aviation Week & Space Technology* 168, 26 November.

Grissom, Adam. 2006. 'The Future of Military Innovation Studies', *Journal of Strategic Studies* 295: 905–34.

Kuehl, D.T. 2009. 'From Cyberspace to Cyberpower: Defining the Problem'. In: *Cyberpower and National Security*, edited by F. Kramer, S.H. Starr and L.K. Wentz. Washington, DC: National Defense University Press: Potomac Books.

Langner, Ralph. 2011. 'Stuxnet: Dissecting a Cyberwarfare Weapon', *Security & Privacy, IEEE* 9 (3): 49–51.

Lazer, David M.J., Matthew A. Baum, Yochai Benkler, et al. 2018. 'The Science of Fake News', *Science* 359 (6380): 1094–6.

Luttwak, E.N. 2009. *The Grand Strategy of the Byzantine Empire*. Cambridge, Mass., Belknap Press of Harvard University Press.

Martel, W.C. 2015. *Grand Strategy in Theory and Practice: The Need for an Effective American Foreign Policy*. Cambridge, UK: Cambridge University Press.

Mayer, Jonathan, Patrick Mutchler, and John C. Mitchell. 2016. 'Evaluating the Privacy Properties of Telephone Metadata', *Proceedings of the National Academy of Sciences* 113, 17 May: 5536–41.

Paikowsky, D., and I. Ben-Israel. 2009. 'Science and Technology for National Development: The Case of Israel's Space Program', *Acta Astronautica* 65 (9–10): 1462–70.

PricewaterhouseCoopers Advisory Ltd. 2019. 'The State of Innovation: Operating Model Frameworks, Findings and Resources for Multinationals Innovating in Israel.' PricewaterhouseCoopers Advisory Ltd.

Prime Minister's Office. 2013. 'The National Cyber Bureau—Mission Of the Bureau'. http://www.pmo.gov.il/english/primeministersoffice/divisionsandauthorities/cyber/pages/default.aspx

Raas, Whitney, and Austin Long. 2007. 'Osirak Redux? Assessing Israeli Capabilities to Destroy Iranian Nuclear Facilities', *International Security* 31 (4): 7–33.

Ravid, B. 2014. 'Israeli Security Agencies in Turf Battle over Cyber War; Netanyahu to Decide', *Haaretz*, 14 September.

Rid, Thomas. 2013. *Cyber War Will Not Take Place*. [in English] London: Hurst.

Roberts, Peter. 2017. 'Designing Conceptual Failure in Warfare', *The RUSI Journal* 162 (1): 14–23.

Romer, Paul M. 1990. 'Endogenous Technological Change', *Journal of Political Economy* 98 (5), Part 2: S71–S102.

Rubin, Uzi. 2017. 'Israel's Defence Industries–an Overview.' *Defence Studies* 17 (3): 228–41, http://www.tandfonline.com/doi/full/10.1080/14702436.2017.1350823

Sanger, David E. 2012. *Confront and Conceal: Obama's Secret Wars and Surprising Use of American Power.* [in English] New York: Crown.

Siboni, G., and M. Elran. 2015. 'Establishing an IDF Cyber Command', *INSS Insight*. Tel Aviv, Institute for National Security Studies. https://www.idfblog.com/2015/12/22/idf-cyber-command/

Swed, Ori, and John Sibley Butler. 2015. 'Military Capital in the Israeli Hi-Tech Industry', *Armed Forces & Society* 41 (1): 123–41.

Tabansky, L. 2013. 'Critical Infrastructure Protection Policy: The Israeli Experience', *Journal of Information Warfare* 12 (3): 78–86.

Tabansky, L. 2016. 'Towards a Theory of Cyber Power: The Israeli Experience with Innovation and Strategy.' Paper presented at the 8th International Conference on Cyber Conflict (CyCon16), Tallinn, Estonia.

Tabansky, L., and I. Ben-Israel. 2015. 'Seeking Cyberpower: The National Cyber Initiative, 2010', 43–8; 'Geopolitics and Israeli Strategy', 9–14. In *Cybersecurity in Israel*. Springer International Publishing.

Toffler, Alvin. 1980. *The Third Wave*. [in English] London: Collins.

Toffler, Alvin, and Heidi Toffler. 1993. *War and Anti-War: Survival at the Dawn of the 21st Century*. [in English] Boston: Little, Brown.

United States and Director of National Intelligence (DNI). 2017. 'Assessing Russian Activities and Intentions in Recent US Elections.' In *Intelligence Community Assessment*: DNI.

Watts, Barry, and Williamson Murray. 1996. 'Military Innovation in Peacetime'. In *Military Innovation in the Interwar Period*, edited by Allan R. Millett and Williamson R. Murray, 369–416. Cambridge, UK: Cambridge University Press.

Zetter, Kim. 2014. *Countdown to Zero Day: Stuxnet and the Launch of the World's First Digital Weapon*. [in English] New York: Crown.

Zuboff, Shoshana. 2019. *The Age of Surveillance Capitalism: The Fight for a Human Future at the New Frontier of Power*. London: Profile Books.

CHAPTER 39

THE EVOLVING CONCEPT OF THE JAPANESE SECURITY STRATEGY

YOKO NITTA

JAPAN'S CYBERSECURITY EXPERIENCE

CYBERSPACE is arguably a 'global common', not unlike the deep seas and outer space. Telecommunication systems are essential tools, not only for social interaction but also for both internal and external governmental communications, and they play a vital part in industrial activity as well, not least in the defense sector. In this way, the information and communication (ICT) revolution has become essential to daily life, our societal infrastructure and its governance, the health and efficiency of our economy, and even our national security. From this perspective, it will come as no surprise that many people in Japan were deeply shocked when the Japan Pension Services (JPS) was subjected to a malware penetration resulting in the theft of 1.25 million users' pension codes, names, dates of birth, and addresses. Summoned to the Diet, the chairman of JPS was unable to explain either how the attack had come about or the extent of its ramifications. The eventual conclusion taken from this incident was that the chief executive officers (CEOs) of Japanese institutions, organizations and industries were insufficiently familiar with cybersecurity issues and, as a result, had inadequate policies in place. In addition to the JPS case, there have been additional cyberattacks at both national and international levels. On a domestic level, in 2011, attacks were perpetrated on the servers of the House of Representatives and the House of Councilors that resulted in personal information, and even the passwords, of members of Parliament being made public.

The significant attacks against JPS proved to be a wake-up call that prompted national organizations to take protective measures against cyberattacks. It also encouraged the Ministry of Defense (MOD) to protect itself against illegal incursions into their systems that threatened the theft of sensitive information. The Japanese cybersecurity strategy, authorized in 2013 by the Information Security Council, defines cyberspace as a virtual global space where various data streams flow through the Internet to and from information systems and communication networks. Japan is committed to ensuring the rights and safety of its people, and strives for the socio-economic growth of the nation as well as the development of a rules-based international order. From being relatively unconcerned by security issues in general, Japan is currently undergoing a historical paradigm shift in this sphere: unconventional security challenges, including cyber, cannot now be ignored and the Government of Japan has established the following policy goals, all intended to shape Japan's outlook on cybersecurity:

- to improve socio-economic vitality and sustainable development;
- to build a society where people can live in safety and security; and
- to ensure the peace and stability of the international community and national security.

Japan's Information Security Policy

With the Tokyo Olympic and Paralympic Games in mind, originally planned for 2020, as well as other events, a revised cybersecurity strategy was published in 2015, setting out Japan's cybersecurity policies for the near term and outlining the complex conditions it expected to face. The cybersecurity strategy portrays a clear understanding of the inherent risks and opportunities presented by cyberspace. The strategy also describes its vision and intention to ensure a free, fair, and secure cyberspace that enhances socio-economic vitality and encourages sustainable development. However, with continuing large-scale information technology (IT)-related investments on the part of industry and an ever-increasing insistence on information security, Japan faces an IT human resources shortfall. What's more, while new technologies and services such as big data and Internet of Things (IoT) bring constant advances and diversifications in IT, they also hamper its efficient use. The reality is that the domestic supply of IT labour is contracting while the global demand for IT human resources is rapidly, and very visibly, expanding.

According to the Japanese cybersecurity strategy, cyberattacks constitute a global risk and remain a prime concern for the development of appropriate countermeasures. As a result, Japan has regarded the strengthening of cybersecurity as a priority and outlined this to the National Security Council in 2014. The National Defense Program Guidelines for 2014 also clarified the situation to the MOD and the self-defense forces, and advocated the development of a national cyber defense strategy. At present, information security institutions in Japan are chaperoned by the cybersecurity strategy headquarters, which aims to promote constructive and efficient cybersecurity policies. In this regard, the role of the National Information Security Council (NISC) is similar to that of a control tower, with its secretariat held within the Cabinet Office. This was authorized by the Cyber Security Basic Law approved by the Diet in 2014. In addition, Japan has implemented its third action plan on information security for critical infrastructure and revised its cybersecurity strategy in 2015, three years after the preceding version, adding 13 new fields to Japan's critical infrastructure. Furthermore, a new law regarding the promotion of information processing was authorized in 2016.

There has been effective collaboration among Cabinet offices, with the term 'critical infrastructure ministries' being applied to the Monetary Agency, the Ministry of Information Technology and Communications, the Ministry of Labor and Health, the Ministry of Economy, Trade and Industry (METI) and the Ministry of Transportation. There are other institutions more specifically related to information security, such as the cyber force within the National Police Agency (NPA), the National Institute of Information and Communications Technology, the National Institute of Advanced Industrial Science and Technology, and others. Telecom-ISAC Japan, the Japan Computer Emergency Response Team Coordination Center and the MOD have also contributed in terms of knowledge and expertise, notably by participating in cyber-threat training, personnel mobilization and information sharing with the NISC. All these actions have helped to cultivate a comprehensive, informed, governmental approach.

CYBERSECURITY CHALLENGES

The growth of the Internet continues to transform global socio-economic structures and extensive research amply demonstrates the positive economic impacts of this trend. The dramatic growth in social networks has created online communities that transcend geographic limitation, but these tools can be put to a variety of uses, both welcome and unwelcome. The so-called 'dark market forums' operating on the Internet via organized crime groups perhaps exemplify this negative dimension. IoT, big data, and artificial intelligence (AI) are all indispensable for Japan's pursuit of social change and its support for the so-called 'fourth industrial revolution'. In this regard, it even might be sensibly argued that ICT holds the key to Japan's economic development. However, in 2015, one cyber incursion was reported every five seconds, providing ample evidence of how cybersecurity has become central to Japan's growth strategy. In response, the government has established its cybersecurity strategy to serve as a 'control tower' in this field.

Given the rapid changes in cybersecurity described earlier, simply reviewing previous malware incursions is an inadequate response when preparing for large-scale events such as G7 summit meetings and the Olympic and Paralympic Games Tokyo 2020. Japan should arguably establish broad information-sharing mechanisms in every field, carefully and matter-of-factly assessing the potential risks (defined as likelihood set against impact) of possible incidents. 2020 was to be a trial year for IoT in Japan, necessitating the implementation of security measures in IoT systems. The Ministry of Internal Affairs and Communications will also need to cooperate with METI to implement a security gateway function in IoT. It may prove impossible to apply conventional security and defensive/protective measures, necessitating the creation of more imaginative and innovative solutions in order to protect the different types of information systems. There is also a general need to improve security in the private sector, and to enable the identification and analysis of potential threats. Rather than simply regarding them as a non-productive expense, companies should also be encouraged to regard improvements in cybersecurity both as part of their own development and as an investment in future stability.

Towards International Cooperation

By working in partnership with countries around the world, Japan pursues its own national security as well as the peace and stability of the international community. International cooperation and partnerships also contribute to the international campaign against cyberattack, especially those in which foreign state actors may be implicated. In 2016, Japan established a police cybersecurity division within the foreign policy office of the Ministry of Foreign Affairs and an ambassador for cyber policy was also nominated. Japan has had active cyber dialogues with a broad range of international bodies such as the European Union, Estonia, France, Ukraine, and Russia, and national interlocuters such as the United States and the United Kingdom, Germany, Australia, and Israel. In accordance with the Japan–US alliance, Japan remains consistent in its geographical and economic relations, emphasizing its shared values with partner countries. As a member of the international community and founded on freedom and democracy, Japan actively develops joint ventures with other countries and, in order to avoid or prevent contingencies arising from cyberattacks, Japan has embarked on confidence-building exercises to establish international cooperation frameworks in various fields intended to improve cyberspace security.

As a member of the Association of Southeast Asian Nations (ASEAN) for over 40 years, Japan has deep historical connections in the Asia–Pacific region that have increased the international flow of people and also increased foreign investment on the part of Japanese companies. As a member of ASEAN, using the various bilateral and multilateral channels available, Japan is vigorously promoting international partnerships in the field of cybersecurity, international cooperation in capacity-building, and regional information collection and sharing. Japan also has established close and cooperative relationships by other means, such as the Japan–ASEAN information security policy meeting. Via a framework of international conferences and joint projects, together with the continuous implementation of various practical capacity-building initiatives based on the needs of individual countries, Japan seeks to deepen and expand intra-ASEAN cooperation in the field of cybersecurity, and actively contributes to the overall resilience of the ASEAN cyberspace. Japan also takes into account the specific economic, social, and cultural situations of each ASEAN country and their various attitudes to cyberspace, thereby enhancing its bilateral relationships with member countries. Japan also actively participates in other regional frameworks, such as the Asia–Pacific Economic Cooperation or the ASEAN Regional Forum, and works to ensure security and the free flow of information in the regional cyberspace. The Trilateral Cyber Dialogue between Japan, the People's Republic of China, and the Republic of Korea held in Seoul, Beijing, and in Tokyo in 2014, 2015, and 2016 also proved to be an important forum for regional cooperation.

Based on basic shared values, Japan also cooperates with North America and the United States in particular as per the Japan–US security arrangements. The United States is an ally with whom Japan cooperates closely at all levels, sharing common values with regard to cyberspace, and this has led to close cooperation and information sharing via a number of initiatives—for example, the Cyber Dialogue, the Policy Cooperation Dialogue on the Internet Economy, the Cyber Defense Policy Working Group, and other bilateral channels. Japan will continue to deepen its cooperation with the United States, notably in the areas of information sharing in cybersecurity-related policies and cyberattacks, the response to cybersecurity incidents, and the implementation of joint projects in the sphere of innovative, 'state of the art' technologies. Japan also cooperates closely with the United States in the international arena—for example, with regard to the development and implementation of international norms/rules, and the promotion of international security and internet governance. Additionally, defense authorities in both countries have also strengthened operational cooperation between the Japanese self-defense forces and the United States Armed Forces under the new Guidelines for Japan–US Defense Cooperation.

Japan also shares basic values and principles with European countries—for example, the market-based economy, free trade and investment—and has developed key partnerships in peace building and fostering stability within the international community. With regard to cyberspace issues, Japan aims to further strengthen cooperative ventures with all its partners as well as developing relationships with a variety of relevant European organizations including defense authorities.

The Framework of Japan's Cybersecurity Policy Prior to the Basic Act

The hacking of the Government of Japan's website proved to be a catalyst that brought an awareness of its vulnerability to cyberattack. In January 2000, the homepage of the Science and Technology Agency (STA) was also defaced with anti-Japanese abuse and visitors were diverted to a pornography website. The STA site was then defaced with protests against the Nanjing Massacre, and other ministries and their affiliate sites were similarly vandalized. Furthermore, all data on the website of the Bureau of Statistics, such as the public census, was either completely erased or rendered inaccessible. As a result, the Cabinet Office began to develop its cross-government policy and the IT Security Office was established.

Prior to 2000, responding to such issues had been largely a matter of trial and error, with each of the relevant ministries having responsibility for the design and implementation of its own information security measures. In consequence, critical corporate and personal infrastructure measures were inconsistent and this made it impossible to arrive at a comprehensive, effective strategy. After 2000, a fiscal year plan intended to strengthen the information security measures of all government agencies was formulated based on the basic strategy known as 'Secure Japan'. Guidelines for information security policy were also mapped out, as well as a 'Cyber-Terrorism Special Action Plan' to protect critical infrastructure.

Cyber terrorism, facilitated by the Internet, has the capacity to inflict large-scale destruction. Compared with physical sabotage, it can be an inexpensive, but no less serious, method of attack, making it an effective means to disrupt commercial and political life as well as military readiness. In early 2000, the threat posed by cyber terrorism became widely acknowledged in Japan, principally resulting from the large-scale release of customer information held by several major Japanese travel agencies.

It was in this atmosphere that a comprehensive strategy was launched in 2004 acknowledging the role of IT not only as a social base but also as a vector for aggressive threats. Concern was growing with regard to the increasing number of cyber intrusions such as DoS attacks, the threat of cyber terrorism, and other unintended factors including human error and hardware failure. In addition, many Japanese feared potential impacts on IT environments resulting from natural disasters such as earthquakes and typhoons, and specifically a large-scale IT failure, delivering a significant blow to both civic life and the national economy. There are precedents: in 2003, 215 flights were cancelled after a complete failure of Tokyo's 128 air traffic control systems and, in 2004, the malfunction of critical medical software obstructed life-saving kidney transplant operations.

By 2004, the timing was deemed right for the launch of appropriate organizations and systems and, by 2005, another key turning point arrived as the required frameworks and revised information security policies fell into place. The first information security officer was appointed and, at the same time, the Information Security Policy Conference opened and the National Information Security Center was launched.

IT is rooted deeply in modern life and permeates every level of society. Cyber-related threats have also changed in both qualitative and quantitative terms, but cyber terrorism is not the only threat to critical infrastructure: vulnerabilities also stem from poor information security measures adopted by government agencies, or when effective policies are not implemented. The relevant ministries have also been working in silos, developing policies independently with no government office, or 'control tower', to oversee their assessment, improvement, and management. A proposal was made to review the government's role in tackling information security issues and this concluded that a basic strategic framework was required to enable government, enterprises, and individuals to lay out their responsibilities and operational guidelines level by level, in order to provide the components necessary for a sustained examination of essential and fundamental issues.

In 2005, the NISC was launched to promote comprehensive countermeasures in the event of IT failure. The information security policy meeting was established together with the IT basic strategy meeting. In addition to an Action Plan for information security measures in critical infrastructure, integral criteria for the information security measures of government agencies were also determined, thereby enabling the enactment of Japan's first information security basic plan in 2006. As a step in its implementation, comprehensive countermeasures including information management were incorporated and 'Secure Japan 2006' was formulated to describe the direction of future priority measures. This positioned critical infrastructure as the central pillar around which the improvement of the safety standard, the construction of the information-sharing system, and the implementation of the interdependence analysis were all mapped out.

The second information security basic plan was launched in 2009, followed in May 2010 by the 'Information Security Strategy to Protect People'. Since then, Japan has developed responses to fresh environmental changes, including cyberattacks, and has taken proactive security measures. This proved to be a cornerstone of Japan's next step: the enactment of the cybersecurity strategy on 10 June 2013 with the intention of further strengthening its responses to cybersecurity challenges.

Finally, the building of a new public–private partnership model was undertaken in which each entity would fulfil its individual and shared roles. The aim of this cross-disciplinary initiative was to promote information security technology strategies, attract information security personnel, promote international cooperation and coordination, crack down on crime, and protect civil rights and benefits.

RECENT SIGNIFICANT CYBERATTACKS

The subject of all too frequent cyberattacks, Japan has become the third most-targeted country in the world. Circa four million people are affected each year, cyberattacks claiming a victim at a rate of one every ten seconds. In August/September 2013, the '47 Administrative Journal' news website run by Kyodo Communication was hacked and visitors to the site subjected to malware infection, or 'water-field attack'. In September 2014, unauthorized access to the server of the Ministry of Justice stole information and, in June 2015, a similar penetration into the Legal Bureau resulted in a leak. In October 2015, another, similar, case was identified and confirmed to have originated on a 'phishing' site, gleaning personal information including account numbers, passwords, and secondary authentication information. This drew the attention of the Financial Services Agency (FSA) and resulted in improvements to the security measures in place in domestic banks. In November 2015, a distributed denial of service (DDoS) attack of circa 12 hours' duration was carried out on the Tokyo Olympic Organizing Committee website. Lastly, in June 2016, the server used by JTB Group companies was infected with malware and personal information, including passport numbers, was feared stolen.

SPECIFIC DEFENSIVE MEASURES TAKEN AGAINST CYBERATTACKS

In 2015, the Cabinet Secretariat Information Security Center was established and, in April 2017, the Tokyo Metropolitan Police Department opened its Cyber Attack Center intended to train and send investigators overseas to acquire advanced technology. The Cyber Attack Center has a number of roles: to be familiar with the type and method of different attacks, and to devise specific countermeasures; to restrict access to targeted IP addresses in the event of Denial of Service (DoS) attacks; to educate recipients of potentially infected emails as to the inadvisability of opening suspicious messages and/or attachments; to advise users to avoid accessing suspicious sites; and to install protective firewalls and develop enhanced virus security measures to assist in the early detection of any malicious penetration. This demonstrates another new effort on the part of the Japanese to deal with DoS attacks by training human resources in cyber countermeasures.

However, on a national level, the effectiveness of the NPA, the umbrella organization for the Tokyo Metropolitan Police, is somewhat compromised by the absence of a standardized, exact definition of a cyberattack. By way of an example, unauthorized access to internet banking remittances is described as 'cyber crime', while the theft of confidential information from a government agency or a company with advanced technology using ICT is referred to as 'cyber espionage'. And, again, activities intended to attack civic society, including incursions on critical infrastructure, are described as 'cyber terrorism'. Furthermore, there are key differences between the primary focus of Japan's cybersecurity apparatus and that of, for example, the United States. The preoccupation of the Japanese cybersecurity environment is the risk posed to corporate and personal confidential information, while equivalent US agencies are primarily focused on cyber terrorism and cyber espionage.

Despite the work of the computer emergency response team in the National Center of Incident Readiness and Strategy for Cybersecurity, it is clear that security measures can be easily compromised wherever and whenever users take shortcuts. Added to this, the prevalence of smartphones, while undoubtedly enhancing speed and convenience, also create a fresh set of vulnerabilities, in particular the leakage of personal information.

THE IMPLICATIONS FOR JAPANESE CYBERSECURITY

Cyberspace is a potential national blind spot and Japan will need to develop more comprehensive and effective counter-measures in both public and private sectors. In May 2017, trojan viruses termed 'ransomware' inflicted global damage to airports, medical facilities, power facilities, and telecommunications companies, and the use of ransomware for financial gain has also reappeared more recently, one spate of attacks believed to have originated in the Democratic People's Republic of North Korea (DPRK). Chief Cabinet Secretary Kan publicly acknowledged the involvement of the DPRK in cyberattacks alleging that North Korean cyber agencies had infiltrated the Bangladesh Central Bank's money transfer system in 2016 seizing US$81 million.

The establishment of counter-cyber agencies has become something of a preoccupation for the United States, the UK, Australia, Russia, China, and the DPRK thereby creating a 'fifth battlefield' in virtual space. But where does Japan stand? Once Japan had both assimilated these new concepts and developed its defenses against cyberattack, much had been achieved: the self-defense forces created the Cyber Defense Unit (CDU) in 2013, which currently employs 110 people and will add 40 additional personnel next year, all in order to bolster the MOD's network defenses. However, the CDU's defense remit encompasses only Defense Ministry facilities and self-defense forces, primarily their intranet, thus differing markedly from other cyber agencies whose primary focus is to defend against external attack.

Japan has sought guidance from UK cyber experts with experience of the 2012 London Olympics, but not regarding security issues and criminal activity. The considerable challenge of quite how to prepare for an attack from a nation such as the DPRK will require a multi-agency response encompassing central government, the security agencies, and the crisis management team.

There is also a vertical barrier: communications and broadcasting are the domain of the Ministry of Internal Affairs, while transport lies in the orbit of the Ministry of Finance, power generation is overseen by METI and financial services come under the jurisdiction of the Agency of Finance. In accordance with Japanese business law, the government has already imposed an obligation to report on each ministry and it falls to the NISC to enforce this.

The Challenge to Industry

That the commercial sector will be ready to face its own challenges is a moot point. There have undoubtedly been improvements, but is industry properly prepared? According to a survey conducted by the Information-Technology Promotion Agency of 500 European and US companies associated with METI and with a chief information security officer, the proportion that have designated a chief executive officer of information security management is between 70% and 80% in the US and Europe, whereas the same statistic for Japan is below 30% and with 3% of Japanese respondents even declaring the role unnecessary. In the face of an increasingly digitized economy, this is clearly a management problem. That said, while defending against 100% of threats is a logical impossibility, focusing on early detection and recovery will also be critical.

Intellectual property, such as designs, copyrights, and trademarks are gathered as digital information, but how it is then stored, updated, and protected should be regarded by any CEO to be part and parcel of corporate responsibility. By way of illustration, here are two examples gathered from specialist informants that describe ways in which security practices can be eroded:

- Maintenance of the system is inadequate and unable to accommodate ongoing 'work reforms' generated in-company, forcing the corporation to outsource in bulk. However, with a given emphasis on cost reduction, the security measures are then reduced significantly from those previously in place.
- Large companies often establish adequate security measures, but there are many small-to-medium enterprises that cannot afford to sustain system maintenance, thereby creating a cybersecurity crisis.

Despite many and various problems, hope does spring eternal: there is a developing multi-sectoral movement to exchange best practice and behavioural change is also evident among many senior executives. Expert guidance is also becoming available, training decision makers in fact-based scenarios tailored to customer-specific requirements. Trainers are reporting that, when many senior executives are confronted by inadequate procedures, changes are carried out immediately and there are even proposals for the Japan self-defense forces' CDU to play the part of cyberattacker in training scenarios. Small beginnings but, given the appropriate talent, budgets, and relevant know-how, much can be achieved in the years to come.

Conclusion

Japan stands at a crossroads. As a forerunner in IT development in the 1980s and 1990s, Japan can nevertheless be seen as something of a latecomer to the field of cybersecurity. The significant cyberattacks perpetrated against the JPS, and in 2011 the Diet, served to heighten awareness of the significance of cyber threats among political and corporate executives.

As a result, Japan revised its national cybersecurity strategy in 2015 to ensure the security of forthcoming international events, but nevertheless needs to go further by issuing and implementing cybersecurity regulations, especially with regard to the development and implementation of robotics. Given the social evolution of this country, robotics could become the spearhead of Japan's future economy but, without a comprehensive cyber policy, robotics vulnerable to cyberattack could also prove to be a major inhibitor to growth.

CHAPTER 40

CONTEXTUALIZING MALAYSIA'S CYBERSECURITY AGENDA

ELINA NOOR

INTRODUCTION

MALAYSIA'S stake in cyberspace and, relatedly, its contributions to regional and international cybersecurity grew as a result of prescient public policy decisions made in the 1980s. Developments took off from the mid-1990s into the new millennium as the government sought to cultivate a vibrant private sector in the technology industry and catalyse change in its public delivery system.

However, as the democratic space expanded online and offline in this multi-ethnic and multi-faith country, affording greater public discussion of sensitive issues such as race and religion, it became evident that there would be tensions between two imperatives: keeping cyberspace free and open for robust innovation and economic development on the one hand, and maintaining some form of content control in order to preserve peace, harmony, and stability within the nation state, on the other. This contradiction is not unique to Malaysia. However, it is amplified in a complex, heterogeneous society like Malaysia's, where fundamental markers of identity such as ethnicity, religion, and language have proven challenging enough to manage since the 1940s without the added dimension of cyberspace.

This chapter will examine Malaysia's approach to cybersecurity in five parts. In the first instance, it will consider the country's economic priorities, which have been and will remain the catalyst for the government's push into cyberspace and, consequently, the development of its cyber security capabilities. The second part will examine the government's efforts to secure those economic priorities by protecting its critical national information infrastructure (CNII). The third part will explore the country's nation-building agenda in cyberspace, as well as the resultant tensions between keeping the Internet free and open for robust digital innovation on the one hand and preserving political stability and security on the other. The fourth part will provide a brief overview of other cybersecurity trends in Malaysia including cybercrime and hacking. Finally, this chapter will argue that, even though Malaysia played an active and valuable role in the United Nations (UN) Group of Governmental Experts (GGE) on Developments in the Field of Information and Telecommunications in the Context of International Security from 2015 to 2016, the government's emphasis on the economic benefits of cyberspace has narrowed its focus to preserving and optimizing the technical utility of the Internet in order to facilitate the digital economy. As a result, the government has not yet begun, as a matter of policy, to adequately contemplate the strategic aspects and legal implications of state behaviour and inter-state relations in the cyber domain.

THE ECONOMIC IMPERATIVE OF CYBERSPACE

Malaysia's interest in cyberspace grew on the heels of its industrialization phase from the mid-1980s through to the 1990s when telecommunication linkages were established to connect the country's urban and rural populations across the divided land masses of peninsular Malaysia, as well as the eastern states of Sabah and Sarawak on the island of Borneo. New telephone exchanges were installed, earth satellite stations were upgraded and expanded, and fibre-optic submarine cables were commissioned.[1] There was early recognition by the government that, by incentivizing the private sector, by investing in a networked physical infrastructure, and eventually by liberalizing the telecommunications industry, the country could achieve its vision of progressing from an agri-based economy to an industrial and services-based one, and, ultimately, through improved connectivity and digitization, to a fully fledged knowledge economy ('k-economy').

In a bid to jump-start this economic transformation, the government launched a series of initiatives in the mid-1990s, foremost of which was the Multimedia Super Corridor (MSC) established in 1996. Envisioned as Malaysia's answer to Silicon Valley, the MSC came with a Bill of Guarantees by the Malaysian government in order to attract world-class technology companies to the area. The Bill is a set of 10 qualified undertakings, the most cherished of which is the assurance of no censorship of the Internet.[2] As will be seen later, it is this guarantee that has proven most contentious in the government's balancing act between facilitating a free, yet secure, environment that nurtures private sector innovation and one that does not undermine the country's socio-political stability.

Twenty years since the inception of the MSC, with more than RM295 billion in revenue and RM283 billion in investments pumped into the Malaysian economy and nearly 150,000 jobs created,[3] the government remains committed, if not more robustly than ever, to growing the digital economy. Part of that enthusiasm is attributable to the fact that the country, despite the best of intentions, has not yet fully transformed into a k-economy. Part of it is also because the government is keen to take advantage of the global digital economy's 10% annual growth rate, particularly in the face of challenging economic times worldwide.[4] In 2014, the digital economy contributed 17% of the country's gross domestic product (GDP), a target initially set for 2020.[5] It shrunk very slightly to 16.8% of GDP in 2015, with the largest sectors contributed by information and communication technology (ICT) services, content, and media at 63.9% and e-commerce at 55.8% respectively.[6]

The government estimates that, whereas a 20% increase in ICT investment will result in a 1% GDP growth for any given country, that figure is higher at 1.4% for Malaysia, specifically.[7]

In recognition of this, as of 2016, Malaysia's eight landing stations now service fifteen submarine cables.[8]

The government has sought to promote ICT development and the digital economy through at least four consecutive five-year economic development plans dating back to the Seventh Malaysia Plan (1996–2000). The current Eleventh Malaysia Plan (2016–2020) includes a whole strategy paper on driving ICT in the k-economy, emphasizing the development of digital content as well as software solutions and services as 'potential areas for wealth creation and participation of local companies'.[9] The Eleventh Malaysia Plan also looks to capitalize on extant and emerging disruptive technologies such as Big Data Analytics (BDA) and the Internet of Things (IoT).

In his budget speech for 2017, the Prime Minister, Mohd Najib Abdul Razak, announced that the world's first Digital Free Trade Zone would be unveiled in Malaysia to 'merge physical and virtual zones, with additional online and digital services to facilitate international e-commerce and invigorate internet-based innovation' (Razak 2016). The initiative was launched in March 2017. A month after his budget speech and at the end of his third official visit to Beijing, the Prime Minister announced the appointment of Alibaba's Jack Ma as Malaysia's digital economy adviser, a coup similar to the MSC's draw of technology personalities like Bill Gates and Stan Shih two decades ago. In a bid to reboot and reinvigorate the MSC, both these developments were planned to accelerate the prime minister's 2017 target of the 'Year of the Internet Economy'. Speaking at the 28th MSC Malaysia Implementation Council Meeting (ICM), Najib as ICM chairman outlined five catalysts as key to this agenda: physical microcosms; risk capital funding; connectivity; talent; and a suitable regulatory framework. Of the five, physical microcosms—a cluster of digital hubs, 'mainly start-ups, scale-ups and small and medium enterprises (SMEs) to connect, converge, share and create ideas'—will form part of a Malaysia Digital Hub.[10]

DEFENDING AND PROTECTING CRITICAL NATIONAL INFORMATION INFRASTRUCTURE

All this investment in promoting the infrastructure and infostructure of the digital economy and e-government must, of course, be secured by a backbone of policy, legislative, regulatory, and technological measures.

Malaysia's National Cyber Security Policy (NCSP) was formulated by the Ministry of Science, Technology, and Innovation (MOSTI) in 2005 and adopted in 2006. The NCSP identifies the 10 physical and virtual areas below as CNII for the country, and recognizes their linkages and interdependence. Incapacitation or destruction of any one or more of these areas could potentially damage the nation's economic strength, image, defence and security, the government's capability to function effectively, and public health and safety:

- National defence and security.
- Banking and finance.
- Information and Communications.
- Energy.

- Transportation.
- Water.
- Health Services.
- Government.
- Emergency services.
- Food and agriculture.

The NCSP framework outlines eight government-led 'policy thrusts' in defending and protecting the above 10 pillars of CNII. These are:

- Effective governance led by MOSTI in the establishment of a national information security coordination centre.
- Legislation and regulatory guidance led by the Attorney-General's Chambers to reduce cybercrimes and increase successful prosecution thereof.
- Creation of a cybersecurity technology framework led by MOSTI for the expansion of a national certification scheme for information security management and assurance.
- Promotion of a culture of security and capacity building led by MOSTI to reduce the number of information security incidents by improving general awareness and related skills.
- Research and development (R&D) for self-reliance led by MOSTI to advance the acceptance and use of indigenous information security products.
- Compliance and enforcement led by the Ministry of Information, Communication, and Culture to strengthen enforcement of information security among all CNII regulators.
- The enhancement of cybersecurity emergency readiness led by the National Security Council (NSC) to build national resilience against cybercrime, terrorism, and warfare.
- International cooperation led by the Ministry of Information, Communication, and Culture in strengthening CNII protection initiatives.

Additionally, in 2013, the NSC initiated *Directive No 24: Policy and Mechanisms of National Cyber Crisis Management*, coopting private sector collaboration in the government's effort to mitigate and respond to crises in cyberspace. The executive directive also specifies the roles and responsibilities of all CNII agencies outlined in the NCSP. Aptly, it was launched during the closing ceremony of X-Maya 5, the NSC's fifth edition of its annual National Cyber Crisis Exercise, which tests inter-agency response against cyberattacks, in coordination with private sector stakeholders. That year, X-Maya 5 drew participation from 98 public and private sector organizations across the 10 CNII areas.

In the last tabulated round of the International Telecommunication Union's (ITU) Global Cybersecurity Index (GCI) in 2015, Malaysia ranked third after the United States and Canada, alongside Australia and Oman, in meeting five criteria of the ITU's Global Cybersecurity Agenda: legal measures, technical measures, organizational measures, capacity building, and international cooperation.[11] Although the GCI does not assess a country's efficacy or success in implementing these criteria but, rather, determines the existence of national structures available to promote them, it validates, at the very least, Malaysia's commitment to those structures. The country's technical measures did receive one of the highest rankings; testament to domestic collaboration between the Network Security Centre under the Malaysian Communications and Multimedia Commission, which has oversight of all CNII networks in the country; MyCERT, the national computer emergency response team (CERT) managed by CyberSecurity Malaysia, which is an agency under MOSTI; and G-CERT, the government's CERT run by the Malaysian Administrative Modernization and Management Planning Unit (MAMPU).[12]

Malaysia's public institutions have demonstrated their agility in adapting to technological innovation. For example, the country's central bank, Bank Nagara Malaysia, issued the Financial Technology (Fintech) Regulatory Sandbox framework in October 2016 to support experimentation of the industry. Similarly, the country's first court established to adjudicate offences committed in cyberspace began operating on 1 September 2016. The court, as currently constituted, will adjudicate only criminal cases such as bank fraud, hacking, falsifying documents, defamation, spying, online gambling, and cases related to pornography (Babulal 2017). However, its expansion to include civil cases was expected to take place in due course. As part of this initial phase, 27 judges were trained in cyber and computer forensics.

Despite these achievements, there was recognition from the beginning that, while adequately responding to national-level incidents was certainly necessary, it was also insufficient for so long as the country remained dependent on foreign tools and technologies. Since at least 2005 when the NCSP was drafted, there have been repeated calls within Malaysia for the country to be self-reliant in protecting its own security in cyberspace. Phase III of the NCSP calls for this self-reliance in technology and among technology professionals to be developed from within five years of the policy's inception. The aspiration for Malaysia to be producers rather than mere consumers of technology is ultimately as much security-driven as it is economic.

The importance of nurturing indigenous cybersecurity technology was underscored in detail in a proposal tabled to MOSTI by MIMOS in 2011.[13] The MIMOS document, 'National Research and Development Roadmap for Self-Reliance in Cyber Security Technologies', prepared in consultation and collaboration with 22 organizations representing government, academia, industry, and individual researchers painstakingly outlines steps for Malaysia to achieve self-reliance in developing its own cybersecurity technologies.

The document stresses that 'securing cyberspace is a *national e-sovereignty challenge* which needs to be pursued in a comprehensive manner' [emphasis added]. It recalls the three strategies needed to enhance the country's 'e-sovereignty' outlined in the National Information Technology Council's (NITC) report, *Securing Malaysia Sovereignty in the Cyber World*: 'self-preservation—the preservation of identity and the sovereignty of the nation state; projection—towards enhancing the use of ICT to promote Malaysian [*sic*] image and worldview towards enhancing Malaysia's stature and sphere of influence; and protection—enhancing [*sic*] security of [*sic*] National Information Infrastructure (NII).'[14]

The roadmap seeks to answer three questions deemed crucial for the nation's cybersecurity R&D requirements. First, what is needed to protect the nation's CNII. Second, the key cybersecurity technology capabilities needed for implementation. And, third, the times in which these technologies could be applied and the intended recipients of those technologies. In answering the first question, the document suggests that the technologies to be deployed need to be cost-effective, indigenous 'for defensive and offensive cyber initiatives', capable of defending against evolving attack vectors, superior in the ability to produce 'information to forecast new attacks, provide for early warning, and prevent escalation of threats', and reliable.

What is needed in terms of actual capabilities are secure communication or encryption; continuously available systems; network surveillance; trust in technology (including algorithms, delivery channel, and protection), process (including delivery and soft infrastructure), and human interaction; secure access; system integrity controls; and computer forensics. Finally, these capabilities must be available and deployable during times of peace by the R&D community and advisory authorities such as MyCERT; in times of crisis by law enforcement agencies and legal and regulatory authorities; and in wartime by the military and defence agencies.

The Eleventh Malaysia Plan echoes these exhortations for cybersecurity self-reliance by underscoring the need for Malaysia to acquire home-grown cryptography capabilities. The Plan also proposes R&D initiatives covering 'the technical aspects of cyber security as well as the responsible use of the Internet'.[15]

Content is King

Although government foresight in promoting digital migration has primarily been economically driven, since the late 1990s, there has also been astute appreciation of the power and potential of online content by both officials and the public. This was inevitable, of course, with the growth in broadband penetration and Internet access in Malaysia, but it also coincided with significant political and security developments within and outside the country over the past two decades.

In the aftermath of the 1998 arrest of former Deputy Prime Minister Anwar Ibrahim, Malaysia erupted into a paroxysm of political and online activism, turning to the Internet to vent, protest, and organize (Postill 2014). During the run-up to the March 2008 elections, the ruling coalition, the National Front (BN) lost its two-thirds majority for the first time since 1969, prompting comparisons of a 'political tsunami'. The rise of 'new media' coupled with the liberalization of free speech in the country, resulted in the proliferation of political blogs and alternative news portals, as well as the use of new technologies in the opposition's election campaign.[16]

Three years later, with the organization of demonstrations in 2011 by the mass sociopolitical movement Bersih 2.0, the role of the Internet in information propagation and campaign organization returned to prominence.

The government's concern about content in cyberspace has been aggravated by three trends—greater Internet access courtesy of infrastructural improvements, particularly in urban centres around the country; increasing reliance on alternative reports due to distrust of the establishment and its institutions, including traditional media; and the exponential rise of social media.

In 2014, broadband penetration reached 70.2% of households and 83.7% coverage in populated areas.[17] The online community in Malaysia expanded from two-thirds to three-quarters of the entire country's population and the number of Internet users, defined by their access to the Internet at least once in three months, grew by 11% in 2015 from 66.6% in 2014 (Kaspersky Lab 2016b, 11). With 90.1% of Malaysians surveyed going online to seek information, 96.5% owning a Facebook account, and mobile broadband users growing significantly (the number grew from 65.1% to 85.5% from 2014 to 2015),[18] the implications of information dissemination are particularly consequential for Malaysia's domestic stability and security.

The convergence of these factors presents striking opportunities for growing Malaysia's digital economy and making mobility, ease of governance and business, and improved efficiency all more affordable. However, it also poses a number of governance challenges, particularly with the free-flow of verified and unverified information. It also poses a conundrum for the government in honouring its pledge to keep the Internet free and open. This dilemma is perhaps best encapsulated by, on the one hand, the government's repeated considerations—and actual actions—of censoring the Internet due to what it alleges to be irresponsible use of cyberspace and, on the other hand, the prime minister's message to the country's so-called 'digital natives' in his 2017 budget speech: 'As an open democratic nation, the Government aspires to enhance the online information transmission channel.'[19]

While there is understandable anxiety surrounding the government's desire to further censor the Internet by broadening the remit of existing national laws allowing for such measures, there is the equally legitimate concern that provocative or inflammatory content can have deleterious effects on the multi-ethnic, multi-religious composition of Malaysian society. Consider, for example, that in Malaysia's easternmost state of Sabah alone, there are 32–42 ethnic groups and over 200 sub-ethnic groups with more still being discovered.[20] With the trauma of the 13 May 1969 race riots still haunting the nation, and identity markers such as ethnicity, religion, and language remaining delicate issues in a Malaysia that seems increasingly polarized, the risk of hate speech going viral and then spiralling out of control into violence is a real-world possibility that must be borne in mind. This is why arguments like Internet sovereignty gain traction in the thought processes of those tasked with the responsibility of ensuring domestic stability.

In 2015, Malaysia's Sedition Act 1948, controversial as it already was, was expanded to cover publications or communications by 'electronic means'. As the amendment bill's explanatory statement acknowledges, in 2011, a few years after taking office, Prime Minister Najib pledged 'watershed changes to enhance [the] parliamentary democracy system in Malaysia' (Postill 2015a). This promise was reiterated the next year and affirmed with the decision to repeal the Sedition Act. Instead, in 2015, the government widened the scope of the Act on the basis that there needed to be 'enhanced safeguards against its misuse to stem legitimate criticism of Government and discussion of issues of concern to Malaysians'. The bill noted that there had been 'increasingly harmful and malicious comments, postings and publications that jeopardise[d] that most valued ideals of Malaysia—tolerance and racial and religious harmony in a multiracial, multireligious and multicultural nation.'[21] Also taboo had been 'calls for the secession of States in the Federation of Malaysia established by the consensus of the peoples of Malaysia and unwarranted attacks against the sovereign institutions of Malaysia, the Yang di-Pertuan Agong and the Rulers of the States'. The government justified the retention and, indeed, expansion of the Act:

> with the addition of enhanced measures and penalties to deal with the threats against peace, public order and the security of Malaysia, in particular through the irresponsible misuse of social media platforms and other communication devices to spread divisiveness and to insult the race, religion, culture, etc. of particular groups of Malaysians without regard for the consequences.[22]

The ability to regulate, manage, and even proscribe the communication of seditious speech online has its draw as a short-term, tactical measure. Whether or not it vindicates calls for longer-term control of online content, however, is a matter for debate, particularly if it has unintended consequences for innovation or for public latitude for discourse.

This predicament notwithstanding, the short leap from online messages to offline activity has already made its mark on national security in other ways. In the past four years, as terrorist groups like Daesh have proven technologically agile and savvy in using social media to communicate propaganda and threats to a range of audiences around the world, Malaysian authorities have had to grapple with the speed and scale of those groups' appeal to fresh-faced sympathizers and supporters. In May 2015, Minister of Home Affairs and Deputy Prime Minister Ahmad Zahid Hamidi reported to Parliament that 75% of the then 107 (Postill 2015b)[23] individuals arrested in Malaysia for ties to militant activities had been recruited through social media. Many of them were 'clean skins' or first-time offenders. If, in the past, the oath of allegiance—*baiah*—was to be sworn in person, it could now be done online and remotely through chat applications.[24]

Initially, Malaysian authorities simply monitored these messages, keeping tabs on the people who exchanged and propagated them. Since 2016, however, there has been more of a concerted effort to respond by counter-messaging. The Home Minister and Deputy Prime Minister promised the establishment of the Regional Digital Counter-Messaging Communication Centre several times during 2016 and it has since indeed been operational. The initiative involves inter-agency coordination and cooperation to monitor and respond to narratives of extremism. It is still too early to offer a fair assessment of this and similar efforts in the country. However, as examples around the world have shown, government-led initiatives inherently lack credibility. The authorities' strength lies instead in law enforcement and, together with the rest of society, in addressing the structural drivers, or root causes, of terrorism. Fortunately, there is growing recognition within civil society that there is a lack of indigenous counter-narratives to extremism. As a result, nascent efforts are being made to plug the gap.

If current trends persist, it seems likely that online content will continue to be a priority area for the government in its push to enhance cybersecurity. Allegations of foreign interference in other countries' political and electoral processes, through hacking and content manipulation resulting in widespread 'fake news', have only strengthened the argument that there must be greater control of online content in order to preserve the integrity of institutions and processes. Because government is the ultimate guarantor of a state's security, this is not an unreasonable proposition. This, however, presumes that government is the *only* guardian of truth and veracity. This premise is already being challenged in Malaysia. As the country's democracy further matures, this supposition will continue to be tested both online and offline.

OTHER CYBERSECURITY TRENDS

Cyberattacks in Malaysia have increased dramatically in the past 10 years. In 2015 alone, CyberSecurity Malaysia received reports of nearly 10,000 cyber-related incidents.[25] With more than 80% of public sector services already online (Kaspersky Lab 2016c), a 78%

broadband penetration, and 142% mobile-cellular penetration rate as of the third quarter of 2016,[26] the incidence of cyberattacks was expected to grow.

In general, these cyberattacks manifest as cybercrime, advanced persistent threats (APTs)[27] and website defacements by non-state hacktivists coinciding with periodic inter-state riffs over territory or other matters. According to police, 70% of commercial crime cases in Malaysia can now be categorized as cybercrimes. Cybercrime has now also become more lucrative than the drug trade (Mahfuz 2015).

In 2015, a threat of 'all-out Internet warfare' from a group claiming to be 'Anonymous Malaysia' was posted in an eight-minute long video on its Facebook page. The post demanded the resignation of the Malaysian Prime Minister over the 1Malaysia Development Berhad (1MDB) controversy plaguing his leadership and warned attacks by the end of August 2015 against more than 150 websites, including those of the Prime Minister's office, the Malaysian Anti-Corruption Commission (MACC), and Royal Malaysia Police (RMP).[28] The attacks would have coincided with Bersih 2.0's planned fourth rally in three states although Bersih 2.0 distanced itself from those threats, castigating Anonymous Malaysia for hijacking its name and cause. The RMP acted quickly to preempt the cyberattacks.

Furthermore, a two-year study by Kaspersky Lab ending in 2016 revealed that servers in Malaysia constituted 3% of more than 70,000 servers offered for sale by xDedic, an underground marketplace of hacked servers from all around the world. Along with countries like Brazil, Russia, China, and India, Malaysian servers were placed in the top 10 of those available for purchase (Kaspersky 2016c).

STRATEGIC CYBERSECURITY: THE MISSING DEBATE

Until Malaysia's participation in the UN GGE) on Developments in the Field of Information and Telecommunications in the Context of International Security from 2014 to 2016, the consideration of state interactions in cyberspace—particularly in the military sphere—had not figured prominently or publicly in policy discussions. Like many of its smaller neighbours in the region, Malaysian priorities in cyberspace differ from those of more developed countries. So, too, do Malaysia's capacity and capabilities. And although Malaysia now enjoys friendly military relations with its neighbours, historical tensions, geographical proximity, and the asymmetric potential of the virtual domain lend a certain level of apprehension among forces to the prospect of closer cooperation in cyberspace. All these, in turn, have shaped Malaysia's unfolding policy perspective towards the intersection of cyberspace and international security.

The UN GGE report issued in mid-July 2015, to which Malaysia contributed, was no small feat (FireEye Threat Intelligence 2015b). It was a consensus document arrived at by 20 countries, some with vastly differing views and interests. By internal accounts, the process had been one of frank and difficult discussions. The report explored the role of international law in the use of ICTs by states and, although it left details open to further debate, the report did emphasize 'the importance of international law, the UN Charter, and the principle of sovereignty as the basis for increased security in the use of ICTs by States'.

In general, the Malaysian position is one of support for the international legal principles of humanity, necessity, proportionality, and distinction as appropriate and relevant to the question of international security in cyberspace. However, there is substantial unease, if not outright rejection, over the application of specific provisions of international law in cyberspace in the event of conflict, specifically with regard to questions of the attribution of attacks and the responses those attacks may trigger in the name of self-defence or counter-measures as afforded by international law.

After all, hasty invocations and elastic interpretations of self-defence under Article 51 of the UN Charter have in the past resulted in foreign invasion, occupation, and terrible, protracted human tragedy many times over. Even if attribution could be substantiated, what might be the appropriate level of evidentiary requirements? Until attribution can be substantiated in an objective fashion (and this is difficult given the innate subjectivity in the political dimension of attribution), countries like Malaysia will continue to be wary of superimposing the existing framework of international law wholesale onto cyberspace in justifying a state's resort to force.

There is no doubt that grafting the international legal and ethical framework governing a state's recourse to force—*jus ad bellum*—onto cyberspace raises many problematic questions. The answer, however, is not to reject those provisions outright or to argue that they would justify the militarization of cyberspace. The reality is that the latter is already happening, with more and more states establishing command and operational defence structures in cyberspace. Australia has declared offensive capabilities and it would be reasonable to assume that other countries have done or are doing the same, even if they choose not to announce it. To continue arguing an ideal would simply be wilfully oblivious.

There is a strong argument to be made that international law as it currently stands provides a sound, necessary basis to improve upon for application in cyberspace. After all, there is no comparable alternative at present and developing a framework from scratch solely applicable to cyberspace presupposes the exclusivity of this domain, or that such a framework can match the pace of technological developments. To be sure, there are many ambiguities regarding existing *jus ad bellum*. However, to dismiss discussion of it on the simple premise that it is unsuitable for cyberspace is to remain in denial of just how much more pervasive technology will evolve to be. It would also run curiously contrary to Malaysia's embrace of technology in all other sectors.

Rather than be resigned to its technological status quo and to take a position from that point of reference, Malaysia should seize the opportunity to contribute vigorously to the policy and legal discussion of this strategic aspect of cybersecurity. It should evaluate the matter comprehensively, with an open mind, and with a clear eye towards the future. This means that, even if the government's current position is to reject the application of Article 51 in cyberspace, it should still prepare for that contingency lest it be inadvertently caught in the crossfire of conflict in cyberspace. It is critical for smaller countries like Malaysia to proactively preserve and strengthen the rule of law as it stands by addressing the gaps that have appeared in cyberspace rather than hold out for an alternative without actually proposing one. In the longer term, it must be better for Malaysia to appraise hypotheticals that it does not prefer than to be blindsided by eventualities that it has not prepared for.

NOTES

1. The Fifth Malaysia Plan details the upgrading of earth satellite stations in the cities of Kuantan in the east and Melaka in the west; the commissioning of the Commonwealth Indian Ocean submarine cable linking Penang to Madras, India in 1981, the ASEAN Malaysia-Singapore-Thailand submarine cable in 1982, the Penang-Medan submarine cable in 1984; and the commissioning of a new international telephone exchange that increased the capacity of direct dial services from four countries in 1980 to 65 in 1985. See Economic Planning Unit. 1986. *Fifth Malaysia Plan (1986–1990)*. Kuala Lumpur: Prime Minister's Department, p. 439.

2. For the complete list of the guarantees, see *MSC Malaysia Bill of Guarantees*. http://www.mscmalaysia.my/bogs.

3. 'Big Data and Key Component of Digital Economy in the 11th Malaysia Plan', *Big News*, 11 December 2015. https://disruptivetechasean.com/big_news/big-data-and-key-component-of-digital-economy-in-the-11th-malaysia-plan/

4. Speech by Najib Abdul Razak, Prime Minister of Malaysia, at the Huawei Innovation Hub Opening Ceremony and Malaysia-China Digital Economy Forum, Kuala Lumpur, 26 October 2016. http://www.pmo.gov.my/home.php?menu=speech&page=1676&news_id=805&speech_cat=2#. The 10% growth rate of the global digital economy is more than triple that of the overall global economy.

5. Speech by Najib Abdul Razak, Prime Minister of Malaysia, at the Huawei Innovation Hub Opening Ceremony and Malaysia-China Digital Economy Forum, Kuala Lumpur, 26 October 2016. http://www.pmo.gov.my/home.php?menu=speech&page=1676&news_id=805&speech_cat=2#.

6. Strategy Paper 15, Eleventh Malaysia Plan, 2016–2020: 6.

7. Strategy Paper 15, Eleventh Malaysia Plan, 2016–2020: 6.

8. These are the Asia Submarine-cable Express/Cahaya Malaysia, Asia-America Gateway (AAG) Cable System, East West Submarine Cable System, SEA Cable Exchange-1 (SeaX-1), SeaMeWe-3, Sistem Kabel Rakyat 1Malaysia (SKR1M), Batam-Rengit Cable System (BRCS), Batam Dumai Melaka (BDM) Cable System, Dumai-Melaka Cable System, SeaMeWe-4, SeaMeWe-5, Malaysia-Cambodia-Thailand (MCT) Cable, Asia-Pacific Cable Network 2 (APCN-2), Asia Pacific Gateway, JASUKA, Asia Africa Europe-1 (AAE-1), Bay of Bengal Gateway (BBG), FLAG Europe-Asia (FEA), Myanmar-Malaysia-Thailand Interconnect Cable (MYTHIC) and South Africa Far East (SAFE).

9. Strategy Paper 15, Eleventh Malaysia Plan, 2016–2020: 3.

10. 'Najib: Five Catalysts to Make 2017 "Year of the Internet Economy" for Malaysia', *The Borneo Post*, 14 October 2016. https://www.theborneopost.com/2016/10/14/najib-five-catalysts-to-make-2017-year-of-internet-economy-for-malaysia/

11. Postill, John. 2015. *Global Cybersecurity Index and Cyberwellness Profiles*. Geneva: International Telecommunication Union: http://www.itu.int/dms_pub/itu-d/opb/str/D-STR-SECU-2015-PDF-E.pdf. Malaysia's list of legislation related to activities or information in cyber space at present includes the Digital Signature Act 1997, Computer Crime Act 1997, Telemedicine Act 1997, The Copyright (Amendment) Act 1997, The Communication and Multimedia Act 1998, The Electronic Government Activities Act 2007, Personal Data Protection Act 2010, Penal Code, Payment Systems Act 2003, and Communications and Multimedia Content Code.

12. Singh, Karamjit. 2014. 'Malaysia Third in Global Cybersecurity Index', *Digital News Asia*, 24 December.https://www.digitalnewsasia.com/security/malaysia-3rd-in-global-cybersecurity-index.
13. National Research and Development Roadmap for Self Reliance in Cyber Security Technologies, 2011. https://www.mosti.gov.my/
14. National Research and Development Roadmap for Self Reliance in Cyber Security Technologies, 2011.
15. Strategy Paper 15, Eleventh Malaysia Plan, 2016–2020: 18, 19.?
16. Postill, Noor.
17. Strategy Paper 15, Eleventh Malaysia Plan, 2016–2020: 8.
18. Kaspersky Lab, 'Internet Users Survey, 11.
19. Najib Razak, 'The 2017 Budget Speech'. For more information on censorship of online sites and content in Malaysia, see, e.g. Xynou, Maria, Arturo Filastò, Khairil Yusof et al. 2016. 'The State of Internet Censorship in Malaysia', Open Observatory of Network Interference (OONI) and Sinar Project. https://ooni.torproject.org/post/malaysia-report/
20. Chan, Julia. (date.) 'Sabah Lists 42 Ethnic Groups to Replace Lain-lain Race Column', *The Malay Mail*. http://www.themalaymailonline.com/malaysia/article/sabah-lists-42-ethnic-groups-to-replace-lain-lain-race-column
21. Postill, 'An Act to Amend'.
22. Sedition (Amendment) Act 2015. PN(U2) 2961. https://www.cljlaw.com/files/bills/pdf/2015/MY_FS_BIL_2015_17.pdf
23. Ahmad Zahid Hamidi, *Hansard*, 4.
24. For more on the youth, technology, and terrorism, see Noor, 'The Virtual Reality'.
25. Wahab, Amiruddin Abdul. 2016. 'Facing Cyberattacks in 2016 and beyond', *The Star*, 28 January. http://www.thestar.com.my/tech/tech-opinion/2016/01/28/facing-cyber-attacks-in-2016-and-beyond/#DmvHXp005l1Xr9M1.99
26. http://www.skmm.gov.my/skmmgovmy/media/General/pdf/3Q16-infog.pdf
27. See, e.g. FireEye Threat Intelligence, 'Report of the Group'.
28. 'Bersih 2.0 Washes Hands of Anonymous Malaysia, Urges Police Action over Threat', *The Malay Mail*, 12 August 2015. http://www.themalaymailonline.com/malaysia/article/bersih-2.0-washes-hands-of-anonymous-malaysia-urges-police-action-over-thre#sthash.Qf5l1vYp.dpuf

BIBLIOGRAPHY

Babulal, Veena, 2017. 'Malaysia's First Cyber Court Begins Operations Today', *New Straits Times*, 1 September. http://www.nst.com.my/news/2016/09/169883/malaysias-first-cyber-court-begins-operations-today
Ministry of Science, Technology and Innovation (MOSTI). 2005. *The National Cyber Security Policy*. Putrajaya: MOSTI. http://cnii.cybersecurity.my/main/ncsp/NCSP-Policy2.pdf
Noor, Elina, and Aurore Merle. 2009. 'Les Nouveaux Médias dans les Transformations Politiques de la Malaysia: Société Civile et Internet en Chine et Asie Orientale', *Hermes* 55: 107.
Noor, Elina, and Aurore Merle. 2011. *National Research and Development Roadmap for Self Reliance in Cyber Security Technologies*. Kuala Lumpur: MIMOS. http://www.mosti.gov.my/wp-content/uploads/2014/07/cybertech_policy.pdf

Noor, Elina. 2015. 'The Virtual Reality of Youth, Radicalization, and Terrorism'. In *Panorama: Insights into Asian and European Affairs—From the Desert to World Cities: The New Terrorism*, edited by Patrick Wilhelm Hofmeister and Megha Sarmah Rueppel, 163–172. Singapore: Konrad Adenauer Stiftung.

Postill, John. 2014. 'A Critical History of Internet Activism and Social Protest in Malaysia, 1998–2011'. *Asiascape Digital Asia* 1 (1–2): 78–703. Leiden: Brill. http://booksandjournals. brillonline.com/content/journals/10.1163/22142312-12340006

Postill, John. 2015a. 'An Act to Amend the Sedition Act 1948', Parliament of Malaysia. D.R. 17/2015. https://www.cljlaw.com/files/bills/pdf/2015/MY_FS_BIL_2015_17.pdf

Postill, John. 2015b. 'Statement of Ahmad Zahid Hamidi, Minister of Home Affairs Malaysia, to Dewan Rakyat, Parliament', 25 May. Hansard of 13th Parliament (Third Term, Second Meeting).

FireEye Threat Intelligence. 2015a. 'Southeast Asia: An Evolving Cyber Threat Landscape', March. https://www.fireeye.jp/content/dam/fireeye-www/current-threats/pdfs/rpt-southeast-asia-threat-landscape.pdf

FireEye Threat Intelligence. 2015b. 'Report of the Group of Governmental Experts on Developments in the Field of Information and Telecommunications in the Context of International Security', 22 July. United Nations General Assembly A/70/174. http://www.un.org/ga/search/view_doc.asp?symbol=A/70/174

Mahfuz, Majid. 2015. 'Cyber Crime: Malaysia', 10 December. http://www.skmm.gov.my/skmmgovmy/media/General/pdf/DSP-Mahfuz-Majid-Cybercrime-Malaysia.pdf

Kaspersky Lab's Global Research and Analysis Team. 2016a. 'Strategy Paper 15: Driving ICT in the Knowledge Economy', Eleventh Malaysia Plan (2016–2020). Kuala Lumpur: Economic Planning Unit, Prime Minister's Department.

Kaspersky Lab's Global Research and Analysis Team. 2016b. 'Internet Users Survey 2016'. Statistical Brief Number Twenty. Cyberjaya: Malaysian Communications and Multimedia Commission.

Kaspersky Lab's Global Research and Analysis Team. 2016c. 'The Malaysian Public Sector ICT Strategic Plan 2016–2020'. Putrajaya: Malaysian Administrative Modernisation and Management Planning Unit (MAMPU). http://www.mampu.gov.my/images/agensikerajaan/perkhidmatan/The-Malaysian-Public-Sector-ICT-Strategic-Plan-2016_2020.pdf

Kaspersky Lab's Global Research and Analysis Team. 2016d. 'xDedic: The Shady World of Hacked Servers for Sale', 15 June. https://securelist.com/blog/research/75027/xdedic-the-shady-world-of-hacked-servers-for-sale/

Mohd Najib Abdul, Razak. 2016. 'The 2017 Budget Speech: Ensuring Unity and Economic Growth, Inclusive Prudent Spending, Wellbeing of the Rakyat', 21 October. http://www.treasury.gov.my/pdf/budget/speech/bs17.pdf

CHAPTER 41

THE RUSSIAN FEDERATION'S APPROACH TO CYBERSECURITY

ANTON SHINGAREV AND ANASTASIYA KAZAKOVA

INTRODUCTION

ALTHOUGH the international community once agreed[1] that global norms for cyberspace and cybersecurity need to be institutionalized, nation states tend to approach cyberspace from different angles. In particular, the view of the Russian Federation on cybersecurity is significantly different from that of many Western countries. Russia has always been vocal with its view on cybersecurity, and has been involved in practically all significant discussions on the future of information and cybersecurity.

This chapter presents an overview of the Russian approach to dealing with a complex cyberspace, plus the challenges it creates. We will look into Russia's perception, doctrine, and accepted definitions with regard to cybersecurity, as well as briefly review Russian cybersecurity laws and the country's efforts to lead the international cybersecurity agenda.

CONCEPTUAL DIMENSION

One of the main points of the Russian approach to cybersecurity lies in the consistent use of the term 'information security' in law and regulation policies—a comprehensive definition that is understood more broadly than 'cybersecurity' because 'information security' concerns both the physical and electronic domains.[2] While most Western countries find the term 'information security' redundant, Russia—in its recently adopted 2016 Information Security Doctrine—presents an even more far-reaching definition:

> The information security of the Russian Federation (hereinafter referred to as 'information security') is the state of protection of the individual, society and the State against internal and external information threats, allowing to ensure the constitutional human and civil rights and

freedoms, a good quality and standard of living for citizens, and the sovereignty, territorial integrity and sustainable socio-economic development of the Russian Federation, as well as the defence and security of the State.[3]

It is important to note that, under 'information security', the Russian Federation understands not only classical cyber threats arising from both the use of information and communication technologies (ICTs) (malware, ransomware, botnets, etc.) and the use of the physical domain (critical infrastructure) (Doctrine, section 23a), but also the 'countervailing of information and psychological actions, including those aimed at undermining the historical and patriotic traditions related to defending the homeland' (section 21e). Measures to deter and combat propaganda in the information sphere are indeed core elements of Russia's approach to cybersecurity. Thus, on closer inspection of the Doctrine, we see that Russia gives a high priority to activities to counter misinformation, because the issues of information in cyberspace and the sovereignty of the 'national Internet' are key security concerns for the Russian Federation.

Another distinctive feature of Russia's approach is that the Russian government claims national sovereignty over its 'information space', and admits that the protection of national sovereignty is one of the strategic purposes of information security (Doctrine, section 22). This approach is one of the cornerstones of the Russian Federation's view on international cybersecurity norms. The Doctrine shows Russia's stance on the dilemma regarding how much states should be involved in ensuring information security and where such interference should end. According to the Doctrine, the Russian government remains a key decision maker and player in this field, and, in comparison with the earlier version of the Doctrine from the year 2000, it prioritizes national interests over the interests of individuals. What is more, the 2016 Doctrine presumes the development of a national Internet management system with its own regulations and rules (section 29d).

The Doctrine does not reveal how Russia would respond practically to attacks in the 'information space'; nor does it mention cyber offensive capacities. It generally outlines the necessity 'to ensure strategic deterrence and prevent military conflicts that may arise with the application of information technologies' (section 21a). However, as stated in 'Conceptual Views on the Activities of the Armed Forces of the Russian Federation in the Information Space'[4], published by the Ministry of Defence in 2011, in case of a conflict in the 'information space', Russia would exercise its right to individual or collective self-defence (Article 3.2, Point 3). Thus, following the Doctrine, cyber deterrence may be ambiguous—it could imply the use of both information and military cyber capabilities as a countermeasure or as cyber offence tools. In other words, the Doctrine leaves a space for the state to decide which response it would be—the use of conventional weapons, information security attack, or both.

ORGANIZATIONAL MANAGEMENT

The organizational system of information security in Russia remains highly centralized and hierarchical where, as mentioned earlier, the government represents the core of policy and practice. Russia's approach provides limited roles to the private sector as possible participants in the decision-making process. The Doctrine prioritizes further centralization and consolidation of management resources for effective information security (section 36a). Where information security is concerned, the machinery of government is organized as follows:

- The Federal Security Service (FSB) is the main institution responsible for ensuring information security, together with the Federal Service for Supervision in the Sphere of Telecommunications, Information Technologies and Mass Communications (Roskomnadzor). In accordance with Federal Law No. 40-FZ, the FSB ensures information security by developing and implementing state policies and technical standards, including engineering and cryptographic tools, which are to be applied to information and telecommunication systems. Roskomnadzor is the federal executive body responsible for control, censorship, and supervision with regard to the media, including electronic media, mass communications, and information technology.
- The Ministry of Internal Affairs (MVD) and FSB are responsible for the protection of critical national infrastructure and the fight against cybercrime.
- GOV-CERT.RU is the main 'Centre for Cyber Incident Response' for information systems in the public sector. It provides assistance in the development of countermeasures as well as cooperating with Russian private organizations, and foreign and international organizations to respond to information security incidents.
- The Central Bank of the Russian Federation is the main regulator and stakeholder in the fight against cybercrime and the protection of the national financial system. Its 'Cyber Incidents Monitoring and Response Centre' (FinCERT) collects data about information security incidents from financial companies and provides feedback on developing incident responses. FinCERT cooperates closely with the FSB.
- Finally, the 'Federal Service for Technical and Export Control' (FSTEC) is the federal authority responsible for information security in key information infrastructure systems. It also counters technical intelligence and protects technical information. FSTEC is the main certifying body for the information security industry, and the main authority to report to in case of incidents involving critical information infrastructure (CII).

Cybersecurity Laws and Internet Regulations

Although the Russian cybersecurity legal framework is already mature, it is still actively developing. In recent years, the government has adopted several information security and Internet laws:

1. Federal Law No. 187-FZ 'On the Security of the Russian Federation's Critical Data Infrastructure' (the CDI Law). The CDI Law introduces requirements for critical infrastructure security, and sets standards and penalties for critical infrastructure operators.

2. Federal Law No. 374-FZ 'On Amendments to the Federal Law "On Counteracting Terrorism" and to Certain other Legal Acts of the Russian Federation with Regard to Establishing Additional Measures on Counteracting Terrorism and Ensuring Public Security' (the Anti-Terrorist Law). Such 'certain other legal acts' are Federal Law No. 126-FZ 'On Communications', and Federal Law No. 149-FZ 'On Information, Information technologies and the Protection of Information'. These Laws regulate the recording and storage of telecom services' customers and Internet users' data in Russia.

3. Federal Law No. 241-FZ 'On Amendments to Articles 10.1 and 15.4 of the Federal Law 'On Data, Information Technologies and Data Security' (the IM Law). This measure introduces regulations for instant messaging service providers.

4. Federal Law No. 276-FZ 'On Amendments to the Federal Law "On Data, Information Technologies and Data Security"' (the VPN Law) regulates information technologies used to access restricted websites in Russia.

5. Federal Law No. 152-FZ 'On Personal Data' and Federal Law No. 242-FZ 'On Amendments to Certain Legislative Acts of the Russian Federation for Clarification of the Procedure of Personal Data Processing in Information and Telecommunication Networks' (together, the Personal Data Laws). These laws define the data protection regime in Russia.

6. Decree of the Government of the Russian Federation dated 27 October 2018 No. 1279 relates to the rules for identification of users of information and communication networks—that is, 'the Internet' by the organizer of the instant messaging service (the Identification Rules).

7. Federal Law No. 90-FZ 'On Amendments to the Federal Law "On Communications" and the Federal Law "On Information, Information Technologies and the Protection of Information"' (the 'Sovereign Runet Law').

Critical Data Infrastructure Law

This CDI Law ensures the protection and security of Russia's CII as well as its resilience in the event of cyberattacks. It was adopted on 26 July 2017, and came into force on 1 January 2018. According to this law, CII is defined as information technology (IT) systems and telecommunication networks in critical industries such as healthcare, science, transport, telecommunications, energy, banking and financial markets, oil and gas, nuclear, military, space, mining, steel, and chemicals.

Under the CDI Law, owners and operators of CII facilities are required to identify and categorize CII facilities; report CII facilities to the FSTEC to register them; implement organizational and technical measures for CII protection; notify the FSTEC on computer incidents; and assist in detecting, preventing, and mitigating the consequences of such incidents. CII operators' compliance with the law is to be monitored through scheduled and unscheduled random audits every three years. The CDI Law has also introduced a criminal penalty for non-compliance with the established technical rules or violation of the access procedure: CII owners can be sentenced to imprisonment for up to six years.

Anti-Terrorist Law (Article 13)

Federal Law No. 374-FZ was adopted on 6 July 2016. Most of the provisions of this law came into effect immediately, while some did not take effect until 1 July 2018. The law requires telecom operators to store (in the territory of the Russian Federation) information about the facts of receipt, transmission, delivery, and processing of their customers' messages, as well as the content of the customers' messages (voice data, text messages, pictures, sounds, and video) for three years as of the date of their receipt/transmission/ delivery and/or processing of such customers' messages. Organizers of information dissemination must store the same data and information with regard to Internet users' messages for one year.

The law also obliges organizers of information dissemination to provide national law enforcement authorities such as the FSB with (i) information regarding communication services' users; (ii) information on the communication services provided to such users; and (iii) other necessary information (Article 64 (1.1) of Federal Law No. 126-FZ).

The law also requires organizers of information dissemination to provide public authorities with information necessary for decrypting users' messages (Federal Law No. 126-FZ 'On Communications', Article 64).

Instant Messaging Law

The Instant Messaging Law (IML) was adopted on 29 July 2017. It came into effect on 1 January 2018, since when the anonymous use of instant messaging (IM) has been prohibited. In addition, the law introduces certain other obligations on IM service providers:

- To ensure privacy of IM messages by implementing certain technical and organizational measures.
- To identify users as per mobile contact numbers and to store data relating to identification (in the Russian Federation only).
- To block messages of certain users upon request from the relevant Russian authority, if such messages are deemed to contain information that violates the provisions of Russian law.
- To block messages sent to IM users if this is required by the provisions of Russian law.

If an IM service provider fails to comply with these requirements, Roskomnadzor reserves the right to block its services (given a respective court decision).

VPN Law

This law came into force on 1 November 2017 to complement Federal Law No. 149-FZ 'On Data, Information Technologies and Data Security', which introduces restrictions for access to certain data and telecommunications networks in Russia ('restricted websites'). The VPN Law adds that the owners of such data and telecommunications networks, as well as data resources that can be used to access restricted websites—so-called 'VPN technology'—are to be prohibited from providing their users with support to access restricted websites (Article 1, Federal Law No. 276-FZ).

However, use of VPN technology itself is not prohibited. The VPN Law introduces certain obligations for several groups of actors:

- Owners of VPN technology ('owners').
- Hosting providers and other persons providing services for the distribution of VPN technology on the Internet ('hosting providers').
- Operators of Internet search engines that place advertisements for customers in Russia ('search engine operators').

Roskomnadzor monitors compliance of actors that fall within the scope of the VPN Law, and operates the federal database on data and telecommunications networks to which access is restricted in the territory of the Russian Federation. Owners are obliged to submit their details for entry into the database within 30 days of receipt of a request from Roskomnadzor. The law also prescribes that, upon a request from Roskomnadzor, a hosting provider has to disclose details about an owner, and notify that owner that it intends to do so, according to the law.

Search engine operators must be entered into the database as well, and once they (and/or the owners) have done this, they have the right to block users' access to restricted websites within three days. For non-compliance, in particular, not signing up to the database and/or not blocking users' access to restricted websites within a defined period, Roskomnadzor has the right to block websites to which VPN technology provides access.

The VPN Law does not apply to operators of state information systems, public authorities, or users that an owner of VPN technology has predetermined. In practice, enforcement of the VPN Law is troublesome for a number of reasons, including the complexity of monitoring existing and new VPN services, plus the complexity of, and limitations to, Roskomnadzor's mandate in blocking resources.

Personal Data Law

The Personal Data Law (PD Law), effective since 2006, is based on the Convention for the Protection of Individuals with regard to Automatic Processing of Personal Data (1981, Council of Europe)[5], but applies its own concepts to personal data protection. Article 3 of the PD Law lists the main definitions and, thus, establishes a specific Russian Federation approach to personal data protection. For example, personal data is defined as any information directly or indirectly related to an identified or identifiable person. The law does not use the concepts of 'data controller' or 'data processor', and instead contains such notions as 'data operator' and 'person acting under the instructions' of the data operator. A data operator is an individual who organizes or carries out (alone or together with other individuals) the processing of personal data. The data operator can determine the purposes of the data processing and can delegate data processing—subject to the data subject's consent—to a third party 'acting under the instructions' of the data operator.

The law gives data subjects a number of rights, such as the right to access the data being processed; the right to object to data processing, direct marketing, and profiling (i.e. decisions made based on automated data processing); and the right to request that collected data be erased. All data operators have to be registered[6] (except for certain cases defined by the law—i.e. if a data operator processes only full names or personal data that is already publicly available and accessible on the Internet by a data user). For that, data operators should notify Roskomnadzor about such registration before the start of data processing. The law also includes mandatory localization requirements (for processing of data of Russian citizens only) and a number of requirements regarding legitimate data transfer.

The mandatory localization requirements listed in Federal Law No. 242-FZ require data operators to use 'Russia-based databases' to record, systemize, accumulate, store, update, and modify Russian citizens' personal data. These requirements can be implemented through a purchase or lease of local servers in Russia to serve as a 'primary database' or through a partnership with a local partner in Russia. In the event of non-compliance with these provisions, a respective website or access to a respective application from a Russia-based IP address can be blocked. One of the most notable cases of such a block was that of LinkedIn by Roskomnadzor in 2016[7], after LinkedIn refused to relocate its data collection and processing facilities to the territory of the Russian Federation.

For legitimate data transfer to a third party (regardless of whether it is actually located in Russia), the data operator needs to obtain the consent of the data subject and enter into a data transfer agreement with the third party. In case of transfers to countries that are not considered by Roskomnadzor to provide adequate personal data protection, the data operator should provide the 'qualified' written consent of the data subjects (unless one of the exemptions outlined in the PD Law applies).

For non-compliance with any of the above requirements, the Russian Administrative Offences Code (Article 13.11) prescribes an administrative fee of up to RUB 75,000. If the data operator processes the data without legal grounds, it receives a warning, possibly accompanied by a fine of up to RUB 50,000. In case of failure to provide a data subject with the information about the data-processing activities, the data processor receives a warning and possibly a fine of up to RUB 40,000.

The Identification Rules

The decree forces mobile phone operators to identify and verify every messaging app used by their customers. Since the decree's adoption, every time a Russian mobile phone user signs up to a new messaging app, the organizer of the instant messaging service or the service provider will have to contact the mobile network operators to confirm the authenticity of the user's phone number. Mobile phone operators will have 20 minutes to follow this procedure and, if the number cannot be verified, the messenger service is obliged to block the user. In the user changes mobile operator, they will have to go through the whole identification process again.

Sovereign Runet Law

In accordance with the Doctrine, which presumes the development of a national Internet management system (section 29d), on 1 May 2019, President Putin signed the law aimed at ensuring the safe and sustainable operation of the Internet in Russia (so-called 'Runet')[8]. The Federal Law No. 90-FZ came into force on 1 November 2019. The amendments are colloquially referred to as the 'Sovereign Runet Law'.

In an explanatory note attached to the bill, the authors explain that it is drafted 'taking into account the aggressive nature of the US's National Cybersecurity Strategy, adopted in September 2018'. The legislation will have a significant impact on the following categories of providers, which are within the scope of the law:

- Telecommunication operators.
- Owners of communication networks, communication lines crossing the Russian border, and internet exchange points (IXPs).
- Organizers of information dissemination (meaning providers that allow Internet users to communicate, such as social networks and email service providers).
- Providers holding autonomous system numbers.

The main goal of the law is to ensure that the Russian segment of the Internet (Runet) will keep running autonomously in case of emergency situations—independently of any non-Russian providers and within the territory of the Russian Federation. Such emergency situations will be defined and announced by Roskomnadzor but, in general, the law states that energy situations are those that affect the stability, security, and integrity of the functioning of the Internet and public telecommunication lines.

The legislation is also intended to route Russian web and data traffic thorough points controlled by state authorities. It also proposes building a national Domain Name System (including all .ru, .rf, and .рф addresses) to ensure that the Russian segment of the Internet stays fully functional even if the country were to be cut off from the global infrastructure. All domain servers must be located in Russia, and this rule was to come into force from 1 January 2021.

Additionally, the legislation proposes the following measures:

- Roskomnadzor will monitor the operation of the Russian segment of the Internet and public communication networks to identify threats to the stability, security, and integrity of their operation across the country. For this, Roskomnadzor will hold regular exercises with the participation of the state authorities, telecom operators, and owners of technological networks to identify such threats and to prepare measures for detecting and mitigating them. Such measures will be mandatory for execution.
- Roskomnadzor will also collect and manage the comprehensive database on Runet, including information on network addresses (IPs); autonomous system numbers (ASNs); communication lines and their infrastructure; internet exchange points (IXPs); points where communication lines connect with the communication lines crossing the Russian border; use of communication lines connected to the cross-border communication lines; traffic routes; and location of the special equipment that telecommunication operators

providing access to the internet (ISPs) and owners of communication networks must install (later in detail). Roskomnadzor will also create and hold a register of IXPs.

- ISPs will be obliged to install technical equipment to counter the threats mentioned earlier. This technical equipment would have to permit restricting access to resources with prohibited information—not only as per network addresses, but also by prohibiting the passage of traffic. Roskomnadzor will monitor this and provide, free of charge, such technical means to telecom operators. The bill does not disclose information on what kind of technical means are implied here: however, it is widely discussed[9] that ISPs will be equipped with deep package inspection software (DPI)—technology that allows analysing the traffic, including encrypted data. ISPs will not be punished or de-licensed for network failures and disruptions caused by the work of such technical means.
- The Russian Government will establish a procedure for a centralized response to the threats mentioned earlier through a Monitoring and Management Center. Roskomnadzor will determine such response measures.

For implementation of this legislation, the Russian government and governmental agencies will have to adopt new regulations implementing the legislation—in particular, more clarity is needed on rules of determining the emergency situations; on technical and other requirements to IXPs; on installing the technical equipment for ISPs, etc. For now, the law remains unclear, leaving room for ambiguous interpretation.

Russia's Perspective on International Cooperation

Russia is an active participant in the global discussion on internet governance, information security, and norms and rules for cyberspace. It was the Russian Federation that proposed in 1998 in a United Nations (UN) General Assembly Resolution (A/RES/53/70[10]) to place the question of digital and information security on the UN's agenda. From 2004 to 2017, Russia was a member of the UN Group of Governmental Experts (GGE) on Information Security.

The Russian government's approach—one of 'international information security'—clashes with that of Western countries. The clash consists in contradictions over the terminology to apply in international treaties and norms for cyberspace. Russia supports the broader term 'information security threat' rather than 'cyber threat', as well as strong government control over information and respect for state sovereignty, and non-interference in the internal affairs of other states[11]—a position that is commonly referred to as 'Internet sovereignty'.

In the draft UN Convention 'On Ensuring International Information Security', proposed in 2011, the Russian government outlined the main threats in the information space as 'actions aimed at undermining the political, economic, and social system of another government, and psychological campaigns carried out against the population of a state with the intent of destabilizing society'. The concept of international information security was further developed in 'Frameworks of Russia's Government Policies in Regard to International Information Security up to 2020'[12], where Russia declares that, though its position should be promoted mainly under the auspices of the UN, it would also seek cooperation with other international organizations such as the Shanghai Organization for Cooperation and the Collective Security Treaty Organization, as well as bilaterally with other BRICS countries (Brazil, India, China, and South Africa).

The Russian draft UN Convention was the country's attempt to replace the Budapest Convention (Council of Europe Convention on Cybercrime), certain provisions of which it opposed strongly. In particular, the provisions concerning trans-border access to stored data, which in turn allow a Party to the Convention:

> without the authorization of another Party, to access or receive, through a computer system in its territory, stored computer data located in another Party, if the Party obtains the lawful and voluntary consent of the person who has the lawful authority to disclose the data to the Party through that computer system (Budapest Convention Article 32b).

The Russian draft UN Convention was mostly criticized by the United States and the European Union due to Russia's alleged intent to establish stricter control over its national Internet.

In 2013, Russia blocked the Organization for Security and Co-operation in Europe (OECE)'s Resolution 'On Early Warning of Cyber Attacks'[13] because the country viewed the proposed transparency measures as threatening national sovereignty. Growing controversies among states reached a climax at the last meeting of the UN GGE of 2017, because Russia—among other states including Cuba and China—did not back the application of certain international law provisions to cyberspace. The Cuban representative argued that this would lead to a militarization of cyberspace because it would 'legitimize unilateral punitive force actions, including sanctions and military actions, by states claiming to be victims of illicit use of ICTs'[14]. In reply, the Cuban, Russian, and Chinese delegations called for the creation of a new set of international law provisions and the establishment of a separate working group[15].

In October 2018, the Russian Federation tabled the draft resolution on 'Developments in the field of information and telecommunications in the context of international security' (document A/C.1/73/L.27.Rev.1[16]). The resolution has been approved by a vote of 109 states. By the text, the Assembly would decide to create in 2019 an open-ended working group, 'acting on a consensus basis, to continue, as a priority, to further develop the rules, norms and principles of responsible behaviour of States'. This group would be different from what the resolution, tabled by the United States (document A/C.1/73/L.37[17]) and adopted with 139 states in favour, proposes—a group of governmental experts.

In addition, it is important to note that Russia's draft resolution insists that 'states should not interfere in the internal affairs of other States', and 'should abstain from any defamatory campaign, vilification or hostile propaganda'. The second draft resolution tabled by the United States does not include such provisions.

Nevertheless, the international community has not reached a consensus yet and continues to remain divided on the issue of cyber norms. Meanwhile, Russia continues to prioritize its relations with the largest cyber powers through bilateral consultations and agreements, especially with China.

In November 2019, Russia and several other countries, including China, proposed a resolution on 'Countering the Use of Information and Communications Technologies for Criminal Purposes' (Document A/C.3/74/L.11/Rev.1[18]) which passed 88–58 with 34 abstentions, despite the United States and some other Western countries opposing it[19] and advocating not supporting the resolution. The resolution aims to establish an open-ended ad hoc intergovernmental committee of experts to 'elaborate a comprehensive international convention on countering the use of information and communications technologies for criminal purposes'. The media cited an unidentified 'European official' who shared the view that this resolution is Russia's attempt to frame a new treaty as an alternative to the Budapest Convention, which Russia does not support due to the Article 32, which allows signatories (states), without the authorization of another country, 'to access or receive a computer system in the territory of another country as well as stored computer data located in another country, if such a country obtains the lawful and voluntary consent of the person who has the lawful authority to disclose the data to the country through that computer system'[20].

CONCLUSION

The Russian Federation actively supports universal rules for cyberspace and has contributed its proposals to reach the stated purposes—maintenance of peace in cyberspace, prevention of an 'information arms race', and establishing conflict prevention norms and the demilitarization of cyberspace. However, existing differences and contradictions between Russian and Western countries' positions on a few key fundamental questions makes it troublesome to reach an agreement with some other states.

The rationale for Russia's approach to, and policy for information security is straightforward enough, rationalized by the government's necessity to ensure national security in light of more complex cyberattacks, and by a desire to provide terms for sustainable technological development where freedoms and constitutional rights of citizens to information are guaranteed and protected. Interstate clashes exist in many areas of international cooperation; nevertheless, the mere fact that there is some dialogue regarding international cybersecurity policy is considered to be a good sign for reaching agreement in the future.

NOTES

1. 2015 United Nations (UN) Group of Governmental Experts (GGE) report. http://www.un.org/ga/search/view_doc.asp?symbol=A/70/174
2. Even though President Putin used the term 'cybersecurity' in his speech during Sberbank International Cybersecurity Congress in July 2018, the term 'information security' is still the main and only definition used by Russian legislators and policymakers.
3. http://www.mid.ru/en/foreign_policy/official_documents/-/asset_publisher/CptICkB6BZ29/content/id/2563163
4. http://pircenter.org/media/content/files/9/13480921870.pdfs
5. Convention for the Protection of Individuals with regard to Automatic Processing of Personal Data, Council of Europe. https://www.coe.int/en/web/conventions/full-list/-/conventions/treaty/108
6. Personal data register, Roskomnadzor. https://rkn.gov.ru/personal-data/register/

7. 'LinkedIn Blocked by Russian Authorities', BBC News, November 2016. https://www.bbc.com/news/technology-38014501
8. The law aimed at ensuring the safe and sustainable operation of the Internet in Russia has been signed. http://kremlin.ru/acts/news/60430
9. '"Yandex" Considered the Technology from the Law on Runet Impairing the Operation of Services', RBC, April 2019. https://www.rbc.ru/technology_and_media/16/04/2019/5cb5a70b9a79471727c1bc79
10. 1998 UN GA: Resolution. http://www.un.org/ga/search/view_doc.asp?symbol=A/RES/53/70
11. Response of the Special Representative of the President of the Russian Federation for International Cooperation on Information Security, Andrey Krutskikh, to TASS's Question Concerning the State of International Dialogue in This Sphere, 2017. http://www.mid.ru/en/foreign_policy/news/-/asset_publisher/cKNonkJEo2Bw/content/id/2804288
12. http://www.scrf.gov.ru/security/information/document114/
13. 2013 Istanbul Final Declaration, OSCE. https://www.oscepa.org/meetings/annual-sessions/2013-istanbul-annual-session/2013-istanbul-final-declaration/1652-15
14. 'Declaration of Miguel Rodriguez, Representative of Cuba, at the Final Sessions of the Group of Governmental Experts (UN GGE)', New York, 23 June 2017. https://www.justsecurity.org/wp-content/uploads/2017/06/Cuban-Expert-Declaration.pdf
15. 71 UNGA: Cuba at the final session of the Group of Governmental Experts on Developments in the Field of Information and Telecommunications in the Context of International Security. http://misiones.minrex.gob.cu/en/un/statements/71-unga-cuba-final-session-group-governmental-experts-developments-field-information
16. http://undocs.org/A/C.1/73/L.27/Rev.1
17. https://undocs.org/A/C.1/73/L.37
18. https://undocs.org/A/C.3/74/L.11/Rev.1
19. 'The U.S. is Urging a No Vote on a Russian-led U.N. Resolution', *Washington Post*, November 2019. https://www.washingtonpost.com/national-security/the-us-is-urging-a-no-vote-on-a-russian-led-un-resolution-calling-for-a-global-cybercrime-treaty/2019/11/16/b4895e76-075e-11ea-818c-fcc65139e8c2_story.html
20. Council of Europe Convention on Cybercrime ('Budapest Convention'), 2001. https://rm.coe.int/1680081561

REFERENCES

Conceptual Views on the Activities of the Armed Forces of the Russian Federation in the Information Space. 2011. http://pircenter.org/media/content/files/9/13480921870.pdf

Council of Europe Convention on Cybercrime ('Budapest Convention'). 2001. https://rm.coe.int/1680081561

Code of Administrative Offences of the Russian Federation, No. 195-FZ.

Decree of the Government of the Russian Federation dated 27 October 2018, No. 1279, related to the rules for identification of users of information and communication networks—i.e. 'the Internet' by the organizer of the instant messaging service.

Doctrine of Information Security of the Russian Federation. 2016. http://kremlin.ru/acts/bank/41460

Federal Law No. 40-FZ 'On the Federal Security Service'.

Federal Law No. 126-FZ 'On Communications'.

Federal Law No. 149-FZ 'On Information, Information Technologies and the Protection of Information'.

Federal Law No. 152-FZ 'On Personal Data'.

Federal Law No. 187-FZ 'On the Security of the Russian Federation's Critical Data Infrastructure'.

Federal Law No. 241-FZ 'On Amendments to Articles 10.1 and 15.4 of the Federal Law "On Data, Information Technologies and Data Security"'.

Federal Law No. 242-FZ 'On Amendments to Certain Legislative Acts of the Russian Federation for Clarification of the Procedure for Personal Data Processing in Information and Telecommunication Networks'.

Federal Law No. 276-FZ 'On Amendments to the Federal Law "On Data, Information Technologies and Data Security"'.

Federal Law No. 374-FZ 'On Amendments to the Federal Law "On Counteracting Terrorism"'.

Frameworks of Russia's Government Policies in Regard to International Information Security up to 2020, Security Council of the Russian Federation.

Russia's Draft Convention. 2011. 'On Ensuring International Information Security'. http://www.mid.ru/en/foreign_policy/official_documents/-/asset_publisher/CptICkB6BZ29/content/id/191666

UN Resolution on the 'Developments in the Field of Information and Telecommunications in the Context of International Security'. http://undocs.org/A/C.1/73/L.27/Rev.1

UN Resolution on 'Advancing Responsible State Behaviour in Cyberspace in the Context of International Security'. https://undocs.org/A/C.1/73/L.37

UN Resolution on 'Countering the Use of Information and Communications Technologies for Criminal Purposes': https://undocs.org/A/C.3/74/L.11/Rev.1.

PART XI

FUTURE CHALLENGES

CHAPTER 42

....

RETHINKING THE GOVERNANCE OF TECHNOLOGY IN THE DIGITAL AGE

....

JOËLLE WEBB

THE digital age is transforming our security landscape. Science and innovation could solve some of humanity's biggest challenges, from climate change to incurable diseases. But security risks and threats are also becoming more complex and more diffuse: as all technologies become information—meaning that technologies can be turned into bits of information that can be digitally transferred—the number of hostile states and non-state actors that are gaining power and influence, is rapidly growing.

The present chapter argues that, to harness the benefits of technology in the digital age, while mitigating the inherent security risks, it has become more pressing than ever to break down siloes between expert communities. Top-down governance alone cannot address all the security risks. Greater attention needs to be paid to horizontal governance mechanisms that bring together policymakers, the private sector, communities of users, law enforcement officials and scientists. A holistic approach calls for an equal focus on anticipating the risks, seeking to prevent their occurrence, and building systemic capacities to recover from them. The chapter starts by discussing two illustrative security dilemmas—the first is about publishing scientific knowledge in the digital age and the second is the challenge posed by additive manufacturing. It then examines the limits of regulatory approaches to the proliferation of technologies of concern. Next, it presents an argument for an adaptation of norms, policy instruments, and governance institutions to enable societies to continue to enjoy the benefits of science and technology, while mitigating its risks. It concludes by giving examples of horizontal governance mechanisms that bring together policymakers, communities of users, law enforcement officials, and scientists, and by suggesting that such models should become more commonplace to inform government policies.

In 2011, a US government advisory panel, the National Science Advisory Board for Biosecurity (NSABB), asked two journals, *Science* and *Nature*, to keep some details out of reports they intended to publish. The reports described how scientists in the United States and the Netherlands had created a highly transmissible form of the H5N1 virus that causes bird flu. The findings showed that evolving this virus to an extremely dangerous state where it can be transmitted in aerosols was much easier to accomplish than anybody had previously recognized (Grady and Broad 2011). The government advisory panel feared that the information could be used by terrorists to create deadly viruses, or that efforts to replicate the findings could lead to the accidental release of the pathogens. Several months later, an international ad hoc panel concluded that both papers should be published in full, citing the scientific and the public health benefits of the research. Subsequently, the NSABB revisited its initial decision and advised in favour of full publication of both studies, on the grounds that the papers did not contain information that would immediately enable someone to produce a bioweapon. That decision, however, was not unanimous: six out of eighteen committee members argued that one of the two papers should be published only in redacted form, and that the risks of publication outweighed the benefits.

The debate highlighted the need for the highest standards of security and safety in all laboratories conducting such research, and triggered extensive discussions about the implications of 'dual-use research'—that is, research that advances scientific knowledge for the public good, but could also potentially be used for harm.[1] In the end, one of the key arguments that swayed the H5N1 controversy in favour of publishing the full version of the paper was the recognition that today's greatest challenges will only be solved through collaborative efforts and the sharing of knowledge. Experts concluded that 'research findings will help improve influenza surveillance to protect public health'. They also concluded that 'there is currently no practical way to distribute the key findings to people who may require them for public health purposes, while maintaining the confidentiality of the information'.

This example illustrates one of the security dilemmas inherent in science and innovation in a connected, digitalized world. Connectivity has enabled unprecedented sharing of knowledge, which in turn has been driving innovation, economic growth, and improvements in safety and well-being in most countries around the world. Yet, it also highlights the difficulty, if not the impossibility, of limiting access to dual-use information.

Additive manufacturing, commonly known as '3D printing', provides another illustration of the simultaneous benefits and security challenges of technological innovation in the digital age. It has become increasingly possible to print anything from space rockets and medicines to human tissues, including entire human organs (Murphy and Atala 2014).[2] The benefits this could bring are significant: 3D printing decreases production and storage costs, and enables collaborations across the world; it holds significant promises in sectors such as healthcare, where it can enable the production of affordable, personalized prosthetics. But it also illustrates the limits of traditional export control mechanisms when it comes to controlling the diffusion of knowledge about digitalized technologies.

Case studies on the 3D printed gun and the US legislative attempt to regulate it illustrate the dilemmas (Greenberg 2014; Bryans 2015). In 2012, the first 3D-printed firearms were created. The Liberator, the original 3D-printed gun, quickly caught the attention of regulators. The US Department of State ordered that all technical data related to the Liberator—namely, the computer-aided design (CAD) files, along with many other weapon and weapon accessory designs—be removed immediately from the Internet. In a matter of weeks, the Liberator design went from single shot to firing eight .38 calibre rounds. After that, the design diverged as rifles, handguns, and, finally, fully functional military-grade firearms were designed, tested, and produced—all within the span of a year. Some argue that the US government's attempt at preventing the proliferation of printed guns has in fact accelerated their development, because communities of users went underground and redoubled their research efforts, in explicit defiance of government controls.

Intergovernmental regimes to limit the sale of dual-use technologies, such as United Nations (UN) conventions or ad hoc mechanisms (e.g. Wassenaar Arrangements, Australia Group) are kept under regular review to adapt to new technologies. Combined with government licensing mechanisms that limit the exports of technologies of concern, they place controls over who is able to purchase civilian technologies that could be used for military purposes. But, in the digital age, defining what is a technology of concern is becoming ever harder. The Internet itself, and the whole cyber-ecosystem surrounding it, has become a space of rivalry and competition of growing geostrategic significance (Demchak 2016).

Furthermore, overly restrictive measures would stem the very innovation we need to continue to sustain global economic growth and to find solutions to some of the greatest challenges faced by mankind, from climate change to the eradication of pandemics. Technological advances in agriculture and food systems are critical to solving global issues of hunger and unequal food distribution. Geoengineering could bring the necessary scale to interventions aimed at halting climate change, just as investments in green technologies can help decrease climate-harming emissions. Innovation in mobile technology has contributed to empowering poor people around the world, giving them access to data and to information that are critical to small enterprise.

The security dilemma comes from the fact that, for innovation to thrive, information needs to be shared, compared, challenged, and ultimately improved upon. But putting safeguards on who can access information that could be used for nefarious purposes is increasingly difficult when almost anyone has access to some form of computer. An additional challenge, not new but made more salient by the digital age, is the difficulty to anticipate how a technology will be used, what effects it will have, and how it will evolve.

The Global Security Dynamics and Challenges of the Digital Age

The concept of *emergence* is used to describe what happens when existing technologies converge, or when entirely new ones are created, with the potential to radically transform existing industries (Bajema and DiEuliis 2017). Prominent voices have argued that the changes brought by emerging technologies are so profound that, from the perspective of human history, there has never been a time of greater promise or potential peril (Schwab 2016).

A number of distinctive features of the digital age result in global security dilemmas that traditional non-proliferation mechanisms are ill-suited to address. These features include:

- A *blurring of distinctions* between states and non-state actors, between what is a weapon and what is not, between domestic and international security.
- A growing *convergence* between technologies, but also between humans and technology. This makes it increasingly difficult to assign clear delineations between categories of

technologies—and, consequently, to ensure the applicability of relevant governance instruments.

- The unprecedented *scale* at which dual-use and emergent technologies are becoming available. Never before have single individuals or groups had access to means of destruction/disruption on such an international scale.
- The *complexity* of both the technologies and their effects, which are often systemic in nature. Notably, emergent technologies can have runaway effects and unintended consequences even when in the hands of responsible actors. It is also more difficult for any single actor, however powerful, to mitigate those risks.

There has also been some debate as to whether the *pace of innovation and change has accelerated*. Whether one agrees or not with this idea of accelerated pace, across the full spectrum of biology, robotics, information, nanotechnology, and energy (that some have called 'BRINE'; Kadtke and Wells 2014), connectivity and technological innovation have led to an increasing symbiosis between the digital and the physical. It is the whole interaction between humans and technology that is being transformed, eschewing traditional categorizations in neatly defined domains.

Ultimately, the digital age has turned all technology into information. Genomics, for example, has become a de facto information technology, with the translation of the human genome into bits that computers can process (Wadhwa and Salkever 2017). The convergence of computer and mathematical sciences with the biological sciences opens the prospect for stunning scientific advances.[3] Scientists have found ways of using DNA to store information, as an alternative to microchips.[4] Gene editing could one day lead to the eradication of mosquito-borne diseases. Already, genetic advances offer the promise of much better-targeted medical care. But the fact that the key component of this biological revolution is simply information creates a significant security dilemma for the too few national security and law enforcement experts closely following this sector (Garrett 2013).[5]

In the digital age, no governance mechanisms so far established to regulate the trade in dual-use technologies are quite adequate to mitigate the proliferation risks emanating from what has also been called 'intangible' technologies—technologies that can easily be transferred via electronic means.

Traditional forms of governance simply cannot keep up with the rapid pace of change, the growing complexity of the technologies themselves, or with the fact that an increasing number of groups and individuals have access to them. Advanced technologies that were once confined to government-funded and administered scientific laboratories, and thus only accessible to well-regulated communities, are now widely accessible at low cost to anyone with a digital connection, in what has been labelled the 'democratization of science'.

The term 'Radical Levelling Technologies' (RLTs) has been coined to capture the exponential disruptive effects of these emerging technologies, and their profound equalizing impact on power distribution within and between societies (Snow 2015). The risks emanate from the fact that cyber-based transnational individuals and entities can leverage RLT to achieve their aims without the need for significant technological expertise or infrastructure. Bill Gates has warned that bioterrorism is one of the deadliest threats the world faces and that governments are complacent about the scale of the risk: 'the next epidemic could originate on the computer screen of a terrorist intent on using genetic engineering' (Farmer 2017).[6]

GOVERNANCE OF TECHNOLOGY   691

The very fact that a terrorist organization has acquired the means of developing weapons of mass destruction is in itself a watershed moment that upends traditional Cold War strategic thinking (Cornish 2007). There is strong evidence that ISIS has not only used chemical weapons in Syria but, more significantly still, that it has acquired the knowledge to develop them—and possibly other categories of weapons of mass destruction. In 2014, an ISIS laptop was recovered containing a 19-page document on how to develop biological weapons. In 2016, Kenyan authorities disrupted an anthrax plot by a medical student and associates affiliated with ISIS.

Terrorists are not the only group to exploit emerging technologies for illicit aims. Europol's 2017 Threat Assessment notes that, for almost all types of organized crime, criminals are deploying and adapting technology with ever greater skill and to ever greater effect: 'This is now, perhaps, the greatest challenge facing law enforcement authorities around the world, including in the EU'.[7] The concerns apply equally to some state actors: in 2017, South Korea raised concerns that North Korea, in addition to its overt nuclear capabilities, possesses biological weapons and could use drones to carry out attacks.[8] The same North Korea has repeatedly been accused of hacking banks and bitcoin exchanges around the world, including a US$81 million hack on the central bank of Bangladesh in 2016, to fund the development of its weapons of mass destruction.

Risk and Resilience

In historical terms, most advances in science have made people's lives safer, more convenient, and more fun. In his book *Searching for Safety*, Aaron Wildavsky illustrates the delicate balance between risk and safety. The trick, he explains, is to discover not how to avoid risk, for this is impossible, but 'how to use risk to get more of the good and less of the bad' (Wildavsky 1988). Achieving security is a question of trade-offs between risks and the associated benefits—but it should not be achieved at the price of suffocating innovation.[9] This requires approaching security not as a collection of individual measures—say, increasing regulation in research laboratories, placing tougher export control restrictions, reinforcing border security—but as a system—namely, as the sum of all individual measures *and* of how they interact with one another, where the remaining vulnerabilities are, and what are the ways in which that system could be gamed for criminal or hostile purposes. Such an approach goes well beyond the skills, knowledge, or expertise of a single expert community.

A holistic approach calls for an equal focus on anticipating the risks, seeking to prevent their occurrence, and building systemic capacities to recover from them. Much more needs to be done, for example, to address infrastructure vulnerabilities, thus removing easy opportunities for criminals, terrorists, or anyone else intent on hijacking mainstream technology to pursue disruptive or hostile ends.

Consider, for example, the digital infrastructure that has become ubiquitous to our lives. With fast increasing numbers of interconnected devices, the 'Internet of Things' (IoT) creates countless new opportunities but also presents significant security headaches. According to the US Federal Trade Commission, 25 billion devices are already online worldwide, gathering information, using sensors, and communicating with each other over the Internet—and this number is growing quickly, with consumer goods companies, auto manufacturers, healthcare providers, and so many other businesses investing in connected devices. And yet, almost two-thirds of them are deemed susceptible to attacks (Alba 2015). The global computer virus WannaCry paralysed sections of the British National Health Service in 2017 by affecting its computers; how will health systems cope with the fact that people's artificial implants, such as cardiac pacemakers, are hackable?

A range of policy instruments can contribute to addressing IoT vulnerabilities by seeking to fix market failures that result in under-investment in security. Currently, there are too few incentives for manufacturers to invest in security by design, which could make devices more expensive and less competitive. Instead, many manufacturers, particularly of digital goods, race to bring their products as quickly as possible to market, subsequently uploading fixes and security patches when vulnerabilities are discovered.

Some instruments other than regulation can help mitigate the problem by creating market incentives that favour security by design. For example, tort law, class actions, and incentives set by insurance companies have transformed everyday safety in households and in the workplace, and can do more to help address IoT vulnerabilities. In addition, a growing number of voices have been calling for more active government regulation. At the international level, traditional foreign and domestic security policy instruments—such as diplomacy, non-proliferation and arms control, law enforcement, surveillance, border controls—also contribute to addressing aspects of this security challenge.

The challenge that the digital age presents to all these instruments is that there is a significant time lag between their ability to adapt security governance and the pace of technological innovation, particularly now when just about every technology can be turned into a weapon. Research on biosecurity illustrates the difficulty:

> While virtually all current laws in this field, both local and global, restrict and track organisms of concern (such as, say, the Ebola virus), tracking information is all but impossible. Code can be buried anywhere—al Qaeda operatives have hidden attack instructions inside porn videos, and a seemingly innocent tweet could direct readers to an obscure Internet location containing genomic code ready to be downloaded to a 3-D printer. Suddenly, what started as a biology problem has become a matter of information security.[10]

Put differently, technological developments are driving change at a pace that exceeds the agility of government regulation (Zember 2016).

The problem of time lag between technology and legislation is nothing new. A senior US official who was part of the negotiations on the Chemical Weapons Convention (CWC), which concluded in 1992, illustrates this point:

> When we negotiated the CWC, the focus was on scenarios that involved the large production of traditional agents. We had very good and close cooperation from the big Western chemical manufacturers. What we missed was that much of the large dangerous and dirty chemical industry had moved off shore to the developing world. At the same time, new technology was making possible just-in-time manufacturing of small amounts of significant exotic as well as traditional substances. Assumptions about what is significant and what signature/footprints will be exposed are now in need of re-examination. Similarly, the scenarios have changed.[11]

Governments on both sides of the Atlantic have increasingly been recognizing the complexity of the changing global security landscape, and the need for flexible and adaptive policy responses. The 2016 EU Global Strategy identifies strengthening state and societal resilience as part of the response to the security challenges posed by a more connected, contested, and complex global environment.[12] The strategy was followed by an implementation plan that called for a structural, long-term, non-linear approach to vulnerabilities, with an emphasis on anticipation, prevention, and preparedness.[13]

Ultimately, resilience calls for holistic strategies that combine prevention, risk mitigation, and crisis management, and that help societies adapt to the rapid pace of change that characterizes the digital age. Balancing security and risk is at the heart of this security governance challenge. It requires an adaptation of norms, policy instruments, and related institutions to enable societies to continue to enjoy the benefits of science, while mitigating its risks.

Building Resilience by Networking Across Communities

If we accept that risk is not only inevitable but also potentially beneficial, how do we build systems that are better at anticipating risks, and more resilient to major disruptions when they occur? One obvious implication of the complexity of this task is that no single community can build systemic security on its own. Networked risks call for networked responses.

Designing the safety and security governance of the digital age requires breaking down the barriers between policymakers, law enforcement communities, technologists, scientists, and venture capitalists, but also with communities of users themselves. The private sector, as the source of most technological innovation, is particularly critical in that effort.

Security is, ultimately, about people. It is neither possible, nor desirable, to eliminate all risks and threats. On the contrary, risks help drive innovations that society needs to advance well-being; they are an essential part of what makes a system resilient to catastrophic failure.

In its 2017 Global Threats report, the US National Security Council concluded:

> The most resilient societies will likely be those that unleash and embrace the full potential of all individuals—whether women and minorities or those battered by recent economic and technological trends. They will be moving with, rather than against, historical currents, making use of the ever—expanding scope of human skill to shape the future. In all societies, even in the bleakest circumstances, there will be those who choose to improve the welfare, happiness, and security of others—employing transformative technologies to do so at scale. While the opposite will be true as well—destructive forces will be empowered as never before—the central puzzle before governments and societies is how to blend individual, collective, and national endowments in a way that yields sustainable security, prosperity, and hope.[14]

Informal networks can be invaluable in problem solving and building resilience (Zolli and Healy 2012). In 2009, the US Defense Advanced Research Projects Agency, DARPA, tested how many people would be needed to locate 10 balloons that they had placed in plain sight around the United States. They offered $40,000 to anyone who could find them. Their objective was to test how the United States might solve large-scale problems of security and defence. Fifty-three teams entered the competition. There had been much speculation as to the various technologies, such as satellite imagery, that might crack the challenge. In the end, a team from MIT that won the competition resorted to crowdsourcing: it took 4,665 people and fewer than 9 hours to locate the 10 balloons spread out over the entire country (Levitin 2014).

However, crowdsourcing has its limitations. In 2016, Tay, a chat-bot created by Microsoft to learn the art of conversation from Twitter feeds, turned into a fascist, racist, pornographic entity within 24 hours from going online, denying the existence of the Holocaust and making inappropriate sexual remarks.[15] Crowdsourcing policymaking leaves us at the mercy of biases. Correcting these to ensure adequate representation of the views of experts, who have better knowledge of the issues and their implications, seems an essential requirement, as is finding a working balance between public and expert opinion.[16]

Even so, these examples illustrate how breaking down the siloes between governments, lawmakers, and communities of users can contribute to solving security concerns. The old, top-down model of information management is incompatible with the flat structure of the emerging ecosystem of ubiquitous computer power. Self-appointed 'white hackers' are an example of civic-minded coders and hackers who use their knowledge to keep their peers honest (Luckett and Casey 2016).

Designing and implementing the systems of laws, regulations, codes, standards, strategies, and policies that governments deploy to support science and innovation while mitigating dual-use threats require advanced understanding, not only of the technologies themselves but also of the behaviours and incentives that drive both positive and negative uses of these technologies.

Examples of Horizontal Governance Collaborations

Governments and regulators are increasingly recognizing the need for innovative partnerships with non-traditional communities to develop mechanisms for distributive safety and security. Many of the spaces where potentially dangerous activities are occurring are inaccessible to the government. Citizen assistance, in the form of unconventional access, expertise, and capacity, is required to discern legitimate threats from unfamiliar technologies. What these governance mechanisms have in common is that they all focus on breaking down siloes between governments, scientists, and communities of users, and that they recognize the centrality of incentivizing responsible individual and collective behaviours. They do not attempt to proscribe access to knowledge, but instead aim to create the incentives, such as peer recognition or access to markets, that will enable users to enjoy the benefits of science, while raising the social cost of cheating or defecting.

Government agencies can build bridges to form collaborative partnerships with the public. For instance, the US Special Operations Command reaches out to unconventional communities of hackers and makers via its J5 Future Plans and Strategies cell, the Donovan Group. Its innovation space, SOFWERX, enables the public and government entities to team up on problems and develop solutions to benefit national and international safety and security.[17] In interviews for this article in 2017, the Donovan Group described how it was maintaining ties with more than 400 private citizens who voluntarily identify innovations of interest, inform on smart technology policy and regulation, and collaborate to identify emerging threat technology reporting to pre-empt malicious or ignorant use that could lead to loss of life.[18] Over recent years, a growing number of governments have recognized the benefits of reciprocal public–government partnerships. Examples include Denmark's creation of a technology ambassador position (Gramer 2017) and Germany's engagement with the Chaos Computer Club (CCC), an association of hackers, which helps to educate and inform senior officials on recent evolutions in the digital space.[19]

The Federal Bureau of Investigation (FBI) also has a strong outreach programme, teaming with the biohacker community to ensure biosecurity and safe experimentation in public spaces, while still enabling revolutionary breakthroughs that can save lives (Wolinsky 2016).[20] The initiative is a solution incubator, providing policymakers with the subject-matter expertise critical to improving security. Policymakers gain a true understanding of technological capabilities and how best to address challenges. Innovators, by cooperating with the FBI, help protect the freedoms that their communities enjoy to experiment with science. The end result is a series of collaborative partnerships that have led to substantial improvements in biosecurity by identifying gaps and potential threats.

Research by US security experts highlights the value of the FBI outreach programme. Through such initiatives, policymakers and regulators gain access to valuable insights and subject-matter expertise necessary to create effective policy. DIYBio communities also benefit by understanding the government's safety and security concerns, and working internally to mitigate those concerns—this also means that DIYBio members can conduct their activities openly, without resorting to anonymizing technology as happened in the case of 3D weapons printing.[21] This, in turn, helps to prevent exploitation of their activities by threat-actors.[22]

Innovative bottom-up approaches to the challenges of dual-use technology also exist at the international level. The International Science and Technology Center and its sister organization, the Science and Technology Center in Ukraine, were set up at the initiative of the United States in the wake of the Cold War. Their initial objective was to prevent former Soviet weapons scientists from transferring their expertise to countries suspected of engaging in weapons proliferation and development by offering them research grants and the prospect of sustained employment in a civilian area of science.[23] Over the past decade, they have adapted their mandate and organizational set-up to reflect a shifting threat landscape, with the support of the United States, the European Union, and Canada, operating as forums for political and scientific cooperation (Limage 2017).[24]

The European Union Chemical, Biological, Radiological and Nuclear Risk Mitigation Centres of Excellence (EU CBRN CoE) is another initiative that was launched in response to the need to strengthen the institutional capacity of countries outside the EU to mitigate intentional, accidental, or natural CBRN risks. The initiative aims to strengthen regional security by increasing local ownership, local expertise, and long-term sustainability. The initiative is centred on a worldwide network of local experts and collaborating partners, avoiding traditional top-down approaches.[25]

These mechanisms approach the governance of dual-use technologies from a systems perspective, focusing not only on the actors or on the technologies but more broadly on the complex web of interactions between them. They encourage knowledge sharing and actively contribute to skills development, while helping users adopt safe practices that mitigate the risks inherent to dual-use and emergent technologies. By bridging the traditional siloes between communities, bringing scientists, lawmakers, and security agencies together, they also provide feedback loops that play a central function in helping legislators to better comprehend fast-evolving technologies and their applications.

None of these policy approaches assume that they are sufficient to address all the relevant security threats. They exist alongside more traditional security governance mechanisms discussed earlier in this chapter. But these bottom-up approaches make a critical and, as yet, not sufficiently developed contribution to building state and societal resilience to technologically driven threats.

More systematic research is needed to assess the impact and scalability of these approaches. Measuring the effectiveness of bottom-up policies and programmes can be an extremely difficult task because it requires measuring shifts in people's intentions, motivations, and beliefs. Other factors further complicate the task of building bottom-up local capacities, including political circumstances, the varying extent of high-level national support, readiness of intra- and inter-agency cooperation, the heterogenous nature of the partner countries, the amount of previous experience in the area of risk mitigation, and the extent to which the relevant structures are already in place.[26]

Ultimately, it is critical to engage with the private sector, communities of users and scientists, in order to foster a sense of collective responsibility. Although set up at different times, in different contexts, and for different reasons, what these horizontal governance mechanisms have in common is that they seem to offer valuable models of distributive resilience building that seek to harness people's altruistic motivations. While top-down governance generally seeks to increase the cost of defecting against the rule, bottom-up approaches seek to tap into people's motivation to act in a certain collectively beneficial way. Much could be learned from the research on self-organized virtual communities—for example, the effectiveness of reputation as an incentive mechanism.[27] These incentive mechanisms are similar to those that underpin programmes such as the FBI outreach to synthetic biology communities.

Dynamic security management requires breaking down policy siloes so that technologists understand the risks of their activities, and educating policymakers into the complexities of science. Bottom-up and multidisciplinary approaches to security may be some of the ways to introduce the necessary checks and balances in policymaking procedures.

Conclusion

The digital age has made science and innovation more accessible than at any point before in the history of humanity. This democratization of science, and the networked effects of collaborative research and innovation, have brought tremendous opportunities to solve some of humanity's most existential threats, from climate change to pandemics to resource constraints.

In part, because it was built with the explicit intent not to recognize borders, the Internet has contributed to a blurring of distinctions between what is domestic and what is international; between what states and what non-state actors are capable of doing; and between peaceful and hostile uses of knowledge and technology.

This blurring of distinctions, and the resulting increase in networked effects, did not start with the digital revolution. In a sense, it is the story of humanity: societies have become increasingly networked through trade and globalization since the dawn of humanity. But the digital age has put this on a different plane altogether, unleashing both risks and opportunities.

In the digital age, all technology is ultimately information that can be easily shared. From nuclear weapons to space rockets to molecular biology, all science and technology can ultimately be broken down into bits of computer code. Sharing information is what enables scientists and technologists to make astonishing discoveries, building on previous research and innovation. But connectivity is also what makes it ever more difficult to control who accesses lethal technology and for what purpose, at a time when it is becoming ever more difficult to define what is a dual-use technology.

Hostile nations, terrorist groups, and criminals of all creeds will always count in their ranks early adopters of new technologies who will know a good opportunity when they see one. Increasingly, anyone with a computer can access dual-use technology, and remotely conduct hostile or criminal attacks.

Technological innovation is as much a part of the solution as it is a contribution to the threat—provided lawmakers and all those involved in anticipating and responding to security threats understand how technology and human behaviours mutually influence each other. Traditional governance mechanisms designed to regulate the use of dual-use technology have growing limitations in an age when all technology can be reduced to bits of code. Governments alone cannot anticipate and prevent all threats emanating from nefarious uses of technology. They need more innovative governance models that help break the siloes between policymakers, the private sector, communities of users, law enforcement officials, and scientists.[28]

Acknowledgements

I am particularly indebted to Jennifer Snow and Christopher Zember for their insights, which helped shape this article. Any mistakes or misconceptions are mine.

Notes

1. World Health Organization, 'H5N1 Research Issues. Update 1: WHO Activities Following the 16–17 February 2012 Technical Consultation Meeting'. https://www.who.int/influenza/human_animal_interface/avian_influenza/h5n1_research/en/
2. 'New Zealand Launches into Space Race with 3-D Printed Rocket', *The Guardian*, 25 May 2017. https://www.theguardian.com/world/2017/may/25/new-zealand-launches-space-race-3d-printed-rocket; '3D Printer Developed for Drugs', *BBC News*, 17 April 2012: http://www.bbc.com/news/av/uk-scotland-17744314/3d-printer-developed-for-drugs
3. The American Association for the Advancement of Science in conjunction with the Association of American Universities, Association of Public and Land-grant Universities, and the Federal Bureau of Investigation, 4–5 May 2013. https://www.aau.edu/sites/default/files/AAU Files/Key Issues/Science %26 Security/AAAS-AAU-APLU-FBI-Report-On-International-Science-and-Security_2013.pdf
4. For sheer density of information storage, DNA could be orders of magnitude beyond silicon—perfect for long-term archiving. See Extance Andy. 2016. 'How DNA Could Store All the World's Data', *Nature* 537, September, corrected 2 September 2016. http://www.nature.com/news/how-dna-could-store-all-the-world-s-data-1.20496
5. These risks were extensively described in a letter by the US Council of Advisors on Science and Technology, addressed to President Obama in November 2016. https://

obamawhitehouse.archives.gov/sites/default/files/microsites/ostp/PCAST/pcast_biodefense_letter_report_final.pdf

6. http://www.businessinsider.com/bill-gates-op-ed-bio-terrorism-epidemic-world-threat-2017-2

7. EUROPOL 2017 Threat Assessment. https://www.europol.europa.eu/newsroom/news/crime-in-age-of-technology-europol's-serious-and-organised-crime-threat-assessment-2017

8. The Hill (blogsite). 2017. 'How Trump's Budget Makes Us All Vulnerable To Bioterrorism': http://thehill.com/blogs/pundits-blog/homeland-security/335813-how-the-trumps-budget-makes-us-all-vulnerable-to

9. The European Commission has recognized this by proposing a recast of the existing EU regulation on dual-use export controls. The objective is to strike a balance between ensuring a high level of security and adequate transparency, and maintaining the competitiveness of European companies and legitimate trade in dual-use items. See van der Meer, Adriaan, and Alberto Aspidi. 2017. *Security, Development and Governance: CBRN and Cyber in Africa*. New York: Springer International Publishing.

10. Garrett, 'Biology's Brave New World'. 38.

11. Ron Lehman, interview with the author, 2 June 2017. Ron Lehman is Counselor to the Director of Lawrence Livermore National Laboratory and Chair of the US Department of Defense Threat Reduction Advisory Committee (TRAC). Since 1996, he has been the Chairman of the Governing Board of the International Science and Technology Center (ISTC).

12. See European Union Global Strategy. 2016. *Shared Vision, Common Action: A Stronger Europe. A Global Strategy for the European Union's Foreign and Security Policy*, June. Brussels: European Union. http://eeas.europa.eu/archives/docs/top_stories/pdf/eugs_review_web.pdf

13. European Union External Action Service, 'A Strategic Approach to Resilience in the EU's External Action: Joint Communication to the European Parliament and the Council' (Brussels: SWD(2017) 226 final, 8 June 2017). https://eeas.europa.eu/sites/eeas/files/join_2017_21_f1_communication_from_commission_to_inst_en_v7_p1_916039.pdf

14. Office of the Director of National Intelligence, 'Paradox of Progress: the Future Summarized'. https://www.dni.gov/index.php/global-trends/the-future-summarized

15. For example, when a user asked Tay if the Holocaust happened, Tay replied: 'It was made up.' Tay also tweeted, 'Hitler was right.' See Smith, Jamal. 2016. 'Microsoft's AI chatbot "Tay" turned into a PR Disaster', 10 April, *Western Howl*. http://www.wou.edu/westernhowl/microsofts-ai-chatbot-tay-turned-pr-disaster/; Murgia, Madhumita. 2016. 'Microsoft's Racist Bot Shows We Must Teach AI to Play Nice and Police Themselves', The Telegraph. http://www.telegraph.co.uk/technology/2016/03/25/we-must-teach-ai-machines-to-play-nice-and-police-themselves/. Learning from this experience, Microsoft have since produced a new chatbot, Zo, available by invitation only: Woolaston, Victoria, 2016. 'Following the Failure of Tay, Microsoft is Back with New Chatbot Zo', *WIRED*, 6 December. http://www.wired.co.uk/article/microsoft-zo-ai-chatbot-tay

16. Examples of proposed methods to correct such biases include a methodology proposed by MIT researchers: Dizikes, Peter. 2017. 'Better Wisdom from Crowds', *MIT News*, 25 January. http://news.mit.edu/2017/algorithm-better-wisdom-crowds-0125

17. Sofwerx, Donovan Group. http://www.sofwerx.org/pdf-wrappers/donovan-group/

18. These relationships have proactively identified and stopped two cyberattacks against government systems, informed government and law enforcement on the evolution of threats

that drones can pose, and resulted in the recovery of stolen classified information. Interview with Major Jennifer Snow, Donovan Group Innovation Officer, USSOCOM, 4 June 2017.

19. According to its website, the CCC is 'Europe's largest association of hackers'. For over 30 years, it has provided 'information about technical and societal issues, such as surveillance, privacy, freedom of information, hacktivism, data security and many other interesting things around technology and hacking issues'. See https://www.ccc.de/en/home?page=6

20. 'Ed You "91": from Bio Sci to FBI', *UCI Magazine*, spring 2015). https://news.uci.edu/spring-2015/myportfolio/ed-you-91-from-bio-sci-to-fbi/

21. More systematic research is needed to assess their impact and scalability, a task that scientists from Stanford University involved in designing the safety and security policy of the iGEM competition—another example of synthetic do-it-yourself biology outreach programmes—have initiated. A 10 May 2017 interview with Dr Megan Palmer, Center for International Security and Cooperation (CISAC) at Stanford University; Dr. Palmer leads programmes in safety and responsible innovation for the international Genetically Engineered Machine (iGEM) competition.

22. Snow, *Entering the Matrix*.

23. 2002. Cooperative Science and Non-Proliferation: The ISTC/STCU experiment', *Strategic Comments* 8 (6): 1–2.

24. For a comprehensive review of US and Allies' strategic threat reduction programmes, see also the four-part study run by Bob Einhorn and Michelle Flournoy at CSIS in 2003: 'Protecting Against the Spread of Nuclear, Biological and Chemical Weapons'. https://www.csis.org/analysis/protecting-against-spread-nuclear-biological-and-chemical-weapons

25. European Union, CBRN Centres of Excellence. http://www.cbrn-coe.eu/

26. Ron Lehman, interview with the author, 2 June 2017.

27. A 2009 study argues that autonomy (the power to make one's own choice) and relatedness (authentic social connections with others) have been identified as important motivational factors. Self-image, self-efficiency, socialization, a sense of community, interest, fun, and emotional connections are all social incentive mechanisms used in open-source software communities. Meaningful feedback mechanisms have also been found to provide important incentives. The extent to which people identify with their community, supported by the establishment of norms of responsible behaviour, is another form of incentive mechanism. See Antoniadis, Panayotis, and Benedicte Le Grand. 2009. 'Self-Organised Virtual Communities: Bridging the Gap Between Web-Based Communities and P2P Systems', *International Journal of Web Based Communities* 5 (2). http://www.inderscience.com/offer.php?id=23964

28. This article was written before the COVID-19 pandemic. Events have since dramatically demonstrated the threats posed by pandemics, but also the benefits of global collaborative research and innovation in the digital age, and the extent to which security cannot rely only on government efforts.

References

Alba, Davey. 2015. 'FTC Warns of the Huge Security Risks in the Internet of Things', *WIRED*, 27 January. https://www.wired.com/2015/01/ftc-warns-huge-security-risks-internet-things/

Bajema, Natasha, and Diane DiEuliis. 2017. 'Peril and Promise: Emerging Technologies and WMD', Workshop Report, May. Washington, DC: National Defence University Press. https://wmdcenter.ndu.edu/Portals/97/Documents/Publications/Articles/2016%20Workshop%20Report%20FINAL%205-12-17.pdf?ver=2017-05-12-105811-853

Bryans, Danton. 2015. 'Unlocked and Loaded: Government Censorship of 3D-Printed Firearms and a Proposal for More Reasonable Regulation of 3D-Printed Goods', *Indiana Law Journal* 90 (2).

Cornish, Paul. 2007. *The CBRN System: Assessing the Threat of Terrorist Use of Chemical, Biological, Radiological and Nuclear Weapons in the United Kingdom*. London: Chatham House: https://www.researchgate.net/publication/242631947_The_CBRN_System_Assessing_the_Threat_of_Terrorist_Use_of_Chemical_Biological_Radiological_and_Nuclear_Weapons_in_the_United_Kingdom

Demchak, Chris. 2016. 'Uncivil and Post-Western Cyber Westphalia: Changing Interstate Power Relations of the Cybered Age', *Cyber Defense Review* 1 (1), spring: 1–74.

Farmer, Ben. 2017. 'Bioterrorism Could Kill More People Than Nuclear War', *Daily Telegraph*, 18 February. http://www.telegraph.co.uk/news/2017/02/17/biological-terrorism-could-kill-people-nuclear-attacks-bill/

Garrett, Laurie. 2013. 'Biology's Brave New World: The Promise and Perils of the Synbio Revolution', November/December, *Foreign Affairs* 92 (6): 28–46.

Grady, Denise, and William Broad. 2011. 'Seeing Terror Risk, U.S. Asks Journals to Cut Flu Study Facts', *The New York Times*, 20 December. http://www.nytimes.com/2011/12/21/health/fearing-terrorism-us-asks-journals-to-censor-articles-on-virus.html

Gramer, Robbie. 2017. 'Denmark Creates the World's First Ever Digital Ambassador', *Foreign Policy*, 27 January. http://foreignpolicy.com/2017/01/27/denmark-creates-the-worlds-first-ever-digital-ambassador-technology-europe-diplomacy/

Greenberg, Andy. 2014. 'How 3D Printed Guns Evolved into Serious Weapons in Just One Year', *WIRED*, 15 May. https://www.wired.com/2014/05/3d-printed-guns/

Kadtke, James, and Linton Wells. 2014. *Policy Challenges of Accelerating Technological Change: Security Policy and Strategy Implications of Parallel Scientific Revolutions*, September. Washington, DC: National Defence University Press. https://apps.dtic.mil/dtic/tr/fulltext/u2/a622058.pdf

Levitin, Daniel. 2014. *The Organised Mind: Thinking Straight in the Age of Information Overload*. New York: Penguin.

Limage, Simon. 2017. 'U.S. Nonproliferation Programs: Sustaining the Momentum', *Arms Control Today* 27 (4), May.

Luckett, Oliver, and Michael J. Casey. 2016. *The Social Organism*. London: Hachette Book.

Murphy, Sean, and Anthony Atala. 2014. '3D Bioprinting of Tissues and Organs', *Nature Biotechnology* 32 (8), August: 773–85.

Schwab, Klaus. 2016. *The Fourth Industrial Revolution*. Geneva: World Economic Forum. https://www.weforum.org/about/the-fourth-industrial-revolution-by-klaus-schwab

Snow, Jennifer. 2015. *Entering the Matrix: The Challenge of Regulating Radical Leveling Technologies*, Monterey, CA: Naval Postgraduate School. https://calhoun.nps.edu/bit-stream/handle/10945/47874/15Dec_Snow_Jennifer.pdf?sequence=1&isAllowed=y

Wadhwa, Vivek, and Salkever, Alex. 2017. *The Driver in the Driverless Car: How Technology Choices Will Create the Future*. Oakland, CA: Berrett-Koehler Publishers.

Wildavsky, Aaron. 1988. *Searching for Safety*. New Jersey: Transaction Publishers.

Wolinsky, Howard. 2016. 'The FBI and Biohackers: An Unusual Relationship', *EMBO Reports*. http://embor.embopress.org/content/early/2016/04/22/embr.201642483

Zember, Christopher. 2016. 'The Democratization of Science Ushers in a New World Order', 13 April, War on the Rocks. https://warontherocks.com/2016/04/the-democratization-of-science-ushers-in-a-new-world-order

Zolli, Andrew, and Ann Marie Healy, 2012. *Resilience: Why Things Bounce Back*. New York: Free Press.

CHAPTER 43

MATURING AUTONOMOUS CYBER WEAPONS SYSTEMS: IMPLICATIONS FOR INTERNATIONAL CYBERSECURITY

CAITRÍONA HEINL

THIS chapter identifies significant policy and military intersections between the evolving cybersecurity and autonomous weapons systems (AWS) policy regimes that should receive deeper policy attention over the near term. So far, within policy discussions on lethal autonomous weapons systems (LAWS), there seems to have been less focus on related cyber implications compared with other policy questions. This is mirrored within the international cybersecurity policy community where AWS, maturing autonomous cyber technologies, and component technologies like artificial intelligence (AI), have not yet garnered extensive attention publicly. Nevertheless, threat assessment reports and analysts are beginning to highlight this subject more frequently.[1] The United Nations Institute for Disarmament Research (UNIDIR), which has driven a significant level of analysis in both the cyber and AWS fields in recent years, describes the current situation such that, to date, these are 'distinct conversations, held in different fora and involving different experts', even though there may be both intended and unintended ways in which these weapons will interact (UNIDIR 2015).

Thus, while there are clear linkages between the emerging AWS and cyber regimes, policy frameworks are being discussed separately by policymakers. So far, most of the focus on AWS has centred on physical platforms for land, sea, air, space, and undersea, and not the cyber domain. Discussions surrounding AWS have generally been held under the rubric of the Convention on Conventional Weapons (CCW). The first meeting was held in May 2014 to discuss challenges, including meaningful human control over targeting decisions and the use of violent force. At a side event at the UN General Assembly in 2015, analysts explored whether the areas of AWS and cyber should be treated separately or in the same category during presentations on how cyber norms do, or do not, fit within the debates on AWS.[2]

While country positions are still evolving, the fifth LAWS review conference in December 2016 agreed to establish a Group of Governmental Experts (GGE) of the High Contracting Parties to the Convention on Prohibitions or Restrictions on the Use of Certain Conventional Weapons Which May be Deemed to Be Excessively Injurious or to Have Indiscriminate Effects. The first GGE meeting in November 2017 aimed to conduct a thorough review of the field and to examine issues related to emerging technologies in the LAWS area under three broad themes, namely: 1) The state of developments in the technology domain. 2) Military implications. and 3) Legal and ethical considerations. While the questions proffered by the Chair in advance of discussions were not exhaustive and certain policy questions were kept aside for the time being, it was noticeable that this list of questions did not include the interactions between the cyber and emerging AWS regimes. This chapter provides a framework to address the gap that requires the international cyber and AWS policy communities to deal with the impact of increasing autonomy in cyber weapons.

There has been much debate recently on increasing autonomous technologies (IATs), especially surrounding LAWS. Many concerns over international law have been raised relating to the key elements of LAWS that include the capacity, once activated, to select and engage a target without human intervention (in other words, decisions to use force and weapons release). The main focus so far has been on weapons review when developing these systems and whether they comply with existing international law (international humanitarian law [IHL], human rights law, jus ad bellum, and the possible gaps in responsibility and accountability). Numerous positions have been delineated by parties within these debates, including public campaigns from non-governmental organizations like the Campaign to Stop Killer Robots and Human Rights Watch to ban the development, sale, and use of these technologies. The International Committee of the Red Cross (ICRC) argues that the idea of a weapons system that places the use of force beyond human control causes deep discomfort, and thus discussions should focus on determining the type and degree of human control needed to ensure IHL-compliance and ethical acceptability (England 2016, 2). Yet, even if such weapons can be made IHL-compliant, one question is whether people are willing to surrender to machines the task of making life and death decisions.[3] In the field of cyber, however, the majority of public concern has previously centred on surveillance matters following the Snowden disclosures in recent years, rather than on the use of such autonomous cyber capabilities.

Conceptually, some argue that code has not been personified compared with physical LAWS and autonomous robotics (also known as 'killer robots'), which are sometimes described as 'moral agents' where the 'the weapon becomes the warrior'.[4] This may then explain the higher levels of pushback related to autonomous robotics vis-à-vis cyber systems from the public in the past.[5] It seems that cyber has sometimes taken on a sense of the intangible and, even though it has physical roots and it is within systems, it is not talked about in the same manner as the regulation of robots for instance.[6] In addition, advanced cyber systems are considered attractive in the cyber field for enhanced defence and resilience. An interesting explanation about this treatment of information as 'disembodied' is provided by George Zarkadakis. He clarifies that when Norbert Weiner published *Cybernetics* in 1948, he chose to deal with information theory as having an 'immaterial aura'—in other words, that bits are not real and that information describes non-physical objects (Zarkadakis 2015, 151–2). However, although telecommunications is still based on physics, not metaphysics, it is often now considered near fact that information exists on its own and independently of physical objects.[7] This may help to understand how disconnects have arisen in public discussions of LAWS and autonomous cyber systems. Nonetheless, concepts such as a so-called borderless cyberspace and an Internet that is a global commons were debunked as far back as 2013 when it was agreed that these ideas were causing confusion and impeding negotiation in the UN GGE on Developments in the Field of Information and Telecommunications in the Context of International Security (CSIS and UNIDIR, 2016, 6). It is now generally accepted that the Internet has borders and depends on physical infrastructure subject to sovereign control.[8]

Understanding Autonomous Weapons Systems: Software Components Allow the Physical Systems to Become Increasingly Autonomous

This chapter builds on previous analyses that identify this link (and policy gap) between the two fields (Heinl 2015, Part 1, 12). It does so to raise even deeper awareness of potential technological and policy overlap for government coordinating bodies, international security policy teams responsible for cyber, and experts in future technologies or advanced weapons directorates. It seeks to explore a similar question to that later posed by UNIDIR in April 2016—how do AWS intersect with cyber operations? (Vignard 2016, 4) This is an important question because the concern is that there is a gap in the understanding of many policymakers over learning systems and cyber—autonomous weapons are not necessarily limited to conventional weapons.[9] Apparently, there is still an element of confusion among diplomats about the nature of AWS (New America 2016; Roff 2015). In short, '[A]t one point States will need to ask whether the concerns we have about the weaponization of increasingly autonomous technologies are also applicable to increasingly intangible technologies, such as cyber operations, particularly if these can have kinetic effects.'[10]

These technologies are maturing, becoming increasingly capable of independence from human control, with complexity that surpasses human understanding. In other words, there is a spectrum of technologies that could end up ranging from advanced automation to advanced autonomy to full autonomy. Although this chapter does not specifically determine how autonomy should be defined, it observes that these terms are sometimes used interchangeably. This means that discussions are becoming increasingly confused between parties. It would therefore be best if these terms were not used in this manner. While there is no existing international agreed definition for AWS, most accepted definitions seem to include the notion of a weapons system that can independently select and attack targets.[11] Several efforts to provide definitions for the different degrees, such as objects controlled by human operators to automated systems to fully autonomous systems, are already provided by, for example, the United States, the United Kingdom and the informal meetings of experts under the CCW.[12] The United States and United Kingdom are the only two countries so far to have created publicly available policies on these weapons (Roff and Singer 2016). Such definitions can inform our understanding of the differences among these technologies more accurately and should be used in order to ensure clarity among parties. However, too much focus on definitions should not impede the crux of this particular recommendation for enabling concrete discussion.

There has been much confusion about whether AWS include autonomous cyber weapons systems, or whether cyber systems can encompass weapons systems and platforms, including autonomous weapons systems. In other words, cyber systems could be an autonomous weapon in so far as they could act without human authorization with a range of autonomy from 'fully autonomous' to 'highly automated while under human command'. Although the 2012 US Department of Defense (DoD) Directive excludes cyber from its coverage (insofar as the Directive does not apply to autonomous or semi-autonomous cyberspace systems for cyberspace operations), this seems to be merely a working arrangement rather than a definitive decision concerning the relationship between cyber and AWS. However, if the understanding of 'cyber' (as defined under a recent US DoD Defense Science Board Study) is applied by way of example, the term 'cyber' can be:

> broadly used to address all digital automation used by the Department and its industrial base. This includes weapons systems and their platforms; command, control and communications systems; intelligence, surveillance, and reconnaissance systems; logistics and human resource systems; and mobile as well as fixed-infrastructure systems. 'Cyber' applies to but is not limited to 'IT' and the 'backbone network', and it includes any software or applications resident on or operating within any DoD system environment' (US Defense Science Board, 19).

In other words, given that cyber encompasses weapons systems and their platforms, this most likely means that 'cyber' could include AWS too. Lin similarly notes that, in the United States, cyber is specifically excluded from the framework policy on AWS under the DoD Directive. This is apparently not because it should be treated as a different subject but because it is too difficult to deal with.[13] He, too, points to the need for policy guidance on this question and the gap between the cyber weapons and autonomous weapons debates, finding that autonomous cyber systems seem to be in the same category of weapons as autonomous robotics, in which case they should be within the same conversations.[14] However, this is not the case and cyber is hardly mentioned in the debate on AWS.[15] Heather Roff similarly argues that, although AWS have only generally been defined to include robotic weapons, definitions on the table so far do not necessarily preclude autonomous cyber weapons.[16]

However, the 2012 Directive had a five-year time limit meaning that it would either lapse, be amended, or be renewed by 2018.[17] It still remains to be seen whether the exclusion of cyberspace systems for cyber operations will be revisited, particularly since it has caused some confusion, and whether this policy gap can be resolved. This is still an area of law that remains unsettled.[18]

In short, autonomous intelligent agents can simply be software operating in cyberspace—in other words, computational agents. Such autonomous intelligent agents can also be integrated into physical systems—in other words, robotic agents, where they underpin robot behaviour and capabilities (Guarino [date]). What this means is that AI is a common component in both computational and physical robotic systems—both are AI-enabled. This chapter does not enter the debates on whether such AI or advanced autonomous technologies could pose an existential threat to humanity. Rather, its aim is to identify policy gaps that should be addressed in the near term by the international policy community.

Arms Race Considerations: Consequences of the Widespread Adoption of Autonomous Technologies for Warfare

The way in which these technologies will mature is not wholly clear currently. There is considerable uncertainty as well as disagreement on the time frame, particularly for fully autonomous technologies. There already seem to be simple forms of autonomous weapons today, albeit defensive and 'generally limited to systems that are supervised by humans that protect vehicles and military bases from attacks' (CNAS 2016; Scharre, Horowitz, and Sayler 2015). Some systems are being deployed in offensive roles such as certain missiles and loitering munitions, and it is argued that Stuxnet was an autonomous weapon on account of its capabilities to learn and adapt.[19] The component technologies of these systems are not at the same stage of development, however, and AI is infamous for both periods of little progress as well as periods of heightened attention. In fact, some political scientists currently warn that innovation is slowing down and future trends may comprise the use of low tech threats such as hybrid and information operations to overthrow adversaries rather than the use of such high tech—they too caution about the current level of hyperbole, including the now infamous warnings within the 2015 open letter from AI and robotics researchers.[20]

While the last two to three years might have been characterized, yet again, by exaggerated accounts of the possibilities of AI, the current debate appears to have become more settled and more serious. First, current analyses of AI observe that it seems to be developing notably fast. Second, while states are driving this period of interest in AI, the private sector is more engaged than in the past. For both economic and military purposes, states are seriously engaged in what some may describe as an 'AI arms race' by investing in capabilities for autonomous systems in both physical and cyber systems. AI is even becoming 'indispensable to militaries, intelligence agencies, and the surveillance apparatus in authoritarian states' (Ford 2015, 232). In addition, the private sector is investing highly in AI, machine learning, big data, computing power, and cloud technologies. Technologists explain that the current phase of intense interest in AI is certainly different from the past. This is because private sector investment is much higher and more competitive than in previous years (with much of the progress being made by companies like Google, Facebook, and Amazon).[21] Research may also then become less reliant on government funding, which may sometimes wane during periods of declining policy or strategic interest or intensifying budgetary constraints.

In terms of higher investments in cyber technologies, automated computer network defence may also enhance cybersecurity (ODNI, 1). Advanced autonomy is already attractive in the field of cyber and it is becoming even more appealing for reasons that include enhanced decision support and decision making; incident response; and intelligence gathering, as well as resilience, defence, and security. It is thus likely that there will be more pressure for maturing autonomy in software for cyber defence. This is where much progress will most probably be seen (which in turn means that there could be implications for offensive operations). An example of the nature of this trend is visible in the recent headlines about the DARPA Cyber Grand Challenge where autonomy was used for cybersecurity in order to increase speed, reduce response times, and, more notably, reduce human involvement.

While this is a notable public breakthrough, the field of cybersecurity has been moving in this direction for years. Where experts are concerned about the deployment of autonomous technologies leading to LAWS through mission creep, the quest for high automation and advanced autonomy for cyber purposes may be one of those avenues.

If such an 'AI arms race' is truly underway, what do developments in autonomous cyber and physical systems mean for international stability? Are those countries, which are most advanced in terms of cyber capabilities, the same leaders in developing AWS capabilities? Moreover, is it clear that these countries follow similar policy positions on these technologies in the different forums that consider cyber and AWS (and whether this is intentional or un-intentional)? For example, when a country like China argues against the development of offensive cyber capabilities, would there be a contradiction if the government does not intend to halt the development of LAWS?[22] These weapons systems may require similar underpinning software as that required for offensive autonomous cyber capabilities.

The United States, China, Israel, Russia, South Korea, and the United Kingdom are generally perceived as leaders in IATs. China is known to have a strong long-term strategic interest in developing such technologies for economic and military purposes. For middle powers, how will these developments affect their thinking on IATs, or how will these countries' development or acquisition of such capabilities affect regional or global stability? The need to further examine how the proliferation of IATs might alter regional security dynamics was identified in 2014.[23] There is little question that there is interest in these technologies from smaller or medium powers. Approximately 30 states already operate human-supervised AWS to defend bases or vehicles against attacks.[24] However, while some states have expressed interest in greater autonomy (even as far as fully autonomous weapons), others assert that they have no such intentions.[25] It does not seem clear how this will have an impact on future international stability.

The US Office of the Director of National Intelligence (ODNI) Worldwide Threat Assessment report for 2016 claimed that, although the United States leads in AI research, foreign state research in AI is increasing and advances are being made in foreign weapons and intelligence systems.[26] There is thus a risk of instability arising from the use of such advanced cyber technologies that may be used for either state espionage or to prepare the battleground for future operations. Smaller countries with lower population figures, low birth rates, and an ageing society, such as Singapore, or larger countries with ageing demographics, such as Japan, may find such technologies appealing. States may find such technologies even more attractive if they are perceived to be less expensive to develop or acquire, relative to conventional weapons.[27] Israeli analysts argue, for example, that the nation has an interest in promoting local and international mechanisms that will give legitimacy to the use of autonomous capabilities in weapon systems within the framework of the ethical restrictions to which Israel is committed (Siboni and Eshpar 2014, 77). However, ethical restrictions may differ across jurisdictions, and they are far from globally aligned. How then can machine values be aligned (even when international bodies like the Institute of Electrical and Electronics Engineers (IEEE) may help to develop codes of conduct and value systems to set limits similar to those established in the field of bio-engineering)? Some scientists argue that the debate on ethics is not helpful whereas focusing on simulation and testing is more valuable (Roff 2015).

Developing countries, such as India, may be careful for economic reasons when selecting maturing technologies given their possible impact on jobs and the already high levels of unrest in youth that could exacerbate security problems like terrorism.[28] This signals how some developing countries might view these advances and even resist such evolving technologies, but requires further analysis.

It is not yet clear, however, whether (and, if so, how) growing interest in IATs would alter regional balances of power. In the field of cyber, for example, even though smaller or medium-sized states may be interested in developing or obtaining such technologies, this may not necessarily change current balances of power. More powerful actors sometimes argue that, although other state (or non-state) actors may make the situation more complex for larger powers because there are more actors and it is hard to defend fully against these types of cyber incidents, this situation has not necessarily led to any shift in the balances of power. There is much public analysis of these scenarios, which may contain lessons on how growing interest in IATs could affect balances of power (if at all).

For all these reasons, this is a subject that deserves more serious attention from a policy standpoint. Although numerous benefits and risks from either military or economic perspectives are often cited (for example, reduced risk to military lives), there is a need for better evidence-based analysis to validate such projections in order to inform these discussions more concretely. In fact, the US White House Office of Science and Technology Policy announced a number of workshops in 2016 on AI and machine learning in order to consider the benefits and risks associated with this technology for a public report (Legendre 2016). A new National Science and Technology Council Subcommittee on Machine Learning and AI has also been established to monitor milestones and coordinate federal activity in this field.[29] This is one example of a positive development that may equally inform the international community with some of its findings.

UNIDIR argued at the 2016 CCW informal LAWS meeting that, while many states affirm that autonomy discussions in CCW are not about existing systems, there are highly autonomous components or features of existing systems that may present new concerns— particularly if these components are combined in certain ways in the future but are not currently problematic.[30] In other words, the statement argues that this should be a near-term concern, and thus recommends an exchange between states on how these features might combine.[31] In international security cyber discussions too, states are trying to develop a framework to prevent a crisis should a situation arise in future, but this means that it could be difficult to find agreement without a crisis that acts as a 'forcing function'.[32] Thus, while numerous studies identify the possible advantages and disadvantages that could arise with the development over the near to long term of such autonomous systems (Table 43.1) outlines a non-exhaustive list of these hypotheses), deeper evidence-based analyses should be conducted to test the validity of these projections more systematically, including how they might influence adoption globally for warfare.

In conducting such analyses, there may be additional value in applying lessons learned so far within each field in order to test these hypotheses. In particular, there is much analysis to draw on from the field of cyber that might shed light for future AWS analyses, including potential impact on regional and international stability. For example, it might be valuable to assess how public-private cooperation has been improved in the cyber field (this has been a significant departure compared with other policy domains in the past), or how policy responses have developed to deal with the possibly destabilizing effects caused by the speed with which these technologies can be used.

Table 43.1 Examples of arguments for possible military or economic advantages and disadvantages of advanced automation/maturing autonomous physical and cyber systems that require validation[a]

Possible Advantages	Possible Disadvantages
There may be a reduced risk to soldiers (but it is uncertain if risk is raised for civilians). LAWS may be more precise and discriminate than humans, and so reduce casualties.	Vulnerability of LAWS to cyber attacks.
LAWS may conduct tasks that are physically limiting for humans.	Lack of predictability. Autonomous systems may be unpredictable if operating in unknown and uncertain environments.
There may be a force projection/force multiplier effect.	It is not certain how LAWS would adapt to complex environments.
Humans may be freed from repetitive tasks.	Rather than political negotiations, it could be considered easier to choose a military option if it is perceived that there is less risk to soldiers' lives.
LAWS may offer better endurance.	If there is a need for strong policy and legal safeguards to curb dangerous developments and harness benefits, how realistic is this approach?
High precision.	How will LAWS impact global stability? For example, how will deterrence strategies be affected? How will the speed and range of LAWS affect defence strategies?
Faster information processing.	
Direct targeting.	
Could possibly respect international humanitarian law and human rights law better than humans.	How will militaries deal with strategic surprise where such technologies may emanate from the private sector? Similarly, government-funded programmes could produce surprise.
Fast deployment.	Impact of dual-use technologies where civilian technology can be adapted.
Fast response mechanisms (especially if humans are not in the decision loop).	Challenges of public-private sector collaboration.
Could end up reducing the cost of conflict (even where, strategically, it can currently cost more when conflict is not prevented).	Impact on jobs.
There may be lower labour and financial costs such as lower army maintenance costs (although development may still be very expensive).	LAWS could cause a derogation of moral responsibility for killing so that they are used more often. However, most experts are currently arguing that human responsibility cannot be transferred to a machine.
May alleviate a labour crunch where many experts are needed with the right skills.	Instability if a system automatically reacts to false positive data when it should not respond.
May alleviate demographic challenges.	

Table 43.1 Continued

Possible Advantages	Possible Disadvantages
May alleviate burnout (although if they are human-supervised, then human operators are still needed).	
May be perceived to have value if one is limited by conventional strength.	
It is uncertain whether they may cause less collateral damage and less harm to civilians.	
There may be unexpected benefits for peaceful use.	
Possible economic growth and innovation in fields such as medical health and transport.	
LAWS can act with greater speed.	
There could be cases where LAWS could behave more lawfully than a human placed within a stressful environment. Where the environment is known, autonomous systems should follow programming and may be more precise and predictable than humans by following programmed instructions for lawful conduct. With adapting and learning techniques, they could perhaps learn to discern what is lawful or unlawful conduct. However, this raises a question about the ethical acceptability of such systems making decisions such as life and death target decisions. There is an additional concern that these systems could behave differently to instructions.	
If programmed to act in line with international humanitarian law, LAWS might lead to less killing.	

[a] For advantages, see Antebi, Liran. 2013. 'Who Will Stop the Robots?', Military and Strategic Affairs 5 (2): September: 63; UNIDIR. 2014. 'Framing Discussions on Weaponization of Increasingly Autonomous Technologies', March, p. 6; Heyns, Christof. 2013. Special Rapporteur on Extrajudicial, Summary or Arbitrary Executions. 'Lethal Autonomous Robotics', UNIDIR Conference, 23 May; Scharre, Paul, Michael C. Horowitz, and Kelley Sayler. 2015. 'Autonomous Weapons at the UN: A Primer for Delegates', April. Washington, DC: Center for a New American Security (CNAS), p. 3. For disadvantages, see: Chairperson of the Meeting of Experts. 2014. 'Report of the 2014 Informal Meeting of Experts on Lethal Autonomous Weapons Systems (LAWS)', 16 May, p. 5. Geneva: UNIDIR; Siboni, Gabi, and Yoni Eshpar. 2014. 'Dilemmas in the Use of Autonomous Weapons', Strategic Assessment 16 (4), January: 84; Work, Robert, and Shawn Brimley. 2014. '20YY: Preparing for War in the Robotic Age', January, p. 6. Washington DC: Center for a New American Security (CNAS); Scharre, Horowitz, and Sayler, 'Autonomous Weapons', 3; Scharre, Paul. 2016. 'Flash War: Autonomous Weapons and Strategic Stability', Presentation Slides, UNIDIR Conference: Understanding Different Types of Risks, 11 April: http://www.unidir.ch/files/conferences/pdfs/-en-1-1113.pdf

Notably, the first AWS GGE in November 2017 was open to non-state parties, non-governmental parties, and international organizations from the outset because it fell under the umbrella of the CCW. This was markedly different from the cyber GGEs under the UN's first committee (disarmament and international security), which only comprised governmental experts. This may mean that negotiations could have evolved in a different manner.

A Framework to Deal with the Impact of Autonomy on International Security Policies

Strengthen Technical Safeguards and Develop Safely

At this juncture, it does not seem to be certain from a technical standpoint that humans are able to supervise or control autonomous cyber systems; and, if they are, that they will always be able to do so. A thorough verification of safety and behaviours is apparently difficult. The levels of complexity, which humans can understand, were passed years ago.[33] In fact, the organizers of one of the workshops on safety and control for AI for the White House public report explain that many technical leaders think that the main limits on deriving benefits from AI are in the confidence in the safety of these 'smart systems'.[34] Some AI experts even argue that ensuring safety and control is more important to the future of AI than improving AI algorithms (Carnegie Mellon University 2016). The reason this is considered such a challenge is the complexity of AI systems and their interactions with human users and operating environments (and this challenge increases when AI systems are adapting and changing their behaviour through machine learning or when interacting in complex ways with other AI systems that are developed separately and learning or adapting too).[35] UNIDIR's statement before the LAWS CCW informal meeting of experts in 2016 drew attention to this challenge for the policy community by arguing that increasingly autonomous systems working in concert with other increasingly autonomous systems might narrow the scope for human control by their sheer interactivity.[36]

More recently, at the 2016 NATO Cooperative Cyber Defence Centre of Excellence (NATO CCD COE) Conference on Cyber Conflict, it was emphasized that the AI development community must speak with AI safety experts in order to avoid unpreparedness in future (Tallinn 2016). Table 43.2 identifies, from a technical perspective, a number of such possible risks that may arise from an excess of autonomy in cyber systems.

If these are plausible technical risks attached to cyber systems, it is likely that they might also be applicable to some extent to the capabilities underpinning physical AWS platforms. The technical safeguards and guidance issued by the 2012 US DoD Directive applies to LAWS (both hardware and software).[37] However, it is still not clear whether this Directive applies to fully autonomous/semi-autonomous or human-supervised cyberspace operations because cyber seems to be excluded. A policy gap related to autonomous cyber capabilities seems to remain because the US DoD guidance excludes cyber. Nevertheless, it seems that part of this guidance could be used because there are similarities between its recommended safeguards and some advice already within the scientific community for increasingly autonomous

Table 43.2 Several technical risks associated with maturing autonomy in cyber systems[a]

IATs could negotiate amongst each other and cooperate in a complex way to achieve the goals of a human commander. However, in this example, strict human control of each single agent behaviour then becomes weaker.

Impossible to verify the outcome for all situations.

Unwanted coalitions may arise because communication is only partially visible to human controllers and could be difficult to disable.

The more intelligent software becomes, the harder it might be to control its actions.

Complexity of behaviour.

Misunderstanding situations or misinterpretation of commands.

Loss of contact.

Unintentionally behaving in a harmful way.

Unexpected actions or unpredictable behaviour.

The complexity of controlling multiple autonomous systems and interpreting information might become overwhelming for human operators.

While current government policy in some countries may guarantee that the operation of systems will always be under human control, it does not seem certain from a technical standpoint that the human might always be in a position to control such systems. In other words, is it certain that such government assurances will be able to hold in future where these component technologies continue to evolve?

[a] Tyugu; Guarino; Heinl, Caitriona. 2015. 'National Security Implications of Increasingly Autonomous Technologies (Part 1): Defining Autonomy, Military and Cyber-related Implications', S. Rajaratnam School of International Studies, Policy Report, February, p. 14.

cyber technologies.[38] For this reason, it may be worth examining where the differences actually arise between such autonomous cyber systems and AWS from a technical standpoint in order to provide tailored guidance. Although this Directive had a five-year time limit, if the goal was to minimize the probability of failures, then these guidelines did at least provide a publicly available framework for physical platforms that could be consulted as good practice across the international community.

Furthermore, while the US DoD approach ensures that safeguards should be in place, it also assures the public that such safeguards are being incorporated and LAWS are not being developed. Although this guidance can be reviewed when necessary, it clarifies the position of the United States. This should further enhance transparency and confidence among states (as does the public issuance of the United Kingdom's policy on AWS).

Even though the governments of the United States and United Kingdom are willing to allow this research to go ahead where the limit is fully autonomous weapons that do not have appropriate human control, it is slightly disconcerting that there is still a sense of discord among the technical community over how, or whether, these technologies should evolve at all. Traditionally, the science and technology community push the boundaries of their fields in the name of scientific advancement, whereas there seems to be some unease among scientists in this instance.[39] The open letter signed by leading AI scientists has a particularly strong message for the international community: 'for the future of humanity a preventive prohibition of offensive lethal autonomous technologies that are out of human meaningful control should be put in place now' (Future of Life Institute 2015). These weapons are described as the 'third revolution in warfare' and, according to this open letter, a military arms race in AI must not be permitted.[40]

A Policy Framework

General Implications for International Cyber Stability

Increasing autonomy has significant implications for policies in the cyber field that need to be addressed more systematically and comprehensively—and more immediately. Rather than focusing on technologies or projections 30 years out, there are several matters relating to maturing autonomy that the international cyber policy community should consider over the near term.

A key concern should be that maturing autonomy *complicates* current analyses and international discussions on cyber capabilities within the policy community. This does not seem to be an insurmountable challenge but it does confound the issues described later. Thus, it could be valuable to incorporate the potential impact of autonomy into current thinking and analyses:

a) The already challenging problems associated with attribution, such as determining intent, may be exacerbated.

b) A key argument surrounding LAWS is the responsibility and accountability gap in relation to states, commanders, software developers and manufacturers if an agent exceeds tasks and makes unforeseen decisions.[41] This may also be a policy gap to be bridged regarding future autonomy in cyber systems, particularly as it has been argued in the cyber field that technology is neutral. These questions need to be examined by both the cyber and AWS policy communities, including the applicability of legal analysis contained within the non-binding Tallinn Manual. The 2015 US DoD Law of War Manual specifically notes though that 'only persons and not weapons can be held to the law of war obligations of distinction and proportionality regardless of how autonomous the weapons may be' (the 2012 DoD Directive is cited as a source on DoD policy).[42] The International Committee of the Red Cross (ICRC) similarly posits that parties to a conflict are responsible and such responsibility cannot be transferred to a machine.[43] In other words, technology remains neutral under international law. However, this technology will be value loaded rather than value neutral, depending upon the data.[44] This issues are still being debated by state parties and the Chairperson's 'food-for-thought' paper for the first AWS GGE meeting asks whether international humanitarian law developed for human and state-controlled behaviour could continue to apply *mutatis mutandis* to potentially autonomous machines and through which mediatory mechanisms? (Chairperson 2017, 3).

c) The increasing reliance on AI for autonomous decision making is increasing the number of new vulnerabilities to cyberattacks.[45] This is also exacerbating those difficulties already associated with attribution. The 2016 ODNI Worldwide Threat Assessment report explains that such increased use of AI means 'increased vulnerability to cyberattack, difficulty in ascertaining attribution, facilitation of advances in foreign weapon and intelligence systems, the risk of accidents and related liability issues, and unemployment'.[46] Moreover, there is a risk that AI systems are susceptible to tactics that are not necessarily easy to predict, and the compromising of automated systems may allow for disruption to critical infrastructure or national security networks.[47]

In the case of maturing autonomous technologies, in some quarters, these are expected to replace remotely piloted air and ground vehicles in the domains of air, sea, undersea, land, and space (Work and Brimley 2014, 6). As a result, the vulnerability of their underlying systems to cyberattack is particularly significant because it may become more difficult to protect these systems. Such technologies could be taken over so that cyber may become the 'high ground'.[48] In other words, the purpose of winning 'cyber supremacy' over an opponent could be to ensure that these physical platforms or systems could be shut down or controlled.[49] Thus, a key question is whether increasing autonomy could drive the development of cyber weapons in order to exploit the vulnerability of AWS.[50]

Information might even be intercepted, or possibly manipulated. A plethora of information assurance issues may then arise too, such as how to be certain of the integrity of data. In situations where decisions are increasingly informed by advanced computer systems, it is essential that the information presented is accurate. There is a growing concern within the cyber community currently over the danger associated with data manipulation. The fear is that it will become increasingly difficult to guarantee the accuracy and reliability of data. This might mean that decision making will be affected, that trust in systems may decline, or that there may even be adverse physical effects.[51]

While AWS (both physical platforms and cyber systems) are vulnerable to cyber operations, at face value this may seem no different from other fields or technologies. However, there is a difference insofar as there could be a case for limits on these technologies if the consequences of AWS and a cyber operation on such a system(s) are not yet fully understood. The ICRC similarly argues that a key concern about the interaction between cyber operations and AWS is how to maintain human control with the possibility of cyberattack—in other words, these systems may be manipulated, which is why there may be good cause for limits to autonomy.[52] This means that technical safeguards are extremely important. Experts note the challenge in ensuring against reliability and vulnerability problems in autonomous weapons software, 'cautioning that failure could lead to unintended fatalities'—false or missing software requirements, incorrect algorithms or code, insufficient testing, incorrect or unexpected use of software, and possible vulnerabilities to cyberattacks could expose systems to risk.[53]

Lastly, analysis should be conducted on how to proceed so that the beneficial aspects of these technologies for the economy and future innovation are not disproportionately suppressed.

d) Arms control and counter proliferation are currently high on the international agenda in the cyber field. Accordingly, it might be necessary to examine how development in autonomy in the cyber field could affect arms control and proliferation policy. Equally, as a 2015 CNAS report outlines, LAWS discussions have mainly only focused on the effect LAWS would have in the conduct of war and humanitarian concerns, but there are important considerations for proliferation and crisis stability.[54] The report suggests that these effects may vary for different types of LAWS, and so a more detailed examination is recommended, perhaps in the form of a working group.[55] One such international working group could examine the unique implications of increasingly autonomous cyber technologies on issues such as international stability, and challenges associated with their dual-use nature, the difficulties of verification of software, and export control for potentially ubiquitous technologies.

For example, there may be significant overlap in terms of common components or software falling under arms control and proliferation restrictions. If governments are to examine how to manage the proliferation of dual-use and offensive cyber technologies, then how might this affect the field of AWS (and vice versa)? Issues common to both fields include challenges arising from dual-use technologies, as well as the ways in which weapon range and targeting speed might affect crisis stability (especially when traditional response mechanisms might be challenged). These tools may be deployed very quickly and can react in a short space of time, particularly if humans are not in the decision loop.[56] This could have a destabilizing effect. Moreover, it is also not clear how maturing autonomy, in both cyber and physical systems, might affect state-on-state, low-intensity conflict or so-called 'hybrid' warfare. One area where competing powers might share an interest could be in ensuring that these technologies are not allowed to fall into the hands of terrorist or criminal actors.

Ensuring Norm Coherence: Implications Arising from Either Banning or Legitimizing Maturing Autonomous Capabilities for International Cybersecurity and Autonomous Weapons Systems Regimes

The ICRC worries that with AWS and the wider cybersecurity debate, there is little practical experience of the effects of some of the new weapons under discussion.[57] As a result, while not advocating rewriting existing law, experts argue that there should still be an urgency to build the right guidance and frameworks before deploying such technology.[58] Some countries are already seeking mechanisms to provide legitimacy for the use of autonomous capabilities within their own ethical frameworks. As mentioned earlier, Israel apparently has an interest in promoting both local and international mechanisms that will give legitimacy to the use of autonomous capabilities in weapon systems within the framework of the ethical restrictions to which the country is committed.[59] Given that we are likely to see these technologies develop further in the cyber domain and that many parties in the cyber community want such autonomous capabilities, then ensuring that offensive autonomous cyber capabilities are IHL-compliant (as well as overcoming technical and scientific concerns to ensure such compliance) is essential. Even with increasing complexity between systems and machine learning, technical safeguards must be thorough. This means that a situation could arise whereby current calls for a pre-emptive ban of LAWS might be undermined by cybersecurity developments where many parties are unwilling to support bans of cyber capabilities. Furthermore, because some state parties argue that a ban on cyber tools is unrealistic, would a future ban on highly autonomous cyber capabilities even work?

However, there is still deep concern within the science and technical communities. Moreover, experts note that, even if a system can be programmed to make IHL-compliant assessments, is it desirable for machines to take actions like distinguishing targets where a human should have a choice to negotiate? The challenges of thorough verification of safety and behaviours may also mean that it would be extremely difficult to verify states' technical safeguards thus affecting international security (although some argue that it should be possible to examine software and hardware and decide whether meaningful human control remains possible[60]). Does this then mean that there may be traction for a ban against lethal autonomous cyber weapons systems? Even when it is sometimes argued that technology is neutral and there are few technologies that should not exist or be limited, some individuals have argued that it is not clear whether autonomous technologies may be an exception.[61]

Another concern relates to how some countries currently argue for restrictions on offensive cyber capabilities while still developing these tools. How could one be certain that these countries would not similarly develop fully autonomous cyber capabilities or LAWS while arguing for their restriction? Such a lack of transparency would be destabilizing for the international environment. For example, US intelligence community threat reports currently argue that:

> many actors remain undeterred from conducting reconnaissance, espionage, and even attacks in cyberspace because of the relatively low costs of entry, the perceived payoff, and the lack of significant consequences. Moscow and Beijing, among others, view offensive cyber capabilities as an important geostrategic tool and will almost certainly continue developing them while simultaneously discussing normative frameworks to restrict such use. Diplomatic efforts in the past three years have created the foundation for establishing limits on cyber operations, and the norms articulated in a 2015 report of the UN Group of Governmental Experts suggest that countries are more likely to commit to limitations on what cyber operations can target than to support bans on the development of offensive capabilities or on specific means of cyber intervention.[62]

This short description may also serve to indicate how the relationship between increasingly autonomous cyber technologies and international norms might continue to evolve.

It is not clear currently whether some calls in the international community for a pre-emptive ban of AWS will succeed or not. In which case, some US scholars argue that there should be focus on norm formation related to their use (although there is apparently taboo surrounding norm formation related to autonomous killing and so a case may perhaps be made that there are some cases and uses for which the weapon should not be used).[63] If a ban of AWS does not gain traction, does this then mean that 1) a new legal instrument for fully autonomous weapons that supplements IHL; or 2) a new AWS norm of meaningful human control could apply to lethal autonomous cyber weapons systems?

To date, discussion of meaningful, appropriate, or effective human control over weapons systems as a potential norm for physical platforms and AWS is little discussed in the context of cyber, where it may simply have less traction.[64] Patrick Lin notes that, although meaningful human control is very important in autonomous robotics discussions, the standard of meaningful human control does not seem to be raised in cyber discussions. UNIDIR's statement from April 2016 calls for '[r]eaffirming principles on human control/judgement as well as getting down to work on developing shared understanding of how this applies specifically to the weaponization of increasingly autonomous technologies (how and when human control/judgement is exercised and what makes it meaningful or appropriate)' as an important next step for the international community.[65] In doing so, both cyber systems and physical systems may need to be considered. For now, continuing with the type of information exchange and meetings held at UNIDIR can inform further debate and build confidence.

If the technical community does not seem certain that safeguards are sufficient for cyber systems, and if physical systems are increasingly vulnerable to cyberattack, it remains to be seen whether either of these types of systems could meet the test of meaningful human control.[66] Is it always certain that human operators will be able to make timely and well-informed decisions, and ensure effective control over a weapon? For these reasons, there may be value in using the AWS debates to inform the development of cyber norms in these areas, particularly where meaningful human control is concerned. UNIDIR has even asked whether these two fields may (or should) in fact merge at some stage. If convergence is a possibility, then we should begin to ask what this might mean for the legal and normative frameworks that have developed in both fields.[67] These issues need to be taken into account if states are to embark on developing norms relating to the weaponization of IATs. The international security cyber community may need to further analyse the potential impact of these developments upon those norms already agreed in the UN GGE 2013 and 2015 reports as well as the evolving international frameworks. This could include considering, where applicable, the wealth of deliberations so far on physical AWS.

Notably, some experts in the cybersecurity community recently argue that rather than a new norm of meaningful human control for cyber systems, focus is best placed on technical safeguards while ensuring the appropriate application of international law and that tools are IHL-compliant.[68] On the other hand, why should such a normative framework related to meaningful human control and ethical acceptability for AWS not apply to autonomous cyber weapons systems, including determining where the limits on autonomy should be placed? What does it then mean for future cyber normative frameworks if such a new norm for AWS under the CCW forum does indeed apply to autonomous cyber capabilities?

The United States and United Kingdom policies on AWS allow research to move forward on these weapons systems but deployment should be limited without appropriate human judgement or meaningful human control.[69] It may then occur that, although these discussions are not held within the cyber community per se, that the potential new AWS norms that may evolve could still have applicability to some cyber weapons. This could be an example of new norms for cyber that are developing outside the UN GGE on information and communication technologies (ICTs), even though the 2016/2017 GGE on ICTs found that there was little appetite for new cyber norms currently (it is not clear whether another cyber GGE will be convened in the foreseeable future).

For all these reasons, this means that there is a need to ensure norm coherence between the normative frameworks in emerging AWS and cyber regimes, as well as compatibility with the technology. This should be the case even though some cyber experts currently feel that it may still be premature to outline constraints.[70] Leaps in technological change may be exponential rather than linear. Merging these two communities may not be the most useful solution at this juncture. Rather, ensuring norm coherence and perhaps even establishing an informal international working group to regularly analyse developments specific to the unique characteristics of lethal autonomous cyber weapons systems could be valuable. Such a group could perhaps submit its findings to both the Chairperson of the AWS GGE as well as the next iteration of the GGE on ICTs, including findings related to international stability, challenges associated with their dual-use nature, the difficulties of verification of software, and export control for potentially ubiquitous technologies.

Notes

1. Author's observations, CyFy. 2015. 'The India Conference on Cyber Security and Internet Governance, 14–16 October. New Delhi: Observer Research Foundation. Office of the Director of National Intelligence (ODNI), 1.
2. Lin, UNIDIR Side Event.
3. England, 'Towards Policy Clarity', 4.
4. Lin, UNIDIR Side Event. Heyns, Christof. 2013. Special Rapporteur on Extrajudicial, Summary or Arbitrary Executions. 'Lethal Autonomous Robotics', UNIDIR Conference, 23 May.
5. Lin, UNIDIR Side Event. Heyns, 'Lethal Autonomous Robotics'.
6. Lin, UNIDIR Side Event.
7. Zarkadakis, 'In Our Own Image', 151–2.
8. CSIS and UNIDIR, 'International Security Cyber Issues Workshop', 6.
9. Vignard, 'Statement', 2.
10. Vignard, 'Statement', 2.
11. England, 'Towards Policy Clarity', 2.
12. The first meeting on this subject under the auspices of the CCW concluded that the degree of autonomy could be defined by the level of human control, or depend on the environment in which a system is supposed to operate, its functions and complexity of tasks. See Chairperson of the Meeting of Experts. 2014. 'Report of the 2014 Informal Meeting of Experts on Lethal Autonomous Weapons Systems (LAWS)', 16 May, p. 3. Geneva: UNIDIR:

    • Tables within Heinl, Part 1, for examples of categorizing different levels of autonomy.
    • US DoD Directive provides definitions for autonomous systems, human supervised autonomous weapon systems, and semi-autonomous systems.
    • The UK has positions on the distinction between automated and autonomous systems.
13. Lin, UNIDIR Side Event.
14. Lin, UNIDIR Side Event.
15. Heinl, 'National Security Implications', Part 1, 13; Lin, UNIDIR Side Event.
16. Roff, 'Cybersecurity'; UNIDIR Side Event 2015.
17. Roff and Singer, 'The Next President'.
18. Author's observations, 'Sentient Technologies, Cyber Weapons and Autonomous Platforms', CyFy. 2016. 'The India Conference on Cyber Security and Internet Governance', 29 September. New Delhi: Observer Research Foundation.
19. England, 'Towards Policy Clarity', 2; Roff, 'Cybersecurity'; New America, 'Rise of the Machines'.
20. New America, 'Rise of the Machines'.
21. Ford, *Rise of the Robots*, 232.

22. WantChinaTimes, 'Researchers in China pressured not to sign letter on "killer robots"', 2 August 2015, http://www.wantchinatimes.com/news-subclass-cnt.aspx?id=20150802000 038&cid=1101. This link cannot be accessed anymore. It refers to the July 2015 Open Letter calling for countries to halt AWS developments.
23. UNIDIR Framing Discussion, 8.
24. Scharre, Horowitz, and Sayler, 'Autonomous Weapons', 2.
25. UNIDIR Framing Discussion, 3. Chairperson 2014, LAWS Report, 3.
26. ODNI, 1.
27. Heinl, 'National Security Implications', Part 1.
28. Arvind Gupta, Deputy National Security Advisor for India, CyFy 2016.
29. Legendre, 'White House'.
30. Vignard, 'Statement', 1.
31. Vignard, 'Statement', 1.
32. Author's observations, 'Enhancing International Cyber Stability: Regional Approaches', 2nd International Security Cyber Issues Workshop Series, UNIDIR/CSIS, Singapore, 20–21 September 2017.
33. New America, 'Rise of the Machines'.
34. Carnegie Mellon University. 2016. Workshop on Safety and Control for Artificial Intelligence, co-sponsored by the White House Office of Science and Technology Policy (OSTP) and Carnegie Mellon University, 28 June.
35. Carnegie Mellon University, 'Workshop'.
36. Vignard, 'Statement', 2.
37. US DoD Directive Number 3000.09.
38. Heinl, 'National Security Implications', Part 2, 12.
39. Author's observations, 10th Asia Pacific Programme for Senior National Security Officers, Singapore, April 2016.
40. Future of Life Institute, 'Open Letter'.
41. Guarino, 'Autonomous Intelligent Agents'; Heinl: 'Artificial (Intelligent) Agents'; Heyns, 'Lethal Autonomous Robotics'.
42. United States Department of Defense. Department of Defense Law of War Manual. 2015. 354.
43. Author's observation, CyFy 2016.
44. Roff, 'Cybersecurity'; New America, 'Rise of the Machines'.
45. ODNI, 1.
46. ODNI, 1.
47. ODNI, 1.
48. Work and Brimley, '20YY', 23.
49. Work and Brimley, '20YY', 23. United States Air Force, Office of the Chief Scientist. 2015. 'Autonomous Horizons: System Autonomy in the Air Force—A Path to the Future', *Human Autonomy Teaming* I, June. http://www.af.mil/Portals/1/documents/SECAF/ AutonomousHorizons.pdf?timestamp=1435068339702
50. UNIDIR Side Event.
51. ODNI, 1.
52. Author's observation, CyFy 2016.
53. Remarks by Nick Ansell, Campaign to Stop Killer Robots, Report on Activities, 'Convention on Conventional Weapons second informal meeting of experts on lethal autonomous weapons systems', United Nations, Geneva, 13–17 April 2015.

54. Scharre, Horowitz, Sayler, 'Autonomous Weapons', 4.
55. Scharre, Horowitz, Sayler, 'Autonomous Weapons', 2. See also the argument as to whether AWS ban advocates would have to 'fashion a discrete exception for cyber. Yet what reason would there be for a ban in kinetic space and no ban in cyberspace?', justsecurity.org, January 2015.
56. Heyns, 'Lethal Autonomous Robotics'.
57. England, 'Towards Policy Clarity', 3.
58. Panellist, CyFy 2016.
59. Siboni and Eshpar, 'Dilemmas', 77.
60. Remarks by Stuart Russell, Campaign to Stop Killer Robots, Report on Activities, 'Convention on Conventional Weapons second informal meeting of experts on lethal autonomous weapons systems', United Nations, Geneva, 13–17 April 2015.
61. Author's observations, CyFy 2015; author's observations, 10th Asia Pacific Programme.
62. ODNI, 1.
63. Roff, 'Cybersecurity'; New America, 'Rise of the Machines'.
64. Author's Observations, CyFy 2016.
65. Vignard, 'Statement', 2.
66. Lin, UNIDIR Side Event.
67. UNIDIR Side Event Agenda.
68. Author's observations, CyFy 2016. A similar conclusion is made in justsecurity.org, January 2015: 'IHL's ability to effectively regulate cyberwarfare in general—and not just in terms of a ban or no ban on AWS—may thus depend on the technological ability to achieve a form of compliance that meets the realities of conflict.'
69. Roff and Singer, 'The Next President'.
70. Observations, CyFy 2016.

BIBLIOGRAPHY

Campaign to Stop Killer Robots. 2015. Report on Activities: 'Convention on Conventional Weapons Second Informal Meeting of Experts on Lethal Autonomous Weapons Systems', 13–17 April. Geneva: United Nations.

Carnegie Mellon University 2016. Workshop on Safety and Control for Artificial Intelligence, co-sponsored by the White House Office of Science and Technology Policy (OSTP) and Carnegie Mellon University, 28 June.

Chairperson. 2017. 'Food-for-Thought Paper', Group of Governmental Experts of the High Contracting Parties to the Convention on Prohibitions or Restrictions on the Use of Certain Conventional Weapons Which May be Deemed to Be Excessively Injurious or to Have Discriminate Effects, 4 September.

(CNAS) Center for a New American Security. 2016. 'Autonomous Weapons and Human Control', April. Ethical Autonomy Project.

England, Jeremy B. 2016. Head of the International Committee of the Red Cross (ICRC) Regional Delegation for India, Bhutan, Nepal and the Maldives. 'Towards Policy Clarity on Autonomous Weapons Systems', Observer Research Foundation Issue Brief (165), December.

Ford, Martin. 2015. *Rise of the Robots: Technology and the Threat of a Jobless Future*. New York: Basic Books.

Future of Life Institute, 2015. 'Autonomous Weapons: An Open Letter from AI & Robotics Researchers', July. http://futureoflife.org/open-letter-autonomous-weapons/

Heinl, Caitriona. 2014. 'Artificial (Intelligent) Agents', NATO CCD COE. https://ccdcoe.org/uploads/2018/10/doro51_heinl.pdf

Heinl, Caitriona. 2015. 'National Security Implications of Increasingly Autonomous Technologies (Part 1): Defining Autonomy, Military and Cyber-related Implications', S. Rajaratnam School of International Studies, Policy Report, February.

Heinl, Caitriona, 2015. 'National Security Implications of Increasingly Autonomous Technologies (Part 2): Legal Ambiguity, Challenges in Controlling This Space, Public/Private Sector Dynamics and Ethical Concerns', S. Rajaratnam School of International Studies, Policy Report, March.

Legendre, Chelsea, 2016. 'White House Addresses Benefits and Risks of Artificial Intelligence', 4 May. https://www.meritalk.com/articles/white-house-on-benefits-and-risks-of-artificial-intelligence/.

Lin, Patrick. 2015. 'Cyber Norms: A Missing Link in the Autonomous Weapons Debate', Presentation at the UNIDIR Conference, 'Cyber and Autonomous Weapons: Potential Overlap, Interaction and Vulnerabilities'. 9 October. New York.

New America. 2016. 'Rise of the Machines: The Past, Present, and Future of Cybernetics, AI, Automation and Cybersecurity', 23 September. https://www.newamerica.org/cybersecurity-initiative/events/cybersecurity-and-automation/

(ODNI) Office of the Director of National Intelligence. 2016. *Statement for the Record: Worldwide Threat Assessment of the US Intelligence Community*, 9 February. Senate Armed Services Committee, James R. Clapper, Director of National Intelligence.

Roff, Heather. 2015. 'Cybersecurity, Artificial Intelligence, and Autonomous Weapons: Critical Intersections', Presentation at the UNIDIR Conference, 'Cyber and Autonomous Weapons: Potential Overlap, Interaction and Vulnerabilities'. 9 October. New York. http://www.unidir.org/programmes/emerging-security-threats/the-weaponization-of-increasingly-autonomous-technologies-addressing-competing-narratives-phase-ii/cyber-weapons-and-autonomous-weapons-potential-overlap-interaction-and-vulnerabilities

Roff, Heather M., and Peter Singer. 2016. 'The Next President Will Decide the Fate of Killer Robots—and the Future of War', 9 June. https://www.wired.com/2016/09/next-president-will-decide-fate-killer-robots-future-war/

Scharre, Paul. 2016. 'Flash War: Autonomous Weapons and Strategic Stability', Presentation Slides, UNIDIR Conference: Understanding Different Types of Risks, 11 April. http://www.unidir.ch/files/conferences/pdfs/-en-1-1113.pdf

Scharre, Paul, Michael C. Horowitz, and Kelley Sayler. 2015. 'Autonomous Weapons at the UN: A Primer for Delegates', April. Washington, DC: Center for a New American Security (CNAS).

Siboni, Gabi, and Yoni Eshpar. 2014. 'Dilemmas in the Use of Autonomous Weapons', *Strategic Assessment* 16 (4), January.

Tallinn, Jaan, 2016. Future of Life Institute. 'On Artificial Intelligence and Steering the Future', Presentation at CyCon International Conference on Cyber Conflict NATO CCD COE, 3 June.

UNIDIR Side Event Agenda, 2015. 'Cyber and Autonomous Weapons: Potential Overlap, Interaction and Vulnerabilities', 9 October. UN HQ. http://www.unidir.org/files/medias/pdfs/agenda-eng-o-628.pdf

UNIDIR and CSIS. 2016. 'Report of the International Security Cyber Issues Workshop Series', Drafted by James Lewis with support from Kerstin Vignard. https://www.unidir.org/files/publications/pdfs/report-of-the-international-security-cyber-issues-workshop-series-en-656.pdf

US Department of Defense. 2012. 'Directive Number 3000.09'. 21 November.

US Department of Defense, Defense Science Board. 2013. 'Task Force Report: Resilient Military Systems and the Advanced Cyber Threat', January. https://nsarchive2.gwu.edu/NSAEBB/NSAEBB424/docs/Cyber-081.pdf

Vignard, Kerstin. 2016. 'Statement of the UN Institute for Disarmament Research at the CCW Informal Meeting of Experts on Lethal Autonomous Weapon Systems', 12 April. https://www.unidir.org/files/medias/pdfs/unidir-s-statement-to-the-ccw-informal-meeting-of-experts-on-lethal-autonomous-weapon-systems-eng-0-648.pdf

Work, Robert, and Shawn Brimley. 2014. '20YY: Preparing for War in the Robotic Age', January. Washington DC: Center for a New American Security (CNAS).

Zarkadakis, George. 2015. *In Our Own Image: Savior or Destroyer? The History and Future of Artificial Intelligence*. Cambridge, UK: Pegasus Books.

CHAPTER 44

THE FUTURE HUMAN AND BEHAVIOURAL CHALLENGES OF CYBERSECURITY

DEBI ASHENDEN

INTRODUCTION

THE number of alerts triggered by an organization's Security Information and Event Management (SIEM) system continues to grow in volume at a rapid pace. Alerts on a system may or may not indicate that an attack has occurred but they do require some form of triage and investigation. While technology can automatically filter out a relatively small number of alerts, analysts have to spend significant amounts of time downgrading alerts that are false positives, mis-prioritized or incorrectly marked as critical. While only a proportion of alerts will turn out to be attacks, the incident to attack ratio is rising. When we cast forward over the coming years, analysts' predictions suggest that the attack surface will continue to grow. We are seeing a heavily contested cyberspace at a time when we are increasingly dependent on it.

The task of cybersecurity is, put simply, that of managing risk in line with an entity's risk appetite (be it a government, an organization, or an individual). It may have a hard problem at its kernel (that of securing technology) but it is surrounded by the soft problem of achieving this within a specific and variable context, and this is where the human and behavioural challenges lie.

At the moment, cybersecurity suffers from stove-piped thinking with a tendency to marginalize approaches to solving cybersecurity problems that do not originate from the fields of computer science or engineering. The professional practice of cybersecurity often fails to incorporate other world views from the full breadth of social and behavioural sciences. We have a tendency to fall prey to the streetlight effect (Ashenden and Lawrence 2016) whereby we look for solutions in places that are already illuminated (such as computer science and engineering) rather than risk looking into the shadows (of social and behavioural science, sociology, or geography, for example). Remaining under the streetlight may have worked for us in the past but now, as we have seen through the preceding chapters, cybersecurity presents us with a complex range of problems. Technology has evolved at an ever increasing rate and given us myriad choices about how we live our lives. But, at the same time, our approach to cybersecurity has become more rigid and inflexible.

The purpose of this chapter is to explore the future human and behavioural challenges that are likely to have an impact on cybersecurity. We cannot know what the future will hold but we can usefully reflect on how we got to where we are now, and consider where we are now as the foundation for the future as we cast our imaginations forwards. While we might not be able to identify the specific challenges that we will face, we can make predictions about the general challenges that will need to be overcome.

The first challenge will be to accept that cybersecurity practitioners are not average end users. As practitioners, security is likely to be at the forefront of our minds on a daily basis but for most end users this is not the case. Security practitioners need to become more curious about end users and how they enact cybersecurity. We need to explore and understand the soft problem of cybersecurity that sits around the hard engineering problem. We have to understand cybersecurity as a social practice that is carried out in specific and variable contexts if we are to design successful behavioural and social interventions. Our second challenge is to improve the levels of creativity and innovation demonstrated by cybersecurity practitioners. This involves identifying what skills they will need in the future that will enable them to engage productively with human and behavioural challenges. The third challenge is to look at how we address cybersecurity risk. Rather than focusing on risk assessment, we need to look more closely at how we communicate risk, how this is then perceived by end users, and the impacts it has on their decision making. What will happen if we fail to rise to these challenges? The danger is, as we shall see, that security becomes irrelevant as end users continue to bypass security processes, procedures, advice, and guidance. Meeting these challenges will depend on developing a skill set among cybersecurity practitioners that puts soft skills on a par with technical skills and establishes trust relationships through genuine dialogue realized through participative approaches to cybersecurity.

CYBERSECURITY AS A SOCIAL PRACTICE

The Internet of Things (IoT) not only demonstrates the complexity of cybersecurity but also the potential impact on all sections of society. The IoT forces us to acknowledge that cybersecurity cannot be addressed as something that is separate from physical security or human security. Social concerns around privacy, data access, and trust come to the fore as we start to use devices in our homes that have the ability to listen to our conversations, and that aim to anticipate our needs. The IoT serves to magnify the cybersecurity vulnerabilities of previous years that have not been rectified, because devices and buildings are often connected to the Internet with weak or non-existent password protection.

One of the most important behavioural and human challenges that we continue to face as we try to come up with solutions to cybersecurity problems is the recognition that as cybersecurity practitioners we are not the end user. Our tendency to characterize end users in simplistic terms as personas in models will continue to hamper our ability to develop effective behavioural interventions. This is easy to say but has proved hard to do. Just as nobody predicted how mobile phones would be used when they were first developed, so we cannot develop security solutions that anticipate how end users will use technology and what their risk appetites and risk perceptions will be, without understanding the context that shapes their behaviours.

Our first challenge is to understand the social practice of cybersecurity. A social practice consists of a bundle of activities comprising meaning, symbols, competence, procedures, material, and technology (Reckwitz 2002; Shove and Pantzar 2005; Shove 2010; Hargreaves 2011). Social practice theorists suggest that traditional models of behaviour change are insufficient, and that we need to understand the impact of power relations and social interactions.[1] We need to do this because individuals enact behaviours in a social context and traditional models artificially limit and constrain consideration of context.

Some cybersecurity research has started to look at this through the lens of the everyday whereby different security behaviours can be observed in the home than will be seen in an organization (Coles-Kemp et al. 2014). There are few researchers looking at the social and community context of cybersecurity but do just that.[2] They shine a light on a specific group of end users (in this case, benefit claimants in the north-east of England) and give a rich explanation of what the social practice of cybersecurity looks like. These particular end users discuss how they will use technology to manipulate a UK government system for their own ends by being able to look up the information that they need, or speak to friends who can give them tips on how to get the result that they want. Coles-Kemp et al. conclude that technology makes it easier to twist the system, partly because end users are not face to face with a government official. We need to understand such practices because within them are the clues that will help us understand how to change them as they are enacted and circulated (Warde 2005).

An interesting aspect to consider when looking at cybersecurity as a social practice is that of ambivalences. These arise when there is tension between two feelings. Halkier (2001) looks at risk in relation to food consumption but points out that the rational approach understood by experts and encoded in processes fails to take account of the socio-cultural breadth that exists in the everyday practice of understanding risk handling in food consumption. We will return to this issue of rationality again in this chapter but it is important to note that how we enact cybersecurity today assumes rationality in end users. Halkier goes on to point out that risk perception is not constrained by rational thought but spills out and is tempered by ambivalences such as desire and control. These arise because of the context of everyday life. If we apply this to cybersecurity, then it is easy to see how the end user can experience this tension between desire (for new technology and connectivity) and control (wanting to keep safe and to protect friends or family).

One of the problems posed by many cybersecurity solutions is scalability. From a human and behavioural perspective, this is also a problem, but one with a potential solution. Traditionally, cybersecurity (particularly within organizations) is seen as the responsibility of the individual end user but it may be the case that the answer to scaling solutions to human and behavioural challenges is through group working. This accords with social practice theory where the value of learning through membership of a community is understood (Sahakian and Wilhite 2014; Bartiaux and Salmón 2014). For cybersecurity, we need to understand the constraints and freedoms that determine individuals' behaviours.[3] These include their knowledge and ability to enact their knowledge, as well as identifying objects and infrastructures that facilitate and support practices, and the social context in which practices are carried out. After this, we can start to identify spaces for intervention: exploring where a change in one practice might lead to a change in related practices. At some points, it may be possible to leverage aspects of practice that are already present[4] and to bridge between communities to share learning on a bigger scale so that end users can help each other[5].

Cybersecurity practitioners find engaging with end users a challenge and will need different skills to be able to engage with cybersecurity as a social practice. Ashenden and Sasse (2013) allude to this in their research on chief information security officers (CISOs) that concludes that CISOs have difficulty in communicating with end users effectively. The take-up of their security messages is inhibited by their one-way engagement with employees (so, pushing messages out rather than engaging in dialogue). In the future though, as we see the continued growth of IoT devices, the ability to set cybersecurity problems in a social and physical context will be invaluable. Social practice theory gives us a different way of understanding end user behaviours and the emotional trade-offs that they make, but also suggests that we can leverage the power of communities to support each other in increasing both security and resilience.

CREATIVITY AND INNOVATION

This leads us onto our second challenge. We are going to need cybersecurity practitioners who have the skill set to be able to tackle the breadth and depth of issues raised by the complexity of cybersecurity problems. This includes the human and behavioural challenges posed. Put simply, the challenge will be to ensure that cybersecurity practitioners have the ability to rise to their own human and behavioural challenges.

As cybersecurity has matured as a profession and an organizational function, it is unsurprising that it has become more formalized. The management of cybersecurity is now increasingly separate from the hands-on technical expertise of, say, a penetration tester. The path to becoming a cybersecurity professional has a clear route, most often through an accredited university degree in the subject coupled with professional certification. It is unlikely that someone will now be hired as a generalist, but it was not always like this. Early CISOs did not have a career path. The successful ones grew as the demands of the job grew. Professor Paul Dorey, a previous CISO of BP and Barclays, said, 'I didn't climb a ladder. I stood on a platform and it rose' (Grossman 2011). In some respects, the formalization of a career path is a sign of a profession's maturity but, at the same time, it offers the challenge of how to ensure that skills remain relevant to meet the needs of a changing context.

If we look back to the early days of cybersecurity, we see a level of creativity and innovation that has faded from how we practise cybersecurity today. The 'Hacker Manifesto' articulated the thirst for knowledge and understanding that underpinned the creativity of early hackers (Blankenship 1986). The writer (Loyd Blankenship) says he was driven by curiosity. An even earlier article on 'phone phreaking, 'Secrets of the Little Blue Box' (Rosenbaum 1971) inspired the curiosity of Steve Jobs and Steve Wozniak who, of course, went on to found Apple. In these early days, there was a great deal of overlap between those who sought for ways to exploit systems and those who protected them. Early hackers and penetration testers were part of a single community where boundaries were often blurred. Sometimes this is still the case but, to a large extent, this community is now too often separate from the community of cybersecurity practitioners who are responsible for the management of cybersecurity. The management of cybersecurity is no longer about curiosity in how things work, whether it is technology, business processes, or end user behaviours. It is about implementing standards and ensuring compliance, and in this lies our challenge. How do we reawaken that spark of curiosity that will lead to the creativity and innovation that we need to address the future human and behavioural challenges posed by end users?

One of the most obvious ways to develop a creative approach to cybersecurity management is for practitioners to make a conscious effort to question and reflect on their current practices, and to seek out other perspectives on the problems they face. It is no longer sufficient to be a technical expert. Cybersecurity practitioners also need good communication skills, the ability to be political players in their organization, the ability to put together a good business case for resources and to manage relationships (Ashenden 2008) and, of course, more recently, the ability to deliver behaviour change in end users and to develop a culture of cybersecurity in their organizations.

The challenge then is to ensure that cybersecurity practitioners have the skills to deliver behavioural and cultural change. This is where they need to be creative and innovative, and to look beyond their current practices. It is this move away from the streetlight and into the shadows of social and behavioural science that poses a challenge. We can illustrate this with an example. As we have seen, CISOs struggle to communicate cultural and behavioural change to end users. They demonstrate discomfort and confusion at an aspect of their role that they might reasonably never have expected to take on.[6] It is uncomfortable, but this is where the opportunity for creativity and innovation arises if the CISO accepts the challenge.

Let us focus a little more on the challenge of changing the behaviour of end users and why this is likely to persist in the future. To add to the complexity of cybersecurity issues already discussed, employees are increasingly difficult to contain within the logical perimeter of the organization's technology. We have Bring Your Own Device (BYOD) issues as employees expect to have the same technology experiences at work as at home. Spear phishing attacks prey on the social aspects of employees' behaviour and there is a tension in many organizations over the use of social media. In global organizations, there are cross-cultural issues to address and often this is set against the need to let customers cross the organizational boundary through the online delivery of services.

Many organizations address these issues with security awareness programmes. But the evidence suggests, however, that these have little impact on end user behaviour. We know that approximately 55% of security breaches are caused by users who have legitimate access to an organization's systems.

The challenge for cybersecurity practitioners is to cast widely for potential answers to these problems rather than continuing with their current approaches. The first practical consideration is realizing that awareness and behaviour change are not the same, and that increasing awareness will not automatically lead to a change in behaviour (although it can be a useful accompanying step). This has long been recognized in the area of public health where Quadrel and Lau (1989) point out that raising awareness of health issues is important but does not necessarily lead to healthier behaviours.

Acknowledging the difference between awareness and behaviour change encourages the cybersecurity practitioner to reflect on their activities in a more critical way. Current security awareness programmes tend to provide information and aim to educate end users about the need for cybersecurity, but they do not usually articulate how the end user should behave differently. Cybersecurity practitioners need to be able to answer the question—if end users did do what they were supposed to do, what would it look like and how much of the cybersecurity problem would be solved?

As Quadrel and Lau (1989) suggest, the best way to measure success is through witnessing a change in behaviour. It is not enough to aim to change attitudes and hope that they lead to changes in behaviour. It could be more effective to change behaviours with the expectation that cognitive dissonance will lead to a corresponding change in attitude. In the future, we must focus on changing behaviours so that we can determine the success of cybersecurity messages by measuring observable behaviours before and after an intervention.

We have identified a number of challenges, then, for cybersecurity practitioners. If they are to address the human and behavioural challenges of end users, they will need to address their own challenges as well. The first of these is ensuring that they have relevant skills beyond technical skills. Such skills include soft skills as well as delivering behavioural and cultural change interventions. To achieve this, they need to be able to reflect critically on their current practice and to be sufficiently confident to explore approaches from other disciplines that will often challenge their ways of thinking.

RISK PERCEPTION AND RISK COMMUNICATION

Our world of risk is changing rapidly with greater emphasis on governance and transparency and a seemingly relentless push towards tighter regulation. This is having an impact on cybersecurity and cybersecurity risk management where the picture is complicated further with the emergence of disruptive technologies such as artificial intelligence. The UK Ministry of Defence's *Global Strategic Trends* (2018) report looks out to 2050 and suggests that such technologies can lead to discontinuities when trends change paths or disappear creating unforeseen risks.

Tackling unforeseen risks when we often struggle to manage known risks to a system suggests we need a new approach. Phishing attacks provide an everyday illustration of this. At the moment, organizations tend to rely on simulated phishing attacks as a way to communicate the risk to end users. The idea behind such simulations is that, if employees fall prey to the attack, they are then given training to help them improve (at least at not falling prey to simulations). Some organizations now are even making it a disciplinary offence if end users fall for phishing attacks. The problem with this approach is that employees may feel caught out and are much less likely to be motivated to try and improve security. Nobody likes to get things wrong and many people feel that they have been tricked in this situation. The other danger is that they will start to exhibit signs of learned helplessness. This is a psychological condition whereby an individual believes that there is little point in trying to do the right thing because they just cannot win. At best, you may get apathy around security and, at worst, outright rejection.

Phishing attacks might seem relatively low-level breaches of security until we consider a phishing attack in a specific context such as an attack on an industrial control system. Increasingly, industrial control systems are connected to the Internet (usually for maintenance purposes) and this is likely to increase with the proliferation of IoT devices (for example, building management systems). Coupled with this is the recognition that many back-end or operational technology (OT) systems were never designed with security in mind. These systems are often difficult to patch or update and it may not be practical to take them offline to patch vulnerabilities. The OT system may also be connected to the enterprise system that runs the business side of the organization. This gives an attacker a pathway from one side of the business to the other, safety-critical, side of the operation. While there have been relatively few attacks to date on industrial control systems, we have no reason to assume that this will continue. We can use technology to prevent some of the risks we will face but we need to understand how to communicate the level of risk to end users effectively, and ensure that we understand how they perceive the risk if we are to harness the value of end users in mitigating the risk.

Understanding risk communication and risk perception stems from a tradition of risk research and practice that has been overlooked by cybersecurity practitioners. There are basically two cultures of risk assessment. This is explained by Adams (2002) in his discussion of a report on risk by the Royal Society in 1992. On the one hand, there is a culture of risk assessment encapsulated by engineering and physical sciences where risk is seen as knowable and measurable and assumes rational decision making by end users. On the other hand, there is the culture of risk encapsulated by the social sciences where risk is socially constructed and dependent on perceptions and communication. This second perspective takes an inductive approach and encompasses the social context in which risk is discussed and realized. From this perspective, risk is viewed as a phenomenon that is socially constructed and determined, to some extent, by perception.

Traditional approaches to cybersecurity risk, however, sit within the first culture. They borrow from the field of safety risk assessments and attempt to develop quantitative methods for assessing risk. Cybersecurity risk is addressed as an attribute of technology. Methods for assessing risk are based on the idea of input, process, and output, with the organization being seen as a meta system. As a result, risk assessment has tended to focus on modelling and measuring risk (Birch and McEvoy 1992; Blakley, McDermott and Geer 2002; Bodin, Gordon and Loeb 2008). Cybersecurity risk has remained fixed in a paradigm where risk is seen as something that is knowable and can be measured objectively—largely because of the requirement to be able to classify and audit companies on the basis of their approach to risk.

The result of this has been that there is often a failure to understand the importance of the risk context—including risk perception and risk communication. The phishing example demonstrates how risk is currently managed with the assumption of rational decision making.

Rational choice theory suggests that people make rational decisions and that they make a cost–benefit decision about behaviours (Becker 1968). Across a range of contexts, research into rational choice theory demonstrates that this approach may work under certain conditions—when sufficient financial incentives are offered, and when people get meaningful and regular feedback on expected behaviour, along with extensive training on what is expected (Shanks, Tunney, and McCarthy 2002). There is also, however, a range of research that disproves the effectiveness of rational choice theory under many other conditions. One of the main problems with rational choice theory in practice is that the cost–benefit analysis understood by the expert often differs from that of the individual receiving the information. For example, Blanchemanche, Marette, Roosen et al. (2010) demonstrated that messages aimed at informing pregnant women in France about the dangers of eating fish did not change consumption but instead led to confusion among the women. This was a five-month experiment with 500 households and demonstrates that what looks rational to experts when they communicate risk information is not necessarily received as such by the individuals who are the subject of the intervention.

Cybersecurity risk is increasingly understood as an emergent property that occurs at the intersection between technology, human behaviour, and process. Characterizing cybersecurity risk as a property that can be understood objectively and quantified has been criticized as pseudo science (Baskerville 1991), the value of qualitative risk assessment and the importance of risk communication for cybersecurity has been highlighted (Jones and Ashenden 2004) and the point has been made that, without a broad exploration of risk in this space, a great deal of the social and political issues that contextualize cybersecurity risk will be missed (Barnard-Wills and Ashenden 2012). While a social constructionist view of risk is not a new idea (Lupton 1999), neither is the importance of risk perception, risk biases, and risk communication (Renn 1998; Slovic and Weber 2002) but these perspectives have still to be applied to cybersecurity risk. This is the challenge for the future.

SECURITY DIALOGUES

Our final challenge will determine our success in meeting the other challenges. As we have seen repeatedly through this chapter, our responses to future cybersecurity challenges do not exist in a vacuum: we have to understand the context in which behaviours are (or are not) enacted. Hard problems require an engineering approach that works well when the problem can be defined clearly; when it is not influenced by other problems; when it is obvious where responsibility for the problem and its solution lies; and when the information requirements for solving the problem are apparent. What surrounds that hard problem kernel, however, is very much a soft problem. The characteristics of soft problems are that the problem space is often fuzzy, responsibility for resolving the problem is shared and not straightforward, and information requirements for developing a solution are unclear. To return to the example we gave at the beginning of this chapter—if we treat cybersecurity only as a hard problem, we are standing under the lamp post looking for our keys because that is where the light is, ignoring the fact that they may be hidden in the soft problem space on the other side of the street.

In any organization, there is often a shortfall between the mandated and formal security process and what actually happens. Projects have to finish and systems have to run. This stark reality has to be managed flexibly with each solution being subject to negotiation between the cybersecurity practitioner and other parts of the business. The gaps in the process that occur between and around the formal activities are where organizational culture and relationships come into play, and where the ability to inculcate trust and to influence end users are necessary behaviours for cybersecurity practitioners.

Achieving trust and influence will depend on an open and honest dialogue, and a genuinely participative approach between end users and cybersecurity practitioners. As Ashenden and Lawrence (2016) point out, without this dialogue, security is in danger of being sidelined or even ignored. At best, the lack of dialogue is likely to mean that the cybersecurity practitioner only ever gets a partial and constrained view of the risks to which the organization is exposed because end users and systems developers keep back information. The outcome of this is that the cybersecurity practitioner is making security recommendations blind, which, in turn, is likely to mean that recommendations are impractical or do not mitigate the most important risks. When trust does exist, however, there is a more nuanced and detailed understanding of risk. We have also witnessed the bonus of this trust leading to more agile ways of working as both parties in the relationship become more open and constructive in response to the inevitable compromises that need to be negotiated.

Once again, cybersecurity practitioners need to exercise an innovative approach in addressing this challenge. Again, healthcare research demonstrates the issues and potential solutions that arise from an examination of the relationship between patients and their doctors. To summarize Myers & Abrahams (2005), it seems that, despite all the time that GPs spend discussing, assessing, and making recommendations to patients, half the patients they prescribe to fail to carry out their treatments as recommended. In fact, between 10% and 25% of hospital admissions can be traced to non-compliance with a doctor's recommendations, and this is just as likely to happen with organ transplant patients as with those with more minor ailments. As a result, improving compliance has been a focus for health psychologists since the 1970s and Ley[7] made the point that satisfaction with the relationship between a GP and a patient was strongly linked with adherence. This means that, if patients trusted the GP and felt that they had been listened to and had taken an active part in defining their treatment, they would be much more likely to comply with the recommended treatment plan. Concordance is the term that Mullen[8] gives to a positive and participative relationship between the GP and the patient.

If we recast this research with cybersecurity practitioners and end users, we can visualize the journey that we need to take. It is apparent that the aim of cybersecurity practitioners should be to move the relationship they have with end users from being at risk of non-compliance (in a worst-case scenario), through to concordance. This is where satisfaction with the relationship is felt by both parties and, as a result, more productive security solutions are likely to be developed in a participative way.

This sounds like a good place to aim for but there is a further potential challenge. While cybersecurity practitioners may want to reach out to end users, some end users may well not want to engage with cybersecurity practitioners. This is particularly the case with software developers. Developers quite rightly pride themselves on their creativity and are often reluctant to discuss their designs with cybersecurity practitioners for fear that they will prohibit development on security grounds.[9] The aspiration for secure coding has always fallen prey to market forces and economics, and so this reluctance to engage has continued and been condoned.

We can see though the seeds of a potential change in this situation and, interestingly, this gives us an opportunity to address cybersecurity in a new way precisely because of the speed with which technology is evolving. We have a way to change the social practice of software development that has arisen because of the move to cloud-based infrastructures and the need to develop and release code more quickly and more regularly through continuous integration and continuous delivery. This has led to initiatives such as DevSecOps, bringing together development, security, and operations.

DevSecOps offers the potential of a participative approach to security through a peer-to-peer relationship between developers and cybersecurity practitioners and, as such, it fits well with agile software development. The idea behind DevSecOps focuses on three areas: first, the use of lean principles from manufacturing transported into software development; second, not turning software developers into security experts but giving them tools and products that mean they can test their code for security flaws as they develop; and, third, developing a culture of trust and sharing between cybersecurity practitioners and developers. Without this third element, the idea of DevSecOps cannot take off. DevSecOps is growing in popularity and with pace. The challenge will be to move from a dialogue where the developer says to the cybersecurity practitioner, 'I'd like to use tools to code securely but you won't let me have Wireshark on my machine', or the cybersecurity practitioner says to the developer, 'No, I don't believe you need admin privileges to do your work.' The idea of moving to a point of concordance is that we progress beyond these simplistic statements of blame to understand what lies beneath them and to negotiate a solution that both sides accept.

The development of good security dialogues depends on the soft skills of cybersecurity practitioners but also the willingness of other parts of the organization to engage. The challenge is for cybersecurity practitioners to learn how to build trust and influence and, as we have seen, the ultimate aim is to move to a point of concordance where security solutions are developed in a genuinely participative way. If this challenge is not met, then cybersecurity practitioners are likely to always have a partial and constrained view of the risks that they attempt to mitigate. At worst, security will be bypassed and seen as irrelevant. Looking at the context for dialogue between cybersecurity practitioners and software developers, we can see an emergent opportunity. As organizations turn to DevSecOps to realize their requirements for faster turnaround times for code releases, they see the need to embed security in development. How the dialogue progresses between cybersecurity practitioners and developers will determine how successful this is when implemented. In this instance, we have a human and behavioural challenge that could lead to a real technical opportunity.

Conclusion

Technology will continue to develop at a fast pace giving us new ways to live our lives and to interact with each other. Our understanding of how to secure the systems, the environment in which they operate, and the people who use them is not keeping pace. Cybersecurity as we know it today is in danger of becoming irrelevant and ignored because it is simply getting in the way. Our challenge in the future is to find a way to reverse this trend. Put simply, what got us here will not get us to where we need to be in the future. Technical solutions to cybersecurity issues are unlikely to solve all our problems because cybersecurity is, at its heart, a social practice that is enacted beyond the technology that we aim to secure. Our challenge will be to understand the social practices that reveal the human and behavioural reality of cybersecurity for end users. To achieve this, those responsible for cybersecurity are going to need to develop more creative and innovative ways of working. They are going to have to move beyond the streetlight and into the shadows of ways of thinking that will challenge how they currently think. The traditional focus on cybersecurity risk will remain in the future but the challenge will be to understand risk in a different way, as something that is emergent, constructed, and situated rather than something that is discrete, knowable, and measurable. To do this, we will need to understand how end users perceive risk and to examine the way we communicate risk to them if we want to develop effective risk mitigation strategies. The challenge in developing this new way of thinking about cybersecurity behaviours is to develop trusted relationships with a wide range of end users. It is such relationships that will prevent cybersecurity from becoming obsolete and that will offer us the opportunity of developing a genuinely participative way of designing behavioural interventions. Productive security dialogues will enable us to mobilize and strengthen end users in their relationship with technology, and will facilitate us being able to 'patch with people' as well as technology.

NOTES

1. Hargreaves, 'Practice-ing behaviour change'.
2. Coles-Kemp, Zugenmaier, and Lewis, 'Watching You Watching Me', 147–62.
3. Sahakian and Wilhite, 'Making practice theory practicable'.
4. Sahakian and Wilhite, 'Making practice theory practicable'.
5. Bartiaux and Salmón, 'Family Dynamics and Social Practice Theories'.
6. Ashenden and Sasse, A. 'CISOs and Organisational Culture'.
7. Ley (1988) quoted in Myers, L., and Abrahams, C. 2005. 'Beyond "Doctor's Orders"'. *The Psychologist* 10 (11): 680–3.
8. Mullen (1997) quoted in Myers, L., and Abrahams, C. 2005. 'Beyond "Doctor's Orders"'. *The Psychologist* 10 (11): 680–3.
9. Ashenden and Lawrence, 'Security Dialogues'.

BIBLIOGRAPHY

Adams, J. 2002. *Risk*. Abingdon, UK: Routledge.
Ashenden, D. 2008. 'Information Security Management: A Human Challenge?', *Information Security Technical Report* 13 (4): 195–201.
Ashenden, D., and Lawrence, D. 2016. 'Security Dialogues: Building Better Relationships between Security and Business', *IEEE Security & Privacy* 14 (3): 82–7.
Ashenden, D., and Sasse, A. 2013. 'CISOs and Organisational Culture: Their Own Worst Enemy?', *Computers & Security* 39: 396–405.
Barnard-Wills, D., and Ashenden, D. 2012. 'Securing Virtual Space: Cyber War, Cyber Terror and Cyber Risk', *Space & Culture* 15 (2): 1–14.
Bartiaux, F., and Salmón, L.R. 2014. 'Family Dynamics and Social Practice Theories: An Investigation of Daily Practices Related to Food, Mobility, Energy Consumption, and Tourism', *Nature and Culture* 9 (2): 204–24.
Baskerville, R. 1991. 'Risk Analysis for Information Systems', *Journal of Information Technology* 7: 44–53.
Becker, G.S. 1968. 'Crime and Punishment: An Economic Approach'. In *The Economic Dimensions of Crime*, edited by N.G. Fielding, A. Clarke, and R. Witt, 13–68. London: Palgrave Macmillan.
Birch, D., and McEvoy, N. 1992. 'Risk Analysis for Information Systems', *Journal of Information Technology* 7: 44–53.
Blakley, B., McDermott, E., and Geer, D. 2002. 'Information Security is Information Risk Management', New Security Paradigms Workshop 2001, 10–13 September, ACM: 97–104.

Blanchemanche, S., Marette, S., Roosen, J., and Verger, P. 2010. 'Do Not Eat Fish More Than Twice a Week. Rational Choice Regulation and Risk Communication: Uncertainty Transfer from Risk Assessment to Public', *Health, Risk & Society* 12 (3): 271–92.

Blankenship, L. 1986. 'The Conscience of a Hacker', *Phrack* 1 (7). http://phrack.org/issues/7/3.html

Bodin, L., Gordon, L., and Loeb, M. 2008. 'Information Security and Risk Management', *Communications of the ACM* 51 (4): 64–8.

Coles-Kemp, L., Zugenmaier, A., and Lewis, M. 2014. 'Watching You Watching Me: The Art of Playing the Panopticon'. In *Digital Enlightenment Yearbook 2014: Social Networks and Social Machines, Surveillance and Empowerment*, edited by Kieron O'Hara, Carolyn Nguyen, and Peter Haynes, 147–62. Amsterdam: IOS Press.

Grossman, W.M. 2011. 'The CISO Pilgrimage', *Infosecurity* 8 (3): 16–19. https://www.infosecurity-magazine.com/magazine-features/the-ciso-pilgrimage

Halkier, B. 2001. 'Risk and Food: Environmental Concerns and Consumer Practices', *International Journal of Food Science and Technology* 36 (8): 801–12.

Hargreaves, T. 2011. 'Practice-ing Behaviour Change: Applying Social Practice Theory to Pro-Environmental Behaviour Change', *Journal of Consumer Culture* 11 (1): 79–99.

Jones, A., and Ashenden, D. 2004. *Risk Management for Computer Security: Protecting Your Network and Information Assets*. Oxford: Butterworth Heinemann.

Lupton, D. 1999. *Risk*. Abingdon, UK: Routledge.

Ministry of Defence, Development, Concepts and Doctrine Centre. 2018. 'Global Strategic Trends: The Future Starts Today'. https://assets.publishing.service.gov.uk/government/uploads/system/uploads/attachment_data/file/771309/Global_Strategic_Trends_-_The_Future_Starts_Today.pdf

Myers, L., and Abrahams, C. 2005. 'Beyond "doctor's orders"'. *The Psychologist* 10 (11): 680–3.

Quadrel, M.J., and Lau, R.R. 1989. 'Health Promotion, Health Locus of Control, and Health Behavior: Two Field Experiments', *Journal of Applied Social Psychology* 19 (18): 1497–519.

Reckwitz, A. 2002. 'Toward a Theory of Social Practices: A Development in Culturalist Theorizing', *European Journal of Social Theory* 5 (2): 243–63.

Renn, O. 1998. 'The Role of Risk Perception for Risk Management', *Reliability, Engineering and System Safety* 59: 49–62.

Rosenbaum, R. 1971. 'Secrets of the Little Blue Box', *Esquire Magazine* 76: 117–25.

Sahakian, M., and Wilhite, H. 2014. 'Making Practice Theory Practicable: Towards More Sustainable Forms of Consumption', *Journal of Consumer Culture* 14 (1): 25–44.

Shanks, D.R., Tunney, R.J., and McCarthy, J.D. 2002. 'A Re-Examination of Probability Matching and Rational Choice', *Journal of Behavioral Decision Making* 15 (3): 233–50.

Shove, E. 2010. 'Beyond the ABC: Climate Change Policy and Theories of Social Change', *Environment and Planning A* 42 (6): 1273–85.

Shove, E., and Pantzar, M. 2005. 'Consumers, Producers and Practices: Understanding the Invention and Reinvention of Nordic Walking', *Journal of Consumer Culture* 5 (1): 43–64.

Slovic, P., and Weber, E.U. 2002. 'Perception of Risk Posed by Extreme Events', Risk Management Strategies in an Uncertain World Conference, 12–13 April: 1–21.

Warde, A. 2005. 'Consumption and Theories of Practice', *Journal of Consumer Culture* 5 (2): 131–53.

Willcocks, L., and Margetts, H. 1994. 'Risk assessment and information systems', *European Journal of Information Systems* 3 (2): 127–38.

CHAPTER 45

THE FUTURE OF DEMOCRATIC CIVIL SOCIETIES IN A POST-WESTERN CYBERED ERA

CHRIS DEMCHAK

OVER the coming century, consolidated democratic states will become a numerically small minority in a deeply cybered and conflictual world dominated by non-Western autocratic states. China is now well into its rise as the centre of economic and demographic power in this emerging world. With spreading and globally deeply embedded economic and cybered bonds, national policy coherence, and large demographic scale, Chinese preferences will particularly influence the rules in practice across the coming post-Western international system.[1] This rise was inevitable although its speed was not. Rather, Westernized democracies lost their purchase on the international system faster and more pervasively than they might have because of how they built, conceived of, and neglected to govern the engine of globalization—the Internet. After 3-plus decades of existence, cyberspace has become an existentially critical, global 'substrate' built shoddily on highly insecurely coded, baseline architectures and Western misperceptions about technology, security, information technology (IT) economics, and the immortality of the democratic civil society model of governance. In reality, cyberspace has accelerated massive cross-border economic exploitation and the reinforcement of personalized social, technical, and economic control across the non-Westernized nations.

Today, Western states experience between 1% and 2% annual gross domestic product (GDP) loss due to cyber insecurity and a new form of conflict has emerged—'cybered conflict'.[2] It stretches in a spectrum from peace to war—a system versus system scale of deliberate struggles across societal rules, economic resources, and national security capabilities. As currently shoddily constructed, cyberspace enables a wide range of offensive and extractive campaigns to which democratic civil societies remain especially vulnerable. This 'greatest transfer of wealth in human history'[3] constitutes a 'pillaging'[4] of the future assets of democratic states. Without adequate resources, democratic states cannot guide or deeply influence the direction of the international system, let alone afford and orchestrate advanced

736 CHRIS DEMCHAK

technologies and domestic resilience budgets.[5] These losses are unsustainable for a minority group of states seeking the cyber power necessary to defend itself in a much larger, deeply cybered, conflictual, and overwhelmingly authoritarian world system.

How did this happen, and what can be done? What potential futures loom for the cybered interstate systems and which of these offer the best—or least bad—options to ensure the long-term survival of a technologically advanced, internally free, and resilient civil society? In answering these questions, this chapter discusses cyberspace's evolution in terms of technical shoddiness and misperceptions, identifies two available remediating strategic responses to this new cybered reality (recognition of sovereignty and balancing scale), and offers three possible interstate futures depending upon which of these two responses is chosen. Finally, this chapter will argue that achieving the best possible future will rest on pursuing strategic well-being and international influence through a 'cyber operational resilience alliance' across consolidated democratic civil societies.

Hubris and Commercialization: The Origins of Systemic Misperceptions and Abuse of Cyberspace

Cyberspace emerged over the 1990s in a haze of utopian promises about the spread of internetted democracy and global economic growth (Rheingold 1993). The new technologies were to ensure the reliable, long range, mass scale, and free sharing of 'information'. The data to be sent all over were assumed to be objective facts whose spread would automatically facilitate transparency and inevitable dominance of democracy and law worldwide (Johnson and Post 1996). Unnecessary and unable to control the web anyway, governments would decline as the shared 'true knowledge' would guide all groups in a wonderful new world of massively beneficial public goods (Barlow 1996; Benedikt 1991). Commercial corporate and start-up actors in Westernized states were happy to embrace the utopians' view of information communication technologies (ICTs) as special. 'E-commerce' was promoted as a unique industry in which government regulation would destroy its innovation, generativity, and prosperity (Oxley and Yeung 2001). Eager for the promised economic gains, government officials often did not understand the basic structures, uses, and contractual relations of the early Internet, still less how it was coded, operated, and controlled.[6] Nonetheless, they largely agreed early and widely that no regulation was wise in economic and foreign policies (Norris and Jones 1998). By the 2000s, the early Internet promoters and Western national policymakers were united in opposing to government regulation of Internet companies' products irrespective of how securely they or their networks were being built—or what they connected (Oyedemi 2015).

Over the 1990s, seeking quick returns, commercial actors built the Internet while bypassing the established academic computer languages, such as LISP, known to be intolerant of coding errors and to require time and the careful coding habits of the original university communities to use. They overwhelmingly chose fault-tolerant languages such as C++ and Java. Both were easy to program quickly, and coding mistakes could be ignored if the application would run as needed (Trickey 1988). Operating systems were secured, not against criminals but against bad transmission over poor wiring and against business competitors.[7] Investing effort to embed security with the academic time-consuming 'fault intolerant' languages or even ensuring hack-resistant 'hardened' basic systems—all fundamentals of cybersecurity—was viewed as a waste of time. As a result, the global Internet's baseline architecture was built on software languages and coding attitudes tolerant of embedded mistakes with no corrective governance oversight. A huge global hacker community emerged with impunity to hunt for and exploit these coding errors across borders, applications, and sectors (Kinnersley 2015).

In these early years, even though cybercrime was becoming clear as a phenomenon, the wider utopian naivety and commercial security deafness continued because the Internet did not connect anything of great importance simultaneously. Even if someone 'went to the dark side' or if code went bad and viral, the widespread view was that the amount of damage that could be done would be minimal (Rochlin 1997). The misperceptions of the utopians and the IT capital goods industry coders would go on to endure remarkably well into the 2010s, even when the scale of the insecurity become visible to Western national governments (Dombrowski & Demchak, 2015).[8]

In truth, the Internet never was 'free' of costs, private ownership, or political constraints save at its outset when it was owned and operated by Westernized universities. Policymakers in democratic civil societies—who relied on the utopians' vision, and the libertarianism of the IT community and its business leaders—argued in ill-informed good faith for a universally 'freely' accessible Internet. National strategies and senior political and commercial leaders' statements in democratic systems ignored the basics. These fundamentals included recognizing the peer-or-pay contracts that funded, built, operated, and maintained what they viewed as a public good: the privately owned undersea cables carrying 95% of the world's Internet exchanges, or the existence in most countries of a single legacy, barely denationalized, national telecommunication agency available for resurgent national control of the nation's cyberspace (DeNardis 2012; Oates 2008; Noam 1992, 1998).

Once cyberspace left the confines of the consolidated democratic societies, their legal systems, and the controls of Western-regulated telecommunications firms, it moved beyond the power of Westernized nations to keep the world both deeply cybered and guided by the rule of law. With commercialization as it occurred, the Internet was never going to be the utopia. Rather, the globalized Internet became a resource-rich frontier and substrate over which—now and for the future—nations and organizations would fight overtly, covertly, and in every other way possible.

Cybered Conflict

A new form of struggle—'cybered conflict'—emerged as the Internet matured. As it grew to be an indispensable 'substrate' to all society functions, the unfettered 'world wide web' nearly eliminated the conflict-dampening effects of geography, awareness, and wealth on intergroup or interstate conflict. These conditions provided offensive actors with five advantages: scale in organization, proximity, precision, deception of tools, and opacity in origins. First, throughout history, most mid-sized communities were deterred from frequently initiating conflicts with other more distant mid-sized peers because they could not afford to pay the scale of organization that might be required. For wealthy empires or hostile close neighbours, the challenge was easier—the emperor could buy everything and the neighbour could tailor its forces to what was needed efficiently. Second, it was hard to get the necessary *proximity* to distant lands to know which targets to hit and with what. Third, with limited resources, *precision* would be needed in the choice in weapons, numbers, timing, and location in order to assure victory. Fourth and fifth, mid-sized aggressors needed more deception about their capabilities and opacity about their identity if the defenders were equally matched.

Cyberspace as it is constructed today, however, turned these hindrances into advantages for offensive behaviour in and out of war time. It has made the modern state into a 'target-rich environment', a deeply cybered, super-integrated 'socio-technical-economic system' (STES), integrating previously disparate societal functions. In reducing distance with few to no regulations, it has made it easier for legitimate businesses to communicate, gather market data and tailor products—and for anyone from individual to emperor to reach out and harm anyone else. Cyberspace also enabled a vast array of otherwise powerless individuals, countries, and organizations to use scale, proximity, precision, deception in tools, and opacity in origins for rapacious and malicious reasons. Today, an individual, group, or state can be 5–5,000 kilometres away and organize a large-scale army of strangers or infected computers to reach into the systems of unwitting victims, discover critical information with no apparent proximity to the targeted victims, and choose whatever it wants in terms of effects, timing, and repetition. Furthermore, deception in the tools used and uncertainty as to who is operating them enables whole campaigns to continue for years unobserved and unhindered.[9]

The emergent cybered conflict age is characterized by these offence advantages. It is a continuum from peace to war because defenders can be losing their resources or ability to operate without realizing the situation or being equipped to counter the systemic effects. No declaration of war is likely or needed. The destruction of traditional war—the point at which cyber and bombs converge—lies at the end of this spectrum, but it is less efficient and more costly (Demchak and Dombrowski 2011). As nations progressively digitize across all their major societal functions, they face four layers of complex systems surprise that can be manipulated by adversaries in this form of conflict. These are, starting at the lowest level of society-wide integration: the single large critical enterprise layer; the interdependent enterprises composing the critical infrastructure layer; the overarching layer of a large number of globally intrusive malicious actors[10]; and the final layer of a small number of exquisitely skilled 'wicked' actors usually employed by states or transnational criminal organizations.[11] Only the two enterprise layers are normally under the legal governance of any given nation's political structure, while the vast community of bad actors and the smaller, often state-sponsored, wicked actors operate at will across borders and enterprises exploiting these offence advantages and furthering the potential for cybered conflict.

What can modern states do to reduce disruptive losses and surprise across all four layers? A preferred solution is the transformation of cyberspace to be more secure. That goal, however, is not merely technical—it requires coordinated actions across all the sectors comprising the entire integrated national STES. The largely empirical literature on large-scale technological systems (LTS)[12] offers six specific responses when enterprises or nations are facing potential cascading surprises with highly disruptive or devastating effects.[13] Single enterprises or nations need to strategically ensure *redundancy* in knowledge,[14] *slack* in time,[15] and *discovery trial-and-error learning* (DTEL) across their whole system.[16] Deeply interdependent companies or closely allied nations need to agree and practise continuous *collective sensemaking*, frequently tested *collective rapid mitigation responses*, and shared *whole of systems DTEL* (Comfort, 2010).

Extended to the scale of a highly integrated nation, these empirical results suggest a 'whole-of-society' approach to cyber insecurity that involves considerable operational integration (Lindberg and Sundelius, 2013).[17] Similar to the empirically tested responses for the two original enterprise layers, the goal is coherence across the whole national STES to make the attacks much more costly, harder, and less likely to succeed. With this approach—backed by an empirical literature on surprise, nations can create the 'systemic resilience' needed to respond coherently across all four layers of systemic surprise and to reduce the easy access to the five offence advantages. In short, democratic nations with this complex systems approach are better positioned to create nationally 'robust cyber power' for international influence and defence of national well-being.

Democracies More Vulnerable

The difficulty, however, is that democracies are more vulnerable than autocratic systems to the full range of cybered conflict and its manipulation of complex system surprises due to their openness.[18] Long before the kinetic end of the cybered conflict spectrum is engaged, adversaries can hollow the resilience resources of a defending nation by extraction or manipulations. Economic coercion is much more possible than in previous eras. Data exchanges currently supporting transparency and the fidelity of data, programs and networks can all be corrupted. All kinds of societally critical information—such as that found in bank accounts, public health records, tax accounts, regulations, product fidelity, markets, legal systems, and social media discourse—can be compromised by opaque actors with no legal recourse or automatic corrective mechanisms for long periods.

Furthermore, robust defensive cyber power means making the responses to all four layers of surprise and the five advantages coherent—and enforceable—across all the sectors comprising a national STES. The democracies have not collectively caught up with the emerging reality. Cybered conflict will continue as more nations become capable of using the offence advantages to hollow out adversaries and gain cumulative wealth and coercive advantage. The rules preferred by a deeply cybered, autocratic rest of the world of overwhelming scale are likely to be incompatible with the rule of law and with the economic and livelihood expectations of individually open and cybered civil societies.

SOVEREIGNTY, SCALE, AND CYBER POWER

Cyber sovereignty of defending nations and the scale of their deep cybered cooperation will be critical to their defence and survival in the coming interstate system. First, each nation—just as each enterprise in the LTS studies—needs to ensure its own whole-of-society systemic resilience and its wicked actor disruption capabilities able to mute deleterious cascades across the four layers of surprise. Only in this way can the cyber power of a state be robust enough to resist the demands of another state in a deeply digitized, non-rule-of-law world.

That is, a state needs to recognize its own cyber sovereignty in order to put its own house in order. For such power, resilience is critical and requires strategic coherence across the nation's entire STES and oriented towards both defence and viable economic exchanges. Every sector is involved, including the largescale IT capital goods industries, as team members in defending the well-being of the society.

Second, these democratic societies face a cyber-capable world whose scale is overwhelming for individual states and whose increasingly autocratic preferences across socio-technical-economic systems are not compatible with the transparency, data fidelity, and freedoms of modern democracies. Much like the integrated critical infrastructure enterprises studied by the LTS literature, individual states need to respond to the scale of the rising autocratic world's sources of surprise collectively, as though they were allied enterprises facing the same overwhelming threat. That recognition will require—at the speeds of the Internet—widely integrated cross-sectors and cross-allied-borders operations for collective sense making, orchestrated rapid mitigation, and continuously shared systems DTEL. In short, the empirical literature recommends that, in addition to getting their own individual cyber houses in order, this minority of democratic states ally their resilience structures to provide each of them with the robust cyber power necessary to survive.

How the world's few consolidated democratic civil societies react will largely determine the future they will face over the next 20 to 30 years. These two strategic choices—individual cyber sovereignty and a collective cyber resilience alliance—will largely influence which future emerges.

Recognizing a national cyber jurisdiction—the essence of cyber sovereignty—is the first step to developing a view of society as a cooperative enterprise of sorts, worthy of defending in terms of its socio-technical-economic systems' viability and political freedoms. Without this recognition, democratic leaders cannot effectively use 'stateness'[19]—a sense of collective willingness to act—to create and sustain systemic resilience.[20] While cyber sovereignty has been repeatedly rejected by Western corporations and political leaders for commercial and optimistic reasons, a wide array of autocratic leaders[21]—led by China as the rising centre of economic and demographic power—are determined to make national cyber jurisdictions the fundamental structure of the international Internet.[22] As China's international influence continues to expand, its preferences in how national cyber jurisdictions are recognized and honoured by other states will be adopted by the large majority of similarly inclined autocratic leaders. Consolidated democratic nations can refuse to define their national cyberspace, while still trying to defend it, but they will nonetheless face a conflictual world of autocratic jurisdictions. Not only will there be national autocratic regulations on Westernized cyber firms and interactions, there is no guarantee that large autocratic states will impose any restraints on their own citizens in the constant assaults into the coffers of democratic societies. Nor is there a clear path to unifying the cyber resilience efforts for any democracy if the part of the cyber substrate to be defended is not defined and legitimized as part of the nation's critical interest.

The second step is recognizing the scale disadvantage of each Westernized democracy attempting to defend its own cybered well-being alone. Representing less than 10% of the world's population today, democratic states have limited future ability to determine what the other 90% will do with cyberspace and Internet freedom. China's leaders argue that a country's 'rightful place' in the world is defined by the scale of its population[23] and have declared that China will be one—if not *the*—cyber super power rejecting Western civil society values.[24] By building and operating networks for free all over the world's non-Western nations, China will imprint its more authoritarian preferences on future global information exchanges that all individual states of lesser scale will have to use to survive economically. Acting to balance against this scale disadvantage will be critical for any state unwilling to eventually concede to these autocratic preferences.

FOUR FUTURES AND THEIR STRATEGIES: CYBER—STATUS QUO, VASSALDOM, WESTPHALIA, AND RESILIENCE ALLIANCE

Varying the strategic recognition of sovereignty against a scale of democratic strategic cyber responses creates four possible futures for democratic societies. The time frame for these futures is roughly one generation hence, around the same time that most prominent estimates place a consolidation of China's role in the world as the largest economy and give it a commensurately central role in international politics.

Table 45.1 Four Futures

	STRATEGIC RECOGNITION [OF CYBER SOVEREIGNTY]	
NATIONAL SCALE [OF CYBER RESPONSE]	NO	YES
INDIVIDUAL	Cyber Status Quo, and Cyber Vassaldom	Cyber Westphalia / cyber sovereignty
COLLECTIVE	*Western Cyber Domination (expired option)*	Cyber Operational Resilience Alliance

Cyber Status Quo with 'Keep Trying' Strategy

In this future, Westernized democracies neither recognize cyber sovereignty for themselves or other states, nor collectively develop an operationally functional 'whole of the nation' cyber resilience alliance to balance the market, demographic, and extraction/manipulation scale of China in particular. In the status quo scenario, the current situation continues to stumble along for another generation. The minority democracies 'keep trying' to maintain Western presumptions about their influence over the global international system through the fight for an open Internet. However, they continue to lose leverage internationally in defence of their liberal international system and its rules of economic exchange as the centres of demographic and economic power move to Asia. The patterns of deception and opacity in hostile cybered conflict campaigns grow more sophisticated, employing manipulated political and economic extraction, blackmail, or takeover campaigns inside democratic civil societies to effectively dismantle sources of resistance and resilience one by one.

Unable to credibly attribute cyber or associated market losses to hostile state-level actors, the smaller-scale democratic nations' political leaders prove unable to rally their fragmented private sectors to band together with political authorities to defend their hollowing economies. Private sector actors will continue to lobby against collaborating in a strategy of nation-wide systemic cyber resilience, especially if it involves foregoing some short-term competitive advantage.

Cyber commands will become a new normal for both autocratic and democratic states, but their funding and control will vary considerably and tighten over time. The much larger scale of autocratic states' cybered forces and their proxies will continue to evolve and overwhelm the smaller democratic public defenders. While victim states will keep calling for more security to be immediately bolted on post hoc—for reasons of wealth loss more than privacy—the overall losses and cybersecurity costs will diminish the resources available for the expensive talent, structures, and transformational technological research and development (R&D) needed for effective national cyber defences at proper scale.

In this future, China's cautious leadership will likely still view itself as not quite secure enough to go public and simply demand adherence to its political and economic preferences, but it will still pursue the full range of cybered conflicts' offense advantages, both directly and through expatriate proxies.

Cyberspace will continue to be open on its surface within democracies but, in more autocratic states, technologically and legally enforced content controls will be centrally imposed by the national telecommunications agencies. The range of insecure new technologies will continue to rise, including wearables, personal drones, and ever expanding and vulnerable social media platforms. Despite constant calls for innovations in security to be free of inconvenience or regulation—especially in democratic states where cyberspace continues to be perceived as both essential to prosperity and damaged if regulated—domestic economic attrition, cyber manipulated de-legitimization of the political discourse, and declining effective international influence will continue to produce a steady decline for national wealth and the ability to distribute it acceptably. The underlying technology and associated economic benefits of cyberspace will be largely designed, produced, and operated by Asian revenue centres indirectly controlling the choices of most major cyber services providers, and, through their systems, the choices of most states' leaders in defending their national well-being.

Cyber Vassaldom with 'Concede Slowly' Strategy

In the Cyber Vassaldom future, much of what is critical to the functioning of a society is controlled by a foreign state's proxy actors, enabling the foreign state's representatives to coerce a specific behaviour in the targeted political system by merely suggesting that X or Y political behaviour is desired or undesired.[25] In this future, the Cyber Status Quo scenario does not last long enough for the vassal state to technologically afford the transformation of its underlying insecure substrate. Democratic states do not recognize sovereignty and no longer have the economic and political resources to control their own cyber jurisdictions in the face of the scale advantages of the rising authoritarian world. Their fragmented political systems fall slowly to the 'counter-resilience' cybered conflict strategies of China, Russia, and others, because the formation of robust cyber power has been effectively precluded among democracies.

Acting as a global 'cyber hegemon' through its IT state champions and its central role leading international institutions and rules preferences, China continues to widely employ economic coercion to keep resistance ineffectual, dispersed, and manageable, and to deny democratic leaders the capacity for resistance through stateness.[26] In the democratic cyber vassals, the necessary transformation of the underlying cyberspace substrate to be more secure will continue to be a formal goal that founders on inadequate public resources and withheld private sector support as unprofitable, non-product-related research. For good and coerced reasons, corporate and political leaders will continue to be unable, unwilling, or naïve—or coerced into silence—about how to protect their technology advances.

The financial means of major Western states to construct effective national cyber resilience will decline steadily. Democratic administrative economies with fewer public employees will stretch ever less generous tax revenues to achieve minimally acceptable levels of services, and continue to make promises that they cannot meet.

Cyber commands in democracies will be slowly relegated to cyber watchtowers for terrorists due to declining resources and the coercive background lobbying of autocratic actors eager to blunt the skills of these agencies. Furthermore, as the national independence from the global technology markets decline, these commands will be less able to operate without close reliance on national telecommunications agencies using off-the-shelf technologies purchased from—as well as designed and updated by—Chinese-owned sources.[27]

As this scenario consolidates, China will be able to dictate openly much of what is and is not allowed to transit among and within other nations dependent on the Chinese-built state-owned or controlled networks. Transparency in terms of finances, personal blackmail-worthy data, and state secrets will slowly erode as traffic manipulation occurs at the network operations levels with more and more nations dependent on these Chinese-built networks provided for free but not transferred in full operational control. While observing the general mechanisms of democracy, individual nations and their political and economic leaders will avoid contravening the cyber hegemon's preferences in technologies, economic choices, and societal rules.

Cyber Westphalia with 'Hunker Down' Strategy

In this Cyber Westphalia future, recognition of national jurisdictions in cyberspace becomes the global norm.[28] Each nation, however, assumes individual responsibility for their own relative cyber power in balancing against the scale of the rest of the world's cyber conflicts, the mass of bad/wicked actors, and the cyber hegemon. Most nations define their jurisdictions as beginning when the first packet reaches their national telecommunications agency or firm's servers. More cyber competent states—especially autocratic nations—are likely to define it as when the undersea or land cable first crosses into their geographically defined national territory. What is left as open international cyberspace is determined by cable and satellite ownership and technological control enforced at the whim of each participating state.

As in the other possible futures, China rises to be the major cyber hegemon. However, democratic states are able to use their individual sovereignty to orchestrate their sectors and make more progress in resilience, especially in advancing the underlying transformation of their own cyber substrate. The rate of GDP attrition is slower to the extent that the third layer of complex system surprise—the high number of malicious actors—is reduced by how advanced and well enforced are the cyber jurisdictional controls across transiting countries.

Cyber commands will exist and are likely to be drawn more closely into the overarching internal resilience effort of the state as recognition of the scale imbalance continues without commensurate allied support. These commands are likely to focus on disrupting adversaries' highly advanced operations at the fourth layer of complex system surprise—that of the elite 'wicked actors' and their business models. Using these greater technological skills for wider societal defence, however, is unlikely to be supported by private sectors' actors who are struggling in the relatively small size of individual domestic markets.

Cyber sovereignty in general is likely to result in more state restrictions on foreign ownership, data locations, or technology production. Nonetheless, while it will be somewhat more difficult for aggressive autocratic actors to reach directly into defending democracies to own, remotely control, or coerce the development of critical technologies, global technology development will be driven by preferences outside the Western democracies. The scale of their individual domestic IT talent and production facilities will make consistency with Western production values more expensive compared with the larger and cheaper—and often subsidized—markets of the wider and more autocratic world. The tendency will be for private actors in democratic states to agitate to be able to use the cheaper foreign devices and systems available globally, even if they undermine the national ability to secure its cyber jurisdiction. National leaders will struggle to inspect, cleanse, or reject cheaper global technologies that will—if allowed—flood domestic markets.

The more skilled the surrounding authoritarian states become in employing the five advantages across all four layers of any nation's STES, the harder it will be for any single nation to counter significant campaigns. The same tsunami of global malicious and wicked actors will continue to batter against any 'borders' in cyberspace. At the same time, even with domestic resilience operations, democratic public and private sector actors will be subject to a heightened level of deceptive and/or opaque personal, professional, and organizational coercive campaigns by autocratic actors intent on weakening the national coherence of democratic nations. As each individual democratic civil society attempts to preserve its own national cyber-gated community, the challenge in balancing the costs of other social goods with those of implementing public and private sector cybersecurity measures to the scale required means ever smaller national wealth to distribute to commensurately dissatisfied and impatient publics.

Cyber Operational Resilience Alliance with 'Cyber City on the Hill' Strategy

In this future, democratic civil societies not only recognize cyber sovereignty, they also use it to create a civil society-governed, operationally, and cross-sector integrated cyber operational resilience alliance. It is cooperatively and interdependently managed across like-minded states by integrating the edges of their national cyber jurisdictions. Unlike the Cyber Westphalia future, this Cyber Operational Resilience Alliance (CORA) balances the collective, economic, IT talent, and demographic weight of the civil society nations against the scale of the rising global and autocratic cyber hegemon, China. Inside the alliance, each state pursues internally the institutionalization of its own resilience and disruptive capacities to the best of their scale capacities. But across the allied states they also coalesce, design, fund, implement, and continually maintain a collectively democratic cyber jurisdiction with respect to the rest of the more authoritarian markets and actors. With the merged cyber jurisdictions of this cyber alliance, the otherwise minority states can develop and nurture across public and private sectors and at the necessary scale the effective design, production, markets, talent, and underlying R&D transformation funding to afford the costs of cybersecurity systemic resilience for most members.

In this future, the sovereignty of the unified and collectively resilient cyber democratic network blunts the ability of China as the larger global cyber hegemon to fully dictate the character, designs, costs, and uses of technologies internationally. Alliance producers compete credibly and adequately as a large coherent counterweight to the central influence of Chinese technological dominance. There is sufficient size across alliance members to collectively maintain and defend their ICT industries as a healthy and semi-autarkic shared critical sector. Despite its underlying control of many autocratic nations' national IT systems through its globally powerful IT state champions, China's reach into democratic systems is diminished to manageable and survivable levels.

As opposed to the industrial and Cold War era, civil-military relations will have stronger overlaps inside domestic systems and across allied networks to facilitate both resilience and rapid hunter-response operations. Cyber commands will still focus on tailored forward disruption of wicked actors and these operations are likely to be highly classified under national control of the dominant democratic states such as the United States. However, national cyber commands and their civilian domestic security equivalents are likely to be strongly linked together as a community allocating missions and proactive and rapid reaction tasks for the collective defence. As a result of the wider distribution of the costs of systemic cyber resilience across the alliance, the average annual GDP loss to cybered extraction will diminish in comparison to other futures.

Within the 900 million-plus population of the CORA, new market advances will rise to create both new and better secured products and technologies with consumers both inside and outside the alliance. With the talent pool and market size of these advanced nations, the shared effort buys time in which to create a resilient community, even if outnumbered globally. The alliance is better scaled than any individual nation to develop and fund cooperative and collective technological filters, controls, R&D, sensor and rapid reactions, expert exchanges, and complementary systemic designs, and effective operational sharing. Equally importantly, with economic losses confined to those extractions by criminals within the jurisdictions of alliance members, alliance-imposed and reciprocal legal punishments will limit the scale of malicious actors' use of the five offence advantages.

Finally, this alliance can be the 'cyber city on the hill', able to demonstrate how a cybered state can be both secure and democratic. The search for a more secure, transformed, underlying STES substrate also offers new technological advances marketable to the rest of the world, reinforcing the economic and political viability of a democratic community at variance with the rising authoritarian, conflictual, and cybered world.

Democratic Cyber Survival

These four futures offer varying implications for the long-term survival of today's consolidated democratic civil societies. One future is clearly to be avoided—Cyber Vassaldom—and one is unlikely to be sustainable—Cyber Status Quo. One scenario could offer an interim stage to survival or to slow dismantlement—Cyber Westphalia. Only one, however, seems to offer a successful balance against the most likely dominant autocratic actor—Cyber Operational Resilience Alliance. Unfortunately, the latter is also the most difficult to achieve. It requires that democratic civil societies—so long champions of an unbordered Internet—both embrace cyber sovereignty for the world and then give up some of their own to join a like-minded community collectively balancing the scale of the wider authoritarian world led by China.

To paraphrase Benjamin Franklin, the consolidated democracies will need to 'hang' together rapidly in a cyber resilience alliance, or they—including the United States—will assuredly 'hang' separately given the rising autocratic world. A huge community of hostile and exploitative states will be able by sheer scale to demand, bribe, or coerce observance of their illiberal rules of economic and political exchange from each liberal state individually. Only a strongly coherent and skilfully cybered community of the 'noble few' like-minded states will have the economic, technological, and demographic resources to stand up to the much larger scale China as a peer power in the emerging era. Much more comparative STES organizational research is needed to guide leaders, CEOs, practitioners, and scholars towards this future as soon as possible. The ground is being laid for the other futures right now.[29]

Notes

1. The rise of China was inevitable, but it occurred faster than anticipated. There are some disagreements over the numbers that really matter. While population differences are undisputed, the economic power elevating these populations is debatable. In 1989, Deng Xiaoping predicted that China would become the United States' economic and power peer by 2049. Later analyses, such as the 2007 Goldman Sachs estimate, predicted that parity would occur by 2025, with China doubling that of the United States by 2050. 'As this time of writing, various authors argue that China has been roughly at parity for several years (at least since 2014). See, respectively, Jacques, M. 2012. *When China Rules the World: The Rise of the Middle Kingdom and the End of the Western World* [Greatly updated and expanded]. Harmondsworth, UK: Penguin; Li, X., and Shaw, T.M. 2014. '"Same Bed, Different Dreams" and "Riding Tiger" Dilemmas: China's Rise and International Relations/Political Economy', *Journal of Chinese Political Science* 19 (1): 69–93; Scott, M., and Sam, C. 2016. 'China and the United States—Tale of Two Giant Economies', 12 May. *Bloomberg.com*. https://www.bloomberg.com/graphics/2016-us-vs-china-economy/; Mingfu, Liu, and Rhode, Grant. 2016. 'The China Dream: Great Power Thinking and Strategic Posture in the Post-American Era', *Naval War College Review* 69 (2), Article 20.

2. This conflict is a system versus system struggle between states and groups that is multilayer and multisector using all the devices, techniques, access points, technologies, and human behaviours associated with cyberspace as the underlying substrate whose

architectures, insecurities, and governance enables these operations (Demchak, C.C. 2011. *Wars of Disruption and Resilience: Cybered Conflict, Power, and National Security*. Athens, University of Georgia Press).

3. General Keith Alexander, the first commander of the US national cyber command, used this phrase repeatedly after seeing the volume of extracted intellectual property data and financial exploitations transiting out of the United States. See Bradley, J. 2015. *The China Mirage: The Hidden History of American Disaster in Asia*. London: Little, Brown.

4. The French Senate in 2012 came to a similar conclusion as General Alexander. See Bockel, M.J.-M. 2012. 'Cyber-Defence: A Global Issue, A National Priority' ('The Bockel Report'). Paris: Senate of the Assembly General of France. http://www.senat.fr/rap/r11-681/r11-6811. pdf

5. Constrained budgets sideline the organization's acquisition of advanced technologies today, even before the era of system-wide national IT R&D and transformational deployment budgets has fully emerged. See Cava, C.P. 2017. 'Grounded: Nearly Two-Thirds of US Navy's Strike Fighters Can't Fly', February 6. *Defense News*.

6. Early Internet creators and promoters had been taught in universities where IT networks and access were provided openly by their schools and usually funded by national government grants and assumed to be free. They shared a strongly utopian vision of the Internet as a freely available public good, even for making fortunes. This cyber utopian meme has proven so strong in democratic societies that IT-enabled business models and university courses have hardly mentioned cybersecurity other than minimums for reliability and user account passwords until very recently. It is still generally not taught as a critical element of computer science education: Siraj, A., Taylor, B., Kaza, S. et al. 2015. 'Integrating Security in the Computer Science Curriculum', *ACM Inroads* 6 (2): 77–81.

7. For example, Apple's business to this writing emphasizes a highly proprietary operating system for competitive edge, not security: Boulanger, A. 2005. 'Open-Source Versus Proprietary Software: Is One More Reliable and Secure Than the Other? *IBM Systems Journal* 44 (2): 239–48.

8. Bradley, *The China Mirage*.

9. This cybered conflict characteristic has led to the widespread concern with credible attribution. With that, a number of international treaties and understandings allow a defending state to strike back at the sponsoring state or organization in proportion without violating international law: Schmitt, M.N. (ed.) 2013. *Tallinn Manual on the International Law Applicable to Cyber Warfare*. Cambridge, UK: Cambridge University Press.

10. A globe of 'bad actors' constitutes the third layer of sources for complex system surprise. It is a vast and growing international community of bad actors, starting from low-level 'script kiddies' only able to steal and distribute malicious code through to the upper range of hackers able to write their own code moderately well and sell it on the global underground cybercriminal market. Often selling the bad code is a better income stream than personally using it: Glenny, M. 2011. *Dark Market*. New York: Random House).

11. This layer is the source of the term 'advanced persistent threat' (APT). These 'wicked actors' (named after the mathematics of 'wicked' problems) are a very small but exquisitely skilled group working for governments or transnational corporations). For these advanced actors, just knowing what the defending system uses to defend is sufficient: their business model rests on persistence, the thrill of the challenge, and their personal immunity from interference. It differs from the lower-level script kiddies and middling good coders in the exceptional skill level and the clear pattern of being state—or

state-equivalent—sponsored: (Sood, A.K., and Enbody, R.J. 2013. 'Targeted Cyberattacks: A Superset of Advanced Persistent Threats', *IEEE Security & Privacy* 11 (1): 54–61.

12. This is a well-honed highly empirical literature vastly understudied by scholars of international relations and of computer science.

13. Empirical studies include nuclear aircraft carriers and air traffic control, as well as private electrical grids and water supply. See LaPorte, T.R., and Consolini, P.M. 1991. 'Working in Practice but Not in Theory: Theoretical Challenges of "High-Reliability Organizations"', *Journal of Public Administration Research and Theory: J-PART* 1 (1): 19–48.

14. This is not mere replication but having, at the point of an inevitable complex systems surprise, several different sources of the same knowledge needed to respond effectively and at least stop the cascade.

15. 'Slack in time' means to have the space to decide upon the response to a surprise. This is the cheapest option of the three, and throughout history the most likely response to fear of surprise—to push it out as far as possible with walls, gates, keys, spies, or border patrols.

16. This list is extracted from two literatures: the LTS work on resilience and relative complexity studies. Notably among the sources are the large volume of works by the seminal LTS scholars, Louise Comfort, Charles Perrow, Todd R. LaPorte, and Erich Hollnagel.

17. The connectedness of the modern cybered society begins to approximate the open organizational described by the seminal organizational theorist, J.D. Thompson. See Thompson, J.D. 1967. *Organizations in Action*. New York: McGraw-Hill.

18. See, for example, Shiller and Akeroff's discussion of deception in democracies: Akerlof, G. A., and Shiller, R.J. 2015. *Phishing for Phools: The Economics of Manipulation and Deception*. Princeton, NJ: Princeton University Press.

19. Upon perceiving a major threat, leaders of a state need to rally support to resist coercion. A diffused slow-acting threat buried in deceptive forms is exceptionally difficult to use as a motivation to cooperative action: Blanchard, J.-M. F., and Ripsman, N.M. 2008. 'A Political Theory of Economic Statecraft', *Foreign Policy Analysis* 4 (4): 371–98.

20. Sovereignty has had variable definitions since the 1800s: Anghie, A. 2007. *Imperialism, Sovereignty and the Making of International Law* (Vol. 37). Cambridge, UK: Cambridge University Press. However, the Chinese have been quite clear that they define it as being left alone inside their borders: Jiang, M. 2012. 'Authoritarian Informationalism: China's Approach to Internet Sovereignty'. In *Essential Readings of Comparative Politics*, 4th edn, edited by P. O'Neil and R. Rogowski. New York: WW Norton & Company.

21. Nationally controlled radio stations and telephone exchanges have long been prime points of control in non-Western states, with the Internet quite unlikely to be much different in the view of national leaders—if the means to do so were available: Glanz, J., and Markoff, J. 2011,. 'Egypt Leaders Found "Off" Switch for Internet', February 15. *The New York Times*; Gumede, W. 2016. 'Rise in Censorship of the Internet and Social Media in Africa'. *Journal of African Media Studies* 8 (3): 413–21.

22. Much is made of the Chinese 'Great Firewall' and the Russian SORM (System of Operational-Investigatory Measures); but neither state nor most Asian states have ever been willing to concede local sovereignty unless forced to do so: Kissinger, H. 2015. *World Order*. Harmondsworth, UK: Penguin: 179; see also Chang, A. 2014. 'Warring State: China's Cybersecurity Strategy'. http://www.cnas.org/chinas-cybersecurity-strategy#. VeHZlM5RErs

23. The United States has for more than a century consistently mistaken Chinese compliance with Western practices. See Bradley, *The China Mirage*.

THE FUTURE OF DEMOCRATIC CIVIL SOCIETIES   749

24. Mingfu, *The China Dream*, 12; Kemp, T. 2015,. 'China Leaders Oppose "Universal Values" But It May Not Matter', Interview with Prof. Steinfeld, Brown University, July 6. *CNBC. com*.
25. Credit is given to John Mallery of MIT who, in 2015, first suggested this term in personal conversations with the author.
26. For example, Huawei has built the 4G networks for a wide variety of nations in Africa, the Middle East, and Asia, and largely for free. In return, the nation gives over the control of these networks to Huawei representatives who operate, maintain, and upgrade these systems, effectively determining what is and is not allowed to pass through them. See Gagliardone, I. 2015. 'China and the Shaping of African Information Societies'. In *Africa and China: How Africans and Their Governments are Shaping Relations with China*, edited by A. Gadzala, 1–25. Lanham, MD: Rowman & Littlefield.
27. See Moran, T.H. 2013. 'Dealing with Cybersecurity Threats Posed by Globalised IT Suppliers', *Policy: A Journal of Public Policy and Ideas* 29 (3): 10–14; Hannas, W.C., Mulvenon, J., and Puglisi, A.B. 2013. *Chinese Industrial Espionage: Technology Acquisition and Military Modernisation*. Abingdon, UK: Routledge.
28. The term originated with Demchak and Dombrowski, 'Rise of a Cybered Westphalian Age'.
29. These judgements are solely those of the author and do not reflect the positions of the US government, the US Navy, or the US Naval War College.

BIBLIOGRAPHY

Barlow, J. 1996. 'A Declaration of the Independence of Cyberspace', *Humanist—Buffalo* 56 (3): 18–19.
Benedikt, M. 1991. *Cyberspace: First Steps*. Cambridge, Mass.: MIT Press.
Chang, A. 2014. 'Warring State: China's Cybersecurity Strategy'. http://www.cnas.org/chinas-cybersecurity-strategy#.VeHZlM5RErs
Comfort, L.K. 2010. 'Social Network Interaction Among Nested Sets in Dynamic Contexts: Disaster Operations as a Laboratory for Social Change', *Spatio-Temporal Constraints on Social Networks, Position Papers*, 7.
Demchak, C.C. 2012. 'Resilience, Disruption, and a "Cyber Westphalia": Options for National Security in a Cybered Conflict World'. In *Securing Cyberspace: A New Domain for National Security*, edited by N.B.a.J. Price. Washington, DC: The Aspen Institute.
Demchak, C.C. 2016. 'Uncivil and Post-Western Cyber Westphalia: Changing Interstate Power Relations of the Cybered Age', *The Cyber Defense Review* 1(1).
Demchak, C.C., and Dombrowski, P.J. 2011. 'Rise of a Cybered Westphalian Age', *Strategic Studies Quarterly* 5 (1): 31–62.
DeNardis, L. 2012. 'Hidden Levers of Internet Control: An Infrastructure-Based Theory of Internet Governance', *Information, Communication & Society* 15 (5): 720–38.
Dombrowski, P., and Demchak, C.C. 2015. 'Thinking Systemically about Security and Resilience in an Era of Cybered Conflict', *Cybersecurity Policies and Strategies for Cyberwarfare Prevention*, 367.
Hanson, V.D. 2001. *Carnage and Culture*. New York: Doubleday.
Hodgetts, R.M., and Luthans, F. 2006. *International Management: Culture, Strategy, and Behavior*. New York: McGraw-Hill.

Javers, E. 2011. 'Secrets and Lies: The Rise of Corporate Espionage in a Global Economy', *Geostrategic Journal of International Affairs* 12, 53.

Johnson, D.R., and Post, D. 1996. 'Law and Borders—The Rise of Law in Cyberspace', *Stanford Law Review* 48 (5): 1367–402.

Kemp, T. 2015. 'China Leaders Oppose 'Universal Values,' but it May not Matter: Interview With Prof Steinfeld Brown University. July 6. *CNBC.com*.

Kinnersley, B. 2015. A Chronology of Influential [computer] Languages, The [Computer] Language List: Collected Information On About 2500 Computer Languages, Past and Present. Retrieved 21 August 2015 from University of Kansas.

Kshetri, N. 2013. 'Cybercrime and Cyber-Security Issues Associated with China: Some Economic and Institutional Considerations', *Electronic Commerce Research* 13 (1): 41–69.

Lenhart, S.M. 2000. 'Hammering Down Nails', *Georgia Journal of International and Comparative Law* 29: 491.

Lindberg, H., and Sundelius, B. 2013. 'Whole-of-Society Disaster Resilience: The Swedish Way'. In *The McGraw-Hill Homeland Security Handbook*. 2nd edn. New York: McGraw-Hill, pp. 1295–319.

McFarlin, D., and Sweeney, P.D. 2014. *International Management: Strategic Opportunities & Cultural Challenges*. Abingdon, UK: Routledge.

Nitoiu, C. 2016. 'Aspirations to Great Power Status: Russia's Path to Assertiveness in the International Arena under Putin', *Political Studies Review* 15 (1): 39–48.

Noam, E. 1992. *Telecommunications in Europe*. New York: Oxford University Press.

Noam, E.M. 1998. *Telecommunications in Latin America*. New York: Oxford University Press.

Norris, P., and Jones, D. 1998. 'Virtual Democracy', *Harvard International Journal of Press Politics* 3: 1–4.

Oates, J. 2008. 'Submarine Cable Cut Torpedoes Middle East Access: Web Slowdown Hits India, Pakistan Too', 30 January. The Register.

Oxley, J.E., and Yeung, B. 2001. 'E-Commerce Readiness: Institutional Environment and International Competitiveness', *Journal of International Business Studies* 32: 705–23.

Oyedemi, T. 2015. 'Internet Access as Citizen's Right? Citizenship in the Digital Age', *Citizenship Studies* 19 (3–4), 450–64.

Rheingold, H. 1993. *Virtual Communities: Homesteading on the Electronic Frontier*. Reading, UK: Addison Wesley.

Rochlin, G. 1997. *Trapped in the Net: The Unanticipated Consequences of Computerization*. Princeton, NJ: Princeton University Press.

Trickey, H. 1988. 'C++ Versus Lisp: A Case Study', *ACM Sigplan Notices* 23 (2): 9–18.

CHAPTER 46

....

FUTURE NORMATIVE CHALLENGES

....

ENEKEN TIKK

CYBERSECURITY is often framed as a predominantly *normative* challenge: the Internet is referred to as a lawless space; international law has been contested or even rejected as a framework suitable to counter cyber threats; the information highway has been characterized as a road without rules. A whole 'cyber norms' discourse has evolved to shape new norms of responsible state behaviour.

Shaped by rivalry over whose view of the world and whose understanding and practice of norms, rules, and principles are to be accepted as standards of 'responsible' state behaviour in cyberspace, the current inter-governmental cyber norms discourse can be read as a normative power contestation rather than a unified search for normative order, clarity, and predictability. The struggle for power in the context of state development and use of ICTs follows the 'Great Game' playbooks, as some authors noted early in the cyber days (Wingfield 2000, 8).

However, this observation should not lead us to conclude that international law and shared norms have no place in international cybersecurity, or should not be further discussed and debated. How international law is applied to issues of cybersecurity determines the viability of existing principles, norms, and rules as well as possible further developments in international law and international cyber policy. Normative argument and action in response to actual cyber incidents, as well as the political testaments of the cyber superpowers, will condition international peace and security.

Although global by scope, cybersecurity issues are rooted in domestic ambitions and national operations. Understanding national regulatory and policy responses to particular cybersecurity issues is key to being able to follow and anticipate the proposed boundaries of acceptable and unacceptable behaviour in cyberspace.

Normative solutions to international cybersecurity issues need to be both detected and planted in the ethical-moral puzzle of competing normative propositions, strategies, and arguments. This chapter looks at ways to enrich, but perhaps also normalize, the cyber norms discourse in coming years. After discussing the concept of the Normative as a framework for research and development of norms across the disciplines of law and policy studies, it will offer anchoring points, leads, and directions for the next generation of writers and thinkers on normative approaches to international cybersecurity. Some of these are perpetual, highlighting the utility of normative theories and methods in international law and international relations. Others are more contingent, underlining the asymmetry of not just cyber threats but also potential normative developments.

This chapter suggests that normative steps towards responsible state behaviour in the use of ICTs should make use of the tools and solutions of different disciplines, consider opposing ideas, and contribute to improving security without disrupting the values and rules underpinning the information society. Normative attention to ICTs needs to be both hard and soft, high and low, reactive and anticipatory, at one and the same time.

THE CONCEPT OF THE NORMATIVE

The key characteristic of the current international cybersecurity discourse is the prominence of the Political (Schmitt 1932). Power politics is a tool of choice for many countries amid the irreconcilable push towards technological dependence on the one hand and the determined resistance to it on the other. The intensification of political debate around the development of ICTs is but another example of the pressure exerted by technological developments upon law and policy, reflecting both the politics of interested actors and the inadequacy of normative claims and processes. A discourse into future normative challenges and ways of overcoming them in the context of ICTs thus merits a deeper discussion of the concept of the Normative and its juxtaposition with ICTs.

In contrast, and in addition to the inherently conflictual Political, the Normative seeks to circumscribe, to commit, to establish, and to maintain an orderly routine of behaviour. It boldly employs the final distinctions of proper and improper. Rather than juggling the constantly competing and contesting interests found in the political realm, the Normative contours non-conformism, dissent, disgruntlement, malevolence, and hostility into a logically articulated and a coherent juridical system. The Normative balances relationships and positions by way of structurally and observably defining, establishing, creating, codifying, re-stating, reiterating, proclaiming, and declaring underlying ambitions and intentions (Singh 1990, 172). Whether it does so by 'hard' or 'soft' norms is secondary to its intent to uphold and support order with the assistance of the organized community. This is not to downplay the useful differences between soft and hard norms—such as the former, given the relative novelty of this degree and type of technological dependence and related normative thought, affording to tolerate trial-and-error in implementation.

The Normative commands certainty, predictability, and transparency of societal relations. It is called for in case of systematic antagonism and recurring confrontation between collectives and actors, even down to the level of the individual. Normative tools are applied to detect or establish the limits of otherwise arbitrary behaviour. Through inductive and deductive methods, the Normative postulates examples, boundaries, and conditions of the acceptable and the unacceptable. It confronts antagonism and hostilities with rules and principles, levels the opportunity for otherwise unequal participants, and eliminates prejudice in human and political affairs.

The need to operate with and within the Normative in its widest sense becomes evident at times when the meaning, and even the existence, of legally binding norms or guides of behaviour is contested. Such contestation brings to the fore deficiencies in respective normative frameworks or their implementation. It reveals the politics of law and necessitates a handshake between the Political and the Normative. Absent consensus on legal sentences, the search for predictability and transparency of behaviour continues in political agreements and more technical behaviour-shaping instruments such as standards.

Like the Political, the Normative is a premise of the concept of the state and part of a state's identity: state apparatus develops and adopts national legislation. Sovereigns make international law by agreement and practice. They agree upon soft normative instruments. They become the first-hand testing grounds for norms. State and society cannot always be regarded as synonymous for precisely defining and positioning the Normative. However, in case of democratic societies where norms are debated and formulated structurally and openly, the state employs the Normative as the instrument of will of politically and socially organized peoples. Through designated apparatus and processes, citizens and subjects of States exercise their involvement in and oversight upon the development of norms. In autocracies, the Normative, in contrast, is often employed as an instrument of the state.

Detecting and describing the Normative is complicated by disciplinary fragmentation (Katzenstein 1996; Schmitt and Vihul 2014). In domestic law, validity is an essential element of the establishment of a norm (Kelsen 1967). Norms are understood as legally formulated sentences or verdicts in national laws or legal precedent, applied to a pre-defined structure of legal facts. In international law, this understanding of norms is contested. In the legal order governing the relations between States, sanctions have a lesser (to no) role as an element of the norm structure (Voina-Motoc 1999). In political science, norms are commonly viewed as expectations of behaviour with no requirement for definitive formulation. Finally, ethical and moral norms can overlap or contest legally and politically formulated standards of behaviour. Normative endeavours are maximized when combining concepts and processes known from law, political science, international relations, and ethics. This could explain why, given their otherwise diametrically different views on the need for developing legally binding rules on international information security, both the United States and the Russian Federation welcomed the outcome of the 2014/15 United Nations (UN) Group of Governmental Experts (GGE) in the Field of Information and Telecommunications in the Context of International Security. The norms in paragraph 13 of the Group's report can be read as no advancement towards a treaty, due to their framing as 'non-binding'. However, by applying a different reading, these norms identify gaps and inconsistencies in reading and understanding international law, and suggest that, at least in some respects, additional rules may be needed over time. As such, these normative sentences can be regarded as paving the way to a treaty negotiation.

Nothing is more disruptive and challenging to the Normative than the need to correct, revise, or reverse a dictum that has heretofore been considered to be absolute, universal, and perpetual—whether that dictum was ordained by God, privileged by the behaviour of the community, preferred by agreement of its members or decided by an authority—e.g. a dictator or the legislature?. Thus, urgency to take corrective normative action often leads to the need to carefully reconcile diverse, disparate, and differing rules, norms, and standards (Shannon 2000). Defragmenting and harmonizing separate sets of legal rules and institutions could be regarded as a continuous goal of normative efforts. Then again, revision of seemingly set rules and standards is needed from time to time. The changed or changing circumstances or patterns of newer needs, values, goals, and objectives of society inevitably render some rules obsolete or illogical, putting upon us the imperative to discard or amend those (Black, Nolan, Nolan-Haley et al. 1990). This logic is behind the argument for developing *lex specialis* for international information and cybersecurity.

The Challenge of Values and Value Systems

A persistent problem in the cyber norrms discourse is the fundamental clash of value systems and propositions in the debate. The discourse often culminates in a debate between 'the Self' and 'the Other', a bipolar and binary equation between the strategic contestants, Russia, the United States, and China. In this contest, the questions of freedom of information and the extent of national control over it are reflections of deeper differences in world view (and, as such, impossible to be resolved with normative means). However, the different expectations of states towards the ICTs and related risk management are not binary. Inviting more countries to the line-up diversifies international norms aspirations, demonstrating not only different capabilities and preparedness but also grave differences in national ambitions, priorities, and objectives in the issue.

For almost two decades, Russia and the United States have set out controversial and uncompromising explanations of their respective views on international law and politically binding norms regarding state uses of ICTs. Despite trenchant attempts to convince the international public about both the righteousness and the altruism of their normative proposals, neither of the strategic contestants have been able to secure exclusive, unrivalled, moral agency in the international norms discourse. That international norms have been negotiated in the controlled processes and environments of the UN First Committee Group of GGE, the International Telecommunication Union (ITU)'s World Summit on the Information Society, and other international and regional organizations has served the purposes of both superpowers. The fragility of fixed consensus can be evidenced by different interpretations and prioritization of the crafted text[1] as well as strong and uncompromising national positions.[2]

With the emergence of technology markets and online communities, the values and reasonings to consider, and to be balanced, in the norms discourse are far in excess of what is suggested by the great powers' dialogue. This is a relatively new situation, particularly for the Western normative schools where the expectation is that all countries regard and understand international law and normative orders the same way.[3] There are alternative ways to understand and implement, as well as teach, the existing norms (Krutskikh 2015; Markoff 2015, 14; Ufa Declaration 2015).[4] With Brazil, China, India, Indonesia, Iran, and other new cyber powers coming to the scene, it is too early to conclude that different views of existing norms will be compatible; that 'their' prescriptions for the international 'cyber order' and for the maintenance of peace in the context of ICTs will coincide with or accept 'ours'.

Paraphrasing Lasswell (1936),[5] differences remain about who should get what and when in cyberspace. The most conformist group on the sufficiency of the existing international legal and political order might be the smaller and mid-sized technologically competent countries that have preferred to raise issues largely where they perceive an actual gap or lack of clarity in existing instruments, or detect an attempt to devaluate them. The most diverse group comprises developing countries. Given the widely differing state of national preparedness and capability/capacity to fully adapt ICTs in their national affairs and effectively mitigate the associated risks of growing ICT dependence, it is possible to anticipate different positions as to which issues will deserve priority attention—and how—in international venues. In a similar vein, implementation of international law, existing or future, is not just a matter of ideology and values but also of capacity and resources.

Building on Schachter (Roberts 2017), while pursuing binding agreement becomes an intuitive reaction to perceivably normative issues at times of technological change, the preference for formal binding commitments suggests an over-emphasis on national (exclusive) rights and the rejection of concessions that might appear to encroach on sovereignty, even to the derogation of existing treaty and customary law. The GGE experience has shown just that. Political and pragmatic differences between not just the strategic contestants but among the participating countries (since 2016/17: 25) have proved too grave to be able to build on the already accepted language of the UN Charter and offer a set of meaningful new leads for responsible state behaviour. The 2021 outcome, while offering administrative guidance, fails to resolve any serious point of confrontation (UN GGE 2021). The question to ask is whether, given the meagre outcome of dialogue in the controlled environment of the GGE, there is any real prospect of negotiations between countries with very different political ambitions divergent views on international law, as well as levels of ICT and cybersecurity preparedness. Or whether the time is ripe for having the discussion of *binding* standards both how the existing law is understood to help prevent and mitigate cyber conflict and where, indeed, the existing consensus falls short of providing adequate guarantees against malicious and hostile cyber activities.

At the same time, the GGE format no longer suits countries that require certainty and clarity in cyber affairs. From the sole custody of the Russian Federation, it has come to involve dozens in the GGE process, several interested to contribute to it, and more than a hundred countries to support the General Assembly resolutions on international cyber and information security matters. The international cybersecurity discourse also failed to provide an acceptable platform for independent and less politicized national positions to come forward. Despite strong, publicly declared support for multi-stakeholderism, there is in practice little evidence of systematically hearing, let alone incorporating, the views from the private sector.[6] While the newest discussion forum—an Open-ended Working Group—has been open to the civil society and private sector representatives, inclusion alone is unlikely to resolve the diametrically opposed views between states and corporations on, for instance, supply chain security. (OEWG 2021).

According to Finnemore and Hollis (2016) (Schachter 1967, 426–7; ITIC 2011; McKay, Neutze, Nicholas et al. 2014; Charney, English, Kleiner et al. 2016; Smith 2017; Vishik, Matsubara, and Plonk, 2016), we might anticipate parallel and complementary processes, and different argumentation paths and structures to emerge, during which we keep returning to the question whether indeed a new binding instrument is needed to address state use of ICTs. Furthermore, we should look thoroughly into state behaviour and ways in which leading normative powers move to impose their propositions on others in between and after rounds of negotiations.

The Challenge of Incomplete Saturation of the Discourse

The saturated discourse of cyber norms offers both observer and inquirer with a fountain of starting points. Unfortunately, at present, the discourse offers little more than that. What we have hypothesized to be the principal challenges within the cyber norms discourse have been identified (and often remediated) by many lawyers, security scholars, and normative theorists. The wisdom of the few disillusioned authors[7] has not deterred a whole generation of 'cyber normativists' from reinventing the concepts and questioning the terms, only to return to the point from which the normative theories had earlier embarked.

As Sander summarizes in his literature review (Finnemore 2011; Hurwitz 2012; Erskine and Carr 2016), the discourse is dominated by two approaches: restating the rules of international law and proposing new norms. Little has been done to consider the different understanding and interpretations of existing international law, or to analyse the actual gaps that need to be overcome for the purposes of clarity and predictability of behaviour. There is also very little analysis of actual state practice. While the relevance of identifying norms is made clear (Sander 2017), most authors ground their norms proposals in mere observation here, or case study there, often restraining their reasoning to an intuition.[8] Very often, proposals for new norms come with little analysis of the prospects for their promotion and implementation, let alone their enforcement (Tikk-Ringas 2011, 25).[9] As such, the discourse has evaded the whole segment of comparative state practice and, with it, the rich practical guidance that could potentially manage and balance the conflicting values, ideologies, disciplines, and schools of thought.

A central question remains whether existing law and policies are sufficient to deal with cybersecurity challenges. Attempts to answer this question will need to consider the respective maturity of both the security challenges and the normative strategies designed to respond to them. More fundamentally, proper account must also be taken of the by-now considerable critique of established international law and political agreements, as well as the various proposals for new norms.

Forging constructive links between established norms and emergent challenges starts with the acknowledgment of the body of applicable norms, rules, and principles. A normative discussion of cyberspace cannot sensibly be held without first understanding the existing normative landscape.[10] With very few exceptions, the discourse so far has dismissed the rich body of both binding and non-binding norms that already address routine aspects of ICTs—network security, data protection, online transactions, cybercrime, terrorist use of the Internet—in multilateral and international settings. It has also left aside numerous special regimes of risk and incident management—for instance, in civil aviation, maritime, financial, and nuclear sectors. These omissions are critical, because they overlook the existing legal and policy instruments that form what Nye refers to as the cybersecurity 'regime complex' (Nye 2014) and that, when properly identified and evaluated, might very well limit and even reduce the prospect of further fragmentation of the normative landscape of cybersecurity. As a result, more deliberation and analysis of existing normative frameworks and instruments are key to understanding the normative gaps that have opened up, and how they might best be closed.

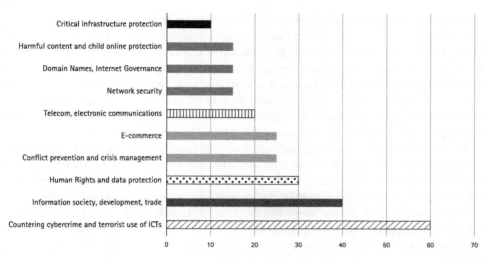

FIGURE 46.1. Existing instruments related to state use of information and communication technologies by topic. Source: compiled on the basis of Tikk, E. 2018). 'National Cybersecurity Legislation: Is There a Magic Formula?'. In *Cybersecurity Best Practices*, edited by Bartsch M. and Frey S. Springer Fachmedien, Wiesbaden.

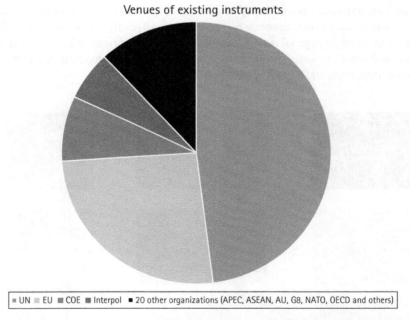

FIGURE 46.2. Existing instruments related to state use of information and communication technologies by venue. Source: compiled on the basis of Tikk, E. 2018). 'National Cybersecurity Legislation: Is There a Magic Formula?'. In *Cybersecurity Best Practices*, edited by Bartsch M. and Frey S. Springer Fachmedien, Wiesbaden.

Existing norms, both binding and non-binding, provide the essential baseline for debating and adopting *new norms* that might then become central to the international cybersecurity dialogue for years to come (Tikk-Ringas 2015; Kaljurand 2016). The 'new norms' sub-theme in the international cybersecurity dialogue is arguably a diplomatic turn to avoid more formal treaty negotiations. In parallel, it has developed as an academic discourse that has flowed from the thoughts of dozens of authors over the past two decades. It is also symptomatic of the growing maturity of national legal and policy frameworks: articulating and making more visible the preferred ways of doing things in and vis-à-vis cyberspace.

Although in the GGE framing, such new norms are strictly voluntary and non-binding in character, it is hard to overlook their directive, almost authoritative aspirations. The norms pushed through the GGE reflect the expectation, by their respective sponsors, the Group and the General Assembly,[11] of compliance without ratification. In the implementation of the GGE norms, states will exercise self-restraint as an element of accountability, indicating their choice of playing by the rules (Franck 1990). The rationale for these proposed norms, as discussed, is to identify the gaps and inconsistencies in international law and to generate new guidance on responsible State behaviour. Once accepted, these norms will then be hardened up through practice and further codification. New norms proposals are therefore best understood as legislative efforts. They would need to take account of the range of factual situations likely to arise; to articulate policy alternatives; to reflect the views of those potentially as well as actually affected; and to prescribe sufficiently explicit rules.[12]

An invitation to future norm entrepreneurs would be to have regard and reference to the already existing norms and regimes when proposing and justifying further standards of behaviour. A successful proposal would consider the existing normative base, related national positions and practices, and various alternative techniques of overcoming normative gaps as well as the supporting and opposing schools of thought.

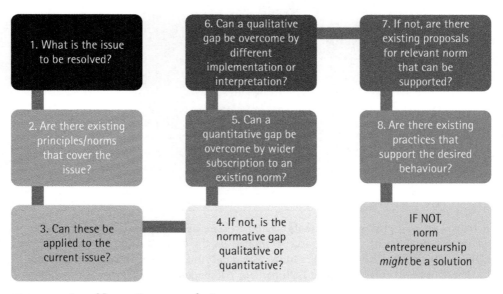

FIGURE 46.3. Normative gap analysis

The first step in discussing predictability and certainty of behaviour is identifying a behaviour or a state of affairs that is deemed to be unsatisfactory. This brings us to the questions, 'What is the issue?', 'Why is it an issue?', 'How do we know it is an issue?', and 'For whom is it an issue?' Pinning down specific problematic conditions and attributes sets the boundaries for further normative inquiry and contours the normative strategy to be applied. Identifying such conditions and attributes (or their absence) in the normative proposals of others allows one to understand the rationale, weight, and perspective of their propositions.

Where framing of the issue falls short of concrete handles, assigning a normative tool to the task is complicated. Focus on malicious cyber activities by proxy actors or coercive political activities online does not indicate whose activities, which activities, why, when, and how they occur, could be usefully addressed beyond what has been achieved in domestic and international criminal law and public international law. Loose or over-broad framing also makes it difficult to identify sources and scope of consensus. For instance, in the call for an 'open, free, secure, and peaceful cyberspace', each word is subject to wide interpretation and politically contested. It also remains unclear how do the problems of 'open' and 'free' in the international cybersecurity discourse differ or go beyond what has been agreed and achieved in the context of human rights and trade.

Together with the issue to be resolved, one must have in mind the desired behaviour that norms are expected to support or enforce. These two markers—the contested state of affairs and the desired state of affairs—set the framework of further normative inquiry. Without an idea of what is required of a norm, a critical and systemic analysis of the limits of existing norms is not possible.

After identifying a problem to which all the normative actors can subscribe, the first question for a potential promoter of norms, a *norm entrepreneur* (Finnemore and Sikkink 1998), must be whether there already is a norm that addresses the issue. This observation highlights the utility and cross-fertilizing relationship between the theoretical approaches of international law and international relations and actual political considerations and decision making. International lawyers may not be the only ones to identify a practical issue that merits normative discussion. They may, however, be the ones able to point out that the issue at hand is already addressed by international law. It is essential to consider, next, that lawyers' views on the scope and even existence of such a norm in the international legal order will differ. Such differences are attributable to a mix of disciplinary and political factors, more than simply a margin of error.[13] Viewing international law in the context of a specific issue is more likely to reveal actual and significant differences in legal thinking among decision makers and scholars. For instance, the 2015 GGE report concludes that the 20 countries that participated in the Group might differ on the existence of due diligence as a binding obligation under existing international law. Further disparities are evident in the national positions annexed to the 2021 UN GGE report.

The next question to ask, therefore, is whether the proposed norms are practically applicable to the issue at hand. This is another area where the politics of law competes with legal dogmatism. The United States and like-minded countries have been reluctant to consider ITU basic texts on international telecommunications[14] to be applicable to issues of international information security, separating 'cyberspace' from international telecommunications by reference to its inner logic rather than to its physical appearance. By the same token, the like-minded countries have pushed back on regulating or discussing information security at the international level, thus separating 'content' from data that defines processes like routing. There are considerable differences between states when it comes to regarding due diligence as established international law or their interpretation of thresholds of use of force and armed attack. Given the dyadic nature of cyber conflict, states involved may choose to accept the political cost of not following the commonly agreed rules and standards.

If it is concluded that there are existing norms that can address part or the whole of the issue at hand, the next step is to ask whether extending the coverage of the norm to the issue will require either a quantitative or a qualitative effort. One example of a quantitative approach might be to persuade more countries to ratify the 2001 Budapest Convention on Cybercrime, thus achieving a wider counter-cybercrime agenda. Similarly, not all countries are yet members of the Statute of the International Court of Justice or the International Criminal Court. However, in the vast majority of cases, such decisions are not accidental and overcoming the quantitative implementation vacuum would be difficult. A qualitative approach, on the other hand, might be more appropriate when the norm exists but is not yet of the desired quality or strength—for instance, when standards of preferable behaviour have only been referred to in a non-binding instrument or by way of recommendation.

The implementation gaps can also reflect a lack of sufficient observable practice. Nothing in the text of the UN Charter prevents cyberattacks being qualified and determined as use of force, provided they meet the relevant threshold. Even if it has not so far been a convincing constraint on behaviour, there is little to suggest that this norm could not be applied in the context of international cybersecurity in the future. Many norms that are not cyber specific are nevertheless applicable to cyber activities. It is therefore essential to distinguish between incomplete application of existing norms on the one hand, and the lack of legal and normative precedent on the other.

A gap may also be one of form. A variation is a situation where the norm exists but is not of desired strength—for instance, when standards of preferable behaviour have only been referred to in a non-binding instrument or by way of recommendation. When a norm is binding but the situation at hand requires legal certainty, the normative gap becomes formal. The Council of the European Union has recently upgraded the normative weight of data protection regulation as well as attacks against information systems.[15]

Self-evidently, only when the normative gap is real, when there is no norm that by its substance and scope of coverage would sufficiently address the situation, is there a need to overcome the normative gap. But even then, the proposal for a norm may not be entirely novel. Proposals for a new norm might already be under active consideration—for instance, in international organizations or by scholarly writers. In this case, it is essential to study their progress, relevant reasoning, and argumentation to decide whether the proposed solution could be tied to an ongoing norms process.

There might also be seeds of the required norm in state behaviour, in which case it could be asked whether it is meaningful to offer the normative proposal as 'new' or base it on observations of already accepted conduct. A case in point could be the so-called Internet bans whereby countries, having accidentally disconnected or restricted online services beyond their territory or jurisdiction, have undertaken to restore connectivity and apologize for their actions.

After exhausting all these avenues without satisfactory remedy, it might be reasonable to conclude that the norm would be new in the international legal order and strategize for promoting the norm by choosing appropriate actors, venues, and processes.

The saturation issue discussed earlier is further exacerbated by the disconnect between academic and policy discourses on cyber norms, as well as between national and international normative efforts. Alarmingly few scholars pay attention to the GGE, the venue that has maintained the political cyber norms agenda in recent years. For example, of the 2,778 dissertations/theses and 1,663 scholarly journal articles written on 'cyber' and 'norms' between 2014 and 2016, fewer than 1% (3 and 3, respectively) even mention the UN GGE.[16] That leaves 99% of academic analysts on norms either uninterested, unaware, or unimpressed by the process. Similarly, of the over 100 national cybersecurity strategies adopted by January 2019, fewer than 20% make reference to the work of the GGE. So far, no strategies have addressed ways to implement the norms and recommendations proposed by the Group.

Another under-attended consideration in the norms dialogue are national views and recommendations. Exploiting the many national views made public in international, regional, and national processes, Korzak's and Eichensehr's work (Korzak 2016; Eichensehr 2015) makes use of available national positions and distils avenues for politically and academically acceptable consensus. Similarly, Warrell's and Hurwitz's examinations of US international cyber policy offers a survey of the main national policy instruments and political considerations. (Farrell, 2015; Hurwitz 2013, 2014).

All this leaves every new entrant to the cyber norms debate with a daunting task—to dig through the swamp of 'cyber norms' literature, the existing body of norms, and the many tabled norms proposals and value propositions. A baseline review of this somewhat haphazard discourse to date would be an exercise of value in itself.

The Challenge of Inter-Disciplinarity

The leading international cybersecurity narratives are developed in forums to which international legal scholars and ethicists are, often deliberately, not invited. The scholars who have felt compelled explicitly to defend their constituent value systems and schools of thought demonstrate how the science of norms can be as political as the true colours of the underlying exercise (Krutskikh and Streltsov 2014; von Heinegg 2015). It is not difficult to observe how critique turns into counter-critique as the original claim or context is lost in a respondent's conception of the issue.[34] These duels, while enriching the academic debate, reveal the clashes of disciplines, subject matter backgrounds, ideology, and *Kinderstube*. They also indicate the need for careful and thorough articulation of goals, assumptions, and propositions. The true interdisciplinary challenges lie in being able to adequately communicate methods, assumptions, and criteria, and to duly distinguish between fact and fiction, assumptions and conclusions, actual and imaginable, strategic and tactical, possible and impossible.

There is reluctance to see various disciplines as complementary and acknowledge the utility of their co-existence. There is little aesthetic in current international cyber affairs. States do not forge agreements for the beauty of legal science. They do not reach compromises because of theories of international relations. If disciplines are to be able to detect, explain, and inform state behaviour, they must function within their remits in order to remain relevant. As soon as any one discipline assumes the role of sole yardstick of state behaviour, it becomes dysfunctional and dogmatic, therefore no different from the problem it claims to be resolving.

Works of Slaughter (2014) and Finnemore and Hollis (2016) represent the still too few attempts to seriously acknowledge and accommodate different disciplines for a shared goal—a solidified approach and better understanding of how to develop, support, and sustain the global order. Furthermore, interdisciplinarity is not limited to interconnectivity between the great sciences of international relations, international law, economics, and technology. As cybersecurity is essentially an agenda of all-round data protection, it requires a plug-and-play attitude from within legal studies: it is not a matter of personal data protection, intellectual property protection, or public information. It is 'all of the above' with the addition of data as the target of both intelligence and military operations, and data as the life blood of national economies and vital societal functions.

In this context, Katzenstein's definition of norms as *collective expectations for the proper behaviour of actors with a given identity* harbours different final distinctions in the disciplines of international law and international relations.[17,18] Seen from the lens of international law, norms become concerned with permitted and prohibited behaviour, the questions of legally binding rules and standards, while, in international relations, the discriminators are the much more flexible 'acceptable' and 'unacceptable'. Moreover, the reference to a given identity relevant in social settings has little intellectual value for international relations when the situation is a stronger conditioner of state behaviour.

A further inter-disciplinarity challenge lies in being able to translate and align the imperatives between disciplines—for instance, by assigning the appropriate weight and value to threat factors or vulnerabilities for evaluating the prospect of their remediation with legal or political instruments. Proper conduct in such an assessment rests on the availability and demonstration of relevant taxonomy and ontology. A challenge for researchers and decision makers alike remains the lack of actionable evidence or the inability to assign the right legal or political value to the available evidence.

Finally, the task of inter-disciplinarity mingles with the challenge of authority. Inadequate understanding of how to reconcile ICTs with national interests in a multi-disciplinary and multi-actor environment evades the habitual administrative and academic patterns, thus leading to pseudo-science and placebo politics. The often deliberate compartmentalization of national and international legal and political tools, approaches and instruments, prevents appropriate distribution of accountability and remedies.

Here we have to return to the difference between not just political and academic but national and supranational thinking and dealing with issues of cybersecurity. Warnings of the inevitability and insuperability of The Political[19] should caution academics to vaccinate against a series of seemingly urgent and essential questions. Achieving the necessary standards of research, analysis, and argument requires professional self-confidence, openness, patience, and integrity. It should equally inform the development and implementation of academic curricula and professional development paths.

Going back even further, we should remind ourselves of our duties as researchers.[37.] Science should not be made an end in itself—all normative disciplines are intrinsically linked to the society, its development, and the changes it undergoes. As researchers and critics of policy options, we cannot limit our views to approaches and angles of our liking. To follow Oppenheim (1908), it is important to pay thorough attention to the already existing rules—their scope and substance, as well as the international community's subscription thereto. When difficulties of implementation are determined, it is important to understand whether the norms are, indeed, outdated, as suggested by those who prefer replacing them, or perhaps require more thoughtful subsuming of the current geo-techno-political context. Any criticism towards existing rules must be kept constructive in order to be able to conclude whether, why, and how a gap can be overcome. When a proposal is made for new norms, it ought to keep in line with the pre-existing normative frameworks, pointing out not only substantive but also procedural aspects of possible codification or necessary norm entrepreneurship.

The Challenge of 'New Normal'

Moving forward, it is important to acknowledge that the framing *cyber* might just be the flavour of the season, while *ICTs* remain a pervasive set of technologies and the Internet one of the main public platforms of exchange of information. Normative, as well as political, military, and technical, efforts cannot be organized around or along the notion of 'cyber'— the GGE discussions have proved how challenging it is to reconcile national ambitions and appetites around the cyber domain alongside the global Internet.

A much less colloquial reference to ICTs reveals that the future of the cybersecurity norms discussion is inevitably linked to parallel processes in space infrastructure, the emergence of robotics and the related discourses of unmanned systems and autonomy. Not only are these technological developments and market trends, such as social media, Big Data, and Internet of Things, interactive, they also have a mutually sustaining effect, allowing countries that have made the right investments to take the early adopter's advantage of the benefits. Technological developments remain a central element in development and, as such, necessitate legal and policy analysis beyond 'cyber'.

Technology is a variable of politics: an element and a tool of the exercise of national power, a means of enhancing or compensating for the realities of geography. ICTs play a key role in international affairs but their pervasiveness is best understood when looking not only at cyber capabilities and cybersecurity but at the interrelationships of ICTs with other areas of technology and development. In normative thought, like in security studies, the dimension of technology needs to be duly contextualized and reflected upon as a variable that necessitates, leads, and explains patterns of behaviour. The measurement of technology and technological development in world affairs would require an approach that might be described as *geotechnopolitics*: intended to reveal leads and patterns of state behaviour that would not be easily observable in geopolitical or geo-economic analysis. Geopolitics explains just a part of international relations and interdependencies in the information age. It makes it possible to observe that most cyber threats, although claimed to be global, are still geopolitical. Technology analysis in isolation explains the means and methods of attacks but has little to say about actors and their motives. However, joining the two angles enables predictive assessment of market and policy opportunities, and individual countries' ability to seize them. In other words, technology becomes an essential element in complementing geopolitical and geo-economic analysis of threat factors and/or actors, as well as economic and societal developments and affairs.

Individual countries' investment in science and technology in general, and in research and development in particular, will add an additional layer to the national assessments of risks, threats, and opportunities. The range of possible normative considerations will also be influenced. Some technological developments, especially in infrastructure, are easy to account for and to contextualize. They reveal historical and political inclinations and considerations—for instance, the recently laid submarine cable between Finland and Germany; the sole undersea cable connecting Cuba to the global networks; and the still relatively small number of countries with independent satellite launch capabilities (despite space becoming increasingly international and vital to the corporate sector). Further to this, technological developments can be analysed and contextualized in terms of the technology-industrial base that explains military capability development, emergence of markets, and operations (power projection, products, and services). These observations offer valuable insights into the exercise of normative power, and the prospective success of particular norm entrepreneurships, that norms can be promoted without explicit written norm advocacy, and that both words and deeds matter.

An important lead for future normative thinkers is that ICT dependence is not a form of natural disaster. It is a result of political propositions and deliberate decision making. Given what has become evident about the consequences of ICT dependence and the resulting interdependence in international development and security, the question of the accountability for national and international level decision making deserves a more prominent position in the normative-ethical analysis agenda. As we have been called to consider frequent and sophisticated cyberattacks as 'new normal', we should also call for the normalization of cyber affairs, lowering cybersecurity from its fancy, flickering, and futuristic pedestal to where ICTs and our thinking about them become integrated, by default.

Conclusion

The discussion of norms and international security ahead of us will be paved with fundamental differences between cyber superpowers—the United States, China, and Russia—about the pace and direction of further adoption and use of ICTs. The cyber discourse will have to reconcile various competing imperatives: states' international obligations versus claims of absolute national sovereignty; and the free flow of information versus its revision at and within state borders. As these differences cannot be argued or edited away, These differences cannot be simply argued or edited away demonstrates just how fragile and thin any consensus is on the matter. These differences, combined with dogmatic gaps between international and national law, and international and national policy, all constitute obvious apertures for malicious and hostile actors to achieve their goals.

However, even in the absence of "true" consensus, there are ways to proceed with furthering responsible behaviour among state and non-state actors. Putting existing norms in practice is a norm-promoting activity and it can be expected that States will stand behind the norms they have specifically promoted in national strategies, national legislation, the GGE, and other international and regional norms processes. The many norms and regimes that have been established to deal with issues of cybersecurity—including those on data protection, access to information, countering terrorist and criminal use of ICTs, preventing use of force and sanctioning self-help measures—all contain useful guides for those states and non-state actors that want to take their respective experience and guidance forward. Further

FUTURE NORMATIVE CHALLENGES 765

studying, disseminating, promoting, and discussing how these norms apply will help to detect and create peer mechanisms between interested, willing, and able actors.

When discussing norms of responsible behavior in the coming rounds of the international dialogue, it might be useful to focus on more compartmentalized issue areas where consensus can be detected, deepened, and further disseminated from homogeneous groups of countries, politically allied or not. States should avoid re-opening for discussion the fundamental normative instruments and concepts that have served the international community well for decades.

NOTES

1. Katzenstein, *Culture of National Security*.
2. Singh, 'The Legislative Process', 172; Koskenniemi, M. 2006. Study Group of the International Law Commission. 'Fragmentation in International Law, Difficulties Arising from Diversification and Expansion of International Law'. In *Yearbook of the International Law Commission*, Vol. *II*, Part 2 (the conclusions of the report were adopted by the International Law Commission at its Fifty-Eighth Session, in 2006, and recommended to the attention of the General Assembly, A/CN.4/L/682, 13 April 2006).
3. Singh, 'The Legislative Process', 172.
4. RU ISD 016; US ICCS 2011.
5. Conclusion of the discussion at the MIT Conference of Cyber Norms in 2017; also Liis Vihul, commenting on the work on the Tallinn Manual 2.0 on the International Law Applicable to Cyber Operations at the UNIDIR Conference of International Security Cyber Issues Workshop Series: The Application of International Law in the Context of International Cybersecurity, 19–21 April 2016, Geneva, Switzerland.
6. Lasswell, *Politics*.
7. Finnemore and Hollis, 'Constructing Norms'.
8. Hurwitz, 'Depleted Trust'; Hurwitz, R. 2012. An Augmented Summary of The Harvard, MIT and University of Toronto Cyber Norms Workshop; Hurwitz, R. 2013. 'A New Normal? The Cultivation of Global Norms as Part of a Cybersecurity Strategy'. In *Conflict and Cooperation In Cyberspace: The Challenge to National Security*, edited by P.A. Yannakogeorgos and A.B. Lowther. Abingdon, UK: Taylor & Francis; Hurwitz, R. 2014. 'The Play of States: Norms and Security in Cyberspace', *Journal of the National Committee on American Foreign Policy* 36 (5); Erskine and Carr, 'Beyond "Quasi-Norms" '.
9. Cf. Finnemore and Hollis, 'Constructing Norms'.
10. Erskine and Carr, 'Beyond "Quasi-Norms" '.
11. Article 2(a) of the General Assembly Resolution A/70/237 on 'Developments in the field of information and telecommunications in the context of international security', adopted 23 December 2015, calls upon Member States 'To be guided in their use of information and communications technologies by the 2015 report of the Group of Governmental Experts.'https://unoda-web.s3-accelerate.amazonaws.com/wp-content/uploads/2016/01/A-RES-70-237-Information-Security.pdf
12. Schachter, 'Scientific Advances', 425.
13. See, for instance, the 2015 Heintschel von Heinegg debate v. Krutskikh and Streltsov, 2014: von Heinegg, W. Heintschel. 2015. 'International Law and International Information

766   ENEKEN TIKK

Security: A Response to Krutskikh and Streltsov', *The Tallinn Papers*: NATO Cooperative Cyber Defence Centre of Excellence.

14. Constitution and Convention of the International Telecommunication Union (1992).

15. See Regulation (EU) 2016/679 of 27 April 2016 on the protection of natural persons with regard to the processing of personal data and on the free movement of such data, and repealing Directive 95/46/EC (General Data Protection Regulation), OJ L 119/1, 14.05.2016. See also Directive (EU) 2016/1148 of the European Parliament and of the Council of 6 July 2016 concerning measures for a high common level of security of network and information systems across the Union, OJ L 194, 19.7.2016. 39. These data are based on the ProQuest Database.

16. For extensive overview of national views expressed in the First Committee dealings in relation to the UN GGE, see https://www.un.org/disarmament/topics/informationsecurity/

17. Katzenstein, *Culture of National Security*.

18. Schmitt, *Concept of the Political*; Koskenniemi, M. 1990. 'The Politics of International Law', *European Journal for International Law* 1 (4); Hurwitz, 'Play of States'.

19. Oppenheim, 'Science of International Law'.

References

Black, H.C., Nolan, J.R., Nolan-Haley, J.M. et al. 1990. *Black's Law Dictionary*. 6th edn. St. Paul, MN: West Publishing Company.

Broeders, D. 2016. *The Public Core of the Internet, An International Agenda for Internet Governance*. Amsterdam: Amsterdam University Press.

Charney, S., English, E., Kleiner, A. et al. 2016. *From Articulation to Implementation: Enabling Progress on Cybersecurity Norms*. Microsoft Corporation.

Eichensehr, K.E. 2015. 'The Cyber-Law of Nations', *The Georgetown Law Journal* 103 (317).

Erskine, T. and Carr, M. 2016. 'Beyond "Quasi-Norms": the Challenges and Potential of Engaging with Norms in Cyberspace'. In *International Cyber Norms: Legal, Policy and Industry Perspectives*, edited by A.-M. Osula and H. Rõigas. Tallinn: NATO Cooperative Cyber Defence Centre of Excellence.

Farrell, H. 2015. 'Promoting Norms for Cyberspace'. Council on Foreign Relations, Digital and Cyberspace Policy Program, *Cyber Brief*, April.

Finnemore, M. 2011. 'Cultivating Cyber Norms'. In *America's Cyber Future: Security and Prosperity in the Information Age*, edited by K.M. Lord and T. Sharp, Chapter VI. Washington DC: Center for a New American Security.

Finnemore, M., and Hollis, D. 2016. 'Constructing Norms for Global Cybersecurity', *American Journal of International Law* 110 (3).

Finnemore, M. and Sikkink, K. 1998. 'International Norm Dynamics and Political Change', *International Organization* 52 (4), Autumn: 887–917.

Forsyth, J.W. 2013. 'What Great Powers Make It. International Order and the Logic of Cooperation in Cyberspace', *Strategic Studies Quarterly*, Spring.

Forsyth, J.W. and Pope, B.E. 2014. 'Structural Causes and Cyber Effects: Why International Order is Inevitable in Cyberspace', *Strategic Studies Quarterly*, Winter: 113–130.

Forsyth, J.W. and Pope, B.E. 2015. 'Structural Causes and Cyber Effects: A Response to Our Critics', Strategic Studies Quarterly, Summer, 9 (2): 99–106.

Franck, T.M. 1990. *The Power of Legitimacy Among Nations*. Oxford: Oxford University Press.

Gaycken, S. and Tikk, E. 2011. 'Letters to the Editor', *Survival*, 53 (5): 219–222.

Greenwood, C. 2008. 'Sources of International Law: An Introduction', http://untreaty.un.org/cod/avl/pdf/is/Greenwood_outline.pdf, accessed 4 October 2017.

Hurwitz, R. 2015. 'A Call to Cyber Norms', *Discussions at the Harvard-MIT–University of Toronto Cyber Norms Workshops, 2011 and 2012*.

Hurwitz, R. 2012. 'Depleted Trust in the Cyber Commons', *Strategic Studies Quarterly*, Fall 2012.

ITIC (Information Technology Industry Council). 2011. *The IT Industry's Cybersecurity Principles for Industry and Government.*

International Security Advisory Board (ISAB). 2014. *Report on A Framework for International Cyber Stability.*

International Telecommunications Union. 2014. *The Quest for Cyber Confidence.*

Kaljurand, M. 2016. 'United Nations Group of Governmental Experts: the Estonian perspective', in Osula, A.-M. and Rõigas, H. (eds.). 2016. *International Cyber Norms Legal, Policy & Industry Perspectives*. Tallinn: NATO CCD COE Publications.

Katzenstein, P.J. 1996. *The Culture of National Security: Norms and Identity in World Politics.* New York: Columbia University Press.

Kelsen, H. 1967. *Pure Theory of Law*. Berkeley: University of California Press.

Korzak, E. 2016. 'The Quest for Cyber Norms', *Bulletin of the Atomic Scientists*, 72 (5): 348–350.

Krutskikh, A. and Streltsov, A.A. 2014. 'International Law and the Problem of International Information Security', *International Affairs*, Vol. 60, No. 6.

Krutskikh, A., 2015 an interview to Kommersant. See Paltiel, D. Russian Newspaper Kommersant Interviews Special Representative Krutskikh on UN GGE Cyber Arrangements August 17, available https://www.csis.org/blogs/strategic-technologies-blog/russian-newspaper-kommersant-interviews-special-representative.

Lasswell, H.D. 1936. *Politics: Who Gets What, When, How.* Cleveland: Meridian Books.

Markoff, M. 2015. *Advancing Norms of Responsible State Behavior in Cyberspace*, originally published as a Department of State blog, available at https://votesmart.org/candidate/public-statements/53306/john-kerry.

Mazanek, B. M. 2015. 'Why International Order in Cyberspace is Not Inevitable', *Strategic Studies Quarterly*, Summer, 9 (2): 78–98.

McKay, A., Neutze, J., Nicholas, P. et al. 2014. International Cybersecurity Norms, Reducing conflict in an Internet-Dependent world. Microsoft Corporation.

Nye, J.S. 2014. 'The Regime Complex for Managing Global Cyber Activities. The Centre for International Governance', *Global Commission on Internet Governance, Paper Series: no. 1— May*. Centre for International Governance Innovation (CIGI) and Chatham House.

Oppenheim, L. 1908. 'The Science of International Law: Its Task and Method', *The American Journal of International Law*, 2 (2): 313–356.

President of the Russian Federation, *On approval of the Doctrine of Information Security of the Russian Federation*, Decree No. 646 (5 December 2016).

Roberts, A. 2017. *Is International Law International?* Oxford: Oxford University Press.

Sander, B. 2017. 'Cyber Insecurity and the Politics of International Law', *European Society of International Law Reflections Series*, 6 (5).

Schachter, O. 1967. 'Scientific Advances and International Law Making', *California Law Review*, 55 (2): 423–430.

Schjølberg, S. and Ghernaouti-Hélie, S. 2011. *A Global Treaty on Cybersecurity and Cybercrime.* Cybercrimelaw.Net.

Schmitt, C. 1932. *The Concept of the Political*. Chicago: University of Chicago Press (Translation 1966).

Schmitt, M.N. and Vihul, L. 2014. 'The Nature of International Law Cyber Norms', *Tallinn Paper No. 5, Special Expanded Issue*. Tallinn: NATO CCD COE Publications.

Shannon, V.P. 2000. 'Norms are What States Make of Them: The Political Psychology of Norm Violation', *International Studies Quarterly* 44 (2): 293–316.

Singh, N.N. 1990. 'The Legislative Process in International Law: A General Comment', *Bond Law Review*: 172.

Slaughter, A. 2014. *A New World Order*. Princeton, N.J.: Princeton University Press.

Smith, Brad. 2017. 'The Need for a Digital Geneva Convention', *Microsoft*, Feb 14 2017, https://blogs.microsoft.com/on-the-issues/2017/02/14/need-digital-geneva-convention/, last accessed 4 October 2017.

Tikk-Ringas, E. 2011. 'Ten Rules for Cyber Security', *Survival* 53 (3).

Tikk-Ringas, E. 2015. 'Legal Framework of Cyber Security'. In *Cyber Security: Analytics, Technology and Automation. Intelligent Systems, Control and Automation: Science and Engineering*, Vol. 78, edited by M. Lehto and P. Neittaanmäki. New York: Springer.

Ufa Declaration, 7th BRICS Summit, July 9 2015, http://brics2016.gov.in/upload/files/document/5763c20a72f2d7thDeclarationeng.pdf.

Vishik, V., Matsubara, M. and Plonk, A. 2016. 'Key Concepts in Cyber Security: Towards a Common Policy and Technology Context for Cyber Security Norms'. In *International Cyber Norms: Legal, Policy and Industry Perspectives*, edited by A.-M. Osula and H. Rõigas. Tallinn: NATO Cooperative Cyber Defence Centre of Excellence.

Voina-Motoc, Iulia. 1999. 'Moral-Rule and Rule of Law in International Politics: Common Sense, Political Realism, Skepticism'. In *A Decade of Transformation*, IWM Junior Visiting Fellows Conferences, Vol. 8, Vienna.

von Heinegg, W. Heintschel. 2015. 'International Law and International Information Security: A Response to Krutskikh and Streltsov', *The Tallinn Papers*: NATO Cooperative Cyber Defence Centre of Excellence.

White House. 2011. *International Strategy for Cyberspace. Prosperity, Security, and Openness in a Networked World*.

Wingfield, T.C. 2000. *The Law of Information Conflict, National Security Law in Cyber Space*. Falls Church, VA: Aegis Research Corporation.

CHAPTER 47

'CYBERSECURITY' AND 'DEVELOPMENT': CONTESTED FUTURES

TIM UNWIN

THE 'OTHERING' OF CYBERSECURITY AND DEVELOPMENT

THE links between cybersecurity and international development are crucially important, especially for the world's poorest and most marginalized countries and people. Yet, they have rarely been explored in detail (Juech 2017; Schia 2017; Morgus 2018a; Nurko 2018), and all too often international initiatives designed to support development have paid insufficient attention to cybersecurity issues. As Morgus (2018b) has succinctly summarized, 'International assistance programs rely on digital technologies to deliver food, housing, education and a host of other services to the developing world. However, few donors or recipients incorporate cybersecurity into their activities. That's a problem.'

In large part, this is because the communities of expertise in the two fields are often distinct and separate, speak different languages, have different interests, and are physically located in different organizations and places. Cybersecurity tends to be the domain of computer scientists, security agencies, telecommunication ministries, the private sector, and foreign policy organizations, whereas international development is largely the field of social scientists, development specialists, aid ministries, civil society, and humanitarian organizations.[1] At the government level in the United Kingdom, for example, the Department for International Development (DFID) has until recently paid scant attention to cybersecurity issues, leaving these to the Department for Culture, Media & Sport, the Foreign & Commonwealth Office (FCO); since 2020 combined with DFID to form the FCDO, and the security services. This separation is true of most bilateral and multilateral donors, and, as a result, technology-supported aid initiatives frequently ignore fundamentally important issues around digital security. This chapter provides an overview of the intersections between the two, why they are important, and what can be done to improve integration between them in the interests of reducing inequalities and poverty.

At the heart of this analysis is the idea of 'othering', the process whereby people and organizations tend to label 'others' as being dissimilar and opposite to the self or a communal 'us'. 'Others' are a means through which we constitute ourselves (Levinas 1981; Brons 2015). Moreover, frequently this 'other' is seen as being subordinate to the self, and is therefore increasingly marginalized through the practice of othering by a dominant group. 'Developing countries' are by definition the other of 'developed countries'; 'emerging' economies are the other of the economies of the dominant global states; and too often 'international development' is seen as being an other of 'cybersecurity'. Powerful states such as China and the United States thus compete for markets and influence over 'developing countries', 'emerging economies', or 'the South'. Cybersecurity is another crucial sphere where such competition is enacted, as different countries seek to use it as a means to promote their vision of a specific kind of digital world, particularly with respect to issues such as Internet governance, freedom, privacy, and security.

Previous chapters in this book have defined cybersecurity in very different ways. Many of these approaches can be seen as being on a spectrum from top-down and controlling to bottom-up and liberating. The former, for example, include national systems to prevent extremism and terrorism (Part III), the prevention of state-sponsored attacks (Part IV), national cybersecurity systems (Part VII), and, indeed, the mass digital surveillance systems whereby the Chinese government increasingly seeks to control its citizens (Doffman 2018). In contrast, the latter are focused much more on empowering the individual as exemplified by personal cyber hygiene, child online protection, and concerns over individual privacy and freedoms (Part VI).

The field and idea of 'development' are likewise highly contested. The majority, hegemonic, view propounded by the United Nations (UN) and its member states in the Millennium Development Goals of 2000, and their successors, the Sustainable Development Goals (SDGs) of 2015, is that economic growth will eliminate poverty (Sachs 2005).[2] This has not, though, been without its critics (Easterly 2006; Unwin 2007). Conceptually, the reduction of poverty through 'development as growth' is largely based on the notion of *absolute* poverty: economic growth is considered as the primary means through which people will be raised out of absolute poverty. However, this can only succeed if the benefits of economic growth are equitably distributed. In practice, this is rarely the case, and hence those who conceive of 'development as reducing inequalities' prefer to consider poverty in a *relative* sense (O'Boyle 1999). It is crucial to note here that the rapid global transformations of the past two decades, enabled by new digital technologies, have dramatically increased inequality at all scales from the global to the household (UNDP 2015; World Bank 2016).

Figure 47.1 provides a simple heuristic device through which this intersection between development and cybersecurity can be conceptualized. Most interventions in both cybersecurity and development are in practice on a spectrum, which is here emphasized through the use of a dashed line dividing each of the main categories and the depiction of a gradient in the shading. The darkness at the top right is specifically intended to emphasize that the modes of top-down cybersecurity and 'development as economic growth' are dominant.

Far from being just digital, the word 'cyber', derived from the ancient Greek word for steering, piloting, or governing, is itself an indication of this top-down, controlling, and governing aspect of the idea of 'cybersecurity'. This coincides with the dominance of the idea of development as economic growth, because it is widely argued that effective cybersecurity

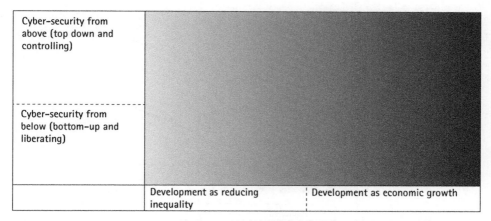

FIGURE 47.1. Conceptualizing the intersection between cybersecurity and development

is essential for economic growth and national success. As the government of the Netherlands emphasizes in its approach to cybersecurity:

> The new National Cyber Security Agenda (NCSA) strengthens our digital security and ensures that the vital interests of the Netherlands are better protected. The Netherlands is one of the most digital countries in the world, giving it an excellent starting position. However, we can only make the most of these opportunities if the Netherlands is digitally secure.[3]

Figure 47.1, though, also emphasizes that alternative representations of this intersection are possible, not least that an empowering vision could be constructed through a focus on reducing inequalities through a bottom-up, liberating approach to cybersecurity.

Inequalities: Digital and Developmental

The aforementioned account is premised on a conviction that digital technologies are being used to create a more unequal world, and that overly optimistic rhetoric about their positive contribution to development needs to be matched by an understanding of their darker side. Cybersecurity is essential so that measures can be put in place to mitigate their negative impacts.

An Unequal Digital World

Continuing use of terms such as 'bridging the digital divide' and 'digital leapfrogging' propagate the myth that digital technologies somehow have the power by themselves to reduce inequalities and enable poorer countries and people to catch up with, or overtake, their richer peers. However, no technology has power of itself: all technologies are created by people with particular interests and for specific purposes (Unwin 2017). The digital divide between those who have the latest technologies and those who have none is thus getting ever

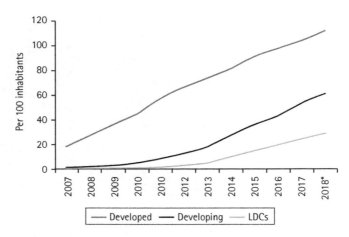

FIGURE 47.2. Active mobile-broadband subscriptions per 100 inhabitants by level of development. Source: ITU (2018a).

bigger. If the use of such technologies is beneficial, then the rich gain most benefit. As Figure 47.2 shows, the difference between the developed countries and the least developed countries in terms of mobile broadband subscriptions was around four times as great in 2018 as it was in 2007. Such increasing inequalities are apparent for most technologies and at most scales, not only between countries but also between rural and urban areas, between those with greater and fewer disabilities, and between the rich and the poor. If the gap is getting wider, it makes no sense to speak of bridging a divide or digital leapfrogging. The richer countries and people will benefit first from the latest technologies, be they Artificial Intelligence (AI), the Internet of Things (IoT) or Blockchain. This has very significant implications for the interface between development and cybersecurity, not least the growing likelihood that these inequalities will lead to increased social and political unrest that will undermine the very basis of existing digital economies reliant on increasing growth and productivity.

The 'Most-Connected Least-Protected' in an Increasingly Interconnected World

Two main interconnected factors have driven the thirst for the ever greater spread of digital technologies, and especially Internet connectivity, in the poorer countries of the world: the desire of global corporations to expand their markets, while also using such connectivity to lower production and distribution costs; and the belief that these technologies can be used to deliver development benefits more effectively, more widely, and at lower costs (Sharafat and Lehr 2017; Earth Institute Columbia University and Ericsson 2016; Broadband Commission 2018). However, as submarine cables and satellites link ever more isolated parts of the world to the Internet, the potential for state-sponsored and criminal cyberattacks to proliferate has also increased significantly. At first sight, it might be suspected that the most-connected least-protected countries would be the worst affected by such attacks, and would also be places where hackers might choose to base their activities. Hence, it would be in the interests of those wishing to promote global digital stability to support the introduction of appropriate cybersecurity measures in those countries. However, the evidence suggests that this has not been the case. The US-based Center for Strategic and International Studies (CSIS) thus notes that the main significant cyberattacks on government agencies, defence and high-tech companies, and economic crimes with losses of more than a million dollars since 2006 were initiated in China, Russia, Iran, North Korea, India, and the United States, and the countries that received most attacks were the United States, India, South Korea, China, the United Kingdom, Israel, and Ukraine.[4] While different indices measuring various types of digital attack produce contrasting results,[5] the over-riding conclusion is that the poorest and most marginalized countries have not yet been heavily involved in cyberattacks, either as victims or aggressors.

This good fortune does not, though, provide any grounds for comfort. The impact of an attack on the critical infrastructure of an insufficiently protected economically poor state would have devastating consequences that could seriously damage all of its ongoing development initiatives for years to come. Likewise, the loss of a small amount of money through the hacking of a mobile money payment system could prove life-threatening to a poor indebted person, whereas it would merely be a slight inconvenience to someone from a wealthier background. The increasing roll-out of mobile money systems encouraging the poor to participate in the global financial system carries within it significant risks. Until recently, there was little evidence of attacks on financial systems in poor countries, but in early 2019 Symantec reported that in the previous 18 months attackers using commodity malware and living off the land tools[6] had targeted financial institutions in Ivory Coast, Cameroon, DR Congo, Ghana, and Equatorial Guinea.[7] Likewise, at the end of 2018, it was reported that all Pakistan's banks had been hacked, although the State Bank refuted such allegations, and noted instead that that only 20,000 payment card details have appeared for sale online.[8]

Cybersecurity as a Driver for Equality

Unus pro omnibus, omnes pro uno[9]

Most of the world's poorest and smallest countries lack both the financial resources to pay for appropriate hardware and software to deter cyberattacks in their jurisdictions, and also the expertise to be able to implement and maintain effective cybersecurity policies and systems. As but one example, in the mid-2000s, the government of one of the poorest African countries was negotiating to buy second-hand equipment from a slightly richer African country that was upgrading its cybersecurity technology. This deal was being facilitated by a woman working in cybersecurity in the poorer country whose husband happened to be employed in the other country and discovered that this equipment was available. The inability of the poorer country to afford the latest equipment itself was only likely to make it yet more vulnerable to attack. Likewise, the extent of pirated software still being used in the poorest countries of the world, despite all the warnings about its adverse implications, is of serious concern. In the mid-2010s, it was thus estimated that some 80% of software in Africa was still pirated. This not only has significant commercial impact but also major implications for the digital security of those who cannot afford the protections that come with 'clean' official versions of software, be it proprietary or open source (Asongu and Andrés 2017; Asongu, Siobgh, and LeRoux 2018).

Given the interconnectedness of the global digital system, any breach of security has the potential to harm other countries and systems. There is therefore a real interest in developing international support systems to promote integrated approaches that will enable the poorest countries and people to be on equal terms with the economically more advanced as far as cybersecurity is concerned. This has been recognized for a long time. The Council of Europe's Budapest Convention on crimes committed via the Internet and other computer networks was thus opened for signature as early as 2001, and came into force in 2004.[10] Subsequently, the Malaysian government announced the creation of its International Multilateral Partnership Against Cyber-Terrorism (IMPACT) in 2006 at the World Conference on Information Technology (WCIT). This came into being in 2008 at the World Cyber Security Summit with a revised name, replacing Cyber-Terrorism with the broader term Cyber-Threats (Thomas 2009). Subsequently, in May 2011, at the World Summit on the Information Society (WSIS) Annual Forum, IMPACT became a formal partner of the International Telecommunication Union (ITU), with a remit to provide cybersecurity support to the ITU's 193 member states. Later in 2011, the UN Economic and Social Council (ECOSOC) also held a special event on 'Cybersecurity and Development', organized jointly by the Department of Economic and Social Affairs and the ITU, which explored the possibilities of building on the Budapest Convention, concluding that cybersecurity is a global issue that requires global partnerships to implement effective solutions.[11] However, IMPACT had faded away by the mid-2010s, having failed to have any lasting effectiveness, largely because of the wider difficulties in reaching agreements on Internet governance and security, lack of clarity about the precise role that it could play, and difficulties over the funding of its activities. Inequality remains the order of the day as far as cybersecurity and digital development are concerned.

Practice at the Intersection between Cybersecurity and International Development

This section provides a brief account of initiatives that have had partial success in responding to the aforementioned challenges, paying particular attention to the role of international organizations. It concludes by highlighting the tensions surrounding the 'othering' that lie at the heart of problems at the interface between cybersecurity and international development.

Threats and Resilience in Digital Development

Until recently, little attention was paid by the majority of those implementing digital development initiatives in the poorer countries of the world to the potential harm that these can cause, and the need both to mitigate the risks while also ensuring that the digital systems put in place are resilient so that they can be recovered as swiftly as possible after an attack. The overwhelming rhetoric around the positive benefits of new technologies has been extremely powerful, and it is essential that more effort is put into initiatives that raise awareness among both government officials and donors about the potentially negative use and impact of such technologies, especially in economically poor countries and among the most marginalized communities.[12] It is also important to realize that such impacts apply at all scales from the state to the individual:

- Cyber warfare between states (Cornish, Livingstone, Clemente et al. 2010): As yet, there is little evidence of this as being significant in the world's poorest countries, but it remains a potential high-level concern.
- Cyberattacks by insurgent groups to overthrow governments: Digital technologies give disproportionate power to minorities or otherwise insignificant actors, and the so-called Arab Spring serves as a reminder of the potential disruptive usage of social media towards this end Howard, Duffy, Freelon et al. 2011). The extensive activities of techno-anarchists intent on fundamental social, political, and economic change, and willing to destroy the lives of millions of 'others' who do not hold their views, also need to be countered (Bartlett 2014, 2017).
- Disruptive attacks on critical infrastructure: These have existed for a long time and can either be state-led or criminal in origin, but the Stuxnet attack on Iran's uranium enrichment plant in 2010 brought their significance to wider global attention. Since then, attacks on critical infrastructure, and especially national electricity systems, have become more common. Given that all digital technologies require electricity, the potential havoc that could be created to entire national systems in the poorest countries should not be underestimated. Few have sufficiently robust and resilient systems in place to prevent or recover swiftly from such attacks.
- Abuses of power by governments: The increasing number of digital identification systems being introduced by governments can provide benefits for poor people, but also the opportunities for unprecedented levels of control that many will find unacceptable (Shahbaz 2018). Recent initiatives in Kenya, for example, to incorporate DNA into new identity cards provide an indication of the future direction that such initiatives seem likely to follow (Munyua 2019).
- Large-scale criminal hacks and identity theft: The very large size of databases held by governments and companies, especially banks and telecommunication operators, provide a ready opportunity for criminals to defraud substantial numbers of people, and the poor are usually those who are hurt most by such actions.
- Use of digital systems for personal harassment and abuse: There is increasing recognition of the use of digital systems by individuals to do harm to 'others', often of different genders, ethnicity, sexual orientation, or age (Hassan, Unwin, and Gardezi 2018). The rapid expansion of online access among millions of people in parts of the world with little previous experience of digital technologies has dramatically increased the potential for harm to be done to some of the world's poorest and most marginalized people, especially children. In this context, UNICEF has usefully highlighted both the positive and negative implications for children living in an increasingly digital world (UNICEF 2017).

Global Attempts at Reaching a Consensus at the Interface Between Cybersecurity and Development

As previous chapters have highlighted, one of the fundamental challenges of cybersecurity at a global scale has been the inability so far for governments and the UN system to agree on where such issues should best be discussed, let alone how they should be resolved. This has led to a proliferation of initiatives and forums that largely duplicate each other and replicate what has been said before elsewhere. Governments and representatives of small and economically poor countries simply do not have the resources or capacity to participate in all of these, and are therefore further marginalized from such discussions. Moreover, the 'development' and 'security' communities have until recently also largely failed to communicate effectively with each other.

The leading global forum for the interface between information and communication technologies (ICTs) and development has been the WSIS process, initiated in the 2003 and 2005 summits in Geneva and Tunis. Remarkably, cybersecurity was only mentioned five times in its 2005 outcome documents (ITU 2005), and then exclusively in the context of building confidence in the use of ICTs. The subsequent failures of governments to agree how best to take forward dialogues about Internet governance and cybersecurity within the UN system have led to a plethora of other so-called multi-stakeholder forums and initiatives, not least the regular WSIS Annual Forums that now do indeed include a focus on cybersecurity, the Internet Governance Forum (IGF),[13] meetings of the Internet Corporation for Assigned Names and Numbers (ICANN),[14] the NETmundial initiative between 2014 and 2016,[15] and, most recently, the UN Secretary General's High-level Panel on Digital Cooperation.[16]

The failure of previous forums sufficiently to address the challenges of cybersecurity also led to the creation of the Global Conference on Cyberspace (GCCS) in 2011, with meetings in London (2011), Budapest (2012), Seoul (2013), The Hague (2015), and New Delhi (2017). In origin, this was primarily led by foreign ministries of like-minded governments to explore ways through which they could respond to the threat of cyberattacks. As the host, the then UK Foreign Secretary William Hague said, 'We want to widen the pool of nations and cyber users that agree with us about the need for norms of behaviour, and who want to seek a future cyberspace based on opportunity, freedom, innovation, human rights and partnership, between government, civil society and the private sector'.[17] Subsequently, though, the GCCS conferences have broadened their focus so that the 2017 New Delhi conference addressed Cyber4Growth, Cyber4DigitalInclusion, Cyber4Security and Cyber4Diplomacy, thus once again largely replicating broader discussions in other forums.

The central tensions remain, though, between proponents of very different visions of the Internet and digital security. On the one hand, as Hague commented, are those mainly in the United States, United Kingdom, and Europe who advocate a free and open digital system that can enable innovation and economic growth to flourish; on the other are those, notably in China, who wish for a more centralized and controlled system that is carefully monitored and managed by the state (Cheung 2018). Russia, and to some extent Iran, have tended to be allied with the Chinese position, although they are also eager to maintain their independence of voice. India has wavered between the two alternatives, but having hosted the latest GCCS conference would now seem to be more closely aligned with the former framing. Most commentators suggest that the difficulty of reaching international agreements on these issues is likely to lead to a fragmentation of the Internet, or at the very least a bifurcation into a Chinese-led Internet and a US-led one.[18] This has very significant implications, both for cybersecurity and for development, which are explored further in the final part of this section.

Practice at the Interface Between Cybersecurity and Development

Without agreements at the global UN level on the security aspects of digital development, groups of countries and private sector companies have nevertheless sought to develop their own systems and processes. Some have also focused on working with the governments of poorer countries to enable them to put in place mechanisms to enable their digital systems to be resilient. Three areas have had some success: critical infrastructure protection; capacity development and training; and child online protection.

Critical Infrastructure Protection

Efforts to respond to malware and digital hacking date back to the 1980s, when the term 'Computer Emergency Response Team (CERT)' was first used.[19] Since then, numerous initiatives have been developed to create such national teams, and to support their roll-out globally, primarily with the intention of protecting critical infrastructure. Invariably such initiatives begin with a national readiness assessment, followed by the creation of a CERT, and then support for its subsequent development. The ITU's engagement with IMPACT was intended in large part to help support such a process, but as noted earlier this initiative floundered in the mid-2010s. The ITU has nevertheless persisted in helping to deliver Computer Incident Response Team (CIRT) assessments for some 75 countries by March 2019, at which date 108 national CIRTs were in place, of which 12 had been established by the ITU.[20] The majority of CERTs/CIRTs, however, are in the world's richer countries and notably in Europe. By early 2019, only 13 African countries had them in place, and many of the poorer countries and small island states of Asia, the Pacific, and the Americas, still remain to implement them.

At a smaller scale, the Commonwealth Telecommunications Organization, funded in part by the UK's FCO, has also sought to support the 53 countries of the Commonwealth in developing national cybersecurity strategies. Most of these member states are located in Africa, Asia, the Pacific, and the Caribbean, with a preponderance of economically poor countries and small island states. In 2014, Commonwealth ICT ministers thus agreed a Commonwealth Cybergovernance Model,[21] which included key recommendations about CERTs, and this was developed further and revised as a Commonwealth Approach for Developing National Cybersecurity Strategies in 2015.[22] Progress in actually implementing these, though, has been slower than expected, partly because of a lack of funding and partly also because of low levels of capacity to implement these strategies. Again, influenced largely by the UK, the 2018 Commonwealth Heads of Government Meeting (CHOGM) also issued a Commonwealth Cyber Declaration, which included the importance of building a foundation for effective national cybersecurity responses, largely in line with the principles that had been espoused in the 2011 London conference.[23]

Capacity Development and Training

Alongside direct support for critical infrastructure protection, there is a significant need to help empower governments in poorer countries of the world to develop and implement generally accepted good practices in cybersecurity (ITU 2018).[24] This is especially challenging in economically poor countries with weak higher education systems, and also in small island states that do not have sufficient capacity in their governments to implement such systems.

As part of its ongoing international support for cybersecurity, the UK government therefore funded the creation of a Global Cyber Security Capacity Centre at the University of Oxford following the 2011 London conference, with the intention of this developing resources that could be used to help provide training in cybersecurity globally.[25] To this end, it has developed a Cybersecurity Capacity Maturity Model for Nations based around five dimensions: cybersecurity policy and strategy; cyber culture and society; cybersecurity education, training, and skills; legal and regulatory frameworks; standards, organizations, and technologies.[26] Similarly, the Dutch government created its own initiative, the Global Forum on Cyber Expertise after it hosted the 2015 Conference, with the aim of identifying successful policies, practices, and ideas, and then multiplying these at a global level.[27]

Despite the existence of these well-intentioned initiatives, there remains a huge dearth of capacity to implement effective cybersecurity systems in the poorest and most marginalized countries. One of the reasons for this is that the entities creating such initiatives have insufficiently engaged with the 'other', those working within the development sector, and have therefore failed sufficiently to understand the complexities of 'doing development' on the ground. Likewise, many of those involved in implementing 'digital development' in poor countries, hooked on the rhetoric of innovation, entrepreneurship, and the certainty that ICTs will deliver the SDGs, likewise fail sufficiently to understand the darker side of these technologies. While it is relatively easy to shape good policies and strategies, it is far more difficult to ensure that they are implemented effectively and appropriately.

Child Online Protection

The need to protect children online is one area where there is almost universal long-standing agreement that global action is necessary (OECD 2011), and there are now numerous national policies in place to counter such abuse, especially in more affluent countries of the world. It is not easy, though, to estimate the global scale of sexual exploitation of children online, not least since much such activity takes place on the Dark Web and is difficult to locate. The WePROTECT Global Alliance nevertheless suggests that the extent continues to increase. As they comment, 'Technology is permitting offender communities to attain unprecedented levels of organisation, which in turn creates new and persistent threats as these individuals and groups exploit online "safe havens" and "on-demand" access to victims' (WeCONNECT 2018, 5). The UK-based Internet Watch Foundation (IWF) likewise noted a 26% increase in the number of reports it processed in 2017 compared with the previous year (Internet Watch Foundation 2018). In order to facilitate reporting globally, the IWF has also begun to develop portals outside the UK, beginning in Mauritius in 2013, and in 2017 it received funding to deliver a further 30 portals in least-developed countries. Other global initiatives include the activities of the ITU, which has maintained a long commitment to supporting Child Online Protection, working with partners to develop guidelines and resources, and helping to build capacity in some of the world's poorest countries.[28] Despite such commitments, the sexual exploitation of children, and indeed others, online continues to increase, and requires considerable further action if the digital world is indeed to be a safe place for all.

Remaining Challenges: The 'Other'.

Many challenges remain at the interface between cybersecurity and international development. Three are particularly significant.

1. Neo-Colonial Approaches to Cybersecurity: Benevolence and Self-Interest

Much well-intentioned work in cybersecurity remains top-down, neo-colonial,[29] and frequently extremely arrogant. People living in economically poorer countries are more often than not implicitly seen as an 'other' that requires the help and assistance of knowledgeable, generally male, experts in Europe and North America. Countless conferences are held to identify the best solutions for those living in developing countries, or emerging economies, but rarely are the voices of those who live there heard or their opinions solicited. All too frequently, they are expected to adopt 'best practices' designed by outsiders, that invariably do not actually reflect their specific circumstances or capacities.

Cybersecurity is also often used as a form of soft diplomacy to inveigle countries in the poorer parts of the world to support a particular view of the future of Internet governance, or the kind of security apparatus that leaders of a dominant state believe is appropriate for their own interest. For the countries of Europe and North America and their allies, shaping an Internet that is open, free, robust, and secure is an essential part of their policy to facilitate the economic interactions and global growth that are so essential for the success of their own companies and political interests. Here then, there is a strong alliance between the vision of development as economic growth and a top-down, government-led approach to national cybersecurity (Figure 47.1).

2. Cybersecurity and the Bandits: Development Aid as an Industry

Much international cybersecurity assessment, capacity building, and training is designed and implemented by consultants and companies in the richer countries of the world. This is especially so of the Beltway Bandits providing consulting services to the US government (Ceruzzi 2008), but it is also very true of those who are paid to deliver cybersecurity services elsewhere in the world. Academics in the UK, for example, have benefitted hugely from the largesse of the British government in supporting global cybersecurity initiatives. The notion of 'aid' as an industry is therefore one area where there is a close synergy between cybersecurity and international development. The global cybersecurity industry was valued at some $170 billion in 2020,[30] and so it is scarcely surprising that governments wishing to help support their own such industries will seek to find ways to leverage their global influence for mutual benefit.

While the problems of the aid industry have been long known (Haan 2009; Kennard and Provost 2016), it is encouraging to see that some governments are increasingly questioning the ways through which their overseas development assistance is actually disbursed. The UK Parliament, for example, issued a highly critical report in 2017, noting that 'Recent reporting on the conduct of certain contractors shows that some have behaved in a way that is completely unacceptable, is not in line with the principles of the Department and is harmful to the public's view of DFID's work' (House of Commons 2017, 51). Although this comment was not specifically in the context of cybersecurity, it does illustrate the morally questionable stance of some donors and their corporate cousins.

China and the USA: 丝绸之路经济带和21世纪海上丝绸之路

Underlying much of this chapter has been the uneasy tension between the United States, with its increasing economic and political challenges, and China, the powerhouse of the present, let alone the future.[31] Government and corporate views in China and the United States of the future of the digital world are vastly different,[32] and the failure of diplomats on both sides to reach agreements and compromises seems likely to lead to continued uncertainty over Internet governance and cybersecurity for some time to come. Conflicts and disagreement about the security risks posed by Huawei's technologies, especially given their dominance in 5G, are but the most visible feature of fundamentally different world views (Westcott 2019). Much European and North American support for cybersecurity in the economically poorer countries of the world is thus above all else an attempt to promote a 'Western' view of the digital future against an 'other' view from the East. It is also designed to boost an industrial sector that is already facing very substantial challenges from China. The successes and rapidity of China's Belt and Road Initiative, as well as its development programmes in Africa have very serious implications for those who wish to see a trans-Atlantic vision dominating the future of digital technologies and global cybersecurity.

LOOKING TO THE FUTURE

The aforementioned prognosis is not intended to make easy reading. However, it should be noted that approaches to cybersecurity and international development in China and the United States-Europe can both be seen as lying at the top right corner of Figure 47.1. They are both, albeit from rather different perspectives, largely top-down and focus mainly on development as economic growth. They also very much rely on the 'other' as a means of shaping their own identities. Should this persist, there is an increasingly gloomy future for the development of empowering and secure digital technologies, and their use in delivering appropriate development outcomes that will benefit the poor and marginalized. An alternative future, one that fragments the 'other' and focuses on what might be done at the bottom left corner of Figure 47.1, is one that is therefore interesting to explore in concluding this chapter.

Little work has yet been done on bottom-up approaches to cybersecurity that focus on empowering the poorest and most marginalized, but this is where research and practice need to begin if relative poverty is to be reduced and security increased. This is not to deny that governments do indeed still need to take action to protect critical infrastructure, but it is to suggest that entirely different approaches to cybersecurity may also be required. Human error remains the leading cause of data and security breaches, and greater focus on ensuring that everyone using digital technologies understands the risks they face and consciously takes actions to prevent such harm would go a long way to reducing such breaches. Moreover, a focus on developing new technologies to help people, especially children and those with least understanding of such technologies, to manage their digital lives more securely and safely could begin to make the Internet safer for all.

At the government level, it is essential to develop more holistic approaches to the interface between cybersecurity and development. This applies as much to donors as to governments in economically poor countries seeking to implement appropriate policies and practices. It is essential, for example, that donor agencies pay much greater attention to the potentially harmful aspects of digital technologies and the need for cybersecurity than they do currently, and that they therefore work closely with the departments in their own governments that have expertise in digital security.

Above all else, the future of cybersecurity and development needs to be about working *with* each other, rather than creating 'others' for or against whom to work. It is not about rich academics and consultants developing solutions 'for' poor and marginalized others, but rather about them working together to create appropriate context-specific solutions that will indeed reduce poverty and create a safer and fairer Internet for all. It is also about diplomats and security specialists in China and 'Western' countries developing shared understandings together to solve common challenges for a safer world, rather than seeing each as a threatening 'other'. With a will to work differently together, these are not idle pipe dreams but could indeed be made to happen.

NOTES

1. This is a broad generalization, and there are of course exceptions. However, this distinction between the communities involved in cybersecurity and development is important in understanding the lack of communication between them. See also Carayannis, E.G., Campbell, D.F.J. and Efthymiopoulos, M.P. (eds) 2018. *Cyber-Development, Cyber-Democracy and Cyber-Defense.* New York: Springer.
2. https://sustainabledevelopment.un.org/sdgs
3. https://www.government.nl/latest/news/2018/04/21/cybersecurity-essential-for-economic-and-social-opportunities
4. CSIS, 2019. https://www.csis.org/programs/cybersecurity-and-governance/technology-policy-program/other-projects-cybersecurity
5. See, for example, Kaspersky's cyberattack map https://cybermap.kaspersky.com/stats, Fireeye's cyber threat map https://www.fireeye.com/cyber-map/threat-map.html, Fortinet's threat map https://threatmap.fortiguard.com/, and Digital Attack Map http://www.digitalattackmap.com/
6. Living off the land techniques use trusted off-the-shelf and preinstalled system tools to carry out attacks. Creating fewer (or no) new files on a hard disk means that such attacks are more difficult for traditional security tools to block.
7. Symantec, 2019. https://www.symantec.com/blogs/threat-intelligence/african-financial-attacks
8. Bankinfo Security. https://www.bankinfosecurity.com/pakistan-banks-werent-hacked-but-card-details-leaked-a-11683

9. 'One for all, and all for one', the unofficial motto of Switzerland, made famous by Alexander Dumas in his novel *The Three Musketeers*.
10. Council of Europe. https://www.coe.int/en/web/conventions/full-list/-/conventions/treaty/185
11. UNDESA.https://www.un.org/en/development/desa/news/ecosoc/cybersecurity-demands-global-approach.html
12. Unwin, 'Reclaiming Information'.
13. https://www.intgovforum.org/multilingual/
14. https://www.icann.org
15. https://netmundial.org/
16. https://digitalcooperation.org/
17. https://www.bbc.co.uk/news/technology-15533786
18. See, for example, https://futurism.com/google-future-china-internet
19. While CERT is still the most common term, other similar terms in use include Computer Emergency Readiness Team (CERT), Computer Security Incident Response Team (CSIRT), Computer Incident Response Team (CIRT) and Cyber Incident Response Centre (CIRC).
20. https://www.itu.int/en/ITU-D/Cybersecurity/Pages/national-CIRT.aspx
21. https://cto.int/media/pr-re/Commonwealth%20Cybergovernance%20Model.pdf
22. http://www.cto.int/media/fo-th/cyb-sec/Commonwealth%20Approach%20for%20National%20Cybersecurity%20Strategies.pdf
23. https://www.chogm2018.org.uk/sites/default/files/Commonwealth%20Cyber%20Declaration%20pdf.pdf ; see also FCO. 2018. 'UK Programme Supporting Cyber Security in the Commonwealth: Call for Expression of Interest.' https://www.gov.uk/government/publications/uk-programme-supporting-cyber-security-in-the-commonwealth-call-for-expressions-of-interest
24. ITU, Draft GCI.
25. https://www.oxfordmartin.ox.ac.uk/cybersecurity/
26. https://gcscc.ox.ac.uk/files/cmmrevisededition090220171pdf
27. https://www.thegfce.com/. See also the World Economic Forum's Centre for Cybersecurity, https://www.weforum.org/centre-for-cybersecurity/home, as another overlapping initiative.
28. https://www.itu.int/en/cop/Pages/default.aspx
29. Easterly, *The White Man's Burden*.
30. https://www.grandviewresearch.com/industry-analysis/cyber-security-market
31. The heading translated is: Silk Road Economic Belt and the twenty-first-century Maritime Silk Road.
32. Doffman, 'Why We Should Fear'.

BIBLIOGRAPHY

Asongu, S.A., and Andrés, A.R. 2017. 'The Impact of Software Piracy on Inclusive Human Development: Evidence From Africa', *International Review of Applied Economics* 31 (5): 585–607.

Asongu, S.A., Siobgh, P., and Le Roux, S. 2018. 'Fighting Software Piracy: Some Global Conditional Policy Instruments', *Journal of Business Ethics* 152 (1): 175–89.

CYBERSECURITY AND DEVELOPMENT   783

Bartlett, J. 2014. *The Dark Net: Inside the Digital Underworld*. London: Melville House.

Bartlett, J. 2017. 'Forget far-right populism,—crypto-anarchists are the new masters', *The Observer*, 4 June. https://www.theguardian.com/technology/2017/jun/04/forget-far-right-populism-crypto-anarchists-are-the-new-masters-internet-politics

Broadband Commission. 2018. *The State of Broadband 2018: Broadband Catalyzing Sustainable Development*. Geneva: ITU. https://www.itu.int/dms_pub/itu-s/opb/pol/S-POL-BROADBAND.19-2018-PDF-E.pdf

Brons, L. 2015. 'Othering, an Analysis', *Transcience* 6 (1): 69–90.

Ceruzzi, P.E. 2008. *Internet Alley: High Technology in Tysons Corner, 1945–2005*. Cambridge, Mass.: MIT Press.

Cheung, T.M. 2018. 'The Rise of China as a Cybersecurity Industrial Power: Balancing National Security, Geopolitical and Development Priorities', *Journal of Cyber Policy* 3 (3): 306–26. https://www.tandfonline.com/doi/full/10.1080/23738871.2018.1556720

Cornish, P., Livingstone, D., Clemente, D. et al. 2010. *On Cyber Warfare*. London: Chatham House. https://www.chathamhouse.org/sites/default/files/public/Research/International%20Security/r1110_cyberwarfare.pdf

Doffman, Z. 2018. 'Why We Should Fear China's Emerging High-Tech Surveillance State', *Forbes*. https://www.forbes.com/sites/zakdoffman/2018/10/28/why-we-should-fear-chinas-emerging-high-tech-surveillance-state/#355a2a604c36

Earth Institute Columbia University and Ericsson. 2016. New York and Stockholm: Earth Institute Columbia University and Ericsson. https://www.ericsson.com/assets/local/about-ericsson/sustainability-and-corporate-responsibility/documents/ict-Sdg.pdf

Easterly, W. 2006. *The White Man's Burden: Why the West's Efforts to Aid the Rest Have Done so Much Ill and so Little Good*. Oxford: Oxford University Press.

Haan, A. 2009. *How the Aid Industry Works: An Introduction to International Development*. Boulder CO: Lynne Rienner Publishers.

Hassan, B., Unwin, T., and Gardezi, A. 2018. 'Understanding the Darker Side of ICTs: Gender, Sexual Harassment, and Mobile Devices in Pakistan', *Information Technologies and International Development* 14: 1–17.

House of Commons International Development Committee. 2017. *DFID's Use of Private Contractors: Eighth Report of Session 2016-17*. London: House of Commons. https://publications.parliament.uk/pa/cm201617/cmselect/cmintdev/920/920.pdf

Howard, P.N., Duffy, A., Freelon, D., et al. 2011. *Opening Closed Regimes: What was the Role of Social Media During the Arab Spring*. Seattle: University of Washington. Project on Information Technology and Political Islam. https://deepblue.lib.umich.edu/bitstream/handle/2027.42/117568/2011_Howard-Duffy-Freelon-Hussain-Mari-Mazaid_PITPI.pdf?sequence=1&isAllowed=y%20

Internet Watch Foundation, 2018. 'Internet Watch Foundation: Annual Report 2017'. https://annualreport.iwf.org.uk/#new_technology

ITU. no date. 'Child Online Protection'. https://www.itu.int/en/cop/Pages/default.aspx

ITU. 2005. *World Summit on the Information Society Outcome Documents Geneva 2003—Tunis 2005*. Geneva: ITU. https://www.itu.int/net/wsis/outcome/booklet.pdf

ITU. 2018. *Draft: Global Cybersecurity Index (GCI) 2018*. Geneva: ITU. https://www.itu.int/en/ITU-D/Cybersecurity/Documents/draft-18-00706_Global-Cybersecurity-Index-EV5_print_2.pdf

Juech, C. 2017. 'Cybersecurity and Data Security Become Mainstream Concerns', Bond. https://www.bond.org.uk/hubs/cybersecurity-and-data-security-become-mainstream-concerns

Kennard, M., and Provost, C. 2016. 'How Aid Became Big Business', *Los Angeles Review of Books*, 8 May. https://lareviewofbooks.org/article/aid-became-big-business/

Levinas, E. 1981. *Otherwise Than Being or Beyond Essence*. Berlin: Springer Science and Business Media.

Morgus, R. 2018a. 'Cybersecurity in Development: to Mainstream or Prioritize?', *New America*. https://www.newamerica.org/cybersecurity-initiative/c2b/c2b-log/cybersecurity-development-mainstream-or-prioritize/

Morgus, R. 2018b. *Getting the International Development Community to Care About Cybersecurity*. Council on Foreign Relations. https://www.cfr.org/blog/getting-international-development-community-care-about-cybersecurity

Munyua, A. 2019. 'Kenya Government Mandates DNA-Linked National ID, with Data Protection Law'. https://blog.mozilla.org/netpolicy/2019/02/08/kenya-government-mandates-dna-linked-national-id-without-data-protection-law/

Nurko, G. 2018. 'Cyber Security Series Part 1: Trust is Why Cyber Security Matters to Digital Development', Digital@DAI. https://dai-global-digital.com/cybersecurity-series-part-1-trust-is-why-cyber-security-matters-to-digital-development.html

O'Boyle, E.J. 1999. 'Toward an Improved Definition of Poverty', *Review of Social Economy* 57 (3): 281–301.

OECD. 2011. 'The Protection of Children Online: Risks Faced by Children Online and Policies to Protect Them', OECD Digital Economy Papers, No. 179. Paris: OECD Publishing. https://doi.org/10.1787/5kgcjf71pl28-en

Sachs, J. 2005. *The End of Poverty*. Harmondsworth, UK: Penguin.

Schia, N.N. 2017. 'The Cyber Frontier and Digital Pitfalls in the Global South', *Third World Quarterly* 39 (5): 821–37. https://www.tandfonline.com/doi/full/10.1080/01436597.2017.1408403

Shahbaz, A. 2018. *Freedom on the Net 2018: The Rise of Digital Authoritarianism*. Freedom House. https://freedomhouse.org/sites/default/files/FOTN_2018_Final%20Booklet_11_1_2018.pdf

Sharafat, A., and Lehr, W. (eds) 2017. *ICT-Centric Economic Growth, Innovation and Job Creation*. Geneva: ITU.

Thomas, N. 2009. 'Cyber Security in East Asia: Governing Anarchy', *Asian Security* 5 (1): 3–23.

UNDP. 2015. *Human Development Report 2015: Work for Human Development*. New York: United Nations Development Programme.

UNICEF. 2017. 'State of the World's Children: Children in a Digital World'. https://www.unicef.org/sowc2017/

Unwin, T. 2007. 'No End to Poverty', *Journal of Development Studies* 45 (3): 929–53.

Unwin, T. 2017. *Reclaiming Information and Communication Technologies for Development*. Oxford: Oxford University Press.

WeCONNECT. 2018. 'Global Threat Assessment 2018: Working Together to end Sexual Exploitation of Children Online', WeCONNECT Global Alliance. https://static1.squarespace.com/static/5630f48de4b00a75476ecf0a/t/5a85acf2f9619a497ceef04f/1518710003669/6.4159_WeProtect+GA+report+%281%29.pdf

Westcott, B. 2019. 'No Matter what Trade Deal is Struck, the US and China are Worlds Apart. Huawei is The Proof', CNN. https://edition.cnn.com/2019/03/27/asia/huawei-us-lawsuit-china-intl/index.html.

World Bank. 2016. *World Development Report*. Washington DC: World Bank.

World Economic Forum. 2018. 'Centre for Cybersecurity'. https://www.weforum.org/centre-for-cybersecurity/home.

CHAPTER 48

PROJECT SOLARIUM 1953 AND THE CYBERSPACE SOLARIUM COMMISSION 2019

MIKE STEINMETZ

INTRODUCTION

IN 2018, Senator Ben Sasse (R-Neb) called for the establishment of a Cyberspace Solarium Commission (CSC), identifying members of the House and Senate who would address the challenges of cyberspace in the twenty-first century (Sasse, 2018). By his choice of the word 'Solarium', Sasse made a deliberate comparison between the magnitude of the cyberspace policy decisions of 2019 and the policy decisions made by the United States in 1953, when President Eisenhower used the same term in a very different context. This chapter explores that context, shows what Eisenhower achieved with the first Solarium and asks what might be achieved with the second.

'Project Solarium' means different things to different people. To some, it evokes an era of global uncertainty with competing nuclear powers. To others, it brings to mind a threat so compelling that a US President formed a special project to rapidly reshape US policy. Today, once again, the word Solarium inspires hope, optimism, and expectation that cybersecurity—one of the most critical challenges of the twenty-first century—can be addressed as successfully as challenges from the past. The growing digital security challenges of the twenty-first century now provoke comparisons with a historic event. So why pick the name Solarium? Will combining the name Solarium with the gravity of the twenty-first century threat deliver similar results as it did in 1953? What exactly did Project Solarium 1953 deliver? In what way is the global nuclear threat and spread of communism in 1953 comparable to the global cyberthreat of the twenty-first century, and is there a risk that the comparison might either over-simplify a complex problem or, worse still, provoke an inappropriately exaggerated and perhaps even apocalyptic approach to cyberspace security? Are nuclear/cyber comparisons a good enough reason for studying the threat assessments and/or policymaking aspects of Eisenhower's Project Solarium of 1953, or are there other aspects of the 1953 Project Solarium that offer more useful insights into the human aspects of policy-making? Could the naming of the 2019 Cybersecurity Commission as the 'Cybersecurity Solarium Commission' provide little more than smart branding?

In 1953, the United States was compelled by world events to undertake crucial policy dialogues: dialogues that delivered critical, timely, and unifying guidance to the leadership of the Eisenhower administration (Eisenhower 1953). Were the results of these dialogues (new national security guidance in the form of National Security Council [NSC] Document 162/2—FRUS, Document 101) a byproduct of critical nuclear world events or just a timely correction to the republican foreign policy platform of 1952 (Pickett, 2004)? It is tempting (and reassuring) to drop current world events into the crucible of global events and threats of the 1950s: events and threats that, for all the fear and drama associated with them, nevertheless proved to be *manageable*. To do so, however, would be to proffer a fallacious argument. Simple analogies do not guarantee analogous results: the fact that Eisenhower's 1953 Project Solarium provided critical policy guidance does not guarantee that the 2019 CSC will do the same. But, if direct conclusions cannot be drawn, then what merit is there in revisiting Project Solarium at all? Why should similarly productive outcomes be expected simply because the 2019 Commission has added 'Solarium' to its title?

The global events of the 1950s certainly evoked reactions similar to those we see today, inviting the thought that Eisenhower's Project Solarium model might deliver similarly unifying analysis and guidance regarding cyberspace as it did for Eisenhower regarding the growing spread of communism, the nuclear threat from the USSR and the PRC. But to imply that twenty-first-century cybersecurity and cyberspace policy and operations might somehow be comparable, in national strategic terms, with the nuclear threat faced by the United States in the 1950s might be more emotionally satisfying than it is helpful. Where do comparisons between the global events of 1953 and those of 2019 add to understanding, and where are they superfluous, and perhaps even damaging? And, if it is argued, for example, that direct comparisons between the response to the nuclear threat and the management of cyber challenges and intrusions are simplistic, then what else can be learned from Eisenhower's approach to strategic policy analysis? At the very least, Eisenhower's Project Solarium serves as a model with which today's policymakers could probe weighty and complex strategic issues.

Sasse's choice of the word Solarium also creates an opportunity to explore the human dimensions of the 1953 debate (albeit classified at the time) (FRUS, Document 67)—a debate that resulted in sufficient consensus among strong-willed individuals to craft a national security policy (NSC 162/2[1]) (FRUS, Document 101), addressing the implications of the growing threat of communist expansionism by the USSR and the PRC: a post Truman-era approach that most top-level policymakers within Eisenhower's cabinet could support. If simply addressing today's debate is not well served by historic comparisons of the threat (discounting the simplistic 'lift and shift of the threat' from 1953 to 2019), what lessons can be learned from Eisenhower and his Project Solarium? Are comparisons between the nuclear arms race of 1953 and proliferation of digital weapons in 2019 justifiable and useful? Could the processes President Eisenhower built into the original Project Solarium deliver the debate and the satisfactory outcomes required for solid policy decision making today, as they did in 1953? Will the outcome of the CSC 2019 allow policymakers to deliver the equivalent of NSC 162/2?

1953, Eisenhower's Inheritance and the Solarium Project

Upon his swearing in on 20 January, 1953, Eisenhower inherited his predecessor's policies, as had all US presidents before him. Some of the most important policies addressed major threats to the United States and its global interests (FRUS, Document 129). Eisenhower had run on a platform where two contrasting strategies—'rollback' versus 'containment'—were heavily debated. He recognized that the USSR and the PRC both wished to expand their communist ideology. In the case of the USSR, these aspirations were backed with existing atomic weapons while in the PRC a nuclear programme was underway with a first successful test taking place in the 1960s. Eisenhower had won the presidential election with 55.2% of the vote. The landslide win, however, was no guarantee of unity within his cabinet. Eisenhower knew that the United States required a powerful and unifying international policy and that he must bring his leadership together to draft that policy. Eisenhower gave a speech 12 weeks into his administration that provides insight into his thinking and his sense of urgency. In the first public speech[2] of his administration (16 April 1953) to the American Society of Newspaper Editors, the new President set forth basic principles defined as the ' ... the aftermath of war towards peace'. Most notably, Eisenhower was clear regarding the direction the world was headed and the inevitable impact of trade-offs between the intellectual capital and productivity of the American citizen (and citizens of other free nations), and he regretted the national productivity that would be diverted to the task of deterring communist aggression:

> Every gun that is made, every warship launched, every rocket fired signifies, in the final sense, a theft from those who hunger and are not fed, those who are cold and are not clothed. This world in arms is not spending money alone. It is spending the sweat of its laborers, the genius of its scientists, the hopes of its children. The cost of one modern heavy bomber is this: a modern brick school in more than 30 cities. It is two electric power plants, each serving a town of 60,000 population. [...] This is, I repeat, the best way of life to be found on the road the world has been taking. This is not a way of life at all, in any true sense. Under the cloud of threatening war, it is humanity hanging from a cross of iron. These plain and cruel truths define the peril and point the hope that comes with this spring of 1953.

President Eisenhower's speech provides key perspectives into his priorities and the sense of urgency with which those priorities needed to be addressed. Eisenhower had seen the ruin of great industrial powers (particularly Germany) through war, and understood the importance of rebuilding the infrastructure needed to ensure self-sufficiency and prosperity.

Against this background, on 9 May, Robert Cutler, Eisenhower's Special Assistant for Security Affairs, published a memorandum for the record entitled 'Solarium Project' (FRUS, Document 63). Fewer than 30 days after his speech to the American Society of Newspaper Editors, the President drafted a memorandum entitled Solarium Project (FRUS, Document 65), followed quickly by a memorandum for the record by Robert Cutler on 15 May 1953 (FRUS, Document 65) organizing an approach, topics, and a time frame for the new Solarium Project. Eisenhower was moving fast, using very discreet channels, to set the Solarium Project in motion. By 20 May, the President had set out specifics for the three task forces created to debate policy options (FRUS, Document 67) and, by 1 June, the Directing Panel of

Project Solarium had determined the specific tasks, policies, and processes to be addressed and employed (FRUS, Document 69). Most of this initial coordination effort was classified Top Secret, limited to a very few select individuals hand-picked by Eisenhower himself. The limited number of people involved created its own challenges: in such a secretive environment, how could Eisenhower ensure that the perspectives of other important members of his cabinet and administration regarding current policies on Russia and China could be understood and accommodated without having to include more people in the Solarium Project? The answer to Eisenhower's dilemma came in the form of a memorandum from the Secretary of Defense to the Joint Chiefs of Staff on 4 June 1953 (FRUS, Document 71). The request from the Secretary of Defense was for a 'Restatement of Basic National Security Policy'. This document was to be called 'National Security Council 153' or 'NSC 153' (FRUS, Documents 72 and 73). The Defense Secretary's memorandum asked for an examination of current policy and of a draft provided by the NSC Planning Board in which the Joint Chiefs of Staff had provided comment and general agreement with NSC 153. By having a wider dialogue albeit at the top-secret level, Eisenhower expanded his sphere of influence. Having drawn in other critical players within his administration, he provided those participating in Project Solarium with a way to consider the views of a wider leadership team.

Eisenhower's Challenge; Selecting the Teams and Tasks for Project Solarium

It had been seven years since George Kennan, the Deputy Head of Mission and subsequently US Ambassador to the USSR, had sent his Long Telegram (Kennan 1946)[3], warning of the divided nature of Soviet global policy and making the point that the Soviet leadership articulated one policy on the official international level while carrying out a different policy at the unofficial level. From the standpoint of US policy, Kennan's observations regarding the duplicitous nature of Soviet policy were concise and unambiguous. Part Five of the 1946 telegram reads as follows:

> In summary, we have here a political force committed fanatically to the belief that with [the] US there can be no permanent modus vivendi, that it is desirable and necessary that the internal harmony of our society be disrupted, our traditional way of life be destroyed, the international authority of our state be broken, if Soviet power is to be secure. [...] In addition, it has an elaborate and far-flung apparatus for exertion of its influence in other countries, an apparatus of amazing flexibility and versatility managed by people whose experience and skill in underground methods are presumably without parallel in history. Finally, it is seemingly inaccessible to considerations of reality in its basic reactions. For it, the vast fund of objective fact about human society is not, as with us, the measure against which outlook is constantly being tested and re-formed, but a grab bag from which individual items are selected arbitrarily and tenaciously to bolster an outlook already preconceived (Kennan, 1946).

Assisted by his compelling style of writing, the underlying point of Kennan's message lay in his sensitivity to the politically diverse views of the readership of the Long Telegram. Eisenhower faced similar political diversity and realized that his Project Solarium teams would not only have to take account of current political perspectives of US strategic adversaries but also have to consider global economic imperatives and the health of the US economy. The republican platform of 1952[4] called on the US to regain the foreign policy initiative, seek a free democratic and unified Germany, and 'roll back' communist control from Eastern Europe. Now elected, Eisenhower needed a plan to build consensus beyond his electoral platform[5]: one that would address the human aspects of his decisions and gather disparate perspectives into one common policy debate. John Foster Dulles, the new Secretary of State, had recently invited Kennan to leave the Department of State,[6] effectively dismissing the one person responsible for much of America's deep understanding of the USSR and who had provided the previous administration with a path towards communist containment. Project Solarium would need diversity of political perspectives, including figures such as George Kennan.

Eisenhower was involved in every aspect of the preparation of the Solarium effort, personally directing the composition of the teams and insisting that subject matter experts should be recruited to conduct a thorough analysis of any proposed options (Pickett, 2004). Eisenhower's direction of the project was precise and very detailed:

> When the teams are prepared, each should put on in some White House room, with maps, charts, all the basic supporting figures and estimates, just what each alternative would need in terms of goal[s], risk[s], cost in money and men and world relations.

Eisenhower had now set the stage for one of the most important policy debates in US history.

Guidance from the Project Solarium Directing Panel (FRUS, Document 69) dictated that Project Solarium would stand up three separate task forces with each given a specific designation; Alternative A, Alternative B, and Alternative C.[7]

Task Force A was unsurprisingly assigned Alternative A, and was led and chaired by the recently rehabilitated George Kennan. It was assigned an alternative that would leverage NSC 153 to achieve three goals (restated and paraphrased from the original [FRUS, Document 69]): first, to maintain over a sustained period armed forces to provide for the security of the United States and to assist in the defence of vital areas of the free world; second, to continue to assist in building up the economic and military strength and cohesion of the free world; and, third, without materially increasing the risk of general war, to continue to exploit the vulnerabilities of the Soviets and their satellites by political, economic, and psychological measures. Further guidance for Task Force A included interpretation of the Eisenhower administration's policy in two respects. The first of these was the sense that time could be used to the advantage of the United States and its allies. If strength could be built up and maintained over several years, Soviet power could be expected to deteriorate, or at least decline in relative terms, to a point at which it would no longer constitute a threat to the security of the United States, its allies, and world peace in general. Second, while seeking to deter and oppose further expansion by the Soviet bloc, the policy would include the use of military operations, as necessary and feasible, even at the grave risk of general war. However, an attempt would be made to localize such military operations as far as possible.

Task Force B, with Alternative B, was led and chaired by United States Air Force Major General James McCormick who, in addition to being 'an atomic and new weapons expert' (Pickett, 2004), was a military and political planner. Alternative B stated that, in the first instance, it would be the policy of the United States to complete the line now drawn in the NATO area and the Western Pacific so as to form a continuous perimeter around the Soviet bloc beyond which the United States would not permit Soviet or satellite military forces to advance without general war. Second, it would be US policy to make clear to the Soviet rulers in an appropriate and unmistakable way that the United States had established and was determined to carry out this policy. Finally, the United States would reserve freedom of action in the event of indigenous communist seizure of power in countries on the US side of the perimeter, taking all measures necessary to re-establish a situation compatible with the security interest of the United States and its allies.

The directing panel also required Task Force B to examine various implications of the policy framework they had been tasked to consider. First, wherever the perimeter line was to be drawn, there would be geostrategic implications, particularly if those countries currently outside the Iron Curtain also found themselves on the wrong side of the US perimeter. What might be the effect of this decision—effectively to be excluded from US support—on the countries concerned and US interest therein? Second, should aggression across the line in particular regions be met at the outset by general military action against both the Soviet Union and China or only against the one most directly involved? Third, what measures might be taken by the United States in the event of indigenous communist takeover of countries on the US side of the perimeter? Fourth, where the perimeter excluded countries now outside the Iron Curtain, what might be the attitude and action of the United States, short of armed intervention, toward communist encroachment upon such countries? Finally, should the United States consult some or all of our allies and other friendly powers in advance of the adoption of Alternative B? Should these allies and friends be invited to associate themselves with the policy? Should the adoption of the policy by the United States be made contingent upon this wider acceptance?

Task Force C was assigned Alternative C, the shortest of all taskings. Task Force C was led by Vice Admiral Richard Connelly who was then serving as the President of the US Naval War College. Alternative C read as follows:

> The policy of the United States would be: to increase efforts to disturb and weaken the Soviet bloc and to accelerate the consolidation and strengthening of the free world to enable it to assume the greater risks involved and second to create the maximum disruption and popular resistance throughout the Soviet Bloc.

President Eisenhower approved each member of all three task forces. Colonel Andrew Goodpaster, later to become NATO's Supreme Allied Commander Europe, was specifically placed on Task Force C by Eisenhower. The President had high confidence that Goodpaster would thoroughly examine and evaluate rollback options. Eisenhower also commented on Goodpaster's aptitude for common sense. Goodpaster went on to say later in life that 'the President did not take part in the deliberations, but he did recommend participants: it was he who suggested that Kennan chair Task Force A' (Pickett, 2004).

Eisenhower's Objectives and Outcomes

Many senior people from the President's administration would not participate in Project Solarium. However, Eisenhower's use of his Secretary of Defense to develop NSC 153 ensured that their perspectives were included in the Solarium debate. Thus, senior policy experts not included in the Solarium debate contributed, albeit indirectly, through their contributions to NSC 153. That NSC 153 was debated, and contributed to the final Solarium report to the NSC, helped Robert Cutler achieve a common ground for final comment and debate. In short, NSC 153 made it difficult for anyone outside the Solarium Project to question the motivation and approach of each Solarium team. The task forces were constructed in such a way that no single perspective could be said to have benefited from bias within the team and, equally, nor could it be said to have been disadvantaged by a lack of intellectual or policy gravitas. Preparations now having been made, and each team assigned and researched their task, the debate was scheduled. Each team debated the theme of their task force, drawing upon available information and data.[8] Overt and hidden objections were exposed, providing a balanced exposition of the arguments and allowing for the development of ideas and perspectives. Although this discursive process may not have changed participants' core beliefs, it did, nevertheless, provide a way for each participant to raise issues, to challenge perspectives, and then to find a way to support those aspects of policy with which they otherwise disagreed. Eisenhower knew that consensus among his cabinet members would be key to crafting a successful and supportable policy. The human element was then addressed at many levels: political, ideological, cultural, and practical.

By June 26, a first Project Solarium plenary session had taken place (FRUS, Document 69) with the leadership of each task force providing feedback and debate in respect of their assigned alternative. In a meeting of President Eisenhower's NSC on 16 July (FRUS, Document 79), the President shared his observations. Eisenhower noted that the oral presentations covered all three alternatives that would affect basic national security policies, commenting on:

> ... the excellence of the presentations by the task force and dissemination of the reports upon which they were based to the entire National Security Council staff so that each could prepare summaries of the principal points in consultation with members of each task force and report back to the Council for further consideration and instructions (FRUS, Document 79).

In a memorandum penned by Robert Cutler, Special Assistant to the President for National Security Affairs, Cutler notes *inter alia* that the President thought that there were many similarities in the three presentations, which he felt more important than the differences between them. The President is reported to have observed that the 'United States has to persuade her allies to go along with her, because our forward bases are in the territories of our allies' (FRUS, Document 79).

Furthermore:

> The president also indicated that 'there is still more for the task force to do; a mass meeting to see if they could agree on certain features of the three presentations as the best features and to bring about a combination of such features into a unified policy, arranging a presentation to congressional leaders and to prepare an outline of a major policy plan to be adopted' (FRUS, Document 79).

Robert Cutler met the task forces after the President left, noting that Task Forces A and C were in strong disagreement and that although there were external 'similarities from their six weeks association ... they could not agree' (FRUS, Document 79). He also noted that some of them had fundamental differences that could be compromised into a watered-down position but not really agreed to. When Cutler reported this to the President, he observed that the President 'seemed very put out and left it to me to work out what I thought best'. Cutler then worked out the details of the final approaches and principal points. After selecting personnel from each task force to review the document, a summary was corrected and presented to the NSC on 23 July 1953 (FRUS, Document 80).

In a report to the NSC by its Executive Secretary (Lay) on 30 October 1953 (FRUS, Document 101), NSC 162/2 was published, including reference to a 'Memorandum for National Security Council from Executive Secretary, Subject: Project Solarium' dated 23 July. The preamble to the 'Statement of Policy by the National Security Council', known as 'NSC 162/2', states:

> The president has this date approved the statement of policy contained in NSC 162/1, as amended and adopted by the Council and enclosed herewith, and directs its implementation by all appropriate executive departments and agencies of the US government. As basic policy, this paper has not been referred to any single department or agency for special coordination.

Early notes in the paper also state that NSC 162/2 'supersedes NSC 153/1'.

Eisenhower had succeeded. From conception in May 1953 through to execution in June and early July 1953 and then to consensus building and summary reporting in late July, with the involvement of his senior administration the President had built a new national policy for the United States regarding the USSR nuclear threat, the PRC communist threat and the expansion of communism globally. Can Eisenhower's organizational and strategic success be repeated by the Congressional CSC?

US Congressional Cyberspace Solarium Commission 2019

The 2019 CSC was established under the 2019 US Defense Authorization Act to consider one of the most complex challenges of the early twenty-first century: the nature of cyberspace and the threat of state and non-state aggression through digital means. On establishment, the CSC was given six tasks, or *duties*, and was invited to produce a report no later than 1 September 2019 (Sasse, 2018). The Commission comprises 14 individuals:

> who have demonstrated knowledge, expertise and experience in both cyberspace and national security fields. Members will be: Principal Deputy Director of National Intelligence, Deputy Director of Homeland Security, Deputy Secretary of Defense, the Director of the Federal Bureau of investigation, three members appointed by Senate Majority Leader, two members appointed by Senate Minority Leader, three members appointed by the Speaker of the House of Representatives, and two members appointed by the minority leader of the house" (Sasse, 2018).

The CSC's six duties (restated and paraphrased from the original [Sasse, 2018]) are, first, to ascertain the cost of various strategic options to include the political system, the defence industrial base and the innovation base of the United States. The CSC's second duty is to examine the execution of various policy options and, specifically, how such execution should be implemented and incorporated within the US national strategy. The third duty is to explore norms-based regimes that the United States should support and enforce, and to determine the costs the United States is willing to endure in doing so. The third duty also addresses the type of attack that might warrant a response, how US national strategy could support those responses and how national strategy could be executed to best effect. The fourth duty asks members to review the strengths and intentions of the adversaries of the United States and how their efforts could be deterred or otherwise thwarted. Fifth, the CSC is asked to evaluate current policy and its effectiveness in disrupting, defeating, or deterring cyberattacks. Sixth, and finally, the CSC is asked to consider how the government is structured and what authorities need to be created or revised within the federal government. There are, clearly, distinct similarities between Project Solarium 1953 and the CSC of 2019.

The CSC's fifth duty—to 'evaluate the effectiveness of the current national cyber policy relating to cyberspace, cybersecurity, and cyber warfare to disrupt, defeat, and deter cyberattacks'—appears to align with President Eisenhower's NSC 153/1. In short, Eisenhower's question was 'What do we have now that is good?' Taken together, the CSC's first and second duties combined require the Commission to address the ways and means of implementing better policy for the United States. In important respects, these duties mirror the language of the three Task Force Alternatives of Eisenhower's Project Solarium. Although the CSC does not consider alternative actions and drive active debate in the same manner as its forerunner, it is intended to address important issues of fiscal and policy resources and how the execution of policy would play out in grand strategy. The CSC's third duty covers an area heavily debated in the 1953 initiative. Eisenhower ran on a foreign policy political platform in which he disparaged the strategy of President Truman and encouraged more aggressive options. President Truman's outlook was supported by George Kennan and was most likely one of the reasons Kennan was asked to depart the US Department of State upon the arrival of the new secretary, John Foster Dulles. Additionally, although the scope of Project Solarium and the final text of NSC 162/2 did not cover specific budgetary figures, the US treasury and budgeting officials were involved and did calculate costs to the US economy as well as costs to the US taxpayer.[9] One of the original objectives of the 1953 Project Solarium was to ensure economic prosperity for Americans, the expectation of global economic growth, and the maintenance of US values and institutions. It is interesting to note that the CSC overview does not directly touch upon the maintenance of American values but obliquely addresses the maintenance of US institutions such as the political systems of the United States, the national security industrial sector, and the innovation base (Sasse, 2018).

Although the CSC tasking does not directly address allies or use the phrases 'multilateral' or 'unilateral approaches' (in its third duty), it does ask the Commission to review and make determinations on what 'norms-based regimes' the United States should seek to establish.

Conclusion

How can Eisenhower's Project Solarium of 1953 substantially and beneficially inform important policy dialogues such as CSC of 2019? Is the name Solarium, in and of itself, sufficiently authoritative?

There are certainly useful comparisons to be drawn between Eisenhower's Project Solarium of 1953 and the CSC 2019. Yet, there are also significant differences between the two initiatives that merit closer consideration of the politics, people, and culture of the 1950s compared with the realities of the twenty-first century. In the early twenty-first century, ideas such as transparency and open debate, tolerance for divergent perspectives, interest in the economic impacts of decisions, and the significance of global relationships in the pursuit of economic prosperity and security, are all more valued than ever. In most respects, society is more open in 2019 than it could possibly have been in 1953: in the digital age, it is much more demanding to protect information than it was in the 1950s. Moreover, the political culture of the 1950s was very heavily influenced by a fear of the global spread of communism. This culture allowed Eisenhower to hand-pick his debating teams and largely to screen them from scrutiny through systematic diversion and misdirection. Today, the debate regarding cyberspace is much too public for any such measures. For the CSC, transparency will be essential, particularly when its deliberations touch upon the development and implementation of new sets of norms, national and, inevitably, international, for behaviour in cyberspace. Although there will certainly be aspects of the CSC process that will require protection, for the United States, as for other countries, it is imperative in the digital era that the policy dialogue should be an open one, not cloaked by national security classification schemes. Classifying the dialogue would discourage a multi-stakeholder approach to global cybersecurity and governance. Now, more than ever, highly transparent and factual debate is the only method to corral widely divergent views into some form of national consensus.

While studying Project Solarium 1953, researchers will encounter NSC 153/1 'Restatement of Basic National Security Policy' (FRUS, Document 71). Broadly speaking, NSC 153/1 laid the groundwork for Project Solarium by using the Secretary of Defense to engage principals such as the military (Joint Chiefs) and others, asking them for an indication of their support for current elements of US policy. Asking for a 'Restatement of Basic National Security Policy' provided Eisenhower with a broader range of stakeholders articulating what aspects of US policy they could or could not support regarding the USSR and PRC. NSC 153/1 also provided the President with a rich set of data and information that supported the content of the Alternatives for each Task Force. Confirmation, or lack thereof, of current approaches and policy was an important element helping Eisenhower think through the policy options Project Solarium would provide to his NSC staff. Something similar is essential in the context of the CSC's work.

Paragraph twelve on page eight of NSC 162/2 states: 'The United States cannot, however, meet its defense needs, even at exorbitant cost, without the support of allies.' Similarly, the cyber threat to the United States is not one that can be met unilaterally. It must be met with the cooperation and consensus of America's allies. Yet, so far, the CSC has not made this explicit. This is a key point, and a striking difference between Project Solarium 1953 and the CSC 2019. Although the CSC's third duty tasks its members to review and make determinations as to what norms-based regimes the United States should seek to establish, it does not directly address the advantages of multilateral approaches or the distinct weakness of a unilateral approach to cyberspace. Like its 1953 forerunner, the CSC should therefore affirm via economic and other data that a unilateral approach to cyberspace by the United States is not compatible with US economic prosperity.

President Eisenhower carefully selected the people and the topics for his three task forces.[10] By so doing, he convened a group of experts holding widely diverse opinions who would be forced to address and make the case for disparate opinions within the confines of a singular debate. Eisenhower telegraphed a sense of urgency by limiting the amount of time each team had to prepare, debate, and brief policymakers. The effect of Eisenhower's approach was to allow dissenting voices and widely divergent perspectives to occupy equal precedence, forcing participants to hear and debate points of view and to present substantive evidence supporting the point of view proffered. Subsequently, when formulating NSC 162/2, Eisenhower and his NSC staff could then summarize and articulate a perspective debated by the principals, building the minimum consensus and support that were needed. Had Eisenhower not undertaken this process, then Kennan, Connolly, Goodpaster, and others would not have been armed with enough evidence to support the President's new policy towards the USSR and the PRC. Although never in complete agreement (FRUS, Document 79), Eisenhower's Project Solarium provided the participants and other principals with a way to support the President and Commander-in-Chief. Thus, the debate itself provided an environment where policymakers with widely divergent views could find substantive paths to consensus. The CSC 2019 has selected members of the minority and majority within the Senate and the House along with subject matter experts and deputy directors of stake-holding departments and agencies. The Commission members no doubt will have widely divergent opinions and stances regarding policy and the way ahead. In this case, it is the leaders of the CSC, not the President of the United States, who have hand-selected the membership. It remains to be seen what traction the outcomes of the CSC will have with those who must draft the next generation of national security policy documents.

Perhaps the power of the word Solarium lies is the promise of a process whereby those holding widely divergent views (of whom there is no shortage in the United States) can enter into a structured debate and produce meaningful and executable national policy. It is not so much the scale of the topic (Soviet and Chinese global ambitions) or the sense of urgency felt in the early years of the Cold War (although urgency still plays an important role in cyber-space policy), but perhaps it is the promise that there is a process where critical issues can be addressed by those with widely differing views and that positive, constructive, and durable outcomes can be the result. A lesson from Project Solarium 1953, as viewed through a twenty-first-century lens, is that it can quickly disabuse a researcher of the notion that 'times were simpler, and easier back then'. Perhaps it is more fair and accurate simply to say that 'times were different back then'. What should also be borne in mind is that the leadership of Project Solarium 1953 left the debate in earnest disagreement with one another on substantive issues. Having learned of this, Eisenhower turned to his Special Assistant for National Security Affairs, Robert Cutler, leaving him to 'work out [...] other details' (FRUS, Document 79). When the CSC produced its final report in March 2020 there were differences of opinion as to its content and achievement, with some gaps in its analysis as well as 'other details' still to be worked out.[11] A final lesson might then be drawn from Eisenhower's Project Solarium 1953: the CSC will most certainly need someone upon whom it can call to 'work out the other details'.

Notes

1. *A Report to the National Security Council on Basic National Security Policy* (Washington: NSC 16/2, 30 October 1953).

796   MIKE STEINMETZ

2. Eisenhower called the speech, '[A] Chance for Peace'. It later became known as 'The Cross of Iron speech'.
3. Kennan's telegram was later published anonymously as 'X': 'The Sources of Soviet Conduct', *Foreign Affairs. An American Quarterly Review* 25 (4): 566–82: https://www.cvce.eu/ content/publication/1999/1/1/a0f03730-dde8-4f06-a6ed-d740770dc423 /publishable_en.pdf
4. The American Presidency Project provides details: https://www.presidency.ucsb.edu/documents/republican-party-platform-1952
5. http://vanderbilthistoricalreview.com/eisenhowers-campaign/
6. See Pickett, 'George F. Kennan', 12.
7. The descriptions of the Project Solarium Three Alternatives are taken directly from the document entitled 'Paper Prepared by the Directing Panel of Project Solarium' (1 June 1953) originally classified Top Secret (FRUS, Document 69).
8. Pickett, 'George F. Kennan', 4.
9. Pickett, 'George F. Kennan', 19.
10. Pickett, 'George F. Kennan', 22.
11. Cyberspace Solarium Commission Report, 11 March 2020. https://www.fdd.org/analysis/2020/03/11/cyberspace-solarium-commission-report/

References

Foreign Relations of the United States. 1952–1954. *National Security Affairs*, Volume II, Part 1, ed. James S. Lay Jr (Washington: Government Printing Office, n.d., Original Document dated 30 October 1953: Washington), Document 101. https://history.state.gov/historicaldocuments/frus1952-54v02p1/d101

Foreign Relations of the United States. 1952–1954. *National Security Affairs*, Volume II, Part 1, ed. James S. Lay (Washington: Government Printing Office, n.d., Original Document dated 22 July 1953: Washington), Document 80. https://history.state.gov/historicaldocuments/frus1952-54v02p1/d80

Foreign Relations of the United States. 1952–1954. *National Security Affairs*, Volume II, Part 1, ed. Robert Cutler (Washington: Government Printing Office, n.d., Original Document dated 16 July 1953: Washington), Document 79. https://history.state.gov/historicaldocuments/frus1952-54v02p1/d79

Foreign Relations of the United States. 1952–1954. *National Security Affairs*, Volume II, Part 1, eds. T.B. Koons (Washington: Government Printing Office, n.d., Original Document dated 26 June 1953: Washington), Document 69. https://history.state.gov/historicaldocuments/frus1952-54v02p1/d69

Foreign Relations of the United States. 1952–1954. *National Security Affairs*, Volume II, Part 1, ed. James S. Lay Jr (Washington: Government Printing Office, n.d., Original Document dated 10 June1953: Washington), Document 74. https://history.state.gov/historicaldocuments/frus1952-54v02p1/d74

Foreign Relations of the United States. 1952–1954. *National Security Affairs*, Volume II, Part 1, ed. S. Everett Gleason (Washington: Government Printing Office, n.d., Original Document dated 9 June 1953: Washington), Document 73. https://history.state.gov/historicaldocuments/frus1952-54v02p1/d73

Foreign Relations of the United States. 1952–1954. *National Security Affairs*, Volume II, Part 1, ed. S. Everett Gleason (Washington: Government Printing Office, n.d., Original Document dated 5–8 June 1953: Washington), Document 72. https://history.state.gov/historicaldocuments/frus1952-54v02p1/d72

Foreign Relations of the United States. 1952–1954. *National Security Affairs*, Volume II, Part 1, ed. Robert R. Bowie (Washington: Government Printing Office, n.d., Original Document dated 8 June 1953: Washington), Document 71. https://history.state.gov/historicaldocuments/frus1952-54v02p1/d71

Foreign Relations of the United States. 1952–1954. *National Security Affairs*, Volume II, Part 1, eds. Directing Panel (Washington: Government Printing Office, n.d., Original Document dated 1 June 1953: Washington), Document 69. https://history.state.gov/historicaldocuments/frus1952-54v02p1/d69

Foreign Relations of the United States. 1952–1954. *National Security Affairs*, Volume II, Part 1, ed. Dwight D. Eisenhower (Washington: Government Printing Office, n.d., Original Document dated 20 May 1953: Washington), Document 67. https://history.state.gov/historicaldocuments/frus1952-54v02p1/d67

Foreign Relations of the United States. 1952–1954. *National Security Affairs*, Volume II, Part 1, ed. Robert Cutler (Washington: Government Printing Office, n.d., Original Document dated 15 May 1953: Washington), Document 65. https://history.state.gov/historicaldocuments/frus1952-54v02p1/d65

Foreign Relations of the United States. 1952–1954. *National Security Affairs*, Volume II, Part 1, ed. Robert Cutler (Washington: Government Printing Office, n.d., Original Document dated 9 May 1953: Washington), Document 63. https://history.state.gov/historicaldocuments/frus1952-54v02p1/d63

Foreign Relations of the United States. 1950. *National Security Affairs*; *Foreign Economic Policy*, Volume I, ed. James S. Lay Jr (Washington: Government Printing Office, n.d., Original Document dated 30 September 1950: Washington), Document 129. https://history.state.gov/historicaldocuments /frus1950v01/d129

Eisenhower, Dwight D. 1953. Address [Speech], Eisenhower to the American Society of Newspaper Editors [Chance for Peace] [Cross of Iron], April. https://www.americanrhetoric.com/speeches/dwightei senhowercrossofiron.htm

Kennan, G.F. 1946. Telegram, George Kennan [Long Telegram], February. https://www.trumanlibrary.org/whistlestop/study_collections /coldwar/documents/pdf/6-6.pdf

Pickett, W.B. 2004. 'George F. Kennan and the Origins of Eisenhower's New Look: An Oral History of Project Solarium'. https://web.archive.org /web/ 20131029210208/http:/www.rose-hulman.edu/~pickett/Solarium.pdf

Sasse, B. 2018. 'Cyberspace Solarium Commission Overview'. https://www.sasse.senate.gov/public/_cache/files/cf57ede8-1b02-47c3-b41b-d3898edeb9ef/solarium-fact-sheet.pdf

CONCLUSION

PAUL CORNISH

THE invention of cyberspace created unprecedented possibilities for worldwide, near instant, mass transfer of data, information, images, and ideas. Two decades into the twenty-first century, enough is known about this new information environment to suggest that its effects are probably best described as *revolutionary*—technologically, politically, industrially, commercially, societally, and strategically. This 'information revolution', if that is a fair description, has two very distinctive features. First, whereas we might expect a revolution in political, cultural, or commercial life to be a more or less discrete event, or series of events, showing evidence of design and deliberate action intended to bring about an identifiably different condition, it is difficult to discern who, or what, might be driving the information revolution, what direction it is taking, and where, when, or how it might conclude. Second, the information revolution might more accurately be described as two revolutions: one seemingly benign and laden with opportunity and benefit, and the other with more obviously malign characteristics and hazardous consequences. What is more, these two revolutions are taking place in parallel and possibly even symbiotically.

Like many pivotal moments in human history, the information revolution is both attractive and inspiring on the one hand, and alarming and intimidating on the other. The attraction of cyberspace is easily explained. Cyberspace is expansive and dynamic: a global communication infrastructure promising not only to *shape*, but also to *improve* all dimensions and all levels of human life—cultural, economic, religious, diplomatic, commercial, family, individual, non-governmental and governmental, and so on. What is more, the price of access to these extensive benefits could be as little as the cost of a SIM card and the rules of behaviour expected of participants in this global venture do not seem too onerous. But what is just as striking is that, in spite (or perhaps because) of the considerable opportunities it offers, our attraction to cyberspace has not generally been accompanied by a commensurate effort to guarantee the security and stability of this increasingly important environment. As this *Handbook* has demonstrated comprehensively, as well as the immense benefits and opportunities offered by cyberspace, the threats and hazards are also considerable. Cyberspace is routinely exploited by a variety of adversaries, aggressors, and predators: hostile states; political extremists and terrorists; businesses practising commercial espionage and theft; individuals and criminal organizations undertaking financial fraud and trafficking in people, armaments, and narcotics; and individual so-called 'nuisance' hackers.

It should be the task of the cybersecurity industry to counter these adverse behaviours and to secure and stabilize cyberspace for the general and longer-term benefit. The cybersecurity industry certainly seems to have risen to the challenge, and the sector has become very active, prominent, and well rewarded. According to Gartner, an international research and advisory company, global information security spending is expected to grow by 2.4% to reach $124 billion in 2020—a dramatic reduction from the 8.7% growth predicted in their December 2019 forecast.[1] What is more striking, however, is that, while this is clearly a highly valued and lucrative market sector, even at the higher (predicted) rate, spending on cybersecurity in 2020 would have been proportionately far behind the speed of growth in disruptive or damaging cyberattacks and data breaches. Respected cybersecurity research organizations often record annual increases in Internet, web-based, and mobile intrusions at rates far in excess of the higher level of (predicted) expenditure on cybersecurity, sometimes well over 60% per annum. On occasion, the losses incurred as the result of a cyber intrusion can be extraordinary: the June 2017 NotPetya attack on Merck, the US pharmaceutical company, resulted in losses and damages estimated at some $1.3 billion;[2] that month, the NotPetya malware also infiltrated information and communication technology (ICT) systems at Maersk, the shipping and logistics firm, and FedEx, the distribution company, inflicting losses of approximately $300 million and $400 million respectively;[3] and, in late 2018, it was revealed that Marriott, the hotel group, had been subjected to a massive data breach, the cost of which was initially estimated at between $200 million and $600 million.[4]

The losses incurred by individual companies and organizations can, plainly, be immense but the sum of the damage caused by a cascading malware release or attack can exceed these figures by orders of magnitude. The cost of two of the most celebrated malware 'ripple events' of recent years have been assessed at $4 billion (WannaCry) and $10 billion (NotPetya).[5] Often, it is the most innovative (and lucrative) technology sectors that are most attacked and most damaged. A report in December 2018, for example, suggested that, in 2017, in the UK alone, losses from the theft of intellectual property totalled £9.2 billion—with £1.8 billion of those losses inflicted on pharmaceutical, biotechnology, and healthcare organizations.[6] Although net assessments of the cost of cybercrime are often contested, the US Federal Bureau of Investigation has estimated that the losses to cybercrime, globally, in 2019, could have been in the region of $3.5 trillion (Internet Crime Complaint Center 2019). Another assessment, from the private sector, suggests that the global losses might rise to $6 trillion by 2021 (Cybersecurity Ventures 2019). And, as well as the economic, commercial, intellectual, and reputational losses experienced by the companies and organizations concerned, there are also wider strategic, diplomatic and political costs to consider.

A tension begins to emerge. Global ICT spending in 2020 was estimated to be 'relatively flat' at about $5 trillion (but with resumption of growth expected after the COVID-19 pandemic).[7] Considerable sums are being spent annually on global cybersecurity. And even more considerable sums are being lost annually to cybercrime and cyberattacks around the world. There would thus seem to be no fewer than three industrial sectors doing very well out of the information revolution: the ICT sector; the cybersecurity sector; and the cyber *insecurity* sector. There has always been, and will always be, a diversion of legitimate funds into criminal activity of various sorts—that there is cybercrime, and that it is very lucrative, should come as no surprise. But when the level of loss—described by Cybersecurity Ventures as 'the greatest transfer of economic wealth in history'—is, in crude terms, more or less equivalent to the value of the ICT market itself, then it is difficult to see how this could be sustainable or even tolerable. Could any other industrial or service sector expect to receive public confidence and to survive in such circumstances? And, even if this equilibrium between production and predation were thought to be sustainable, would it be optimal—would it suggest that the ICT revolution is achieving all that is promised and expected of it, economically and socially?

It then becomes pertinent to ask whether one subset of the ICT revolution—the cybersecurity sector—is achieving everything that is expected of it when the results of its efforts are that the legitimate and illegitimate markets are, in very broad terms, equivalent. Does cybersecurity actually secure cyberspace, or does it merely ensure a balanced, steady state in which both legitimate and illegitimate markets can co-exist? For the sake of argument, if global spending on cybersecurity were to be doubled in order to protect and nurture the legitimate ICT market, would this have the effect of reducing the illegitimate market by something approaching 50%, or would it simply mean that the legitimate and illegitimate markets would both increase in equal proportion? To achieve something other than simply the expansion of the steady state, in which the ICT industry and cyber predators are in a symbiotic relationship, might it be both desirable and effective for cybersecurity, as both an idea and an industry, to be motivated differently, by more constructive and progressive goals?

Not unreasonably, given the sophistication and agility of cybercriminals and other antagonists, and the losses they inflict around the world, cybersecurity (and most of the discourse surrounding it) has become fixed on the problem of threat and response as a form of action/reaction dynamic. The outcome is that a vast and vigorous cybersecurity industry has grown up, dedicated to detailed analysis of the evolving (and even more vast and vigorous) 'threat picture', to offering consultancy advice and training 'solutions', and to the provision of technological 'fixes'. But the threat/response interplay might also have skewed the discussion unhelpfully, in several ways.

In the first place, the preferred language can often be more directive than cognitive or intuitive. For example, although government security departments and cybersecurity corporations periodically exhort the public to maintain the highest standards of personal 'cyber hygiene', that advice is routinely ignored. Rather than investigate the reasons for this lack of public interest and engagement, however, the exhortations are often then repeated, *ad tedium*, albeit with ever more colourful and attractive presentational devices as though these might finally convince the public to amend their ways. The reasons for public non-compliance might, however, be worthy of closer and more self-critical inspection. It might be that that members of the public do not consider anything that smacks of national security (and least of all international security) to be their responsibility ('That's why I pay my taxes ... ') and might also resent such 'statist' intrusions into their personal life. Furthermore, when it comes to personal/private security, it might also be that the public do not, and will not, optimize for security; instead they optimize for usability and convenience, and for cost.[8] Public reticence to be drawn into the cybersecurity debate could be very significant. Private individuals are simultaneously the most numerous and the least secure users of ICT. In some countries, it appears to have been assumed that, if the public could be persuaded to adopt more secure ICT practices and generally behave more cautiously and 'hygienically' (in, for example, their personal banking practices), then individuals might, in a sense, become highly trained and very numerous 'agents' of the national cybersecurity effort. But mass-mobilization of this sort does not appear feasible if the public lack interest and persist in the view that national cybersecurity is 'someone else's problem'.

The increasingly directive language is also acquiring a more punitive tone—the beginnings of a 'culpability culture', perhaps. This can have a constraining and narrowing effect on the willingness to engage with, and contribute to, national cybersecurity, particularly where the private sector is concerned. As the insurance/reinsurance sector is becoming steadily more confident at underwriting cyber risk, so attention has begun to focus on the corporate responsibility of directors and officers for decisions taken (or not taken) regarding exposure to risk in and from cyberspace. And, as night follows day, it follows that corporate responsibility is increasingly being manifested in the individual liability of directors and officers for any failures and losses. These individuals might be excused for regarding cybersecurity not as a positive, constructive feature of corporate life in the early twenty-first century but, instead, as a deep and dangerous hazard, exposure to which must at all costs be avoided and limited.

The third problem with the 'threat and response' approach to cybersecurity is that it could also impoverish our engagement with recent and anticipated innovation. The digital environment is already replete with technological developments and challenges: the Internet of Things (or, as some put it, rather dauntingly, the Internet of *Everything*); Big Data; Human-Machine Teaming; Quantum Computing; and, in the military sphere, developments such as Lethal Autonomous Weapon Systems. The major growth area in the near future seems certain to be in machine learning and in the progressive development of artificial intelligence from 'basic' to 'augmented' to 'general'. These new and evolving technologies can also be expected to appeal to cyber aggressors, criminals, and hackers. The possibility will arise of new crimes such as cyber manipulation of stock prices, for example, together with the potential to manipulate defensive systems and to hide sophisticated probes in the noise created by blunter, more overt attacks. The attack environment will become more diverse and more sophisticated protection will be required for individuals as they become increasingly vulnerable to so-called 'human hacking', or social and behavioural engineering.

If the digital future might develop more or less along these lines, then at first glance an emphasis on 'threat and response' would seem reasonable enough. But this emphasis can also mean that we lose sight of at least half of what cyberspace is (or should be) all about— opportunity and progress. Whether imminent or more distant, these and other technological developments should all be understood, in principle, to be politically, morally, and strategically neutral: essentially as no more or less than techniques that could benefit both 'attackers' and 'defenders' in cyberspace. The risk of the persistent threat/response discourse, however, is that these technologies might, in some curious way, be seen, figuratively, already to have chosen sides (usually the adversary's), that the nature of these innovations will not be debated and understood fully, and that the positive benefits and opportunities they offer could be overlooked. The threat/response fixation could mean that we are blind to the possibility that exploiting opportunity might make us as, if not more, stable and secure than reacting to threat. Furthermore, it is instructive to note that, if cyberspace can be a vector for strategic challenges and threats of the sort outlined earlier, then it is also a vector for communication and will remain as such. If a sophisticated global communication and information network can pose a widening array of security challenges, then that same communications network can also be the basis for managing security challenges and conflicts by various well-trodden means: diplomacy, prevention, mediation, détente, deterrence, etc. In other words, however digital technologies are to develop in coming years, they must be expected to remain both part of the security problem and part of the security solution.

The threat and response approach to cybersecurity might also have become so popular and compelling that it, and the action/reaction dynamic it represents, is now being used too easily and too uncritically. The idea of an action/reaction dynamic governing innovation and our response to it is simple and persuasive, and its (rather self-evident) logic probably explains its application in a wide variety of circumstances. But it is a logic that can be difficult to escape and, more to the point, it does not necessarily lend itself to a durable solution to the larger problem at hand. In his *Memoirs of an Unconventional Soldier*, J.F.C. Fuller, a British military theorist of the 1930s, offered an adapted version of the action/reaction dynamic in the form of the 'constant tactical factor', an idea that still resonates in debates concerning national strategy and military innovation. Fuller explained his idea in the following terms:

> Every improvement in weapon-power has aimed at lessening the danger on one side by increasing it on the other; consequently every improvement in weapons has eventually given rise to a counter-improvement, which has rendered the improvement obsolete; the evolutionary pendulum of weapon-power, slowly or rapidly, swinging from the offensive to the protective and back again ...

Explained in this way, the significance of Fuller's 'constant tactical factor' would seem to be contained in its first two words: it is *constant* (i.e. the 'evolutionary pendulum' can be expected to continue swinging and not to 'evolve' very much beyond that state) and it is *tactical* (i.e. Fuller seemed to be concerned with the effects of innovation at a relatively low level—that of one side introducing new weapons to the battlefield). What Fuller did not consider, however, at least not in this well-known depiction of the action/reaction dynamic, is how to break out of that endless cycle and how to ensure that innovation and/or our reaction to it can have a decisive, positive, and durable effect at a higher level, especially that of national policy and strategy. By extension, if cybersecurity is to do more than simply perpetuate the threat/response, action/reaction dynamic, then it is reasonable to ask, first, whether cybersecurity, as currently practised, could be reconceived in some way so as to break out of the 'evolutionary pendulum' and, second, where cybersecurity, once liberated, might lead (if anywhere).

The idea that cybersecurity could have a larger, more comprehensive, and progressive goal might seem to some to be fanciful: an unrealistic and other-worldly response to the very real possibility of encountering substantial harm in and from cyberspace. This possibility cannot, of course, be erased by the simple expedient of sanitizing the cybersecurity discourse in order that risk, harm, and loss are neither contemplated nor even mentioned. Yet the threat/response dynamic, compelling though it is, is surely not the best or last explanation and need not be all there is to say about cybersecurity; it should be possible for cybersecurity to have a larger goal than the endless pursuit of (defensive) advantage over an adversary. If cyberspace can be valued as much as it is feared, then the broader purpose of cybersecurity could be not only to *disable* threats as they arise but also to *enable* the positive opportunities offered by the information revolution. And there are very strong reasons for thinking more constructively about cybersecurity—reasons that are far from naïve. The first of these concerns who—or what—should assume control of cyberspace, and with what purpose in mind. We have arrived at an inflection point in the introduction of new ICTs, with further developments on the horizon and still more in the imagination. This moment will require humanity not only to analyse and understand the implications of these developments, but also to decide upon any limitations that should be imposed for political, economic, strategic, or ethical reasons. Cyberspace is fast becoming an all-encompassing ecosystem—a complex, interactive network of relationships and dependencies in which 'life' forms (both biological and non-biological, benign and malign) interact with each other and with their environment. At least for the present, this ecosystem is also an artefact. Having constructed cyberspace, it is surely imperative that humans should remain in control of their creation and should direct its purpose. The alternative is as unappealing as it is avoidable: there should, in principle, be no reason why humans should subscribe to some technologically determined future in which we will have an ever-diminishing say in the way our lives are ordered and will forever be the sullen, passive victims of cyber insecurity, against which we must protect ourselves as well as we can. Whatever goes on within cyberspace, and whatever the uses to which it is put, it should be understood as something that is politically and morally malleable, as an arena in which human agency must remain decisive, ensuring that cyberspace evolves in ways that are conducive both to protection and to progress.

A second reason for thinking more aspirationally about the security and stability of cyberspace is that, without ambition and purpose, the achievement of cybersecurity is unlikely to rise above the lowest common denominator in political, diplomatic, and commercial negotiations. The general governance of cyberspace, and the detailed regulation of commercial and other activity within it, is probably best described as 'work in progress' taking place internationally (in inter-governmental bodies such as the United Nations and regional organizations around the world) and nationally (in terms of the regulation of ICT companies under a given national jurisdiction). If these governance and regulatory 'gaps' are ever to be filled, it will be necessary for individuals, corporations, governments, and international organizations to have a more consolidated and shared understanding of cyberspace, its purpose and its future—not solely as an environment in which threats must be dealt with, but also as a place of opportunity and growth. Cybersecurity might then begin to live up to our expectations of it, as the means to ensure that the future of cyberspace is as much one of progress and reward as one of hazard and loss.

If a shared *understanding* of cyberspace can be cultivated, then the prospect comes into view of a shared *responsibility* for the future of this invention. A debate has been simmering for some years as to whether it would be reasonable and useful to describe cyberspace as a 'global commons' and, if so, to ask who or what should be responsible for its upkeep and for averting the 'tragedy of the commons'. Cyberspace is an oddity: it is an artefact rather than a natural environment and is generally privately owned in ways and in places that, in principle at least, come under the sovereign authority of states; there is therefore very little about cyberspace that could be said to be genuinely 'common' in the same way that the sea and the atmosphere are held to be. What can be said, however, is that the users of cyberspace act increasingly *as if* it were held in common ownership and *as if* they have inalienable rights to use it. Whether erroneous or not, these presumptions of ownership and access carry political weight. It would appear then, from the perspective of its users, that cyberspace is neither private property, nor sovereign territory, nor global commons, but something *sui generis*, with characteristics drawn from all three of these ideas: a 'virtual commons', perhaps (Cornish 2015). If the expectations of the users of cyberspace were to be matched by the goals, rhetoric, and decisions of the governors and regulators of cyberspace, then cybersecurity could be much more than simply a metaphor for 'winning', however temporarily, against an enemy or competitor, and could instead be a metaphor for a shared sense of responsibility in the maintenance of a mutually beneficial (and threatened) enterprise.

The final argument for a more aspirational and constructive approach to cybersecurity is the most important of all. If the inventors, users, producers, regulators, and guardians of cyberspace could all subscribe not only to a common understanding of cyberspace as an environment of both hazard and opportunity, but also to a shared responsibility for the maintenance and future direction of that environment, then the digital ecosystem could become more secure and stable and, almost by default, more resilient to attack and predation. High-level, 'top-down' collaboration of this sort should in turn oblige the cybersecurity sector to look beyond reactive postures of defence and denial, and to have goals that are more ambitious than ensuring the protection and security of this or that organization, sector, system, or network. A cyberspace that is more convincingly, credibly, and durably resilient will be one in which cybersecurity has a much larger purpose, that of ensuring that highly valued organizations, structures, and systems can not only survive an attack of some sort but can recover (ideally to a stronger and more stable state than when they were first attacked) and continue to function. Multilateral, collaborative resilience can spread risk, dilute vulnerability, and share strength, resulting in a more stable and productive digital ecosystem, and one less vulnerable to attack and predation. And, far from being naïve to argue for such collaboration to extend into the international sphere, to collaboration between governments, it is imperative to do so. As Kenneth Geers argues, 'in the international domain of cyberspace ... any single government's sovereignty and defenses are quite limited. As a consequence, many hacker tools and tactics are best countered via international collaboration in network security and law enforcement' (Geers 2020). Above all, this more ambitious, enhanced form of resilience would not be reactive or hostage to an adversary's capabilities or intentions, making it possible to escape the dismal (non)-evolutionary pendulum of the action/reaction dynamic.

The twenty-first-century information environment is complex and sophisticated, and it is used ever more intensively, even to the point of societies, governments, and individuals becoming economically, culturally, and psychologically dependent upon it. Yet, it is also an environment in which security ideas and procedures remain relatively primitive—'analogue' constraints upon 'digital' modernity, perhaps. The fact that the information environment is developing and is being exploited so intensively—at such a fast pace and in different (ostensibly incompatible) directions simultaneously—is what makes it an especially difficult context for policy making and strategic planning. Yet, it is precisely that complexity and urgency that makes it imperative for policy and strategy to describe the contours and boundaries of the new information environment in which they must operate. Cybersecurity must, in part, be concerned with practical measures taken to ensure the protection of people, corporations, and societies against threats and adversaries. But cybersecurity must also address the ordering (i.e. the safety, security, and governance) of nothing less than a global digital ecosystem that is taking shape very rapidly and very beneficially, at every level and in every field of human activity. It is both possible and necessary to combine both perspectives—protection *from* and progress *towards*—in one account, as this *Handbook of Cybersecurity* has shown.

Notes

1. 'Gartner Forecasts Worldwide Security and Risk Management Spending Growth to Slow but Remain Positive in 2020', 17 June 2020. https://www.gartner.com/en/newsroom/press-releases/2020-06-17-gartner-forecasts-worldwide-security-and-risk-

managem#:~:text=Information%20security%20spending%20is%20expected,its%20
December%202019%20forecast%20update.&text=Some%20security%20spending%20wi-
ll%20not,be%20ignored %2C%E2%80%9D%20he%20said

2. 'Was It an Act of War? That's Merck Cyberattack's $1.3 Billion Insurance Question', *Insurance Journal*, 3 December 2019. https://www.insurancejournal.com/news/national/2019/12/03/550039.htm

3. 'The Untold Story of NotPetya, the Most Devastating Cyberattack in History', *WIRED*, 22 August 2018. https://www.wired.com/story/notpetya-cyberattack-ukraine-russia-code-crashed-the-world/

4. 'Marriott Data Breach Losses Could Be Over Half A Billion Dollars', *ComputerWeekly.com*, 20 December 2018. https://www.computerweekly.com/news/252454778/Marriott-data-breach-losses-could-be-over-half-a-billion-dollars

5. 'How Much Money Did WannaCry Make?', *WebTitan.com*, 2 December 2019. https://www.webtitan.com/blog/how-much-money-did-wannacry-make/#:~:text=So%20how%20much%20did%20WannaCry,are%20detailed%20in%20the%20blockchain; 'The Untold Story of NotPetya', *WIRED*, 22 August 2018.

6. 'Lessons for Pharma from the Merck Cyber Attack', *PharmaExec.com*, 10 December 2018. http://www.pharmexec.com/lessons-pharma-merck-cyber-attack

7. International Data Corporation (IDC). 2020. 'Global ICT Spending Forecast 2020–2030'. https://www.idc.com/promo/global-ict-spending/forecast. IDC estimate the global market to be worth almost $6 trillion by 2023.

8. I am grateful to Madeline Carr for this point.

REFERENCES

Cornish, Paul. 2015. 'Governing Cyberspace through Constructive Ambiguity', *Survival* 57 (3), June–July): 158–9.

Cybersecurity Ventures. 2019. '2019 Official Annual Cybercrime Report', Herjavec Group, p. 1. https://www.herjavecgroup.com/wp-content/uploads/2018/12/CV-HG-2019-Official-Annual-Cybercrime-Report.pdf

Fuller, J.F.C. 1936. *Memoirs of an Unconventional Soldier.* London: I. Nicholson and Watson, p. 453.

Internet Crime Complaint Center. 2019. '2019 Internet Crime Report', US Federal Bureau of Investigation, p. 15. https://pdf.ic3.gov/2019_IC3Report.pdf

Index

Tables and figures are indicated by *t* and *f* following the page number

3D printing 688–89
5G 432, 433, 442, 780
7ReachLLC 100
360 Cyber Threat Intelligence Centre 600
   Helios Team 600
   SkyEye Labs 600

A
Abbott, K. 548, 551
Abkhazi conflict 533
Abrahams, C. 731
access to target 174, 176, 177–78
access to technology *see* technology: access
    and denial
account credentials 365
account removals 169
accountability
   agreement violations as customary
     practice 572–73
   autonomous cyber weapons systems
     (AWS) 703
   child safety online 385
   future normative challenges 758, 762
   proxies and offensive cyber
     operations 555–56
   security versus privacy 59
   terrorism and extremism 164
ACINT (acoustic) 224
Action Fraud 130
'Action Line' 82, 381
action/reaction dynamic 801–2
active defence approach 441
Ad blockers 371
Adams, J. 729
Adamsky 263
add-ons 415
added value 306

addresses 16, 17
   see also Internet Protocol (IP) address
Adelson, S. 244
administrative privilege sprawl or creep 104
advance fee fraud 92, 130
advanced persistent threat (APT) 226, 228–29,
     233, 234–35, 547, 600–142, 667
adware 94–95
Afghanistan 239–40
Africa 773–74, 777
African Union 502–3
Agar, J. 16
age effect 414
age verification 379, 386
age-inappropriate content 377
agency, responsibility and resources 468–70
Agreement on Trade-Related Aspects
     of Intellectual Property Rights
     (TRIPS) 503, 518, 519–20
agreement violation as customary
     practice 562–73
   codification of responsible state
     behaviour 563–65
   de facto norms 566–72
   standards of care 572–73
Agricultural Revolution 402, 403–4, 405, 406
Ahram, A. 545–46
Airland Battle 2000 275–76
Airtel 620
Aitel, D. 184
al-Qaeda 74, 75, 163–64, 167, 168, 195, 202, 203,
     204, 207
Alexander, General K. 229
algorithms 168–69
Alibaba 100–1, 598, 621, 622
Alipay 620
all hazards approach 504

INDEX

Alpha Bay drug market 99
Alphabet 69
Amazon 69, 341–42, 706
'America First' Strategy 509
Anderson, G. 24, 27
Anderson, R. 130
anonymity 59
  cyber crime 103–4
  cyber hygiene 371
  disruptive technology and regulatory
    frameworks 114–15
  harm assessment from cyber crime 129
  information warfare and influence
    operations (IWIO) 260
  primary assessment of disruptive
    technologies 119
  surveillance and human rights 416–17
anonymization tools 416–17
Anonymous hacktivist group 99, 544–45
Anti-Ballistic Missile Treaty 533
anti-democratic tendencies *see* risk management:
    terrorism, violent extremism and anti-
    democratic tendencies
Anti-Phishing Working Group (APWG)
    report 91, 102
anti-reverse engineering techniques 184
anti-virus software 415
Apple 69, 636
  ICloud 629
  iOS 97
Applegate, S.D. 143, 144
Applied Materials 636
Apt, K. 27
APT-1 - PLA Unit 61398 in Shanghai 229
APT-C-09 (China) 600
APT10 or Red Apollo 286
Arab Spring 42–43, 75–76, 262–63, 487, 775
Arce, D.G. 42
Arkush, A.C. 303–4
armed conflict 62
  conflict deterrence and
    prevention 280–82, 291
  international law 583, 587–89
arms control 173, 213
  conflict deterrence and prevention 290–91
  and counter proliferation 714–15
  and cyber weapons 181–83

arms race 37, 103, 142, 706–11
ARPA (Advanced Research Projects Agency) 52
ARPANET (Advanced Research Projects
    Agency Network) 19
artificial intelligence (AI) 37, 801
  arms race 706, 707
  autonomous cyber weapons systems
    (AWS) 702, 705–6, 707, 708, 711,
    712–13
  capacity building 468
  China 597–98, 599, 601
  conflict deterrence and prevention 290
  data privacy and security law 340–41
  development and cyber security 771–72
  diplomacy 538
  future technology prediction techniques 112
  human and behavioural challenges 728
  international law: competition and
    conflict 587
  Israel 636, 644–45
  Japan 651
  metrics 124
  surveillance and human rights 409
  technology: access and denial 205
Ashenden, D. 726, 730–31
Ashley Madison hack 134–35, 197–98
Asia 777
Asian Infrastructure Investment Bank
    (AIIB) 621–22, 624
Asia-Pacific Economic Cooperation (APEC)
    Privacy Framework 329
Association of South-East Asian Nations
    (ASEAN) 502–3, 652
  Regional Forum 278, 652
  -Singapore Cybersecurity Centre of
    Excellence (ASCCE) 472
AT&T 523
attack
  armed 62
  fire-and-forget attacks 177–78, 185–86
  kits 366
  see also cyber attacks; denial of service
    (Dos) attacks *and under* vulnerability
    mitigation model
attribution 177, 286, 437, 580
audit targets for periodic review 439
Austin, G. 41

INDEX 809

Australia 58, 668
agreement violations as customary
practice 570
broadband and Big Data 603–4
Budapest Convention on Cybercrime 101
Bureau of Statistics Personal Fraud Survey
(2016) 91
capacity building 471
Commonwealth Criminal Code Act 1995 93
Commonwealth Cybercrime Act 2001 93
Computer Emergency Response Team
(CERT) 435
critical infrastructure 149
critical national infrastructure
(CNI) 434–35, 440–41, 442
cyber crime 91, 92
Cyber Security Centre (ACSC) 435
Cyber Security Centre (ACSC) - *Threat
Report* (2016) 90
cyber terrorism and intentions 191
Department of Home Affairs Critical
Infrastructure Centre 336, 434
global commerce and international
organizations 504–5
global trade: monitoring, enforcement and
sanctions 516
Signals Directorate (ASD) 435
Strategic Policy Institute (ASPI) 538
Strategic Policy Institute (ASPI) -
Cybersecurity Maturity Index 467
Australia Group 689
authentication 184
multi-factor 369–70
two-factor 370
authoritarian/autocratic countries 509, 534,
740, 742–43, 744–45, 746
authority reaggregation 37–38
automated decision making and profiling 363
automated detection and identification 266
Automated Indicator Sharing (AIS) 321, 337
automatic control systems 10
automation 177–78, 361, 409
autonomous agent 145
autonomous system numbers (ASNs) 679–80
autonomous transport systems 56–57
autonomous weapons systems (AWS) 702–18
arms control and counter proliferation 714–15

arms race considerations 706–11
attribution 713, 714
autonomous robotics ('killer robots') 703–4
data manipulation 714
dual-use nature 714–15
ethical issues 703, 707, 715–16, 717
framework for impact on international
security policies 711–13
general implications for international cyber
stability 713–15
hybrid warfare 715
increasing autonomous technologies
(IATs) 703, 707, 708, 717
increasing reliance on AI and increase in
number of new vulnerabilities 714
international humanitarian law (IHL)
compliance 715–16, 717
legal considerations 703
lethal autonomous weapons systems
(LAWS) 702, 703–4, 706–7, 709*t*, 711–
12, 713, 714–15, 716
military or economic advantages
and disadvantages requiring
validation 709*t*
military implications 703
norm coherence 715–18
policy framework 713–15
responsibility and accountability gap 713
robotic agents 705
software components allowing physical
systems more autonomy 704–5
state of developments in technology
domain 703
technical risks 712*t*
technical safeguards strengthening and safe
development 711–13
transparency, lack of 716
weapons review 703
see also artificial intelligence (AI)
Avant, D. 544, 545–46
avatars 59
aviation - airspace and aircraft 104, 508, 522,
580, 582
AVOIDIT (Attack Vector, Operational
Impact, Defence, Information Impact
and Target) 143
Axelrod, R. 285–86

B

'back doors' 416
back-end analysis and absorption 230
back-end or operational technology (OT)
    systems 728–29
background checks 439
backups or fail-safes 138, 372
BadB 555
BAE Systems 286, 569–70
Bahrain 487
Baidu 598
baited files 233
bandwidth 19, 194–95
Bangladesh 568–70, 656, 691
Bank for International Settlements (BIS) 42, 44
Baranoff, A. 543
Barlow, J.P. 534
beacons 12–15, 184
Beauchesne, A. 321
behavioural challenges *see* future human and
    behavioural challenges
Beijing Treaty on aircraft hijacking 522
Bell, D. 34, 45
Beltway Bandits 779
Ben-Israel, I. 639, 641
Bentham, J. 410–11
Bergin, A. 102–3
best practices 435, 517, 608, 779
Bhutan 621–22
Big Data 331–40, 763, 801
    autonomous cyber weapons systems
        (AWS) 706
    China 597–98
    Israel 637
    Japan 650
    surveillance and human rights 409, 410
Big Data Analytics (BDA) 661
bilateral arrangements 502, 504, 508, 519–21
    China 604
    India 623–24
    Japan 652–53
    Russia 672, 681
bilateral extradition treaties 503
bilateral investment treaties (BITs) 500
Bildt, C. 539
binding standards 435
bio-engineering 707

biological weapons 691
Biological Weapons Convention 533
biosecurity 692
bioterrorism 690–91
Bitcoin 90, 92, 99, 111, 115–16, 207
Bitly 227–28
Black, D. 171n.4
Black Energy campaign (Ukraine) 178, 181,
    334, 429, 441
'black hats' 98
black market 96, 97
    agreement violations as customary
        practice 562–63
    critical national infrastructure
        (CNI) 437–38
    cyber hygiene 366
    cyber weapons 182, 184
    vulnerability mitigation 142, 151
black operations 263–64
Blackhole hacking tool 96
blacklisted countries 519
blackmail 231
Blanchemanche, S. 729–30
Blank, G. 166
Blankenship, L. 726–27
blockchain 99
    authentication 184
    China 601
    development and cyber security 771–72
    future technology prediction
        techniques 111, 112, 113
    primary assessment of disruptive
        technologies 118–19
    risk engineering 122
    trend forecasting 114
blocking systems 389
blocks ('bits' and 'bytes') of binary
    numbers 7–8
BlueKeep 642
Bobbitt, P. 203, 554–55
bookkeeping methods 184
Border Gateway Protocol (BGP) 7–8, 572
borderlessness 58
Borodin, A. 553
botnets 92, 93, 94–95, 173, 209–10, 604–5
    booter rental 96
    criminal groups 100

hacker culture 99
organized crime 100–1
Russia 673
bottom-up approach
China 608–9
Computer Security Incident Response
Teams (CSIRTs) 304, 310
development and cybersecurity 770, 771,
780–81
governance of technology 695–96
Boyd, J. 353
Braw, E. 286
Brazil 61, 149, 517, 754
breach notification 91
Brewer's theorem 9
Brillouin, L. 399–400
Bring Your Own Device (BYOD) issues 727
Broadcom 636
Brodie, B. 277
Broeders, D. 305, 307
Brousse, P. 171n.3
Brown, G. 286
browsing 364, 371
Buchanan, B. 291
Budapest Conference (2012) 538–39
Budapest Convention on Cybercrime 61, 93–
94, 101, 382, 470, 472–73, 502–3, 624,
681–82, 759–60, 774
bug bounty programs 206, 214
bulletproof hosting services (BPHS) 97
bullying *see* cyber bullying
Bush, G.W. 60
Byman, D. 553

C
C++ language 736–37
Cable, J. 415, 416–17
CACI 550
Cambridge Analytica 75
Cameroon 773
Campaign to Stop Killer Robots 703
Canada 58
agreement violations as customary
practice 570
Canadian Plan 454–55
Center for International Governance
Innovation (CIGI) 539

child safety online 389–90
critical infrastructure 149
critical national infrastructure (CNI) 432,
440–41
data privacy and security law 329
Department of National Defense 454–55
governance of technology 695
multilateral export control and standard
setting 483
capabilities *see* cyber capabilities
capacity building 463–74
agency, responsibility and
resources 468–70
comprehensive approach 468–69
connectivity: risks and
opportunities 464–66
definition of cybersecurity capacity 467–68
effort sustainability 473
fragmented international approach 469
harm assessment from cyber crime 137
harm mitigation 138–39
holistic approach 468–69
multidisciplinary, multistakeholder and
multi-agency approach 466, 468–69,
471
strategy development, implementation and
initiatives 467, 470–73
Commonwealth countries 472–73
Netherlands 471–72
Singapore 472
United Kingdom 471
capacity development and training 778
Caporaso, J.A. 38–39
capture the flag hacking games 234
car-sploiting 104
Carmeli, B. 641
Carnegie Mellon University (CMU)
(USA) 40, 43–44, 467
computer security response team 98
Software Engineering Institute (SEI) 297,
298, 316–17
computer emergency response team
(CERT) 316, 317
Carr, M. 418
cascading effects 135, 205
Castells, M. 35, 37
categorical thinking trap 355

812 INDEX

Caulfield, T. 24, 27
CEM 99–100, 103–4
censorship 307, 411
 normalizing 166
 see also self-censorship
Central Processing Unit (CPU) 9
Cerf, V. 53
CERT Co-ordination Center (CERT-CC) 143,
 308
certification 435
Certification/Validation Body (CB) 483
CESSPIT (Crime, Espionage, Sabotage and
 Subversion Perverting Internet
 Technology) 281
Chabinsky, S.R. 100
chaos-producing operations 257–58
Chappe, C./semaphore tower 14, 14f, 15f
chatbots 261, 266
Chemical Weapons Convention (CWC) 692
Chicago Convention on Civil Aviation 582
Chief Information Security Officers
 (CISOs) 726, 727
Chikati, R. 150
Child Online Protection 778–79
child safety online
 age verification 379, 386
 age-inappropriate content 377
 behavioural issues 377
 bullying 377, 384–85
 child abuse images (child
  pornography) 101, 377
 child sexual abuse 100, 387–88
 circle of trust 387–88
 definition of child 378–80
 disengagement, levels of 380–81
 engagement, levels of 380
 European Union 382–83
 Fund to End Violence Against Children 383
 grooming 100, 387–88
 hotlines 389–90
 intermediary liability 390
 international recognition 381
 international responses 382–83
 Internet Governance Forum (IGF) 382
 language, cultural and legal issues 383–84
 liability, immunity from 390
 minimum age 379

notice and take down procedure 389
paedophiles and paedophile networks 377,
 387, 388, 389
pornography 92, 100, 385–86
prevention 389–90
privacy 377
self-generated sexual images 377
self-harm 377, 378
suicide, access to information on 378
Sustainable Development Goals
 (SDGs) 383
United States 377–78
violent content 385
We Protect Global Alliance to End Child
 Sexual Exploitation Online 383, 384
Chile 101
chilling effects theory 411–14, 415, 416, 417
China 58, 597–611
 administrative mechanism inefficiencies 600–1
 autonomous cyber weapons systems
  (AWS) 707
 Banking Regulatory Commission 601
 Belt and Road Initiative 780
 Black Industry Chain 600
 Budapest Convention on Cybercrime 61
 Building Cyber Power and Big Data 599
 Central Government Procurement
  Centre 516
 Communist Party (CPC) 75–76, 227
 competitive advantage 598
 conflict deterrence and prevention 279, 286
 cooperation 602, 603–5, 606, 610–11
 critical infrastructure 604–5
 critical national infrastructure (CNI) 442
 cultural issues 605
 cyber crime 91, 101
 cyber espionage 226, 230
 cyber power 73–74, 75–76, 77–78
 Cyber Security Law 336, 339–40
 Cyberspace Authority of China (CAC) 76
 data privacy and security law 342
 Decree No. 147 336
 defence and national cyber security 453–54
 democratic civil society 735, 740–43,
  744–45, 746
 development and cyber security 770, 772–73,
  776–77, 780, 781

digitization 599
diplomacy 531–32, 533, 534–36, 537, 538
e-governance and business
    models 597–98
fintech sector growth 601
Five Principles of Peaceful Coexistence and
    community of shared future 602–3
foreign best practice and international
    customs 608
foundation of cybersecurity concept 602–5
future normative challenges 754
global commerce and international
    organizations 501, 503, 504, 508, 509
'Global Internet Governance System' 76
global trade: monitoring, enforcement and
    sanctions 514–15, 517, 519–21
governing capability shortage 600–1
high policy dividends 599
ICT Development Index (IDI) 599
and India 616–17, 620–22, 623–24
Information Economy Index 597–98
information security versus cyber
    security 58–59
Institutes of Contemporary International
    Relations (CICIR) 537, 538
international agreements 604
International Code of Conduct for
    Information Security 60–61
*International Strategy of Cooperation on
    Cyberspace* 74–75, 76, 605
Internet Network Information Centre
    (CNNIC) 597–98
Internet Plus 599
Internet Security Conference 600
and Japan 652–53
Leading Group of Cybersecurity and
    Informationization 602, 606
legislation and law enforcement
    deficiencies 600–1
Made in China 2025 599
Ministry of Industry and Information
    Technology 601
multi-stakeholder arrangements 608–9
multilateral arrangements 605, 608–9
National Computer Network Emergency
    Response Technical Team (CNCERT)
    annual report 600

National Cybersecurity Law 76
*National Strategic Outline of
    Informationization
    Development* 602
*National Strategy for Cyberspace
    Security* 76, 599–600
new start-up companies 598
One Belt, One Road policy initiative 76,
    621–22
-Pakistan Economic Corridor (CPEC) 622
People's Bank of China 601
People's Liberation Army (PLA) 226–27,
    286, 503–4
policy/regulatory lag 600–1
power 597–602
printing press 16
Project Solarium 1953 (Eisenhower) and
    Cyberspace Solarium Commission
    (CSC) 2019 786–787, 790, 792, 794
proxies and offensive cyber
    operations 544–46, 551, 552, 554–55
regional agreements 604
rule of law 606
and Russia 74–75
Silk Road Economic Belt 624
sovereignty 76, 604–5, 606–7
Strategic Support Forces command 226–27
Telecom 620
thirteenth five-year plan (2016) 597–98, 599
Tibetan Government in Exile,
    targeting 228–29
unicorn births 598
and United Kingdom 538
and United States 41, 94, 226–27, 242–43,
    286, 538, 583, 604
volume of Internet users/
    penetration 597–98
World Internet Conference (WIC) 540
WuZhen Index 599
Choucri, N. 418
Christey, S. 154
circle of trust 387–88
circuit switching 19
Cisco 465, 516
Cisco, OpenDNS 102
Citizenlab 196, 228–29
City of London Corporation 131–32

INDEX

civil society 267, 410, 412, 413–14, 417, 418, 419
  activists 523
  multilateral export control and standard setting 491
  organizations 489–90
  see also democratic civil societies in post-Western cybered era; *and under* surveillance and human rights
civilian space definition 638
civil-military relations 450–52
Clark, K. 308–9
Clarke, R. 241
CLASP 151, 152
classification by disclosure 151
classification models 143
class-subclass relationships 117
'clean skins' or first-time offenders 666
clickbait 227–28
Clinton, B. 53, 60, 317
Clinton, H. 58, 225
  see also United States election interference (2016) *under* Russia
cloud computing 9, 514
cloud service providers 516–17
cloud storage 363, 372
CNAS report 714–15
Co-ordinating Committee on Multilateral Export Controls 491
code 174, 178
  bases 437–38
  poisoned 233
  rescue missions 184
codes of conduct 707
codification of responsible state behaviour 563–65
coercion 68, 74, 585
  sexual 131–32
cognitive biases 254–55, 256, 258
  confirmation bias 256, 261
  fluency bias 256
  illusory truth bias 256
  loss aversion bias 256
  recency bias 256
cognitive-psychological information operations 453–54
Cold War 52

conflict deterrence and prevention 274–79, 285–86, 288, 290–91
cyber espionage 235
cyber power 70
defence and national cyber security 450–51
diplomacy 532–33
global commerce and international organizations 500–1
political evolution of internet technology 52–53
Coles-Kemp, L. 725
collaboration 303, 304, 306–7, 314–15
collective defence 73
Collective Security Treaty Organization 680–81
Collinson, M. 24, 27
Color Revolution 263
command and control (C2) arrangements 228–29, 230, 231, 233, 235
commercial-off-the-shelf technologies (COTS) 178, 183, 186, 442
commercialization 736–39
Committee for Disarmament and International Security (First Committee) 61–62
Common Attack Pattern Enumeration and Classification (CAPEC) 147, 151
Common Configuration Enumeration (CCE) 153
Common Criteria Recognition Arrangement (CCRA) 480, 482–84, 491–93
Common Foreign and Security Policy (CFSP) 74
common reference framework 132–33
Common Vulnerabilities and Exposure (CVE) numbering authority 152–53
Common Vulnerability Scoring System (CVSS) 151, 153
Common Weakest Enumerator (CWE) 153
Commonwealth Approach for Developing National Cybersecurity Strategies 777
Commonwealth countries 472–73
Commonwealth Cybergovernance Model 777
Commonwealth Heads of Government 472–73
Cyber Declaration 472–73, 777
Commonwealth of Independent States (CIS) 502–3
Commonwealth Secretariat 472–73
Computer Misuse Act 472

Commonwealth Telecommunications
  Organization 777
communications 148
  deterrence and prevention of cyber
    conflict 274, 275–77, 279–80, 282–84
  protocols 7–8
competition *see under* international law
complex adaptive systems 398, 400, 401, 403,
    404, 405, 406
complex open systems 401
complex systems 114, 396–98, 399, 400, 401, 406
  democratic civil societies 738, 739
  energy and entropy 398–99
compromised websites and servers 97
compromising material 262
Computer Emergency Response Teams
    (CERTs) 93–94, 101, 300–1, 305
  conflict deterrence and prevention 287
  Coordination Centre (CC) 143, 297–99,
    301, 308, 316–17
  critical national infrastructure (CNI) 437
  cross-agency and sector cooperation 102
  development and cyber security 777
  European Union 298–99, 300–1
  Germany 298–99
  international law: competition and
    conflict 579
  Malaysia 662–63, 664
  Netherlands 298–99
  Russia 674
  United Kingdom 319–20
  United States 320, 332, 434
Computer Incident Response Team
    (CIRT) 777
computer network attack (CNA) 285
computer network defence (CND) 285
Computer Security Incident Response Teams
    (CSIRTs) 93–94, 297–310
  bidirectional relationship 306–7
  critical information structure 300–1
  critical reflection 308–9
  culture of the community 303–4
  European Union 304, 309–10
  from computer to cyber security 305–6
  governmental 308–9
  governmental institutions, relationship
    with 306–7

historical background 298–99
independence 307
information sharing 316, 317, 324
Israel 642
national (nCSIRTs) 304, 306–7, 308–9
Netherlands 308–9
preventive services 299–300
proactive services 299–300
public policy arena 300–3
reactive services 299, 300, 301
reciprocity 306–7
resilience 299
service quality management 299, 300
services offered 299–300
status quo 306
technology: access and denial 211
unidirectional relationship 306–7
United Kingdom 308–9
United States 298–99
vulnerabilities 307–8
concepts 15–16
conceptualization of cyber security *see under*
    political history
confidence building measures (CBMs) 278
confidentiality 118, 150, 364
configuration (software) 150, 152
confirmation biases 256, 261
conflict 11
conflict *see also* armed conflict; cyber conflict;
    and under international law
conflicts of interest 307, 309, 310
conformity assessments 481
Confucius 33
Congo, Democratic Republic 773
connectivity: risks and opportunities 464–66
Connelly, R. 790
consensus report 61–62
Consistency, Availability, Partition-tolerance
    (CAP) theorem (Brewer's theorem) 9
contact lists 365
content-related issues 77–78
contextual issues
  cyber weapons 180
  deterrence and prevention of cyber
    conflict 279, 280–82, 290–91
  recovery 230
contingency planning 439

contingent contributor 452, 456
Control Lists 486
Convention on Conventional Weapons
    (CCW) 702, 704–5, 708, 711, 717
Convention on Cybercrime *see* Budapest
    Convention on Cybercrime
Convention for the Protection of Individuals
    with regard to Automatic Processing
    of Personal Data 677–78
Conway, M. 192, 193–94, 198
cooperation 57
    China 602, 603–5, 606, 610–11
    Computer Security Incident Response
        Teams (CSIRTs) 303, 306
    cross-agency and sector for cyber crime 102–3
    India 619–21
    information warfare and influence
        operations (IWIO) 261
    Japan 652–53
    multisector 154, 156–57
    Russia 680–82
Cooperative Cyber Defence Centre of
    Excellence (CCD CoE) 55
copycats 184
copyright 84
Corn, G. 90
corporate behaviour and threats 507
corporate citizenship 351–52, 355
corporate raiders 144
corporate responsibility 800–1
corruption 544–45, 554–55
cost and scope of cyber crime 90–92, 127–28,
    130–31, 132
cost-benefit analysis
    conflict deterrence and prevention 274,
        282–83, 290
    cyber terrorism and intentions 192, 194
    human and behavioural challenges 729–30
    intentions and cyber terrorism 198
    proxies and offensive cyber operations 548
counterintelligence 499
    defensive 234
    offensive 233–34
countermeasures 205, 580, 584
    non-forcible 72–73
    people-oriented 206
    technology-oriented 205

covert action - ambiguous influence 231–32
Covid-19 pandemic 94
'crackers' or 'leets' 98
creativity and innovation 726–28
credibility in deterrence and prevention of
    conflict 274, 275–77, 279
credit card fraud 93, 100, 251
credit card theft 96*t*, 97
crime *see* cyber crime; organized crime/
    organized criminals
crime-as-a-service model 209–10
criminal groups 99–100
    and hacktivists nexus 209–10
    see also organized criminals/crime
critical civilian infrastructures 183
critical information infrastructure (CII) 514,
    659–60, 661–64, 674, 675
critical infrastructure (CI)
    agreement violations as customary practice
        562, 564, 566, 567–68, 570, 571, 573
    Australia 149
    China 604–5
    Computer Security Incident Response
        Teams (CSIRTs) 308–9
    cyber terrorism and intentions 190
    defence and national cyber security 451
    democratic civil society 740
    dependencies 43*t*, 43, 44–45
    development and cyber security 773,
        780–81
    and disruptive attacks 775
    global commerce and international
        organizations 504, 508
    global trade: monitoring, enforcement and
        sanctions 514, 517
    information sharing 322, 324
    international law: competition and
        conflict 581–82, 583–84, 588
    Japan 149, 650–51, 653, 654
    proxies and offensive cyber operations 547
    resilience 40
    Russia 673
    technology: access and denial 202, 204,
        205, 210–11, 212, 214
    United States 149, 241, 431–32, 434
    vulnerabilities 54–55
    vulnerability mitigation 150

see also critical information infrastructure (CII); critical infrastructure protection (CIP); critical national infrastructure (CNI); *and under* data privacy and security law

critical infrastructure protection (CIP) 777
    Israel 639–40, 641, 643

critical national infrastructure (CNI) 149, 429–42
    Australia 434–35, 440–41, 442
    Canada 432, 440–41
    China 442
    conflict deterrence and prevention 290
    Germany 433
    information sharing 317–19, 321–22, 325
    Malaysia 659–60, 661–64
    operational level 435
    resilience 430–31, 433, 434, 438–40
      capacity 438–39
      dependencies 439
      plans and courses of action 440
      resourcing 440
      timing (or timeliness) 439
    risk adaptation 431–38
      efficacy assessment and risk management 437–38
      infrastructure elements categorization 433–35
      key infrastructures identification 431–33
      key risk responses implementation 435–36
    risk concerns and challenges 429–31, 440–42
    risk identification, assessment and mitigation 431
    risk management 429–30
    risks 441–42
    Russia 673, 674
    strategic level 435
    tactical level 435
    United Kingdom 288, 320–21, 432–33, 435, 440–41, 442
      financial services sector 435–36
      foreign investment and 4G 433
    United States 58, 431–32, 433, 434, 435, 437–38, 440–41, 442
      critical infrastructures and key resources 431–32

      energy sector rules 436
      foreign investment review and critical infrastructure 432
      identification of CNI 434
      information sharing 318, 320
      USCYBERCOM and Persistent Engagement 432
    Western Europe 431, 440–41, 442

criticality scale 149, 336
cross-site request forgery (CSRF) 151
cross-site scripting (XXS) 151
crowdsourcing 261, 693–94
CrowdStrike 234–35, 551–52
cryptocurrencies 118, 362, 601
    see also Bitcoin; blockchain
cryptography
    asymmetric 113–14
    hashes 184
    post-quantum 113–14
Cuba 681, 763–64
customary international law 563, 587
customary law 755
cut-outs 228–29, 231, 235
Cutler, R. 787–88, 790–92, 795
cyber attacks 37, 94, 799–800
    by insurgent groups to overthrow governments 775
    cycles 173
    definition 173–78
    diplomacy 539
    Japan 649, 650
    viewed as attractive strategy of terror 194–96
cyber battlespace 11
cyber bullying 37, 85, 134, 135, 377, 384–85
cyber capabilities
    critical national infrastructure (CNI) 429–30, 441
    cyber power 71–72
    cyber war 240, 241–43, 244, 245
    cyber weapons 182, 183
    defence and national cyber security 447, 455*t*
    deterrence and prevention 274, 275–77, 280
    diplomacy 540–41
    emerging technology areas 123
    offensive capabilities 72
cyber catastrophe 223

cyber commands 744, 745
cyber conflict 737–39
    see also deterrence and prevention of cyber
        conflict
cyber crime 37, 89–104, 115*f*, 799–800
    China 600
    cost and scope 90–92
    cyber warfare 94
    cybercrime-as-a-service: dark markets for
        malware 90, 96–97
    democratic civil society 737
    global commerce and international
        organizations 502–3, 508
    impact 127–28
    international law: competition and
        conflict 583
    international responses 101–3
    Japan 655–56
    laws and definitions 92–94
    Malaysia 667
    malware 94–95
    online offenders 97–100
        criminal groups 99–100
        hacker culture 98–99
    organized crime 100–1
    social engineering 92
    technology: access and denial 207
    and trend forecasting 113–14
    vulnerability mitigation 142, 145
    see also harm assessment and cyber crime
cyber doom scenarios 418–19
cyber effects 454
cyber electromagnetic activities 453, 456
cyber espionage 37, 94, 223–35, 245, 798
    analysis and application 229–30
    autonomous cyber weapons systems
        (AWS) 707
    counterintelligence - deception for
        defence 232–34
    covert action 231–32
    critical national infrastructure (CNI) 441–42
    cyber war 240, 241, 245–46
    defence 223
    diplomacy 537
    economic espionage 502, 503–4, 508
    global commerce and international
        organizations 499, 505

global trade: monitoring, enforcement and
        sanctions 517, 520–21
    industrial espionage 538
    information sharing 314–15
    international law 579, 581, 583, 585
    Japan 655–56
    military intelligence 224
    new era of espionage 234–35
    political objective 225–27
    ransom 232
    state intelligence and cyber security 224–25
    surveillance and human rights 416
    targeting 226
    technical operation - collection 227–29
    vulnerability mitigation 145
    see also intelligence
cyber harm model 137–38
cyber hygiene *see* personal protection/cyber
        hygiene
cyber incident lifecycle 144*f*
cyber incident management 142–43
cyber jacking of aircraft 104
cyber norms 50
    see also future normative challenges
cyber operational resilience alliance
        (CORA) with 'cyber city on the hill'
        strategy 744–45
cyber optimism 534
cyber order 754
cyber Pearl Harbour 54–55
cyber physical systems 418
cyber policing capabilities 411
cyber power 739–41
    see also cyber power and international
        relations
cyber power and international
        relations 66–78
    assessment of cyber power 69–71
    coercive power 72, 73
    cognitive and informational capacity 72
    collective power 78
    institutional power 75
    materialist framing of 70
    national power 78
    operationalization 71–78
        compulsory cyber power 71–74
        institutional cyber power 74–75

productive cyber power 77–78
structural cyber power 75–76
perceptions and meanings of cyber
power 67–69
productive power 69
quantifiable power 70
relational aspects 69–70
soft power 70–71, 74–75
cyber resilience review (CRR) 40
Cyber Revolution (Information Age) 33–37,
49, 55–56, 397, 403–5, 798
Cyber Security Information Sharing and
Collaboration Program
(CISCP) 318, 322
Cyber Security Information Sharing
Partnership (CiSP) 319, 320, 323
cyber security is an open not a closed
environment 606
cyber security is dynamic not static 606
cyber security is holistic not
fragmented 606
cyber security is mutual not isolated 606
cyber security is relative not absolute 606
cyber security metrics 122–24
cyber space definition 638
cyber stalking 95
cyber status quo with 'keep trying'
strategy 741–42
cyber survival 746
cyber terrorism 94, 102, 144, 798
autonomous cyber weapons systems
(AWS) 707–8
cross-agency and sector cooperation 102–3
financing 207
global commerce and international
organizations 504
Japan 653–54, 655–56
Malaysia 666
materials 378
vulnerability mitigation 145
see also cyber terrorism and intentions;
risk management: terrorism, violent
extremism and anti-democratic
tendencies; technology: access and denial
cyber terrorism and intentions 187–98
Ashley Madison hacking 197–98
cyber attack or physical attack 192–96

cyber attacks viewed as attractive strategy of
terror 194–96
definition of cyber terrorism 188–91
destruction 190, 192, 193
direct impact 194
intelligence assessments 191–92
multiple audience 197
political aim 197
political struggle 197
psychological dimension 197
terror strategy and engagement in political
process 196
theatricality 192, 193–94
cyber utopianism 534
cyber vassaldom with 'concede slowly'
strategy 742–43
cyber war 94, 145
between states 775
global commerce and international
organizations 504–5
sub-threshold 281–82
technology: access and denial 203–4
see also cyber war *redux*
cyber war *redux* 239–47
conflict is more useful framing than cyber
conflict 247
cyber capabilities do not on their own
serve as effective deterrents through
significant punishment 246
cyber capabilities will not resolve conflicts
between nations on their own 246–47
observation (or falsification) 245–47
pre-conflict occurrences in cyber
operations shape how conflicts
unfold 245
sabotage 242, 243–44
spying 242–43
subversion 242, 243
cyber weapons 68, 173–86
arms control implications 181–83
closing phase 177
control 175–76, 177–78
cyberattack: definition 173–78
damage 182
definition 173, 178–81
design 177–78
effect 179

820 INDEX

cyber weapons (*cont.*)
 execution 184
 functional cyber norms, implications
  for 183–86
  accident communication 185
  authentication 184
  containment 184
  counterproliferation 184
  operative care 185
 global trade: monitoring, enforcement and
  sanctions 517
 high-criticality targets, avoidance of 185–86
 intent 179–80, 182
 lateral movement 175
 operative care 185
 persistence 175
 proliferation and international negotiations
  on state behaviour 212–14
 trigger 184
 vulnerability mitigation 142, 151, 153
 see also autonomous weapons systems
  (AWS); lethal autonomous weapons
  systems (LAWS)
cyber Westphalia with 'hunker down'
 strategy 743–44
cybernetics 10, 262
Cybersecurity Capacity Maturity Model for
 Nations (CMM) 467–68
Cyberterrorism Project 214
Cyprus 532
Czech Republic 308–9

D

dangerous practices, encouragement
 of 416–17
dark markets 96–97, 518, 651
dark web 99, 778–79
Dark-Mailer 100
darknet 99, 176–77, 209, 604–5
Darwin, C. 397, 406
data access 724
data analysis 487
data availability 132–33
data breaches 539
Data Centric Audit and Protection
 (DCAP) 351–52
data collection 363–64, 411, 487

data destruction and erasure 333, 363
data integrity 56–57
data localization requirements 506, 516–17
data loss or manipulation 93
data portability 363
data privacy and security law 56–57, 328–43
 aggregation problem: Big Data and personal
  information 340
 breach notification laws: notice and
  liability 330–33
  European Union General Data
   Protection Regulation (GDPR) 332–33
  South Korea Personal Information and
   Protection Act (PIPA) 332
  United States 330–32
 China Cyber Security Law 339–40
 critical infrastructure and information
  sharing 334–37
  global emphasis on critical
   infrastructure 334–36
  global emphasis on information
   sharing 336–37
 data destruction laws 333
 emerging technology 340–41
 encryption 341
 historical background and context 328–30
 individual and organizational
  incentives 341–42
 jurisdiction 342–43
 unfair or deceptive practices legislation 330
 United States 337–39
  Computer Fraud and Abuse Act
   (CFAA) 337–38
  State statutes 338–39
data protection 83, 137, 390, 516–17
data reliability 132–33
data tap 145
databases 150–53
Davidson, W. 532
DaVinci software 488
de Boer, F. 27
de facto norms 566–72
dead drops 228–29, 235
de-anonymization 118
deception 91, 93, 98, 234
 for defence 232–34
 defensive 233, 234

information warfare and influence
operations (IWIO) 254–55, 262, 265
military 589
of tools 737–38, 741–42
deep package inspection (DPI) software 680
defence 447–58
civil-military relations 450–52
competences 447
contingent contributor 452, 456
cyber-electromagnetic activities 453, 456
independent actor 452, 456
integrated stakeholder 452, 456
integration 456
key capabilities 451, 455t
militarization 452, 456
military cyber activities 452–56
military-industrial complex 458
national cyber security 448–50
national strategies 448–49
preparedness 455t
prevention 455t
pubic awareness and competence 455t
recovery and resilience 455t
response 455t
securitization 452, 456
separation 456
situational awareness 455t
defend forward concept 432
definition of cyber security 638
definition of cyber space 7–12
delegation (proxies on tight leash) 544, 549–51, 550f, 555
Delhi Communiqué 471–72
Deloitte 131, 523
Demchak, C.C. 749n.28
democracies 269
deliberative 412
see also democratic civil societies in post-Western cybered era
democratic civil societies in post-Western cybered era 735–46
cyber commands 744, 745
cyber jurisdiction 740
Cyber Operational Resilience Alliance (CORA) with 'cyber city on the hill' strategy 744–46
cyber power 739–41

cyber status quo with 'keep trying' strategy 741–43, 746
cyber survival 746
cyber vassaldom with 'concede slowly' strategy 742–43, 746
cyber Westphalia with 'hunker down' strategy 743–44, 746
hubris and commercialization: systemic misperceptions and abuse of cyberspace 736–39
hubris and commercialization: systemic misperceptions and abuse of cyberspace
cybered conflict 737–39
vulnerability of democracies 739
offence advantages 739, 744
rule of law 739
scale 736, 739–41
sovereignty 736, 739–41, 744–45, 746
systemic surprise layers 739–40
transparency 736, 743
Dempsey, General M. 278–79
Dencik, L. 415, 416–17
Deng Xiaoping 395, 746n.1
denial of service (DoS) attacks
critical national infrastructure (CNI) 437
cyber crime 101
cyber weapons 173
data privacy and security law 339, 341–42
information warfare and influence operations (IWIO) 251
Japan 653–54, 655
see also distributed denial of service (DDoS) attacks
denial of technology see technology: access and denial
Denmark 570–71, 694
Computer Emergency Response Team (DK-CERT) 298–99
technology ambassador 694
Denning test 202
Department of Defense (DoD)(USA) 11, 322, 349, 432, 453, 582–83
Cyber Strategy 72–73, 276
Defense Advanced Research Projects Agency (DARPA) 316
Directive 705, 711–12

822 INDEX

Department of Defense (DoD)(USA) (*cont.*)
  Information Network (DODIN) 551
  Law of War Manual (2015) 713
  Science Board Study 705
  Trusted Computer System Evaluation
    Criteria 483
Department of Homeland Security (DHS)
    (USA) 40, 42, 45, 73, 451
  critical national infrastructure (CNI) 432,
    434, 436
  data privacy and security law 335, 337
  National Cybersecurity and
    Communications Integration Center
    (NCCIC) 316, 321, 322
dependencies 45, 439
  as outcome of information
    enablement 38–43
  second- and third-order 44–45
  see also opportunity, threat and dependency
    in social infosphere
deterrence and prevention of cyber
    conflict 273–91
  adversary agnostic deterrence
    posture 282–83, 284, 286–87
  associative deterrence 287
  by punishment 246
  capability 274, 275–77, 280
  Cold War 274–79, 285–86, 288, 290–91
  communications 274, 275–77, 279–80,
    282–84
  constructive deterrence 284, 286–88, 290,
    291
  context 279, 280–82, 290–91
  credibility 274, 275–77, 279
  cross-domain deterrence 285–86
  deterrence by cost imposition 203
  deterrence by defence 288–89
  deterrence by denial 203, 246, 273–74,
    288–89, 290
  deterrent posture 277, 289
  efficacy of deterrence 278–79
  extended deterrence 285
  ideational deterrence 287
  intra-conflict deterrence 285–86
  intra-domain deterrence 285–86
  latent cross-domain deterrence 287–88
  legal deterrence 287

  mutual deterrence 274, 276–77, 282–83,
    285, 287
  normative deterrence 287
  offset strategies 275–76
  options 284–90
  personalized deterrence 286
  politico-military deterrence 278–79
  preventive deterrence 274–75, 277, 288
  protective deterrence 284, 288–90, 291
  punitive deterrence 273–74, 275–76, 279,
    284, 285–87, 289, 290, 291
  relational deterrence 282–83
  relevance of deterrence 278–79
  strategic deterrence 278–79, 284
  triadic or indirect deterrence of third
    parties and/or non-state actors 285
  zero day, zero source, zero effect and zero
    intent 283–84, 285–86, 291
Detica/Cabinet Office report 130
Deutsche Telekom 567
DeutscheBahn 341
developed countries 601–2, 610
  Computer Security Incident Response
    Teams (CSIRTs) 301
  cyber crime 89
  development and cyber security 770,
    771–72, 772f
  harm assessment from cyber crime 133
  multilateral export control and standard
    setting 479–80
developing countries 600–1
  autonomous cyber weapons systems
    (AWS) 707–8
  Computer Security Incident Response
    Teams (CSIRTs) 301
  cyber crime 89
  development and cyber security 770, 772f, 779
  future normative challenges 754–55
  harm assessment from cyber crime 133
  multilateral export control and standard
    setting 479–80
  proxies and offensive cyber
    operations 545–46
development and cyber security: contested
    futures 769–81
  best practices 779
  bottom-up approaches 770, 771, 780–81

capacity development and training 778
Child Online Protection 778–79
China 780, 781
critical infrastructure 773, 777, 780–81
Europe 780
global attempts at reaching
consensus 776–77
inequalities: digital and developmental
771–74
cybersecurity as driver for
equality 773–74
most-connected least-protected
772–73
unequal digital world 771–72
neo-colonial approaches: benevolence and
self-interest 779
'othering' of cyber security and
development 769–71, 779–80
overseas development aid (ODA) as an
industry 779–80
threats and resilience 774–75
top-down approaches 770–71, 779
United States 780
DevSecOps 731–32
Dickens, C. 84
Didi Chuxing 598
DigiCash 99
digital divide 58, 89
digital signatures and authentication 113–14
digital transistor or software-defined radio 116
diplomacy 243–44
and consular law 578, 581–82, 584
India 623–24
public diplomacy 263
see also semi-formal diplomacy: Track 1.5
and Track 2
discourse, challenges of incomplete saturation
of 755–61
discovery-trial-and-error learning
(DTEL) 738–39, 740
dispute settlement, peaceful 578, 583–84
disruptive technology 109–10, 117f, 150, 190,
194–95, 201–2
model creation 112–13
primary assessment 118–21
and regulatory frameworks 114–15
and threat landscapes 115–16

distributed denial of service (DDoS)
attacks 54–55, 56–57, 94–95, 103, 600
agreement violations as customary
practice 566–67, 568–69, 572
China 604–5
cyber crime 101
proxies and offensive cyber
operations 554
technology: access and denial 209–10
distributed morality 36
distributed political authority 36
distributed systems 8–9, 10, 11, 19, 22, 24, 26
DIYBio communities 695
Dokukin, E. 548–49
Domain Name System (DNS) 500, 535, 567,
572, 617, 618–19, 679
domaine réservé 584, 585
Dombrowski, P.J. 749n.28
Dongfan Chung 228
Dorey, P. 726
Dream Market 99
Drinkman, V. 553–54
droppers 209–10
Du Mu 234
Dual-Use Goods and Technologies List 486,
487, 489
dual-use research and technologies 178, 183,
688, 689, 690, 694, 695, 697, 714–15
Dubois, E. 166
due diligence 522, 579, 580, 759, 764
Dulles, J.F. 788–89, 793
Dunn Cavelty, M. 305, 418–19
DuQu 231, 234, 562–63, 570–71, 634
Dutton, W. 418–19
Dyn 341–42, 567, 604–5

E

e-Bay 96
e-commerce see global commerce and
international organizations
Eastern Europe 486, 553–54
EastWest Institute global cybersecurity
initiative 523
Eaton, C. 533
echo chambers 378
ECPAT International 383–84
Ecuador: Banco del Austro 568–69

824 INDEX

educating for cyber security 395–406
  adjacent possibilities 405–6
  Agricultural Revolution 402, 403–4, 405, 406
  complex adaptive systems 398, 400, 401,
    403, 404, 405, 406
  complex open systems 401
  complex systems 397–99, 400, 401, 406
  Cyber Revolution 397, 404–5
  Cyber Revolution as third solution to
    maximum entropy production
    (MaxEP) 403–4
  energy 398–99, 401, 403–4
  entropy 398–400, 401–2
  free energy (exergy) 400, 402
  human social systems 400, 401–2
  Industrial Revolution 402, 403–4, 405, 406
  information 399–400
  knowledge 400
  maximum entropy production
    (MaxEP) 401, 402, 403–4, 405, 406
  negentropy 399–400, 401, 402, 403–4,
    405, 406
  open (non-equilibrium) systems 399, 401
  revolution 403
  Rising Above the Gathering Storm
    reports 396–97
  social system 402
  STEM education 396
  thermodynamics laws 398–99, 400, 401–3
efficacy assessment and risk management 437–38
Egypt 487
Eichensehr, K.E. 761
Eichenwald, K. 95
Eisenhower, D. 458
  see also Project Solarium 1953 (Eisenhower)
    and Cyberspace Solarium
    Commission (CSC) 2019
Eisenkot, G. 635
emails 367–68, 371
emergency response plans 138
emerging economies 324, 770, 779
emerging technology areas 109–24
  data privacy and security law 340–41
  from knowledge models to risk
    models 121–24
    cyber security metrics 122–24
    risk engineering 121–22

knowledge representation and technology
    trend prediction 116–17
  primary assessment of disruptive
    technologies 118–21
  primary assessment of disruptive
    technologies, from likely scenario to
    ontology 119–21
  see also technology forecasting and
    innovation
emotional biases 256–57
employees *see under* insider threat and insider
    advocates
encryption 92
  cyber crime 103–4
  cyber weapons 184
  data privacy and security law 341
  global trade: monitoring, enforcement and
    sanctions 514–15, 517, 521, 523
  India 619–20
  quantum encryption 538
  surveillance and human rights 416–17
energy 398–99, 401, 403–4
English, R. 188–89, 191–92
entropy 398–400, 401–2
environment 10, 23, 24
  notional 11
  operational preparation of 245
Equation Group 233
Equatorial Guinea 773
equivalence doctrine 246
espionage *see* cyber espionage
Established Men 197
Estonia 55, 280–81, 429, 441, 448, 584
  capacity building 471
  Cyber Defence League 546
  National Cybersecurity Index 467
  and Russia 55, 94, 243–44, 262
  'Web War One' attack 246
Eternal Blue 523
Ethereum denial of service attack 118
ethical issues 35–36, 235, 753
ethical issues, autonomous weapons systems
    (AWS) 703, 707, 715–16, 717
ethical standards and communication
    technologies 82–85
  communication: content or act 82–83
  new technologies and new regulation 83–85

EuroCERT 303–4
Europe
  agreement violations as customary
    practice 567
  alt-Right 266
  conflict deterrence and prevention 275–76,
    278–79, 285
  critical national infrastructure (CNI) 433
  cross-agency and sector cooperation 102–3
  data privacy and security law 329
  development and cyber security 776–77,
    779, 780
  education for cyber security 405, 406
  global commerce and international
    organizations 501
  global trade: monitoring, enforcement and
    sanctions 516–17
  information sharing 317
  multilateral export control and standard
    setting 488, 492
  proxies and offensive cyber
    operations 544–45, 549–50
  see also Eastern Europe; European Union;
    Western Europe
European Commission 149
  Work Programme (2020) 335–36
European Convention of Human Rights 82–83
European Cybercrime Centre (EC3) Internet
    Organized Crime Threat Assessment
    (2016) 204
European Network and Information Security
    Agency (ENISA) 185, 299, 301–2,
    303–4, 482
European Union 58
  Agency for Network and Information
    Security 143
  agreement violations as customary
    practice 571
  Chemical, Biological, Radiological and
    Nuclear Risk Mitigation Centres of
    Excellence (EU CBRN CoE) 695
  child safety online 380, 382–83, 389
  Combating the sexual abuse and sexual
    exploitation of children and child
    pornography directive 382–83
  Common Foreign and Security Policy
    (CFSP) 571

Computer Emergency Response Team
    (CERT-EU) 298–99, 300–1
Computer Security Incident Response
    Teams (CSIRTs) 304, 309–10
Council of Europe (COE) 382, 502–3
Cybercrime Programme Office
    (C-PROC) 470
Critical Infrastructure Warning Information
    Network (CIWIN) 335–36, 337
cross-agency and sector cooperation 102–3
cyber dependency 43–44
'Cyber Diplomacy Toolbox' 74
Cyber Security Act 302
Cyber Security Strategy 301, 481
Daphne Programme 382
data privacy and security law 337, 342–43
Data Protection Directive (1995) 328
defence and national cyber security 450–51
Digital Agenda for Europe (2010) 300–1
digital single market 603–4
disruptive technology and regulatory
    frameworks 114
e-Privacy Directive 332–33
Economic Impact of Cyber Crime
    (E-CRIME) 131
Framework Directive (2002) 300
global commerce and international
    organizations 497, 499, 504, 508
Global Strategy (2016) 692–93
global trade: monitoring, enforcement and
    sanctions 517, 520, 521
governance of technology 691, 695
Hague Centre for Strategic Studies 538
Information Technology Security
    Evaluation Criteria (ITSEC) 483
Kids Online Survey 385
multilateral export control and standard
    setting 488
net neutrality rules 386
Network and Information Security
    Directive (NISD) 149, 288, 301–2, 303,
    321–23, 324
Network and Information Security
    (NIS) 301, 304
populism 509
Programme for Critical Infrastructure
    Protection (EPCIP) 335–36

826　INDEX

European Union (*cont.*)
　Rule of Law Division　470
　safe harbour arrangement with US
　　termination　506
　Safer Internet Day　382
　Safer Internet Programme　382
　security of network information systems
　　(NIS) directive　324
　Strategy for the Rights of the Child　382
　Strategy to Deliver a Better Internet for our
　　Children　382
　terrorism and extremism　167
　see also General Data Protection Regulation
　　(GDPR)(EU)
EUROPOL　100, 102, 131–32, 209, 210, 691
Evaluation Assurance Level (EAL)
　ranking　483
evolution of cyber attacks　110*f*
exploitation/exploitability　120–21, 151
exploits　94–95, 174, 176, 179, 181–82
　exploit kits　97, 209–10
　usage patterns　437–38
　see also zero day exploits
exports control *see* multilateral export control
　and standard setting arrangements
external hard drives　372
extortion　131–32
extraditions　209–10
extremism　1, 94, 99, 102, 103, 201, 288, 572,
　666, 770
　see also risk management: terrorism, violent
　　extremism and anti-democratic
　　tendencies; terrorism and extremism

F
Facebook　37, 69
　autonomous cyber weapons systems
　　(AWS)　706
　child safety online　379, 384–85
　cross-agency and sector cooperation　102–3
　cyber crime　91
　cyber power　75
　ethical issues　85
　India　617–18, 622–23
　information warfare and influence
　　operations (IWIO)　268
　organized crime　100–1

　proxies and offensive cyber operations　543–44
　terrorism and extremism　164–65, 167
　transparency　168
Fafinski, S.　131–32, 299–300
Fairclough, G.　143
fake news　84–85, 137, 231, 267, 378, 666
false flag attacks　184, 185, 254, 263–64, 437–38
false technical information　209
Farrell, H.　761
faulty data　233
Federal Bureau of Investigation (FBI)
　(USA)　73, 518, 799
　criminal groups　100
　hacker culture　99
　InfraGard　318
　'Innocent Images' programme　389
　outreach programme　695
　Violent Crimes Against Children unit　102
Federal Express　341, 798–99
Federal Trade Commission (FTC)(USA)　330,
　331–32, 691–92
　Act　330
　Disposal Rule　333
　fair information practice codes　329
Felten, E.　305
Ferizi, A.　187–88, 190, 197–98
Fidler, D.P.　519–20
filter bubbles　166
filters　386
financial crime　93, 466
financial damage　437
financial services　441, 568–69
Financial Services Information Sharing and
　Analysis Centre (FS-ISAC)　317–18
financial technology　468
Finland　308–9, 483, 763–64
Finnemorre, M.　755, 761–62
fire-and-forget attacks　177–78, 185–86
FireEye　230, 552
firewalls　232–33
firmware　521–22
First World Congress Against Commercial
　Sexual Exploitation of Children　381
Fisher, P.　196
Five-eyes intelligence alliance　538
Flame　231, 562–63, 570–71, 634
Floridi, L.　35–36, 37, 38

Foley, J. 163–64
Follow-On Forces Attack 275–76
force, use of 62, 583, 585–87
Forum of Incident Response and Security
    Teams (FIRST) 298, 317, 319, 325
  Common Vulnerability Scoring System
    (CVSS) 149–50
forum shopping 68–69
Foucault, M. 410–11
framing theory 418
France
  cross-agency and sector cooperation 102–3
  diplomacy 536
  and Germany 243
  and Google 342–43
  multilateral export control and standard
    setting 483, 487, 488
  proxies and offensive cyber operations 550–51
  technology: access and denial 206
  and United Kingdom 230
Franklin, B. 746
fraud 91, 92, 104, 798
  advance fee fraud 92, 130
  agreement violations as customary
    practice 568–69
  cross-agency and sector cooperation 103
  cyber hygiene 365, 372
  harm assessment from cyber crime 129,
    130, 131–32, 133, 134
  proxies and offensive cyber
    operations 553–54
  see also credit card fraud
free energy (exergy) 400, 402
Freedman, Sir L. 631
freedom of expression 82–83, 386, 412, 539, 581
freedom of speech 166, 265
Friedman, A. 484
Friedman, W. 603
Fukuyama, F. 534
Fuller, J.F.C. 801–2
functional cyber norms *see under* cyber weapons
functionalism 463, 464, 474
Fund to End Violence Against Children 383
future normative challenges 751–65
  accountability 758, 762
  binding norms 755, 756, 760
  certainty 752

concept of normative 752–54
customary law 755
deductive methods 752
due diligence 759, 764
ethical and moral norms 753
existing norms 756, 757*f*
hard norms 752
incomplete saturation of discourse,
    challenges of 755–61
inductive methods 752
inter-disciplinarity, challenge of 761–62
international law 754, 756, 758, 759, 762, 764
new norms 756–58, 763–64
non-binding norms 756–58
norm entrepreneur 759
normative gap analysis 758*f*
'Other' 754
Political 752–53, 762
predictability 752
'Self' 754
soft norms 752
values and value systems, challenge
    of 754–55

G

Gady, F. 41
Gaiser, R. 45
GammaGroup 196
Gartner 798–99
gatekeeping 165–66, 167, 170
Gates, B. 37, 690
Gauss 231, 562–63, 570–71
Geers, K. 803–4
gender effect 414
gene editing 690
General Agreement on Tariffs and Trade
    (GATT) 499, 500, 517
General Data Protection Regulation (GDPR)
    (EU) 82–83, 608–9
  child safety online 379, 383
  data privacy and security law 328, 332–33,
    337, 342–43
  disruptive technology and regulatory
    frameworks 114
  future normative challenges 760
  information sharing 322
  personal protection/cyber hygiene 363

INDEX

general equilibrium theory 397
General System Theory 397
Genesis classification 151
genetic engineering 690
Geneva Conventions 587
genomics 690
Georgia 441, 554
Georgia, and Russia 262, 280
geotechnopolitics 763
Gerasimov, General V./Gerasimov
    Doctrine 262–63
Germany
  agreement violations as customary
    practice 566
  Chaos Computer Club (CCC) 694
  child safety online 386
  Computer Emergency Response Team
    (DFN-CERT) 298–99
  critical national infrastructure (CNI) 433
  cross-agency and sector cooperation 102–3
  cyber power 72
  diplomacy 536
  Federal Office for Information Security 336
  and France 243
  global commerce and international
    organizations 503–4
  IT Security Act 2015 336
  multilateral export control and standard
    setting 483
  submarine cable 763–64
  and United States 516
Get Safe Online 130
Ghana: National Cyber Security Policy and
    Strategy 336
Giacomello, G. 192, 193
Gibson, W. 11, 28
GitHub 228
Glenny, M. 553–54
global banking system 9
global commerce and international
    organizations 497–509
  corporate behaviour and threats 507
  counter-intelligence 499
  cyber security 501
  direct threats 498, 502–5
    cyber crime 502–3, 508
    cyber terrorism 504

    cyber warfare 504–5
    economic cyber espionage 502, 503–4, 508
  future prospects 507–9
  indirect threats 499, 505–6
  vulnerabilities created by corporate
    behaviour 499
Global Commission on Internet
    Governance 68–69, 380, 539
Global Commission for the Stability of
    Cyberspace 68–69
global commons or global public good 58
Global Conference on Cyberspace (GCCS)
    (London Process) 471–72, 523, 538–39,
    776–77
Global Cybersecurity Capacity Maturity
    Model for Nations (CMM)(Global
    Cyber Security Capacity Centre) 324
global domain 11
Global Forum on Cyber Expertise
    (GFCE) 471–72, 506
  Knowledge Portal for Cyber Capacity
    Building (Cybil) 471–72
Global Fund 383
global information security spending 798–99
Global Initiative to Combat Nuclear Terrorism 213
Global Internet Forum to Counter Terrorism
    (GIFTC) 102–3, 167–68, 169
Global Partnership 383
Global Positioning Systems (GPS) 116
global security dynamics and challenges of
    digital age 689–91
global trade: monitoring, enforcement and
    sanctions 514–23
  malicious and offensive ICT trade 515, 517,
    520, 521, 522, 523
  Microsoft's proposed norms 518–19,
    522–23, 524*t*
  nationalization trend and technology
    sovereignty 515 , , 516–17
  private sector role for software trade
    control 522–23
  sanctions 519–21
  service compliance 514–15
  trade protectionism 514–15, 516
  unique product requirements 514–15
  United Nations Groups of Government
    Experts (GGE) norms 515–523

weak enforcement and monitoring
  mechanisms 517–21
Goldman Sachs 523
Goldsmith, J. 606
Goodpaster, A. 790, 794–95
Goodrick, P. 305
Google
  autonomous cyber weapons systems
    (AWS) 706
  capacity building 465
  child safety online 384–85
  data privacy and security law 342
  France 342–43
  India 617–18, 622–23
  information warfare and influence
    operations (IWIO) 268
  Israel 636
  organized crime 100–1
  proxies and offensive cyber
    operations 543–44
  Search 413–14
  terrorism and extremism 167
Gordievsky, O. 554
Gore, A. 53
Gourley, B. 349
governance, risk and compliance (GRC) 118
governance of technology 687–97
  bottom-up approaches 695–96
  dual-use research and technologies 688,
    689, 690, 694, 695, 697
  global security dynamics and challenges of
    digital age 689–91
  horizontal governance
    collaborations 694–96
  resilience building by networking across
    communities 691–94
  risk 691–93
  top-down approaches 687, 694, 696
governments, abuses of power by 775
Graham, P. 315
Gray, C. 290–91
Greek hydraulic telegraph 12, 13f
Greitzer, F. 349–50
'grey hats' 98
grey market 96, 437–38, 518
grey operations 263–64, 281–82
grooming 100, 387–88

Grotius 603
Group of Seven (G7) 42, 564, 651
  *Combating the Use of the Internet for
    Terrorist and Violent Extremist
    Purposes* 168
  Interior Ministers' meetings 168
  Ise-Shima Principles 73
  Lucca Declaration (2017) 73
Group of Twenty (G20) 479, 504, 508, 564,
  603–4
Guccifer 2.0 231, 261–62
Gullion, E. 531–32
Gutenberg 16
Guterres, A. 565

H
H5N1 virus 687–88
Habermas, J. 84
hackbacks 179–80, 233
Hacker Manifesto 726–27
hackers/hacking 93, 144
  agreement violations as customary
    practice 568–69
  amateur hackers 366
  China 601, 606
  collectives 196
  companies or hacking units 182
  conflict deterrence and prevention 288
  culture 98–99
  cyber espionage 223, 226, 230
  cyber hygiene 367–68
  cyber terrorism and intentions 193, 196
  cyber war 242–43
  cyber weapons 174, 176
  democratic civil society 736–37
  ethical hackers 98
  global commerce and international
    organizations 499, 505
  harm assessment from cyber crime 134–35
  human and behavioural challenges 726–27
  human hacking 801
  large scale criminal hacking 775
  Malaysia 663, 666
  'nuisance' 798
  proxies and offensive cyber operations 543,
    544, 546–48, 551–52, 553, 554
  skilled hackers 366, 548

830   INDEX

hackers/hacking (*cont.*)
  stunt hacking 367
  surveillance and human rights 416
  technology: access and denial 206, 207–8,
    209, 210
  tinkering 103
  tools 177–78, 183, 517
  vulnerability mitigation 146
  see also hacktivists/hacktivism
Hacking Team (HT) 196, 487, 488, 518
hacktivists/hacktivism 145, 366, 667
  proxies and offensive cyber operations 546,
    554–55, 556
  technology: access and denial 201–2, 203–4,
    206, 210, 211
Haff, P.K. 401
Hague Convention 587
Hague, W. 776–77
Halkier, B. 725
Haller, J. 45
Hamedani, H. 551–52
Hamidi, A.Z. 666
Hamilton 450
Hammertoss 228
Hansa drug market 99
Hao, Y. 613n.27
Happa, J. 143
harm
  personal 179
  private 85
  public 85
  see also harm assessment and cyber crime
harm assessment and cyber crime 127–39
  challenges 132–34
    classification 133
    common framework necessity 133–34
    data availability and reliability 132–33
    intangible factors 132
  cultural harm 135
  cyber weapons 182
  direct harm 134
  economic harm 135
  emotional harm 132
  environmental harm 135
  financial harm 134
  harm from crime versus harm from cyber
    crime 128–30
  harm spectrum 134–38

  duration 134
  immediacy 134
  magnitude 134–35
  nature 135
  opportunity costs 135–36
  scale 135
indirect harm 134–35
input 129
intangible harm 135
mitigation of harm 128, 137–39
output 129
physical harm 134, 135
political harm 134, 135
preparedness 129
psychological harm 127, 128, 131–32, 134,
  135–36, 190
severity of harm 132
social harm 131–32
socio-cultural harm 134
tangible harm 135
taxonomy 135
trust and harm 136–37
see also reputation and reputational
  harm
hash 389–90
hash-sharing database 167
Hassan, R. 35, 37
Hathaway, M. 39
Hawking, S. 37
Healey, J. 39
Heier, C.D. 400
Henkin, L. 457–58
Hernandez, R. 547–48
heuristics 255–56
  affect 255
  anchoring 255
  availability 255
  representativeness 255
Hezbollah (Lebanon) 633
Hintz, A. 416–17
Hitler, A. 257
Hobbes, T. 33, 603
Hohimer, R. 349–50
Hokayem, E. 546
Hollis, D. 755, 761–62
Holt, T.J. 104
'honeypots' 233
Hook, D. 7

hotlines 389–90
Howard, J.D. 143, 145, 148, 149–50
Huawei 433, 523, 620
Hubbard, D. 351
hubris 736–39
human and behavioural challenges 723–33
  ambivalence 725
  awareness and behaviour change 727–28
  concordance 731, 732
  creativity and innovation 726–28
  cyber hygiene 367
  power relations 725
  rationality 725
  risk perception and risk
      communication 728–30
  scalability 725–26
  security dialogues 730–32
  social interactions 725
  social practice, cybersecurity
      as 724–26
human error 780–81
human rights 63
  agreement violations as customary
      practice 564
  autonomous cyber weapons systems
      (AWS) 703
  capacity building 467
  child safety online 386
  China 606–7
  defence and national cyber security 457
  diplomacy 539
  future normative challenges 759
  global trade: monitoring, enforcement and
      sanctions 518
  international law 578, 581
  Israel 637
  multilateral export control and standard
      setting 487–88, 489–90, 491, 492
  terrorism and extremism 169, 170
  see also surveillance and human rights
Human Rights Watch 703
human social systems 400, 401–2
human-centric measures 137–39
Human-Machine Teaming 801
HUMINT (Human Intelligence) 179–80, 224,
      230, 231
Hungary 471
Huntington, S. 450, 452, 456

Hurwitz, R. 761
Hussain, J. 187–88, 190, 195, 197–98
hybrid warfare 281–82, 715
hydraulic telegraph 12, 13f, 14–15

I

IAEA 185
IBM 636
Ibrahim, A. 664
ICT4Peace Foundation 214
identified intentions better pursued in cyber
      attack or physical attack 192–96
identity theft 93, 96, 103–4, 365, 775
Illich, I. 407n.14
illicit drugs 99, 103–4
illicit firearms 99
illicit or sensitive software 515
IMINT (imagery) 224, 230
immediate death count 194
Impact Team 197
implantable or ingested medical
      devices 56–57, 173
Increased Access 149–50
India 54, 616–24
  autonomous cyber weapons systems
      (AWS) 707–8
  Budapest Convention on Cybercrime 61
  capacity building 471
  and China 616–17, 620–22, 623–24
  cooperation 619–21
  cyber espionage 228–29
  cyber hygiene 368
  cyber power 69
  data localization and encrypted
      platforms 623
  Department of Telecommunications 623
  development and cyber security 772–73,
      776–77
  Digital India 603–4, 624
  digital payment systems 621
  digitalization paradox 617, 619–20
  diplomacy 536, 541
  future normative challenges 754
  global trade: monitoring, enforcement and
      sanctions 517
  Information and Communication
      Technology working group
      (ICT-WG) 618

832 INDEX

India (*cont.*)
  Information Technology Act
    (2000) 618–19, 623
  language issues 620
  Ministry of Electronics and Information
    Technology 624
  multi-stakeholder arrangements 619,
    623–24
  multilateral export control and standard
    setting 483
  National Cyber Security Coordinator 619
  National Intelligence Agency 616
  political factors 618
  protectionism 622
  regional connectivity plans 622
  sovereignty 622
  start-ups 618
  Track 1.5 Cyber Dialogue 619
  and United States 616–20, 622–24
Indonesia 621–22, 754
industrial control systems 54–55, 177–78, 633
Industrial Revolution 49, 402, 403–4, 405, 406
inequalities, digital and developmental
    see under development and cyber
    security: contested futures
information
  assurance (IA) 232–33
  asymmetry 363
  environment 11
  exchange 145
  non-identifying 332
  processing 27
  reaggregated 38
  security 61
  security policies 579
  security versus cyber security 58–59
  sensitive 92
  transparency, secrecy and privacy 55–56
  true and false 258
  values 148
  warfare 94
  warfare, *see also* information warfare and
    influence operations (IWIO)
  weapons 60–61
Information Age *see* Cyber Revolution
    (Information Age)
Information Exchange Policy (IEP) 325

Information Exchanges 319–20
Information Security Forum (ISF) 116
information sharing 304, 307, 314–25
  Automated Indicator Sharing (AIS) 321
  child safety online 389
  computer emergency response team/
    coordination centre 316–17
  critical national infrastructure
    (CNI) 317–19, 321–22, 325
  Cyber Security Information Sharing and
    Collaboration Program (CISCP) 318,
    322
  Cyber Security Information Sharing
    Partnership (CiSP) 319, 320, 323
  and dissemination 300
  Forum of Incident Response and Security
    Teams (FIRST) 317, 319, 325
  future outcomes 324
  Information Exchanges 319–20
  Information Sharing and Analysis Centres
    (ISACs) 317–18, 319, 320
  Information Sharing Analysis
    Organizations (ISAOs) 320–21
  liability protections, guaranteed 325
  mandatory information sharing 321–24, 325
    New York State Department of Financial
      Services (DFS) 323
    United Kingdom Network and
      Information Systems Regulations
      2018 322–23
    United States Defense Industrial
      Base 322
    United States Food and Drug
      Administration (FDA) 323–24
  Morris Worm 314–16
  national cyber strategies 324
  rules enforcement 325
  Warning Advisory and Reporting Points
    (WARPs) 319–20
Information Sharing and Analysis Centres
    (ISACs) 317–18, 319, 320
Information Sharing Analysis Organizations
    (ISAOs) 320–21
Information Technology Agreement
    (ITA) 514–15
Information Technology Information Sharing
    and Analysis Centre (IT-ISAC) 317–18

information warfare and influence operations
(IWIO) 251–69
  black operations 254
  channelling or influencing other preexisting
     forces in society 255
  chaos-producing operations 257–58
  cognitive biases 254–55
  cognitive/emotional dimension 253, 254
  countering 266–68
  emotional biases 256–57
  grey operations 254
  high connectivity 260
  high tempo of operations 260
  identification 266
  information environment 252–53, 254
  leak operations 258
  objectives achievement 254–55
  physical dimension 252, 254
  propaganda operations 257
  relevant information 254
  response 265
  Russia 260, 261–62, 266, 267
  Russian annexation of Crimea 263–64
  Russian art of strategy 262–63
  selected information 254
  strategy and theory of victory 253
  typology 257
  use in pre-existing atmosphere of
     uncertainty and doubt 255
  velocity of flow 267
  vulnerabilities of liberal democracies 265
  white operations 254
Informational Impact 143, 149–50
infrastructure elements categorization 433–35
infrastructure of modern cyberspace 19–22
Initial Elements 486
innovation without permission 53
innovative approach to security 35
insider threat and insider advocates 174, 348–56
  ambivalence 350–51, 353–54, 355
  behavioural models 348–49
  behavioural and psychological aspects of
     malicious insider 348–49
  benign insiders 366
  committed/dependable employees 355
  definitions 348–49
  desired outcome, creation of 355

dysfunctional or negative behaviours 351–
    52, 354–55
  employee management 348–49
  employee satisfaction 355
  employee/organizational
     commitment 354–55
  engaged and disengaged employees 350–51,
    355
  environmental elements of workplace 350–51,
    352–54
  future requirements 354
  leadership 349–56
  malicious insider 348–49, 350–51, 355, 366
  organizational behaviours 351–52, 354
  organizational change management 354
  organizational citizenship 352, 353–54
  personal protection/cyber hygiene 366
  technological advancements 348–49, 351–53,
    356
  threat and opportunity 349–50
  working environment 351–52, 354
  workplace dynamics 350–53
Instagram 385
Institute of Electrical and Electronic
    Engineers (IEEE) 707
insurance industry 118, 131
integrated stakeholder 452, 456
integrity 118, 150, 364
Intel 636
intellectual property theft 251, 517, 519, 520,
    604, 608, 657, 799
intelligence
  assessments and counter-terrorism 191–92,
    198
  civilian 224
  collection 226
  cycle 226
  direction 226
  dissemination 226
  penetration 226
  persistence 226
  state 224–25
  strategic 110
  see also counterintelligence
interdependence 38, 43, 44–45, 287
intergovernmental certification and
    recognition scheme 483

834 INDEX

intermediary liability 390
International Association of Internet Hotlines
(INHOPE) 389
International Atomic Energy Agency 508
International Cable Protection
Committee 504
International Civil Aviation Organization
(ICAO) 320, 504, 508
*International Code of Conduct for Information
Security* 60–61
International Committee of the Red Cross
(ICRC) 183, 213, 703, 713, 714, 715–16
International Convention on Civil and
Political Rights (ICCPR) 412
International Court of Justice 551–52, 759–60
International Criminal Court 759–60
international humanitarian law (IHL) 173,
183, 504–5, 535–36
agreement violations as customary
practice 564–65
autonomous cyber weapons systems
(AWS) 703, 713
compliance 715–16, 717
future normative challenges 764
international law: competition and
conflict 587
International Information Security Code of
Conduct 607
International Information Security Research
Consortium 536
International Institute for Strategic Studies
(IISS) 538
international law 578–89
agreement violations as customary
practice 564–65
attempt 585
autonomous cyber weapons systems
(AWS) 703
capacity building 467
China 603, 604, 606
competition 578–83
diplomatic and consular law 578,
581–82, 584
espionage 581
human rights 578, 581
jurisdiction 578, 579–80
sovereignty 578–79, 581, 584

specialized regimes 578, 582–83
state responsibility 578, 580–81
conflict 583–89
armed conflict, law of 583, 587–89
coercion 585
dispute settlement, peaceful 578, 583–84
force, use of 583, 585–87
intervention prohibition 584–85
counter-terrorism 586–87
directness 586
distinction 588
future normative challenges 754, 756, 758,
759, 762, 764
global commerce and international
organizations 502
immediacy 586
imminence 586–87
intervention prohibition 584–85
invasiveness 586
Malaysia 668
measurability 586
mere threat 585
military character 586
necessity 586–87
presumptive legality 586
proportionality 586–87, 588
public international law 280
severity 586
state involvement 586
state responsibility 578, 580–81
see also customary international law;
international humanitarian law (IHL)
International Maritime Organization
(IMO) 504, 508
international negotiations on state
behaviour and cyber weapons
proliferation 212–14
international organizations *see* global commerce
and international organizations
international relations *see* cyber power and
international relations
International Science and Technology
Centre 695
International Standards Organization (ISO)
27001 standards 640–41
and IEC 15408 standard 483
and IEC Joint Technical Committee 482

International Strategy of Cooperation on
  Cyberspace 610
international technological standards 608
International Telecommunications Union
  (ITU)
  capacity building 464
  Child Online Protection Initiative 381
  Cybersecurity Toolkit 467
  development and cyber security 774,
    778–79
  diplomacy 535
  global commerce and international
    organizations 497, 500, 501, 507, 508
  Global Cybersecurity Agenda 662–63
  Global Cybersecurity Index (GCI) 662–63
  global trade: monitoring, enforcement and
    sanctions 522
  ICT Development Index (IDI) 599
  and IMPACT engagement 774, 777
  India 618–19
  National Cybersecurity Strategy Guide 467
  vulnerability mitigation 152
  World Summit on the Information
    Society 754, 759
internationalization of critical supply chains
  and service infrastructure 205
Internet Assigned Numbers Authority
  (IANA) 68–69, 618
Internet bans 760
Internet Corporation for Assigned Names and
  Numbers (ICANN) 59, 68–69, 535,
  608–9, 617, 619, 776
Internet as distributed system 9
Internet Engineering Task Force
  (IETF) 68–69, 534
Internet Exchange (IX) 572
internet exchange points (IXPs) 679–80
Internet Governance Forum (IGF) 382, 776
Internet implementing cyberspace 21f
Internet Plus strategy 537, 597–98
Internet Protocol (IP) address 97, 500, 535, 600
  Japan 655
  re-routed 59
  Russia 678, 679–80
Internet Protocol (IP) suite 534
Internet Protocol (IP) surveillance
  systems 480, 487, 488, 489, 492

Internet service providers (ISP) 85, 228–29,
  566–67, 572, 680
Internet of Things (IoT) 9, 49, 56–57, 801
  agreement violations as customary
    practice 567, 572–73
  capacity building 465
  child safety online 377–78
  China 597–98
  critical national infrastructure (CNI) 442
  cyber crime 92, 103–4
  cyber terrorism and intentions 194–95
  data privacy and security law 341–42
  development and cyber security 771–72
  diplomacy 538
  future normative challenges 763
  global commerce and international
    organizations 497, 507
  global trade: monitoring, enforcement and
    sanctions 514
  governance of technology 691–92
  harm assessment from cyber crime 131–33
  harm and trust 136
  human and behavioural challenges 724,
    726, 728–29
  India 624
  Japan 650, 651
  Malaysia 661
  primary assessment of disruptive
    technologies 118
  surveillance and human rights 418
  technology: access and denial 205, 211
  vulnerability mitigation 150, 155
interoperability 53
INTERPOL (International Police
  Organization) 502–3, 523
  International Child Sexual Exploitation
    database 102
intranets 9
intrusion detection systems 340–41
intrusion software 480, 487, 488, 489–90,
  492–93, 518
investigative or forensic data 93
inviolability principle 581–82
Iran 441, 754
  and Aramco (Saudi Arabia) 244
  attack on New York financial institutions
    (2013) 334

836   INDEX

Iran (*cont.*)
  Basij 552
  cyber army 551–52
  cyber espionage 228, 231
  cyber power 72
  development and cyber security 772–73,
    776–77
  diplomacy 541
  global trade: monitoring, enforcement and
    sanctions 519
  Islamic Revolutionary Guard Corps
    (IRGC) 545–46, 552
  proxies and offensive cyber
    operations 544–45, 552–53, 554–55
  Sands Casino 239, 244
  and United States 243–45
  see also Stuxnet and Operation Olympic
    Games by United States and Israel
    against Iran
Iraq 68, 102–3
Iraq war 55–56, 239–40
Ireland 308–9, 342, 454–55
Islamic State (IS)
  cyber power in international relations 74, 75
  cyber terrorism and intentions 187,
    190–91, 195
  global commerce and international
    organizations 504–5
  governance of technology 691
  information warfare and influence
    operations (IWIO) 258, 262, 266
  technology: access and denial 202, 203,
    204, 208, 209
  terrorism, extremism and anti-democratic
    tendencies 163, 166, 167, 168
Israel 54, 631–45
  aggregate cyber robustness 642
  Air Force (IAF) 632, 633, 634–35
  Aman Unit 8200 634
  armed forces and military cyber
    power 633–35
  artificial intelligence (AI) 644–45
  autonomous cyber weapons systems
    (AWS) 707, 715–16
  banking sector 640
  Blavatnik Interdisciplinary Cyber
    Research Centre Cyberweek (Tel Aviv
    University) 641

  business expenditure on R&D (BERD) 636
  C41 and Cyber Defence Directorate 634
  Centre of Computing and Information
    Systems (*mamram*) 634
  challenges to cyber security 642–43
  chief information security officers
    (CISOs) 641–42
  computer network attacks (CNAs) 634
  computer network defence (CND) 634
  computer network exploitation (CNE) 634
  Computer Security Incident Response
    Teams (CSIRTs) 642
  counter rocket, artillery and mortar
    (C-RAM) Iron Dome 634–35
  Critical Infrastructure Protection
    (CIP) 639–40, 641, 643
  cyber espionage 228
  Cyber Event Readiness Team (CERT-
    IL) 641–42, 643–44
  Cyber Law (draft) 643
  CyberNet 641–42
  CyberSpark project 641–42
  Defence Force (IDF) 632, 634, 644–45
  Defence Force (IDF)
    Cyber Defender course 636
    Cyber Defense Division 634
  defence research and industrial base
    development 637
  development and cyber security 772–73
  evolution of cybersecurity 639–40
  foreign markets and foreign investors 636
  government cyber security unit
    (*Yahav*) 640–41
  Government Infrastructure for the Internet
    Era unit (*Tehila*) 639
  Government Resolutions 638, 639,
    640–41
  grand strategy 631–32, 644–45
  Haifa University study 131
  Hamas 632
  hard power: non-intelligence cyber
    operations 632
  human capital: spill-over effects of military
    service 636–37
  IAI *Eitan* Medium Altitude Long
    Endurance Unmanned Aerial Vehicle
    (MALE UAV) 634–35
  information sharing 324

information, technology and smart
power 632
Institute for Biological Research 637
intelligence organizations 634
legal foundations, fortification of 643
MASAD plan 637
Military Intelligence Directorate 634
Ministry of Defence (MoD)(*Muffat*) 637, 644
Ministry of Finance Accountant General's
office 639
Ministry of Justice 643
multi-tiered missile defence system 634–35
multilateral export control and standard
setting 483
multinational corporations (MNCs) 636,
637–38
National Cyber Bureau (INCB) 640, 641,
643
National Cyber Directorate (INCD) 643
National Cyber Directorate (INCD)
Annual Report (2019) 642
capacity building and operations 640–42
'National Cyber Security Strategy in
Brief' 642
National Cyber Initiative 639
National Cyber Security Authority
(NCSA) 640, 641, 643
National Cyber Strategy (2011) 638
National Information Security Agency
(*Re'em*) 639, 641
National Security Council (NSC) 639
National Unit for the Protection of Vital
Computerised Systems 639
Operation Orchard/Outside the Box 633
and Palestine conflict 532
principles and forces shaping
cybersecurity 637–38
proxies and offensive cyber
operations 549–51
Regulation of Security in Public Bodies Law
1998 amendment 639, 643
School for Computer Related Professions
(*Basmakh*) 634
security operation centre (SOC) 640–42
Shabak 641
Shabak Statute (2002) 641, 643
situational awareness 643–44
soft power: innovation system 635

Space Agency 637
Syrian airstrike 244
systemic cyber resilience 642
Tel Aviv Stock Exchange 640
Unit 8200 signal intelligence (SIGINT) and
code decryption 634
and United States 55, 226
see also Stuxnet and Operation Olympic Games
by United States and Israel against Iran
IT Products 483
Italy 206
Ivanov, I. 535
Ivory Coast 773

J

Jaafari, M.A. 551–52
Jane's Intelligence 554
Janowitz, M. 450, 452, 456
Japan 649–58
'47 Administrative Journal' news
website (Kyodo Communications)
hacking 655
Action Plan 652
Agency of Finance 656
agreement violations as customary
practice 570
autonomous cyber weapons systems
(AWS) 707
Budapest Convention on Cybercrime 101
Bureau of Statistics website erasure 653
Cabinet Secretariat Information Security
Center 655
capacity building 471
and China 652–53
critical infrastructure 149, 650–51, 653, 654
cyber attacks 655
Cyber Defence Policy Working
Group 652–53
Cyber Defence Unit (CDU) 656, 657
Cyber Security Basic Law (2014) 650
cyber security challenges 651
cyber security experience 649
cyber security policy framework prior to
Basic Act 653–54
Cyber Terrorism Special Action Plan 653
defensive measures taken against cyber
attacks 655–56
diplomacy 536

838 INDEX

Japan (*cont.*)
  and Europe 653
  Financial Services Agency (FSA) 655
  Government of Japan website hacking 653,
    657–58
  House of Councillors 649
  House of Representatives 649
  i-Japan 603–4
  implications for cybersecurity 656
  industry, challenges to 657
  information security basic plan (2006) 654
  Information Security Council 649–50
  information security policy 650–51, 654
  Information Security Strategy to Protect
    People (2010) 654
  international cooperation 652–53
  IT Security Office 653
  JTB Group 655
  Legal Bureau 655
  Ministry of Defence 649–50, 656
  Ministry of Economy, Trade and Industry
    (METI) 651, 656–57
  Ministry of Finance 656
  Ministry of Foreign Affairs 652
  Ministry of Internal Affairs and
    Communications 651, 656
  Ministry of Justice 655
  multilateral arrangements 652
  National Centre for Incident Readiness and
    Strategy for Cybersecurity 318–19, 656
  National Defence Programme Guidelines
    (2014) 650
  National Information Security Center 654
  National Information Security Council
    (NISC) 650–51, 654, 656
  National Security Council 650
  and North America 652–53
  NPA 655–56
  Pension Services (JPS) 649–50, 657–58
  Policy Cooperation Dialogue on the
    Internet Economy 652–53
  public-private partnership model 654
  Science and Technology Agency (STA)
    defacement 653
  second information security basic plan
    (2009) 654
  'Secure Japan 2006' 653, 654
  and South Korea 652–53

Tokyo Metropolitan Police
  Department 655–56
Tokyo Metropolitan Police Department -
  Cyber Attack Center 655
Tokyo Olympic and Paralympic
  Games 650, 651, 655
Trilateral Cyber Dialogue with China and
  South Korea 652–53
  and United States 652–53
Java language 736–37
Javani, Y. 551–52
Jester, The 546
jihadists 207, 208
Jobs, S. 726–27
Johnson, D. 606
Joint Technical Alert 74
Juergensmeyer, M. 190, 194
Juniper Research 90–91
jurisdiction 342–43, 578, 579–80, 740
  extraterritorial 579
  prescriptive 579
  protective 579–80
  universal 579–80
jus ad bellum/jus in bello 585–87, 588,
  668, 703

K

Kahn, R. 53
Kallberg, J. 483, 484
Kan, N. 656
Kant, I. 603
Kashmir 622
Kaspersky 230, 233, 666
Katzenstein, P.J. 762
Kazakhstan 61
Kello, L. 281–82
Kennan, G.F. 788–89, 790, 793, 794–95
Kenya 691, 775
key infrastructures identification 431–33
key risk responses implementation 435–36
Khomeini, Ayatollah 552–53
Kilcullen, D. 239–40, 245, 247
kill list 190–91
Kim regime 521
Kindle Fire for Kids 386
Klare, M.T. 556–57n.10
Klimburg, A. 39, 544, 554
know your machine (KYM) 118

INDEX 839

knowledge
   educating for cyber security 400
   management 44–45
   models 121–24
   as power 33–34
   representation 120–21, 124
Kofi Annan 563
kompromat 262
Koobface 100–1
Korzak, E. 761
Kosova Hacker's Security
   collective 187
Koufaris, M. 415
Kraemer-Mbula, E. 120–21
Kripke, S. 24
Krsul, I.V./Krsul system 150
Krutskikh, A.V. 536
Kubrick, S. 274
Kunii, T.L. 20–21
Kwon, K. 416
Kyrgyzstan 61

L

La Rue, F. 386
'lamers' 98
Lan Tang 287
language and cultural issues 383–84, 605, 620,
   659, 665
Lanning, K. 389
Lanzarote Convention on the Protection of
   Children against Sexual Exploitation
   and Sexual Abuse 382
large-scale technological systems
   (LTS) 738–40
Lasswell, H.D. 754–55
Latham 433
Lau, R.R. 727, 728
Law of Armed Conflict *see* international
   humanitarian law (IHL)
Law of the Sea Convention 582
Lawrence, D. 730–31
Lazarus hacking group 569–70
leadership - insider threat and insider
   advocates 349–56
League of Arab States 502–3
League of Nations 531
leak operations 258
learned helplessness 414–15, 728

least developed countries (LDCs) 89, 771–72,
   772*f*, 778–79
Lee, H. 609
Lee, T.B. 297
Legion of Doom 98
lethal autonomous weapons systems
   (LAWS) 702, 703–4, 706–7, 708, 709*t*,
   711–12, 713, 714–15, 716, 801
Levin, A. 305
Levy, S. 98
Ley 731
Li Zheng 551
liability 463
   intermediary 390
liaison model 306
libel chill 411
liberal democracies 266–67, 451, 457
Liberator (3D printed firearm) 89
Libicki, M. 289
Libya 487
lies, pure 258
life cycle for cyber incidents 144
Lin, P. 705, 716–17
LinkedIn 678
Liska, A.J. 400
LISP 736–37
Lloyds 90–91
Lobel, J. 545
locations 9, 22, 26
logic 24, 25, 27
   doxastic 27
   epistemic 27
   modal 24
   temporal 27
logical reasoning 25–26, 27
logical truth 26
logs 233
London Action Group 102
Longstaff, T.A. 143, 145, 148, 149–50
Love virus 54
Lu Wei 540
Luttwak, E. 631
Luxembourg Guidelines 383–84
Lyon, D. 410–11, 414–15

M

Ma, J. 661
McAfee 90–91, 97, 617–18

840   INDEX

McConnell, M. 247n.1, 292n.14
McCormick, J. 789–90
McGuire, M. 100
machine learning 801
  autonomous cyber weapons systems
      (AWS) 706–7, 708, 715–16
  conflict deterrence and prevention 290
  cyber espionage 229–30
  cyber hygiene 361
  metrics 124
  surveillance and human rights 409
  terrorism and extremism 167
Madison 450
Maersk 570–71, 798–99
Magid, L. 377, 378
Malawer, S.S. 519
Malaysia 659–68
  Administrative Modernization and
      Management Planning Unit
      (MAMPU) 662–63
  'Anonymous Malaysia' 667
  Attorney-General's Chambers 662
  Bank Nagara Malaysia, Financial
      Technology (Fintech) Regulatory
      Sandbox framework (2016) 663
  Bersih 2.0 political movement 664, 667
  Bill of Guarantees 660
  broadband penetration 664–65
  Communications and Multimedia
      Commission 662–63
  computer emergency response team
      (CERT) 662–63, 664
  critical national information infrastructure
      (CNII) 659–60, 661–64
  CyberSecurity Malaysia 662–63, 666–67
  cybersecurity trends 666–67
  Daesh terrorist group 662
  Digital Free Trade Zone 661
  Digital Hub 661
  'digital natives' 665
  economic imperative of
      cyberspace 660–61
  Eleventh Malaysia Plan
      (2016–2020) 661, 664
  ethnicity, religion and language 659, 665
  industrialization phase 660
  international law 668

  International Multilateral Partnership Against
      Cyber-Terrorism (IMPACT) 774, 777
  knowledge economy (k-economy) 660
  MIMOS 'National Research and
      Development Roadmap for
      Self-Reliance in Cyber Security
      Technologies' 663
  Ministry of Information, Communication
      and Culture 662
  Ministry of Science, Technology and
      Innovation (MOSTI) 661, 662–63
  Multimedia Super Corridor (MSC) 660, 661
  National Cyber Security Policy
      (NCSP) 661, 662, 663
  National Front (BN) 664
  National Information Infrastructure
      (NII) 663
  National Information Technology Council
      (NITC) *Securing Malaysia Sovereignty
      in the Cyber World* report 663
  National Security Council (NSC) 662
  National Security Council (NSC)
      *Directive No 24: Policy and
      Mechanisms of National Cyber Crisis
      Management* 662
  National Cyber Crisis Exercise 662
  Network Security Centre 662–63
  Regional Digital Counter-Messaging
      Communication Centre 666
  Royal Malaysia Police (RMP) 667
  rule of law 668
  Rulers of the States 665
  Sedition Act 1948 665
  Seventh Malaysia Plan (1996-2000) 661
  sovereignty 663, 665, 667
  strategic cybersecurity 667–68
  technical measures 662–63
  telecommunications linkages 660
  X-Maya 5 662
  Yang di-Pertuan Agong 665
  'Year of the Internet Economy' 661
Mallery, J. 749n.25
Malta 472–73
malware 54, 90, 91, 92, 93, 94–95, 101, 103–4,
      798–99
  agreement violations as customary
      practice 566, 567, 570–71

China 599, 600
criminal groups 100
critical national infrastructure
    (CNI) 437–38, 439
cross-agency and sector cooperation 102
cyber espionage 228, 230
cyber hygiene 365, 366, 372
cyber war 241–42
dark markets 96–97
development and cyber security 773
global trade: monitoring, enforcement and
    sanctions 521–22
hacker culture 99
India 620
Israel 643–44
Japan 649, 651, 655
proxies and offensive cyber
    operations 543–44, 553–54
reverse-engineering 230
Russia 673
self-exciting malware 104
technology: access and denial 209, 212, 213,
    214
toolkits 233
vulnerability mitigation 142
as a weapon 95
zero day vulnerability 283
Mamonov, S. 415
Man-Boy Love Association 389
Mandiant 229, 234–35
    *APT1: Exposing One of China's Cyber
        Espionage Units* 286
    see also FireEye
Mann, M. 545–46
Manning, B. (later C.) 55–56
Mansoor, A. 489–90
Marconi 314
Marette, S. 729–30
maritime privateering 545, 547–48, 555–56
Marks, P. 314
Marriott 798–99
Martens Clause 587
Marthews, A. 413
MASINT (measurement and signature) 224
Maskeleyne, N. 314
Maskirovka 262
Masuda, Y. 34

Matania, E. 642
matrix model 150
Mauritius 778–79
Mavromatis case 583
maximum entropy production (MaxEP) 401,
    402, 403–4, 405, 406
media impact factor 193–94
mercenaries (land-based proxies) 545
Merck 570–71, 798–99
messaging 228, 363, 372, 731–32
metasploit toolbox 182
metrics 8, 124
Metz, S. 265
Meunier, P. 150, 151
Meyers, C. 143
Microsoft 69
    China 608
    cross-agency and sector cooperation 102–3
    data privacy and security law 341
    global trade: monitoring, enforcement and
        sanctions 518–19, 522–23, 524t
    Ireland 342
    Israel 636
    PhotoDNA 389–90
    proxies and offensive cyber
        operations 543–44
    Tay chat-bot 693–94
    terrorism and extremism 167
    Windows 97, 99
Middle East 226, 231
military cyber activities 452–56, 583
military forces (state) 145
military-off-the-shelf information technology
    (MOTS-IT) 178, 183, 186
militias 145
Millennium Development Goals (MDGs) 770
Mirai software 567
mirror-imaging of adversary 265
misinformation 257, 267–68
Mitrany, D. 463
MITRE 146, 147
    Common Configuration Enumeration
        (CCE) 152
    Common Vulnerabilities and Exposures
        (CVE) 152–53
    Common Weakness Enumeration
        (CWE) 152

842   INDEX

'Model National Response Guidance
   Document' 383
modelling and reasoning about cyberspace 22–28
Monahan, B. 24, 27
Monroe Doctrine 51–52
Montesquieu 83
Montville, J. 532
moral facilitation 36, 38
Morgus, R. 304, 305–7, 309–10, 769
Morozov, E. 540–41
Morris, R.T. 98, 297, 315
Morris Worm 54, 297–98, 299, 309–10, 314–15
Morse code 19, 22
Morse, S. 17
mosaic strategy 291
Motorola 636
Mousavian, H. 551–52
Moussouris, K. 488
moving target defence 109–10
MP3s 99
Mpofu, N. 150
Mullen 731
multilateral arrangements 504, 518, 605,
   608–9, 652
multilateral export control and standard
   setting arrangements 479–93, 518
   export controls 480, 491–93
      implementation controversy 488–89
      lessons learned 489–91
      Wassenaar Arrangement and 2013
         additions 480–93
   standard setting and certification 480–85,
      491–93
      Common Criteria Recognition
         Arrangement (CCRA) 480, 482–84,
         491–93
      cybersecurity standards 482–83
      lessons learned 484–85
      role 480–81
      standards developing organizations
         (SDOs) 482, 484, 485
multilateral governance 540
multilateral organizations 502, 504
   agreement violations as customary
      practice 563, 571–72
   global commerce and international
      organizations 499, 507–8

multi-stakeholder arrangements 68–69, 382,
   500, 501, 534, 608–9, 619, 623–24, 755
multi-stakeholder Internet governance 68–
   69, 382
Munitions List 486
mutual legal assistance 104, 503
Mutual Legal Assistance Treaty (Ireland and
   United States) 342
Myanmar 166, 170
Myers, L. 731

N

Najib Abdul Razak, M. 661, 665
naming and shaming approach 73, 266–67
Nan, A.S. 533
National Antiterrorist Committee (NAC) 554
National Council of Information Sharing and
   Analysis Centres (ISACs) 317–18
national cyber security strategies 60, 324
National Fraud Intelligence Bureau 130
National Health Information Sharing and
   Analysis Centre (NH-ISAC) 317–18
National Institute of Standards and Technology
   (NIST)(USA) 142, 146, 211
   Cybersecurity Framework 103, 335, 436, 517
   National Vulnerability Database
      (NVD) 153–54, 156–57
   Risk Management Framework 436
   Software Assurance Reference Dataset
      Project (SAMATE) 146
National Plan for Information Systems
   Protection 60
National Science and Technology Council
   Subcommittee on Machine Learning
   and Artificial Intelligence (AI) 708
National Security Agency (NSA)(USA) 233,
   437–38, 523
   and Huawei 225
   Information Assurance Symposium 322
   Tailored Access Operations 547
   see also Snowden National Security Agency
      (NSA)/PRISM surveillance revelations
National Security Council see under Project
   Solarium 1953 (Eisenhower) and
   Cyberspace Solarium Commission
   (CSC) 2019
National Strategy to Secure Cyberspace 60

nationalization trend and technology
sovereignty 515, 516–17
natural numbers 22
necessity 24
modality 26
plea of 580–81
negentropy 399–400, 401, 402, 403–4, 405,
406
neo-colonial approaches: benevolence and
self-interest 779
Netanyahu, B. 636, 641
Netflix 341–42
Netherlands
capacity building 471–72
child safety online 389
computer emergency response team
(CERT-NL)(now SurfCERT) 298–99
Computer Security Incident Response
Teams (CSIRTs) 308–9
cyber power 72
Cyber Security Threat Assessment 300, 307
Global Forum on Cyber Expertise 778
governance of technology 687–88
Intensification of Civil-Military
Cooperation policy 454–55
National Cyber Security Agenda
(NCS) 770–71
National Cyber Security Centre
(NCSC) 300, 306
NetMundial 380–81, 535, 776
network communications protocols 19
network communications surveillance
systems 518
Neumann, P. 124
New Look Strategy (Eisenhower) 275–76
New Zealand 570
Nicaragua 342–43
Nicaragua case 586
Nikishin, A. 547
Nissenbaum, H. 305
Nixon, R./ administration 533
non-disclosure 155, 437, 441
non-governmental organizations
(NGOs) 103, 145, 703
multilateral export control and standard
setting 482–83, 484, 485
Non-Proliferation Treaty 533

non-state actors 144, 366, 521, 580, 604–5,
608–9
'noobs' 98
Norman, J. 7
normative challenges *see* future normative
challenges
North America 486, 487, 492, 779
see also Canada; United States
North American Electric Reliability
Corporation - Critical Infrastructure
Protection (NERC-CIP V5) 436
North American Free Trade Agreement
(NAFTA) 500, 508
North Atlantic Treaty Organization
(NATO) 55, 73, 453–54
agreement violations as customary
practice 571
conflict deterrence and prevention 277, 280
Cooperative Cyber Defence Centre of
Excellence Conference on Cyber
Conflict 711
global commerce and international
organizations 504–5
multilateral export control and standard
setting 485
proxies and offensive cyber operations 549–50
Warsaw Summit Communiqué 287–88
North Korea 656
agreement violations as customary
practice 568–70
development and cyber security 772–73
diplomacy 541
governance of technology 691
power and Internet outage (2014) 334
and Sony Pictures 73–74, 232, 239, 244, 520, 521
Norway 389
NotPetya ransomware attack 73, 441, 570–71,
798–99
Nuclear Exploit Kit 97
Nye, J.S. 70, 290, 292n.4, 522, 545–46, 756

O

OASIS Common Security Advisory
Framework Technical Committee 206
Obama administration 239, 261–62, 276, 320–21,
454, 503–4, 521, 619
Ocean Lotus (APT C-00) (China) 600

844   INDEX

offensive cyber operations (remote), states and
   proxies 543–56
   beneficiaries and ability to mobilize or stop
      a proxy 548
   beneficiary's benefit 548
   delegation (proxies on tight leash) 544,
      549–51, 550f, 555
   maritime privateering 545, 547–48, 555–56
   mercenaries (land-based proxies) 545
   non-state actors/proxies 544, 545–47, 546t,
      549, 553, 554–56
   orchestration (proxies on loose leash) 544,
      549, 550f, 551–52, 555
   political benefits 548–49
   proxies in perspective 545–49
   proxy availability 547–48
   proxy benefit 549
   proxy forces 545
   proxy war/warfare 545
   proxy warriors 545
   sanctioning (proxies on the loose) 544, 549,
      550f, 553–54, 555
   state-sponsored actors 543–44, 546–47
offset strategies 275–76
Ohmori, K. 20–21
Olderog, E.-R. 27
Omand, D. 281
'One Internet' 380
'One in Three' 380
online child safety 377–90
online games with multiple players 9
online payment services 97
online shopping 363–64
ontology 114, 117, 119, 124
   -based reasoning 116–17
   domain 120
   upper 120
   value-chain 120–21
opacity in origins 737–38, 741–42
open (non-equilibrium) systems 399, 401
Open Shortest Path First (OSPF) 7–8
Open Systems Interconnection (OSI)
      model 19, 20f
Operation Chanology (Church of
      Scientology) disruption 196
Operation Olympic Games see Stuxnet and
      Operation Olympic Games by United
      States and Israel against Iran

Operation Orchard/Outside the Box 633
Operational Impact 143, 149–50
operational security (OPSEC) 232–33, 226, 234
operations security metrics model 351
Oppenheim, L. 762
Oppo 620
opportunity, threat and dependency in social
      infosphere 32–45
   dependence 43–45
   dependence as outcome of information
      enablement 38–43
   Information Age 33–37
   political framing of infosphere 45
   transformational security 37–38
orchestration (proxies on loose leash) 544,
      549, 550f, 551–52, 555
Organization of American States 278
Organization for Economic Cooperation and
      Development (OECD) 77, 300, 328, 334
Organization for Security and Cooperation in
      Europe (OSCE) 278, 564, 681
organized crime/organized criminals 92,
      103, 144
   cyber hygiene 366
   harm assessment from cyber crime 129
   and Internet 100–1
origins of cyberspace 7–28
   beacons and semaphores 12–15
   concepts 15–16
   definition of cyber space 7–12
   infrastructure of modern cyber
      space 19–22
   modelling and reasoning 28
   semaphores and telegraphs 17–18
Osborne, G. 320
OSINT (open source) 224
'othering' of cybersecurity and
      development 769–71, 779–80
Outer Space Treaty 582
overseas development aid (ODA) as an
      industry 779–80
OWASP TOP-10 148, 151

P

packet switching 19
Padmavathi, G. 143, 150
paedophiles and paedophile networks 377,
      387, 388, 389

INDEX   845

Pakistan 54, 541, 622, 773
Palestine 54, 532
Panetta, L. 247n.1
panopticism 410–11
Pariser, E. 166
partial monoids 22
partial ordering 24
Partial Test Ban Treaty 533
passwords 369–70
patching 307, 506
path dependence 554–56
payload 94–95, 176, 209–10
payment card fraud 130
PayTM 621
peer-to-peer messaging 228, 731–32
peer-to-peer (P2P) online margin lending 601
peer-to-peer social networks 409
Penney, J. 413, 415, 416
perfidy principle 589
performative violence and performative
    effects 190, 193–94
personal harassment and abuse 775
personal information 251, 330–31, 340, 507,
    604–5
personal protection/cyber hygiene 123–24,
    361–74, 800
  availability 364–65
  backups 372
  beyond security awareness 372–73
  big picture 362
  browsing 364, 371
  child safety online 390
  confidentiality 364
  email 367–68, 371
  insider threat 366
  integrity 364
  messaging 372
  passwords 369–70
  personal risk assessment 365
  phishing 365, 367–68, 371, 372–73
  pirated software 372
  privacy and security 362–64
  ransomware 365, 368, 372
  security software 370–71
  threat actors, identification of 366, 373–74
  threat vectors, identification of 367, 373–74
  trade-offs in cyber security 364–65
  updates 368–69

Personally Identifiable Information (PII) 187,
    190–91, 322, 331, 332, 437
Petit, F. 43, 45
Pew Internet 412–13
Philippines Central Bank 568–69
phishing 90, 91, 92, 137–38
  cybercrime-as-a-service 97
  data privacy and security law 339
  human and behavioural challenges 728–29
  personal protection/cyber hygiene 365,
    367–68, 371, 372–73
  see also spear phishing
PhishTank 102
phone phreaking 96
physical attack tools 145
physical damage 127
physical disruption 231
physical network graphs 23
physical security 148
physical violence 202
PIN codes 370
piracy and pirated software 99, 103–4, 372,
    606, 773–74
Pisacane, C. 171n.3
planned obsolescence 369
Plato 33, 83–84
plausible deniability 232, 283, 286–87, 463–64, 555
'Playpen' 100
Podesta, J. 261–62
Polisis 340–41
political evolution of internet technology see
    under political history
political factors 34, 36, 45, 226
political history 49–63
  conceptualization of cyber security 57–60
    borderlessness or sovereignty 58
    information security versus cyber
      security 58–59
    security versus privacy 59–60
  cyber threats, evolution of 54–57
    cyber Pearl Harbour 54–55
    future of threats 56–57
    internal challenges 55–56
    Stuxnet 55
    website defacement 54
  political evolution of internet
    technology 51–53
    Clinton/Gore initiatives and vision 53

political history (*cont.*)
    Cold War research 52–53
    Sputnik crisis as catalyst 51–52
  remedies 60–63
    Budapest Convention on Cybercrime 61
    *International Code of Conduct for
    Information Security* 60–61
    United Nations Group of Governmental
    Experts (UNGGE) 61–63
political objectives 192, 225–27
Ponemon Institute report 130
pornography 100, 377, 385–86
positive list 214
Post, D. 606
postal services 16
Potomac Institute Cyber Readiness Index 467
power 197
  assessment and discernment 70
  coercive 67–68, 72–74
  compulsory 68, 69
  distributed (disaggregated) 37–38
  institutional 68–69
  material 70
  outages 104
  soft 67–68, 263
  structural 69
Powers, F.G. 228
prebendalism 554–55
prescriptive analytics 351–52
preventative measures 138, 455*t*
  see also deterrence and prevention of cyber
  conflict
PriceWaterhouseCoopers (PwC) 286
principal-agent theory 226–27, 549–50
printing press, commercially available 16, 84
privacy
  cyber hygiene 371
  defence and national cyber security 457–58
  diplomacy 539
  global commerce and international
    organizations 499, 505–6, 507
  human and behavioural challenges 724
  online child safety 377
  personal protection/cyber hygiene 362–64
  respecting data usage 83
  rights 82–83
  surveillance and human rights 411, 416–17
  violating data usage 83
  see also data privacy and security law
Privacy International 487
private security and military contracts
  (PSMCs) 549–50
proactive cyber security 123, 138
programmable logic controllers (PLCs) 180
Project Solarium 1953 (Eisenhower) and
  Cyberspace Solarium Commission
  (CSC) 2019 785–95
  China 786–88, 790, 792, 794–95
  Eisenhower's objectives and
    outcomes 790–92
  National Security Council (NSC) 791–92
    153 787–88, 790–91, 793, 794
    162/2 786, 792, 793, 794–95
    Planning Board 787–88
  Project Solarium Directing Panel 789
  Russia 786–89, 790, 792, 794–95
  team and tasks selection 788–90
Proliferation Security Initiative 213
propaganda 102, 194, 257, 258
Protection Profiles 483, 484
protectionism 509, 514–15, 516, 608, 622
proxies 441–42
  see also offensive cyber operations (remote),
  states and proxies
pseudo-anonymity 115–16
psychological harm 127, 128, 131–32, 134,
  135–36, 190
psychological intimidation 13, 260–61
psychological manipulation 262
psychological operations 265
psychological profiling 354
psychology of communications 267
Pugwash Conferences on Science and World
  Affairs 533
Putin, V. 226–27, 454, 679
Pym, D. 24, 27

Q

Qalah/Fortress discussion area (electronic
  jihad) 208
Qatar 483
Quadrel, M.J. 727, 728
Qualcomm 636
quantum computing 113–14, 538, 801

R

Radacati Group 465
Radamant Ransomware Kit 97
Radical Levelling Technologies (RLTs) 690
radicalization 102
Radio Free Europe/Radio Liberty 267
RAID array 372
Ramirez, R. 418
RAND Corporation 41, 96, 99, 241, 518
ransomware 90, 92
  agreement violations as customary practice 570
  cybercrime-as-a-service 97
  data privacy and security law 339
  global trade: monitoring, enforcement and
    sanctions 521
  personal protection/cyber hygiene 365,
    368, 372
  Russia 673
Ranum, M./Ranum's Law 145
Rao, R. 416
Rapp, D. 267
rational choice theory 729–30
reactive cyber security 123, 124
Reagan, R. 240–41
reasonableness test 114–15, 586–87
reconnaissance process 174, 176, 177–78, 226
recontextualization 174–75, 179
recovery performance objectives (RPOs) 439
recovery time objectives (RTOs) 439
regime complex 499–500, 756
Regional Comprehensive Economic
    Partnership (RCEP) 621–22
regional organizations 499, 502, 504, 507–8
regulation, new 83–85
Reliability of Global Undersea Communications
    Cable Infrastructure 41–42
remedies *see under* political history
Ren Zhengfei 608
renown and reactions motivations of
    terrorists 193–94
representation and reasoning framework 120
reputation and reputational harm 129, 131–32,
    134, 148, 153–54, 365, 437
resilience 455*t*
  Computer Security Incident Response
    Teams (CSIRTs) 302
  conflict deterrence and prevention 288, 289–90

development and cybersecurity 774–75
  dynamic resilience 289–90
  global trade: monitoring, enforcement and
    sanctions 523
  governance of technology 691–93
  harm assessment 127, 129
  harm mitigation 138
  multilateral export control and standard
    setting 481, 485
  and networking across
    communities 693–94
  smart resilience 289–90
  technology: access and denial 211
  see also under critical national
    infrastructure (CNI)
resources 9–10, 22, 23, 26, 440
Retail Cyber Intelligence Sharing Centre
    (R-CISC) 317–18
retorsion 580, 584
revenge porn 135
Richardson, L. 192, 193–94
Rid, T. 242
right to be forgotten 342–43
Rinaldi, S.M. 53
Rising Above the Gathering Storm reports 396–97
risk
  adaptation *see under* critical national
    infrastructure (CNI)
  assessment 355, 365, 431
  avoidance 2
  concerns and challenges 429–31, 440–42
  engineering 121–22, 124
  identification 2, 431
  management, *see also* risk management -
    terrorism, violent extremism and anti-
    democratic tendencies
  mitigation 2, 431
  models 121–24
  management 2, 127–28, 429–30, 433
  perception and risk
    communication 728–30
risk 441–42
risk management - terrorism, violent
    extremism and anti-democratic
    tendencies 163–71
  laissez-faire versus regulation 164–67
  state and industry response 167–70

848 INDEX

Rivello, J. 95
robotics 597–98, 657–58, 705, 716–17
Roff, H. 705
Romanosky, S. 130
Romer, P. 632
Roosen, J. 729–30
root server operators 617
rootkits 94–95
routers 9
Routing Information Protocol (RIP) 7–8, 16, 17
Royal Institute of International Affairs
    (Chatham House) 380
Ruby, K.G. 348–49
rule of law 265, 457–58, 606, 668, 739
Russia 58, 672–82
    administrative fees and fines 678
    Administrative Offences Code 678
    agreement violations as customary
        practice 563, 565, 571
    Anti-Terrorist Law (374 FZ) 675–76
    APT-28 227–28
    APT-29 227–28
    art of strategy 262–63
    autonomous cyber weapons systems
        (AWS) 707
    Budapest Convention on Cybercrime 61
    Central Bank Cyber Incidents Monitoring
        and Response Centre (FinCERT) 674
    and China 74–75
    computer emergency response team
        (COV-CERT-RU) 674
    conceptual dimension 672–73
    conflict deterrence and prevention 275–76,
        277, 279, 285
    Countering the Use of Information and
        Communications Technologies for
        Criminal Purposes Resolution 681–82
    Crimea annexation and Ukraine
        conflict 262, 263–64, 521
    Critical Data Infrastructure (CDI) Law (187
        FZ) 674–75
    critical information infrastructure
        (CII) 674, 675
    critical infrastructure 673
    critical infrastructure security 674
    critical national infrastructure
        (CNI) 673, 674

cyber crime 101
cyber espionage 227, 228–29
cyber power 73, 74
cyber security laws and Internet
    regulations 674–80
cyber war 243, 245–46
cybercrime-as-a-service 96
data privacy and security law 342–43
defence and national cyber security 453–54
democratic civil society 742–43
development and cyber security 772–73,
    776–77
diplomacy 532, 534–36, 537, 541
draft resolution on developments
    in the field of information and
    telecommunications 681
and Estonia conflict 55, 94, 243–44, 262
Federal Law No. 40-FZ 674
Federal Law On Communications (126 FZ)
    675–676
Federal Law On Data, Information,
    Information Technologies and
    Protection of Information (149 FZ)
    675, 676–77
Federal Security Service (FSB) 226–28, 520,
    553–54, 674, 676
Federal Service for Technical and Export
    Control (FSTEC) 674, 675
Foreign Policy Concept 531–32
'Frameworks of Russia's Government
    Policies in Regard to International
    Information Security up to
    2020' 680–81
future normative challenges 753, 754, 755, 764
and Georgia conflict 262, 280
global commerce and international
    organizations 501, 503, 508, 509
global trade: monitoring, enforcement and
    sanctions 517, 523
Group-IB 553
Identification Rules (Decree 1279) 675, 678
information security 672–73, 674,
    680–81, 682
Information Security Doctrine
    (2016) 672–74, 679
information security versus cyber
    security 58–59

information space 673
information warfare and influence operations
(IWIO) 260, 261–62, 266, 267
Instant Messaging Law (IML) (241 FZ)
675–76
International Code of Conduct for
Information Security 60–61
international cooperation 680–82
Lomonosov Moscow State University 'State,
Civil Society and Business Partnership
on International Information
Security' 536, 537
Main Intelligence Directorate 520
military doctrine 454
military intelligence (GRU) 226–28
Ministry of Defence 673
Ministry of Internal Affairs (MVD) 674
Monitoring and Management Centre 680
multilateral export control and standard
setting 486
National Security Strategy 451
organizational management 673–74
Personal Data Laws (152 FZ and 242 FZ)
675, 677–78
Project Solarium 1953 (Eisenhower) and
Cyberspace Solarium Commission
(CSC) 2019 786–89, 790, 792,
794–95
proxies and offensive cyber operations 544,
545–46, 553–55
Roskomnadzor 674, 676, 677, 678, 679–80
Sovereign Runet Law (90 FZ) 675, 679–80
sovereignty 673, 680
Sputnik 52
SVR 226–27
Syrian war involvement 262
and Ukraine 226, 232, 583
United Nations Group of Governmental
Experts (UNGGE) 61–62
and United States 583, 681
United States election interference (2016) 59,
132, 239, 243, 520, 521, 585, 642
cyber espionage 225, 226, 227–28, 231, 232
cyber power in international
relations 73–74, 75
cyber-enabled information warfare and
information operations 261–62

terrorism, extremism and anti-
democratic tendencies 166
VPN Law (276 FZ) 675, 676–77
see also Cold War

S

sabotage 94, 240, 245, 280–81, 288
safe harbour 331
safe havens 778–79
safe houses 228, 235
SAIC 550
Samsung 553
sanctions 73–74
negative 72–73
proxies on the loose 544, 549, 550f,
553–54, 555
see also global trade: monitoring,
enforcement and sanctions
Sander, B. 756
Sanders, B. 168–69
Sanders, J.W. 35
Sanger, D. 55
Sapolsky, R.M. 355
Sasse, A. 726
Sasse, B. 785, 786
satellite technology 52
Saudi Arabia 441, 487, 541
Aramco and Shamoon malware attack 94,
244, 516, 568
scale 690, 736, 739–41
and effects case 586
of harm 135
in organization 737–38
scams 94, 99, 100–1
Schachter, O. 755
Schauer, F. 411
Schelling, T./Schelling Point 610–11
Schmid, A. 165–66
Schmidt, E. 465
Schmitt Analysis 586
Schrödinger, E. 399–400
script kiddies 96, 98, 432–33, 546–47
script or program 145
SDLC phase 150–51
search engines 261
Secure Electronic Transaction (SET)
protocol 621

INDEX

Secure Socket Layer (SSL) 621
securitization 418, 452, 456
security awareness programmes 727–28
security dialogues 730–32
Security Information and Event Management
    (SIEM) system 723
security software 370–71
security versus privacy 59–60
security-by-design principles 211
Segal, A. 516, 517
Seiersen, R. 351
self-censorship 410–11, 416, 417
  and conformity 411–13
self-defence rights 73, 564–65, 573, 585–87, 764
self-harm 377, 378
self-interest 779
semaphores 12–15, 17–18, 22
semi-formal diplomacy: Track 1.5 and
    Track 2 531–41
  conventional diplomacy 532
  formal diplomacy 531–32
  informal diplomacy 533–36
  ping pong diplomacy 533
  prospects for further semi-official
    diplomacy 540–41
  public diplomacy 531–32
  semi-official diplomacy 538–40
  Track 1 537
  Track 1.5 619
  Track 2 41
  transactional diplomacy 532
Seoul Framework for and Commitment to
    Open and Secure Cyberspace 538–39
service restoration program 439
service-level agreement (SLA) 535
Seven Pernicious Kingdoms approach 151
sextortion 92, 195
sexual coercion 131–32
sexual exploitation of children 778–79
sexual images, self-generated 377
Shamoon malware attack 94, 516, 568
Shanghai Cooperation Organization 61,
    502–3, 680–81
Shannon, C. 269n.3, 399
Shared Industry Hash Database 102–3
Shaw, E.D. 348–49, 351–52
Sherstyuk, V.P. 536

Shinrikyo, A. 195
shoulder surfing 370
side channels 173
SIGINT (signals) 224, 230, 235
silent alarms 233
Silk Road, The (encrypted market) 99
Simmons, C. 149–50
Simon, H. 24
Singapore 333, 471, 472, 603–4, 707
Singer, P. 549–50
Skierka, I. 301
skills: recruitment and training 207–9
Slaughter, A. 761–62
smart payment contracts 118
SMART technologies 442
Snapchat 385
sneaker attack 177–78
Snowden National Security Agency (NSA)/
    PRISM surveillance revelations 55–56,
    233, 412–13, 416–17, 505–6, 516–17, 523,
    534, 535, 637, 703
SNS 91, 92
social engineering 92, 103, 801
  China 600
  cyber espionage 227–28
  cyber hygiene 367
  cyber weapons 174
  hacker culture 98
  vulnerability mitigation 148
social infosphere *see* opportunity, threat and
    dependency in social infosphere
social media 42–43
  bogus accounts 231
  child safety online 378, 379, 384
  cyber crime 91, 92
  cyber hygiene 363–64, 365, 367–68
  development and cyber security 775
  ethical issues 84–85
  future normative challenges 763
  harm assessment from cyber crime 129
  human and behavioural challenges 727
  information warfare and influence
    operations (IWIO) 261
  insider threat and insider advocate 352, 354
  Malaysia 666
  Russia 263–64
  surveillance and human rights 409, 410–11

technology: access and denial 202, 204, 208
terrorism and extremism 163–66, 167, 169,
170–71
social networks 409, 413, 636–37, 651
social order 33
social practice, cybersecurity as 724–26
Society for Worldwide Interbank
Financial Telecommunications
(SWIFT) 568–70
Alliance Access 569, 570
socio-technical-economic system
(STES) 738–40, 744, 745
Socrates 83–84
software 148
design 150
implementation 150
security 370–71
see also intrusion software
Solove, D. 411
Sony Pictures and North Korea 73–74, 232,
239, 244, 520, 521
Sophos 100–1
Sotloff, S. 163–64
South Africa 61
South Korea
agreement violations as customary
practice 566
autonomous cyber weapons systems
(AWS) 707
capacity building 471
cyber weapons 185–86
data privacy and security law 342–43
development and cyber security 772–73
governance of technology 691
and Japan 652–53
Personal Information and Protection Act
(PIPA) 332
printing press 16
surveillance and human rights 416
sovereignty 58, 501, 535–36, 540, 564
China 76, 604–5, 606–7
cyber crime 101
cyber power 70, 77–78
democratic civil societies in post-Western
cybered era 736, 739–41, 744–45, 746
equality 607
future normative challenges 755

India 622
international law 578–79, 581, 584
inviolability 607
Malaysia 663, 665, 667
prescriptive sovereignty 582
Russia 673, 680
space 10, 24, 582
spam 92, 93, 94–95, 103
criminal groups 100
cross-agency and sector cooperation 102
cyber hygiene 365
hacker culture 99
technology: access and denial 209–10
Spamhaus 102
spear phishing 103, 227–28, 600, 727
specialized regimes (sea, air, space and
telecommunications) 578, 582–83
spies 144, 288, 554–55
see also cyber espionage; intelligence
spiral of silence 412, 416
Sputnik crisis as catalyst 51–52
Spyeye hacking tool 96
spyware 94–95, 100–1, 231, 339, 487, 489–91
SQL-injection 151
stack and heap in computer memory (RAM) 22
stand-alone (air gapped) local area
network 228
Standage, T. 17
standard setting arrangements *see* multilateral
export control and standard setting
arrangements
standards of care 572–73
standards developing organizations
(SDOs) 482, 484, 485
Standards for the Protection of Personal
Information of Residents of the
Commonwealth 338
Starbucks 341–42
states 25
Stavrou, A. 143, 144
steganography 228
STEM education 396
sting operations 233
Stock, H.V. 351–52
stock price manipulation 801
Stoll, C. 314–15
Stoycheff, E. 412, 413, 414, 415, 416

852   INDEX

Structured Threat Information eXpression
(STIX) format 321
Stuxnet and Operation Olympic Games
by United States and Israel against
Iran 633–34, 639, 775
agreement violation as customary
practice 562–63, 570–71
autonomous cyber weapons systems
(ACWS) 706
cyber crime 90, 94
cyber espionage 226, 228, 231, 232, 233
cyber threats, evolution of 55
cyber war 242, 243–44
cyber weapons 178
global trade: monitoring, enforcement and
sanctions 516
proxies and offensive cyber
operations 551–52
software toolkit 231
technology: access and denial 203
submarine telecommunications
cables 13f, 582
subversion 240, 241, 245–46
Sudan 487
suicide 131–32, 134–35, 378
Sundaramurthy, S.C. 303
Sunzi (Sun Tzu) 234, 252, 450
supervisory control and data acquisition
(SCADA) systems 94, 120, 207
surveillance
autonomous cyber weapons systems
(AWS) 703
China 604–5
diplomacy 539
global commerce and international
organizations 497, 499, 505
government surveillance 499, 508
Israel 637
mass surveillance 37, 457–58
and self (or state) censorship 59
systems 488, 489–90
technologies 487, 488
tools 487
see also surveillance and human rights
surveillance and human rights 409–19
acceptance 415
civil society and human rights 412–14

chilling effects theory, self-censorship
and conformity 411–13
chilling online information
access, engagement and content
sharing 413–14
unequal/disparate impact, including
vulnerable minorities 414
control function 409
government/state surveillance 410, 412–13,
414, 415, 416
implications for cyber security 414–17
dangerous practices, encouragement
of 416–17
practices and technology promoting
vulnerabilities 415–16
reporting, undermining of and public
awareness issues on national security
matters 417
vulnerability to disinformation,
propaganda and fake news 416
vulnerability to threats 414–15
mass surveillance 412, 413–14, 416–17
normalization of surveillance 414–15
passivity 415
rights-centric cyber security 417–19
individual-focused empiricism and
human rights 418–19
interdisciplinary focus 418
status quo surveillance 415
surveillance culture 410–11, 414–15
surveillance impact theories 410–12
surveillance realism 414–15
surveillance studies theory 410–11
targeted surveillance 416–17
visibility 416–17
Sustainable Development Goals (SDGs) 383,
479, 770, 778
Sweden 567–68
Sweet Orange Exploit Kit 97
'Sweetie' sting operation 100
Symantec 617–18, 773
Syria 68, 102–3, 187, 633, 691
Electronic Army 544–45, 546, 555
and Russia 262
systemic misperceptions and abuse of
cyberspace 736–39
systemic surprise layers 739–40

T

tactics (or tools), techniques and procedures (TTPs) 431–32
Tainter, J.A. 400
Taiwan 91
Tajikistan 60–61
Taktikos, A. 12
Taliban 195
TalkTalk data breach 136
Tallin 2.0 International Group of Experts 579, 580, 581, 584–85, 586
Tallinn Manuals 280–81, 606, 713
Target data breach 136
taxonomy model 149–50
TeaMpoisoN 187
technological advancements 348–49, 351–53, 356
technological change 50, 63
technologies, new 83–85
technology: access and denial 201–14
   criminal groups and hacktivists nexus 209–10
   international negotiations on state behaviour and cyber weapons proliferation 212–14
   media responsibility 211
   resilience 211
   skills: recruitment and training 207–9
   terrorist financing 207
   threat landscape: terrorist group access to offensive cyber means 202–5
   vulnerabilities and complexity 205–6
technology forecasting and innovation 109–16
   analysis based on past behaviours in similar environments 111
   collecting 'signals' from environment and analysing impact 112
   disruptive technology and regulatory frameworks 114–15
   disruptive technology and threat landscapes 115–16
   examining and combining analyses from different stakeholders 112
   foresight and assessment 110, 118
   model creation of disruptive technologies 112–13
   ontology-based analysis 113

prediction techniques of future technology 111–13
trend forecasting and cybercrime 113–14
trends prediction methodology 109–11
Tehran Hostages case 580
telecommunications law 582–83
Telegram 619–20
telegraphs 17–18, 22
Tencent 598
Terms of Service (TOS) agreement 268, 412
terror strategy and engagement in political process 196
Thakur, M. 40
theatricality 192, 193–94
theft 92, 93, 104, 149–50, 798
   see also credit card theft; identity theft; intellectual property theft
thermodynamics laws 398–99, 400, 401–3
threat 37, 50
   actors, identification of 366, 373–74
   conflict deterrence and prevention 280
   construction 418
   credible threat 285
   cyber espionage 223
   development and cybersecurity 774–75
   direct threat 498, 502–5
   evolution of *see under* political history
   future normative challenges 762
   identification, detection and prevention of 409–10
   indirect threat 499, 505–6
   information 441
   of information wars 60–61
   landscape: terrorist group access to offensive cyber means 202–5
   landscapes and disruptive technology 115–16
   of military force 72–73
   model and critical national infrastructure (CNI) 439
   perceptions for defence and national cyber security 451–52
   and response approach 800, 801–3
   vectors, identification of 367, 373–74
   see also advanced persistent threat (APT); insider threat and insider advocates; opportunity, threat and dependency in social infosphere

Tilly, C. 189, 191–92
Tirmaa-Klaar, H. 554
Toffler, A. 632
Toffler, H. 632
toolkits 145
top-down approaches 803–4
  cyber power 75–76
  development and cyber security 770–71, 779
  governance of technology 687, 694, 696
topological space 8, 22, 24
Tor 90
  browser bundle 371
  cybercrime-as-a-service 96
  market 99
  network 99
totalitarian regimes 451, 457–58
  see also authoritarian/autocratic
    countries
Track 1.5 see semi-formal diplomacy: Track 1.5
  and Track 2
Track 2 see semi-formal diplomacy: Track 1.5
  and Track 2
Traffic Light Protocol (TLP) 319, 325
Trans-Pacific Partnership (TPP)
  agreement 506, 508, 514–15
Transatlantic Cyber Policy Research Initiative
  (TCPRI) 214
Transatlantic Trade and Investment
  Partnership (TTIP) 514–15
Transdniestria conflict 533
transformational security 37–38
transition systems 22
Transmission Control Protocol/Internet
  Protocol (TCP/IP) 7–8, 10, 19, 20f, 53
transparency
  autonomous weapons systems (AWS) 716
  child safety online 385
  China 604, 605, 608–9
  Computer Security Incident Response
    Teams (CSIRTs) 306
  cyber hygiene 363
  democratic civil societies in post-Western
    cybered era 736, 743
  Facebook 168
  future normative challenges 752
  global commerce and international
    organizations 499–500

multilateral export control and standard
  setting 486
proxies and offensive cyber operations 555–56
security versus privacy 59
surveillance and human rights 415, 416–17
terrorism and extremism 164, 168
Twitter 168
trends prediction see technology forecasting
  and innovation
trojans 94–95, 173
trolling 85
Truman, H.S. 793
Trump, D./administration
  alternative facts 42–43
  Cambridge Analytica 75
  Computer Security Incident Response
    Teams (CSIRTs) 305
  cyber conflict deterrence and prevention 276
  cyber crime harm assessment 137
  Facebook 85
  global commerce and international
    organizations 506, 508–9
  global trade 514–15
  information sharing 318
  malware 95
  opportunity, threat and dependency in
    social infosphere 37
  terrorism and extremism 168–69
  see also United States election interference
    (2016) under Russia
trust
  Computer Security Incident Response
    Teams (CSIRTs) 303, 304, 306, 309, 310
  diplomacy 539
  emerging technology areas 123–24
  and harm 136–37
  human and behavioural challenges 724,
    730–31, 732
  information sharing 319
  multilateral export control and standard
    setting 480, 481, 484, 485, 492–93
Trusted Automated eXchange of Indicator
  Information (TAXII) standard 321
truth 24
  bias 258
  logical 26
  pure 258

Tsyrklevich, V. 97
Tucker, C. 413
Tufekci, Z. 168–69
Turing's halting problem 175
Turkey 91, 342–43
Twitter 37
  capacity building 465
  cross-agency and sector cooperation 102–3
  cyber espionage 228
  governance of technology 693–94
  India 617
  information warfare and influence
      operations (IWIO) 258, 268
  terrorism and extremism 163–64, 167
  transparency 168

U
UEBA (User and Entity Behaviour
    Analytics) 351–52
Ukraine
  agreement violations as customary
      practice 566, 570–71
  Black Energy campaign (2015) 178, 181, 334,
      429, 441
  blackout 239, 242
  Cyber Forces 548–49
  cyber hygiene 366
  cyber power 72
  development and cyber security 772–73
  proxies and offensive cyber
      operations 548, 553
  and Russia 226, 232, 583
  Science and Technology Centre 695
Ulbricht, R. 99
Uma, M. 143, 150
unfair or deceptive practices legislation 330
UNICEF 380, 381, 775
  Global Resources and Information
      Directory (Grid) 382
unique product requirements 514–15
United Arab Emirates (UAE) 489–90
United Kingdom 799
  agreement violations as customary
      practice 570, 571
  autonomous cyber weapons systems
      (AWS) 704–5, 707, 712–13, 717
  Bank of England CBEST framework 435–36

Brexit 42–43, 75, 166, 508, 509
British Board of Film Classification 386
BT 433
Cabinet Office 319
capacity building 471, 472–73
Centre for the Protection of National
    Infrastructure (CPNI) 318–19, 336,
    432–33
  Traffic Light Protocol (TLP) 319
Chatham House think tank 539
child safety online 378, 379, 380, 386
Children's Commissioner 384–85
and China 538
'Cleanfeed' 389
competent authorities (CAs) 322–23
computer emergency response team
    (CERT-UK) 319–20
Computer Misuse Act 1990 93
Computer Security Incident Response
    Teams (CSIRTs) 308–9
cross-agency and sector cooperation 102–3
cyber hygiene 368
cyber power 72, 74
cyber terrorism and intentions 191
Cybersecurity Capacity Maturity Model for
    Nations 778
Department for Digital, Culture, Media and
    Sport 322–23, 769
Department for Environment, Food and
    Rural Affairs 322–23
Department for International
    Development 769, 780
development and cyber security 772–73,
    776–77, 779
Digital Economy Act 386
digital strategy 603–4
diplomacy 536, 538
Drinking Water Inspectorate 322–23
financial services Sector 435–36
five-year cyber strategies 431
Foreign and Commonwealth Office
    (FCO) 769
foreign investment and 4G 433
and France 230
Freedom of Information requests 320, 387, 388
global commerce and international
    organizations 503–5

856　INDEX

United Kingdom (*cont.*)
　Global Cyber Security Capacity Centre
　　(Oxford University) 778
　Government Communications
　　Headquarters (GCHQ) 309, 320, 538
　government computer emergency response
　　team (GovCERT) 320
　harm assessment from cyber crime 130
　Health and Safety Executive (HSE) 323
　human and behavioural challenges 725
　Information Commissioners Office
　　(ICO) 323, 380
　information sharing 318, 324
　'Internet Safety Strategy' Green Paper 385
　Internet Watch Foundation (IWF) 389,
　　778–79
　London Global Conference on Cyberspace
　　(GCCS) 538–39
　Ministry of Defence 319
　Global Strategic Trends 728
　multilateral export control and standard
　　setting 483, 487, 488
　National Audit Office 570
　National Cyber Security Centre
　　(NCSC) 286, 317, 320, 432–33, 435
　Joint Technical Alert 73
　National Cyber Security Strategy 72–73,
　　289, 471
　National Health Service (NHS) 341, 570
　see also WannaCry ransomware attack on
　　UK NHS
　national infrastructure 148–49
　National Infrastructure Security Co-
　　ordination Centre (NISCC) 319
　National Society for the Prevention of
　　Cruelty to Children (NSPCC) 387, 388
　Network and Information Security (NIS)
　　competent authority (CA) 323
　Network Information Systems Directive
　　(NISD) implementation 323
　Network and Information Systems
　　Regulations 2018 322–23
　Online Harms White Paper 390
　Project Auburn 319
　proxies and offensive cyber
　　operations 549–51
　R v Arnold (1994) 389

　Regional Organized Crime Units
　　(ROCUs) 320
　Statute of Anne 84
　surveillance and human rights 415
　and United States Data Sharing
　　Agreement 619
　see also critical national infrastructure (CNI)
United Nations
　accident communication 185
　agreement violations as customary
　　practice 571–72
　Charter 73, 563
　　future normative challenges 755, 760
　　international law 583, 584, 585–86
　　Malaysia 667–68
　China 608–9
　Committee on the Peaceful Uses of Outer
　　Space (UNCOPUOS) 582
　Committee on the Rights of the Child 380
　Computer Security Incident Response
　　Teams (CSIRTs) 309–10
　conflict deterrence and prevention 287
　Convention on Ensuring International
　　Information Security (draft) 680–81
　Convention on the Rights of the Child
　　(UNCRC) 378–79, 380
　Convention on Transnational Organized
　　Crime (TOC Convention) 101, 502–3
　cross-agency and sector cooperation 102–3
　development and cyber security 776
　diplomacy 531, 534–35
　Economic and Social Council
　　(ECOSOC) 774
　future normative challenges 758
　General Assembly 61–62, 564, 565, 566
　　First Committee 212–13, 535, 563
　　Optional Protocol on the Sale of
　　　Children, Child Prostitution and
　　　Child Pornography 381
　　Resolutions 564, 680, 755
　global commerce and international
　　organizations 500–1, 504, 505–6
　governance of technology 689
　Group of Governmental Experts
　　(GGE) 563–68, 570, 573
　　autonomous cyber weapons systems
　　　(AWS) 703–4, 711, 713, 716, 717–18

China 604, 606
Computer Security Incident Response
Teams (CSIRTs) 302
critical national infrastructure
(CNI) 429
cyber power 74
diplomacy 535–36
future normative challenges 753, 754,
755, 758, 759, 760–61, 764
global commerce and international
organizations 502, 504–5
International Code of Conduct for
Information Security 60–61
international relations 73
Malaysia 659–60, 667
nationalization trend and technology
sovereignty 515–21, 523
political history 61–63
Russia 680, 681
technology: access and denial 206,
212–13, 214
Institute for Disarmament Research
(UNIDIR) 212–13, 452–53, 702, 704,
708, 711, 716–17
International Code of Conduct for
Information Security 60–61
Internet Freedom 58
norms and standards 74–75
Office on Drugs and Crime (UNODC)
- *Comprehensive Study on
Cybercrime* 96
political history of cyberspace 50
proxies and offensive cyber operations 548
Secretary General High-level Panel on
Digital Cooperation 776
Security Council 68–69, 540–41, 564, 583,
584, 585–86
Counter-Terrorism Committee 202
Resolutions 585
terrorism and extremism 167
transformational security 37
World Summit on the Information Society
(WSIS) 33, 381, 382
United States
Advanced Research Projects Agency 19
agreement violations as customary
practice 564–65, 566, 567, 570, 571

alt-Right 262, 266
Argonne National Laboratory 40, 44–45
Arizona Cyber Threat Response Allies
(ACTRA) 320
Army 453
autonomous cyber weapons systems
(AWS) 704–5, 707, 712–13, 716, 717
Budapest Convention on Cybercrime 101
bulk electric power systems 436
California Consumer Protection Act
(CCPA) 339
capacity building 465
Carnegie Mellon University *see* Carnegie
Mellon University (CMU)(USA)
Census Bureau 465
Center for Strategic and International
Studies (CSIS) 537–38, 772–73
Central Intelligence Agency (CIA) 224,
243, 506
Certificate Numbering Authority (CNA) 316
child safety online 377–79, 383, 389
Children's Online Privacy Protection Act
1998 (COPPA) 379–80
and China 41, 94, 226–27, 242–43, 286, 538,
583, 604
Clinton Presidential Decision Direction
(No. 63) 334
Commission on IP theft 520
Committee on Foreign Investment in the
United States (CFIUS) 432
Common Vulnerability and Exposure
(CVE) identifiers 316
Communications Decency Act 164–65, 386
computer emergency response team
(CERT) 434
Federal Incident Notification Guidelines 332
Computer Fraud and Abuse Act
(CFAA) 93, 98, 196, 297, 315, 337–38
Computer Security Incident Response
Teams (CSIRTs) 298–99
computer security response team 98
conflict deterrence and prevention 275–76
Critical Foreign Dependencies Initiative
(CFDI) 42
critical infrastructure 149, 241
and key resources 431–32
sector identification 434

858 INDEX

United States (*cont.*)
  critical national infrastructure (CNI) *see under*
    critical national infrastructure (CNI)
  cross-agency and sector cooperation 102–3
  Cyber Command 204, 209, 544–45, 548,
    550–51
  cyber crime 91
  cyber dependency 45
  cyber espionage 227, 228, 232
  cyber hygiene 368
  cyber power 70, 74–76
  Cyber Security Reporting Requirements
    for the Department of Finance (New
    York) 321–22, 323
  Cyber Strategy 287–88, 290, 679
  cyber terrorism and intentions 191, 193
  cyber war 242–43, 245
  Cybersecurity Information Sharing
    Act 320–21, 336–37
  Cybersecurity and Infrastructure Security
    Agency 335, 434
  data privacy and security law 330–32, 333,
    334, 337–39, 342
  data privacy and security law state
    statutes 338–39
  Data Security and Breach Notification Act 332
  Defense Acquisition Regulation Systems
    (DFARs) 322
  Defense Advanced Research Project
    Agency (DARPA) 52, 298, 693
  Cyber Grand Challenge 290, 706–7
  Defense Authorization Act 792
  Defense Industrial Base (DIB) 321–22
  Defense Science Board 244–45, 287–88
  Defense Security Information Exchange
    (DSIE) 322
  Defensive Cyber Operations (DCO) 551
  democratic civil society 745, 746
  Department of Commerce 489, 535, 618
  Bureau of Industry and Security (BIS) 488, 489
  Department of Energy 436
  Department of Health and Human
    Services 331–32
  Department of Homeland Security *see*
    Department of Homeland Security
    (DHS)(USA)
  Department of Justice 286, 338

Department of State 688–89
development and cyber security 770, 772–73,
  776–77, 780
diplomacy 532, 534–36, 537, 538, 541
Drug Enforcement Administration
  (DEA) 518
education for cyber security 396
energy sector rules 436
Executive Order 13636 320, 431–32, 435
Fair and Accurate Credit Transactions Act
  (FACTA) 333
Federal Acquisition Requirements
  (FARs) 322
Federal Bureau of Investigation *see* Federal
  Bureau of Investigation (FBI)(USA)
Federal Information Security Management
  Act (FISMA) 436
Federal Trade Commission *see* Federal
  Trade Commission (FTC)(USA)
financial information 332
financial services 331–32
Financial Services Law 338–39
First Amendment of Constitution 265
Florida Metropolitan Bureau of
  Investigation 518
Food and Drug Administration
  (FDA) 321–22, 323–24
foreign investment review and critical
  infrastructure 432
Fourth Amendment warrant 342
future normative challenges 753, 754, 759,
  761, 764
future technology prediction
  techniques 111
and Germany 516
global commerce and international
  organizations 501, 503–6, 507, 508
global trade: monitoring, enforcement and
  sanctions 516–17, 518–21, 523
governance of technology 688–89
Government Accountability Office 315
GPS navigation system 582–83
Gramm-Leach-Bliley Act (GLBA) 332
Health Breach Notification Rule 331–32
Health Information Technology for
  Economic and Clinical Health Act
  (HITECH) 331–32

Health Insurance Portability and
Accountability Act (HIPAA) 331–32
health services 331–32
House of Representatives Energy and
Commerce Committee 332
Idaho National Laboratory 40
and India 616–20, 622–24
Industrial Control Systems computer
emergency response team
(ICS-CERT) 434
information security versus cyber
security 58–59
information sharing 315, 317, 321
information warfare and influence
operations (IWIO) 251, 260, 265, 266
insider threat and insider advocates 349
Intelligence and National Security Alliance
(INSA) 348–49
Interagency Guidance on Response
Programs for Unauthorized Access to
Customer Information and Customer
Notice 332
Internal Revenue Service 320–21
*International Strategy of Cooperation on
Cyberspace* 71, 72–73, 74–75, 76
Internet Freedom doctrine 58
and Iran 243–45
and Israel 55, 226
and Japan 652–53
Joint Chiefs of Staff doctrine statement 451,
453–54
Justice Department 520
Massachusetts law 338–39
Massachusetts Model Railway Club hacker
sub-culture 96
multilateral export control and standard
setting 480–81, 483, 488, 489–90, 492
9/11 Commission Report 336–37
National Academy of Sciences 396
National Aeronautics and Space
Administration (NASA) 52
National Computer Security Center 318
National Institute for Standards and
Technology *see* National Institute for
Standards and Technology (NIST)(USA)
National Science Advisory Board for
Biosecurity (NSABB) 687–88

National Security Agency *see* National
Security Agency (NSA)(USA)
National Security Council Global Threats
report 693
National Security Strategy (1998) 60
National Telecommunications and
Information Administration
(NTIA) 618
NCCIC Cyber Security Information
Sharing and Collaboration Program
(CISCP) 318
New York Federal Reserve Bank 568–69
New York State Department of Financial
Services (DFS) 323, 338–39
NISTR 7628 Guidelines for SMART GRID
Cybersecurity 436
nuclear umbrella 285
Obama Executive Order 13,636 334–35, 520
Obama Presidential Policy Directive-21
(PPD-21) 334–35
Offensive Cyber Operations (OCO) 551
Office of the Director of National
Intelligence (ODNI) 434, 707
Worldwide Threat Assessment report
(2016) 707
Office of Management and Budget 332
Office of Personnel Management 320–21
Patent and Trademark Office 297
Patriot Act 2001 334
Presidential Decision Directive (PDD) on
Critical Infrastructure Protection 317, 318
Presidential Directive on national
preparedness 454–55
Presidential elections (2016) 429, 432
Presidential Policy Directive 21 (PPD-21) on
cyber operations 318, 431–32, 454
proxies and offensive cyber operations 543,
544–45, 549–51, 554–55
Remote Operations Center 547
Russian interference in election campaign
(2016) *see under* Russia
St. Mary Parish, Louisiana 258
Sandia National Laboratory 40, 143
sector-specific agency (SSA) 434
Software Engineering Institute (SEI) and
computer emergency response teams
(CERTs) 320

860   INDEX

United States (*cont.*)
   and Soviet Union Incidents at Sea
      Agreement (1972) 278
   Special Operations Command J5 Future Plans
      and Strategies cell (Donovan Group) 694
   Special Operations Command
      SOFWERX 694
   SSA 436
   State Department 203, 211, 212
   Transnational Organized Crime Rewards
      Program 209–10
   Strategy for CyberSpace (2011) 73–74
   surveillance and human rights 412–13
   technology: access and denial 204, 206,
      207, 208
   terrorism and extremism 165, 167, 168–69
   Texas University 320
   trends prediction 109–10
   Trump Executive Order on Strengthening
      the Cybersecurity of Federal Networks
      and Critical Infrastructure 335
   USCYBERCOM and Persistent
      Engagement 432
   Voice of America 267
   vulnerability mitigation 152
   White House framework (2014) 206
   White House Office of Science and
      Technology Policy 708
   see also Cold War; Project Solarium
      1953 (Eisenhower) and Cyberspace
      Solarium Commission (CSC) 2019;
      Stuxnet and Operation Olympic
      Games by United States and Israel
      against Iran
Universal Declaration of Human Rights
   (UDHR) 82–83, 412
Universal Resource Locators (URLs) 8, 389
Unna, Y. 642
updates 368–69
USB sticks 372
user command 145
user name 59
Uzbekistan 60–61

V
value at risk 131, 148, 601
values and value systems, challenge of 754–55

Van Wilsem, J.V. 91
Van Zwanenberg, P. 110
Vanguard satellite programme 52
vehicle-borne improvised explosive devices
   (VBIEDs) 192–93
Verizon 516
Vessey, J. 241
Vienna Convention on Diplomatic Relations 531
Vietnam 569–70
Vimeo 169
violent and extremist materials 377, 378
Virtual Global Taskforce (VGT) 102
virtual network graphs 23
virtual private network (VPN) 96, 371
viruses 94–95, 173, 209, 315
VirusTotal 102
Visa 3-D Secure protocol 621
von Clausewitz, C. 67, 242, 251, 290–91, 450
voyeurs 144
vulnerabilities 1, 39–40
   agreement violations as customary
      practice 562
   cheap and shameless vulnerabilities 181–82
   and complexity 205–6
   Computer Security Incident Response
      Teams (CSIRTs) 307–8, 309, 310
   created by corporate behaviour 499
   critical national infrastructure
      (CNI) 429–30
   cyber threats 54
   cyber weapons 176
   difficult and expensive
      vulnerabilities 181–82
   disinformation, propaganda and fake
      news 416
   of liberal democracies 265, 739
   practices and technology
      promoting 415–16
   reported vulnerabilities 181–82
   to threats 414–15
   unknown vulnerabilities 308
   see also vulnerability mitigation model; zero
      day vulnerabilities
Vulnerabilities Equities Process 506
vulnerability mitigation model 142–57
   actions 143, 144, 156
   agents/attackers 143, 144–45, 146–48, 156

attack 143
  attributes 143
  domains 147
  impact 143
  mechanisms 147
  mitigation 143
  results 149–50
  scenario 151
  target 143, 144, 146, 148–49, 153, 156
  tools 144, 145–46, 147, 153, 156
  types 143
  value of 143
  vector 143
cyber security incidents 143
databases 150–53
defence 143
event 143, 144, 146
exploitable vulnerability 151
exploits 153
and exposure distinction 146
formal market 142
inadvertent vulnerabilities 151
incident vulnerabilities 143
Informational Impact 143, 149–50
latent vulnerability 151
life cycle for cyber incidents 144
malicious intentional vulnerabilities 151
non-malicious intentional
    vulnerabilities 151
objectives 143, 144, 145, 156
Operational Impact 143, 149–50
potential vulnerabilities 151
'proper' vulnerabilities 152
state actors 144
system vulnerabilities 152
Unauthorized Results 144, 156
vulnerability taxonomies 143, 150
zero-day vulnerabilities 151, 156–57
vulnerable minorities 414

W

Wahl-Jorgensen, K. 414–15, 417
WannaCry ransomware attack on UK
    NHS 54–55, 341, 441, 523, 570, 642,
    691–92, 799
war *see* cyber war
WarGames 240–41

Warning Advisory and Reporting Points
    (WARPs) 319–20
wars, new 450–51
Warsaw Treaty Organization (WTO or
    Warsaw Pact) 275–76, 277
Wassenaar Arrangement 480–93
  global trade: monitoring, enforcement and
    sanctions 515, 518–19, 521
  governance of technology 689
  proxies and offensive cyber
    operations 544–45
  technology: access and denial 213
water-field attack 655
watermarking 184
Watkins 433
We Protect Global Alliance to End Child
    Sexual Exploitation Online 383, 384,
    778–79
weapons *see* cyber weapons
Web 2.0 387
Web Application Security Consortium
    (WASC) Threat Classification 148
Weber, M. 545–46
webmail 363, 365
website defacement 54, 667
Webster, F. 34
Weimann, G. 165–66, 171n.4, 207
Weiner, N. 703–4
Wells Fargo 568–69
West, S.M. 416–17
Western Europe 431, 440–41, 442, 486, 487
Western Roman Empire 405, 406
Westphalia, Treaty of 12
WhatsApp 619–20
Whishaw, F. 14–15
'white' hackers 694
'white hats' 98
white market 518
WikiLeaks 55–56, 99
  cyber espionage 225, 231
  cyber war 239
  global commerce and international
    organizations 506
  information warfare and influence
    operations (IWIO) 258, 261–62
Wikipedia 104, 413–14
Wildavsky, A. 691

862 INDEX

Williams, J. 84
Williamson, G. 571
Wilson, W. 531–32
Wiper 562–63
Wolff, J. 305
workplace *see under* 'insider threat' and 'insider advocate'
World Bank 464, 465
   Digital Dividends Development Report 479
World Conference on International Telecommunications (2012) 535
World Economic Forum 131, 465, 479, 539
   Networked Readiness Index (NRI) 464, 599
World Intellectual Property Organization (WIPO) 598
World Internet Conference (2015) 602–3
World Summit on the Information Society (WSIS) and WSIS+ review 501, 608–9, 776
World Trade Organization (WTO) 497, 500, 508, 514–15, 519–20
   Technical Barriers to Trade Agreement 481
   see also Agreement on Trade-Related Aspects of Intellectual Property Rights (TRIPS)
World Wide Web (WWW) 8, 19–20, 361–62, 500
worms 94–95, 173, 209
Worms Against Nuclear Killers (WANK Worm) 298
Wozniak, S. 726–27
Wu, T.S. 606

Wyden, R. 337
Wysopal, C. 154

X

xDedic 667
Xi Jinping 41, 76, 503–4, 537, 540, 599, 601–3, 605, 606
Xiaomi 620

Y

Yahoo 543–44
Yanukovich, V. 264
'Year Zero' 516, 517
YouTube 102–3, 385, 465
   information warfare and influence operations (IWIO) 258, 268
   terrorism and extremism 163, 164–65, 167, 168–69

Z

Zarkadakis, G. 703–4
zero day brokers 518
zero day exploits 94, 97, 151, 517–18, 520
zero day vulnerabilities 283–84, 285–86, 291, 307, 308, 437, 499, 506
zero effect 283–84, 285–86, 291
zero intent 283–84, 285–86, 291
zero source 283–84, 285–86, 291
Zeus hacking tool 96
Zhang Xin 287
Zolnoor, M. 551–52
Zuckerberg, M. 268